# Frommer's®
# California

# My California

by Matthew Richard Poole

**I'VE BEEN TRAVELING THROUGHOUT CALIFORNIA SINCE MY DAD** bought a shiny new wood-paneled station wagon in 1967 and I still haven't seen every destination in this guidebook. In fact, this state is so huge and diverse that it takes a team of Frommer's travel writers to cover it from end to end. So if you're planning a vacation to California, you're going to have to make some tough decisions.

Obviously you can't see everything in a single trip, but how can you choose to visit Yosemite instead of Lake Tahoe? Or the Wine Country instead of Gold Country? San Francisco rather than San Diego? Disneyland over SeaWorld? It's the kind of conundrum that only a state as incredibly varied as California can create.

The beautiful images in the following pages will only make your decision more difficult, because it probably didn't occur to you that California's desert regions are a major international attraction (Germans love Death Valley's blistering heat), that you can hug the world's largest (by volume) tree (Sequoia National Park) and the world's tallest tree (Redwoods National and State Parks), or that you can still find plenty of fat nuggets to pan for in the Gold Country.

My advice? Quit your job, buy a VW camper, and spend the next few years exploring California, one of the most alluring places on earth.

© Stephen Wilkes/Getty Images

My all-time favorite LA activity is to take a leisurely ride on the 8-mile **BEACHSIDE BIKE PATH (left)** that runs along Santa Monica and Venice Beach. Here, everyone appears healthy and happy as they jog, skate, walk, and ride in the sunshine as a cool breeze blows in off the Pacific.

Some of the biggest stars in show business have their noses (Bob Hope), hair (Whoopi Goldberg), cigars (George Burns), wheels (R2-D2), hands, feet, and signatures immortalized at the famous **ENTRY COURT TO SID GRAUMAN'S CHINESE THEATER (above)**, in Los Angeles. I drop by once in a while just to admire Betty Grable's gams.

The unique warming temperatures of the desert create air currents perfect for hot-air ballooning. At each sunrise and sunset, these quiet vehicles rise into the sky, offering unparalleled views of the **COACHELLA VALLEY (left)** and the nearby Santa Rosa Mountains. Those interested in romance should choose the special champagne flight.

Along with the most famous amusement park in the world—the Disneyland Resort—the LA region hosts three other destinations for thrill-seekers: Six Flags California, Universal Studios, and **KNOTT'S BERRY FARM (below)**. That's 4 days of guaranteed fun in the sun.

Established in 1789, the **MISSION BASILICA SAN DIEGO DE ALCALA** (above) is California's oldest mission and an active Catholic Parish; mass is conducted here daily. If these walls could talk, they would tell stories of the bitter disputes between the natives and the Spanish missionaries.

San Diego's beach scene consists of a variety of outdoor activities, like jogging, biking, and **BEACH VOLLEYBALL** (right). On any given sunny day, dozens of volleyball games pepper San Diego's beaches. Remember, you don't have to play to enjoy this game—half the fun is in people-watching or applauding a smooth slide in the sand.

© Brett Shoaf/San Diego CVB

If you've seen the lines to board
**SAN FRANCISCO'S CABLE CARS** (above)
you can guess why most locals don't
take them with regularity. But riding
one is an instant reminder of why they
are so fun—and romantic, thrilling, and
even a bit death defying—as they
slowly lunge down the city's steep hills.
Seriously, this is a must-do.

Like most cities, gentrification continues to encroach on San Francisco's
diversity. But the colorful **MISSION
DISTRICT** (right) still celebrates its Latin
community, especially through its
preservation and recognition of its
hundreds of murals.

*Opposite page: © Chad Ehlers/Index Stock*

Whether you walk it, bike it, drive it, or view it from a distance, San Francisco's most famous landmark, the **GOLDEN GATE BRIDGE,** commands attention. The bridge is a visual wonder. But its flanking backdrop of the woodsy Presidio to the south, rugged Marin Headlands to the north, and glistening waters of the Golden Gate below make it downright magical to behold.

To see the largest living thing in the world—that's one reason why you should make the drive to **SEQUOIA NATIONAL PARK (above).** The General Sherman Tree is so massive that its branches are more than 7 feet thick. This remote region offers the most pristine wilderness in the Sierra Nevada, with 75 groves of mind-blowingly big sequoias, granite walls that rise thousands of feet, and the deepest canyon in the United States. Bring a very wide-angle lens.

When it's time to hang up my keyboard, I'm going to retire in **LAKE TAHOE (right).** If there's a more beautiful place to live that offers as many outdoor activities, please let me know. Surrounded by the majestic peaks of the Sierra Nevada, Lake Tahoe is the largest alpine lake in North America and the best year-round playground in California. Spend a few days here and you too will consider purchasing some Sierra Nevada real estate.

The **WINE COUNTRY** (right) is all about great wine and food and leisure pursuits. Go to Napa or Sonoma to sip through a few wineries, sit down at a bucolic restaurant, and linger over a bottle of wine and a ridiculously good meal. This is about as good as life gets.

There aren't enough adjectives to describe the sensation of seeing **YOSEMITE VALLEY** (below) for the first time. Among the most beautiful and popular of America's National Parks, Yosemite is home to the highest waterfall in North America, the tallest and largest granite monolith in the world, and one of the world's largest trees.

© Charles O'Rear/Corbis

© Mike Roessler/Index Stock

If all you think of is football when some-one mentions the Forty-Niners, then spend some time touring California's rugged **GOLD COUNTRY (left)**, where many of the historic mining towns, saloons, and gold mines date back to the mid-1800s. One of the most underrated tourist desti-nations in California, the Gold Country provides the ideal vacation combination of historical interest, gorgeous scenery, cozy B&Bs, and such entertaining activi-ties as exploring active gold mines, white-water rafting, and panning for real gold (yes, you get to keep it).

One of the last great estates of America's Gilded Age, **HEARST CASTLE (below)** is among the most elaborate (and excessive) buildings on earth. This over-the-top estate of publishing magnate William Randolph Hearst is one of those you-have-to-see-it-to-believe-it kind of places, where a 100-plus-room mansion and the Greco-Roman Neptune pool (pictured here) are just part of the tour package.

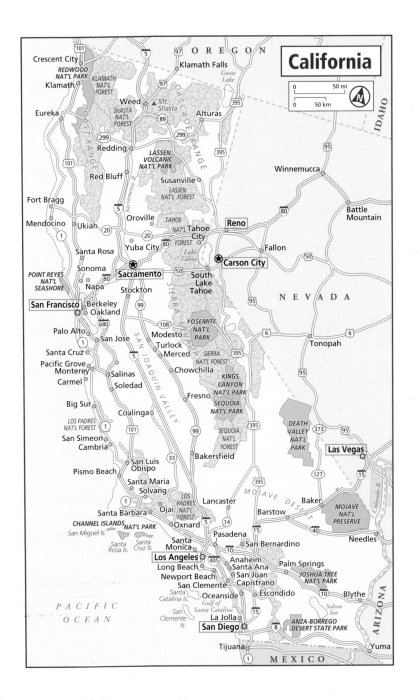

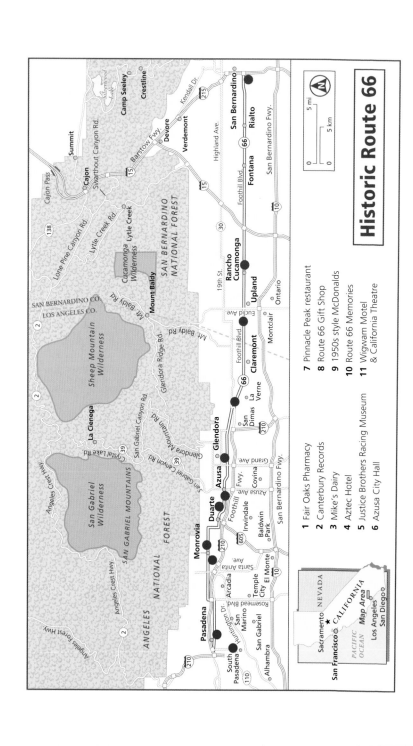

# Historic Route 66

1 Fair Oaks Pharmacy
2 Canterbury Records
3 Mike's Dairy
4 Aztec Hotel
5 Justice Brothers Racing Museum
6 Azusa City Hall
7 Pinnacle Peak restaurant
8 Route 66 Gift Shop
9 1950s style McDonalds
10 Route 66 Memories
11 Wigwam Motel & California Theatre

0 — 5 mi
0 — 5 km

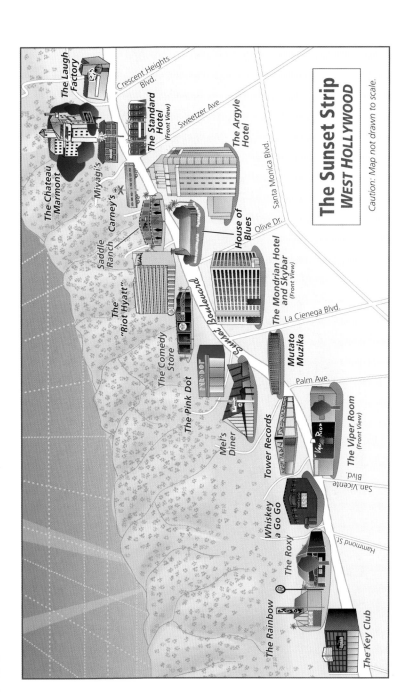

# The Sunset Strip
## *WEST HOLLYWOOD*

Caution: Map not drawn to scale.

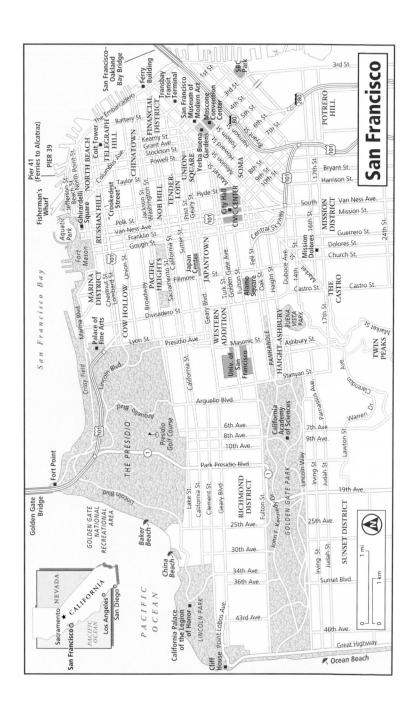

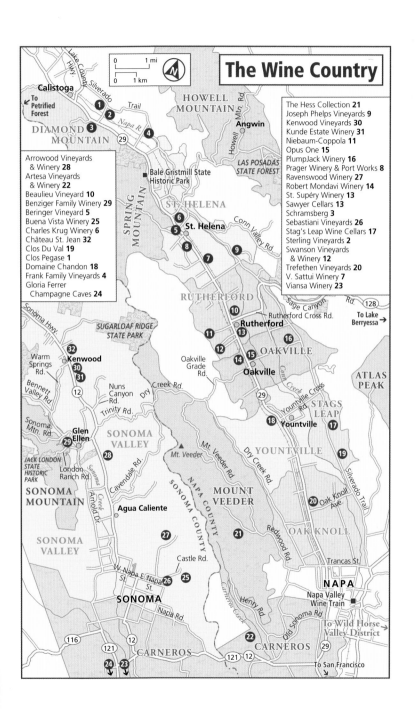

# The Wine Country

The Hess Collection **21**
Joseph Phelps Vineyards **9**
Kenwood Vineyards **30**
Kunde Estate Winery **31**
Niebaum-Coppola **11**
Opus One **15**
PlumpJack Winery **16**
Prager Winery & Port Works **8**
Ravenswood Winery **27**
Robert Mondavi Winery **14**
St. Supéry Winery **13**
Sawyer Cellars **13**
Schramsberg **3**
Sebastiani Vineyards **26**
Stag's Leap Wine Cellars **17**
Sterling Vineyards **2**
Swanson Vineyards
  & Winery **12**
Trefethen Vineyards **20**
V. Sattui Winery **7**
Viansa Winery **23**

Arrowood Vineyards
  & Winery **28**
Artesa Vineyards
  & Winery **22**
Beaulieu Vineyard **10**
Benziger Family Winery **29**
Beringer Vineyard **5**
Buena Vista Winery **25**
Charles Krug Winery **6**
Château St. Jean **32**
Clos Du Val **19**
Clos Pegase **1**
Domaine Chandon **18**
Frank Family Vineyards **4**
Gloria Ferrer
  Champagne Caves **24**

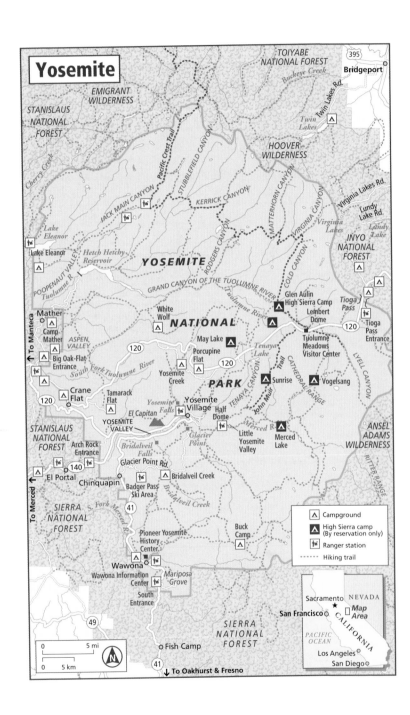

# Frommer's®

# California

# 2006

### by Harry Basch, Mark Hiss,
### Erika Lenkert & Matthew Richard Poole

WILEY

Wiley Publishing, Inc.

Published by:

## Wiley Publishing, Inc.

111 River St.
Hoboken, NJ 07030-5774

ISBN-13: 978-0-7645-9549-3
ISBN-10: 0-7645-9549-0

Editor: Maureen Clarke
Production Editor: Ian Skinnari
Cartographer: Tim Lohnes
Photo Editor: Richard Fox
Production by Wiley Indianapolis Composition Services

Back cover photo: Anza-Borrego Desert State Park: Dune Evening Primrose and Desert Sand Verbena in bloom

For information on our other products and services or to obtain technical support, please contact our Customer Care Department within the U.S. at 800/762-2974, outside the U.S. at 317/572-3993 or fax 317/572-4002.

Wiley also publishes its books in a variety of electronic formats. Some content that appears in print may not be available in electronic formats.

Manufactured in the United States of America

5   4   3   2   1

# Contents

## 12 The Monterey Peninsula & the Big Sur Coast    360

*by Matthew Richard Poole*

## 13 The Central Coast    405

*by Matthew Richard Poole*

## 14 Los Angeles    456

*by Matthew Richard Poole*

# List of Maps

## About the Authors

**Harry Basch** is the author of *Frommer's Exploring America by RV* and *RV Vacations For Dummies,* and a contributor to *Frommer's USA.* His books, articles, and photographs—many of which he produced in collaboration with his late wife, Shirley—have been published internationally for more than 25 years.

**Mark Hiss** is a San Diego–based writer and photographer, and a third generation Southern Californian.

A native San Franciscan, **Erika Lenkert** spends her time traipsing through San Francisco and across the globe in search of adventure and great food. She has written for *Travel + Leisure, Food & Wine, Bride's, Wine Country Living, San Francisco Magazine, Los Angeles Magazine,* and *Time Out.* Her latest work is an entertaining and cooking guide called *The Last-Minute Party Girl: Fashionable, Fearless, and Foolishly Simple Entertaining* (www.lastminutepartygirl.com), which mixes fun, humor, and recipes into a tasty, useful guide to living large, Bay Area–style.

**Matthew Richard Poole,** a native Californian, has authored more than two dozen travel guides to California, Hawaii, and abroad. A regular contributor to radio and television travel programs, he has made numerous guest appearances on the award-winning *Bay Area Backroads* television show, among other broadcast outlets. Before becoming a full-time travel writer and photographer, he worked as an English tutor in Prague, ski instructor in the Swiss Alps, and scuba instructor in Maui and Thailand. Highly allergic to office buildings and mortgage payments, he spends most of his time traveling the globe in search of new adventures. His other Frommer's titles include *California from $70 a Day, San Francisco from $70 a Day, Los Angeles, Portable Los Angeles,* the *Irreverent Guide to San Francisco,* and *Portable Disneyland*®.

## An Invitation to the Reader

In researching this book, we discovered many wonderful places—hotels, restaurants, shops, and more. We're sure you'll find others. Please tell us about them, so we can share the information with your fellow travelers in upcoming editions. If you were disappointed with a recommendation, we'd love to know that, too. Please write to:

*Frommer's California 2006*
Wiley Publishing, Inc. • 111 River St. • Hoboken, NJ 07030-5774

## An Additional Note

Please be advised that travel information is subject to change at any time—and this is especially true of prices. We therefore suggest that you write or call ahead for confirmation when making your travel plans. The authors, editors, and publisher cannot be held responsible for the experiences of readers while traveling. Your safety is important to us, however, so we encourage you to stay alert and be aware of your surroundings. Keep a close eye on cameras, purses, and wallets, all favorite targets of thieves and pickpockets.

---

## Other Great Guides for Your Trip:

*Frommer's California from $70 a Day*

*California For Dummies*

*The Unofficial Guide to California with Kids*

*Frommer's California's Best-Loved Driving Tours:
25 Unforgettable Itineraries*

*Frommer's Portable California Wine Country*

*Frommer's San Francisco*

*Frommer's Los Angeles*

*The Unofficial Guide to Disneyland®*

## Frommer's Star Ratings, Icons & Abbreviations

Every hotel, restaurant, and attraction listing in this guide has been ranked for quality, value, service, amenities, and special features using a **star-rating system.** In country, state, and regional guides, we also rate towns and regions to help you narrow down your choices and budget your time accordingly. Hotels and restaurants are rated on a scale of zero (recommended) to three stars (exceptional). Attractions, shopping, nightlife, towns, and regions are rated according to the following scale: zero stars (recommended), one star (highly recommended), two stars (very highly recommended), and three stars (must-see).

In addition to the star-rating system, we also use **seven feature icons** that point you to the great deals, in-the-know advice, and unique experiences that separate travelers from tourists. Throughout the book, look for:

| | |
|---|---|
| **Finds** | Special finds—those places only insiders know about |
| **Fun Fact** | Fun facts—details that make travelers more informed and their trips more fun |
| **Kids** | Best bets for kids and advice for the whole family |
| **Moments** | Special moments—those experiences that memories are made of |
| **Overrated** | Places or experiences not worth your time or money |
| **Tips** | Insider tips—great ways to save time and money |
| **Value** | Great values—where to get the best deals |

The following **abbreviations** are used for credit cards:

| | | | | | |
|---|---|---|---|---|---|
| AE | American Express | DISC | Discover | V | Visa |
| DC | Diners Club | MC | MasterCard | | |

## Frommers.com

Now that you have the guidebook to a great trip, visit our website at **www.frommers.com** for travel information on more than 3,000 destinations. With features updated regularly, we give you instant access to the most current trip-planning information available. At Frommers.com, you'll also find the best prices on airfares, accommodations, and car rentals—and you can even book travel online through our travel booking partners. At Frommers.com, you'll also find the following:

- Online updates to our most popular guidebooks
- Vacation sweepstakes and contest giveaways
- Newsletter highlighting the hottest travel trends
- Online travel message boards with featured travel discussions

# What's New in California

*Frommer's California 2006* features a new, 16-page section of enticing photographs, as well as handy color maps of our favorite things to see and do in the Golden State. We're also launching a new chapter of suggested itineraries for your trip, to help you make the most of your vacation time. Think of them as insiders' guides to memorable road trips in California, complete with detailed maps and recommended hotels and restaurants along the route. See chapter 4 for more details.

**SAN FRANCISCO** We have some good news and some bad news regarding the City by the Bay. The bad news is that the dip in tourism and the economy—which made hotels and restaurants cheaper and more readily available—is officially a thing of the past. The good news is that the city, post-recovery, is much more exciting. If you're headed here anytime soon, check out this lengthy list of the latest developments, to make the most of your trip. See chapter 5 for details.

**Where to Stay** Many hotels in town have been upgrading their rooms in recent years, making a stay by the Bay that much more comfortable. But 2005 was the year of the *new* hotel—from rock-bottom budget lodgings to the most highfalutin' luxury accommodations. On the less expensive end of the spectrum is **Elements Hotel,** 2524 Mission St. (© **866/327-8407** or 415/647-4100), the Mission District's stylish new youth hostel, as vibrant and heterogeneous as the

nightlife and restaurants in this traditionally funky, increasingly more upscale neighborhood. Although it hit the scene more than a year ago, **Hotel Carlton,** 1075 Sutter St. (© **800/922-7586** or 415/673-0242) made this list because it's a wee bit off the tourist trail. In the dreary outskirts of Union Square and Civic Center, it's an attractive and extremely well-priced option.

**Where to Dine** 2005 also marked the resurgence of fancy destination restaurants, the most chichi of which is **Michael Mina,** 335 Powell St. (© **415/397-9222**). As this book goes to press, the Westin St. Francis's new dining room is the sexiest hot spot in town—with lush, glamorous cream-on-cream surroundings; a lengthy, pricey wine list; and small plates that let diners experience 18 minicourses during what is technically a three-course meal. (Alas, fans of the Compass Rose, the tearoom formerly on the premises, may miss their Earl Gray and finger sandwiches, but so far the locals aren't complaining.) My favorite new fine dining spot downtown is **Campton Place,** 340 Stockton St. (© **415/955-5555**). And I'm not alone in my estimation: Daniel Humm, the young chef behind Campton's exquisite European cuisine, was a 2005 *Food & Wine* Best New Chef award winner, and nominated for a James Beard award as well. Across Market Street at **Fifth Floor,** 12 Fourth St. (© **415/348-1555**), three gals have taken this excellent restaurant to new heights since the departure of chef Laurent Gras. One of them is chef Melissa Perello, from Charles Nob Hill, who has garnered two James Beard nominations in the past two years; the second is Marika Doob, one of the city's very best pastry chefs; and the third is Emily Wines, who appropriately oversees the wine list. One of my favorite casual newcomers is **Levende Lounge,** 1710 Mission St. (© **415/864-5585**). The Mission's hottest thing going, it combines small plates worthy of a more serious setting with DJ music and a jumping bar scene.

**What to See and Do**    After closing for several years to await construction of a new building, the **de Young Museum,** 50 Hagiwara Tea Garden Dr. (© **415/682-2481**) is scheduled to reopen in Golden Gate Park in October 2005. The excellent collection includes American paintings, African arts, sculptural and decorative arts, and textiles.

**Shopping**    As if San Francisco didn't already offer enough reasons to beg your credit card company to up your limit, consider the latest addition to the Hayes Valley: At **R.A.G.,** 541 Octavia St. (© **415/621-7718**), you can snag affordable, one-of-a-kind female fashions made by up-and-coming local designers.

**THE WINE COUNTRY  Calistoga Ranch,** 580 Lommel Rd., Calistoga (© **707/254-2800**), integrates individual luxury cabins into a stunning canyon setting. In the more affordable category, retro motel and spa **Dr. Wilkinson's Hot Springs,** 1507 Lincoln Ave., Calistoga (© **707/942-4102**), opened a new facial cottage. It's sweet, private, and secluded. Best of all, the facials are superb. See chapter 7.

**THE NORTHERN COAST**    For just $75 you can spend the night in a rustic, romantic redwood cabin steps away from a small secluded beach. **Steep Ravine**

**Environmental Cabins** (© **415/388-2070**), near Stinson Beach, sleep up to five in quarters with only the most basic amenities: a wood-burning stove, platform beds, running water, and an outhouse. Four other new, reasonably priced accommodations warrant mention as well. In the tiny town of Elk, the **Griffin House Inn,** 5910 Hwy. 1 (© **707/877-3422**), has several romantic, cliffside cottages, and a terrific Irish pub on the premises. The best B&B in Point Reyes for the money, **Bear Valley Inn Bed & Breakfast,** 88 Bear Valley Rd., (© **415/663-1777**), is a two-story farmhouse from 1919, with rooms starting at $110. In Bodega Bay, the **Bodega Harbor Inn,** 1345 Bodega Ave. (© **707/875-3594**), offers rooms, cottages, and rental homes overlooking Bodega Bay. Way up north, in Eureka, the **Bayview Motel,** 2844 Fairfield St. (© **866/725-6813**), is one of the nicest, best landscaped motels I've ever seen. See chapter 8 for more details.

**THE FAR NORTH**    As South Lake Tahoe becomes more like Aspen each year, it's getting harder to find unique, affordable lodging. I did manage to discover the **Fireside Lodge,** 515 Emerald Bay Rd. (© **800/692-2246**), a small, log cabin-style inn that sits at the edge of the National Forest, with quick access to a public beach and miles of hiking and biking trails.

I've added a couple Lake Tahoe classics to this year's restaurant list: **Rosie's Café,** 571 North Lake Blvd., (© **530/583-8504**), is Tahoe City's most popular stop for comfort food in a cozy setting. And **Ernie's Coffee Shop,** 1146 Emerald Bay Rd. (© **530/541-2161**), is the undisputed king of South Lake Tahoe cafes. (I'm addicted to their milkshakes.) See chapter 9 for more details.

**THE HIGH SIERRA**    I've updated this entire chapter, with dozens of new attractions, restaurants, lodgings, and travel tips to Yosemite and Sequoia national parks. In addition to more than a dozen new dining options within Yosemite Valley, I've added new golf courses, whitewater rafting trips, ranger tours, and horseback riding. I've also included nearly a dozen new places to stay, ranging from romantic cabins in the woods to creekside B&Bs, rustic mountain lodges, and inexpensive tent cabins. One of my favorites is the **Evergreen Lodge** in Groveland (33160 Evergreen Rd.; © 800/935-6343), on the border of Yosemite National Park. Evergreen has 68 cozy cabins, scattered throughout a wooded grove of towering pines, and offers guided hikes, river rafting, horseback riding, and mountain biking throughout Yosemite. It also hosts campfire stories and serves pitchers of cold beer at the classic old bar. It's the ideal Yosemite experience without the maddening crowds. See chapter 10 for more details.

**SACRAMENTO & THE GOLD COUNTRY** For those of you who won't leave home without your canine pal, I've added the **Grass Valley Courtyard Suites**, 210 N. Auburn St. (© 530/272-7696), to our roster of accommodations. The selection of rooms is great; they have a swimming pool, spa, and sauna; and they serve a generous continental breakfast. Plus, they'll supply your "best friend" with a fuzzy little blanket. No bones about it.

When you're heading to **Volcano,** that most authentic ghost town in the central Sierras, be sure to visit the **Black Chasm,** 15701 Pioneer-Volcano Rd. (© 866/762-2837), a cave with stalactites, stalagmites, and rare crystals. A new visitors center explains the cave's history, contents, and mysterious connection to *The Matrix* movies (we're sworn to silence on this; you'll have to visit). Year-round, they run guided tours of the cave throughout the day. Above ground, kids can mine for gemstones.

The **Gate House Bed and Breakfast Inn**, 1330 Jackson Gate Rd., Jackson (© 800/841-1072), is a beautiful, historic mansion with a variety of accommodations, in the main house and in several cottages on the landscaped grounds. You'll waddle away after breakfast here, so save up your calories. In fact, don't plan to eat anything for the rest of the day, while you tour the surrounding area, so you can dine at **Buscaglia's Ristorante,** 1218 Jackson Gate Rd., Jackson (© 209/223-9992). A wide selection of hearty Italian dishes guarantees something for everybody in the family. See chapter 11 for more details.

**THE MONTEREY PENINSULA** I've added three fantastic new lodgings in Santa Cruz, the Carmel Valley, and Pinnacles National Monument. **Pleasure Point Inn,** 2-3665 East Cliff Dr. (© 831/475-4657), is the Santa Cruz seaside vacation house you've always wanted—complete with a rooftop deck overlooking the ocean, with an eight-person hot tub, surround-sound music, and chaise longues. Farther south in Carmel Valley, the **Bernardus Lodge,** 415 Carmel Valley Rd. (© 888/648-9463), is rated one of the top hotels in the country. With luxurious, adobe-style guesthouses, a championship golf course, a full spa, a meditation garden, a croquet lawn and bocce court, two tennis courts, and a top-ranked restaurant, it's a tough place to leave. I've also added new information about **Pinnacles National Monument** (one of my favorite Central Coast escapes)—including tips on spotting the elusive California condor, and a review of the new **Inn at the Pinnacles,** 32025 Stonewall Canyon Rd. (© 831/678-2400). The park's only lodgings, this hacienda-style, six-room inn offers private patios with gas grills and unblemished views of rolling vineyards. See chapter 12 for more details.

**THE CENTRAL COAST** This year, I spent 3 weeks traveling up the Central Coast and found so much new material I could write an entire guidebook about it.

Highlights include a complete overhaul of the **Hearst Castle** section, including expanded reviews, new places to stay and dine in Cambria, and a side trip to an elephant seal rookery. I've also added a daytrip to the **Golden Sand Dunes of Gaudalupe,** the largest and most diverse coastal dune–lagoon ecosystem on the planet ((C) **805/343-2455;** www.dunes center.org). In Paso Robles, I had a pleasant stay at **Villa Toscana Bed & Breakfast,** 4230 Buena Vista Dr. ((C) **805/238-5600)**—a new all-suites inn fashioned after a lavish Spanish villa, with views of surrounding vineyards from every room. I also found a great place to buy picnic supplies for a day of wine tasting: **Odyssey World Café,** 1214 Pine St. ((C) **805/237-7516),** in downtown Paso Robles.

The section on **Solvang** ("More Danish than Denmark") was a bit anemic in the last edition, so I've added several pages on the Central Coast's most popular bakeries, shops, museums, and side trips to quiet wine country towns. The section on **Los Olivos** has new reviews of **Fess Parker's Wine Country Inn & Spa,** 2860 Grand Ave. ((C) **800/446-2455)** and **Los Olivos Café,** 2879 Grand Ave. ((C) **805/688-7265).**

If you prefer seaside accommodations, I highly recommend the new **The Brakey House Bed & Breakfast,** 411 Poli St. ((C) **805/643-3600),** in Ventura. On a hill overlooking the town and ocean, this 1890 Cape Cod–style home is made for couples, with king-size beds, Jacuzzi tubs, and cast-iron fireplaces. And it's a short stroll to the shops and restaurants along Main Street. See chapter 13 for more details.

**LOS ANGELES Where to Dine** In the past 12 months, so many excellent restaurants have opened in L.A. they're calling it the city's Golden Age of dining. I've included several of the best, such as **Grace,** 7360 Beverly Blvd. ((C) **323/934-4400),** my new favorite. Executive chef

and co-owner Neal Fraser is destined to be L.A.'s next celebrity chef. (I'm still swooning from his pumpkin risotto with sea urchin and sweet Maine shrimp.) A close second for best newcomer is **Beacon,** 3280 Helms Ave., Culver City ((C) **310/838-7500),** where Spago-trained chef Kazuto Matsusaka thrills his fans with reasonably priced Asian-fusion dishes such as warm crispy oysters set in cool lettuce cups, and miso-marinated black cod. Executive Chef Josef Centeno's globally inspired cuisine at the stylish new **Meson G,** 6703 Melrose Ave. ((C) **323/525-1415),** is sensational: a series of small plates ranging from Maine scallop ceviche to foie gras *panna cotta.* **Ortolan,** 8338 W. Third St. ((C) **323/653-3300),** is another hit newcomer, a glamorous venue with velvet curtains, crystal chandeliers, and superb French cuisine by Executive Chef Christophe Emé. With its hip atmosphere and übertender steaks, **Boa,** 101 Santa Monica Blvd., Santa Monica ((C) **310/899-4466),** has quickly become one of L.A.'s most "in" restaurants. **Locanda del Lago,** 231 Arizona Ave., Santa Monica ((C) **310/451-3525),** on the other hand, has been popular for nearly 15 years, but I wish I'd known about it the day it opened. Their pappardelle tossed in a duck ragout was the best pasta dish I've ever had, and the *osso bucco* is also outstanding.

**What To See & Do** This edition features all sorts of exciting new things to see and do in L.A. **Universal Studios Hollywood** ((C) **800-UNIVERSAL)** has a new thrill ride called **Revenge of the Mummy,** a hyper high-tech indoor roller coaster with creepy animatronic "warrior mummies." They also just opened the *Fear Factor Live* show, where park guests compete against each other in a progression of extreme stunts.

The **Getty Museum** ((C) **310/440-7300)** now offers free GettyGuides, a handheld multimedia system at the information desk. The nifty orange iPod-like device tracks a visitor's location within the huge museum and provides various tours for immediate use, with in-depth information on specific art objects.

I've also added an outrageous new **Celebrity Helicopters** (© 877/999-2099) product: The fly-and-dine Night Tour begins with a 25-minute aerial city tour and ends with a landing atop a Downtown skyscraper, where dinner is served. (How cool is that?) And **Segway L.A.,** 1660 Ocean Ave., Santa Monica (© 310/395-1395), is providing yet more fun in the sun, with those goofy, two-wheeled "Human Transporter" scooters. They're a blast to ride along the paved shoreline path at Venice Beach and the Santa Monica Pier. And *everyone* checks you out.

In Marina del Rey, Captain Larry of **Free Spirit Sailing Adventures** (© 310/780-3432) will lead you on a full-day coastal outing aboard the *Carmina Mare,* a 46-foot cutter-rigged motorsailor.

In case you've always wanted to watch a polo match, I've included information about the **Will Rogers Polo Club** (© 310/573-5000). Matches take place on weekends at Will Rogers State Park from mid-April through early October.

**Shopping** Resident L.A. shopping expert Tracy Larrua filled me in on the hottest new stores. The new entries are too numerous to list here, but highlights include: **A.B.S. by Allen Schwartz,** 1533 Montana Ave. (© 310/393-8770), which carries inexpensive knock-offs of celebrity award show getups; **DNA Clothing Co.,** 411 Rose Ave. (© 310/399-0341), an invaluable resource for film and television stylists and costumers; and my favorite, **Panty Raid,** 2378½ Glendale Blvd. (© 323/668-1888), a sexy boutique for designer lingerie and hanky panky accessories.

**After Dark** You won't get into this year's hottest clubs unless you're on a list.

**Whiskey Blue,** 930 Hilgard Ave. (© 310/443-8232), at the W Hotel in Westwood, is *the* scene where Westside glitterati come to *be* seen. **White Lotus,** 1743 N. Cahuenga Blvd. (© 323/463-0060), is another restaurant/nightclub where celebrity limos regularly clog the street outside.

If you think waiting in line is for losers, you'll be happier (and stand a better chance of gaining entry) at the new **Star Shoes** club in Hollywood, 6364 Hollywood Blvd. (© 323/462-7827). Trendy young partiers pack this combination shoe store/dance club. If you hate all that überhip dig-me crap, head to **King King,** 6555 Hollywood Blvd. (© 323/960-9234), a poser-free venue that feels more like SoHo than L.A.

In the same Hollywood area, **Cine-Space,** 6356 Hollywood Blvd. (© 323/817-3456), is a stylish Hollywood supper club that serves great food—and stiff cocktails—while screening recent hits, indies, classics, and shorts.

If single-malt whiskey and fine cigars are essential to your idea of a great night out, don't miss the **Lone Wolf Cigar Company** in Santa Monica, 223-B Broadway Blvd. (© 800/577-9653). You can enjoy a rare indoor, guilt-free smoke here, on soft leather couches.

If you need passes to an L.A. event of any kind, turn to **Good Time Tickets** (© 800/464-7383; www.goodtime tickets.com). Based in Hollywood for more than 30 years, this private company specializes in ticket sales to sporting, theater, music, and other entertainment events throughout the city.

See chapter 14 for more details.

**SIDE TRIPS FROM L.A.** This big chapter includes dozens of new additions (far too many to list here)—from **Monarch Adventures** (© 949/254-8139), a surfing school along the Orange Coast to the **Cape Canyon** backcountry tours of Catalina (© **800/626-1496**) and a fantastic new accommodation called **The Avalon Hotel,** 124 Whittley Ave. (© **310/510-7070**). Disney parks worldwide continue to celebrate the 50th anniversary of the original **Disneyland,** 1300 South Harbor Blvd., Anaheim (© **714/781-7290**), with an 18-month tribute featuring new shows, parades, rides, and fireworks. The Disneyland Resort's hottest new attraction is the **Twilight Zone Tower of Terror,** where you board an elevator only to plunge 13 stories to the fifth dimension and beyond. See chapter 15 for more details.

## SOUTHERN CALIFORNIA DESERT

Are you ready for a $1,000 caviar and lobster omelet? Then get thee to **Le Parker,** Palm Springs newest luxury resort, on the premises of the former Gene Autry Melody Ranch and Merv Griffin's Givenchy Resort and Spa. If you knew those properties in the past, you won't recognize the Parker, after $27 million's worth of renovations (4200 E. Palm Canyon Dr.; © **760/770-5000;** www.the parkerpalmsprings.com).

Under new management, the **Villa Royale,** 1620 Indian Trail, Palm Springs (© **800/245-2314**) has merely tweaked the original resort—subtly improving every aspect of a desert oasis known for its quiet charm. The Villa Royale's glorious restaurant, **Europa,** is hardly the least of its charms. See chapter 16.

## SAN DIEGO & ENVIRONS

Old Town State Historic Park, California's most-visited state park, showcases San Diego's past and now also hosts one of its newest attractions, **Plaza del Pasado,** 2754 Calhoun St. (© **619/297-3100;** www.plazadelpasado.com). This shopping and dining complex features 11 retail stores, 3 restaurants, and 1 boutique hotel. All adhere to an early California motif (circa 1821–72), with employees in period costume. Strolling musicians,

special events and activities, and an education center round out the scene.

Another San Diego attraction celebrating the past, the **Maritime Museum,** 1492 N. Harbor Dr. (© **619/234-9153;** www.sdmaritime.org), has added to its collection of historic vessels with the acquisition of a B-39 Soviet attack submarine. The 300-foot-long Cold War relic, which was built in 1971 and decommissioned in 1994, joins—among other big boats—the Star of India, the world's oldest active ship (built in 1863), and the H.M.S. *Surprise,* a replica of an 18th-century Royal Navy frigate used in the film *Master and Commander: The Far Side of the World.*

San Diego, especially the downtown Gaslamp Quarter, is experiencing an explosion of new clubs, restaurants, and hotels. A long-promised **House of Blues,** 1055 Fifth Ave. (© **619/299-2583**), finally opened, featuring an eclectic lineup of top rock, blues, and world-music acts, as well as Southern-inspired cuisine. HOB's collection of outsider and folk art is reason alone to visit.

New downtown hotels are getting in on the act, too, with the **San Diego Marriott Gaslamp Quarter,** 660 K St. (© **619/696-0234;** www.sandiegogas lamphotel.com), and **Hotel Solamar,** 435 Sixth Ave. (© **877/230-0300;** www.hotel solamar.com)—both of which are launching hot nightspots. The Marriott's roof-top **Altitude** (660 K St.; © **619/ 696-0234**) sits 22 stories above the city, offering stellar views of the Coronado Bridge, the Convention Center and PETCO Park, home of Major League Baseball's San Diego Padres; while Solamar debuted **Jbar** (616 J St.; © **619/ 531-8744**), another open-air, rooftop space, on the less vertigo-inducing fourth floor. Jbar offers draped cabanas, fire pits, and menu selections from the downstairs restaurant, **Jsix.**

See chapter 17 for details.

# 1

# The Best of California

*by Harry Basch, Mark Hiss, Erika Lenkert & Matthew Richard Poole*

In my early 20s, I took the requisite college student's pilgrimage to Europe, exploring its finer train stations and sleeping on the premier park benches from London to Istanbul. I was relatively anonymous—just another tanned and skinny, blond and blue-eyed American with a backpack. That is, until I crossed into the former Eastern Bloc.

The reaction there was dramatic, almost palpable. Like Moses parting the sea, I wandered the crowded streets of Prague and citizens would stop, stare, and step aside as if I bore a scarlet letter "A" across my chest. It wasn't until a man with faltering English approached me that I discovered the reason for my newfound celebrity status.

"Eh, you. Where you from? No, no. Let me guess." He stepped back and gave a cursory examination, followed by a pregnant pause. "Ah. I've got it! California! You're from California, no?" His eyes gleamed as I told him that, yes, he was quite correct. "Wonderful! Wonderful!" A dozen or so pilsners later with my loquacious new friend, and it all became clear to me: To him, I was a celebrity—a rich, convertible-driving surfer who spent most his days lazing on the beach, fending off hordes of buxom blondes while arguing with his agent via cellphone. The myth is complete, I thought. I *am* the Beach Boys. I *am* *Baywatch*. Status by association. The tentacles of Hollywood have done what no NATO pact could achieve—they've leapfrogged the staid issues of capitalism versus communism by offering a far more potent narcotic: the mystique of sun-drenched California, of movie stars strolling down Sunset Boulevard, of beautiful women in tight shorts and bikini tops roller-skating along Venice Beach. In short, they've bought what the movie industry is selling.

Of course, the allure is understandable. It *is* warm and sunny most days of the year, movie stars *do* abound in Los Angeles, and you can't swing a cat by its tail without hitting a rollerblading babe in Venice Beach. This part of the California mystique, however exaggerated, *does* exist, and it's not hard to find.

But there's more—a lot more—to California that isn't scripted, sanitized, and squeezed through a cathode-ray tube to the world's millions of mesmerized masses. Beyond the Hollywood glitter is a wondrously diverse state that, if it ever seceded from the Union, would be one of the most productive, powerful nations in the world. We've got it all: misty redwood forests, an exceptionally verdant Central Valley teeming with agriculture, the mighty Sierra Nevada Mountain Range, eerily fascinating deserts, a host of world-renowned cities and, of course, hundreds of miles of stunning coastline.

And despite the endemic crime, pollution, traffic, and bowel-shaking earthquakes for which California is famous, we're still the golden child of the United States, America's spoiled rich kid, either loved or loathed by everyone else. (Neighboring Oregon, for example, sells lots of license-plate rims that proudly state, "I hate California.") Truth be told, however, we don't care what anyone thinks of us. Californians *know* they live in one of the most diverse and interesting places in the world, and we're proud of the state we call home.

Granted, we can't guarantee that you'll bump into Arnold Schwarzenegger or learn to surf, but if you have a little time, a little money, and an adventurous spirit, then Harry, Mark, Erika, and I will help guide you through one of the most fulfilling vacations of your life. The four of us travel the world for a living, but we *choose* to live in California—simply because no other place on earth has so much to offer.

—*Matthew Richard Poole*

## 1 The Best of Natural California

- **Redwood National & State Parks:** Acres of inconceivably massive redwood trees, up to 350 feet tall, tower over thick, lush, oversized ferns, mosses, and wild orchids in the old-growth forests along the Northern California coast. Walking through these groves is an unforgettably humbling, serene experience. See "Redwood National & State Parks" in chapter 8.

- **Lake Tahoe:** One of the world's most magnificent bodies of fresh water, sparkling Lake Tahoe contains close to 40 trillion gallons—enough to cover the entire state of California to a depth of 14½ inches. See "Lake Tahoe" in chapter 9.

- **Yosemite National Park:** You're in for the ultimate treat at Yosemite. Nothing in the state—maybe even the world—compares to this vast wilderness and its miles of rivers, lakes, peaks, and valleys. With 3 of the 10 tallest waterfalls on earth, the largest granite monolith anywhere, and some of the world's largest trees, Yosemite is one of the most superlative natural places on the planet. See "Yosemite National Park" in chapter 10.

- **Big Sur:** Sloping redwood forests and towering cliffs pounded by the Pacific create one of the world's most dramatic coastal panoramas. See "The Big Sur Coast" in chapter 12.

- **Point Reyes National Seashore:** This extraordinarily scenic stretch of coast and wetlands is one of the state's best bird-watching spots for waterfowl, shorebirds, songbirds, osprey, and red-shouldered hawks. You might even catch a glimpse of a whale from the Point Reyes Lighthouse. See "Point Reyes National Seashore" in chapter 8.

- **Mount Shasta:** The mighty volcano Mount Shasta, a solitary tower of rock and snow, rises thousands of feet above the valley floor. If you're in good shape, it makes for an exhilarating climb as well. See "Mount Shasta & the Cascades" in chapter 9.

- **Channel Islands National Park:** This is California in its most virginal state. Paddle a kayak into sea caves; camp among indigenous island fox and seabirds; and swim, snorkel, or scuba dive tide pools and kelp forests teeming with wildlife. The channel waters are prime for whale-watching, and winter brings elephant-seal–mating season, when you'll see them and their sea-lion cousins sunbathing on cove beaches. See "Channel Islands National Park" in chapter 13.

- **Joshua Tree National Park:** You'll find awesome rock formations; groves of flowering cacti and gnarly, eerily beautiful Joshua trees; ancient Native American petroglyphs; and shifting sand dunes in this desert wonderland. If you choose to camp here, you'll sleep under a brilliant night sky. See "Joshua Tree National Park" in chapter 16.

- **Anza-Borrego Desert State Park:** The largest state park in the lower 48 attracts the most visitors during the spring wildflower season, when a kaleidoscopic carpet blankets the desert. Others come year-round to hike more than 100 miles of trails. See "Anza-Borrego Desert State Park" in chapter 16.

- **Torrey Pines State Reserve:** On a cliff above the Pacific Ocean, this state park is set aside for the most rare pine trees in North America. The reserve has short trails that immerse hikers into a delicate and beautiful coastal environment. See chapter 17.

## 2 The Best Beaches

- **Sonoma Coast State Beaches:** Stretching 10 miles from Bodega Bay to Jenner, these beaches draw more than 300 bird species. Look for osprey from December to September, seal pups from March to June, and gray whales from December to April. See "Along the Sonoma Coast" in chapter 8.

- **Santa Cruz's Beaches:** Santa Cruz has 29 miles of beaches, varied enough to please surfers, swimmers, fishers, sailboarders, the sand-pail-and-shovel set, and the bikini-and-biceps crowd. For starters, walk down the steps from the famous Santa Cruz Beach Boardwalk to the mile-long Main Beach, complete with summer lifeguards and golden-oldie tunes drifting over the sand. See "Santa Cruz" in chapter 12.

- **Pismo Beach:** Pismo's 23-mile stretch of prime beachfront has been an annual destination for generations of California families. Fishing, shopping, surfing, and renting dune buggies are just a few of the many outdoor activities here. Even dogs are welcome to play on the beach. See "Pismo Beach" in chapter 13.

- **Santa Barbara's East Beach:** This wide swath of white sand hosts beach umbrellas, sandcastle builders, and volleyball games. On Sundays, local artists display their wares beneath the palm trees. See "Santa Barbara" in chapter 13.

- **Malibu's Legendary Beaches:** Zuma and Surfrider beaches inspired the 1960s surf music that embodies the Southern California coast experience. Surfrider, just up from Malibu Pier, is home to L.A.'s best waves. Zuma is loaded with amenities, including snack bars, restrooms, and jungle gyms. The beach hosts some of the state's best sunbathing and allows you to stroll in front of the Malibu Colony, a star-studded enclave of multimillion-dollar homes. See "L.A.'s Beaches & Coastal Attractions" in chapter 14.

- **La Jolla's Beaches:** "La Jolla" may be misspelled Spanish for "the jewel," but *this* is no mistake: The bluff-lined beaches here are among the state's most beautiful. Each has a distinct personality: Surfers love Windansea's waves; harbor seals have adopted the Children's Pool; La Jolla Shores is popular for swimming, sunbathing, and kayaking; while the Cove is a top snorkeling spot—and the best place to spot the electric-orange California state fish, the garibaldi. See "Beaches" in chapter 17.

## 3 The Best Golf Courses

- **Pebble Beach Golf Links:** The famous 17-Mile Drive is the site of 10 national championships and the celebrity-laden AT&T Pebble Beach National Pro-Am. The nearby Pacific and a backdrop of the Del Monte

Forest *almost* justify the astronomical greens fees. See "Pebble Beach & the 17-Mile Drive" in chapter 12.

- **Poppy Hills** (Pebble Beach): *Golf Digest* has called this Robert Trent Jones, Jr.–designed course one of the world's top-20 greens. Cutting through the pines of Del Monte Forest, it's maintained in state-of-the-art condition. Unlike some of its competitors, it's rarely crowded. See "Pebble Beach & the 17-Mile Drive" in chapter 12.

- **PGA West TPC Stadium Course** (La Quinta): The par-3 17th hole has a tiny island where Lee Trevino made Skins Game history with a hole in one. The rest of Pete Dye's 7,261-yard design is flat with huge bunkers, lots of water, and severe mounding throughout. See "The Palm Springs Desert Resorts" in chapter 16.

- **Torrey Pines Golf Course** (La Jolla): Two 18-hole championship courses overlook the ocean and provide players with plenty of challenges. In February, the Buick Invitational Tournament takes place here. The rest of the year, these popular municipal courses are open to everybody. See "Outdoor Pursuits" in chapter 17.

## 4 The Best Californian Travel Experiences

- **Hot-Air Ballooning over Napa Valley:** Sure, you have to rise at dawn to do it, but drifting over the Napa Valley's vineyards in a balloon is the best way to view the verdant, undulating hills, meticulously striped with vines and bordered by mountains. Flights run in the morning on clear days, when the air is calm and cool. You can book a trip through your hotel or with **Bonaventura Balloon Company** (© **800/FLY-NAPA**) or **Adventures Aloft** (© **800/944-4408**). See "Hot-Air Ballooning over the Valley" in chapter 7.

- **Wine Tasting in Napa or Sonoma:** You don't have to be a connoisseur to appreciate a day or two on the wine trail. All you need is a decadent streak and a designated driver. Sniff and sip at a few wineries, take in the bucolic views, and see why this region is not only one of the country's hottest destinations, but also a place to sample some of the world's best wines right at the source. See chapter 7.

- **Rafting Scenic Northern California Rivers:** You can white-water raft through thrilling cascades of raging Class IV waters or float tranquilly under blue skies, through deep forests, past all sorts of wildlife. Depending on the river and the time of year, some trips are okay for children over age 6. See chapters 9, 10, and 11.

- **Exploring a Real Gold Mine:** Don your hardhat, "tag in," board the mine shuttle, and experience what it's like to be a gold miner. The **Sutter Gold Mine** tour company (© **866/762-2837**) takes you deep into a mine that's loaded with gold deposits. You'll have the chance to sluice for some real gold. See p. 345.

- **Taking a Studio Tour:** Studio tours are an opportunity to see the actual stage sets for shows such as *ER* and *The West Wing,* and you never know who you're going to spot emerging from his or her star wagon. See "Exploring the City" in chapter 14.

- **Visiting Venice Beach's Ocean Front Walk:** You haven't visited L.A. properly until you've rented some skates in Venice and taken in the human carnival around you. Nosh on a Jody Maroni's haute dog; buy some cheap sunglasses, silver jewelry, or ethnic garb, and relish the wide beach, blue sea, and performers along the boardwalk. See "L.A.'s Top Attractions" in chapter 14.

- **Flying a World War II Fighter Aircraft:** Don your parachute, strap yourself into the 600-horsepower fighter aircraft, and prepare to blow your mind as you (yes, *you*) perform aerobatic maneuvers—loops, rolls, and lazy-8s—high above the Carlsbad coastline, accompanied (but not driven) by a pilot from Biplane, Air Combat & Warbird Adventures (© **800/SKY-LOOP**). It's an experience you'll never forget. See p. 622.

- **Explore Wreck Alley** (San Diego): Five drowned vessels sit on the sea floor, 2 miles off Mission Beach, providing certified divers the chance to investigate an exciting nautical graveyard, which includes a 366-foot Canadian destroyer, the *Yukon* (intentionally sunk in 2000). See "Outdoor Pursuits" in chapter 17.

## 5 The Best of Small-Town California

- **St. Helena:** In the heart of the Napa Valley, St. Helena is known for its Main Street. In a horse and buggy, Robert Louis Stevenson and his bride once made their way down this thoroughfare lined with Victorian homes. The Painted Ladies remain, but now they're stores for designer clothing, hardware, bath products, you name it. Come for the old-time, tranquil mood and the food. See "Napa Valley" in chapter 7.

- **Mendocino:** An artists' colony with a New England flavor, Mendocino served as the backdrop for *Murder, She Wrote.* On the cliffs above the Pacific Ocean, it's filled with small art galleries, general stores, weathered wooden houses, and organically inclined restaurants. See "Mendocino" in chapter 8.

- **Arcata:** If you're losing faith in America, restore it by spending a few days in this Northern California coastal town. Arcata has it all: its own redwood forest and bird marsh, a charming town square, great family-owned restaurants, even its own minor-league baseball team, which draws the whole town together on many an afternoon. See "Eureka & Environs" in chapter 8.

- **Nevada City:** The entire town is a national historic landmark and the best place to understand Gold Rush fever. Settled in 1849, it offers fine dining and shopping and a stock of the multigabled Victorian frame houses of the Old West. Relics of the Donner Party are on display at the 1861 Firehouse No. 1. See "The Gold Country" in chapter 11.

- **Pacific Grove:** You can escape the Monterey crowds by heading 2 miles west to Pacific Grove, known for its tranquil waterfront and unspoiled air. Thousands of monarch butterflies flock here between October and March. See "Pacific Grove" in chapter 12.

- **Ojai:** When filmmakers needed a Shangri-La for the movie *Lost Horizon,* they drove to Ojai Valley, with its unspoiled eucalyptus groves and small ranches nestled in soft, green hills. Ojai is the amiable village at the valley's heart. It's a mecca for artists, free spirits, and weary city folk in need of a restful weekend in the country. See "The Ojai Valley" in chapter 13.

- **Santa Catalina Island:** A day trip to the small town of Catalina makes for a most indulgent day: Take a scenic boat ride, shop, snorkel and dive, golf, hike, lick ice cream, get a sunburn, and barhop sans fear of a DUI.

*Tip:* The helicopter taxi is cheaper than you'd expect. See "Santa Catalina Island" in chapter 15.

- **Julian:** This old mining town in the Cuyamaca Mountains near San Diego has long been known for its apple harvest, its apple pies, and its charming bed-and-breakfasts. Forest fires in October 2003 shook Julian and the surrounding communities, but from a touring standpoint, most of the area is back to normal. There's plenty of pioneer legacy here, including a local-history museum, an 1888 schoolhouse, and mining demonstrations. See "Julian: Gold, Apple Pies & a Slice of Small-Town California" in chapter 17.

## 6 The Best Family Vacation Experiences

- **San Francisco:** The City by the Bay will please every member of the family. If you're traveling with kids, ride the cable cars that "climb halfway to the stars," visit the Exploratorium, the Metreon, the zoo, the ships at the National Maritime Museum, Golden Gate Park, and more. See chapter 5.

- **Lake Tahoe:** Lake Tahoe has fun activities galore for families: skiing, snowboarding, hiking, tobogganing, swimming, fishing, boating, water-skiing, mountain biking, etc. The possibilities seem endless. See "Lake Tahoe" in chapter 9.

- **Yosemite National Park:** Camping or sleeping in a cabin in Yosemite is one of California's premier attractions for families. Sites lie scattered over 17 campgrounds, surrounded by the rugged Sierra Nevadas. During the day, families can pack their schedule with hiking, bicycling, white-water rafting, scaling snowy peaks, and more. See "Yosemite National Park" in chapter 10.

- **Santa Cruz:** This funky bayside town has everything you need for an ideal family vacation: surfing, sea kayaking, hiking, fishing, and shopping. And those fantastic beaches and the legendary amusement park on the boardwalk will please travelers of all ages. See "Santa Cruz" in chapter 12.

- **Disneyland Resort:** The "Happiest Place on Earth" is enhanced by its sister theme park, **Disney's California Adventure.** Whether you're wowed by Disney animation, thrilled by the roller-coaster rides, or interested in the history and secrets of this pop-culture juggernaut, you won't walk away disappointed. Get a FASTPASS to skip those long lines! See "The Disneyland Resort" in chapter 15.

- **San Diego Zoo, Wild Animal Park, & SeaWorld:** San Diego boasts three of the world's best animal attractions. At the zoo, animals live in naturalistic habitats such as Monkey Trails and Forest Tails (the most elaborate enclosure it has ever created), and it's one of only four zoos in the U.S. with giant pandas. At the Wild Animal Park, most of the 3,500 animals roam freely over a 1,800-acre spread. And Sea-World, with its water-themed rides, flashy animal shows, and detailed exhibits, is an aquatic wonderland of pirouetting dolphins and 4-ton killer whales with a penchant for drenching visitors. See "The Three Major Animal Parks" in chapter 17.

## 7 The Best Architectural Landmarks

- **The Golden Gate Bridge** (San Francisco): More tomato red than golden, the famous bridge remains the cheery hallmark of the San Francisco skyline.

It's also an excellent expanse to walk. See "The Top Attractions" in chapter 5.

- **California State Capitol** (Sacramento): The Golden State's dazzling white capitol was built in 1869 and renovated in 1976. Its dome, which looks like a Faberge egg from inside, and original statuary along its eaves remain, and antiques from the original offices furnish its historic rooms. The collection of California governors' portraits is strangely compelling. See "Sacramento" in chapter 11.

- **Mission San Carlos Borromeo del Río Carmelo** (Carmel): The second mission founded in California, in 1770 by Father Junípero Serra, is perhaps the most beautiful. Its stone church and tower dome have been restored, and a garden of poppies adjoins the church. See "Carmel-by-the-Sea" in chapter 12.

- **Hearst Castle** (San Simeon): This 165-room estate of publishing magnate William Randolph Hearst is one of the last great estates of America's Gilded Age. It's an astounding, over-the-top monument to unbridled wealth and power. See "San Simeon: Hearst Castle" in chapter 13.

- **Walt Disney Concert Hall:** You would have to fly to Spain to see Frank Gehry's other architectural masterpiece, and this one is sufficiently awe-inspiring. And the dramatically curvaceous stainless-steel exterior houses one of the most acoustically perfect concert halls in the world. See p. 527.

- **The Gamble House** (Pasadena): The Smithsonian Institution calls this Pasadena landmark, built in 1908, "one of the most important houses in the United States." Architects Charles and Henry Greene created a masterpiece of the Japanese-influenced Arts and Crafts movement. Visitors can tour the spectacular interior—designed by the Greenes down to the last piece of teak furniture and coordinating Tiffany lamps, and executed with impeccable craftsmanship. See p. 540.

- **Balboa Park** (San Diego): The Spanish Revival–style buildings along El Prado were built as temporary structures for the Panama-California Exposition (1915–16). The ornately decorated and imposing facades create a sort of romantic fantasia amid the beautifully landscaped mesas and canyons that constitute one of the country's finest city parks, home to many of the city's top museums. See "Exploring the Area" in chapter 17.

## 8 The Best Museums

- **California State Railroad Museum** (Sacramento): Old Sacramento's biggest attraction, the 100,000-square-foot museum was once the terminus of the Transcontinental and Sacramento Valley railways. It displays nearly two dozen locomotives and railroad cars, among other attractions. See p. 330.

- **J. Paul Getty Museum at the Getty Center** (Los Angeles): Designed by Richard Meier and completed in 1997 to the tune of $1 billion, the Getty Center is a striking, starkly futuristic architectural landmark, with panoramic views of the city and ocean. The building itself is enough reason to visit, but so is the permanent collection, the crown jewel of which is Van Gogh's "Irises," which the museum paid $53.9 million to acquire. See p. 519.

- **Petersen Automotive Museum** (Los Angeles): This museum is a natural for Los Angeles, a city whose personality and history is so entwined with the popularity of the automobile. Impeccably restored vintage autos are displayed in life-size dioramas accurate to the last period detail (including an authentic 1930s-era service station). Upstairs galleries house movie star and motion-picture vehicles, car-related artwork, and exhibits. See p. 530.

- **The Museums of Balboa Park** (San Diego): Balboa's museums afford a variety of cultural experiences in a relaxed, verdant setting. My favorites include the Aerospace Museum, the Museum of Photographic Arts, the Model Railroad Museum, the Botanical Building, the Timken Museum of Art, and the Mingei International Museum of Folk Art. Check in at the House of Hospitality for a map and "Passport to Balboa Park," a low-cost combination pass to the museums. See p. 713.

## 9 The Best Luxury Hotels & Resorts

- **The Ritz-Carlton** (© 800/241-3333): Two blocks from the top of Nob Hill, San Francisco's Ritz is world-renowned for its accommodating staff, luxurious amenities, and top-rated restaurant. Another bonus is the most lavish brunch in town, served on Sundays in the Terrace Room or on the patio amid blooming rose bushes. See p. 94.

- **Calistoga Ranch** (© 707/254-2800): Napa Valley's latest upscale hotel blows away the competition, with individual luxury cabins stocked with every imaginable luxury. In a secluded canyon, it's where nature meets nurture with a fabulous pool, spa, gym, and guest-only restaurant overlooking a lake. See p. 178.

- **Château du Sureau** (Oakhurst; © 559/683-6860): Close to Yosemite, the Château du Sureau and Erna's Elderberry House restaurant stand out for their subtle European attention to quality and detail. Furnishings are exquisite in the individually decorated rooms, and the cuisine is worthy of the stars. See p. 289.

- **Casa Palmero Resort** (Pebble Beach; © 800/654-9300): A small, ultraluxury resort on the first tee of the Pebble Beach Golf Course, Casa Palmero has 24 cottages and suites, all very intimate and private. In addition, the splendors of Pebble Beach will amuse you. See p. 384.

- **Post Ranch Inn** (Big Sur; © 800/527-2200): Twelve-hundred feet above the sea, the elevated wood-and-glass guest cottages at this romantic cliffside retreat give guests the illusion that they're living at cloud level. See p. 398.

- **Four Seasons Resort Santa Barbara Biltmore** (Santa Barbara; © 800/819-5053): Open since 1927, this Four Seasons operation (often known as "the Biltmore," on the grounds of the historic Biltmore Hotel), has palm-studded formal gardens and a prime beachfront location along "America's Riviera." Meander through the elegant Spanish-Moorish arcades and walkways, accented by exquisite Mexican tile, and then play croquet on manicured lawns, or relax at the Coral Casino Beach and Cabana Club. The rooms are the epitome of refined luxury. See p. 441.

- **Shutters on the Beach** (Santa Monica; © 800/334-9000) and **Casa del Mar** (Santa Monica; © 800/898-6999): If an oceanfront room at either of these hotels doesn't put a spring in your love life, it's hard to imagine what will. Which one is best for you depends on your taste: Shutters is dressed up like a rich friend's contemporary-chic beach house, while glamorous Casa del Mar is an impeccably restored Deco-era delight. See p. 479 and 478.

- **Beverly Hills Hotel and Bungalows** (Beverly Hills; © 800/283-8885): A deep dent in your credit card is a small price to pay for the chance to take afternoon tea next to Ozzy Osbourne in the Polo Lounge, swim laps in the same pool Katharine Hepburn once dove into fully clothed, and eat pancakes in the fabled Fountain Coffee Shop. See p. 483.

- **La Quinta Resort & Club** (La Quinta; © 800/598-3828): This luxury resort, set in a grove of palms at the base of the Santa Rosa Mountains, is surrounded by some of the desert's best golf courses. Single-story, Spanish-style cottages are set amid gardens and 24 "private" swimming pools. The lounge and library in the original hacienda remain unaltered, hearkening back to the days when Clark Gable, Greta Garbo, and other celebrities escaped to the seclusion of La Quinta. See p. 647.

- **The Lodge at Torrey Pines** (La Jolla; © 800/656-0087): You don't need to know much about Craftsman-style architecture to appreciate the taste and artistry that went into creating this luxury resort. The lodge sits next to the Torrey Pines Golf Course, and you can enjoy a fireplace in your room, sunset ocean views from your balcony, and superb meals at the hotel's A.R. Valentien restaurant. See p. 690.

## 10  The Best Affordable Small Hotels & Inns

- **St. Orres** (Gualala; © 707/884-3303): Designed in a Russian style—complete with two Kremlinesque, onion-domed towers—St. Orres offers secluded accommodations constructed from century-old timbers salvaged from a nearby mill. One of the most eye-catching inns on California's North Coast. See p. 211.

- **Albion River Inn** (Albion; © 800/479-7944): One of the best rooms-with-a-view on the coast, the Albion River Inn is on a cliff overlooking a rugged stretch of shoreline. Most of the luxuriously appointed rooms have Jacuzzi tubs for two, elevated to window level. Add champagne and you're guaranteed to have a night you won't soon forget. See p. 219.

- **River Ranch Lodge** (Lake Tahoe; © 800/535-9900): Alongside the Truckee River, the River Ranch has long been one of our favorite affordable inns around Lake Tahoe. It has everything you'd want in a mountain lodge: rustic decor, a great bar and outdoor deck overlooking the river, and a restaurant serving wood-oven-roasted Montana elk loin and other hearty dishes. See p. 260.

- **Evergreen Lodge** (Yosemite; © 800/935-6343): Scattered through a grove of towering pines near the entrance to Yosemite, Evergreen's rustic cabins, with a beautiful old bar and restaurant, afford easy access to dozens of outdoor adventures. Enjoy a pitcher of beer and a game of Ping-Pong on the patio, or sit around the campfire telling stories and roasting marshmallows; it's all part of the Evergreen experience. See p. 285.

- **The Mosaic** (Beverly Hills; © 800/463-4466): This Beverly Hills boutique is an ideal blend of art, luxury, service, location, and value. Huge rainforest showerheads, Frette linens, Bulgari bath products, Wolfgang Puck refreshments, and piles of pillows will leave you wondering if you checked in at the pearly gates. See p. 486.

- **Casa Malibu** (Malibu; ✆ **800/831-0858**): This beachfront motel will fool you from the front; its humble entrance on the Pacific Coast Highway belies the quiet, restful haven within. Bougainvillea vines festoon the rooftops and balconies of the motel's 21 rooms around a courtyard garden. Many rooms have private decks above the sand, and one suite was reportedly Lana Turner's favorite. See p. 482.

- **Olallieberry Inn** (Cambria; ✆ **888/927-3222**): This 1873 Greek Revival house, furnished in a floral-and-lace Victorian style, is an ideal base for exploring Hearst Castle. The gracious innkeepers provide everything from directions to Moonstone Beach to restaurant recommendations—and a scrumptious breakfast in the morning. See p. 412.

- **Casa Cody** (Palm Springs; ✆ **800/231-2639**): You'll feel more like a houseguest than a client at this 1920s Spanish-style *casa* blessed with peaceful, blossoming grounds and two swimming pools. The Southwestern-style rooms are large and equipped for extended stays, and the hotel is just a couple of easy blocks from the heart of the action. See p. 645.

- **La Pensione Hotel** (San Diego; ✆ **800/232-4683**): In Little Italy, on the fringe of downtown San Diego, this find feels like a small, modern European hotel, with tidy lodgings at bargain prices. Great dining options abound in the surrounding blocks, and you'll be perfectly situated to explore the rest of the city and region by car. The immediate neighborhood is filled with art galleries and some of the city's most dashing new architecture. See p. 682.

## 11 The Best Places to Stay with the Kids

- **KOA Kamping Kabins** (Point Arena; ✆ **800/562-4188**): Once you see the adorable log cabins at this KOA campground, you'll have to admit that this is one cool way to spend the weekend on the coast. Primitive is the key word: mattresses, a heater, and a light bulb are the standard amenities. All you need is some bedding (or sleeping bags), cooking and eating utensils, and charcoal for the barbecue out front. See p. 213.

- **City Hotel** and **Fallon Hotel** (Columbia; ✆ **800/532-1479**): Some parents may roll their eyes at this preserved Gold Rush town, but it's rather remarkable. Visitors can ride a 100-year-old stagecoach, visit a blacksmith shop, and view lots of mining artifacts. And these reasonably priced Victorian hotels dish up a great buffet breakfast. Cars are barred from the dusty main street. See p. 352.

- **Camping at Yosemite's Tuolumne Meadows** (✆ **800/436-7275**): At an elevation of 8,600 feet, this is the largest alpine meadow in the High Sierra and a gateway to the "high country;" it's especially memorable in late spring, when it's carpeted with wildflowers. Park authorities run the large campground and a full-scale naturalist program, but hardcore adventurers can backpack into the wilderness. See p. 301.

- **Disneyland Resort Hotels** (Anaheim; ✆ **714/956-MICKEY**): The Holy Grail of Disney lovers has always been the "Official Hotel of the Magic Kingdom," the original **Disneyland Hotel** (p. 605). The newer **Paradise Pier Hotel** (p. 605) and **Grand Californian** (p. 604) are also an easy monorail or tram ride to Disneyland's gates (the Grand Californian opens directly into California Adventure). See p. 604.

- **Marriott's Desert Springs Spa & Resort** (Palm Desert; ℭ **800/331-3112**): In the spirit of Disney-esque resorts, this oasis welcomes guests with a "rainforest" lobby featuring tropical birds and gondolas that ferry guests to their rooms. Once settled,

kids will revel in the lag and play areas (with sup dren's programs). And grov luxuriate on the golf cour ennis court, or in the 30,000-square-foot day spa. See p. 647.

- **Crystal Pier Hotel** (San Diego; ℭ **800/748-5894**): On a historic pier that extends into the Pacific Ocean, this property affords guests the experience of sleeping *over* the ocean in a cottage. Ideal for beach-loving families, who can enjoy the sound of waves or head out for boardwalk action; beach gear is available for rental. See p. 686.

## 12 The Best Restaurants

- **San Francisco's Finest:** In this town, it's sacrilege to *attempt* naming the "top" restaurant. For a perfect combo of food and atmosphere, though, we count on **Campton Place** (ℭ **415/955-5555**; p. 99), **Restaurant Gary Danko** (ℭ **415/749-2060;** p. 110), and **Zuni Café** (ℭ **415/552-2522;** p. 114).

- **Chez Panisse** (Berkeley; ℭ **510/548-5525**): This is the domain of Alice Waters, "the queen of California cuisine." Originally inspired by the Mediterranean, her kitchen has found its own style, and her food captivates the senses as well as the imagination. Chez Panisse's delicacies include dishes such as grilled fish wrapped in fig leaves with red-wine sauce, and Seckel pears poached in red wine with burnt caramel. See p. 146.

- **Bistro Don Giovanni** (Napa; ℭ **707/224-3300**): In this large, cheery Napa Valley dining room you can get an incredible Italian meal without a reservation. Just drop in and wait at the bar for a seat. See p. 183.

- **Terra** (Napa; ℭ **707/963-8931**): One of the best choices in the state,

this small restaurant affords its patrons intimacy, outstanding food by Hiro Sone (one of California's best chefs), great wine, heavenly desserts, and complete freedom from pretense. See p. 183.

- **Restaurant 301** (Eureka; ℭ **800/404-1390**): A recipient of *Wine Spectator's* Grand Award, Mark Carter is passionate about food and wine, and it shows: His hotel restaurant is considered the best on the Northern Coast. Most of the herbs and many vegetables served are picked fresh from the hotel's organic gardens. Indulge in the five-course fixed-price dinner menu; Carter pairs each course with an excellent wine, available by the glass, or as part of a wine flight. See p. 230.

- **Erna's Elderberry House** (Oakhurst; ℭ **559/683-6800**): Erna's shines like a beacon across the culinary wasteland around Yosemite. The six-course menu, which changes nightly, is an ideal blend of Continental and Californian cuisine. Portions are bountiful, and the European ambience is elegant. See p. 289.

- **bouchon** (Santa Barbara; Ⓒ 805/730-1160): With an intriguing seasonal menu derived from Santa Barbara County's wine country, this intimate restaurant (whose name means "wine cork") is hidden behind a shrubbery portal in the heart of downtown. The food and service are impeccable, and an experienced staff stands ready to help coordinate by-the-glass (or even half-glass) wines for each course. See p. 443.

- **The Hump** (Santa Monica; Ⓒ 310/313-0977): The chefs here are deadly serious about their sushi. Flown in daily from Tokyo's Tsukijii and Fukuoka fish markets in oxygen-filled containers, it's so fresh a sign at the entrance warns the faint-of-heart that the meat's still moving. See p. 498.

- **Koi** (West Hollywood; Ⓒ 310/659-9449): One of L.A.'s hottest restaurants has A-list celebrities arriving nightly for addictive dishes such as baked crab rolls with edible rice paper. Koi is a killer combo of good feng shui and superb Asian fusion cuisine. See p. 507.

- **Bertrand at Mister A's** (San Diego; Ⓒ 619/239-1377): With the city's most delectable views, this longtime San Diego institution was reborn in 2000 after a reported $1-million makeover. The owners molded a very old-school, vaguely campy space into an elegant, bright, sophisticated dining destination with excellent American-Mediterranean fare. See p. 697.

## 13 The Best Culinary Experiences

- **Grazing at San Francisco's Farmers Market:** In 2003, San Francisco's favorite outdoor culinary fair moved to the Ferry Building Marketplace, where some of the best artisan food producers and restaurants have storefronts. Stop by anytime to peruse the exceptional, abundant selection of gourmet shops and restaurants, or join the locals during open-air market days—Tuesday and Thursday—to feast on the freshest vegetables, fruits, and prepared foods from beloved restaurants. See "The Top Attractions" in chapter 5.

- **A Decadent Meal in the Wine Country:** As a setting, the Wine Country is a better backdrop for indulgent dining than any other place in the state. Add the best wines and some of the most talented chefs in the nation, and you've got what we consider the ultimate dining experience. Diners with deep pockets must reserve an evening meal at **The French Laundry** in St. Helena (Ⓒ 707/944-2380); see p. 182. More moderately priced memories can be made at aforementioned **Terra** (Ⓒ 707/963-8931; p. 183).

- **Tomales Bay Oysters: Johnson's Oyster Farm** (Ⓒ 415/669-1149) sells its farm-fresh oysters—by the dozen or the hundreds—for a fraction of the price you'd pay at a restaurant. See "Point Reyes National Seashore" in chapter 8.

- **A Date with the Coachella Valley:** Some 95% of the world's dates are farmed here. While the groves of date palms make evocative scenery, it's their fruit that draws visitors to the National Date Festival in Indio each February. Amid the Arabian Nights Parade and camel races, you can feast on an array of plump Medjool, amber Deglet Noor, caramel-like Halawy, and buttery Empress dates. The rest of the year, date farms and markets sell dates from the season's harvest, as well as date milkshakes, date coconut rolls, and more. See "Sweet Treat of the Desert: The Coachella Valley Date Gardens" in chapter 16.

## 14 The Best of the Performing Arts & Special Events

- **The San Francisco Opera** (© 415/ 864-3330): This world-class company performs at the War Memorial Opera House, modeled after the Opéra Garnier in Paris. The season opens with a gala in September and runs through December. This was the first municipal opera in the United States, and its productions and members have been acclaimed throughout the world. See p. 135.

- **The San Francisco Symphony** (© 415/864-6000): The symphony is such a hot ticket, it's hard to get a seat in advance. If your concierge doesn't have any tricks up his or her sleeve, you can always try to buy tickets at the door, and someone is usually attempting to sell theirs at the last second. See p. 136.

- **The American Conservatory Theater** (San Francisco; © 415/749-2ACT): The A.C.T. is one of the nation's leading regional theaters. It has been called the American equivalent of the British National Theatre, the Berliner Ensemble, and the Comédie Française in Paris. See p. 135.

- **The Monterey Jazz Festival** (© 831/ 373-3366): When the third weekend of September rolls around, the Monterey Fairgrounds draws jazz fans from around the world. The 3-day festival (which usually sells out a month in advance) is known for the sweetest jazz west of the Mississippi. See "Calendar of Events" in chapter 2.

- **The Hollywood Bowl** (Los Angeles; © 323/850-2000): This iconic outdoor amphitheater is the summer home of the Los Angeles Philharmonic, a stage for visiting virtuosos—including the occasional pop star—and the setting for splendid fireworks shows throughout the summer. See p. 569.

- **Festival of Arts/Pageant of the Masters** (Laguna Beach): These events draw crowds to the Orange County coast every July and August. Begun in 1932 by a handful of painters, the festival has grown to showcase hundreds of artists. In the evening, crowds marvel at the Pageant of the Masters' *tableaux vivants,* in which costumed townsfolk pose inside a giant frame and depict famous works of art, accompanied by music and narration. See "The Orange Coast" in chapter 15.

- **The Old Globe** (San Diego; © 619/ 239-2255): This Tony Award–winning, three-theater complex, fashioned after Shakespeare's original stage, celebrated its 70th anniversary in 2005. It has launched Broadway hits such as *Dirty Rotten Scoundrels, The Full Monty,* and *Into the Woods,* and has billed such notable performers as John Goodman, Hal Holbrook, and Ellen Burstyn. In 2004, the theater revived its outdoor summer Shakespeare Festival, featuring three of the Bard's plays in nightly rotation. See p. 726.

# 2

# Planning Your Trip to California

*by Matthew Richard Poole*

In the pages that follow, we've compiled everything you need to know to handle the practical details of planning your trip—from making campsite reservations to finding great deals on the Internet, plus a calendar of events and much more.

## 1 Visitor Information

### VISITOR INFORMATION

For information on the state as a whole, see the **California Tourism** website at www.visitcalifornia.com. Residents of the United States and Canada can receive free travel planning information in the mail by calling © **800/862-2543** (an operator will ask for your mailing address). In addition, almost every city and town in the state has a tourist bureau or chamber of commerce that will send you information on its particular area. These are listed under the appropriate headings in the geographically organized chapters that follow.

International travelers should also see chapter 3 for entry requirements and other pertinent information.

**PARK INFORMATION** To find out more about California's national parks, contact the **Pacific West Region Information Center,** National Park Service, 1111 Jackson St., Suite 700, Oakland, CA

94607 (© **510/817-1300;** www.nps.gov). Reservations can be made at national park campsites by calling © **800/365-CAMP** (800/436-PARK for Yosemite) or logging on to http://reservations.nps.gov from 7am to 7pm (PST).

For information on state parks, contact the **Department of Parks and Recreation,** P.O. Box 942896, Sacramento, CA 94296-0001 (© **800/777-0369;** http://cal-parks.ca.gov). Thousands of campsites are on the department's reservation system and can be booked up to 8 weeks in advance by calling **Park-Net** at © **800/444-PARK.** You can also get reservations information online at www.reserveamerica.com.

For information on fishing and hunting licenses, contact the **California Department of Fish and Game,** License and Revenue Branch, 3211 S St., Sacramento, CA 95816 (© **916/227-2245;** www.dfg.ca.gov).

## 2 Money

### ATMs

The **Cirrus** (© **800/424-7787;** www.mastercard.com) and **PLUS** (© **800/843-7587;** www.visa.com) automated teller machine networks span the globe;

look at the back of your bank card to see which network you're on, then call or check online for ATM locations at your destination. Be sure you know your personal identification number (PIN) before you leave home and find out your daily withdrawal limit before you depart. Keep in mind that many banks impose a fee every time you use their card at a different bank's ATM, and that fee can be higher for international transactions (up to $5 or more) than for domestic ones. On top of this, the bank from which you withdraw cash may charge its own fee. To compare banks' ATM fees within the U.S., use www.bankrate.com. For international withdrawal fees, ask your bank.

You can also get cash advances on your credit card at an ATM. Keep in mind that credit card companies try to protect themselves from theft by limiting the funds people can withdraw outside their home country, so call your credit card company before you leave home. And keep in mind that you'll pay interest from the moment of your withdrawal, even if you pay your monthly bills on time.

## TRAVELER'S CHECKS

Traveler's checks are something of an anachronism from the days before the ATM made cash accessible at any time. Keep in mind, however, that you will likely be charged an ATM withdrawal fee if the bank is not your own, so if you're withdrawing money every day, you might be better off with traveler's checks—provided that you don't mind showing identification every time you want to cash one.

You can get traveler's checks at almost any bank. **American Express** offers denominations of $20, $50, $100, $500, and (for cardholders only) $1,000. You'll pay a service charge ranging from 1% to 4%. You can also get American Express traveler's checks over the phone by calling ℂ **800/221-7282;** Amex gold and platinum cardholders who use this number are exempt from the 1% fee.

**Visa** offers traveler's checks at Citibank locations nationwide, as well as at several other banks. The service charge ranges between 1.5% and 2%; checks come in denominations of $20, $50, $100, $500, and $1,000. Call ℂ **800/732-1322** for information. AAA members can obtain Visa checks for a $9.95 fee (for checks up to $1,500) at most AAA offices or by calling ℂ **866/339-3378. MasterCard** also offers traveler's checks. Call ℂ **800/223-9920** for a location near you.

**Foreign currency traveler's checks** are useful if you're traveling to one country, or to the euro zone; they're accepted at locations such as bed-and-breakfasts where dollar checks may not be, and they minimize the amount of math you have to do at your destination. **American Express, Thomas Cook, Visa,** and **MasterCard** offer foreign currency traveler's checks. You'll pay the rate of exchange at the time of your purchase (so it's a good idea to monitor the rate before you take the plunge), and most companies charge a transaction fee per order (and a shipping fee if you order online).

If you choose to carry traveler's checks, be sure to keep a record of their serial numbers separate from your checks in the event that they are stolen or lost. You'll get a refund faster if you know the numbers.

## CREDIT CARDS

Credit cards are a safe way to carry money: They also provide a convenient record of all your expenses, and they generally offer relatively good exchange rates. You can also withdraw cash advances from your credit cards at banks or ATMs, provided you know your PIN. If you've forgotten yours, or didn't even know you had one, call the number on the back of your credit card and ask the bank to send it to you. It may take 5 to 7 business days.

Some companies ask that you notify them of an impending trip so they don't suspect fraud and block your charges. If you skip this step, carry the card's toll-free emergency number with you (see "Fast Facts," p. 47), separate from your card, so you can call if a charge is refused. Most importantly, carry more than one card; one might not work for any number of reasons, so it's best to have a backup.

For tips and telephone numbers to call if your wallet is stolen or lost, go to "Lost & Found" in the "Fast Facts" section of this chapter.

## 3 When to Go

### CLIMATE

California's climate is so varied that it's impossible to generalize about the state as a whole.

San Francisco's temperate marine climate means relatively mild weather year-round. In summer, temperatures rarely top 70°F (21°C; pack sweaters, even in Aug), and the city's famous fog rolls in most mornings and evenings. In winter the mercury seldom falls below freezing, and snow is almost unheard of. Because of the fog, summer rarely sees more than a few hot days in a row. Head a few miles inland, though, and it's likely to be clear and hot.

The Central Coast shares San Francisco's climate, although it gets warmer as you get farther south. Seasonal changes are less pronounced south of San Luis Obispo, where temperatures remain relatively stable year-round. The Northern Coast is rainier and foggier; winters tend to be mild but wet.

Summers are refreshingly cool around Lake Tahoe and in the Shasta Cascades—perfect for hiking, camping, and other outdoor activities and a popular escape for residents of the sweltering deserts and valleys who are looking to beat the heat. Skiers flock to this area for terrific snowfall from late November to early April.

Southern California—including Los Angeles and San Diego—is usually much warmer than the Bay Area, and it gets significantly more sun. Even in winter, daytime temperatures regularly reach into the 60s (15°C–20°C) and warmer. Summers can be stifling inland, but Southern California's coastal communities are always comfortable. The area's limited rainfall is generally seen between December and mid-April, and is rarely intense enough to be more than a slight inconvenience. It's possible to sunbathe throughout the year, but only die-hard enthusiasts and wet-suited surfers venture into the ocean in winter. The water is warmest in summer and fall, but even then, the Pacific is too chilly for many.

The deserts, including Palm Springs and the desert national parks, are sizzling hot in summer; temperatures regularly

### San Francisco's Average Temperatures

|  | Jan | Feb | Mar | Apr | May | June | July | Aug | Sept | Oct | Nov | Dec |
|---|---|---|---|---|---|---|---|---|---|---|---|---|
| Avg. High (°F) | 56 | 59 | 60 | 61 | 63 | 64 | 64 | 65 | 69 | 68 | 63 | 57 |
| Avg. High (°C) | 13 | 15 | 16 | 16 | 17 | 18 | 18 | 18 | 21 | 20 | 17 | 14 |
| Avg. Low (°F) | 46 | 48 | 49 | 49 | 51 | 53 | 53 | 54 | 56 | 55 | 52 | 47 |
| Avg. Low (°C) | 8 | 9 | 9 | 9 | 11 | 12 | 12 | 12 | 13 | 13 | 11 | 8 |

### Los Angeles's Average Temperatures

|  | Jan | Feb | Mar | Apr | May | June | July | Aug | Sept | Oct | Nov | Dec |
|---|---|---|---|---|---|---|---|---|---|---|---|---|
| Avg. High (°F) | 65 | 66 | 67 | 69 | 72 | 75 | 81 | 81 | 81 | 77 | 73 | 69 |
| Avg. High (°C) | 18 | 19 | 19 | 21 | 22 | 24 | 27 | 27 | 27 | 25 | 23 | 21 |
| Avg. Low (°F) | 46 | 48 | 49 | 52 | 54 | 57 | 60 | 60 | 59 | 55 | 51 | 49 |
| Avg. Low (°C) | 8 | 9 | 9 | 11 | 12 | 14 | 16 | 16 | 15 | 13 | 11 | 9 |

top 100°F (38°C). Winter is the time to visit the desert resorts (and remember, it gets surprisingly cold at night in the desert).

## AVOIDING THE CROWDS

The period between Memorial Day and Labor Day is the height of the tourism season virtually everywhere—except for desert areas like Palm Springs and Death Valley, where sizzling temperatures keep all but the hardiest bargain hunters away. California's pleasant summer weather (with relatively low humidity) has a lot to do with these numbers, but the season is also popular simply because that's when most people, especially families with kids, get to take that precious vacation time. So, naturally, prices are highest between Memorial Day (late May) and Labor Day (early Sept) in much of the state, and can fall dramatically outside of that period—exceptions to this rule include the aforementioned deserts and winter ski resorts. *Insider tip:* Californians know the best time to travel the state is autumn. That's roughly from late September to early December, when crowds drop off, "shoulder season" rates kick in, and before winter rains loom on the horizon.

## CALENDAR OF EVENTS

### January

**Tournament of Roses,** Pasadena. A spectacular parade marches down Colorado Boulevard, with lavish floats, music, and extraordinary equestrian entries, followed by the Rose Bowl football game and a nightlong party along Colorado Boulevard. Call © **626/449-4100** or see www.tournamentof roses.com for details. January 1.

### February

**AT&T Pebble Beach National Pro-Am,** Pebble Beach. A PGA-sponsored tour where pros team up with celebrities to compete on three famous golf courses. Call © **800/541-9091** or 831/649-1533, or visit www.attpbgolf.com. Early February.

**Chinese New Year and Golden Dragon Parade,** Los Angeles. Dragon dancers and martial arts masters parade through the streets of Downtown's Chinatown. Chinese opera and other events are scheduled. For this year's schedule, contact the Chinese Chamber of Commerce at © **213/617-0396** or visit www.lachinesechamber.org. Late January or early February.

**National Date Festival,** Indio. Crowds gather to celebrate the Coachella Valley desert's most beloved cash crop with events like camel and ostrich races, the Blessing of the Date Garden, and Arabian Nights pageants. Plenty of date-sampling booths are set up, along with rides, food vendors, and other county-fair trappings. Call © **800/811-3247** or 760/863-8247, or visit www.datefest.org. Two weeks mid-February.

**Mardi Gras,** West Hollywood. You'll find the food and festivities along Santa Monica Boulevard, from Doheny Drive to La Brea Avenue, and in the alley behind Santa Monica Boulevard. Call the West Hollywood Convention & Visitors Bureau at © **800/368-6020** for details. Late February or early March.

**Mustard Festival,** Napa Valley. Celebrating the blossom of yellow-petaled mustard flowers, which coat the valley during February and March, the event was conceived to drum up visitors during this once-slow season. The festival has evolved into 6 weeks of events from a kickoff gourmet gala to a wine auction, recipe and photography competitions, and plenty of food and wine. For information and a schedule, call © **707/259-9020** or 707/938-1133, or visit www.mustardfestival.com. February and March.

## March

**Santa Barbara International Film Festival.** For 10 days each March, Santa Barbara does its best impression of Cannes. There's a flurry of foreign and independent film premieres, appearances by actors and directors, and symposia on cinematic topics. For a rundown of events, call ✆ **805/963-0023.** Early to mid-March.

**Return of the Swallows,** San Juan Capistrano. Each St. Joseph's Day, visitors flock to this charming village for the arrival of the mission's loyal flock of swallows that nest and remain until October. The celebration includes a parade, dances, and special programs. Call ✆ **949/234-1300** for details. March 19.

**Kraft Nabisco Championship,** Rancho Mirage. This 33-year-old LPGA golf tournament takes place near Palm Springs. After the celebrity Pro-Am early in the week, the best female pros get down to business. For further information, call ✆ **760/324-4546** or visit www.nabiscochampionship.com. Other special-interest events for women usually take place around the tournament, including the country's largest annual lesbian gathering. Last week of March.

**Redwood Coast Dixieland Jazz Festival,** Eureka. Three days of jazz featuring a dozen or so of the best Dixieland groups. Call ✆ **707/445-3378.** Late March.

## April

**San Francisco International Film Festival.** One of the nation's oldest film festivals, featuring more than 100 films and videos from 30-plus countries. Tickets are inexpensive, and screenings accessible to the general public. Call ✆ **415/931-FILM** or visit www.sffs.org. Mid-April to early May.

**Toyota Grand Prix,** Long Beach. An exciting weekend of Indy-class auto racing and entertainment in downtown Long Beach draws world-class drivers from the United States and Europe, plus many celebrity contestants and spectators. Contact the Grand Prix Association at ✆ **888/82-SPEED** or www.longbeachgp.com. Mid-April.

**Renaissance Pleasure Faire,** San Bernardino. This annual event in the relatively remote Glen Helen Regional Park is one of America's largest Renaissance festivals. It features an Elizabethan marketplace with costumed performers. The fair provides an entire day's activities, including shows, food, and crafts. You're encouraged to come in period costume. For ticket information, call ✆ **800/52-FAIRE,** or log onto the national website, http://renaissance-faire.com. Weekends from late April to Memorial Day.

**ArtWalk,** San Diego. This free, 2-day festival in stylish Little Italy is the largest art event in the San Diego/Tijuana region, with some 70,000 people each year. It features visual and performing arts—painting, photography, music, and drama—in outdoor venues, galleries, artist studios, and businesses. The event also offers hands-on art experiences for kids. Call ✆ **619/615-1090** or visit www.artwalkinfo.com. Late April.

## May

**Cinco de Mayo.** A weeklong celebration of one of Mexico's most jubilant holidays takes place throughout Los Angeles near May 5. Large crowds, live music, dances, and food create a carnival-like atmosphere. The main festivities are held in El Pueblo de Los Angeles State Historic Park, with other events around the city. Call ✆ **213/485-6855** for information.

There's also a Cinco de Mayo celebration in Old Town, San Diego, featuring folkloric music, dance, food, and historical reenactments. Call ✆ **619/296-3161** for more information.

**Calaveras County Fair and Jumping Frog Jubilee,** Angels Camp. Inspired by Mark Twain's "The Celebrated Jumping Frog of Calaveras County," this race draws entrants and frogs and their guardians from all over. Call ✆ **209/736-2561** or see www.frogtown.org. Third weekend in May.

**Paso Robles Wine Festival.** What began as a small, neighborly gathering has grown into the largest outdoor wine tasting in California. The 3-day event features winery open houses and tastings, a golf tournament, 5K run and 10K bike ride, and concerts, plus a festival in downtown's City Park. For a schedule, call ✆ **800/549-WINE** or visit www.pasowine.com. Third weekend in May.

**Bay to Breakers Foot Race,** San Francisco. One of the city's most popular annual events, it's more fun than run. Thousands of entrants show up dressed—or undressed—in their best costumes for the 7.5-mile run. Call ✆ **415/777-7770** or log on to www.baytobreakers.com. Third Sunday of May.

**Carnival,** San Francisco. The Mission District's largest annual event is a 2-day series of festivities that culminates with a parade on Mission Street over Memorial Day weekend. More than half a million spectators line the route, and the samba musicians and dancers continue to play on 14th Street, near Harrison, at the end of the march. Call the hot line at ✆ **415/920-0125** or visit www.carnavalsf.com. Memorial Day weekend.

**June**

**San Francisco Lesbian, Gay, Bisexual, Transgender Pride Parade.** It's celebrated over various weekends throughout the state in June and July, but San Francisco's party draws up to half a million participants. The parade heads west from Market Street and Beale to Market and Eighth Street, where hundreds of food, art, and information booths are set up around several stages. Call ✆ **415/864-3733** or visit www.sfpride.org for info. Usually the third or last weekend of June.

**Ojai Music Festival.** This event has been drawing world-class classical and jazz personalities to the open-air Libbey Bowl since 1947. Past events have featured Igor Stravinsky, Aaron Copland, and the Juilliard String Quartet. Seats (and local lodgings) fill up quickly; call ✆ **805/646-2094** for more information, or log on to www.ojaifestival.org. Early June.

**Mariachi USA Festival,** Los Angeles. For this 2-day family-oriented celebration of Mexican culture at the Hollywood Bowl, festival-goers pack their picnic baskets and enjoy music, folkloric ballet, and related performances by top groups. The all-day, all-night celebration is one of the largest mariachi festivals in the world. For tickets, call ✆ **800-MARIACHI** or 323/850-2000 (the Hollywood Bowl), or log onto www.mariachiusa.com.

**San Diego County Fair.** Referred to as the Del Mar Fair by locals, this is the other big happening (besides horse racing) at the Del Mar Fairgrounds. The whole county turns out for the 3-week event, with livestock competitions, rides, flower and garden shows, food and craft booths, carnival games, and home-arts exhibits; concerts by name performers are included with admission.

Call ✆ **858/793-5555,** or check www. sdfair.com. Mid-June through early July.

## July

**Mammoth Lakes Jazz Jubilee.** A 4-day festival featuring 20 bands on 10 different stages, plus food, drink, and dancing—all under the pine trees and stars. Call ✆ **760/934-2478** or see www.mammothjazz.org. Second weekend in July.

**World Championship Over-the-Line Tournament,** San Diego. The beach softball event dates from 1953 and is renowned for boisterous, beer-soaked, anything-goes behavior—over 1,000 three-person teams compete, and upwards of 50,000 attend. It's a heap of fun for the open-minded but a bit much for small kids. It takes place on Fiesta Island in Mission Bay; admission is free. For more details, call ✆ **619/688-0817** or visit www.ombac.org. Mid-July.

**Gilroy Garlic Festival.** A gourmet food fair with more than 85 booths serving garlicky food from almost every ethnic background, plus close to 100 arts, crafts, and entertainment booths. Call ✆ **408/842-1625** or visit www.gilroygarlicfestival.com. Last full weekend in July.

**Thoroughbred Racing Season,** Del Mar. The "turf meets the surf" during the thoroughbred racing season at the Del Mar Race Track. Post time is 2pm most days; the track is dark on Tuesdays. Keep your eyes out for the occasional celebrity. For this year's schedule, call ✆ **858/792-4242.** Mid-July to mid-September.

**Beach Festival,** Huntington Beach. Two weeks of fun in the sun featuring two surfing competitions—the U.S. Open of Surfing and the world-class Pro of Surfing—plus extreme sports like BMX biking, skateboarding, and

more. The festival includes entertainment, food, tons of product booths and giveaways—and plenty of tanned, swimsuit-clad bodies of both sexes. For more information, call ✆ **714/969-3492** or log onto www.hbvisit.com. End of July.

**U.S. Open Sandcastle Competition,** San Diego. The quintessential beach event: a parade and children's castle-building contest on Saturday, followed by the adult event on Sunday. Creations of astounding complexity are plundered after the awards ceremony. For details, visit www.usopensandcastle.com or call ✆ **619/424-6663.** Late July.

## August

**Old Spanish Days Fiesta,** Santa Barbara. The city's biggest annual event, this 5-day festival features a parade with horse-drawn carriages, music and dance performances, marketplaces, and a rodeo. Call ✆ **805/962-8101** or visit www.oldspanishdays-fiesta.org. Early August.

**Nisei Week Japanese Festival.** This weeklong celebration of Japanese culture and heritage is held in the Japanese American Cultural and Community Center Plaza in Little Tokyo. Festivities include parades, food, music, arts, and crafts. Call ✆ **213/687-7193.** Mid-August.

## September

**Los Angeles County Fair,** Pomona. Horse racing, arts, agricultural displays, celebrity entertainment, and carnival rides are among the attractions at one of the largest county fairs in the world, held at the Los Angeles County Fair and Exposition Center. Call ✆ **909/623-3111** or visit www.fair plex.com for information. Throughout September.

**Long Beach Blues Festival.** Great performances by blues legends such as

Etta James, Dr. John, the Allman Brothers, and Ike Turner make this an event you won't want to miss if you love the blues. In the middle of the athletic field at Long Beach State, the event serves cold beer, wine, and food. Call © **562/985-5566** or log onto www.kkjz.org. Labor Day weekend.

**Sausalito Art Festival.** A juried exhibit of more than 180 artists. It's accompanied by music provided by Bay Area jazz, rock, and blues performers and international cuisine enhanced by wines from some 50 Napa and Sonoma producers. Call © **415/331-3757** or log on to www.sausalitoartfestival.org for information. Labor Day weekend.

**Monterey Jazz Festival.** Features top names in traditional and modern jazz. One of the oldest annual jazz festivals in the world. Call © **831/373-3366** or see www.montereyjazzfest.com for more info. Mid-September.

**Danish Days, Solvang.** Since 1936 this 3-day event has been celebrating old-world customs and pageantry with a parade, gymnastics exhibitions by local schoolchildren, demonstrations of Danish arts and crafts, and plenty of *aebleskivers* (Danish fritters) and *medisterpolse* (Danish sausage). Call © **800/468-6765** for more information or see www.solvangusa.com. Mid-September.

**Watts Towers Day of the Drum Festival,** Los Angeles. Celebrating the historic role of drums and drummers, this event features a variety of unique performances, from Afro-Cuban *folklóricos* to East Indian tabla players. Call © **213/847-4646.** Late September.

**October**

**Catalina Island Jazz Trax Festival.** Contemporary jazz artists travel to the island to play in the legendary Avalon Casino Ballroom. The festival is held over two consecutive 3-day weekends.

Call © **760/323-1171** or visit www.jazztrax.com for advance ticket sales and a schedule of performers. Early October.

**Sonoma County Harvest Fair,** Sonoma County Fairgrounds. A 3-day celebration of the harvest with exhibitions, art shows, and annual judging of the local wines. Call © **707/545-4203.** Dates vary.

**Hollywood Film Festival.** More than 50 films from the U.S. and abroad are screened, amid celebrities galore. Actors and filmmakers will find a variety of workshops and marketplaces. Call © **310/288-1882** or visit www.hollywoodawards.com for info and tickets. Mid-October.

**The Half Moon Bay Art & Pumpkin Festival,** Half Moon Bay. The festival features a Great Pumpkin Parade, pie-eating contests, a pumpkin-carving competition, arts and crafts, and all manner of squash cuisine. The highlight of the event is the Giant Pumpkin weigh-in. For exact date and details, call the Pumpkin Hot Line at © **650/726-9652.**

**Western Regional Final Championship Rodeo,** Lakeside. Cowboys compete in calf roping, barrel racing, bull riding, steer wrestling, and other events. At the Lakeside Rodeo Grounds, at Hwy. 67 and Mapleview Avenue in Lakeside. Call © **619/561-4331.** Mid-October.

**Halloween,** San Francisco. A fantastic parade starts at Market and Castro, and a mixed gay-straight crowd revels in extraordinarily imaginative costumes. October 31.

**West Hollywood Halloween Costume Carnaval.** This is one of the world's largest Halloween parties. Over 400,000 people, many dressed in outlandish drag couture, party all night

along Santa Monica Boulevard. Call
© **310/289-2525** or see www.visitwest
hollywood.com for info. October 31.

### November

**Catalina Island Triathlon.** This is one
of the top triathlons in the world. Participants run on unpaved roads, swim
in the cleanest bay on the West Coast,
and bike on challenging trails. Call
Pacific Sports at © **714/978-1528** or
visit www.pacificsportsllc. com. Early
November.

**Doo Dah Parade,** Pasadena. This outrageous spoof of the Rose Parade features such participants as the Briefcase
Precision Drill Team and a kazoo-
playing marching band. Call © **626/
440-7379** or visit www.pasadenadoo
dahparade.com. Near Thanksgiving.

**Hollywood Christmas Parade.** This
star-studded parade marches through
the heart of Hollywood. For information, call © **323/469-2337.** Sunday
after Thanksgiving.

### December

**Balboa Park December Nights,** San
Diego. The city's urban park is decked
out in holiday splendor for a weekend
of evening events, including a candlelight procession, caroling and baroque
music, craft displays, ethnic food, and
hot cider. The event and the park's 13
museums are free these evenings. For
more information, call © **619/239-
0512** or visit www.balboapark.org.
First weekend in December.

**Christmas Boat Parade of Lights.**
Following long-standing tradition,
sailors decorate their crafts with colorful lights. Several Southern California
harbors hold nighttime parades to
showcase the creations, which range
from tiny dinghies draped with a single
strand of lights to showy yachts with
entire Nativity scenes twinkling on
deck. Contact the following for schedules and information: Ventura Harbor,
© **805/382-3001;** Long Beach,
© **562/435-4093;** Huntington Harbor, © **714/840-7542,** and **San Diego
Bay** (www.sdparadeoflights.org).

**New Year's Eve Torchlight Parade,**
Big Bear Lake. Watch dozens of nighttime skiers follow a serpentine path
down Snow Summit's ski slopes bearing glowing torches—it's one of the
state's loveliest traditions. Afterward,
the party continues indoors with live
bands and plenty to eat and drink. For
more information: © **909/866-5766**
or www.bigbearmountainresorts.com.

## 4 Travel Insurance

Check your existing insurance policies
and credit card coverage before you buy
travel insurance. You may already be covered for lost luggage, canceled tickets, or
medical expenses.

The cost of travel insurance varies
widely, depending on the cost and length
of your trip, your age and health, and the
type of trip you're taking; expect to pay
5% and 8% of the vacation itself.

**TRIP-CANCELLATION INSURANCE**
Trip-cancellation insurance helps you get
your money back if you have to back out

of a trip, if you have to go home early, or if
your travel supplier goes bankrupt.
Allowed reasons for cancellation can range
from sickness to natural disasters to the
State Department declaring your destination unsafe for travel (see http://travel.
state.gov). (Insurers usually won't cover
vague fears, though, as many travelers discovered who tried to cancel their trips in
October 2001 because they were wary
of flying.) In this unstable world, trip-
cancellation insurance is a good buy if
you're purchasing tickets well in advance

(who knows what the state of the world, or of your airline, will be in 9 months?). Insurance policy details vary, so read the fine print—and make sure that your airline or cruise line is on the list of carriers covered in case of bankruptcy. A good resource is **"Travel Guard Alerts,"** a list of companies considered high-risk by Travel Guard International (see website below). Protect yourself further by buying the insurance with a credit card—by law, consumers can get their money back on goods and services not received if they report the loss within 60 days after the charge is listed on their credit card statement.

*Note:* Many tour operators, particularly those offering trips to remote or high-risk areas, include insurance in the cost of the trip or can arrange insurance policies through a partnering provider, a convenient and often cost-effective way for the traveler to obtain insurance. Make sure the tour company is a reputable one, however: Some experts suggest you avoid buying insurance from the tour or cruise company you're traveling with, saying it's better to buy from a "third party" insurer than to put all your money in one place.

For more information, contact one of the following recommended insurers: **Access America** (✆ 866/807-3982; www.accessamerica.com); **Travel Guard International** (✆ 800/826-4919; www.travelguard.com); **Travel Insured International** (✆ 800/243-3174; www.travelinsured.com); and **Travelex Insurance Services** (✆ 888/457-4602; www.travelex-insurance.com).

**MEDICAL INSURANCE**    Most health insurance policies cover you if you get sick away from home—but check before you leave, particularly if you're insured by an HMO.

**LOST-LUGGAGE INSURANCE**    On domestic flights, checked baggage is covered up to $2,500 per ticketed passenger. On international flights (including U.S. portions of international trips), baggage coverage is limited to about $9.07 per pound, up to about $635 per checked bag. If you plan to check items more valuable than the standard liability, see if your valuables are covered by your homeowner's policy, get baggage insurance as part of your comprehensive travel-insurance package, or buy Travel Guard's "BagTrak" product. Don't buy insurance at the airport, as it's usually overpriced. Be sure to take any valuables or irreplaceable items with you in your carry-on luggage, as many valuables (including books, money, and electronics) aren't covered by airline policies.

If your luggage is lost, immediately file a lost-luggage claim at the airport, detailing the luggage contents. For most airlines, you must report delayed, damaged, or lost baggage within 4 hours of arrival. The airlines are required to deliver luggage, once found, directly to your house or destination free of charge.

## 5 Health & Safety

### WHAT TO DO IF YOU GET SICK AWAY FROM HOME

In most cases, your existing health plan will provide the coverage you need. But double-check, and bring your insurance ID card with you when you travel.

If you suffer from a chronic illness, consult your doctor before your departure. For conditions like epilepsy, diabetes, or heart problems, wear a **MedicAlert Identification Tag** (✆ 888/633-4298; www.medicalert.org), which will alert doctors to your condition and give them access to your records through MedicAlert's 24-hour hot line.

Pack **prescription drugs** in your carry-on luggage, in their original containers, with pharmacy labels—otherwise they won't make it through airport security. And bring copies of your prescriptions in case you lose your pills or run out. Don't forget an extra pair of contact lenses or eyeglasses.

## STAYING SAFE

An unscientific survey indicates that the issue most on the minds of would-be visitors to California is earthquakes, but in fact, the incidence of earthquakes is far surpassed by the paranoia. Refer to "Earthquakes" in "Fast Facts," later in this chapter, for general tips on what to do in the event of an earthquake, but avoid letting these fears dominate your thoughts before or during a California vacation. Major quakes are rare, and they're localized enough that it is highly unlikely you will ever feel one.

Driving perils in California include winter driving on mountain roads. Chains may be required in the Sierras during icy weather at elevations above 3,000 feet. The **California Department of Transportation** provides 24-hour info at ⓒ **916/445-1534.**

Conversely, driving in desert areas carries its own hazards: Always be aware of the distance to the next gas station. In some areas, they may be 50 miles apart, and summer temperatures well above 100°F (38°C) can turn a scenic drive into a disaster.

Penalties in California for drunk driving are among the nation's toughest. The legal limit is .08% blood alcohol level. In some areas, freeway speed limits are aggressively enforced after dark, as a pretext for nabbing drivers who might have imbibed.

## 6 Specialized Travel Resources

### TRAVELERS WITH DISABILITIES

California's spirit of tolerance has made it a welcoming place for travelers with disabilities. Building codes make most public facilities and attractions accessible (though some historic sites and older buildings can't accommodate drastic remodeling), and the state provides many services for those with disabilities.

The U.S. National Park Service offers a **Golden Access Passport** that gives free lifetime entrance to all properties administered by the National Park Service— national parks, monuments, historic sites, recreation areas, and national wildlife refuges—for persons who are visually impaired or permanently disabled, regardless of age. You may pick up a Golden Access Passport at any NPS entrance fee area by showing proof of medically determined disability and eligibility for receiving benefits under federal law. Besides free entry, the Golden Access Passport also offers a 50% discount on federal-use fees charged for such facilities as camping, swimming, parking, boat launching, and

tours. For more information, go to www. nps.gov/fees_passes.htm or call ⓒ **888/ 467-2757.**

Many travel agencies offer customized tours and itineraries for travelers with disabilities. **Flying Wheels Travel** (ⓒ **507/ 451-5005;** www.flyingwheelstravel.com) offers escorted tours and cruises that emphasize sports and private tours in minivans with lifts. **Access-Able Travel Source** (ⓒ **303/232-2979;** www.access-able. com) offers extensive access information and advice for traveling around the world with disabilities. **Accessible Journeys** (ⓒ **800/846-4537** or 610/521-0339; www.disabilitytravel.com) caters to slow walkers and wheelchair travelers and their families and friends.

**Avis Rent a Car** has an "Avis Access" program that offers such services as a dedicated 24-hour toll-free number (ⓒ **888/ 879-4273**) for customers with special travel needs; special car features such as swivel seats, spinner knobs, and hand controls; and accessible bus service.

Organizations that offer assistance to disabled travelers include **MossRehab** (www.mossresourcenet.org), with its online library of accessible-travel resources; **SATH (Society for Accessible Travel & Hospitality)** (© 212/447-7284; www.sath.org; annual membership fees: $45 adults, $30 seniors and students), which offers a wealth of travel resources for all types of disabilities and informed recommendations on destinations, access guides, travel agents, operators, vehicle rentals, and companion services; and the **American Foundation for the Blind (AFB)** (© 800/232-5463; www.afb.org), a referral resource for the visually impaired with information on traveling with Seeing Eye dogs.

For more information specifically targeted to travelers with disabilities, the community website **iCan** (www.icanonline.net/channels/travel/index.cfm) has destination guides and several regular columns on accessible travel. Also check out the quarterly magazine **Emerging Horizons** ($15 per year, $20 outside the U.S.; www.emerginghorizons.com); and *Open World* magazine, published by SATH (see above; subscription: $13 per year, $21 outside the U.S.).

## GAY & LESBIAN TRAVELERS

California is one of the country's most progressive states when it comes to antidiscrimination legislation and workplace benefits for domestic partners. The gay and lesbian community spreads well beyond the famed enclaves of San Francisco, West Hollywood, and San Diego's Hillcrest. Gay travelers (especially men) will find a number of gay-owned inns in Palm Springs and the Russian River, north of the Bay Area.

The **International Gay & Lesbian Travel Association (IGLTA)** (© 800/448-8550 or 954/776-2626; www.iglta.org) is the trade association for the gay and lesbian travel industry, and offers an online directory of gay- and lesbian-friendly travel companies.

Many agencies offer tours and travel itineraries specifically for gay and lesbian travelers. **Above and Beyond Tours** (© 800/397-2681; www.abovebeyondtours.com) is the exclusive gay and lesbian tour operator for United Airlines. **Now, Voyager** (© 800/255-6951; www.nowvoyager.com) is a well-known San Francisco–based gay-owned and -operated travel service.

*Out and About* (© 800/929-2268; www.outandabout.com) offers guidebooks and a newsletter ($20 per year for 10 issues) with solid information on the gay and lesbian travel scene.

The *Damron* guides (www.damron.com), with separate, annual books for gay men and lesbians, offer state-by-state listings and resources. *Gay Travel A to Z: The World of Gay & Lesbian Travel Options at Your Fingertips* by Marianne Ferrari (Ferrari International; Box 35575, Phoenix, AZ 85069) is also a very good gay and lesbian guidebook series.

## SENIOR TRAVEL

Mention the fact that you're a senior citizen when you make your travel reservations. Although all of the major U.S. airlines except America West have canceled their senior discount and coupon-book programs, many hotels still offer discounts for seniors. In most cities, people over the age of 60 qualify for reduced admission to theaters, museums, and other attractions, as well as discounted fares on public transportation.

Members of **AARP** (formerly known as the American Association of Retired Persons), 601 E St. NW, Washington, DC 20049 (© 888/687-2277; www.aarp.org), get discounts on hotels, airfares, and car rentals. AARP offers members a wide range of benefits, including *AARP: The Magazine* and a monthly newsletter. Anyone over 50 can join.

The **U.S. National Park Service** offers a **Golden Age Passport** that gives seniors 62 years or older lifetime entrance to all properties administered by the National Park Service—national parks, monuments, historic sites, recreation areas, and national wildlife refuges—for a one-time processing fee of $10, which must be purchased in person at any NPS facility that charges an entrance fee. Besides free entry, a Golden Age Passport also offers a 50% discount on federal-use fees charged for such facilities as camping, swimming, parking, boat launching, and tours. For more information, go to www.nps.gov/ fees_passes.htm or call © **888/467-2757.**

Many reliable agencies and organizations target the 50-plus market. **Elder-hostel** (© **877/426-8056;** www.elder hostel.org) arranges study programs for those age 55 and over (and a spouse or companion of any age) in the U.S. and in more than 80 countries around the world. Most courses last 5 to 7 days in the U.S. (2–4 weeks abroad), and many include airfare, accommodations in university dormitories or modest inns, meals, and tuition. **ElderTreks** (© **800/741-7956;** www.eldertreks.com) offers small-group tours to offbeat or adventure-travel locations, restricted to travelers 50 and older. **INTRAV** (© **800/456-8100;** www. intrav.com) is a high-end tour operator that caters to mature, discerning travelers (not necessarily seniors) with trips around the world including guided safaris, polar expeditions, private-jet adventures, and small-boat cruises down jungle rivers.

Recommended publications for senior travel resources and discounts include: the quarterly *Travel 50 & Beyond* (www. travel50andbeyond.com); *Travel Unlimited: Uncommon Adventures for the Mature Traveler* (Avalon); *101 Tips for Mature Travelers,* from Grand Circle Travel (© **800/221-2610** or 617/350-7500; www.gct.com); and *Unbelievably Good Deals and Great Adventures That You Absolutely Can't Get Unless You're Over 50* (McGraw-Hill), by Joann Rattner Heilman.

## FAMILY TRAVEL

If you have enough trouble getting your kids out of the house in the morning, dragging them thousands of miles away may seem like an insurmountable challenge. But family travel can be immensely rewarding, giving you new ways of seeing the world through smaller pairs of eyes.

**Familyhostel** (© **800/733-9753;** www.learn.unh.edu/familyhostel) takes the whole family, including kids ages 8 to 15, on moderately priced domestic and international learning vacations. Lectures, field trips, and sightseeing are led by academics.

Recommended family travel Internet sites include **Family Travel Forum** (www.familytravelforum.com), a comprehensive site that offers customized trip planning; **Family Travel Network** (www. familytravelnetwork.com), an award-winning site that offers travel features, deals, and tips; **Traveling Internationally with Your Kids** (www.travelwithyourkids.com), a comprehensive site offering sound advice for long-distance and international travel with children; and **Family Travel Files** (www.thefamilytravelfiles.com), which offers an online magazine and a directory of off-the-beaten-path tours and tour operators for families.

Several books offer tips on traveling with kids. *Family Travel* (Lanier Publishing International) and *How to Take Great Trips with Your Kids* (The Harvard Common Press) are full of good general advice. *The Unofficial Guide to California with Kids* (Wiley Publishing, Inc.) is an excellent resource that covers the entire state. It rates and ranks attractions for each age group, lists dozens of family-friendly accommodations and restaurants, and suggests lots of beaches and activities that are fun for the whole clan.

## 7 Planning Your Trip Online

### SURFING FOR AIRFARES

The "big three" online travel agencies, **Expedia.com, Travelocity,** and **Orbitz,** sell most of the air tickets bought on the Internet. (Canadian travelers should try expedia.ca and travelocity.ca; U.K. residents can go for expedia.co.uk and opodo.co.uk.). Each has different business deals with the airlines and may offer different fares on the same flights, so it's wise to shop around. Expedia.com and Travelocity will also send you **e-mail notification** when a cheap fare becomes available to your favorite destination. Of the smaller travel agency websites, **SideStep** (www.sidestep.com) has gotten the best reviews from Frommer's authors. It's a browser add-on that purports to "search 140 sites at once," but in reality only beats competitors' fares as often as other sites do.

Also remember to check **airline websites,** especially for low-fare carriers such as Southwest, JetBlue, AirTran, WestJet, or Ryanair; their fares are often misreported or unrepresented by travel agency websites. With major airlines, you can shave a few bucks by booking directly through the airline and avoiding a travel agent's fee. But you'll get these discounts only by **booking online:** Most airlines now offer online-only fares that even their phone agents don't know about. For the websites of airlines that service your destination, go to "Getting There," p. 37.

Great **last-minute deals** are available through free weekly e-mail services provided directly by the airlines. Most of these are announced on Tuesday or Wednesday and must be purchased online. Most are only valid for travel that weekend, but some (such as Southwest's) can be booked weeks or months in advance. Sign up for weekly e-mail alerts at airline websites or check megasites that compile comprehensive lists of last-minute specials, such as **Smarter Living** (smarter living.com). For last-minute trips, **site59. com** and **lastminutetravel.com** in the U.S. and **lastminute.com** in Europe often have better air-and-hotel package deals than the major-label sites. A website listing numerous bargain sites and airlines around the world is **www.itravelnet.com**.

If you're willing to give up some control over your flight details, use what is called an **"opaque" fare service** like **Priceline** (www.priceline.com; www.price line.co.uk for Europeans) or its smaller competitor **Hotwire** (www.hotwire.com). Both offer rock-bottom prices in exchange for travel on a "mystery airline" at a mysterious time of day, often with a mysterious change of planes en route. The mystery airlines are all major, well-known carriers—and the possibility of being sent from Philadelphia to Chicago via Tampa is remote; the airlines' routing computers have gotten a lot better than they used to be. But your chances of getting a 6am or 11pm flight are pretty high. Hotwire tells you flight prices before you buy; Priceline usually has better deals than Hotwire, but you have to play their "name our price" game. (Helpful staff members at **Bidding ForTravel.com** will help demystify Priceline's prices and strategies for newcomers.) Priceline and Hotwire are great for flights within North America and between the U.S. and Europe. But for flights to other parts of the world, consolidators will almost always beat their fares. *Note:* In 2004 Priceline added nonopaque service to its roster. You now have the option to pick exact flights, times, and airlines from a list of offers—or opt to bid on opaque fares as before.

### SURFING FOR HOTELS

Shopping online for hotels is generally done one of two ways: by booking through the hotel's own website or through an independent booking agency (or a fare-service agency like Priceline; see below). These Internet hotel agencies have multiplied in mind-boggling numbers of late, competing for the business of millions of consumers surfing for accommodations around the world. This competitiveness can be a boon to consumers who have the patience and time to shop and compare the online sites for good deals—but shop they must, for prices can vary considerably from site to site. And keep in mind that hotels at the top of a site's listing may be there for no other reason than that they paid money to get the placement.

Of the "big three" sites, **Expedia.com** offers a long list of special deals and "virtual tours" or photos of available rooms so you can see what you're paying for (a feature that helps counter the claims that the best rooms are often held back from bargain booking websites). **Travelocity** posts unvarnished customer reviews and ranks its properties according to the AAA rating system. Also reliable are **Hotels.com** and **Quikbook.com.** An excellent free program, **TravelAxe** (www.travelaxe.net), can help you search multiple hotel sites at once, even ones you may never have heard of—and conveniently lists the total price of the room, including the taxes and service charges. Another booking site, **Travelweb** (www.travelweb.com), is partly owned by the hotels it represents (including the Hilton, Hyatt, and Starwood chains) and is therefore plugged directly into the hotels' reservations systems—unlike independent online agencies, which have to fax or e-mail reservation requests to the hotel, a good portion of which get misplaced in the shuffle. More than once, travelers have arrived at the hotel, only to be told that they have no reservation. To be fair, many of the major sites are undergoing improvements in service and ease of use, and Expedia.com will soon be able to plug directly into the reservations systems of many hotel chains—none of which can be bad news for consumers. In the meantime, it's a good idea to **get a confirmation number** and **make a printout** of any online booking transaction.

In the opaque website category, **Priceline** and **Hotwire** are even better for hotels than for airfares; with both, you're allowed

---

## Frommers.com: The Complete Travel Resource

For an excellent travel-planning resource, we highly recommend **Frommers. com** (www.frommers.com), voted Best Travel Site by *PC Magazine*. We guarantee you'll find the travel tips, reviews, monthly vacation giveaways, bookstore, and online-booking capabilities indispensable. Special features include our popular **Destinations** section, with expert travel tips and hotel and dining recommendations for more than 3,500 destinations around the globe; the **Frommers.com Newsletter,** with the latest deals, travel trends, and money-saving secrets; our **Community** area featuring **Message Boards,** where Frommer's readers post queries and share advice, and our authors sometimes answer questions; and our **Photo Center,** under Tips & Tools, where you can post and share vacation snapshots. When your research is done, the **Online Reservations System** (www.frommers.com/book_a_trip) takes you to Frommer's preferred online partners for booking your vacation at affordable prices.

to pick the neighborhood and quality level of your hotel before offering up your money. Priceline's hotel product even covers Europe and Asia, though it's much better at getting five-star lodging for three-star prices than at finding anything at the bottom of the scale. On the down side, many hotels stick Priceline guests in their least desirable rooms. Be sure to go to the BiddingForTravel website (see above) before bidding on a hotel room on Priceline; it features a fairly up-to-date list of hotels that Priceline uses in major cities. For both Priceline and Hotwire, you pay upfront, and the fee is nonrefundable. *Note:* Some hotels do not provide loyalty program credits or points or other frequent-stay amenities when you book a room through opaque online service.

## SURFING FOR RENTAL CARS

For booking rental cars online, the best deals are usually found at rental-car company websites, although all the major online travel agencies also make rental-car reservations. Priceline and Hotwire work well for rental cars, too; you won't know which major rental company you're getting until you book, but for most travelers the difference between Hertz, Avis, and Budget is negligible.

## 8 The 21st-Century Traveler

### WEB ACCESS ON THE ROAD

Travelers have any number of ways to check their e-mail and access the Internet on the road. Of course, using your own laptop—or even a PDA (personal digital assistant) or electronic organizer with a modem—gives you the most flexibility. But if you don't have a computer, you can still access your e-mail and even your office computer from cybercafes.

### WITHOUT YOUR OWN COMPUTER

It's hard nowadays to find a city that *doesn't* have a few cybercafes. Although there's no definitive directory for cybercafes, you can start looking at **www.cyber captive.com** and **www.cybercafe.com**.

Aside from formal cybercafes, most **youth hostels** nowadays have at least one computer you can get to the Internet on. And most **public libraries** across the world offer Internet access free or for a small charge. Avoid **hotel business centers** unless you're willing to pay exorbitant rates.

Most major airports now have **Internet kiosks** scattered throughout their gates. These kiosks, which you'll also see in shopping malls, hotel lobbies, and tourist information offices around the world, give you basic Web access for a per-minute fee that's usually higher than cybercafe prices. They're clunky and costly, however, so avoid them when possible.

To retrieve your e-mail, ask your **Internet Service Provider (ISP)** if it has a Web-based interface tied to your existing e-mail account. If your ISP doesn't have such an interface, you can use the free **mail2web** service (www.mail2web.com) to view and reply to your home e-mail. For more flexibility, you may want to open a free, Web-based e-mail account with **Yahoo! Mail** (http://mail.yahoo.com). (Microsoft's Hotmail is another popular option, but Hotmail has severe spam problems.) Your home ISP may be able to forward your e-mail to the Web-based account automatically.

If you need to access files on your office computer, look into a service called **GoToMyPC** (www.gotomypc.com). The service provides a Web-based interface for you to access and manipulate a distant PC from anywhere—even a cybercafe—provided your "target" PC is on and has an always-on connection to the Internet (such as with Road Runner cable). The service offers top-quality security, but if you're worried about hackers, use your own laptop rather than a cybercafe computer to access the GoToMyPC system.

## WITH YOUR OWN COMPUTER

Travelers can now get high-speed "Wi-Fi" (wireless fidelity) connection—without cable wires, networking hardware, or a phone line (see below)—from more and more hotels, cafes, and retailers. You can get Wi-Fi connection one of several ways. Many laptops sold in the last year have built-in Wi-Fi capability (an 802.11b wireless Ethernet connection). Mac owners have their own networking technology, Apple AirPort. For those with older computers, an 802.11b/**Wi-Fi card** (around $50) can be plugged into your laptop. You sign up for wireless access service much as you do cellphone service, through a plan offered by one of several commercial companies that have made wireless service available in airports, hotel lobbies, and coffee shops, primarily in the U.S. (followed by the U.K. and Japan). **T-Mobile Hotspot** (www.t-mobile.com/hotspot) serves up wireless connections at more than 1,000 Starbucks coffee shops nationwide. **Boingo** (www.boingo.com) and **Wayport** (www.wayport.com) have set up networks in airports and high-class hotel lobbies. IPass providers (see below) also give you access to a few hundred wireless hotel lobby setups. Best of all, you don't need to be staying at the Four Seasons to use the hotel's network; just set yourself up on a nice couch in the lobby. The companies' pricing policies can be Byzantine, with a variety of monthly, per-connection, and per-minute plans, but in general you pay around $30 a month for limited access—and as more and more companies jump on the wireless bandwagon, prices are likely to get even more competitive.

There are also places that provide **free wireless networks** in cities around the world. To locate these free hotspots, go to **www.personaltelco.net/index.cgi/Wireless Communities**.

If Wi-Fi is not available at your destination, most business-class hotels throughout the world offer dataports for laptop modems, and a few thousand hotels in the U.S. and Europe now offer free high-speed Internet access using an Ethernet network cable. You can bring your own cables, but most hotels rent them for around $10. **Call your hotel in advance** to see what your options are.

In addition, major Internet Service Providers (ISP) have **local access numbers** around the world, allowing you to go online by placing a local call. Check your ISP's website or call its toll-free number and ask how you can use your current account away from home, and how much it will cost.

If you're traveling outside the reach of your ISP, the **iPass** network has dial-up numbers in most of the world's countries. You'll have to sign up with an iPass provider, who will then tell you how to set up your computer for your destination(s). For a list of iPass providers, go to www.ipass.com and click on "Individuals Buy Now." One solid provider is **i2roam** (www.i2roam.com; ✆ **866/811-6209** or 920/235-0475).

Wherever you go, bring a **connection kit** of the right power and phone adapters, a spare phone cord, and a spare Ethernet network cable—or find out whether your hotel supplies them to guests.

## USING A CELLPHONE ACROSS THE U.S.

Just because your cellphone works at home doesn't mean it'll work elsewhere in the country (thanks to our nation's fragmented cellphone system). It's a good bet that your phone will work in major cities. But take a look at your wireless company's coverage map on its website before heading out—T-Mobile, Sprint, and Nextel are particularly weak in rural areas. If you need to stay in touch at a destination where you know your phone won't work, **rent** a phone that does from **InTouch USA** (℡ **800/872-7626;** www. intouchglobal.com) or a rental car location, but beware that you'll pay $1 a minute or more for airtime.

If you're venturing deep into national parks, you may want to consider renting a **satellite phone ("satphones"),** which are different from cellphones in that they connect to satellites rather than ground-based towers. A satphone is more costly than a cellphone but works where there's no cellular signal and no towers. Unfortunately, you'll pay at least $2 per minute to use the phone, and it only works where you can see the horizon (i.e., usually not indoors). In North America, you can rent Iridium satellite phones from **RoadPost** (www.roadpost.com; ℡ **888/290-1606** or 905/272-5665). InTouch USA (see above) offers a wider range of satphones but at higher rates.

If you're not from the U.S., you'll be appalled at the poor reach of our **GSM (Global System for Mobiles) wireless network,** which is used by much of the rest of the world. Your phone will probably work in most major U.S. cities; it definitely won't work in many rural areas. (To see where GSM phones work in the U.S., check out www.t-mobile.com/coverage/national_popup.asp) And you may or may not be able to send SMS (text messaging) home—something Americans tend not to do anyway, for various cultural and technological reasons. (International budget travelers like to send text messages home because it's much cheaper than making international calls.) Assume nothing—call your wireless provider and get the full scoop. In a worst-case scenario, you can always rent a phone; InTouch USA delivers to hotels.

## DIGITAL CAMERAS

Digital cameras offer travelers many advantages. They'll free you from lugging film, and airport X-rays will leave them relatively unscathed. You don't even need to carry your laptop to download the day's images and make room for more. With a **media storage card,** sold by all major camera dealers, you can store hundreds of images in your camera. These "memory" cards come in different configurations—memory sticks, flash cards, secure digital cards—with various storage capacities, and they range in price from $30 to over $200. (*Note:* Each camera model works with a specific type of card, so you'll need to determine which is compatible with your camera.) When you get home, you can print the images on your own color printer or take the storage card to a camera store, drugstore, or chain retailer. A service like **Snapfish** (www. snapfish.com) will develop them online for about 25¢ a shot.

## 9 Getting There

### BY PLANE

All major U.S. carriers serve the San Francisco, Sacramento, San Jose, Los Angeles, John Wayne (Orange County), and San Diego airports. They include **American** (℡ 800/433-7300; www.aa. com), **America West** (℡ 800/235-9292; www.americawest.com), **Continental** (℡ 800/525-0280; www.continental. com), **Delta** (℡ 800/221-1212; www. delta.com), **JetBlue** (℡ 800/538-2583; www.jetblue.com), **Northwest** (℡ 800/ 225-2525; www.nwa.com), **Southwest** (℡ 800/435-9792; www.southwest.com), **United** (℡ 800/241-6522; www.united. com), and **US Airways** (℡ 800/428-4322; www.usairways.com). The lowest round-trip fares to the West Coast from New York fluctuate between about $350 and $500; from Chicago, they range from

$300 to $400. International travelers should also see "Getting to the U.S." in chapter 3 for information on overseas flights into California. For details on air travel within California, see "Getting Around," later.

## GETTING THROUGH THE AIRPORT

Since the federalization of airport security, security procedures at U.S. airports are more consistent than ever. Generally, you'll be fine if you arrive at the airport **1 hour** before a domestic flight and **2 hours** before an international flight; if you show up late, tell an airline employee and he or she will probably whisk you to the front of the line.

Bring a **current, government-issued photo ID** such as a driver's license or passport. Keep your ID handy at check-in, the security checkpoint, and the gate. (Children under 18 do not need government-issued photo IDs for domestic flights, but they do for international flights to most countries.)

In 2003, the Transportation Security Administration (TSA) phased out **gate check-in** at all U.S. airports. Passengers with e-tickets can beat the ticket-counter lines by using airport **electronic kiosks** or even **online check-in** from a home computer. Online check-in involves logging on to your airlines' website, accessing your reservation, and printing out your boarding pass. The airline may even offer you bonus miles to do so! If you're using a kiosk at the airport, bring the credit card you used to book the ticket or your frequent-flier card. Print out your boarding pass from the kiosk and proceed to the security checkpoint with your pass and a photo ID. Most kiosks also allow you to check bags or reserve an exit-row seat. Even the smaller airlines are employing the kiosk system, but always call your airline to make sure these alternatives are available. **Curbside check-in** is another

good way to avoid lines, although a few airlines still ban this procedure; call before you go.

Security checkpoint lines are getting shorter than they were during 2001 and 2002, but some doozies remain. If you have trouble standing for long periods of time, tell an airline employee; the airline will provide a wheelchair. Speed up security by **not wearing metal objects** such as big belt buckles. If you've got metallic body parts, a note from your doctor can prevent a long chat with the security screeners. Keep in mind that only **ticketed passengers** are allowed past security, except for folks escorting disabled passengers or children.

Federalization has stabilized **what you can carry on** and **what you can't.** The general rule is that sharp things are out, nail clippers are okay, and food and beverages must be passed through the X-ray machine—but that security screeners can't make you drink from your coffee cup. Bring food in your carry-on rather than checking it, as explosive-detection machines used on checked luggage have been known to mistake food (especially chocolate, for some reason) for bombs. Travelers in the U.S. are allowed one carry-on bag, plus a "personal item" such as a purse, briefcase, or laptop bag. Carry-on hoarders can stuff all sorts of things into a laptop bag; as long as it has a laptop in it, it's still considered a personal item. The TSA has issued a list of restricted items; for details, see its website (www.tsa.gov/public/index.jsp).

Airport screeners may decide that your checked luggage needs to be searched by hand. You can now purchase luggage locks that allow screeners to open and re-lock a checked bag if hand-searching is necessary. Look for Travel Sentry–certified locks at luggage or travel shops and Brookstone stores (you can buy them online at www.brookstone.com). These locks, approved by the TSA, can be opened by luggage inspectors with a special code or key. For more information on the locks, visit www.travelsentry.org. If you use something other than TSA-approved locks, your lock will be cut off your suitcase if a TSA agent needs to hand-search your luggage.

## FLY FOR LESS: HOW TO GET THE BEST AIRFARE

Passengers sharing the same airplane cabin rarely pay the same fare. Travelers who need to purchase tickets at the last minute, change their itinerary at a moment's notice, or fly one-way often get stuck paying the premium rate. Here are ways to keep your costs down.

- Passengers who can book their ticket **long in advance,** who can **stay over Saturday night,** or who **fly midweek** or **at less-trafficked hours** may pay a fraction of the full fare. If your schedule is flexible, say so, and ask if you can secure a cheaper fare by changing your flight plans.
- You can also save on airfares by keeping an eye out in local newspapers for **promotional specials** or **fare wars,** when airlines lower prices on their most popular routes. You rarely see fare wars offered for peak travel times, but if you can travel in the off-months, you may snag a bargain.
- Search **the Internet** for cheap fares (see "Planning Your Trip Online").
- Try to book a ticket **in its country of origin.** For instance, if you're planning a one-way flight from Johannesburg to Bombay, a South Africa–based travel agent will probably have the lowest fares. For multileg trips, book in the country of the first leg; for example, book New York–London–Amsterdam–Rome–New York in the U.S.
- **Consolidators,** also known as bucket shops, are great sources for international tickets, although they usually can't beat the Internet on fares within North America. Start by looking in Sunday newspaper travel sections; U.S. travelers should focus on the *New York Times, Los Angeles Times,* and *Miami Herald.* For less-developed destinations, small travel agents who cater to immigrant communities in large cities often have the best deals. ***Beware:*** Bucket shop tickets are usually nonrefundable or rigged with stiff cancellation penalties, often as high as 50% to 75% of the ticket price, and some put you on charter airlines, which may leave at inconvenient times and experience delays. Several reliable consolidators are worldwide and available on the Net. **STA Travel** is now the world's leader in student travel, thanks to its purchase of Council Travel. It also offers good fares for travelers of all ages. **ELTExpress (Flights.com) (© 800/ TRAV-800;** www.eltexpress.com) started in Europe and has excellent fares worldwide, but particularly to that continent. It also has "local" websites in 12 countries. **FlyCheap (© 800/FLY-CHEAP;** www.1800 flycheap.com) is owned by package-holiday megalith MyTravel and so has especially good access to fares for sunny destinations. **Air Tickets Direct (© 800/778-3447;** www. airticketsdirect.com) is based in Montreal and leverages the currently weak Canadian dollar for low fares; it'll also book trips to places that U.S. travel agents won't touch, such as Cuba.
- Join **frequent-flier clubs.** Accrue enough miles, and you'll be rewarded with free flights and elite status. It's free, and you'll get the best choice of seats, faster response to phone inquiries, and prompter service if your luggage is stolen, your flight is canceled or delayed, or if you want to change your seat. You don't need to

## Travel in the Age of Bankruptcy

Airlines go bankrupt, so protect yourself by **buying your tickets with a credit card,** as the Fair Credit Billing Act guarantees that you can get your money back from the credit card company if a travel supplier goes under (and if you request the refund within 60 days of the bankruptcy). **Travel insurance** can also help, but be sure it covers against "carrier default" for your provider. Know that if a U.S. airline goes bust midtrip, a 2001 federal law requires other carriers to take you to your destination (on a space-available basis) for a fee of no more than $25, provided you rebook within 60 days of the cancellation.

fly to build frequent-flier miles— **frequent-flier credit cards** can provide thousands of miles for doing your everyday shopping.

- For many more tips about air travel, including a rundown of the major frequent-flier credit cards, pick up a copy of *Frommer's Fly Safe, Fly Smart* (Wiley Publishing, Inc.).

## LONG-HAUL FLIGHTS: HOW TO STAY COMFORTABLE

Long flights can be trying; stuffy air and cramped seats can make you feel as if you're being sent parcel post in a small box. But with a little advance planning, you can make an otherwise unpleasant experience almost bearable.

- Your choice of airline and airplane will definitely affect your leg room. Find more details at www.seatguru. com, which has extensive details about almost every seat on six major U.S. airlines. For international airlines, research firm Skytrax has posted a list of average seat pitches at www.airlinequality.com.
- Emergency exit seats and bulkhead seats typically have the most legroom. Emergency exit seats are usually held back to be assigned the day of a flight (to ensure that the seat is filled by someone able-bodied); it's worth getting to the ticket counter early to snag one of these spots for a long flight. Many passengers find that bulkhead seating (the row facing the

wall at the front of the cabin) offers more legroom, but keep in mind that bulkheads are where airlines often put baby bassinets, so you may be sitting next to an infant

- To have two seats for yourself in a three-seat row, try for an aisle seat in a center section toward the back of coach. If you're traveling with a companion, book an aisle and a window seat. Middle seats are usually booked last, so chances are good you'll end up with three seats to yourselves. And in the event that a third passenger is assigned the middle seat, he or she will probably be more than happy to trade for a window or an aisle.
- Ask about entertainment options. Many airlines offer seatback video systems where you get to choose your movies or play video games—but only on some of their planes. (Boeing 777s are your best bet.)
- To sleep, avoid the last row of any section or a row in front of an emergency exit, as these seats are the least likely to recline. Avoid seats near highly trafficked toilet areas. Avoid seats in the back of many jets—these can be narrower than other coach seats. You also may want to reserve a window seat so that you can rest your head and avoid being bumped in the aisle.
- Get up, walk around, and stretch every 60 to 90 minutes to keep your blood flowing. This helps avoid **deep vein thrombosis,** or "economy-class

syndrome," a potentially deadly condition that can be caused by sitting in cramped conditions for too long. Other preventative measures include drinking lots of water and avoiding alcohol (see next bullet).

- Drink water before, during, and after your flight to combat the lack of humidity in airplane cabins—which can be drier than the Sahara. Bring a bottle of water on board. Avoid alcohol, which will dehydrate you.

- If you're flying with kids, don't forget to carry on toys, books, pacifiers, and chewing gum to help them relieve ear pressure buildup during ascent and descent. Let each child pack his or her own backpack with favorite toys.

## BY CAR

If you're planning a road trip, it's a good idea to be a member of the **Automobile Association of America (AAA).** Members (who carry their cards with them) receive free roadside assistance, and have access to a wealth of free travel information, including detailed maps. Also, many hotels and attractions throughout California offer discounts to AAA members—always ask. Call © **800/922-8228** or visit www.aaa. com for membership details.

Here are some handy driving times if you're on one of those see-the-USA car trips. From Phoenix, it's about 6 hours to Los Angeles on I-10. Las Vegas is 265 miles northeast of Los Angeles (about a 4-hr. drive).

San Francisco is 227 miles southwest of Reno, Nevada, and 577 miles northwest of Las Vegas. It's a long day's drive 640 miles south from Portland, Oregon, on I-5. The drive between San Francisco and L.A. takes about 6 hours on I-5, closer to 8 hours on the more scenic U.S. 101.

## BY TRAIN

**Amtrak** (© **800/USA-RAIL;** www. amtrak.com) connects California with about 500 American cities. The Sunset Limited is Amtrak's regularly scheduled transcontinental service, originating in Florida and making 52 stops along the way as it passes through Alabama, Mississippi, Louisiana, Texas, New Mexico, and Arizona before arriving in Los Angeles 2 days later. The train, which runs three times weekly, features reclining seats, a sightseeing car with large windows, and a full-service dining car. Round-trip coach fares begin at around $300; several varieties of sleeping compartments are also available for an extra charge.

## 10  Packages for the Independent Traveler

Before you start your search for the lowest airfare, consider booking your flight as part of a travel package. Package tours are not the same thing as escorted tours. Package tours are simply a way to buy the airfare, accommodations, and other elements of your trip (such as car rentals, airport transfers, and sometimes even activities) at the same time and often at discounted prices—kind of like one-stop shopping. Packages are sold in bulk to tour operators—who resell them to the public at a cost that usually undercuts standard rates.

One good source of package deals is the airlines themselves. Most major airlines offer air/land packages, including **American Airlines Vacations** (© 800/321-2121; www.aavacations.com), **Continental Airlines Vacations** (© 800/301-3800; www.coolvacations.com), **Delta Vacations** (© 800/221-6666; www.delta vacations.com), **Southwest Airlines Vacations** (© 800/423-5683; www. southwest.com and www.swavacations. com), and **United Vacations** (© 888/854-3899; www.unitedvacations.com). And don't forget to look at the local websites: For instance, the **San Diego Convention & Visitors Bureau** (© 800/350-6205; www.sandiego.org) has its own booking engine for packages incorporating air, hotel, and activities. Also note that the **Walt Disney Travel Company** (© 877/700-DISNEY; www.disney.com) is one of the state's largest tour operators, featuring packages that go well beyond the Magic Kingdom.

Several big **online travel agencies**— Expedia.com, Travelocity, Orbitz, Site59, and Lastminute.com—also sell a lot of packages. If you're unsure about a smaller packager, check with the Better Business Bureau, or go online at www.bbb.org. If a packager won't tell you where it's based, don't fly with it.

Travel packages are also listed in the travel section of your Sunday newspaper. Or check ads in travel magazines such as *Arthur Frommer's Budget Travel, Travel & Leisure, National Geographic Traveler,* and *Condé Nast Traveler.*

Package tours can vary by leaps and bounds. Some offer a better class of hotels than others. Some offer the same hotels for lower prices. Some offer flights on scheduled airlines, while others book charters. Some limit your choice of accommodations and travel days. You are often required to make a large payment upfront. On the plus side, packages can save you money, offering group prices but allowing for independent travel. Some even let you add on a few guided excursions or escorted day trips (also at prices lower than if you booked them yourself) without booking an entirely escorted tour.

Before you invest in a package tour, get some answers. Ask about the **accommodations choices** and prices for each. Then look up the hotels' reviews in a Frommer's guide and check their rates for your specific dates of travel online. You'll also want to find out what **type of room** you get. If you need a certain type of room, ask for it; don't take whatever is thrown your way. Request a nonsmoking room, a quiet room, a room with a view, or whatever you fancy.

Finally, look for **hidden expenses.** Ask whether airport departure fees and taxes, for example, are included in the total cost.

## 11 Getting Around

### BY CAR

California's freeway signs frequently indicate direction by naming a town rather than a point on the compass. If you've never heard of Canoga Park, you might be in trouble—unless you have a map. The best state road guide is the comprehensive *Thomas Guide California Road Atlas,* a 300-plus-page book of maps with schematics of towns and cities statewide. It costs about $25, a good investment if you plan to do a lot of exploring. Smaller, accordion-style maps are handy for the state as a whole or for individual cities and regions; you'll find a very useful one inserted in the back of this book.

If you're heading into the Sierra or Shasta-Cascades region for a winter ski trip, top up on antifreeze and carry snow chains for your tires. (Chains are mandatory in certain areas.)

See the full-color driving distance chart inside the front cover of the book for an idea of the distance between the state's popular destinations.

**DRIVING RULES** California law requires both drivers and passengers to wear seat belts. A law that took effect January 1, 2004, requires an approved safety seat for children under 6 or weighing less than 60 pounds. Motorcyclists must wear helmets. Auto insurance is mandatory; the car's registration and proof of insurance must be carried in the car.

You can turn right at a red light, unless otherwise indicated—but be sure to come to a complete stop.

Many California freeways have designated carpool lanes, also known as high-occupancy vehicle (HOV) lanes or "diamond" lanes. Some require two passengers, others three. Most on-ramps are metered during even light congestion to regulate the flow of traffic onto the freeway; cars in HOV lanes can pass the signal without stopping. All other drivers are required to observe the stoplights—fines begin at around $271.

**CAR-RENTAL AGENCIES** California is one of the cheapest places in the United States to rent a car. The best-known firms, with locations throughout the state and at most major airports, include **Alamo** (✆ 800/462-5866; www.alamo.com), **Avis** (✆ 800/230-4898; www.avis.com), **Budget** (✆ 800/527-0700; www.budget.com), **Dollar** (✆ 800/800-3665; www.dollar.com), **Hertz** (✆ 800/654-3131; www.hertz.com), **National** (✆ 800/227-7368; www.nationalcar.com), and **Thrifty** (✆ 800/847-4389; www.thrifty.com).

Many rental agencies have begun offering a variety of essential or just helpful extras, such as cellphones, child seats, and specially equipped vehicles for travelers with disabilities.

**DEMYSTIFYING RENTER'S INSURANCE** Before you drive off in a rental car, be sure you're insured. Hasty assumptions about your personal auto insurance or a rental agency's additional coverage could end up costing you tens of thousands of dollars—even if you're involved in an accident that was clearly the fault of another driver.

If you already hold a **private auto insurance** policy, you are most likely covered in the United States for loss of or damage to a rental car, and liability in case of injury to any other party involved in an accident. Be sure to find out whether you're covered in the area you're visiting, whether your policy extends to all persons who will be driving the rental car, how much liability is covered in case an outside party is injured in an accident, and whether the type of vehicle you are renting is included under your contract. (Rental trucks, sport-utility vehicles, and luxury vehicles or sports cars may not be covered.)

Most **major credit cards** provide some degree of coverage as well—provided they were used to pay for the rental. Terms vary widely, however, so be sure to call your credit card company directly before you rent.

If you're **uninsured,** your credit card may provide primary coverage as long as you decline the rental agency's insurance. This means that the credit card may cover damage or theft of a rental car for the full cost of the vehicle. (In a few states, however, theft is not covered; ask specifically about state law where you will be renting and driving.) If you already have insurance, your credit card may provide secondary coverage—which basically covers your deductible.

Credit cards **will not cover liability,** or the cost of injury to an outside party and/or damage to an outside party's vehicle. If you do not hold an insurance policy, you may want to consider purchasing additional liability insurance from your rental company. Be sure to check the terms, however: Some rental agencies only cover liability if the renter is not at fault.

The basic insurance coverage offered by most car-rental companies, known as the **Loss/Damage Waiver (LDW)** or **Collision Damage Waiver (CDW),** can cost as much as $20 per day. It usually covers the full value of the vehicle with no deductible if an outside party causes an accident or other damage to the rental car. Liability coverage varies according to the company policy and state law, but the minimum is usually at least $15,000. If you are at fault in an accident, however, you will be covered for the full replacement value of the car but not for liability. In California, you can buy additional liability coverage for such cases. Most rental companies will require a police report in order to process any claims you file, but your private insurer will not be notified of the accident.

## BY PLANE

In addition to the major carriers listed earlier in this section, several airlines provide service within the state, including **American Eagle** (© 800/433-7300), **Southwest** (© 800/435-9792), **United Express** (© 800/241-6522), and **US Airways Express** (© 800/428-4322). The round-trip fare between Los Angeles and San Francisco ranges from $79 to $200. See "Orientation" or "Getting There," in some of the city chapters, for further information

## BY TRAIN

**Amtrak** (© 800/USA-RAIL; www.amtrak.com) runs trains up and down the California coast, connecting San Diego, Los Angeles, and San Francisco, and all points in between. There are multiple trains each day, and rates fluctuate according to season and special promotions. One-way fares for the most popular segments can range from $17 (L.A.–Santa Barbara), to $24 (L.A.–San Diego), to $46 to $78 (San Francisco–L.A.).

## 12 Tips on Accommodations

The **rack rate** is the maximum rate that a hotel charges for a room. Hardly anybody pays this price, however, except in high season or on holidays. To lower the cost of your room:

- **Ask about special rates or other discounts.** Always ask whether a room less expensive than the first one quoted is available, or whether any special rates apply to you. You may qualify for corporate, student, military, senior, or other discounts. Mention membership in AAA, AARP, frequent-flier programs, or trade unions, which may entitle you to special deals as well. Find out the hotel policy on children—do kids stay free in the room or is there a special rate?
- **Dial direct.** When booking a chain hotel room, you'll often get a better deal by calling the individual hotel's reservation desk rather than the chain's main number.
- **Book online.** Many hotels offer Web-only discounts, or supply rooms to Priceline, Hotwire, or Expedia.com at lower rates than you'd get through the hotel itself. Shop around. And if you have special needs—a quiet room, a room with a view—call the hotel directly and make your needs known after you've booked online.
- **Remember the law of supply and demand.** Resort hotels are most crowded and therefore most expensive on weekends, so discounts are usually available for midweek stays. Business hotels in downtown locations are busiest during the week, so you can expect big discounts on weekends. Many hotels have high-season and low-season prices, and booking the day after "high season" ends can mean big discounts.
- **Look into group or long-stay discounts.** If you come as part of a large group, you should be able to negotiate a bargain rate, since the hotel can then guarantee occupancy in a number of rooms. Likewise, if you're planning a long stay (at least 5 days), you might qualify for a discount. As a general rule, expect 1 night free after a 7-night stay.

- **Avoid excess charges and hidden costs.** When you book a room, ask whether the hotel charges for parking. Use your own cellphone, pay phones, or prepaid phone cards instead of dialing direct from hotel phones, which usually have exorbitant rates. And don't be tempted by the room's minibar offerings: Most hotels charge through the nose for water, soda, and snacks. Finally, ask about local taxes and service charges, which can increase the cost of a room by 15% or more. If a hotel insists upon tacking on a surprise "energy surcharge" that wasn't mentioned at check-in or a "resort fee" for amenities you didn't use, you can often make a case for getting it removed.
- **Book an efficiency.** Rooms with kitchenettes let you to shop for groceries and cook your own meals. This is a big money saver, especially for families.
- **Consider enrolling in hotel "frequent-stay" programs,** which reward repeat customers who accumulate enough points or credits to earn free hotel nights, airline miles, complimentary in-room amenities,

or merchandise. These are offered by many chains (Hilton H-Honors and Marriott Rewards, to name a couple) and some inns and B&Bs.

## LANDING THE BEST ROOM

Somebody has to get the best room in the house. It might as well be you. Start by joining the hotel's frequent-guest program, which may make you eligible for upgrades. A hotel-branded credit card usually gives its owner free "silver" or "gold" status in frequent-guest programs. Ask for a corner room. They're often larger and quieter, with more windows and light, and they often cost the same as standard rooms. When you make your reservation, ask if the hotel is renovating; if it is, request a room away from the construction. Ask about nonsmoking rooms, rooms with views, rooms with twin, queen- or king-size beds. If you're a light sleeper, request a quiet room away from vending machines, elevators, restaurants, bars, and discos. Ask for a room that has been most recently renovated or redecorated.

If you aren't happy with your room when you arrive, ask for another one. Most lodgings will be willing to accommodate you.

## 13 Recommended Reading

There's no shortage of reading material about the history and culture of California, one of the most romanticized places on earth. Almost from the beginning, novelists and poets were part of California's cultural mosaic, and the works they've created offer a fascinating window into the lives and legends of the huge, diverse state and its state of mind.

### HISTORICAL PERSPECTIVES

When it comes to fictionalized accounts of California's pioneers, readers have lots of choices. Salinas native John Steinbeck, one of the state's best-known authors,

paints a vivid portrayal of proletarian life in the early to mid-1900s. His *Grapes of Wrath* remains the classic account of itinerant farm laborers coming to California in the midst of the Great Depression. *Cannery Row* has forever made the Monterey waterfront famous, and *East of Eden* offers insight into the way of life in the Salinas Valley.

Famed humorist and storyteller Mark Twain penned vivid tales during California's Gold Rush era, including one of his most popular works, "The Celebrated Jumping Frog of Calaveras County" (an annual Gold Country competition that still has legs). Other good Gold Rush reads include Bret Harte's *The Luck of Roaring Camp,* a sentimental tale of hard-luck miners and their false toughness, and J. S. Holliday's *The World Rushed In,* one of the finest nonfiction accounts of the Gold Rush still in print.

San Francisco was also a popular setting for many early works, including Twain's *San Francisco,* a collection of articles that glorified "the liveliest, heartiest community on our continent." It was also the birthplace of Jack London, who wrote several short stories of his younger days as an oyster pirate on the San Francisco Bay, as well as *Martin Eden,* his semiautobiographical account of life along the Oakland shores.

An excellent anthology containing selections from writers representing all the varied cultures in California's diverse history, *The Literature of California: Writings from the Golden State,* from the University of California Press, represents writers from the various cultures in state history.

Finally, for what some critics consider the best novel ever written about Hollywood, turn to Nathanael West's *The Day of the Locust,* a savage and satirical look at 1930s life on the fringes of the film industry.

## MYSTERY & MAYHEM

For you mystery buffs headed to California, two must-reads include Frank Norris's *McTeague: A Story of San Francisco,* a tale of love and greed set at the turn of the 20th century, and Dashiell Hammett's *The Maltese Falcon,* a detective novel that captures the seedier side of San Francisco in the 1920s. Another favorite is Raymond Chandler's *The Big Sleep,* in which Philip Marlowe explores the darker side of Los Angeles in the 1930s.

California has always been a hotbed for alternative—and, more often than not, controversial—literary styles. Joan Didion, in her novel *Slouching Toward Bethlehem,* and Hunter S. Thompson, in his columns for the *San Francisco Examiner* (brought together in the collection *Generation of Swine*), both used a "new journalistic" approach in their studies of San Francisco in the 1960s. Tom Wolfe's early work *The Electric Kool-Aid Acid Test* follows the Hell's Angels, the Grateful Dead, and Ken Kesey's Merry Pranksters as they ride through the hallucinogenic 1960s. Meanwhile, in "Howl" and *On the Road,* Beat writers Allen Ginsberg and Jack Kerouac, respectively, were penning protests against political conservatism—and promoting their bohemian lifestyle.

## CONTEMPORARY FICTION

If you're interested in a contemporary look back at four generations in the life of an American family, you can do no better than Wallace Stegner's *Angle of Repose.* The winner of the Pulitzer Prize in 1971, this work chronicles the lives of pioneers on the Western frontier. Among Stegner's many other works of fiction and nonfiction about the West is his novel *All the Little Live Things,* which is set in the San Francisco Bay Area of the 1960s.

## SPECIAL-INTEREST READS

Geology buffs will want to pack a copy of *Assembling California,* John McPhee's observation of California's geological history. Mike Davis's *City of Quartz* and *Ecology of Fear* offer a critical perspective on the social and natural history of Los Angeles.

Outdoor enthusiasts have dozens of sporting books to choose from, but most comprehensive is Foghorn Press's outdoor series—*California Camping, California Fishing, California Golf, California Beaches,* and *California Hiking.*

## FAST FACTS: California

*Earthquakes* In the rare event of an earthquake, if you're in a **tall building,** don't run outside; instead, move away from windows and toward the building's center. Crouch under a desk or table, or stand against a wall or under a doorway. If you're in bed, get under the bed, stand in a doorway, or crouch under a sturdy piece of furniture. When exiting the building, use stairwells, *not* elevators. If you're in your **car,** pull over to the side of the road and stop, but wait until you're away from bridges or overpasses, as well as telephone or power poles and lines. Stay in your car. If you're **outside,** stay away from trees, power lines, and the sides of buildings.

*Emergencies* To reach the police, ambulance service, or fire department, dial © **911.** No coins are needed at pay phones for 911 calls.

*Liquor Laws* Liquor and grocery stores, as well as some drugstores, can sell packaged alcoholic beverages between 6am and 2am. Most restaurants, nightclubs, and bars are licensed to serve alcoholic beverages during the same hours. The legal age for the purchase and consumption of alcoholic beverages is 21; proof of age is strictly enforced.

*Lost & Found* Be sure to tell all of your credit card companies the minute you discover your wallet has been lost or stolen and file a report at the nearest police precinct. Your credit card company or insurer may require a police report number or record of the loss. Most credit card companies have an emergency toll-free number to call if your card is lost or stolen; they may be able to wire you a cash advance immediately or deliver an emergency credit card in a day or two. Visa's U.S. emergency number is © **800/847-2911** or 410/581-9994. American Express cardholders and traveler's check holders should call © **800/221-7282.** MasterCard holders should call © **800/307-7309** or 636/722-7111. For other credit cards, call the toll-free number directory at © **800/555-1212.**

If you need emergency cash over the weekend when all banks and American Express offices are closed, you can have money wired to you via **Western Union** (© **800/325-6000;** www.westernunion.com).

Identity theft or fraud are potential complications of losing your wallet, especially if you've lost your driver's license too. Notify the major credit-reporting bureaus immediately; placing a fraud alert on your records may protect you against liability for criminal activity. The three major U.S. credit-reporting agencies are **Equifax** (© **800/766-0008;** www.equifax.com), **Experian** (© **888/397-3742;** www.experian.com), and **TransUnion** (© **800/680-7289;** www.transunion.com). If you've lost all your photo ID, call your airline and explain; they might allow you to board the plane if you have a copy of your passport or birth certificate and a copy of the police report you've filed.

*Passports* **For Residents of the United States:** Whether you're applying in person or by mail, you can download passport applications from http://travel.state.gov, the U.S. State Department website. To find your regional passport office, either check the U.S. State Department website (**http://travel.state.gov**) or call the

**National Passport Information Center** toll-free number (© **877/487-2778**) for automated information.

**For Residents of Canada:** Passport applications are available at travel agencies throughout Canada or from the central **Passport Office,** Department of Foreign Affairs and International Trade, Ottawa, ON K1A 0G3 (© **800/567-6868;** www.ppt.gc.ca).

**For Residents of the United Kingdom:** To pick up an application for a standard 10-year passport (5-yr. passport for children under 16), visit your nearest passport office, major post office, or travel agency or contact the **United Kingdom Passport Service** at © **0870/521-0410** or search its website at www.ukpa.gov.uk.

**For Residents of Ireland:** You can apply for a 10-year passport at the **Passport Office,** Setanta Centre, Molesworth Street, Dublin 2 (© **01/671-1633;** www.irlgov.ie/iveagh). Those under age 18 and over 65 must apply for a €12 3-year passport. You can also apply at 1A South Mall, Cork (© **021/272-525**) or at most main post offices.

**For Residents of Australia:** You can pick up an application from your local post office or any branch of Passports Australia, but you must schedule an interview at the passport office to present your application materials. Call the **Australian Passport Information Service** at © **131-232,** or visit the government website at www.passports.gov.au.

**For Residents of New Zealand:** You can pick up a passport application at any New Zealand Passports Office or download it from their website. Contact the **Passports Office** at © **0800/225-050** in New Zealand or 04/474-8100, or log on to www.passports.govt.nz.

*Taxes* California's state sales tax is 7.25%. Some cities include an additional percentage or fraction, so the tax varies throughout the state; for example, it's 7.75% in San Diego, 8.25% in Los Angeles, and 8.5% in San Francisco. Hotel taxes are almost always higher than tariffs levied on goods and services.

*Time Zone* California and the entire West Coast are in the Pacific Standard Time zone, 3 hours earlier than the East Coast.

# 3

# For International Visitors

Whether it's your 1st visit or your 10th, a trip to the United States may require advance planning. This chapter will provide you with essential information, helpful tips, and advice for the more common problems that international visitors may encounter while vacationing in California.

## 1 Preparing for Your Trip

### ENTRY REQUIREMENTS

Check at any U.S. embassy or consulate for current information and requirements. You can also obtain a visa application and other information online at the **U.S. State Department**'s website, at **www.travel.state.gov**.

**VISAS** The U.S. State Department has a **Visa Waiver Program** allowing citizens of the following countries (at press time) to enter the United States without a visa for stays of up to 90 days: Andorra, Australia, Austria, Belgium, Brunei, Denmark, Finland, France, Germany, Iceland, Ireland, Italy, Japan, Liechtenstein, Luxembourg, Monaco, the Netherlands, New Zealand, Norway, Portugal, San Marino, Singapore, Slovenia, Spain, Sweden, Switzerland, and the United Kingdom. Citizens of these nations need only a valid passport and a round-trip air or cruise ticket upon arrival. If they first enter the United States, they may also visit Mexico, Canada, Bermuda, and/or the Caribbean islands and return to the United States without a visa. Further information is available from any U.S. embassy or consulate. Canadian citizens may enter the United States without visas; they need only proof of residence.

Citizens of all other countries must have (1) a valid passport that expires at least 6 months later than the scheduled end of their visit to the United States, and (2) a tourist visa, which may be obtained without charge from any U.S. consulate.

**To obtain a visa,** the traveler must submit a completed application form, with a 1½-inch-square photo, and demonstrate binding ties to a residence abroad. Usually you can obtain a visa at once or within 24 hours, but it may take longer during the summer rush from June through August. If you cannot go in person, ask the nearest U.S. embassy or consulate about applying by mail. Your travel agent or airline office may also be able to provide you with visa applications and instructions. The U.S. consulate or embassy that issues your visa will determine whether you will be issued a multiple- or single-entry visa and any restrictions regarding the length of your stay.

**British** subjects can obtain up-to-date visa information by calling the **U.S. Embassy Visa Information Line** (② **0891/200-290**) or by visiting the "Visas to the U.S." section of the American Embassy London's website at www.usembassy.org.uk.

**Irish** citizens can obtain up-to-date visa information through the **Embassy of the USA Dublin,** 42 Elgin Rd., Dublin 4, Ireland (② 353/1-668-8777; or by checking the "Consular Services" section of the website at http://dublin.usembassy.gov.

**Australian** citizens can obtain up-to-date visa information from the **U.S. Embassy Canberra,** Moonah Place, Yarralumla, ACT 2600 (② 02/6214-5600) or by checking the U.S. Diplomatic Mission's website at http://usembassy-australia.state.gov/consular.

Citizens of **New Zealand** can obtain up-to-date visa information by contacting the **U.S. Embassy New Zealand,** 29 Fitzherbert Terrace, Thorndon, Wellington (② 644/472-2068), or get the information directly from the "For New Zealanders" section of the website at http://usembassy.org.nz.

**MEDICAL REQUIREMENTS**  Unless you're arriving from an area known to be suffering from an epidemic (particularly cholera or yellow fever), inoculations or vaccinations are not required for entry into the United States. If you have a medical condition that requires **syringe-administered medications**, carry a valid signed prescription from your physician—the Federal Aviation Administration (FAA) no longer allows airline passengers to pack syringes in their carry-on baggage without documented proof of medical need. If you have a disease that requires treatment with **narcotics,** you should also carry documented proof with you—smuggling narcotics aboard a plane is a serious offense that carries severe penalties in the U.S.

For **HIV-positive visitors,** requirements for entering the United States are somewhat vague and change frequently. According to the latest publication of *HIV and Immigrants: A Manual for AIDS Service Providers,* the Immigration and Naturalization Service (INS) doesn't require a medical exam for entry into the United States, but INS officials may stop individuals because they look sick or because they are carrying AIDS/HIV medicine. For up-to-the-minute information, contact **AIDSinfo** (② 800/448-0440 or 301/519-6616 outside the U.S.; www.aidsinfo.nih.gov) or the **Gay Men's Health Crisis** (② 212/367-1000; www.gmhc.org).

**DRIVER'S LICENSES**  Foreign driver's licenses are usually recognized in the U.S., but you should get an international one if your home license is not in English.

## PASSPORT INFORMATION

Safeguard your passport in an inconspicuous, inaccessible place like a money belt. Make a copy of the critical pages, including the passport number, and store it in a safe place, separate from the passport itself. If you lose your passport, visit the nearest consulate of your native country as soon as possible for a replacement. Passport applications are downloadable from the websites listed below.

*Note:* The International Civil Aviation Organization has recommended a policy requiring that *every* individual who travels by air have a passport. Many countries are now requiring that even children have their own passports to travel internationally.

### FOR RESIDENTS OF CANADA

You can pick up a passport application at any of 28 regional passport offices or most travel agencies. Canadian children who travel must have their own passport. However, if you hold a valid Canadian passport issued before December 11, 2001, that bears the name of your child, the passport remains valid for you and your child until it expires. Passports cost C$87 for those 16 years and older (valid 5 years), C$37 children 3 to 15 (valid 5 years), and C$22, children under 3 (valid 3 years). Applications, which must be accompanied by two identical passport-sized photographs and proof of Canadian citizenship, are available at travel agencies throughout Canada or from the central **Passport Office,** Department of Foreign Affairs and International Trade, Ottawa, ON K1A 0G3 (✆ **800/567-6868;** www.dfait-maeci.gc. ca/passport). Processing takes 5 to 10 days if you apply in person, or about 3 weeks by mail.

## FOR RESIDENTS OF THE UNITED KINGDOM

To pick up an application for a standard 10-year passport (5-year passport for children under 16), visit the nearest passport office, major post office, or travel agency. You can also contact the **United Kingdom Passport Service** at ✆ **0870/571-0410** or visit its website at www.passport. gov.uk. Passports are £42 for adults and £25 for children under 16, with another £30 fee if you apply in person at a passport office. Processing takes about 2 weeks (1 week if you apply at the passport office).

## FOR RESIDENTS OF IRELAND

You can apply for a 10-year passport (€57), at the **Passport Office,** Setanta Centre, Molesworth Street, Dublin 2 (✆ **01/671-1633;** www.irlgov.ie/iveagh). Those under age 18 and over 65 must apply for a €12 3-year passport. You can also apply at 1A South Mall, Cork (✆ **021/ 272 525-**) or over the counter at most main post offices.

## FOR RESIDENTS OF AUSTRALIA

You can get an application from your local post office or any branch of Passports Australia, but you must schedule an interview at the passport office to present your application materials. Call the **Australian Passport Information Service** at ✆ **131-232,** or visit the government website at www.passports.gov.au. Passports for adults are A$150 and for those under 18 are A$75.

## FOR RESIDENTS OF NEW ZEALAND

You can pick up a passport application at any New Zealand Passports Office or download it from their website. Contact the **Passports Office** at ✆ **0800/225-050** in New Zealand or 04/474-8100, or log on to www.passports.govt.nz. Passports for adults are NZ$71 and for children under 16 NZ$36.

## CUSTOMS
### WHAT YOU CAN BRING IN

Every visitor more than 21 years of age may bring in, free of duty, the following: (1) 1 liter of wine or hard liquor; (2) 200 cigarettes, 100 cigars (but not from Cuba), or 3 pounds of smoking tobacco; and (3) $100 worth of gifts. These exemptions are offered to travelers who spend at least 72 hours in the United States and who have not claimed them within the preceding 6 months. It is altogether forbidden to bring into the country foodstuffs (particularly fruit, cooked meats, and canned goods) and plants (vegetables, seeds, tropical plants, and the like). Foreign tourists may carry in or out up to $10,000 in U.S. or foreign currency with no formalities; larger sums must be declared to U.S. Customs on entering or leaving, which includes filing form CM 4790. For details regarding U.S. Customs and Border Protection, consult your nearest U.S. embassy or consulate, or **U.S. Customs** (✆ **202/927-1770;** www.customs.ustreas.gov).

### WHAT YOU CAN TAKE HOME

**U.K. citizens returning from a non-EU country** have a customs allowance of: 200 cigarettes; 50 cigars; 250g of smoking tobacco; 2 liters of still table wine; 1 liter of spirits or strong liqueurs (over 22% volume); 2 liters of fortified wine, sparkling wine or other liqueurs; 60cc (ml) perfume; 250cc (ml) of toilet water; and £145 worth of all other goods, including gifts and souvenirs. People under 17 cannot have the tobacco or alcohol allowance. For more information, consult **HM Customs & Excise** at (C) **0845/010-9000** (from outside the U.K., 020/8929-0152), or http://customs. hmrc.gov.uk

For a clear summary of **Canadian** rules, request the booklet *I Declare,* from the **Canada Customs and Revenue Agency** ((C) **800/461-9999** in Canada, or 204/ 983-3500; www.cra-arc.gc.ca). Canada allows its citizens a C$750 exemption, and you're allowed to bring back duty-free one carton of cigarettes, one can of tobacco, 40 imperial ounces of liquor, and 50 cigars. Canadian citizens under 18 or 19, depending on their province, cannot have the tobacco or alcohol allowance. In addition, you're allowed to mail gifts to Canada valued at less than C$60 a day, if they're unsolicited and don't contain alcohol or tobacco (write on the package "Unsolicited gift, under $60 value"). All valuables should be declared on the Y-38 form before departure from Canada, including serial numbers of valuables you already own, such as expensive foreign cameras. *Note:* The C$750 exemption can only be used once a year and only after an absence of 7 days.

The duty-free allowance in **Australia** is A$900 or, for those under 18, A$450. Citizens age 18 and over can bring in 250 cigarettes or 250 grams of loose tobacco, and 2.25 liters of alcohol. If you're returning with valuables you already own, such as foreign-made cameras, you should file form B263. A helpful brochure available from Australian consulates or Customs offices is *Know Before You Go.* For details, consult the **Australian Customs Service** at (C) **1300/363-263** or www.customs.gov.au.

The duty-free allowance for **New Zealand** is NZ$700. Citizens over 17 can bring in 200 cigarettes, 50 cigars, or 250 grams of tobacco (or a mixture of all three if their combined weight doesn't exceed 250g); plus 4.5 liters of wine and beer, or 1.125 liters of liquor. New Zealand currency does not carry import or export restrictions. Fill out a certificate of export, listing the valuables you are taking out of the country; that way, you can bring them back without paying duty. Most questions are answered in a free pamphlet available at New Zealand consulates and Customs offices: *New Zealand Customs Guide for Travellers, Notice no. 4.* For more information, contact **New Zealand Customs,** The Customhouse, 17–21 Whitmore St., Box 2218, Wellington ((C) **0800/428-786** or 04/473-6099; www.customs.govt.nz).

## HEALTH INSURANCE

Although it's not required of travelers, health insurance is highly recommended. Unlike many European countries, the United States does not usually offer free or low-cost medical care to its citizens or visitors. Doctors and hospitals are expensive, and in most cases will require advance payment or proof of coverage before they render their services. Policies can cover everything from the loss or theft of your baggage and trip cancellation to the guarantee of bail in case you're arrested. Good policies will also cover the costs of an accident, repatriation, or death. Packages such as **Europ Assistance's "Worldwide Healthcare Plan"** are sold by European automobile clubs and travel agencies at attractive rates. **Worldwide Assistance Services, Inc.** ((C) **800/777-8710;** www.worldwide assistance.com) is the agent for Europ Assistance in the United States.

Though lack of health insurance may prevent you from being admitted to a hospital in nonemergencies, don't worry about being left on a street corner to die: The American way is to fix you now and bill the living daylights out of you later.

**INSURANCE FOR BRITISH TRAVELERS** Most big travel agents offer their own insurance and will probably try to sell you their package when you book a holiday. Think before you sign. **Britain's Consumers' Association** recommends that you insist on seeing the policy and reading the fine print before buying travel insurance. **The Association of British Insurers** (✆ **020/7600-3333;** www.abi.org.uk) gives advice by phone and publishes *Holiday Insurance,* a free guide to policy provisions and prices. You might also shop around for better deals: Try **Columbus Direct** (✆ **0870/033-9988;** www.columbusdirect.net).

**INSURANCE FOR CANADIAN TRAVELERS** Canadians should check with their provincial health plan offices or call **Health Canada** (✆ 866/225-0709; www.hc-sc.gc.ca) to find out the extent of their coverage and what documentation and receipts they must take home in case they are treated in the United States.

## MONEY

**CURRENCY** The U.S. monetary system is very simple: The most common **bills** are the $1 (a "buck"), $5, $10, and $20 denominations. There are also $2 bills (seldom encountered), $50 bills and $100 bills (the last two are usually not welcome as payment for small purchases). All the paper money was recently redesigned, making the faces on them disproportionately large, but the old-style bills are still legal tender.

Coins come in seven denominations: 1¢ (1 cent, or a penny); 5¢ (5 cents, or a nickel); 10¢ (10 cents, or a dime); 25¢ (25 cents, or a quarter); 50¢ (50 cents, or a half dollar); the gold-colored Sacagawea coin, worth $1; and the rare silver dollar.

*Note:* The "foreign-exchange bureaus" so common in Europe are rare even at airports in the U.S., and nonexistent outside major cities. It's best not to change foreign money (or traveler's checks denominated in a currency other than U.S. dollars) at a small-town bank, or even a branch in a big city; in fact, leave any currency other

than U.S. dollars at home—it may prove a greater nuisance to you than it's worth.

**TRAVELER'S CHECKS** Traveler's checks are widely accepted, but make sure that they're denominated in U.S. dollars; foreign-currency checks are often difficult to exchange. The three traveler's checks that are most widely recognized—and least likely to be denied—are **Visa, American Express,** and **Thomas Cook.** Be sure to record the numbers of the checks, and keep that information in a separate place in case they get lost or stolen. Most California businesses are pretty good about taking traveler's checks, but you're better off cashing them in at a bank (in small amounts, of course) and paying in cash. Remember: You'll need identification, such as a driver's license or passport, to change a traveler's check.

**CREDIT CARDS & ATMs** Credit cards are the most widely used form of payment in the United States: **Visa** (Barclaycard in Britain), **MasterCard** (EuroCard in Europe, Access in Britain, Chargex in Canada), **American Express, Diners Club,** and **Discover.** There are, however, a handful of stores and restaurants in California that do not take credit cards, so be sure to ask in advance. Most businesses display a sticker near their entrance to let you know which cards they accept. (*Note:* Businesses may require a minimum purchase, usually around $10, to use a credit card.)

It's highly recommended that you bring at least one major credit card. You must have one to rent a car, and hotels and airlines usually require a credit card imprint as a deposit against expenses. And in an emergency, a credit card is invaluable.

You'll find automated teller machines (ATMs) in just about every town in California, and on every block in the business districts of the big cities. Some ATMs will allow you to draw U.S. currency against your bank and credit cards. Check with

> **Travel Tip**
> Keep a copy of all your travel papers separate from your wallet or purse, and
> leave a copy with someone at home in case of an emergency.

your bank before leaving home, and remember that you will need your personal identification number (PIN) to do so. Most accept Visa, MasterCard, and American Express, as well as ATM cards from other U.S. banks. Expect to be charged up to $3 per transaction, however, if you're not using your own bank's ATM.

One way around these fees is to ask for "cash back" at grocery stores that accept ATM cards and don't charge usage fees. Of course, you'll have to purchase something first. The same is true at most U.S. post offices.

ATM cards with major credit card backing, known as "debit cards," are now a commonly acceptable form of payment in most stores and restaurants. Debit cards draw money directly from your checking account. Some stores enable you to receive "cash back" on your debit-card purchases as well.

## SAFETY

**GENERAL SUGGESTIONS** Although California's tourist areas are generally safe, U.S. urban areas tend to be less safe than those in Europe or Japan. You should always stay alert. This is particularly true of large American cities. If you're in doubt about which neighborhoods are safe, don't hesitate to make inquiries with the hotel front desk staff or the local tourist office.

Avoid deserted areas, especially at night, and don't go into public parks after dark unless there's a concert or similar occasion that will attract a crowd.

Avoid carrying valuables with you on the street, and keep expensive cameras or electronic equipment bagged up or covered when not in use. If you're using a map, try to consult it inconspicuously—or

better yet, study it before you leave your room. Hold on to your pocketbook, and place your billfold in an inside pocket. In theaters, restaurants, and other public places, keep your possessions in sight.

Always lock your room door—don't assume that once you're inside the hotel you are automatically safe and no longer need to be aware of your surroundings.

**DRIVING SAFETY** Driving safety is important, too, and carjacking is not unprecedented. Question your rental agency about personal safety and ask for a traveler-safety brochure when you pick up your car. Obtain written directions— or a map with the route clearly marked— from the agency showing how to get to your destination. (Many agencies now offer the option of renting a cellphone for the duration of your car rental; check with the rental agent when you pick up the car. Otherwise, contact **InTouch USA** at ✆ **800/872-7626** or www.intouch usa.com for short-term cellphone rental.) And, if possible, arrive and depart during daylight hours.

If you drive off a highway and end up in a dodgy-looking neighborhood, leave the area as quickly as possible. If you have an accident, even on the highway, stay in your car with the doors locked until you assess the situation or until the police arrive. If you're bumped from behind on the street or are involved in a minor accident with no injuries, and the situation appears to be suspicious, motion to the other driver to follow you. Never get out of your car in such situations. Go directly to the nearest police precinct, well-lit service station, or 24-hour store.

Park in well-lit, busy areas when possible. Always keep your car doors locked, even if the vehicle is attended. Never leave any packages or valuables in sight. If someone attempts to rob you or steal your car, don't try to resist the thief/carjacker. Report the incident to the police department immediately by calling ✆ **911.**

## 2 Getting to the U.S.

**AIRLINES**   In addition to the domestic U.S. airlines listed in chapter 2, many international carriers serve LAX and other U.S. gateways. These include, among others: **Aer Lingus** (✆ 01/886-8888 in Dublin; www.aerlingus.ie), **Air Canada** (✆ 800/776-3000; www.aircanada.ca), **British Airways** (✆ 0845/7733-377 in the U.K.; www.british-airways.com), **Canadian Airlines** (✆ 800/426-7000), **Japan Airlines** (✆ 0354/89-1111 in Tokyo; www.jal.co.jp), **Qantas** (✆ 13-13-13 in Australia; www.qantas.com.au), and **Virgin Atlantic** (✆ 01293/747-747 in the U.K.; www.fly.virgin.com). British Airways and Virgin Atlantic offer direct flights to San Francisco and Los Angeles from London. **Air New Zealand** (✆ 73-7000 in New Zealand; www.airnewzealand.co.nz) also flies direct to California.

**AIRLINE DISCOUNTS**   Smart travelers can reduce the price of a plane ticket by shopping around. Overseas visitors, for example, can take advantage of the APEX (Advance Purchase Excursion) reductions offered by all major U.S. and European carriers. For more money-saving airline advice, see "Getting There," in chapter 2. For the best rates, compare fares and be flexible with the dates and times of travel.

**IMMIGRATION AND CUSTOMS CLEARANCE**   Visitors arriving by air, no matter what the port of entry, should cultivate patience and resignation before setting foot on U.S. soil. Clearing immigration control can take as long as 2 hours, especially on summer weekends, so carry this guidebook or other reading material. This is especially true in the aftermath of the September 11, 2001, terrorist attacks, when U.S. airports have considerably beefed up security clearances. People traveling by air from Canada, Bermuda, and certain Caribbean countries can sometimes clear Customs and Immigration at the point of departure, which is much faster.

*Tips*  **Prepare to Be Fingerprinted**

As of January 2004, many international visitors traveling on visas to the United States will be photographed and fingerprinted at Customs in a new program created by the Department of Homeland Security called **US-VISIT.** Non-U.S. citizens arriving at airports and on cruise ships must undergo an instant background check as part of the government's efforts to deter terrorism by verifying the identity of incoming and outgoing visitors. Exempt from the extra scrutiny are visitors entering by land or those (mostly in Europe; see p. 49) that don't require a visa for short-term visits. For more information, go to the Homeland Security website at **www.dhs.gov/dhspublic.**

## 3 Getting Around the U.S.

**BY PLANE** Some large airlines offer transatlantic or transpacific passengers special discount tickets under the name **Visit USA,** which allows mostly one-way travel from one U.S. destination to another at very low prices. Unavailable in the U.S., these discount tickets must be purchased abroad in conjunction with your international fare. This system is the easiest, fastest, cheapest way to see the country. Obtain information well in advance from your travel agent or the airline, since the conditions attached to these discount tickets can be changed without advance notice.

**BY TRAIN** International visitors (excluding Canadians) can also buy a **USA Rail Pass,** good for 15 or 30 days of unlimited travel on **Amtrak** (© 800/ **USA-RAIL;** www.amtrak.com). The pass is available through many overseas travel agents. Prices valid for travel across the United States in 2005 for a 15-day pass were $295 off-peak, $440 peak; a 30-day pass costs $385 off-peak, $550 peak. Fares are significantly cheaper, however, within particular regions. See Amtrak's website for the cost of travel within the western, eastern, or northwestern United States. With a foreign passport, you can also buy passes direct from some Amtrak locations, including San Francisco, Los Angeles, Chicago, New York, Miami, Boston, and Washington, D.C. Reservations are generally required and should be made as early as possible. Regional rail passes are also available.

**BY BUS** Bus travel is often the most economical form of public transit for short hops between U.S. cities, but it can also be slow and uncomfortable—certainly not an option for everyone (particularly when Amtrak, which is far more luxurious, offers similar rates). **Greyhound/Trailways** (© **800/231-2222;** www.greyhound.com), the sole nationwide bus line, offers an **International Ameripass** that must be purchased before coming to the United States, or by phone through the Greyhound International Office at the Port Authority Bus Terminal in New York City (© **212/971-0492**). The pass can be obtained from foreign travel agents or through Greyhound's website (order at least 21 days before your departure to the U.S.) and costs less than the domestic version. 2005 passes cost as follows: 4 days ($179), 7 days ($239), 10 days ($289), 15 days ($349), 21 days ($419), 30 days ($479), 45 days ($529), or 60 days ($639). You can get more info on the pass at the website, or by calling © **402/330-8552.** In addition, special rates are available for seniors, students, and children.

**BY CAR** Unless you plan to spend the bulk of your vacation in a city where walking is the best way to get around (read: New York City or New Orleans), the most cost-effective way to travel the United States—especially California and Los Angeles—is by car. The interstate highway system connects cities and towns all over the country, with an extensive network of federal, state, and local highways and roads as well. California has only a couple of obscure toll roads, though it does charge a toll at many major bridges. Some of the national car-rental companies with offices in California include **Alamo** (© 800/462-5266; www.alamo.com), **Avis** (© 800/230-4898; www.avis.com), **Budget** (© 800/527-0700; www.budget.com), **Dollar** (© 800/800-3665; www.dollar.com), **Hertz** (© 800/654-3131; www.hertz.com), and **National** (© 800/227-7368; www.nationalcar.com).

If you plan to rent a car in the United States, you probably won't need the services of an additional automobile organization. If you're planning to buy or borrow a car, automobile-association membership is recommended. **AAA, the American Automobile Association** (© 800/222-4357; http://travel.aaa.com), is the country's largest auto club and supplies its members with maps, insurance, and, most important, emergency road service. The cost of joining runs from $63 for singles to $87 for two members, but if you're a member of a foreign auto club with reciprocal arrangements, you can enjoy free AAA service in America. See "Getting There" in chapter 2 for more information.

## FAST FACTS: For the International Traveler

*Automobile Organizations*  Auto clubs will supply maps, suggested routes, guidebooks, accident and bail-bond insurance, and emergency road service. The **American Automobile Association (AAA)** is the major auto club in the United States. If you belong to an auto club in your home country, inquire about AAA reciprocity before you leave. You may be able to join AAA even if you're not a member of a reciprocal club; to inquire, call AAA (© 800/222-4357). AAA is actually an organization of regional auto clubs, so look under "AAA Automobile Club" in the White Pages of the telephone directory. AAA has a nationwide emergency road service telephone number (© 800/AAA-HELP).

*Business Hours*  Offices are usually open weekdays from 9am to 5pm. Banks are open weekdays from 9am to 3pm or later and sometimes Saturday mornings. Stores typically open between 9 and 10am and close between 5 and 6pm from Monday through Saturday. Stores in shopping complexes or malls tend to stay open late: until about 9pm on weekdays and weekends, and many malls and larger department stores are open on Sundays.

*Currency & Currency Exchange*  See "Entry Requirements" and "Money" under "Preparing for Your Trip," earlier.

*Drinking Laws*  The legal age for purchase and consumption of alcoholic beverages is 21; proof of age is required and often requested at bars, nightclubs, and restaurants, so it's always a good idea to bring ID when you go out. Supermarkets and convenience stores in California sell beer, wine, and liquor.

Do not carry open containers of alcohol in your car or any public area that isn't zoned for alcohol consumption. The police can fine you on the spot. And nothing will ruin your trip faster than getting a citation for DUI ("driving under the influence"), so don't even think about driving while intoxicated.

*Electricity*  Like Canada, the United States uses 110 to 120 volts AC (60 cycles), compared to 220 to 240 volts AC (50 cycles) in most of Europe, Australia, and New Zealand. If your small appliances use 220 to 240 volts, you'll need a 110-volt transformer and a plug adapter with two flat parallel pins to operate them here. Downward converters that change 220–240 volts to 110–120 volts are difficult to find in the United States, so bring one with you.

*Embassies & Consulates*  All embassies are located in the nation's capital, Washington, D.C. Some consulates are located in major U.S. cities, and most nations have a mission to the United Nations in New York City. If your country isn't listed below, call for directory information in Washington, D.C. (© 202/555-1212) or log on to www.embassy.org/embassies.

The embassy of **Australia** is at 1601 Massachusetts Ave. NW, Washington, DC 20036 (© 202/797-3000; www.austemb.org). There are consulates in New York, Honolulu, Houston, Los Angeles, and San Francisco.

The embassy of **Canada** is at 501 Pennsylvania Ave. NW, Washington, DC 20001 (© 202/682-1740; www.canadianembassy.org). Other Canadian consulates are in Buffalo (New York), Detroit, Los Angeles, New York, and Seattle.

The embassy of **Ireland** is at 2234 Massachusetts Ave. NW, Washington, DC 20008 (© 202/462-3939; www.irelandemb.org). Irish consulates are in Boston, Chicago, New York, San Francisco, and other cities. See website for complete listing.

The embassy of **Japan** is at 2520 Massachusetts Ave. NW, Washington, DC 20008 (© 202/238-6700; www.embjapan.org). Japanese consulates are located in many cities, including Atlanta, Boston, Detroit, New York, San Francisco, and Seattle.

The embassy of **New Zealand** is at 37 Observatory Circle NW, Washington, DC 20008 (© 202/328-4800; www.nzemb.org). New Zealand consulates are in Los Angeles, Salt Lake City, San Francisco, and Seattle.

The embassy of the **United Kingdom** is at 3100 Massachusetts Ave. NW, Washington, DC 20008 (© 202/588-7800; www.britainusa.com). Other British consulates are in Atlanta, Boston, Chicago, Cleveland, Houston, Los Angeles, New York, San Francisco, and Seattle.

*Emergencies* Call © **911** to report a fire, call the police, or get an ambulance anywhere in the United States. This is a toll-free call (no coins are required at public telephones).

If you encounter traveler's problems, call the Los Angeles chapter of the **Traveler's Aid Society** (© 310/646-2270; www.travelersaid.org), a nationwide, nonprofit, social service organization that helps travelers in difficult straits. Its services might include reuniting families separated while traveling, providing food and/or shelter to people stranded without cash, and even emotional counseling.

*Gasoline (Petrol)* Petrol is known as gasoline (or simply "gas") in the United States, and petrol stations are known as both gas stations and service stations. At press time, the cost of gasoline in the U.S. is abnormally high ($3 a gallon) and fluctuating drastically, on the rise. Taxes are already included in the printed price. One U.S. gallon equals 3.8 liters or .85 imperial gallons.

*Holidays* Banks, government offices, post offices, and many stores, restaurants, and museums are closed on the following legal national holidays: January 1 (New Year's Day), the third Monday in January (Martin Luther King, Jr., Day), the third Monday in February (Presidents' Day), the last Monday in May (Memorial Day), July 4 (Independence Day), the first Monday in September (Labor Day), the second Monday in October (Columbus Day), November 11 (Veterans' Day/Armistice Day), the fourth Thursday in November (Thanksgiving Day), and December 25 (Christmas). The Tuesday after the first Monday in November is Election Day, a federal government holiday in presidential-election years (held every 4 years, and next in 2008).

*Legal Aid*  If you are "pulled over" for a minor infraction (such as speeding), never attempt to pay the fine directly to a police officer; this could be construed as attempted bribery, a much more serious crime. Pay fines by mail, or directly into the hands of the clerk of the court. If accused of a more serious offense, say and do nothing before consulting a lawyer. Here the burden is on the state to prove a person's guilt beyond a reasonable doubt, and everyone has the right to remain silent, whether he or she is suspected of a crime or actually arrested. Once arrested, a person can make one telephone call to a party of his or her choice. Call your embassy or consulate.

*Mail*  If you aren't sure what your address will be in the United States, mail can be sent to you, in your name, c/o General Delivery at the main post office of the city or region where you expect to be. (Call ℰ **800/275-8777** for information on the nearest post office.) The addressee must pick up mail in person and must produce proof of identity (driver's license, passport, etc.). Most post offices will hold your mail for up to 1 month, and are open Monday to Friday from 8am to 6pm, and Saturday from 9am to 3pm.

Generally found at intersections, mailboxes are blue with a red-and-white stripe and carry the inscription U.S. MAIL. If your mail is addressed to a U.S. destination, don't forget to add the five-digit postal code (or zip code), after the two-letter abbreviation of the state to which the mail is addressed. This is essential to prompt delivery.

At press time, domestic postage rates were 37¢ for a large postcard and 37¢ for a letter. For international mail, a first-class letter of up to ½ ounce costs 80¢ (60¢ to Canada and Mexico); a first-class postcard costs 70¢ (50¢ to Canada and Mexico); and a preprinted postal aerogramme costs 70¢. For more information, see http://pe.usps.gov.

*Measurements*  See the chart on the inside front cover of this book for details on converting metric measurements to U.S. equivalents.

*Smoking*  Heavy smokers have it rough in California: Smoking is banned in public buildings, sports arenas, elevators, theaters, banks, lobbies, restaurants, offices, stores, bed-and-breakfasts, most small hotels, and bars. As of January 1, 1998, you can't even smoke in a bar in California (the only exception being bars where drinks are served solely by the owner). You will find, however, that many neighborhood bars turn the other cheek and pass you an ashtray.

*Taxes*  The United States has no value-added tax (VAT) or other indirect tax at the national level. Every state, county, and city may levy its own local tax on all purchases, including hotel and restaurant checks and airline tickets. These taxes will not appear on price tags. Sales tax in California is generally around 8%. Hotel tax applies to the room tariff only (which is not subject to sales tax); it's set by the city, ranging from 12% to 17% throughout California.

*Telephone, Telegraph, Telex & Fax*  Private corporations run the telephone system in the U.S., so rates can vary widely, especially for long-distance service and operator-assisted calls. Generally, hotel surcharges on long-distance and local calls are astronomical, so you're better off using a **public pay telephone,** which you'll find clearly marked in most public buildings and private establishments, as well as on the street. Convenience grocery stores and gas stations almost always have them. Many convenience groceries and packaging services sell **pre-paid calling cards** in denominations up to $50; these can be the least expensive way to call home. Many public phones at airports now accept American Express, MasterCard, and Visa credit cards. **Local calls** made from public pay phones in most locales cost either 25¢ or 35¢. Pay phones do not accept pennies, and few will take anything larger than a quarter.

You may want to look into leasing a cellphone for the duration of your trip.

Most long-distance and international calls can be dialed directly from any phone. **For calls within the United States and to Canada,** dial 1 followed by the area code and the seven-digit number. **For other international calls,** dial 011 followed by the country code, city code, and the number you are calling.

Calls to area codes **800, 888, 877,** and **866** are toll-free. However, calls to area codes **700** and **900** (chat lines, bulletin boards, "dating" services, and so on) can be very expensive—usually a charge of 95¢ to $3 or more per minute, and they sometimes have minimum charges that can run as high as $15 or more.

For **reversed-charge or collect calls,** and for person-to-person calls, dial the number 0 then the area code and number; an operator will come on the line, and you should specify whether you are calling collect, person-to-person, or both. If your operator-assisted call is international, ask for the overseas operator.

For **local directory assistance** ("information"), dial 411; for long-distance information, dial 1, then the appropriate area code and 555-1212.

**Telegraph and telex services** are provided primarily by Western Union. You can bring your telegram to the nearest Western Union office or dictate it by phone (📞 **800/325-6000**). You can also telegraph money, or have it telegraphed to you, very quickly over the Western Union system, but this service can cost as much as 15 to 20 percent of the amount sent.

Most hotels have **fax machines** available for guest use (be sure to ask about the charge to use it). Many hotel rooms are even wired for guests' fax machines. A less expensive way to send and receive faxes may be at stores such as **The UPS Store** (formerly Mail Boxes Etc.), a national chain of retail packing service shops. (Look in the Yellow Pages directory under "Packing Services.")

The U.S. has two kinds of telephone directories. The **White Pages** list private households and business subscribers in alphabetical order. The inside front cover lists emergency numbers for police, fire, ambulance, poison-control center, crime-victims hot line, and so on. The first few pages will tell you how to make long-distance and international calls, complete with country codes and area codes. Government numbers are usually printed on blue paper within the White Pages. Printed on yellow paper, the so-called **Yellow Pages** list all local services, businesses, industries, and houses of worship according to activity with an index at the front or back. (Drugstores/pharmacies and restaurants are also listed by geographic location.) The Yellow Pages also include city plans or detailed area maps, postal ZIP codes, and public transportation routes.

*Time* The continental United States is divided into **four time zones:** Eastern Standard Time (EST), Central Standard Time (CST), Mountain Standard Time (MST), and Pacific Standard Time (PST). Alaska and Hawaii have their own zones. For example, when it's 9am in Los Angeles (PST), it's 7am in Honolulu (HST),10am in Denver (MST), 11am in Chicago (CST), noon in New York City (EST), 5pm in London (GMT), and 2am the next day in Sydney.

**Daylight saving time** takes effect at 2am the first Sunday in April until 2am the last Sunday in October, except in Arizona, Hawaii, most of Indiana, the U.S. Virgin Islands, and Puerto Rico. Daylight savings moves the clock 1 hour ahead of standard time. (A new law will extend daylight saving in 2007; clocks will change the second Sunday in March and the first Sunday in November.)

For the correct time, call "POP CORN" (© 767-2676) anywhere in California.

*Tipping*  Tips are a very important part of certain workers' income, and gratuities are the standard way of showing appreciation for services provided. (Tipping is certainly not compulsory if the service is poor!) In hotels, tip **bellhops** at least $1 per bag ($2–$3 if you have a lot of luggage) and tip the **chamber staff** $1 to $2 per day (more if you've left a disaster area for him or her to clean up). Tip the **doorman** or **concierge** only if he or she has provided you with some specific service (for example, calling a cab for you or obtaining difficult-to-get theater tickets). Tip the **valet-parking attendant** $1 every time you get your car.

In restaurants, bars, and nightclubs, tip **service staff** 15% to 20% of the check, tip **bartenders** 10% to 15%, tip **checkroom attendants** $1 per garment, and tip **valet-parking attendants** $1 per vehicle.

As for other service personnel, tip **cab drivers** 15% of the fare; tip **skycaps** at airports at least $1 per bag ($2–$3 if you have a lot of luggage); and tip **hairdressers** and **barbers** 15% to 20%.

*Toilets*  You won't find public toilets or "restrooms" on the streets in most California cities (except San Francisco), but they can be found in hotel lobbies, bars, restaurants, museums, department stores, railway and bus stations, and service stations. Large hotels and fast-food restaurants are often the best bet for clean facilities. If possible, avoid the toilets at parks and beaches, which tend to be dirty; some may be unsafe. Restaurants and bars in resorts or heavily visited areas may reserve their restrooms for patrons. Some establishments display a notice indicating this. You can ignore this sign or, better yet, avoid arguments by paying for a cup of coffee or a soft drink, which will qualify you as a patron.

# 4

# Suggested Itineraries

*by Matthew Richard Poole, Erika Lenkert & Harry Basch*

Because California is so vast and geographically varied—from misty redwood forests to eerily beautiful deserts, gold-sand beaches, and rugged mountain ranges—it would take months to see all its major attractions. We're guessing you don't have that much vacation time, so we're recommending the following itineraries. Essentially, we're divulging how we, as the authors, would spend our own week-long California dream vacations. We've divided the chapter into our four favorite regions—with our favorite sites, hotels, restaurants, and scenic drives. Skim the following trips and decide which one piques your wanderlust. We've allowed leeway to stray from the route, but we've also mapped out enough details to guide you through entire journeys.

As you choose a route, be sure to consider the importance of timing. If you don't care to learn what it's like to drive through an Easy-Bake oven, skip the Southern California Desert itinerary in mid-July. Conversely, Yosemite and Lake Tahoe are best avoided in winter, however,

when several access roads close down due to heavy snowfall. The Wine Country is best in spring, when the Napa and Sonoma valleys are abloom and the summer crowds haven't yet arrived, or during the heady fall grape crush. As for cruising the Pacific Coast Highway, any time of the year is fine, as long as the sun is out and the convertible top is down.

For all of the itineraries in this chapter you'll need a car, so fly into the largest city near each itinerary region, and rent a vehicle for a week. See "Getting There" and "Getting Around," in chapter 2, for information about California's airports, driving rules, and rental-car companies. You'll also need a detailed map and some Dramamine if you're prone to road sickness, because most of these itineraries take you down windy roads. And since it's almost always sunny in California, splurge on a convertible Mustang—it will turn the mundane task of driving into one of the highlights of your vacation.

*—Matthew Richard Poole*

## 1 The Pacific Coast Highway in 1 Week (San Francisco to Big Sur)

If you've ever wondered why it's outrageously expensive to buy a home in California, this seaside journey by car will resolve the mystery: Superlatives don't do justice to the views you'll see while twisting and turning, climbing and descending along the Pacific Coast Highway (Hwy. 1) from San Francisco to Big Sur. It's one of the most thrilling roads in the country, gripping the mountainside while it passes through some of the most dramatic scenery in the world—from coastal redwood forests to ocean cliffs and secluded coves battered by the dazzling, formidable Pacific Ocean.

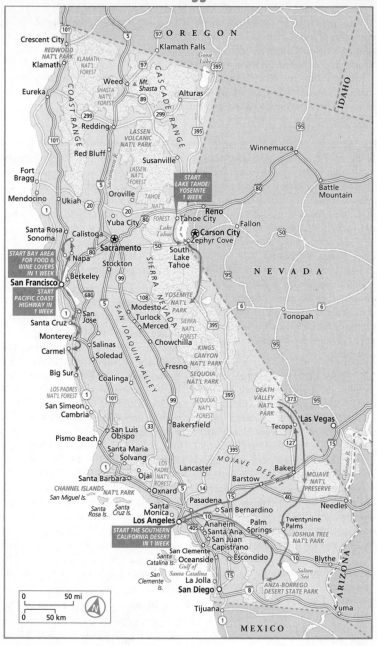

The trek begins with a half-day's leisurely drive from San Francisco to Santa Cruz, then continues south past Monterey and Carmel into thickly forested Big Sur. Not a single part of this drive lacks interesting sights; even the acres of artichokes around the farming town of Castroville are pretty, and it's a wonder the ocean views around Big Sur don't cause hundreds of car wrecks a day.

Heavy traffic can afflict Carmel and Big Sur on summer weekends. Try planning your trip to avoid the congestion,so you can cruise at a 55 miles per hour from town to town—with the top down and your spirits up.

---

### Day ❶: Santa Cruz & Boardwalk

From San Francisco take Highway 1 south and follow the signs to Pacifica. Continue along Highway 1 for about 60 miles to Santa Cruz. Check into the **Pleasure Point Inn** ✮✮ (p. 365) and make a reservation for the **Bittersweet Bistro** ✮✮ (p. 365). Spend some time on the **Santa Cruz Beach Boardwalk** ✮✮ (p. 361) and be sure to ride the wooden Giant Dipper roller coaster and the old-school carousel. The **Seymour Marine Discovery Center** (p. 362) is also worth a visit, especially for kids. Have dinner in Aptos at the **Bittersweet Bistro** and head back to the inn.

### Day ❷: Monterey Bay Aquarium

Sleep in, sip coffee on the roof deck, and admire the ocean view until checkout (11am), or walk along the coastal path to **Capitola** ✮ (p. 362) for a bloody mary. Back in the car, head south on Highway 1 to Monterey, about a 1-hour drive. Check into the **Seven Gables Inn** ✮✮✮ (p. 379) or **Martine Inn** ✮✮ (p. 379) for 2 nights, and make a dinner reservation for **Montrio** restaurant ✮✮ (p. 376) for this evening, and **Fandango** restaurant ✮✮ (p. 381) and **Monterey Bay Kayaks** tour (p. 372) for tomorrow. Drive to the **Monterey Bay Aquarium** ✮✮✮ (p. 372), the world's finest. Spend 2 to 3 hours here, then stroll **Cannery Row** (briefly if you loath tourist schlock; p. 372). Drive or walk to **Montrio** for dinner.

### Day ❸: Kayaking & Sea Otters

Breakfast at the inn, then drive to Del Monte Beach for a leisurely **kayak tour of**

**Monterey Bay.** Watching sea otters and sea lions play from the water is an unforgettable experience, requiring no kayaking expertise. Afterward, stroll along **Old Fisherman's Wharf** (p. 376) and snack on all those small cups of fresh seafood offered at the numerous faux fish markets. Return to the car for an afternoon/sunset drive along **17-Mile Drive** ✮✮ (p. 383). Dine at **Fandango** and return to the B&B.

### Day ❹: Seafood & Beer in Carmel

Eat breakfast, check out, and drive to Carmel. Check in to the **Mission Ranch** ✮✮ (p. 388) for 2 nights, and make a reservation for the **Flying Fish Grill** ✮✮ (p. 390) for tonight and **The Restaurant at Mission Ranch** ✮✮ (p. 391) tomorrow night. Apply sunscreen, pack a jacket, and walk along the coastal path to downtown **Carmel** for window-shopping—a beloved Carmel pastime—and a burger and beer at **The Hog's Breath Inn** (p. 391). If it's Saturday, take the 2pm **Carmel Walking Tour** (p. 386); otherwise, pick up a free map at the **Carmel Business Association** (p. 385) and check out the **San Carlos Mission** ✮✮ (p. 386) and **Tor House** ✮ (p. 386) on your own. Have dinner at the **Flying Fish Grill,** then stroll back to the **Mission Ranch bar** for an Irish whisky and piano tunes.

### Day ❺: Chillin' at the Beach

Take the day off. Sleep in, stock up on picnic stuff at **Neilsen Brothers Market** (p. 393), and devote the day to **Carmel Beach** ✮✮ (p. 385)—a welcoming stretch of pristine white sand and cypress trees.

Head back to your hotel room in the late afternoon, clean up, and walk to the hotel restaurant for a fat steak dinner.

### Day 6: Big Sur
Check out, have breakfast at **the Little Swiss Cafe** (p. 392), and top off the fuel tank. Drive south on Highway 1 deep into **Big Sur** ★★★, and make various stops along the way to photograph the spectacular coastline. Have lunch at either **Nepenthe** or **Café Kevah** (in the same building, one level below; p. 400), then check into either **Deetjen's Big Sur**

**Inn** ★ (p. 401) if you like extrarustic lodgings, or splurge at the **Post Ranch Inn** ★★★ (p. 398).

### Day 7: Hiking & Home
Check out, then drive to **Julia Pfeiffer Burns State Park** ★★ (p. 397) and hit the trail from the parking area to **McWay Waterfall** (it's an easy trek). Hop back in the car and return to San Francisco via Highway 1, if you have the time, or via Highway 101 near Salinas, a much faster route.

## 2 Lake Tahoe & Yosemite National Park Adventure in 1 Week

This weeklong excursion covers two of my favorite places on the planet: Lake Tahoe and Yosemite National Park. I've visited both countless times, yet each time I'm awestruck by the beauty of these mountain regions. I'd go so far as to credit them for my choice of career; the opportunity to explore natural wonders such as these is what compelled me to be a travel writer.

The trip starts in North Lake Tahoe, winds its way to South Lake Tahoe, then veers southeast along Highway 395 to Mono Lake. From there, it cuts westward on Highway 120 and heads up, up, up to the famed Tioga Pass and into Yosemite National Park. In winter months, the scenery is even more spectacular, but Tioga Pass is usually closed due to snow. The inland route, via Highway 49, will get you there in winter, but it adds about 4 hours driving time.

The quickest way to cover this ground is to fly into Reno-Tahoe International Airport and rent a car; otherwise, take Interstate 80 east from the San Francisco or Sacramento airports to Truckee. From there it's a short drive southward on Highway 89 to the north shore of Lake Tahoe. From Yosemite National Park, it's about a 3½-hour drive back to San Francisco.

Be sure to pack comfortable hiking shoes, a swimsuit, a small backpack, plenty of sunscreen, a wide-brimmed hat, and spare cash for the casinos.

### Day 1: Bike Ride & Slot Machines
From Tahoe City head south on West Lake Boulevard for a few miles to **Sunnyside Lodge** ★★ (p. 260). Check in for 2 nights, make dinner reservations for tonight at the **Wild Goose** restaurant ★★★ (p. 264) and **Gar Woods Grill & Pier** ★ (p. 264) tomorrow night, then have lunch on the deck at Sunnyside and soak in the view. Drive back to Tahoe City to the **Olympic Bike Shop** (p. 248). Rent a bike for a few hours and take the scenic paved bike path that follows West Lake

Boulevard and the Truckee River. Return the bikes then drive to **Wild Goose.** Plan to arrive about an hour before your reservation, so you can knock down a few top-shelf margaritas while watching the sunset from the lakeside deck. After dinner, drive to the **Cal-Neva Casino** ★ (p. 259) for some evening entertainment, and then head back to the hotel.

### Day 2: Rafting & Lakeside Dining
Eat breakfast at the **Fire Sign Café** ★ (p. 265) down the street, and then drive

to **Truckee River Raft Rental** (p. 250) in Tahoe City. After a leisurely raft trip down the mostly calm, always beautiful Truckee River, have a burger and beers on the riverside deck at the **River Ranch Lodge & Restaurant** ✦✦ (p. 260) while waiting for the return shuttle. Next, drive to **Squaw Valley** ✦✦✦ (p. 246) and ride the cable car to **High Camp** ✦✦ (p. 246), where you can explore numerous hiking trails or just relax at the **Poolside Café** and admire the view. Either walk or take the cable car back to the parking lot, then drive to **Gar Woods Grill & Pier** for dinner. (Leave time to arrive before sunset.) If you're not ready to retire after dinner, drive to the **Pierce Street Annex** (p. 266), a local hangout for drinks and dancing.

**Day ❸: Picnic Lunch, Beachside Mai Tais & More Gambling**
Sleep in, grab breakfast at the hotel, and check out. Stock up on sandwiches and drinks at the local deli, stuff them into a small backpack, and head south on Highway 89 toward South Lake Tahoe. Park at **Emerald Bay** ✦✦ (p. 251) and walk down to **Vikingsholm** ✦ (p. 251) for a lakeside picnic lunch. (I recommend the hike to **Eagle Lake** as well; p. 249.) Back in the car to **South Lake Tahoe,** drive through town (heading east on Lake Tahoe Blvd./Hwy. 50) into Nevada, and check into a lakeside cabin at **Zephyr Cove** ✦ (p. 257) for 2 nights. Drink a mai tai at the **beachside bar,** and then drive back toward the casinos for either Italian food at **Ivano's** ✦✦ (p. 262), or sushi at **The Naked Fish** ✦✦ (p. 263). Spend the evening at the **casinos** (p. 266).

**Day ❹: Gondola Ride & Lobster**
Sleep in, have breakfast at **Zephyr Cove Restaurant** (p. 257), then walk to the pier and board the **MS *Dixie II*** (p. 250) for a 2-hour cruise to Emerald Bay. Return to the beachside bar for another mai tai, and then relax at the gold-sand

beach right in front of your cabin. If you can water-ski or wakeboard, consider renting a boat or jet ski. Around 4pm, hop in the car and head to the **Heavenly Resort** ✦✦ (p. 245) for a **gondola** ride (p. 253) to the **viewing platform** before sunset (wow). For dinner, drive to **Fresh Ketch** ✦ (p. 262) for oysters, steak, and lobster. Then win your money back at the casinos and/or see a show.

**Day ❺: Mono Lake & Yosemite**
Today's itinerary entails lots of driving, so rise early, eat breakfast at Zephyr Cove Restaurant, gas up the car, and take the Kingsbury Grade to Highway 395 (it's a bit confusing to find, so bring a map). Head south to **Mono Lake** ✦ (p. 310), spend an hour or so at the excellent Visitors Center, then head east on Hwy 120 into **Yosemite National Park** ✦✦✦ (p. 291) toward **Yosemite Valley.** Be sure to stretch your legs at **Tuolumne Meadows** ✦✦ (p. 298) and walk around a bit, admiring the view. If you can afford it, check into the legendary **Ahwahnee Hotel** ✦✦✦ (p. 301) for 2 nights; otherwise, stay at the **Wawona Hotel** ✦ (p. 302) or just outside the park entrance at my favorite place to stay in Yosemite, the **Evergreen Lodge** ✦✦ (a bit of a drive from Yosemite Valley but worth the trip; p. 285). Dine at the hotel and call it a night.

**Day ❻: Tours, Biking, More Views & Alpenglow**
Sleep in, eat breakfast at the hotel, and take the 2-hour **Valley Floor Tour** (p. 295) in an open-air tram. Next, rent bikes at **Yosemite Lodge** or **Curry Village** (p. 302) and ride the paved trail through the valley. When you return the bikes, purchase the *Map and Guide to Yosemite Valley,* which describes an assortment of hikes and short nature walks. Plan tomorrow's hike while you lunch at one of the cafes in Curry Village (although all are mediocre and overpriced). Save your energy for the long

hike for tomorrow, and stroll eastward at a leisurely pace into the valley on the **John Muir Trail** ★★ (p. 296) along the Merced River toward Vernal falls—one of the most scenic trails in Yosemite. Make sure you have a clear view of the valley at sunset to witness the **alpenglow** (p. 321). Back to the hotel for dinner.

### Day ❼: Hiking & Drive Home

Rise early, catch a light breakfast, check out (but leave your luggage at the hotel), and unfold your *Map and Guide to Yosemite Valley* to see which hike best fits your schedule and endurance level. Some of my favorites are the **Upper Yosemite Fall Trail** ★ (a real thigh-burner but very rewarding; p. 296) or the **Mist Trail** ★★ (p. 296) to Nevada Falls. Alas, after your hike, it's time to head home. If you're heading to the Bay Area or Sacramento, take Highway 120 toward Groveland and follow the signs.

## 3 The Bay Area for Food & Wine Lovers in 1 Week

San Francisco and its environs are the nation's top destination for **world-class food and wine.** The city's **culinary diversity** began with the Gold Rush of the mid-1880s, when men from all over the world migrated to the region to strike it rich. Having left behind their wives and mothers who cooked for them, miners turned to the settlers who replicated and sold the flavors of home through local food shops and restaurants.

California's impressive concentration of **superfresh ingredients,** from the sea and from the farms and gardens of Central and Northern California, enhanced the region's culinary diversity. Over time, the general population came to live for the next great food and wine experience, which enticed **aspiring and top chefs** to settle here as well.

Given the bounty of **farmers markets** selling **organic produce, meats, and fowl;** small **neighborhood gem restaurants** with every type of cuisine imaginable; and the nation's most established wine region, in **Napa and Sonoma counties,** you're in for more good food than you can handle. A week of gluttony in the San Francisco Bay area demands stamina, but with careful pacing and a little exercise worked into your route, you can savor the region and still fit in your pants by the time you head home.

*Note:* Because some of the following attractions operate only on certain days, you may need to rearrange the itinerary based on opening hours. It's also important to make restaurant reservations; the places recommended here are popular on the foodie circuit.

### Day ❶: Alfresco Noshing By Day & Fine Dining By Night

Start your movable feast in San Francisco at the **Ferry Building Marketplace Farmers Market** ★, at the foot of Market Street in the Embarcadero (p. 120). From November through March, when produce is less abundant, the market takes place Tuesday and Saturday mornings; the rest of the year, it's open on Thursday and Sunday mornings as well. Join more than 10,000 locals around the Ferry Building Marketplace to browse stalls abundant with organic goods from local artisan farms, snack on specialty foods, and mingle in the bayfront air. Inside, shop or simply gawk at delicacies from the city's finest gourmet chocolatiers, bread bakers, fish and meat mongers, and tea merchants. Have Vietnamese food for lunch at **The Slanted Door** ★★ (p. 105; reservations a must). Afterward, work off some calories with a walk along the Embarcadero to Fisherman's Wharf. If you're exceptionally energetic, continue up to Fort Mason and the Marina (a 20- to 30-minute walk uphill, at a brisk pace, from Fisherman's Wharf) for more classic views of the bay

(p. 129). Rest in the late afternoon to revitalize yourself in time for a French feast at one of the city's finest dining rooms, **Restaurant Gary Danko** ★★★ (p. 110). Or opt for more affordable, nonetheless delicious contemporary Italian fare at **A16** ★★ (p. 112). Advance reservations are required for both restaurants.

### Day ❷: North Beach Treats & Chez Panisse

Pace yourself. Start with coffee and a light breakfast at one of the **cafes** in **North Beach** (p. 108). Wander the streets suffused with **Italian heritage** and the aromas of garlic and pizza. Drop by **Biordi Art Imports** to pick up some **Italian pottery** (p. 134). Lunch at **Piperade** ★★, for dishes from the Basque region of Spain served in a casual, warm setting (p. 109), or **L'Osteria del Forno** ★★ for classic Italian fare at reasonable prices served in a shoebox-size dining room (p. 109). Then find your way to Berkeley, to learn how chocolate is made on **Scharffen Berger Chocolate Maker**'s 1-hour tour (p. 144). From the city it's a 20-minute drive, traffic permitting (you can also take BART; call for directions ℂ **510 465-2278**); follow Columbus Avenue south and follow signs to I-80 east, which will take you across the Bay Bridge. Take the Ashby Avenue exit, turn left at Seventh Street (the first signal), go to the second light, and the factory is on your right, at the corner of Seventh and Heinz. Then dine at one of the nation's most famous, influential restaurants. **Chez Panisse** ★★★—run by Alice Waters, the mother of contemporary California cuisine—is a requisite pilgrimage stop for any food lover (p. 146). If the skies are clear on the drive back to San Francisco, revel in the **city views** from the East Bay.

### Day ❸: Eating Your Way Through Chinatown

Kick off another delicious day in San Francisco with the "**I Can't Believe I Ate My Way Through Chinatown**" excursion—led by knowledgeable local celebrity Shirley Fong-Torres (ℂ **650/ 355-9657;** www.wokwiz.com). Part variety show, part feast, the Chinatown food tour takes place every Saturday and the occasional Sunday; call for details. If you're visiting on a weekday, try Fong-Torres's standard Chinatown tour, an equally authentic introduction to delicacies in the vicinity. Work off lunch (which is included in the tour price) with a visit to **Golden Gate Park** (p. 120), where you can explore, lounge in the grass, or ride a paddle boat. Head to the bustling Mission District for dinner at **Delfina** ★★, one of the city's best Italian restaurants, with its hip, young, fun patrons and casual setting (p. 116).

### Day ❹: Union Square

Spend your last day in the city **shopping at Union Square** department stores and boutiques. Lunch at the elegant **Campton Place** restaurant ★★, where Swiss chef Daniel Humm creates gorgeous European cuisine in a sophisticated, quiet, yet comfortable setting (p. 99). Devote the afternoon to last-ditch sightseeing and visit **Alcatraz** ★★★ (p. 117) or the city's best museums (p. 124). Or pamper yourself—before dinner and the following day's push to the wine country—with a pay-per-view movie in bed, or with a spa treatment. In the evening, either go for a wildly intricate, lengthy, multicourse feast at **Michael Mina** ★★ (p. 102), a refined dinner at **Fifth Floor** ★★★ (p. 105), a relaxed but opulent meal at **Grand Café** ★★ (p. 103), or budget exotic fare at **Burma Superstar** ★★ (p. 115), in the Richmond District—provided you entered your name on the waiting list early. If you've still got energy after dinner, head downtown for wine tasting at **First Crush** (p. 139) or for champagne at **The Bubble Lounge** (p. 139).

## Day ⑤: Napa Wine Tasting

Get an early start and take the scenic Highway 101 to 37 to 12/121 to **Napa** (p. 164), which crosses the Golden Gate Bridge and offers the most rural landscape on the drive up. You'll need a car for this portion of the trip, which should take about 1 ½ hours. If you'd rather skip the scenery and make tracks, take I-80; it will shave 15 to 20 minutes off your trip, traffic permitting. Make **Artesa Vineyards & Winery** ★★ your first wine-tasting stop, as it's known for its beautiful views and contemporary architecture, as well as for its Carneros District pinot noirs (p. 169). If a cooking demo is underway, make a reservation to participate at **Copia: The American Center for Wine, Food & the Arts** (p. 167). Next, stop at **Bistro Don Giovanni** ★★★ for an excellent Italian lunch (don't skip the pasta); if the weather's good, reserve a patio table overlooking the garden, whimsical fountain, and vineyards (p. 183). If you're visiting during the week, make **Shafer Vineyards'** exclusive tour and tasting (p. 130) your next sipping stop. If it's the weekend, take the scenic drive to **The Hess Collection** winery and art gallery ★★ (p. 169) instead. If you're booking your trip months in advance, make a reservation to splurge at **The French Laundry** ★★★ (p. 182), one of the world's top restaurants. (If you're traveling at the last minute, you can show up at the restaurant before 10am to register for the waiting list and hope other guests cancel during your stay.) Otherwise, you'll be equally satiated at **Terra** ★★★ (p. 183), one of Northern California's best restaurants. Shack up at any B&B hotel you can afford that can accommodate you.

## Day ⑥: Sparkling Wine, Hand-Dug Caves & Hot Springs

We know. You're getting tired—and full. So take it easy on the morning meal and have coffee and pastries; ask your concierge for the best place near you. Then head north on Highway 29 to **Schramsberg** ★★ in Calistoga (about ½ hr. from downtown Napa and 15 min. from St. Helena) for a tour of their sparkling winemaking process and hand-dug caves, followed by a tasting (p. 136). Stop for lunch, with a huge wine selection, at **All Seasons Café** ★★ in downtown Calistoga (p. 183). Then browse the **boutiques** on the one commercial strip in town. Spend the rest of the afternoon visiting other wineries in the area, including Francis Ford Coppola's **Niebaum-Coppola** ★ (p. 173) and **Swanson Vineyards** ★ (p. 172). Or relax with spa treatments at funky-cool **Dr. Wilkinson's Hot Springs** ★, one of Calistoga's numerous spas (p. 181). Dine at the festive French brasserie **Bouchon** ★★ (p. 184) Day 7: Food & Wine Gifts, Picnic & Pétanque

## Day ⑦: Food and Wine Gifts, Picnic & Pétanque

Reserve the day for shopping. Start with a light breakfast near your hotel. Then head to St. Helena for the Main Street boutiques. Grab mementos and gifts from **Napa Valley Olive Oil Manufacturing Company** (p. 174), follow your nose at the culinary emporium **Dean & DeLuca** (p. 185), and buy a picnic lunch from **Oakville Grocery** (p. 185). Picnic, taste wines, and play the French lawn-bowling game *pétanque* at **Clos Du Val** winery (p. 169). Then head out of town to wherever you're going next. If you're bound for San Francisco, consider taking scenic U.S. 101. If you have time, you can stop in downtown **Sonoma** (p. 188) to meander around its square, or make one last sip-stop at **Buena Vista Winery** (p. 188).

## 4 Driving the Southern California Desert in 1 Week

The California desert encompasses distinct arid regions: **Death Valley's** low desert, with its infernal heat; the **Mojave's** high desert, with its ghost towns and mines; vast **Anza-Borrego,** the biggest state park in California, with 600,000 acres of cactus and canyons near Mexico; and **Joshua Tree National Park.**

And then there's **"The Desert."** Palm Springs and vicinity is the civilized desert—where celebrities pay big money to desiccate, and where more than 10,000 swimming pools and countless lawn sprinklers, water slides, and misting outdoor air-conditioners work to provide a little moisture for everyone else.

Winter is the best time to explore California's desert country, when days are balmy and nights are cool. The heat is bearable in early spring and late autumn as well. Summer in the low desert, however, is for mad dogs and Englishmen (as well as the many Germans, Swiss, and Japanese travelers who inexplicably gravitate to Death Valley in August, when the temperature can top 115°F/46°C).

A lazy loop around the region takes about a week. If you allow a little more time, you can also explore some of the alternate side trips recommended below.

### Day ❶: Baker & Death Valley

The loop begins in **Los Angeles,** heading east on I-10 to I-15, en route to **Baker.** If you begin in **San Diego,** head north on I-15 to Baker. From Pasadena, you can take legendary **Route 66** to I-15 (which can add a couple of hours to your trip). In Baker, 113 miles from L.A. you can stay overnight at the **Bun Boy Motel** (p. 665), next to the largest thermometer in the world, then get an early start into Death Valley. Check out the **Mad Greek** for falafel sandwiches with tahini or gyros cooked by Mexicans (p. 665).

If you want to press on to **Death Valley** ★★ (p. 666), 116 miles away, head up Highway 127 to **Tecopa Hot Springs.** Top off your gas tank here; although prices seem high, in the valley they're even worse. The most scenic entrance to the valley is via Highway 178, 1 mile north of Tecopa (marked TO BADWATER AND DEATH VALLEY). The faster route is Highway 190, which brings you into Death Valley Center.

If you're in an RV, you're in luck; the area has nine campgrounds. If you're traveling by car, consider staying at the **Furnace Creek Inn** ★★ (p. 671), an oasis in the desert with red-tiled roofs and a mineral-fed swimming pool. The **Furnace Creek Ranch** near the village is less expensive. **Stovepipe Wells Village** and **Panamint Springs Resort** (p. 670 and p. 670) are other alternatives. Reservations are imperative; in the winter, rooms sell out well in advance.

### Day ❷: Desert Culture & Canyons

Use the day to explore sites in the valley, such as **Harmony Borax Works, Badwater** at 282 feet below sea level, **Zabriskie Point** at sunrise, and **Dante's View** for an overview of the desert (p. 669). Drive through the 9-mile loop of **Artists Drive** (RVs prohibited) and head north to **Scotty's Castle & the Gas House Museum** for a 1-hour tour (p. 669). Biking and hiking trails afford a variety of terrain, from the 14-mile **Telescope Peak Trail** to the 2.5-mile trek into **Mosaic Canyon** near Stovepipe Wells (p. 670).

### Day ❸: Mojave & the Kelso Dunes

This is a touring day, from Death Valley into the **Mojave** desert (p. 662). Take Highway 190 back to **Tecopa Hot Springs** and go left into **Tecopa.** Head southeast on the back road through the

Kingston range and bear right at the fork to head south to Valley Wells and I-15. Continue past the freeway on the Cima road to Cima, center of the largest, densest Joshua tree forest. You will soon reach Kelso Depot, where you can explore the Kelso Dunes—a 45-square-mile formation of sculptured sand famous for reverberating, or "booming," every time a person steps on the sand (p. 663). Heading south out of Kelso, continue past I-40 and turn right to Amboy. The road south out of Amboy goes through Bristol Dry Lake and swings around to Twentynine Palms. Stay at the 29 Palms Inn (p. 658) and visit Western-style Pappy and Harriet's Pioneer-town Palace (© 760/365-5956) for steaks and honky-tonk entertainment.

### Day ④: Joshua Tree & Salton Sea Wildlife Refuge

Twentynine Palms is at the northern entrance into Joshua Tree National Park ⚘ (p. 653). The park headquarters has maps and information about hiking and rock climbing. Continue on the road through the park past Jumbo Rocks (which captures the essence of the park), the Cholla Cactus Garden, and through the Pinto Basin to Cottonwood Springs (p. 657). Exit at I-10. Just east of this junction, (General) George S. Patton Memorial Museum (© 760-227-3483), built on the site of a World War II desert training center, has a great collection of war memorabilia, open daily 9:30am to 4:30pm.

Backtrack to the junction of I-10 and the Joshua Tree road, exit, go southwest through Mecca, and take Highway 195 to U.S. 86 south. Within a few miles, you will reach the Salton Sea Wildlife Refuge

(© 760/348-5278), rich with Canada geese, snowy egrets, snow geese, and pelicans. You will have to leave the main road, at one of the numerous turnoffs, to visit the nearby lake. Midway along the lake, turn right onto County Road S22 into Borrego Springs and the Anza-Borrego State Park ⚘ (p. 658). Book a room at La Casa del Zorro Desert Resort ⚘⚘ or The Palms at Indian Head ⚘⚘ (p. 660 and 661).

### Day ⑤: Anza-Borrego State Park

Hop to the Red Ocotillo for an old-fashioned, hearty breakfast (p. 662). If you plan to hike, stop at the Borrego Springs Chamber of Commerce (p. 659), a block from the restaurant, for information about the area. Then head for the Visitors Center on County Road S22 (p. 659). There, you can find maps for trails, including a 1.5-mile path that leaves from the nearby campground. Be sure to carry a hat, sunscreen, and plenty of water when hiking in the desert.

### Day ⑥: Palm Springs

Return to U.S. 68 and head north to Indio and the Palm Springs area. Running along Highway 111 for miles, this group of small communities (La Quinta, Indian Wells, Palm Desert, Cathedral City, Rancho Mirage, and Palm Springs) has grown into a metropolis of golf courses, high-rise resorts, elite hideaways, and small motels. By day, play a round of golf, relax in the pool, or visit the nearby tourist attractions. At night, take in the nightlife.

### Day ⑦: The Journey Home

Relax in the morning then head to I-10 for the 2-hour drive back to L.A.

# 5

# San Francisco

*by Erika Lenkert*

After starting this chapter the past few years with the announcement that San Francisco is still recovering from the dot.com crash, the terrorist attacks of September 11, 2001, a dramatic influx of new residents (up 13% since the '90s), and the general economic strains of 2002 and 2003, we have some great news: San Francisco is definitely on an upswing!

No indicator better defines the city's mood than the local restaurant scene, and after a rather boring couple of years, during which our dining rooms played it safe, closed, or cut back while awaiting more freewheeling times, it is smooth sailing once again. Restaurants all over town are abuzz with chatter and clinking of wineglasses, and swank new spots are popping up faster than a maitre d' can say, "Sorry, we only have tables at 9."

Sure, even during harder times, the City by the Bay was still a fantastic place to visit, with all the classic pleasures that have made it the number-one U.S. city for *Condé Nast Traveler* readers for the past 12 years: stunning bay vistas, Victorian architecture, swank boutiques, killer restaurants, walkable beaches, ever-charming cable cars, the trademark dash of liberalism, and the sort of social trailblazing found only in San Francisco (remember the gay marriages of 2004?)—all tightly tucked into about 7 miles squared. For us locals, though, the change underfoot is obvious and welcome: The city feels exciting again.

So, what can you expect from the country's most romantic European-style city, founded on the pioneers' boom-or-bust way of life? Whatever your heart desires: Feel the cool blast of salt air as you stroll across the Golden Gate, stuff yourself on dim sum, walk along the beach, pierce your nose, see a play, rent a Harley. Like an eternal world's fair, it's all happening in San Francisco—and everyone's invited.

## 1 Orientation

### GETTING THERE
#### BY PLANE

Two major airports serve the Bay Area: San Francisco International and Oakland International. All the major car-rental companies have desks at the airports; see "Getting Around," later in this chapter, for details on car rentals.

**SAN FRANCISCO INTERNATIONAL AIRPORT** San Francisco International Airport (© 650/821-8211; www.flysfo.com), 14 miles south of downtown on U.S. 101, is served by almost four dozen major scheduled carriers and several budget airlines (AirTran, Independence Air, Song, and WestJet). Travel time to downtown during rush hours is about 40 minutes; at other times it's about 20 to 25 minutes. The airport offers a hot line for information on ground transport (℡ **415/817-1717**), and each of the three main terminals has a transportation information desk.

A cab from the airport to downtown will cost $30 to $35, plus tip. **SuperShuttle** (℡ **415/558-8500;** www.supershuttle.com) will take you anywhere in the city, charging $15 to a residence or business, plus $8 for each additional person, and $65 to charter a van for as many as seven people. Keep in mind that this shuttle demands they pick you up 2 hours before your flight (3 hr during holidays).

For budget travelers, **BART** (Bay Area Rapid Transit; ℡ **415/989-2278;** www.bart. gov) runs from the airport to downtown. Rates are about $5 per person, depending on where you're bound, and the trip takes just less than half an hour.

The San Mateo County Transit system, **SamTrans** (℡ **800/660-4287** in Northern California, or 650/508-6200; www.samtrans.com), runs two buses between the airport and the Transbay Terminal at First and Mission streets. Bus no. 292 costs $1.25 and makes the trip in 55 minutes. The KX bus costs $3.50 and takes 35 minutes but permits only one carry-on bag. Both buses run daily. The 292 starts at 5:25am Monday through Friday and at 5:31am on weekends; daily it runs twice an hour from about 6:30am until 6:30pm, then once an hour until about 1am; see website for details. The KX starts at 5:55am and ends at 10:31pm Monday through Friday. On weekends, service runs from 7:11am to 9:30pm, twice an hour until 6:30pm, then hourly.

**OAKLAND INTERNATIONAL AIRPORT**    About 5 miles south of downtown Oakland, at the Hagenberger Road exit off Highway 17 (I-880), Oakland International Airport (℡ **510/563-3300;** www.oaklandairport.com) primarily serves passengers with East Bay destinations. Many San Franciscans, however, prefer this less-crowded, accessible airport served by a dozen carriers, including discount airlines JetBlue, America West, Southwest, and SunTrips. In the absence of traffic, a car or taxi ride to the airport from downtown takes 20 to 30 minutes; with traffic, give yourself at least an hour. It's also accessible by BART (see below for details), which is unaffected by traffic congestion.

Taxis from the Oakland airport to downtown San Francisco are expensive, costing approximately $50, plus tip.

**Bayporter Express** (℡ **877/467-1800** or 415/467-1800) shuttle service is $26 for the first person, $12 for each additional person, to downtown San Francisco; it costs more to the city's outlying neighborhoods. Children under 12 ride for $7. Independently owned shuttles, usually located to the right of the airport exit, will take you to the city for around $20 per person. Prices vary, so ask questions and negotiate (which is sometimes possible) before you ride.

The cheapest way to downtown San Francisco (and the easiest during traffic snarls) is the shuttle bus from the airport to **BART** (Bay Area Rapid Transit; ℡ **510/464-6000;** www.bart.gov). The **AirBART** shuttle bus runs about every 15 minutes Monday through Saturday from 6am to 11:30pm, and Sunday from 8:30am to 11:30pm. It makes pickups in front of terminals 1 and 2 near the ground transportation signs. Passengers must purchase tickets prior to boarding from airport vending machines. The 10-minute ride to BART's Coliseum station in Oakland is $2. BART fares vary, depending on your destination; the trip to downtown San Francisco costs $3.15 and takes 15 minutes once you're on board. The entire excursion should take around 45 minutes.

## BY CAR

San Francisco is accessible via several major highways: **U.S. 101** and **Highway 1** from the north and south, and **I-80** and **I-580** from the northeast and east, respectively. If you drive from Los Angeles, you can either take the longer coastal route along Highway 1/U.S. 101 (437 miles, 11 hr.), or the inland route along I-5 to I-580 (389 miles, 6½ hr.). From Mendocino, it's a little more than 3 hours along Highway 1, and about 3¼ hours along U.S. 101; and from Sacramento, it's 88 miles, or 1½ hours, along I-80.

## BY TRAIN

San Francisco–bound **Amtrak** trains (℡ 800/USA-RAIL; www.amtrak.com) leave from New York and cross the country via Chicago. The journey takes about 3½ days, and seats sell quickly. At this writing, the lowest round-trip fare starts at $268 from New York and $245 from Chicago. Round-trip tickets from Los Angeles cost as little as $100. Trains arrive in Emeryville, just north of Oakland, and connect with regularly scheduled buses to San Francisco's Ferry Building and Caltrain station downtown.

**Caltrain** (℡ **800/660-4287** or 415/546-4461; www.caltrain.com) operates train service between San Francisco and other towns on the peninsula. The city depot is at 700 Fourth St., at Townsend Street.

## VISITOR INFORMATION

The **San Francisco Visitor Information Center,** Hallidie Plaza, 900 Market St. (at Powell St.), Lower Level, San Francisco, CA 94102 (℡ **415/391-2000;** www.sf visitor.org), is the best source for any kind of specialized information about the city. Even if you don't have a specific question, you may want to request the free *Visitors Planning Guide* or the *San Francisco Visitors Kit.*

## CITY LAYOUT

San Francisco sits at the tip of a 32-mile-long peninsula between San Francisco Bay and the Pacific Ocean. Its land area measures about 46 square miles. Twin Peaks, in the geographic center of the city, is more than 900 feet high.

San Francisco may seem confusing at first, but it quickly becomes easy to negotiate. The city's downtown streets are laid out in a simple grid pattern, with the exception of Market Street and Columbus Avenue, which cut across the grid at right angles to each other. Hills appear to distort this pattern and can be disorienting; as you learn your way around, though, these same hills will become your landmarks and reference points.

**MAIN ARTERIES & STREETS**   **Market Street** is San Francisco's main thoroughfare. Most city buses travel it en route to the Financial District from the outer neighborhoods to the west and south. The tall office buildings clustered downtown are on the northeast end of Market; 1 block beyond lie the Embarcadero and the San Francisco Bay.

The **Embarcadero** curves along San Francisco Bay from south of the Bay Bridge to the northeast perimeter of the city, and terminates at Fisherman's Wharf, the famous tourist-oriented pier. Aquatic Park, Fort Mason, and the Golden Gate National Recreation Area are farther around the bay, occupying the northernmost point of the peninsula.

From the eastern perimeter of Fort Mason, **Van Ness Avenue** runs due south, back to Market Street.

# NEIGHBORHOODS IN BRIEF

**Union Square** Named for a series of violent pro-Union demonstrations held here on the eve of the Civil War, Union Square is the city's commercial hub. Most major hotels and department stores are crammed into the surrounding area, with a plethora of boutiques, restaurants, and galleries tucked between the larger buildings.

**Nob Hill/Russian Hill** Bounded by Bush, Larkin, Pacific, and Stockton streets, Nob Hill is the city's most genteel, well-heeled district, occupied by power brokers and the neighborhood businesses they frequent. Russian Hill extends from Pacific to Bay and from Polk to Mason streets. It's marked by steep hills, lush gardens, and high-rises occupied by both moneyed and more bohemian residents.

**SoMa** In the mid-'90s, this once-desolate area, demarcated by the Embarcadero, U.S. 101, and Market Street, grew to be the hub of dot-commercialization, new hotels, $950,000 lofts, and urban entertainment à la Yerba Buena Gardens and the Museum of Modern Art. It's also home to the Giants baseball stadium and many of the city's nightclubs.

**Financial District** East of Union Square, this area bordered by the Embarcadero and Market, Third, Kearny, and Washington streets is the city's business district and stomping grounds for major corporations. The TransAmerica Pyramid, at Montgomery and Clay streets, is one of the area's most conspicuous features. To its east stands the sprawling Embarcadero Center, an 8½-acre complex housing offices, shops, and restaurants. Farther east is the World Trade Center, standing adjacent to the old Ferry Building, the city's prebridge transportation hub.

Ferries to Sausalito and Larkspur still leave from this point.

**Chinatown** The official entrance to Chinatown is marked by a large red and green gate on Grant Avenue at Bush Street. Beyond lies a 24-block labyrinth, bordered by Broadway, Bush, Kearny, and Stockton streets, filled with restaurants, markets, temples, and shops—and a substantial percentage of San Francisco's Chinese residents. Chinatown is a great place for urban exploration, especially along Stockton, Grant, Portsmouth Square, and the alleys that lead off them, like Ross and Waverly. This area is jam-packed, so don't even think about driving around here.

**North Beach** The Italian quarter, which stretches from Montgomery and Jackson to Bay Street, is one of the best places in the city to grab some coffee, pull up a cafe chair, and do some serious people-watching. Nightlife also abounds: Restaurants, bars, and clubs along Columbus and Grant avenues attract folk from all over the Bay Area who fight for parking in order to romp through this festive neighborhood. Down Columbus toward the Financial District are the remains of the city's Beat generation landmarks, including Lawrence Ferlinghetti's City Lights Bookstore and Vesuvio bar. Broadway—a short strip of sex joints and restaurants—cuts through the heart of the district. Telegraph Hill looms over the east side of North Beach, topped by Coit Tower, one of San Francisco's best vantage points.

**Fisherman's Wharf** North Beach runs into Fisherman's Wharf, which was once the busy heart of the city's great harbor and waterfront industries. Today

# San Francisco at a Glance

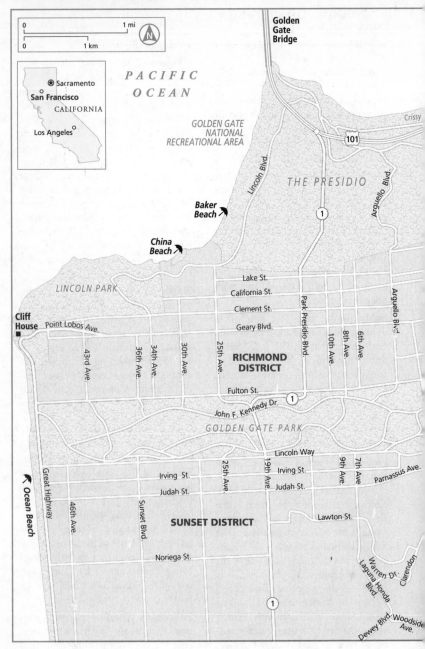

PACIFIC OCEAN

Golden Gate Bridge

Sacramento
San Francisco
CALIFORNIA
Los Angeles

GOLDEN GATE NATIONAL RECREATIONAL AREA

Crissy

101

THE PRESIDIO

Lincoln Blvd.

Arguello Blvd.

Baker Beach

China Beach

1

LINCOLN PARK

Lake St.
California St.
Clement St.
Geary Blvd.

Cliff House
Point Lobos Ave.

43rd Ave.
36th Ave.
34th Ave.
30th Ave.
25th Ave.

RICHMOND DISTRICT

Park Presidio Blvd.

10th Ave.
8th Ave.
6th Ave.

Arguello Blvd.

Fulton St.

1

John F. Kennedy Dr.

GOLDEN GATE PARK

Lincoln Way

Ocean Beach

Great Highway

46th Ave.

Sunset Blvd.

25th Ave.

19th Ave.

Irving St.
Judah St.

Irving St.
Judah St.

9th Ave.
7th Ave.

Parnassus Ave.

Lawton St.

SUNSET DISTRICT

Noriega St.

Warren Dr.
Laguna Honda Blvd.
Clarendon

1

Dewey Blvd.
Woodside Ave.

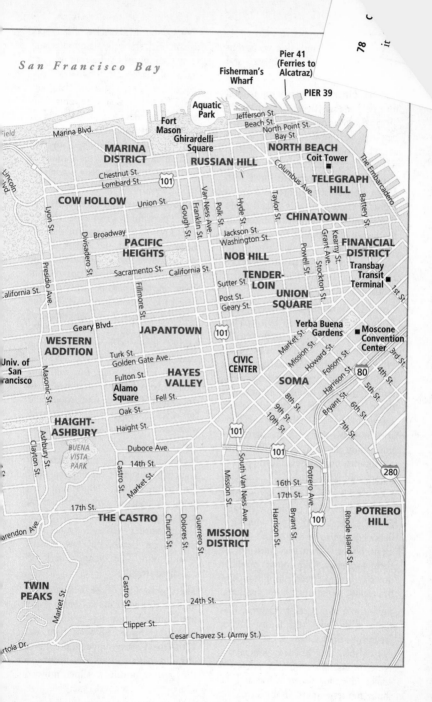

San Francisco Bay

Pier 41
(Ferries to
Alcatraz)

Fisherman's
Wharf

PIER 39

Aquatic
Park

Jefferson St.
Beach St.
North Point St.
Bay St.

Fort
Mason
Ghirardelli
Square

Marina Blvd.

MARINA
DISTRICT

RUSSIAN HILL

NORTH BEACH
Coit Tower

TELEGRAPH
HILL

The Embarcadero

Chestnut St.
Lombard St.

101

COW HOLLOW

Union St.

CHINATOWN

Broadway

PACIFIC
HEIGHTS

Jackson St.
Washington St.

NOB HILL

FINANCIAL
DISTRICT

Transbay
Transit
Terminal

Sacramento St.

California St.

TENDER-
LOIN

UNION
SQUARE

Sutter St.

Post St.
Geary St.

Geary Blvd.

JAPANTOWN

101

Yerba Buena
Gardens

Moscone
Convention
Center

WESTERN
ADDITION

Turk St.
Golden Gate Ave.

CIVIC
CENTER

Market St.
Mission St.
Howard St.
Folsom St.

Univ. of
San
Francisco

Fulton St.

HAYES
VALLEY

SOMA

Harrison St.

Alamo
Square

Oak St.

Fell St.

Bryant St.

80

HAIGHT-
ASHBURY

Haight St.

Duboce Ave.

101

BUENA
VISTA
PARK

14th St.

280

17th St.

THE CASTRO

16th St.
17th St.

POTRERO
HILL

MISSION
DISTRICT

101

Rhode Island St.

TWIN
PEAKS

24th St.

Clipper St.

Cesar Chavez St. (Army St.)

s a tacky but attractive tourist area with little if any authentic waterfront life, except for recreational boaters and some friendly sea lions.

**Marina District** Created on landfill for the Panama-Pacific Exposition of 1915, the Marina boasts some of the best views of the Golden Gate, as well as grassy fields along San Francisco Bay (check out newly restored Crissy Fields). Streets are lined with Mediterranean-style homes and apartments, where the city's well-to-do singles and families live. Here, too, are the Palace of Fine Arts, the Exploratorium, and Fort Mason Center. The main street is Chestnut between Franklin and Lyon, which is lined with shops and cafes.

**Cow Hollow** West of Van Ness Avenue, between Russian Hill and the Presidio, this flat area supported 30 dairy farms in 1861. Today, Cow Hollow is largely residential and occupied by the city's young and upwardly mobile. Its two primary commercial thoroughfares are Lombard Street, known for its many relatively inexpensive motels, and Union Street—a flourishing shopping sector filled with restaurants, pubs, cafes, and shops.

**Pacific Heights** The mansions and homes of Pacific Heights are peopled by ultraelites such as the Gettys and Danielle Steel, and those who were lucky enough to buy in before the real estate boom. When they steal out of their fortresses, they often meander down to Union Street, a long stretch of boutiques, restaurants, cafes, and bars.

**Japantown** Bounded by Octavia, Fillmore, California, and Geary streets, Japantown shelters only a small percentage of the city's Japanese population. Nevertheless, it's a cultural experience to explore these few square blocks and the shops and restaurants within them.

**Civic Center** Millions have been spent here on brick sidewalks, lampposts, and street plantings, but the southwestern section of Market Street remains dilapidated. The Civic Center, at the "bottom" of Market, is an exception. This complex includes the domed City Hall, the Opera House, Davies Symphony Hall, the Asian Art Museum, and the main public library. The plaza connecting the buildings has been the site of many a political demonstration.

**Haight-Ashbury** Part trendy, part nostalgic, part funky-gritty, the Haight, as it's known, was the soul of the psychedelic '60s and the center of the counterculture movement. Today the neighborhood straddling upper Haight Street, on the eastern border of Golden Gate Park, is more gentrified, but the commercial area still harbors all walks of life. Leftover hippies mingle outside Ben & Jerry's with grungy, begging street kids, marijuana dealers, and people with Day-Glo hair. But you don't need to be a freak or wear tie-dye to enjoy the Haight: The food, shops, and bars cover all tastes. From Haight Street, walk south on Cole Street for a more peaceful neighborhood experience.

**Richmond & Sunset Districts** San Francisco's answer to the suburbs, these districts are the city's largest and most populous, consisting mainly of homes, shops, and restaurants. Both neighborhoods border Golden Gate Park and Ocean Beach, but few tourists venture into "The Avenues," as locals call these areas.

**The Castro** One of the liveliest streets in town, Castro is the epicenter of gay tradition in San Francisco. At the end of Market Street, between 17th and 18th, the Castro supports dozens of shops, restaurants, and bars catering to the gay community. Open-minded straight people are welcome, too.

**Mission District** Now known as the Mission Deluxe, this is another area greatly affected by the city's new wealth. The Mexican and Latin American populations—along with their cuisine, traditions, and art—still make the Mission District a vibrant area to visit. Some parts of the neighborhood are still poor and sprinkled with homeless people, gangs, and drug addicts, but young urbanites have been heavily infiltrating, forging the oh-so-hot restaurants and bars that stretch from 16th Street and Valencia to 25th and Mission streets. Less adventurous tourists still duck into Mission Dolores, cruise by a few of the 200-plus amazing murals, and head back downtown. Visitors should still use caution here at night.

## 2 Getting Around

### BY PUBLIC TRANSPORTATION

The San Francisco Municipal Railway, better known as **Muni** (© **415/673-6864;** www.sfmuni.com), operates the city's cable cars, buses, and Metro streetcars. These public transportation services crisscross the city, making all its neighborhoods accessible to everyone. Buses and Metro streetcars cost $1.25 for adults, 35¢ for children ages 5 to 17 and seniors over 65. Cable cars cost $3 for people over 5 years old ($1 for seniors after 9pm). They're packed primarily with tourists. Exact change is required on all vehicles except cable cars.

For detailed route information, phone Muni or consult the bus map at the front of the Yellow Pages. If you plan to make extensive use of public transportation, you may want to invest in a comprehensive route map ($2), sold at the San Francisco Visitor Information Center (see "Visitor Information" in "Orientation," earlier in this chapter) and in many downtown retail outlets.

Muni **discount passes,** called "Passports," entitle holders to unlimited rides on buses, Metro streetcars, and cable cars. A Passport is $9 per day, and $15 or $20 for 3 or 7 consecutive days. Muni's City Pass, which is $40 for adults, $31 for seniors over 65 and kids 5 to 17, entitles you to unlimited rides for 7 days and admission to the California Academy of Sciences, Museum of Modern Art, Exploratorium, Palace of the Legion of Honor, and Blue & Gold Fleet Bay Cruise. You can buy a Passport or City Pass at the San Francisco Visitor Information Center, the Holiday Inn Civic Center, and the Tix Bay Area booth at Union Square. For the Blue & Gold Fleet tour to be included, you must purchase tickets from the Blue & Gold Fleet at © **415/705-5555** and pay a $2.25 fee.

**BY CABLE CAR** San Francisco's cable cars may not be the most practical means of transport, but these rolling historic landmarks sure are fun to ride. The city has only three lines, concentrated in the downtown area. The most scenic and exciting is the **Powell-Hyde line,** which follows a zigzag route from the corner of Powell and Market streets, over both Nob Hill and Russian Hill, to a turntable at gaslit Victorian Square in front of Aquatic Park. The **Powell-Mason line** starts at the same intersection and climbs over Nob Hill before descending to Bay Street, just 3 blocks from Fisherman's Wharf. The least scenic is the **California Street line,** which begins at the foot of Market Street and runs a straight course through Chinatown and over Nob Hill to Van Ness Avenue. All riders must exit at the last stop and wait in line for the return trip. The cable-car system operates daily from approximately 6:30am to 12:50am.

**BY BUS**   Buses service almost every corner of San Francisco and travel over the bridges to Marin County and Oakland. All are numbered and display their destinations on the front. Stops are designated by signs, curb markings, and yellow bands on utility poles. Most bus shelters post Muni's transportation map and schedule. Many buses travel along Market Street or near Union Square and run daily from about 6am to midnight, after which infrequent, all-night "Owl" service commences. For safety's sake, however, avoid taking buses late at night.

Popular tourist routes are nos. 5, 7, and 71, all of which run to Golden Gate Park; 41 and 45, which travel along Union Street; and 30, which runs between Union Square and Ghirardelli Square.

**BY METRO STREETCAR**   Five of Muni's seven Metro streetcar lines—designated F, J, K, L, M, N, and S—run underground downtown and on the street in the outer neighborhoods. The sleek railcars make the same stops as the BART trains (see below) along Market Street, including Embarcadero Station (in the Financial District), Montgomery and Powell streets (both near Union Sq.), and the Civic Center (near City Hall). Past the Civic Center, the routes branch off in different directions: The J line will take you to Mission Dolores; the K, L, and M lines run to Castro Street; and the N line parallels Golden Gate Park and now extends all the way to the Embarcadero. Streetcars run about every 15 minutes (more frequently during rush hours) Monday through Friday from 5am to 12:45am; on Saturday from 6am to 12:45am; and on Sunday from 8am to 12:20am. The L and N lines operate all day and all night.

The most recent streetcar additions are not newcomers at all, but refurbished classics from the 1930s. The beautiful, multicolored cars on the F Market line run along the Embarcadero from Fisherman's Wharf to Market Street, and then to the Castro and back. They're a quick and charming way to get uptown and downtown without any hassle.

**BY BART**   BART—an acronym for **Bay Area Rapid Transit** (© 415/989-2278; www.bart.gov)—is a high-speed rail network that connects San Francisco and the airport with the East Bay towns of Oakland, Richmond, Concord, and Fremont. Four stations are located along Market Street (see "By Metro Streetcar," above). Fares range from $1.25 to $7.45, depending on how far you go. Machines in the stations dispense tickets, encoded with a dollar amount, and computerized exits deduct the correct fare. Children 4 and under ride free. Trains run every 15 to 20 minutes, Monday through Friday from 4am to midnight; Saturday from 6am to midnight; and Sunday from 8am to midnight.

*Note:* The $2.5-billion, 33-mile BART extension, which debuted in mid-2003, includes a southern line that extends to San Francisco International Airport.

## BY TAXI

If you're downtown during rush hour or leaving from a major hotel, it won't be hard to hail a cab—just look for the lighted sign on the roof indicating which cars are available. Otherwise, it's a good idea to call one of the following companies to arrange a ride: **Veteran's Cab** (© 415/552-1300), **Luxor Cabs** (© 415/282-4141), or **Yellow Cab** (© 415/626-2345). Rates are approximately $2.85 for the first mile and $2.25 for each mile thereafter.

## BY CAR

In this crowded and compact city, a car can be your worst nightmare. You're likely to end up stuck in traffic with lots of aggressive and frustrated drivers (especially downtown),

### Curb Your Wheels!

When parking on a hill, drivers are required by law to apply the hand brake, put the car in gear, and *curb their front wheels*—toward the curb when facing downhill, away from it when facing uphill. Failure to curb your wheels, preventing a possible "runaway," will result in a pricey ticket—an expensive fine that is aggressively enforced.

pay upward of $40 a day in parking, and spend a good portion of your vacation looking for a parking space. But if you want to range outside of the city, driving is the best way to go.

**RENTALS**    Some of the national car-rental companies operating in San Francisco include **Alamo** (© 800/327-9633; www.alamo.com), **Avis** (© 800/331-1212; www.avis.com), **Budget** (© 800/527-0700; www.budget.com), **Dollar** (© 800/800-4000; www.dollar.com), **Enterprise** (© 800/325-8007; www.enterprise.com), **Hertz** (© 800/654-3131; www.hertz.com), **National** (© 800/227-7368; www.nationalcar.com), and **Thrifty** (© 800/367-2277; www.thrifty.com).

**PARKING**    If you want to have a relaxing vacation, don't even attempt to find street parking downtown or in Nob Hill, North Beach, Chinatown, by Fisherman's Wharf, or on Telegraph Hill. Park in a garage or take a cab or a bus. If you do find street parking, pay attention to street signs that explain when you can park and for how long. Be especially careful not to park in zones that become tow areas during rush hours.

## *FAST FACTS:* San Francisco

*American Express*    For travel arrangements, traveler's checks, currency exchange, and other member services, visit the office at 455 Market St., at First Street (© **415/536-2600**), in the Financial District, open Monday through Friday from 9am to 5:30pm and Saturday from 10am to 2pm. To report lost or stolen traveler's checks, call © **800/221-7282.** For **American Express Global Assist,** call © **800/554-2639.**

*Dentists*    In the event of a dental emergency, see your hotel concierge or contact the **San Francisco Dental Office,** 131 Steuart St., Suite 323 (© **415/777-5115**), between Mission and Howard streets, which offers emergency service and comprehensive dental care Monday and Tuesday from 8am to 4:30pm, Wednesday and Thursday from 10:30am to 6:30pm, and Friday from 8am to 4:30pm.

*Doctors*    **Saint Francis Memorial Hospital,** 900 Hyde St., between Bush and Pine streets on Nob Hill (© **415/353-6000**), provides emergency service 24 hours a day; no appointment is necessary. The hospital also operates a **physician-referral service** (© **800/333-1355** or 415/353-6566).

*Drugstores*    **Walgreens** pharmacies are all over town, including the one at 135 Powell St. (© **415/391-4433**). The store is open Monday through Friday from 7am to midnight and Saturday and Sunday from 8am to midnight; the pharmacy is open Monday through Friday from 8am to 9pm, and Saturday from

9am to 5pm; it's closed on Sunday. The branch on Divisadero Street at Lombard (© **415/931-6415**) has a 24-hour pharmacy.

*Earthquakes* California will always have earthquakes, most of which you'll never notice. In case of a significant shaker, however, visitors should know a few basic precautions. When you are inside a building, seek cover; do not run outside. Stand under a doorway or against a wall, and stay away from windows. If you exit a building after a substantial quake, use stairwells, not elevators. If you are in your car, pull over to the side of the road and stop—but not until you are away from bridges, overpasses, telephone poles, and power lines. Stay in your car. If you're out walking, stay outside and away from trees, power lines, and the sides of buildings. If you're in an area with tall buildings, find a doorway in which to stand.

*Internet Access* Surprisingly, San Francisco has very few Internet cafes. Other establishments around town, however, afford online access, perhaps with a sandwich and a cup o' joe. You can do your laundry, listen to music, dine, and check your stocks online at SoMa's **Brainwash,** 1122 Folsom St., between Seventh and Eighth streets (© **415/861-FOOD**). It's open Monday through Friday from 7am to 11pm, and Saturday and Sunday from 7:30am to noon; rates are $3 for 20 minutes. Without the rock and suds, **Copy Central,** 110 Sutter St., at Montgomery Street (© **415/392-6470**), provides access cards for 20¢ per minute. It's open Monday through Thursday from 8am to 8pm, and Friday from 8am to 7pm. **Kinko's,** 1967 Market St., near Gough Street (© **415/252-0864**), charges 25¢ per minute. Both companies have numerous locations around town.

*Police* For emergencies, dial © **911** from any phone; no coins are needed. For other matters, call © **415/553-0123.**

*Post Office* The city has dozens of post offices. The closest branch to Union Square is in Macy's, 170 O'Farrell St. (© **800/275-8777**).

*Safety* Few locals would recommend walking alone late at night in certain areas, particularly the Tenderloin, between Union Square and the Civic Center. Compared to dodgy neighborhoods in other cities, however, even this section of San Francisco is relatively tranquil. You should also be alert in the Mission District, around 16th and Mission streets; the lower Fillmore area, around lower Haight Street; and SoMa (south of Market St.).

*Taxes* An 8.5% sales tax is added at the register for all goods and services purchased in San Francisco. The city hotel tax is a whopping 14%.

*Transit Information* For live help, call **Muni** (© **415/673-6864**) Monday through Friday between 7am and 5pm, and Saturday and Sunday between 9am and 5pm. Recorded information is available at other times.

*Useful Telephone Numbers* **Tourist information** (© **415/283-0176**); **highway conditions** (© 800/427-7623); **Moviefone** (© **415/777-FILM**).

*Weather* Call © **831/656-1725** or visit www.nws.noaa.gov to find out when the next fog bank is rolling in.

## 3 Where to Stay

San Francisco is an extensive—and expensive—hotel town, especially considering its relatively small size. I can't cover all the options in this guide; for a larger selection, check out *Frommer's San Francisco 2006* and *Frommer's San Francisco from $70 a Day,* which detail dozens of other choices.

Most of the hotels listed below are within walking distance of Union Square and accessible via cable car. Union Square is near the city's major shops, the Financial District, and all transportation. Prices listed below do not include state and city taxes, which total 14%.

The price categories below reflect the prices of double rooms during the high season, which runs approximately April through September. (In reality, rates vary greatly these days.) So remember: These are "rack" (or published) rates; you can almost always get a much better deal if you inquire about promotions, packages, weekend discounts, corporate rates, and family plans. Call the hotel directly, rather than a number for the entire chain.

**San Francisco Reservations,** 360 22nd St., Suite 300, Oakland, CA 94612 (© **800/ 677-1500** or 510/628-4450; www.hotelres.com), arranges reservations at more than 150 of San Francisco's hotels and often offers discounted rates.

In addition to the hotels below, I also recommend those represented by the reasonably priced and fashionable **Joie de Vivre** chain (© 800/SF-TRIPS; www.sftrips.com) and **Personality Hotels** (© 800/553-1900; www.personalityhotels.com), which spiffs up older buildings in central locales. Pricier options include the **Donatello** (© 800/227-3184) and the **Kimpton Group,** which operates the **Juliana Hotel** (© 800/328-3880) and the **Hotel Serrano** (© 415/885-2500). The **Hilton San Francisco** (© 800/HILTONS) and **San Francisco Marriott** (© 800/228-9290) both have convention-hotel ambience, but they're conveniently located, with enough rooms to sleep thousands. Along the same lines, the **Pan Pacific** (© 800/533-6465) exudes elegance despite its enormous size.

## UNION SQUARE
### VERY EXPENSIVE
**Campton Place Hotel** ★★★   This luxury boutique hotel offers some of the best— not to mention the most expensive—accommodations in town. During a $15-million room renovation completed in 2001, rooms were gutted and appointed with limestone, pear wood, and Italian-modern furnishings. The two executive suites and one luxury suite are outrageously posh. The hotel's many discriminating repeat guests return again and again for the superlative service, extralarge beds, exquisite bathrooms, bathrobes, top-notch toiletries, slippers, and many other extras. The downside is that rooms can be small.

Chef Daniel Humm delights diners with delicately prepared, highly sculpted cuisine at the excellent **Campton Place** restaurant (p. 99).

340 Stockton St. (between Post and Sutter sts.), San Francisco, CA 94108. © **800/235-4300** or 415/781-5555. Fax 415/955-5536. www.camptonplace.com. 110 units. $340–$475 double; $575–$2,000 suite. American breakfast $17. AE, DC, MC, V. Valet parking $38. Cable car: Powell-Hyde or Powell-Mason lines (1 block west). Bus: 2, 3, 4, 30, 38, or 45. Streetcar and BART: Market St. **Amenities:** Restaurant; outdoor fitness terrace; concierge; secretarial services; 24-hr. room service; laundry service; same-day dry cleaning. *In room:* A/C, TV w/pay movies, dataport, T1 line, minibar, hair dryer, iron, safe.

# San Francisco Accommodations

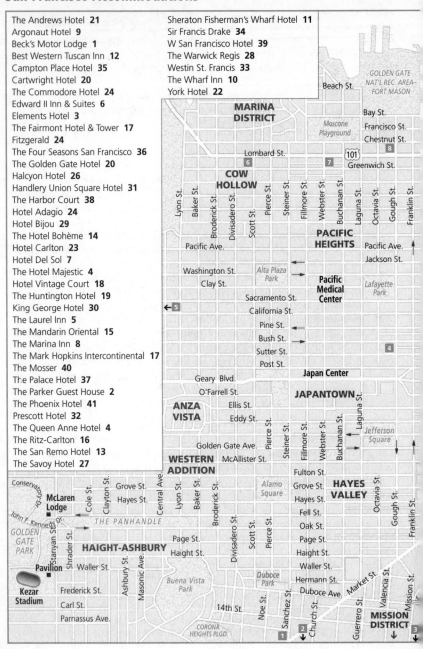

The Andrews Hotel  **21**
Argonaut Hotel  **9**
Beck's Motor Lodge  **1**
Best Western Tuscan Inn  **12**
Campton Place Hotel  **35**
Cartwright Hotel  **20**
The Commodore Hotel  **24**
Edward II Inn & Suites  **6**
Elements Hotel  **3**
The Fairmont Hotel & Tower  **17**
Fitzgerald  **24**
The Four Seasons San Francisco  **36**
The Golden Gate Hotel  **20**
Halcyon Hotel  **26**
Handlery Union Square Hotel  **31**
The Harbor Court  **38**
Hotel Adagio  **24**
Hotel Bijou  **29**
The Hotel Bohème  **14**
Hotel Carlton  **23**
Hotel Del Sol  **7**
The Hotel Majestic  **4**
Hotel Vintage Court  **18**
The Huntington Hotel  **19**
King George Hotel  **30**
The Laurel Inn  **5**
The Mandarin Oriental  **15**
The Marina Inn  **8**
The Mark Hopkins Intercontinental  **17**
The Mosser  **40**
The Palace Hotel  **37**
The Parker Guest House  **2**
The Phoenix Hotel  **41**
Prescott Hotel  **32**
The Queen Anne Hotel  **4**
The Ritz-Carlton  **16**
The San Remo Hotel  **13**
The Savoy Hotel  **27**

Sheraton Fisherman's Wharf Hotel  **11**
Sir Francis Drake  **34**
W San Francisco Hotel  **39**
The Warwick Regis  **28**
Westin St. Francis  **33**
The Wharf Inn  **10**
York Hotel  **22**

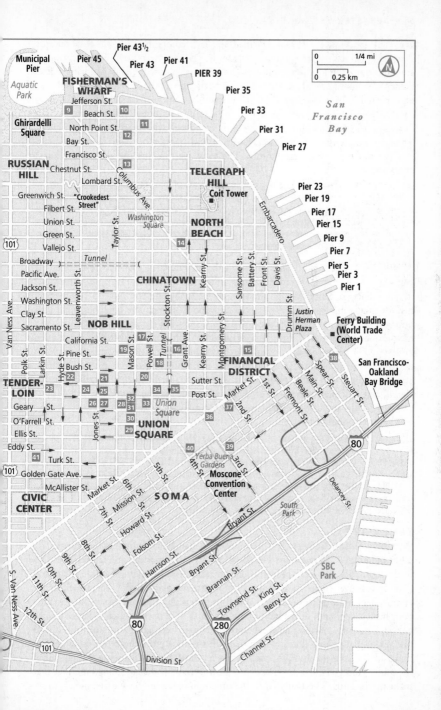

Municipal
Pier

*Aquatic
Park*

Pier 45

Pier 43¹/₂

Pier 43

Pier 41

PIER 39

Pier 35

*San
Francisco
Bay*

FISHERMAN'S
WHARF

Jefferson St.

Pier 33

Ghirardelli
Square

Beach St.

Pier 31

North Point St.

Pier 27

Bay St.

Francisco St.

RUSSIAN
HILL

Chestnut St.

TELEGRAPH
HILL

Pier 23

Coit Tower

Pier 19

Lombard St.

Greenwich St.

"Crookedest
Street"

Pier 17

Filbert St.

NORTH
BEACH

Pier 15

Union St.

*Washington
Square*

Pier 9

Green St.

Pier 7

Vallejo St.

Pier 5

Broadway

*Tunnel*

Pier 3

Pacific Ave.

Pier 1

Jackson St.

CHINATOWN

Washington St.

Clay St.

Sacramento St.

NOB HILL

*Justin
Herman
Plaza*

California St.

Ferry Building
(World Trade
Center)

Pine St.

Bush St.

San Francisco-
Oakland
Bay Bridge

TENDER-
LOIN

Sutter St.

FINANCIAL
DISTRICT

Post St.

Geary St.

O'Farrell St.

Ellis St.

*Union
Square*

Eddy St.

UNION
SQUARE

Turk St.

*Yerba Buena
Gardens*

Golden Gate Ave.

McAllister St.

Moscone
Convention
Center

CIVIC
CENTER

SOMA

*South
Park*

Howard St.

Folsom St.

Harrison St.

Bryant St.

Brannan St.

SBC
Park

Townsend St.

King St.

Berry St.

Division St.

Channel St.

85

**Prescott Hotel** ★★  It may be small and lack common areas, but the boutique Prescott Hotel has some big things going for it. The staff treats you like royalty, rooms are handsome, the location is ideal (a block from Union Sq.), and Wolfgang Puck's **Postrio** restaurant provides the room service—though it's somewhat limited, and only higher-paying, "concierge-level" guests receive free continental breakfast and evening cocktails and hors d'oeuvres. In each of the soundproof rooms, Ralph Lauren fabrics in dark tones of green, plum, and burgundy blend well with cherrywood furnishings. The bathrooms, though tiny, come stocked with terry robes and Aveda products, and the suites have Jacuzzi bathtubs. The view, alas, doesn't live up to this hotel's other assets.

545 Post St. (between Mason and Taylor sts.), San Francisco, CA 94102. ✆ **800/283-7322** or 415/563-0303. Fax 415/563-6831. www.prescotthotel.com. 164 units. $235–$340 double; $270 concierge-level double (including breakfast and evening cocktail reception); from $365 suite. AE, DC, DISC, MC, V. Valet parking $38. Cable car: Powell-Hyde or Powell-Mason lines (1 block east). Bus: 2, 3, 4, 30, 38, or 45. **Amenities:** Restaurant; bar; small exercise room; concierge; limited courtesy car; limited room service. *In room:* TV w/pay movies and video games, dataport, high-speed wireless Internet access, minibar, hair dryer, iron, safe.                •

**Westin St. Francis** ★★ *Kids*  Although the St. Francis is too massive to offer the personal service you get at smaller deluxe hotels, its majestic aura is almost unrivaled in San Francisco. Stroll through the vast, ornate lobby and you can feel 100 years of history emanating from its hand-carved redwood paneling. The hotel has spent millions on major renovations in the last 8 years, gussying up the lobby, restoring the facade, and replacing all the guest-room carpeting, furniture, and bedding in the main building. The rooms in the Tower, which was built in the 1970s and renovated in 2001, have a contemporary design, but the main building retains its high ceilings, crown molding, and other traditionally elegant details. Unfortunately, the tearoom closed, but **Michael Mina**—a new fancy restaurant by the famed chef of Aqua— debuted on the premises in 2004 (p. 102). The Westin Kids Club program entitles children to a goodie bag.

335 Powell St. (between Geary and Post sts.), San Francisco, CA 94102. ✆ **800/WESTIN-1** or 415/397-7000. Fax 415/774-0124. www.westin.com. 1,195 units. Main building $199–$499 double; Tower (Grand View) $219–$549 double; from $550 suite (in either building). Extra person $30. Continental breakfast $15–$18. AE, DC, DISC, MC, V. Valet parking $42. Cable car: Powell-Hyde or Powell-Mason lines (direct stop). Bus: 2, 3, 4, 30, 38, 45, or 76. Pets under 40 lb. accepted (dog beds available on request). **Amenities:** 2 restaurants; elaborate health club and spa; concierge; car-rental desk; business center; 24-hr. room service. *In room:* A/C, TV, dataport, high-speed Internet access ($15), minibar, fridge on request, hair dryer, iron/board, cordless phones.

## EXPENSIVE

**Handlery Union Square Hotel** ★ *Value*  A half-block from Union Square, the 1906 building that houses the Handlery and its more modern annex underwent an overhaul in 2002. Now the rooms, which are tasteful and modern, if a little sedate and dark, feature every amenity, including new mattresses, alarm radios, voice mail, refrigerators, light fixtures, paint, carpets, and furnishings. Additional perks include an outdoor heated pool and, in the newer building, club-level options such as larger rooms, a complimentary morning newspaper, turndown service, bathroom scale, robes, two phones, and adjoining doors, which make this hotel a great choice for families. The downsides? Given the price, the place wants for direct light and a sense of grandeur in the lobby. And you'll have to trek if you want to traverse the adjoining buildings that make up the hotel. **The Daily Grill,** the American restaurant on the premises, is so-so.

351 Geary St. (between Mason and Powell sts.), San Francisco, CA 94102. ✆ **800/843-4343** or 415/781-7800. Fax 415/781-0269. www.handlery.com. 377 units. $194–$294 historic section; club section from $249 double, from $294 suite. Extra person $10. AE, DC, DISC, MC, V. Parking $29. Cable car: Powell-Hyde or Powell-Mason lines (direct stop). Bus: 2, 3, 4, 30, 38, or 45. **Amenities:** Restaurant; heated outdoor swimming pool; access to nearby health club ($10 per day); sauna; barber shop; room service (7am–10pm); babysitting; same-day laundry. *In room:* A/C, TV w/Nintendo and pay movies, dataport, wireless Internet access, fridge, complimentary coffee and tea makers, hair dryer, iron, safe, voice mail.

**Hotel Adagio** ★★   After an $11-million renovation in 2003, this 1929 Spanish Revival hotel has a gorgeous modern style to reflect its youthful, fashionable clientele. Local hip hotelier Joie de Vivre swathed the 171 large, bright guest rooms in a chocolate brown and mocha palette, and appointed them with chic, dark-wood furnishings, firm mattresses, double-paned windows that open, and voice mail. Bathrooms are old but clean, and most have tubs. Corporate units, on the 12th and 16th floors, include irons, robes, and free continental breakfast. Feel like splurging? Go for one of the five penthouse-level suites, which have lovely terraces with a New York vibe. Or step into **Cortez** at night, the on-site restaurant with a full, chic bar and good "small plates" to go with your cocktails. *Tip:* Rooms above the ninth floor have good southern views of the city.

550 Geary St., San Francisco, CA 94102. ✆ **800/228-8830** or 415/775-5000. www.thehoteladagio.com. 171 units. $209 double. AE, DISC, MC, V. Valet parking $29. Bus: 2, 3, 4, 30, 38, or 45. **Amenities:** Restaurant; bar; fitness center; concierge; business center w/free wireless Internet; room service; laundry service; dry cleaning; luggage storage room. *In room:* TV w/pay movies and Nintendo, dataport, complimentary high-speed Internet access, minibar, fridge, hair dryer, iron, safe, CD player.

**Sir Francis Drake** ★★   The Sir Francis Drake, whose owners have spent millions on renovations over the past decade, is a glorious, 21-story historic hotel. For visitors willing to trade chipped bathroom tiles or mismatched furniture for the chance to vacation in grand fashion, it's a fine choice. Allow Tom Sweeny, the ebullient (and legendary) Beefeater doorman, to handle your bags as you enter the elegant lobby. Sip cocktails or swing dance to a live orchestra at the chic retro Starlight Room, overlooking the city. Or dine at **Scala's Bistro** (p. 103), one of the most festive restaurants downtown.

450 Powell St. (at Sutter St.), San Francisco, CA 94102. ✆ **800/227-5480** or 415/392-7755. Fax 415/391-8719. www.sirfrancisdrake.com. 417 units. $219–$259 double; $500–$700 suite. AE, DC, DISC, MC, V. Valet parking $35. Cable car: Powell-Hyde or Powell-Mason lines (direct stop). Bus: 2, 3, 4, 45, or 76. **Amenities:** 2 restaurants; bar; exercise room; concierge; 24-hr. room service; same-day laundry service/dry cleaning. *In room:* A/C, TV w/pay movies and Nintendo, dataport, minibar, hair dryer, iron.

## MODERATE

A few worthy hotel companies operate properties throughout the city. **Holiday Inn** (✆ **800/465-4329;** www.holiday-inn.com) has several locations.

**The Andrews Hotel** ★   For location and price, the Andrews is a safe bet for an enjoyable stay. Two blocks west of Union Square, the Andrews was a Turkish bath before its conversion in 1981. As is typical in Euro-style hotels, the rooms are small but well maintained and comfortable, with nice touches like lace curtains and fresh flowers. Upgrades in 2002 and 2003 included new mattresses, carpets (in most rooms), and fresh paint in the bathrooms.

624 Post St. (between Jones and Taylor sts.), San Francisco, CA 94109. ✆ **800/926-3739** or 415/563-6877. Fax 415/928-6919. www.andrewshotel.com. 48 units (some w/shower only). $109–$139 double; $139–$179 superior rooms. Rates include continental breakfast and evening wine. AE, DC, MC, V. Valet parking $25. Cable car: Powell-Hyde

or Powell-Mason lines (3 blocks east). Bus: 2, 3, 4, 30, 38, or 45. **Amenities:** Restaurant; access to nearby health club; concierge; room service (5:30–10pm); babysitting; nearby self-service laundromat; laundry service; dry cleaning, coffee in lobby. *In room:* TV/VCR w/video library, dataport, wireless high-speed Internet access ($10 per day), fridge and CD player in suites only, hair dryer on request, iron.

### The Cartwright Hotel ★★
Remarkably quiet, despite its convenient location near one of the busiest downtown corners, this eight-story hotel still looks much as it did when it opened more than 80 years ago. High-quality antiques, collected for decades, furnish the lobby and the individually decorated rooms. Some guest quarters are very small, but all of them were gussied up with new paint and furniture in 2004. *Tip:* Request a room with a view of the backyard; they're the quietest. Complimentary wine is served in the small library each night, and afternoon tea and cookies are a daily treat, as are the apples and hot beverages in the lobby. The breakfast room, added in 2004, serves a complimentary, expanded continental breakfast.

524 Sutter St. (at Powell St.), San Francisco, CA 94102. ✆ **800/919-9779** or 415/421-2865. Fax 415/398-6345. www.cartwrighthotel.com. 114 units. $99–$159 double; $189–$259 family/business suite (sleeps 4). Rates include 24-hr. tea, coffee, and apples in the lobby, continental breakfast, nightly wine hour, weekday newspapers, and afternoon cookies. AE, DC, DISC, MC, V. Valet parking $35; self-parking $25. Cable car: Powell-Hyde or Powell-Mason lines (direct stop). Bus: 2, 3, 4, 30, or 45. **Amenities:** Access to nearby health club for $15; concierge; free wireless Internet access. *In room:* TV, dataport, free wireless Internet access, fridge upon request, hair dryer, iron.

### The Commodore Hotel ★★
If you're looking for a little fun and fantasy in your vacation, check out this six-story, low-budget, trendy spot. The Neo-Deco rooms feature bright colors, whimsical furnishings, and tasteful artwork. The Red Room—a swank, dim bar and lounge that's redder than Dorothy's ruby slippers—steals the show. The new **Canteen** restaurant, adjacent to the hotel, features Franco-American cuisine.

825 Sutter St. (at Jones St.), San Francisco, CA 94109. ✆ **800/338-6848** or 415/923-6800. Fax 415/923-6804. www.thecommodorehotel.com. 110 units. $125–$169 double. AE, DC, DISC, MC, V. Parking $25. Bus: 2, 3, 4, 27, 19, 47, or 49. **Amenities:** Restaurant; bar; access to nearby health club ($15 per day); concierge; Internet access in lobby. *In room:* TV w/pay movies, dataport, wireless Internet, minifridge, coffeemaker, hair dryer, iron.

### Hotel Carlton (Value)
If you're looking for attractive, clean, cheap accommodations, and you don't mind being in midtown (read: in the middle of nowhere), book a room here. Joie de Vivre hotel group was behind the May 2004 renovation of this 163-room, 1927 hotel. Revamped in international vintage decor, the interior is wonderful, with travel photographs from the American Himalayan Foundation, tribal figurines, Oriental rugs, a vibrant sarilike color scheme and, in the guest rooms, imported, hand-painted Moroccan tables and cool Lucite-beaded table lamps. The surrounding neighborhood is drab, but it's only a 7-block walk to Union Square. With doubles starting at $99, you can splurge for a taxi with the money saved.

1075 Sutter St., San Francisco, CA 94109. ✆ **800/922-7586** or 415/673-0242. Fax 415/929-8788. www.jdvhospitality. com. 163 units. $99–$119 double. Rates include evening wine hour. AE, MC, V. Valet $25, self $20. Bus: 2, 3, 4, 19, or 76. **Amenities:** Concierge, laundry, dry cleaning. *In room:* TV w/pay per view, Internet access in deluxe rooms, coffeemaker, hair dryer, iron, safe.

### Hotel Vintage Court ★★ (Value)
Consistent personal service and great value attract the loyal clients who swear by this European-style hotel, 2 blocks north of Union Square. You'll be tempted to wallow away your time in the recently renovated lobby with comfy couches—especially when the bartenders are pouring free California wines every evening from 5 to 6pm. Even after happy hour, the hotel stays under the influence: The tidy rooms, each named after a winery, have a modern country look, decorated in greens and

other earth tones, with cream duvets and lovely mahogany-slat blinds. The deluxe, two-room penthouse suite, called the Niebaum-Coppola (after the winery owned by the movie maverick), has an original 1912 stained-glass skylight, a wood-burning fireplace, whirlpool tub, entertainment center, and panoramic views of the city. *Note:* Smoking is prohibited in all rooms. **Masa's,** which has long been one of the city's top (and priciest) contemporary French restaurants, is off the lobby. They've just changed chefs as this book goes to press, however, so it's too soon to tell whether a meal here is worth the high prices.

650 Bush St. (between Powell and Stockton sts.), San Francisco, CA 94108. © **800/654-1100** or 415/392-4666. Fax 415/433-4065. www.executivehotels.net/vintagecourt. 107 units. $139–$199 double; $325–$350 penthouse suite. Rates include continental breakfast and evening wine service. AE, DC, DISC, MC, V. Valet parking $37; self-parking $27. Cable car: Powell-Hyde or Powell-Mason lines (direct stop). Bus: 2, 3, 4, 30, 45, or 76. **Amenities:** Restaurant; access to off-premises health club ($14 per day); concierge; in-room massage; same-day laundry service/dry cleaning. *In room:* A/C, TV w/video games, dataport, wireless Internet, minibar, coffeemaker, hair dryer, iron.

**King George Hotel** ★★ *Value*    Built in 1914 for the international Panama-Pacific Exhibition, this delightful hotel has continued to draw a mostly European clientele over the years. Surrounded by cable-car lines, the Theater District, Union Square, and dozens of restaurants, its location is superb. And the rooms are surprisingly quiet for such a busy area (although thin walls can make interior noise audible). The very clean rooms can be small, but they're efficiently appointed, with new mattresses, desks, a handsome, studylike ambience, and new textiles. The hotel's English afternoon tea is a big hit, served in the Windsor Tea Room Saturday, Sunday, and holidays from 1 to 4:30pm. Recent additions include a pub, 24-hour business center, and an upgraded "executive" level.

334 Mason St. (between Geary and O'Farrell sts.), San Francisco, CA 94102. © **800/288-6005** or 415/781-5050. Fax 415/835-5991. www.kinggeorge.com. 153 units. $165 double; $165 queen; $185 suite. Continental breakfast $12–$15. Special-value packages available seasonally. AE, DC, DISC, MC, V. Valet parking $25; self-parking $23. Cable car: Powell-Hyde or Powell-Mason lines (1 block west). Bus: 1, 2, 3, 4, 5, 7, 30, 38, 45, 70, or 71. **Amenities:** Tearoom; evening lounge/bar; $10 access to health club ½ block away; concierge; 24-hr. business center; wireless Internet access in lobby; secretarial services; 24-hr. room service; same-day laundry service/dry cleaning. *In room:* TV w/pay movies and Nintendo, dataport, complimentary wireless high-speed Internet access, hair dryer, iron, safe.

**The Savoy Hotel** ★★ *Value*    The European-style Savoy is one of my favorite moderately priced downtown hotels (the Warwick Regis is my other top pick). Given the cozy, apartment-like feel of each room, appointed with featherbeds and goose-down pillows, it's easy to relax here. Rooms can be small, but each has 18th-century period furnishings, 400-thread-count sheets, full-length mirrors, two-line telephones, and clean old bathrooms with original tile work. Guests also enjoy round-the-clock concierge service and access to the newly relocated **Millennium** restaurant, the city's only gourmet vegan dining room.

580 Geary St. (between Taylor and Jones sts.), San Francisco, CA 94102. © **800/227-4223** or 415/441-2700. Fax 415/441-0124. www.thesavoyhotel.com. 82 units. $119–$169 double; $149–$169 suite. Complimentary wine and cheese 4–6pm daily. Ask about packages; full continental breakfast $5. Government, AAA, senior, and corporate rates. AE, DC, DISC, MC, V. Valet parking $30. Bus: 2, 3, 4, 27, or 38. **Amenities:** Restaurant; 24-hr. concierge; free high-speed Internet stations; laundry service; dry cleaning. *In room:* TV, dataport, hair dryer, iron, safe.

**The Warwick Regis** ★★ *Value*    Louis XVI might have been a rotten monarch, but he certainly had taste. Fashioned in the style of pre-Revolutionary France, the Warwick is awash with French and English antiques, Italian marble, chandeliers, four-poster beds, hand-carved headboards, and the like. The result is an expensive-looking hotel that, for all its perks, is surprisingly affordable compared to its Union Square contemporaries. Rooms can be on the small side, but they're among the city's most charming. Bathrooms are also winning but small. Honeymooners should splurge on the fireplace rooms with canopy beds. Adjoining the lobby is **La Scene Restaurant and Bar,** a beautiful place to start your day with a latte, and end it with a nightcap.

490 Geary St. (between Mason and Taylor sts.), San Francisco, CA 94102. © **800/827-3447** or 415/928-7900. Fax 415/441-8788. www.warwicksf.com. 74 units. $129–$199 double; $159–$269 suite. AE, DC, DISC, MC, V. Parking $29. Cable car: Powell-Hyde or Powell-Mason lines. Bus: 2, 3, 4, 27, or 38. **Amenities:** Restaurant; access to nearby health club ($15 per day); concierge; business center; secretarial services; 24-hr. room service; babysitting; laundry service; dry cleaning. *In room:* TV, dataport, wireless Internet access, minibar, hair dryer, iron, safe.

**The York Hotel** ★★  Even as a local, I stop by the York because it's home to **The Empire Plush Room,** the city's best jazz and cabaret club, which also features a new vaudeville show. For the out-of-town visitor, this 1922 hotel, featured in Hitchcock's *Vertigo,* is simply a great deal. Awarded Three Diamonds by AAA, the hotel has a helpful staff, a workout room, and promotional rates, which include continental breakfast served in the lobby. Rooms are cheery, swathed in terra cotta and green, and loaded with nice touches like dark-wood writing desks; newly upholstered, comfy chairs; Internet access; tub/showers; and walk-in closets.

940 Sutter St. (between Leavenworth and Hyde sts.), San Francisco, CA 94109. © **800/808-9675** or 415/885-6800. Fax 415/885-2115. www.yorkhotel.com. 96 units. $119–$149 double. Rates include continental breakfast. AE, DISC, MC, V. Valet parking $35, self parking $25. Bus: 2, 3, or 4. **Amenities:** Jazz club; bar; workout room; valet laundry. *In room:* TV w/pay movies, high-speed wireless Internet access (free in the Superior King rooms), coffeemaker, hair dryer, iron on request, safe.

### INEXPENSIVE

**The Fitzgerald** ★  A perfect example of "you get what you pay for," The Fitzgerald's guest quarters have newish furniture, sweet striped wallpaper, bright bedspreads, and patterned carpets, but some of the rooms are really small. (At least one has a dresser less than a foot from the bed.) Of course, the $80-a-night rate leaves little room for complaining, but do ask for a larger room. If you can live without a sizable closet, you'll find that the price, breakfast (home-baked breads, muffins, juice, tea, and coffee), and cleanliness make it a good value.

620 Post St. (between Jones and Taylor sts.), San Francisco, CA 94109. © **800/334-6835** or 415/775-8100. Fax 415/775-1278. www.fitzgeraldhotel.com. 47 units. $65–$125 double. Rates include continental breakfast. Lower rates in winter. AE, DC, DISC, MC, V. Self-parking $24, valet for $34. Cable car: Powell-Hyde or Powell-Mason lines. Bus: 2, 3, 4, or 27. **Amenities:** Free access to a nearby exercise room; pay Internet access in lobby; same-day dry cleaning. *In room:* TV, dataport, hair dryer.

**The Golden Gate Hotel** ★★  Among the city's small hotels in historic buildings, the Golden Gate is a hidden gem. Its greatest strength is that it's family run: John and Renate Kenaston and daughter Gabriele are hospitable innkeepers who take pleasure in making their guests comfortable. Each individually decorated room has antique furnishings (plenty of wicker), quilted bedspreads, and fresh flowers; some have clawfoot tubs. The hotel is very well located, 2 blocks north of Union Square and 2 blocks from the crest of Nob Hill, with cable-car stops at the corner for easy access to Fisherman's Wharf and Chinatown. Theaters and the best restaurants are within walking distance. Guests are welcome to complimentary afternoon tea, served daily from 4 to 7pm, and free use of the house fax and computer with wireless DSL.

775 Bush St. (between Powell and Mason sts.), San Francisco, CA 94108. © **800/835-1118** or 415/392-3702. Fax 415/392-6202. www.goldengatehotel.com. 25 units, 14 w/bathroom. $85 double without bathroom; $130 double

w/bathroom. Rates include continental breakfast and afternoon tea. AE, DC, MC, V. Self-parking $16. Cable car: Powell-Hyde or Powell-Mason lines (1 block east). Bus: 2, 4, 30, 38, or 45. BART: Powell or Market. **Amenities:** Access to health club 1 block away; activities desk; business services (fax, copier, laptop available for free on 1-hr. basis); laundry service/dry cleaning next door. *In room:* TV, dataport, wireless Internet access, hair dryer and iron upon request.

**Halcyon Hotel** *★* *(Value*   Inside this small, four-story brick building is a penny pincher's dream come true: all the comforts of home, in the heart of Union Square, for a fair price. The small but very clean studio guest rooms have microwave ovens, refrigerators, flatware and utensils, toasters, and voice mail. Guests have access to the coin-operated washer and dryer in the basement, with free laundry soap and use of irons. You also get your own doorbell and mailbox. The owners are usually on hand to offer friendly, personal service, making this option an unbeatable deal. Be sure to ask about special rates for weekly stays.

649 Jones St. (between Geary and Post sts.), San Francisco, CA 94102. (℃) **800/627-2396** or 415/929-8033. Fax 415/441-8033. www.halcyonsf.com. 25 units. $79–$129 double year-round, $510–$590 weekly. Minimum length of stay Oct–Apr is 7 days. AE, DC, DISC, MC, V. Parking garage nearby $14–$16 per day. Bus: 2, 3, 4, 9, 27, or 38. **Amenities:** Access to nearby health club; concierge; tour desk; car-rental booklet and accessible rentals within walking distance; laundry facilities, free fax available in lobby. *In room:* Dataport, kitchen, fridge, coffeemaker, hair dryer, iron, safe, voice mail.

**Hotel Bijou** *★* *(Value*   Although it's on the periphery of the gritty Tenderloin (3 blocks off Union Sq.), this 1911 hotel is cheery, clean, and cheap, with a little style, too. Lively decor, a Deco theater theme, and vibrant paint disguise the hotel's age. Off the small lobby is a "theater" where guests can watch San Francisco–based movies nightly (on old-fashioned theater seating in front of a TV showing videos). Upstairs, the rooms—which are named after local films—are small but colorful, painted in shades like buttercup, burgundy, and purple. And they fit all the essential amenities, from dressers and small desks to tiny private bathrooms. Some mattresses could be firmer, however, and the only elevator is small and slow.

111 Mason St., San Francisco, CA 94102. (℃) **800/771-1022** or 415/771-1200. www.hotelbijou.com. 65 units. $95–$139 double. Rates include continental breakfast. AE, DC, DISC, MC, V. Valet parking $25. Streetcar: Powell St. station. Bus: All Market St. buses. **Amenities:** Concierge, DSL Internet access in lobby for $4 for 20 mins; limited room service, same-day laundry service/dry cleaning. *In room:* TV, dataport, high-speed Internet, hair dryer, iron.

## SOMA
### VERY EXPENSIVE

**The Four Seasons Hotel San Francisco** *★★★*   Sophisticated and hip, Four Seasons does everything right, despite its lack of grand public areas. Take the elevators up to the lobby and you're surrounded by calm, cool, collected hotel perfection and a sexy cocktail lounge that's sure to be your second home in San Francisco. Not too trendy, not too traditional, the rooms are just right, with original artwork, huge, luxury marble bathrooms, and deep tubs. Custom-made mattresses and pillows guarantee a great night's sleep. Many of the oversize rooms (starting at 460 sq. ft., including 46 suites) overlook Yerba Buena Gardens. Other perks include free access to the building's huge **Sports Club L.A.,** round-the-clock business services, and a 2-block walk to Union Square and the Moscone Convention Center.

757 Market St. (between Third and Fourth sts.), San Francisco, CA 94103. (℃) **800/332-3442** or 415/633-3000. Fax 415/633-3001. www.fourseasons.com/sanfrancisco. 277 units. $469–$600 double; $800 executive suite. AE, DC, DISC, MC, V. Parking $39. Streetcar: F, and all underground streetcars. BART: All trains. Bus: All Market St. buses. **Amenities:** Restaurant; bar; huge fitness center; spa; concierge; high-tech business center; wireless in lobby; secretarial services; salon; 24-hr. room service; in-room massage; overnight laundry and dry-cleaning service. *In room:* AC, TV w/pay movies, fax, dataport, minibar, hair dryer, safe.

**The Palace Hotel** 💥   To walk through the doors of the 1875 Palace Hotel, rebuilt after the 1906 quake, is to experience the majesty of old luxury. The most spectacular attributes are the regal old lobby and the Garden Court, a San Francisco landmark restored to its original grandeur. The rooms recently underwent renovations as well, with mahogany four-poster beds, warm gold paint and upholstery, and tasteful artwork.

2 New Montgomery St. (at Market St.), San Francisco, CA 94105. ℂ **800/325-3589** or 415/512-1111. Fax 415/543-0671. www.sfpalace.com. 552 units. $550–$650 double; from $775 suite. Extra person $40. Children under 18 sharing existing bedding stay free in parent's room. Weekend rates and packages available. AE, DC, DISC, MC, V. Parking $40. Bus: All Market St. buses. Streetcar: All Market St. streetcars. **Amenities:** 4 restaurants; bar; health club w/skylit, heated lap pool; spa; Jacuzzi; sauna; concierge; business center; conference rooms w/wireless Internet access, wireless Internet in lobby (for fee); 24-hr. room service; laundry service; dry cleaning. *In room:* A/C, TV w/pay movies, dataport, high-speed access for $16 per day, minibar, hair dryer, iron, safe.

**W San Francisco Hotel** 💥💥💥   This 31-story, 423-room property, adjacent to the San Francisco Museum of Modern Art, is one of the most hip hotels in town. Sleek and stylish, its octagonal, three-story glass entrance and lobby give way to a great lounge and two bars. The guest rooms have a residential feel, "luxury" featherbeds with goose-down comforters and pillows, oversized dark-wood desks, upholstered chaise lounges, and louvered blinds that open to exceptional city views. Rooms also feature a compact media wall with CD and videocassette players, an extensive CD library, 27-inch color TV, and Internet service via an infrared keyboard and portable two-line phones. Bathrooms are stocked with Bliss products, to match the new Bliss Spa that opened here in mid-2005.

181 Third St. (between Mission and Howard sts.), San Francisco, CA 94103. ℂ **877/WHOTELS** or 415/777-5300. Fax 415/817-7823. www.whotels.com/sanfrancisco. 410 units. $469–$550 double; $800–$1,800 suite. AE, DC, DISC, MC, V. Valet parking $40. Streetcar: J, K, L, or M to Montgomery. Bus: 15, 30, or 45. **Amenities:** Restaurant; 2 bars; heated atrium pool and Jacuzzi; fitness center; spa; concierge; business center; Wi-Fi in public spaces; secretarial services; 24-hr. room service; same-day laundry service/dry cleaning. *In room:* A/C, TV/VCR w/pay movies and high-speed Internet access, fax in some rooms, dataport, minibar, coffeemaker, hair dryer, iron, safe, CD player.

### EXPENSIVE

**The Harbor Court** 💥💥   Just off the Embarcadero at the edge of the Financial District, this former YMCA with bayfront views books a lot of corporate travelers. It will satisfy anyone, however, who appreciates a lively scene and stylish, high-quality accommodations, with half-canopy beds, large armoires, writing desks, and soundproof windows. ***Note:*** You'll pay extra for a room with a view.

165 Steuart St. (between Mission and Howard sts.), San Francisco, CA 94105. ℂ **800/346-0555** or 415/882-1300. Fax 415/882-1313. www.harborcourthotel.com. 131 units. $165–$399 double. Continental breakfast $10. AE, DC, MC, V. Parking $35. Streetcar: Embarcadero. Bus: 14 or 80x. Pets accepted. **Amenities:** Access to adjoining health club and large, heated indoor pool; courtesy car weekday mornings; room service (breakfast only); same-day laundry service/dry cleaning; safe. *In room:* A/C, TV, dataport, minibar, hair dryer, iron.

### MODERATE

**The Mosser** 💥💥 *Value*   The Mosser is hip on the cheap—a budget hotel that combines Victorian architecture with modern interior design. It opened in 1913 as a luxury hotel, but a major multimillion-dollar renovation in the fall of 2001 transformed this aging charmer into a sophisticated, stylish, yet affordable option. In the guest rooms, original Victorian flourishes (such as bay windows, high ceilings, and hand-carved moldings) are the backdrop for contemporary, custom-designed furnishings, granite showers, stainless-steel fixtures, ceiling fans, Frette linens, and modern electronics. The least expensive rooms have shared bathrooms, but rates start at $60. The location is also excellent—3 blocks from Union Square, 2 blocks from MOMA and Moscone Convention Center, and half a block from the cable-car turnaround.

54 Fourth St. (at Market St.), San Francisco, CA 94103. ℂ **800/227-3804** or 415/986-4400. Fax 415/495-7653. www.themosser.com. 166 units, 112 w/bathroom. $159–$249 double w/bathroom; $69–$89 double without bathroom. Rates include safe deposit boxes and mail services. AE, DC, DISC, MC, V. Parking $29 plus $10 for oversize vehicles. Streetcar: F, and all underground Muni and BART. **Amenities:** Restaurant; bar; 24-hr. concierge; same-day laundry service/dry cleaning. *In room:* TV, dataport, TFI and DSL for $10 per day, hair dryer, iron/ironing board, ceiling fan, AM/FM stereo w/CD player, voice mail.

## FINANCIAL DISTRICT
### VERY EXPENSIVE

**The Mandarin Oriental** ★★★ *Finds*   The common areas here are limited, but the rooms are lavishly appointed and the views divine, making this a top choice for luxury travelers. The larger rooms, between the 38th and 48th floors, afford extraordinary views. Not all units have tub-side views (get one that does and you'll never forget it!), but all have well-stocked marble bathrooms with terry- and cotton-cloth robes, makeup mirrors, and silk slippers. The less opulent rooms are done in a kind of reserved contemporary decor with Asian accents. Don't miss the Asian teatime, complete with a bento box of uncommonly delicious goodies.

222 Sansome St. (between Pine and California sts.), San Francisco, CA 94104. ℂ **800/622-0404** or 415/276-9888. Fax 415/433-0289. www.mandarinoriental.com. 158 units. $260–$750 double; $450–$750 signature rooms; from $1,400 suite. Continental breakfast $21; American breakfast $32. AE, DC, DISC, MC, V. Valet parking $36. Streetcar: J, K, L, or M to Montgomery. Bus: All Market St. buses. **Amenities:** Restaurant; bar; fitness center; concierge; car rental; business center; free wireless; 24-hr. room service; in-room massage; laundry service; same-day dry cleaning. *In room:* A/C, TV w/pay movies, fax on request, dataport, high-speed Internet access $13 per day, minibar, hair dryer, iron, safe, CD player.

## NOB HILL
### VERY EXPENSIVE

**The Fairmont Hotel & Tower** ★★   The granddaddy of Nob Hill's ritzy hotels, the Fairmont has the most awe-inspiring lobby in San Francisco. Even if you're not staying here, it's worth a trip to gape at its massive marble columns, vaulted ceilings, velvet chairs, gilded mirrors, and spectacular wraparound staircase. Thanks to an $85-million renovation in 2001, the glamour extends to the guest rooms, where everything is new and opulent, yet tasteful. In addition to the expected luxuries, you'll find goose-down pillows, electric shoe buffers, walk-in closets, and multiline phones with voice mail. Whatever you do, try to visit the **Tonga Room** (p. 139), a fantastically kitschy tropical bar and restaurant where happy hour hops and rain falls into a pool every 20 minutes.

950 Mason St. (at California St.), San Francisco, CA 94108. ℂ **800/441-1414** or 415/772-5000. Fax 415/772-5086. www.fairmont.com. 591 units. Main building $289–$319 double, from $500 suite; tower $349–$379 double, from $750 suite; penthouse $12,500. Extra person $30. AE, DC, DISC, MC, V. Parking $39. Cable car: California St. line (direct stop). **Amenities:** 2 restaurants/bars; health club ($15 daily); concierge; tour desk; car-rental desk; business center; wireless Internet in lobby; shopping; salon; 24-hr. room service; massage; babysitting; same-day laundry service/dry cleaning. *In room:* A/C, TV w/pay movies and PlayStation and Nintendo, dataport, high-speed Internet access, kitchenette in some units, minibar, hair dryer, iron, safe.

**The Huntington Hotel** ★★★   The Huntington has long been a favorite retreat for Hollywood stars and VIPs who desire privacy and security. Family-owned since 1924— a rarity among large hotels—this place eschews pomp and circumstance; absolute privacy and unobtrusive service are its mainstays. Though the 19th-century-style lobby is rather petite, the apartment-like guest rooms are large and feature Brunschwig and Fils fabrics, antiques, and city views.

1075 California St. (between Mason and Taylor sts.), San Francisco, CA 94108. ℂ 800/227-4683 or 415/474-5400. Fax 415/474-6227. www.huntingtonhotel.com. 135 units. $339–$399 single or double; $490–$1,120 suite. Continental breakfast $14. Special packages available. AE, DC, DISC, MC, V. Valet parking $29. Cable car: California St. line (direct stop). Bus: 1. **Amenities:** Restaurant; lounge; indoor heated pool (ages 16 and up); health club; spa; Jacuzzi; steam room; sauna; concierge; massage; babysitting; same-day laundry service/dry cleaning; yoga and Pilates room; sun deck. *In room:* A/C, TV w/pay movies, fax, dataport, free high-speed DSL Internet, kitchenettes in some units, minibar, fridges in some units, hair dryer, iron, safe.

**The Mark Hopkins Intercontinental** ★★    Built in 1926 on the spot where railroad millionaire Mark Hopkins' turreted mansion once stood, this 19-story landmark is one of the city's most classy historic hotels. A renovation in 2000 resulted in exceedingly comfortable neoclassical rooms with all the amenities you'd expect from a worldclass hotel, including custom furniture, plush fabrics, sumptuous bathrooms, and extraordinary city views. Luxury suites, added in 2001, are twice the size of most San Francisco apartments and cost close to a month's rent per night. The **Top of the Mark**—a fantastic bar and lounge, where Pacific-bound servicemen went to toast good-bye to the States during World War II—is an extremely romantic place to sip cocktails, dance to live jazz or swing, or have brunch backed by superb city views.

1 Nob Hill (at California and Mason sts.), San Francisco, CA 94108. ℂ 800/327-0200 or 415/392-3434. Fax 415/421-3302. www.markhopkins.net. 380 units. $395–$525 double; from $650 suite; from $3,000 luxury suite. Continental breakfast $20; breakfast buffet $25. AE, DC, DISC, MC, V. Valet parking $44, some oversize vehicles prohibited. Cable car: California St. or Powell sts (direct stop). Bus: 1. **Amenities:** 2 restaurants; bar; exercise room; concierge; business center; secretarial services; 24-hr. room service; babysitting; laundry service; dry cleaning; concierge-level floors. *In room:* A/C, TV w/pay movies, VCR/DVD in suites only, dataport, Wi-Fi in all rooms for nominal fee, minibar, coffeemaker, hair dryer, iron, safe.

**The Ritz-Carlton** ★★★    Ranked among the top hotels in the world (and the city's number one) by readers of *Condé Nast Traveler,* the Ritz-Carlton has been the standard for San Francisco luxury hotels since it opened in 1991. A Nob Hill landmark, it's outfitted with opulent public areas—including spots for afternoon tea, cocktails, and fancy dinners at one of the city's finest French restaurants, The Dining Room at the Ritz-Carlton. Rooms offer every amenity and service, from Italian-marble bathrooms with double sinks and plush terry robes to the finest furnishings, fabrics, and artwork. The more expensive rooms offer good views of the city. Club rooms have a dedicated concierge, separate elevator-key access, and complimentary buffet meals throughout the day.

600 Stockton St. (between Pine and California sts.), San Francisco, CA 94108. ℂ 800/241-3333 or 415/296-7465. Fax 415/986-1268. www.ritzcarlton.com. 336 units. $425–$460 double; $580–$830 club-level double; $730–$830 executive suite. Buffet breakfast $32; champagne brunch on Sun $65. Weekend discounts and packages available. AE, DC, DISC, MC, V. Parking $50. Cable car: California St. (direct stop). **Amenities:** 2 restaurants; 3 bars; indoor heated pool; outstanding fitness center; Jacuzzi; steam room; concierge; courtesy car; business center; secretarial services; 24-hr. room service; in-room massage and manicure; babysitting; same-day laundry service/dry cleaning. *In room:* A/C, TV w/pay movies, dataport, high-speed Internet access $13 for 24 hrs, minibar, hair dryer, iron, safe.

## NORTH BEACH
### MODERATE
**Hotel Bohème** ★★ *Finds*    Romance awaits you at the Bohème. In the center of North Beach, this hotel's style and demeanor are reminiscent of a prestigious home in upscale Nob Hill. The decor evokes the Beat generation, which flourished here in the

1950s; rooms are small but hopelessly romantic, with gauze-draped canopies and walls accented with lavender, sage green, black, and pumpkin. The staff is ultrahospitable, and bonuses include free sherry in the lobby each afternoon. *Take note:* The bathrooms are sweet but tiny, without tubs. *Tip:* Request a room off the street side; they're quieter.

444 Columbus Ave. (between Vallejo and Green sts.), San Francisco, CA 94133. ℂ 415/433-9111. Fax 415/362-6292. www.hotelboheme.com. 15 units. $149–$169 double. Rates include afternoon sherry. AE, DC, DISC, MC, V. Parking $12–$31 at nearby public garages. Cable car: Powell-Mason line. Bus: 12, 15, 30, 41, 45, or 83. **Amenities:** Concierge. *In room:* TV, dataport, free Wi-Fi, hair dryer, iron.

### INEXPENSIVE

**The San Remo Hotel** ★★ *Value*  In a quiet North Beach neighborhood within walking distance of Fisherman's Wharf, this small, European-style *pensione* is one of the best budget hotels in San Francisco. The rooms are small and bathrooms are shared, but all will be forgiven when the bill arrives. Rooms are decorated in a cozy country style with brass and iron beds, armoires, and wicker furnishings; most have ceiling fans. The shared bathrooms are immaculately clean, with tubs and brass pull-chain toilets with oak tanks and brass fixtures. If the penthouse is available, book it: You won't find a more romantic place to stay in San Francisco for so little money (with your own bathroom, TV, fridge, and patio).

2237 Mason St. (at Chestnut St.), San Francisco, CA 94109. ℂ 800/352-REMO or 415/776-8688. Fax 415/776-2811. www.sanremohotel.com. 62 units, 61 w/shared bathroom. $55–$95 double; $155–$175 penthouse suite. AE, DC, MC, V. Self-parking $10–$14. Cable car: Powell-Mason line. Streetcar: F. Bus: 10, 15, 30, or 47. **Amenities:** Access to nearby health club; two massage chairs; self-service laundry; TV room; dataport. *In room:* Ceiling fan.

## FISHERMAN'S WHARF
### VERY EXPENSIVE

**Argonaut Hotel** ★★ *Kids*  The Kimpton Hotel Group is behind Fisherman's Wharf's best hotel, which opened in 2003 at the San Francisco Maritime National Historic Park (p. 125). Half a block from the bay (yet miraculously quiet), the four-story, timber-and-brick, 1909 landmark building is now a boutique gem. Its 239 rooms and 13 suites emulate a luxury cruise ship, decorated in cheerful nautical blue, white, red, and yellow. Luxury touches include flatscreen TVs, DVD and CD players, and Aveda toiletries. Suites have killer views, telescopes, and spa tubs. And kids get to pick a toy from the hotel "treasure chest." *Tips:* Get a room with a view of the wharf or bay; some even offer fabulous views of Alcatraz. And ask the concierge for tickets to tour the infamous island-prison; they seem to be able to snag them when they're sold out.

495 Jefferson St (at Hyde St.), San Francisco, CA 94109. ℂ 866/415-0704 or 415/563-0800. Fax 415/345-5513. www.argonauthotel.com. 252 units. $159–$339 double; $249–$599 suite. Rates include evening wine in the lobby, daily newspaper, and kid-friendly perks like cribs and strollers. AE, DC, DISC, MC, V. Parking $36. Bus: 10, 30, or 47. Cable car: Powell-Hyde line. Streetcar: F. **Amenities:** Restaurant; bar; fitness center; concierge; laundry service; dry cleaning; yoga video and mats. *In room:* TV w/pay movies, DVD player, Nintendo, Web TV, free high-speed Internet access, minibar, coffeemaker, hair dryer, iron, safe.

**Best Western Tuscan Inn** ★★  The Tuscan is one of the best midrange options at Fisherman's Wharf. An island of respectability in a sea of touristy schlock, it offers far more style and comfort than its neighbors. Splurge on parking—cheaper than the wharf's outrageously priced garages—then make your way toward the plush lobby, warmed by a grand fireplace. The rooms, with writing desks and armchairs, are also a cut above what's available in competing neighborhood hotels. The only caveat is the lack of views—a small price to pay for a good hotel in a popular location. The adjoining **Cafe Pescatore** serves lovely Italian fare in an airy setting.

425 North Point St. (at Mason St.), San Francisco, CA 94133. ⓒ **800/648-4626** or 415/561-1100. Fax 415/561-1199. www.tuscaninn.com. 221 units. $189–$269 double; $229–$369 suite. Rates include coffee, tea, and evening fireside wine reception. AE, DC, DISC, MC, V. Parking $28. Cable car: Powell-Mason line. Bus: 10, 15, or 47. Pets welcome for $50 fee. **Amenities:** Access to nearby gym; concierge; courtesy car; secretarial services; limited room service; same-day laundry service/dry cleaning. *In room:* A/C, TV w/pay movies and Nintendo, dataport, free wireless Internet, mini-bar, coffeemaker, hair dryer, iron.

### EXPENSIVE

**Sheraton Fisherman's Wharf Hotel** ⭐ Built in the mid-1970s, this contemporary, four-story hotel offers the reliable comforts of a Sheraton in San Francisco's most popular tourist area. In other words, the clean, modern rooms are comfortable and well equipped but not unique to the city. The Corporate Floor caters exclusively to business travelers.

2500 Mason St. (between Beach and North Point sts.), San Francisco, CA 94133. ⓒ **800/325-3535** or 415/362-5500. Fax 415/956-5275. www.sheratonatthewharf.com. 529 units. $239–$279 double; $550–$1,000 suite. Extra person $20. Continental breakfast $11. AE, DC, DISC, MC, V. Valet parking $32. Cable car: Powell-Mason line (1 block east, 2 blocks south). Streetcar: F. Bus: 10 or 49. **Amenities:** Restaurant; bar; outdoor heated pool; exercise room; concierge; car-rental desk; business center; limited room service; laundry; dry cleaning. *In room:* A/C, TV, fax (in suites only), dataport, high-speed Internet access $9.95 for 24 hr., coffeemaker, hair dryer.

### MODERATE

**The Wharf Inn** ⭐⭐ *(Value)* The top value in this part of town, the Wharf Inn offers above-average accommodations at one of the world's most popular tourist attractions. Completely refurbished from 2002 through 2005, handsome, earth-toned rooms (painted in muted greens, burnt orange, and sandy colors) have brand new carpets, installed in 2005. The well-stocked rooms are well-situated—smack-dab in the middle of the wharf, 2 blocks from PIER 39 and the cable car turnaround, within walking distance of the Embarcadero and North Beach. And parking is free, which saves you $25 a day off the bat.

2601 Mason St. (at Beach St.), San Francisco, CA 94133. ⓒ **800/548-9918** or 415/673-7411. Fax 415/776-2181. www.wharfinn.com. 51 units. $95–$199 double; $299–$449 penthouse. AE, DC, DISC, MC, V. Free parking. Cable car: Powell-Mason or Powell-Hyde lines. Bus: 10, 15, 39, or 47. Streetcar: F. **Amenities:** Access to nearby health club ($10 per day); concierge; tour desk; car-rental desk; complimentary coffee/tea and newspapers. *In room:* TV, dataport, hair dryer and iron on request.

## COW HOLLOW/PACIFIC HEIGHTS

### MODERATE

**Hotel Del Sol** ⭐⭐ *(Value)* A hip, two-level motor lodge, Hotel Del Sol attracts a youngish clientele. Two blocks off busy, bland Lombard Street, Del Sol is nevertheless festive, with a centerpiece courtyard and pool and a Miami Beach–style vibrant exterior, painted yellow, red, orange, and blue. The 57 spacious rooms also boast colorful (read: loud) interior decor and fun extras such as CD players, Aveda products, DVD players and minifridges in suites, and brochures on local events and shopping. Sorry, smokers, you'll have to step outside to puff.

3100 Webster St. (at Greenwich St.), San Francisco, CA 94123. ⓒ **877/433-5765** or 415/921-5520. Fax 415/931-4137. www.thehoteldelsol.com. 57 units. $119–$189 double; $169–$229 suite. Rates include continental breakfast and complimentary newspapers in the lobby. AE, DC, DISC, MC, V. Free parking. Bus: 22, 28, 41, 43, 45, or 76. **Amenities:** Heated outdoor pool; same-day dry cleaning. *In room:* TV/VCR, dataport, wireless high-speed Internet access ($10 per day), kitchenettes in 3 units, iron, CD player, DVD and fridge in suites only.

**The Laurel Inn** ★★  If you don't mind lodging beyond the downtown area, you'll find this motel to be one of the most tranquil, lovely, and affordable places to rest your head. Tucked beyond the southernmost tip of the Presidio, with its winding roads shaded by eucalyptus, the outside isn't impressive. Inside, however, it's *très* chic and modern, with Zen-like influences. Some rooms have excellent views and all have CD players, VCRs, and spiffy bathrooms. All this is topped off by concierge services, 24-hour coffee and tea service, pet-friendly rooms, free parking, and a hip bar/lounge called **G.**

444 Presidio Ave. (at California Ave.), San Francisco, CA 94115. © 800/552-8735 or 415/567-8467. Fax 415/928-1866. www.thelaurelinn.com. 49 units. $155–$190 double. Rates include continental breakfast and afternoon lemonade and cookies. AE, DC, DISC, MC, V. Free parking. Bus: 1, 3, 4, or 43. Pets accepted. **Amenities:** Adjoining bar; access to mind-blowing new JCC gym across the street at $10 per day; concierge; same-day laundry/dry cleaning. *In room:* TV/VCR, dataport, wired and wireless Internet, kitchenette in some units, hair dryer, iron, CD player.

### INEXPENSIVE

**Edward II Inn & Suites** ★★  This three-story, self-styled "English Country" inn has a room for almost anyone's budget, ranging from *pensione* rooms with shared bathrooms to luxuriously appointed suites and cottages with living rooms, kitchens, and whirlpool tubs. Originally built for houseguests who attended the 1915 Pan-Pacific Exposition, it's now a good place to shack up in clean, comfortably appointed rooms with antique furnishings. The only drawback is its traffic-congested Lombard Street location. Nearby Chestnut and Union streets, however, offer some of the best shopping and dining in the city. The adjoining pub serves evening drinks.

3155 Scott St. (at Lombard St.), San Francisco, CA 94123. © 800/473-2846 or 415/922-3000. Fax 415/931-5784. www.edwardii.com. 32 units, 21 w/bathroom. $83–$89 double w/shared bathroom; $115–$129 double w/private bathroom; $185–$249 suite. Extra person $25. Rates include continental breakfast and evening sherry. AE, DISC, MC, V. Self-parking $12 1 block away. Bus: 28, 30, 43, or 76. **Amenities:** Pub; computer station (for nominal fee). *In room:* TV, free high-speed and wireless Internet, hair dryer and iron available on request.

**The Marina Inn** ★★ *Value*  The Marina Inn is one of the best low-priced hotels in San Francisco. Each guest room in this 1924 four-story Victorian looks like something from a country furnishings catalog, complete with rustic pinewood furniture, a four-poster bed with silky-soft comforter, pretty wallpaper, and soothing rose, hunter green, and pale yellow interiors—all for as little as *$65 a night!* Combine that with continental breakfast, friendly service, and an armada of shops and restaurants within easy walking distance, and there you have it: the top choice for best overall value. (*Note:* Traffic can be a bit noisy here, so the hotel added double-paned glass on windows facing the street.)

3110 Octavia St. (at Lombard St.), San Francisco, CA 94123. © 800/274-1420 or 415/928-1000. Fax 415/928-5909. www.marinainn.com. 40 units. Nov–Feb $65–$105 double; Mar–May $75–$125 double; June–Oct $85–$135 double. Rates include continental breakfast. AE, DC, DISC, MC, V. Bus: 28, 30, 43, or 76. *In room:* TV, hair dryer, iron on request.

## JAPANTOWN & ENVIRONS

### MODERATE

**The Hotel Majestic** ★★ *Value*  The Majestic, built in 1902, meets every professional need while retaining the opulence of a luxurious old-world boutique hotel. The lobby will sweep you back to another era with its tapestries, brocades, Corinthian columns, and intricate details. Rooms are furnished with French and English antiques: mirrored armoires, antique reproductions and, in each room, a four-poster canopy bed. Extras include a well-lit desk, bathrobes, fireplaces (in some rooms), and easy access to a fantastic, intimate bar.

1500 Sutter St. (between Octavia and Gough sts.), San Francisco, CA 94109. ℂ 800/869-8966 or 415/441-1100. Fax 415/673-7331. www.thehotelmajestic.com. 58 units. $115–$150 double; $175–$250 suite. Rates include complimentary continental breakfast in lobby 7–10am and wine and appetizers 4–6pm. Group, government, corporate, and relocation rates available. AE, DC, DISC, MC, V. Valet parking $19. Bus: 2, 3, 4, 47, or 49. **Amenities:** Bar; access to nearby health club ($10 per day); concierge; 24-hr. room service; in-room massage; babysitting; same-day laundry service/dry cleaning; complimentary laptop use. *In room:* TV, dataport, free wireless Internet access, fridge in some rooms, hair dryer, iron.

### MODERATE

**The Queen Anne Hotel** ★★ *Value*   This majestic, 1890 Victorian boutique hotel remains true to its heritage, and emulates San Francisco's golden days. The lavish "grand salon" greets you with oak paneling and antiques; rooms follow suit with armoires, marble-top dressers, and other period pieces. Some have corner turret bay windows that overlook tree-lined streets, separate parlor areas, and wet bars; others have cozy reading nooks and fireplaces. All rooms have phones in the bathroom, computer hookups, and fridges. You can relax in the parlor, with its floor-to-ceiling fireplace, or in the hotel library. Amenities include complimentary afternoon tea and sherry.

1590 Sutter St. (between Gough and Octavia sts.), San Francisco, CA 94109. ℂ 800/227-3970 or 415/441-2828. Fax 415/775-5212. www.queenanne.com. 48 units. $99–$199 double; $169–$350 suite. Extra person $10. Rates include continental breakfast on weekday mornings, local complimentary limousine service, afternoon tea and sherry, and morning newspaper. AE, DC, DISC, MC, V. Parking $14. Bus: 2, 3, or 4. **Amenities:** Access to nearby health club for $15; 24-hr. concierge; business center; same-day dry cleaning; front desk safe. *In room:* TV, dataport, complimentary wired and wireless Internet, hair dryer, iron.

## CIVIC CENTER

### MODERATE

**The Phoenix Hotel** ★   On the fringes of the less-than-pleasant Tenderloin District, this retro, 1950s-style hotel is a gathering place for visiting rockers, writers, and filmmakers who crave a connection to Southern California during their visits to San Francisco. The focal point of the pastel-painted Palm Springs–style hotel is a heated, paisley-muraled pool in a modern-sculpture garden. The rooms, while more pop than plush, are comfortably equipped with bright festive furnishings and original local art. In addition, the hotel offers VCRs and movies on request, not to mention a party vibe that's unique to hotels in this town. Additional bonuses include free parking and the hotel's groovy new restaurant and club, the **Bambuddha Lounge** (ℂ **415/885-5088**), which serves Southeast Asian cuisine with cocktail-lounge flair.

601 Eddy St. (at Larkin St.), San Francisco, CA 94109. ℂ 800/248-9466 or 415/776-1380. Fax 415/885-3109. www.thephoenixhotel.com. 44 units. $149–$169 double; $219–$279 suite. Rates include continental breakfast. AE, DC, MC, V. Free parking. Bus: 19, 31, 38, or 47. **Amenities:** Bar; heated outdoor pool; concierge; tour desk; in-room massage; same-day laundry service/dry cleaning. *In room:* TV, VCR on request, dataport, high-speed and Wi-Fi Internet for fee, fridge and microwave in some rooms, hair dryer, iron.

## THE CASTRO

### MODERATE

**Beck's Motor Lodge** ★   A run-of-the-mill motel swathed in vibrant color, Beck's ultratidy rooms are standard but contemporary with recently updated motel furnishings, a sun deck overlooking the action on upper Market Street, and free parking. Unless you're into B&Bs, this is really your only choice in the area; fortunately, it's very well maintained.

2222 Market St. (at 15th St.), San Francisco, CA 94114. ℂ 800/227-4360 in the U.S., except Calif.(800/955-2325 or 415/621-8212). Fax 415/241-0435. 58 units. $104–$145 double. AE, DC, DISC, MC, V. Free parking. Streetcar: F. Bus: 8 or 37. **Amenities:** Coin-operated washing machines. *In room:* TV, dataport, fridge, coffeemaker.

**Finds   Hip New Hostel**

Good news for hip hostelers: The newly deluxe Mission District finally has budget lodgings: **Elements Hotel** (2524 Mission St., between 21st and 22nd sts.; ℰ **866/327-8407** or 415/647-4100; www.elementssf.com; single $25–$30, except holidays). Opened in 2004, this brightly painted crash pad announces itself from the outside with orange and yellow squares. Inside, options include private rooms (with TVs), shared dorms, and double-bed and twin-bunk rooms, all with private bathrooms. Add to that Wi-Fi Internet access throughout the hotel, luggage storage areas and laundry facilities, a (free) high-speed Internet lounge, rooftop parties, and nearby restaurants and bars, and you've got it made—provided you don't mind hunkering down with traveling party people.

**The Parker Guest House** ★★   This is the Castro's best B&B, and a top pick in the entire city. This gay-friendly, 5,000-square-foot, beautifully restored Edwardian home is a few blocks from the heart of the neighborhood. The cheery urban compound has period antiques, and the spacious guest rooms are wonderfully appointed with smart, patterned furnishings, voice mail, robes, and a spotless private bathroom (plus amenities) en suite or across the hall. A fire burns nightly in the cozy living room, and guests are welcome to make themselves at home in the wood-paneled common library (with fireplace and piano) or sunny breakfast room overlooking the garden with fountains and a steam room.

520 Church St. (between 17th and 18th sts.), San Francisco, CA 94114. ℰ **888/520-7275** or 415/621-3222. Fax 415/621-4139. www.parkerguesthouse.com. 21 units. $119–$200 double; $199 junior suite. Rates include extended continental breakfast and evening wine and cheese. AE, DISC, MC, V. Self-parking $15. Streetcar: J Church. Bus: 22 or 33. **Amenities:** Access to nearby health club; steam room; concierge; wireless Internet access. *In room:* TV, dataport, free Wi-Fi, hair dryer, iron.

## 4  Where to Dine

San Francisco's dining scene is one of the best in the world. Below is a cross section of the city's best restaurants in every price range. For a greater selection of reviews, see *Frommer's San Francisco 2006* or *Frommer's San Francisco from $70 a Day.*

### UNION SQUARE
#### VERY EXPENSIVE
**Campton Place** ★★★  CONTEMPORARY EUROPEAN   Campton Place is everything a fine-dining establishment should be. Intimate with well-spaced tables that allow for easy conversation, warm beige surroundings, and a knowledgeable, relaxed staff, it sets the perfect stage for the exceptional cuisine of award-winning Swiss chef Daniel Humm. Appetizers such as heirloom tomato-and-watermelon salad with basil, sea salt, and almond-vanilla vinaigrette, or foie gras six ways are inventive, beautifully presented, and tasty. The entrees solidify Humm's superiority. Think light but decadent dishes such as delicate salt-crusted and baked *branzino* with olive oil–and-lemon confit, or Sonoma squab shrouded by a hand-woven dome of zucchini strips,

# San Francisco Dining

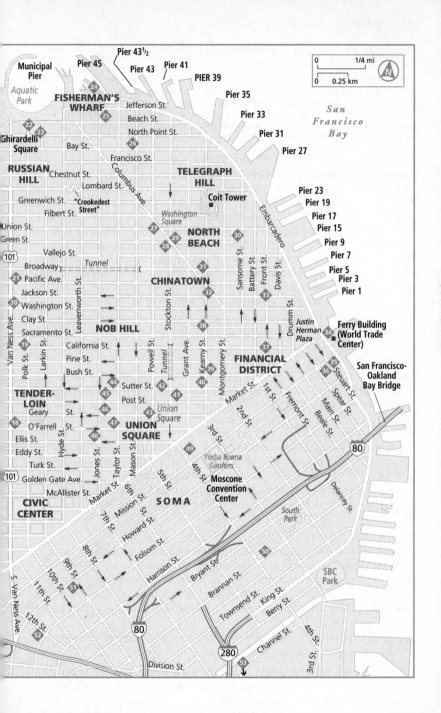

Municipal
Pier

Aquatic
Park

Ghirardelli
Square

RUSSIAN
HILL

Pier 45          Pier 43½
          Pier 43     Pier 41
                      PIER 39
                           Pier 35
FISHERMAN'S   Jefferson St.        Pier 33
WHARF                              Pier 31
         Beach St.            Pier 27
         North Point St.
Bay St.
         Francisco St.
Chestnut St.        TELEGRAPH
Lombard St.          HILL
Greenwich St.  "Crookedest    Coit Tower
Filbert St.     Street"
                Washington
Union St.       Square
Green St.                    NORTH
Vallejo St.                  BEACH
Broadway    Tunnel
Pacific Ave.
Jackson St.           CHINATOWN
Washington St.
Clay St.
Sacramento St.  NOB HILL
California St.
Pine St.
Bush St.

San
Francisco
Bay

Pier 23
Pier 19
Pier 17
Pier 15
Pier 9
Pier 7
Pier 5
Pier 3
Pier 1

Sutter St.
Post St.
TENDER-
LOIN     Geary    St.
O'Farrell   St.
Ellis St.
Eddy St.
Turk St.
Golden Gate Ave.
McAllister St.
CIVIC
CENTER

Union
Square
UNION
SQUARE

Yerba Buena
Gardens
Moscone
Convention
Center

SOMA
Howard St.
Folsom St.
Harrison St.

South
Park

Justin
Herman
Plaza

Ferry Building
(World Trade
Center)

FINANCIAL
DISTRICT

San Francisco-
Oakland
Bay Bridge

SBC
Park

Division St.

0          1/4 mi
0    0.25 km

**101**

served with niçoise olive–and–thyme sauce. They also serve a great breakfast, lunch, and Sunday brunch.

340 Stockton St. (between Post and Sutter sts.). © **415/955-5555**. www.camptonplace.com. Reservations recommended. Lunch 2-course $34, 3-course $39, 4-course $49; dinner 3-course fixed-price $65, 4-course $78; chef's tasting menu $98. AE, DC, MC, V. Mon–Thurs 7–10:30am, 11:30am–2pm and 5:30–9:30pm; Fri 7–10:30am, 11:30am–2pm and 5:30–10pm; Sat 8–11am, noon–2pm and 5:30–10pm; Sun 8am–1:45pm and 5:30–10pm. Valet parking $8 for 1st hour; $1.75 for each additional hour. Cable car: Powell-Hyde or Powell-Mason lines (1 block west). Bus: 2, 3, 4, 30, 38, or 45. Streetcar and BART: Market St.

**Michael Mina** ★★ AMERICAN    Chef Michael Mina, who once presided over Aqua, takes the small-plate dining concept to extremes at this swank spot (previously the Compass Rose tearoom in the Westin St. Francis). The cream-on-cream room—with deep leather lounge chairs and tables that are too wide for romance—sets the scene for the formal, prix-fixe affair. Courses arrive as a trio of renditions on the same theme (with three sides to match) on custom, Mina-designed modular china. That's six different preparations per dish, for a total of 18 flavors over the course of an evening! It's a bit fussy for anyone who prefers to order a few things that sound good and eat substantial portions of them. But if the idea of sampling lots of styles and flavors appeals you, don't miss the food case studies served here. Some dishes hit, some miss, but in any case, it's *the* place to be at the moment, with an incredible wine list by Raj Parr.

335 Powell St. (at Geary St.). © **415/397-9222**. Reservations recommended. 3-course tasting menu $78; seasonal classic tasting menu $120. AE, DC, DISC, MC, V. Sun–Thurs 5:30–10 pm; Fri–Sat 5:30–11pm. Valet parking $17. Bus: 2, 3, 4, 30, 38, 45, or 76.

## EXPENSIVE

**Le Colonial** *Finds* VIETNAMESE    With its slowly spinning ceiling fans and French Colonial decor, this French Vietnamese restaurant is one of the sexiest bar lounges in town. Romance reigns in the upstairs lounge, once it opens, at 4:30pm: A crowd of swank professionals kicks back in cozy couches for cocktails and yummy Vietnamese treats such as coconut-crusted crab cakes and spring rolls. In the tiled downstairs dining room, and along the stunning heated front patio, guests savor the vibrant flavors of dishes like coconut curry with black tiger prawns, mangos, eggplant, and Asian basil, or tender wok-seared beef tenderloin with watercress onion salad.

20 Cosmo Place (off Taylor St., between Post and Sutter sts.). © **415/931-3600**. www.lecolonialsf.com. Reservations recommended. Main courses $18–$33. AE, DC, MC, V. Sun–Wed 5:30–10pm; Thurs–Sat 5:30–11pm. Public valet parking $6 1st hr., $2 each additional ½ hr. Bus: 2, 3, 4, or 27.

## MODERATE

**Café Claude** ★ FRENCH    European transplants love Café Claude, a crowded, lively restaurant on a narrow side street with an old-world feel, near Union Square. Every table, spoon, saltshaker, and waiter seems to be imported from France. The menu features classics like steak tartare, steamed mussels, duck confit, escargot, steak with spinach gratin and crisp potatoes, and quail stuffed with pine nuts, sausage, and

---

> *Tips* **Make Reservations in Advance**
>
> If you want a table at a top restaurant, make your reservation weeks in advance—perhaps through **www.opentable.com**, which provides real-time reservations to many Bay Area establishments.

wild rice. With prices topping out at about $20, Café Claude offers an affordable slice of Paris in the City by the Bay, with live jazz on Thursdays, Fridays, and Saturdays from 7:30 to 10:30pm. Atmospheric sidewalk seating is available for 30 diners when weather permits.

7 Claude Lane (off Sutter St.). ℂ 415/392-3515. www.cafeclaude.com. Reservations recommended. Lunch $8–12; dinner $14–$20. AE, DC, DISC, MC, V. Mon 11:30am–5:30pm; Tues–Wed 11:30am–10pm; Thurs–Sat 11:30am–10:30pm. Cable car: Powell-Mason. Bus: 30.

**Grand Café** ★★ CONTEMPORARY FRENCH   My current top downtown pick, this stunning restaurant has the most, well, *grand* dining room in the city. This turn-of-the-20th-century, Art Nouveau ballroomlike dining oasis is festive and casually glamorous, with a great cocktail and appetizer area called the Petite Café, which serves Fridays and Saturdays until midnight. What really gets me excited about this place is the 2005 appointment of Executive Chef Fabrice Roux, a star in the making who worked under previous bosses here for the past 5 years. One bite of his deconstructed cassoulet (duck confit, baby back ribs, and turkey-artichoke sausage on white beans in a delicate tomato sauce) will prove my point. Ditto for the vanilla-and-rum-infused foie gras *au torchon* with mango-pineapple chutney, the vegetarian lasagna, and the hanger steak with roasted shallots, spinach, and fries. If you're dining downtown and want a great, moderately priced, memorable meal, this should be your first pick. It's great for larger parties, too.

501 Geary St. (at Taylor St., adjacent to the Hotel Monaco). ℂ **415/292-0101.** Reservations recommended. Main courses $16–$26. AE, DC, DISC, MC, V. Mon–Thurs 7:30–10:30am, 11:30am–2:30pm and 5:30–10pm; Fri 7:30–10:30am, 11:30am–2:30pm and 5:30–11pm; Sat 8–10:30am, 11:30am–2:30pm and 5:30–11pm; Sun 9am–2:30pm and 5:30–10pm. Valet parking $15 for 3 hr, $3 each additional ½ hr. Bus: 2, 3, 4, 27, or 38.

**Scala's Bistro** ★ FRENCH/ITALIAN   This polished Italian dining room with high ceilings and big booths is a downtown favorite. The Parisian bistro atmosphere balances elegance with informality, which means it's okay to have some fun here (and apparently most people do). The menu, which features an array of Italian and French dishes, includes a yummy Earth and Surf calamari appetizer, rich duck-leg confit, and seared salmon.

In the Sir Francis Drake hotel, 432 Powell St. (at Sutter St.). ℂ **415/395-8555.** www.scalasbistro.com. Reservations recommended. Breakfast $7–$10; main courses $12–$24. AE, DC, DISC, MC, V. Daily 8–10:30am and 11:30am–midnight. Cable car: Powell-Hyde line. Bus: 2, 3, 4, 30, 45, or 76.

**INEXPENSIVE**

**Dottie's True Blue Café** ★ *Kids* AMERICAN/BREAKFAST   This family-owned breakfast restaurant is one of my favorite downtown diners. It's the kind of place you'd expect to see off Route 66. Most customers are on a first-name basis with staff members, who welcome every guest with a hearty hello and steaming mug of coffee. Dottie's serves above-average American morning fare (big portions of French toast, pancakes, bacon and eggs, omelets, and the like), delivered on rugged, diner-quality plates, to tables laminated with old movie-star photos. Orders arrive with delicious homemade bread, muffins, or scones, as well as homemade jelly. The menu also features daily specials and vegetarian dishes.

In the Pacific Bay Inn, 522 Jones St. (at O'Farrell St.). ℂ **415/885-2767.** Reservations not accepted. Breakfast $5–$11. DISC, MC, V. Wed–Mon 7:30am–3pm. Cable car: Powell-Mason line. Bus: 2, 3, 4, 27, or 38.

**Mocca** ⭐ ITALIAN    If you can't be bothered with a long lunch when you've got serious shopping to do, head to this classic Italian deli on Maiden Lane, where vehicle traffic is prohibited. Here it's counter service and cash only for sandwiches, *caprese* (Italian tomato-and-mozzarella salad), and big leafy salads. You can enjoy them at one of the few indoor tables or the pedestrian-only street-front tables, shaded by umbrellas, that look onto Union Square.

175 Maiden Lane (at Stockton St.). ℭ **415/956-1188**. Reservations not accepted. Main courses $7–$13. No credit cards. Pastry and coffee daily 10:30am–5:30pm; lunch daily 11am–5:30pm. Bus: All Union Square buses.

**Pho Hoa** ⭐ *(Value)* VIETNAMESE    For the brave, this simple, cafeteria-like restaurant in the Tenderloin District promises huge, killer bowls of Vietnamese soup with all the classic fixings (basil, bean sprouts, and the like) at absurdly low prices. (The walk there is an adventure that can include encounters with crack-smoking loiterers, but the food and prices make it worth the trip.) The menu features dozens of selections—both rice and rice noodle dishes served with beef, chicken, vegetables, and other staples—each of which is a meal in itself. My favorite is the seafood soup with rice noodles. Other favorites are deep-fried egg rolls, barbecued pork, and intensely strong iced coffee.

431 Jones St. (between O'Farrell and Ellis sts.). ℭ **415/673-3163**. Reservations accepted. Soups and main courses $5–$8. No credit cards. Daily 8am–7pm. Bus: 27, 31, or 38.

**Sanraku Japanese Restaurant** ⭐ *(Value)* JAPANESE/SUSHI    Great Japanese dishes and sushi at bargain prices make this bright, busy restaurant one of my favorites. A box lunch might include a California roll, soup, seaweed salad, deep-fried salmon roll, and beef with noodles and steamed rice, all for just $8.50. The main menu features irresistible sesame chicken with teriyaki sauce and rice, tempura, a vast selection of rolls, and delicious combination plates that mix sushi, sashimi, and teriyaki. Business is brisk during lunch and dinner, but a table or two always seems to be available.

704 Sutter St. (at Taylor St.). ℭ **415/771-0803**. www.sanraku.com. Main courses $7.25–$13 lunch, $10–$23 dinner; 7-course fixed-price menu $55. AE, DC, DISC, MC, V. Daily 11am–10pm. Cable car: Powell-Mason line. Bus: 2, 3, 4, 27, or 38.

## SOMA
### EXPENSIVE

**bacar** ⭐ AMERICAN BRASSERIE    No other dining room makes wine as integral to the meal as popular bacar—with 1,300 vintages to choose from (about 100 by the glass, 2-ounce pour, or 250- or 500-milliliter decanter). An eclectic mix of up to 250 fashionable diners pack this warehouse-restaurant for chef Arnold Eric Wong's "American Brasserie" cuisine (that is, French Bistro with a California twist). I'm a fan of the creamy salt-cod and crab *brandade* (purée) or the zesty roasted mussels with a chile-and-garlic sauce that begs to be soaked up by the accompanying grilled bread (the same goes for the braised beef short ribs). If you want a festive night out, this is the place—especially when jazz is playing, Monday through Saturday eves.

448 Brannan St. (at Third St.). ℭ 415/904-4100. www.bacarsf.com. Reservations recommended. Main courses $14–$17 lunch, $22–$38 dinner. AE, DC, DISC, MC, V. Sun 5:30–11pm; Mon–Sat 5:30pm–midnight; Fri 11:30am–2:30pm. Valet parking (Mon–Sat beginning at 6pm) $10. Bus: 15, 30, 45, 76, or 81.

**Boulevard** ⭐⭐⭐ *(Finds)* AMERICAN    Master restaurant designer Pat Kuleto and chef Nancy Oaks are behind one of the city's all-time favorite restaurants. What's the winning combination? The dramatic Belle Epoque interior combined with Oaks' mouthwatering dishes. Starters alone could make a perfect meal, especially the sweet-breads wrapped in prosciutto on watercress and Lola Rose lettuce with garlic croutons and a whole-grain mustard vinaigrette; and Sonoma foie gras with elderberry syrup, toast, and Bosc pear salad. The main courses are equally creative and might include pan-roasted, miso-glazed sea bass with asparagus salad, Japanese rice, and shiitake-mushroom broth, or the spit-roasted, cider-cured pork loin with sweet-potato–swirled mashed potatoes and sautéed baby red chard. Vegetarian items, such as wild-mushroom risotto with fresh chanterelles and Parmesan, are also available. Three dining areas—bar, open kitchen, or main dining room—allow for three levels of formality.

1 Mission St. (between Embarcadero and Steuart sts.). ℂ **415/543-6084.** Reservations recommended. Main courses $9–$17 lunch, $24–$32 dinner. AE, DC, DISC, MC, V. Mon–Fri 11:30am–2:15pm; Sun–Thurs 5:30–10pm; Fri–Sat 5:30–10:30pm. Valet parking $12 lunch, $10 dinner. Bus: 15, 30, 32, or 45.

**Fifth Floor Restaurant** ★★★ FRENCH  Two-time James Beard nominee Melissa Perello (previously of Charles Nob Hill), sommelier Emily Wines (yes, that is her given last name), and truly exceptional pastry chef Marika Doob are the all-female culinary dream team behind one of the city's finest restaurant experiences. The decor—rich colors and fabrics, burgundy velvet banquettes, Frette linens, zebra-striped carpeting, and a clublike atmosphere—is as luxurious as the perfectly executed, wonderfully fresh menu, which might include Alaskan halibut *en cocotte* with aspara-gus, spring onions, and lemon, or veal rib-eye with wilted baby spinach, apricots, and chanterelle mushrooms. The wine program also reigns, with one of the most presti-gious, expensive lists around and a team of consummate professionals serving it.

In the Hotel Palomar, 12 Fourth St. (at Market St.). ℂ **415/348-1555.** www.fifthfloor.citysearch.com. Reservations recommended. Main courses $26–$45; tasting menu $75–$115. AE, DC, DISC, MC, V. Mon–Thurs 5:30–9:30pm; Fri–Sat 5:30–10:30pm. Valet parking $12 w/validation. Bus: All Market St. buses.

## MODERATE

**The Slanted Door** ★★ *Finds* VIETNAMESE  The likes of Mick Jagger and former president Bill Clinton have dined at the previous location of this extremely popular spot for impeccably fresh and flavorful (albeit relatively expensive) Vietnamese food. It's even more of a hot spot since its April 2004 relocation to a beautiful, bay-inspired, custom-designed space in the Ferry Building Marketplace. Pull up a chair and order anything from clay-pot catfish or green papaya salad to one of the lunch rice dishes, which come in a large ceramic bowl topped with such options as grilled shrimp and stir-fried eggplant. Dinner items, which change seasonally, might include beef with garlic and organic onions, grapefruit, and jícama salad. Finish off your meal with an eclectic collection of teas, which come by the pot for $4 to $6.

1 Ferry Plaza (at The Embarcadero and Market). ℂ **415/861-8032.** www.slanteddoor.com. Reservations recom-mended. Lunch main courses $8.50–$17, 7-item fixed-price lunch $38; most dinner dishes $15–$27, 7-item fixed-price dinner $45 (parties of 8 or more only). AE, MC, V. Mon–Sat 11am–2:30pm; Mon–Thurs 5:30–10pm; Fri–Sat 5:30–10:30pm. Bus: All Market Street buses. Streetcar: F or N-Judah line.

**Yank Sing** ★★ CHINESE/DIM SUM  Loosely translated as "a delight of the heart," cavernous Yank Sing is the best dim sum restaurant downtown. Confident, experienced servers aptly guess your gastric threshold as they wheel carts of exotic dishes past each table. Most dim sum dishes are dumplings, filled with tasty concoctions of pork, beef, fish, or vegetables. *Congees* (porridges), spareribs, stuffed crab claws, scallion pancakes, shrimp balls, pork buns, and other palate-pleasers complete the menu. While the food is delicious, the location makes this the most popular tourist spot and weekday lunch spot; at other times, residents generally head to **Ton Kiang** (p. 115), the undisputed top choice for these Chinese delicacies. A second location, open weekdays for lunch only, is at 49 Stevenson St., off First Street (✆ **415/541-4949**).

101 Spear St. (at Mission St. at Rincon Center). ✆ **415/957-9300**. Dim sum $3.50–$8 for 2–4 pieces. AE, DC, MC, V. Mon–Fri 11am–3pm; Sat–Sun, holidays 10am–4pm. Validated parking in Rincon Center Garage. Cable car: California St. line. Bus: 1, 12, 14, or 41. Streetcar: F. BART: Embarcadero.

### INEXPENSIVE

**AsiaSF** ✪ CALIFORNIA/ASIAN   At AsiaSF, Asian men in drag lip-sync show tunes as they serve excellent grilled shrimp–and-herb salad, Asian-influenced hamburgers, potstickers, duck quesadillas, and chicken satay. Fortunately, the food and the atmosphere are as colorful as the staff, which means a night here is more than a meal—it's an event.

201 Ninth St. (at Howard St.). ✆ **415/255-2742**. www.asiasf.com. Reservations recommended. Main courses $9–$19. 3-course fixed-price menu Sun–Thurs $32, Fri–Sat $37. AE, DISC, MC, V (Mon–Wed $25 minimum). Sun–Thurs 6–10pm; Fri–Sat 5–10pm. Bus: 9, 12, or 47. Streetcar: Civic Center on underground streetcar. BART: Civic Center.

**Manora's** ✪ THAI   Ever-bustling Manora's cranks out dependable Thai to a mix of local diners. It's perpetually packed (unless you come early), so you'll be crammed like sardines at a small but well-appointed table. During the dinner rush, the din can make conversation among larger parties almost impossible; the food is so good, though, you'll be content to stuff your face in silence. Start with tangy soup or chicken satay. Follow with any of the wonderful dinner dishes—which should be shared—and a side of rice. The options seem endless, including a vast array of vegetarian plates. *Tip:* Come before 7pm or after 9pm if you don't want a loud, rushed meal.

1600 Folsom St. (at 12th St.). ✆ **415/861-6224**. Reservations recommended for 4 or more. Main courses $7–$12. MC, V. Mon–Fri 11:30am–2:30pm; Mon–Sat 5:30–10:30pm; Sun 5–10pm. Bus: 9, 12, or 47.

## FINANCIAL DISTRICT
### EXPENSIVE

**Aqua** ✪✪ SEAFOOD   At San Francisco's finest seafood restaurant, heralded chef Laurent Manrique dazzles customers with a bewildering juxtaposition of earth and sea treats. Although he's changed my all-time favorite *ahi* tartare appetizer (introduced by previous chef George Morrone) to include a heavenly combo of pears, pine nuts, quail egg, and spices, you can still request the original. Entrees are decadent, such as the lobster casserole with roasted squash, *cippolini* onions, and truffle chantilly, or their famed whole seared foie gras with seasonal garnishes. Desserts are equally impressive. Alas, the large dining room with high ceilings, three big floral arrangements, and otherwise stark decor can be seriously loud. That doesn't stop power-lunchers from pow-wowing by day and well-dressed gourmands from feasting at night. Keep in mind that there's no valet or street parking at lunch, so you'll have to pull into one of The Embarcadero lots 2 blocks away.

252 California St. (near Battery). ✆ **415/956-9662**. www.aqua-sf.com. Reservations recommended. Main courses $29–$39; 6-course tasting menu $95; vegetarian tasting menu $65. AE, DC, DISC, MC, V. Mon–Fri 11:30am–2pm; Mon–Sat 5:30–10:30pm; Sun 5:30–9:30pm. Bus: All Market St. buses. Valet parking (dinner only) $8.

### MODERATE

**Kokkari** ✪✪ (Value) GREEK   Kokkari (Ko-*car*-ee) takes Greek food to delicious contemporary heights—both in decor and flavor. The dining area is like a rustic living room, with a commanding fireplace and oversize furnishings. Delicious, traditional

---

**Finds** **Dine in the Sunshine at Belden Place**

---

San Francisco has always been lacking in the alfresco dining department. One exception, however, is Belden Place, an adorable brick alley in the Financial District closed to everything but foot traffic. When the weather is agreeable, the restaurants here break out the umbrellas, tables, and chairs, à la Boulevard St-Michel and *voilà*—a bit of Paris just off Pine Street.

A handful of adorable cafes line Belden Place and offer a wide variety of cuisine. There's **Cafe Bastille,** 22 Belden Place (© **415/986-5673**), your classic French bistro and fun speakeasy basement serving excellent crepes, mussels, and French onion soup, along with live jazz on Fridays; **Cafe Tiramisu,** 28 Belden Place (© **415/421-7044**), a stylish Italian hot spot serving addictive risottos and gnocchi; and **Plouf,** 40 Belden Place (© **415/986-6491**), which specializes in big bowls of mussels slathered in a choice of seven sauces, as well as fresh seafood. **B44,** 44 Belden Place (**415/986-6287**), serves a revered paella and other seriously zesty Spanish dishes. Come at night for a Euro-speakeasy vibe with your dinner.

---

Aegean dishes include a moussaka (eggplant, lamb, potato, and béchamel) that's to die for, or the quail stuffed with winter greens served on oven-roasted leeks, orzo, and wild-rice *pilafi.*

200 Jackson St. (at Front St.). © **415/981-0983.** www.kokkari.com. Reservations recommended. Main courses $14–$23 lunch, $19–$35 dinner. AE, DC, DISC, MC, V. Lunch Mon–Fri 11:30am–2:30pm; bar menu 2:30–5:30pm; dinner Mon–Thurs 5:30–10pm, Fri 5:30–11pm, Sat 5–11pm. Valet parking (dinner only) $8. Bus: 12, 15, 41, or 83.

**Sam's Grill & Seafood Restaurant** ★ *Finds* SEAFOOD   Sam's has done a brisk business with Financial District suits since—get this—1867. Even if you're not carrying a briefcase, this time capsule of old San Francisco is a rare treat. Pass the crowded entrance and small bar to reach the main dining room—packed almost exclusively with men—kick back, and watch yesteryear play out again today. Tuxedo-clad waiters race around, doling out big crusty cuts of sourdough and salads overflowing with fresh crab and Roquefort vinaigrette; towering plates of seafood pasta with marinara; charbroiled fish; roasted chicken; and old-school standbys like calves' liver with bacon and onions, Salisbury steak, and creamed spinach. Mildly salty service makes the excellent food taste even better. If you need privacy, slither into a curtained booth.

374 Bush St. (between Montgomery and Kearny sts.). © **415/421-0594.** www.samsgrill.citysearch.com. Reservations recommended for dinner and for 6 or more at lunch. Main courses $12–$24. AE, DC, DISC, MC, V. Mon–Fri 11am–9pm. Bus: 15, 45, or 76, all Market St. buses.

## CHINATOWN
### INEXPENSIVE
**Brandy Ho's Hunan Food** ★ *Kids* CHINESE   Fancy black-and-white granite tabletops and a large, open kitchen are the first clues that the food at this casual, fun restaurant is a cut above the usual Hunan fare. Take my advice and start immediately with fried dumplings (in sweet-and-sour sauce) or cold chicken salad, and then move on to fish-ball soup with spinach, bamboo shoots, noodles, and other goodies. The best main course is Three Delicacies, a combination of scallops, shrimp, and chicken with

onion, bell pepper, and bamboo shoots, seasoned with ginger, garlic, and wine, and served with black-bean sauce. Most dishes are hot and spicy, but the kitchen will adjust the level of heat to your specifications. A full bar includes Asian food-friendly libations like plum wine and sake, from 11:30am to 11pm.

217 Columbus Ave. (at Pacific Ave.). (© 415/788-7527. www.brandyhos.com. Reservations recommended. Main courses $8–$13. AE, DC, DISC, MC, V. Sun–Thurs 11:30am–11pm; Fri–Sat 11:30am–midnight. Paid parking available at 170 Columbus Ave. Bus: 15 or 41.

**R&G Lounge** ★★ CHINESE   If you want a sure thing in Chinatown, go to R&G Lounge. During lunch, both newly redecorated levels are packed with neighborhood workers, who go straight to the $5 rice-plate specials. You can also order from the dinner menu, which features legendary (though very greasy and rich) deep-fried salt-and-pepper crab. My favorites include R&G's melt-in-your-mouth Special Beef, which explodes with the tangy flavor of the accompanying sauce; savory seafood in a clay pot; and delicious classic roast duck.

631 Kearny St. (at Clay St.). (© 415/982-7877. Reservations recommended. Main courses $9–$30. AE, DC, DISC, MC, V. Mon–Thurs 11am–9:30pm; Fri 11am–10pm; Sat 11:30am–10pm; Sun 11:30am–9:30pm. Parking validated across the street at Portsmouth Sq. garage or Holiday Inn after 5pm. Bus: 1, 9AX, 9BX, 12, or 15.

## NOB HILL/RUSSIAN HILL
### EXPENSIVE
**House of Prime Rib** ★★ STEAKHOUSE   Anyone who loves a huge slab of meat and old school–style dining will feel right at home at this shrine to prime rib. It's a fun, crowded affair within the men's clublike dining rooms (with fireplaces), where drinks are stiff, waiters are loose, and all the beef is roasted in rock salt, sliced tableside, and served with salad dramatically tossed tableside, followed by creamed spinach and either mashed potatoes or baked potato and Yorkshire pudding, which accompany the entree. To placate those who don't eat meat, they offer a fish-of-the-day special. Another bonus: Kids' prime rib dinners are a mere $9.45.

1906 Van Ness Ave. (near Washington St.). (© 415/885-4605. Reservations recommended. Complete dinners $26–$32. AE, MC, V. Mon–Thurs 5:30–10pm; Fri 5–10pm; Sat 4:30–10pm; Sun 4–10pm. Valet parking: $7. Bus: 47 or 49.

### INEXPENSIVE
**Swan Oyster Depot** ★★ (Finds) SEAFOOD   The 94-year-old Swan Oyster Depot is a classic San Francisco dining experience you shouldn't miss. Opened in 1912, this tiny hole-in-the-wall, run by the city's friendliest servers, is little more than a narrow fish market that decided to slap down some bar stools—only about 20 of them, jammed cheek-by-jowl along a long marble bar. Most patrons come for a quick cup of chowder or a plate of oysters on the half shell chilled on crushed ice. The menu is limited to fresh crab, shrimp, oyster, clam cocktails, a few types of smoked fish, Maine lobster, and Boston-style clam chowder, all of which are exceedingly fresh. *Note:* Don't let the lunchtime line dissuade you; it moves fast.

1517 Polk St. (between California and Sacramento sts.). (© 415/673-1101. Reservations not accepted. Seafood cocktails $7–$15; clams and oysters on the half shell $7.50 per half dozen. No credit cards. Mon–Sat 8am–5:30pm. Bus: 1, 19, 47, or 49.

## NORTH BEACH
### MODERATE
**Enrico's** ★ CALIFORNIA   Enrico's is the most fun sidewalk-restaurant/supper-club destination on North Beach's Broadway strip. Anyone with an appreciation for live

jazz (featured nightly), late-night noshing, and people-watching from the outdoor patio will be content to spend an evening alfresco, under the heat lamps (though the best view of the band is inside). I tend to drop by and snack on wine and addictive, deep-fried olives or pizza Margherita, and move on. But when I linger for dinner, entrees are usually satisfying, ranging from roasted chicken under a brick with mashed potatoes, to flat-iron steak or butternut-squash ravioli. The best part? No cover charge.

504 Broadway (at Kearny St.). (C) 415/982-6223. www.enricossidewalkcafe.com. Reservations recommended. Main courses $7–$12 lunch, $11–$23 dinner. AE, MC, V. Sun–Thurs 11:30am–11pm; Fri–Sat 11:30am–midnight; bar daily 11:30am–1:30am or earlier, depending on patronage. Valet parking (dinner only) $10. Bus: 9X, 12, or 15.

**Piperade** 🌟🌟 WEST COAST BASQUE   This casual spot on the outskirts of North Beach is the place for an outstanding Basque dinner. Chef Gerald Hirigoyen sets a comfy scene with a wood-beam-lined ceiling, oak floors, and soft sconce lighting. More importantly, he satisfies the stomach with delicious dishes such as crabmeat coddled in a paper-thin crepe with mango-and–red pepper salsa; a bright, simple salad of giant white beans, egg, chives, and marinated anchovies; and braised seafood-and-shellfish stew with sweet and savory red-pepper sauce. Do yourself a favor: Save room for orange blossom beignets. Light and airy with a delicate, moist web of dough within and a kiss of orange essence, it's dessert at its finest. *Note:* The wine list has an apt selection of vintages available by the bottle or glass, and a community table caters to drop-in diners.

1015 Battery St. (at Green St.). (C) 415/391-2555. www.piperade.com. Reservations recommended. Main courses $15–$18. AE, DC, DISC, MC, V. Mon–Fri 11:30am–3pm; Mon–Sat 5:30–10:30pm. Bus: 10, 12, 30, or 82x.

### INEXPENSIVE

**L'Osteria del Forno** 🌟🌟 ITALIAN   L'Osteria del Forno might be slightly larger than a walk-in closet, but it's one of the top three authentic Italian restaurants in North Beach. Peer in the window facing Columbus Avenue, and you'll probably see two Italian women with their hair up, sweating from the heat of the brick-lined oven, which cranks out the best focaccia in the city. There's no pomp or circumstance here: Locals come strictly to eat. The menu features a variety of superb pizzas, salads, soups, and fresh pastas, plus a good selection of daily specials (pray for the roast pork braised in milk), which include a roast of the day, pasta, and ravioli. Small baskets of warm focaccia keep you going until the entrees arrive. Good news for folks on the go: Pizza comes by the slice.

519 Columbus Ave. (between Green and Union sts.). (C) 415/982-1124. Reservations not accepted. Sandwiches $6–$7; pizzas $10–$18; main courses $6–$14. No credit cards. Sun–Mon and Wed–Thurs 11:30am–10pm; Fri–Sat 11:30am–10:30pm. Bus: 15, 30, 41, or 45.

**Mario's Bohemian Cigar Store** 🌟 *Finds* ITALIAN   Across the street from Washington Square is one of North Beach's most popular neighborhood hangouts. The century-old bar—small, well worn, and always busy—is best known for its focaccia sandwiches, including meatball and eggplant. Wash it all down with an excellent cappuccino or a house Campari as you watch the tourists stroll by. And no, they do not sell cigars.

566 Columbus Ave. (at Union St.). (C) 415/362-0536. Sandwiches $6.75–$7.25. MC, V. Daily 10am–11pm. Closed Dec 24–25 and Jan 1. Bus: 15, 30, 41, or 45.

**Pasta Pomodoro** 🌟🌟 *Kids* *Value* ITALIAN   If you're looking for a good, cheap meal in North Beach—or anywhere else in town, for that matter—this San Francisco chain can't be beat. You'll usually wait 20 minutes for a table, but after you're seated, you'll be surprised by how promptly you're served. Every dish is fresh and sizable. Best of all, they cost a third of what you'd pay elsewhere. Winners include the spaghetti *frutti di mare,* made with calamari, mussels, scallops, tomato, garlic, and wine; or *cavatappi pollo* with roast chicken, sun-dried tomatoes, cream, mushrooms, and Parmesan. Both dishes are less than $8. There are seven other locations, including 2304 Market St., at 16th St. (℗ **415/558-8123**); 3611 California St. (℗ **415/831-0900**); and 816 Irving St., between 9th and 10th sts. (℗ **415/566-0900**).

655 Union St. (at Columbus Ave.). ℗ **415/399-0300**. www.pastapomodoro.com. Reservations not accepted. Main courses $6–$12. AE, MC, V. Sun–Thurs 11am–10:30pm; Fri–Sat 11am–11pm. Cable car: Powell-Mason line. Bus: 15, 30, 41, or 45.

**Tommaso's** ★★ *(Kids* ITALIAN   From the street, Tommaso's looks unappealing—a drab brown facade sandwiched between sex shops. Then why the perpetual line out the door? Tommaso's been packing them in since 1935. The center of attention in the dining room is the chef, who continuously tosses huge hunks of garlic and mozzarella onto pizzas before sliding them into the brick oven. Nineteen toppings make pizza the dish of choice, even though Italian classics such as veal Marsala, chicken cacciatore, lasagna, and calzones are available. Tommaso's also offers half-bottles of house wines, homemade manicotti, and Italian coffee. If you can overlook the seedy surroundings, this fun, boisterous restaurant is a great place to take the family.

1042 Kearny St. (at Broadway). ℗ **415/398-9696**. www.tommasosnorthbeach.com. Reservations not accepted. Pasta and pizza $14–$24; main courses $11–$18. AE, DC, DISC, MC, V. Tues–Sat 5–10:30pm; Sun 4–9:30pm. Closed Dec 15–Jan 15. Bus: 15 or 41.

## FISHERMAN'S WHARF
### EXPENSIVE

**A. Sabella's** ★★ *(Finds* SEAFOOD   The Sabella family has operated this restaurant since 1920, catering heavily to the tourist trade. The menu offers something for everyone—steak, lamb, seafood, chicken, and pasta, all made from scratch with fresh local ingredients. Where A. Sabella's really shines, however, is in the shellfish department. Its 1,000-gallon saltwater tank allows for fresh crab, abalone, and lobster year-round. No restaurant in the city can touch A. Sabella's when it comes to fresh Dungeness crab and abalone out of season. Such luxuries, of course, are anything but cheap. But on the bright side, with Sabella's kids' menu, you can fill up tots' tummies for a mere $7.50. Added bonuses: The third-floor restaurant overlooks the wharf, and the wine list offers many tasty choices.

Fisherman's Wharf, 2766 Taylor St. (at Jefferson St.), 3rd floor. ℗ **415/771-6775**. www.asabellas.com. Reservations recommended. Most main courses $16–$28. AE, DC, DISC, MC, V. Daily 5–10pm. 2-hr. validated parking at the Wharf Garage, 350 Beach St. Cable car: Powell-Mason or Powell-Hyde lines. Streetcar: F.

**Restaurant Gary Danko** ★★★ *(Finds* MODERN CLASSIC   Gary Danko, who received the James Beard Foundation award for best chef in California, makes for one of my favorite fancy dining experiences. The three- to five-course fixed-price menu is freestyle, so whether you want a sampling of appetizers or a flight of meat courses, you need only ask. Top picks? Glazed oysters with leeks and intricately carved "zucchini pearls"; seared foie gras with peaches, caramelized onions, and *verjus* sauce; and Moroccan spiced squab with *chermoula* (a thick, spicy sauce) and orange-cumin carrots. Diners at the bar may order a la carte, and everyone has access to the stellar though expensive wine list. Diners with the will power to eschew the cheese cart or desert receive a complimentary plate of petit fours with the check.

800 North Point St. (at Hyde St.). ℂ **415/749-2060**. www.garydanko.com. Reservations required. Walk-in bar. 3- to 5-course fixed-price menu $59–$79. AE, DC, DISC, MC, V. Daily 5:30–10pm. Bar opens 5pm. Valet parking $10. Cable car: Hyde. Bus: 10. Streetcar: F.

**Scoma's** ⭐ SEAFOOD   A throwback to the dining traditions of yesteryear, Scoma's eschews trendier trout preparations and fancy digs for huge portions of old-fashioned seafood served in a casual, waterfront setting. Gourmands should skip this one. But if your idea of heaven is classic, straightforward sea fare like fried calamari, raw oysters, pesto pasta with rock shrimp, and lobster thermidor served with old-time hospitality, this is as good as tourist restaurants get. Unfortunately, they charge the same as some of the finest restaurants in town. I'd rather splurge at Gary Danko or Masa's, but many of my guests from out of town insist we meet at Scoma's. It's a change of pace from today's chic urban restaurants, and parking is free.

Pier 47 and Al Scoma Way (between Jefferson and Jones sts.). ℂ **415/771-4383**. www.scomas.com. Reservations not accepted. Most main courses $18–$35. AE, DC, DISC, MC, V. Sun–Thurs 11:30am–10pm; Fri–Sat 11:30am–11pm. Hours change seasonally so call to confirm. Complimentary valet parking. Bus: 10 or 47. Streetcar: F.

## MODERATE

**Ana Mandara** ⭐⭐ VIETNAMESE   In a shuttered room with mood lighting, palms, and Vietnamese-inspired decor, diners (mostly tourists) splurge on Vietnamese delights such as spring rolls; Dungeness crab with lemon sauce; Chilean sea bass, wrapped and steamed in banana leaf with shiitake mushrooms and miso sauce; lobster with sweet-and-sour sauce and black sticky rice; and wok-charred tournedos of beef tenderloin with sweet onions and peppercress.

891 Beach St. (at Polk St.). ℂ **415/771-6800**. www.anamandara.com. Reservations recommended. Main courses $17–$32. AE, DISC, DC, MC, V. Mon–Fri 11:30am–2pm; Sun–Thurs 5:30–9:30pm; Fri–Sat 5:30–10:30pm (bar open until 1am). Valet parking Tues–Sun $9. Bus: 19, 30, or 45.

**Cafe Pescatore** ⭐ ITALIAN   This cozy trattoria with an open kitchen is one of the better bets in Fisherman's Wharf. Two walls of sliding glass doors offer pseudo-sidewalk seating when the weather's warm, although heavy vehicular traffic can detract from the alfresco experience. All the classics are well represented here: crisp Caesar salad, fried calamari, bruschetta, cioppino, pastas, chicken Marsala, and veal medallions with mushrooms, caramelized onions, sage, and veal sauce. The consensus is that anything cooked in the wood-fired oven is worth ordering, such as pizza (Margherita), roasts (sea bass with pine-nut crust, sun-dried tomato pesto, and roasted veggies), or panini (lunch only; grilled chicken or grilled eggplant). They serve darned good breakfasts, too.

2455 Mason St. (at North Point St., adjoining the Tuscan Inn). ℂ **415/561-1111**. www.cafepescatore.com. Reservations recommended. Main courses $6–$12 breakfast, $8.50–$17 lunch and dinner. AE, DC, DISC, MC, V. Daily 7am–10pm. Cable car: Powell-Mason line. Bus: 15, 39, or 42. Streetcar: F.

## MARINA DISTRICT, COW HOLLOW & PACIFIC HEIGHTS
### VERY EXPENSIVE

**Harris'** ⭐⭐ STEAKHOUSE   Every big city has a great steak restaurant, and in San Francisco it's Harris'. It's comfortably elegant, with a wood-paneled dining room, high-backed booths, banquettes, high ceilings, and hunting murals. But the real point, of course, is steak—dry aged, filet mignon, whatever you like—served with a baked potato and seasonal vegetables. You'll also find options for meat-challenged diners, as well as classic French onion soup, spinach and Caesar salads, and sides of delicious creamed spinach, sautéed shiitake mushrooms, or caramelized onions. Desserts, such as a sculptural beehivelike baked Alaska, are surprisingly good. The adjacent bar is convivial, with live jazz Thursday through Saturday. A meat counter services carnivores on the go.

2100 Van Ness Ave. (at Pacific Ave.). ⓒ 415/673-1888. www.harrisrestaurant.com. Reservations recommended. Most main courses $17–$40. AE, DC, DISC, MC, V. Mon–Thurs 5:30–9:30pm; Fri 5:30–10pm; Sat 5–10pm; Sun 5–9:30pm. Valet parking $7. Bus: 12, 47, or 49.

## MODERATE

**A16** ★★ ITALIAN   Thanks to chef Christophe Hille, this contemporary, casual, convivial spot is one of the city's best Italian restaurants, featuring Neapolitan-style pizza and cuisine from the Campania region. Don't miss the insanely good braised pork breast with olives, herbs, and caramelized chestnuts, but start by sharing dried fava beans with fennel salad and tuna *conserva* with braised dandelion greens and crunchy bread crumbs. Definitely ask Shelley Lindgren for wine recommendations—she's got some little-known winners on her list, which features 40 options by the half-glass, glass, and carafe.

2355 Chestnut St. (between Divisadero and Scott sts.). ⓒ 415/771-2216. www.a16sf.com. Reservations recommended. Main courses $8–$13 lunch, $14–$20 dinner. AE, DC, MC, V. Wed–Fri 11:30am–2:30pm; Sun–Thurs 5–10pm; Fri–Sat 5–11pm. Bus: 22, 30, or 30X.

**Ella's** ★★ *Kids* AMERICAN/BREAKFAST   This place is widely known for serving the best breakfast in town, so you're likely to wait up to an hour to get in on weekends. Midweek and in the wee hours, though, it's possible to slide into a counter or table seat in the colorful dining room and lose yourself in outstanding, generous servings of chicken hash, crisped to perfection and served with eggs any way you like them, with fluffy buttermilk biscuits. Pancakes, omelets, and the short list of other essentials are equally revered. Service can be slow, but the busboys are quick to fill coffee cups. Come lunchtime, solid entrees like salads or grilled salmon with mashed potatoes remind you what's great about good old American cooking.

500 Presidio Ave. (at California St.). ⓒ 415/441-5669. www.ellassanfrancisco.com. Reservations accepted for lunch. Main courses $5.50–$10 breakfast, $6–$12 lunch. AE, DISC, MC, V. Mon–Fri 7am–5pm; Sat–Sun 8:30am–2pm. Bus: 1, 3, or 43.

**Greens Restaurant** ★★ *Finds* VEGETARIAN   Knowledgeable locals swear by Greens, where Executive Chef Annie Somerville (author of *Fields of Greens*) cooks with the seasons, using produce from local organic farms. In an old warehouse, with enormous windows overlooking the bridge and the bay, the restaurant is a legendary pioneer. A weeknight dinner might start with mushroom soup with Asiago cheese and tarragon, or grilled portobello and endive salad. Entrees run from pizza with wilted escarole, red onions, lemon, Asiago, and Parmesan, to Vietnamese yellow curry or risotto with black trumpet mushrooms, leeks, savory spinach, white-truffle oil, Parmesan Reggiano, and thyme. A four-course dinner is served on Saturday. Adjacent to the restaurant, **Greens to Go** bakery sells homemade breads, sandwiches, soups, salads, and pastries.

Building A, Fort Mason Center (enter Fort Mason opposite the Safeway at Buchanan and Marina sts.). ⓒ 415/771-6222. www.greensrestaurant.com. Reservations recommended. Main courses $9.50–$14 lunch, $15–$20 dinner; fixed-price dinner $46; Sun brunch $8–$14. AE, DISC, MC, V. Tues–Sat noon–2:30pm; Sun 10:30am–2pm; Mon–Sat 5:30–9pm. Greens to Go Mon–Thurs 8am–8pm; Fri–Sat 8am–5pm; Sun 9am–4pm. Free parking (but rumor has it they're going to start charging soon). Bus: 28 or 30.

### INEXPENSIVE

**Andale Taquería** ★★ *Kids* *Value* MEXICAN   Andale (Spanish for "hurry up") offers incredibly high-end fast food for the health-conscious and the plain hungry in an attractive, casual setting. Lard, preservatives, or canned items are eschewed for salad dressings made with virgin olive oil; vegetarian beans (not refried); skinless chicken; salsas and *aguas frescas* (fruit drinks) made from fresh fruits and veggies; and mesquite-grilled meats. Factor in the great location (on a sunny shopping stretch), sophisticated decor, full bar, and patio seating (with a corner fireplace), and it's no wonder so many fitness-obsessed residents of the Marina consider this place home. Cafeteria-style service keeps prices low.

2150 Chestnut St. (between Steiner and Pierce sts.). ℂ 415/749-0506. Reservations not accepted. Most dishes $4.25–$11. MC, V. Sun–Thurs 11am–10pm (until 9pm in the winter); Fri–Sat 11am–10:30pm. Bus: 22, 28, 30, 30X, 43, 76, or 82X.

**Chez Nous** ★★ FRENCH   Diners are crammed into the 45-seat dining area of this cheery small dining room, but the French tapas are so delicious and affordable no one seems to care. Indeed, this friendly, fast-paced neighborhood haunt has become a blueprint for other restaurants that understand the allure of small plates. But Chez Nous stands out as more than a petite-portion trendsetter; most of its Mediterranean dishes taste so clean and fresh you can't wait to come back again. Start with the soup, whatever it is; don't skip tasty french fries with *harissa* aioli; savor the lamb chops with lavender sea salt; and save room for their famed dessert, the mini custard cake–like *canneles de Bordeaux.*

1911 Fillmore St. (between Pine and Bush sts.). ℂ 415/441-8044. Reservations recommended. Main courses $5–$12. AE, MC, V. Daily 11:30am–2:45pm and 5:30–10pm (Fri–Sat until 11pm). Bus: 22, 41, or 45.

**Eliza's** ★★ *Value* CHINESE   Despite the incongruous design of modern architecture, glass art, and color, this packed neighborhood haunt serves some of the freshest, best-tasting California-influenced Chinese food in town. Unlike most comparable options, the presentation and unintentionally funky atmosphere reflect the food. The fantastically fresh soups, salads, seafood, pork, chicken, duck, and specials such as spicy eggplant are outstanding, served on beautiful Italian plates. (Get the sea bass with black-bean sauce and go straight to heaven!) I often come at midday and order the Kung Pao chicken lunch special: a mixture of tender chicken, peanuts, chile peppers, subtly hot sauce, and perfectly crunchy vegetables. It's 1 of 32 main-course choices that come with rice and soup for around $6. The place is jumping at night, so prepare to stand in line.

2877 California St. (at Broderick St.). ℂ 415/621-4819. Reservations accepted for parties of 4 or more. Main courses $5.30–$6.15 lunch, $7.15–$15 dinner. MC, V. Mon–Thurs 11am–3pm and 5–9:30pm; Fri 11am–3pm and 5–10pm; Sat 4:30–10pm; Sun 4:30–9pm. Bus: 1 or 24.

**Mel's Drive-In** ★ *Kids* AMERICAN   Sure, it's contrived, touristy, and nowhere near healthy, but when you get that urge for a chocolate shake and banana cream pie at midnight—or when you want to entertain the kids—no other place comes through like Mel's Diner. Modeled after a 1950s diner, down to the jukebox at each table, Mel's harks back to the days when cholesterol and fried foods didn't jab your conscience with every greasy, wonderful bite. Too bad the prices don't reflect the '50s: A burger with fries and a Coke runs about $9.50.

There's another Mel's at 3355 Geary St., at Stanyan Street (ℂ 415/387-2244); it's open from 6am to 1am Sunday through Thursday, and 6am to 3am Friday and

Saturday. Additional locations, at 1050 Van Ness (🕿 **415/292-6857**) and at 801 Mission St (🕿 **415/227-4477**), are open Sunday through Thursday 6am to 3am, and Friday and Saturday 6am to 4am.

2165 Lombard St. (at Fillmore St.). 🕿 **415/921-3039**. www.melsdrive-in.com. Main courses $6.50–$12 breakfast, $7–$10 lunch, $8–$15 dinner. MC, V. Sun–Wed 6am–2am; Thurs 6am–3am; Fri–Sat 24 hr. Bus: 22, 30, or 43.

## CIVIC CENTER
### MODERATE

**Zuni Café** ★★★ *Finds* MEDITERRANEAN   Delicious, trendsetting Zuni Café is and probably always will be a local favorite. Its expanse of windows and lower Castro location guarantee good people-watching, but even better is the action within: 30- and 40-somethings crowding in for the flavors of chef Judy Rodgers's satisfying Mediterranean-influenced menu. For the full effect, stand at the copper-topped bar and order a glass of wine and a few oysters from the oyster menu (a dozen or so varieties are on hand). Then take a seat amid the two-level maze of little dining rooms with exposed brick. Although the changing menu always includes meat (such as New York steak with Belgian endive gratin) and fish (grilled or braised in the kitchen's brick oven), the proven winners are Rodgers's brick oven-roasted chicken for two with Tuscan-style bread salad, the polenta with mascarpone, and the hamburger on grilled rosemary focaccia bread.

1658 Market St. (at Franklin St.). 🕿 **415/552-2522**. Reservations recommended. Main courses $10–$19 lunch, $15–$29 dinner. AE, MC, V. Tues–Sat 11:30am–midnight; Sun 11am–11pm. Valet parking $8 (dinner only). Streetcar: All Market St. streetcars. Bus: 6, 7, or 71.

## HAIGHT-ASHBURY
### INEXPENSIVE

**Cha Cha Cha** ★★ *Value* CARIBBEAN   Put your name on the mile-long list, crowd into the tiny bar, and drink sangria while you wait. When you finally get seated, you'll dine in a loud—and I mean *loud*—dining room with Santería altars, banana trees, and plastic tablecloths. Do as I do and order from the tapas menu, sharing some of the city's best fried calamari, fried new potatoes, Cajun shrimp, and mussels in saffron broth, all served with luscious sauces. This is the kind of place where you can come in a partying mood, let your hair down, and make an evening of it. If you want the flavor without the festivities, come during lunch. A second, larger location is open in the Mission at 2327 Mission St., between 19th and 20th streets (🕿 **415/648-0504**).

801 Haight St. (at Shrader St.). 🕿 **415/386-7670**. www.cha3.com. Reservations not accepted. Tapas $5–$9; main courses $12–$15. MC, V. Daily 11:30am–4pm; Sun–Thurs 5–11pm; Fri–Sat 5–11:30pm. Streetcar: N. Bus: 6, 7, or 71.

## RICHMOND & SUNSET DISTRICTS
### MODERATE

**Aziza** ★★ MOROCCAN   If you're looking for something really different, or a festive spot for a large party, head deep into the Avenues for an exotic taste of Morocco. Chef-owner Mourad Lahlou creates an excellent dining experience through colorful and distinctly Moroccan surroundings and his modern, nonetheless authentic take on the food of his homeland. In any of the three opulently adorned dining rooms (front room features private booths, the middle room is more formal, and the back has lower seating and a Moroccan lounge feel), you can indulge in the affordable, five-course tasting menu ($39) or individual treats such as kumquat-enriched lamb shank, saffron Cornish hen with preserved lemon and olives, or lavender honey-braised squab. Finish off with my favorite dessert: rhubarb galette with rose- and geranium-scented crème fraîche, vanilla aspic, and rhubarb consommé.

5800 Geary Blvd. (at 22nd Ave.). ✆ **415/752-2222**. www.aziza-sf.com. Reservations recommended. Main courses $10–$20; 5-course menu $39. MC, V. Wed–Mon 5:30–10:30pm. Valet parking: $8 weekdays, $10 weekends. Bus: 29 or 38.

**Kabuto A&S** ⭑⭑ JAPANESE/SUSHI    In a town overflowing with seafood and pretentious diners, you'd think it would be easier to find great sushi. The truth is, finding an outstanding sushi restaurant in San Francisco is more challenging than spotting a parking space in Nob Hill. Chopsticking these fish-and-rice delicacies is one of the most joyous and adventurous ways to dine, and Kabuto is one of the best (and most expensive) places to do it. Chef Sachio Kojima, who presides over the small, crowded sushi bar (which moved into an even tinier space across the street from its old location in 2003), constructs each dish with smooth, lightning-fast movements known only to master chefs. If you're big on wasabi, ask for the stronger stuff Kojima serves on request.

5121 Geary Blvd. (at 16th Ave.). ✆ **415/752-5652**. www.kabutosushi.com. Reservations not accepted. Sushi $2–$10; small plates $5–$12; main courses $15–$20. MC, V. Tues–Sat 5:30–10:30pm.

### INEXPENSIVE

**Burma Superstar** ⭑⭑ *Value* BURMESE    Despite its gratuitous name, this restaurant works hard to offer exceptional Burmese food at rock-bottom prices. Unfortunately, the allure of their tea-leaf salad, clay-pot chicken curry, and sweet-tangy sesame beef is one of the city's worst-kept secrets. Given the no-reservations policy, you can count on waiting in line for up to an hour. (FYI, parties of two are seated more quickly than larger groups, and it's less crowded at lunch.) A smart approach is to pencil your cellphone number onto the waiting list and browse the Clement Street shops until you receive a call.

309 Clement St. (at Fourth Ave.). ✆ **415/387-2147**. www.burmasuperstar.com. No reservations. Main courses $8–$16. MC, V. Mon–Thurs 11am–9:30pm; Fri–Sat 11am–10pm; Sun 11am–9:30pm. Bus 4, 38, or 44.

**Ton Kiang** ⭑⭑ *Kids* *Finds* CHINESE/DIM SUM    Ton Kiang is the number-one place in the city to do dim sum. Wait in line (which runs out the door anytime between 11am and 1:30pm), get a table on the first or second floor, and say yes to dozens of delicacies, which are brought to the table for your approval. Every tray of morsels coming from the kitchen is a delight—from stuffed crab claws, roast Peking duck, and a gazillion dumplings (scallop and vegetable, shrimp, beef, and more) to rarer treats like *doa miu* (snow pea sprouts flash-sautéed with garlic and peanut oil), shark-fin soup, and mango pudding. It's hard to get past the dim sum, served all day every day, but the full menu of Hakka cuisine is also worth investigating. This is one of my favorite places to do lunch, and staff members happen to be unusually friendly.

5821 Geary Blvd. (between 22nd and 23rd aves.). ✆ **415/387-8273**. www.tonkiang.net. Reservations accepted for parties of 8 or more. Dim sum $2–$5.50; main courses $8.50–$14. AE, DC, DISC, MC, V. Mon–Thurs 10am–10pm; Fri 10am–10:30pm; Sat 9:30am–10:30pm; Sun 9am–10pm. Bus: 38.

## THE CASTRO

### MODERATE

**Mecca** ⭑⭑ *Finds* AMERICAN    In 1996, Mecca entered the scene in a decadent swirl of chocolate-brown velvet, stainless steel, cement, and brown leather. This industrial-chic supper club that makes you want to order a martini just so you'll blend in. An eclectic mix of urbane patrons (with a heavy dash of same-sex couples) mingle at the oval centerpiece bar, where a live DJ spins hot grooves. Classic American fare, prepared by chef Stephen Barber and served at tables tucked into several nooks, includes oysters on the half shell, seared ahi tuna, and wood-oven roasted pork tenderloin. The food is very good, but it's that quintessential San Francisco vibe that makes this place the hot spot in the Castro.

2029 Market St. (by 14th and Church sts.). ℭ **415/621-7000.** www.sfmecca.com. Reservations recommended. Main courses $18–$29. AE, DC, MC, V. Tues–Thurs 5:30–10pm; Fri–Sat 6–10:30pm (bar remains open later); Sun 5–9:30pm. Valet parking $10. Streetcar: F, K, L, or M. Bus: 8, 22, 24, or 37.

## INEXPENSIVE

**Chow** ★★ *Value* AMERICAN   Chow claims to serve American cuisine, though the standard fare is not exactly meatloaf and apple pie. But what's not to like about starting with a Cobb salad and moving on to Thai-style noodles with steak, chicken, peanuts, and spicy lime-chile garlic broth, or linguine with clams? Especially when everything except the fish of the day costs less than $15. The daily sandwich specials are more traditional, served with salad, soup, or fries. While the food and prices alone are good reason to come here, the beer on tap, great, inexpensive wine selection, and the fun, tavernlike environment clinch the deal. A second location, **Park Chow,** is at 1240 Ninth Ave. (ℭ **415/665-9912**). You can't make reservations for parties of fewer than eight, but if you're on your way, you can call ahead to place your name on the wait list, which is advisable.

215 Church St. (near Market St.). ℭ **415/552-2469.** Reservations not accepted. Main courses $7–$15. DISC, MC, V. Mon–Thurs 11am–11pm; Fri 11am–midnight; Sat 10am–midnight; Sun 10am–11pm. Streetcar: F, J, K, L, or M. Bus: 8, 22, or 37.

# MISSION DISTRICT
## MODERATE

**Delfina** ★★ *Finds* SEASONAL ITALIAN   Delfina eschews bells, whistles, big-time design, and fancy preparations for something that used to be characteristic of San Francisco restaurants: chic but straightforward simplicity and a small-business feel. Unpretentious atmosphere, reasonable prices, and chef and co-owner Craig Stoll's ultrafresh seasonal Italian cuisine mean you're in for a reasonably priced, delicious experience. Try the slow-roasted pork shoulder, gnocchi with squash and chestnuts, sand dabs with frisée, fingerling potatoes and lemon-caper butter, or lamb with polenta and sweet peas.

3621 18th St. (between Dolores and Guererro sts.). ℭ **415/552-4055.** Reservations recommended. Main courses $13–$22. MC, V. Sun–Thurs 5:30–10pm; Fri–Sat 5:30–11pm. Parking lot at 18th and Valencia sts. next to Sharin's Appliances, $8. Bus: 26 or 33. Streetcar: J.

**Levende Lounge** ★★ CALIFORNIA/AMERICAN   The city's hottest new cocktail spot for young singles is an exemplar of warehouse chic, with brick walls and brown leather couches and banquettes. It's also a fine place to eat—provided you come early, or enjoy noshing while revelers crowd the bar, flirt, and groove to the DJ's mixes. Twenty-nine-year-old chef Jamie Lauren's small-plate fare is so pristine and balanced I'm curious to see how long she'll stick around before landing a gig that's more strictly about the cuisine. Hopefully she'll stay put long enough for you to taste her frisée salad with baby leek vinaigrette, bacon, and a fried quail egg; mini lamb burgers; slow-cooked baby back ribs; and duck confit tacos with dried cherry mole. Desserts are less special.

1710 Mission St. (at Duboce St.) ℭ **415/864-5585.** www.levendelounge.com. Reservations recommended. Tapas: $8–$18. AE, MC, V. Tues–Sat 5:30–11pm. Street parking only. Bus: 14, 33, or 49.

NEW
REVENGE OF THE
**MUMMY**
THE RIDE

**STUDIO TOUR**

**UNIVERSAL STUDIOS**
**HOLLYWOOD**

WORLD'S LARGEST
MOVIE STUDIO AND THEME PARK℠

# STAR IN
# EXTREME
# ACTION!

- Tour behind the scenes and on the sets where today's hottest movies are being made. (And keep your eyes peeled for stars!)

- Put yourself to the test and stare fear in the eye with extreme stunt challenges in the all-new Fear Factor Live.

- Escape into the thrilling worlds of The Mummy, Jurassic Park, Shrek and other hit movies.

It can only happen in Hollywood...
Universal Studios Hollywood℠

For tickets and information, see
your hotel front desk or concierge.
1-800-UNIVERSAL

PRINT
@HOME
TICKETS

PRINT YOUR THEME PARK TICKETS AT HOME AT
www.UniversalStudiosHollywood.com

**Now Open**
**Fear factor** NEW!
**LIVE**

## 5 The Top Attractions

## TOP SAN FRANCISCO SIGHTS

**Alcatraz Island** ★★★    Visible from Fisherman's Wharf, Alcatraz (aka "The Rock") has a checkered history. Juan Manuel Ayala, who named it after the pelicans that nested on the island, discovered it in 1775. From the 1850s to 1933, when the army vacated the island, it served as a military post protecting the bay shoreline. In 1934, the buildings were converted into a maximum-security prison—believed to be escape-proof, given the sheer cliffs, treacherous currents, and frigid water temperatures. Alcatraz's most infamous inmates included Al Capone, Robert Stroud (the so-called Birdman of Alcatraz), Machine Gun Kelly, and Alvin Karpis. In 1963, however, after an apparent escape in which no bodies were recovered, the government closed the prison and, in 1969, a group of American Indians chartered a boat and symbolically reclaimed the island for the Indian people, occupying it until 1971. In 1972, The Rock became part of the Golden Gate National Recreation Area. The wildlife driven away during the military and penitentiary years has started returning; black-crested night heron and other seabirds nest here again, and visitors can view them from a nature trail that runs through the island. Park rangers lead entertaining tours through the prison block as well, including an audio tour and slide show.

It's a ridiculously popular excursion and space is limited, so purchase tickets as far in advance as possible, from **Blue & Gold Fleet** (© **415/705-5555;** www.blueand goldfleet.com). You can also buy tickets in advance from the Blue & Gold ticket office on Pier 41. Wear comfortable shoes; bring snacks (none are for sale on the island, and the snacks aboard the boat are scarce and junky); take a heavy sweater or windbreaker (even when the sun's out, it's cold); and prepare yourself to climb a lot of steep steps.

Pier 41, near Fisherman's Wharf. © 415/773-1188 (info only). Admission (includes ferry trip and audio tour) $16 adults w/headset, $12 without; $14 seniors 62 and older w/headset, $9.75 without; $11 children 5–11 w/headset, $8.25 without. Winter daily 9:30am–2:15pm; summer daily 9:30am–4:15pm. Ferries depart 15 and 45 min. after the hour. Arrive at least 20 min. before sailing time. Thurs–Mon night tour at 4:20, adults $24, seniors and juniors ages 12–17 $21, kids $14.

**Cable Cars** ★★★    Designated historic landmarks by the National Park Service in 1964, San Francisco's beloved cable cars clank across the hills like mobile museum pieces. Each weighs about 6 tons and runs on a cable under the street in a center rail. They move at a constant 9½ mph—never more, never less. This may strike you as slow, but it doesn't feel that way when you're cresting an almost perpendicular hill and looking down at what seems like a bobsled dive into the ocean. In spite of the thrills, though, they're perfectly safe.

Powell-Hyde and Powell-Mason lines begin at the base of Powell and Market sts.; California St. line begins at the foot of Market St. $3 per ride.

**Coit Tower** ★★    In a city known for its panoramic views and vantage points, Coit Tower is "The Peak." If it's a clear day, it's wonderful to walk up the Filbert Steps to get here (thereby avoiding nightmarish traffic), then take in the panoramic views of the city and bay at the base of the tower. (In fact, I'd recommend against paying the admission to go to the top; the view is just as good from the parking area, and you can see the murals for free.) Completed in 1933, the tower is the legacy of Lillie Hitch-cock Coit, a wealthy eccentric who left San Francisco a $125,000 bequest. Inside the base of the tower are the WPA murals titled *Life in California, 1934,* completed

# Top San Francisco Sights

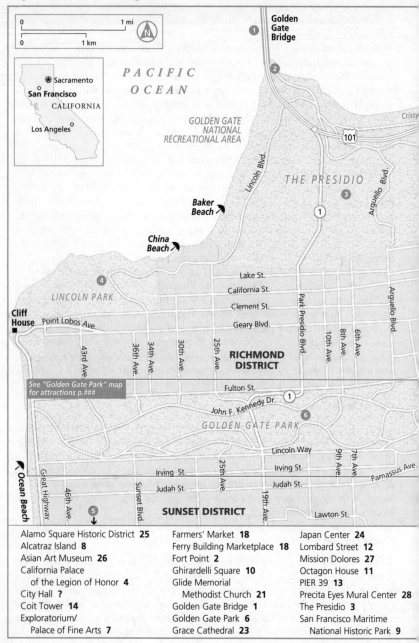

Alamo Square Historic District **25**
Alcatraz Island **8**
Asian Art Museum **26**
California Palace
   of the Legion of Honor **4**
City Hall **?**
Coit Tower **14**
Exploratorium/
   Palace of Fine Arts **7**
Farmers' Market **18**
Ferry Building Marketplace **18**
Fort Point **2**
Ghirardelli Square **10**
Glide Memorial
   Methodist Church **21**
Golden Gate Bridge **1**
Golden Gate Park **6**
Grace Cathedral **23**
Japan Center **24**
Lombard Street **12**
Mission Dolores **27**
Octagon House **11**
PIER 39 **13**
Precita Eyes Mural Center **28**
The Presidio **3**
San Francisco Maritime
   National Historic Park **9**

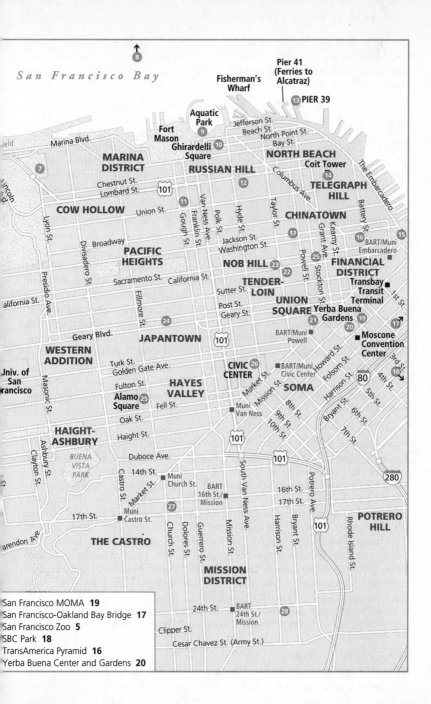

San Francisco Bay

↑ 8

Pier 41
(Ferries to
Alcatraz)

Fisherman's
Wharf

13 PIER 39

Aquatic
Park
9

Jefferson St.
Beach St.
North Point St.
Bay St.

Fort
Mason

Ghirardelli
Square 10

NORTH BEACH

Coit Tower

14

MARINA
DISTRICT

RUSSIAN HILL

Columbus Ave.

TELEGRAPH
HILL

The Embarcadero

Marina Blvd.

12

Chestnut St.
Lombard St.

101

11

Van Ness Ave.

Polk St.

Hyde St.

Taylor St.

CHINATOWN

Battery St.

COW HOLLOW

Union St.

Franklin St.

Gough St.

17

Kearny St.

Grant Ave.

16 BART/Muni
Embarcadero

15

Broadway

Jackson St.
Washington St.

Powell St.

Stockton St.

25

FINANCIAL
DISTRICT

PACIFIC
HEIGHTS

NOB HILL 23

Sacramento St.

California St.

22

Transbay
Transit
Terminal

1st St.

Fillmore St.

TENDER-
LOIN

Sutter St.

UNION
SQUARE

Yerba Buena
Gardens 19

Divisadero St.

Presidio Ave.

alifornia St.

Lyon St.

24

Post St.

Geary St.

21

20

17

Geary Blvd.

JAPANTOWN

101

BART/Muni
Powell

Moscone
Convention
Center

3rd St.

WESTERN
ADDITION

Turk St.
Golden Gate Ave.

CIVIC
CENTER 26

BART/Muni
Civic Center

Howard St.

Folsom St.

80

4th St.

18

Univ. of
San
Francisco

Masonic St.

Fulton St.

HAYES
VALLEY

Market St.

Mission St.

SOMA

Harrison St.

5th St.

Alamo
Square 25

Fell St.

Muni
Van Ness

8th St.

9th St.

10th St.

Bryant St.

6th St.

7th St.

HAIGHT-
ASHBURY

Oak St.

Haight St.

280

Clayton St.

Ashbury St.

BUENA
VISTA
PARK

Duboce Ave.

101

Masonic St.

14th St.

Castro St.

Market St.

Muni
Church St.

BART
16th St./
Mission

South Van Ness Ave.

16th St.

17th St.

Potrero Ave.

POTRERO
HILL

arendon Ave.

17th St.

Muni
Castro St.

27

Church St.

Dolores St.

Guerrero St.

Mission St.

Harrison St.

Bryant St.

101

Rhode Island St.

THE CASTRO

MISSION
DISTRICT

San Francisco MOMA  **19**
San Francisco-Oakland Bay Bridge  **17**
San Francisco Zoo  **5**
SBC Park  **18**
TransAmerica Pyramid  **16**
Yerba Buena Center and Gardens  **20**

24th St.

BART
24th St./
Mission

28

Clipper St.

Cesar Chavez St. (Army St.)

7

lincoln
d.

field

during the New Deal by more than 25 artists, many of them pupils of master muralist Diego Rivera.

Telegraph Hill. ℂ **415/362-0808**. www.coittower.org. Admission to the top $3.75 adults, $2.50 seniors, $1.50 children 6–12. Daily 10am–6pm. Bus: 39 ("Coit").

**Farmers Market** 🌟 *Finds*    Several days per week around the Ferry Building Marketplace, San Francisco foodies and chefs peruse alfresco stands hawking the finest Northern California fruits, vegetables, breads, dairy products, flowers, and readymade snacks by local restaurants. You'll be amazed at the variety and quality, and the crowded scene itself is something to behold. You can also pick up locally made vinegars and oils; they make wonderful gifts. Drop by on Saturday from 10am to 2pm for the "Shop with the Chef" excursion, led by a different local food pro every week, who interview local farmers and perform cooking demonstrations.

The Embarcadero, at Market St. ℂ **415/291-3276**. Apr–Nov Sat 8am–2pm; Tues, Thurs, and Sun 10am–2pm; Dec–Mar Tues 10am–2pm and Sat 8am–2pm. www.cuesa.org.

**Ferry Building Marketplace** 🌟🌟 *Finds*    For gourmets, the recently renovated Ferry Building, open daily, is a must. Tenants include many of Northern California's finest gourmet food purveyors: Cowgirl Creamery's Artisan Cheese Shop, Recchiuti Confections (amazing!), Scharffen Berger Chocolate, Acme breads, Wine Country's gourmet diner Taylor's Refresher, famed Vietnamese restaurant The Slanted Door, and myriad other restaurants, food shops, and wine bars. Check out the Imperial Tea Court and learn the traditional Chinese way to steep and sip, buy cooking items at the Sur La Table shop, grab a bite and savor the bayfront views from outdoor tables, or browse the farmers market when it's up and running (see above). Whatever you do, you'll be doing it with a swarm of San Franciscans who can't get enough of this place.

The Embarcadero, at Market St. Most stores open daily 10am–6pm. Restaurant hours vary. www.ferrybuilding marketplace.com.

√ **Golden Gate Bridge** 🌟🌟🌟    Construction on San Francisco's most famous landmark began in 1933 and cost $35 million by the time it opened, in May 1937. Contrary to pessimistic predictions, the bridge neither collapsed in an earthquake nor proved to be a white elephant. What it did was change the Bay Area's economic life, encouraging the development of regions north of San Francisco, and providing a symbol of hope when widespread unemployment afflicted the nation. The mile-long steel link is even longer if you factor in the approach, and it reaches a height of 746 feet above the water. Though it's usually windy and cold, walking even a short distance onto the span is one of the best ways to experience the immense scale of the structure. To cross on foot, as millions do every year, you can either park in the lot at the foot of the bridge on the city side or venture out from Marin's Vista Point, at the bridge's northern end, which affords one of the most famous urban vistas in the world.

Hwy. 101 N. www.goldengatebridge.org. $5 cash toll collected when driving south. Bridge-bound Golden Gate Transit buses (ℂ **415/923-2000**) depart every 30–60 min. during the day for Marin County, starting from the Transbay Terminal (Mission and First sts.) and stopping at Market and Seventh sts., at the Civic Center, and along Van Ness Ave. and Lombard St.

√ **GOLDEN GATE PARK**

From the Conservatory of Flowers near the eastern end, to Ocean Beach on the western border, Golden Gate Park is an interactive, 1,017-acre botanical symphony—and anyone who likes can play in the orchestra. Spend a sunny day lounging on the grass along JFK Drive, have a good read in the Shakespeare Garden, or stroll around Stow Lake, and you will understand the allure.

The park is made up of hundreds of gardens and attractions linked by wooded paths and roads. The park has infinite hidden treasures, beyond its immediate appeal, so make your first stop the **McLaren Lodge and Park Headquarters** (© **415/831-2700**) for a detailed overview of information.

The best gardens, among dozens in the park, are the aforementioned Conservatory of Flowers, Rhododendron Dell, the Rose Garden, the Strybing Arboretum (see below) and, at the western edge in spring, the thousands of tulips and daffodils around the Dutch windmill. The AIDS Memorial Grove is a special, low-key place for reflection, near the northeastern side of the park.

The park also contains recreational facilities such as tennis courts; playing fields for baseball, soccer, and polo; a golf course; riding stables; and fly-casting pools. Bus: 16AX, BX, 5, 6, 7, 66, or 71.

## OTHER PARK HIGHLIGHTS

**BEACH CHALET**    First listed on the National Register of Historic places in 1981, the Spanish-Colonial Beach Chalet, 1000 Great Hwy., at the west end of Golden Gate Park near Fulton Street (© **415/386-8439**), was a popular stopover for generations of beachgoers. Designed by Willis Polk in 1925, the chalet features a 200-seat restaurant upstairs and a public lounge and changing rooms on the first floor. In the 1930s, the Works Progress Administration (WPA) commissioned Lucien Labaudt (who also painted the Coit Tower frescoes) to create frescoes, mosaics, and wood carvings of San Francisco life. After decades of use, the chalet grew old and worn, forcing its closure in 1981. In 1996, it reopened, to continue celebrating the city's heritage with original mosaics as well as new literature and plays. The upstairs restaurant, though modern, is a great place to stop for a house-made brew and a glimpse of the expansive Pacific.

**CONSERVATORY OF FLOWERS (1878)**    This striking assemblage of glass and iron, modeled on the glass house at Kew Gardens in London, exhibits a rotating display of plants and shrubs, including an astounding variety of orchids. After years of remodeling, it opened in 2003 and is one of the park's must-see attractions. If you're around during summer and fall, don't miss the Dahlia Garden to the right of the entrance in the center of what was once a carriage roundabout. The conservatory is open Tuesday through Sunday from 9am to 4:30pm; closed Mondays. Admission is $5 for adults; $3 for children 12 to 17 years of age, seniors, and students with ID; $1.50 for children 5 to 11, free to children 4 and under and to all visitors the first Tuesday of the month. For more information, visit www.conservatoryofflowers.org or call © **415/666-7001.**

**DE YOUNG MUSEUM**    After closing for several years, San Francisco's oldest museum, the **de Young Museum,** 50 Hagiwara Tea Garden Dr. (© **415/682-2481**), is scheduled to reopen in October 2005, with a new, state-of-the-art facility in Golden Gate Park. The de Young's vast collections include American paintings, decorative arts and crafts, and arts from Africa, Oceania, and the Americas, as well as Western and non-Western textiles. The de Young is beloved for its excellent exhibitions and educational arts programs for both children and adults. Fees and hours have yet to be established as this book goes to press, but you can find out more—and learn about upcoming shows— by visiting www.thinker.org.

**JAPANESE TEA GARDEN (1894)** Developed for the 1894 Midwinter Exposition, this garden would be a quiet place with cherry trees, shrubs, and bonsai, crossed by winding paths and high-arched bridges—were it not for the hordes of tourists and screaming children. Come early to enjoy the places for contemplation, including the bronze Buddha cast in Japan in 1790 and donated by the Gump family; the Buddhist pagoda; and the Wishing Bridge, which looks as though it completes a circle when it's reflected in the water. The garden is open daily November through February from 8:30am to 5pm (teahouse 10am–4:30pm), March through October from 8:30am to 6pm (teahouse 10am–5:30pm). For admission **information,** call ✆ **415/752-4227.** For the **teahouse,** call ✆ **415/752-1171.**

**STOW LAKE & STRAWBERRY HILL** ⭐ *Kids* Rent a paddleboat, rowboat, or motorboat and cruise around the circular lake where turtles bathe on rocks and logs, ducks waddle around awaiting handouts, painters render still lifes, and joggers work out along the shoreline. Strawberry Hill, the artificial, 430-foot-high island at the center of Stow Lake, is a great picnic spot, with a waterfall, peace pagoda, and bird's-eye view of San Francisco and the bay. For the **boathouse,** call ✆ **415/752-0347.** Boat rentals are available daily from 10am to 4pm, weather permitting; four-passenger rowboats go for $13 per hour, and four-person paddleboats run $17 per hour; fees are cash only.

**STRYBING ARBORETUM & BOTANICAL GARDENS** Some 6,000 plant species grow here, including rare breeds, ancient plants in the "primitive garden," and a grove of California redwoods. Strybing is open Monday through Friday from 8am to 4:30pm, and Saturday, Sunday, and holidays from 10am to 5pm. Free admission. For more information, call ✆ **415/661-1316** or visit www.strybing.org.

## 6 Exploring the City

### MORE POINTS OF INTEREST

**Lombard Street** *Overrated* Known (erroneously) as the "crookedest street in the world," the switchback block of Lombard between Hyde and Leavenworth puts smiles on the faces of thousands of visitors each year. So steep it bows like a river to make descent possible, this short stretch is one-way, downhill, and fun to drive. Take the curves slowly and in low gear, and expect daunting crowds and delays during the weekend. Save your film for the bottom; if you're lucky, you'll find a parking space where you can photograph the spectacle. You can also take straight staircases up or down either side of the street.

Between Hyde and Leavenworth sts.

**Mission Dolores** ⭐ This is the oldest structure in the city, dedicated in June 1776 at the northern terminus of El Camino Real, the Spanish missionary road that runs from Mexico to California. Founded by Father Francisco Palou, on the order of Franciscan Father Junípero Serra, Mission Dolores was constructed from 36,000 sun-baked bricks. It's a serene place to visit, with its cool, thick adobe walls and the cemetery and gardens where the early settlers are buried.

16th St. (at Dolores St.). ✆ **415/621-8203.** $3 adults, $2 children. Daily 9am–4pm; Good Friday 9am–noon. Closed Easter, Thanksgiving, Christmas Day. Bus: 14, 26, or 33 to Church and 16th sts. Streetcar: J.

**Yerba Buena Center for the Arts & Yerba Buena Gardens** ⭐ *Kids* An interactive wonderland across from the Museum of Modern Art, Yerba Buena could keep you busy all day with its 5-acre garden, cafes, and art-related attractions. The **Center for the Arts** showcases music, theater, dance, and visual arts; **Galleries and Arts Forum** features three galleries and a dance space; **Zeum** (✆ 415/777-2800; www.zeum.org) is a children's addition with a cafe, interactive cultural center, ice-skating rink, fabulous 1906 carousel, and interactive learning garden. You'll also find Sony's futuristic retail-and-entertainment mecca **Metreon Entertainment Center** (✆ 415/537-3400; www.metreon.com), a 350,000-square-foot complex of cinemas, including an **IMAX** theater, small restaurants, shops, and interactive attractions.

701 Mission St. ✆ 415/978-ARTS (box office). www.ybca.org. Admission for gallery $6 adults, $3 seniors, teachers, and students. Free to all 1st Tues of each month; every Thurs free for seniors and students w/ID. Tues–Wed and Sun noon–5pm; Thurs–Sat noon–8pm. Streetcar: Powell or Montgomery. Bus: 5, 9, 14, 15, 30, or 45.

## ARCHITECTURAL HIGHLIGHTS

The **Alamo Square Historic District** has one of the largest concentrations of the city's 14,000 **Painted Ladies,** or Victorian homes restored and ornately painted by residents. The area is small and easy to walk—bordered by Divisadero Street on the west, Golden Gate Avenue on the north, Webster Street on the east, and Fell Street on the south, about 10 blocks west of Civic Center. From Alamo Square at Fulton and Steiner streets, you'll see one of the most famous views of San Francisco, reproduced on postcards and posters around town—sharp-edged Financial District skyscrapers towering above a row of Victorians.

**City Hall** and the **Civic Center** are part of a "City Beautiful" complex built in 1881, in the Beaux Arts style, designed by Brown and Bakewell. The newly renovated City Hall dome rises to 308 feet outside, ornamented with *oculi* (round windows) and topped by a lantern. The rotunda, which soars 112 feet, is finished in oak, marble, and limestone, with a marble staircase leading to the second floor.

The **Flood Mansion,** 1000 California St., at Mason Street, was built between 1885 and 1886 for James Clair Flood—who, thanks to the Comstock Lode, rose from being a bartender to one of the city's wealthiest men. The house cost $1.5 million; the fence alone was $30,000! It was designed by Augustus Laver and modified by Willis Polk to accommodate the Pacific Union Club.

The **Octagon House,** 2645 Gough St., at Union Street (✆ 415/441-7512), is an eight-sided, cupola-topped house from 1861. Its circular staircase, ceiling medallion, and other features are extraordinary, and the furniture, silverware, and American pewter date from the colonial and Federal periods. The historic document collection includes the signatures of 54 (of 56) signers of the Declaration of Independence. Even if you're not able to visit during opening hours, this strange structure is worth a look from outside. It's open February through December on the second Sunday, and the second and fourth Thursdays of each month from noon to 3pm; it's closed January and holidays.

The **Palace of Fine Arts,** on Baker between Jefferson and Bay streets, is the only building to survive from the Pan-Pacific Exhibition of 1915. Constructed by Bernard Maybeck, it was rebuilt in concrete using molds taken from the original in the 1950s. It now houses the **Exploratorium** (p. 124).

The **TransAmerica Pyramid,** 600 Montgomery St., between Clay and Washington streets, is the tallest structure in San Francisco's skyline. It's 48 stories tall, capped by a 212-foot spire.

Although the **San Francisco–Oakland Bay Bridge** is visually less appealing than the Golden Gate Bridge, it's more spectacular in many ways. Opened in 1936 (a year before the Golden Gate), it's one of the world's longest steel bridges, at 8¼ miles long. A dovetailed series of spans joined midbay by one of the world's widest tunnels, at Yerba Buena Island, it's not really a single bridge: West of Yerba Buena, it's two separate suspension bridges, joined at a central anchorage; east of the island, it's a 1,400-foot cantilever span, followed by a succession of truss bridges.

## A ROUSING CHURCH EXPERIENCE

**Glide Memorial United Methodist Church** ★ *Moments*    This Tenderloin-area church would be nothing special if not for its pastor, Cecil Williams. Williams has attracted national fame with his enthusiasm, uplifting preaching and singing, and outreach work with poor and homeless people in the neighborhood. Visit Sunday morning for an exhilarating experience.

330 Ellis St. (west of Union Sq.). © 415/771-6300. Services Sun at 9 and 11am. Bus: 37. Streetcar: Powell.

## MUSEUMS

**Asian Art Museum** ★    Reopened in March 2003, in its new Civic Center home renovated by Italian architect Gae Aulenti, the Asian Art Museum is one of the Western world's largest institutions devoted to Asian art. Its collection boasts more than 13,000 art objects, including world-class sculptures, paintings, bronzes, ceramics, jades, and decorative objects representing 6,000 years of history and various regions of South Asia, West Asia, Southeast Asia, the Himalayas, China, Korea, and Japan. Previously in Golden Gate Park, the museum now resides in the city's Beaux Arts–style central library—with 29,000 square feet of permanent gallery space, able to showcase 2,500 objects at any given time. Add temporary exhibitions, live demonstrations, learning activities, and a new cafe and store, and you've got one very good reason to head to the Civic Center.

200 Larkin St. (between Fulton and McAllister sts.). © 415/581-3500. www.asianart.org. Admission $10 adults, $7 seniors 65 and over, $6 youths 12–17, free for children under 12, $5 flat rate after 5pm Thurs. Free 1st Tues of the month. Tues–Wed and Fri–Sun 10am–5pm; Thurs 10am–9pm. Bus: All Market St. buses. Streetcar: Civic Center.

**California Palace of the Legion of Honor** ★★    One of San Francisco's most beautiful sites, the Palace of the Legion of Honor was designed as a memorial to California's World War I casualties. The neoclassical structure is an exact replica of the Legion of Honor Palace in Paris, down to the inscription HONNEUR ET PATRIE above the portal. Reopened after a 2-year, $29-million renovation and upgrading project, which was stalled by the discovery of almost 300 coffins, the collection holds paintings, sculpture, and decorative arts from Europe, as well as tapestries, prints, and drawings. The chronological display of more than 800 years of European art includes a collection of Rodin sculptures. The expansive, grassy surrounds afford astounding views of the Golden Gate.

In Lincoln Park (34th Ave. and Clement St.). © 415/750-3600, or 415/863-3330 (recorded information). www.thinker.org. Admission $8 adults, $6 seniors 65 and over, $5 youths 12–17, free for children under 12. Fees may be higher for special exhibitions. Free to all on Tues. Tues–Sun 9:30am–5pm. Bus: 18.

**The Exploratorium** ★ *Kids*    This fun, hands-on science fair hosts hundreds of exhibitions exploring everything from color theory to Einstein's theory of relativity. Booths demonstrate optics, for example, with a statue in three dimensions: When you try to touch it, you discover it isn't there. In another booth, when you stretch your hand forward in a mirror, a hand comes out to touch you, but the hands miss each other in the air. You can also whisper into a concave reflector, so a friend can hear you 60 feet away, or you use sound waves to design your own animated, abstract art. The museum is at the **Palace of Fine Arts** 𝄐, the only building left standing from the Panama-Pacific Exposition of 1915. The adjoining park and lagoon are the perfect place for an afternoon picnic. And they're home to ducks, swans, seagulls, and grouchy geese, so bring extra bread!

3601 Lyon St., in the Palace of Fine Arts (at Marina Blvd.). ℂ 415/563-7337, or 415/561-0360 (recorded information). www.exploratorium.edu. Admission $12 adults; $9.50 seniors, youth 13–17, visitors w/disabilities, and college students w/ID; $8 children 4–12; free for children under 4. Free 1st Wed of each month. Groups of 10 or more must make advance reservations. AE, MC, V. Tues–Sun 10am–5pm. Closed Mon except Martin Luther King, Jr., Day, Presidents' Day, Memorial Day, and Labor Day. Free parking. Bus: 28, 30, or Golden Gate Transit.

### San Francisco Maritime National Historical Park 𝘒𝘪𝘥𝘴

Shaped like an Art Deco ship, near Fisherman's Wharf, the National Maritime Museum is filled with sailing, whaling, and fishing artifacts. Exhibitions include model boats, scrimshaw, and a collection of shipwreck photographs and historic marine scenes—including an 1851 snapshot of hundreds of abandoned ships, deserted en masse by crews dashing off to participate in the Gold Rush. Finely carved, painted wooden figureheads from old windjammers line the museum walls.

Two blocks east, at Aquatic Park's Hyde Street Pier, several historic ships are open to the public. The *Balclutha,* one of the last surviving square-riggers, was built in Glasgow in 1886, and carried grain from California around Cape Horn at a near-record speed of 300 miles a day; it rounded the treacherous cape 17 times in its career. Visitors are invited to spin the wheel, squint at the compass, and imagine they're weathering a mighty storm. Kids can climb into the bunking quarters, visit the "slop chest" (galley to you, matey), and read the sea chanteys (clean ones only) that decorate the walls.

For San Franciscans, the 1890 *Eureka* still carries a cargo of nostalgia. The last of 50 paddle-wheeled ferries that regularly plied the bay, it made its final trip in 1957. Restored to its original splendor, the side-wheeler is loaded with deck cargo, including antique cars and trucks.

At the pier's small-boat shop, visitors can follow the restoration of historic boats from the collection. It's behind the maritime bookstore on your right as you approach the ships.

At the foot of Polk St. (near Fisherman's Wharf). ℂ **415/561-7100.** www.nps.gov/safr. Museum free; tickets to board ships $5, free for children under 16. Museum daily 10am–5pm. Ships on Hyde St. Pier Memorial Day to Oct 15 daily 9:30am–5:30pm; Oct 16 to day before Memorial Day daily 9:30am–5pm. Cable car: Powell-Hyde St. line to the last stop. Bus: 19, 30, or 47.

### San Francisco Museum of Modern Art (SFMOMA) 𝄐

Although it doesn't compare with similar institutions in New York City, SFMOMA is a fine museum, with more than 23,000 works to its name. One of the first museums to recognize photography as a major art form, SFMOMA holds more than 12,000 photographs, by notables such as Ansel Adams, Alfred Stieglitz, Edward Weston, and Henri Cartier-Bresson. Its painting and sculpture departments encompass nearly 5,000 works, by Henri Matisse, Jackson Pollock, Willem de Kooning, Diego Rivera, Georgia O'Keeffe, Paul Klee, the Fauvists, Richard Diebenkorn, and others. Alas, the museum displays only a small amount of its holdings at any given time. Phone for details of special exhibitions, and whatever you do, check out the fabulous MuseumStore and cafe.

151 Third St. (2 blocks south of Market St., across from Yerba Buena Gardens). ℂ **415/357-4000.** www.sfmoma.org. Admission $10 adults, $7 seniors, $6 students over 12 w/ID, free for children 12 and under. Half-price for all Thurs 6–9pm; free to all 1st Tues of each month. Thurs 11am–8:45pm; Fri–Tues 11am–5:45pm. Closed major holidays. Streetcar: J, K, L, or M to Montgomery. Bus: 15, 30, or 45.

## NEIGHBORHOODS WORTH SEEKING OUT

For self-guided walking tours of San Francisco's neighborhoods, pick up a copy of *Frommer's Memorable Walks in San Francisco.*

**THE CASTRO** Castro Street around Market and 18th streets is the hub of the city's gay community, catered to by the many stores, restaurants, bars, and other institutions here. Among the landmarks are Harvey Milk Plaza and the Castro Theatre, a 1920s movie palace.

**CHINATOWN** California Street to Broadway, and Kearny to Stockton Street are the boundaries of today's Chinatown. While San Francisco is home to the second-largest community of Chinese in the U.S., the majority do not live and work in these 24 blocks, but they do return to shop and dine here on weekends.

The gateway at Grant and Bush marks the entry to the neighborhood. Walk up Grant, the tourist face of Chinatown, to California Street and Old St. Mary's. The heart of the district is at **Portsmouth Square,** where you'll find Chinese-American locals playing board games (often gambling) or just sitting quietly. This square was the center of early San Francisco and the spot where the American flag was first raised on July 9, 1846. From the square, Washington Street leads up to Waverly Place, where you can see three temples.

Explore the area at your leisure, or see "Organized Tours," below if you'd like to join a special-interest walking tour.

**FISHERMAN'S WHARF & THE NORTHERN WATERFRONT** Few cities in America are as adept at wholesaling their historical sites as San Francisco, which has converted Fisherman's Wharf into one of the world's most popular tourist destinations. Unless you arrive really early, you won't find any traces of the city's historic waterfront tradition; the only serious fishing going on now is for tourist dollars. A fleet of fewer than 30 boats still operates from here, but basically today's Fisherman's Wharf is one long shopping mall stretching from Ghirardelli Square at the west end to PIER 39 at the east. Some love it; others can't get far enough away from it. Most agree, however, that Fisherman's Wharf, for better or for worse, should be seen at least once.

**PIER 39,** on the waterfront at Embarcadero and Beach Street (© **415/981-8030**), is a 4½-acre waterfront complex a few blocks east of Fisherman's Wharf. Ostensibly a re-creation of an early-20th-century street scene, it features walkways of aged, weathered wood salvaged from demolished piers. But don't expect a slice of old-fashioned maritime life. This is the busiest mall of the group, with more than 100 touristy stores and about 20 restaurants and snack outlets, some with good views of the bay.

In recent years, some 600 California **sea lions** have taken up residence on the adjacent floating docks. They sun themselves and honk and bellow. The latest addition to Fisherman's Wharf is **Aquarium of the Bay,** a $38-million, 1-million-gallon tank filled with sharks, stingrays, and more—all witnessed from a moving footpath that transports visitors through clear acrylic tunnels.

The shops are open daily from 10:30am to 8:30pm. Take the Powell-Mason cable-car line to Bay Street.

**THE MISSION DISTRICT** Once inhabited almost entirely by Irish immigrants, the Mission—an oblong area stretching roughly from 14th to 30th streets between Potrero Avenue in the east and Dolores on the west—is now the center of the city's Latino community and dot-com industry. The heart of the community lies along 24th Street between Van Ness and Potrero, where dozens of ethnic restaurants, bakeries, bars, and specialty stores attract a hip crowd from all over the city. Some of San Francisco's finest Victorians still stand in the outer limits. At night, stroll through the Mission District with caution, though by day the neighborhood is quite safe and highly recommended.

The city's oldest building and the district's namesake is the **Mission San Francisco de Assisi** (aka **Mission Dolores;** p. 122), at 16th and Dolores.

The **Precita Eyes Mural Arts Center,** 2981 24th St., between Harrison and Alabama streets (© **415/285-2287**), runs 1½-hour tours of nearby murals, on Saturday and Sunday at 11am and 1:30pm, for $10 for adults, $8 for students with ID, $5 for seniors, and $2 for under-18s. You'll see 85 murals in an 8-block walk. Every year, the center holds a Mural Awareness Month (usually in May) with daily tours. Most tours leave from 2981 24th St.; call ahead to confirm.

**NOB HILL**   When cable cars debuted in San Francisco, in 1873, this hill became the most exclusive residential area in the city. The Big Four and the Comstock Bonanza kings built their mansions here, but the 1906 earthquake and fire destroyed most of the structures. Only the Flood Mansion, which serves today as the Pacific Union Club, and the Fairmont (still under construction when the earthquake struck) were spared. Now, the area is home to some of the city's most upscale hotels, as well as Grace Cathedral, on the Crocker Mansion site. Stroll around and enjoy the views, and pay a visit to Huntington Park.

**NORTH BEACH**   In the late 1800s, an influx of Italian immigrants into North Beach established this aromatic district as San Francisco's "Little Italy." Today, dozens of Italian restaurants and coffeehouses continue flourishing in what is still the center of the city's Italian community. Walk down Columbus Avenue any given morning, and the wonderful aromas of roasting coffee and savory pasta sauces will overwhelm you. North Beach is not without interesting shops and bookstores either, but it's the old world cafes, delis, bakeries, and coffee shops that give this neighborhood its Italian-bohemian character.

## FLORA AND FAUNA

In addition to **Golden Gate Park** and **Golden Gate National Recreation Area** and the **Presidio** (see "Golden Gate National Recreation Area & the Presidio," below), San Francisco boasts more than 2,000 additional acres of parkland, most of which is perfect for picnicking. **Lincoln Park,** at Clement Street and 34th Avenue, on 270 acres in northwestern San Francisco, is home to both the California Palace of the Legion of Honor (see "Museums," above) and an 18-hole municipal golf course. The park's most dramatic features, however, are the 200-foot cliffs overlooking the Golden Gate Bridge and San Francisco Bay. Take bus no. 38 from Union Square to 33rd and Geary streets, and then transfer to bus no. 18 into the park.

**The San Francisco Zoo & Children's Zoo**   In the city's southwest corner between the Pacific Ocean and Lake Merced, the city zoo is underfunded and tired-looking. But if the kids must see animals, they can see more than 1,000 here, in landscaped enclosures guarded by concealed moats. The Primate Discovery Center is noteworthy for its many rare and endangered species, including ruffed-tailed lemurs, black-and-white colobus monkeys, patas monkeys, and emperor tamarins (pint-size primates with long, majestic mustaches). Other highlights include Koala Crossing, where kangaroos, emus, and walleroos also dwell; Gorilla World, one of the world's largest exhibitions of these gentle giants; and Penguin Island, with its large breeding colony of

Magellanic penguins. The Feline Conservation Center is a wooded sanctuary and breeding facility for the zoo's endangered snow leopards, Persian leopards, and other jungle cats. The Lion House is home to rare Sumatran and Siberian tigers, a rare white Bengal tiger, and the African lions (you can observe feeding hour at 2pm Tues–Sun). The latest exhibit, which opened in mid-2004, is African Savanna, a 3-acre mixed-species habitat with giraffes, zebras, antelope, and birds.

At the Children's Zoo, adjacent to the main park, the barnyard is alive with domestic animals such as sheep, goats, ponies, and a llama. And the Insect Zoo showcases myriad species, including the hissing cockroach and walking sticks.

Sloat Blvd. and 47th Ave. and Great Hwy. ⓒ 415/753-7080. www.sfzoo.org. Admission to main zoo and Children's Zoo $11 adults, $8 seniors 65 and over and youth 12–17, $5 children 3–11, free for children 2 and under accompanied by an adult; discounted admission for residents; $1 discount w/valid Muni transfer. Free to all 1st Wed of each month, except $2 fee for Children's Zoo. Carousel $2. Main zoo daily 10am–5pm; Children's Zoo Mon–Fri 11am–4pm, weekends and summer 10:30am–4:30pm. Streetcar: L from downtown Market St. to the end of the line.

## 7 Organized Tours

### ORIENTATION TOURS

### THE 49-MILE SCENIC DRIVE ★★

This self-guided, 49-mile drive is an easy way to orient yourself and grasp the beauty of San Francisco and its location. Beginning in the city, it follows a rough circle around the bay and passes the best-known sights: from Chinatown and the Golden Gate Bridge to Ocean Beach, Seal Rocks, Golden Gate Park, and Twin Peaks. Originally designed for the benefit of visitors to the 1939 and 1940 Golden Gate International Exposition, the route is designated with blue-and-white seagull signs. Although it makes an excellent half-day tour, if can easily take longer—if you decide, for example, to walk across the Golden Gate Bridge, or to have tea in Golden Gate Park's Japanese Tea Garden.

The San Francisco Visitor Information Center, at Powell and Market streets, distributes free route maps. Since a few of the Scenic Drive marker signs are missing, the map will come in handy. Try to avoid the downtown area during the weekday rush hours from 7 to 9am and from 4 to 6pm.

### BOAT TOURS

One of the best ways to view San Francisco is from the water. The **Blue & Gold Fleet,** PIER 39, Fisherman's Wharf (ⓒ **415/773-1188;** www.blueandgoldfleet.com), tours the bay year-round in a sleek, 350-passenger sightseeing boat, complete with food and beverage facilities. The fully narrated, 1-hour cruise passes beneath the Golden Gate Bridge and comes within yards of Alcatraz Island. For the best experience, don a jacket, bring the camera, and make sure it's a clear day. Frequent daily departures from PIER 39's West Marina begin at 10:45am on weekdays, at 10am on weekends and holidays during winter months; and at 10am daily in the summer. Tickets cost $20 for adults, $16 for seniors over 62 and juniors 12 to 18, and $12 for children 5 to 11; children under 5 are admitted free. Tickets ordered by phone are an extra $2.25; discounts are available online at blueandgoldfleet.com.

The **Red & White Fleet,** Pier 43½ (ⓒ **415/447-0597;** www.redandwhite.com), offers daily Bay Cruises tours that leave from Pier 43½. The tour boats cruise along the city waterfront, beneath the Golden Gate Bridge, past Angel Island, and around Alcatraz. Narrations are available in eight languages. Prices are $21 for adults, $17 for seniors and teens 12 to 17, and $13 for children 5 to 11. Online purchases are discounted.

## 8 Golden Gate National Recreation Area & the Presidio

## GOLDEN GATE NATIONAL RECREATION AREA

One could easily contend that no urban shoreline is as stunning as San Francisco's. Wrapping around the northern and western edges of the city, the Golden Gate National Recreation Area is run by the National Park Service, which lets visitors fully enjoy it as a park. Several landmarks line the shore, from which visitors have views of both the bay and the ocean. Muni runs service to most sites, including Aquatic Park, the Cliff House, and Ocean Beach. For more information, see "Outdoor Pursuits," below, or contact the **National Park Service** (© 415/561-4700).

Here's a brief rundown of the park's major features, starting at the northern section and moving westward around the coast:

**Aquatic Park,** adjacent to the Hyde Street Pier, is a small swimming beach, although it's not that appealing and the water is unbearably cold.

**Fort Mason Center** runs from Bay Street to the shoreline and encompasses several buildings and piers used during World War II. Today, a variety of museums, theaters, and organizations occupies the complex. **Greens Restaurant** (p. 112) is among the best, affording views of the Golden Gate Bridge. For information on Fort Mason Center events, call © 415/441-5706.

Farther west along the bay, at the northern end of Fillmore, **Marina Green** is an optimum spot for flying kites or watching the sailboats on the bay. Next stop along the bay is the St. Francis Yacht Club and the start of the paved, 3.5-mile **Golden Gate Promenade,** a favorite biking-and-hiking path defining the outer limits of the Presidio (see below). The path leads to the fantastic, recently reestablished marshland preserve **Crissy Field,** the city's latest favorite playground. Make a point of seeing this spectacular destination, complete with sandy beach, lots of native birds, and jogging paths.

A national historic site under the Golden Gate Bridge, **Fort Point** (© 415/556-1693) was built in 1853 to protect the entrance to the harbor. Film buffs will recognize it from Alfred Hitchcock's *Vertigo.* During the Civil War, 140 men and 90 pieces of artillery armed the brick fort to prevent a Confederate takeover of California. Rangers in Civil War regalia lead regular tours and sometimes fire the old cannons.

**Lincoln Boulevard** sweeps around the western edge of the bay to two of the city's most popular beaches. **Baker Beach,** a small, beautiful strand where the waves roll ashore. A fine spot for sunbathing, walking, or fishing, it's packed on sunny days; you'll likely see some nude sunbathers here. Because of the cold water and roaring currents that pour from the bay twice daily, swimming here is risky for all but the most competent. Here you can pick up the **Coastal Trail,** which leads through the Presidio (see below). A short distance from Baker, **China Beach** is a small cove where swimming is permitted. Changing rooms, showers, a sun deck, and restrooms are available.

A little farther around the coast, **Land's End** looks out to Pyramid Rock. A lower and an upper trail provide varied hiking options amid wind-swept cypress trees and pines on the cliffs above the Pacific.

**Point Lobos,** the **Sutro Baths,** and the **Cliff House** lie still farther along the coast. The latter, slated to undergo renovation in the coming year, has been serving refreshments to visitors since 1863. Here you can view the **Seal Rocks,** home to a colony of sea lions and marine birds. Only traces of the Sutro Baths remain today, northeast of the Cliff House. This popular swimming facility accommodated as many as 24,000 people before it burned down in 1966. A little farther inland, at the western end of California Street, **Lincoln Park** is home to a golf course and the Palace of the Legion of Honor.

From the Cliff House, the Esplanade continues south along the 4-mile-long **Ocean Beach,** which is unsuitable for swimming. At the southern end of Ocean Beach, around **Fort Funston,** an easy loop trail runs across the cliffs; for information, call the ranger station (© **415/239-2366**). Here, too, you can watch the hang gliders taking advantage of the high cliffs and strong winds.

Farther south along I-280, **Sweeney Ridge** is accessible only by car but affords sweeping views of the coastline from the many trails that crisscross these 1,000 acres of land. From here, in 1769, the expedition led by Don Gaspar de Portolá first laid eyes on San Francisco Bay. In Pacifica, the ridge is accessible via Sneath Lane off Highway 35 (Skyline Blvd.) in San Bruno.

## THE PRESIDIO

When the U.S. Army transferred the Presidio to the National Park Service in 1994, it became one of a handful of urban national parks that combine historical, architectural, and natural elements—not to mention a formerly private golf course and a home for George Lucas's production company—into one arboreal expanse.

These 1,480 acres include a variety of terrain, such as coastal scrub, dunes, and prairie grasslands that shelter many rare plants and more than 150 bird species, some of which nest here. The property also encompasses more than 350 historic buildings and a national cemetery. The National Park Service operates walking and biking tours around the Presidio, including the 2-mile **Ecology Loop Trail** through some of the Presidio's 60,000 trees, such as redwoods, spruce, cypress, and acacias; and the 2.5-mile **Coastal Trail,** from the bluff top from Baker Beach to the southern base of the Golden Gate Bridge. Reservations are required.

A former airfield, **Crissy Field** in recent years has become known as a hot arena for California's windsurfers. Between March and October, hundreds come to ply the waters, as well as to see and be seen. The beach affords easy water access and plenty of room to rig up, but is not recommended for the inexperienced. Crissy Field is also a popular route for joggers circuiting the Marina District to Fort Point and back, with great picnic spots and a sweet cafe along the path to Fort Funston. A pier at the west end of Crissy Field is popular for fishing and crabbing.

The Presidio is currently undergoing major changes so that it may pay for its upkeep. For schedules, maps, and updates on ongoing developments, the best source is the **Golden Gate National Recreation Area Headquarters** at Fort Mason, Building 102, San Francisco, CA 94123 (© **415/561-4700**). For additional information, call the **Presidio Visitor Center** at © **415/561-4323.** Take the no. 28, 45, 76, or 82X bus.

## 9 Outdoor Pursuits

The prime places for recreational activities in San Francisco were described earlier in this chapter. See "The Top Attractions" (p. 117) for a complete description of Golden Gate Park, and "Golden Gate National Recreation Area & the Presidio," above, for complete details on these sites.

**BEACHES**    Only two beaches in San Francisco are safe for swimming: **Aquatic Park,** a patch of sand adjacent to the Hyde Park Pier, and **China Beach,** a small cove on the western edge of the South Bay. Even here, you must dip in at your own risk; no lifeguards monitor the painfully cold waters.

**Baker Beach,** a small, beautiful strand outside the Golden Gate, has strong currents that rule out swimming, but it's still great for sunning, walking, or fishing. You'll climb down a long flight of stairs from the street to reach the sand. It's wonderful to sit here with a prime view of the bridge on a sunny day.

**Ocean Beach,** at the end of Golden Gate Park, on the westernmost side of the city, is San Francisco's largest beach, at 4 miles long. Shorebirds and a large colony of barking sea lions inhabit the jagged Seal Rocks offshore at the beach's northern end, in front of the Cliff House. Bring binoculars for a close-up view. Ocean Beach is for strolling or sunning, but don't swim here—tides are tricky, and bathers and surfers drown every year in the rough waters.

**BICYCLING**    The Recreation and Parks Department maintains two city-designated bike routes. One winds for 7½ miles through Golden Gate Park to Lake Merced; the other traverses the city, starting in the south and continuing over the Golden Gate Bridge. The San Francisco Visitor Information Center and bike shops all around town provide route maps.

A massive new seawall—constructed to buffer Ocean Beach from storm-driven waves—doubles as a public walk and bikeway along 5 waterfront blocks of the Great Highway, between Noriega and Santiago streets. It's an easy ride from the Cliff House or Golden Gate Park.

The Presidio also affords great biking, and you can venture from there across the Golden Gate Bridge and into the Marin hills.

**Avenue Cyclery** at 756 Stanyan St., at Waller Street (© **415/387-3155**), rents bikes for $5 per hour or $25 per day. The shop is open daily April through September from 10am to 7pm, and October through March from 10am to 6pm.

**CITY STAIR-CLIMBING**    You don't need a StairMaster in San Francisco. The **Filbert Street Steps,** 377 of them between Sansome Street and Telegraph Hill, scale the eastern face of Telegraph Hill, from Sansome and Filbert past 19th-century cottages and lush gardens. Napier Lane, a wooden plank walkway, leads to Montgomery Street. Turn right and follow the path to the end of the cul-de-sac, where another stairway continues to Telegraph's panoramic summit.

Another historic stairway street, the **Lyon Street Steps,** between Green Street and Broadway, comprise four steep sets of stairs, totaling 288 steps. Begin at Green Street and climb all the way up, past manicured hedges and flower gardens, to an iron gate that opens into the Presidio. A block east, on Baker Street, another set of 369 steps descends to Green Street.

**GOLF**    **Golden Gate Park Golf Course,** 47th Avenue and Fulton Street (© **415/751-8987;** www.goldengateparkgolf.com), is a 9-hole, par-27 course over 1,357 yards. All holes are par 3, tightly set, and well trapped with small greens. Greens fees are very reasonable: $13 per person Monday through Friday, and $17 Saturday and Sunday. The course is open daily from 6:30am to dusk.

**Lincoln Park Golf Course,** 34th Avenue and Clement Street (© **415/221-9911**), San Francisco's prettiest municipal course, has terrific views and fairways lined with Monterey cypress trees. Its 18 holes encompass 5,081 yards, for a par 68. Greens fees are $31 per person Monday through Friday, and $35 Saturday and Sunday, with rates decreasing after 2pm. The course is open daily from daybreak to dusk.

**Presidio Golf Course** (© **415/561-4664;** www.presidiogolf.com), one of the city's finest, charges $42 Monday through Thursday, $52 on Friday, and $72 Saturday and Sunday; carts are included and rates decrease later in the day.

**SKATING**   Although people skate in Golden Gate Park all week, Sunday is best, when John F. Kennedy Drive, between Kezar Drive and Transverse Road, is closed to cars. Check out the disco skaters who congregate near the Eighth Avenue park entrance.

## 10 Shopping

Store hours vary, but most are open Monday through Saturday from 10am to 6pm, and Sunday from noon to 5pm. Most department stores stay open later, as do shops around Fisherman's Wharf. Sales tax in San Francisco is 8.5%. If you live out of state and buy an expensive item, consider asking the store to ship it home for you. You'll have to pay for transport, but you'll evade the sales tax.

**UNION SQUARE & ENVIRONS**   San Francisco's most popular, congested shopping mecca centers around Union Square. Most of the big department stores and many high-end specialty shops are in this area. Be sure to venture to Grant Avenue, Post and Sutter streets, and Maiden Lane.

If you're into art, pick up *The San Francisco Gallery Guide,* a comprehensive, bimonthly publication listing the city's current shows (most of which are downtown). It's available free by mail; send a self-addressed stamped envelope to San Francisco Bay Area Gallery Guide, 1369 Fulton St., San Francisco, CA 94117 (© **415/921-1600**). You can also pick one up at the San Francisco Visitor Information Center at 900 Market St. (at Powell St.).

One of my favorite galleries is the **Catharine Clark Gallery,** on the second floor at 49 Geary St., between Kearny and Grant streets (© **415/399-1439;** www.cclark gallery.com). It exhibits the work of up-and-coming, pop culture–inspired artists (mainly from California), and nurtures novice collectors through an unusual, interest-free purchasing plan.

Century-old **Gump's,** 135 Post St., between Kearny Street and Grant Avenue (© **415/982-1616;** www.gumps.com), is a must-visit. A virtual treasure trove of household items and gifts, the shop purveys a collection of Asian antiquities, contemporary art glass, exquisite jade and pearl jewelry, and more. Unfortunately, staff members can often be stuffy.

Music aficionados will revel in **Virgin Megastore,** 2 Stockton St., at Market Street (© **415/397-4525**), with thousands of CDs (including an impressive collection of imports), videos, laser discs, and a multimedia department. Its literary equivalent is nearby **Borders Books & Music,** 400 Post St., at Powell (© **415/399-1633**), with thousands of titles and a cafe.

While the department stores have plenty of clothes, real fashion fiends will want to check out the boutiques. For men, **Cable Car Clothiers,** 200 Bush St., at Sansome Street (© **415/397-4740**), is popular for traditional attire, such as three-button suits with natural shoulders, Aquascutum coats, McGeorge sweaters, and Atkinson ties.

**Wilkes Bashford,** 375 Sutter St., at Stockton Street (© **415/986-4380**), is one of the most well-known, expensive clothing boutiques in the city, with fashions for both sexes. It stocks only the finest clothes (often worn by former mayor Willie Brown and current Mayor Gavin Newsom), including men's Kiton and Brioni suits (some of the most expensive in the world, at $2,500 and up).

For fabulous, expensive women's fashions, check out **Métier,** 355 Sutter St., between Grant and Stockton streets (© **415/989-5395;** www.metiersf.com). Its inventory of European ready-to-wear lines is in the best taste; featured designers include Italian designer Anna Molinari Hache and Blue Marine, as well as a distinguished collection of antique-style, high-end jewelry from L.A.'s Cathy Waterman and ultrapopular custom-designed poetry jewelry by Jeanine Payer.

**SOMA**   Although this area is too big and shops are too scattered to be suitable for strolling, you'll find good discount shopping, along with a few great regular retail shops, in warehouse spaces south of Market. Most major hotels carry discount-shopping guides. Many buses pass through this area, including nos. 9, 12, 14, 15, 19, 26, 27, 30, 42, 45, and 76.

The **SFMOMA MuseumStore,** 151 Third St., 2 blocks south of Market Street, across from Yerba Buena Gardens (© 415/357-4035; www.sfmoma.org), is a favorite among locals. The shop's art cards and books, as well as jewelry, housewares, and knickknacks are well designed. For visitors, the San Francisco mementos here are much more tasteful than those sold in Fisherman's Wharf.

Fashionable bargain hunters head to **Jeremys,** 2 S. Park, at Second Street between Bryant and Brannan streets (© 415/882-4929; www.jeremys.com), where top designer fashions, from shoes to suits, sell at rock-bottom prices. Another worthy stop is the **Wine Club San Francisco,** 953 Harrison St., between 5th and 6th streets (© 415/512-9086), with bargain prices on more than 1,200 domestic and foreign wines; bottles run from $4 to $1,100.

**HAYES VALLEY**   Most neighborhoods cater to either trendy or conservative shoppers, but lower Hayes Street, between Octavia and Gough, celebrates anything vintage, artistic, and funky. Although the neighborhood is still in transition, it's definitely the most interesting place to shop—with modern and retro furniture stores, trendy shoe stores, and hip men's and women's clothiers. For fashionable classic clothing for men and women check out **MAC,** 387 Grove St., at Gough Street (© 415/863-3011). Nearby, **R.A.G.,** 541 Octavia St. at Hayes Street (© 415/621-7718; www.ragsf.com) showcases very affordable trendy fashions from upcoming local designers. My contemporary favorite furniture store, **Propeller,** 555 Hayes St., between Laguna and Octavia streets (© 415/701-7767; www.propeller-sf.com) is here, too. Lots of great antiques shops are south on Octavia and on nearby Market Street. Bus lines include nos. 16AX, 16BX, and 21.

If you're afflicted with a shoe fetish, check out **Bulo,** 437A Hayes St., at Gough Street (© 415/864-3244; www.buloshoes.com). Their Italian men's and women's shoes run the gamut from casual to dressy, reserved to wildly funky. **Gimme Shoes,** 416 Hayes St. (© 415/864-0691; www.gimmeshoes.com), is ultrahip but expensive. Ferret out the sale items unless you're ready to drop around $200 per pair.

**THE CASTRO**   You could spend a day wandering the Castro's housewares and men's clothing shops. Buses serving the area are nos. 8, 24, 33, 35, and 37.

**Citizen Clothing,** 536 Castro St., between 18th and 19th streets (© 415/575-3560), is a popular shop for stylish casual clothing.

**Joseph Schmidt Confections,** 3489 16th St., at Sanchez Street (© 415/861-8682; www.josephschmidtconfections.com), adds another dimension to designer chocolate: Sinfully luscious sweets take on sculptural shapes so exquisite you'll be reluctant to bite into them. Prices are remarkably reasonable.

**CHESTNUT STREET**   Parallel to Union Street, a few blocks north, Chestnut likewise has endless shopping and dining choices—as well as a population of superfit, postgraduate singles who hang around cafes and eye each other. The area is serviced by bus lines 22, 28, 30, 41, 42, 43, and 76.

**FISHERMAN'S WHARF & ENVIRONS**   The tourist-oriented malls—Ghirardelli Square, PIER 39, the Cannery at Del Monte Square, and the Anchorage—run along Jefferson Street and include hundreds of shops, restaurants, and attractions. That said, they're not particularly impressive.

Locals tend to avoid this part of town, but do venture to **Cost Plus World Market,** 2552 Taylor St., between North Point and Bay streets (© 415/928-6200), a vast warehouse crammed to the rafters with Chinese baskets, Indian camel bells, Malaysian batik scarves, innumerable items from Algeria to Zanzibar, and a decent wine section. Adjoining is a **Barnes & Noble** "superstore," at 2550 Taylor St., between Bay and North Point (© 415/292-6762).

**FILLMORE STREET**   Some of the best women's clothes shopping in town is packed into 5 blocks of Fillmore Street in Pacific Heights, from Jackson to Sutter streets. This area is also the perfect place to grab a bite and peruse the boutiques, crafts shops, and housewares stores. It's serviced by bus lines 1, 2, 3, 4, 12, 22, and 24.

One of my favorite stops is **Zinc Details,** 1905 Fillmore St., between Bush and Pine streets (© 415/776-2100; www.zincdetails.com). They ply an amazing collection of modern and contemporary handcrafted glass vases, pendant lights, ceramics, and furniture.

**HAIGHT STREET**   Green hair, spiked hair, no hair, or mohair—even the hippies look conservative next to Haight Street's dramatic fashion freaks. The shopping in the 6 blocks of upper Haight Street, between Central Avenue and Stanyan Street, reflects its clientele and offers everything from incense to furniture and from European street styles to vintage and übertrendy clothing and shoes—all at reasonable prices. Bus lines 7, 66, 71, and 73 run down Haight Street. The Muni Metro N line stops at Waller Street and at Cole Street.

**Recycled Records,** 1377 Haight St., between Central and Masonic streets (© 415/626-4075; www.recycled-records.com), is easily one of the best used-record stores in the city. This loud shop has a good selection of promotional CDs, and cases of used classic rock LPs. You can also buy sheet music, tour programs, and old *TV Guides* here.

**NORTH BEACH**   Grant and Columbus avenues cater to their hip clientele with great coffee shops and a small but worthy selection of boutiques and specialty shops. You can pick up a great gift for yourself or anyone else at **Biordi Art Imports,** 412 Columbus Ave., at Vallejo Street (© 415/392-8096; www.biordi.com). Its Italian Majolica pottery is both exquisite and unique. Join the funky literary types who browse **City Lights Booksellers & Publishers,** 261 Columbus Ave., at Broadway (© 415/362-8193; www.citylights.com), the famous bookstore owned by Beat poet Lawrence Ferlinghetti. The shelves here are stocked with a comprehensive collection of art, poetry, and political paperbacks, as well as more mainstream books.

## 11 San Francisco After Dark

For up-to-date nightlife information, turn to the *San Francisco Weekly* and the *San Francisco Bay Guardian,* which contain comprehensive, current listings. They're free at bars and restaurants, and from street-corner boxes around the city. *Where,* a free tourist monthly, also details programs and performance times; it's available in most fine hotels. The Sunday edition of the *San Francisco Chronicle* also features a "Datebook" section, on pink paper, with information and listings.

**GETTING TICKETS**   **Tix Bay Area** (℅ 415/433-7827; www.tixbayarea.org) sells half-price tickets to theater, dance, and music performances on the day of the show only; tickets for Sunday and Monday events, if available, are sold on Saturday and Sunday. Tix also peddles advance, full-price tickets for most performance halls, sporting events, concerts, and clubs. They levy a service fee, from $2 to $5, on each ticket, payable by American Express, MasterCard, and Visa. Tix, located on Powell Street between Geary and Post, is open Tuesday through Thursday from 11am to 6pm, Friday and Saturday from 11am to 7pm, and Sunday from 11am to 3pm. Tickets to most theater and dance events are available through **City Box Office,** 180 Redwood St., Suite 100, between Golden Gate and McAllister streets off Van Ness Avenue (℅ 415/ 392-4400; www.cityboxoffice.com). MasterCard and Visa are accepted.

**Tickets.com** (℅ 415/478-2277 or 510/762-2277; www.tickets.com) sells computer-generated tickets to concerts, sporting events, plays, and special events. Beware, though, that this service imposes a hefty service charge of $3 to $19 per ticket. Call for the local office nearest you.

For information on local theater, check out **www.bayareatheatre.org**.

## THE PERFORMING ARTS

**American Conservatory Theater (A.C.T.)**   A.C.T. made its debut in 1967 and quickly established itself as the city's premier resident theater group. The highly venerated troupe has been compared to the superb British National Theatre, the Berliner Ensemble, and the Comédie Française. The A.C.T. season runs September through July and features both classical and experimental works. Performing at the Geary Theater, 415 Geary St. (at Mason St.). ℅ 415/749-2ACT. www.act-sfbay.org. Tickets $11–$68.

**The Magic Theatre**   After nurturing the talents of luminary playwrights such as Sam Shepard, whose Pulitzer Prize–winning *Buried Child* premiered here, the acclaimed Magic Theatre continues its commitment to the work of new writers. The season usually runs from October through July, with performances Tuesday through Sunday. At Building D, Fort Mason Center, Marina Blvd. (at Buchanan St.). ℅ 415/441-8822. www. magictheatre.org. Tickets $20–$53. Discounts for students and seniors.

**Philharmonia Baroque Orchestra**   This "early music" orchestra performs throughout the Bay Area. The season runs from September to April. At Herbst Theater, 401 Van Ness Ave. ℅ 415/392-4400 (box office) or 415/252-1288 (administrative offices). www. philharmonia.org. Tickets $28–$62.

**San Francisco Ballet**   Founded in 1933, the San Francisco Ballet is the oldest professional ballet company in the United States and one of the country's finest, with an eclectic repertoire of full-length, neoclassical, and contemporary ballets. The season runs February through May; the company performs *The Nutcracker* in late November through most of December. The San Francisco Ballet Orchestra accompanies all performances. War Memorial Opera House, 301 Van Ness Ave. (at Grove St.). ℅ 415/865-2000 for tickets and information. Tickets $10–$165.

**San Francisco Opera**   The second municipal opera in the United States, the San Francisco Opera is one of the city's cultural icons. All productions have English supertitles. The season starts in September, lasts 14 weeks, takes a break for a few months, then picks up again in June and July. During the interim winter period, future opera stars are featured in showcases and recitals. Performances are held most evenings, except Monday, with matinees on Sundays. Tickets go on sale as early as June for subscribers, and in August for the general public. The best seats sell out quickly, but unless Domingo is in town, some less-coveted seats are usually available until curtain time. War Memorial Opera House, 301 Van Ness Ave. (at Grove St.). ℭ **415/864-3330** (box office). www. sfopera.com. Tickets $24–$235. Standing room $10 (no credit cards).

**San Francisco Symphony** Founded in 1911, the internationally respected San Francisco Symphony has long been an important part of this city's cultural life, under legendary conductors such as Pierre Monteux and Seiji Ozawa. In 1995, Michael Tilson Thomas took over from Herbert Blomstedt and has led the orchestra to new heights, crafting an exciting repertoire of classical and modern music. The season runs September through June. Tickets are hard to come by, but you can usually find someone trying to sell their tickets, outside the theater, on the night of the show. At Davies Symphony Hall, 201 Van Ness Ave. (at Grove St.). ℭ **415/864-6000** (box office). www.sfsymphony.org. Tickets $12–$103.

## COMEDY & CABARET

**Beach Blanket Babylon** *(Moments)* Now a San Francisco tradition, *Beach Blanket Babylon* is best known for its outrageous costumes and oversize headdresses. It's been playing almost 32 years, and nearly every performance still sells out. It's wise to write for tickets at least 3 weeks in advance, or buy them through Tix (ℭ **415/433-7827**). At Club Fugazi, Beach Blanket Babylon Blvd., 678 Green St. (between Powell St. and Columbus Ave.). ℭ **415/421-4222**. Tickets $25–$75.

## THE CLUB & MUSIC SCENE

### ROCK & BLUES CLUBS

**Biscuits & Blues** This basement-cum-supper-club is the best place in town for the blues—with its crisp, booming sound system (ear plugs are a requisite); its New Orleans–speakeasy appeal (though it's perfectly legal); and live entertainment nightly. 401 Mason St. (at Geary St.). ℭ **415/292-2583**. www.biscuitsandblues.com. Cover $5–$20.

**Cafe du Nord** *(Finds)* In operation since 1907, this restaurant club rightfully proclaims itself as the place for a "slightly lurid indie pop scene set in a beautiful old speakeasy." The club draws a diverse mix of typically younger patrons to dine on American fare, listen to live music in the back room, and crowd the front-room bar. 2170 Market St. (at Sanchez St.). ℭ **415/861-5016**.

**Lou's Pier 47 Club** You won't find many locals in the place, but Lou's is still good, old-fashioned fun. It's a casual spot with Cajun seafood (downstairs) and live blues

---

*Tips* **Teatro ZinZanni**

Hungry for dinner and a damned good time? It ain't cheap, but Teatro ZinZanni makes for a rollicking ride—purveying food, drama, song, and whimsy within an elegant, 1926 tent on the Embarcadero. Part musical theater and part comedy, the 3½-hour show includes a four-course meal served by dozens of performers who incorporate audience members and astounding physical acts (think Cirque du Soleil) into their wacky, playful world. Shows are Wednesday through Sunday, and tickets are $110 to $135 including dinner. The tent is at Pier 29 on the Embarcadero at Battery Street. Call ℭ **415/438-2668** or visit www.teatrozinzanni.org for more details.

bands (upstairs). Patrons who are primarily on vacation make the place one of the more, um, jovial spots near the wharf. They charge a $3 to $5 cover to hear live music between 4 and 7pm; and a $5 to $10 cover for shows at 8pm, 9pm, midnight, and 1am. 300 Jefferson St. (at Jones St.). ✆ 415/771-5687. www.louspier47.com. Cover $5–$10.

**Pier 23** Embarcadero's Pier 23 is an anchor for local party people. Part ramshackle patio spot, part dance floor, with a heavy dash of dive bar, it's all about fun at this well-worn box of a restaurant and tented patio with a startlingly diverse clientele. By day, it's a prime sunny-day social spot for white collars, but on weekends, it's a straight-up people zoo, where patrons of every age and persuasion coexist more peacefully than the cast in a McDonald's commercial. Expect to boogie down shoulder-to-shoulder to live bands playing blues or funk. Pier 23, at the Embarcadero and Greenwich St. ✆ 415/362-5125. www.pier23cafe.com. Cover $5 to $8 during performances.

## JAZZ CLUBS

**Jazz at Pearl's** One of the best venues for jazz in the city, this place serves ribs and chicken with the sounds, too. Prices range from $6 to $14, and live jams last until 1:30am nightly. 256 Columbus Ave. (at Broadway). ✆ 415/291-8255. www.jazzatpearls.com. No cover. 2-drink minimum.

## DANCE CLUBS

**Nickie's Bar-be-cue** Don't come here for dinner; the only hot thing you'll find is the small, crowded dance floor. But don't let that stop you from checking it out. Every time I visit, old-school hits are playing full force, casually dressed dancers are losing all inhibitions, and all types of friendly San Franciscans are mixing in the crowd. This place is perpetually hot, so dress accordingly. And don't expect to pay for top-shelf liquors by credit card; it's beer, wine, and cash only. 460 Haight St. (between Fillmore and Webster sts.). ✆ 415/621-6508. www.nickies.com. Cover $5.

**Paradise Lounge** Labyrinthine Paradise features three dance floors that vibrate simultaneously to different beats. Smaller, auxiliary spaces host private parties, with rentable tables, and poetry readings. Open Thursday through Saturday only. Dress code enforced. 1501 Folsom St. (at 11th St.). ✆ 415/621-1911. www.paradiselounge.com. Cover $5–$20.

**Ruby Skye** Downtown's most glamorous and gigantic nightspot is aglitter thanks to a dramatic renovation and the addition of killer light and sound systems within the 1890s Victorian playhouse previously known as The Stage Door. Inside, hundreds of partiers boogie on the ballroom floor, mingle on the mezzanine, and puff freely in the smoking room while DJs or live music bring the dancing house down Thursday through Saturday. Big spenders should book the VIP lounge, which offers a glitzy place to kick it, and bird's-eye views of the whole club scene. 420 Mason St. (between Geary and Post sts.). ✆ 415/693-0777. www.rubyskye.com. Cover $10–$25.

## SUPPER CLUBS

In San Francisco, if you can eat dinner, listen to live music, and dance in the same room, it's a supper club.

**Harry Denton's Starlight Room** Come dressed to the nines or in casual attire to this old-fashioned cocktail lounge turned nightclub, where tourists and locals sip drinks at sunset and boogie down to live '70s and '80s music, Motown covers, jazz, and funk Friday through Tuesday nights; live salsa on Thursday nights; and the DJs' hip hop and Top-40 tunes after dark on Wednesdays. The room is classic 1930s San Francisco, with red-velvet banquettes, chandeliers, and fabulous views. Crowds of all ages come for a night of drinking and unrestrained dancing. Atop the Sir Francis Drake hotel, 450 Powell St., 21st floor. ℂ **415/395-8595.** www.harrydenton.com. Cover $10 Wed after 7pm; $10 Thurs–Fri after 8pm; $15 Sat after 8pm.

## DESTINATION BARS WITH DJ GROOVES

**Bambuddha Lounge** *Finds* The hottest place for the young and the trendy to feast, flirt, and be fabulous is this restaurant/bar adjoining the funky-cool Phoenix Hotel. It's an "it" joint of the moment—with a 20-foot reclining Buddha on the roof, ultra-modern San Francisco–meets–Southeast Asian decor, inexpensive Southeast Asian cuisine served late into the night, and a state-of-the-art sound system streaming ambient, down-tempo, soul, funk, and house music. 601 Eddy St. (at Larkin St.). ℂ **415/885-5088.** www.bambuddhalounge.com. Cover $5–$10 Thurs–Sat.

**The Bliss Bar** Surprisingly trendy for sleepy, family-oriented Noe Valley, this small, stylish, and friendly bar is a great place to stop for a varied mix of locals, colorful cocktail concoctions, and a DJ spinning at the front window from 9pm to 2am every night except Monday. Take your cocktail into the too-cool back Blue Room, if it's open. And if you're on a budget, stop by from 4:30 to 7pm when martinis, lemon drops, cosmos, watermelon cosmos, and apple martinis are $4. 4026 24th St. (between Noe and Castro sts.) ℂ **415/826-6200.** www.blissbarsf.com.

**Levende Lounge** A fusion of great food and cocktails, 2004's hottest Mission addition was recently voted best bar for singles, romance, bar food, and a slew of other accolades by CitySearch.com. And chef Jamie Lauren was chosen as one of the city's Rising Star Chefs of 2005 by the *San Francisco Chronicle.* Drop in early for a meal of California-style tapas (small plates). Later, management switches the tables for lounge furnishings, for late-night noshing and grooving. *Tip:* A cover is charged on some nights, but you can avoid the fee with a dinner reservation; food is served until 11pm. 1710 Mission St. (at Duboce St.). ℂ **415/864-5585.** www.levendesf.com.

**The Monkey Club** Casual and tucked away in a quiet section of the Mission, this hip local bar draws mostly 20- and 30-somethings. It's an ever-fun, rather red spot to kick back on plush, comfy couches backed by giant picture windows; nibble on decent, inexpensive appetizers; and down stiff drinks while a DJ spins grooving house, jazz, and world music It's open Wednesday through Sunday. 2730 21st St. (at Bryant St.). ℂ **415/647-6546.**

**Wish Bar** This somewhat mellow, narrow bar, in the popular night-crawler area around 11th and Folsom streets, promises flirtation, fun, and a very attractive staff. Swathed in burgundy and black, with exposed cinderblock walls and cement floors, the place glows with candlelight and red-shaded sconces. With a bar in the front, DJ spinning upbeat lounge music in the back, and cushy leather couch seating in between, it's often packed with a surprisingly diverse (albeit youthful) crowd, and ever filled with eye candy. 1539 Folsom St. (between 11th and 12th sts.). ℂ **415/278-9474.** www.wishsf.com.

## RETRO CLUB

**Club Deluxe** Deluxe and its fedora-wearing patrons had been celebrating the 1940s era for years before it became a citywide trend. Fortunately, even with all the popular retro-hype, the vibe here hasn't changed. Expect a mix of throwbacks and generic San Franciscans in the intimate bar and adjoining lounge, and live jazz or swing most nights. Although many regulars dress the part, they don't have an attitude about it, so come as you like. 1511 Haight St. (corner of Ashbury St.). ℂ **415/552-6949**. www.clubdeluxesf.com.

## THE BAR SCENE

Finding your idea of a comfortable bar has a lot to do with picking a neighborhood filled with your kind of people and investigating the vicinity. San Francisco has hundreds of bars, and although many are obscurely located, beyond clearly defined neighborhood boundaries, the following list is an attempt to classify bar crowds by district:

- **Chestnut and Union Street** bars tend to attract a post-collegiate crowd.
- Young alternatives and hipsters frequent **Mission District** haunts.
- **Upper Haight** caters to eccentric neighborhood cocktailers.
- **Lower Haight** is skate- and snowboarder grungy.
- Tourists mix with theatergoers and businesspeople **downtown.**
- **North Beach** serves all types.
- **Castro** caters to gay locals and tourists.
- **South of Market (SoMa)** draws a mixed crowd.

### WINE BARS

**The Bubble Lounge** Toasting the town is a nightly event at this two-level champagne bar. With 300 champagnes (around 30 by the glass), brick walls, couches, and velvet curtains, this fizzy lounge has plenty of pop. 714 Montgomery St. (at Columbus Ave.). ℂ **415/434-4204**. www.bubblelounge.com.

**First Crush** If you're staying downtown and want to sip through regional specialties, stop by this wine-centric restaurant and bar. The food is "progressive American" and the wine list includes an outstanding selection of California vintages, including three dozen excellent choices by the glass. 101 Cyril Magnin St. (aka Fifth St. just north of Market, at Ellis St.). ℂ**415/982-7874**. www.firstcrush.com.

**Nectar Wine Lounge** Catering to the Marina's young and beautiful, this ultrahip place to sip—and snack—pours an exciting and well-edited wine selection (plus 800 choices by the bottle) along with creative small plates (pairings optional). Industrial-slick decor includes cube chairs, a long bar, and lounge areas that are often packed with 20- through 40-somethings. 3330 Steiner St. (at Chestnut St.). ℂ **415/345-1377**. www.nectar winelounge.com.

### OTHER BARS

**Spec's** An incognito location on Saroyan Place (a tiny alley at 250 Columbus Ave.), makes Spec's less of a walk-in bar and more of a lively locals hangout. Funky decor—maritime flags hanging from the ceiling, exposed-brick walls lined with posters and photos—lend it plenty of character. A "museum," displayed under glass, contains memorabilia and items brought back by seamen who drop in between sails, and the clientele is funky enough to keep you entertained while you drink a beer. 12 Saroyan Place (off Columbus Ave.). ℂ **415/421-4112**.

**The Tonga Room & Hurricane Bar** *Finds* It's kitschy as all get out, but there's no denying the goofy Polynesian pleasures of the Fairmont Hotel's tropical oasis. Drop in and join the crowds for an umbrella drink, a simulated thunderstorm and downpour, and a heavy dose of whimsy (which escapes most San Francisco establishments). If you're on a budget, stop by for the weekday happy hour from 5 to 7pm, when you can graze at the all-you-can-eat bar-grub buffet (chicken wings, chow mein, potstickers) for $7 and the cost of one drink. Settle in and you'll catch live top-40s music after 8pm, when a $3 to $5 cover charge takes effect. In the Fairmont Hotel, 950 Mason St. (at California St.). ℂ 415/772-5278. www.tongaroom.com.

**Toronado**   Lower Haight isn't exactly a charming street, but for the beer aficionado it's heaven—thanks to the 50-plus microbrews on tap and 100 bottled beers served in this dark, casual, cool bar. The brooding atmosphere matches the surroundings: an aluminum bar, a few tall tables, dark lighting, and a back room packed with tables and chairs. Happy hour runs 11:30am to 6pm daily, with $1 off draft beers. 547 Haight St. (at Fillmore St.). ℂ 415/863-2276. www.toronado.com.

**Tosca** *Finds*   Open Tuesday through Sunday from 5pm to 2am, Tosca is a low-key, spacious, popular watering hole for local politicos, writers, media types, visiting celebrities (such as Johnny Depp and Nicolas Cage), and other cognoscenti. With dim lights, red leather booths, and high ceilings, it's everything you'd expect an old, North Beach legend to be. 242 Columbus Ave. (between Broadway and Pacific Ave.). ℂ 415/986-9651.

**Vesuvio**   Along Jack Kerouac Alley across from the City Lights Bookstore, this beatnik hangout isn't just riding its historic reputation. Popular with writers, artists, songsters, and wannabes, Vesuvio is crowded with self-proclaimed philosophers, along with everyone else from longshoremen and cab drivers to businesspeople. 255 Columbus Ave. (at Broadway). ℂ 415/362-3370.

### BREWPUBS

**San Francisco Brewing Company**   The bar is one of the city's few remaining old saloons, aglow with stained-glass windows, tile floors, skylights, a mahogany bar and, running the length of the bar, a massive overhead fan—a bizarre contraption crafted from brass and palm fronds. Menu items range from $3.70 (for *edamame*, or soybeans) to $20 for a full rack of baby back ribs with all the fixings. The happy-hour special, a dollar per 8.5-ounce microbrew beer (or $2.50 a pint), runs daily from 4 to 6pm and midnight to 1am. 155 Columbus Ave. (at Pacific St.). ℂ 415/434-3344. www.sfbrewing.com.

**Thirsty Bear Brewing Company**   Seven superb, handcrafted varieties of beer are always on tap at this stylish brick edifice with high ceilings. The Spanish food is excellent too. Upstairs, patrons can play pool or darts and hear live flamenco music on Sunday nights. 661 Howard St. (1 block east of the Moscone Center). ℂ 415/974-0905. www.thirstybear.com.

### COCKTAILS WITH A VIEW

In addition to these options, see p. 137 for a full review of **Harry Denton's Starlight Room.**

**The Carnelian Room**   On the 52nd floor of the Bank of America building, the Carnelian Room offers uninterrupted views of the city. From a window-front table, you feel as if you can reach out, pluck up the TransAmerica Pyramid, and stir your martini with it. *Note:* The restaurant has the most extensive wine list in the city, with 1,600 selections. 555 California St., in the Bank of America Building (between Kearny and Montgomery sts.). ℂ 415/433-7500. www.carnelianroom.com. Jacket and tie required for men.

**Cityscape**   Sitting under the glass roof here to sip a drink is like being out under the stars, with views of the bay. Dinner is served nightly, with a live DJ and dancing from 10:30pm. Mirrored columns and floor-to-ceiling draperies lend the place an elegant, romantic ambience. *FYI:* They also serve a champagne brunch with live jazz on

# The San Francisco Bay Area

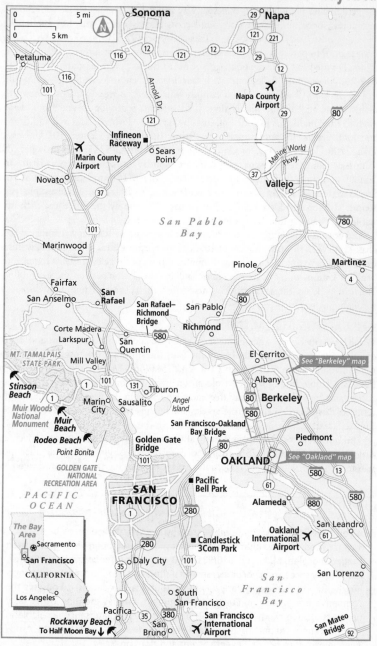

the action takes place between Bancroft Way and Ashby Avenue, where coffeehouses, restaurants, book and record stores, and crafts booths swarm with life. Bibliophiles shouldn't miss **Cody's Books,** 2454 Telegraph Ave. (© **510/845-7852;** www.codys books.com), to peruse its huge selection of titles, independent-press books, and magazines. For used and antique books, stop by **Moe's Books,** 2476 Telegraph Ave. (© **510/ 849-2087;** www.moesbooks.com), with four floors of new, used, and out-of-print titles.

**UC Berkeley** is a beautiful old campus with plenty of woodsy paths, noteworthy architecture, and 33,000 highly diversified students scurrying to and from classes. Architectural highlights include buildings by Bernard Maybeck, Bakewell and Brown, and John Galen Howard. Contact the **Visitor Information Center,** 101 University Hall, 2200 University Ave., at Oxford Street (© **510/642-5215;** www.berkeley.edu/ visitors), to join a free campus tour. Tours are Monday through Saturday at 10am, and Sunday at 1pm. Additional tours are available March 15 through April 30 at 1pm Monday through Friday. Electric cart tours are $25 with advance reservations year-round, save for mid-December to mid-January. Or stop by the office and pick up a self-guided walking-tour brochure or a free Berkeley map.

The university's southern entrance is at the north end of Telegraph Avenue, at Bancroft Way. Walk through the main entrance into **Sproul Plaza.** When school is in session, you'll have to make your way through a throng of Berkeley students to reach the **Student Union,** with a bookstore, cafes, and an information desk on the second floor. You can pick up the local student newspaper there; it's also found in dispensers throughout campus.

## OFF-CAMPUS ATTRACTIONS

**PARKS**    Berkeley has some of the most extensive and beautiful parks around. If you enjoy hiking, getting a breath of California air, and sniffing a few roses, jump in your car and make your way to **Tilden Park** ⚓ (© **510/562-PARK**). You'll find plenty of flora and fauna, hiking trails, an old steam train and merry-go-round, a farm and nature area for kids, and a chilly tree-encircled lake. On the way, stop at the colorful terraced **Rose Garden** in north Berkeley on Euclid Avenue between Bay View and Eunice Street.

The **University of California Botanical Garden,** in Strawberry Canyon on Centennial Drive (© **510/643-2755;** http://botanicalgarden.berkeley.edu), is another great nature excursion, with its vast collection of plant life, ranging from cacti to redwoods.

---

### ⟨*Finds* **Sweet Sensations at Berkeley's Chocolate Factory**

If you haven't had chocolate nibs—crunchy roasted, shelled cocoa beans—you haven't lived. At least that's what chocoholics will say upon visiting **Scharffen Berger Chocolate Maker** (© **510/981-4050;** www.scharffenberger.com). California's highly successful chocolatier invites visitors to taste the "nibs" while touring the facility, during regularly scheduled tours (call for details), to observe the company's use of vintage European equipment. Besides the nibs, other tasty products include candy bars, cocoa powder, and chocolate sauce, available in the retail shop. The factory is at 914 Heinz Ave.; from I-80 East, take the Ashby Avenue exit, turn left on Seventh Street and right on Heinz.

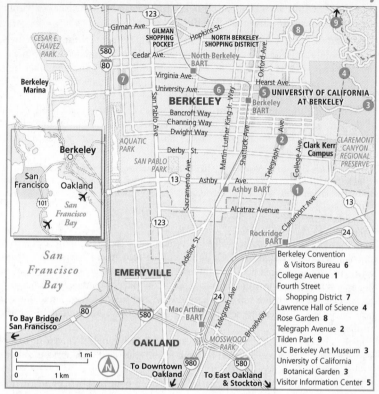

Berkeley Convention
& Visitors Bureau **6**
College Avenue **1**
Fourth Street
Shopping District **7**
Lawrence Hall of Science **4**
Rose Garden **8**
Telegraph Avenue **2**
Tilden Park **9**
UC Berkeley Art Museum **3**
University of California
Botanical Garden **3**
Visitor Information Center **5**

**SHOPPING**   If you're itching to exercise your credit cards, head to one of two places. **College Avenue** from Dwight to the Oakland border is crammed with boutiques, antiques shops, and restaurants. The other option is **Fourth Street** in west Berkeley, 2 blocks north of the University Avenue exit off I-80. Once there, grab a cup of java, read the paper at a patio table, and then hit the **Crate & Barrel Outlet,** 1785 Fourth St., between Hearst and Virginia (*©* **510/528-5500**), where retail prices are reduced 30% to 70%. Or wander into any of the small, wonderful stores crammed with imported and locally made housewares. Nearby is **REI,** the Bay Area's favorite outdoor outfitter, at 1338 San Pablo Ave., near Gilman Street (*©* **510/527-4140**).

## WHERE TO STAY

Berkeley's not a good hotel town. Most accommodations are basic motels and funky B&Bs. The exception is **The Claremont Resort & Spa,** 41 Tunnel Rd., Berkeley (*©* **800/551-7266** or 510/843-3000; www.claremontresort.com)—a grand Victorian hotel with modern rooms, a spa and gym, a hip bar, and grandiose surroundings. Although it's the most luxurious thing going in town, it's overpriced, and rooms aren't nearly as charming as the exterior. Prices range from $290 to $450 double occupancy. Another option is to call the **Berkeley & Oakland Bed and Breakfast Network**

(📞 **510/547-6380;** www.bbonline.com/ca/berkeley-oakland), which books visitors into homes and apartments in the East Bay.

**Rose Garden Inn**    A favorite among visiting grandparents and vacationing retirees, this 40-room, five-building compound with two landmark mansions is overrun with pink and green in every pattern, dolls over the mantle, floral print, and other frills. Outside, the expansive garden explodes with rose bushes, hydrangeas, and other flora and fauna; you'll forget you're on a stretch of Telegraph devoid of character, a few blocks from the student hub. Rooms, many of which have fireplaces, cable TVs, and all the basic amenities, show some wear and tend to be a little dark. Despite signs of age in some of the bathroom nooks and crannies, the rooms are spacious, partially updated, and very clean.

2740 Telegraph Ave. (at Stuart St.), Berkeley. 📞 **510/549-2145.** www.rosegardeninn.com. $115–$265 double. AE, DC, DIS, MC, V. **Amenities:** Wireless Internet, full breakfast, coffee, and afternoon cookies included. *In room:* TV, high-speed Internet in most rooms, hair dryer, iron upon request.

## WHERE TO DINE
### EXPENSIVE

**Chez Panisse**  ★★★ CALIFORNIA    No chef in the state is more recognized for contributing to the evolution of California cuisine than Alice Waters. Here, at this restaurant, she introduced her vastly influential, trademark style of cooking based on the freshest ingredients (organic whenever possible), culled from the region's best producers. Decades later, Alice still tends her redwood-and-stucco cottage restaurant with great integrity and ingenuity, serving simple but innovative Mediterranean-inspired cuisine.

In the upstairs cafe, the menu might feature delicately smoked gravlax or roasted eggplant soup with pesto, followed by lamb ragout garnished with apricots, onions, and spices, served with couscous.

The cozy downstairs restaurant, strewn with floral bouquets, is a warm environment for indulging in the $65 fixed-price, four-course gourmet dinner, served Tuesday through Thursday; Friday and Saturday, it's $75 for four courses; and Monday is bargain night, with a three-course dinner for $50.

The restaurant posts the following week's menu every Saturday. The wine list is excellent, with bottles ranging from $28 to $300.

1517 Shattuck Ave. (between Cedar and Vine). 📞 **510/548-5525,** or 510/548-5049 cafe reservations. Fax 510/548-0140. www.chezpanisse.com. Reservations required. Restaurant fixed-price menu $50–$75; cafe main courses $15–$25. AE, DC, DISC, MC, V. Restaurant seatings Mon–Thurs 5:30–6pm and 8–8:45pm; Fri–Sat 6–6:30pm and 8:30–9:30pm. Cafe Mon–Thurs 11:30am–3pm and 5–10:30pm; Fri–Sat 11:30am–3:30pm and 5–11:30pm. BART: Downtown Berkeley. From I-80 north, take the University Ave. exit and turn left onto Shattuck Ave.

### MODERATE

**Cafe Rouge** ★ MEDITERRANEAN    After cooking at San Francisco's Zuni Café for 10 years, chef-owner Marsha McBride launched her own restaurant, a sort of Zuni East. She brought some of Zuni's former staff and dishes with her, and she now serves salads, rotisserie chicken with oil and thyme, grilled lamb chops, steaks, and homemade sausages from a loftlike dining room. East Bay carnivores are happy with the top-notch burger.

1782 Fourth St. (between Delaware and Hearst). 📞 **510/525-1440.** www.caferouge.net. Reservations recommended. Main courses $9.50–$24. MC, V. Daily 11:30am–3pm; Tues–Sat 3–4:30pm (w/interim bar menu available); Tues–Thurs 5:30–9:30pm; Fri–Sat 5:30–10:30pm; Sun 5–9:30pm.

**O Chamé** ★★ JAPANESE   With ocher-colored walls etched with patterns, this spot has a spare, meditative air, which complements the traditional yet experimental, fresh, clean Japanese-inspired cuisine. The menu, which changes daily, offers meals in a bowl for $9 to $13: soba or udon noodles in a clear soup with a variety of toppings—from shrimp and *wakame* seaweed to beef with burdock root and carrot. Appetizers include a melding of grilled shiitake mushrooms, as well as portobello mushrooms and green-onion pancakes. Their entrees always include delicious roasted salmon.

1830 Fourth St. (near Hearst). ✆ 510/841-8783. Reservations recommended Fri–Sat dinner. Main courses $9–$19 lunch, $18–$24 dinner. AE, MC, V. Mon–Sat 11:30am–3pm; Mon–Thurs 5:30–9pm; Fri–Sat 5:30–9:30pm.

**Rivoli** ★★★ *Finds* CALIFORNIA   Rivoli offers top-notch food at amazingly reasonable prices. In an architecturally uninteresting space, the owners have created a warm, intimate dining room overlooking a sweet little garden. The menu changes every 3 weeks, save for a few house favorites, to feature whatever's freshest and in season—think chicken with prosciutto di Parma, wild-mushroom chard and ricotta cannelloni, Marsala *jus,* snap peas, and baby carrots; artichoke lasagna with ricotta, mint salsa, and tomato sauce; and braised lamb shank with green garlic risotto, sautéed spinach, and oven-dried tomatoes. The wine list follows suit with around 10 options available by the glass, handpicked to complement the food, from the wine bar near the entrance. Finish the evening with an assortment of cheeses or a warm chocolate truffle torte with hazelnut ice cream, orange *crème anglaise,* and chocolate sauce.

1539 Solano Ave. ✆ 866/496-2489 or 510/526-2542. www.rivolirestaurant.com. Reservations recommended. Main courses $16–$22. AE, DC, DISC, MC, V. Mon–Thurs 5:30–9:30pm; Fri 5:30–10pm; Sat 5–10pm; Sun 5–9pm.

## 2 Oakland

10 miles E of San Francisco

Although it's fewer than a dozen miles from San Francisco, Oakland is worlds apart from its sister city. Originally a cluster of ranches and farms, its size and stature exploded practically overnight in 1869, as the last mile of transcontinental railroad track was laid. Major shipping traffic soon followed, and to this day Oakland is one of the busiest industrial ports on the West Coast.

The price for all this success, however, has been Oakland's reputation as a working-class city famous for its crime and forever in the shadow of its chic neighbor to the west. Certain areas of town are still plain, but "Oaktown" is in a renaissance, with far more inviting housing prices and weather than San Francisco. For visitors who know where to venture, it holds plenty of pleasant surprises. Rent a sailboat on Lake Merritt, stroll the waterfront, or explore the fantastic Oakland Museum. They're all great reasons to hop the bay and spend a fog-free day in one of California's largest and most ethnically diverse cities.

### ESSENTIALS

**GETTING THERE   Bay Area Rapid Transit (BART)** makes the trip from San Francisco to Oakland through one of the longest underwater transit tunnels in the world. Fares range from $1 to $4, depending on your station of origin; children 4 and under ride free. BART trains operate Monday through Friday from 4am to midnight, Saturday from 6am to midnight, and Sunday from 8am to midnight. Exit at the 12th Street station for downtown Oakland.

**By car** from San Francisco, take I-80 across the San Francisco–Oakland Bay Bridge and follow the signs to downtown Oakland. Exit at Grand Avenue South for the Lake Merritt area.

**VISITOR INFORMATION**  A calendar of events and a free copy of the 60-page *Destination Oakland* guide are available online or by mail from the **Oakland Convention and Visitors Bureau,** 463 11th St., Oakland, CA 94607 (℧ **510/839-9000;** www. oaklandcvb.com). The city sponsors free guided tours, including African-American Heritage and neighborhood tours; call ℧ **510/238-3234** for details.

**CITY LAYOUT**  Downtown Oakland is bordered by Grand Avenue on the north, I-980 on the west, Inner Harbor on the south, and Lake Merritt on the east. Downtown landmarks include three BART stations (12th St., 19th St., and Lake Merritt), City Hall, the Oakland Museum, Jack London Square, and other sights.

## WHAT TO SEE & DO

**Lake Merritt** is Oakland's primary tourist attraction, along with Jack London Square (see below). Three and a half miles in circumference, the tidal lagoon was bridged and dammed in the 1860s and now serves as a refuge to flocks of migrating ducks, herons, and geese. The 122-acre Lakeside Park—a popular place to picnic, feed the ducks, and escape the fog—surrounds the habitat on three sides. At the **Municipal Boathouse** (℧ **510/238-2196**) along the north shore, you can rent sailboats, rowboats, pedal boats, and canoes for $6 to $12 per hour (cash only). Another option is to take an hour-long gondola ride with **Gondola Servizio** (℧ **510/663-6603;** www.gondo laservizio.com). Experienced gondoliers will serenade you as you glide across the lake; the hourly rate for two varies from $45 for your basic Venetian fling, to $225 for a customized photo-op package for weddings and other celebrations.

Another worthy site is Oakland's **Paramount Theatre,** 2025 Broadway (℧ **510/ 893-2300;** www.paramounttheatre.com), an outstanding example of Art Deco architecture and decor. Built in 1931 and restored in 1973, it's the city's main performing-arts center, with acts such as Smokey Robinson and Alicia Keys, gospel music, symphonies, and classic movies. Guided tours of the 3,000-seat theater take place the first and third Saturdays of each month, excluding holidays. Reservations are not necessary; just show up at 10am at the box-office entrance on 21st Street at Broadway. Cameras are allowed, and admission is $1.

If you're a diehard Jack London fan, or if you just take pleasure in strolling sailboat-filled wharves, visit **Jack London Square** (℧ **866/295-9853;** www.jacklondonsquare. com). As of 2005, it's undergoing a 5- to 10-year, $300-million site-by-site renovation and expansion. In the meantime, Oakland's only designated tourist area is a low-key version of San Francisco's Fisherman's Wharf.

The Oakland wharf shamelessly plays up the fact that Jack London spent most of his youth along the waterfront. The square that fronts the harbor, however, houses a tacky complex of boutiques and restaurants that couldn't be farther from London's "call of the wild." Most are open Monday through Saturday from 10am to 7pm; some restaurants stay open later.

In the center of the square is a small, reconstructed version of the Yukon cabin in which Jack London lived while prospecting in the Klondike during the Gold Rush of 1897. In Jack London Square, you'll find a more authentic memorial, **Heinold's First and Last Chance Saloon** (℧ **510/839-6761**)—a funky, friendly bar and landmark. London did some writing and most of his drinking here; the corner table he used has

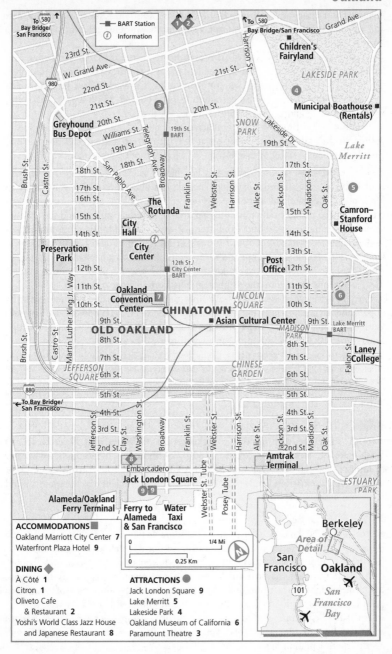

**BART Station**

*i* **Information**

To 580
Bay Bridge/
San Francisco

To 580
Bay Bridge/San Francisco

Grand Ave.

23rd St.

W. Grand Ave.

21st St.

22nd St.

21st St.

20th St.

20th St.

Greyhound
Bus Depot

Williams St.

19th St.

18th St.

17th St.

16th St.

15th St.

14th St.

Preservation
Park

12th St.

11th St.

10th St.

9th St.

8th St.

7th St.

6th St.

5th St.

4th St.

3rd St.

2nd St.

Children's
Fairyland

LAKESIDE PARK

Municipal Boathouse
(Rentals)

SNOW
PARK

19th St.

Lake
Merritt

17th St.

19th St.
BART

Camron–
Stanford
House

Telegraph Ave.

Broadway

The
Rotunda

City
Hall

City
Center

Franklin St.

Webster St.

Harrison St.

Alice St.

Jackson St.

Madison St.

Oak St.

15th St.

14th St.

13th St.

Post
Office

12th St.

11th St.

LINCOLN
SQUARE

10th St.

Oakland
Convention
Center  7

CHINATOWN

OLD OAKLAND

Asian Cultural Center

9th St.

MADISON
PARK

Lake Merritt
BART

Lincoln Dr.

Lakeside Dr.

Harrison St.

San Pablo Ave.

Brush St.

Castro St.

Martin Luther King Jr Way

King St.

12th St./
City Center
BART

JEFFERSON
SQUARE

CHINESE
GARDEN

Laney
College

Fallon St.

To Bay Bridge/
San Francisco

Jefferson St.

Clay St.

Washington St.

Broadway

Franklin St.

Webster St.

Harrison St.

Alice St.

Jackson St.

Madison St.

Oak St.

Amtrak
Terminal

ESTUARY
PARK

Embarcadero

Jack London Square  8

9  9

Alameda/Oakland
Ferry Terminal

Ferry to
Alameda
& San Francisco

Water
Taxi

Webster St. Tube

Posey Tube

Berkeley

Area of
Detail

San
Francisco

Oakland

101

San
Francisco
Bay

## ACCOMMODATIONS
Oakland Marriott City Center  7
Waterfront Plaza Hotel  9

## DINING
À Côté  1
Citron  1
Oliveto Cafe
  & Restaurant  2
Yoshi's World Class Jazz House
  and Japanese Restaurant  8

0                    1/4 Mi
0          0.25 Km

## ATTRACTIONS
Jack London Square  9
Lake Merritt  5
Lakeside Park  4
Oakland Museum of California  6
Paramount Theatre  3

remained as it was nearly a century ago. The square is also the resting place of the mast and nameplate from the **USS *Oakland,*** a ship that saw extensive action in the Pacific during World War II.

Locals come to the Oakland wharf mostly for the Farmers Market, year-round on Sunday from 10am to 2pm, and on Wednesdays, as well, from May through October. One of the best nearby dining establishments is **Yoshi's World Class Jazz House & Japanese Restaurant** *✦*, 510 Embarcadero W. (*℃* **510/238-9200;** www.yoshis.com), with decent sushi and, as you might have guessed, live jazz.

The square is at Broadway and Embarcadero. Take I-880 to Broadway, turn south, and go to the end. Via BART, get off at the 12th Street station, walk south along Broadway (about ½ mile) or take bus no. 51a to the foot of Broadway.

**Oakland Museum of California** *✦*    Two blocks south of Lake Merritt, the Oakland Museum of California's holdings include just about everything you'd want to know about the state and its people, history, culture, geology, art, environment, and ecology. Inside a low, modern building set among sweeping gardens and terraces, it's actually three museums in one: exhibitions of works by California artists from Bierstadt to Diebenkorn; collections of historic artifacts, from Pomo Indian basketry to Country Joe McDonald's guitar; and re-creations of California habitats from the coast to the mountains. The museum holds major exhibitions of California artists and art movements, and frequently shows photographs from its huge collection.

Forty-five-minute guided tours leave from the information desks on request or by appointment. The grounds include a cafe, a **gallery** (*℃* **510/834-2296**) that sells work by California artists, and a museum shop. The cafe is open Wednesday through Friday from 10:30am to 4:30pm, Saturday from 1:30 to 4:30pm.

1000 Oak St. (at 10th St.). *℃* **888/625-6873,** or 510/238-2200 for recorded information. www.museumca.org. Admission $8 adults; $5 students and seniors; free for children under 6. 2nd Sun of the month is free. Wed–Sat 10am–5pm; Sun noon–5pm; open until 9pm 1st Fri of the month. Closed Jan 1, July 4, Thanksgiving, Dec 25. BART: Lake Merritt station; walk 1 block north. From I-880 north, take the Oak St. exit; the museum is 5 blocks east. Or take I-580 to I-980 and exit at the Jackson St. ramp.

## WHERE TO STAY

Two fine midrange hotel options in Oaktown are the **Waterfront Plaza Hotel,** 10 Washington St., Jack London Square (*℃* **800/729-3638** or 510/836-3800; www.water frontplaza.com), and the **Oakland Marriott City Center,** 1001 Broadway (*℃* **510/ 451-4000;** www.marriott.com). Most major budget motel chains have locations around town and near the airport.

## WHERE TO DINE

**Citron** *✦* FRENCH/CALIFORNIA    This adorable French bistro was a smash when it opened in 1992. And it continues to earn raves for its small, enticing menu, which uses fresh California produce but draws on the flavors of France, Italy, and Spain—with results you likely haven't tasted elsewhere. The menu changes every few weeks, but dishes might range from aioli-breadcrumb-crusted Sonoma rack of lamb atop grilled ratatouille; spicy bayou seafood stew brimming with fried oysters, shrimp, snapper, and bell-pepper-and-tomato sauce; or rich saffron artichoke risotto. *A word of advice:* If you're into classic foods you can identify by name, head elsewhere; it's all about experimentation here.

5484 College Ave. (north of Broadway between Taft and Lawton sts.). *℃* **510/653-5484.** www.citron-acote.com. Reservations recommended. Main courses $20–$26; 3- to 5-course fixed-price menu (Sun–Fri only) $35–$46. AE, DC, DISC, MC, V. Mon–Tues 5:30–9pm; Wed–Thurs 5:30–9:30pm; Fri 5:30–10pm; Sat 5–10pm; Sun 5–9pm.

**Oliveto Cafe & Restaurant** ★★ ITALIAN    Paul Bertolli presides over one of the Bay Area's top Italian restaurants (certainly the best in Oakland). During the week, it's a madhouse at lunchtime, when local workers pile in for the wood-fired pizzas and tapas in the lower-level cafe. The upstairs restaurant—with neo-Florentine decor—is packed nightly with fans of Bertolli's house-made pastas, sausages, and prosciutto. Oliveto has a wood-burning oven, flame-broiled rotisserie, and a good wine list. An assortment of pricey grills, braises, and roasts anchor the daily changing menu, and the heavenly pastas that will send you into orbit. The Arista (classic Italian pork with garlic and rosemary and pork *jus*) is insanely good; and no one does fried calamari, onion rings, and lemon slices better than Oliveto. *Tip:* You can park free in the lot at the rear of the Market Hall building. Right outside, along College Avenue and in the building housing the restaurant, you'll find great gourmet food and boutique shopping.

Rockridge Market Hall, 5655 College Ave. (off the northeast end of Broadway at Shafter/Keith St., across from the Rockridge BART station). © 510/547-5356. www.oliveto.com. Reservations recommended for restaurant. Main courses cafe $2.50–$12 breakfast, $4–$8 lunch, $12–$15 dinner; restaurant $11–$15 lunch, $16–$30 dinner. AE, DC, MC, V. Cafe Mon 7am–9pm; Tues–Fri 7am–10pm; Sat 8am–10pm; Sun 8am–9pm. Restaurant Mon–Fri 11:30am–2pm; Tues–Wed 5:30–9:30pm; Thurs–Sat 5:30–10pm; Sun–Mon 5–9pm.

## MODERATE

**À Côté** ★★ FRENCH TAPAS    Stop here for killer rustic, Mediterranean-inspired small plates served amid loud, festive, warmly lit surroundings. A "no reservations" policy usually guarantees a long wait during prime dining hours. Once you're seated, however, you can graze with the locals on the likes of *croque-monsieur; pommes frites* with aioli; wood-oven-cooked mussels in Pernod; grilled pork tenderloin with creamy polenta; *traviso* cheese; and pancetta. Wash it down with excellent wines (by the glass or bottle), Belgian ales, or perky cocktails. *Note:* The heated, covered outdoor seating area tends to be quieter.

5478 College Ave. (at Taft Ave.). © 510/655-6469. www.citron-acote.com. Reservations not accepted except for parties of 10 or more. Small plates $5–$14. MC, V. Sun–Tues 5:30–10pm; Wed–Thurs 5:30–11pm; Fri–Sat 5:30pm–midnight.

## 3 Sausalito

5 miles N of San Francisco

Just off the northern end of the Golden Gate Bridge, Sausalito feels like St. Tropez on the French Riviera—minus the starlets and the European aristocracy. It has its quota of paper millionaires, but the town is still slightly bohemian and nonchalant, albeit a little cheesy with touristy boutiques and restaurants luring sun-seeking visitors to the main drag, Bridgeway. With approximately 8,000 residents, it's sort of an adjunct to San Francisco, across the Bay, but with scenery and sunshine: Once you cross the Golden Gate Bridge, the San Francisco fog patch usually gives way to blue California skies.

## ESSENTIALS

**GETTING THERE**    The **Golden Gate Ferry Service** fleet, Ferry Building (© **415/ 923-2000;** www.goldengateferry.org), operates between the San Francisco Ferry Building, at the foot of Market Street, and downtown Sausalito. Service runs at frequent intervals every day except January 1, Thanksgiving, and December 25. Phone for an exact schedule. The ride takes a half-hour, and one-way fares are $6.15 for adults and $4.60 for kids 6 to 12. Seniors and those with disabilities ride for $3.05; children 5 and under ride free. Family rates are available on weekends.

**Blue & Gold Fleet** ferries (© **415/705-5555;** www.blueandgoldfleet.com) leave from Pier 41 (Fisherman's Wharf); one-way is $7.25 for adults, $4 for kids 5 to 11. Boats run on a seasonal schedule; phone for departure information.

**By car** from San Francisco, take U.S. 101 north, then the first right after the Golden Gate (Alexander exit). Alexander becomes Bridgeway in Sausalito.

## EXPLORING THE TOWN

Sausalito is a magnet for shoppers. The town's best stores are in the alleys, malls, and second-floor boutiques reached by steep, narrow staircases on and off **Bridgeway,** Sausalito's main touring strip, along the water. Those in the know detour to **Caledonia Street,** which runs parallel to Bridgeway, 1 block inland. Not only is it less congested, but the selection of cafes and shops is better.

**Bay Model Visitors Center** *(Kids)* The U.S. Army Corps of Engineers once used this high-tech, 1½-acre model of San Francisco's bay and delta to analyze problems and observe the impact of changes in water flow. The model reproduces (in scale) the rise and fall of tides, the flows and currents of water, and the mixing of fresh and salt water, and indicates trends in sediment movement. You can view a 10-minute film or take a 1-hour tour (free; book a reservation), but the most interesting time to visit is when the center is in use, so call ahead.

2100 Bridgeway. © 415/332-3871. www.spn.usace.army.mil/bmvc. Free admission. Labor Day to Memorial Day (winter hours) Tues–Sat 9am–4pm; Memorial Day to Labor Day (summer hours) Tues–Fri 9am–4pm, Sat–Sun and holidays 10am–5pm.

## WHERE TO STAY

**Casa Madrona** *★★* A hideaway by the bay built in 1885 by a lumber baron, this rambling, New England–style structure, high on the hillside, is now a historic landmark. The place offers individually decorated and themed rooms, suites, and cottages, accessed by steep, landscaped pathways. The older buildings have the most personalized character and charm, decorated in a variety of styles. Some have Jacuzzis and others have fireplaces. The 16 freestanding units recently underwent contemporary makeovers, and were appointed with four-poster beds and marble bathrooms. The more recently designed rooms—on Bridgeway, in a brand new building that also houses the spa and the town's most contemporary and elaborately adorned restaurant, Poggio (see below)—offer modern luxury with deep tubs, fancy new decor in rich earth tones, and fabulous views of the water, San Francisco skyline, and bay.

801 Bridgeway, Sausalito, CA 94965. © 415/332-0502. Fax 415/332-2537. www.casamadrona.com. 63 units. $295–$450 double; $550 suite. AE, DC, DISC, MC, V. Valet parking $20. Ferry: Walk across the street from the landing. From U.S. 101 north, take the 1st right after the Golden Gate Bridge (Alexander exit); Alexander becomes Bridgeway. **Amenities:** Restaurant; concierge; room service; babysitting; laundry service; dry cleaning. *In room:* TV, VCR upon availability, minibar, coffeemaker, hair dryer, robes.

**The Inn Above Tide** *★★* Elevated on well-grounded pilings over the Bay, this former luxury apartment complex underwent a $4-million transformation into one of Sausalito's finest accommodations. It's the view that clinches it: Every room comes with a panorama of the San Francisco Bay, with the city glimmering in the distance. Should you manage to tear yourself away from your private deck, you'll find that 23 of the sumptuously appointed rooms have a romantic little fireplace; some have a vast sunken tub with Jacuzzi jets, remote-control air-conditioning, and wondrously comfortable queen- or king-size beds. Soothing earth tone shades highlight the decor, which blends in well with the bay landscape outside. Be sure to request that your breakfast and newspaper be delivered to your deck, and then cancel your early appointments: On sunny mornings, nobody checks out early.

30 El Portal (next to the Sausalito Ferry Landing), Sausalito, CA 94965. © **800/893-8433** or 415/332-9535. Fax 415/332-6714. www.innabovetide.com. 29 units. $265–$865 double. Rates include continental breakfast and evening wine and cheese. AE, DC, MC, V. Valet parking $12. **Amenities:** Concierge; in-room massage; same-day laundry service/dry cleaning; complimentary shoeshine. *In room:* A/C, heat, TV w/DVD player, dataport, free high-speed wireless Internet access, minibar, fridge, hair dryer, CD player.

## WHERE TO DINE
### EXPENSIVE

**Poggio** ★★ ITALIAN  Poggio—a loose Italian translation for "special hillside place"—does more than live up to its name. Floor-to-ceiling doors open to an interior with arches and earthen colors, mahogany accents, and well-directed light. A fine wine cellar, terra cotta–tiled floors, comfy mohair banquettes, and white linen-draped tables enhance the dining experience. A cadre of chefs tends the centrally located wood oven, and executive chef and co-owner Christopher Fernandez ensures the food is as elegant as the decor. His endive, Gorgonzola, walnut, fig, and honey salad is superb; and his pizza and pastas are addictive (try the spinach ricotta gnocchi with beef ragout). Entrees include roasted halibut with faro, snap peas, mushrooms, and spring-onion broth or grilled lamb chops with roasted fennel and *gremolata*. With a full bar, great, well-priced wine list, and tasty desserts, this is one of Sausalito's top dining destinations.

777 Bridgeway (at Bay St.). © **415/332-7771**. www.casamadrona.com. Continental breakfast a la carte $2.50–$5.50; main courses lunch $8–$18, dinner $10–$25. AE, DC, DISC. MC, V. Daily 6:30–11am and 11:30am–5:30pm; Sun–Thurs 5:30–10pm; Fri–Sat 5:30–11pm. Free valet parking.

### MODERATE

**Guernica** ★ FRENCH/BASQUE  Established in 1974, Guernica is one of those funky old restaurants that you'd probably pass up for something more chic and modern if you didn't know better. What? You don't know about Guernica's legendary paella Valenciana? Well, now you do, so call ahead and order it in advance, and bring a partner because it's served for two and will amply feed three. Begin with an appetizer of mussels or escargots. Other main courses include grilled lamb shank and roasted duckling with orange sauce. Rich desserts include specialties such as crème brûlée, bread pudding, and crème caramel.

2009 Bridgeway. © **415/332-1512**. Reservations recommended. Main courses $12–$18. AE, DC, MC, V. Daily 11:30am–4pm and 5–10pm. From U.S. 101 north, take the 1st right after the Golden Gate Bridge (Alexander exit); Alexander becomes Bridgeway in Sausalito.

**Sushi Ran** ★★ SUSHI/JAPANESE  San Franciscans often cross the bridge just to cram into the bar, window seats, and more roomy back dining area of this top-quality favorite. They journey here for the standard rolls (yellowtail, *unagi, maguro,* and the like) or the specialty rolls (crab, avocado, and beyond). You'll also find a slew of creative dishes, such as generously sized, unbelievably moist and buttery miso-glazed black cod, oysters on the half shell with *ponzu* sauce and *tobiko,* and a Hawaiian-style *ahi* (tuna) poke salad with seaweed dressing. Pay the extra $2.50 or so for fresh wasabi, select from the fine sake and wine list, and don't miss dessert, because they're more creative and delicious than most served at Japanese restaurants.

107 Caledonia St. (℃ **415/332-3620.** www.sushiran.com. Reservations recommended. Sushi $5–$14; main courses $8.50–$16. AE, MC, V. Mon–Fri 11:45am–2:30pm; Mon–Sat 5:30–11pm; Sun 5–10:30pm. From U.S. 101 north, take the 1st right after the Golden Gate Bridge (Alexander exit); Alexander becomes Bridgeway in Sausalito. At Johnson St. turn left, then right onto Caledonia.

## 4 Angel Island

8 miles N of San Francisco

A federal and state wildlife refuge, **Angel Island** is the largest of the San Francisco Bay's three islets (the others being Alcatraz and Yerba Buena). The island has been a prison, a quarantine station for immigrants, a missile base, and a site for duels. Nowadays, though, most of the people who visit here are content to picnic on the large green lawn that fronts the docking area. Loaded with the necessary recreational supplies, they claim a barbecue, plop their fannies down on the lush green grass, and while away the afternoon free of televisions and traffic. Hiking, mountain biking, and guided tram tours are also popular activities.

### ESSENTIALS

**GETTING THERE    Blue & Gold Fleet** ferries (℃ **415/705-5555;** www.blueand goldfleet.com) leave from Pier 41 (Fisherman's Wharf) and travel to both Angel Island and Tiburon. Boats run on a seasonal schedule; phone for departure information. The round-trip fare is $12 to Angel Island or Tiburon, $6.50 for kids ages 6 to 11, and free for kids under 6. Tickets are available at Pier 41 or over the phone.

**By car** from San Francisco, take U.S. 101 to the Tiburon/Highway 131 exit, then follow Tiburon Boulevard downtown, a 30-minute drive from San Francisco. Catch the **Tiburon–Angel Island Ferry** (℃ **415/435-2131;** www.angelislandferry.com) to Angel Island from the dock at Tiburon Boulevard and Main Street. The 15-minute round trip costs $10 for adults, $7.50 for children 5 to 11, and $1 for bikes. Boats run on a seasonal schedule, but usually depart hourly from 10am to 4pm. Call ahead or look online for departure information. One child under 4 is admitted free of charge with each paying adult. Tickets can only be purchased when boarding.

Passengers disembark from the ferry at **Ayala Cove,** a small marina abutting a huge lawn area equipped with tables, benches, barbecue pits, and restrooms. Ayala Cove also has a small store, gift shop, cafe (with surprisingly good grub), and an overpriced mountain-bike rental shop (helmets included).

Angel Island has 12 miles of hiking and mountain-bike trails. **Perimeter Road,** for one, is a partly paved path that circles the island and winds its way past old troop barracks, former gun emplacements, and other military buildings; several turnoffs lead up to the top of Mount Livermore, 776 feet above the bay.

Sometimes referred to as the "Ellis Island of the West," from 1910 to 1940 Angel Island was used as a holding area for Chinese immigrants awaiting their citizenship papers. You can still see some faded Chinese characters on the walls of the barracks where the immigrants were held. During the warmer months, you can camp at a limited number of sites; reservations are required and can be obtained by calling **ReserveAmerica** at ℃ **800/444-7275** (www.reserveamerica.com).

**Sea Trek** ⚲ (℃ **415/332-8494;** www.seatrekkayak.com) offers guided **sea-kayak tours**. The all-day trips, which include a catered lunch, combine the thrill of paddling stable kayaks for one, two, or three people with a naturalist-led tour that encircles the island (conditions permitting). All equipment is provided, kids are welcome, and no experience is necessary. Rates run about $110 per person; a shorter trip takes 2½ hours and costs $75 per person.

The 1-hour **Angel Island Tram Tour** (© **415/897-0715;** www.angelisland.com) costs $13 for adults, $11 for seniors, and $7.50 for children ages 6 to 12; children under 6 ride free. For information on **Angel Island State Park,** call © **415/435-1915.**

## 5 Muir Woods & Mount Tamalpais

12 miles N of the Golden Gate Bridge

Muir Woods, in a remote ravine on the flanks of Mount Tamalpais, escaped destruction while the rest of Marin County's redwood forests were devoured to feed the building spree in San Francisco around the turn of the 20th century.

### MUIR WOODS

Although the Pacific Coast's magnificent redwoods have been transplanted to five continents, their homeland is a 500-mile strip along the mountainous shoreline of southwestern Oregon and Northern California. The coast redwood, or *Sequoia sempervirens,* is the tallest tree in the region; the largest-known specimen, in the Redwood National Forest, towers 368 feet high. Seeing it, soaring upward like a wooden cathedral, is an experience you won't soon forget.

Muir Woods is tiny compared to the Redwood National Forest farther north, but you can still get a good idea of what it must have been like when these giants dominated the coastal region. What's amazing is that they exist a mere 6 miles (as the crow flies) from San Francisco; close enough, unfortunately, that tour buses arrive in droves on the weekends. You can avoid the masses by hiking up the **Ocean View Trail** and returning via the **Fern Creek Trail**—a moderate hike that shows off the woods' best sides and leaves the tour-bus crowd behind.

To reach Muir Woods from San Francisco, cross the Golden Gate Bridge heading north on U.S. 101, take the Stinson Beach/Highway 1 exit heading west, and follow the signs. The park is open daily from 8am to sunset; the entrance fee is $3 per person 17 years or older. Stop by the gift shop and educational displays, or take one of the docent-led tours. For more information, call the **Muir Woods information line** (© **415/388-2595;** www.visitmuirwoods.com).

If you don't have a car, you can book a bus trip with the **Red & White Fleet** (© **877/855-5506** or 415/447-0597; www.redandwhite.com), which takes you to Muir Woods via the Golden Gate Bridge, and on the way back makes a short stop in Sausalito. The 3½-hour tours run several times daily and are $39 for adults, $20 for children ages 5 through 11, and free for kids under 5. Call for more information and specific departure times.

### MOUNT TAMALPAIS

The birthplace of mountain biking, "Mount Tam" is the most dominant mountain in the region and the most popular for biking. Most every local has his or her secret trail and scenic overlook, as well as an opinion on the dilemma between mountain bikers and hikers (a touchy subject around here). The main trails—mostly fire roads—see a lot of foot and bicycle traffic on the weekends, particularly on clear, sunny days when you can see a hundred miles in all directions, from the foothills of the Sierra to the western horizon. It's a great place to escape from the city for a leisurely hike and to soak in the breathtaking views of the bay.

To get to Mount Tamalpais **by car,** cross the Golden Gate Bridge heading north on U.S. 101 and take the Stinson Beach/Highway 1 exit. Follow the shoreline highway about 2½ miles and turn onto the Panoramic Highway heading west. After about 5½ miles, turn onto Pantoll Road and continue for about a mile to Ridgecrest Boulevard. Ridgecrest winds to a parking lot below East Peak. From here, it's a 15-minute hike to the top.

## 6 Half Moon Bay

28 miles SW of San Francisco

A 45-minute drive from the teeming streets of San Francisco is a heavenly little hamlet called Half Moon Bay, one of the finest—and friendliest—small towns on the California coast. While other communities like Bolinas make tourists feel unwelcome, Half Moon Bay residents are disarmingly amicable, bestowing greetings on anyone and everyone who stops for a visit.

Half Moon Bay has only recently begun to capitalize on its beaches, mild climate, and proximity to San Francisco, so it's still not tourist-tacky. Visitors will find it a peaceful slice of classic California: pristine beaches, redwood forests, nature preserves, fishing harbors, horse ranches, organic farms, and a host of superb inns and restaurants—everything for the perfect weekend getaway.

*Note:* Temperatures rarely venture past the 70s (20s Celsius) in Half Moon Bay, so be sure to pack for cool (and often wet) weather.

### ESSENTIALS

**GETTING THERE** No public transportation runs from San Francisco to Half Moon Bay, but you can get there two ways by car. To save time, take Highway 92 west from I-280 or U.S. 101 out of San Francisco, which will take you over a small mountain range and drop you into Half Moon Bay. The prettier route is Highway 1, which starts at the south end of the Golden Gate Bridge and veers southwest to the shoreline a few miles south of Daly City. Both routes to Half Moon Bay are clearly marked, so don't worry about getting lost.

Downtown Half Moon Bay, however, is easy to miss since it's not on Highway 1, but a few hundred yards inland. Head 2 blocks up Highway 92 from the Highway 1 intersection, then turn south at the Shell gas station onto Main Street until you cross a small bridge. For more information, call the **Half Moon Bay Coastside Chamber of Commerce** (© 650/726-8380; www.halfmoonbaychamber.org).

### EXPLORING HALF MOON BAY & ENVIRONS

A wonderful **paved beach trail** winds 5 miles from Half Moon Bay to Pillar Point Harbor, where you can watch trawlers unload their catch. Be sure to keep a lookout for dolphins and whales as you walk, bike, jog, or skate along this path.

Half Moon Bay is also known for its organically grown produce, and the best place to stock up on fruits and vegetables is the **Andreotti Family Farm,** 329 Kelly Ave., off Highway 1 (© 650/726-9151), an old-fashioned outfit in business since 1926. Every Friday, Saturday, and Sunday, a member of the Andreotti family slides open the door to their old barn at 10am sharp to reveal a cornucopia of strawberries, artichokes, cucumbers, and more. Head toward the beach and you'll see the barn on your right-hand side. It's open until 6pm year-round.

**BEACHES & PRESERVES** The 4-mile arc of golden sand that rings Half Moon Bay is actually three state-run beaches—Dunes, Venice, and Francis—all part of **Half Moon Bay State Beach** (© 650/726-8820). All three levy a $5-per-vehicle entrance fee. Surfing is allowed, but swimming isn't a good idea unless you happen to be cold-blooded. You can reserve campgrounds here by contacting © 800/444-PARK or visiting www.parks.ca.gov.

About 7 miles farther north on Highway 1 is the **Fitzgerald Marine Reserve** (© 650/728-3584), one of the most diverse tidal basins on the West Coast, as well as one of the safest, thanks to a wave-buffering rock terrace 50 yards from the beach. Call before coming to find out when it's low tide (all the sea creatures are hidden at high tide) and to get information on the docent-led tour schedules (usually offered on Saturday). Rubber-soled shoes are recommended. The reserve is at the west end of California Avenue off Highway 1 in Moss Beach. Reservations are required for all groups of 10 or more; call © 650/363-4021. *Note:* Dogs, open fires, or barbecue pits are prohibited, as is collecting of any kind.

Sixteen miles south of Half Moon Bay on Highway 1 (at the turnoff to Pescadero) is the **Pescadero Marsh Natural Preserve,** one of the few remaining natural marshes on the central California coast. Part of the Pacific flyway, it's a resting stop for nearly 200 bird species, including great blue herons that nest in the northern row of eucalyptus trees. Passing through the marsh is the mile-long **Sequoia Audubon Trail,** accessible from the parking lot at Pescadero State Beach on Highway 1. (The trail starts below the Pescadero Creek Bridge.)

From December through March, the **Año Nuevo State Reserve** is home to one of California's most amazing animal attractions: the breeding grounds of the northern elephant seal. Every winter, people reserve tickets for a chance to witness a fearsome clash between the 2½-ton bulls over mating privileges among the females. Reservations are required for the 2½-hour naturalist-led tours (held rain or shine Dec 15–Mar 31). For tickets, which cost $5 per person (free for children under 3), and information, call © 800/444-4445 or visit www.anonuevo.org. Even if it's not mating season, you can still see the elephant seals lolling around the shore almost year-round, particularly between April and August when they come ashore to molt.

**OUTDOOR PURSUITS** One of the most popular activities in town is horseback riding along the beach. **Sea Horse Ranch** (aka Friendly Acres Horse Ranch), on Highway 1 a mile north of Half Moon Bay (© 650/726-9903), offers kids' pony rides and guided and unguided rides along the beach or on well-worn trails, starting at $45. A $35 "early-bird special" includes a 2-hour ride from 8 to 10am. Hours are daily from 8am to 6pm.

Golfers can choose from two courses at **Half Moon Bay Golf Links,** 2000 Fairway Dr., at the south end of Half Moon Bay next to the Half Moon Bay Lodge (© 650/726-4438; www.halfmoonbaygolf.com). The 18-hole "Old Course," designed by Arnold Palmer, has been rated among the top 100 courses in the country, as well as the best in the Bay Area. The newer Arthur Hills–designed course is oceanside. Greens fees range from $145 to $170 (but you'll save $5 if you book online). Reserve your tee time as far in advance as possible.

**SHOPPING** Main Street is a shopper's paradise. Dozens of small stores and boutiques line the quarter-mile strip, selling everything from feed and tack to custom furniture and camping gear. From north to south, must-see stops include the **Buffalo Shirt Company,** 604 Main St. (℅ **650/726-3194**), which carries a fine selection of casual wear, Indian rugs, and outdoor gear, and **Half Moon Bay Feed & Fuel,** 331 Main St. (℅ **650/726-4814**), a great place to pick up a treat for your pet. **Cunha's Country Store,** 448 Main St. (℅ **650/726-4071**), the town's beloved grocery and general store that was rebuilt in 2004 after a fire tore through the place, is a mandatory stop for visitors from the Bay Area. Half Moon Bay also has a good bookstore, **Coastside Books,** 432B Main St. (℅ **650/726-5889**), which carries a fair selection of children's books and postcards. End your shopping spree with a stop at **Cottage Industries,** 621 Main St. (℅ **650/712-8078**), to marvel at the high-quality handcrafted furniture.

## WHERE TO STAY

**Beach House Inn** ✦ Although the facade has a rather unimaginative Cape Cod look, the rooms at this three-story hotel are surprisingly well designed and decorated with modern prints, stylish furnishings (replaced in 2004), soothing yellow and blue or red and tan tones, and spectacular views of the bay and harbor. Every room comes fully loaded with a wood-burning fireplace, king-size bed and sleeper sofa, large bathroom, and stereo with CD player. Wait, there's more: Private patio or deck access, two color TVs, *four* telephones with dataports and voice mail, and a kitchenette with microwave and fridge. Opt for one of the corner rooms, which offer a more expansive view for the same price.

4100 N. Cabrillo Hwy. (Hwy. 1), Half Moon Bay, CA 94019. ℅ **800/315-9366** or 650/712-0220. Fax 650/712-0693. www.beach-house.com. 54 units. $175–$355 double. Rates include continental breakfast and Fri–Sat evening wine hour. AE, DC, DISC, MC, V. From Half Moon Bay, go 3 miles north on Hwy. 1. **Amenities:** Heated outdoor pool; exercise room; oceanview whirlpool; concierge; in-room massage; same-day laundry/dry cleaning. *In room:* TV, free high-speed Internet access, kitchenette, minibar, fridge, coffeemaker, hair dryer, iron, CD player.

**Cypress Inn on Miramar Beach** ✦✦ A favorite place to stay in Half Moon Bay, this three-building compound is free of Victorian charm (nary a lace curtain in *this* joint). Instead you have one modern, artistically designed and decorated building infused with colorful folk art and rustic furniture made of pine and heavy wicker. Each room in the main building has a feather bed, private balcony, gas fireplace, private bathroom, and unobstructed ocean view. Adjacent is the Beach House building, which has rooms equipped with built-in stereo systems and hidden TVs, though they lack the Santa-Fe-meets-California effect that I adore in the main house (also a few rooms don't have ocean views and one lacks a deck). In 2002, six new Lighthouse rooms were added, complete with whirlpool spas. This is one of the only B&Bs right on the beach.

407 Mirada Rd., Half Moon Bay, CA 94019. ℅ **800/83-BEACH** or 650/726-6002. Fax 650/712-0380. www.cypress inn.com. 18 units. $225–$385 double. Rates include breakfast; tea, wine, and hors d'oeuvres; and after-dinner treats. AE, DISC, MC, V. From the junction of Highways 92 and 1, go 3 miles north, then turn west and follow Medio to the end; hotel is at Medio and Mirada. **Amenities:** Room service (breakfast only). *In room:* TV, VCR, coffeemakers in some rooms, hair dryer, iron/ironing board, CD player, robes.

**Seal Cove Inn** ✦✦ Before Karen Herbert and her husband, Rick, opened this topnotch B&B, she was the writer and publisher of *Karen Brown's Guides,* so she knows what it takes to create and run a superior bed-and-breakfast. The result is a stately,

---

*Tips*  **Best Brunch**

One of Half Moon Bay's biggest recent arrivals is the stunning Ritz-Carlton. On a bluff above the Pacific, the six-story structure has the most luxurious tempo-rary digs in the region, a fantastic spa, tennis courts, and all the usual five-star amenities—not to mention instant access to the Half Moon Bay Golf Links. But most important for San Francisco day-trippers and those from farther afield, it's also the place to indulge in an insanely opulent all-you-can-eat brunch. Held every Sunday in the stately open-kitchen restaurant Navio, which also has ocean views, brunch includes an endless array of gourmet edibles—including sushi, dim sum, soufflés, a raw bar, classic breakfast dishes (including great blintzes), tarts, salads, cheeses, a meat-carving station (think rack of lamb), veggies, pas-tas, and desserts. The feast will set you back $75 per adult (half price for kids 5–12 and free for those under 5). Reservations are a must. The resort is located at 1 Miramontes Point Road, Half Moon Bay (© **650/712-7000**). Be sure to make reservations; brunch always sells out.

---

sophisticated B&B that blends California, New England, and European influences in a spectacular setting. All rooms have fireplaces, antiques, watercolors, grandfather clocks, hidden televisions with VCRs, and refrigerators stocked with free beverages. The rooms overlook distant cypress trees and a colorful half-acre wildflower garden dotted with birdhouses. You'll find coffee and a newspaper outside your door in the morning, wine, appetizers, brandy, and sherry by the living-room fireplace in the evening, and chocolates beside your turned-down bed at night. The ocean is just a short walk away.

221 Cypress Ave., Half Moon Bay, CA 94038. © **650/728-4114.** Fax 650/728-4116. www.sealcoveinn.com. 10 units. $200–$300 double. Rates include breakfast, wine and snacks, and sherry. AE, DISC, MC, V. The inn is 6 miles north of Half Moon Bay off Hwy. 1; follow signs to Moss Beach Distillery. **Amenities:** Concierge. *In room:* TV/VCR, minibar, fridge, hair dryer, robes.

## WHERE TO DINE

Downtown's Main Street—with a handful of good restaurants, many of which don't require reservations—makes for a pleasant stroll. If you're not in the mood for Italian, cruise the street and pick a spot you like.

**Cetrella Bistro & Café** ⭐ MEDITERRANEAN   Cetrella is as close to big-city dining as Half Moon Bay gets. Within warm, chic dining rooms—with a centerpiece fireplace—locals and visitors mingle over dishes ranging from hearts of romaine salad with toasted capers, ricotta di Pecora, and niçoise olive dressing to mesquite-grilled dry-aged prime Angus rib-eye steak service for two, served with *pommes frites* and chicory with balsamic. Bonuses include a killer cheese program, small $5 kids menu, and live evening jazz Thursday through Saturday. Attached is the more casual, cheaper cafe, which offers the likes of small plates (pizza, soups, salads) and entrees like burg-ers, steamed mussels, and cassoulet. Brunch is decadent and gourmet—think brioche French toast with huckleberries and chantilly cream, Tuscan-style baked eggs, or a nice juicy burger with grilled onions and arugula and crisp fries. If you're in the neighbor-hood, check it out, but make reservations first; everyone from *Gourmet* to *San Fran-cisco Chronicle* have trumpeted this small-town gem, so it's no secret.

845 Main St. (at Monte Vista Lane). ℂ **650/726-4090**. www.cetrella.com. Reservations recommended. Most main courses bistro dinner $19–$27, main courses café dinner $10–$15; brunch $10–$16. Bistro: Sun 10:30am–2pm; Sun–Thurs 5:30–9:30pm; Fri–Sat 5:30–10pm. Cafe: Sun–Tues 5:30–10pm; Wed–Sat 5pm–midnight.

**Pasta Moon** ✮ ITALIAN   Nouveau Italian Pasta Moon makes everything from scratch and uses only fresh ingredients. Pasta dishes, which are always freshly made and perfectly cooked, earn the highest recommendations. They include house-made linguine with Manila clams, pancetta, leeks, garlic, red-pepper flakes, and clam broth; and semolina gnocchi with sweet peppers, *piopinni* mushrooms, and pesto. For dessert, try the wonderful tiramisu, with its layers of espresso-soaked ladyfingers and creamy mascarpone.

315 Main St., Half Moon Bay. ℂ **650/726-5125**. Reservations recommended. Main courses $10–$23 lunch, $15–$25 dinner. AE, DC, DISC, MC, V. Mon–Fri 11:30am–2:30pm; Sat noon–3pm; Sun–Thurs 5:30–9:30pm; Fri–Sat 5:30–10pm.

## 7 San Jose

45 miles SE of San Francisco

The San Jose of yesteryear—a sleepy town of orchards, crops, and cattle—is long gone. Founded in 1717, and hidden in the shadows of San Francisco, San Jose is now Northern California's largest city. Today the prosperity of Silicon Valley has transformed what was once an agricultural backwater into a thriving network of restaurants, shops, a state-of-the-art light-rail system, a sports arena (go Sharks!), and a reputable art scene. And despite all the growth, a number of surveys declare it one of the safest and sunniest cities in the nation.

### ESSENTIALS

**GETTING THERE   BART** (ℂ **510/465-2278;** www.bart.gov) travels from San Francisco to Fremont in 1¼ hours; you can take a bus from there. **Caltrain** (ℂ **800/ 660-4287;** www.caltrain.com) operates frequently from San Francisco and takes about 1 hour and 25 minutes.

**VISITOR INFORMATION**   Free visitors guides, published by the **San Jose Convention & Visitors Bureau,** 408 Almaden Blvd. (ℂ **800/SAN-JOSE** or 408/295-9600), are available at kiosks within the **San Jose McEnery Convention Center,** 150 W. San Carlos St., San Jose, CA 95113 (ℂ **408/277-5277**). You can request information live at the visitors bureau, or log onto www.sanjose.org to receive a free visitors guide by mail.

**GETTING AROUND   Light Rail** (ℂ **408/321-2300**) is the best transportation option in town. A ticket is good for 2 hours, and stops include Paramount's Great America, the convention center, and downtown museums. Fares are $1.75 for adults, $1.50 for children ages 5 to 17, 75¢ for seniors and travelers with disabilities, and children age 4 and under ride for free. Day passes are $5.25 for adults, $4.50 for children, $2.25 for seniors.

### MUSEUMS WORTH SEEKING OUT

**Children's Discovery Museum** *Kids*   Children will find shows, workshops, and more than 150 interactive exhibitions exploring the sciences, humanities, arts, and technology. **ZOOMZone** consists of science and art activities designed by kids for kids; **Bubbalogna,** an exhibit that explores the chemistry and physics of bubbles, draws rave reviews. Smaller kids will love dressing up in costumes and playing on the fire truck.

180 Woz Way. (*C*) **408/298-5437**. www.cdm.org. Admission $7 children and adults, $6 seniors 60 and up, free for children under 1. Tues–Sat 10am–5pm; Sun noon–5pm.

**Rosicrucian Egyptian Museum & Planetarium**    The Rosicrucian is associated with an ancient Egyptian educational organization that strongly advocated belief in the afterlife and reincarnation. Permanent exhibitions display human and animal mummies, funerary boats, canopic jars, and a replica of a noble Egyptian's tomb. Less morbid artifacts include Egyptian jewelry, pottery, and bronze tool collections. *Note:* In March 2004, the planetarium reopened after 8 years of renovation and features shows at 2pm Tuesday through Sunday. A second show on Saturday and Sunday begins at 3:30pm. If you're here on a Monday, call to see if they're open; rumor has it they'll be open daily soon.

1342 Naglee Ave. (*C*) **408/947-3636**. www.egyptianmuseum.org. Museum admission $9 adults, $7 seniors and students, $5 children 5–10, free for children under 5. Planetarium free admission. Tues–Fri 10am–5pm; Sat–Sun 11am–6pm. Closed major holidays.

**San Jose Historical Museum**    Twenty-six restored original and replica buildings, on 25 acres in Kelley Park, recreate life in 1880s San Jose. The usual cast of 19th-century characters is here—the doctor, the printer, the postmaster—with an occasional local surprise, such as the 1888 Chinese temple and the original Stevens fruit barn. If you want to peek inside, come on the weekend or during summer months, when docents offer interior tours daily.

1650 Senter Rd. (*C*) **408/287-2290**. Free admission. Tues–Sun noon–5pm.

**San Jose Museum of Art** ☆    This contemporary art museum features revolving exhibitions of post-1980 works plus older 20th-century art from the permanent collection. The Historic Wing includes a cafe, bookstore, and education center. From Tuesday to Sunday, tours begin at 12:30 and 2:30pm; for group tours, call for reservations at least 1 week in advance. Docents will also sign tours for deaf and hearing-impaired visitors with 72 hours notice.

110 S. Market St. (*C*) **408/294-2787** or 408/271-6840. www.sjmusart.org. Free admission. Tues–Sun 11am–5pm. Closed major holidays.

**Tech Museum of Innovation** ☆ *Kids*    In a 132,000-square-foot facility, the Tech Museum allows visitors to experience a world of phenomena: Create your own virtual roller-coaster ride, survive an earthquake on a giant shake table, operate an underwater ROV (remotely operated vehicle), ride the same virtual bobsled used to train Olympic competitors, and play with lots of other cool high-tech gizmos. A genetics gallery explores DNA politics as well as science. The museum also features an IMAX Dome Theater.

201 S. Market St., downtown at the corner of Park and Market sts. (*C*) **408/294-TECH**. www.thetech.org. Admission $9.50 adults, $8 seniors 65 and over, $7 children 3–12, free for children under 3; additional fee for IMAX shows; combo ticket (IMAX and museum) $16 adults, $13 children, and $15 seniors. Daily 10am–5pm. IMAX has extended hours on weekends.

## THEME-PARK THRILLS

It's a 10-minute drive from downtown San Jose to **Paramount's Great America,** 100 acres of family entertainment on the Great America Parkway (off U.S. 101), in Santa

## The Winchester House: A Monument to Paranoia

Begun in 1884, the **Winchester Mystery House,** 525 S. Winchester Blvd., at the intersection of I-280 and Highway 17, San Jose (© **408/247-2101;** www. winchestermysteryhouse.com), is the legacy of Sarah L. Winchester, widow of the famous Winchester rifle magnate's son. After her husband and baby daughter died young, Mrs. Winchester consulted with a seer. The psychic proclaimed that the family was haunted by the fatal victims of Winchester rifles, and nothing would appease the evil spirits but perpetual construction on the Winchester mansion. To spare her own life, the widow used much of her $20-million inheritance to finance construction work 24 hours a day, 7 days a week, 365 days a year, for 38 years.

As you can probably guess, this is no ordinary home. With 160 rooms, it sprawls across half a dozen acres. And it's full of disturbing features: a stair-case leading nowhere, a Tiffany window with a spider's web design, doors that open onto blank walls, and bizarre building patterns based on the number 13: The estate has 13 bathrooms, 13 windows and doors in the old sewing room, 13 palms lining the main driveway, 13 hooks in the séance room, and chandeliers with 13 lights. The heiress designed these schemes to confound the spirits that, she imagined, sought her demise.

Sixty-five-minute tours of the mansion and grounds are $20 for adults, $17 for seniors age 65 and over, $14 for children 6 to 12, and free for kids under 6; a 55-minute tour behind the scenes (for a separate fee of $17 for adults, $16 kids and seniors) is available for guests over 10. The 2½-hr. Estate Tour—which includes the mansion and behind-the-scenes itineraries—costs $25 for adults, $22 for kids 10 to 12 and seniors. Tours leave about every 20 to 30 minutes. The house is open daily from 9am to 7pm in the summer; winter hours vary, so call ahead.

Clara (© **408/988-1776;** www.pgathrills.com). A pretty cool place to lose your lunch, the park includes such favorites as the *Top Gun* suspended jet coaster; a 3-acre Nickelodeon Center for children; Drop Zone, the world's tallest free-fall ride; the Xtreme Skyflyer, which combines skydiving with hang gliding; and the new Pyscho Mouse roller coaster and go-carts. Check for concerts and special events, too. Crocodile Dundee's Boomerang Bay, a 3-acre water park with 11 slides and a "lazy river," is included in the general admission; it's $50 for adults and children ages 7 to 59, $40 for seniors age 60 and over, $34 for children 3 to 6, and free for children under 2. Check the website for discounted tickets. Parking is $10 per vehicle. It's open daily June through August; opening hours, and opening days from September through May, vary according to season and the weather, so call for details. From San Francisco, take U.S. 101 south for about 45 miles to the Great America Parkway exit.

## AN EXCELLENT SHOPPING & DINING EXCURSION

With 66 restaurants, 18 shops, and 5 spas organized in one glamorous alfresco mall, **Santana Row,** at Winchester and Stevens Creek boulevards, is *the* hotbed for dining, shopping, and strolling in San Jose. Check out your options by visiting www.santana row.com, calling ✆ **408/551-4600,** or dropping by for a lazy afternoon. Stores range from Urban Outfitters to Gucci. Two of the many good dining bets include super-casual, fun New England seafood house **Yankee Pier** and Asian-inspired, flavorful, and creative **Strait's Café.**

## WHERE TO STAY

**The Fairmont San Jose**   In a landmark building near the San Jose McEnery Convention Center and the Center of Performing Arts, the Fairmont is a popular spot for afternoon tea or cocktails, and the lobby attracts many shoppers who are just passing through. For guests, the hotel places an emphasis on comfort: The guest rooms, located in two 13-story towers, feature high-tech amenities such as fax and high-speed modem lines. Other luxuries include 24-hour room service and a fourth-floor rooftop pool surrounded by tropical foliage. The most high-end restaurant of the four on the premises is **The Grill** steakhouse. The other options are an Asian Fusion restaurant with a sushi lounge, an upscale seafood restaurant, and a coffee shop accented with a massive marble soda fountain.

170 S. Market St., San Jose, CA 95113. ✆ **800/527-4727** or 408/998-1900. Fax 408/287-1648. www.fairmont.com. 805 units. $270–$400 double; $350–$1,800 suite. AE, DC, DISC, MC, V. **Amenities:** 4 restaurants and a sushi bar; bar; heated outdoor pool; health club; spa; sauna; concierge; car-rental desk; business center; secretarial services; 24-hr. room service; in-room massage; same-day laundry service/dry cleaning. *In room:* A/C, TV w/pay movies, VCR and fax in suites, high-speed Internet access, minibar, hair dryer, iron, safe in tower rooms.

## WHERE TO DINE

**Emile's** ⭐⭐ CONTEMPORARY EUROPEAN   A source of exceptional, ever-evolving contemporary cuisine since 1973, this fancy restaurant still ranks among the Bay Area's best. Mirrors, recessed lighting, and large, bold floral arrangements create an elegant atmosphere. To start, try *torchon* of foie gras with a dried fruit compote and brioche toast, or sautéed prawns Bordelaise with butter, white wine, garlic, and lemon juice over a grilled polenta crouton. Follow with beef filet in a Madagascar pepper sauce, on a bed of spinach mashed potato, served with a vegetable medley. For dessert, go with the Grand Marnier soufflé. Emile's offers "small plate" versions of entrees; a "taste" costs about two-thirds of the entree price and allows diners to snack their way through the menu.

545 S. Second St. ✆ **408/289-1960.** www.emiles.com. Reservations recommended. Main courses $17–$32. AE, DC, DISC, MC, V. Tues–Sat 6–10pm.

**Paolo's** ⭐ NORTHERN ITALIAN   Paolo's attracts a business crowd at lunchtime and a cultured crowd in the evening. The cuisine is refined northern Italian, with innovative flourishes. Appetizers include tuna carpaccio or breadcrumb-crusted prawns with white wine, garlic, lemon, parsley, and butter. The main dishes range from *pappardelle* with fresh saffron egg pasta ribbons and traditional Bolognese-style meat sauce; to braised chicken with artichokes, mixed herbs, and soft polenta; and grilled dry-aged angus rib-eye chop, roasted root vegetable mash, and braised winter greens. Desserts also stretch typical Italian favorites to limits: Tuscan doughnuts, filled with chocolate, in a pomegranate glaze, for example. The extensive wine list features more than 600 selections.

333 W. San Carlos St. ✆ **408/294-2558.** www.paolosrestaurant.com. Reservations recommended. Main courses $15–$22 lunch, $18–$34 dinner. AE, DC, DISC, MC, V. Mon–Fri 11am–2:30pm; Mon–Sat 5:30–10pm.

# 7

# The Wine Country

*by Erika Lenkert*

California's Napa and Sonoma valleys are two of the most famous wine-growing regions in the world, and two of my favorite places in the state. In fact, I liked Napa so much I moved there. The valleys that provide a way of life for thousands of vintners are also the ultimate retreat for wine and food lovers and romantics. Hundreds of wineries are nestled among the vines, and most are open to visitors. Even if you're a teetotaler, the country air, rolling countryside, and world-class restaurants and spas are reasons enough to visit. If you can, plan to spend a couple of days just to get to know one of the valleys. No matter how long you stay, you'll probably never get enough of the romantic, indulgent way of life.

While Napa and Sonoma are close to each other (about 30 min. apart by car), each is attraction-packed enough that your best bet is to focus on just one of the valleys, especially if your time is limited. I recommend that you read about each below, and then decide which one is right for you—unless, of course, you're lucky enough to have time to explore both.

## 1 Napa Valley

Size is the most obvious distinction between the two valleys—Napa dwarfs Sonoma Valley in population, number of wineries, and sheer tourist volume (and, in summertime, vexing traffic). Napa is definitely the more commercial of the two, with dozens more wineries, spas, and a far superior selection of fine restaurants, hotels, and quintessential Wine Country activities such as hot-air ballooning, set amid mustard flower–covered hills and vast stretches of vineyards. If your goal is to learn about winemaking, world-class wineries such as Sterling and Robert Mondavi offer the most interesting and edifying wine tours in North America, if not in the world. Napa's attractions make it the place to visit for the ultimate Wine Country experience.

Napa Valley is relatively condensed. It's just 35 miles long, which means you can venture from one end to the other in around half an hour (traffic permitting). Conveniently, most of the large wineries—as well as most of the hotels, shops, and restaurants—line a single road, Highway 29, which starts at the mouth of the Napa River, near the north end of San Francisco Bay, and continues north to Calistoga and the top of the growing region. Every Napa Valley town and winery can be reached from this main thoroughfare.

## ESSENTIALS

**GETTING THERE**   From San Francisco, cross the Golden Gate Bridge and head north on U.S. 101. Turn east on Highway 37 (toward Vallejo), then north on Highway 29, the main road through Napa Valley. Or take the scenic route: Highway 37 to Highway 121/12, following the signs toward Napa, turn left onto Highway 29.

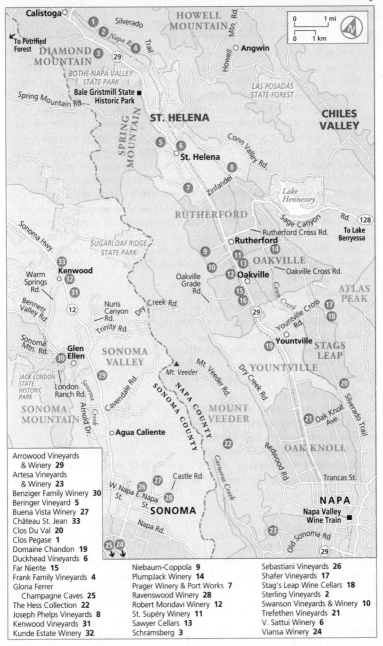

# The Wine Country

Calistoga

0        1 mi

0        1 km

HOWELL
MOUNTAIN

To Petrified
Forest

DIAMOND
MOUNTAIN

Silverado

Napa Rd.

Silverado Trail

Howell Mtn. Rd.

Angwin

LAS POSADAS
STATE FOREST

29

BOTHE-NAPA VALLEY
STATE PARK

Spring Mountain Rd.

Bale Gristmill State
Historic Park

CHILES
VALLEY

SPRING MOUNTAIN

ST. HELENA

St. Helena

Conn Valley Rd.

Zinfandel

Lake
Hennessey

RUTHERFORD

Sage Canyon

Rd.

128

To Lake
Berryessa

Sonoma Hwy.

SUGARLOAF RIDGE
STATE PARK

Rutherford Cross Rd.

Rutherford

OAKVILLE

Kenwood

Warm
Springs
Rd.

Oakville
Grade
Rd.

Oakville

Oakville Cross Rd.

ATLAS
PEAK

Conn Creek

Bennett
Valley Rd.

12

Nuns
Canyon
Rd.

Dry Creek Rd.

Trinity Rd.

29

Yountville Cross
Rd.

Sonoma
Mtn. Rd.

Glen
Ellen

SONOMA
VALLEY

Mt. Veeder

Mt. Veeder Rd.

Yountville

STAGS
LEAP

JACK LONDON
STATE
HISTORIC
PARK

London
Ranch Rd.

Sonoma Creek

Arnold Dr.

Cavendale Rd.

SONOMA COUNTY

NAPA COUNTY

Dry Creek Rd.

YOUNTVILLE

Silverado Trail

SONOMA
MOUNTAIN

Agua Caliente

MOUNT
VEEDER

Oak Knoll Ave.

OAK KNOLL

20

Carneros Creek

Redwood Rd.

Trancas St.

W. Napa St.

E. Napa St.

Castle Rd.

NAPA

SONOMA

Napa Rd.

Napa Valley
Wine Train

Old Sonoma Rd.

29

## Winery List

Arrowood Vineyards
  & Winery **29**
Artesa Vineyards
  & Winery **23**
Benziger Family Winery **30**
Beringer Vineyard **5**
Buena Vista Winery **27**
Château St. Jean **33**
Clos Du Val **20**
Clos Pegase **1**
Domaine Chandon **19**
Duckhead Vineyards **6**
Far Niente **15**
Frank Family Vineyards **4**
Gloria Ferrer
  Champagne Caves **25**
The Hess Collection **22**
Joseph Phelps Vineyards **8**
Kenwood Vineyards **31**
Kunde Estate Winery **32**

Niebaum-Coppola **9**
PlumpJack Winery **14**
Prager Winery & Port Works **7**
Ravenswood Winery **28**
Robert Mondavi Winery **12**
St. Supéry Winery **11**
Sawyer Cellars **13**
Schramsberg **3**

Sebastiani Vineyards **26**
Shafer Vineyards **17**
Stag's Leap Wine Cellars **18**
Sterling Vineyards **2**
Swanson Vineyards & Winery **10**
Trefethen Vineyards **21**
V. Sattui Winery **6**
Viansa Winery **24**

## *Tips* The Ins & Outs of Shipping Wine Home

Perhaps the only thing more complex than that $800 case of cabernet you just purchased are the rules and regulations about shipping it home. Wine shipping is limited by widely varying state regulations. Shipping rules also vary from winery to winery. Hence, depending on which state you live in, sending even a single bottle of wine can be a Kafkaesque experience.

To avoid major hassles, before you buy talk to the wineries and the shipping companies below about whether they can ship. Be skeptical of any winery that tells you it can ship to nonreciprocal states: If they run into problems, you'll never get your wine. Find out if you can order the wine on the Internet. If you have to find a shipping company yourself, keep in mind that it's technically illegal to box your own wine and send it to a nonreciprocal state; the shippers could lose their license, and you could lose your wine. If you do get stuck shipping illegally (I'm not recommending you do that but, FYI, people do it all the time), you might want to disguise your box and head to a post office, UPS, or other shipping company outside the Wine Country; it's far less obvious that you're shipping wine from, say, Vallejo or San Francisco than from Napa Valley.

**Shipping from Napa Valley**
**The UPS Store,** at 3212 Jefferson St. in the Grape Yard Shopping Center (✆ **707/259-1398**), packs and ships anything anywhere ($25 per case, ground shipping, to L.A.; $64 to New York).

**St. Helena Mailing Center,** 1241 Adams St., St. Helena (✆ **707/963-2686**), packs and ships to reciprocal states (prewrapped shipments $30 per case, ground shipping, to L.A.; $92 to New York).

**Shipping From Sonoma**
The **Wine Exchange of Sonoma,** 452 First St. E., Sonoma (✆ **707/938-1794**), will ship your purchases, but you must buy an equal value of wine at the store ($20 per case to L.A., $50 to the East Coast).

**Mail Boxes, Etc.,** 19229 Sonoma Hwy., Sonoma (✆ **707/935-3438**), ships a lot of wine and claims it will ship to any state ($22 per case to L.A., $73 to the East Coast, $140 to Hawaii and Alaska).

**VISITOR INFORMATION** Once in Napa Valley, stop first at the **Napa Valley Conference & Visitors Bureau,** 1310 Town Center Mall, Napa, CA 94559 (✆ **707/ 226-7459**), and pick up the *Napa Valley Guide,* or call in ahead to order the $10 package—the guide plus a bunch of brochures, a map, and *Four Perfect Days in the Wine Country* itinerary. If you don't want to pay for the official publications, point your browser to **www.napavalley.org**, the NVCVB's official site, which has much of the same information for free.

**WHEN TO GO** The beauty of the valley is striking any time of year, but it's most memorable in September and October—harvest season, when the wineries are in full production. Another great time to visit is the spring, when the mustard flowers are in full bloom and the tourist season hasn't yet begun; you'll find less traffic and fewer crowds at the wineries and restaurants, and better deals on hotel rooms. Winter is still beautiful and promises the best budget rates, but the vines are dormant and rain is likely, so bring appropriate shoes and an umbrella. And in summer? Say hello to hot weather, traffic, crowds, and an expensive good time.

## TOURING THE VALLEY & WINERIES

The Napa Valley has more than 280 wineries—each with distinct wines, atmosphere, and experience—so touring the valley takes a little planning. Decide what interests you most and chart your path from there. Ask locals which vintners have the type of experience you're looking for. And don't plan to visit more than four wineries in a day. Above all, take it slowly. The Wine Country should never be rushed; like a great glass of wine, it should be savored.

Most wineries are open 10am to 5pm (some have extended hours during summer; most are closed on major holidays). Many offer tours daily from 10am to 4:30pm, which usually chart the entire winemaking process—from grafting and harvesting the vines, to pressing the grapes, to blending and aging the juice in oak casks. Tours vary in length and formality; most are free.

The towns and wineries below are organized geographically, from south to north along Highway 29, from Napa village to Calistoga. I've included a handful of my favorites below; for a complete list, be sure to pick up one of the free guides to the valley (see "Essentials," above).

### NAPA
55 miles N of San Francisco

The city of Napa serves as the commercial center of the Wine Country and the gateway to Napa Valley. Most visitors whiz right past it on their way to the heart of the valley, but if you do veer off the highway, you'll be surprised to discover a small but burgeoning community of nearly 73,000 residents and some of the most affordable accommodations in the area. It is also in the process of gentrification, thanks to relatively affordable housing, an old-fashioned downtown, and new restaurants and attractions. From the city of Napa, northbound Highway 29 or the Silverado Trail lead you to wineries and the more quintessential Wine Country landscape of vineyards and wide-open country views.

A top visitor stop is **Copia: The American Center for Wine, Food & the Arts** ⍟, 500 First St. (© **707/259-1600;** www.copia.org), which explores how wine and food influence our culture. This $50-million, multifaceted facility tackles the topic in myriad ways—with rotating art exhibitions, vegetable and herb gardens, culinary demonstrations, wine classes, concerts, and opportunities to dine and drink on the

---

*Tips* **Reservations at Wineries**

While plenty of wineries are open to everyone between 10am and 4:30pm, most require reservations, because of local permitting laws. A few wineries limit guests to create a more intimate experience but, in many cases, they'll be happy to see you if you arrive unannounced. It's always best to call ahead if you have your heart set on a winery that prefers you make reservations.

premises. Truth is, for drop-by visitors to the art galleries, there's not a lot of "there" there. But if you're interested in watching a cooking demonstration with a famous chef (for an extra fee), exploring organic gardens, browsing the gift shop, or catching a great evening movie (on Friday) or an alfresco musical performance (on Mon during summer months; bring a lawn chair and blanket), you can find it here. Check the schedule in advance and book a class (they often sell out), so you know what you're in for. You can also grab gourmet picnic items, taste wines, or dine in the adjoining California-French restaurant, **Julia's Kitchen,** named after Julia Child. (Personally, I'd skip it—the food's second-rate and overpriced.) Or make like a local and drop by Tuesday morning from April through November for the outdoor farmers market.

Copia admission is $13 for adults, $10 for seniors 62 and over, $7.50 for students of any age, $5 for young adults 13 to 20, and free for children under 13. The center is open Wednesday through Monday from 10am to 5pm. The restaurant stays open until 9:30pm Thursday through Sunday. Wednesday admissions are half price for Napa and Sonoma residents.

Anyone with an appreciation for art must visit the **di Rosa Preserve** ★★, which through a private tour explores the collection and 215-acre grounds of Rene and Veronica di Rosa, who have been collecting contemporary American art for more than 40 years. Their world-renowned collection features 2,000-plus works in all media by more than 900 Greater Bay Area artists. Treasures are on display practically everywhere—from along the shores of their 30-acre lake to each nook and cranny of their century-old winery-turned-residence, adjoining building, two additional galleries, and gardens. It's at 5200 Sonoma Hwy. (Hwy. 121/12). Tours are by appointment only; they'll guide a maximum of 25 guests through the preserve. Each tour lasts 2 to 2½ hours and costs $12 per person on weekdays, $15 per person on Saturday (free at 10am every Wed). Call © **707/226-5991** for reservations.

Discount shoppers should pull off Highway 29 at Napa's First Street exit to find the **Napa Premium Outlets** (© **707/226-9876;** www.premiumoutlets.com). Shoppers will find multiple places to part with their money including Barneys New York, Tse (cashmere at basement prices!), Nine West, Jones New York, BCBG, kitchenware shops, a food court, and a decent but expensive sushi restaurant. The shops are open Monday through Saturday from 10am to 8pm, and Sunday from 10am to 6pm.

South of downtown Napa, 1⅓ miles east of Highway 29 on Highway 12, the **Chardonnay Golf Club** (© **707/257-8950**) is a 36-hole land-links golf complex with first-class service. Three 9s of equal difficulty start at the clubhouse, so you can play the 18 holes of your choice. You pay just one fee, which makes you a member for the day.

---

## *Tips* Sip Tip

You can cheaply sip your way through downtown Napa without ever getting behind the wheel with the new "Taste Napa Downtown" wine card. For a mere $15 you get 10¢ tasting privileges in 10 local wine-centric watering holes and tasting rooms, all of which are within walking distance of each other. Plus you'll get 10% discounts at tasting rooms and free admission to Copia. Available at the **Napa Valley Conference & Visitors Bureau** (1310 Town Center, off First Street (© **707/226-7459**); and Copia (see above). Learn more at www.napa downtown.com.

---

Privileges include the use of a golf cart and the practice range (including a bucket of balls), and access to services usually found only at a private club. Starting times can be reserved up to 2 weeks in advance. Greens fees (including mandatory cart and practice balls) are $55 Monday through Friday, $80 weekends and holidays before 12:30pm; at 12:30pm, fees go down to around $45 on weekdays and $55 on weekends.

**Artesa Vineyards & Winery** ★★ *Finds*    Views, modern architecture, seclusion, and region-specific pinot noirs are the reasons Artesa is one of my favorite stops. Arrive when the wind is blowing less than 10 mph, and the fountains are captivating (they automatically shut off with higher winds). Inside the fescue grass-covered winery is a tasteful gift shop, a room outlining history and details on the Carneros region, and a long bar where $5 to $8 tastes include everything from chardonnays and pinot noirs to sauvignon blanc, cabernet sauvignon, zinfandel, and sparkling wine. Sorry, but their permits don't allow for picnicking. To find the winery, turn north on Dealy Lane from Old Sonoma Road off Highway 12/121 and turn right on Henry Road.

1345 Henry Rd., Napa. © 707/224-1668. www.artesawinery.com. Daily 10am–5pm; tours daily at 11am and 2pm.

**The Hess Collection** ★★ *Finds*    No place in the valley brings together art and wine better than this combination winery and art gallery on the side of Mount Veeder. Swiss art collector Donald Hess acquired the old Christian Brothers Winery in 1978 and funded a huge restoration and expansion project to honor wine and the fine arts. The result is a working winery interspersed with gloriously lit rooms displaying his stunning art collection; the free, self-guided tour takes you through the galleries as it introduces you to the winemaking process.

For a $5 tasting fee, you can sample the winery's current cabernet and chardonnay, as well as one other featured wine. By the bottle, prices start at $10 for the second-label Hess select brand; most other choices range from $15 to $40.

4411 Redwood Rd., Napa. © 707/255-1144. www.hesscollection.com. Daily 10am–4pm, except some holidays. From Hwy. 29 north, exit at Redwood Rd. west, and follow Redwood Rd. for 6½ miles.

**Trefethen Vineyards**    Listed on the National Register of Historic Places, the vineyard's main building was built in 1886 and is Napa's only wooden, gravity-flow winery. Although Trefethen is one of the valley's oldest wineries, it didn't produce its first chardonnay until 1973—but thank goodness it did; the award-winning whites and reds here are a pleasure to the palate. Tastings are $10 for four estate wines; if you want to sample a reserve wine, it will cost you $20.

1160 Oak Knoll Ave. (east of Hwy. 29), Napa. © 707/255-7700. www.trefethen.com. Daily 10am–4:30pm. From Hwy. 29 north, take a right onto Oak Knoll Ave.

**Clos Du Val**    This winery's ivy-covered building and well-manicured rose garden set the scene for a romantic wine-tasting experience. Bordeaux-born founder and winemaker Bernard Portet and his newer, younger counterpart, John Clews, are responsible for the output; Portet has garnered a reputation for his cabernet, which makes up 70% of the winery's production. Other varietals include chardonnay, pinot noir, and merlot. You can try them all in the basic tasting room, although they charge a $5 tasting fee (refunded with purchase) for their most exclusive wines. The grassy nooks along the grounds include facilities for picnics and the game *pétanque*, which is played in parks all over France.

5330 Silverado Trail (north of Oak Knoll Ave.), Napa. © 707/259-2200. Daily 10am–5pm. Tours by appointment only.

---

**Tips** **Paying to Taste**

It used to be out of the norm to charge for wine tasting, and when the tides first started changing, I didn't like it. Over the past decade, however, sipping has become such a popular pastime that in the free or cheap tasting spots, you'll often find yourself jockeying for room and your host's attention at the bar. As a result, I've changed my view on paying a premium to taste. With the flash of a $10 or $20 per person, you avoid crowding in with the hundreds of tipsy souls who come for the cheap buzz. You also get a more intimate experience, with more attention from the staff, more educational information, and far more exclusive surroundings—maybe even a seat.

---

**Stag's Leap Wine Cellars**    Founded in 1972, Stag's Leap shocked the oenological world 4 years later, when its 1973 cabernet won first place over French wines in a Parisian blind tasting. Visit the charmingly landscaped, unfussy winery and its cramped "tasting room." For $10 per person, you can judge the four to six current releases for yourself; for up to $30, you can try estate samples as well. The 1-hour tour and tasting runs through everything from the vineyard and production facilities to the swank, $5-million wine caves (to store and age wine), which premiered in mid-2001.

5766 Silverado Trail, Napa. © 707/944-2020. www.cask23.com. Daily 10am–4:30pm. Tours by appointment only. From Hwy. 29, go east on Trancas St. or Oak Knoll Ave., then north to the cellars.

**Shafer Vineyards** *Finds*    For an intimate experience off the beaten track, reserve a tour and tasting at this Stag's Leap District destination. Unlike many Napa wineries, this one is family owned—by John Shafer, who after 23 years in publishing bought 209 hillside acres and planted vines on 50 of them. Today, he and his son Doug, joined by winemaker Elias Fernandez, use sustainable farming and solar energy to make exceptional chardonnay, merlot, sangiovese-cab blend (their answer to a Super Tuscan and my personal favorite!), cabernet sauvignon, and syrah. Although they only produce 34,000 cases per year, their wines are well known and highly regarded. What's more, they share their output and their winemaking philosophy during a relaxed, enjoyable 1½-hour tour and tasting. The bright, homey tasting room has a long wooden table, a fireplace, a pitched ceiling, and windows overlooking vineyards from every angle. Most wines go for $37 to $60, but their Hillside Select cabernet is $150.

6154 Silverado Trail, Napa. © 707/944-2877. www.shafervineyards.com. By appointment only Mon–Fri 10:30am–1:30pm.

## YOUNTVILLE
70 miles N of San Francisco

The town of Yountville was founded by the first white American to settle in the valley, George Calvert Yount. While it lacks the small-town charm of neighboring St. Helena and Calistoga—primarily because its main street is rather sprawling and sprinkled with shops and restaurants rather than sites—it does serve as a good base for exploring the valley. And it's home to a handful of excellent wineries, inns, boutiques, and a small stretch of fabulous restaurants, including the world-renowned French Laundry.

Shoppers with an eye for contemporary, feminine house and garden wares should browse **Mosswood Collection**'s perky, hand-painted martini glasses, wall tapestries, and fabulous food-and-wine etchings. You'll also find antique corkscrews, garden art, tabletop items, children's toys, and a wide selection of ribbons. It's open daily 10am to 5pm (6550 Washington St.; ℂ 707/944-8151).

**Domaine Chandon** ★★ Finds   Founded in 1973 by French champagne house Moët et Chandon, Domaine Chandon is the valley's most renowned sparkling winery. Manicured gardens showcase locally made sculpture, guests linger with snacks and bubbly on the shaded patio, and in the restaurant diners indulge in formal, French-inspired cuisine (reservations recommended). Champagne tastings, served with complimentary bread and spread, are $9 to $14. The comprehensive tour of the facilities is interesting, very informative, and friendly. The complex includes a shop and revolving art exhibitions, with works for sale. Check the website for events; Chandon often hosts live music and extends its salon hours during the summer.

1 California Dr. (at Hwy. 29), Yountville. ℂ 707/944-2280. www.chandon.com. Daily 10am–6pm; hours vary by season, so call to confirm. Call for free tour schedules.

## OAKVILLE
68 miles N of San Francisco

Driving farther north on the St. Helena Highway (Hwy. 29) brings you to the Oakville Cross Road and the famous **Oakville Grocery Co.** (see "Gourmet Picnics, Napa-Style" on p. 185), a favorite for picnic fare.

**PlumpJack Winery**   If most wineries are like a Brooks Brothers suit, PlumpJack stands out as the Todd Oldham of wine tasting: chic, colorful, a little wild, and popular with a young, hip crowd as well as with a growing number of more mature aficionados. Like the franchise's PlumpJack restaurant and wine shop in San Francisco, as well as its resort in Lake Tahoe, this mock-medieval winery is a welcome diversion.

---

### ⟨ Moments  Hot-Air Ballooning over the Valley

Napa Valley is the busiest hot-air balloon "flight corridor" in the world. Northern California's temperate weather allows for ballooning year-round, and on summer mornings in the valley, it's a rare day when you don't see at least one of the colorful airships floating above the vineyards.

Trips depart early in the morning, when the air is cooler and the balloons have better lift. (*Note:* When weather conditions aren't optimal, balloon companies often launch flights from locations up to an hour's drive outside the valley. You won't know until the morning of the flight, but you should be able to cancel on the spot if you desire.) Flight paths vary with the direction and speed of the changing breezes, so "chase" crews on the ground must follow the balloons to their undetermined destinations. Most flights last about an hour and end with a traditional champagne celebration and breakfast. Reservations are required and should be made far in advance. Prices run close to $200 per person for the basic package, which includes shuttle service from your hotel. Wedding, wine tasting, picnic, and lodging packages are also available. For more information or reservations, call Napa's **Bonaventura Balloon Company** (ℂ 800/FLY-NAPA) or **Adventures Aloft** (ℂ 800/944-4408 or 707/944-4408; www.nvaloft.com).

Formerly the Villa Mt. Eden winery, it's now backed by Getty bucks, and the ample budget is in evidence beyond the atmosphere: Some serious winemaking goes down here, too. For $5 you can sample the cabernet, merlot, and chardonnay. The facility wants for tours or picnic spots; nevertheless, you'll want to hang out for a while at this refreshingly stylized, friendly facility.

620 Oakville Cross Rd. (just west of the Silverado Trail), Oakville. © 707/945-1220. www.plumpjack.com. Daily 10am–4pm.

**Far Niente** This stone winery, straight out of a storybook, is a serious treat for lovers of wine, gardens, and/or classic cars. Founded in 1885, it was abandoned for 60 years around Prohibition. Gil Nickel (also of nearby Nickel & Nickel winery) purchased it in 1979 and, in spring 2004, opened it to the public. The tour includes a walk of the historic stone property, caves, private car collection, and azalea garden. It culminates with a sampling of five wines, including a delicious chardonnay, cabernet sauvignon, and Dolce—their sensational semillon and sauvignon blanc dessert blend, sure to make converts of even sweet-wine debunkers. Tastings are $40, by appointment only. Wines aren't cheap; they range from around $52 for the chardonnay to $110 for their estate cabernet sauvignon.

1350 Acacia Dr, Oakville. © 800/FN-DOLCE or 707/944-2861. www.farniente.com. Tours and tastings by appointment only Mon–Sat 10am–4pm.

**Robert Mondavi Winery** ★ *Finds* The Mission-style Mondavi winery offers the most comprehensive tours in the valley. Basic jaunts—which last about an hour and cost $20—lead you through the vineyards and their newest winemaking facilities. (Ask the guides anything about the process; they know a lot.) After the tour, you can taste a selection of current wines. To learn even more, ask about the in-depth tours. Mondavi offers a wide variety, including the "essence tasting" tour ($50), during which you compare wine with the scents of fruits, spices, nuts, and more. You can also sample wines without taking the tour, for $5 per glass or $30 per flight.

My favorite attraction at Mondavi is their summer concert series. Tickets are expensive, but the talent is usually world-renowned, and the crowd really gets into the picnic-party spirit of these events. Call about upcoming artists.

7801 St. Helena Hwy. (Hwy. 29), Oakville. © 800/MONDAVI or 707/226-1395. www.robertmondaviwinery.com. Daily 10am–4pm (5pm in summer). Reservations recommended for guided tour; book 1 week ahead, especially for weekend visits.

## RUTHERFORD
3 miles N of Oakville

If you blink after Oakville, you're likely to overlook Rutherford, the next small town that borders on St. Helena. Rutherford has its share of spectacular wineries, but you can't see most of them while driving along Highway 29.

**Swanson Vineyards & Winery** ★ *Finds* Swanson runs the valley's most posh and unique wine tastings, for $25 or $55, with reservations required. Here, tastings are more like a private party, known on the premises as a "SA-lon." You and up to seven other guests will sit at a round table in a coral parlor adorned with huge paintings, seashells, and a fireplace; the atmosphere is uncommonly refined yet whimsical. The table appears to be set for a dinner party rather than a tasting—with Reidel stemware, slivers of a fine cheese or two, crackers, and one superb chocolate Alexis ganache-filled bonbon (more of which are available for purchase on the premises). Over the course of the hour-plus event, a winery host will pour four to seven wines and discuss the history and fine points of each—in between casual sessions of banter among guests, of course. Expect a bright pinot grigio, rich merlot, and hearty Alexis, their signature cab-syrah blend. If you can afford it, don't miss this place.

1271 Manley Lane, Rutherford. ⓒ 707/967-3500. www.swansonvineyards.com. Appointments available Wed–Sun 11am, 1:30pm, and 4pm.

**Sawyer Cellars** *(Finds)*   The most attractive thing about Sawyer, besides its clean, tasty, extremely high-quality wines, is its humble, accommodating attitude. Step into the simple, restored 1920s barn to see what I mean. Whatever your request, they do their best to accommodate it. Want to picnic on the back patio overlooking the vineyards? Be their guest. Like to participate in a grape crushing? Come on over and get your hands dirty. Fancy their wine library for a private luncheon? Pay a minimal fee and make yourself at home. You can tour the property on a little tram or learn more about winemaker Brad Warner, who spent 30 years at Mondavi before embarking on this exclusive endeavor. Plunk down $5 to taste delicious estate-made wines: sauvignon blanc, merlot, cabernet sauvignon, and Meritage ($16–$46 for current releases), which some contend are worth twice the price. With a total production of only 4,200 cases and a friendly attitude, this winery is a rare treat.

8350 St. Helena Hwy. (Hwy. 29), Rutherford. ⓒ 707/963-1980. www.sawyercellars.com. Tastings and tours by appointment.

**St. Supéry Winery** *(Kids)*   The outside looks like a modern corporate office building, but inside you'll find a functional, welcoming winery that encourages first-time tasters to learn more about oenology. On the self-guided tour, you can wander through the demonstration vineyard, where you'll learn about growing techniques. Inside, kids gravitate toward coloring books and "SmellaVision," an interactive display that teaches you how to identify different wine ingredients. The adjacent Atkinson House chronicles more than 100 years of winemaking history. For $10, you'll get lifetime tasting privileges and a tour, which includes samples of delicious sauvignon blanc, chardonnay, cab, and more. Even the prices make visitors feel at home: Bottles start at $19, although the tag on their high-end red Bordeaux blend is $50.

8440 St. Helena Hwy. (Hwy. 29), Rutherford. ⓒ 800/942-0809 or 707/963-4507. www.stsupery.com. Daily 10am–5pm (until 5:30pm in summer). $10 tour at 1 and 3pm daily.

**Niebaum-Coppola** *(★)*   Hollywood meets Napa Valley at Francis Ford Coppola's Inglenook Vineyards, now known as Niebaum-Coppola (*Nee*-bom *Coh*-pa-la). From the outside, the 1880s ivy-draped stone winery and grounds have an historic grandeur. From the inside, it's one big retail center promoting Coppola's wines and, more subtly, his films. Academy Awards and memorabilia from *The Godfather* and *Bram Stoker's Dracula* are on display. The Centennial Museum chronicles the history of the estate, its winemaking tradition and, last but not least, Coppola's films. Wine, food, and gift items dominate the cavernous tasting area, where visitors may sample four wines—such as the estate-grown blend, the cabernet Franc, merlot, chardonnay, zinfandel, or the vintage made from organically grown grapes—for $15 (price includes a souvenir glass). Bottles range from $19 to more than $100. The château and garden tour is $25 a pop, and the 1½-hour journey includes a private tasting and a memento glass.

1991 St. Helena Hwy. (Hwy. 29), Rutherford. ⓒ 707/968-1100. www.niebaum-coppola.com. Daily Sept–May 10am–5pm; June–Aug 10am–6pm. Tours daily at 10:30am, 12:30pm, and 2:30pm.

## ST. HELENA

73 miles N of San Francisco

This quiet little town, 17 miles north of Napa on Highway 29, is home to lots of beautiful old houses and first-rate restaurants, accommodations, and shops. The former Seventh-day Adventist village manages to maintain a pseudo Old West feel while catering to upscale shoppers with deep pockets. Hence it's *the* destination for retail-therapy seekers. On St. Helena's **Main Street** ★, between Pope and Pine streets, you'll find trendy fashions at **Pearl,** 1428 Main St. (© 707/963-3236); Jimmy Choo shoes at **Footcandy,** 1239 Main St. (© 707/963-2040); chic pet gifts at **Fideaux,** 1312 Main St. (© 707/967-9935); custom-embroidered French linens at **Jan de Luz,** 1219 Main St. (© 707/963-1550); estate jewelry at **Patina,** 1342 Main St. (© 707/ 963-5445); and European home accessories, sample holiday table settings, and free gift-wrapping at **Vanderbilt and Company,** 1429 Main St. (© 707/963-1010). Most stores are open 10am to 5pm Monday through Sunday.

Shopaholics should also take the sharp turn off Highway 29, 2 miles north of downtown St. Helena, to the **St. Helena Premier Outlets** (© **707/963-7282;** www. sthelenapremieroutlets.com). Featured designers include Escada, Coach, Tumi, and Movado. The stores are open daily from 10am to 6pm.

One last favorite stop: **Napa Valley Olive Oil Manufacturing Company,** 835 Charter Oak Ave. (© **707/963-4173**), at the end of the road behind Tra Vigne restaurant. The tiny market presses and bottles its own oils and sells them at a fraction of the price you'd pay elsewhere. It also has an extensive selection of Italian cooking ingredients, imported snacks, great deals on dried mushrooms, and a picnic table in the parking lot. You'll love the age-old method for totaling the bill—which you must discover for yourself. (I won't spoil the surprise.)

If you'd like to go **bicycling,** the quieter, northern end of the valley is an ideal place to rent a set of wheels and pedal the Silverado Trail. **St. Helena Cyclery,** 1156 Main St. (© **707/963-7736**), rents bikes for $7 per hour or $30 a day, including rear rack, helmet, and picnic bag.

**V. Sattui Winery** *Kids* As one of the only wineries allowed to sell food in the valley, this winery and huge deli (pronounced "Vee Sa-*too*-ee") has become the top picnic spot in the valley. Mobs cluster here for feasts in the grass. Their gourmet store stocks more than 200 cheeses, sandwich meats, breads, exotic salads, and delicious desserts, such as a white-chocolate cheesecake. Meanwhile, the long wine bar in the back offers everything from chardonnay, sauvignon blanc, Riesling, cabernet, and zinfandel to a Madeira and a muscat dessert wine. Their wines aren't distributed (nor are they particularly noteworthy), so if you taste something you simply must have, buy it. Wine prices start around $9, with many in the $15 range; reserves top out at around $75. V. Sattui's expansive, lively, and grassy picnic facilities make this a favorite for families. *Note:* To use the facilities, you must purchase your food and wine here.

1111 White Lane (at Hwy. 29), St. Helena. © **707/963-7774.** www.vsattui.com. Winter daily 9am–5pm; summer daily 9am–6pm.

**Joseph Phelps Vineyards** ★ Visitors interested in intimate, comprehensive tours and a knockout tasting should make a reservation at this stellar winery. Founded in 1973, it has since become a major player in both the region and the worldwide wine market. Phelps himself is credited with a long list of valley firsts—launching the syrah varietal in the valley, for instance, and extending the 1970s Berkeley food revolution (led by Alice Waters) up to the Wine Country, by founding the **Oakville Grocery Co.** (see "Gourmet Picnics, Napa-Style,"p. 185). The tour and tasting are only available via reservation, and the location—a quick, unmarked turn off the Silverado Trail in Spring Valley—is impossible to find unless you're looking for it.

Those in the know come to this modern, state-of-the-art winery and find an air of seriousness that hangs heavier than harvest grapes. Fortunately, the mood lightens as the well-educated tour guide explains the details of what you're tasting while pouring samples of five to six wines, which may include sauvignon blanc, viogner, syrah, chardonnay, merlot, and cab. Unfortunately, some wines are so popular they sell out quickly; come late in the season and you may not be able to taste or buy them. The three best-located picnic tables—on the terrace overlooking the valley—are available to those who join their wine club, Phelps Preferred; call for details.

200 Taplin Rd. (off the Silverado Trail), P.O. Box 1031, St. Helena. 🕐 800/707-5789. www.jpvwines.com. Mon–Sat 9am–5pm; Sun 10am–4pm. $20 seminars and tastings by appointment only; $10 per person for 2-oz. pour of Insignia.

**Beringer Vineyards** 🐸  You won't have the most personal experience at this tourist-heavy stop, but you will find a regal 1876 estate, founded by brothers Jacob and Frederick, and hand-dug tunnels in the hillside. The oldest continually operating winery in Napa Valley, Beringer managed to stay open even during Prohibition by making "sacramental" wines. White zinfandel is the winery's most popular seller, but plenty of other varietals are available. Tastings of current vintages ($5–$16) are conducted in new facilities, where a large selection of bottles sell for less than $20. Reserve wines are available for tasting in the remarkable Rhine House, and tours range from the $5 standard or $18 historical to the $30 1½-hour vintage legacy tour. Check the website for current tour prices; rumor has it they're changing.

2000 Main St. (Hwy. 29), St. Helena. 🕐 707/963-7115. www.beringer.com. Off season daily 10am–5pm (last tour 3:30pm); summer 10am–6pm (last tour 3:30pm).

## CALISTOGA
81 miles N of San Francisco

This last tourist town in Napa Valley was named by Sam Brannan, entrepreneur extraordinaire and California's first millionaire. After making a bundle supplying miners during the Gold Rush, he took advantage of the natural geothermal springs at the north end of Napa Valley, by building a hotel and spa in 1859. Flubbing up a speech in which he compared this natural California wonder to New York State's Saratoga Springs resort, he serendipitously coined the name "Calistoga," and it stuck. Today, this small, simple resort town—with 5,190-plus residents and an old-time main street (no building along the 6-block stretch is more than two stories high)—is popular with city folk who come here to unwind. Calistoga is a great place to relax and indulge in mineral waters, mud baths, Jacuzzis, massages and, of course, wine. The vibe is more casual—and a little groovier—than you'll find in neighboring towns to the south.

**NATURAL WONDERS   Old Faithful Geyser of California,** 1299 Tubbs Lane (🕐 707/942-6463; www.oldfaithfulgeyser.com), is one of only three "old faithful" geysers in the world. It has been blowing off steam at regular intervals for as long as anyone can remember. The 350°F (176°C) water spews at a height of about 60 feet every 40 minutes, day and night. The performance lasts about 3 minutes, and you can bring a picnic lunch to munch on between spews. An exhibit hall, gift shop, and snack bar are open every day. Admission is $8 for adults, $7 for seniors, $3 for children 6 to 12, and free for children under 6. The geyser is open daily from 9am to 6pm (to 5pm in winter). To get there, follow the signs from downtown Calistoga; it's between highways 29 and 128.

You won't see thousands of stone trees, but you'll still find many petrified specimens at the **Petrified Forest,** 4100 Petrified Forest Rd. (© **707/942-6667;** www.petrified forest.org). Volcanic ash blanketed this area after an eruption near Mount St. Helena 3 million years ago. You'll find redwoods that have turned to rock through the slow infiltration of silicas and other minerals, as well as petrified seashells, clams, and marine life indicating that water covered this area before the redwood forest appeared. Admission is $6 for adults, $5 for seniors and youths 12 to 17, $3 for children 6 to 11, and free for children under 6. The forest is open daily from 9am to 6pm (to 5pm in winter). Heading north from Calistoga on Highway 128, turn left onto Petrified Forest Road, just past Lincoln Street.

Cyclists can rent bikes from **Getaway Adventures BHK** (Biking, Hiking, and Kayaking), 1117 Lincoln Ave. (© **800/499-BIKE** or 707/763-3040; www.getaway adventures.com). Full-day tours are $105 including lunch and four or five wineries; downhill cruises (about half the price) are available for people who hate to pedal. Bike rental costs $28 per day plus a $20 delivery fee.

If you like horses and venturing through cool, misty forests, then $90 will seem like a bargain for a 2-hour ride with a friendly tour guide and owner, Midori, from the **Napa Valley Trailrides and Sonoma Cattle Company,** P.O. Box 6883, Napa, CA 94581 (© **707/255-2900;** www.napavalleytrailrides.com). After a lesson in basic horse handling, at the stable, they'll lead you on a leisurely stroll through Skyline Park in Napa. The price includes photos and refreshments.

**Frank Family Vineyards** ★ *Finds* "Wine dudes" Dennis, Tim, Jeff, Grant, and Pat will do practically anything to maintain their rightfully self-proclaimed reputation as the "friendliest winery in the valley." The name may have changed from Kornell Champagne Cellars to Frank-Rombauer to Frank Family, but the atmosphere remains the same; it's all about down-home fun: no muss, no fuss, no intimidation. At Frank Family, you're part of their family—no joke. They'll greet you like a long-lost relative and serve you all the bubbly you want (three to four varieties: *blanc de blanc, blanc de noir,* and reserve *rouge,* at $20–$70 a bottle). Still-wine lovers can slip into the casual back room to sample well-received chardonnay and a cabernet sauvignon. Behind the tasting room, a choice picnic area is situated under the oaks, overlooking the vineyards.
1091 Larkmead Lane (just off the Silverado Trail), Calistoga. © **707/942-0859.** Daily 10am–5pm.

**Schramsberg** ★★ *Finds* One of the valley's all-time best places to explore, this 217-acre, landmark champagne estate has a wonderful old-world feel. Schramsberg is the label that presidents serve when toasting dignitaries from around the globe—with a bevy of historic memorabilia in the front room to prove it. But the real mystique begins when you enter the champagne caves, partly hand-carved by Chinese laborers in the 1800s, which wind for 2 miles—reputedly making them the longest in North America. The caves have an authentic Tom Sawyer ambience, complete with dangling cobwebs and seemingly endless passageways; you can't help but feel you're on an adventure. The comprehensive, unintimidating tour ends in the tasting room, where you'll sit around a big table and sample four surprisingly varied selections of bubbly. Tastings are $20 per person, but it's money well spent. Tastings are offered only to those who take the free tour, and you must make reservations in advance.
1400 Schramsberg Rd. (off Hwy. 29), Calistoga. © **707/942-2414.** www.schramsberg.com. Daily 10am–4pm. Tours and tastings by appointment only.

**Sterling Vineyards** ⚡ *Kids* *Finds*   You don't need climbing shoes to reach this dazzling white Mediterranean-style winery, 300 feet up, on a rocky knoll. Just fork over $15 ($10 for kids, which includes a goodie bag) and take the aerial tram, which yields stunning bucolic views along the way. Once you're back on land, follow the self-guided tour (one of the most comprehensive in the Wine Country) of the winemaking process. The tram fare includes tastings of four varietals, in the panoramic tasting room. Limited release wines or reserve flights will set you back anywhere from $3 to $25 respectively. Expect to pay anywhere from $14 to $75 for a souvenir bottle ($20 is the average).

1111 Dunaweal Lane (off Hwy. 29, just south of downtown Calistoga), Calistoga. © 707/942-3344. www.sterling vineyards.com. Daily 10:30am–4:30pm.

**Clos Pegase** ⚡ *Finds*   Michael Graves designed this otherworldly oasis—which integrates artwork, 20,000 square feet of aging caves, and a luxurious private hilltop home. Viewing the art is as much the point as tasting the wines—which, by the way, don't come cheap: Prices range from $13 for the 2000 Vin Gris to as much as $75 for the 1998 Hommage Artist Series Reserve, an extremely limited blend of the winery's finest lots of cabernet sauvignon and merlot. Tasting current releases costs $5 for samples of three premium wines. The grounds at Clos Pegase (Clo Pey-*goss*) feature an impressive sculpture garden as well as scenic picnic spots.

1060 Dunaweal Lane (off Hwy. 29 or the Silverado Trail), Calistoga. © 707/942-4981. www.clospegase.com. Daily 10:30am–5pm. Tours daily at 11am and 2pm.

## WHERE TO STAY

Accommodations here run the gamut from motels and B&Bs to world-class luxury retreats, and all are accessible from the main highway. While I recommend the more romantically pastoral areas such as St. Helena, you're definitely going to find better deals in the towns of Napa or laid-back Calistoga.

Keep in mind that during high season—between June and November—most hotels charge peak rates and sell out completely on weekends; many have a 2-night minimum. If you need help organizing your Wine Country vacation, contact one of the following companies: **Accommodation Referral Bed & Breakfast Exchange**

---

*Moments*  **Find the New You—in Mud**

People in Calistoga have been taking mud paths for the last 150 years. Local volcanic ash, imported peat, and naturally boiling, mineral hot springs are mulled together to produce a thick, natural mud that simmers at a temperature of about 104°F (40°C). Follow your soak with a warm mineral-water shower, a whirlpool bath, a visit to the steam room, and a relaxing blanket-wrap. Emerge rejuvenated, revitalized, and squeaky clean.

Indulge yourself at any of these Calistoga spas: **Dr. Wilkinson's Hot Springs,** 1507 Lincoln Ave. (© 707/942-4102); **Golden Haven Hot Springs Spa,** 1713 Lake St. (© 707/942-6793); **Calistoga Spa Hot Springs,** 1006 Washington St. (© 707/942-6269); **Calistoga Village Inn & Spa,** 1880 Lincoln Ave. (© 707/942-0991); **Indian Springs Resort,** 1712 Lincoln Ave. (© 707/942-4913); or **Roman Spa Motel,** 1300 Washington St. (© 707/942-4441).

(📞 **800/240-8466** or 707/965-3400; www.accommodationsreferral.com), which also represents hotels and inns, will ask for dates, price range, and accommodations type before coming up with recommendations; **Bed & Breakfast Inns of Napa Valley** (📞 **707/944-4444**), an association of B&Bs, provides descriptions and makes reservations; **Napa Valley Reservations Unlimited** (📞 **800/251-NAPA** or 707/252-1985; www.napavalleyreservations.com) is also a source for booking everything from hot-air balloon to wine-tasting tours by limousine.

## VERY EXPENSIVE

**Calistoga Ranch** ★★★   Napa Valley's hottest new luxury resort is my very favorite. Tucked into the eastern mountainside, on 157 pristine hidden-canyon acres, each of the 46 rural-chic freestanding cottages may cost more than $525 per night. But the property combines the best of sister establishment Auberge du Soleil and rival Meadowood, it's beautifully decorated, and it's packed with every conceivable amenity (including fireplaces, outdoor patios along a wooded area, and cushy outdoor furnishings). Reasons not to leave include a giant swimming pool, reasonably large gym, beautifully designed indoor-outdoor spa with a natural thermal pool and individual pavilions with private-garden soaking tubs, and a breathtaking restaurant with stunning views of the property's Lake Lommel.

580 Lommel Rd., Calistoga, CA 94515. 📞 **707/254-2800.** Fax 707/942-4706. www.calistogaranch.com. 46 cottages. $450–$1,025 double. AE, DC, DISC, MC, V. **Amenities:** Restaurant; large heated outdoor pool; gym; spa; Jacuzzi; steam room; concierge; 24-hr. room service; massage; laundry service; next-day dry cleaning. *In room:* A/C; TV/VCR w/DVDs; fax upon request; dataport; 1 room w/full kitchen; minibar; fridge; coffeemaker; hair dryer; iron; safe.

**Cottage Grove Inn** ★★   Standing in two parallel rows at the end of the main strip in Calistoga is an ideal retreat: Although a paved road runs between the two rows of these adorable cottages on a residential street, they seem removed from the action once you've stepped across the threshold. Each compact guesthouse has a wood-burning fireplace, homey furnishings, cozy quilts, and an enormous bathroom with a skylight and a deep, two-person Jacuzzi tub. Guests enjoy such niceties as gourmet coffee, a stereo with CD player, a VCR (the inn has a video library), and a wet bar. Several major spas are within walking distance. This is a top pick if you want to do the Calistoga spa scene in comfort and style—especially since bicycles are provided for cruises around town and guests have access to complimentary tasting passes to more than a dozen nearby wineries. Smoking is allowed only in the gazebos.

1711 Lincoln Ave., Calistoga, CA 94515. 📞 **800/799-2284** or 707/942-8400. Fax 707/942-2653. www.cottagegrove. com. 16 cottages. $250–$325 double. Rates include continental breakfast and evening wine and cheese. AE, DC, DISC, MC, V. *In room:* A/C, TV/DVD, dataport, wet bar, fridge, coffeemaker, hair dryer, iron, safe, robes, 40 digital music channels.

**Meadowood Napa Valley** ★★★ *Finds*   Meadowood is summer camp for wealthy grownups. On 250 acres of pristine mountainside amid a forest of madrone and oak trees, this resort is quiet and exclusive enough to make you forget that busy wineries are just 10 minutes away. Rooms, furnished with American country classics, have beamed ceilings, private patios, stone fireplaces, and wilderness views; many are individual suite-lodges so far removed from the common areas that you must drive to get to them (lazier folks can opt for more centrally located accommodations). You can spend your days playing golf, tennis, or croquet; lounging around the pools or spa; or hiking the area. Those who actually want to leave the property to do some wine tasting can check in with the hotel's wine tutor.

900 Meadowood Lane, St. Helena, CA 94574. © 800/458-8080 or 707/963-3646. Fax 707/963-3532. www.meado wood.com. 85 units. $475–$825 double; $775–$1,250 1-bedroom suite; $1,275–$2,075 2-bedroom suite; $1,775–$2,900 3-bedroom suite; $2,275–$3,725 4-bedroom suite. Ask about promotional offers and off-season rates. 2-night minimum stay on weekends. AE, DC, DISC, MC, V. **Amenities:** 2 restaurants; 2 large heated outdoor pools; golf course; 7 tennis courts; health club and full-service spa; Jacuzzi; sauna; concierge; business center; secretarial services; 24-hr. room service; same-day laundry service/dry cleaning weekdays only; 2 croquet lawns. *In room:* A/C, TV, dataport, free high-speed Internet access, kitchenette in some rooms, minibar, coffeemaker, hair dryer, iron.

**Napa Valley Lodge** ★★ *(Finds*    Many frequent guests compare this contemporary hotel to the nearby upscale Vintage Inn, but they note that Napa Valley Lodge is even more personable and accommodating. It's off Highway 29, beyond a wall that does a good job of disguising the road. Guest rooms are large, ultraclean, and better appointed than many in the area. Many have vaulted ceilings, and 39 have fireplaces. Each comes with a king- or queen-size bed, wicker furnishings, robes, and a private balcony or a patio. The least expensive units, at ground level, are smaller with less sunlight than those on the second floor. Extras include a concierge, afternoon tea and cookies in the lobby, Friday-evening wine tasting in the library, and a full champagne breakfast. It's no wonder AAA gave the Napa Valley Lodge the Four Diamond award for excellence. Ask about winter discounts (as high as 30%).

2230 Madison St., Yountville, CA 94599. © 800/368-2468 or 707/944-2468. Fax 707/944-9362. www.napavalley lodge.com. 55 units. $252–$475 double. Rates include champagne breakfast buffet, afternoon tea and cookies, and Fri-evening wine tasting. AE, DC, DISC, MC, V. **Amenities:** Heated outdoor pool; small exercise room; spa; Jacuzzi; redwood sauna; concierge; free wireless in lobby and conference rooms. *In room:* A/C, TV w/pay movies, high-speed Internet access, minibar, coffeemaker, hair dryer, iron, ceiling fans.

## MODERATE

**Cedar Gables Inn** ★★ *(Finds*    This grand, romantic B&B in Old Town Napa is in a stunning Victorian built in 1892. Rooms reflect that era, with rich tapestries and stunning gilded antiques; four have fireplaces, five have whirlpool tubs, and all feature queen-size brass, wood, or iron beds. Guests meet each evening in front of the roaring fireplace in the lower "tavern" parlor for wine and cheese. At other times, the family room is a perfect place to cuddle up and watch the large-screen TV. Bonuses include a gourmet breakfast each morning, port in every room, and VIP treatment at many local wineries.

486 Coombs St. (at Oak St.), Napa, CA 94559. © 800/309-7969 or 707/224-7969. Fax 707/224-4838. www.cedar gablesinn.com. 9 units. $189–$319 double. Rates include full breakfast, evening wine and cheese, and port. AE, DISC, MC, V. From Hwy. 29 north, exit onto First St. and follow signs to downtown; turn right onto Jefferson, and left on Oak; house is on the corner. **Amenities:** Dataport (in the shared living room). *In room:* A/C, free wireless Internet, hair dryer, iron/ironing board, deluxe robes.

**Christopher's Inn** ★ *(Kids*    Ten years of renovations and expansions by architect-owner Christopher Layton have turned these sweet old homes in downtown Calistoga into hotel rooms with pizzazz. Options range from simple but tasteful quarters (colorful, with impressive antiques and small bathrooms) to huge, lavish abodes (with four-poster beds, rich fabrics and brocades, and sunken Jacuzzi tubs facing a gas fireplace). Most rooms have gas fireplaces, and some have flatscreen TVs and DVDs (with cable). Those who prefer homey accommodations will feel comfortable here, since the property doesn't have corporate polish or big-business blandness. The two plain but very functional two-bedroom units are ideal for families, provided you're not expecting the Ritz. An extended continental breakfast is delivered to your room daily.

1010 Foothill Blvd., Calistoga, CA 94515. (C) **866/876-5755** or 707/942-5755. Fax 707/942-6895. www.christophers inn.com. 24 units. $150–$475 double; $330–$350 house sleeping 5 or 6. Rates include continental breakfast. AE, MC, V. *In room:* TV, dataport, Wi-Fi wireless, free computer hookups, massage.

**Maison Fleurie** ★★   One of the prettiest garden-set B&Bs in the Wine Country, this inn comprises a trio of beautiful 1873 brick-and-fieldstone buildings overlaid with ivy. The main house—a charming Provençal replica with thick brick walls, terra-cotta tile, and paned windows—holds seven rooms; the rest are in the old bakery building and the carriage house. Some feature private balconies, patios, sitting areas, Jacuzzi tubs, and fireplaces. An above-par breakfast is served in the little dining room; afterward, you're welcome to wander the landscaped grounds or hit the wine-tasting trail, returning in time for afternoon hors d'oeuvres and wine.

6529 Yount St. (between Washington St. and Yountville Cross Rd.), Yountville, CA 94599. (C) **800/788-0369** or 707/944-2056. Fax 707/944-9342. www.maisonfleurienapa.com. 13 units. $120–$285 double. Rates include break-fast and hors d'oeuvres. AE, DC, DISC, MC, V. **Amenities:** Heated outdoor pool; Jacuzzi; free bike use. *In room:* A/C, TV, dataport, hair dryer, iron.

**Rancho Caymus Inn** ★   Heiress sculptor Mary Tilden Morton (of Morton Salt) was the creator of this cozy, Spanish-style hacienda. Two floors open onto wisteria-covered balconies, and guest rooms surround a garden courtyard with a huge outdoor fireplace. Morton fancied each room a work of art, so she employed the most skilled craftspeople she could find, designed adobe fireplaces in 22 of 26 rooms, and added artifacts she gathered in Mexico and South America.

The mix-and-match decor in the decent-sized guest rooms is on the funky side, with braided rugs and overly varnished, imported carved-wood furnishings. It's hard to balk, though, when the rooms include wet bars, sitting areas with sofa beds, small private patios, and new beds and wall paint added in 2005. Most suites have fireplaces, one has a kitchenette, and five have whirlpools. Breakfast, served in the dining room, includes fresh fruit, granola, orange juice, and pastries. Fancy, formal, French-influenced La Toque restaurant is next door.

1140 Rutherford Rd., P.O. Box 78, Rutherford, CA 94573. (C) **800/845-1777** or 707/963-1777. Fax 707/963-5387. www.ranchocaymus.com. 26 suites. $145–$300 double; $185–$400 master suite; $265–$440 2-bedroom suite. Rates include continental breakfast. AE, MC, V. From Hwy. 29 north, turn right onto Rutherford Rd./Hwy. 128 east.; the hotel is on your left. **Amenities:** Restaurant. *In room:* A/C, TV, dataport, kitchenette in 1 room, minibar, fridge, coffeemaker, hair dryer, iron in some rooms, microwaves in master suites.

**Wine Country Inn** ★★   Just off the highway, behind Freemark Abbey vineyard, is one of Wine Country's most personable choice of accommodations. This attractive, wood and stone, family-run inn, complete with a French-style mansard roof and tur-ret, overlooks a pastoral landscape of vineyards. Inside, individually decorated rooms contain antique furnishings and handmade quilts; most have fireplaces and private terraces overlooking the valley, and others have private hot tubs. Five luxury cottages include king-size beds as well as a single bed (perfect for the tot in tow), sitting areas, fireplaces, private patios, and two-person Jacuzzi tubs. One of the inn's best fea-tures (besides the absence of TVs) is the heated outdoor pool. Another outstanding feature is the selection of suites, which come with stereos and plenty of space and pri-vacy. The owners make every guest feel welcome, serving wine and appetizers nightly, greeting guests hospitably in the warm living room, and offering a full buffet break-fast as well.

1152 Lodi Lane, St. Helena, CA 94574. ℭ **888/465-4608** or 707/963-7077. Fax 707/963-9018. www.winecountry inn.com. 29 units, 12 w/shower only. $195–$525 double; $495–$555 for cottages. Rates include breakfast and appetizers. MC, V. **Amenities:** Heated outdoor pool; Jacuzzi; concierge; free Internet access at a computer station, big-screen TV in common room. *In room:* A/C, hair dryer, iron.

## INEXPENSIVE

In addition to the listings below, I highly recommend **Napa Valley Railway Inn,** 6503 Washington St., Yountville, adjacent to the Vintage 1870 shopping complex (ℭ **707/944-2000**), which rents private railway cars converted into adorable hotel rooms.

### Calistoga Spa Hot Springs ⭐ Kids Value
Calistoga Spa Hot Springs is one of very few hotels in the Wine Country that caters specifically to families with children. They classify themselves as a family resort and accommodate visitors of all ages. In any case, it's a great bargain, with unpretentious yet comfortable rooms and a plethora of spa facilities. All of Calistoga's best shops and restaurants are within easy walking distance, and you can whip up your own grub at the barbecue grills near the large pool and patio area.

1006 Washington St. (at Gerrard St.), Calistoga, CA 94515. ℭ **866/822-5772** or 707/942-6269. www.calistoga spa.com. 57 units. Winter $104–$185 double, summer $127–$185 double. MC, V. **Amenities:** 3 heated outdoor pools; kids' wading pool; exercise room; spa. *In room:* A/C, TV, kitchenette, fridge, coffeemaker, hair dryer, iron.

### Chablis Inn ⭐
There's no way around it: If you want to sleep cheaply in a town where the *average* room rate tops $200 per night in high season, you're destined for a motel. But look on the bright side: Your room is likely to be little more than a crash pad, anyway, after a full day of eating and drinking. A clean bed and a remote control are all you'll really need, and Chablis offers much more than that. All of the motel-style rooms are superclean, and some are even equipped with kitchenettes or whirlpool tubs. Guests have access to an outdoor heated pool and hot tub as well.

3360 Solano Ave., Napa, CA 94558. ℭ **707/257-1944.** Fax 707/226-6862. www.chablisinn.com. 34 units. May to mid-Nov $99–$165 double; mid-Nov to Apr $79–$150 double. AE, DC, DISC, MC, V. **Amenities:** Heated outdoor pool; Jacuzzi. *In room:* A/C, satellite TV, dataport in some rooms, kitchenette in some rooms, fridge, coffeemaker, hair dryer.

### Dr. Wilkinson's Hot Springs Resort ⭐
This spa/"resort" in the heart of Calistoga is one of the best deals in Napa Valley. Rooms range from attractive Victorian-style accommodations to modern, cozy, recently renovated guest rooms in the main 1950s-style motel. All are spiffier than most in the area, with surprisingly tasteful textiles and basic motel-style accoutrements. Larger rooms have refrigerators and/or kitchens. Facilities—which are the highlight of a Calistoga visit—include three mineral-water pools (two outdoor and one indoor), a Jacuzzi, a steam room, and mud baths. All kinds of body treatments are available in the spa, including famed mud baths, steams, and massage—all of which I highly recommend. Be sure to inquire about their excellent midweek packages and their new, fantastic facial performed in a private cottage.

1507 Lincoln Ave. (Hwy. 29, between Fairway and Stevenson aves.), Calistoga, CA 94515. ℭ **707/942-4102.** www.drwilkinson.com. 42 units. $109–$199 double. Weekly discounts and packages available. AE, MC, V. *In room:* A/C, TV, dataport, coffeemaker, hair dryer.

### El Bonita Motel ⭐ Kids Value
This 1930s Art Deco motel is a bit too close to Highway 29 for comfort, but the 2½ acres of beautifully landscaped gardens away from the road help even the score. The rooms are small and basic as can be, but spotlessly clean, decorated with newer furnishings and kitchenettes; some have a whirlpool bathtub. It ain't heaven, but it's cheap for St. Helena.

195 Main St. (at El Bonita Ave.), St. Helena, CA 94574. (C) **800/541-3284** or 707/963-3216. Fax 707/963-8838. www.elbonita.com. 41 units. $89–$259 double. Rates include continental breakfast. AE, DC, DISC, MC, V. **Amenities:** Heated outdoor pool; spa; Jacuzzi; free high-speed Internet access in lobby. *In room:* A/C, TV, free wireless Internet, fridge, coffeemaker, hair dryer, iron, microwave.

**White Sulphur Springs Retreat & Spa** ★  If your idea of the ultimate vacation is a cozy cabin on 45 acres, paradise is a short, winding drive away from downtown St. Helena. Established in 1852, the property features a creek, a waterfall, a naturally heated sulfur hot spring, and redwood, madrone, and fir trees. Guests stay in either creekside cabins of varying sizes, the inn, or the Carriage House. Cabins are decorated with simple, homey furnishings; no. 9 has two queen-size beds and a kitchenette. From here, you can take a dip in the natural hot sulfur spring; lounge by the large outdoor unheated pool; sit under a tree and watch for deer, fox, raccoon, spotted owl, or woodpecker; or schedule a day of massage, aromatherapy, and other treatments in their spa, completed in early 2001. (The massage is fantastic.) *Note:* No RVs are allowed. All rooms are nonsmoking. Call well in advance; the resort is often rented by large groups.

3100 White Sulphur Springs Rd., St. Helena, CA 94574. (C) **800/593-8873** in California, or 707/963-8588. Fax 707/963-2890. www.whitesulphursprings.com. 37 units, 14 w/shared bathroom; 9 cottages. Carriage House (shared bathroom) $95–$120; small creekside cottages $170–$190; large cottages $185–$200; cottage no. 9 $190–$210. Rates include continental breakfast. 2-night minimum stay on weekends Apr–Oct and all holidays. AE, DC, DISC, MC, V. **Amenities:** Heated outdoor pool; soaking pool; full-service spa; Jacuzzi; free Internet hook-up in hospitality room. *In room:* A/C in some rooms, fridge, hair dryer, iron in large cottage.

**Wine Valley Lodge** ★ *Value*  Dollar for dollar, the Wine Valley Lodge is a great deal. At the south end of town in a quiet, residential neighborhood, the Mission-style motel is extremely well kept and accessible, just a short drive from Highway 29 and the wineries to the north. The reasonably priced two-bedroom deluxe units are great for families.

200 S. Coombs St. (between First and Imola sts.), Napa, CA 94559. (C) **800/696-7911** or 707/224-7911. www.wine valleylodge.com. 54 units. $89–$124 double; $150–$165 deluxe. AE, DC, DISC, MC, V. **Amenities:** Heated outdoor pool (closed during the winter). *In room:* A/C, TV.

## WHERE TO DINE

To best enjoy Napa's restaurant scene, keep one thing in mind: You'll need reservations—especially for tables in renowned establishments.

### EXPENSIVE

**The French Laundry** ★★★ CLASSIC AMERICAN/FRENCH  Thomas Keller is the chef-owner behind this discreet restaurant that regularly ranks as one of, if not *the*, best restaurant in the world. Plainly put, a meal at the French Laundry is unlike any other dining experience. Part of its unique character has to do with the intricate preparations, often finished tableside, presented with uncommon artistry and detail—from the food itself to the surface on which it's delivered. Other distinguishing features include the intimate environment; the service, which is superfluous, formal, and attentive (one course, for example, comes with a *selection* of salts in a fancy box); and the sheer length of time it takes to ride Keller's culinary magic carpet. The atmosphere is as serious as the diners who quietly swoon over the ongoing parade of bite-size delights. Seating is available downstairs, upstairs, and at garden tables in clement weather. The prix-fixe menu offers a choice of seven or nine courses. A vegetarian menu is available, but signature dishes include Keller's "tongue in cheek" (a marinated, braised round of sliced lamb tongue and tender beef cheeks) and "macaroni and cheese" (sweet, butterpoached Maine lobster with creamy lobster broth and orzo with mascarpone cheese).

The staff is well acquainted with the prestigious wine selection; they charge a $50 corkage fee if you bring your own bottle. On warm summer nights, request a table in the flower-filled garden. *Hint:* If you can't get a reservation, try walking in—on occasion folks don't keep their reservation and tables open up, especially during lunch on rainy days. Reservations are accepted 2 months in advance of the date, starting at 10am; anticipate hitting redial many times for the best chance. Also, insiders tell me that fewer people call on weekends, so you have a better chance at getting through the busy signal on Saturdays and Sundays.

6640 Washington St. (at Creek St.), Yountville. ✆ 707/944-2380. Reservations required. Vegetarian menu $80; 5-course menu $105; chef's tasting menu $175. AE, MC, V. Fri–Sun 11am–1pm; daily 5:30–9pm. Enforced dress code: no jeans, shorts, or tennis shoes; men should wear jackets.

**Terra** ★★★ CONTEMPORARY AMERICAN    Terra is one of my favorite restaurants because it manages to stay humble even though it serves some of the most extraordinary food in Northern California. Terra is the creation of Lissa Doumani and her husband, Hiro Sone, a master chef and James Beard Award–winner from Japan, who met more than 15 years ago when they worked together at Spago in L.A. The menu reflects Sone's full use of the region's bountiful fresh ingredients, and his formal training in classic European and Japanese cuisine. All the dishes here are good beyond belief, but they can be understated and refined, as in the broiled sake-marinated cod with shrimp dumplings and *shiso* broth, or outrageously flavorful, as in the petit ragout of sweetbreads, prosciutto, mushroom, and white truffle oil. I cannot express the importance of saving room for dessert (or forcing it down even if you overate). Doumani's recipes—which include tiramisu and a heavenly orange risotto in a brandy snap cookie with passion-fruit sauce—are some of the best I've ever tasted. The dining room, with fieldstone walls, is at once rustic and romantic.

1345 Railroad Ave. (between Adams and Hunt sts.), St. Helena. ✆ 707/963-8931. www.terrarestaurant.com. Reservations recommended. Main courses $19–$29. AE, DC, MC, V. Wed–Mon dinner starts at 6pm. Closed 2 weeks in early Jan.

## MODERATE

**All Seasons Café** ★★ CALIFORNIA    The best restaurant in downtown Calistoga balances homey charm with sophisticated, seasonally inspired dishes. Vibrant bouquets, large framed watercolors, and windows overlooking busy Lincoln Avenue soften the look of the black-and-white checkered flooring, brick red ceiling, and long, black wine bar. The laid-back service makes what arrives on the plate—such as crispy skin chicken with black truffle chicken *jus* or herb-roasted monkfish with fennel *nage*—that much more of a delicious surprise. More than 400 wines are available from their adjoining wine shop. (Buy next door, pay the $15 corkage fee, and you're still drinking for far less than at most restaurants.) Alas, the kitchen was a wee slow on my last visit, but all was forgiven when the food far surpassed my expectations.

1400 Lincoln Ave. (at Washington St.), Calistoga. ✆ 707/942-9111. Reservations recommended on weekends. Main courses $9–$11 lunch, $19–$28 dinner. DISC, MC, V. Lunch Fri–Sun noon–2:30pm; dinner nightly 6–9pm.

**Bistro Don Giovanni** ★★★ *Value* REGIONAL ITALIAN    Donna and Giovanni Scala own this bright, bustling, cheery Italian restaurant, which happens to be one of my favorites in Napa Valley. The menu features pastas, risottos, pizzas (baked in a wood-burning oven), and a half-dozen other main courses. Every time I grab a menu, I can't get past the beet and *haricots verts* salad and pasta with duck Bolognese. On the rare occasion that I venture from my favorite dishes here, I am equally smitten. The thin-crust pizzas fresh from the wood-burning oven, the seared salmon filet on buttermilk mashed potatoes, and the steak *frites* are excellent. On warm sunny days, I highly recommend dining alfresco on the patio.

4110 Howard Lane (at St. Helena Hwy.), Napa. (© **707/224-3300.** Reservations recommended. Main courses $12–$24. AE, DC, DISC, MC, V. Sun–Thurs 11:30am–10pm; Fri–Sat 11:30am–11pm.

**Bistro Jeanty** ⊕ FRENCH BISTRO  This casual, warm bistro—with muted buttercup walls, patio seats, and two dining rooms divided by the bar—is French chef Phillipe Jeanty's ode to rich French comfort food. The all-day menu includes tomato soup in puff pastry, foie gras pâté, steak tartare, and house-smoked trout with potato slices. No meal should start without a paper cone filled with fried smelt, and none should end without the crème brûlée, made with a thin layer of chocolate cream between classic vanilla custard and a caramelized sugar top. In between, prepare yourself for a rib-gripping free-for-all, including coq au vin, cassoulet, and juicy, thick-cut pork chop with *jus,* spinach, and mashed potatoes. Alas, quality has suffered since Jeanty branched out to three restaurants, but when the kitchen is on, it's still a fine place to sup.

6510 Washington St., Yountville. (© **707/944-0103.** www.bistrojeanty.com. Reservations recommended. Appetizers $8.50–$13; most main courses $15–$29. AE, MC, V. Daily 11:30am–10:30pm.

**Bouchon** ⊕⊕ FRENCH BISTRO  Appeasing the crowds who never manage to get a reservation at The French Laundry, Thomas Keller opened this far more casual, very sexy French brasserie with a raw bar. Expect superb renditions of steak *frites,* mussels *meunière,* grilled-cheese sandwiches, and other heavenly French classics (try the expensive and rich foie gras pâté, made on the premises). My favorite dishes include the bibb lettuce salad (seriously, trust me on this), french fries (perhaps the best in the valley), and roasted chicken bathed in wild mushroom ragout. Late hours are a bonus, although the menu is more limited after the crowds dwindle.

6534 Washington St. (at Humbolt), Yountville. (© **707/944-8037.** Reservations recommended. Main courses $15–$27. AE, MC, V. Daily 11:30am–12:30am.

**Tra Vigne Restaurant** ⊕ *Overrated* ITALIAN  As much as I want to love everything about this famous, absurdly scenic restaurant, I can't anymore; it's just not the sure thing it used to be. After an excessive number of chef changes over the years, meals can range from stupendous to barely so-so. Despite the inconsistency, however, you can still count on Tra Vigne for one thing: If you sit in the Tuscan-style courtyard, you will have a great time, regardless of whether the kitchen is on the money or missing the mark. (Inside, the bustling, cavernous dining room and happening bar is fine for chilly days and evenings, but it's not nearly so magical as the outdoor dining area.) You can also count on wonderful bread (served with house-cured olives), a menu of robust California dishes, cooked Italian-style, a daily oven-roasted pizza special, lots of pastas, and tried-and-true standbys such as short ribs, *fritto misto,* and whole roasted fish.

1050 Charter Oak Ave., St. Helena. (© **707/963-4444.** Reservations recommended. Main courses $13–$22. DC, DISC, MC, V. Daily 11:30am–10pm.

## INEXPENSIVE

**Market** AMERICAN  In past editions, I've highly recommended this upscale but cheap ode to American comfort food. Ever since the chef departed to open a superb, high-end sister restaurant—Cyrus, in Healdsburg—the food here has gone downhill. Still, if you're in expensive St. Helena and want some casual glamour with your burger, visit Market, with fancy stone walls, a Brunswick bar, clunky steak knives, and simple

> **Tips** Gourmet Picnics, Napa-Style
>
> You could plan your whole trip around Napa restaurants, but the valley is also an ideal place for a picnic. One of the finest gourmet food stores in the Wine Country, if not the state, the **Oakville Grocery Co.**, 7856 St. Helena Hwy., at Oakville Cross Road (✆ **707/944-8802**) is the best place to fill a basket. The store is crammed with the very best breads, cheeses, pâtés, cold cuts, fresh foie gras, smoked Norwegian salmon, fresh caviar (beluga, sevruga, osetra), and prepared foods; its selection of California wines is also exceptional. Assemble your own picnic or let the staff prepare a basket for you, with 24-hours notice. The Grocery Co. is open daily from 9am to 6pm; it also has an espresso bar (Mon–Fri 7am–6pm, Sat–Sun 8am–6pm), with breakfast and lunch fare, including homemade pastries.
>
> **Palisades Market**, 1506 Lincoln Ave., Calistoga (✆ **707/942-9549**), serves the best sandwiches I've ever had outside of Italy. You can also drop in for wine, juice, soda, cheese, tamales, green salads, lasagna, soup, and other treats. Hours are Sunday through Wednesday from 7:30am to 6pm and Thursday through Saturday from 7:30am to 7pm.
>
> A Manhattan import, **Dean & Deluca**, 607 S. Main St. (Hwy. 29), north of Zinfandel Lane and south of Sulphur Springs Road in St. Helena (✆ **707/967-9980**) is like a world's fair of beautifully displayed foods, often painfully pricey. Check out the 200 domestic and imported cheeses; tapenades, pastas, oils, hand-packed dried herbs and spices, chocolates, sauces, and cookware; an espresso bar; one heck of a bakery section; and more. The wine shop boasts a 1,200-label collection. It's open daily from 9am to 7pm (the espresso bar opens Mon–Sat at 7:30am and Sun at 9am).

white-plate presentations. Skip the lame chopped salad and go for meatloaf with barbecue sauce over gravy, mashed potatoes, and carrots; or s'mores you can toast yourself on crisp, homemade graham crackers. At lunch, you can opt for a three-course meal—a steal at $15.

1347 Main St., St. Helena. ✆ **707/963-3799**. Most main courses $7–$17. AE, MC, V. Daily 11:30am–10pm.

**Taylor's Automatic Refresher** *(Overrated* DINER  Buyer beware: This gourmet roadside burger shack, built in 1949, is another winner that has slipped to mediocrity. The last few meals I had there left me knowing my money would have been better spent at the Oakville Grocery deli. The burger, onion rings, and fries were fair to middling, and the iceberg salad was unwieldy. Only the shake left me satisfied—and how hard is it to make a great shake? Perhaps the trouble is that the owners now keep a closer watch on their San Francisco outpost—which is great, by the way. In any case, it's still the only casual burger joint in St. Helena, with *ahi* tuna burgers and various tacos and salads as well. And it still draws huge lines of tourists, who love ordering at the counter or feasting alfresco.

933 Main St., St. Helena. ✆ **707/963-3486**. www.taylorsrefresher.com. Main courses $4–$13. AE, MC, V. Daily 11am–8pm (9pm in summer).

**ZuZu** ☆☆ TAPAS   ZuZu lures neighborhood regulars with its no-reservation policy, its cramped but friendly wine and beer bar, and its affordable Mediterranean small plates, meant to be shared. The comfortable, warm atmosphere is anything but corporate. Equally casual and personal, the menu includes sizzling miniskillets of tangy, fantastic paella; addictive prawns with pimento dipping sauce for bread; light and delicate sea scallop ceviche salad; and Moroccan barbecued lamb chops with a sweet-and-spicy sauce. Desserts aren't as good, but with more tasty plates than you can possibly devour, who cares?

829 Main St., Napa. ℂ 707/224-8555. Reservations not accepted. Tapas $3–$13. MC, V. Mon–Thurs 11:30am–10pm; Fri 11:30am–midnight; Sat 4pm–midnight; Sun 4–9pm.

## 2 Sonoma Valley

Sonoma is often regarded as the "other" Wine Country, forever in the shadow of Napa Valley. The truth, however, is that it's a distinct experience. Sonoma still manages to feel like backcountry, thanks to its lower density of wineries, restaurants, and hotels; because it's far less traveled than Napa, it offers a more genuine escape. Small, family-owned wineries are its mainstay—as in the early days of California winemaking, when everyone started with the intention of going broke and loving every minute of it. Unlike the rigidly structured tours at many of Napa Valley's corporate-owned wineries, tastings and tours on the Sonoma side of the Mayacamas Mountains are usually free and low-key, with plenty of friendly banter between the winemakers and their guests.

### ESSENTIALS

**GETTING THERE**   From San Francisco, cross the Golden Gate Bridge and head north on U.S. 101. Exit at Highway 37; after 10 miles, turn north onto Highway 121. After another 10 miles, turn north onto Highway 12 (Broadway), which will take you directly into the town of Sonoma.

**VISITOR INFORMATION**   The **Sonoma Valley Visitors Bureau,** 453 First St. E. (ℂ 707/996-1090; www.sonomavalley.com) is open daily from 9am to 6pm. An additional **visitors bureau** is located a few miles south of the square at 25200 Arnold Dr. (Hwy. 121), at the entrance to Viansa Winery (ℂ 707/935-4747); it's open daily from 9am to 5pm (6pm in summer).

If you prefer some advance information, you can contact the Sonoma Valley Visitors Bureau to order the free *Sonoma Valley Visitors Guide,* which lists most lodgings, wineries, and restaurants in the valley.

**WHEN TO GO**   See the Napa section, earlier in this chapter.

### TOURING THE VALLEY & WINERIES

Sonoma Valley is currently home to about 35 wineries (including California's first, Buena Vista, founded in 1857) and 13,000 acres of vineyards, which produce more than five million cases a year of 25 types of wine.

The towns and wineries covered below are organized geographically from south to north, starting at the intersection of Highway 37 and Highway 121 in the Carneros District and ending in Kenwood. The wineries here tend to be a little more spread out than they are in Napa, but they're easy to find. Still, it's best to decide which wineries interest you most, and devise a touring strategy before you set out, so you don't find yourself backtracking a lot.

I've reviewed some my favorite Sonoma Valley wineries here—more than enough to keep you busy tasting wine for a long weekend. For a complete list, pick up one of the free guides to the valley available at the Sonoma Valley Visitors Bureau (see "Visitor Information," above).

## THE CARNEROS DISTRICT

As you approach the Wine Country from the south, you must pass through the Carneros District, a cool, wind-swept region that borders the San Pablo Bay and marks the entrance to both Napa and Sonoma valleys. Until the latter part of the 20th century, this mixture of marsh, sloughs, and hills was mainly used as sheep pasture (*carneros* means "sheep" in Spanish). After experimental plantings yielded slow-growing yet high-quality grapes—particularly chardonnay and pinot noir—several Napa and Sonoma wineries expanded here, eventually establishing the Carneros District as an American Viticultural Appellation.

**Viansa Winery and Italian Marketplace** *Finds* The first major winery as you enter Sonoma Valley from the south, this Tuscan-style villa sprawls over a knoll overlooking the entire lower valley. Viansa is the brainchild of Sam and Vicki Sebastiani (*Viansa* is a contraction of "Vicki and Sam"), who left the family winemaking dynasty to create their own temple to food and wine.

It's one of the few Sonoma wineries that sells deli items; the focaccia sandwiches are especially delicious. The deli is a large room crammed with a cornucopia of high-quality condiments, prepared foods, Italian tableware, cookbooks, and wine-related gifts—not to mention copious tasting opportunities. You can dine alfresco under the grape trellis while you admire the bucolic view.

The winery, which does an extensive mail-order business through The Tuscan Club, has established a favorable reputation for its Italian varietals. Tastings, which cost $5 to $20 per person, take place at the east and west end of the marketplace. A self-guided tour includes a trip through the underground barrel-aging cellar, adorned with colorful hand-painted murals. Guided tours, held at 11am and 2pm, will set you back $5.

25200 Arnold Dr. (Hwy. 121), Sonoma. © 800/995-4740 or 707/935-4700. www.viansa.com. Daily 10am–5pm. Daily self-guided tours. Guided tours daily 11am and 2pm for $5.

**Gloria Ferrer Champagne Caves** *Finds* When you have had it up to here with chardonnays and pinots, it's time to pay a visit to Gloria Ferrer, the grande dame of the Wine Country's sparkling-wine producers. Gloria is the wife of José Ferrer, whose family has made sparkling wine for 5 centuries. The family business, Freixenet, is the largest producer of sparkling wine in the world; Cordon Negro is its most popular brand. That legacy amounts to big bucks, and certainly a good chunk of change went into building this palatial estate. It glimmers like Oz, high atop a gently sloping hill, overlooking the verdant Carneros District. On a sunny day, enjoying a glass of dry *brut* while soaking in the magnificent views is a must.

If you're unfamiliar with the term *méthode champenoise,* be sure to take the free, 30-minute tour of the fermenting tanks, bottling line, and caves brimming with racks of yeast-laden bottles. Afterward, retire to the elegant tasting room, order a glass of one of seven sparkling wines ($4–$10 per glass) or tastes of their eight still wines ($2–$3 per taste), find an empty chair on the veranda, and say, "Ahhh. *This* is the life." You can sit at outdoor picnic tables, but it's usually too windy for comfort, and you must buy a glass of sparkling wine or a bottle (from around $18–$40) to reserve a table.

23555 Carneros Hwy. (Hwy. 121), Sonoma. ℂ **707/996-7256**. www.gloriaferrer.com. Daily 10am–5:15pm. Tours daily; call day of visit to confirm schedule.

## SONOMA

Sonoma, at the northern boundary of the Carneros District along Highway 12, is the centerpiece of the valley. The midsize town owes much of its appeal to Mexican general Mariano Guadalupe Vallejo, who fashioned this pleasant, slow-paced community after a typical Mexican village—right down to its central plaza, Sonoma's geographical and commercial center. The plaza sits at the top of a T formed by Broadway (Hwy. 12) and Napa Street. Most of the surrounding streets form a grid pattern around this axis, making Sonoma easy to negotiate. The plaza's Bear Flag Monument marks the spot where the crude Bear Flag was raised in 1846, signaling the end of Mexican rule; the symbol was later adopted by the state of California and placed on its flag. The 8-acre park at the center of the plaza, complete with two ponds populated by ducks and geese, is perfect for an afternoon siesta in the cool shade.

The best way to see the town is to follow the **Sonoma Walking Tour** map, provided by the Sonoma League for Historic Preservation. Highlights include General Vallejo's 1852 Victorian-style home; the Sonoma Barracks, erected in 1836 to house Mexican army troops; and the Blue Wing Inn, an 1840 hostelry built to accommodate new settlers, as well as travelers such as John Fremont, Kit Carson, and Ulysses S. Grant. You can purchase the $3 map at the Mission (see below).

The **Mission San Francisco Solano de Sonoma,** on Sonoma Plaza, at the corner of First Street East and Spain Street (ℂ **707/938-9560**), was founded in 1823. It was the northernmost mission built in California. It was also the only one established on the Northern Coast by Mexican rulers, who wished to protect their territory from Russian fur traders. It's now part of Sonoma State Historic Park. Admission is $2 for adults, free for children ages 16 and under. It's open daily from 10am to 5pm except Thanksgiving, Christmas, and New Year's Day.

**Sebastiani Vineyards & Winery**   The name Sebastiani is practically synonymous with Sonoma. What started in 1904, when Samuele Sebastiani began producing his first wines, has in three generations grown into a small empire, producing some 200,000 cases annually. After a few years of seismic retrofitting, a face-lift, and a temporary tasting room, the original 1904 winery is now open to the public with more extensive educational tours ($5 per person), an 80-foot, S-shaped tasting bar, and an extensive gift shop. In the contemporary tasting room's minimuseum area, you can see the company's original turn-of-the-20th-century crusher and press, as well as the world's largest collection of oak-barrel carvings, crafted by bygone local artist Earle Brown. The winery offers one complimentary glass of wine and tasting menus for $8 or $18 (for the fancy stuff and a keepsake glass). Bottle prices are reasonable, ranging from $13 to $75. A picnic area adjoins the cellars, but a far more scenic spot is across the parking lot in Sebastiani's Cherryblock Vineyards.

389 Fourth St. E., Sonoma. ℂ **800/888-5532** or 707/933-3200. www.sebastiani.com. Daily 10am–5pm. Tours winter daily 11am and 3pm; summer 11am, 1pm, and 3pm.

**Buena Vista Winery**   Count Agoston Haraszthy, the Hungarian émigré regarded as the father of California's wine industry, founded Buena Vista in 1857. A close friend of General Mariano Vallejo, Haraszthy returned from Europe in 1861 with 100,000 of the finest vine cuttings, which he made available to all growers. Although Buena

Vista's winemaking now takes place at an ultramodern facility in the Carneros District, the winery maintains a tasting room inside the restored 1862 Press House. The beautiful, stone-crafted room brims with wines, wine-related gifts, and accessories.

Tastings are $5 for four wines and $10 for a flight of three library wines. You can take the self-guided tour any time during operating hours; a Historical Tour and Tasting, daily at 11am and 2pm, details the life and times of Count Haraszthy and includes a viticultural tour, as well as a wine and food pairing. If you drop by on a Saturday, you can opt for the $35 wine-and-cheese tasting. After tasting, grab your favorite bottle, a selection of cheeses from the Sonoma Cheese Factory, salami, bread, and spreads (all available in the tasting room), and plant yourself at one of the many picnic tables in this lush, verdant setting.

18000 Old Winery Rd. (off E. Napa St., just northeast of downtown), Sonoma. ✆ **800/926-1266** or 707/265-1472. www.buenavistawinery.com. Nov–May daily 10am–5pm; June–Oct 10am–5:30pm.

**Ravenswood Winery**   Ravenswood established itself as the *sine qua non* of zinfandel, the versatile grape that's gaining ground on cabernet sauvignon. In fact, Ravenswood was the first winery in the United States to focus primarily on zins, about three-quarters of the company's 500,000-case production; it also produces merlot, cabernet sauvignon, and a small amount of chardonnay.

The winery is smartly designed—recessed into the hillside to protect its treasures from the simmering summer heat. Tours ($10 per person) follow the winemaking process from grape to glass, and include a visit to the aromatic oak-barrel aging rooms. You're welcome to bring your own picnic basket to any of the tables, but if you're coming on the weekend from Memorial Day to Labor Day, consider joining one of the winery's famously fun barbecues (call for details). Tastings are $5 for four wines, which is refundable with purchase.

18701 Gehricke Rd. (off Lovall Valley Rd.), Sonoma. ✆ **888/NO-WIMPY** or 707/933-2332. www.ravenswood-wine. com. Labor Day to Memorial Day 10am–4:30pm; Memorial Day to Labor Day 10am–5pm). Tours by reservation only at 10:30am.

## GLEN ELLEN

Although Glen Ellen is a fraction of the size of Sonoma, about 7 miles to the south, it's home to several of the valley's finest wineries, restaurants, and inns. Aside from the addition of a few new restaurants, this charming Wine Country town hasn't changed much since the days when Jack London settled on his Beauty Ranch, about a mile west. If you haven't yet decided where you want to set up camp during your visit to the Wine Country, I highly recommend this lovable little town.

Hikers, horseback riders, and picnickers will enjoy **Jack London State Historic Park,** 2400 London Ranch Rd., off Arnold Drive (✆ **707/938-5216**). Within its 800 acres, which were once home to the renowned writer, you'll find 9 miles of trails, the remains of London's burned-down dream house, preserved structures, a museum, and plenty of ideal picnic spots. The park is open daily from 9:30am to 5pm. Admission is $6 per car or $5 per seniors' car.

**Arrowood Vineyards & Winery**   This winery stands on a gently rising hillside lined with manicured vineyards. Tastings take place in the Hospitality House, the newer of Arrowood's two gray-and-white buildings. They're fashioned after New England farmhouses, complete with wraparound porches. The focus here is on making world-class wine with minimal intervention, and results have scored very well with the likes of *Wine Spectator* critics. Mind you, excellence doesn't come cheap: A taste is $5 or $10 for limited-production wines, but if you're curious about what near-perfection tastes like, it's worth it. *Note:* No picnic facilities are available here.

14347 Sonoma Hwy. (Hwy. 12), Glen Ellen. ℂ 707/935-2600. www.arrowoodvineyards.com. Daily 10am–4:30pm. Tours by appointment only, daily 10:30am and 2:30pm.

**Benziger Family Winery** ⭐ *Finds* At any given time, two generations of Benzigers (*Ben*-zig-ger) may be running around tending to chores, and they instantly make you feel as if you're part of the clan. The pastoral, user-friendly property features an exceptional self-guided tour ("The most comprehensive tour in the wine industry," according to *Wine Spectator*), gardens, a spacious tasting room staffed by amiable folk, and an art gallery. The fun, informative 40-minute tram tour ($10), pulled by a beefy tractor, winds through the estate vineyards and into caves, and ends with a tasting of one estate wine. *Tip:* Tram tickets—a hot item in the summer—are available on a first-come, first-served basis, so either arrive early, or stop by in the morning to pick up tickets for the afternoon.

Tastings for standard-release wines are $5. Tastes of limited-production, reserve, or estate wines cost $10. The winery has several picnic spots.

1883 London Ranch Rd. (off Arnold Dr., on the way to Jack London State Historic Park), Glen Ellen. ℂ 800/989-8890 or 707/935-3000. www.benziger.com. Tasting room daily 10am–5pm. Tram tours daily (weather permitting) $10 adults and $5 children at 11:30am, 12:30, 1:30, 2:30, and 3:30pm.

## KENWOOD

A few miles north of Glen Ellen along Highway 12 is the tiny town of Kenwood, the northernmost outpost of the Sonoma Valley. The town itself consists of little more than a few restaurants, wineries, and modest homes recessed into the wooded hillsides.

**Kunde Estate Winery** Expect a friendly welcome at this scenic winery, run since 1904 by the Kunde family (pronounced "*Kun*-dee"), now in its fourth generation of winemaking. One of the largest grape suppliers in the area, the Kundes converted 800 acres of their 2,000-acre ranch to grounds for ultrapremium grapes, distributed to about 30 Sonoma and Napa wineries. Hence, all their own wines are "estate," made from grapes grown on their property. The $5 new-release tastings and $10 reserve (with glass) are offered in a 17,000-square-foot winemaking facility. Private tours are available by appointment only, but you can make use of the picnic tables and pond any time during opening hours. Tasting fees are refunded with purchases.

10155 Sonoma Hwy., Kenwood. ℂ 707/833-5501. www.kunde.com. Tastings daily 10:30am–4pm. Cave tours Mon–Thurs 11am and Fri–Sun approximately every half-hour 11am–3pm.

**Kenwood Vineyards** Kenwood dates to 1906, when the Pagani Brothers Winery sold wine on the premises straight from the barrel into the jug. In 1970, the Lee family bought the property and dumped a fortune into converting the aging winery into a modern, high-production facility (most of it cleverly concealed in the original barnlike buildings). Since then, Kenwood has earned a solid reputation for consistent quality with each of its varietals: cabernet sauvignon, chardonnay, zinfandel, pinot noir, merlot, and sauvignon blanc, its most popular—a crisp, light wine with hints of melon. (Gary Heck is now the owner, not the Lees, but the wine quality has remained steady.)

Although the winery looks modest in size, its output is staggering: nearly 500,000 cases of ultrapremium wines, fermented in steel tanks and French and American oak barrels. Popular with collectors is winemaker Michael Lee's Artist Series cabernet sauvignon; a limited production from the winery's best vineyards, its labels feature original artwork by renowned artists. The tasting room, housed in one of the old barns, sells $2 to $5 tastings of most varieties as well as gift items.

9592 Sonoma Hwy. (Hwy. 12), Kenwood. © 707/833-5891. www.kenwoodvineyards.com. Daily 10am–4:30pm.

**Château St. Jean** ★ *Finds* Château St. Jean is notable for its exceptionally beautiful buildings, expansive landscaped grounds, and gourmet market–like tasting room. Among California wineries, it's a pioneer in vineyard designation—the procedure of making wine from, and naming it for, a single vineyard. A private drive takes you to what was once a 250-acre country retreat built in 1920; a well-manicured lawn overlooking the meticulously maintained vineyards is now a picnic area, complete with a fountain and picnic tables.

In the huge tasting room—with a charcuterie shop and plenty of housewares for sale—you can sample Château St. Jean's wide array of wines. They range from chardonnays and cabernet sauvignon to fumé blanc, merlot, Johannesburg Riesling, and Gewürztraminer. Tastings are $5 per person; $10 per person for reserve wines.

8555 Sonoma Hwy. (Hwy. 12), Kenwood. © 800/543-7572 or 707/833-4134. www.chateaustjean.com. Tasting daily 10am–5pm. Tours 11am and 3pm. At the foot of Sugarloaf Ridge, just north of Kenwood and east of Hwy. 12.

## WHERE TO STAY

If you're having trouble finding a vacancy, try calling the **Sonoma Valley Visitors Bureau** at © **707/996-1090** (www.sonomavalley.com). They'll try to refer you to establishments with a room to spare, but they won't make reservations for you. Another option is the **Bed and Breakfast Association of Sonoma Valley** (© **800/ 969-4667**), which will refer you to a member B&B and make reservations for you.

### VERY EXPENSIVE

**Fairmont Sonoma Mission Inn & Spa** ★★★ As you drive through Boyes Hot Springs, you may wonder why someone decided to build a multimillion-dollar spa resort in this ordinary little town. There's no view to speak of, and it certainly isn't within walking distance of any wineries or fancy restaurants. So what's the deal? It's the naturally heated artesian mineral water, piped from directly underneath the spa into the temperature-controlled pools and whirlpools. Set on 12 meticulously groomed acres, the Sonoma Mission Inn consists of a massive, three-story replica of a Spanish mission, built in 1927; an array of satellite wings with numerous superluxury suites; and world-class spa facilities. It's a popular retreat for the wealthy and well known, so don't be surprised if you see a famous face (I bumped into Tiffany Amber Thiessen of *90210* in the spa dressing room during my last visit). Since the resort underwent new ownership in 2000, it has gained 60 suites, updated its spa to the tune of $20 million, and completed a $62-million renovation, which included completely redoing the Heritage Rooms in understated country elegance. The resort also has the Sonoma Golf Club, home to the PGA championship every October.

Corner of Boyes Blvd. and Hwy. 12, P.O. Box 1447, Sonoma, CA 95476. © 800/441-1414 or 707/938-9000. Fax 707/938-4250. www.fairmont.com/sonoma. 226 units. $199–$1,000 double. Rates include free wine tasting 4:30–5:30pm. AE, DC, MC, V. Valet parking free for day use (spa-goers) and $14 for overnight guests. From central Sonoma, drive 3 miles north on Hwy. 12 and turn left on Boyes Blvd. **Amenities:** 2 restaurants; 2 large heated outdoor pools; golf course; health club and spa; Jacuzzi; sauna; bike rental; concierge; business center; salon; room service (6am–11pm); babysitting; same-day laundry service/dry cleaning. *In room:* A/C, TV, dataport, high-speed Internet access ($13 per day), minibar, hair dryer, iron, safe, complimentary bottle of wine upon arrival.

**Gaige House Inn** ★★★ *(Finds)*   The Gaige House is the best B&B I've ever stayed in. The inn's owners, Ken Burnet, Jr., and Greg Nemrow, turned a great bed-and-breakfast into the Wine Country's finest by offering a level of service, amenities, and decor normally associated with outrageously expensive resorts (without the snobbery). A chef featured at the James Beard House, in 2001, prepares breakfast and appetizers with herbs from the garden. Silk-soft linens and premium down comforters grace firm mattresses, and even the furniture and artwork are of museum quality. Behind the inn is a 1½-acre oasis with perfectly manicured lawns, a 40-foot-long swimming pool, and a creekside hammock under a Heritage oak. All rooms, designed in a plantation theme with Asian and Indonesian influences, have private bathrooms and king- or queen-size beds; two rooms have Jacuzzi tubs, and several have fireplaces. The eight new, super-fancy spa garden suites have, among other delights, granite soaking tubs. On sunny days, breakfast is served at individual tables on the large terrace. Evenings are best spent sipping premium wines in the reading parlor.

Greg and Ken also manage four long-term rentals (private guesthouses on private estates) for those who want more privacy and fewer services.

13540 Arnold Dr., Glen Ellen, CA 95442. ℂ **800/935-0237** or 707/935-0237. Fax 707/935-6411. www.gaige.com. 23 units. Summer $275–$375 double, $395–$550 suite; winter $150–$275 double, $325–$525 suite. Rates include full breakfast and evening wines. AE, DC, DISC, MC, V. **Amenities:** Large heated pool; 2 outdoor hot tubs; free wireless Internet access; in-room massage. *In room:* A/C, TV/DVD, dataport, DSL, fridge in some rooms, hair dryer, iron, safe.

**Kenwood Inn & Spa** ★★   Inspired by the villas of Tuscany, the Kenwood Inn's honey-colored, Italian-style buildings, flower-filled flagstone courtyard, and pastoral views of vineyard-covered hills are enough to make any northern Italian homesick. The friendly staff and restful surroundings made this California girl feel right at home. What's not to like about a spacious room, lavishly and exquisitely decorated with imported tapestries, velvets, and antiques, plus a fireplace, balcony (except on the ground floor), feather bed, CD player, and down comforter? With no TV in the rooms, relaxation is inevitable—especially if you book treatments at the spa, which gets creative with its program. A minor drawback is road noise, which you're unlikely to hear from your room, although it can be slightly audible around the courtyard and pool. Anyone with a hefty credit card limit can buy complete seclusion by renting the inn's new, private, two-bedroom villa nearby.

An impressive, three-course gourmet breakfast is served in the courtyard or in the Mediterranean-style dining room.

10400 Sonoma Hwy., Kenwood, CA 95452. ℂ **800/353-6966** or 707/833-1293. Fax 707/833-1247. www.kenwood inn.com. 30 units. Apr–Oct $400–$725 double; Nov–Mar $375–$675 double, $800–$1,000 villa. Rates include gourmet breakfast and bottle of wine. 2-night minimum on weekends. AE, MC, V. **Amenities:** 2 heated outdoor pools; full-service spa; concierge. *In room:* High-speed Internet access, hair dryer, iron, CD player.

## MODERATE
**Beltane Ranch** ★ *(Finds)*   The word *ranch* conjures up a big ol' two-story house amid hundreds of rolling acres—the kind of place where you laze away the day watching the grass grow or pitching horseshoes in the garden. Well, friend, you can have all that and more at the well-located Beltane Ranch, a century-old buttercup-yellow manor that has been everything from a bunkhouse to a brothel to a turkey farm. You simply can't help but feel your tensions ease away as you prop up your feet on the shady, wrap-around porch overlooking the quiet vineyards, and sip a cool, fruity chardonnay while reading *Lonesome Dove* for the third time. Each room is uniquely decorated with

American and European antiques; all have sitting areas and separate entrances. A big, creative country breakfast is served in the garden or on the porch overlooking the vineyards. For exercise, you can play tennis on the private court or hike the trails meandering through the 105-acre estate. The staff here is knowledgeable and helpful. *Tip:* Request one of the upstairs rooms, which have the best views.

11775 Sonoma Hwy./Hwy. 12. (P.O. Box 395) Glen Ellen, CA 95442. ✆ 707/996-6501. www.beltaneranch.com. 5 units, 1 cottage. $140–$190 double; $220 cottage. Rates include full breakfast. No credit cards; personal checks accepted. **Amenities:** Outdoor, unlit tennis court. *In room:* No phone.

**Glenelly Inn** ✦  The rates are reasonable, particularly when you factor in the breakfast and afternoon snacks included in the price. More importantly, this former railroad inn, built in 1916, is bathed in a sense of serenity. Well off the main highway on an oak-studded hillside, the peach-and-cream property comes with everything you would expect from a country retreat. Long verandas with wicker chairs offer views of the Sonoma hillsides; a country breakfast is served beside a cobblestone fireplace; and bright, immaculate units contain old-fashioned claw-foot tubs, Scandinavian down comforters, and ceiling fans. The staff understands that the little things make the difference; hence, the good reading lights and simmering hot tub in a grapevine- and rose-covered arbor. All rooms, decorated with antiques and country furnishings, have queen beds, terry robes, and private entrances. My favorites are the Vallejo and Jack London family suites, both with large private patios, although I also like the rooms on the upper veranda—particularly in the spring, when the terraced gardens below are in full bloom. The new, freestanding garden cottages are worth a splurge.

5131 Warm Springs Rd. (off Arnold Dr.), Glen Ellen, CA 95442. ✆ 707/996-6720. Fax 707/996-5227. www.glenelly. com. 10 units. $150–$185 double/suite; $250 cottage. Rates include full breakfast. AE, DISC, MC, V. **Amenities:** Outdoor Jacuzzi; free Internet access at computer stations; TV in common room.

## INEXPENSIVE

**Sonoma Hotel** ✦✦  This historic hotel on Sonoma's tree-lined town plaza is defined by 19th-century elegance and comfort. Built in 1880 by German immigrant Henry Weyl, it has attractive guest rooms in early California style, with French country furnishings and antique beds. Modern luxuries include private bathrooms, cable TV, phones with dataports, and air-conditioning. Perks include fresh coffee and pastries in the morning and evening wine. The lovely restaurant, **the girl & the fig** (p. 194), serves California-French cuisine.

110 W. Spain St., Sonoma, CA 95476. ✆ 800/468-6016 or 707/996-2996. Fax 707/996-7014. www.sonomahotel.com. 16 units. Summer $110–$245 double; winter $95–$195 double. 2-night minimum required for summer weekends. Rates include continental breakfast and evening wine. AE, DC, MC, V. *In room:* A/C, TV, dataport.

**Victorian Garden Inn** ✦✦  Proprietor Donna Lewis runs what is easily the cutest B&B in Sonoma Valley. A small picket fence, a wall of trees, and an acre of gardens enclose an adorable Victorian garden brimming with violets, roses, camellias, and peonies, all shaded under flowering fruit trees. It's a marvel in spring. The Victorian theme continues in the guest units—three in the century-old water tower, one in the main building (an 1870s Greek Revival farmhouse), and a cottage—with white wicker furniture, floral prints, padded armchairs, and claw-foot tubs. The most popular units are the Top o' the Tower and the Woodcutter's Cottage. Each has its own entrance and a garden view; the cottage has a sofa and armchairs in front of the fireplace. After a hard day of wine tasting, spend the afternoon cooling off in the pool or soaking in the sweet garden smells on the shaded wraparound porch. *New parents, take note:* The property recommends you leave young tots behind.

316 E. Napa St., Sonoma, CA 95476. 𝒞 **800/543-5339** or 707/996-5339. Fax 707/996-1689. www.victoriangardeninn.com. 3 units, 1 cottage. $139–$259 double. Rates include continental breakfast. AE, DC, MC, V. **Amenities:** Outdoor pool; hot tub; concierge; business center w/free Internet access; laundry service. *In room:* A/C, fireplaces in some rooms.

## WHERE TO DINE

Though Sonoma Valley has far fewer visitors than Napa Valley, its restaurants are often equally crowded, so be sure to make reservations in advance.

### EXPENSIVE

**the girl & the fig** ⋆⋆ COUNTRY FRENCH    Matt Murray orchestrates the French-influenced nouveau country cuisine at this well-loved restaurant owned by Sondra Bernstein. She would be the girl and, yes, figs are sure to be on the menu in one form or another. The wonderful winter fig salad contains arugula, pecans, dried figs, Laura Chenel goat cheese, and fig-and-port vinaigrette. Murray uses garden-fresh produce and local meats, poultry, and fish whenever possible, in dishes such as grilled pork chops or duck confit. For dessert, try lavender crème brûlée, a glass of Jaboulet muscat, and a sliver of *raclette* from the cheese list. Sondra knows her wines, features Rhone varietals, and will be happy to choose the best accompaniment for your meal. Looking for brunch? Head here on Sunday, until 3pm.

110 W. Spain St., Sonoma. 𝒞 707/938-3634. www.thegirlandthefig.com. Reservations suggested. Main courses $13–$24. AE, DISC, MC, V. Mon–Sat 11:30am–11pm; Sun 10am–11pm.

**Harmony Club** ⋆ CONTINENTAL    With its elegant, Italianate dining room with dark woods, high ceilings, marble flooring, and a wall of giant doors opening to sidewalk seating and Sonoma's plaza, the Harmony Club is a real looker that also delivers great food and live entertainment. Drop in anytime after their gourmet breakfast for the seasonal menu. In winter, hearty rib-gripping specials include veal *osso bucco* with creamy roast garlic–mushroom polenta and braised greens; warm weather specials include cumin-crusted ahi tuna with beluga lentils, roasted vegetables, and red-wine sauce. Go for sidewalk seating during warmer weather (they also have heat lamps). If you choose to sit inside, at a private table or the carved wood bar, you'll want to face the piano when the nightly performer sings and plays jazz standards. Alas, the only weakness is the limited wine list: Owned by Steve Ledson of Ledson Winery, the restaurant sells only Ledson wines.

480 First St. E. (at the plaza), Sonoma. © **707/996-9779.** Reservations accepted. Entrees $14–$26. AE, MC, V. Wed–Mon 11:30am–10pm.

## MODERATE

**Cafe La Haye** ✦✦ ECLECTIC    Well-prepared and wholesome food, an experienced waitstaff, friendly owners, a soothing atmosphere, and reasonable prices—including a modestly priced wine list—make La Haye a favorite. In truth, everything about this cafelike restaurant is winning. With hardwood floors, an exposed-beam ceiling, and revolving contemporary artwork, the small, split-level dining room is smart and intimate. It's clearly a small business—a welcome departure from Napa Valley's conspicuously corporate restaurants. The straightforward, seasonally inspired cuisine, which chefs bring forth from the tiny open kitchen, is delicious and wonderfully well priced. Expect a risotto special; pasta such as fresh *tagliarini* with butternut squash, prosciutto, sage, and garlic cream; and pan-roasted chicken breast, perhaps with goat cheese–herb stuffing, caramelized shallot *jus,* and fennel mashed potatoes. The filet of beef seared with black pepper-lavender sauce, served with Gorgonzola-potato gratin, is sure to please meat lovers.

140 E. Napa St., Sonoma. © **707/935-5994.** Reservations recommended. Main courses $14–$24. AE, MC, V. Tues–Sat 5:30–9pm.

**Della Santina's** ✦ TUSCAN    Follow the locals to this friendly, traditional Italian restaurant. How traditional? Ask father-and-son team Dan and Robert, who will point out Signora Santina's hand-embroidered linen doilies and proudly tell you about her Tuscan recipes. (Heck, even the dining room looks like an old-fashioned Italian living room.) And their pride is merited: Dishes are authentic and well flavored, without overbearing sauces or one *hint* of California pretension. Be sure to start with traditional antipasti, especially sliced mozzarella and tomatoes, or delicious white beans. The nine pasta dishes are, again, wonderfully authentic (gnocchi lovers, rejoice!). The spit-roasted meat dishes are a local favorite; for those who can't choose between chicken, pork, turkey, rabbit, or duck, one menu option offers a choice of three. Don't worry about breaking your bank on a bottle of wine, because many choices here go for less than $40. Portions are huge, but be sure to save room for the creamy *panna cotta.*

133 E. Napa St. (just east of the square), Sonoma. © **707/935-0576.** Reservations recommended. Main courses $10–$20. AE, DISC, MC, V. Daily 11:30am–3pm and 5–9:30pm.

**Swiss Hotel** ✦ CONTINENTAL/NORTHERN ITALIAN    With its slanting floors and beamed ceilings, the historic Swiss Hotel, in the town center, is a Sonoma landmark and the local favorite for fine food at reasonable prices. The turn-of-the-20th-century oak bar is adorned with black-and-white photos of pioneering Sonomans. The white dining room and sidewalk patio seats are a pleasant place to enjoy lunch specials such as penne with chicken, mushrooms, and tomato cream; hot sandwiches; and California-style pizzas fired in a wood-burning oven. But the secret spot is the very atmospheric back garden patio—a secluded oasis shaded by a wisteria-covered trellis and adorned with plants, a fountain, gingham tablecloths, and a fireplace. Dinner might start with a warm winter salad of radicchio and frisée with pears, walnuts, and bleu cheese. My favorite main courses include linguine and prawns with garlic, hot pepper, and tomatoes; the filet mignon wrapped in bleu-cheese crust; and roasted rosemary chicken. The food is all very simply satisfying.

18 W. Spain St (at First St. W.), Sonoma. 🕾 **707/938-2884.** Reservations recommended. Main courses lunch $8.50–$16, dinner $10–$24. AE, MC, V. Daily 11:30am–2:30pm and 5–9:30pm. Bar daily 11:30am–2am.

**Wolf House** ⭐ ECLECTIC   The most polished-looking dining room in Glen Ellen is elegant yet relaxed, whether you're seated in the handsome dining room—smartly adorned with maple floors, gold walls, dark-wood wainscoting, and a corner fireplace—or outside, on the multilevel terrace, under the trees, with serene views of the adjacent Sonoma Creek. The lunch menu adds fancy finishes to old favorites such as the excellent chicken Caesar salad, fresh grilled ahi tuna niçoise sandwich, or a juicy half-pound burger with Point Reyes Original bleu cheese. During dinner, head straight for seared Roasted Liberty Farms duck breast with pecan and dried-cherry strudel with sautéed cider cabbage and braised kumquat demi, or pan-seared day-boat scallops with heirloom tomatoes and avocado-cucumber emulsion. The reasonably priced wine list offers many options by the glass, as well as a fine selection of Sonoma wines. Locals love the brunch, complete with huevos rancheros, steak and eggs, omelets, and brioche French toast. During my visits, service was rather languid, but well meaning.

13740 Arnold Dr. (at London Ranch Rd.), Glen Ellen. 🕾 **707/996-4401.** www.jacklondonlodge.com/rest.html. Reservations recommended. Main courses $8–$15 brunch and lunch, $15–$25 dinner. AE, MC, V. Brunch Sat–Sun 10am–3pm; lunch Mon–Fri 11am–3pm; dinner nightly 5:30–9:30pm.

**INEXPENSIVE**

**Black Bear Diner** 𝘒𝘪𝘥𝘴 DINER   When you're craving a classic Americana breakfast, with all the cholesterol and the fixings, make a beeline to this old-fashioned diner. One, it's fun—with its over-the-top bear paraphernalia, gazette-style menu listing local news from 1961 and every possible diner favorite, and absurdly friendly waitstaff. Two, it's darned cheap. Three, helpings are huge. Four, it appeals to all ages: Kids get a kick out of the coloring books, old-timers reminisce over Sinatra on the jukebox, and everyone leaves stuffed on omelets, scrambles, and pancakes. Lunch and dinner feature steak sandwiches, salads, and comfort foods such as barbecued pork ribs, roast beef, fish and chips, and spaghetti with meat sauce. You can fill up here on the cheap, especially since dinners come with salad or soup, bread, and two sides; seniors can order from a specially discounted menu.

201 West Napa St. (at Second St.), Sonoma. 🕾 **707/935-6800.** Main courses breakfast $5–$8.50, lunch and dinner $5.50–$17. AE, DISC, MC, V. Sun–Thurs 6am–10pm; Fri–Sat 6am–midnight.

# 8

# The Northern Coast

*by Matthew Richard Poole*

North from San Francisco, the coast bears little resemblance to the southern part of the state. The landscape, climate, flora, and fauna are distinct, and you can forget about surfing and bikinis; instead, you'll find miles of rough shoreline with broad beaches and tiny bays harboring fantastic rock formations—from chimney-stacks to bridges and blowholes—carved by the ocean waves.

You may think you've arrived in Alaska when you hit the beaches of Northern California. Take a dip and you'll soon agree with the locals: The Arctic waters along the Northern Coast are best left to the sea lions. That doesn't mean you can't enjoy the beaches, though, whether by strolling along the water or taking in the views of towering cliffs and seascapes. And unlike their southern counterparts, the

beaches here are not likely to be crowded, even during summer months.

The best season to visit is spring—when wild poppy, iris, and sea foam carpet the headlands, or fall, when the sun shines clear and bright. Summers are typically cool and windy, and the ubiquitous fog burns off by afternoon.

The most scenic way to reach Stinson Beach, Mendocino, and points north is to drive Highway 1 along the coast. U.S. 101 runs inland, much more quickly, through Healdsburg and Cloverdale, but it doesn't provide the spectacular coastal views. A good compromise if you're headed to, say, Mendocino, is to take U.S. 101 to Cloverdale, then cut over to the coast on Highway 128.

And one last thing: Dress warmly.

## 1 Point Reyes National Seashore *(★(★(★*

35 miles NW of San Francisco

The government created the national seashore system to protect rural and undeveloped stretches of coastline from population growth and soaring real-estate values. Nowhere is the success of this system more evident than at Point Reyes. Residents of the surrounding towns—**Inverness, Point Reyes Station,** and **Olema**—have steadfastly resisted runaway development. You won't find strip malls or fast-food here—just laid-back coastal towns with cafes and country inns where gentle living prevails.

The park—a 71,000-acre hammer-shaped peninsula jutting 10 miles into the Pacific and backed by Tomales Bay—abounds with wildlife, ranging from tule elk, birds, and bobcats to gray whales, sea lions, and great white sharks. Aside from its scenery, it also boasts historical treasures that open a window into California's coastal past, including lighthouses, dairies and ranches, the site of Sir Francis Drake's 1579 landing, plus a replica of a coastal Miwok Indian village.

Though the peninsula's people and wildlife live in harmony above the ground, the situation beneath the soil is more volatile. The San Andreas Fault separates Point Reyes—the northernmost landmass on the Pacific Plate—from the rest of California, which rests on the North American Plate. Point Reyes is making its way toward Alaska at a rate of about 2 inches per year, but it has moved faster at times. In 1906 Point Reyes jumped north almost 20 feet in an instant, leveling San Francisco and jolting the rest of the state. The half-mile **Earthquake Trail,** near the Bear Valley Visitor Center, illustrates this geological drama with a loop through an area torn by the fault. Shattered fences, rifts in the ground, and a barn knocked off its foundation illustrate how alive the earth is here. If that doesn't convince you, the seismograph in the visitor center will.

## ESSENTIALS

**GETTING THERE** Point Reyes is 35 miles northwest of San Francisco, but it takes at least 90 minutes to reach by car (the small towns slow you down). The easiest route is via Sir Francis Drake Boulevard from U.S. 101 south of San Rafael; it takes its time to Point Reyes, but does so without detours. For a longer, more scenic route, take the Stinson Beach/Highway 1 exit off U.S. 101 just south of Sausalito and follow Highway 1 north.

**VISITOR INFORMATION** As soon as you arrive at Point Reyes, stop at the **Bear Valley Visitor Center** (② 415/464-5100; www.nps.gov/pore, www.pointreyes.net, or www.pointreyes.org) on Bear Valley Road (look for the small sign just north of Olema on Hwy. 1) and pick up a free Point Reyes trail map. The rangers are helpful and can answer your questions about the national seashore. Be sure to check out the great natural history and cultural displays as well. It's open Monday through Friday from 9am to 5pm, Saturday and Sunday from 8am to 5pm.

**FEES & PERMITS** Entrance to the park is free. Camping is $12 per site per night all year, and permits are required; reservations can be made up to 3 months in advance at ② **415/663-8054,** Monday through Friday from 9am to 2pm.

## WHAT TO SEE & DO

When heading out to any part of the Point Reyes coast, expect to spend the day surrounded by nature. The park encompasses several surf-pounded beaches, bird estuaries, open swaths of land with roaming elk, and the Point Reyes lighthouse—a favorite among visitors who are awestruck by the spectacular views of the coast. Bear in mind, however, that as beautiful as the wilderness can be, it's also untamable. Waters in these areas are not only bone chilling and home to a vast array of sea life, including sharks, but they're also unpredictable and dangerous, with strong waves and riptides, untended by lifeguards; in other words, swimming is inadvisable. Pets are not permitted on any of the area's trails.

The most popular attraction at Point Reyes National Seashore is the venerable **Point Reyes Lighthouse** ⚓, at the westernmost tip. Even if you plan to forego the 308 steps down to the lighthouse, it's worth the visit just to marvel at the scenery, which includes thousands of common murres and prides of sea lions basking on the rocks far below (binoculars come in handy). The lighthouse visitor center (② 415/669-1534) is open Thursday through Monday from 10am to 4:30pm, weather permitting.

The lighthouse is also the top spot on the California coast to see **gray whales** as they make their southward and northward migrations along the coast from January to April. The annual round-trip is 10,000 miles—one of the longest mammal migrations

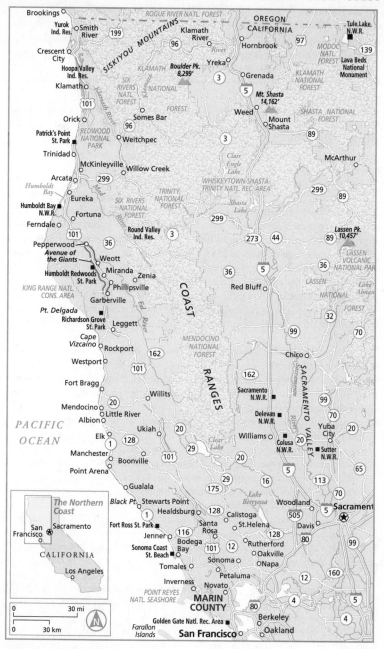

> ⌒*Tips* **Whale Sightings**
>
> Rangers suggest that during the southern migration (Jan), you should go to the lighthouse for the best view, and during the northern migration (Mar), you can see the whales from any of the area's beaches.

known. The whales head south in December and January, and return north in March. *Tip:* If you plan to drive out to the lighthouse to whale-watch, arrive early as parking is limited. If possible, come on a weekday. On a weekend or holiday from December to April (weather permitting), it's wise to park at the Drake's Beach Visitor Center and take the shuttle bus to the lighthouse, which is $3.50 for adults and free for kids age 12 and under. Dress warmly—it's often quite cold and windy—and bring binoculars.

Whale-watching is far from the only activity offered. Rangers conduct many different tours on weekends: You can walk along the **Bear Valley Trail** and spot the wildlife at the ocean's edge; see the waterfowl at **Fivebrooks Pond;** explore tide pools; view some of North America's most beautiful ducks in the wetlands of **Limantour;** hike to the promontory overlooking **Chimney Rock** to see the sea lions, elephant seals, harbor seals, and seabirds; or take a self-guided walk along the **San Andreas Fault** to observe the epicenter of the 1906 earthquake and learn about the regional geology. Since tours vary seasonally, you can either call the **Bear Valley Visitor Center** (② 415/464-5100) or request a copy of *Park Paper,* which includes a schedule of activities and other useful information. Many of the tours are suitable for travelers with disabilities.

North and South **Point Reyes beaches** face the Pacific and withstand the full brunt of ocean tides and winds—so much so that the water is far too rough for even wading. Until a few years ago, entering the water was illegal, but persistent surfers went to court for their right to shred the mighty waves. Today the park service strongly advises against taking on the tides, so play it safe and content yourself to stroll the coastline. Along the southern coast, the waters of **Drake's Beach** ✿ can be as tranquil and serene as Point Reyes's are turbulent. Locals come here to sun and picnic; occasionally a hearty soul ventures into the cold waters. Keep in mind, though, that storms generally come inland from the south and almost always hit Drake's before moving north or south. A powerful weather front can turn wispy waves into torrential tides.

Some of the park's best and least crowded highlights are accessible only on foot, such as **Alamere Falls** ✿, a freshwater stream that cascades down a 40-foot bluff onto Wildcat Beach, or **Tomales Point Trail** ✿, which passes through the Tule Elk Reserve, a protected haven for roaming herds of tule elk that once numbered in the thousands. Hiking most of the trails usually ends up being an all-day outing, however, so it's best to split a 2-day trip within Point Reyes National Seashore into a "by car" day and a "by foot" day.

If you're a bird-watcher, don't miss the **Point Reyes Bird Observatory** ✿ (② 415/868-1221; www.prbo.org), one of the few full-time ornithological research stations in the U.S., at the southeast end of the park on Mesa Road. Ornithologists here keep an eye on more than 400 species. Admission to the visitor center and nature trail is free, and visitors may observe the tricky process of catching and banding the birds. It's open daily from 15 minutes after sunrise until sunset. Banding hours vary seasonally; call ② 415/868-0655 for times.

# Point Reyes National Seashore & Bodega Bay

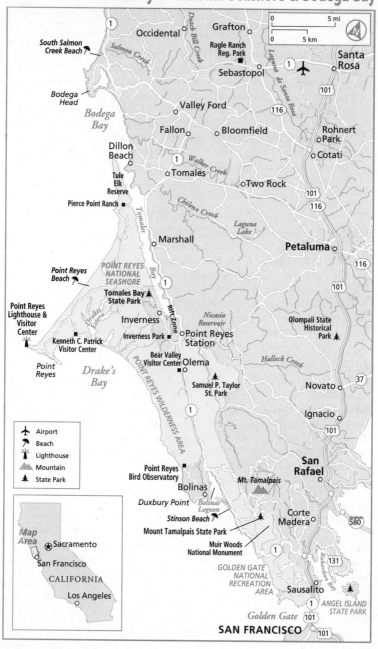

South Salmon Creek Beach

Occidental

Grafton

Ragle Ranch Reg. Park

Sebastopol

Santa Rosa

Bodega Head

Bodega Bay

Valley Ford

Fallon

Bloomfield

Rohnert Park

Cotati

Dillon Beach

Tule Elk Reserve

Tomales

Two Rock

Pierce Point Ranch

Chileno Creek

Laguna Lake

Marshall

Petaluma

POINT REYES NATIONAL SEASHORE

Point Reyes Beach

Tomales Bay State Park

Point Reyes Lighthouse & Visitor Center

Inverness

Nicasio Reservoir

Olompali State Historical Park

Kenneth C. Patrick Visitor Center

Inverness Park

Point Reyes Station

Point Reyes

Drake's Bay

Bear Valley Visitor Center

Olema

Halleck Creek

Novato

Samuel P. Taylor St. Park

Ignacio

POINT REYES WILDERNESS AREA

- ✈ Airport
- 🏖 Beach
- Lighthouse
- ▲ Mountain
- 🌲 State Park

Point Reyes Bird Observatory

Mt. Tamalpais

San Rafael

Bolinas

Duxbury Point

Bolinas Lagoon

Stinson Beach

Corte Madera

Mount Tamalpais State Park

Muir Woods National Monument

Map Area

Sacramento

San Francisco

CALIFORNIA

Los Angeles

GOLDEN GATE NATIONAL RECREATION AREA

Sausalito

ANGEL ISLAND STATE PARK

Golden Gate

SAN FRANCISCO

*Finds* **Johnson's Oyster Farm**

One of my favorite things to do in Point Reyes is swing by **Johnson's Oyster Farm,** buy a sack of oysters fresh from the water and a bottle of "Johnson's Special Sauce," head to one of the beaches, whip out the folding chair, crack an ice-cold beer, prop up my feet, and chow down. The oyster farm is within Drakes Estero, a large saltwater lagoon on the Point Reyes peninsula that produces nearly 20 percent of California's commercial oyster yield. It's off Sir Francis Drake Boulevard about 6 miles west of Inverness; you'll know you've found it when you smell a cluster of odiferous oyster tanks surrounded by huge piles of oyster shells. It's open 8am to 4pm Tuesday through Sunday (© 415/669-1149).

One of my favorite things to do in Point Reyes is paddle through placid Tomales Bay, a haven for migrating birds and marine mammals. **Tamal Saka Tomales Bay Kayaking** ∗ (© 415/663-1743; www.tamalsaka.com) organizes kayak trips, including 3-hour sunset outings, 3½-hour full-moon paddles, yoga tours, day trips, and longer excursions. Instruction, clinics, and boat delivery are available, and all ages and levels are welcome. Prices for tours start at $65. Rentals begin at $35 for one person, $50 for two. Don't worry—the kayaks are very stable, and the water is without waves. The launching point is on Highway 1 at the Marshall Boatworks in Marshall, 8 miles north of Point Reyes Station. Open daily from 9am to 6pm and by appointment.

## WHERE TO STAY
If you're having trouble finding vacancies, **Inns of Marin** (© 800/887-2880 or 415/663-2000; www.innsofmarin.com) and **West Marin Network** (© 415/663-9543) are reputable services that will help you find accommodations, from one-room cottages to inns and vacation homes. The **West Marin Chamber of Commerce** (© 415/663-9232; www.pointreyes.org) is also a good source for lodging and visitor information. Keep in mind that many places here require a 2-night minimum stay, but in slow season they may make exceptions. They'll also refer you to restaurants, hiking trails, and other attractions in the area.

### EXPENSIVE
**Blackthorne Inn** ∗∗    This redwood home with its octagonal widow's walk, spiral staircase, turrets, and multiple decks looks more like a deluxe treehouse than a B&B. My favorite unit (also the priciest) is the Eagle's Nest, an octagonal room enclosed by glass and topped with a sun deck, with a catwalk leading to the bathroom. The largest room is the Forest View, a two-room suite with a deck, a private entrance, and a sitting area facing the woods; it's furnished with wicker and natural rattan, and decorated with floral fabrics and modern lithographs. All units have private bathrooms. The main sitting room in the house features a stone fireplace, skylight, wet bar, and stained-glass windows, and it's surrounded by a huge deck. A country buffet breakfast, included in the room rate, is served on the upper deck when the sun's out.

266 Vallejo Ave. (off Sir Francis Drake Blvd., south of Inverness), Inverness Park (P.O. Box 712), Inverness, CA 94937. © 415/663-8621. Fax 415/663-8635. www.blackthorneinn.com. 4 units. $225–$325 double. Rates include buffet breakfast. MC, V. **Amenities:** Nearby golf course; Jacuzzi. *In room:* Coffeemaker.

**Manka's Inverness Lodge** ★★★   A former hunting and fishing lodge, Manka's Inverness looks like something out of a Hans Christian Andersen fairy tale, down to the tree-limb bedsteads and cooks roasting venison sausage over the hearth. It's all romantic in a Jack London sort of way, and tastefully done. The lodge consists of an excellent restaurant on the first floor (see "Where to Dine" below), four rooms upstairs (nos. 1 and 2 come with large, private decks), four rooms in the Redwood Annex, and two spacious, one-bedroom cabins behind the lodge. For the ultimate romantic splurge, inquire about these secluded cabins: Fishing and Manka's, or at the water's edge, the Boathouse and Chicken Ranch.

30 Callendar Way (on Argyle St. off Sir Francis Drake Blvd., 1½ blocks north of downtown Inverness), P.O. Box 1110, Inverness, CA 94937. ℭ 415/669-1034. Fax 415/669-1598. www.mankas.com. 12 units. $185–$465. MC, V. **Amenities:** Restaurant; bike rental; limited room service; in-room massage. *In room:* TV in some units, kitchenette, fridge, coffeemaker, hair dryer, no phone.

## MODERATE

**Bear Valley Inn Bed & Breakfast** ★   This two-story 1919 farmhouse has survived everything from a major earthquake to a recent forest fire, but you'd be hard-pressed to find a better B&B for the price in Point Reyes. Loaded with charm, down to the profusion of flowers and vines outside and comfy chairs fronting a toasty woodstove inside, it's in a great location, too, with two good restaurants within walking distance and the national seashore at its doorstep. One unit is a private cottage with two futons in the living area, suitable for children.

88 Bear Valley Rd., Olema, CA 94950. ℭ 415/663-1777. www.bearvinn.com. 4 units. $110–$135 double; $140–$185 cottage. Rates include breakfast. AE, DISC, MC, V. *In room:* A/C, TV, kitchen in cottage, some units w/coffeemaker, hair dryer, iron, wireless access.

**Olema Inn & Restaurant** ★★   Built in 1876, the pretty Olema Inn has an interesting history. It opened on July 4, 1876, as a gathering place for farmers and ranchers, was lost in gambling debt, and survived the 1906 earthquake (Olema was the epicenter). Today it still retains much of its period charm, combining modern luxuries such as European Sleepworks mattresses, down comforters, large tub showers, and

---

*Finds*  **Steep Ravine Environmental Cabins**

How's this for a great deal? For $75, you and four of your best friends can stay the night in a redwood cabin on a bluff overlooking the ocean with nearby access to hiking trails and a small, secluded beach. Mount Tamalpais State Park rents 10 cabins that were once the private retreats of Bay Area politicians. The cabins, all of which have gorgeous ocean views, are now available to anyone stubborn enough to get a reservation. Wood-burning stoves, platform beds, running water, and outhouses are provided, but you must bring your own sleeping bag and lantern, there's no electricity, and firewood costs extra. Each cabin sleeps up to five, but only one car per cabin is allowed. The cabins are off Highway 1, a mile south of Stinson Beach; look for a paved turnout and a brown metal sign. The cabins are very popular, so be sure to reserve one as far in advance as possible (you can book them up to 7 months prior). For reservations call ℭ **800/444-7275** or reserve online at www.reserveamerica.com. For more information about the cabins, call the **Mount Tamalpais State Park** at ℭ **415/388-2070.**

Ralph Lauren linens with antique furniture and light fixtures, Victorian-style white porcelain and chrome bathrooms, and those great high ceilings you find in old Bay Area buildings. The decor is simple and elegant—pastels, beige wool carpeting, and floral patterns. Views are of the beautiful back garden—site of many weddings—and Olema Valley. After checking in, take a stroll on the stone pathways behind the inn to the orchard and flower gardens. The inn's romantic candle-lit restaurant features local produce and meats such as Bellweather Farms ricotta gnocchi with pine nuts and sage brown butter, pan-roasted Sonoma duck breast with a crispy potato galette, and a grilled, center-cut Niman Ranch pork chop with cider glaze and a side of crispy corn cake. Much of the restaurant's produce is grown at the inn's organic garden and orchard. *Tip:* Try to reserve room no. 3—the quietest, overlooking the garden.

10000 Sir Francis Drake Blvd., Olema, CA 94950. (✆) **415/663-9559.** Fax 415/663-8783. www.theolemainn.com. 6 units. $145–$185 double. Rates include continental breakfast. AE, MC, V. Checks accepted. Dogs are welcome at no extra charge. **Amenities:** Restaurant; gardens.

**Point Reyes Country Inn & Stables** (★)   Are you and your horse dreaming of a country getaway? Then book a room at Point Reyes Country Inn & Stables, a ranch-style home on 4 acres with pastoral accommodations for two- and four-legged guests (horses only), plus access to plenty of hiking and riding trails. Each of the six B&B rooms has a private bathroom and either a balcony or a garden. The innkeepers have also added two studios (with kitchens) above the stables, plus they rent out two cottages on Tomales Bay with decks, stocked kitchens, fireplaces, and a shared dock.

12050 Hwy. 1 (P.O. Box 501), Point Reyes Station, CA 94956. (✆) **415/663-9696.** Fax 415/663-8888. www.ptreyes countryinn.com. 10 units. $95–$115 studio; $110–$170 double; $190–$200 cottage. $10–$15 per horse. Rates include breakfast in the B&B rooms, breakfast provisions in the cottages. MC, V. **Amenities:** Nearby golf course. *In room:* No phone.

### INEXPENSIVE

**Motel Inverness** (Kids)   Finding an inexpensive place to stay in Point Reyes is next to impossible, because hoity-toity B&Bs reign supreme. One exception is Motel Inverness, a homey, well-maintained lodging fronting Tomales Bay. For the outdoor adventurer who plans to spend as little time indoors as possible, it's the perfect place

---

(Moments  **Low-Tech Life at Point Reyes Station**

Progress is taking its sweet time at Point Reyes Station, a tiny West Marin community across the bay from the national seashore. When you stroll along the 3-block-long Main Street of this former rail town, it's not hard to imagine what it was like when it was founded in the 1890s. Toby's Feed Barn emits that comforting aroma of hay, feed, and horse tack. The hard-working gals at the Cowgirl Creamery make organic handcrafted cheeses the old-school way, from local dairy milk. The cook rises early at the Pine Cone Diner to whip up biscuits and gravy every morning. Brawls still spill into the street once in a while at the Western Saloon, where townies and ranch hands shoot pool in the back. Yep, you sure ain't in the city anymore, so turn off that damn cellphone, mosey on up to the old oak bar at the saloon, and order a Bud (hold the glass).

## Point Reyes Mountain Biking

Marin was the birthplace of mountain biking, so it's no surprise that miles of meandering mountain-bike trails crisscross Point Reyes National Seashore. The challenge level varies from easy to daunting, with mostly fire roads and a few single-track trails winding through densely forested knolls and sunny meadows with pretty ocean views. Because many of the hiking trails are off limits to bikes, you'll need a bike map to figure out which ones are bike-legal. They're available for free at the Bear Valley Visitor Center (p. 198). To rent a bike, call David Barnett at **Cycle Analysis** (② **415/663-9164** or 415/663-1645; www.cyclepointreyes.com).

to hole up. Attached to the hotel is a giant great room, complete with fireplace and pool table to distract the kids; parents can relax on the back lawn overlooking the bay, bird sanctuary, and rolling green hills beyond. The two-bedroom suite with a kitchenette is ideal for families, as is the Dacha cottage, on the water, with three bedrooms.

12718 Sir Francis Drake Blvd., Inverness, CA 94937. ② **888/669-6909** or 415/669-1081. www.motelinverness.com. 8 units. $99–$175 double; $400–$500 suite. MC, V. *In room:* TV, coffeemaker.

**Point Reyes Hostel** *Kids*   Deep within Point Reyes National Seashore, this beautiful, old, ranch-like complex has 44 dormitory-style accommodations, including one room reserved for families (with at least one child 5 years old or younger). The two common rooms are warmed by wood-burning stoves on chilly nights, and guests can share a fully equipped kitchen, barbecue (BYO charcoal), and patio. If you don't mind sharing your sleeping quarters with strangers, this is a deal that can't be beat. Reservations (and earplugs) are strongly recommended.

Off Limantour Rd. (P.O. Box 247), Point Reyes Station, CA 94956. ② **415/663-8811**. www.norcalhostels.org. 44 bunks, 1 private unit. $16 per adult, $9 per child under 17 w/parents. 5 nights out of 30 maximum stay. MC, V. Reception hours 7:30–10am and 4:30–9:30pm daily.

## WHERE TO DINE

**Manka's Inverness Lodge** *★★* CALIFORNIA/WILD GAME   Manka's reputation rests largely on its restaurant, which dominates the bottom floor. The dinners are prix fixe, and the house specialty is fire-grilled wild game, although if you call ahead, you may be able to arrange something tamer. The seasonal menu features items such as pheasant with a Madeira *jus,* mashed potatoes, and a wild-huckleberry jam; black buck antelope chops with sweet-corn salsa; or everybody's favorite, pan-seared elk tenderloin. The restaurant claims the majority of the fish, fruits, and vegetables are grown and raised or caught within 15 minutes of its kitchen. The wine cellar features more than 150 selections.

On Argyle St. (off Sir Francis Drake Blvd., 1½ blocks north of downtown Inverness), Inverness. ② **415/669-1034**. www.mankas.com. Reservations recommended. Prix-fixe menu Sun–Fri $58 per person; Sat $88 per person. MC, V. Daily 6–9pm (hours may vary; call ahead).

**Station House Café** *★★* AMERICAN   For more than 2 decades, the Station House Café has been a favorite pit stop for Bay Area residents headed to and from Point Reyes. It's a friendly, low-key place with an open kitchen, an outdoor garden

_Finds_ **Stinson Beach: The Bay Area's Best**

One of the most popular beaches in Northern California, this 3-mile-wide stretch of sand, at the western foot of Mount Tamalpais, is packed with Bay Area residents (and their dogs) on those rare, fog-free summer weekends. Granted, it lacks Southern California's hard bodies and soft golden sand, but it still makes for an enjoyable day trip via the scenic drive on Highway 1. Although swimming is allowed and lifeguards are on duty from May to mid-September, notices about riptides and the cold water usually discourage beach-goers from venturing too far into the surf. Adjoining the beach is the small town of Stinson Beach, where you can have an enjoyable alfresco lunch at the numerous cafes along Highway 1.

To reach Stinson Beach from San Francisco, cross the Golden Gate Bridge heading north on U.S. 101, take the Stinson Beach/Highway 1 exit heading west, and follow the signs (it's a 20-mile trip full of curves). The beach is open daily from 9am to 10pm, and admission is free. For more information, contact the Stinson Beach ranger and lifeguard station at ✆ **415/868-0942.**

dining area (key on sunny days), and live music on weekend nights. Breakfast dishes include a Hangtown omelet with local oysters and bacon, and eggs with creamed spinach and mashed-potato pancakes. Lunch and dinner specials might include fettuccine with fresh local mussels steamed in white-wine-and-butter sauce, two-cheese polenta served with fresh spinach sauté and grilled garlic-buttered tomato, or a daily fresh salmon special—all made from local produce, seafood, and organically raised Niman Ranch beef. The cafe has an extensive list of fine California wines and local as well as imported beers.

Main St., Point Reyes Station. ✆ **415/663-1515.** www.stationhousecafe.com. Reservations recommended. Breakfast $4.50–$8.50; main courses $7–$11 lunch, $9–$25 dinner. DISC, MC, V. Sun–Tues and Thurs 8am–9pm; Fri–Sat 8am–10pm.

**Taqueria La Quinta** _Value_ MEXICAN   Fresh, fast, good, and cheap: What more could you ask for in a restaurant? Taqueria La Quinta has been one of my favorite lunch stops in downtown Point Reyes for years. A huge selection of Mexican-American dishes are posted above the counter. My favorite is chile verde in a spicy tomatillo sauce with a side of handmade corn tortillas. Those in the know inquire about the seafood specials. Since it's all self-serve, you can skip the tip, but watch out for the salsa—that sucker's _hot._

11285 Hwy. 1 (at Third and Main sts.), Point Reyes Station. ✆ **415/663-8868.** Main courses $5–$9. No credit cards. Wed–Mon 11:30am–7:30pm.

## 2 Along the Sonoma Coast

### BODEGA BAY

Beyond the tip of the Point Reyes peninsula, the road curves around toward the coastal village of Bodega Bay, which supports a fishing fleet of around 300 boats. It's a good place to stop for lunch or a stroll. Despite the droves of tourists on summer weekends,

Bodega Bay is mostly a working-class fishing town, where most locals start their day before dawn mending nets, rigging fishing poles, and talking shop. Several shops and galleries are interesting, but the best show in town—especially for kids—is at **Tides Wharf,** where the fishing boats dock, unload their catch, gut it, and pack it in ice.

**Bodega Head State Park** ⭐ is a great vantage point for whale-watching during the migration from January to April. At **Doran Beach,** a large bird sanctuary is home to willets, curlews, godwits, and more. Next door, the **UC Davis Bodega Bay Marine Laboratory** (℃ 707/875-2211; www.bml.ucdavis.edu) conducts guided tours of its lab projects on Friday afternoons between 2 and 4pm. (Suggested donation is $2.)

The **Bodega Harbour Golf Links,** at 21301 Heron Dr. (℃ 707/875-3538; www.bodegaharbourgolf.com), is an 18-hole, Scottish-style course designed by Robert Trent Jones, Jr., in an oceanside setting. A warm-up center and practice facility is free for registered golfers. Rates range from $60 with cart Monday through Thursday, $70 on Friday, and $90 on weekends. You can also ride horseback through spectacular scenery through **Chanslor Horse Stables** (℃ 707/875-3333; www.chanslor.com), which also has pony rides for kids. It's open daily from 9am to 5pm.

One of the bay's major events is the **Fisherman's Festival** in April. Local fishing boats, decked with ribbons and banners, sail out for a Blessing of the Fleet, while up to 25,000 landlubbers partake of music, a lamb-and-oyster barbecue, and an arts-and-crafts fair. For more information about this festival and other events, consult the **Sonoma Coast Visitors Center,** 860 Hwy. 1, Bodega Bay, CA 94923 (℃ 707/875-3866; www.bodegabay.com or www.visitsonomacoast.com). Open daily, it has lots of brochures about the area, including maps of the Sonoma Coast State Beaches and the best fishing spots.

A few miles inland on Highway 1 (toward Petaluma) is the tiny town of **Bodega** (pop. 100), famous as the setting of Alfred Hitchcock's *The Birds,* filmed here in 1961. Fans will want to visit the Potter School House and St. Teresa's Church.

## WHERE TO STAY
### Expensive
**Bodega Bay Lodge & Duck Club Restaurant** ⭐⭐    Near Doran Beach State Park, this is the best hotel in Bodega Bay. Each room has plush furnishings, a fireplace, and a private balcony with sweeping views of the bay and bird-filled marshes. If you can afford it, opt for one of the large luxury suites. Guests have complimentary access to a fitness center and sauna, as well as to a fieldstone spa and heated pool above the bay, surrounded by gardens. The lodge's **Duck Club Restaurant** enjoys a reputation as Bodega Bay's finest. Picture windows take advantage of the bay view, a romantic setting for Sonoma County cuisine such as roasted Petaluma duck and fresh fish caught by the Bodega fleet.

103 Hwy. 1, Bodega Bay, CA 94923. ℃ 800/368-2468 or 707/875-3525. Fax 707/875-2428. www.bodegabaylodge. com. 84 units. Sun–Thurs $210–$240 double, $400 suite; Fri–Sat $235–$285 double, $450 suite. 2-night minimum on weekends. AE, DC, DISC, MC, V. **Amenities:** Restaurant; heated outdoor pool w/ocean view; nearby golf course; full-service spa and fitness center; concierge; room service; in-room massage; babysitting; coin-op laundry. *In room:* A/C, TV w/pay movies, fax, dataport, minibar, fridge, coffeemaker, hair dryer, iron, safe.

### Moderate
**Inn at the Tides** ⭐    The larger of Bodega Bay's two upscale lodgings (the other being Bodega Bay Lodge), the Inn at the Tides consists of a cluster of condolike wood complexes on the side of a gently sloping hill. The selling point is the view; each unit

is staggered just enough to guarantee a view of the bay across the highway. The rooms are modern and the inn's amenities are first-rate, such as the attractive indoor-outdoor pool, but I would only stay here if I couldn't get a room at the Bodega Bay Lodge. The **Bay View Restaurant** is open Wednesday through Sunday for dinner only, with ocean views, a well-prepared albeit traditional choice of entrees, and a romantic, somewhat formal ambience. Be sure to check the website for special package deals.

800 Coast Hwy. 1 (P.O. Box 640), Bodega Bay, CA 94923. © 800/541-7788 or 707/875-2751. Fax 707/875-3285. www.innatthetides.com. 86 units. Summer Sun–Thurs $169–$249; Fri–Sat $199–$284; winter rates drop about 20%. Rates include continental breakfast. Golf packages available. AE, DC, DISC, MC, V. **Amenities:** Restaurant; indoor-outdoor heated pool; nearby golf course; exercise room; Jacuzzi; Finnish sauna; room service; in-room massage; babysitting (w/notice); self-service laundry. In room: TV w/pay movies, minibar, coffeemaker, hair dryer, iron.

## Inexpensive

### Bodega Harbor Inn ★ Value
Thank Poseidon for the Bodega Harbor Inn, with some of the best lodging bargains on the North Coast. On a small bluff over the bay, the inn consists of four single-story clapboard buildings surrounded by well-maintained lawns and gardens. The rooms, though small, are impeccably neat and tastefully decorated with unpretentious antiques; double beds, private bathrooms, and cable TV are standard. (The best rooms are nos. 12 and 14, which come with small decks and partial ocean views.) The clincher, though, is the inn's private lawn area overlooking the water. On sunny days, there's no better way to enjoy an afternoon in Bodega Bay than parking in one of the lawn chairs and watching the fishing boats bring in their daily catch. Families should inquire about the seven vacation homes the inn rents for as little as $110 per night.

1345 Bodega Ave., Bodega Bay, CA 94923. © 707/875-3594. www.bodegaharborinn.com. 14 units, 7 houses. $65–$95 double; $110–$285 house. Rates include continental breakfast. MC, V. In room: TV.

## WHERE TO DINE

In addition to the following, see the Duck Club Restaurant in "Where to Stay," above.

### Lucas Wharf Deli ★ Value  DELI
I always stop here when I pass through Bodega Bay. Most visitors don't even give it a glance as they head into the adjacent restaurant, but that's because they don't know about the big bowls of fresh, tangy crab cioppino doled out, in season, for about $5.50 a pint—a third of the restaurant price. It's a messy affair, best devoured at the nearby picnic tables. Great fish and chips are available year-round. The deli is also open for breakfast.

595 Hwy. 1, Bodega Bay. © 707/875-3562. Deli items $4–$10. MC, V. Sun–Thurs 9am–6pm; Fri–Sat 9am–7pm.

### Tides Wharf Restaurant  SEAFOOD/PASTA
In summer, as many as 1,000 diners a day pass through the Tides Wharf. In the early '60s, it was a set for Hitchcock's *The Birds,* but don't expect the weather-beaten, board-and-batten luncheonette you saw in the movie—a $6-million renovation gentrified, enlarged, and redecorated the place

---

### ⎰ Fun Fact  Hitchcock Haunt

Alfred Hitchcock fans will want to make the pilgrimage to Bodega, located off Highway 1 a few miles southeast of Bodega Bay. Drive past the roadside shops, turn the corner, look right, and *voilà:* a bird's-eye view of the hauntingly familiar Potter School House and St. Teresa's Church, both immortalized in Hitchcock's *The Birds,* filmed here in 1961.

beyond recognition. The best tables have ocean views, and the fare is what you might expect: oysters on the half shell, clam chowder, and all the fish that the owners can dredge up from the cold blue waters (they send their own boat out into the Pacific every day). Prime rib, pasta, and poultry are available as well. Next to the restaurant are a fish-processing plant, snack bar, and gift shop.

835 Hwy. 1. ⓒ 707/875-3652. www.innatthetides.com/tideswharf.html. Main courses $14–$37. AE, DISC, MC, V. Mon–Fri 7:30am–9pm; Sat–Sun 7am–9:30pm.

## THE SONOMA COAST STATE BEACHES, JENNER & FORT ROSS STATE HISTORIC PARK ⭑⭑

Along 13 winding and picturesque miles of Highway 1—from Bodega Bay to Goat Rock Beach in Jenner—stretch the Sonoma Coast State Beaches. These beaches are ideal for walking, tide pooling, abalone picking, fishing, and bird-watching for species such as great blue heron, cormorant, osprey, and pelican. Each beach is clearly marked from the road, and numerous pullouts are available for parking. Even if you don't stop at any of the beaches, the drive alone is spectacular.

At **Jenner,** the Russian River empties into the ocean. **Penny Island,** in the river's estuary, is home to otters and many species of birds; a colony of harbor seals lives out on the ocean rocks. **Goat Rock Beach** is a popular breeding ground for the seals; pupping season begins in March and lasts until June.

From Jenner, an 11-mile, dramatic coastal drive brings you to **Fort Ross State Historic Park** (ⓒ 707/847-3286; www.parks.sonoma.net), a reconstruction of the fort established in 1812 by the Russians as a base for seal and otter hunting (a post they abandoned in 1842). At the visitor center, you can view the Russians' samovars and table services. The compound contains several buildings, including the first Russian Orthodox church on the North American continent outside Alaska. A short history lesson about the fort takes place at 11:30am, 1:30pm, and 3:30pm between Memorial Day and Labor Day, and at noon and 2pm the rest of the year. Call ahead to be sure. The park also offers beach trails and picnic grounds on more than 1,000 acres. Admission to the park is $2 per car per day.

North from Fort Ross, the road continues to **Salt Point State Park** (ⓒ 707/847-3221). This 3,500-acre expanse encompasses 30 campsites, 14 miles of trails, dozens of tide pools, and old Pomo village sites. Your best bet is to pull off the highway any place that catches your eye and start exploring. At the north end of the park, head inland on Kruse Ranch Road to the **Kruse Rhododendron Reserve** (ⓒ 707/847-3286), a forested grove of wild pink and purple flowers where the *Rhododendron californicum* grow up to a height of 18 feet under the redwood-and-fir canopy. Admission to the park is $2 per car per day.

## WHERE TO STAY

**Jenner Inn & Cottages** ⭑    The worst-kept secret on the Northern Coast is Jenner Inn, a hodgepodge of individually designed and decorated houses and cottages along the coast and inland along the Russian River. Couples from the Bay Area who want to stay along the coast for a night, but dread the long drive to Mendocino, wend their way here. Most of the houses are subdivided into suites, while second honeymooners vie for the ultraprivate oceanfront cottages. Wicker furniture, wood paneling, and private bathrooms and entrances are standard, though each lodging has its own personality: Some have kitchens, while others have fireplaces, porches, or private decks. The private cottages overlooking the Pacific are the priciest, but for about $130, most people are content with one of the small suites. The inn offers yoga classes several times weekly and has a small meditation cabin. A complimentary full breakfast is served in the main lodge. In addition to the B&B accommodations, the inn rents vacation homes along the river, within Jenner Canyon, or overlooking the ocean.

10400 Hwy. 1 (P.O. Box 69), Jenner, CA 95450. (©) 800/732-2377 or 707/865-2377. Fax 707/865-0829. www.jenner inn.com. 20 units (plus several vacation homes). $95–$375 double. Rates include full breakfast. AE, MC, V. *In room:* Kitchen in some units, fridge, coffeemaker, hair dryer, iron, phones in cottages only.

## WHERE TO DINE

River's End ★ INTERNATIONAL    Established in 1927, this unpretentious yet urbane seaside restaurant offers a rugged setting, with big windows overlooking the coast (seals and sea lions might happen to be cavorting offshore). The menu, which changes monthly, offers everything from coconut shrimp, pheasant breast, racks of elk, seafood, and steaks. Whenever possible, the chef uses local Sonoma products—game, lamb, poultry, vegetables, microbrews, and wines. After dinner, take the remainder of your wine to the deck and watch the sun set. *Note:* The hours tend to vary as much as the menu, so call ahead or check the website if you're planning to dine here.

Hwy. 1, Jenner. (©) 707/865-2484. www.ilovesunsets.com. Reservations recommended. Main courses $13–$28. MC, V. Summer daily noon–3:30pm and 5–9pm.

Sizzling Tandoor *Value* INDIAN    Along a desolate stretch of Highway 1 between Bodega Bay and Jenner, the Sizzling Tandoor serves huge, inexpensive plates of Indian cuisine. The lonely location, though peculiar, is superb: High atop a wind-swept hill, the restaurant has an exquisite view of the Russian River far below. The large array of curries and kabobs are accompanied by soup, vegetables, *pulao* rice, and the best *naan* (Indian bread) I've ever had. Even if you're not hungry, order some *naan* to go—it makes the perfect road snack.

9960 Hwy. 1 (at the south end of the Russian River Bridge), Jenner. (©) 707/865-0625. Main courses $9–$14. AE, DISC, MC, V. Mon–Thurs 11:30am–9pm; Fri–Sun 11:30am–9:30pm.

## GUALALA & POINT ARENA

Back on Highway 1 heading north, you'll pass through Sea Ranch, a series of condominium beach developments, before you reach the small coastal community of Gualala (pronounced "Wah-*la*-la"). In the old days, Gualala was a vivacious logging town. A few real-life, suspender-wearing lumberjacks still end their day at the Gualala Hotel's saloon, but for the most part the town's chief function is to provide gas, groceries, and hardware for area residents. Several parks, hiking trails, and about 10 ideal sunbathing beaches lie just outside town.

The **Gualala River,** adjacent to the town of the same name, is suitable for canoeing, rafting, and kayaking, because powerboats and jet skis are forbidden. Along its banks you're likely to see osprey, herons, egrets, and ducks; steelhead, salmon, and river otters make their homes in the waters. You can rent canoes and kayaks in Gualala for 2 hours, a half-day, or a full day from **Adventure Rents** ((©) **888/881-4386** or 707/884-3386; www.adventurerents.com), in downtown Gualala on Highway 1, north of the Chevron. Prices range from $25 for a few hours on a river canoe to $70 for a full day on a tandem ocean kayak.

Point Arena is a few miles north of Gualala. Most folk stop here for the view at the **Point Arena Lighthouse** ★ ((©) **707/882-2777**; www.mcn.org/1/palight), which was built in 1870 after 10 ships ran aground here one night in a storm. A $5-per-person fee ($1 for children under 12) covers parking, entrance to the lighthouse museum, and

## Tips   Renting a Home at the Beach

If you're taking the family for a vacation along the coast—or if you really want to impress your partner—consider renting a furnished home at the Sea Ranch, one of the most beautiful seaside communities around. All the low-swept buildings are designed to blend in with the surrounding forest, meadows, and ocean bluffs; many have outdoor hot tubs, and almost all have wood-burning fireplaces or stoves. About 300 homes are available as rentals with prices starting at about $150 per night. Rentals include use of the community's three outdoor heated swimming pools, tennis courts, and recreation center. The Sea Ranch also has a Scottish-style 18-hole public golf course, a fine-dining restaurant, and private access to 10 miles of coastline and several secluded beaches. For more information, log on to www.sea ranchvillage.com or call **Sea Ranch Rentals** at © 888/732-7262.

a surprisingly interesting tour of the six-story, 145-step lighthouse (the view through the dazzling 6-ft.-wide, lead-crystal lens is worth the hike alone). The lighthouse is open daily 10am to 4:30pm April to September and 10am to 3:30pm October to March; the half-hour tours take place every 20 minutes.

### WHERE TO STAY

**St. Orres** ★★ *Finds*   An extraordinary Russian-style building—complete with two onion-domed towers—St. Orres lies 1½ miles north of Gualala. The complex was built in 1972 with century-old timbers salvaged from a nearby mill. It offers cottage-style accommodations on 42 acres, as well as eight rooms in the main building (these rooms are handcrafted and share three bathrooms decorated in brilliant colors). Other units are very private. Some have wet bars, sitting areas with Franklin stoves, and French doors leading to decks with a distant ocean view. Seven cottages border St. Orres Creek and have exclusive use of a spa facility that includes a hot tub, sauna, and sun deck. The most luxurious is Pine Haven, with two bedrooms, two redwood decks, two bathrooms, a tiled breakfast area, a beach-stone fireplace, and a wet bar. The Black Chanterelle is as exotic as it sounds, with domes, a sauna and Jacuzzi, a fireplace, and an ocean view. Full breakfast is delivered to the cottages. The hotel's restaurant (see review below), open for dinner only, is in a dramatic setting below one of the main building's domes. Light filters through stained-glass windows onto strands of ivy that cascade down from the balcony. The menu is inspired by Pacific Northwest cuisine and includes wild boar, pheasant, venison, quail, and rack of lamb.

36601 Hwy. 1 (P.O. Box 523), Gualala, CA 95445. © **707/884-3303.** Fax 707/884-1840. www.saintorres.com. 8 units (sharing 3 bathrooms), 13 cottages. $80–$95 double; cottage $110–$235 double. Rates include full breakfast. MC, V. **Amenities:** Restaurant; bar; nearby golf course; Jacuzzi; sauna; bike rental; in-room massage; babysitting. *In room:* Kitchenette in some units, fridge, coffeemaker, hair dryer, iron.

**Whale Watch Inn By the Sea** ★★   Ninety feet above the water, in five contemporary buildings on 2 cliffside acres, this inn has one of the best views of the Northern Coast. Private guest rooms all have ocean views, decks, and fireplaces. Room styles range from traditional bed-and-breakfast style to French Provençal to contemporary casual;

check out the pictures on the website before you reserve one. For a closer encounter with nature, take the private stairway that leads to a half-mile long beach with tidal pools. The Whale Watch building has a common room with a circular fireplace, floor-to-ceiling windows, and a wraparound deck for prime viewing.

35100 Hwy. 1, Gualala, CA 95445. © **800/942-5342** or 707/884-3667. Fax 707/884-3667. www.whale-watch.com. 18 units. $180–$300 double. Rates include full breakfast delivered to room at prearranged time. AE, MC, V. **Amenities:** Nearby golf course. *In room:* Kitchen, fridge, and coffeemaker in some units, hair dryer, phone upon request.

## WHERE TO DINE

**St. Orres Restaurant** ★★ NORTH COAST CUISINE   Self-taught chef Rosemary Campiformio has been wowing fans and food writers for years with her version of North Coast cuisine, which favors local organic meats and produce and wild game in dark, fruity sauces. Every day fishermen and farmers deliver their best goods to Rosemary's kitchen door, so you never know what will be on her prix-fixe dinner menu, but it'll probably go something like this: an appetizer of pheasant and venison pâté with a huckleberry glaze and Rosemary's mustard, followed by a garden-fresh salad and an entree of grilled veal chop with garlic mashed potatoes, foie gras, and truffle Madeira sauce (it's either that or the pan-roasted fresh wild salmon with zucchini cakes and wasabi lime and ginger). For dessert, it's a tossup between the bread pudding with homemade nutmeg ice cream and caramel sauce, or the freshly baked individual apple pie with St. Orres cinnamon ice cream. The wine cellar stores a suitable selection of reds that pair well with the hearty entrees. If you're staying at the St. Orres Inn (see review above), it's a short walk from your cabin to this rustic, romantic restaurant situated under the main lodge's distinctive onion dome.

36601 Hwy. 1 (St. Orres Inn), Gualala. © **707/884-3335.** www.saintorres.com. Reservations recommended. Prix-fixe dinner menu $40; appetizers and desserts a la carte. Beer and wine only. MC, V. Checks accepted. Dinner daily 6–9:30pm (winter schedule varies).

## NORTH FROM POINT ARENA

Driving north from Point Arena, you'll pass Elk (a good place to stop for lunch), Manchester, Albion, and Little River on your way to Mendocino.

## WHERE TO STAY

**Greenwood Pier Inn & Cafe** ★   On the edge of a dramatic bluff, the Greenwood Pier Inn is a New Age sort of complex encompassing a cafe, country store, garden shop, and accommodations that range from cabins to rooms in the main inn building. It's the unique domain of owner-operator Kendrick Petty, an artist and gardener whose collages, tiles, and marble work are on display throughout the premises, including the gardens. The Cliffhouse is my favorite unit here: a seaside redwood cabin with a fireplace, a large deck, and an upper-level bathtub with ocean views. All the rooms are within 100 feet of the cliff edge with private decks, fireplaces or wood burners. A beautiful building called The Tower has three levels: a two-person Jacuzzi at the bottom, a deck overlooking the ocean on the second level and, up a library ladder, a full-size bed facing an ocean view. A continental breakfast is delivered to your room; breakfast, lunch, and dinner—roast pork loin, grilled rack of lamb, grilled Chilean sea bass—are served daily in the Greenwood Pier Cafe.

5928 Hwy. 1 (P.O. Box 336), Elk, CA 95432. © **707/877-9997.** Fax 707/877-3439. www.greenwoodpierinn.com. 12 units. $130–$300 double. Rates include continental breakfast. AE, MC, V. Pets accepted in some units for $15 per night. **Amenities:** Restaurant; nearby golf course; oceanview Jacuzzi; in-room massage. *In room:* Fridge, coffeemaker, hair dryer in some units, no phone.

**Griffin House Inn** ★★ *Finds*   I love this unpretentious, peaceful little inn with it's eight cozy cottages, friendly tavern, reasonable rates, and gorgeous views of the rugged coastline. The tiny village of Elk isn't as gentrified as Mendocino up the coast, but those yearning for a calmer commune with nature will love it here. The inn's most coveted cottages are cliffside, with private decks for soaking in the splendor of Greenwood Cove (the Matson Cottage is my favorite). The cottages in the garden setting—sans ocean view—are cheaper but still pleasant. The cottages are individually decorated in a sort of austere Cape Cod style with a mix of pine and mahogany furnishings, stained glass, French doors, and claw-foot tubs; all come with private baths and wood-burning stoves. On the premises is Bridget Dolan's Pub, which serves good, hearty comfort food and plenty of fine wine and cold beer. A full hot breakfast is even delivered to your door. What more could you ask for?

5910 Hwy. 1, P.O. Box 172, Elk, CA 95432. ⓒ **707/877-3422.** Fax 707/877-1853. www.griffinn.com. 7 cottages. $118–$218 cottage. Rates include full breakfast. AE, DISC, MC, V. *In room:* Hair dryer.

**Harbor House Inn & Restaurant** ★★   Built in 1916 by the president of the Goodyear Redwood Lumber Co. as a hideaway for corporate executives, this beautiful, redwood-sided, two-story inn offers 3 acres of gardens, access to a private beach, and views overlooking the Pacific. None of the units has a TV or phone, and that's how guests like it. Five of the rooms in the traditional main building have their own fireplaces, many are furnished with antiques purchased by the lumber executives, and all have private bathrooms. The four cottages tend to be small but have fireplaces and private decks. Set dinners, included in the rates, change nightly and feature California and Pacific Northwest cuisines, making use of seafood harvested from local waters, local herbs, freshly baked breads, and vegetables from the inn's gardens.

5600 S. Hwy. 1 (P.O. Box 369), Elk, CA 95432. ⓒ **800/720-7474** or 707/877-3203. Fax 707/877-3452. www.theharbor houseinn.com. 10 units. $295–$470 double (winter rates considerably less). Extra person $100. Rates include full breakfast and 4-course dinner. AE, MC, V. **Amenities:** Restaurant; nearby golf course; in-room massage. *In room:* A/C, coffeemaker, hair dryer, iron in cottages, no phone.

**INEXPENSIVE**

**KOA Kamping Kabins** *Kids*   "What? You expect me to stay at a Kampgrounds of America?!" You bet. Once you see these neat little log "kabins," you'll admit they're a great way to spend a weekend on the coast. The cabins sleep four to six, with one or two bedrooms and log-frame double beds or bunk beds for the kids. Mattresses, a heater, and a light bulb are your standard amenities. Beyond that, you're on your own; you'll need bedding or a sleeping bag, cooking and eating utensils, and a bag of charcoal for the barbecue in front. Enjoy your meal at the picnic table or on the front porch in the log swing. If this is a little too spartan for you, opt for one of the fully furnished "kottages," both decked out with private bathrooms, fireplaces, comfy beds, and other creature comforts. Hot showers, bathrooms, laundry facilities, a small store, and a swimming pool are a short walk away, as is Manchester Beach. It's kid heaven.

On Kinney Rd. (off Hwy. 1, 5 miles north of Point Arena). ⓒ **800/562-4188** or 707/882-2375. Fax 707/882-3104. www.manchesterbeachkoa.com. 24 cabins, 2 cottages. $52–$72 cabin (up to 6 people); $135–$165 cottage (up to 4 people). AE, DISC, MC, V. **Amenities:** Heated outdoor pool (seasonal); spa; children's center and playground; coin-op laundry. *In room:* TV and kitchenette in cottages, no phone.

**WHERE TO DINE**

**Ledford House Restaurant** ★ NEW AMERICAN   If James Beard were alive today, he'd feel right at home at this innovative but simply decorated restaurant overlooking the pounding surf of the Pacific from a bluff above. The kitchen offers self-styled "New American cuisine," experimenting with the bounty of the Golden State to fashion rich combinations and harmonious flavors. One part of the menu is reserved primarily for the pastas and hearty stews suitable to this far-northern setting, such as their award-winning Antoine's cassoulet, a jumble of pork, lamb, garlic sausage, and duck confit slowly cooked with white beans. Although the menu changes seasonally, for a taste of California, try the salmon primavera with lemon-caper butter, or the crisp-roasted duckling with wild-huckleberry sauce. Evenings bring live jazz in the cocktail lounge.

3000 N. Hwy. 1, Albion. 𝄐 707/937-0282. www.ledfordhouse.com. Reservations recommended. Main courses $22–$26. AE, MC, V. Wed–Sun 5–9pm.

## 3 Mendocino ★★★

166 miles N of San Francisco

Mendocino is, to my mind, *the* premier destination on California's Northern Coast. Despite (or because of) its relative isolation, it emerged as one of Northern California's major centers for the arts in the 1950s. It's easy to see why artists were—and still are—attracted to this idyllic community, a cluster of New England–style captains' homes and stores on headlands overlooking the ocean.

At the height of the logging boom, Mendocino was an important and active port. Its population was about 3,500 residents, who constructed eight hotels, 17 saloons, and more than a dozen bordellos. Today, it has only about 1,000 residents, and most reside on the north end of town. On summer weekends, the population seems more like 10,000, as hordes of tourists drive up from the Bay Area. Despite the crowds, however, Mendocino manages to retain its charm.

### ESSENTIALS

**GETTING THERE**   The fastest route from San Francisco is via U.S. 101 north to Cloverdale. Then take Highway 128 west to Highway 1, and then go north along the coast. It's about a 4-hour drive. (You could also take U.S. 101 all the way to Ukiah or Willits, and cut over to the west from there.) The most scenic route, if you have the time and your stomach doesn't mind the twists and turns, is to take Highway 1 north along the coast the entire way; it's at least a 5- to 6-hour drive.

**VISITOR INFORMATION**   You can stock up on lots of free brochures and maps at the **Fort Bragg/Mendocino Coast Chamber of Commerce,** 332 N. Main St. (P.O. Box 1141), Fort Bragg, CA 95437 (𝄐 800/726-2780 or 707/961-6300; www.mendocinocoast.com). Pick up a copy of the center's monthly magazine, *Arts and Entertainment,* which lists upcoming events throughout Mendocino. It's available at numerous stores and cafes, including the Mendocino Bakery, Gallery Bookshop, and Mendocino Art Center.

### EXPLORING THE TOWN

Stroll through town, survey the architecture, and browse through the dozens of galleries and shops. My favorites include the **Highlight Gallery,** 45052 Main St. (𝄐 707/ 937-3132), for its handmade furniture, pottery, and other craft work; and the **Gallery Bookshop & Bookwinkle's Children's Books,** at Main and Kasten streets (𝄐 707/ 937-2665; www.gallerybooks.com), one of the best independent bookstores in Northern California, with a wonderful selection of books for children and adults.

Another popular stop is **Mendocino Jams & Preserves,** 440 Main St. (© **800/ 708-1196** or 707/937-1037; www.mendojams.com), which offers free tastings, on little bread chips, of its natural, locally made gourmet fruit spreads.

After exploring the town, walk out onto **Mendocino Headlands State Park** ⚘, which wraps around the town. (The park visitor center is in the Ford House on Main St.; © **707/937-5397.**) Three miles of trails, with panoramic views of sea arches and hidden grottoes, wind through the park. At the right time of year, wildflowers blanket the area; when I last stopped by, I picked blackberries beside the trails. The headlands are home to many unique bird species, including black oystercatchers. Behind the Mendocino Presbyterian Church on Main Street, a trail leads to stairs that take you down to the beach, a small but picturesque stretch of sand where driftwood formations have washed ashore.

On the south side of town, **Big River Beach** is accessible from Highway 1; it's good for picnicking, walking, and sunbathing.

In town, stop by the **Mendocino Art Center,** 45200 Little Lake St. (© **707/937-5818;** www.mendocinoartcenter.org), the town's unofficial cultural headquarters. It's also known for its gardens, galleries, and shops that display and sell local fine arts and crafts. Admission is free; it's open daily from 10am to 5pm.

After a day of hiking, head to **Sweetwater Spa & Inn,** 955 Ukiah St. (© **800/ 300-4140** or 707/937-4140; www.sweetwaterspa.com), which offers group and private saunas and hot-tub soaks by the hour. Additional services include Swedish or deep-tissue massages. Reservations are recommended. Private tub prices are $12 per person per half-hour, $16 per person per hour. Group tub prices are $10 per person with no time limit. Special discounts are available on Wednesdays. The spa is open Monday through Thursday from 1 to 10pm, Friday and Sunday from noon to 10pm, and Saturday and holidays from noon to 11pm.

## OUTDOOR PURSUITS

Explore the Big River by renting a canoe, kayak, or outrigger from **Catch a Canoe & Bicycles Too** (© **707/937-0273;** www.stanfordinn.com), open daily from 9am to sunset and located on the grounds of the Stanford Inn by the Sea (see "Where to Stay" below). If you're lucky, you'll see some osprey, blue herons, harbor seals, deer, and wood ducks. These same folks will also rent you a mountain bike (of much better quality than your usual bike rental), so you can head up Highway 1 and explore the nearby state parks on two wheels.

Visitors can ride horseback (both English and Western-style) on the beach and into the woods through **Ricochet Ridge Ranch,** 24201 N. Hwy. 1, Fort Bragg (© **888/873-5777** or 707/964-PONY; www.horse-vacation.com). Prices range from $40 for a 1½-hour beach ride to $205 for an all-day beach-and-redwoods trail ride.

In addition to Mendocino Headlands State Park (see "Exploring the Town," above), several other state parks are within an easy drive or bike ride from Mendocino. The brochure *Mendocino Coast State Parks,* available from the visitor center in Fort Bragg, has information on all the parks, with maps of each. These areas include **Manchester State Park,** where the San Andreas Fault sweeps to the sea; **Jughandle State Reserve;** and **Van Damme State Park** ⚘, with a sheltered, easily accessible beach.

My favorite, on Highway 1 just north of Mendocino, is **Russian Gulch State Park** ⚘⚘. It's one of the region's most spectacular parks, where waves crash against the cliffs that protect the park's California coastal redwoods. The most popular attraction

---

**Tips** Mendocino Nightlife

Typical of a small town, the nightlife scene in Mendocino is like molasses in winter. Visitors have three options: 1) Have a casual cocktail in the elegant bar and lounge at the **Mendocino Hotel** (see review below); 2) Knock down a few Buds with the locals at **Dick's Place** (45080 Main St.; © 707/937-5643), the town's oldest bar; or 3) Get in the car and head up Highway 1 a bit to the **Caspar Inn,** the best nightclub on the North Coast. Everything from rock and jazz to reggae and blues is played live Thursday through Saturday nights starting at 9:30pm. Check its website calendar for upcoming shows and bring a designated dancer and driver. It's located at 14957 Caspar Rd. (take the Caspar Rd. exit off Hwy. 1, ¼ mile north of Mendocino; © 707/964-5565; www.casparinn.com).

---

is the **Punch Bowl,** a collapsed sea cave that forms a tunnel through which waves crash, creating throaty echoes. Inland, visitors can pedal along a scenic, paved bike path, or hoof it on miles of hiking trails, including a gentle, well-marked 3-mile **Waterfall Loop** that winds past tall redwoods and damp green foliage to a 36-foot-high waterfall. Admission is $2 and camping is $12 per night. Call © **800/444-7275** for reservations; for general state park information, call © **707/937-5804** or visit www.cal-parks.ca.gov.

Fort Bragg is a short distance up the coast; deep-sea fishing charters are available from its harbor.

## WHERE TO STAY

### EXPENSIVE

**Stanford Inn by the Sea** ✦✦　Just south of Mendocino, this rustic but sumptuous lodge is on 11 acres of land abutting the Big River. The grounds are captivating, with tiers of gardens, a pond for ducks and geese, and fenced pastures of horses, llamas, and old gnarled apple trees. The solarium-style indoor hot tub and pool surrounded by tropical plants are gorgeous. The luxurious rooms come with thick robes, down comforters, fresh flowers, and works by local artists. All units have fireplaces or stoves and private decks from which you can gaze on the Pacific. Second honeymooners should inquire about the romantic River Cottage; families will want the big renovated barn. Pets are welcome and receive the royal treatment. The inn also has a small massage studio, individual and group yoga lessons, and **The Raven's Restaurant,** the only totally vegetarian restaurant on the Mendocino coast, which has become a big hit with both guests and locals.

N. Hwy. 1 and Comptche Ukiah Rd. (P.O. Box 487), Mendocino, CA 95460. © 800/331-8884 or 707/937-5615. Fax 707/937-0305. www.stanfordinn.com. 33 units. $235–$295 double; $310–$720 suite. Rates include breakfast. AE, DC, DISC, MC, V. Pets accepted w/$25 fee. **Amenities:** Vegetarian restaurant; nearby golf course; exercise room; solarium-style pool, spa, and sauna; kayak and canoe rental; complimentary bikes; concierge; courtesy car; business center; secretarial services; evening room service; in-room massage. *In room:* TV/VCR w/pay movies, dataport, kitchenette and minibar in some units, fridge, coffeemaker, hair dryer, iron.

### MODERATE

**Agate Cove Inn** ✦✦　Good luck trying to find an accommodation with a more beautiful coastal setting than Agate Cove Inn's. Words can barely convey the splendor of the view from the front lawn—a sweeping, unfettered vista of the sea and its surging waves crashing onto the bluffs. Situate yourself on one of the Adirondack chairs with a good book, and you'll never want to leave. The inn consists of a main house trimmed in blue and white, surrounded by a bevy of single and duplex cottages. All but 1 of the 10 spacious units have views of the ocean, king- or queen-size beds, down comforters, fireplaces, and private decks. In the morning, a fantastic country breakfast is served in the main house's enclosed porch (yes, with the same ocean view).

11201 N. Lansing St. (P.O. Box 1150), Mendocino, CA 95460. © 800/527-3111 or 707/937-0551. Fax 707/937-0550. www.agatecove.com. 10 units. $119–$269 double. Rates include full breakfast. AE, MC, V. **Amenities:** Nearby golf course; concierge; activities desk; in-room massage. *In room:* TV/VCR w/complimentary videos, hair dryer, iron, CD player, no phone.

**Brewery Gulch Inn** ★★   I've never met anyone as passionate about the intricacies of virgin redwood than Dr. Arky Ciancutti, the owner, builder, and visionary behind the Brewery Gulch Inn, a beautiful three-story inn high on a bluff overlooking Mendocino's Smuggler's Cove. A "self-confessed wood freak," Arky salvaged more than 100,000 board feet of century-old redwood logs that were embedded in the silty bottom of Mendocino's Big River, then carefully milled the 12-foot-thick trunks to obtain the finest cuts of redwood lumber to build his dream inn. Spend a few minutes talking wood with Arky and you too will marvel at the subtle red, purple, and blond tones that swirl throughout the redwood beams, doors, and decks. The inn was constructed in a clean-lined Arts and Crafts style, with a massive, centerpiece steel-and-glass fireplace and 10 soundproofed guest rooms. Rooms are luxuriously appointed with down comforters, gas-lit fireplaces, hardwood furnishings, leather club chairs, CD players, and private bathrooms with heated flooring; most have Jacuzzis or soaking tubs for two, as well as private decks with expansive views of the ocean and hundreds of acres of unoccupied meadow and forest. An in-house chef prepares the gourmet organic country breakfast with eggs from Arky's chicken coop, and herbs and fruit from the inn's gardens and orchards; hors d'oeuvres and Mendocino wines are offered in the evening as well. *Tip:* Check the website for tempting packages such as the "Marry Me!" and "Ocean Kayaking" deals.

9401 Coast Hwy. 1 N., Mendocino, CA 95460. © **800/578-4454** or 707/937-4753. Fax 707/937-1279. www.brewery gulchinn.com. 10 units. $150–$350. Rates include organic gourmet country breakfast and evening wine tasting w/hors d'oeuvres. AE, MC, V. **Amenities:** Concierge service; gift shop; telescope; daily newspaper and turndown service; common room w/fireplace; library w/wide selection of books, CDs, and videos. *In room:* TV/VCR, phone w/dataport, hair dryer, CD player, fireplace, fresh-cut flowers, private deck, soaking tub for 2, robes.

**Joshua Grindle Inn** ★★   When it was built in 1879, this stately Victorian was one of the most impressive houses in Mendocino, owned by the town's wealthiest banker. Now the oldest B&B in Mendocino, it features redwood siding, a wraparound porch, and emerald lawns. From its prettily planted gardens, the view across the village reaches all the way to the distant bay. The main house has five rooms, with two more in the cottage, and three in the water tower. All have well-lit, comfortably arranged sitting areas, some offer fireplaces, three have deep-soak tubs, and three have whirlpool tubs. Each is individually decorated: The Library Room has a New England feel, with its four-poster pine bed, floor-to-ceiling bookcase, and 19th-century tiles around the fireplace depicting Aesop's fables. Sherry, sweets, and tea are served in the parlor in front of the fireplace; breakfast is in the dining room. The proprietors also have a beautiful two-bedroom, two-bathroom oceanview rental home with floor-to-ceiling windows, a large kitchen, and a wood-burning fireplace. It's a few minutes north of Mendocino, and rates range from $245 to $375, depending on occupancy.

44800 Little Lake Rd. (P.O. Box 647), Mendocino, CA 95460. ℂ **800/GRINDLE** or 707/937-4143. www.joshgrin.com. 10 units. June–Oct $130–$245 double; Nov–May Mon–Thurs $115–$195 double, Fri–Sun $130–$245 double. Rates include full breakfast, afternoon tea, and wine. MC, V. **Amenities:** Nearby golf course; concierge. *In room:* TV/DVD in some units, hair dryer, no phone.

**MacCallum House Inn & Restaurant** ⭐⭐ A historic 1882 gingerbread Victorian mansion, MacCallum House is one of Mendocino's top accommodations. Originally owned by Daisy MacCallum, the daughter of the town's richest lumber baron, the inn remained in the family until 1974, when it became a B&B. Current owners Melanie and Joe Redding preserved the home's original furnishings and contents—right down to Daisy's Christmas cards and books of pressed flowers. With the occasional Tiffany lamp or Persian carpet, each uniquely decorated guest room is furnished with many original pieces—a Franklin stove, a handmade quilt, a cushioned rocking chair, or a child's cradle. All have private bathrooms, many with claw-foot or spa tubs for two. The luxurious barn suite with a stone fireplace can accommodate up to six. The popular restaurant on the premises serves sophisticated North Coast cuisine ranging from pan-seared Sonoma duck breast with huckleberry-honey-vinegar sauce, to roasted Pacific salmon with saffron-pistachio risotto and arugula pesto.

45020 Albion St. (P.O. Box 206), Mendocino, CA 95460. ℂ **800/609-0492** or 707/937-0289. Fax 707/964-2243. www.maccallumhouse.com. 19 units. $120–$195 double. Extra person $15. AE, MC, V. **Amenities:** Restaurant; cafe; bar; concierge. *In room:* Fridge, coffeemaker in some units.

**Mendocino Hotel & Garden Suites** ⭐ In the heart of town, this 1878 hotel evokes California's Gold Rush era. Beveled-glass doors open into a Victorian-style lobby and parlor. Furnishings include antiques and reproductions, such as the oak reception desk from a demolished Kansas bank, Remington paintings, stained-glass lamps, and Persian carpets. Guest rooms feature hand-painted French porcelain sinks with floral designs; old-fashioned wallpaper, beds, and armoires; and photographs and memorabilia of historic Mendocino. About half the rooms are located in four handsome small buildings behind the main house. Many of the deluxe rooms have fireplaces, modern bathrooms, and good views. Suites have an additional parlor, as well as a fireplace or balcony.

45080 Main St. (P.O. Box 587), Mendocino, CA 95460. ℂ **800/548-0513** or 707/937-0511. Fax 707/937-0513. www.mendocinohotel.com. 51 units, 37 w/private bathroom. $95 double w/shared bathroom, $120–$215 double w/private bathroom; $275 suite. Extra person $20. AE, MC, V. **Amenities:** 2 restaurants; 2 bars; nearby golf course; access to nearby health club ($5); room service. *In room:* TV, hair dryer.

## INEXPENSIVE

**Mendocino Village Inn & Spa** ⭐ This historic Victorian inn is across the street from the headlands, overlooking the ocean and the Big River beach. A garden of flowers, plants, and frog ponds fronts the blue-and-white guesthouse, built in 1882 by a doctor and later occupied by famed local artist Emmy Lou Packard. Each room is individually decorated, and many have fireplaces and Jacuzzi tubs. The Queen Anne Room features a four-poster canopy bed and other Victorian furnishings, and the sentimental Madge's Room is named for a child who etched her name in the window glass almost a century ago (you can still see it). All but two attic units have private bathrooms, and four rooms have private outside entrances. Complimentary beverages are served in the evening, and guests have privileges at the nearby Sweetwater Spa.

44860 Main St. (P.O. Box 626), Mendocino, CA 95460. ℂ **800/882-7029** or 707/937-0246. www.mendocinoinn.com. 12 units, 10 w/private bathroom. $85–$95 double w/shared bathroom; $125–$195 double w/private bathroom; $165 Water Tower suite. Winter midweek discounts. Rates include full breakfast and evening refreshments. MC, V. **Amenities:** Spa privileges and massage discount at adjacent Sweetwater Spa.

## IN NEARBY ALBION & LITTLE RIVER

**Albion River Inn and Restaurant** ★★    A quarter-mile north of Albion (or 6 miles south of Mendocino), this modern, beautiful inn overlooks the mouth of the Albion River from a bluff some 90 feet above the Pacific. The view is, of course, spectacular. A plaintive harbor horn in the area adds to the seaside atmosphere. (Earplugs are provided for light sleepers.) The rooms are decorated in a contemporary style with comfortable furnishings; all have ocean views, and most have decks. You'll find wingbacks in front of the fireplaces, down comforters on the queen- and king-size beds, well-lit desks, binoculars for wildlife viewing, and bathrobes. *Insider tip:* If you really want to impress your sweetie, reserve one of the rooms with a spa tub for two, which has a picture window with dazzling views of the coast. The menu at the on-site restaurant changes daily, featuring fresh local produce whenever possible, but the view from the tables remains the same: stellar. The award-winning wine list is also impressive. In the evening, piano music adds to the romantic atmosphere.

3790 N. Hwy. 1 (P.O. Box 100), Albion, CA 95410. © 800/479-7944 or 707/937-1919. Fax 707/937-2604. www.albionriverinn.com. 20 units. $200–$250 double; $290–$310 spa suite. Rates include full breakfast. AE, DC, DISC, MC, V. **Amenities:** Restaurant. *In room:* Fridge, coffeemaker, hair dryer, iron, CD player.

**Glendeven** ★★    Named one of the 12 best inns in America by *Country Inns* magazine, this 1867 farmhouse is a place of exceptional style and comfort. Accommodations spread across 2½ acres, encompassing the main house, the Carriage House Suite, and an addition known as Stevenscroft. Each room is individually decorated with a balanced mix of antiques, contemporary pieces, and original art. Most have ocean views, fireplaces, and porches. Etta's Suite in the Farmhouse has an antique walnut bed, while the Eastlin and Carriage House suites have king-size feather beds. The four rooms in the Stevenscroft annex are also spacious and beautifully furnished. A vacation rental house, La Bella Vista, has two bedrooms, two bathrooms, a kitchen, Jacuzzi, and a beautiful view of the ocean and surrounding gardens. Adjacent to the inn, numerous fern-lined canyon trails lead to the ocean and beaches of Van Damme State Park.

8205 N. Hwy. 1, Little River, CA 95456. © 800/822-4536 or 707/937-0083. Fax 707/937-6108. www.glendeven.com. 10 units. Weekend and summer rates $145–$250. Ask about off-season midweek specials. Rates include full breakfast. AE, DISC, MC, V. **Amenities:** In-room massage (w/notice). *In room:* Hair dryer, no phone.

**Heritage House Inn & Restaurant** ★★    The setting of the movie *Same Time, Next Year,* this country club–style property features rooms with great views of the ocean and coastline. Thirty-seven seafront acres of lush gardens encompass a variety of accommodations, from the attractive to the outright lush. The ivy-covered, New England–style main building has three guest rooms; the others are grouped, two to four, in cottages. Rooms are individually decorated with original antiques and locally made furnishings, with every kind of amenity, including bathrobes, umbrellas, wine splits, and newspapers. Most have wood-burning fireplaces or stoves, private decks, sitting areas, and ocean views; several suites have wet bars and Jacuzzis. Wooded trails wind along the coastline, offering spectacular scenery. The Heritage House dining room is in a magnificent setting overlooking the ocean, with a seasonal menu and a highly touted wine cellar.

5200 N. Hwy. 1, Little River, CA 95456. © 800/235-5885 or 707/937-5885. Fax 707/937-0318. www.heritagehouse inn.com. 66 units. Summer $150–$500 double; winter $150–$425 double. Extra person $20. Rates include full breakfast for 2. AE, MC, V. **Amenities:** Restaurant; concierge; tour and activities desk; in-room massage. *In room:* Fax, dataport, fridge, coffeemaker, hair dryer, iron, no phone.

## WHERE TO DINE

In addition to the following, see "Where to Stay," above, for hotel restaurants.

### EXPENSIVE

**Café Beaujolais** ★★ AMERICAN/FRENCH    This is one of Mendocino's top dining choices. For a time, it was one of the most celebrated restaurants in Northern California and a pioneer in using locally grown organic produce, meat from humanely raised animals, and fresh locally caught seafood. Though Café Beaujolais started out as a breakfast-and-lunch place, it's strictly a dinner house now. The French country–style tavern is set in an early 1900s house; rose-colored carnival-glass chandeliers add a burnish to the oak floors and heavy oak tables adorned with flowers. The menu changes weekly and usually lists about five main courses. A typical dinner may start with a warm free-range duck confit salad in raspberry vinaigrette with fresh raspberries and toasted walnuts on mixed greens, followed by a Washington sturgeon filet, pan-roasted with truffle emulsion sauce and served with house-made tagliatelle, wild mushrooms, beets, and snap peas. For dessert, order the lemon-glazed persimmon cake with vanilla-bean *panna cotta* and red-currant sauce. On warm summer nights, request a table at the enclosed deck overlooking the gardens. *Note:* The restaurant usually closes for most of December.

> *Fun Fact*  **Bread Winner**
>
> Few tourists know that Café Beaujolais's renowned "brickery breads" are sold daily from 11am to around 5pm at their Brickery bakery on Ukiah Street, just east of the restaurant.

961 Ukiah St. ℂ **707/937-5614**. Fax 707/937-3656. www.cafebeaujolais.com. Reservations recommended. Main courses $21–$28. AE, DISC, MC, V. Daily 5:30–9pm.

**The 955 Ukiah Street Restaurant** ★★ NORTH COAST CUISINE    Shortly after this building's construction in the 1960s, Emmy Lou Packard commandeered the premises as an art studio for the creation of a series of giant murals. Today it's a large, surprisingly cozy restaurant, accented with railway ties and vaulted ceilings. Ask for a window table overlooking the gardens. The cuisine is creative and reasonably priced, a worthy alternative to the perpetually booked Café Beaujolais next door. It's hard to pick a favorite dish, although the phyllo-wrapped red snapper with pesto and lime has a zesty tang, and the crispy duck with ginger, apples, and Calvados sauce would garner enthusiasm in Normandy.

955 Ukiah St. ℂ **707/937-1955**. www.955restaurant.com. Reservations recommended. Main courses $12–$26. MC, V. Wed–Sun 6–10pm.

### MODERATE

**Bay View Café** ★ AMERICAN    This reasonably priced cafe is one of the most popular in town. The second-floor dining area affords a sweeping view of the Pacific and faraway headlands; to reach it, climb a flight of stairs outside the town's antique water tower, then detour sideways. Surrounded by dozens of ferns suspended from the ceiling, you'll find a menu with Southwestern selections (the marinated chicken breast is very popular), a good array of sandwiches (my favorite is the hot crabmeat with avocado slices), fish and chips, and the fresh catch of the day. Breakfast ranges from the basic bacon and eggs to eggs Florentine and honey-wheat pancakes.

45040 Main St. ℂ **707/937-4197**. Reservations not accepted. Main courses $6–$15. No credit cards. Summer daily 8am–9pm; winter Mon–Thurs 8am–3pm, Fri–Sun 8am–9pm.

**The Moosse Café** ⋆ CALIFORNIA BISTRO   This petite cafe in a New England–style home is another one of Mendocino's most popular. In 1995, the place was gutted and redone with an attractive, modern interior. The menu changes seasonally, with many local items such as organic herbs and vegetables, as in the outstanding Caesar salad. I also enjoyed the roast chicken with garlic mashed potatoes and the swordfish special, which came with a pile of fresh vegetables. Other popular entrees are the mixed seafood cakes over basmati rice with a roasted-red-pepper rémoulade, and the lavender-smoked double-thick pork chop served with roasted yam and apple purée. Service is friendly; my only complaint is that the tables are a bit too close together, especially if it's crowded.

390 Kasten St. (at Albion St.). © 707/937-4323. Reservations recommended for dinner. Main courses $13–$19. MC, V. Daily 11:30am–3:30pm; Sun–Thurs 5:30–9pm; Fri–Sat and holidays 5:30–10pm.

### INEXPENSIVE

You'd be surprised what $5 will get you for lunch if you know where to go. **Tote Fete Bakery** (© 707/937-3140) has a wonderful carryout booth at the corner of Albion and Lansing streets. I like the foil-wrapped barbecued-chicken sandwiches, but the pizza, focaccia, and twice-baked potatoes are also great. Eat at the stand-up counter or pack a picnic for the headlands down the street.

**Mendo Burgers** (© 707/937-1111) is arguably the best burger joint on the Northern Coast, with patties of all stripes—beef, chicken, turkey, or veggie. A side of thick, fresh-cut fries is mandatory, as is a pile of napkins. Hidden behind the Mendocino Bakery and Café at 10483 Lansing St., it's a little hard to find, but well worth searching out.

In the back of the **Little River Market** (© 707/937-5133), directly across from the Little River Inn on Highway 1, a trio of small tables overlooks the beautiful Mendocino coastline. Order a tamale, sandwich, or whatever else is on the menu at the tiny deli inside the market, or buy a loaf of Café Beaujolais bread sold at the front counter and your favorite spread.

## 4 Fort Bragg

10 miles N of Mendocino; 176 miles N of San Francisco

As the Mendocino coast's commercial center—hence the site of most of the area's fast-food restaurants and supermarkets—Fort Bragg is far more down-to-earth than Mendocino. Inexpensive motels and cheap eats used to be its only attractions, but over the past few years, gentrification has spread throughout the town, as the logging and fishing industries have steadily declined. With no room left to open new shops in Mendocino, many gallery, boutique, and restaurant owners have moved up the road. The result is a huge increase in Fort Bragg's tourist trade, particularly during the Whale Festival in March and Paul Bunyan Days over Labor Day weekend.

To explore the town properly, get a free walking-tour map from the **Fort Bragg/ Mendocino Coast Chamber of Commerce,** 332 N. Main St. (P.O. Box 1141), Fort Bragg, CA 95437 (© 800/726-2780 or 707/961-6300; www.mendocinocoast.com). The friendly staff can answer most questions about Mendocino, Fort Bragg, and the surrounding region.

### SHOPPING & EXPLORING THE AREA

Fort Bragg doesn't boast as many high-end stores and galleries as its dainty cousin to the south, but it does have some worthwhile shopping spots. **Antiques shops** line

Franklin Street between Laurel and Redwood (aka Antiques Row), and several boutiques are housed within the newly refurbished **Union Lumber Company Store,** an impressive edifice built almost entirely with handcrafted redwoods (on the corner of Main and Redwood sts.).

**For the Shell of It,** 344 N. Main St. (© **707/961-0461**), stocks handmade jewelry, chimes, and collectibles made of shells or designed around a nautical theme, as well as rocks, gems, minerals, and fossils. The **Hot Pepper Jelly Company,** 330 N. Main St. (© **866/737-7379;** www.hotpepperjelly.com), is famous for its assortment of Mendocino food products—dozens of pepper jelly varieties, plus local mustards, syrups, and biscotti, hand-painted porcelain bowls, baskets, and more. The **Mendocino Chocolate Company,** 542 N. Main St. (© **707/964-8800**), makes and sells homemade chocolates and truffles, which it ships all over the world. Painters, jewelers, sculptors, weavers, potters, woodworkers, and other local artists display their works at **Northcoast Artists,** 362 N. Main St. (© **707/964-8266**). **Windsong,** 324 N. Main St. (© **707/964-2050**), is predominantly a nice used-book store, but you'll also find a clutter of colorful kites, cards, candles, records, and other gifts.

Fort Bragg is also the home of the **Mendocino Coast Botanical Gardens,** 18220 N. Hwy. 1 (© **707/964-4352;** www.gardenbythesea.org), about 7 miles north of Mendocino. This cliff-top public garden, set among the pines along the coast, nurtures rhododendrons, fuchsias, azaleas, and a multitude of flowering shrubs. The area has bridges, streams, canyons, dells, picnic areas, and trails for easy walking. Admission is $7.50 for adults, $6 for seniors ages 60 and over, $3 for children 13 to 17, $1 for children 6 to 12, and free for 5 and under. (Children under 18 must be accompanied by an adult.) The gardens are open daily March through October from 9am to 5pm, November through February from 9am to 4pm.

The **North Coast Brewing Company,** 455 N. Main St. (© **707/964-2739;** www.northcoastbrewing.com), is also worth investigating. Free tours begin at 1pm Monday through Friday. Across the street, the Brewing Company's pub is open for lunch and dinner (see "Where to Dine," below).

## OUTDOOR PURSUITS

Fort Bragg is the county's sport-fishing hub. South of town, **Noyo Fishing Center,** 32440 N. Harbor, Noyo (© **707/964-3000;** www.fortbraggfishing.com), is a good place to buy tackle, and the best source of information on local fishing boats. Lots of party boats leave from the town's harbor, as do whale-watching tours.

**Lost Coast Kayaking,** in Van Damme State Park (© **707/937-2434;** www.lostcoastkayaking.com), offers guided kayak tours of the numerous sea caves on the coast. All the necessary equipment is provided; all you need to bring is a bathing suit and $45 for the 2-hour tour (closed in winter).

Three miles north of Fort Bragg, off Highway 1, **MacKerricher State Park** (© **707/937-5804**), is a popular place for biking, hiking, and horseback riding. This 1,700-acre park has 142 campsites and 8 miles of shoreline. For a true biking or hiking venture, travel the 8-mile-long "Haul Road"—an old logging road (partly washed out, but safe) with fine ocean vistas all the way to Ten Mile River. Harbor seals make their home at the park's Laguna Point Seal Watching Station.

## WHERE TO STAY

**Beachcomber Motel** *Value*   If the room rates in Mendocino have you reconsidering a visit, the Beachcomber Motel may be just what you seek. Granted, the plain guest rooms are bereft of the antiques and lace you'll find at most B&Bs in the area, but they are spacious, comfortable, and equipped with the necessities. None of this matters, anyway, because you'll be spending most of your time either on the huge back deck overlooking the Pacific, or in MacKerricher State Park's miles of beaches and dunes, across from the motel. If you want to save even more, book a room with a kitchenette, stockpile groceries, and cook your own food, in the barbecue area. Low-end rates are for a standard room with no ocean view, and the top rate is for the deluxe suite with king bed, Jacuzzi, fireplace, and ocean view. Three units are wheelchair accessible.

1111 N. Main St., Fort Bragg, CA 95437. © **800/400-7873** or 707/964-2402. Fax 707/964-8925. www.thebeach combermotel.com. 75 units. $79–$250 double. Rates include continental breakfast. AE, DC, DISC, MC, V. Pets accepted w/$10 fee. **Amenities:** Exercise room. *In room:* TV/VCR, dataport, kitchenette in suites, fridge, coffeemaker.

**Colombi Motel** *Value* A room here costs about a quarter of the average room in Mendocino. For 50 bones, you get a lot at this little motel just off Fort Bragg's main strip: It's clean and neat, with all the essentials (including kitchens in some rooms), and you get your own carport. Families will want to reserve one of the two-bedroom units that sleep up to six. Across the street is a laundromat, a cafe with good Mexican food, and the Colombi Market, where motel guests check in and get free ice and coffee.

600 E. Oak St., Fort Bragg, CA 95437. © **707/964-5773** or 707/964-8015. Fax 707/964-5627. 22 units. Winter $35–$85 double; summer $40–$95 double. MC, V. *In room:* TV, kitchen in some units, fridge.

**Grey Whale Inn** *Kids* In downtown Fort Bragg, a short walk from the beach, this B&B was built as a hospital in 1915—hence the wide hallways and large guest rooms. The redwood building is now a well-run, relaxed inn, with antiques, handmade quilts, and plenty of local art. Each room is unique: Two have ocean views, four have fireplaces, one has a whirlpool tub, three have private decks, and one has a shower with wheelchair access. My favorite is the spacious, elegant Campbell Suite, with a king bed, TV with VCR, and marble gas-log fireplace. The buffet breakfast, served in the Craftsman-style breakfast room (with trays for carrying your food back to bed, if you prefer) includes a hot entree, homemade bread or coffee cake, and fresh fruit. Kids will appreciate the game room with a pool table and foosball.

615 N. Main St., Fort Bragg, CA 95437. © **800/382-7244** or 707/964-0640. Fax 707/964-4408. www.grey whaleinn.com. 14 units. $130–$230 double. Discounted winter rates available midweek Nov–Mar. Rates include buffet breakfast. AE, MC, V. **Amenities:** Access to nearby health club; game room; in-room massage. *In room:* TV, some units w/VCR, kitchenette, fridge, hair dryer, iron.

## WHERE TO DINE

**North Coast Brewing Company** *AMERICAN* Since it opened in 1988, this homey brewpub has been the most happening place in town—especially during happy hour, when boisterous locals take over the bar and dark-wood tables. The brewery's proudest achievement: when the Beverage Testing Institute ranked it one of the 10 best breweries in the world, in 1998. The building that houses the pub is a century-old redwood structure, which in previous lives functioned as a mortuary, an annex to the local Presbyterian church, an art studio, and administration offices for the College of the Redwoods. Nine types of beer are available (to go, even) year-round, in addition to seasonal brews. Standard fare such as burgers and barbecued-chicken sandwiches are supplemented by more substantial dishes, ranging from beef Romanov made with braised sirloin tips, fresh mushrooms, and Russian Imperial Stout, to genuine Carolina barbecued pork served with corn cakes and slaw, and a roast Cornish game hen with a raspberry-balsamic glaze. After your meal, browse the shop or take a free tour of the brewery (see "Shopping & Exploring the Area," above).

455 N. Main St. ℂ **707/964-3400.** www.northcoastbrewing.com. Reservations accepted for large parties only. Main courses $7–$22. DISC, MC, V. Daily 11:30am–11pm.

**The Restaurant** *Kids* PACIFIC NORTHWEST/CALIFORNIA  One of the oldest family-run restaurants on the coast, this unpretentious Fort Bragg landmark is known for its good dinners and Sunday brunches. The menu includes dishes from just about every corner of the planet: New York strip steak, a Provençal-style seafood stew, and a few less expensive options such as the Asian noodle bowl filled with bay shrimp and fresh vegetables. My favorite is the superfresh blackened rockfish. A few vegetarian specialties include grilled polenta with melted mozzarella and sautéed mushrooms, topped with tomato-herb sauce and Parmesan cheese. A nicely priced kids' menu is available as well. The booth section is the best place to sit if you want to keep an eye on the entertainment—courtesy of ebullient chef Jim Larsen—in the kitchen.

418 N. Main St. ℂ **707/964-9800.** www.therestaurantfortbragg.com. Reservations recommended. Dinner $13–$22; Sun brunch $5–$10. MC, V. Thurs–Tues 5–9pm; Sun brunch 10am–1pm.

**Viraporn's Thai Café** THAI  Born in northern Thailand, Viraporn Lobell attended cooking school and apprenticed in restaurants there before coming to the United States. After working at Mendocino's Café Beaujolais, she opened her own restaurant in Fort Bragg in 1991, giving local Thai-food fans good reason to cheer. Viraporn works wonders with staple dishes such as pad Thai, lemon-grass soup, spring rolls, and satays, all of which balance the five traditional Thai flavors of tart, bitter, hot, sweet, and salty. Viraporn also whips up good curry dishes, best washed down with a cool, supersweet Thai iced tea.

500 S. Main St. (across from PayLess drugstore off Hwy. 1). ℂ **707/964-7931.** Main courses $3.95–$9.95. No credit cards. Wed–Mon 11:30am–2:30pm and 5–9pm.

## 5 The Avenue of the Giants ★★

From Fort Bragg, Highway 1 continues north along the shoreline for about 30 miles before turning inland to Leggett and the Redwood Highway (U.S. 101), which runs north to Garberville. Six miles beyond Garberville, the **Avenue of the Giants** (Hwy. 254) begins around Phillipsville. The Avenue of the Giants is one of the most spectacular routes in the West, cutting along the Eel River through the 51,000-acre Humboldt Redwoods State Park. It roughly parallels U.S. 101, with about a half-dozen interchanges between the two roads, in case you don't want to drive the whole thing. The avenue ends just south of Scotia; from here, it's only about 10 miles to the turnoff to Ferndale, about 5 miles west of U.S. 101.

For more information or a detailed map of the area, go to the **Humboldt Redwoods State Park Visitor Center** in Weott (ℂ **707/946-2263;** www.humboldtredwoods.org), in the center of the Avenue of the Giants.

### TOURING THE AVENUE

Thirty-three miles long, the Avenue of the Giants was left intact for sightseers when the freeway was built. The giants are the majestic coast redwoods *(Sequoia sempervirens);* more than 50,000 acres of them make up the most outstanding display in the redwood belt. Their rough-bark columns alone climb 100 feet or more and branches soar to more than 340 feet. With their fire-resistant bark and immunity to insects, they have survived for thousands of years. The oldest dated coast redwood is more than 2,200 years old.

Sadly, the route has several tacky attractions that attempt to turn the trees into some kind of freak show. My suggestion is to skip these and take advantage of the trails and campgrounds off the beaten path. As you drive along, you'll see many parking areas with short loop trails leading into the forest. From south to north, the first of these "attractions" is the **Chimney Tree,** where J. R. R. Tolkien's Hobbit is rumored to reside. This living, hollow redwood is more than 1,500 years old. Nearby are a gift shop and a burger place. Then there's the **One-Log House,** a small apartment-like dwelling built inside a log. You can also drive your car through a living redwood at the **Shrine Drive-Thru Tree,** at Myers Flat midway along the avenue.

A few miles north of Weott is **Founders Grove,** named in honor of those who established the Save the Redwoods League in 1918. Farther north, close to the end of the avenue, stands the 950-year-old **Immortal Tree,** just north of Redcrest. Near Pepperwood at the end of the avenue, the **Drury Trail** and the **Percy French Trail** are two great short hikes. The park itself is also good for mountain biking. Ask the rangers for details. For more information, contact **Humboldt Redwoods State Park** (𝒞 **707/ 946-2409;** www.humboldtredwoods.org).

The state park has three **campgrounds** with 248 campsites: Hidden Springs, half a mile south of Myers Flat; Burlington, 2 miles south of Weott, near park headquarters; and Albee Creek State Campground, 5 miles west of U.S. 101 on the Mattole Road north of Weott. Reservations are advised in summer; you can make them online via **ReserveAmerica** at www.reserveamerica.com or call 𝒞 **800/444-7275.** Remaining sites are on a first-come, first-served basis. You'll also come across picnic and swimming facilities, motels, resorts, restaurants, and rest areas with parking lots.

## WHERE TO STAY & DINE NEAR THE SOUTHERN ENTRANCE

**Benbow Inn** ⭐    This elegant National Historic Landmark, overlooking the Eel River and surrounded by gardens, has housed notable guests such as Eleanor Roosevelt, Herbert Hoover, and Charles Laughton. Constructed in 1926 in a mock-Tudor style, it's named after the family who built it. Guests enter through a grand hall and into the lobby with its huge fireplace surrounded by cushy sofas, grandfather clocks, Oriental carpets, and cherrywood wainscoting. Rooms vary in size and amenities, though all are decorated with period antiques; the deluxe units have fireplaces, Jacuzzis, private entrances, and patios. The Honeymoon Cottage is the most popular accommodation, with vaulted ceilings, a canopy bed, wood-burning fireplace, and private patio overlooking the river. A comfortable annex with elegant woodwork was added in the 1980s. Beautiful Benbow Lake State Park is right out the front door. Complimentary afternoon tea and scones are served in the lobby at 3pm, hors d'oeuvres in the lounge at 5pm, and port wine at 9pm—all very proper, of course. The dramatic, high-ceilinged dining room opens onto a spacious terrace and offers internationally inspired (and expensive) main courses. *Tip:* Ask that the housekeeping staff go light on the "air freshener," which smells nothing like fresh air.

445 Lake Benbow Dr., Garberville, CA 95542. 𝒞 **800/355-3301** or 707/923-2124. Fax 707/923-2122. www.benbow inn.com. 55 units. $130–$275 double; $350 cottage. AE, DISC, MC, V. **Amenities:** Restaurant; bar; nearby golf course; complimentary bikes; courtesy car; babysitting (w/advance notice); guided day hikes. *In room:* A/C, coffeemaker, hair dryer, iron; some units w/TV/VCR, minibar, fridge.

## FERNDALE ★

The village of Ferndale, beyond the Avenue of the Giants and west of U.S. 101, is a National Historic Landmark because of its Victorian homes and storefronts, including a smithy and saddlery. About 5 miles inland from the coast and close to the redwood belt, Ferndale is one of the best-preserved Victorian hamlets in Northern California. Despite its unbearably cute shops, it is nonetheless a vital part of the Northern Coastal tourist circuit.

What's less known about this small town is that it has a number of artists in residence. It's also home to one of California's oddest happenings, the **World Championship Great Arcata to Ferndale Cross-Country Kinetic Sculpture Race,** which draws more than 10,000 spectators every Memorial Day weekend. For 38 miles, over land, sand, mud, and water, participants race in whimsically designed, handmade, people-powered vehicles that have to be seen to be believed—dragons, Christmas trees, flying saucers, and pyramids, to mention but a few. Awards range from Best Art to Best Engineering to Best Bribe. And as the grand prizes are worth about $15, inspired madness is the only incentive. Stop at the museum at 780 Main St. if you want to see a few past race entries, but bear in mind it's nothing like seeing these contrivances in glorious action.

### WHERE TO STAY

**Gingerbread Mansion** ★★  This peach-and-yellow structure with stained glass and other fine details is one of Ferndale's most frequently photographed Victorians. Built in 1899 for a doctor and his family, it's now run by Ken Torbert, who keeps the place furnished with beautiful antiques. Some of the large guest rooms have two old-fashioned claw-foot tubs for double bubble baths, and others have fireplaces. My favorite is the attic-level Empire Suite, with Ionic columns, a massage-jet shower, two fireplaces, and a king-size bed draped with Royal Sateen fabric. The ultraluxurious Veneto Room is also impressive. Guests receive bathrobes and thick, extra-large towels. Staff members turn down the beds, leave hand-dipped chocolates on the nightstand, and deliver coffee or tea to your door in the morning, to sustain you until your breakfast of fruit, cheese, muffins, breads, cakes, and a baked egg dish. Afternoon tea features sandwiches, pastries, and fresh fruit. *Tip:* Even if you're not staying in Ferndale, it's worth stopping by for a tour, scheduled from noon to 4pm daily.

400 Berding St. (P.O. Box 40), Ferndale, CA 95536. Ⓒ **800/952-4136** or 707/786-4000. Fax 707/786-4381. www. gingerbread-mansion.com. 11 units. $150–$210 double; $170–$385 suite. Extra person $40. Rates include full breakfast and afternoon tea. AE, MC, V. **Amenities:** Concierge; activities desk. *In room:* Hair dryer, no phone.

**Shaw House Inn Bed and Breakfast** ★★  Modeled after Hawthorne's House of the Seven Gables, this gorgeous B&B is the oldest structure in Ferndale, the oldest B&B in California, and one of the prettiest Victorian homes I've ever seen (and I've seen a *lot* of B&Bs). It was built in 1854 by Ferndale founder Seth Louis Shaw, who had a penchant for jutting gables, bay windows, balconies, and gazebos. Each of the eight individually decorated guest rooms is handsomely furnished with period antiques, plush fabrics, and private bathrooms (rare for a 19th-century B&B). Four rooms have private entrances, and three have private balconies overlooking the garden. My favorite is the romantic Fountain Suite, with its own fireplace, parlor, and claw-foot tub. The immaculate flower-filled lawns and fishpond are shaded by 25 varieties of majestic trees, and the restaurants and shops along Main Street are a short walk away.

703 Main St., Ferndale, CA 95536. ℂ **800/557-SHAW** or 707/786-9958. Fax 707/786-9758. www.shawhouse.com. 8 units. $85–$225 Nov–Mar; $100–$245 Apr–Oct. Rates include breakfast and afternoon tea. DISC, MC, V. Checks accepted. **Amenities:** 1-acre garden; gift shop; game table. *In room:* Wireless Internet access; private bathroom, antique furnishings.

## WHERE TO DINE

**Curley's Grill** ✦ CALIFORNIA GRILL   This bright, lively restaurant specializes in California-inspired grilled foods, but don't think for a moment that the menu is limited to its steaks, prime rib, and baby back ribs that fall off the bone. Owner Curley Tait also grills items such as portobello-mushroom towers, pork loin with caramelized onion sauce, polenta with a sausage-tomato sauce, crab cakes, and some of the freshest seafood and vegetables on the coast. Curley has added homemade breads and desserts to the menu as well. Curley's also offers an interesting selection of California wines, with a Victorian-style full bar area. On sunny afternoons, request a seat on the shaded back patio.

400 Ocean St., inside the Victorian Inn. ℂ **707/786-9696.** www.restaurant.com/curleysgrill. Main courses $9–$18. DISC, MC, V. Daily 11:30am–9pm; breakfast Sat–Sun 8–11am.

## 6 Eureka & Environs ✦

296 miles N of San Francisco

### EUREKA

At first glance, Eureka (pop. 27,000) looks unappealing: Fast-food restaurants, cheap motels, and shopping malls predominate on the main thoroughfare. But if you turn west off U.S. 101 anywhere between A and M streets, you'll discover **Old Town Eureka** along the waterfront, which is worth exploring. It has a large number of Victorian buildings, a museum, and some good-quality stores and restaurants.

The city's newest development is a waterfront boardwalk between C and F streets, adjacent to the Old Town historic district. This section of the waterfront, previously closed to the public, now offers sweeping views of the harbor and bay.

For more visitor information, contact or visit the **Eureka/Humboldt County Convention and Visitors Bureau,** 1034 Second St., Eureka, CA 95501 (ℂ **800/346-3482** or 707/443-5097; www.redwoodvisitor.org), or the **Eureka Chamber of Commerce,** 2112 Broadway, Eureka, CA 95501 (ℂ **800/356-6381** or 707/442-3738; www. eurekachamber.com).

### WHAT TO SEE & DO

The **Clarke Memorial Museum,** 240 E St. (ℂ **707/443-1947**), has a fine collection of Native American baskets and other artifacts. The other popular attraction is the **Carson Mansion** ✦ (on the corner of Second and M sts.), built from 1884 to 1886 for lumber baron William Carson. A three-story conglomeration of ornamentation, its design is a mélange of styles—Queen Anne, Italianate, Stick, and Eastlake. It took 100 men more than 2 years to build it. Today it's a private club, so you can only marvel at the exterior of this 18-room mansion—said to be the most photographed Victorian home in the U.S. Across the street stands the **Pink Lady,** designed for William Carson as a wedding present for his son. Both buildings testify to the wealth that was once made in Eureka's lumber trade. As early as 1856, seven sawmills produced 2 million board feet of lumber per month. A restored building now houses the **Morris**

**Graves Museum of Art,** 636 F St. (© 707/442-0278; www.humboldtarts.org), with four galleries showcasing local artists as well as traveling exhibitions.

For a good read, drop in at the **Booklegger,** 402 Second St., at E St. (© 707/445-1344), a fantastic bookstore in Old Town with thousands of used paperbacks (especially mysteries, westerns, and science fiction), children's books, and cookbooks.

Humboldt Bay, where the town stands, was discovered by settlers in 1850. To protect the fledgling community from local Native Americans, the government established Fort Humboldt three years later. Ulysses S. Grant was stationed here for 5 months until he resigned after disputes with his commanding officer about his drinking. Troops abandoned the fort in 1870. Today, a self-guided trail takes visitors past a series of logging exhibits, a reconstructed surgeon's quarters, and a restored fort hospital, now a museum of Native American artifacts and military and pioneer paraphernalia. **Fort Humboldt State Historic Park** is at 3431 Fort Ave. (© 707/445-6567). Admission is free; it's open daily from 8am to 5pm.

## OUTDOOR PURSUITS

Humboldt Bay supplies a large portion of California's fish, and Eureka has a fishing fleet of about 200 boats. For an optimal view of the bay and surrounding waters, board skipper Leroy Zerlang's *Madaket*—a state historic landmark and the oldest passenger-carrying vessel in continuous service in the United States—for a 75-minute narrated **Humboldt Bay Harbor Cruise.** Tours depart from the foot of L Street in downtown Eureka daily at 1 and 2:30pm. Tickets are $15 per person, free for children ages 4 and under. The *Madaket* also has the smallest licensed bar in California, and the hour-long casual Cocktail Cruise celebrates this fact Tuesday through Saturday at 5:30pm. Look into the Sunday Champagne Brunch Cruise as well. Call © 707/445-1910 for a recorded departure schedule.

For more water recreation, you can rent kayaks, canoes, and sailboats from **Hum Boats** Friday through Monday from 9am to 5pm at the foot of F Street (© 707/444-3048; www.humboats.com). Tours and lessons are also available.

Humboldt County is suitable for biking because it's relatively uncongested. You can rent bikes from **Pro Sport Center,** 508 Myrtle Ave. (© 707/443-6328). Fishing, diving, biking, and hiking information are also available here.

Humboldt Bay, an important stopover point along the Pacific Flyway, is the winter home for thousands of migratory birds. South of town, the **Humboldt Bay National Wildlife Refuge** ✸, 1020 Ranch Rd., Loleta (© 707/733-5406), provides an opportunity to see many of the 200 or so species that live in the marshes and willow groves—including Pacific black brant, western sandpiper, northern harrier, great blue heron, and green-winged teal. The egret rookery on the bay, best viewed from Woodley Island Marina across the water, is spectacular. Peak viewing for most water birds and raptors is between September and March. The entrance is off U.S. 101 north at the Hookton Road exit. Cross the overpass and turn right onto Ranch Road.

## WHERE TO STAY
### Moderate

**Abigail's Elegant Victorian Mansion Bed & Breakfast** ✸  For owners Doug and Lily Vieyra, the restoration and upkeep of this 1888 house, a National Historic Landmark, is a labor of love. They combed the country for the fabrics and designs that provide the most authentic Victorian atmosphere I have encountered in the U.S. The wallpapers are extraordinary—brilliant blues, golds, jades, and reds in patterns that feature peacocks and mythological figures. Doug pays attention to every detail, from the butler who greets you in morning dress, to the silent movies, to period music on the phonograph. Each unit is individually furnished: The Van Gogh room contains the Belgian bedroom suite of Lily's mother. The Lily Langtry room, named after the actress and king's mistress who stayed here when she performed locally, features a four-poster bed and Langtry memorabilia. Guests can play croquet on the beautifully manicured lawn, where the staff serves ice-cream sodas and lemonade in the afternoon.

1406 C St. (at 14th St.), Eureka, CA 95501. © **707/444-3144.** Fax 707/442-3295. www.eureka-california.com. 4 units. $95–$215 double. Additional person $40–$50. Rates include breakfast. MC, V. **Amenities:** Sauna; complimentary bikes; massage; laundry service. *In room:* A/C.

### Hotel Carter, Carter House, Bell Cottage, and Carter Cottage ★★★ 
At the north end of Eureka's Old Town, the Carter House launched Mark Carter's renowned hostelry empire. Mark Carter built this copy of an 1884 San Francisco Victorian as a family home in 1982. Soon afterwards, he and his wife, Christi, began taking guests, and before long they also built the stately hotel across the street, the Hotel Carter. Later, they acquired the pretty Victorian Bell Cottage and the ultraluxurious Carter Cottage as well.

The 23 rooms in the large, full-service Hotel Carter have beautiful modern furnishings and pine four-posters. The suites have luxury appointments such as fireplaces and Jacuzzis with distant views of the waterfront. The original Carter House has seven rooms, furnished with antiques, Oriental rugs, and modern artwork. Rooms in the Bell Cottage are also individually decorated in grand Victorian fashion. If you want to splurge, reserve the Carter Cottage, a small home that was converted into one of the most luxurious lodgings in Northern California—a minimansion with a chef's kitchen, two fireplaces, a grand bathroom with a whirlpool tub for two, a private deck, and a wine cellar. The Carters offer an array of luxury accommodations, ranging from classic Victorian in the house and cottage to a softer, brighter, more contemporary look in the hotel. The ground level of the Hotel Carter houses one of Eureka's finest restaurants, **Restaurant 301** (see "Where to Dine" below), where a full breakfast (included in the room rate) is served each morning.

301 L St., Eureka, CA 95501. © **800/404-1390** or 707/444-8062. Fax 707/444-8067. www.carterhouse.com. 32 units. $125–$187 double; $297–$326 suite; $497 Carter Cottage. Rates include full breakfast. Packages available. AE, DC, DISC, MC, V. From U.S. 101 north, turn left onto L St. to Third St. **Amenities:** Restaurant; nearby golf course; activities desk; in-room massage; babysitting; laundry service; wine shop. *In room:* A/C, TV/VCR w/pay movies, kitchen in some units, hair dryer, iron.

### Inexpensive
### Bayview Motel *Value* 
Although it's not nearly so opulent as Abigail's Elegant Victorian Mansion, the modern Bayview Motel soundly takes the prize for price and privacy. In fact, it's one of the cleanest, most meticulously landscaped motels I've ever seen. Atop a small knoll on the south side of Eureka, it *does* have a bay view, but you have to peer through a seedy industrial area to see it; the gardens actually make for the better view. All rooms are minisuites with standard motel amenities, including queen-size beds. If you feel like splurging, request a Romantic Getaway room complete with a Jacuzzi and fireplace. Family units are also available, and small pets are welcome.

2844 Fairfield St. (corner of Hwy. 1 and Henderson St.), Eureka, CA 95501. © **866/725-6813** or 707/442-1673. Fax © 707/268-8681. www.bayviewmotel.com. 17 units. $85–$150 double. AE, DISC, MC, V. *In room:* TV, fax, dataport, fridge, coffeemaker, hair dryer, iron.

## WHERE TO DINE

**Ramone's Bakery & Cafe** *Value* BAKERY    Ramone's has a bakery on one side and a small dining room on the other. The baked items are extraordinary—croissants, danishes, cinnamon rolls, truffles, and muffins made from scratch every morning without preservatives or dough conditioners. The bakery also prepares soups, salads, and huge sandwiches, plus a few lunch specials such as lasagna and quiche. Any time of the day, it's a great place to stop for a light, inexpensive meal and cup of coffee. Ramone's has other locations, at 2223 Harrison St., in Eureka, and in Arcata at 747 13th St., at Wildberries Marketplace.

209 E St. (in Old Town). © **707/445-2923.** www.ramonesbakery.com. Main courses $4–$6. No credit cards. Mon–Sat 7am–6pm; Sun 7am–4pm.

**Restaurant 301** ★★★ CALIFORNIA    This is the best restaurant in the area. The large, airy dining room adjacent to the hotel lobby has tall windows overlooking the waterfront. At dinner, patrons may order a la carte or off the highly recommended Discovery Menu—a five-course, prix-fixe feast that pairs each course with suggested wines by the glass. A typical dinner might begin with an artichoke, green lentil, and fennel salad, followed by a warm chèvre cake appetizer, followed by a grilled duck breast with a seasonal fruit and zinfandel sauce. The chef picks most of the herbs and many of the vegetables fresh from organic gardens across the street, and the cuisine displays Asian accents, as in the chicken with spicy peanut sauce, or the tiger prawns with sesame, ginger, and soy. If you love oysters, start with a few Humboldt Bays roasted with barbecue sauce. Courtesy of the hotel's 301 Wine Shop, the wine bar features an excellent, extensive list that garnered *Wine Spectator's* Grand Award.

In the Hotel Carter, 301 L St. © **800/404-1390** or 707/444-8062. www.carterhouse.com. Reservations recommended. Main courses $18–$26. AE, DC, DISC, MC, V. Daily 7:30–10am and 6–9pm.

**Samoa Cookhouse** ★ *Finds* AMERICAN    During the lumber industry's heyday, cookhouses like this one—the last of its kind in the West, dating from 1885—were common, serving as community centers. The mill men and longshoremen chowed down on three hot meals before, during, and after their 12-hour workday. The food is still hearty (though not necessarily healthy by today's standards), served family-style at long tables covered with red-checkered cloths. The price includes soup, salad, fresh-baked bread, the main course, and dessert (usually pie). And the lunch-and-dinner menu still features a daily dish—roast beef, fried or barbecued chicken, ham, or pork chops. Breakfast typically includes eggs, potatoes, sausage, bacon, pancakes, and bottomless orange juice and coffee. Adjacent to the dining room, a small museum features memorabilia from the lumbering era. Bring the kids before this place vanishes into history.

Cookhouse Rd., Samoa. © **707/442-1659.** www.humboldtdining.com/cookhouse. Reservations accepted for large groups only. Main courses $7.45–$12. AE, DISC, MC, V. Mon–Sat 7am–3:30pm and 5–10pm; Sun 7am–10pm (closes 1 hr. earlier in winter). From U.S. 101, take Samoa Bridge to the end and turn left on Samoa Rd., then take the 1st left.

## ARCATA ★

From Eureka, it's 7 miles to Arcata, one of my favorite towns on the Northern Coast. Sort of a cross between Mayberry and Berkeley, it has an undeniable small-town flavor—right down to the bucolic center square—yet it possesses that intellectual and environmentally conscious esprit de corps so characteristic of university towns (Arcata is the home of Humboldt State University).

Family-type activities abound. On Wednesday, Friday, and Saturday evenings between June and July, Arcata's semipro baseball team, the **Humboldt Crabs,** plays at Arcata Ballpark (✆ **707/822-3619**), at Ninth and F streets. Also check out the kid-friendly **Humboldt State University Natural History Museum,** 1315 G St. (✆ **707/826-4479**), open Tuesday through Saturday from 10am to 5pm; **Tin Can Mailman,** at 10th and H streets (✆ **707/822-1307**), a used-book store with more than 130,000 titles; **Redwood Park** (east end of 11th St.), with an outstanding playground for kids and miles of forested hiking trails; and the **Humboldt Brewing Company,** 10th and I streets (✆ **707/826-BREW**), creators of the heavenly Red Nectar Ale (call for tour information).

Home to northern California's indigenous people, the Hoopa Indian Reservation is some 40 miles east of Eureka, and a few miles north of Willow Creek. In the Hoopa Shopping Center, the **Hoopa Tribal Museum** (✆ **530/625-4110**) archives Hoopa culture and history, including ceremonial regalia, basketry, canoes, and tools. By appointment, the museum organizes guided tours of Hoopa Valley historic sites, including the traditional village of Takimildiñ. Hours are Monday through Friday from 8am to noon and 1 to 5pm year-round, and in summer on Saturday from 10am to noon and from 1 to 4pm.

## OUTDOOR PURSUITS

The **Arcata Marsh and Wildlife Sanctuary** ⭐, at the foot of South I Street (✆ **707/826-2359**), is a thought-provoking excursion. The 154-acre sanctuary—which doubles as Arcata's integrated wetland wastewater treatment plant—is a stopover for marsh wrens, egrets, and other waterfowl, including the rare Arctic loon. Every Saturday at 8:30am and 2pm, free 1-hour guided tours start at the cul-de-sac at the foot of South I Street. Or just pick up a free self-guided walking tour map of the preserve, available at the **Arcata Chamber of Commerce,** 1062 G St., at 11th St. (✆ **707/822-3619**). Locals are proud of their town's wastewater solution, boasting "Arcata Residents Flush with Pride."

Heading east from Arcata, Highway 299 leads to the Trinity River in **Six Rivers National Forest.** Willow Creek and Somes Bar are the area's recreational centers. Visitors can sign up for canoeing, rafting, and kayaking trips with outfitters such as **Aurora River Adventures,** in Willow Creek (✆ **800/562-8475** or 530/629-3843). The offbeat, educational excursions are great for kids, and gnarly Class-V trips are for the more daring. They also rent equipment for self-guided adventures.

## WHERE TO STAY

**Hotel Arcata** *Value*    This is the town's most prominent hotel, with many guests visiting their children at Humboldt State University. If you're not inclined to stay at the fancier Lady Anne B&B (see review below), this is definitely the next best choice. On the northeast corner of the town plaza, the Hotel Arcata has a handsome early-1900s brick facade and an appealing lobby. The individually decorated rooms range from small, inexpensive singles to large executive suites that overlook the plaza. The minisuites are the quietest—a bargain at about $90. **Tomo,** the Japanese restaurant on the premises, is under different management.

708 Ninth St., Arcata, CA 95521. ✆ **800/344-1221** or 707/826-0217. Fax 707/826-1737. www.hotelarcata.com. 32 units. $66–$110 double; $116–$138 executive suite. Rates include continental breakfast. AE, DC, DISC, MC, V. Pets accepted w/$5-a-day fee and $50 deposit. **Amenities:** Restaurant; free passes to nearby indoor pool and health club; salon; executive suites. *In room:* TV, dataport, coffeemaker.

**The Lady Anne Bed & Breakfast Inn** ✦   Easily Arcata's finest lodging, this Queen Anne–style bed-and-breakfast is kept in top-notch condition by innkeepers Sharon Ferrett and Sam Pennisi, who also served a term as Arcata's mayor. The large, cozy guest rooms are individually decorated with antiques, lace curtains, Oriental rugs, and English stained glass. For second honeymooners, the Lady Sarah Angela Room is ideal, with a four-poster bed and bay view. Breakfast (request the Belgian waffles) is served in the grand dining room, warmed on winter mornings by a toasty fire. On summer afternoons you can lounge on the veranda or play a game of croquet on the front lawn. Several good dining options are only a few blocks away at Arcata Plaza.

902 14th St., Arcata, CA 95521. ℂ 707/822-2797. www.arcataplaza.com/lodging. 5 units. $100–$120 double. Rates include breakfast. MC, V. In room: Hair dryer, iron, no phone.

## WHERE TO DINE

**Abruzzi** ✦ ITALIAN   The best way to review your dining options in Arcata is to stroll to Jacoby's Storehouse, a mid-19th-century brick warehouse at the southwest corner of the town plaza, and ponder the menus posted outside Abruzzi and Plaza Grill (see below). Abruzzi is considered the best Italian restaurant in town (it certainly smells good when you walk in). It's also romantic, with dark woods and dim lighting. Meals begin with a basket of warm bread sticks, focaccia, and a baguette from a local bakery. Specialties include range-fed veal piccata, well-seasoned filet steaks, and sea scallops with langoustines tossed with cheese tortellini. The standout dessert is the chocolate *paradiso,* a dense chocolate cake in a pool of champagne *mousseline.*

Jacoby's Storehouse (at the corner of Eighth and H sts.). ℂ 707/826-2345. www.abruzzicatering.com. Reservations recommended. Main courses $9–$22. AE, DISC, MC, V. Daily 5:30–9pm.

**Folie Douce** ✦ BISTRO   Humboldt Hip meets Cuisine Chic at Folie Douce, the most energized, inventive restaurant in town. Designer wood-oven-fired pizza is its mainstay, like the grilled duck sausage fennel, chèvre, and sun-dried tomato pizza, or the spicy shrimp with fontina, mozzarella, and scallion combo. Appetizers and entrees are equally intriguing; the highlight of your vacation may well be the artichoke-heart cheesecake appetizer, followed by a plate of grilled wild-rice polenta in a light cream sauce. Other heartier menu items range from brandy-flambéed filet mignon topped with Roquefort cheese and green peppercorns, to the rosemary and mustard grilled lamb chops topped with a roasted garlic and red-wine demi-glace. The restaurant has a serious wine list. This small, festive eatery is extremely popular, so make reservations.

1551 G St. (between 15th and 16th sts.). ℂ 707/822-1042. www.holyfolie.com. Reservations suggested. Main courses $9–$27. AE, DISC, MC, V. Tues–Thurs 5:30–9pm; Fri–Sat 5:30–10pm.

**Plaza Grill** *Kids* AMERICAN   If the prices at Abruzzi are a bit more than you care to spend, consider the Plaza Grill, directly upstairs. Despite efforts to make it more upscale, it can't seem to shake its image as a college-student burger joint, albeit a nice one. The menu is more substantial than you'd think, with a choice of salads, sandwiches, burgers, fish platters, chicken specialties, steaks, and all kinds of coffee drinks. The children's menu is very reasonably priced.

Jacoby's Storehouse (at the corner of Eighth and H sts.). ℂ 707/826-0860. Main courses $7–$17. AE, DISC, MC, V. Sun–Thurs 5–8:30pm; Fri 5–11pm; Sat 5–10:30pm.

## TRINIDAD & PATRICK'S POINT STATE PARK ✦

Back on U.S. 101 north of Arcata, you'll come to **Trinidad,** a tiny coastal fishing village of 400 people. One of the smallest incorporated cities in California, it's on a peninsula 25 miles north of Eureka. If you're not into fishing, there's little to do in town except poke around at the handful of shops, walk along the busy pier, and wish you owned a house here.

Five miles north of Trinidad takes you to the 640-acre **Patrick's Point State Park** ★, 4150 Patrick's Point Dr. ((℃) **707/677-3570**), which has one of the finest ocean access points in the north at **Agate Beach.** It's suitable for driftwood picking, rock hounding, and camping on a sheltered bluff. The park contains a re-creation of a Sumeg village, which is used by the Yurok people and neighboring tribes. A self-guided tour takes you to replicas of family homes and sweat houses.

## WHERE TO STAY

**The Lost Whale Bed & Breakfast Inn** ★★ (Kids) This modern version of a blue-and-gray Cape Cod–style house is on 4 acres of seafront studded with firs, alders, spruces, and redwoods. Its very friendly owners welcome children (there's a play-ground and playhouse on the lawn) as much as romantically inclined couples (a very inviting Jacuzzi on the back deck offers a view of the sea). They claim their hotel is the only one in California with a private beach featuring tide pools and sea lions. Five of the inn's eight soundproof rooms have private balconies or sitting alcoves with views of the Pacific, two rooms have separate sleeping lofts, and all have private bathrooms and queen-size beds. In the morning, you'll marvel at the huge breakfasts, prepared by the resident cook: casseroles, quiches, home-baked muffins, fresh fruit, and locally smoked salmon.

3452 Patrick's Point Dr., Trinidad, CA 95570. (℃) **800/677-7859** or 707/677-3425. Fax 707/677-0284. www.lost whaleinn.com. 8 units. Summer $170–$200 double; winter $140–$170 double. Rates include country breakfast and afternoon tea. AE, DISC, MC, V. **Amenities:** Oceanview Jacuzzi; children's playground and playhouse; game room; business center. *In room:* No phone.

**Trinidad Bay Bed & Breakfast** ★ Set 175 feet above the ocean, all the rooms at this Cape Cod–style home have sweeping views of Trinidad Bay. On a clear day, you can see up to 65 miles of rugged coastline. Your hosts are Corlene and Don Blue (Cordon Blue to their friends), two innkeepers who have created what many visitors think is the most charming inn around. All the rooms have private bathrooms, which is rare for an older B&B. Decor throughout is a mix of New England–style antiques, featuring a collection of antique clocks. If it's available, opt for the Mauve Fireplace Suite, with its wraparound window, wood-burning fireplace, king-size bed, and private entrance. A full breakfast, served at 8:30am, includes French toast puff and Italian egg pie served with fruit, fresh and baked, and homemade breads. *Note:* The inn is open daily March through November, on weekends and for special events only December through February.

560 Edwards St. (P.O. Box 849), Trinidad, CA 95570-0849. (℃) **707/677-0840.** Fax 707/677-9245. www.trinidad baybnb.com. 4 units. Summer $150–$180 double; winter $135–$165 double. Rates include breakfast. MC, V. *In room:* Fridge, coffeemaker, hair dryer, iron, no phone.

**Trinidad Inn** (Value) You'll find a bevy of inexpensive motels in these parts, but the Trinidad Inn is the best of the lot. It's 2 miles north of Trinidad on a serene stretch of road dwarfed by redwoods. Both the motel's exterior—trimmed in shades of white and blue—and guest rooms are impeccably maintained. Each room is unique: Some are family units that hold up to four persons, while others offer a comfortable queen bed and private bathroom for as little as $70 per night (access to the adjoining kitchen is an extra $10). A good room for couples is no. 10, an adorable little cottage complete with a full kitchen, living room, private bathroom, bedroom, and small patio. Each morning fresh coffee, tea, and homemade raspberry scones and muffins are served under the gazebo in the flower-filled garden. Guests are free to use the picnic table and barbecue, or wander through the adjacent forest to the beaches a short stroll away.

1170 Patrick's Point Dr., Trinidad, CA 95570. (℃ **707/677-3349.** www.trinidadinn.com. 10 units. $70–$130 double. Rates include continental breakfast. AE, DC, DISC, MC, V. From U.S. 101, take the Trinidad exit and head 2 miles north on Patrick's Point Dr. Pets accepted w/$10 fee and $20 deposit. *In room:* TV, no phone.

## WHERE TO DINE

**Larrupin Café** ★★ AMERICAN   On a quiet country road 2 miles north of Trinidad, this popular, beautifully decorated restaurant sports a blend of Indonesian and African artifacts mingled with colorful urns full of exotic flowers and candlelit tables. The patio with a reflecting pool and bamboo fencing is a charmer, as is the wood-burning fireplace in winter. Dinner starts with an appetizer board stocked with gravlax, pâté, dark pumpernickel, apple slices, and sauce, followed by a red- and green-leaf salad tossed with a Gorgonzola vinaigrette. Many menu items are barbecued over mesquite fires, such as the hefty cut of halibut basted with lemon butter and served with mustard-flavored dill sauce, or pork ribs with a side of sweet-and-spicy barbecue sauce. Another recommended dish is the barbecued Cornish game hen with an orange-and-brandy glaze. For appetizers, go with the barbecued oysters. For dessert, it's either a slice of pecan-chocolate pie topped with hot buttered rum sauce, or the sinfully good triple-layer chocolate cake layered with caramel and whipped cream. *Note:* They don't take credit cards and the hours tend to vary seasonally, so be sure to call ahead and bring plenty of cash.

1658 Patrick's Point Dr. (℃ **707/677-0230.** Reservations recommended. Main courses $15–$22. No credit cards. Thurs–Mon 10am–2pm (coffee and light dishes only) and 5–9pm.

**The Seascape Restaurant** *Finds* CALIFORNIA   Established in the 1940s, this place is an unpretentious cross between a cafe and a diner, with three dining rooms, ocean views, overworked but cheerful waitresses, and a nostalgic aura. People pop in for coffee or snacks from early morning until after sundown, but by far the biggest seller here is the Trinidad Bay Platter ($18). Heaped with halibut, scallops, and shrimp, and accompanied by salad and rice pilaf, it's even more popular than the excellent prawn brochette. How fresh is the fish? As the menu states, "Availability of seafood depends on Season, Weather conditions, Regulations and Luck." Halibut, rock cod, sole, and other local catches come charbroiled, sautéed in garlic, onions, and mushrooms, or prepared in four other styles. For you late risers, breakfast is served until 4pm.

Beside the pier at the foot of Bay St. (℃ **707/677-3762.** Full dinners $9.50–$22. DISC, MC, V. Daily 7am–9pm.

## 7 Crescent City

79 miles N of Eureka; 375 miles N of San Francisco

Crescent City has little to offer, but it makes a good base for exploring Redwood National Park and the Smith River, one of the great recreational rivers of the West. The **Battery Point Lighthouse,** at the foot of A Street (℃ **707/464-3089;** www.light housefriends.com), which is accessible on foot only at low tide, houses a museum with exhibits on the coast's history. Tours of the lighthouse ($2 for adults, 50¢ for children 12 and under) are offered Wednesday through Sunday from 10am to 4pm, tides permitting, April through September.

Another draw is the **Smith River National Recreation Area** ✿, east of Jedediah Smith State Park and part of Six Rivers National Forest. The Area Headquarters is at 10600 U.S. 199, Gasquet (© **707/457-3131**), reached via U.S. 199 from Crescent City (about a 30-min. drive). You can get maps of the forest at the Supervisor's Office in Eureka, or at either of the Redwood National Park centers in Orick and Crescent City.

The 300,000-plus acres of wilderness have five small campgrounds (with fewer than 50 sites) along the Smith River. Sixteen trails draw hikers from across the country. The easiest short trail is the **McClendon Ford,** which is 2 miles long and drops from 1,000 to 800 feet in elevation to the river. Other activities include mountain biking, whitewater rafting, kayaking, and fishing for salmon and trout.

For information, contact the **Crescent City–Del Norte County Chamber of Commerce,** 1001 Front St., Crescent City, CA 95531 (© **800/343-8300** or 707/464-3174; www.northerncalifornia.net).

## WHERE TO STAY

**Crescent Beach Motel** *Value*    Crescent City doesn't have any fancy hotels or B&Bs, but it does have lots of modestly priced motels—the best of which is the Crescent Beach, which is also the only one on the bay. Near the highway, about a mile south of town, this single-story structure is freshly remodeled, with clean and simple refurbished rooms. Four of the units face the highway; try to get one of the others, all of which have sliding glass doors to decks and a small lawn area overlooking the water. One of the city's most popular restaurants, the **Beachcomber** (see "Where to Dine" below), is next door.

1455 Redwood Hwy. S. (U.S. 101), Crescent City, CA 95531. © 707/464-5436. www.crescentbeachmotel.com. 27 units. Summer $73–$85 double; winter $50–$59 double. AE, DISC, MC, V. *In room:* TV, no phone.

**Curly Redwood Lodge** *Value*    This is a blast from the past, the kind of place where you might have stayed as a kid during a cross-country vacation in the family station wagon. It was built in 1957 on grasslands across from the harbor, and it's trimmed with lumber from a single ancient redwood. Although they're not full of high-tech gadgets, the bedrooms are among the largest and best-soundproofed in town, and certainly the most evocative of a bygone age. In winter about a third of the rooms (the ones upstairs) are locked and sealed. Overall, the aura is more akin to Oregon than what you might imagine in California. I still prefer the rooms on the beach at the Crescent Beach Motel, but the Curly is a solid bet for a clean, comfortable, and inexpensive hotel room.

701 Redwood Hwy. S. (U.S. 101), Crescent City, CA 95531. © 707/464-2137. Fax 707/464-1655. www.curly redwoodlodge.com. 36 units. Summer $60–$86 double; winter $39–$68 double. Winter rates include breakfast. AE, DC, MC, V. *In room:* TV.

## WHERE TO DINE

**Beachcomber** SEAFOOD    The decor is as nautical as this restaurant's name, with rough-cut planking and a scattering of driftwood, fishnets, and buoys dangling above a dimly lit space. The restaurant is beside the beach, 2 miles south of Crescent City's center. The cuisine is a joy for fish lovers who prefer not to mask the flavor of their seafood with complicated sauces. Most of the dishes are grilled over madrone-wood barbecue pits, a technique perfected since this place was established in 1975. Freshly harvested Pacific salmon, halibut, lingcod, shark, sturgeon, Pacific snapper, oysters, and steamer clams have visitors lining up, especially on weekends. The Beachcomber also serves great flame-broiled steaks; thick cuts of prime rib are the special every Saturday and Sunday.

1400 U.S. 101. © 707/464-2205. Reservations recommended. Main courses $6–$15. MC, V. Thurs–Tues 5–9pm. Closed Dec–Jan and part of Feb.

**Harbor View Grotto Restaurant & Lounge** SEAFOOD/STEAKS    This friendly local restaurant has been specializing in fresh seafood at market prices since 1961. The food is not as good as the Beachcomber's, but it's a little less expensive, it's open for lunch, and it's far less crowded on weekend nights. The "light eaters" menu includes either a cup of white chowder (made fresh daily) or salad, a main course, and vegetables; heartier eaters can choose from among three different cuts of prime rib. Menu items include fresh, locally caught fish such as Pacific snapper and salmon. Crab or shrimp Louis, as well as crabmeat or shrimp sandwiches, are popular in season.

150 Starfish Way. ℭ 707/464-3815. Reservations recommended. Main courses $4–$9 lunch, $6–$20 dinner. DISC, MC, V. Daily 11:30am–9pm (later in the summer months).

## 8  Redwood National & State Parks ★★

40 miles N of Eureka; 336 miles N of San Francisco

It's difficult to explain the feeling you get in the old-growth forests of Redwood National and State Parks without citing *Alice in Wonderland*. Like a jungle, the redwood forest is a multistoried affair, and the tall trees are just the top layer. Everything seems big and misty, from another era—flowering bushes cover the ground, 10-foot-tall ferns line the creeks, and the smells are rich and musty. It's so outsized and primeval, you half expect to turn the corner and see a dinosaur.

When Archibald Menzies first noted the botanical existence of the coast redwood in 1794, more than 2 million acres of redwood forest carpeted California and Oregon. By 1965, heavy logging had reduced that to 300,000 acres, and it was obvious something had to be done if any were to survive. The state had created several parks around individual groves in the 1920s, and in 1968 the federal government created Redwood National Park. In May 1994, the National Park Service and the California Department of Parks and Recreation signed an agreement to manage these conservation areas cooperatively.

Although logging of old-growth redwoods in the region is still a major bone of contention among the government, private landowners, and environmentalists, it's auspicious that contention even exists—a sign that perhaps we have all learned to see the forest *and* the trees for what they are: the monarchs of all living things, a link to the age of the dinosaurs, and a humble reminder that mankind is but a hiccup in time compared to the venerable *Sequoia sempervirens*.

### ESSENTIALS

**GETTING THERE**    The southern gateway to the Redwood National and State Parks is the town of Orick. U.S. 101 runs right through the middle of town. The northern gateway to the park is Crescent City, your best bet for a cheap motel, gas, fast food, and outdoor supplies.

**VISITOR INFORMATION**    In Orick, you'll find the **Redwood Information Center,** P.O. Box 7, Orick, CA 95555 (ℭ **707/464-6101,** ext. 5265), one of California's rare examples of well-placed tax dollars. Stop here and pick up a free map; it's open daily from 9am to 5pm. If you missed the Orick center, don't worry: About 10 miles farther north on U.S. 101 is the **Prairie Creek Visitor Center** (ℭ **707/464-6101,** ext. 5300), which carries all the same maps and information. It's open daily from 9am to 5pm in summer, daily from 10am to 4pm (sometimes later) in winter.

# Redwood National & State Parks

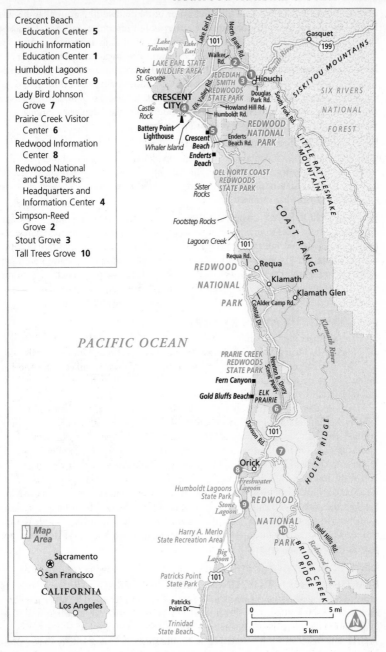

Before touring the park, pick up a free guide at the **Redwood National and State Parks Headquarters and Information Center,** 1111 Second St. (at K St.), Crescent City, CA 95531 (© **707/464-6101,** ext. 5064). It's open daily from 9am to 5pm.

If you happen to be arriving via U.S. 199 from Oregon, the rangers manning the **Hiouchi Information Station** (© **707/464-6101,** ext. 5067) and **Jedediah Smith Visitor Center** (© **707/464-6101,** ext. 5113) can also supply you with the necessary maps and advice. Both are open daily in summer from 9am to 5pm, and in winter when staffing is available. For more information about the Redwood National and State Parks, visit the website at **www.nps.gov/redw**.

**FEES & PERMITS**    Admission to the national park is free, but to enter any of the three state parks (which contain the best redwood groves), you'll pay a $6 day-use fee, which gains you entry into all three. The camping fee is $15 to $20 per night for drive-in sites. (Reservations are highly recommended in summer.) Walk-in sites are free, though a permit is required.

**RANGER PROGRAMS**    The park service runs interpretive programs—covering phenomena from trees to tide pools, legends to landforms—at the Hiouchi, Crescent Beach, and Redwood information centers in summer months, and year-round at the park headquarters in Crescent City. State rangers lead campfire programs and other activities throughout the year as well. Call the **Parks Information** service for both the national and state parks (© **707/464-6101,** ext. 5265) to get information on current schedules and events.

## EXPLORING THE PARKS BY CAR

If you're approaching the park from the south, take the detour along U.S. 101 called the **Newton B. Drury Scenic Parkway** ✮, which passes through groves of redwoods and elk-filled meadows before leading back onto the highway 8 miles later. Another spectacular route is the **Coastal Drive** ✮, which winds through stands of redwoods and offers grand views of the Pacific.

The most amazing car-friendly trail in the Redwood National and State Parks is the hidden, well-maintained gravel **Howland Hill Road** ✮✮, which winds for 12 miles through Jedediah Smith Redwoods State Park. It's an unforgettable journey through spectacular old-growth redwoods—considered by many to be one of the most beautiful areas in the world. To get here from U.S. 101, keep an eye out for the 76 gas station at the south end of Crescent City; just before the station, turn right on Elk Valley Road, and follow it to Howland Hill Road, which will be on your right. After driving through the park, you'll end up at U.S. 199 near Hiouchi, and from here it's a short jaunt west to get back to U.S. 101. Plan at least 2 to 3 hours for the 45-mile round-trip, or all day if you want to do some hiking or mountain biking. This drive is not recommended for trailers and RVs.

## SPORTS & OUTDOOR PURSUITS

**BEACHES, WHALE-WATCHING & BIRD-WATCHING**    The park's beaches vary from long, white-sand strands to cobblestone pocket coves. The water temperature is in the high 40s to low 50s (low 10s Celsius) year-round; it's often rough, so swimmers and surfers should be prepared for adverse conditions.

**Crescent Beach** is a long sandy beach 2 miles south of Crescent City that's popular with beachcombers, surf fishermen, and surfers. Just south of Crescent Beach is **Endert's Beach,** a protected spot with a hike-in campground and tide pools at the southern end of the beach.

High coastal overlooks (such as Klamath and Crescent Beach overlooks) make great whale-watching outposts during the southern migration in December and January and the return migration in March and April. The northern sea cliffs also provide valuable nesting sites for marine birds like auklets, puffins, murres, and cormorants. Birders will thrill at the park's freshwater lagoons as well. These coastal lagoons are some of the most pristine shorebird and waterfowl habitats left, and they're chock-full of hundreds of different species.

**HIKING**   The park's official map and guide, available at any of the information centers, provides a fairly good layout of hiking trails within the park. Regardless of how short or long your hike may be, dress warmly and bring plenty of water and sunscreen. Pets are prohibited on all of the park's trails.

The most popular walk is the short, heavily traveled **Fern Canyon Trail** ✯, which leads to a lush grotto of lady, deer, chain, sword, five-finger, and maidenhair ferns clinging to 50-foot-high vertical walls divided by a brook. It's only about a 1.5-mile walk from Gold Bluffs Beach, but be prepared to scramble across the creek several times on your way via small footbridges.

The **Lady Bird Johnson Grove Loop** ✯ is an easy, 1-hour self-guided tour that loops 1 mile around a glorious lush grove of mature redwoods. It's the site where Mrs. Johnson dedicated the national park in 1968. The **Yurok Loop Nature Trail** at Lagoon Creek is also an easy trek. The 1-mile self-guided trail gradually climbs to the top of a rugged sea bluff (with wonderful panoramic views of the Pacific) before looping back to the parking lot. If someone's willing to act as shuttle driver, have him or her meet you at the Requa Trail Head and take the 4-mile coastal trail to the mouth of the Klamath. And for the whiner in your group, there's **Big Tree Trail,** a quarter-mile paved trail leading to a big tree.

**Tall Trees Trail** leads to one of the world's tallest trees—perhaps 365 feet tall, 14 feet in diameter, and more than 600 years old. It was once touted as the world's tallest tree, but new candidates keep popping up, and this proud giant has lost a couple of feet to time. Now, who knows? It's still worth it to see the contender. Go to the Redwood Information Center near Orick (see "Essentials," above) for a free map and permit to drive to the trail head. The park issues 50 permits per day, on a first-come, first-served basis. After driving to the trail head, walk a steep 1.3 miles down into the grove. The trail is 3.3 miles round-trip.

**WILDLIFE VIEWING**   One of the most striking aspects of Prairie Creek Redwood State Park is its 200- to 300-strong herd of **Roosevelt elk** ✯, usually found in the appropriately named Elk Prairie, in the southern end of the park. These beasts can weigh 1,000 pounds, and the bulls carry huge antlers from spring to fall. You can also spot elk at Gold Bluffs Beach; it's a rush to come upon them out of the fog or after a turn in the trail. Nearly a hundred **black bears** also call the park home but they're seldom seen. Unlike the bears at Yosemite and Yellowstone, these are still afraid of people. Keep them that way by giving them a wide berth, observing food-storage etiquette while camping, and disposing of garbage properly.

## WHERE TO STAY

The national park proper has five small campgrounds. Four of the walk-in (more like backpack-in) camps are free—Little Bald Hills, Nickel Creek, Flint Ridge, and Butler Creek. Only one (the Redwood Creek Gravel Bar) requires a permit from the visitor center in advance.

Most car campsites are in the **Prairie Creek** and **Jedediah Smith state parks,** entirely inside the national park. Prairie Creek has two campgrounds, at Elk Prairie and Gold Bluffs Beach. Sites are $12 per night and can be reserved via ReserveAmerica (© **800/444-7275;** www.reserveamerica.com). It helps to know which campground and, if possible, which site you would like.

If these camping areas are filled, try the **Mill Creek Campground,** in Del Norte Coast Redwoods State Park (part of Redwood National and State Parks), 7 miles south of Crescent City on U.S. 101, which has 145 tent or RV sites. The walk-in tent sites are quite nice, in the forest. Fees are $15 per night. The ReserveAmerica system (see above) handles reservations for this campground as well.

You'll find a number of bed-and-breakfasts and funky roadside motels in the surrounding communities of Crescent City, Orick, and Klamath. The **Crescent City/ Del Norte Chamber of Commerce** (© **800/343-8300**) can probably steer you toward the proper match.

**Hostelling International—Redwood National Park** *(Value)*　The only lodging in the park itself, this settler's homestead was remodeled in 1987 to accommodate 30 guests dormitory-style (in bunks with shared bathrooms), from March through December. The location is optimal—100 yards from the beach, and surrounded by hiking trails leading along the Redwood Coast (the staff lead nature walks and are well versed in local history). A couple's room is available for an additional $10, with advance notice, and the hostel takes reservations by credit card (strongly recommended in the summer). The nightly rate includes use of the showers, common room with VCR and videos, redwood deck, help-yourself common kitchen, laundry room, dining room, pellet stove, and bicycle storage.

14480 U.S. 101 (at U.S. 101 and Wilson Creek Rd., across from False Klamath Cove), Klamath, CA 95548. © 800/ 295-1905, ext. 74, or 707/482-8265. Fax 707/482-4665. www.norcalhostels.org. 30 bunks, 1 couple's room ($42). $16 adults, $8 children ($3 additional for non-AYH/HI members). Closed daily 10am–5pm. Closed Dec–Feb, except for groups of 15-plus. MC, V. **Amenities:** On-site parking; information desk; baggage check; groceries/snacks available.

# 9

# The Far North: Lake Tahoe, Mount Shasta & Lassen Volcanic National Park

*by Matthew Richard Poole*

Dominated by snowcapped Mount Shasta, visible for 100 miles on a clear day, California's upper northern territory is among the least-visited parts of the state. Often called "the Far North," this region stretches from the rice fields north of Sacramento to the Oregon border. The area is so immense that the state of Ohio would fit comfortably within its borders.

For the adventurous traveler, the Far North is a superlative destination for outdoor sports such as hiking, climbing, skiing, white-water rafting, and mountain biking. Other attractions, both artificial and natural, range from the Shasta Dam, the highest overflow dam in the world; to Lava Beds National Monument, which

has dozens of caves to explore; to Lassen Volcanic National Park, a towering laboratory of volcanic phenomena.

South of the Cascade Range is one of the most popular recreational regions in the Golden State: Lake Tahoe, straddling the border between California and Nevada, at 6,225 feet above sea level. Although the lake has been marred by overdevelopment—particularly along the casino-riddled southern shore—the western and eastern coastlines are still quiet havens for hiking, cycling, and watersports. The surrounding Sierra Nevada mountains offer some of the best skiing in the United States, with more than a dozen resorts.

## 1 Lake Tahoe ★★★

107 miles E of Sacramento; 192 miles E of San Francisco; 45 miles SW of Reno, NV

Lake Tahoe is an American national treasure. It's stunningly beautiful, the air is crisp and clear, and the sun shines 80% of the time. In summer, you can partake of boating and watersports, sandy beaches, bicycling, golf, tennis, hiking, camping, ballooning, horseback riding, rock climbing, bungee jumping, parasailing, skating, and so on, with seemingly endless possibilities. In winter, with an average snowfall of 409 inches, Lake Tahoe is one of the nation's premier ski destinations, with 15 downhill resorts, 10 cross-country ski centers, and facilities for snowboarding, ice-skating, snowshoeing, snow-mobiling, sleigh riding, sledding, and snow play as well. Year-round diversions include fishing, Vegas-style gambling, and big-name entertainment in the casinos.

Then there's the lake; it's hard to imagine one as captivating. When Mark Twain first saw it, he declared it "the fairest picture the whole earth affords." It's famed for its crystal-clear water (a white dinner plate at the depth of 75 ft. would be visible from the

> ### *Tips*  A Tale of Two Shores
>
> Before you visit Tahoe for the first time, it's important to understand the distinction between the North and South shores. Don't let the "City" in the North Shore's "Tahoe City" fool you; you can drive through it in a couple of minutes. To the contrary, South Lake Tahoe is brimming with high-rise casinos, motels, and minimalls. Where you choose to stay is important because driving from one end of the lake to the other takes an hour or more in summer and can be downright treacherous in the winter.
>
> So which side is for you? If you're here for gambling or entertainment, go south: The selection of casinos is better, with more action and more lodgings, often at better rates. If you seek a relaxing, outdoor retreat, head to the North Shore, which has a better selection of high-quality resorts and vacation rentals. The woodsy West Shore has the most camping spots, and the East Shore, protected from development, has no commercial activity.
>
> Wherever you stay, you'll find no shortage of water and mountain sports. The lake is crowded during the summer and ski seasons, so plan far ahead. It's much easier to get reservations for the spring and fall, and the rates are significantly lower. Numerous vacation homes and condominiums are available to rent; call the visitor-center bureaus or visit the websites listed below under "Visitor Information" for a list of rental agents.

surface) and its size (at 22 miles long and 12 miles wide, it's the largest alpine lake in North America). Its average depth is 989 feet, with the deepest point being 1,645 feet, containing enough water to cover the entire state of California to a depth of 14½ inches. Surrounded by the imperious peaks of the Sierra Nevada, its waters soak up the colors of the sky and the mountains, creating a kaleidoscope of sparkling blues, greens, and purples—a sight that will lure you back year after year.

## ESSENTIALS

**GETTING THERE**    It's a 4-hour drive from San Francisco; take I-80 east to Sacramento, then U.S. 50 to the South Shore, or I-80 east to Highway 89 or Highway 267 to the North Shore. Be prepared for snow in the winter. During heavy storms, you won't be permitted to pass the CHP (California Highway Patrol) checkpoints without four-wheel-drive or chains. From Los Angeles, it's a 9-hour drive; take I-5 through the Central Valley to Sacramento, and then follow the directions above.

Reno-Tahoe International Airport (45 min. to North Shore, 90 min. to South Shore; www.renoairport.com) offers regular service by 10 major airlines, including **American** (© 800/433-7300), **Delta** (© 800/221-1212), and **United** (© 800/241-6522). Rent a car or take a shuttle up to the lake: **No Stress Express** (© 888/4-SHUTTLE;** www.nostressexpress.com) serves the North and West shores; **Tahoe Casino Express** (© 800/446-6128;** www.southtahoeexpress.com) serves the South Shore (1-day advance reservations recommended). To get to the lake, take U.S. 395 South to Route 431 for the North Shore or U.S. 50 for the South Shore. Although all the roads leading to the lake are scenic, the panorama as you descend into the Lake Tahoe Basin from Route 431 is spectacular. Pull into the overlook and enjoy the view.

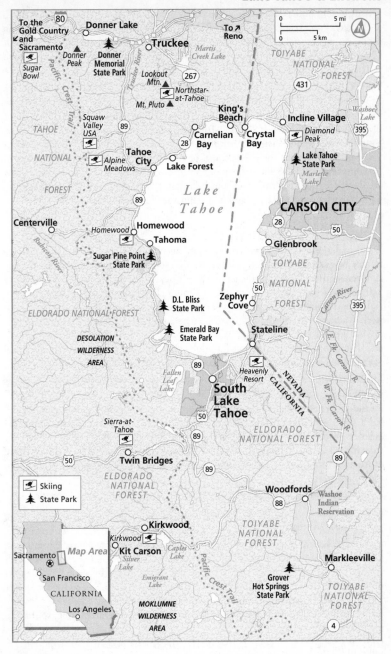

To the Gold Country and Sacramento

Donner Lake

To Reno

Donner Peak

Donner Memorial State Park

Truckee

Martis Creek Lake

Sugar Bowl

Pacific Crest Trail

Lookout Mtn.

267

TOIYABE NATIONAL FOREST

431

Northstar-at-Tahoe

Mt. Pluto

King's Beach

Incline Village

Washoe Lake

Squaw Valley USA

89

Carnelian Bay

Crystal Bay

Diamond Peak

395

TAHOE

28

NATIONAL

Alpine Meadows

Tahoe City

Lake Forest

Lake Tahoe State Park

FOREST

Marlette Lake

89

Lake Tahoe

CARSON CITY

Centerville

Homewood

Homewood

28

50

Tahoma

Glenbrook

Rubicon River

Sugar Pine Point State Park

TOIYABE

ELDORADO NATIONAL FOREST

D.L. Bliss State Park

50

NATIONAL

Carson River

395

Zephyr Cove

FOREST

DESOLATION WILDERNESS AREA

Emerald Bay State Park

Stateline

NEVADA

CALIFORNIA

E. Fk. Carson

89

Heavenly Resort

Fallen Leaf Lake

South Lake Tahoe

W. Fk. Carson R.

50

ELDORADO NATIONAL FOREST

89

Sierra-at-Tahoe

89

50

Twin Bridges

ELDORADO NATIONAL FOREST

89

Woodfords

Washoe Indian Reservation

88

Skiing

State Park

Kirkwood

TOIYABE NATIONAL FOREST

Kirkwood

Kit Carson

Caples Lake

Silver Lake

Markleeville

Sacramento

Map Area

Emigrant Lake

Grover Hot Springs State Park

San Francisco

CALIFORNIA

Pacific Crest Trail

TOIYABE NATIONAL FOREST

Los Angeles

MOKLUMNE WILDERNESS AREA

4

0    5 mi

0    5 km

**Amtrak** (✆ **800/USA-RAIL;** www.amtrak.com) stops in Truckee, 10 miles north of the lake. Public transportation (TART or Truce Trolley) is available from the train depot, or you can take a taxi to the North Shore. **Greyhound Bus Lines** (✆ **800/ 229-9424;** www.greyhound.com) serves both Truckee and South Lake Tahoe with daily arrivals from San Francisco and Sacramento.

**VISITOR INFORMATION** In Tahoe City, stop by the **Visitor Service Center,** 245 North Lake Blvd. (✆ **888/434-1262** or 530/583-3494; www.tahoefun.org). In Incline Village, go to the **Incline Village/Crystal Bay Visitors Center,** 969 Tahoe Blvd. (✆ **800/468-2463** or 775/832-1606; www.gotahoe.com). In South Lake Tahoe, go to the **Lake Tahoe Visitors Authority,** 1156 Ski Run Blvd. (✆ **800/288-2463** or 530/544-5050; www.virtualtahoe.com), or to the **South Lake Tahoe Chamber of Commerce,** 3066 Lake Tahoe Blvd. (✆ **530/541-5255;** www.tahoeinfo.com). Many other websites offer information about Lake Tahoe, including www.skilaketahoe.com, www.laketahoeconcierge.com, and www.tahoevacationguide.com.

## WHAT TO SEE & DO
### SKIING & SNOWBOARDING

With the largest concentration of ski resorts in North America, Lake Tahoe is California's best skiing destination. The ski season typically lasts from November to May and frequently extends into the summer. Lift tickets last winter ranged from $40 to $70 per day for adults, and from free to $35 for children, with special rates for teens and seniors. Ticket prices rise every year, but bargains are available, particularly midweek. Many resorts, hotels, and motels offer ski packages. Contact the visitor centers or visit the websites listed under "Visitor Information," above, to look for these values. The resorts offer instruction for adults and children, equipment rental, special courses for snowboarding, and restaurants. Most have free shuttles.

**Alpine Meadows** ★★ *Kids* With more than 100 runs over 2,400 acres, Alpine has something for everyone: kids' programs and a family ski zone, as well as its "wild side" for the double black diamond crowd. In addition to its 14 lifts, this low-key resort also has a beginner surface lift designed especially for children, novice skiers, and snowboarders. You can get a great bargain through its Bed and Board package, which provides lift tickets and lodging (✆ **800/949-3296**). Alpine also offers ski and snowboard instruction for all ages, excellent snowboarding-terrain parks, snowshoe rentals, and snow-play areas.

2600 Alpine Meadows Rd., Tahoe City, CA 96145. ✆ 800/441-4423 or 530/583-4232. www.skialpine.com.

**Diamond Peak** ★ *Kids* *Value* In the heart of the quiet, upscale community of Incline Village, this is a great choice for a low-key, less crowded, less expensive, nonetheless beautiful skiing adventure, with spectacular lake views. Smaller than most resorts in the area, it's also a premier destination for families. Skiing and snowboarding options for kids abound, with a snowboard park and sledding area, and a snow-play program to entertain the younger ones who aren't quite ready to hit the slopes. The Diamond Peak Cross Country and Snowshoe Center (same telephone number), east of Incline Village on NV Route 431, is gorgeous and even allows dogs to share in the fun in the afternoon.

1210 Ski Way, Incline Village, NV 89451. ✆ 775/832-1177 or 775/831-3249. www.diamondpeak.com.

**Heavenly Resort** ★★ *Kids*   This hugely popular resort—the only one on the South Shore—has the highest elevation (10,067 ft.) of any resort at the lake. Skiers and snowboarders of all levels will find something to challenge them, including 3 snowboard parks, 4,800 skiable acres, 30 lifts (including a 50-passenger aerial tram), and 86 runs. Heavenly is also the only resort with day care for infants as young as 6 weeks (up through 6 years of age), child care and ski combinations for toddlers 3 to 5, and full-day programs for older kids. With arcades, recreation centers, bowling alleys, and movie theaters nearby, it's a great choice if you have teenagers or if you want to visit the big casinos at night. The latest addition here is the $20-million **Heavenly Gondola**—cars that can transport up to eight passengers from the South Shore casino area up to an observation deck at 9,200 feet on Heavenly Mountain—a 2½-mile journey. The resort also recently invested nearly $30 million in improvements to the mountain, including two new high-speed lifts and a new 15-acre beginner's area.

P.O. Box 2180 (on Ski Run Blvd.), Stateline, NV 89449. ℭ 775/586-7000. www.skiheavenly.com.

**Homewood Mountain Resort** ★ *Kids* *Value*   Homewood is one of my favorite small ski areas, a homey little resort with 1,260 acres, 56 runs, 8 lifts, and spectacular lake views. It's a good family resort with child care for ages 2 to 6 and ski schools for ages 4 to 12. Lift tickets were only $44 last winter, and children under 10 skied free when accompanied by an adult.

5145 W. Lake Blvd., Homewood, CA 96141 (6 miles south of Tahoe City and 19 miles north of South Lake Tahoe on Hwy. 89). ℭ 530/525-2992. www.skihomewood.com.

**Kirkwood** ★★ *Kids*   Kirkwood's only drawback is that it's 30 miles south of South Lake Tahoe; otherwise, it's one of the top ski areas in Tahoe, with lots of snow and excellent spring skiing. It has 2,300 skiable acres, 12 lifts, and 65 trails. Many programs cater to children, including child care for the younger ones (ages 2–6). The **Cross Country Ski Center** (ℭ 209/258-7248) is one of the best around, with lessons for all ages, and spectacular scenery. Kirkwood is also ideal for summertime hiking, horseback riding, mountain biking, and rock climbing. With ample lodging (ℭ 800/967-7500) and dining options, this is a great year-round destination. The shuttle service to South Lake Tahoe is free.

Off Hwy. 88 at Carson Pass (P.O. Box 1), Kirkwood, CA 95646. ℭ 209/258-6000. www.kirkwood.com.

**Northstar-at-Tahoe** ★★ *Kids*   With 70 runs covering 2,420 acres on two mountains, Northstar is consistently rated among the top western resorts. Its sophisticated series of lifts, including an express gondola, ensure speedy access to the slopes and short lift lines. Whatever your age or experience level, you'll find what you're looking for here. Backcountry terrain on Saw Tooth Ridge will test the skills of expert skiers and snowboarders on 200 acres of ungroomed, out-of-boundary terrain. The Learning Center offers coaching in skiing, snowboarding, cross country, and the new snow toys. Child care (ages 2–6) is available, as well as instruction—including the "magic carpet" lift and special Paw Parks, Northstar's pint-size obstacle courses. Other outdoor pastimes include cross-country skiing, telemarking, snowshoeing, sleigh rides, tubing, and ice-skating in the heart of Northstar's new Village. Check out the snow toys, such as the snowscoot, the skifox, the snowbike, and the snowskate, a skateboard deck without wheels. See p. 258 for a full review of Northstar-at-Tahoe.

P.O. Box 129, Truckee, CA 96160 (6 miles north of Kings Beach). ℭ 800/466-6784 or 530/562-1010. www.northstarattahoe.com.

**Sierra-at-Tahoe** ✦ *Kids*    Tahoe's third-largest ski area is a great all-around resort, with slightly lower rates than most comparable places in the area. With more than 2,000 acres of slopes, from bunny to expert, Sierra-at-Tahoe features four terrain parks for both boarders and skiers, and 200 acres of backcountry terrain for steeps and deeps. The runs are very wide and well groomed, giving skiers plenty of room to fly down the mountain. On a powder day, don't miss skiing the trees. If you're staying on the South Shore, it's a good alternative to Heavenly Ski Resort. Free ski shuttle service is available from about 40 locations in South Lake Tahoe.

1111 Sierra at Tahoe Rd., Twin Bridges, CA 95735 (off Hwy. 50, 12 miles west of South Lake Tahoe). ✆ **530/659-7453**. www.sierraattahoe.com.

**Squaw Valley USA** ✦✦✦ *Kids*    Site of the 1960 Olympic Winter Games, Squaw is one of the world's finest year-round resorts. Skiing is spread across six peaks with one of the most advanced lift systems in the world providing access to more 4,000 acres of skiable terrain—70% geared toward beginners and intermediates and 30% for the advanced, expert, and/or insane. Children's World offers child care (reservations required; call ✆ **530/581-7280** 1–4pm) and snow school. For nonskiers and skiers alike, High Camp, at the top of the cable car, has the Olympic Ice Pavilion (year-round ice-skating), a swimming lagoon and spa (spring and summer), snow tubing, snowboarding school, bungee jumping, restaurants, and bars. Squaw also has an arcade, cinema, climbing wall, and Central Park (a snowboarder's dream). The Cross-Country Ski Center (✆ **530/583-6300**) has 400 acres of groomed trails. For those who can't get enough of a good thing, Squaw offers free night skiing with the purchase of a full-day lift ticket. Children ages 12 and under ski for only $5. See p. 258 for a full review of The Resort at Squaw Creek.

Olympic Valley, CA 96146 (6 miles north of Tahoe City). ✆ **800/545-4350** or 530/583-6985. www.squaw.com.

**Sugar Bowl** ✦✦ *Kids*    Sugar Bowl is an excellent place to ski—especially if you are driving from the Bay Area or Sacramento on I-80 and don't want to drive all the way to Tahoe. This medium-size resort (13 lifts, 1,500 skiable acres) offers child care, ski school, snowboard parks, and lodging at the foot of the mountains. It was a popular getaway for the Hollywood set in the 1940s and '50s.

P.O. Box 5, Norden, CA 95724 (3 miles east of the Soda Springs/Norden exit of I-80). ✆ **530/426-9000**. www.sugarbowl.com.

## MORE WINTER FUN

**CROSS-COUNTRY SKIING**    In addition to the major resorts, here are some other excellent establishments: **Royal Gorge Cross-Country Ski Resort** ✦✦✦, Soda Springs, near Sugar Bowl (✆ **800/666-3871**; www.royalgorge.com), is one of the largest and best cross-country resorts anywhere, with 90 trails, including 28 novice trails, and 4 ski lifts. For North Shore visitors, **Tahoe Cross Country Ski Area** ✦, 925 Country Club Dr., Tahoe City (✆ **530/583-5475**; www.tahoexc.org), is a small (14 trails), full-service ski center run by a nonprofit community group. A quiet, full-service ski center off the beaten path, **Spooner Lake Cross Country Ski Area** ✦, near the intersection of Highway 28 and U.S. 50 on the East Shore (✆ **888/858-8844**; www.spoonerlake.com), offers some of the most scenic skiing at the lake.

**ICE-SKATING**    Accessible only by a tram ride (included in the admission fee of $20 for adults, $10 for children under 12), **Squaw Valley's High Camp** ✦✦

(☎ 530/583-6985) has one of the world's most beautiful, yet unusual, ice rinks. It's open daily from 11am to 9pm (11am–4pm Apr 14–June 22).

**SNOWMOBILING**    Snowmobile rental and tours are available at several locations in the Lake Tahoe Area. Call ahead for reservations and directions. The **Zephyr Cove Snowmobile Center** ✮, 760 U.S. 50, about 4 miles northeast of the casinos (☎ 775/589-4908), offers several exciting tours daily for all experience levels. They're loads of fun, especially if you've never been on a snowmobile in your life. The cost for a 2-hour tour is about $94 for a single rider, $139 for two. **Snowmobiling Unlimited** (☎ 530/583-7192; www.snowmobilingunlimited.com) offers 2-hour backcountry tours from Brockway Summit, about 3 miles north of Kings Beach on Highway 267; prices are $90 for one, $120 for two. **TC Snomos,** 205 River Rd., Tahoe City (☎ 530/581-3906; www.snowmobilelaketahoe.com), starts its tours in Tahoe City, and charges $80 for one and $110 for two.

**SNOW PLAY**    For snow play beyond the big resorts, try the **North Tahoe Regional Park,** at the top of National Avenue off Highway 28, Tahoe Vista (☎ 530/546-0605). This ultimate snow-play hill charges a $5 fee that includes a choice of sled, tube, or saucer. **Taylor Creek Snow Park** off Highway 89 in South Lake Tahoe is run by the U.S. Forest Service. Bring your own equipment for sledding and tubing. For information about all the California Sno Park locations, call the **Sno Park Hot Line** at ☎ 916/324-1222.

## SUMMER ACTIVITIES

**BALLOONING**    See the lake and mountains from 8,000 to 10,000 feet above them, with **Lake Tahoe Balloons** (☎ 800/872-9294; www.laketahoeballoons.com in South Lake Tahoe. A 1-hour tour and brunch costs about $195 per person.

**BEACHES**    Here are a few popular spots around the lake. All have sandy beaches, picnic areas, and restrooms; many have playgrounds. Remember that this is an alpine lake so the water is *very* cold.

- **Baldwin Beach:** Highway 89, 4 miles north of South Lake Tahoe
- **Commons Beach Park:** Downtown Tahoe City, free movie (Fri at dusk)
- **Connolly Beach:** U.S. 50 at Timber Cove Lodge; boat launches
- **D. L. Bliss State Park:** South of Meeks Bay on Highway 89; camping, trails
- **El Dorado Beach:** Between Rufus Allen and Lakeview in South Lake Tahoe
- **Kings Beach State Recreation Center:** Highway 28 in Kings Beach
- **Pope Beach:** Highway 89, 2 miles north of South Lake Tahoe
- **Sand Harbor:** 4 miles south of Incline Village on Highway 28; lifeguards
- **Sugar Pine Point:** Highway 89, just south of Tahoma; camping, trails, pier
- **Zephyr Cove Beach:** U.S. 50 at Zephyr Cove

**BICYCLING**    Miles of paved bicycle paths surrround the lake. Incline Village has a scenic, easy, 2½-mile path along Lakeshore Boulevard. This is a safe choice for younger children. In Tahoe City you can follow the path in three directions. The one that follows Truckee River is a relaxing, beautiful ride. On the South Shore, the Pope-Baldwin bike path runs parallel to Highway 89 through Camp Richardson and the Tallac Historic Site. Nearby, in South Lake Tahoe, a paved pathway runs from El Dorado Beach along the lake, paralleling U.S. 50. The Tahoe City trails are my personal favorites, especially the Truckee River section. You can rent a bicycle from any of the shops listed below.

Mountain biking is big at Lake Tahoe. A dizzying choice of trails awaits even serious bikers. At both **Northstar-at-Tahoe** (℅ **530/562-1010;** p.245) and **Squaw Valley USA** (℅ **530/583-6985;** p. 246), you can take the cable car (Squaw) or chairlift (Northstar) up with your bike and ride the trails all the way down. For other trails, check with one of the bicycle-rental shops for maps and information. In North Tahoe, try **The Back Country,** 255 N. Lake Blvd., Tahoe City (℅ 530/581-5861); **Olympic Bike Shop,** 620 N. Lake Blvd., Tahoe City (℅ 530/581-2500); **Tahoe Bike & Ski,** 8499 N. Lake Blvd., Kings Beach (℅ 530/546-7437); or **Porter's Sports Shop,** 885 Tahoe Blvd., Incline Village (℅ 775/831-3500). In South Tahoe, try **Anderson's Bike Rental,** 645 Emerald Bay Rd. (℅ 530/541-0500), or **Lakeview Sports,** 3131 Hwy. 50 at El Dorado Beach (℅ 530/544-0183).

Another great choice is **Cyclepaths Mountain Bike Adventures,** 1785 W. Lake Blvd. in Tahoe Park, a few miles south of Tahoe City (℅ **800/780-BIKE;** www.cycle paths.com), where you can arrange a guided off-road tour. Whether you're into hard-core downhill single track or easy-going scenic outings, the expert guides will provide you with the necessary gear, food, and transportation. They offer day tours ($29 and up), weekenders ($199), and 3- and 5-day adventure camps (rates vary).

**BOATING, WATERSPORTS & PARASAILING**   Nothing beats actually getting out on the water. Take a guided tour, go off on your own, or just paddle around. Here are a few reliable choices: **Zephyr Cove Marina** (℅ **775/588-3833;** www.tahoedixie2.com) is the lake's largest marina. It's the home of the paddle-wheeler MS *Dixie II* and the catamaran *Woodwind II.* Here you can parasail (℅ **775/588-3530**), charter sport-fishing trips (℅ **775/586-9338**), or take guided tours. You can also rent motorized boats, pedal boats, kayaks, canoes, water-ski equipment, and jet skis. **Tahoe City Marina** (℅ **530/583-1039**), 700 N. Lake Blvd., Tahoe City, rents motorized boats, sailboats, and fishing boats. Sailboat cruises are available. This is also the location for **Lake Tahoe Parasailing** (℅ **530/583-7245**).

**Lighthouse Water Sports,** 950 N. Lake Blvd., Tahoe (℅ **530/583-6000**), rents jet skis, paddleboats, and canoes. **Tahoe Paddle and Oar,** North Lake Beach Center, 7860 N. Lake Blvd., Kings Beach (℅ **530/581-3029**), is a good place to rent kayaks, canoes, pedal boats, and windsurfing equipment. Paddling around in the clear waters of Crystal Bay is great fun. **Action Water Sports** rents boats, kayaks, jet skis, paddleboats, and other water toys; parasailing and guided tours are also available. Action Water Sports has two locations: 3411 Lake Tahoe Blvd. at Timber Cove Marina, South Lake Tahoe (℅ **530/544-2942**); and across from the Hyatt in Incline Village (℅ **775/831-4386**). **Camp Richardson Marina,** 1900 Jameson Beach Rd., off Highway 89 on the South Shore (℅ **530/542-6570**), on a long sandy beach, rents power- and ski boats, jet skis, kayaks, and paddleboats. It also offers fishing charters, ski school, cruises on the *Woodwind I* sailboat, and raft and kayak tours to Emerald Bay. **SunSports,** 3564 Lake Tahoe Blvd., South Lake Tahoe (℅ **530/541-6000**), provides rentals, tours, and lessons for kayaking, rafting, sailing, and scuba diving.

**CAMPING**   If you have an appetite for the great outdoors, here are a few of the many good campgrounds at Tahoe:

**D. L. Bliss State Park,** on the western shore (℅ **530/525-7277**), has 168 campsites, fine beaches, and hiking trails.

**Sugar Pine Point State Park,** open year-round on the western shore (℅ **530/525-7982**), has 175 campsites, a picnic area, a beach, a nature center, and cross-country skiing.

**Campground by the Lake,** 1150 Rufus Allen Blvd., South Lake Tahoe (© **530/ 542-6096**), features 170 campsites, a boat ramp, a gym, and a history museum.

**Zephyr Cove RV Park and Campground,** located at Zephyr Cove Resort on U.S. 50 (© **775/589-4907**), has a beach, a marina, and complete facilities.

**FISHING** The cold, clear waters of Lake Tahoe are home to kokanee salmon and rainbow, brown, and Mackinaw trout. Fishing here is a challenge in the deep water. Many anglers opt to use a guide or charter boat. Dozens of charter companies offer daily excursions. Rates run about $65 for a half-day to $95 for a whole day (bait, tackle, fish cleaning, and food included). On the North Shore, try **Mickey's Big Mack Charters** at the Sierra Boat Company in Carnelian Bay (© 530/546-4444; www.mickeysbig mack.com) or **Reel Deal Sportfishing,** Tahoe City (© 530/581-0924). On the South Shore, try **Avid Fisherman,** Zephyr Cove (© 775/588-7675); **Blue Ribbon Fishing Charters,** Tahoe Keys Marina (© 530/541-8801); or **Tahoe Sportfishing,** 900 Ski Run Blvd. (© 800/696-7797 or 530/541-5448).

**FITNESS CENTERS & SPAS** The **Incline Recreation Center,** 980 Incline Way, Incline Village (© **775/832-1310**), is an impressive facility with a heated indoor Olympic-size swimming pool, aerobics, basketball, cardiovascular fitness room, lounge, fireplace, and on-site child care. The fee is $13 for adults and $8 for children.

**GOLF** With its world-class golf courses, mild summer weather, and magnificent scenery, Lake Tahoe is a golfer's paradise. All of the following courses are very busy in the summer so call *far* in advance for tee times. For more information about Tahoe-area golf courses, log on to **www.tahoesbest.com/Golf**.

The north end of the lake has four highly rated courses: **Incline Village Championship Course,** 955 Fairway Blvd., and the smaller **Incline Village Mountain (Executive) Course,** 690 Wilson Way (© 775/832-1144 for both); **Northstar-at-Tahoe** (© 530/562-2490; p. 258); and **The Resort at Squaw Creek** (© 800/327-3353; p. 258).

In the south, **Edgewood,** U.S. 50 at Lake Parkway, Stateline (© 775/588-3566), is home of the Celebrity Golf Championship; **Lake Tahoe Golf Course,** 2500 Emerald Bay Rd., South Lake Tahoe (© 530/577-0788), also has some good 9-hole municipal courses. There's also **Old Brockway Golf Course,** 7900 N. Lake Blvd., Kings Beach (© 530/546-9909); **Tahoe City Golf Course,** 251 N. Lake Blvd., Tahoe City (© 530/ 583-1516); and **Bijou Municipal Golf Course,** 3436 Fairway Ave., South Lake Tahoe (© 530/542-6097).

**HIKING** Hiking trails for all levels of experience crisscross the mountains surrounding Lake Tahoe. Before setting out, you may wish to contact the local visitor centers or sporting-goods shops for a map and more in-depth information on particular trails, or hire a guide. Try **Tahoe Trips & Trails** (© **530/583-4506**; www.tahoe trips.com) for short and long guided hikes. Everything is provided: food, drinks, transportation, and information about the lake. Going on your own? Some of the most popular short hikes in the area are:

**Eagle Falls/Eagle Lake.** This moderately easy trail is well marked and begins at Eagle Picnic Area, across Highway 89 from Emerald Bay. It's only about a third of a mile to the steel footbridge overlooking the falls and 2 miles round-trip (1½–2 hr.) to Eagle Lake. Be sure to sign in at the self-registration station at the trail head.

**Emerald Bay/Vikingsholm.** The trail starts at the parking area on the north side of Emerald Bay, on Highway 89. It's a wide, well-maintained trail but fairly steep, about 2.5 miles round-trip. At the bottom of the trail is a picnic area, as well as world-famous Vikingsholm, a replica of a Scandinavian castle.

**Nevada Shoreline.** Begin at the paved parking lot on the west side of Highway 28, 3 miles south of Sand Harbor. The trail drops to the beach and follows the shoreline, passing Chimney Beach, Secret Harbor, and Whale Beach. The trail eventually connects to a service road that can be followed back up to the parking area. It's an easy 4-mile hike, with a vertical climb of only 300 feet.

**Shirley Lake.** This trail leads to Shirley Lake, then down to Shirley Canyon. Take the tram at Squaw Valley up to High Camp and hike down, or vice versa. The trail begins at the end of Squaw Creek Road, next to the cable-car building. It's a 4-mile hike, easy to moderate in difficulty, with some steep sections.

**HORSEBACK RIDING** Most stables offer a variety of guided trail rides and lessons for individuals, families, and groups. Choose the one that appeals to your sense of adventure: 1- to 2-hour trail rides; breakfast, lunch, or dinner rides; half-day, full-day, overnight, and extended pack trips. Expect to pay $20 to $25 for a 1-hour ride, $6 for a half-hour pony ride. Saddle up and savor the scenery. Try **Alpine Meadows Stables,** Alpine Meadows Road, Tahoe City (② 530/583-3905); **Northstar Stables,** Highway 267, 6 miles north of Kings Beach (② 530/562-2480); **Squaw Valley Stables,** 1525 Squaw Valley Rd., north of Tahoe City (② 530/583-7433); **Camp Richardson Corral,** Highway 89, South Lake Tahoe (② 530/541-3113); or **Zephyr Cove Stables,** Zephyr Cove Resort, U.S. 50 at Zephyr Cove (② 775/588-5664).

**RIVER RAFTING** For a swift but gentle ride down the Truckee River (the lake's only outlet), try **Truckee River Raft Rental,** 185 River Rd., Tahoe City (② **530/583-0123;** www.truckeeriverraft.com). Only available in the summer, the rates are $25 for adults and $20 for children (12 and under).

**TENNIS** The mild summer weather at Lake Tahoe is perfect for great tennis. If you want to sharpen your skills, **Northstar-at-Tahoe** (② **530/562-0321;** p. 245 and 258) offers several excellent tennis packages for its guests only. **Squaw Creek** (② **530/ 581-6694;** p. 258) tennis courts are open to the public for $12 an hour. **Kirkwood** (② **209-258-6000;** p. 245), **Caesars Tahoe** (② **775/588-3515;** p. 253), and **Harveys Casino Resort** (② 775/588-2411; p. 254) all feature tennis courts for a fee.

Budget-minded players looking for good local courts should visit Tahoe Lake School on Grove Street in Tahoe City, or Tahoe Regional Park, at the end of National Avenue in Tahoe Vista. South Tahoe Intermediate School on Lyons Avenue has eight lighted courts and charges a manageable $3 per hour. South Tahoe High School, 1735 Lake Tahoe Blvd., has free courts.

## LAKE CRUISES

If you can possibly fit a cruise into your vacation plans, you won't regret it. It's one of the best ways to see the lake. **MS _Dixie II,_** Zephyr Cove Marina, 4 miles north of the casinos on U.S. 50 (② **800/238-2463;** www.zephyrcove.com), is a 570-passenger vessel with bars, a dance floor, and a full dining room. Emerald Bay scenic cruises cost $26 for adults, $9 for children. They also have champagne-brunch and breakfast cruises ($30), dinner cruises ($44), and sunset dinner-dance cruises ($55).

**Hornblower's _Tahoe Queen_** (② **800/238-2463** or 530/541-3364; www.hornblower.com), departing from the Marina Village at Ski Run Boulevard in South Lake Tahoe, is an authentic paddle-wheeler with a capacity of 500. It offers Emerald Bay sightseeing tours ($26 adults, $9 children) and dinner/dance cruises ($53 adults, $29 children), as well as full-service charters. Live music, buffet breakfast, dinner, and appetizers are all available onboard. The **Hornblower Ski Shuttle** ($129, including lift ticket, snacks, and ground transportation) is the world's only waterborne ski shuttle. On the way to Squaw Valley, you can have a breakfast buffet, and on the way home, enjoy an après-ski party. This ski shuttle allows skiers staying on the South Shore an opportunity to ski on the North Shore without having to drive over. Buses pick up passengers from their hotels in the morning and drop them off at night.

The *Tahoe Gal* (© 800/218-2464 or 530/583-0141; www.tahoegal.com), departing from the Lighthouse Marina (behind Safeway) in Tahoe City, is the only cruise boat on the North Shore. Cruises include Scenic Shoreline ($21 adults, $10 children), Emerald Bay ($26 adults, $14 children), Happy Hour (4:30–6pm; $22 for two adults, $8 children), and Sunset Dinner ($22 adults, $12 children). *Note:* Prices are for the cruise only; food and beverages cost extra.

**Woodwind Sailing Cruises** (© 888/867-6394; www.sailwoodwind.com) runs daily sightseeing cruises ($26 adults, $23 seniors, $12 children 3–12), sunset champagne cruises ($32), weddings, and charters. The Woodwind fleet includes the *Woodwind I,* a 30-passenger Searunner trimaran sailing to Emerald Bay from Camp Richardson Marina in South Lake Tahoe, and the *Woodwind II,* a 50-passenger Searunner catamaran sailing from Zephyr Cove Marina.

## A DRIVE AROUND THE LAKE

Overwhelmed by the choices? Get in your car and take a leisurely drive around the lake. It's only 72 miles, but plan on expending several hours, even in the best of weather. In the worst of weather, don't try it! Parts of the road, if not closed, can be icy and dangerous. On a mild day, it will be a memorable experience. If your car has a tape deck, consider buying *Drive Around the Lake,* a drive-along audio cassette that contains facts, legends, places of interest, and just about everything else you might want to know about the lake. It's available at many gift shops or at the **South Lake Tahoe Chamber of Commerce,** 3066 Lake Tahoe Blvd. (© 530/541-5255; www. tahoeinfo.com), which is closed on Sundays.

We'll start at the California-Nevada border in South Lake Tahoe and loop around the western shore on Highway 89 to Tahoe City and beyond. U.S. 50, which runs along the South Shore, is an ugly, overdeveloped strip that obliterates any view of the lake. Keep heading west and you will be free of this boring stretch.

First stop is the **Tallac Historic Site,** site of the former Tallac Resort and a cluster of 100-year-old mansions that provide a fascinating glimpse into Tahoe's past. In its heyday, the resort included two large hotels, a casino, and numerous outbuildings. Throughout the summer the **Valhalla Festival of Arts and Music** (© 888/632-5859 or 530/541-4975; www.valhalla-tallac.com) showcases jazz, bluegrass, rock, mariachi, and classical music. Summer highlights include June's Valhalla Renaissance Festival, July's Native American Fine Arts Festival, and August's Great Gatsby Festival.

From here the highway winds north along the shore until you reach **Cascade Lake** on the left and **Emerald Bay** ★★ on the right. The Emerald Bay Lookout is a spectacular picture-taking spot. Emerald Bay's deep green water is the site of the only island in Lake Tahoe, Fannette Island. The small structure atop the island is the teahouse, built by Ms. Lora Knight, who also constructed **Vikingsholm** ★ (© 530/541-3030), a 38-room Scandinavian castle built in 1929, located at the head of Emerald

Bay. Tours of this unique structure are available from mid-June to Labor Day every half-hour from 10am to 4pm. Even if you don't want to take the tour, it's a pleasant walk from the parking area down to the beach and the mansion's grounds. Just remember that you have to walk back up. Across the highway, there's another parking area. From here, it's a short, steep .25-mile hike to a footbridge above **Eagle Falls.** Then it's about a mile farther up to **Eagle Lake.**

Continuing on, it's only about 2 miles to **D. L. Bliss State Park** (© 530/525-7982), where you'll find one of the lake's best beaches. It gets crowded in the summer, so arrive early to get a parking place. The park also contains 168 campsites and several trails, including one along the shoreline.

In about 7 miles you will reach **Sugar Pine State Park** (© 530/525-7232), the largest (2,000 acres) of the lake's parks and also the only one that has year-round camping. In summer you can visit its beaches, plus a nature center and miles of trails; in winter you can cross-country ski on well-maintained trails.

Continuing on through the town of **Homewood** (site of the ski resort), **Sunnyside,** on the right, is a pleasant place to stop for a lakeside lunch. Or, if you feel like taking a stroll, drive on to Tahoe City with its beautiful paved path along the Truckee River. Check out the big trout at **Fanny Bridge** ⋆ first. If you would like to see **Squaw Valley** and **Alpine Meadows,** take a left at Highway 89. A ride on the Squaw Valley cable car (© 530/583-6985) will reward you with incredible vistas from 2,000 feet above the valley floor. It runs year-round and costs $17 for adults, $14 for seniors, and $5 for children under 13. Back on Highway 28, as you leave **Tahoe City,** you will pass a string of small malls at 700 through 850 North Lake Blvd. If you like to wander around, this is a good area to stop and eat, watch the activity at the **Tahoe City Marina** (parasailing, cruises on the *Tahoe Gal,* and boat rental), or visit the shops.

Continuing around the lake on Highway 28, you'll reach Carnelian Bay, Tahoe Vista, and Kings Beach before crossing the state line into Nevada. **Kings Beach State Recreation Area** ⋆ (© 530/546-7248) is a long, wide beach and picnic area. It is jammed in the summer with sunbathers and swimmers. As you approach **Crystal Bay,** you will immediately know, by the string of small casinos that suddenly appear, that you have crossed the state line. The **Cal-Neva Resort, Spa & Casino** (p. 259) on the right was once owned by Frank Sinatra and has a twinkly, celebrity-studded history. The state line goes right through the lodge, and gambling is allowed only on the Nevada side. This is worth stopping to see.

Your journey next takes you to woodsy Incline Village, arguably the most beautiful community on the lake. Take a right on Lakeshore Boulevard to view the elegant estates. Lunch or dinner time? The **Lone Eagle Grille** (p. 258), at the Hyatt Regency Lake Tahoe, offers panoramic lake views as well as superb food.

The east shore of the lake is largely undeveloped and very scenic. Drive about 4 miles south of Incline Village to **Sand Harbor** ⋆ (© 775/831-0494), one of the lake's best-loved beaches, and home to the very popular **Lake Tahoe Shakespeare Festival** (© 800/747-4697; www.tahoebard.com) every mid-July through August. In addition to turquoise blue water dotted with big boulders and a wide sandy beach, you'll find nature trails, picnic areas, and boating.

Going south you will come to an outcropping called **Cave Rock** where the highway passes through 25 yards of solid stone. Farther along is **Zephyr Cove Resort and Marina,** home to the MS *Dixie II* and a beehive of watersports activity. You'll then return to Stateline and South Lake Tahoe, your original starting point.

*Moments* **Gondola to Heaven**

If you want a preview of heaven, take a ride on the Heavenly Valley Ski Resort gondola. At a cost of a mere $20 million, the gondola consists of state-of-the-art "cars" that whisk you from South Shore's downtown area up the mountain to Heavenly Resort's 14,000-square-foot observation deck. Each car holds up to eight people. The 2½-mile ride rises to an elevation of 9,123 feet, offering passengers shore-to-shore views of Lake Tahoe, Carson Valley to the east, and Desolation Wilderness to the west (all best seen at sunset).

The gondola is a half block west of Stateline, an easy walk from the downtown hotels. It's open year-round Monday through Friday from 10am to sunset, and Saturday and Sunday from 9am to sunset. Tickets are $20 for adults, $12 for children ages 6 to 12, and free for kids 5 and under.

## WHERE TO STAY
### SOUTH SHORE & SOUTH LAKE TAHOE
**Expensive**

**Black Bear Inn Bed & Breakfast** ★★    Within a wooded acre near Heavenly Ski Resort, this beautiful neorustic lodge offers luxury accommodations in a tranquil setting and convenient location (though not the prettiest in town). The great room, with its beamed ceilings, grand piano, early American antiques, three-story rock fireplace, and complimentary evening hors d'oeuvres, offers a relaxing environment after a long day of outdoor activities. Or better yet, soak your tired body in the sheltered Jacuzzi. Breakfast—included in the room rate—is an event, with fresh-baked muffins, eggs Benedict, omelets, and other hearty fare. Each of the spacious guest rooms has an artful blend of modern and authentic Old West furnishings, including a king-size bed, private bathroom, and gas fireplace. For additional privacy, request one of the three cabins behind the inn, and ask for breakfast to be delivered to your door.

1202 Ski Run Blvd., South Lake Tahoe, CA 96150. © **877/232-7466** or 530/544-4451. www.tahoeblackbear.com. 5 lodge rooms, 3 cabins. $205–$245 lodge rooms; $265–$475 cabins. Rates include full breakfast. MC, V. **Amenities:** Nearby golf course; Jacuzzi. *In room:* A/C, TV/VCR, dataport, kitchenette, fridge, coffeemaker, hair dryer in cabins.

**Caesars Tahoe** ★    This 16-story hotel, built in the early 1980s, has the same glitter, glitz, and campy references to Roman mythology that Caesars Palace in Las Vegas has perfected. The guest rooms, many of which offer beautiful views of the lake, are furnished with contemporary hardwood pieces and equipped with extralarge tubs (Roman-style, of course). The gamut of suites ranges from executive-style quarters to lavishly appointed, themed suites with Roman tubs. Highlights include a full casino with sports booking, the Circus Maximus showroom with top-name performers, a lagoon-style indoor pool, and indoor and outdoor wedding chapels. **Club Nero** has live music and the biggest dance floor around. You can even indulge yourself in Caesars' full-service spa.

55 U.S. 50 (P.O. Box 5800), Lake Tahoe, NV 89449. © **800/648-3353** or 775/588-3515. www.caesars.com. 440 units. $79–$300 double; $370–$950 suite. Packages available. AE, DC, MC, V. **Amenities:** 6 restaurants; 4 lounges; indoor pool; 3 outdoor tennis courts; health club; spa; Jacuzzi; sauna; ski rental; bike rental; video arcade; activities desk; car-rental desk; business center; shopping arcade; salon; 24-hr. room service; in-room massage; babysitting; dry cleaning; executive-level rooms. *In room:* A/C, TV, dataport, kitchenette and minibar in suites, fridge upon request, hair dryer, iron, safe.

**Embassy Suites Resort** ⭐ *Kids*  On the edge of the state line, steps away from the Heavenly Gondola, this is the only major noncasino hotel on Tahoe's South Shore. It earns its keep by luring the upscale gambling crowd and the convention business with uncommonly large suites. The nine-story château-style hotel has a roofline pierced with a double layer of dormers; equally impressive is the massive inner atrium filled with plants. The one- and two-bedroom suites all have a separate living room with sofa bed, armchair, a well-lit dining/work table, a microwave, and a wet bar. Complimentary breakfasts, cooked to order, are served in a garden atrium. The resort's fine-dining restaurant, **Echo,** serves superb New American cuisine developed by award-winning chef Roy Choi. **Turtles Sports Bar & Dance Emporium,** which opens onto an outdoor deck, serves great pizzas during the day and turns into a dance club later in the evening. In the summer all guests have access to a private beach, and family skiers fill up the place in winter, partly because kids 18 and under stay free.

4130 Lake Tahoe Blvd., South Lake Tahoe, CA 96150. ℂ 800/362-2779 or 530/544-5400. Fax 530/544-4900. www. embassy-suites.com. 400 suites. $149–$359 double. Rates include full breakfast and evening cocktail reception. Special packages available. Children 18 and under stay free in parent's room. AE, DC, DISC, MC, V. **Amenities:** Restaurant; pizzeria; sports bar; indoor pool; outdoor sun deck; health club; spa; Jacuzzi; dry sauna; watersports equipment rental; concierge; car-rental desk; limited room service; in-room massage; babysitting; same-day dry cleaning; executive-level rooms. *In room:* A/C, TV/VCR, dataport, minibar, fridge, coffeemaker, hair dryer, iron.

**Harrah's Lake Tahoe** ⭐ *Kids*  Understatement is not a word that crosses your mind at Harrah's, the most luxurious and glitzy of Tahoe's casinos. Harrah's takes great pride in its special blend of luxury, beauty, unparalleled guest service, and casino entertainment. The large rooms have two bathrooms (each with its own TV and telephone so you won't miss any action while bathing), with those thick, fluffy, white towels Sinatra always demanded. Most have bay windows overlooking the lake or the mountains. The casino has an enormous fun center for kids, with the latest in video and arcade games, virtual reality, and an indoor "playscape" for young children. Weddings and parties can be scheduled aboard the private yacht, the *Tahoe Star.* The legendary **South Shore Room** hosts showbiz stars and—last but by no means least—the casino is a gambler's dream.

P.O. Box 8, Stateline, NV 89449. ℂ 800/427-7247 or 775/586-6607. Fax 775/586-6601. www.harrahs.com/our_ casinos/tah/index.html. 525 units. $109–$229 double; $229–$399 suite. Packages available. AE, DC, DISC, MC, V. **Amenities:** 3 restaurants; cafe; deli; coffeehouse; indoor pool; full-service health club/spa; family center; game room; shopping arcade; salon; 24-hr. room service; in-room massage; same-day dry cleaning. *In room:* A/C, TV/VCR, coffeemaker, hair dryer, iron, safe.

**Harveys Lake Tahoe Casino & Resort** *Kids*  With its two massive towers and 740 rooms, Harveys is the largest (and possibly the ugliest) hotel in Tahoe. It features an 88,000-square-foot casino, eight restaurants (including a Hard Rock Cafe), and a cabaret with some of the most glittering, bespangled shows in town. Harveys is like a city unto itself, with a children's day camp, beauty and barbershops, and even a wedding chapel, should you get the urge. Heck, you never have to see the real world again. **Tip:** Try to get a room between the 15th and 19th floors in the Lake Tower, where every unit has a view of both Lake Tahoe and the surrounding Sierra.

U.S. 50 at Stateline Ave. (P.O. Box 128), Stateline, NV 89449. ℂ 800/HARVEYS or 775/588-2411. Fax 775/588-6643. http://www.harrahs.com/our_casinos/hlt/index.html. 740 units. $89–$299 double; $299–$699 suite. AE, DC, DISC, MC, V. **Amenities:** 8 restaurants; 10 bars; outdoor heated pool; nearby golf course; health club; spa; Jacuzzi; sauna; watersports equipment rental; children's day camp; video arcade; concierge; car-rental desk; business center; shopping arcade; salon; 24-hr. room service; in-room massage; laundry service; same-day dry cleaning. *In room:* A/C, TV w/pay movies, dataport, minibar, coffeemaker, hair dryer, iron, safe.

**Tahoe Seasons Resort**   Big, modern, and loaded with luxuries, the Tahoe Seasons lies in a relatively uncongested residential neighborhood at the base of the Heavenly Valley Ski Resort, 2 miles from Tahoe's casinos. Every unit here is a spacious, attractive suite, sleeping up to four in the smaller one and six in the larger one. Most have gas fireplaces, and all have huge whirlpool spas complete with shoji screens (in case you plan to lose your shirt in more ways than one). Skiing isn't the only activity around here: Play a round of tennis on the roof or hop aboard the free casino shuttles.

3901 Saddle Rd., off Ski Run Blvd. (P.O. Box 5656), South Lake Tahoe, CA 96157. ✆ 800/540-4874 or 530/541-6700. Fax 530/541-7342. www.tahoeseasons.com. 160 suites. Summer $170–$240 double; winter $180–$250 double; spring and fall $122–$200 double. Seasonal packages available. AE, MC, V. **Amenities:** Restaurant; pub; outdoor heated pool; nearby golf course; 2 rooftop tennis courts; complimentary use of health club at Harveys Resort; game room; concierge; tour and activities desk; courtesy car; room service; in-room massage; same-day dry cleaning. *In room:* A/C, TV/VCR, dataport, fridge, coffeemaker, hair dryer on request, iron.

### Moderate

**Best Western Station House Inn** *Value*   Ensconced amid towering pines but just 3 blocks from the casinos, the Best Western Station House Inn, built in the late 1970s, is one of the few hotels in town that still has its own private "gated" beach on the lake. The decor is corporate dull, but the location is ideal, the large swimming pool and hot tub are a huge bonus, and **LewMarNel's,** the on-site restaurant, won a *Wine Spectator* award. The complimentary breakfast, cooked to order, and free shuttle service make staying here a particularly good value.

901 Park Ave., South Lake Tahoe, CA 96150. ✆ 800/822-5953 or 530/542-1101. Fax 530/542-1714. www.stationhouseinn.com. 100 units. $98–$138 double; $135–$165 suite; $200–$300 cabin. Rates include full breakfast. Packages available. AE, DC, DISC, MC, V. **Amenities:** Restaurant; heated outdoor pool; Jacuzzi; babysitting. *In room:* A/C, TV, coffeemaker, hair dryer.

**Camp Richardson Resort** *Kids*   If you are planning a family vacation, a reunion, or just a weekend getaway, Camp Richardson has it all. (I *love* this place.) On a long

## Village People

That sprawling "alpine village" next to the casinos is the new 464-room **Marriott's Timber Lodge & Grand Residence Club** (4100 Lake Tahoe Blvd; ✆ 800/845-5279; www.marriottvillarentals.com). It's the first phase of a massive redevelopment project slated for Stateline that will level most of the old, inexpensive motels with nickel-slotters and replace them with that expensive corporate faux-village thing that's taking over the world's tourist destinations. The two adjacent vacation ownership resorts also sell rooms on a per-night basis, but it's only a good deal if your family takes full advantage of the resort amenities: restaurants, bars, an ice-skating rink, two pools, a movie theater, a ski gondola, an arcade, and an alpine-style retail minimall. The silver lining? The new building codes are fiercely pro-environment: Holding and treatment ponds are now required to prevent polluted snowmelt and rainwater from dumping straight into the lake, and the central ski gondola and high-tech bus system are two new eco-friendly means of luring people away from their SUVs.

sandy beach on the southwest shore, this woodsy retreat offers a wide array of activities and several lodging and dining options. Its two restaurants offer lakeside dining, but there are also more informal dining options, plus a general store, a candy store, and an ice-cream parlor. The sports center rents all the seasonal equipment you'll need. You can ski right along the shore, scale the rock-climbing wall, or visit the stable, for horseback riding. The full-service marina rents power- and ski boats, jet skis, kayaks, and paddleboats, and offers guided tours, cruises, and chartered fishing trips. Lodging options include a hotel, cabins, a beachside inn, a marina duplex, tent campgrounds, and an RV park. The children will fall into bed exhausted at night with all of the organized activities available. Cabins rent only by the week in summer and fill up quickly. *Tip:* Check their website for seasonal money-saving packages.

Jameson Beach Rd. (P.O. Box 9028), South Lake Tahoe, CA, 96158. ℂ 800/544-1801 or 530/541-1801. Fax 530/541-1802. www.camprichardson.com. $65–$175 hotel; $90–$170 cabins per day, $565–$1,625 per week in summer. Camping or RV hookup $17–$26 per day. DISC, MC, V. **Amenities:** 2 restaurants; deli; cafe; Jacuzzi; sports center w/bike, snowshoe, and ski rental; children's program; tour and activities desk; marina. *In room:* TV in inn and duplex rooms; kitchen in cabin; coffeemaker; no phone in hotel and cabin units.

**Fireside Lodge** 🐾 *Kids* If you're more into outdoor recreation than roulette, on the opposite side of town from the big casinos is the Fireside Lodge, a small log cabin-style inn that sits on the edge of the National Forest, affording easy access to a public beach and miles of hiking and biking trails. It's owned and run by the local family that also owns the Inn at Heavenly, and the location is unbeatable—close to some great restaurants and the kid-friendly facilities at Camp Richardson, but far enough from the main drag to keep your mind on the mountains. The nine recently renovated country-pine suites are cozy (read small), but well equipped with river-rock fireplaces and kitchenettes. After a hike in the woods, relax in the hot-tub room, play some pool in the rec room, and then have a barbecue outside. Dogs and kids are welcome, and the staff will even lend you bicycles, float tubes, and free videos.

515 Emerald Bay Rd., South Lake Tahoe, CA 96150-6505. ℂ 800/692-2246 or 530/544-5515. www.tahoefireside lodge.com. 9 rooms. $89–$135 double. Rates include continental breakfast and afternoon wine service. AE, DISC, MC, V. **Amenities:** Hot tub; rec room; barbecue facilities. *In room:* TV/VCR, dataport, fridge, coffeemaker, microwave.

**Horizon Casino Resort** *Value* This massive resort hotel, next to the even larger Harveys, charges less for basically the same facilities. The lobby is a cheesy sea of white marble and mirrors, and the standard rooms are bland but innocuous (although the suites are far racier). The upper floors of the two towers naturally open onto the best views of mountains and the lake. Besides the 42,000-square-foot gaming room, the resort has a multiplex movie theater, cabaret, lounge, nightclub, the largest outdoor pool in Tahoe, and restaurants ranging from buffet to gourmet.

U.S. 50 (P.O. Box C), Lake Tahoe, NV 89449. ℂ 800/648-3322 or 775/588-6211. Fax 775/588-0349. www.horizon casino.com. 539 units. $119–$169 double summer; $99–$169 winter; $250–$500 suite. Children 11 and under stay free in parent's room. Packages available. AE, DC, DISC, MC, V. **Amenities:** 3 restaurants; large heated outdoor pool; nearby golf course; health club; 3 Jacuzzis; bike and ski rental; video arcade; concierge; car-rental desk; business center; shopping arcade; salon; 24-hr. room service; in-room massage; babysitting; laundry service; same-day dry cleaning; executive-level rooms. *In room:* A/C, TV w/pay movies, dataport, minibar, fridge, coffeemaker, hair dryer, iron in suites.

**Lakeland Village Beach & Mountain Resort** 🐾 *Kids* This condominium resort is a good choice for families. Clustered on 19 lightly forested acres of shoreline property, the half residential condo/half holiday resort complex, built in the 1970s, is a labyrinth of redwood buildings that blend into the surrounding landscape. The only drawback is the proximity to traffic headed into Lake Tahoe, although some units are quieter than those in the main lodge, adjacent to the road. The units, ranging from studios to four-bedroom lakeside apartments, have streamlined California architecture, and many have upstairs sleeping lofts. All rooms come with fully equipped kitchens and fireplaces. Perks include a large private beach directly on the lake, access to a boat dock, and free shuttle service to Heavenly and the casinos.

3535 Lake Tahoe Blvd., South Lake Tahoe, CA 96150. ℂ 800/822-5969 or 530/544-1685. Fax 530/541-6278. www. lakeland-village.com. 212 condo units. $88–$290 double; $135–$975 for a 1- to 4-bedroom town house. Children stay free in parent's room. AE, DISC, MC, V. **Amenities:** 2 heated outdoor pools; nearby golf course; 2 outdoor tennis courts; 2 Jacuzzis; sauna; children's play area and wading pool; seasonal concierge; room service; laundry service; same-day dry cleaning. *In room:* TV/VCR, dataport, kitchen, fridge, coffeemaker, hair dryer, iron.

### Inexpensive

**Viking Motor Lodge** *(Value)*    You get a lot for your money here: agreeable accommodations, access to a private beach, and an easy walk to the casinos and the Heavenly Gondola. It's nothing fancy, but the rooms are clean and pleasant, with all the standard conveniences. If you're traveling with kids, you may want one of the units with a kitchen. Be sure to inquire about the ski and golf packages.

4083 Cedar Ave., South Lake Tahoe, CA 96150. ℂ 800/288-4083 or 530/541-5155. Fax 530/541-5643. www.tahoe viking.com. 76 units. $49–$110 double. Children 11 and under stay free in parent's room. Rates include continental breakfast. Packages available. AE, DC, DISC, MC, V. **Amenities:** Outdoor heated pool; nearby golf course; Jacuzzi. *In room:* TV/VCR, dataport, kitchen in 14 units, fridge on request, coffeemaker, hair dryer, iron.

**Zephyr Cove** ★ *(Value)* *(Kids)*    This is a great place for families in Lake Tahoe—the other being the historic Camp Richardson Resort (see review above). A lakeside bargain in a shady grove of tall pines, about 4 miles from the casinos, this Nevada-side resort has everything you need for a relaxing vacation: a beautiful gold-sand beach, volleyball courts, a beachside bar with strong mai tais, and water toys for rent: pedal boats, kayaks, canoes, and ski boats. Zephyr Cove's pier is also the launching point for cruises on the MS *Dixie II* paddle-wheeler and the *Woodwind II* catamaran. The resort's 28 cabins range in size from studios and cottages to four-bedroom cabins sleeping up to 10. The decor is low-grade Levitz, but all units are very clean with well-equipped kitchens and a front porch with patio furniture. Even in the winter, it's fun to stay here: The resort's snowmobile tours are fantastic, and the Heavenly ski resort is only a 10-minute drive away. The **Zephyr Cove Restaurant** serves hearty American fare for breakfast, lunch, and dinner daily. A free shuttle runs to the restaurants and casinos down the road.

Hwy. 50 at Zephyr Cove, NV 89448. ℂ 775/589-4907. www.zephyrcove.com. 28 cabins. $119–$469 summer; $69–$399 off season. AE, DISC, MC, V. Pets are allowed w/$15 charge per pet, per night. **Amenities:** Restaurant; bar; gift shop; watersports; sailing; beach; volleyball court; horseback riding; snowmobiling. *In room:* TV w/cable and HBO, Internet access, kitchen (w/fridge, oven, microwave, coffeemaker, cookware, dishes, and utensils), private bathroom.

## NORTH SHORE/TAHOE CITY
### Expensive

**Hyatt Regency Lake Tahoe** ★ *(Kids)*    If you like to gamble but hate gauche, glitzy casinos, you'll like the Hyatt in Incline Village. Amid towering pines and mountains on the lake's pristine northeast shore, it's far classier and quieter than the casino hotels you'll find along Stateline. The private beach, loaded with water toys—catamaran cruises, boat rentals, jet skis, parasailing—is available only to guests. The adjoining Lakeside Cottages are a wee bit o' heaven for families or honeymooners who want beachfront access and large, comfortable rooms with unobstructed panoramas of the lake. Popular Camp Hyatt affords kids aged 3 to 12 a break from their parents for the day. The **Lone Eagle Grille,** one of several on-site restaurants, has one of the most beautiful dining rooms on the lake. Be sure to take a walk (or a jog) down Lakeshore Boulevard to see the magnificent estates fronting the water. The latest addition is a 15,000-square-foot spa facility with a multitiered swimming pool and an entire 150-room wing of Spa Terrace guest rooms.

Country Club at Lakeshore, 111 Country Club Dr., Incline Village, NV 89451. (C) **888/899-5019** or 775/832-1234. Fax 775/831-7508. www.laketahoehyatt.com. 405 units, 24 cottages. $160–$330 double; $405–$1,385 cottage. Packages available. AE, DC, DISC, MC, V. **Amenities:** 4 restaurants; 4 lounges; nearby golf course; watersports equipment rental; bike rental; children's program; video arcade; concierge; tour and activities desk; car-rental desk; business center; room service; in-room massage; laundry service; same-day dry cleaning; executive-level rooms. In room: A/C, TV w/pay movies, dataport, minibar, fridge, coffeemaker, hair dryer, iron, safe.

**Northstar-at-Tahoe** ★★★ *Kids*   The owners of Northstar continue to come up with more ways to have fun year-round—the list of activities here is mind-boggling. Northstar prides itself on being the ultimate self-contained family destination, and it's even better now, since completion of the new Village—seven buildings, with 213 new luxury ski-in-ski-out condominium residences, stylish boutiques, outdoor restaurants, an ice rink, and a pedestrian plaza. The Village is surrounded by a honeycomb of fully equipped redwood condos and vacation homes, all nestled among the pines. Lodging options range from a hotel room in the lodge to a five-bedroom house, with every size in between. Summer activities include golf, swimming, tennis, mountain biking, hiking, fly-fishing, rock climbing, rope courses, and horseback riding. See "Skiing & Snowboarding," earlier in this chapter, for winter activities.

Off Hwy. 267, Box 129, Northstar-at-Tahoe, CA 96160. (C) **800/466-6784** or 530/562-1010. Fax 530/562-2215. www.northstarattahoe.com. 100 condominiums plus 262 existing units. $209–$349 double in lodge; $178–$989 condos, homes. Packages available. AE, DISC, MC, V. **Amenities:** 2 restaurants; cafe; deli; bar; 3 pools (outdoor heated, indoor heated, children's); golf course; 10 tennis courts; health club; 3 outdoor Jacuzzis; sauna; bike rental; children and teen center; game room/video arcade; tour and activities desk; business center; babysitting; laundry facilities; ice rink. In room: TV/VCR, kitchen in condos, coffeemaker, hair dryer, iron.

**PlumpJack Squaw Valley Inn** ★★★   Part ski chalet, part boutique hotel, PlumpJack Squaw Valley Inn is among Tahoe's most refined, elegant lodgings. Granted, it lacks the fancy toys offered by its competitor across the valley, The Resort at Squaw Creek (see below), but the PlumpJack is unquestionably more genteel, a tribute to the melding of artistry and hostelry. The hotel is draped in muted, earthy tones, with swirling sconces and sculpted metal accents. Rooms have thick hooded robes, terrycloth slippers, down comforters atop expensive mattresses, and mountain views. The inn's equally fine restaurant, **PlumpJack Café,** is reviewed on p. 264.

1920 Squaw Valley Rd. (P.O. Box 2407), Olympic Valley, CA 96146. (C) **800/323-7666** or 530/583-1576. Fax 530/583-1734. www.plumpjack.com. 61 units. Summer $145–$370; winter $175–$545. Rates include continental breakfast. AE, DISC, MC, V. **Amenities:** Restaurant; bar; heated outdoor pool (seasonal); nearby golf course; 2 Jacuzzis; bike rental; concierge; room service; in-room massage; laundry service; same-day dry cleaning; executive-level rooms. In room: TV w/pay movies, dataport, minibar, fridge, coffeemaker in suites, hair dryer, 1 unit available w/kitchenette.

**The Resort at Squaw Creek** ★★★ *Kids*   The most deluxe resort on the lake is the $130-million Resort at Squaw Creek, a paradise for skiers, golfers, and tennis players. It's ranked among the top 50 resorts in North America by *Conde Nast Traveler.* You can't beat the resort's ski-in/ski-out access to Squaw Valley slopes; the chairlift lands just outside the door. Don't ski? Don't worry. Lots of other sports facilities will divert you, including 20 miles of groomed cross-country skiing trails (marked for hiking and biking in the summer), sleigh and dogsled rides, an ice-skating rink and, in summer, a world-class golf course and an equestrian center with riding stables. Trained counselors lead a Mountain Buddies program for kids ages 4 to 13, with different activities every day. The standard guest rooms are not particularly spacious, but they're well equipped with attractive furnishings, original artwork, and windows that open, with beautiful views. Suites come in all different sizes and configurations. *Tip:* Be sure to ask about the money-saving midweek package deals.

400 Squaw Creek Rd., Olympic Valley, CA 96146. ℂ 800/403-4434 or 530/583-6300. Fax 530/581-6632. www.squaw creek.com. 403 units. $250–$395 double; $450–$1,900 suite. Packages available. AE, DC, DISC, MC, V. Valet parking $15; free self-parking. **Amenities:** 4 restaurants; deli; 4 bars; 3 pools (1 heated); golf course; 2 outdoor tennis courts; health club; region's largest spa; indoor and outdoor Jacuzzis; dry saunas; bike rental; children's program; video arcade; concierge; activities desk; courtesy car; business center; secretarial services; shopping arcade; salon; room service; in-room massage; babysitting; laundry service; same-day dry cleaning. *In room:* A/C, TV w/pay movies, dataport, kitchen in some units, minibar, coffeemaker, hair dryer, iron.

**The Shore House** 🎔🎔    This romantic little bed-and-breakfast inn, right on the lake, is a real charmer. Each individually decorated room has its own entrance, handmade log furniture, knotty-pine walls, a gas-log fireplace, and a blissfully comfortable feather bed. Guests have access to a private beach and landscaped lawn that overlook the lake and an in-house spa. Boat owners can even make use of the inn's six buoys and private dock. If you're planning to tie the knot, the charming hosts will provide everything you need for a beautiful ceremony, including an outdoor lakeside setting and a honeymoon cottage with a two-person spa tub.

7170 N. Lake Blvd. (P.O. Box 499), Tahoe Vista, CA 96148. ℂ 800/207-5160 or 530/546-7270. Fax 530/546-7130. www.shorehouselaketahoe.com. 8 units, 1 cottage. $160–$240 double; $225–$285 cottage. Rates include full breakfast. DISC, MC, V. **Amenities:** Jacuzzi; massage. *In room:* A/C, fridge, hair dryer, no phone.

**Moderate**

**Cal-Neva Resort, Spa & Casino** 🎔    You might guess from the name of this place that the state line literally runs right through it, but you might never imagine its colorful, sometimes scandalous history. It's here that Marilyn Monroe allegedly had her rendezvous with John F. Kennedy (you can even see the secret tunnel), and ownership passed around to moguls with names like Pretty Boy, Babyface, and Sinatra, who built the famed Celebrity Room. Respectability has since laid claim to the Cal-Neva, however, and it's now a popular, reputable lakeside resort. Almost all the elegantly decorated rooms have lake views. Besides the casino (on the Nevada side of the hotel, of course), the Cal-Neva offers a full array of sport and spa options, a complete wedding-planning service, and two wedding chapels. Even if you don't stay here, stop by and take a look.

2 Stateline Rd. (Box 368), Crystal Bay, NV 89402-0368. ℂ 800/225-6382 or 775/832-4000. Fax 775/831-9007. www.calnevaresort.com. 188 units, 9 chalets, 3 bungalows. $79–$189 double; $179–$269 suite, chalet, or bungalow. Packages available. AE, DC, DISC, MC, V. **Amenities:** Lakeview restaurant; heated outdoor pool; nearby golf course; 2 outdoor tennis courts; full-service European health spa; Jacuzzi; large video arcade; concierge; business center; salon; room service. *In room:* A/C, TV, fax, dataport, coffeemaker, hair dryer, iron.

**Meeks Bay Resort** 🎔    Ten miles south of Tahoe City, rustic Meeks Bay Resort is one of the oldest hostelries on the lake and something of a historical landmark. Opened as a public campground in 1920, its sweeping lakefront location has one of the finest beaches on the lake. During the next 50 years, the resort grew to include cabins and other improvements, and attracted many celebrities from Southern California. Acquired by the U.S. Forest Service in 1974, the property is open during summers only. Most rentals are on a weekly basis and consist of motel lodging or modest wood cabins near the lake. Facilities include a full marina with boat rentals, a campground with RV access ($20 a night, 4-night minimum), a beachfront snack bar, a playground, and a visitor center with a cultural display, coffee bar, and retail store. The Kehlet House, set on a rock that juts into the lake, is the resort's prime accommodation. Owned at one time by William Hewlett, co-founder of the Hewlett-Packard Corporation, and later the summer residence of billionaire Gordon Getty, it has seven bedrooms, three bathrooms, a large kitchen, a living room, and water on three sides. The entire house is rented by the week, sleeps a dozen, and costs $3,850. Make all reservations here early.

P.O. Box 787, Tahoma, CA 96142. 📞 877/326-3357 or 530/525-6946. Fax 530/525-4028. www.meeksbayresort. com. 21 units, 28 campsites. $85–$195 double per night, $770–$1,650 per week. AE, MC, V. Open May–Nov only. **Amenities:** Watersports gear rental. *In room:* Kitchen in log cabins.

### River Ranch Lodge & Restaurant ★★

The River Ranch Lodge has long been one of my favorite places to stay in Lake Tahoe. Alongside the Truckee River, the lodge is minutes away from Alpine Meadows and Squaw Valley ski resorts, and a short drive (or ride along the bike path) into Tahoe City. The best rooms have balconies overlooking the river. All have a handsome mountain-home decor, lodgepole-pine furniture, and down comforters. Room nos. 9 and 10, the farthest from the road, are my top choices. In summer, guests relax under umbrellas on the huge patio overlooking the river, working down burgers and beer while watching the rafters float by. During ski season, the River Ranch's spectacular circular cocktail lounge and dining area, which cantilevers over the river, is a popular après-ski hangout. Another big hit is the handsome **River Ranch Lodge Restaurant,** which serves fresh seafood, thick steaks, rack of lamb, and more exotic meats, such as wood-oven roasted Montana elk loin with a dried-cherry/port sauce.

On Hwy. 89, at Alpine Meadows Rd. (P.O. Box 197), Tahoe City, CA 96145. 📞 800/535-9900 or 530/583-4264. Fax 530/583-7237. www.riverranchlodge.com. 19 units. $100–$160 double. Rates include continental breakfast. Packages available. AE, MC, V. **Amenities:** Restaurant; bar; golf course nearby; concierge. *In room:* TV, dataport, iron.

### Sunnyside Lodge ★★

Built as a private home in 1908, this hotel and restaurant is one of the few grand old lodges left on the lake. Two miles south of Tahoe City, it looks very much like a giant, sophisticated wood cabin, complete with dormers, steep pitched roofs, and natural-wood siding. Stretching across the building, a large deck fronts a tiny marina and gravel beach. The Lakefront rooms (suites 30 and 31 and rooms 32 to 39) are the most desirable and go for about $20 more than the others—well worth the added expense. Five units have rock fireplaces. Most of the lodge's ground floor is dominated by the popular **Sunnyside Restaurant** (p. 265).

1850 W. Lake Blvd. (P.O. Box 5969), Tahoe City, CA 96145. 📞 800/822-2754 or 530/583-7200. Fax 530/583-2551. www.sunnysideresort.com. 23 units. $100–$250 double. Rates include continental breakfast. Packages available. AE, MC, V. **Amenities:** Restaurant; bar; nearby golf course; watersports equipment rental; room service. *In room:* TV/VCR, fridge in some units, hair dryer, iron.

### Tahoma Meadows Bed & Breakfast ★ (Kids)

This historic bed-and-breakfast consists of cute red cabins nestled on a gentle forest slope surrounded by flowers and sugar pines. The units are individually decorated with paintings of bucolic settings, a private bathroom, and a comfy king- or queen-size bed; four units have gas-log fireplaces. The largest cabins, Treehouse and Sugar Pine, sleep up to six, ideal for families. The excellent **Stoneyridge Café,** in the main lodge, serves breakfast daily (included in the room rate) and dinner Thursday through Saturday. Nearby activities include ski-ing at Ski Homewood (including shuttle service) and sunbathing at the lakeshore across the street. The friendly owners, Ulli and Dick White, will happily give advice on the best nearby hiking and fishing spots (Dick's an avid fly-fisherman).

6821 W. Lake Blvd. (P.O. Box 810), Homewood, CA 96141. © 800/355-1596 or 530/525-1553. www.tahomameadows. com. 14 units. $95–$295 double. Rates include full breakfast. AE, DISC, MC, V. 8½ miles from Tahoe City; Pets accepted in some units w/$25 fee. **Amenities:** Cafe; nearby golf course. *In room:* TV/VCR, kitchen in some units, no phone.

## Inexpensive

### Ferrari's Crown Resort (Value)

If you're looking for convenient lakefront accom-modations at a reasonable price, this family-operated motel is a great choice. The Ferraris have proudly extended a warm welcome to guests, children included, since 1957. Family suites, completely equipped with kitchenettes and gas fireplaces, can sleep up to seven. It's nothing fancy, but it's well run, the rooms are very inviting, and you can't beat the location. Plan a trip during the off season to take advantage of their great bargain rates.

8200 N. Lake Blvd. (P.O. Box 845), Kings Beach, CA 96143. © 800/645-2260 or 530/546-3388. Fax 530/546-3851. www.tahoecrown.com. 45 units. $45–$95 double; $70–$210 2-bedroom suites or lakefront rooms. Packages avail-able. AE, DISC, MC, V. **Amenities:** Heated outdoor pool (seasonal); nearby golf course; free passes to nearby health club; Jacuzzi. *In room:* A/C, TV, stocked kitchenette, fridge, coffeemaker, hair dryer, iron in some units.

### Lake of the Sky Motor Inn

This remodeled 1960s-style A-frame motel in the heart of Tahoe City offers clean, quiet, inexpensive accommodations in a central location—only steps away from shops and restaurants and a main stop for the ski shuttles. You'll get just the basics here—TV, phone, bathroom—so plan on spending most of your time outdoors. Some rooms have lake views, and the landscaped picnic and barbecue area is attractive.

955 N. Lake Blvd. (P.O. Box 227), Tahoe City, CA 96145. © 530/583-3305. Fax 530/583-7621. www.lakeofthe skyinn.com. 23 units. $59–$129 double. Children 11 and under stay free in parent's room. Rates include continental breakfast. AE, DC, DISC, MC, V. **Amenities:** Heated outdoor pool (seasonal); nearby golf course. *In room:* TV, data-port, fridge in some units.

### Tamarack Lodge 🟊

Tamarack is one of the oldest lodges on the North Shore—so old it was a favorite haunt of Clark Gable and Gary Cooper. Now, it's one of the best bets for the frugal traveler. Hidden among a 4-acre cadre of pines just east of Tahoe City, the Tamarack Lodge consists of a few old cabins, five "poker rooms," and a modern (and far less nostalgic) motel unit. The rooms in the motel unit are the least appealing, but they're certainly clean and comfortable. The cabins all have kitchenettes and can hold up to four guests, but the most popular rooms by far are the original poker rooms (where Gable and Cooper used to play cards) lined with gleaming knotty pine. Complimentary coffee and tea are served in the lobby, and rollaway beds are available for only $5 extra. The beach is within walking distance, but you'll need a car to make forays into town.

2311 N. Lake Blvd. (P.O. Box 859), Tahoe City, CA 96145. © 888/824-6323 or 530/583-3350. Fax 530/583-3531. www.tamarackattahoe.com. 17 units, 4 cabins. $54–$145 double. DISC, MC, V. *In room:* TV.

## WHERE TO DINE

### SOUTH SHORE & SOUTH LAKE TAHOE

#### Expensive

##### Evan's American Gourmet Café 🟊🟊 AMERICAN/CONTINENTAL

This restaurant's impeccable service, award-winning wine list, and unyielding attention to detail serve as a perfect backdrop for the creative culinary artistry of Candice or Evan

Williams. The philosophy here is to use only the finest, freshest ingredients and not overwhelm them with heavy sauces or overstylized culinary technique. The cuisine is an original blend of styles from around the world, with each dish being an artistic creation. For appetizers, typical choices are sautéed Dungeness crab cakes on roasted red-pepper purée with crème fraîche or seared Sonoma foie gras with curried ice cream and roast pineapple. Entrees might include house-smoked-duck-breast salad with microgreens and papaya vinaigrette, or roast Cevena venison with balsamic roast cherries, fresh tarragon, and lacquered root vegetables. If you have room, the desserts are luscious and beautiful. Seats are limited in this cozy little restaurant so be sure to call ahead for reservations.

536 Emerald Bay Rd., South Lake Tahoe. ⓒ 530/542-1990. www.evanstahoe.com. Reservations required (must confirm by 4pm). Main courses $18–$25. DISC, MC, V. Daily 5:30–9:30pm.

**Fresh Ketch** ⭐ SEAFOOD   In a small marina at the foot of Tahoe Keys Boulevard, Fresh Ketch has long been regarded as South Lake's premier seafood restaurant. Try for a window table so you can watch the marina activities. For starters, I always order half a dozen oysters and the seared *ahi* tuna with ponzu and wasabi dipping sauces. Then it's on to the sautéed sea bass encrusted with pistachio, herbs, and garlic, or the big Alaskan king crab, steamed in the shell and served with drawn butter. The menu also includes a modest selection of meat and poultry dishes, such as the great surf and turf of petite mignon and lobster. For dessert, the calorie fest continues with a big slice of Kimo's Hula Pie. Prices are a bit steep, but you can also belly up with the locals and order from the extensive bar menu, with everything from blackened mahimahi to fresh-fish tacos and fish and chips for under $10. Live music acts perform Friday and Saturday evenings.

2433 Venice Dr. ⓒ 530/541-5683. www.thefreshketch.com. Reservations recommended. Main courses $17–$24; market price for crab and lobster. AE, DC, DISC, MC, V. Daily 11:30am–10pm (bar until 10pm).

### Moderate

**Cantina Bar & Grill** ⭐ MEXICAN   The Cantina Bar & Grill is a favorite local hangout and serves the best Mexican food in South Lake. With friendly service, sports on three TVs, and 30 kinds of beer, joviality reigns. The menu is well priced and extensive, offering Cal-Mex specialties such as tacos, burritos, and enchiladas along with a half-dozen Southwestern dishes such as smoked chicken polenta and grilled pork chops with jalapeño mashed potatoes. The steak fajitas get a thumbs-up, as do the barbecued baby back ribs. To demonstrate their sense of whimsy and ethnic appeal, they offer an Oriental chicken salad and a Southwestern Reuben sandwich, as well as a few vegetarian selections.

765 Emerald Bay Rd. ⓒ 530/544-1233. www.cantinatahoe.com. Main courses $8–$15. MC, V. Daily 11:30am–10:30pm (bar until midnight).

**Ivano's** ⭐⭐ *Finds* ITALIAN   Although Ivano Costantini is well known among South Lake's connoisseurs of authentic Italian cuisine, his bistro is easy to miss. On Nevada's southeastern shoreline, it's recessed into a tiny business complex off the highway. But follow the aromas of garlic, olive oil, and fresh basil, and you'll find the front door. Ivano, the charismatic owner and maitre d', is usually there to greet guests and escort them to his intimate dining room adorned with crisp white tablecloths, fresh flowers, and framed paintings of Italian coastal towns. Entrees range from reasonably priced pasta standards such as *tortellini di Parma,* linguine *puttanesca,* and *fettuccini al Bolognese,* to well-prepared *secondi* classics. My favorite dish is the *filetto di Giovanni,* thinly sliced tenderloin marinated in olive oil, vinegar, and rosemary, then quickly seared to lock in the juices (no fusion confusion at this restaurant). The *scaloppine parmigiana* (veal with fresh tomato sauce, prosciutto, and mozzarella) is also quite good. The lengthy wine list features more than 100 wines from Italy and California.

605 Hwy. 50, #4, Zephyr Cove. 🕿 775/586-1070. Reservations recommended. Entrees $10–$19. AE, DISC, MC, V. Daily 5–10pm.

**The Naked Fish** ★★ SUSHI   The Naked Fish in South Lake is the best sushi bar in Tahoe. I can never understand a word the Japanese chefs are saying to me, but I'm not paying much attention; the warm-butter-soft *hamachi nigiri* (yellowtail) has made my toes curl again. The colorful aquamarine theme with mermaids floating across the walls adds to the laid-back atmosphere of this locally owned Japanese restaurant. Before you open the menu, read the "specials" board above the sushi bar—this is the *really* fresh stuff, such as the deftly shelled live scallop sashimi that's still moving as the chef artfully carves it. In the spirit of an authentic sushi bar, the chefs are friendly and talkative, particularly if you buy them a beer. Wimps can order cooked dinners such as sesame-crusted halibut and teriyaki chicken, but it's the flavorful rolls, tender cuts of nigiri, and festive bar that sushi hounds will appreciate.

3940 Lake Tahoe Blvd. (at the junction of Hwy. 50 and Pioneer Trail). 🕿 530/541-3474. Reservations recommended for parties of 6 or more. Main courses $14–$23; sushi $4–$11. AE, DC, DISC, MC, V. Lunch Sat–Sun 11:30am–2pm; dinner daily 5–9pm.

## Inexpensive

**Ernie's Coffee Shop** DINER   The undisputed king of coffee shops in South Lake Tahoe is Ernie's, which has been serving huge plates of good old American, cholesterol-laden grub to locals since the Nixon administration. The food is far from original (omelets, bacon and eggs, pancakes), so it must be the perpetually friendly service, low prices, and huge portions that attract the steady stream of customers. Another good reason to come here is that Ernie's is located next to the cheapest gas station in town, so you can top off your appetite and your tank in one stop. The milkshakes are great, too.

1146 Emerald Bay Rd./Hwy. 89. 🕿 530/541-2161. Main dishes $5–$9. No credit cards. Daily 6am–2pm.

**Sprouts Natural Foods Café** *Value* HEALTH FOOD/JUICES   Sprouts owner Tyler Cannon has filled a much-needed niche in South Lake, serving wholesome food that looks good, tastes good, and *is* good. Most everything is made in-house, including the soups, smoothies, and fresh-squeezed juices. Menu items range from rice bowls to sandwiches (try the Real Tahoe Turkey), huge burritos, coffee drinks, muffins, fresh-fruit smoothies, and a marvelous mayo-free tuna sandwich made with yogurt and packed with fresh veggies. Order from the counter, then scramble for a vacant seat (outdoor tables are coveted). This is also an excellent place to pack a picnic lunch.

3123 Harrison Ave. (at U.S. 50 and Alameda St., next to Lakeview Sports). 🕿 530/541-6969. Meals $4.50–$6.75. No credit cards. Daily 8am–9pm.

**Yellow Sub** *Value* SANDWICHES   When it comes to picnic supplies, the competition is stiff in South Lake Tahoe; this block alone has three sandwich shops. Still, my favorite is Yellow Sub, voted best deli sandwich shop by readers of the *Tahoe Daily Tribune* for 9 years straight. It sells 21 versions of overstuffed subs—made in 6-inch and 12-inch varieties—as well as several kinds of wraps. The shop is in a small shopping center across from the El Dorado Campground.

983 Tallac Ave. (at U.S. 50). 🕿 530/541-8808. Sandwiches and wraps $3.20–$7.15. No credit cards. Daily 10:30am–10pm.

## NORTH SHORE/TAHOE CITY
### Expensive

**PlumpJack Café** ★★ MODERN AMERICAN Squaw Valley investors have spent oodles of money trying to turn the ski resort into a world-class destination, and one big step in the right direction is the sleek, sexy PlumpJack Café. Although dinner prices have dropped slightly (guests balked at the original rates), none of PlumpJack's standards have diminished. Expect impeccable service regardless of your attire (this is, after all, a ski resort). Menu choices range from spicy Maine soft-shell crab with pickled ginger vinaigrette and chili *tobiko* to milk-brined, double-cut pork chop with Yorkshire pudding and summer vegetables, plus a fabulous dish of braised oxtail paired with horseradish mashed potatoes and carrots. Those familiar with PlumpJack in San Francisco know that the reasonably priced wine list is among the nation's best.

In the PlumpJack Squaw Valley Inn, 1920 Squaw Valley Rd., Squaw Valley. ② **530/583-1576.** www.plumpjack.com. Reservations recommended. Main courses $17–$20. AE, MC, V. Daily 7–10am, 11:30am–2:30pm, and 6–10pm.

**Wild Goose** ★★★ CONTEMPORARY AMERICAN Without question, Wild Goose is the finest restaurant in Lake Tahoe and one of my favorites in all of California. It offers the best of everything: a panoramic view of the lake, sleek yet warmly textured modern design elements, and contemporary American cuisine on par with the Bay Area's finest. The restaurant is fashioned after those classic lake cruisers of the 1920s with a profusion of finely polished mahogany and metal; large picture windows overlook a terraced patio dining area with a postcard view. The beautifully arranged presentations are expertly prepared and presented by a well-trained staff. A recent meal started with a fried-squash-blossom appetizer stuffed with herbed goat cheese, followed by curried blue claw crab with mango crème fraîche. The main courses we ordered were superb: wild mushroom-crusted halibut with purslane salad and creamy mashed potatoes, and hoisin-barbecued salmon with braised bok choy and shiitake mushrooms, topped with a coconut–green curry sauce. In the winter, request a table near the custom-built fireplace, and be sure to arrive before the sun sets.

7320 N. Lake Blvd, Tahoe Vista. ② **530/546-3640.** www.wildgoosetahoe.com. Reservations recommended. Entrees $10–$29. AE, DISC, MC, V. Daily 5–10pm.

**Wolfdale's** ★★ CALIFORNIA/JAPANESE Wolfdale's has long been one of Tahoe's finest restaurants, where everything from focaccia to sausages, smoked fish, and desserts is prepared in-house. Chef-owner Douglas Dale knows how to put an international spin on regional ingredients, fusing flavors and textures of the East and the West. Although the menu changes frequently, dinner might begin with soft-shell crab tempura, vegetable spring roll with a Thai curry-ginger sauce, or spinach salad tossed with smoked local trout, olives, and grated eggs. Main courses are equally inventive, such as roasted quail stuffed with fennel sausage and onions served on a bed of kale, or grilled Columbia River sturgeon with mushroom *duxelles* and tomato coulis. I prefer to dine at the small bar, but if it's nice out, request a table on the outdoor deck.

640 N. Lake Blvd., Tahoe City. ② **530/583-5700.** www.wolfdales.com. Reservations recommended. Main courses $18–$24. DISC, MC, V. Wed–Mon 6–10pm (daily July–Aug).

### Moderate

**Gar Woods Grill & Pier** ★ AMERICAN Named after the builder of those beautiful mahogany race boats that used to grace the lake in the 1930s and 1940s, Gar Woods attempts to evoke and pay homage to that era. Whether folks are watching *Monday*

*Night Football* or drinking a famous Wet Woody, it seems as though something is always going on in the bar. On a sunny day, it's great fun to sit on the lakeside deck to enjoy the good food and good cheer. The menu is wide-ranging, covering everything from a shrimp-and-lobster bisque to a pepper-and-garlic turkey burger with curly fries. Appetizers go from beer-battered coconut prawns to sashimi. Dinner entrees include nothing out of the ordinary, but the preparation is good and the service is friendly. Try the sumptuous Sunday brunch; it's more food than you could ever imagine for $26.

5000 N. Lake Blvd., Carnelian Bay. ✆ **800/BY-TAHOE** or 530/546-3366. www.garwoods.com. Lunch $9–$14; dinner $14–$27; brunch $26. AE, DISC, MC, V. Mon–Sat 11:30am–10pm; Sun 10:30am–10pm.

### Sunnyside Restaurant ★ CALIFORNIA

In summer when the sun's shining, the most highly coveted tables in Tahoe are those on Sunnyside's lakeside veranda. Guests can also dine in the lodge's more traditional Chris Craft Dining Room with its 1930s aura. Nothing is extraordinary here: The lunch menu has fresh pastas, burgers, chicken, and fish sandwiches, together with a variety of soups and salads. Dinners are fancier, with main courses such as Australian lobster tail, lamb chops with roasted-garlic chutney butter, and fresh salmon oven-baked on a cedar plank. In the winter, the bar has a lively après-ski scene where both tourists and locals come to watch ski flicks on the big screen and refuel on inexpensive appetizers.

At the Sunnyside Lodge, 1850 W. Lake Blvd., Tahoe City. ✆ **800/822-2754** or 530/583-7200. www.sunnyside resort.com. Main courses $14–$24. AE, DISC, MC, V. Oct–June daily 4–9:30pm; July–Sept Sun–Thurs 11am–9:30pm, Fri–Sat 11am–10pm; year-round Sun brunch 9:30am–2pm.

## Inexpensive

### Bridgetender Tavern and Grill (Value) PUB GRUB

Although it's in one of the most popular tourist areas in North Lake, the Bridgetender is a locals' hangout through and through. Still, they're surprisingly tolerant of out-of-towners, who come for the cheap grub and huge selection of draft beers. Big burgers, salads, pork ribs, and fish and chips round out the menu. It's all very filling and inexpensive. In summer, dine at the patio among the pines.

65 W. Lake Blvd. (at Fanny Bridge), Tahoe City. ✆ **530/583-3342**. Burgers, salads, and ribs $5–$8. DISC, MC, V. Daily 11am–2am.

### Fire Sign Café ★ (Value) AMERICAN

Choosing a place to have breakfast in North Tahoe is a no-brainer. Since the late 1970s, the Fire Sign Café has been the locals' choice—which explains the lines out the door on weekends. Just about everything is made from scratch, such as the delicious coffee cake that accompanies the big plates of bacon and eggs, or blackberry-buckwheat pancakes. Even the salmon for chef and owner Bob Young's legendary salmon omelet is smoked in-house. Lunch—burgers, salads, sandwiches, burritos, and more—is also quite popular, particularly when the outdoor patio is open.

1785 W. Lake Blvd., Tahoe City. ✆ **530/583-0871**. Breakfast and lunch $4–$9. MC, V. Daily 7am–3pm.

### Rosie's Café ★ (Kids) AMERICAN

Two floors' worth of tables usually ensures a short wait—if one at all—at this shingled, lodge-style restaurant in the heart of downtown Tahoe City. Family-owned and operated, Rosie's has been serving quality comfort food to legions of vacationers since it opened in 1980. It's noisy and casual, perfect for families (with children's menus and free balloons even), and servings are plentiful. A big menu offers breakfasts designed to carbo-load skiers, as well as hamburgers, grilled chicken sandwiches, and chef-type salads for lunch. The two-course dinners mostly star fish and meat (the Yankee pot roast with mashed potatoes and gravy is hard to resist on a cold night). You won't mistake it for gourmet, but you'll like the value and ethos.

571 North Lake Blvd., Tahoe City. © 530/583-8504. www.rosiescafe.com. Reservations accepted for dinner. Main courses $5–$10 lunch, $10–$20 dinner. DISC, MC, V. Daily 6:30am–10pm.

## TAHOE AFTER DARK

Tahoe is not known for its nightlife, although something is always going on in the showrooms of the major casinos on the South Shore. Call **Harrah's** (© 775/588-6611), **Harveys** (© 775/588-2411), **Caesars** (© 775/588-3515), and the **Horizon** (© 775/588-6211) for current show schedules and prices. Most cocktail shows cost $15 to $45. On the North Shore, **Bullwhackers Pub,** at the Resort at Squaw Creek (© 530/583-6617; p. 258), hosts live music nightly. The **Pierce Street Annex,** 850 N. Lake Blvd. (© 530/583-5800), behind the Safeway in Tahoe City, has pool tables, shuffleboard, and DJ dancing every night. It's one of the livelier places around. If it's just a casual cocktail you're after, my favorite spot is the cozy fireside lounge at **River Ranch Lodge,** which cantilevers over a turbulent stretch of the Truckee River, on Highway 89 at the entrance to Alpine Meadows (© **530/583-4264**).

## 2 Mount Shasta & the Cascades 🌟🌟

274 miles N of San Francisco

Chances are, your first glimpse of Mount Shasta's majestic, snowcapped peak will result in a twang of awe. A dormant volcano with a 17-mile-diameter base, it stands in virtual isolation 14,162 feet above the sea. When John Muir first saw Shasta from 50 miles away in 1874, he wrote: "[I] was alone and weary. Yet my blood turned to wine, and I have not been weary since." He went on to describe it as "the pole star of the landscape," which indeed it is.

Keep in mind, however, that dining and lodging in these parts lean more toward sustenance than indulgence: It's the fresh air, not fresh fish, that lures visitors this far north. You can leave the dinner jacket at home—all that's really required when visiting the Far North are a pair of broken-in hiking boots, binoculars (the bald eagle is a common sight in these parts), some warm clothing, and an adventurous spirit.

## ESSENTIALS

**GETTING THERE** From San Francisco, take I-80 to I-505 to I-5 to Redding. From the coast, pick up Highway 299 East north of Arcata, to Redding.

**Redding Municipal Airport,** 6751 Woodrum Circle (© **530/224-4321**), is serviced by **United Express** (© 800/241-6522) and **Horizon Air** (© 800/547-9308). **Amtrak** (© 800/USA-RAIL) stops in Dunsmuir and Redding.

**VISITOR INFORMATION** Regional information can be obtained from the following organizations: **Shasta Cascade Wonderland Association,** 1699 Hwy. 273, Anderson, CA 96007 (© 800/474-2782 or 530/365-7500; www.shastacascade.org); **Mount Shasta Visitors Bureau,** 300 Pine St., Mount Shasta, CA 96067 (© 800/926-4865 or 530/926-4865; www.mtshastachamber.com); **Redding Convention & Visitors Bureau,** 777 Auditorium Dr., Redding, CA 96001 (© 800/874-7562 or 530/225-4100; www.visitredding.org); and **Trinity County Chamber of Commerce,** 210 N. Main St., P.O. Box 517, Weaverville, CA 96093 (© 800/487-4648 or 530/623-6101; www.trinitycounty.com).

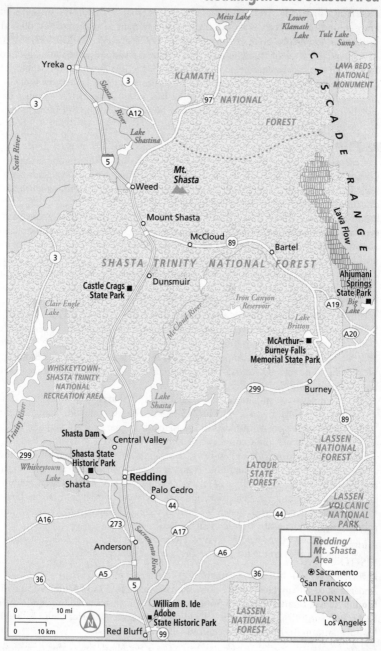

Meiss Lake

Lower Klamath Lake

Tule Lake Sump

Yreka

CASCADE RANGE

LAVA BEDS NATIONAL MONUMENT

KLAMATH

3

Shasta River

A12

97

NATIONAL

FOREST

Lake Shastina

5

Mt. Shasta

Scott River

Weed

Lava Flow

Mount Shasta

McCloud

89

Bartel

3

SHASTA TRINITY NATIONAL FOREST

Ahjumani Springs State Park

Castle Crags State Park

Dunsmuir

Iron Canyon Reservoir

A19

Big Lake

Clair Engle Lake

McCloud River

Lake Britton

A20

McArthur–Burney Falls Memorial State Park

WHISKEYTOWN–SHASTA TRINITY NATIONAL RECREATION AREA

Lake Shasta

299

Burney

89

Trinity River

LASSEN NATIONAL FOREST

Shasta Dam

Central Valley

LATOUR STATE FOREST

299

Shasta State Historic Park

Whiskeytown Lake

Shasta

Redding

Palo Cedro

44

LASSEN VOLCANIC NATIONAL PARK

A16

273

Sacramento River

A17

44

A6

Anderson

36

A5

5

36

LASSEN NATIONAL FOREST

0    10 mi
0    10 km

N

William B. Ide Adobe State Historic Park

Red Bluff

99

Redding/ Mt. Shasta Area

Sacramento

San Francisco

CALIFORNIA

Los Angeles

## THE REPUBLIC OF CALIFORNIA

En route to Mount Shasta from the south, you may want to stop near Red Bluff at **William B. Ide Adobe State Historic Park,** 21659 Adobe Rd. (© **530/529-8599**), for a picnic along the Sacramento River and a visit to an adobe home dating back to 1852. The 4-acre park commemorates William B. Ide, the Republic of California's first and only president. (The Republic of California was proclaimed on June 14, 1846, following the Bear Flag Rebellion, and lasted only 3 weeks.) In summer the park is open from 8am to sunset, and the house from noon to 4pm; call ahead in winter. Parking is $3 per vehicle.

## REDDING

The major town and gateway to the area is Redding, the hub of the panoramic Shasta-Cascade region, at the top of the Sacramento Valley. From here, you can turn westward into the wilderness forest of Trinity and the Klamath Mountains, or north and east into the Cascades and Shasta Trinity National Forest.

In Redding, with its fast-food joints, gas stations, and cheap motels, summer heat generally hovers around 100°F (38°C). A city of some 80,000, Redding is the transportation hub for the upper reaches of Northern California. It has little of interest; it's mainly useful as a base for exploring the natural wonders nearby. Information is available from the **Redding Convention & Visitors Bureau,** 777 Auditorium Dr., Redding, CA 96001 (© **800/874-7562** or 530/225-4100; www.visitredding.org), west of I-5 on Highway 299. It's open Monday through Friday from 8am to 5pm. Ahead and northeast, Mount Shasta rises to a height of more than 14,000 feet. From Redding, I-5 cuts north over the Pit River Bridge, crossing Lake Shasta and leading eventually to the mount itself. Before striking north, however, you may want to explore **Lake Shasta** and see **Shasta Dam.** Another option is to take a detour west of Redding to Weaverville, Whiskeytown–Shasta Trinity National Recreation Area, and Trinity Lake (see "Whiskeytown National Recreation Area" below).

About 3 miles west, stop at the old mining town of **Shasta,** which has been converted into a state historic park (© **530/243-8194**). Founded on gold, Shasta was the "Queen City" of the northern mines in the Klamath Range. Its life was short, and it expired in 1872, when the Central Pacific Railroad bypassed it in favor of Redding. Today the business district is a ghost town, complete with a restored general store and a Masonic hall. The **1861 courthouse** is now a museum where you can view the jail and a gallows out back, as well as a remarkable collection of California art assembled by Mae Helen Bacon Boggs. The collection includes works by Maynard Dixon, Grace Hudson, and many others. It's open Wednesday through Sunday from 10am to 5pm. Admission is $2 for adults; children visit for free.

Continue along Highway 299 west to Highway 3 north, which will take you to Weaverville and then to the west side of the lake and Trinity Center.

### WHERE TO STAY

In addition to Tiffany House (see below), Redding has a **Red Lion Hotel,** 1830 Hilltop Drive, Redding (© **800/733-5466** or 530/221-8700; www.redlion.com) and a **La Quinta Inn,** 2180 Hilltop Drive, Redding (© **866/725-1661** or 530/221-8200; www.laquinta.com). Both are fine choices.

**Tiffany House Bed and Breakfast Inn**   On a hill above town, this beautifully refurbished Cape Cod–style inn has a sweeping view of the Lassen Mountain Range, visible from every guest room and cottage, as well as from the oversize deck above the garden in back. Common areas include the music room with a piano, and the Victorian parlor with a fireplace, games, and puzzles. Each guest room is appointed with a queen-size bed and antique furnishings, and all have private bathrooms and soft robes. Lavinia's Cottage is our top choice, with a 7-foot spa tub, sitting area, and magnificent laurel-wreath iron bed.

1510 Barbara Rd., Redding, CA 96003. ℭ 530/244-3225. www.tiffanyhousebb.com. 4 units. $90–$110 double; $140 cottage. Rates include full breakfast. AE, DISC, MC, V. **Amenities:** Outdoor pool; nearby golf courses; Jacuzzi; game room. *In room:* A/C, hair dryer, no phone.

## WHERE TO DINE

**Buz's Crab Stand** ★★ *(Finds)* SEAFOOD    Don't let the Naugahyde booths and Formica tables fool you: This funky fish joint is one of the best roadside seafood stands in Northern California. What's been drawing fans here from all over the state for more than 30 years are the "seafood baskets," packed with crisp potato rounds, fresh-baked sourdough bread, and whatever's in season: prawns, oysters, scallops, clam strips, calamari, catfish, even Cajun halibut. The fish and chips are also excellent. From December to May, crab's the hot ticket, served freshly boiled from the crab pots on the patio and served with drawn butter and cocktail sauce. *Tip:* Visit Buz's website and print the fantastic cioppino recipe—I've slayed 'em at dinner parties with this one.

2159 East St., at Cypress Ave. ℭ 530/243-2120. www.buzscrab.com. Main courses $2.50–$10. MC, V. Daily 11am–9pm.

**Jack's Grill** ★ STEAKHOUSE    This building was originally constructed in 1835 as a secondhand-clothing store. The second floor served as a brothel in the late 1930s, and an entrepreneur named Jack Young set up the main floor as a steakhouse (his establishment serviced all of a body's needs, you might say). Today it's a local favorite. Waiting for a table over drinks in the bar is part of the fun. Good old-fashioned red meat—thick 1-pound steaks, tender brochettes, fat steak sandwiches—is supplemented by a couple of seafood dishes, such as deep-fried jumbo prawns and ocean scallops. It's a very fetching spot, with good, honest tavern food and a jovial crowd. Be prepared to wait on weekends.

1743 California St. ℭ 530/241-9705. www.jacksgrillredding.com. Reservations not accepted. Main courses $9.15–$22. AE, DISC, MC, V. Mon–Sat 4–11pm.

## WEAVERVILLE

Weaverville was a gold mining town in the 1850s, and the **Jake Jackson Memorial Museum–Trinity County Historical Park,** 508 Main St. (ℭ 530/623-5211), captures part of its history. The collection, from firearms to household items, tells an interesting story about the residents—Native Americans, miners, pioneers, especially the Chinese. In the Gold Rush era, the town was half Chinese, with a Chinatown of about 2,500 residents. Admission is free, but a donation of $1 is suggested.

Across the parking lot, you can view the oldest continuously used Taoist temple in California at the **Joss House State Historic Park** (© 530/623-5284). This well-preserved temple was built by immigrant Chinese miners in 1874. Admission is $2 for adults, free for children ages 16 and under.

## WHERE TO DINE

**LaGrange Café** ★★ *Finds* CREATIVE TRADITIONAL CUISINE  Weaverville isn't exactly a star in the culinary firmament, but there is one bright spot, far and away the best food in town. Heck, it would be considered really good in Redding, Sacramento, or Tahoe. In Weaverville's historic district, two adjoining buildings were combined and stripped to the original brick walls to make a spacious, attractive dining area with a sitdown bar. Chef and owner Sharon Heryford's menu includes the local favorite—chicken enchiladas with marinated tri-tip—plus seasonal items such as the local rabbit braised with mushrooms, fresh herbs, and white wine. The tender Duane's Chicken served with wheat pilaf is also popular. The interesting menu includes other things such as buffalo steaks, venison bratwurst, and wild-boar sausages. Heryford's buffalo ragout won third place in a national contest. The 135-plus selections on the wine list make it one of the strongest in Northern California. Desserts, like a sinfully rich banana cream pie and that quintessential comfort food, bread pudding, are all made on the premises.

226 Main St. © 530/623-5325. Main courses $10–$25. AE, DISC, MC, V. Mon–Thurs 11am–9pm; Fri–Sun 11am–10pm.

## THE TRINITY ALPS

West of Weaverville stretch the Trinity Alps, with Thompson Peak rising to more than 9,000 feet. The second-largest wilderness area in the state lies between the Trinity and Salmon rivers and contains more than 55 lakes and streams. Its alpine scenery makes it popular with hikers and backpackers. You can access the **Pacific Crest Trail** west of Mount Shasta at Parks Creek, South Fork Road, or Whalen Road, and also from Castle Crags State Park. For trail and other information, contact the forest service at Weaverville (© 530/623-2121).

**The Fifth Season,** 300 N. Mount Shasta Blvd. (© 530/926-3606; www.thefifth season.com), offers mountaineering and backpack rentals and will provide trail maps and other information concerning Shasta's outdoor activities.

**Living Waters Recreation** (© 800/994-RAFT or 530/926-5446; www.living watersrec.com) offers half-day to 2-day rafting trips on the Upper Sacramento, Klamath, Trinity, and Salmon rivers. **Trinity River Rafting Company,** on Highway 299W in Big Flat (© 800/30-RIVER or 530/623-3033; www.trinityriverrafting.com), also operates local white-water trips.

For additional outfitters and information, contact the **Trinity County Chamber of Commerce,** 210 N. Main St. (P.O. Box 517), Weaverville, CA 96093 (© 800/487-4648 or 530/623-6101; www.trinitycounty.com).

## WHISKEYTOWN NATIONAL RECREATION AREA

In adjacent Shasta County, Whiskeytown National Recreation Area is on the eastern shore of quiet, relatively uncrowded Trinity Lake, with 157 miles of shoreline. This reservoir was originally named Clair Engle, after the politician who created it. Locals insist on calling it Trinity, however, after the river that used to rush through the region past the towns of Minersville, Stringtown, and an earlier Whiskeytown. When they dammed the river, however, they also destroyed the three towns, which now lie submerged beneath the lake's glassy surface.

Both Trinity Lake and the Whiskeytown National Recreation Area are in the Shasta Trinity National Forest, 1.3 million acres of wilderness with 1,269 miles of hiking trails. For information on trails, contact **Shasta Trinity National Forest** (© 530/244-2978; www.fs.fed.us/r5/shastatrinity).

## LAKE SHASTA

Heading north on I-5 from Redding, travel about 12 miles and take the Shasta Dam Boulevard exit to the **Shasta Dam and Power Plant** ★ (© 530/275-4463; www.shastalake.com/shastadam), which has an overflow spillway that is three times higher than Niagara Falls. The huge dam—3,460 feet long, 602 feet high, and 883 feet thick at its base—holds back the waters of the Sacramento, Pit, and McCloud rivers. A dramatic sight indeed, it is a vital component of the Central Valley water project. At the visitor center is a series of photographs and displays covering the dam's construction. You can either walk or drive over the dam, but it's far more interesting to take the **free, 1-hour tours** that run on the hour daily from 9am to 5pm in summer, and at 10am, noon, and 2pm Labor Day to Memorial Day. The guided tour takes you deep within the dam's many chilly corridors (not a good place for claustrophobes) and below the spillway. It's an entertaining way to beat the summer heat. *Note:* Tours may be canceled due to security reasons, so call ahead first.

Lake Shasta has 370 miles of shoreline and attracts anglers (bass, trout, and king salmon), water-skiers, and other boating enthusiasts—two million, in fact, in summer. The best way to enjoy the lake is aboard a houseboat; you can rent them from several companies, including **Antlers Resort & Marina,** P.O. Box 140, Antlers Road, Lakehead, CA 96051 (© 800/238-3924 or 530/238-2553; www.shastalakevacations.com); and **Packers Bay Marina,** 16814 Packers Bay Rd., Lakehead, CA 96051 (© 800/331-3137 or 530/275-5570; www.packersbay.com). There is a 1-week minimum during the summer, and a 3- to 4-day minimum during the off season.

While you're here, you can visit **Lake Shasta Caverns** (© 800/795-CAVE or 530/238-2341; www.lakeshastacaverns.com). These caves contain 20-foot-high stalactite and stalagmite formations—60-foot-wide curtains of them adorn the great Cathedral Room. To see the caves, drive about 15 miles north of Redding on I-5 to the O'Brien/Shasta Caverns exit. A ferry will take you across the lake and a short bus ride will follow to the cave entrance for a 2-hour-long tour. Admission is $18 for adults, $9 for children ages 4 to 12, and free for kids under 4. The caverns are open daily from 9am to 3pm year-round.

For information about the Lake Shasta region, contact the **Redding Convention & Visitors Bureau,** 777 Auditorium Dr., Redding, CA 96001 (© 800/874-7562 or 530/225-4100; www.visitredding.org), west of I-5 on Highway 299. It's open Monday through Friday from 8am to 5pm.

## MOUNT SHASTA ★★★

A volcanic mountain with eight glaciers, **Mount Shasta** is a towering peak of legend and lore. It stands alone, always snowcapped, unshadowed by other mountains—visible from 125 miles away. Although it has been dormant since 1786, eruptions cannot be ruled out, and hot sulfur springs bubble at the summit. The springs saved John Muir on his third ascent of the mountain in 1875. Caught in a severe snowstorm, he and his partner took turns submersing themselves in the hot mud to survive.

Many New Agers are convinced that Mount Shasta is the center of an incredible energy vortex. These devotees flock to the foot of the mountain. In 1987, the foothills were host to the worldwide Harmonic Convergence, calling for a planetary union and a new phase of universal harmony. Yoga, massage, meditation, and metaphysics are all the rage here. These New Agers seem to coexist harmoniously with those whose metaphysical leanings begin and end with Dolly Parton song lyrics.

Those who don't want to climb can drive up to about 7,900 feet. From the town of Mount Shasta, drive 14 miles up the Everitt Memorial Highway to the end of the road near Panther Meadow. At the **Everitt Vista Turnout,** you'll be able to stop and see the Sacramento River Canyon, the Eddy Mountains to the west, and glimpses of Mount Lassen to the south. You can also take the short hike through the forests to a lava outcrop overlooking the McCloud area.

Continue on to **Bunny Flat,** a major access point for climbing in summer and also for cross-country skiing and sledding in winter. The highway ends at the Old Ski Bowl Vista, providing panoramic views of Mount Lassen, Castle Crags, and the Trinity Mountains.

While in Mount Shasta, visit the **Fish Hatchery** at 3 N. Old State Rd. (© **530/926-2215**), which was built in 1888. Here you can observe rainbow and brown trout being hatched to stock rivers and streams statewide—millions are born here annually. You can feed them via coin-operated food dispensers, and observe the spawning process on certain Tuesdays during the fall and winter. Admission is free; hours are daily from 8am to sunset. Adjacent to the hatchery is the **Sisson Museum** (© **530/926-5508**), which displays a smattering of local-history exhibits. It's open daily year-round, from 10am to 4pm in summer, from 1 to 4pm in winter; admission is free.

## OUTDOOR PURSUITS

**GOLF & TENNIS**   Golfers should head for the 27-hole Robert Trent Jones, Jr., golf course at **Lake Shastina Golf Resort,** 5925 Country Club Dr., Weed (© **800/358-4653** or 530/938-3205; www.shastinagolf.com), or the 18-hole course at **Mount Shasta Resort,** 1000 Siskiyou Lake Blvd., Mount Shasta (© **800/958-3363** or 530/926-3030; www.mountshastaresort.com). The Mount Shasta resort also has tennis courts.

**MOUNTAIN CLIMBING**   Mount Shasta attracts thousands of hikers from around the world each year, from timid first-timers to serious mountaineers who search for the most difficult paths up. The hike isn't technically difficult, but it's a demanding ascent that takes about 8 hours of continuous exertion, particularly when the snow softens up. (*Tip:* Start early, while the snow is still firm.) Before setting out, hikers must secure a permit by signing in at the trail head or at the **Mount Shasta Ranger District** office, which also gives out plenty of good advice for amateur climbers. The office is at 204 W. Alma St., off North Mount Shasta Boulevard in Mount Shasta (© **530/926-4511**). Be sure to wear good hiking shoes and carry crampons and an ice ax, a first-aid kit, a quart of water per person, and a flashlight in case it takes longer than anticipated. Sunblock is an absolute necessity. All the requisite equipment can be rented at **The Fifth Season,** 300 N. Mount Shasta Blvd. (© **530/926-3606;** www.the fifthseason.com). Mere mortals who don't feel compelled to summit can merely hike on the various low-elevation trails.

Weather can be extremely unpredictable, and every year hikers die on this dormant volcano, usually from making stupid mistakes. For **weather and climbing conditions,** call © **530/926-5555** for recorded information. Traditionally, climbers make the ascent from the Sierra Lodge at Horse Camp, accessible from the town of Mount Shasta via Alma Street and the Everitt Memorial Highway or from Bunny Flat.

For more information as well as supervised trips, contact **Shasta Mountain Guides,** 1938 Hill Rd. (© **530/926-3117;** www.shastaguides.com). This outfitter offers a 2-day climb along the traditional John Muir route for $395. It also offers a glacier climb and rock climbing in Castle Crags State Park, backpacking trips, plus cross-country and telemark skiing. The basic rock-climbing course is $120, the mountaineering course is $100, and each of the 3-day ski and snowboard descents is $495.

Also nearby is **Castle Crags State Park** (© **530/235-2684**), a 4,300-acre park with 64 campsites and 28 miles of hiking trails. Here, granite crags formed 225 million years ago tower more than 6,500 feet above the Sacramento River. The park is filled with dogwood, oak, cedar, and pine as well as tiger lilies, azaleas, and orchids in summer. You can walk the 1-mile Indian Creek nature trail or take the easy 1-mile Root Creek Trail. The entrance fee is $4 per vehicle per day. Castle Crags is off I-5, about 50 miles north of Redding.

**OTHER WARM-WEATHER ACTIVITIES**    Mount Shasta offers some excellent **mountain biking.** In the summer, ride the chairlifts to the top of Mount Shasta Ski Park and bike down the trails. An all-day chairlift pass is $15 (© **530/926-8600;** www.skipark.com). Another good source for mountain bike rentals and trail information is **Shasta Cycling** (© **530/938-3002**).

For fishing information or guided trips, call **Jack Trout Flyfishing Guide** (© **530/ 926-4540**). Two other recommended sources are **Mount Shasta Fly Fishing** (© **530/ 926-6648**) and **Hart's Guide Service** (© **530/926-2431**).

**SKIING**    In winter, visitors can ski at **Mount Shasta Board & Ski Park,** 104 Siskiyou Ave., Mount Shasta (© **800/SKI-SHASTA** or 530/926-8610; www.skipark.com), which has 31 runs with 80% snowmaking, three triple chairlifts, and a surface lift. Lift tickets are $35. The Nordic ski center has 16 miles of groomed trails, and Terrain Park is geared toward snowboarders. The Learning Center offers instruction for adults and children. In summer you can ride the chairlifts to scenic views, mountain-bike down the trails (an all-day pass is $15), or practice on the two-story climbing wall. Access to the park is 10 miles east of Mount Shasta (the town) on Highway 89.

**WATERSPORTS**    The source of the headwaters of the Sacramento River accumulates in **Lake Siskiyou,** a popular spot for boating, swimming, and fishing—and a great vantage point for photographs of Mount Shasta and its reflection. Water-skiing and jet-skiing are not allowed, but windsurfing is, and boat rentals are available at **Lake Siskiyou Camp Resort,** 4239 W. A. Barr Rd., Mount Shasta (© **888/926-2618** or 530/926-2618; www.lakesis.com).

## WHERE TO STAY

**Best Western Tree House Motor Inn**    Just off the main highway, this motor inn is one of the better places to stay in the town of Mount Shasta, and it keeps its prices low. The lobby and refurbished rooms, some with decks and fridges, are pleasant enough, and the huge indoor pool is usually deserted, making this a family favorite. Downhill and cross-country ski areas are 10 miles away.

111 Morgan Way (at I-5 and Lake St.), Mount Shasta, CA 96067. © **800/780-7234** or 530/926-3101. Fax 530/926-3542. www.bestwestern.com. 95 units. $82–$125 double. AE, DC, DISC, MC, V. **Amenities:** Restaurant; bar; indoor pool; nearby golf course; exercise room; Jacuzzi; video arcade; business center; secretarial services. *In room:* A/C, TV, fridge, coffeemaker, hair dryer, iron.

**Mount Shasta Ranch B&B** ★ *Kids*    One of the country's most famous horse trainers and racing tycoons, H. D. ("Curley") Brown, conceived and built Mount Shasta as the centerpiece of a private retreat and thoroughbred-horse ranch. Despite the encroachment of nearby buildings, the main two-story house and its annex are a cozy B&B with touches of nostalgia, the occasional antique, and spectacular views of Mount Shasta. Four bedrooms with private bathrooms are in the main house; the remaining five share two bathrooms, in the carriage house. It's a 3-minute trek to the shores of nearby Lake Siskiyou (15 min. to the ski slopes), or you could stay here to enjoy the Jacuzzi, Ping-Pong tables, pool table, darts, and horseshoes. Unlike at most B&Bs, kids are welcome

1008 W. A. Barr Rd., Mount Shasta, CA 96067. (© **530/926-3870.** Fax 530/926-6882. www.stayinshasta.com. 10 units, 5 w/private bathroom; 1 cottage. $60–$80 double w/shared bathroom; $110 double w/private bathroom; $115 cottage for 2. Rates include country breakfast (except cottage). AE, DISC, MC, V. Take Central Mount Shasta exit off I-5 to W. A. Barr Rd. Pets accepted w/$10 fee. **Amenities:** Nearby golf course; game room. *In room:* A/C, TV, kitchen in 2 units, no phone.

**Railroad Park Resort** *(Kids)*   A quarter of a mile from the Sacramento River, this is an offbeat place kids will love. It's at the foot of Castle Crags with a campground and RV park, four rustic cabins, and the Caboose Motel. The guest rooms are railroad cabooses from the Southern Pacific, Santa Fe, and Great Northern Railroads, with their pipes, ladders, and lofts left in place. Surrounding the fenced-in, kidney-shaped pool, they're furnished with modern king- or queen-size brass beds, table and chairs, and dressers; most have small bay windows or rooftop cupolas. The restaurant and lounge are also in vintage railroad cars.

100 Railroad Park Rd., Dunsmuir, CA 96025. (© **530/235-4440.** Fax 530/235-4470. www.rrpark.com. 27 units. $75–$100 double; $10 less off season. Extra person $10. AE, DISC, MC, V. Take Railroad Park exit off I-5, 1 mile south of Dunsmuir. Pets accepted w/$10 fee. **Amenities:** Restaurant; lounge; outdoor pool; Jacuzzi; game room; coin-op laundry. *In room:* A/C, TV, fridge, coffeemaker; minibar and microwave in some units.

**Stewart Mineral Springs Resort** *(Finds)*   Stewart Mineral Springs is one of the most unusual health spas in California, rich with lore and legends. Above cold-water springs that Native Americans valued for their healing powers, the place is deliberately primitive, with as few intrusions from the urban world as possible. Don't expect anything approaching a European spa or big-city luxury here. Designed in a somewhat haphazard compound of about a dozen buildings, 4 miles west of a town called Weed, it occupies a 37-acre site of sloping, forested land accented with ponds, gazebos, and decorative bridges. The grounds are riddled with hiking and nature trails, freshwater streams, and a swimming hole.

Activities revolve around hiking, nature-watching, and the healing waters of the legendary springs. The bathhouse is the resort headquarters, with 13 private rooms where springwater is heated and run into tubs for soaking. A staff member will describe the rituals for you: A 20-minute soak is followed by a visit to a nearby sauna and an immersion in the chilly waters of Parks Creek, just outside the bathhouse. Other options include massages ($30 per 30-min. session). On Saturdays, medicine man Walking Eagle guides guests on a spiritual journey within the Native American Purification Sweat Lodge. They even have a juice bar. If you opt for treatment and R&R here, you won't be alone. The place is popular with young Hollywood types, including soap actors, San Francisco 49ers football players, and local newscasters.

4617 Stewart Springs Rd., Weed, CA 96094. (© **530/938-2222.** Fax 530/938-4283. www.stewartmineralsprings.com. 6 tepees (for up to 4 persons), 4 motel rooms, 6 apt units, 5 cabins w/kitchens, and a large A-frame house (suitable for 10 persons). $24 double tepee; $45–$79 double in motel, apts, and cabins; $325 for house. $5 for each extra person. DISC, MC, V. Leashed pets accepted w/$3-per-day fee. **Amenities:** Restaurant (closed in winter); spa; sauna; massage. *In room:* Kitchen and coffeemaker in cabins and some units, no phone.

## WHERE TO DINE

**Café Maddalena** ★★ *Finds* WORLD CUISINE   The smells wafting from this restaurant are enough to draw you into the refurbished old railroad quarter of Dunsmuir. The seasonal menu features authentic dishes from southern France, Spain, and North Africa: couscous with a *tagine* of yam, carrots, and prunes; *zarzuela* (a Spanish shellfish stew in tomato-saffron broth); herb-roasted lamb rack with ratatouille. Everything is fresh, including the breads and desserts. During the summer months, request a table outside under the grape arbor.

5801 Sacramento Ave., Dunsmuir. ✆ 530/235-2725. Reservations recommended. Main courses $10–$19. MC, V. Thurs–Sun 5–10pm. Closed mid-Dec to mid-May.

**Lily's** ★ WORLD CUISINE   In a white clapboard, early 1900s house in a residential neighborhood south of the town center, this friendly little restaurant has a front porch, a picket fence, a back garden, and dining in two rooms inside and two patios out. It's popular for breakfast, with chunky breads, omelets, and cheesy polenta fritters. Lunch and dinner dishes—tamale pie, chicken curry, *scampi al roma,* and Kung Pao shrimp salad—span the globe. Popular dishes include the enchiladas *suizas* stuffed with shrimp, crab, and fresh spinach, and Chicken Rosie, a tender breast of chicken simmered with raspberries, hazelnut liqueur, and cream.

1013 S. Mount Shasta Blvd., Mount Shasta. ✆ 530/926-3372. www.lilysrestaurant.com. Reservations recommended. Breakfast $7–$11; lunch $8–$12; dinner $14–$23. AE, DISC, MC, V. Mon–Fri 7am–9pm; Sat–Sun 7am–9:30pm.

## MCARTHUR–BURNEY FALLS MEMORIAL STATE PARK ★

On its way to Lassen Volcanic National Park (see below) from Mount Shasta, Highway 89 east loops back south to the 910-acre **McArthur–Burney Falls Memorial State Park** (✆ 530/335-2777). One of its most spectacular features is **Burney Falls** ★★, an absolutely gorgeous waterfall that cascades over a 129-foot cliff. Theodore Roosevelt once called the falls "the eighth wonder of the world." Giant springs a few hundred yards upstream feed the falls and keep them flowing—100 million gallons every day—even during California's dry spells.

The .5-mile **Headwater Trail** will take you to a good vantage point above the falls. If you're lucky, you can observe the black swifts that nest in the mossy crevices behind the cascade. Other birds to look for include barn and great horned owls, the belted kingfisher, the common flicker, and even the Oregon junco. The year-round park also has 5 miles of nature trails, 128 campsites, picnicking grounds, and good fishing for bass, crappie, and brown, rainbow, and brook trout. For **camping reservations,** call ✆ 800/444-PARK (7275).

From here, Lassen Volcanic National Park lies about 40 miles south.

## 3 Lassen Volcanic National Park ★

45 miles E of Redding; 255 miles NE of San Francisco

In the far northeastern corner of California, Lassen Volcanic National Park is a remarkable reminder that North America is still forming, and that the ground below is alive with the forces of creation and, sometimes, destruction. Lassen Peak is the southernmost in a chain of volcanoes (including Mount Saint Helens) that stretches all the way from British Columbia.

Although it's dormant, 10,457-foot **Lassen Peak** is still very much alive. It last awakened in May 1914, beginning a cycle of eruptions that spit lava, steam, and ash until 1921. The eruption climaxed in 1915 when Lassen blew its top, sending a cloud of ash 7 miles high, visible from hundreds of miles away. The peak has been dormant for more than three-quarters of a century now, but the area still boils with a ferocious intensity: Hot springs, fumaroles, geysers, and mud pots are all indicators that Lassen hasn't had its last word. Monitoring of geothermal features in the park shows that they are getting hotter, not cooler, and some scientists take this as a sign that the next big eruption in the Cascades is likely to happen here.

Until then, the park gives visitors an interesting chance to watch a landscape recover from the massive destruction brought on by an eruption. To the north of Lassen Peak is the aptly named **Devastated Area,** a huge swath of volcanic destruction steadily repopulating with conifer forests. Forest botanists have revised their earlier theories that forests must be preceded by herbaceous growth after watching the Devastated Area immediately revegetate with a diverse mix of eight different conifer species, four more than were present before the blast.

The 108,000-acre park is a place of great beauty. The flora and fauna are an interesting mix of species from the Cascade Range, which stretches north from Lassen, and species from the Sierra Nevada Range, which stretches south. The blend accounts for an enormous diversity of plants: 715 species have been identified in the park. Although it is snowbound in winter, Lassen is a summer feeding ground for transient herds of mule deer and numerous black bears.

In addition to the volcano and all its geothermal features, Lassen Volcanic National Park includes miles of hiking trails, 50 beautiful alpine lakes, large meadows, cinder cones, lush forests, cross-country skiing, and great backcountry camping. In fact, three-quarters of the park is designated wilderness.

And crowds? Forget it. Lassen is one of the least-visited national parks in the lower 48 states, so crowd control isn't as big a consideration here as in other places. Unless you're here on the Fourth of July or Labor Day weekend, you won't encounter anything that could rightly be called a crowd. Even then, you can escape the hordes simply by skipping the popular sites like Bumpass Hell or the Sulphur Works and heading a few miles down any of the backcountry trails.

## ESSENTIALS

**GETTING THERE** One of the reasons Lassen Volcanic National Park is one of the least visited national parks is its remote location. The most foolproof route here is Highway 44 east from Redding, which leads directly to the northern gateway to the park. A shortcut if you're coming from the south along I-5 is Highway 36 in Red Bluff, which leads to the park's southern gateway. If you're arriving from the east via I-80, take the U.S. 395 turnoff at Reno and head to Susanville. Depending on which end of the park you're shooting for, take either Highway 44 (to the northwest entrance) or Highway 36 (to the southwest entrance) from Susanville. The $10-per-car entrance fee, valid for a week, comes with a copy of the *Lassen Park Guide,* a handy little newsletter listing activities, hikes, and points of interest. Camping fees range from $10 to $16.

Only one major road, Highway 89 (aka the Park Rd.), crosses the park, in a 39-mile half-circle with entrances and visitor centers at either end.

Most visitors enter the park at the southwest entrance station, drive through the park, and leave through the northwest entrance, or vice versa. Two other entrances lead to remote portions of the park. Warner Valley is reached from the south on the road from Chester. The Butte Lake entrance is reached by a cut-off road from Highway 44 between Highway 89 and Susanville.

# Lassen Volcanic National Park

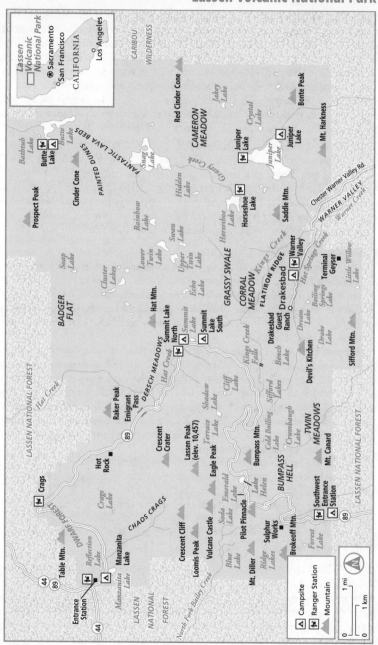

**VISITOR INFORMATION** **Ranger stations** are clustered near each entrance and provide the full spectrum of interpretive displays, ranger-led walks, informational leaflets, and emergency help. The largest **visitor center** is located just inside the northwest entrance station at the Loomis Museum. The park information number for all requests is ✆ **530/595-4444**, or you can visit www.nps.gov/lavo or write Lassen Volcanic National Park, P.O. Box 100, Mineral, CA 96063-0100.

Because of the dangers posed by the park's thermal features, rangers ask that you remain on trails at all times. Fires are allowed in campgrounds only; please make sure they're dead before leaving. Mountain bikes are prohibited on all trails.

**WEATHER** Lassen Volcanic National Park is in one of the coldest places in California. Winter begins in late October and doesn't release its grip until June. Even in the summer, you should plan for possible rain and snow. Temperatures at night can drop below freezing at any time. Winter, however, shows a different and beautiful side of Lassen that more people are starting to appreciate. Since most of the park is over a mile high and the highest point is 10,457 feet, snow accumulates in incredible quantities. Don't be surprised to find snow banks lining the Park Road into July.

## EXPLORING THE PARK

The highlight of Lassen is, of course, the volcano and all of its offshoots: boiling springs, fumaroles, mud pots, and more. You can see many of the most interesting sites in a day, making it possible to visit Lassen as a short detour from I-5 or U.S. 395 on the way to or from Oregon. Available at park visitor centers, the *Road Guide to Lassen Park* is a great traveling companion that will explain a lot of the features you'll see as you traverse the park.

**Bumpass Hell** 🦖, a 1.5-mile walk off the Park Road in the southern part of the park, is Lassen's largest single geothermal site—16 acres of bubbling mud pots reeking with the rotten-egg-like stench of sulfur. The hike leads you through a quiet, peaceful meadow of wildflowers and birds before it reaches the geothermal site—the name of which derives from an early Lassen hunter who lost a leg after he took a shortcut through the area and plunged into a boiling pool. Stay on the wooden catwalks that safely guide visitors past the pyrite pools, steam vents, and noisy fumaroles and you won't follow in Bumpass's footsteps.

**Sulphur Works** 🦖 is another stinky, steamy example of Lassen's residual heat. Two miles from the southwest park exit, the ground roars with seething gases escaping from the ground.

**Boiling Springs Lake** and **Devil's Kitchen** are two of the more remote geothermal sites; they're located in the Warner Valley section of the park, which can be reached by hiking from the main road or entering the park through Warner Valley Road from the small town of Chester.

## OUTDOOR PURSUITS

In addition to the activities below, free naturalist programs are offered daily in the summer, highlighting everything from flora and fauna to geologic history and volcanic processes. For more information, call the **park headquarters** at ✆ **530/595-4444.**

**CANOEING & KAYAKING** Paddlers can take canoes, rowboats, and kayaks on any of the park lakes except Reflection, Emerald, Helen, and Boiling Springs. Motors, including electric motors, are strictly prohibited on all park waters. Park lakes are full of trout, and fishing is popular. You must have a current California fishing license, which you can obtain in Red Bluff at **Lassen Ranch and Home Store,** 22660 Antelope Rd. (© **530/527-6960**).

**CROSS-COUNTRY SKIING**    The park road usually closes due to snow in November, and most years it doesn't open until June, so cross-country skiers have their run of the park. Snowmobiles were once allowed but are now forbidden. Marked trails of all skill levels leave from Manzanita Lake at the north end of the park and Lassen Chalet at the south. Most visitors come to the southwest entrance, where the ski chalet offers lessons, rental gear, and a warm place to stay. Popular trips are the beginners' trails to Lake Helen or Summit Lake. More advanced skiers can make the trek into Bumpass Hell, a steaming valley of sulfuric mud pots and fumaroles.

You can also ski the popular 30-mile course of the Park Road in an overnight trek, but doing this involves a long car shuttle. For safety reasons, the park requires all skiers to register at the ranger stations before heading into the backcountry, whether for an overnight or just the day. For more information, contact the **park headquarters** at © **530/595-4444.**

**HIKING**    Most Lassen visitors drive through in a day or two, see the geothermal hot spots, and move on. That leaves 150 miles of trails and expanses of backcountry to the few who take the time to get off-road. The *Lassen Trails* booklet at the visitor centers gives good descriptions of some of the most popular hikes and backpacking destinations. Anyone spending the night in the backcountry must have a wilderness permit, issued at the ranger stations. And don't forget to bring plenty of water, sunscreen, and warm clothing.

The most popular hike in the park is the **Lassen Peak Trail** ⚡, a 2.5-mile climb from the Park Road to the top of the peak. The trail may sound short, but it's steep and covered with snow until late summer. At an elevation of 10,457 feet, though, you'll get a view of the surrounding wilderness that's worth every step of the way. On clear days, you can see south all the way to Sutter Buttes near Yuba City and north into the Cascades. The round-trip takes about 4 to 5 hours.

Running a close second in popularity is **Bumpass Hell Trail.** This 1.5-mile walk off the Park Road in the southern part of the park deposits you right in the middle of the largest single geothermal site in the park. (See "Exploring the Park," above.)

The **Cinder Cone Trail,** in the northeast corner of the park, is another worthy hike, best reached from Butte Lake Campground at Lassen's far northeast corner. If 4 miles seems too short, you can extend the hike (and shorten the drive) by walking in about 8 miles from Summit Lake on the Park Road. Now dormant, Cinder Cone is generally accepted as the source of mysterious flashing lights that were seen by early settlers in the 1850s. Black and charred-looking, Cinder Cone is bereft of any life and surrounded by dunes of multihued volcanic ash.

**SNOWSHOEING**    From January to March, park naturalists give free 2-hour eco-adventure snowshoe hikes across Lassen's snowpacked hills. The tours take place on Saturdays at 1:30pm at the Lassen Chalet, at the park's southwestern entrance. You must be at least 8 years old, dress warmly, and wear boots. Snowshoes are free of charge on a first-come, first-served basis, although a $1 donation is requested for upkeep. For more details, call park headquarters (© **530/595-4444,** ext. 5133).

# CAMPING

Car campers have their choice of seven park campgrounds with 375 sites, more than enough to handle the trickle of visitors who come to Lassen every summer. In fact, so few people camp in Lassen that the park is without a reservations system, except at the **Lost Creek Group Campground,** and stays there are granted a generous 14-day limit. Sites do fill up on weekends, so get to the park early on Friday to secure a place. If the park is packed, the surrounding Lassen National Forest has 43 campgrounds, so you're bound to find a site somewhere.

By far the most "civilized" campground in the park is at **Manzanita Lake,** where you can find hot showers, electrical hookups, flush toilets, and a camper store. When Manzanita fills up, rangers open the **Crags Campground** overflow camp—about 5 miles away and much more basic. Farther into the park along Highway 89 is **Summit Lake Campgrounds,** on the north and south ends of Summit Lake. It's a pretty spot, often frequented by deer, and it's a launching point for some excellent day hikes.

On the southern end of the park, you'll find **Southwest Campground,** a walk-in camp directly adjacent to the Lassen Chalet parking lot.

The two remote entrances to Lassen and Warner Valley have their own primitive campgrounds with pit toilets and no water, but the price is right—free.

Backcountry camping is allowed almost everywhere, and traffic is light. Ask about closed areas when you get your wilderness permit, which are issued at the ranger stations and required for anyone spending the night in the backcountry.

## WHERE TO STAY

### INSIDE THE PARK

**Drakesbad Guest Ranch** ★★★   Lassen Park's only lodge is Drakesbad Guest Ranch, hidden in a high mountain valley surrounded by meadows, lakes, and streams. It's famous for its rustic cabins, lodge, and steaming thermal swimming pool (where they offer massage service), fed by a natural hot spring and open 24 hours a day. Drakesbad is as deluxe as a place with some electricity and no phones can be, with handmade quilts on every bed and kerosene lamps for reading. Full meal service is available, and it's very good. Because the lodge is very popular and only open from June to mid-October, reservations are booked as far as 2 years in advance (although May or June are good times to call to take advantage of cancellations).

c/o California Guest Services, 2150 N. Main St., no. 5, Red Bluff, CA 96080. ☎ **530/529-1512.** Fax 530/529-4511. www.drakesbad.com. 19 units. $115–$140 per person, double occupancy. Rates include meals. DISC, MC, V. **Amenities:** Restaurant; hot-spring-fed pool; children's center. *In room:* No phone.

### NEAR THE PARK

**The Bidwell House Bed and Breakfast Inn** ★★ *Kids*   In 1901, General John Bidwell, a California senator who made three unsuccessful bids for the U.S. presidency, built a country retreat and summer home for his beloved young wife, Annie. After her death, when Chester had developed into a prosperous logging hamlet, the building, with its farmhouse-style design and spacious veranda, was converted into the headquarters for a local ranch. Today it's one of the most charming B&Bs in the region, with a yard of aspens and cottonwoods and sprawling views of mountain meadows and pretty Lake Almanor. The 14 individually decorated guest rooms are furnished with antiques, most have private bathrooms, a few have wood-burning stoves, and seven have Jacuzzi tubs. A cottage that sleeps up to six is ideal for families.

Breakfast is presented with fanfare and many gourmet touches, including home-baked breads (the inn's manager is a creative pastry chef) and delicious omelets.

1 Main St. (P.O. Box 1790), Chester, CA 96020. (C) **530/258-3338.** www.bidwellhouse.com. 14 units, 12 w/private bathroom. $75–$150 double; $165 for cabin (sleeps 6). Rates include full breakfast. MC, V. **Amenities:** Nearby golf course. *In room:* TV.

**Lassen Mineral Lodge** *Kids*　A mere 9 miles south of Lassen Volcanic National Park's southern entrance, the Lassen Mineral Lodge offers 20 motel-style accommodations in a forested setting. In summer, the lodge is almost always bustling with guests and customers who venture into the gift shop, ski shop, general store, and full-service restaurant and bar. This is probably the best lodging option for families in the Lassen area.

On Hwy. 36E (P.O. Box 160), Mineral, CA 96063. (C) **530/595-4422.** Fax 530/595-4452. www.minerallodge.com. 20 units. $65–$85 double. AE, DISC, MC, V. **Amenities:** Restaurant; saloon; coin-op laundry. *In room:* Kitchens in some units, no phone.

**Mill Creek Resort** ★　Deep in the forest next to ol' Mill Creek, the Mill Creek Resort is that rustic mountain retreat you've always dreamed of while slaving away in the office. A homey country general store and coffee shop serve as the resort's center, a good place to stock up on food while exploring Lassen Volcanic National Park. Nine housekeeping cabins, available on a daily or weekly basis, are clean, cute, and outfitted with vintage 1930s and 1940s furniture, including kitchens (a good thing, since restaurants are scarce in this region). Pets are welcome, too.

1 Hwy. 172 (3 miles south of Hwy. 36), Mill Creek, CA 96061. (C) **888/595-4449** or 530/595-4449. www.millcreek resort.net. 9 units. $75–$100 per cabin. No credit cards. Pets accepted. **Amenities:** Bike rental; coin-op laundry (open May–Oct). *In room:* Kitchen, coffeemaker, no phone.

## WHERE TO DINE
### INSIDE THE PARK

The only restaurant within Lassen Volcanic National Park (besides the Drakesbad Guest Ranch; see above) is the **Summer Chalet Café** ((C) **530/595-3376**), which serves inexpensive, basic breakfasts, as well as sandwiches and burgers for lunch. At the park's south entrance, it's open daily from 8am to 6pm (grill closes at 4pm) from mid-May to mid-October, weather permitting.

### NEAR THE PARK

When you're this far into the wilderness, the question isn't *which* restaurant to choose, but *whether* there is a single restaurant at all. If bacon and eggs, sandwiches, steaks, chicken, burgers, pizza, and salads aren't part of your diet, you're in big trouble unless you packed your own grub.

Deciding where you're going to eat near Lassen Volcanic National Park depends mostly on which side you're on, north or south. At the south entrance to the park, the closest restaurant is the **Lassen Mineral Lodge** (see "Where to Stay" above) in the town of Mineral, which serves the usual uninspired American fare. The best approach, however, is to stay at a B&B or lodge that offers meals to its guests—such as the **Bidwell House** or **Drakesbad Guest Ranch**—or at least provides a kitchen to cook your own meals, such as the **Mill Creek Resort** (see above). Food and camping supplies are available at the **Manzanita Lake Camper Store** ((C) **530/335-7557;** open mid-May to mid-Oct), at the north entrance to the park, or **Lassen Mineral Lodge,** on Highway 36 in Mineral, at the southern end of the park ((C) **530/595-4422**). They also sell or rent just about every outdoor toy you'd ever want to play with in Lassen Park, including cross-country and alpine ski equipment.

## 4 Lava Beds National Monument

324 miles NE of San Francisco; 50 miles NE of Mount Shasta

Lava Beds takes a while to grow on you. It's a seemingly desolate place with high plateaus, cinder cones, and hills covered with lava cinders, sagebrush, and twisted junipers. Miles of land just like it cover most of this corner of California. So why, asks the first-time visitor, is this a national monument? The answer lies underground.

The earth here is like Swiss cheese, so porous in places that it actually makes a hollow sound. When lava pours from a shield volcano, it doesn't cool all at once; the outer edges cool first and the core keeps flowing, forming underground tunnels like a giant pipeline system.

More than 330 lava-tube caves lace the earth at Lava Beds—caves open to the public to explore on their own or with park rangers. Whereas most caves fuel visitors' fear of getting lost within their huge chambers, multiple entrances, and bizarre topography, these tunnels are simple and relatively easy to follow. Once inside, you'll feel that this would be a great place for a game of hide-and-seek.

### ESSENTIALS

**GETTING THERE**   The best access to the park is from Highway 139, 4 miles south of Tulelake.

**VISITOR INFORMATION**   Call the **Lava Beds National Monument** (© 530/667-2282; www.nps.gov/labe) for information on ranger-led hikes, cave trips, and campfire programs. The visitor center is at the southern end of the park.

**ENTRY FEES**   The entry fee is $10 per vehicle for 7 days, $5 per bike or walk-in, and $10 a day for camping.

**WHEN TO GO**   Park elevations range from 4,000 to 5,700 feet, and this part of California can get cold any time of year. Summer is the best time to visit, with average temperatures in the 70s (20s Celsius); winter temperatures plunge down to about 40°F (4°C) in the day and as low as 20°F (–7°C) by night. Summer is also the best time to participate in ranger-led hikes, cave trips, and campfire programs.

### EXPLORING THE PARK

A hike to **Schonchin Butte** (.75 miles each way) will give you a good perspective on the stark beauty of the monument and nearby Tule Lake Valley. Wildlife lovers should keep their eyes peeled for terrestrial animals like mule deer, coyote, marmots, and squirrels, while watching overhead for bald eagles, 24 species of hawks, and enormous flocks of ducks and geese headed to the Klamath Basin, one of the largest waterfowl wintering grounds in the Lower 48. Sometimes the sky goes dark with ducks and geese during the peak migrations.

The caves at **Lava Beds** are open to the public with little restriction. All you need to see most of them are a good flashlight or headlamp, sturdy walking shoes, and a sense of adventure. Many of the caves are entered by ladders or stairs, or by holes in the side of a hill. Once inside, walk far enough to round a corner, and then shut off your light—a chilling experience, to say the least.

One-way **Cave Loop Road,** just southwest of the visitor center, is where you'll find many of the best cave hikes. About 15 lava tubes have been marked and made accessible. Two are ice caves, where the air temperature remains below freezing year-round and ice crystals form on the walls. If exploring on your own gives you the creeps, check out **Mushpot Cave.** Almost adjacent to the visitor center, this cave has been outfitted with lights and a smooth walkway; you'll have plenty of company.

Hardened spelunkers will find enough remote and relatively unexplored caves to keep themselves busy. Many caves require specialized climbing gear.

Above ground, several trails crisscross the monument. The longest of these, the **Lyons Trail** (8.25 miles one-way), spans the wildest part of the monument, where you are likely to see plenty of animals. The **Whitney Butte Trail** (3 miles one-way) leads from Merill Cave along the shoulder of 5,000-foot Whitney Butte to the edge of the Callahan Lava Flow and monument boundary.

## PICNICKING, CAMPING & ACCOMMODATIONS

The 43-unit **Indian Well Campground** near the visitor center has spaces for tents and small RVs year-round, with water available only during the summer. The rest of the year, you'll have to carry water from the nearby visitor center.

Two **picnic grounds,** Fleener Chimneys and Captain Jacks Stronghold, have tables but no water; open fires are prohibited.

The monument grounds have no hotels or lodges, but many services are available in nearby Tulelake and Klamath Falls. For more information, call or write **Lava Beds National Monument,** P.O. Box 867, Tulelake, CA 96134 (© **530/667-2282**).

# 10

# The High Sierra: Yosemite, Mammoth Lakes & Sequoia/Kings Canyon

*by Matthew Richard Poole*

The national parks of California's Sierra lure travelers from around the globe. The big attraction is Yosemite, of course, but the region abounds with other natural wonders as well. John Muir found in Yosemite "the most songful streams in the world . . . the noblest forests, the loftiest granite domes, the deepest ice-sculpted canyons." Few visitors would disagree with Muir's early impressions as they explore this land of towering cliffs, alpine lakes, river beaches, and dazzling fields of snow in winter.

Yosemite Valley, lush with waterfalls and regal peaks, is the most central and accessible part of the park, stretching for some 7 miles from Wawona Tunnel in the west to Curry Village in the east. If you visit during spring or early fall, you'll encounter fewer problems with crowds and have a more intimate experience of Yosemite's splendors.

Across the heart of the Sierra Nevada, in east-central California, Sequoia and Kings Canyon national parks comprise a vast, mountainous region that stretches some 1,300 square miles, taking in the giant sequoias for which they're fabled. This is a land of alpine lakes, deep canyons, and granite peaks, including Mount Whitney—at 14,495 feet, the highest point in the lower 48 states.

Another big attraction is Mammoth Lakes, a popular playground for California residents. Glaciers carved out much of this panoramic region, where you can partake of all sorts of recreational activities against a backdrop of lakes, streams, waterfalls, and meadows.

Because of the vast popularity of the parks, facilities can be strained at peak visiting times. Always make your reservations in advance if possible (for camping as well as for hotel stays).

## 1 Yosemite's Gateways

The three most popular entrances to Yosemite (there are five total) are **Big Oak Flat** (via Hwy. 120), the west entrance, 88 miles east of Manteca and the best passage in from San Francisco; **Arch Rock** (via Hwy. 140), 75 miles northeast of Merced and the easiest route from central California; and the **South Entrance** at Wawona (via Hwy. 41), 64 miles north of Fresno and the best inroad from Southern California. Should you need to reserve accommodations outside Yosemite, it's wise to book a place near the gateway that affords you easiest access to the park.

Towns on the periphery of each gateway are built around the tourism industry, with plenty of places to stay and eat, and natural wonders of their own. The drawback is that if you stay outside Yosemite, reaching any point within the park requires at least a half-hour drive, which is especially frustrating during high season, when motor homes and congestion slow traffic to a snail's pace.

A controversial park plan would restore 180 acres to their natural state and eliminate a 3¼-mile section of road to make way for a foot-and-bike trail, but it would do so by cutting the number of day-use parking spots in Yosemite from 1,600 to 550, encouraging bus and shuttle usage, and reducing lodging rooms from 1,260 to 981.

The plan is still under debate, but various public transportation options are already in effect, allowing you to leave your car behind. You can enter Yosemite on convenient, inexpensive buses and then move around the valley floor on free shuttles. The **Yosemite Area Regional Transit System (YARTS)** (② 877/989-2787; www.yarts.com) provides round-trip transit from communities within Mariposa, Merced, and Mono counties to Yosemite. The Merced route along Highway 140 operates year-round, although the winter schedule is limited. Fares for riding YARTS vary, but generally range from $7 to $15 round-trip for adults, including entrance to the park, with discounts for children and seniors. Summer routes originate at Coulterville, Mammoth Lake and Lee Vining, and Wawona. For information on the Highway 120 east service (Mammoth Lakes to Yosemite Valley) call ② 800/427-7623 from May until it snows (typically Sept or Oct).

## BIG OAK FLAT ENTRANCE

The Big Oak Flat entrance is 150 miles east of San Francisco and 130 miles southeast of Sacramento. Among the string of small communities along the way is **Groveland** (24 miles from the park's entrance)—a throwback to gold-mining days, with some semblance of a town and the oldest saloon in the state. It will take around an hour to reach the park entrance from Groveland, but at least you'll find extracurricular activity there if you're planning to stay in the area for a while. Big Oak Flat has a few hotels as well, but no town. Call the visitor information number below for details.

**GETTING THERE**   If you're driving from San Francisco, take I-580 (which turns into I-205) to Manteca, then Highway 120 east.

**VISITOR INFORMATION**   Contact the **Highway 120 Chamber of Commerce** (② 800/449-9120; www.groveland.org) for an exhaustive list of hotels, motels, cabins, RV parks, and campsites in the area.

### WHERE TO STAY & DINE

Great dining options are scarce in these parts. For options beyond the places mentioned below, ask around town for further recommendations—just don't expect to discover the next Chez Panisse.

**Evergreen Lodge** ★★ *Kids*   If you are looking for *the* classic Yosemite experience at any time of the year, you'll want to book a cabin at the Evergreen Lodge. This idyllic, affordable, and crowd-free hideaway has it all, just 40 minutes east of Groveland right next to Yosemite: cozy cabins in the woods, an historic, well-stocked bar, a great restaurant, a recreation center and library, guided trips, and evening programs including campfires, movies, and music. The 68 cabins are scattered throughout groves of towering pines and come with private bathrooms, decks, sitting areas, and quilted beds. In the evenings, you can enjoy a pitcher of beer and a game of Ping-Pong, pool, or horseshoes, sit around the campfire while roasting marshmallows, or plan your next day's outing in the recreation center. During the day, you'll have proximity to all parts of Yosemite—particularly the beautiful and crowd-free Hetch Hetchy area—and access to numerous hiking and biking trails and swimming holes near the lodge. "Evergreen Dan" Braun, an Evergreen owner and a leading Yosemite expert, runs the outdoor programs—be sure to reserve space on one of Evergreen's guided hiking, biking, fishing, or sightseeing tours before you arrive. All sorts of fun programs for kids are available as well. *Tip:* Request one of the newer cabins; they're well worth the extra few dollars per night.

33160 Evergreen Rd. (at Hwy. 120), Groveland, CA 95321. ℂ **800/935-6343** or 209/379-2606. Fax 209/379-2607. www.evergreenlodge.com. 68 units. Open year-round. Rates vary w/season and cabin size: $79–249 for 1- and 2-bedroom cabins. AE, DISC, MC, V. From San Francisco, take I-580 east (which turns into I-205) to Manteca; take Hwy. 120 east through Groveland; turn left at Hetch Hetchy/Evergreen Rd. **Amenities:** Restaurant; bar; beer garden; recreation center; free wireless Internet and long-distance phone service; general store; meeting hall; campfire area; group tent campground; lake, pool, and tennis courts at neighboring Camp Mather for day-use fee (summer only). *In room:* Minifridge, CD player, fans.

**The Groveland Hotel** ★   Constructed in 1849 from adobe, this California landmark is one of the oldest buildings in the region and loaded with 19th-century character. The guest rooms are cozily appointed with down comforters, private bathrooms, and attractive European antiques. The best rooms are the two-room suites equipped with spa tubs and fireplaces. Along with an authentic Gold Rush–era saloon, the hotel has a restaurant serving baby back ribs, rack of lamb, fresh fish, and pasta, and a wine list that's a recipient of *Wine Spectator*'s Award of Excellence. Be sure to visit the hotel's website for money-saving package deals.

18767 Main St. (P.O. Box 289), Groveland, CA 95321. ℂ **800/273-3314** or 209/962-4000. Fax 209/962-6674. www.groveland.com. 17 units. $145–$175 double; $225–$275 suite. Rates include extended continental breakfast. AE, DC, DISC, MC, V. Pets accepted w/$10 fee per night. **Amenities:** Restaurant; nearby golf course; small game room; concierge; business center; secretarial services; limited room service; babysitting; laundry service. *In room:* A/C, TV/VCR in some units, dataport, minibar, coffeemaker, hair dryer, iron.

---

⟨**Fun Fact**  **Burgers & Bullets: the Iron Door Saloon**

Walk through the English iron doors that were shipped around the Horn, and you'll step into a saloon that has been serving shots of whiskey to thirsty travelers for more than 150 years. Built from solid blocks of granite, the Iron Door Saloon is a must-stop on your way to Yosemite, if only to gawk at the thousands of dollar bills tacked to the ceiling. They say the infamous Black Bart enjoyed a tumbler here now and again, and even put a few bullet holes in the walls to keep the locals jumpy (keep looking). A stuffed buffalo's head hangs on the wall to remind guests of the house special—a thick, juicy, charbroiled buffalo burger served with pickles, tomato, onions, and house-made coleslaw. Espressos, cappuccinos, and lattes are available as well, in case you need a boost from the long drive. At 18763 Main St. in downtown Groveland, it's open daily for lunch and dinner and for breakfast Friday through Sunday (ℂ **209/962-6244;** www.iron-door-saloon.com). Live music acts (with both local and national artists) regularly play at the saloon—a remnant perk from the days when the owners used to work for concert promoter Bill Graham.

**Hotel Charlotte**   Walking into the Charlotte is like stepping back in time. Built in 1918 by an Italian immigrant, and listed on the National Register of Historic Places, it's warm, comfortable, and no-nonsense—a quintessential historic Western hotel. On the outside, it looks like a gentrified saloon. Inside, the 10 individually decorated, recently refurbished rooms (most on the second floor) are cheerily painted or wallpapered. Rooms are small, quaint, and basic (with phones but not TVs), with twin, double, or queen-size beds. Several units adjoin one other with connecting bathrooms (perfect for families). Two units have showers only; the rest have shower/claw-foot tub combos. Guests can choose between two common television rooms. The continental breakfast is great, featuring strong coffee, fresh warm muffins, cereals, fruit, and juices.

18736 Main St. (Hwy. 120), Groveland, CA 95321. (C) **800/961-7799** or 209/962-6455. Fax 209/962-6254. www. hotelcharlotte.com. 10 units. $96–$119 double. Rates include buffet breakfast. Extra person $20. AE, DISC, MC, V. Pets accepted w/$10 fee. **Amenities:** Restaurant; full bar; game room, Internet access.

## ARCH ROCK ENTRANCE

This is the most heavily used park entrance, offering easy access to the valley.

**GETTING THERE**   Arch Rock is 75 miles northeast of Merced. If you're driving from central California, take I-5 to Highway 99 to Merced, then Highway 140 east through El Portal.

Greyhound ((C) **800/229-9424;** www.greyhound.com) and **Amtrak** ((C) **800/USA-RAIL;** www.amtrak.com) have routes to Fresno from many cities. **VIA Adventures** ((C) **800/VIA-LINE** or 209/384-1315; www.via-adventures.com) offers service from Merced Amtrak Passenger Station to Yosemite Valley Visitor Center and Yosemite Lodge. Coaches, which can be wheelchair-lift equipped with advance notice, provide several round-trips daily between Merced and Yosemite.

## WHERE TO STAY

**The Yosemite Bug Lodge** ★ *Kids*   Twenty-five miles from Yosemite Valley, the Bug is a cross between a mountain lodge and summer camp, complete with a big sun deck and swimming hole. Accommodations are simply but pleasantly furnished (even the tent cabins have real beds and linens) and come in multiple configurations: antique-filled private cabins with bathrooms, B&B-style private rooms with shared bathrooms in the main lodge, Yosemite-style wood-frame tent cabins, and campsites. The on-site **Cafe at the Bug** serves good California-American fare—seared yellowtail tuna with a sesame crust, roast pork with almonds and cilantro—along with beer, wine, vegan dishes, and box lunches to go. The cafe also doubles as the lodge's communal lounge. Other perks include hiking trails on the property, a game room with a pool table, a kitchen for hostel guests, and organized outings.

6979 Hwy. 140 (P.O. Box 81), Midpines, CA 95345. (C) **209/966-6666.** Fax 209/966-6667. www.yosemitebug.com. Private rooms w/private bathroom $55–$115; family and private rooms w/semiprivate bathroom $40–$70; dorm beds w/semiprivate bathrooms $16; tent cabins $30–$50; 2 campsites $17 w/grill and table. DISC, MC, V. **Amenities:** Restaurant; bike rentals; game room; wireless Internet; coin-op laundry. *In room:* A/C, no phone.

**Yosemite View Lodge**   It's shocking to drive onto this gargantuan compound, perpetually under construction, amid the otherwise pristine natural surroundings, practically at the park gate. The busloads of tourists need to stay somewhere, however, and this 279-room megamotel is scheduled to eventually offer around 500 rooms. The motel-style units include fridges, microwaves, and HBO; some offer kitchenettes, river views, balconies, and fireplaces. The indoor pool is popular with kids. There's also a general store. The restaurant provides decent food, but it would be pricey for a family. If this place is booked, ask about their other properties in the vicinity, although they're not nearly so close to the park entrance. Call ahead for information or check out the website, which also provides weather and road conditions.

11136 Hwy. 140 (P.O. Box D), El Portal, CA 95318. © 888/742-4371 or 209/379-2681. Fax 209/379-2704. www.yosemite-motels.com. 279 units. Apr–Oct $125–$155 double; Nov–Mar $82–$155 double. 2-night minimum during holidays. MC, V. Pets accepted w/$10 fee per night. **Amenities:** Restaurant; pizza parlor; lounge; indoor and outdoor heated pools; 4 Jacuzzis; tour and activities desk. *In room:* A/C, TV, kitchenette in some units, fridge.

## SOUTH ENTRANCE

The South Entrance is 332 miles north of Los Angeles, 190 miles east of San Francisco, 59 miles north of Fresno, and 33 miles south of Yosemite Valley. Fish Camp and Oakhurst are the closest towns to the South Entrance at Wawona. This entrance to the valley leads through the Wawona Tunnel to the **Tunnel View** where you *must* stop to admire the panorama; if you've never been to Yosemite before, I promise you this is a view you'll never forget.

**GETTING THERE**    If you're driving from Los Angeles, take I-5 to Highway 99 north, then Highway 41 north. **Fresno-Yosemite International Airport** (© 559/621-4500; http://www.fresno.gov/flyfresno), in nearby Fresno, is 93 miles south of Yosemite Village. The airport is served by Alaska Airlines, America West, American, Continental, Delta, Horizon, United, and all the major car-rental companies. From the airport, take Highway 41 north to the South Entrance.

**VISITOR INFORMATION**    Ask the **Yosemite Sierra Visitors Bureau,** 40637 Hwy. 41, Oakhurst, CA 93644 (© 559/683-4636; www.yosemitethisyear.com), for a helpful brochure on the area, and be sure to check out its excellent online guide.

### WHERE TO STAY & DINE

If you can't afford to eat at the opulent Erna's Elderberry House in Oakhurst (see below), try the pleasant **Three Sisters Café,** 40291 Junction Dr., Suite 3, off Highway 49 (© 559/642-2253). For more dining and lodging options, contact the visitors bureau (see above).

**Big Creek Inn** ★★    A mere 2 miles from the South Entrance to Yosemite National Park, this immaculate B&B is run by owner/innkeeper Pamela Salisbury. Near the banks of Big Creek, it has everything you could want from a mountain lodging: easy access to Yosemite, great fishing right outside the front door, a balcony for reading, sounds of the creek from every room, a telescope for stargazing, an outdoor spa tub overlooking the creek, complimentary sunset wine and hors d'oeuvres, and even spa services—facials, body wraps, foot care—offered in the privacy of your own room. (After climbing Half Dome, you'll need a massage!) The game room is filled with books, maps, and board games, Internet access is free, and more than 300 movies are available for in-room viewing. The three guest rooms have private balconies with French doors and forest views, large bathrooms with Neutrogena bath products, and cozy comforters; two come with gas fireplaces and bistro-style dining tables. A hearty, homemade breakfast is served in the dining room or, if you're getting up early for a hike, Pamela will deliver a continental breakfast to your room.

1221 Hwy. 41 (P.O. Box 39), Fish Camp, CA 93623. © 559/641-2828. Fax 559/641-2727. www.bigcreekinn.com. 3 units. $149–$189 double. Rates include continental breakfast, wine, and hors d'oeuvres. AE, DC, DISC, MC, V. **Amenities:** Nearby golf course and ski areas; spa services; game room w/refreshments; Internet access; state-of-the-art robotic telescope. *In room:* TV/VCR/DVD, CD player, ceiling fan, private balcony, complimentary local calls.

**Château du Sureau** ★★★    Its kudos say it all: five diamonds, five stars, hailed by *Zagat* as one of the top three small hotels in the United States. The domain of Vienna-born Erna Kubin-Clanin, the Elderberries estate (*sureau* is French for elderberry) is the sine qua non of luxurious lodging, decadent dining, and exclusivity. The château—"built to look old"—dates from 1991 and is set back off the road on a hill. From the renowned restaurant, a pathway leads through gardens to the house, which resembles a French château, with turret and terra-cotta-tile roof. The interior is exquisitely appointed with antique furnishings, rugs, and fabrics. Each individually decorated room has a wood-burning fireplace and a wrought-iron balcony. Canopy beds are covered in Italian linens and goose-down comforters; several rooms have whirlpool tubs. Celebrities fleeing Los Angeles are fond of the $2,800-per-night Villa Sureau, a two-bedroom, two-bathroom luxury villa with a library, full kitchen, and 24-hour butler service (the price drops to $2,500 without the butler). The restaurant, **Erna's Elderberry House** (© **559/683-6800**), is well known for its impeccable food and service. The six-course, prix-fixe menu changes daily.

48688 Victoria Lane (P.O. Box 577), Oakhurst, CA 93644. © **559/683-6860**. Fax 559/683-0800. www.chateaudu sureau.com. 10 units. $350–$550 double. Rates include full European breakfast. Extra person $75. AE, DISC, MC, V. **Amenities:** Restaurant; bar; outdoor pool; nearby golf course; spa services; concierge; activities desk; 24-hr. room service; in-room massage; laundry service; same-day dry cleaning. *In room:* A/C, TV/VCR on request, hair dryer, CD player.

**The Homestead** ★    Secluded on 160 acres of woodland with plenty of trails, this establishment is a gem, off the beaten path. The wonderful cottages are rustic yet modern, with four-poster log beds, *saltillo* tile floors, stone fireplaces, and separate sitting and dining areas, with the convenience of TV and air-conditioning. Each cabin has a unique bent, from the romantic Garden Cottage to the rugged Ranch Cottage (which is the only family-friendly option at this adult-oriented getaway). Kitchens are part of the package in all rooms except the cozy Star Gazing Loft, which is smaller but an astronomy buff's dream. Families should inquire about the Ranch House, a two-bedroom/two-bathroom accommodation that sleeps up to six guests, and children are welcome. The top-rated River Creek Golf Club is just a mile away.

41110 Rd. 600, Ahwahnee, CA 93601. © **800/483-0495** or 559/683-0495. Fax 559/683-8165. www.homestead cottages.com. 5 cottages, 1 guest house. $145–$349 double; $25 per additional person. DISC, MC, V. 4½ miles north of Oakhurst on Hwy. 49, then south on Rd. 600 for 2½ miles. *In room:* A/C, cable TV, kitchen, hair dryer, iron, no phone.

**Hound's Tooth Inn** ★    This immaculate bed-and-breakfast is well located, 12 miles from Yosemite's South Entrance. It has comfortable, pretty rooms (some with spas or fireplaces), individually decorated in a Victorian style with a mix of reproductions and antiques, wallpaper, lace valances, and original art. My favorite rooms are the Hound's Tooth, with a king-size bed, fireplace, and view of the Sierra; and the Victorian Tower, with sheer white netting, rattan chairs, and a spa. Kids are welcome by prior arrangement (rooms are set up for two people, so additional bedding must be brought in). The private garden area below is the ideal spot for a relaxing read.

42071 Hwy. 41, Oakhurst, CA 93644. © **888/642-6610** or 559/642-6600. Fax 559/658-2946. www.houndstooth inn.com. 12 units, 1 cottage. $110–$175 double; $225 cottage. Extra person $20. Rates include full breakfast. AE, DC, DISC, MC, V. *In room:* A/C, TV/VCR, hair dryer, iron; kitchenette, minibar, fridge, and coffeemaker in some units.

**The Narrow Gauge Inn**    If you want to stay in a place that celebrates its mountainous surrounds, book a room at this friendly inn, 4 miles south of the park entrance. All of the motel-style units have a luxury cabin feel, with A-frame ceilings, little balconies or decks, antiques, quilts, and lace curtains; some have wood paneling.

(*Moments*  **White-Water Rafting on the Tuolumne**

One of the most depressing facts about Yosemite tourism is that few visitors do more than get out of their car, take a brief walk around the valley floor, "ooh" and "ah," snap some photos, and go back to their hotel. But if you really want to experience the wonders of the outdoors, contact **Ahwahnee Whitewater**, P.O. Box 1161, Columbia, CA 95310 (© **800/359-9790** or 209/533-1401; www.ahwahnee.com). Its rafting trips are one of the most direct ways to interact with nature—especially if you're not the type to throw on a backpack and hoof it. The 1- to 3-day trips are ideal for white-water rebels in the spring (when the melting snow makes the ride most exciting) and for families later in the season. Although the trip doesn't go through the park, it's still an all-wilderness adventure—but they make the arrangements, provide and cook the food (gourmet by camping standards), steer the rafts, and practically hand you an experience you'll never forget. All you need to do is reserve well in advance, and if you're going on an overnight trip (highly recommended!), bring a tent, sleeping bag, and a few other camping accouterments—and get ready for a great time.

The higher the price of the room, the cuter it gets. (Nos. 16–26 are the best and most secluded; they look directly into forest.) Hiking trails run through the property, and the old-fashioned, lodge-style restaurant and buffalo bar serves "Old California Rancho Cuisine"; it's open daily in season from 5:30 to 9pm.

48571 Hwy. 41, Fish Camp, CA 93623. © **888/644-9050** or 559/683-7720. Fax 559/683-2139. www.narrowgauge inn.com. 26 units. Apr–Oct $120–$195 double; Nov–Mar $89–$109 double. Extra person $10. Children under 6 stay free in parent's room. Rates include continental breakfast. DISC, MC, V. Pets accepted w/$25 fee. **Amenities:** Restaurant (seasonal); bar; outdoor heated pool (seasonal); Jacuzzi (seasonal). *In room:* TV, dataport, coffeemaker.

**Tenaya Lodge** ★★ *Kids*  Tenaya Lodge is a large, full-service resort that's particularly idyllic for families. The three- and four-story complex is set amid 35 acres of forest a few miles outside the park. Inside, the decor is a cross between an Adirondack hunting lodge and a Southwestern pueblo, with a lobby dominated by a massive riverrock fireplace rising three stories. The modern guest rooms are done in a tasteful Southwestern decor with quality furnishings and roomy, well-appointed bathrooms. At the Guest Experience Center on the premises, you can sign up for tours of Yosemite, white-water rafting, mountain-bike rentals, rock climbing, horseback riding, and other outdoor activities. The lodge's Camp Tenaya for Kids program offers nature hikes, arts and crafts, games, and music 7 days a week from Memorial Day to Labor Day. It's available Friday and Saturday evenings year-round, except when winter weather conditions preclude outdoor activities.

1122 Hwy. 41, Fish Camp, CA 93623. © **888/514-2167** or 559/683-6555. Fax 559/683-8684. www.tenayalodge.com. 244 units. Winter from $169 double; summer from $259 double. Buffet breakfast $15 per person. Children 17 and under stay free in parent's room. AE, DC, DISC, MC, V. **Amenities:** 2 restaurants; deli; indoor and outdoor pools; 2 nearby golf courses; exercise room; full-service spa; indoor and outdoor Jacuzzis; bike rental; children's program; game room; video arcade; activities desk; business center; secretarial services; 24-hr. room service; massage; babysitting; laundry service; dry cleaning. *In room:* A/C, TV w/pay movies, dataport, minibar, fridge on request, coffeemaker, hair dryer, iron, safe.

## 2 Yosemite National Park ★★★

Yosemite is a place of record-setting statistics: the highest waterfall in North America and 3 of the world's 10 tallest waterfalls (Upper Yosemite Fall, Ribbon Fall, and Sentinel Falls); the tallest and largest single granite monolith in the world (El Capitan); the most recognizable mountain (Half Dome); one of the world's largest trees (the Grizzly Giant in the Mariposa Grove); and thousands of rare plant and animal species. But trying to explain its majesty is impossible; you simply must experience it firsthand.

What sets the valley apart is its geology. The Sierra Nevada was formed between 10 million and 80 million years ago, when a tremendous geological uplift pushed layers of granite beneath the ocean up into a mountain range. Cracks and rifts in the rock gave erosion a start at carving canyons and valleys. During the last ice age, at least three glaciers flowed through the valley, shearing vertical faces of stone and hauling away the rubble. The last glacier retreated 10,000 to 15,000 years ago, but it left its legacy in the incredible number and size of the waterfalls pouring into the valley from hanging side canyons. From the 4,000-foot-high valley floor, the 8,000-foot tops of El Capitan, Half Dome, and Glacier Point look like the top of the world, but they're small in comparison to the highest mountains in the park, some of which reach more than 13,000 feet. The 7-square-mile valley acts like a huge bathtub drain for the combined runoff of hundreds of square miles of snow-covered peaks (which explains why the valley flooded during the great storm of 1997).

High-country creeks flush with snowmelt catapult over the abyss left by the glaciers and form an outrageous variety of falls, from tiny ribbons that never reach the ground to the torrents of Nevada and Vernal falls. Combined with the shadows and lighting of the deep valley, the effect of all this falling water is mesmerizing. Hundreds of visitors flock to the park for some of the finest climbing anywhere.

The valley is also home to beautiful meadows and the Merced River. When the last glacier retreated, its debris dammed the Merced and formed a lake. Eventually, sediment from the river filled the lake and created the rich, level valley floor we see today. Tiny Mirror Lake was created later by rockfall that dammed up Tenaya Creek; the addition of a man-made dam in 1890 made it more of a lake than a pond. Rafters and inner-tubers enjoy the slow-moving Merced during the heat of summer.

**Deer** and **coyote** frequent the valley, often causing vehicular mayhem as one heavy-footed tourist slams on brakes to whip out the camera while another rubbernecker drives right into him. Metal crunches, tempers flare, and the deer daintily hops away.

**Bears,** too, are at home in the valley. Grizzlies are gone from the park now, but black bears are plentiful—and hungry for your food. Bears will rip into cars that have even the smallest treats inside, including things you think are safe in your trunk. Each year as many as 500 bear-eats-car incidents occur, and several bears have had to be killed when they became too aggressive and destructive. If that's not enough to deter you from tempting the bears, know park officials levy a fine of up to $5,000 for feeding park animals, and they can also impound your car. Food storage lockers are available throughout the park—please use them.

In the middle of the valley's thickest urban cluster is the **Yosemite Valley Visitor Center** (© 209/372-0200; www.nps.gov/yose), with exhibitions about the park's glacial geology, history, and flora and fauna. Check out the **Yosemite Museum** next door for insight into what life in the park was once like; excellent exhibits explore the Miwok and Paiute cultures that thrived here. The **Ansel Adams Gallery** (© 209/372-4413;

www.adamsgallery.com) features the famous photographer's prints as well as the work of other artists. You'll also find much history and memorabilia regarding nature writer John Muir, one of the founders of the conservation movement.

It's easy to let the beauty of the valley monopolize your attention, but remember that 95% of Yosemite is wilderness. Of the four million visitors who come to the park each year, few venture more than a mile from their cars. That leaves most of Yosemite's 750,000 acres open for anyone adventurous enough to hike a few miles. Even though the valley is the hands-down winner for drama, the high country offers a more subtle kind of beauty: glacial lakes, rivers, and miles of granite spires and domes. In the park's southwest corner, the Mariposa Grove is a forest of rare sequoias, the world's largest trees, as well as several meadows and the south fork of the Merced River.

Tenaya Lake and Tuolumne Meadows are two of the most popular high-country destinations, as well as the starting points for many trails to the backcountry. Since this area is under snow November through June, summer is more like spring. From snowmelt to the first snowfall, the high country explodes with wildflowers and wildlife trying to make the most of the short season.

## ESSENTIALS

**ENTRY POINTS**    The park has four main entrances. Most valley visitors enter through the **Arch Rock Entrance** on Highway 140. The best entrance for Wawona is the **South Entrance** on Highway 41 from Oakhurst. If you're going to the high country, you'll save a lot of time by coming in through the **Big Oak Flat Entrance,** which puts you straight onto Tioga Road without forcing you to deal with the congested valley. The **Tioga Pass Entrance** is open only in summer, and it's only relevant if you're coming from the east side of the Sierra (in which case it's your only option). A fifth, little-used entrance is the **Hetch Hetchy Entrance** in the euphonious Poopenaut Valley, on a dead-end road.

**FEES**    It costs $20 per car per week to enter the park, or $10 per person per week. Annual Yosemite Passes are a steal at $40. Wilderness permits are free, but reserving them requires a $5 fee per person. If you are 62 or older you may purchase a lifetime Golden Age Passport for $10. With reasonable proof of age, you can apply for this passport here (or at any other national park or national forest).

**GAS**    Yosemite Valley has no gas stations, so fill up before entering.

**VISITOR CENTERS & INFORMATION**    For general information, you can either call the central, 24-hour recorded information line for the park (© **209/ 372-0200)** or log onto the park's main website (www.nps.gov/yose). All visitor-related service lines, including hotels and information, can be accessed by touch-tone phone at © **209/372-1000,** or at www.yosemitepark.com. Another good resource is **Yosemite Area Travelers Information** (© 209/723-3153; www.yosemite.com). For details on much of the lodging within Yosemite National Park, contact **Yosemite Reservations,** 5410 E. Home Ave., Fresno, CA 93727 (© **559/252-4848;** www.yosemitepark.com).

The biggest visitor center is the **Valley Visitor Center** (© 209/372-0200). The **Wawona Information Station** (© 209/375-9501) also gives general park information (closed in winter). For trail advice and biological and geological displays about the High Sierra, the **Tuolumne Meadows Visitor Center** (© 209/372-0263) is great (closed in winter). All can provide you with maps, plus more newspapers, books, and photocopied leaflets than you'll ever read.

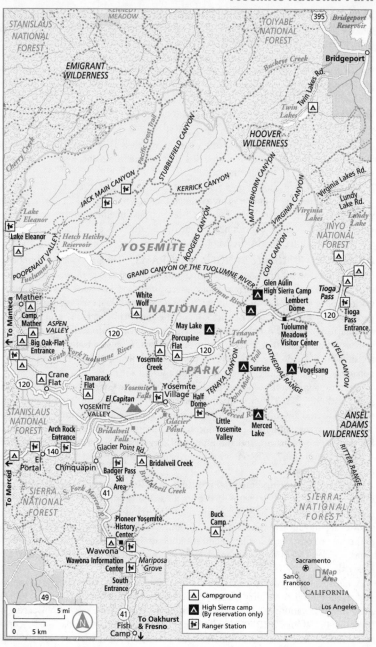

STANISLAUS NATIONAL FOREST

KENNEDY MEADOW

395

Bridgeport Reservoir

TOIYABE NATIONAL FOREST

**Bridgeport**

EMIGRANT WILDERNESS

Buckeye Creek

Twin Lakes Rd.

Cherry Creek

Pacific Crest Trail

Twin Lakes

HOOVER WILDERNESS

Lake Eleanor

JACK MAIN CANYON

STUBBLEFIELD CANYON

KERRICK CANYON

MATTERHORN CANYON

VIRGINIA CANYON

Virginia Lakes Rd.

Lundy Lake Rd.

Lake Eleanor

Hetch Hetchy Reservoir

POOPENAUT VALLEY

Tuolumne R.

YOSEMITE

RODGERS CANYON

Virginia Lakes

COLD CANYON

Lundy Lake

INYO NATIONAL FOREST

GRAND CANYON OF THE TUOLUMNE RIVER

Glen Aulin High Sierra Camp

Tioga Pass

To Manteca

Mather

Camp Mather

ASPEN VALLEY

Big Oak-Flat Entrance

White Wolf

NATIONAL

Tuolumne River

Lembert Dome

Tuolumne Meadows Visitor Center

120

Tioga Pass Entrance

120

South Fork Tuolumne River

May Lake

Porcupine Flat

120

Tenaya Lake

LYELL CANYON

Crane Flat

Yosemite Creek

Tamarack Flat

TENAYA CANYON

Sunrise

Vogelsang

CATHEDRAL RANGE

120

El Capitan

Yosemite Falls

Yosemite Village

Half Dome

John Muir Trail

PARK

STANISLAUS NATIONAL FOREST

YOSEMITE VALLEY

Bridalveil Falls

Glacier Point

Little Yosemite Valley

Merced R.

Merced Lake

ANSEL ADAMS WILDERNESS

Arch Rock Entrance

140

El Portal

Chinquapin

Glacier Point Rd.

Badger Pass Ski Area

Bridalveil Creek

RITTER RANGE

To Merced

SIERRA NATIONAL FOREST

S. Fork Merced R.

41

Bridalveil Creek

Buck Camp

SIERRA NATIONAL FOREST

Pioneer Yosemite History Center

Wawona

Wawona Information Center

Mariposa Grove

South Entrance

49

41

Fish Camp

To Oakhurst & Fresno

| △ | Campground |
| △ | High Sierra camp (By reservation only) |
| ⚐ | Ranger Station |

Sacramento

San Francisco

Map Area

CALIFORNIA

Los Angeles

0    5 mi
0    5 km

**REGULATIONS** Rangers in the Yosemite Valley spend more time being cops than rangers. They even have their own jail, so don't do anything you wouldn't do in your hometown. Despite the pressure, park regulations are pretty simple: Permits are required for overnight backpacking trips; fishing licenses are required; utilize proper food-storage methods in bear country; don't collect firewood in the valley; no off-road bicycle riding; dogs are allowed in the park but must be leashed and kept off trails; and *don't feed the animals.*

**SEASONS** Winter is my favorite time to visit the valley. It isn't crowded, as it is in summer, and a dusting of snow provides a stark contrast to all that granite. To see the waterfalls at their best, come in spring when snowmelt is at its peak. Fall can be cool, but it's beautiful and much less crowded than summer. Sunshine seekers will love summer—if they can tolerate the crowds.

The high country is under about 20 feet of snow November through May, so unless you're snow camping, summer is pretty much the only season to pitch a tent. Even in summer, thundershowers are a frequent occurrence, sometimes with a magnificent lightning show. Mosquitoes can be a plague during the peak of summer, but the situation improves after the first freeze.

**ORGANIZED TOURS & RANGER PROGRAMS** The park offers a number of ranger-guided walks, hikes, and other programs. Check at one of the visitor centers or in the *Yosemite Guide* for current topics, start times, and locations. Walks may vary from week to week, but you can always count on nature hikes, evening discussions on park anomalies (floods, fires, or critters), and the sunrise photography program aimed at replicating some of Ansel Adams's works. The sunrise photo walk always gets rave reviews from the early risers who venture out at dawn. All photo walks require advance registration. (Get details at the visitor centers.) The living history evening program outside at Yosemite Lodge is great for young and old alike.

Several organizations also host guided trips. **Yosemite Guides** ★★ (© 877/425-3366 or 209/379-2231; www.yosemiteguides.com) leads tours to lesser-known areas of the park and fly-fishing trips for all levels. The **Yosemite Institute** ★ (© 209/379-9511; www.yni.org/yi) is a nonprofit organization with a unique environment for learning about nature and the human history of the Sierra Nevada. **Incredible Adventures** (© 800/777-8464; www.incadventures.com) runs 3-day hikes in Yosemite from San Francisco.

**Yosemite Sightseeing Tours** (© 559/658-TOUR; www.yosemitetours.com) conducts scheduled as well as customized trips. Costs range from $76 to $86, depending on the season. Tours are operated on air-conditioned buses with picture windows. The sightseeing includes Mariposa Grove, Yosemite Valley, and Glacier Point. Guides point out geology, flora, and fauna and schedule stops for lunch, shopping, and photo opportunities. Pickup can be arranged from various motels throughout Oakhurst and Bass Lake.

A variety of **guided bus tours** are also available. You can buy tickets at Yosemite Lodge, the Ahwahnee, Curry Village, or beside the Village Store in Yosemite Village. Advanced reservations are suggested for all tours; space can be reserved in person or by phone (© 209/372-1240). Always double-check for updated departure schedules and prices. Most tours depart from Yosemite Lodge, the Ahwahnee, or Curry Village, and prices range from about $20 for adults for a 2-hour tour, to about $50 for adults for full-day trips. Children's rates are usually 40% to 50% less, and most tours offer discounts for seniors.

---

*Tips*  **The Bear Necessities**

In one recent year, bears broke into more than 1,100 cars in Yosemite National Park. If you'd like your vehicle left intact during your visit, never leave food inside your car; use the storage facilities in the park.

---

The 2-hour **Valley Floor Tour** is a great way to get acclimated to the park, with a good selection of photo ops, including El Capitan, Tunnel View, and Half Dome. This ride is also available on nights when the moon is full or near full. It's an eerie but beautiful scene when moonlight illuminates the valley's granite walls. Blankets and hot cocoa are included, but dress warmly, because it can get mighty chilly after the sun goes down. Purchase tickets at valley hotels or call ✆ **209/372-1240** for reservations.

The **Glacier Point Tour** is a 4-hour scenic bus ride through the valley to Glacier Point. Tours also depart from Yosemite Valley to **Mariposa Grove.** The Mariposa Grove trip takes 6 hours, includes the Big Trees tram tour that winds through the grove, and stops for lunch at Wawona. (Lunch is not provided.) You can combine the trip to Glacier Point and Mariposa Grove in an 8-hour bus ride.

If you're staying in the valley, the **Park Service** and **Yosemite Concession Services** present evening programs on park history and culture. Past summer programs have included discussions on early expeditions to Yosemite, the park's flora and fauna, geology, global ecology, and the legends of the American Indians who once lived here. Other programs have focused on Mark Wellman's courageous climb of El Capitan—he made the ascent as a paraplegic—and threats to Yosemite's environment.

**AVOIDING THE CROWDS**     Popularity isn't always the greatest thing for wild places. Over the last 20 years, Yosemite Valley has set records for the worst crowding, noise, crime, and traffic in any California national park.

The park covers more than 1,000 square miles, but most visitors flock to the floor of Yosemite Valley, the 1-mile-wide, 7-mile-long glacial scouring that tore a deep and steep valley from the solid granite of the Sierra Nevada. It becomes a total zoo between Memorial Day and Labor Day. Cars line up bumper to bumper on almost any busy weekend. In 1995, Yosemite's superintendent closed the entrances to the park 11 times between Memorial Day and mid-August, when the number of visitors reached the park's quota; she turned away 10,000 vehicles.

Our best advice is to visit before Memorial Day or after Labor Day. If you must go in summer, do your part to help out. It's not so much the numbers of people that are ruining the valley but their insistence on driving through it. Once you're here, park your car, then bike, hike, or ride the shuttle buses. You can rent bicycles at **Curry Village** (✆ **209/372-8319**) and **Yosemite Lodge** (✆ **209/372-1208**) in summer. It may take longer to get from point A to point B, but you're in one of the most gorgeous places on earth—so why hurry?

## EXPLORING THE PARK
### THE VALLEY

First-time visitors are often dumbstruck as they enter the valley from the west. The first two things you'll see are the delicate and beautiful **Bridalveil Fall** and the immense face of **El Capitan** , a stunning 3,593-foot-tall solid-granite rock. A short trail leads to the base of Bridalveil, which at 620 feet tall is only a medium-size fall by park standards, but one of the prettiest.

This is a perfect chance to get those knee-jerk tourist impulses under control early: Resist the temptation to rush around to see everything. Instead, take your time and look around. One of the best things about the valley is that many of its most famous features are visible from all over. Instead of rushing to the base of every waterfall or famous rock face and getting a crick in your neck from staring straight up, go to the visitor center and spend a half-hour learning something about the features of the valley. Buy the excellent *Map and Guide to Yosemite Valley* for $2.50; it describes many hikes and short nature walks. Then go take a look. Walking and biking are the best ways to get around. To cover longer distances, the park shuttles run frequently around the east end of the valley.

Three-quarters of a mile from the visitor center is **The Ahwahnee Hotel** (p. 301). Unlike the rest of the hotel accommodations in the park, the Ahwahnee lives up to its surroundings. The native granite-and-timber lodge, built in 1927, reflects an era when grand hotels were, well, grand. Fireplaces bigger than most Manhattan studio apartments warm the immense common rooms. Parlors and halls are filled with antique Native American rugs. Don't worry about what you're wearing unless you're going to dinner—this is Yosemite, after all.

The best view in the valley is from **Sentinel Bridge** ✪ over the Merced River. At sunset, Half Dome's face functions as a projection screen for the many hues of the sinking sun—from yellow to pink to dark purple, and the river reflects it all. Ansel Adams took one of his most famous photographs from this very spot.

The **Nature Center at Happy Isles** ✪ has great hands-on nature exhibitions for kids, plus a wheelchair-accessible path along the banks of the Merced River.

**VALLEY WALKS & HIKES**   Yosemite Falls is within a short stroll of the visitor center. You can see it better elsewhere in the valley, but it's impressive to stand at the base of all that falling water. The wind, noise, and spray generated when millions of gallons catapult 2,425 feet through space onto the rocks below are sometimes so overwhelming you can barely stand on the bridge.

The **Upper Yosemite Fall Trail** ✪ zigzags 3.5 miles from Sunnyside Campground to the top of Upper Yosemite Fall. This trail gives you an inkling of the weird, vertically oriented world that climbers enter when they scale Yosemite's sheer walls. As you climb this narrow switchback, the valley floor drops away until people below look like ants, but the top doesn't appear any closer. It's unnerving at first, but rewarding in the end. Plan on spending all day on this 7-mile round-trip trail because of the incredibly steep climb.

A mile-long trail leads from the Valley Stables (take the shuttle; no car parking) to **Mirror Lake** ✪. The already tiny lake is gradually becoming a meadow as it fills with silt, but the reflections of the valley walls and sky on its surface remain one of the park's most unforgettable sights.

Also accessible from the Valley Stables or nearby Happy Isles is the best valley hike of all—the **John Muir Trail** ✪✪ to Vernal and Nevada falls. It follows the Sierra crest 200 miles south to Mount Whitney, but you only need go 1.5 miles round-trip to get a great view of 317-foot Vernal Fall. Add another 1.5 miles and 1,000 vertical feet for the climb to the top of Vernal Fall on the **Mist Trail** ✪, where you'll get wet as you climb alongside the falls. On top of Vernal and before the base of Nevada Fall is a beautiful valley and deep pool. For an outrageous view of the valley and one heck of a workout, continue up the Mist Trail to the top of Nevada Fall. From 2,000 feet above Happy Isles, where you began, it's a dizzying view straight down the face of the fall. To the east is an interesting profile perspective of Half Dome. Return either by the Mist Trail or the slightly easier John Muir Trail for a 7-mile round-trip hike.

**Half Dome** may look insurmountable to anyone but an expert rock climber, yet thousands take the strenuous yet popular cable route up the backside every year. It's almost 17 miles round-trip and a 4,900-foot elevation gain from Happy Isle on the John Muir Trail. Many do it in a day, starting at first light and rushing home to beat nightfall. A more relaxed strategy is to camp in the backpacking campground in Little Yosemite Valley just past Nevada Fall. From here, the summit is within easy striking distance of the base of Half Dome. If you plan to spend the night, you need a Wilderness Pass (see "Camping" below). You must climb up a very steep granite face using steel cables installed by the park service. In summer, rangers also install boards as crossbeams, but they're still far apart. Wear shoes with lots of traction and bring your own leather gloves for the cables (your hands will thank you). Given any chance of a thunderstorm, the trail closes; that cable turns into a lighting rod, so they don't take any risks. The summit yields unbeatable views of the high country, Tenaya Canyon, Glacier Point, and the awe-inspiring abyss of the valley. When you shuffle up to the overhanging lip for a look down the face, be extremely careful not to kick rocks or anything else onto the climbers below, who are earning this view the hard way.

## THE SOUTHWEST CORNER

This corner of the park is densely forested and gently sculpted, in comparison to the stark granite that makes up so much of Yosemite. Coming from the valley, Highway 41 takes you to **Tunnel View**, site of a famous Ansel Adams photograph, and the best scenic outlook of the valley accessible by car. Virtually the whole valley is laid out below: Half Dome and Yosemite Falls straight ahead in the distance, Bridalveil to the right, and El Capitan to the left.

A few miles past the tunnel, Glacier Point Road turns off to the east. Closed in winter, this winding road leads to a picnic area at **Glacier Point**, site of another fabulous view of the valley, this time 3,000 feet below. Schedule at least an hour to drive here from the valley and an hour or two to absorb the view. This is a good place to study the glacial scouring of the valley; the Glacier Point perspective makes it easy to picture the landscape below filled with sheets of ice.

Some 30 miles south of the valley on Highway 41 are the **Wawona Hotel** (p. 302) and the **Pioneer Yosemite History Center.** The Wawona, built in 1879, is the oldest hotel in the park. Its Victorian architecture evokes a time when travelers spent days in horse-drawn wagons to get here. The Pioneer Center is a collection of early homesteading log buildings across the river from the Wawona.

One of the primary reasons Yosemite was set aside as a park was the **Mariposa Grove** of giant sequoias. (Many trails lead through it.) These huge trees have personalities to match their gargantuan size. Single limbs on the biggest tree in the grove, the Grizzly Giant, are 10 feet thick. The tree itself is 209 feet tall, 32 feet in diameter, and more than 2,700 years old. Totally out of scale with the size of the trees are the tiny sequoia cones. Smaller than a baseball and tightly closed, the cones won't release their cargo of seeds until opened by fire.

## THE HIGH COUNTRY ★★★

Yosemite's high country is stunning. Dome after dome of crystalline granite reflects the sunlight above deep-green meadows and icy-cold rivers.

**Tioga Pass** is the gateway to the high country. At times, it clings to the side of steep rock faces; in other places, it weaves through canyon bottoms. Several good campgrounds make it a pleasing overnight escape from summertime crowds in the valley, although use is increasing here, too. **Tenaya Lake ★** is popular for windsurfing, fishing, canoeing, sailing, and swimming, but the water is chilly. Many good hikes lead into the high country from here, and the granite domes surrounding the lake are popular with climbers. Fishing varies greatly from year to year.

**Tuolumne Meadows ★★** is near the top of Tioga Pass. Covering several square miles, this meadow is bordered by the Tuolumne River on one side and granite peaks on the other. The meadow is cut by many trout streams, and herds of mule deer are almost always present. The **Tuolumne Meadows Lodge** and store are a welcome counterpoint to the overdeveloped valley. In winter, they remove the canvas roofs and the buildings fill with snow. You can buy last-minute backpacking supplies here, or grab burgers and fries at the on-site café.

**TUOLUMNE MEADOWS HIKES & WALKS**   So many hikes lead from here into the backcountry that it's impossible to do them justice. A good trail passes an icy-cold spring and traverses several meadows.

On the far bank of the Tuolumne from the meadow, a trail leads downriver, eventually passing through the grand canyon of the Tuolumne and exiting at Hetch Hetchy. Shorter hikes will take you downriver past rapids and cascades.

An interesting geological quirk is the **Soda Springs** on the far side of Tuolumne Meadow from the road. This bubbling spring gushes carbonated water from a hole in the ground; a small log cabin marks its site.

For a selection of Yosemite high-country hikes and backpacking trips, consult some of the guidebooks to the area. Two of the best are published by Wilderness Press: *Tuolumne Meadows,* a hiking guide by Jeffrey B. Shaffer and Thomas Winnett; and *Yosemite National Park,* by Thomas Winnett and Jason Winnett.

## SPORTS & OUTDOOR PURSUITS

**BICYCLING**   With 10 miles of bike paths in addition to the valley roads, biking is an ideal way to get around the park. You can rent them at the **Yosemite Lodge** (© 209/372-1208) or **Curry Village** (© 209/372-8319) for about $6 per hour or $20 per day. You can also rent bike trailers for little kids at $11 per hour or $33 per day. All trails in the park are closed to mountain bikes.

**FISHING**   Trout season begins on the last Saturday in April and continues through November 15. The Merced River from Happy Isles downstream to the Pohono Bridge is catch-and-release only for native rainbow trout, and barbless hooks are required. Everyone 16 years old or more must display a California license to fish. Get licenses at the Yosemite Village Sport Shop (© 209/372-1286). Guided fly-fishing trips in Yosemite for all levels are available from **Yosemite Guides** (© 877/425-3366 or 209/ 379-2231; www.yosemiteguides.com). *Note:* Yosemite Valley has special fishing regulations; get information at the visitor centers.

**HORSEBACK RIDING**   Three stables offer day rides and multiday excursions in the park. **Yosemite Valley Stables** (© 209/372-8348) is open spring through fall.

The other two—**Wawona** (✆ 209/375-6502) and **Tuolumne Stables** (✆ 209/372-8427)—operate only in summer. Day rides run from about $55 to $95, depending on length. Multiday backcountry trips cost roughly $100 per day and must be booked almost a year in advance. The park wranglers can also be hired to make resupply drops at any of the High Sierra Camps if you plan an extended trip. Log on to www.yosemiteparktours.com (click on "Summer") for more information.

**GOLF**    The park has one golf course and several others nearby. **Wawona** (✆ 209/375-6572) sports a 9-hole, par-35 course that alternates between meadows and fairways. Just outside the park, the **River Creek Golf Course** (✆ 559/683-3388) is a 9-hole greens in the small hamlet of Ahwahnee (not at the hotel); and the 18-hole **Sierra Meadows Ranch Course** (✆ 559/642-1343) is in Oakhurst. Call for current fees and other information.

**RAFTING**    Rafting 3 leisurely miles down the Merced River is one of the most refreshing ways to see Yosemite Valley's spectacular scenery. At the raft rental shop in Curry Village (✆ 209/372-8341), daily fees are a mere $14 for adults and $12 for children under 13. Fees include a raft, paddles, mandatory life preservers, and transportation from Sentinel Beach to Curry Village. Swift currents and cold water can be deadly to young kids, so children under 50 pounds are not permitted in rental rafts. Log on to www.yosemiteparktours.com (click on "Summer") for more information.

**ICE-SKATING**    The **Curry Village Ice Rink** (✆ 209/372-8319) is fun in winter. It's outdoors, however, and melts quickly when the weather warms up. Rates are $6.50 for adults and $5 for children under 12. Skate rentals are $3.25.

**ROCK CLIMBING**    Much of the most technical advancement in rock climbing grew out of the highly competitive Yosemite Valley climbing scene of the 1970s and 1980s. Other places have since stepped into the limelight, but Yosemite is still one of the most desirable climbing destinations in the world.

The **Yosemite Mountaineering School** (✆ 209/372-8344; www.yosemitemountaineering.com) runs classes for beginning through advanced climbers. Considered one of the best climbing schools in the world, it offers private lessons that will teach you basic body moves and rappelling, and will take you on a single-pitch climb. Classes run from early spring to early October in the valley, and during summer in Tuolumne Meadows.

**SKIING & SNOWSHOEING**    Opened in 1935, **Badger Pass** (✆ 209/372-8430; www.yosemitepark.com) is the oldest operating ski area in California and great for families. Four chairs and one rope tow cover a compact mountain, with beginner and intermediate runs. At $35 for adults and $19 for children under 12, it's a great place to learn how to ski or snowboard. Naturalists lead special winter children's programs, and the facility provides babysitting.

Yosemite is also a popular destination for **cross-country skiers and snowshoers.** Both the Badger Pass ski school and the mountaineering school run trips and lessons for all abilities, ranging from basic technique to trans-Sierra crossings. Two ski huts can accommodate anyone taking guided cross-country tours, including the spiffy **Glacier Point Hut** (✆ 209/372-8444) with its massive stone fireplace, beamed ceilings, and bunk beds; and the **Ostrander Hut** (✆ 209/372-0740) with 25 bunks. You have to pack in your own supplies, however. If you're on your own, Crane Flat is a good place to go, as is the groomed track up to Glacier Point, a 20-mile round-trip self-guided tour.

## CAMPING

Campgrounds in Yosemite can be reserved up to 5 months in advance through the **National Park Reservation Service** (© 800/436-7275; http://reservations.nps.gov). *Be warned:* During busy season, all valley campsites sell out within hours of becoming available on the service.

Backpacking into the wilderness and camping there is the least crowded option and takes less planning than reserving a campground. If you plan to camp in the wilderness, you must get a free **Wilderness Pass** (and pay the park entrance fee). At least 40% of each trail-head quota is allocated up to 24 hours in advance; the rest is available by mail. Write to the Wilderness Center, P.O. Box 545, Yosemite, CA 95389, specify the dates and trail heads of entry and exit, the destination, number of people, and any accompanying animals; include a $5 per person advance-registration fee. You may also call © 209/372-0740 for a pass.

### VALLEY CAMPGROUNDS

Until January 1997, the park had five car campgrounds that were always full except in the dead of winter. Now the park has half the number of campsites, and getting a reservation on short notice takes a minor miracle. (Yosemite Valley lost almost half of its 900 camping spaces in a freak winter storm in 1997 that washed several campsites downstream and buried hundreds more beneath a foot of silt.)

The two-and-a-half remaining campgrounds—**North Pines, Upper Pines,** and half of **Lower Pines**—charge $18 per night. All have drinking water, flush toilets, pay phones, fire pits, and heavy ranger presence. Showers are available for a small fee at Curry Village. Upper Pines, North Pines, and Lower Pines allow small RVs (less than 40 ft. long). If you're expecting a real nature experience, skip camping in the valley unless you like doing so with 4,000 strangers.

**Camp 4** (previously named Sunnyside campground) is a year-round, walk-in campground that fills quickly since it's only $5 per night. Hard-core climbers used to live here for months at a time. The park service has stopped them, but this site still has a more bohemian atmosphere than any of the other campgrounds.

### CAMPGROUNDS ELSEWHERE IN THE PARK

Outside the valley, things open up for campers. Two-car campgrounds near the South Entrance of the park, **Wawona** and **Bridalveil Creek,** offer a total of 210 sites with all the amenities. Wawona is open year-round, and reservations are required May through September; otherwise, it's first-come, first-served. Family sites at Wawona are $18 per night, and group sites, which hold up to 30 people, are $40 per night. Because it sits well above the snow line, at more than 7,000 feet, Bridalveil is open only in

---

*Tips* **Securing Accommodations**

All hotel reservations can be made exactly 366 days in advance. Call **Yosemite Concessions Services** at © 559/252-4848 in the morning 366 days before your intended arrival for the best chance of securing a spot. If you don't plan that far in advance, it's still worth calling, because cancellations may leave new openings. You may also book reservations online through **www.yosemitepark.com**. Keep in mind that reservations held without deposit must be confirmed on the scheduled day of arrival by 4pm. Otherwise, you'll lose your reservation.

summer. Rates are $12 per night for first-come, first-served sites, and $40 for group sites.

Crane Flat, Hodgdon Meadow, and Tamarack Flat are all in the western corner of the park near the Big Oak Flat Entrance. **Crane Flat** is the nearest to the valley, about a half-hour drive away, with 166 sites, water, flush toilets, and fire pits. Its rates are $18 per night, and it's open June through September. **Hodgdon Meadow** is directly adjacent to the Big Oak Flat Entrance at 4,800 feet elevation. It's open year-round, charges $18 per night, and requires reservations May through September, through the National Park Reservation Service. Facilities include flush toilets, running water, a ranger station, and pay phones. It's one of the least crowded low-elevation car campgrounds, but you won't find lots to do here. **Tamarack Flat** is a waterless, 52-site campground with pit toilets. Open June through October, it's a bargain at $8 per night.

Tuolumne Meadows, White Wolf, Yosemite Creek, and Porcupine Flat are all above 8,000 feet and open only in summer. **Tuolumne Meadows** 🌲 is the largest campground in the park, with more than 300 spaces. It absorbs the crowd well and has all the amenities, including campfire programs and slide shows in the outdoor amphitheater. You will, however, feel sardine-packed between hundreds of other visitors. Half of the sites are reserved in advance; the rest are set aside on a first-come, first-served basis. Rates are $15 per night.

**White Wolf,** west of Tuolumne Meadows, is the other full-service campground in the high country, with 87 sites available for $18 per night for family sites, $40 for group sites. It offers a drier climate than the meadow and doesn't fill up as quickly. Sites are available on a first-come, first-served basis.

Two primitive camps, **Porcupine Flat** and **Yosemite Creek,** are the last to fill up in the park. Both have pit toilets but no running water, and charge $8 per night on a first-come, first-served basis.

## WHERE TO STAY IN THE PARK

**Yosemite Concessions Services,** 5410 E. Home Ave., Fresno, CA 93727 (✆ **559/252-4848**), operates all accommodations within the park and accepts all major credit cards. The reservations office is open Monday through Friday from 7am to 6pm, Saturday and Sunday from 8am to 5pm (PST). For more lodging options and information, or to make an online reservation request, visit **www.yosemitepark.com**.

Bridging the gap between backpacking and hotel stays are Yosemite's five backcountry **High Sierra Camps** (✆ **559/253-5674**). The camps—Glen Aulin, May Lake, Sunrise, Lake Merced, and Vogelsang—are good individual destinations. Or you can link several together, because they're arranged in a loose loop about a 10-mile hike from one another. Guests bunk dormitory-style in canvas tents; each camp has bathrooms and showers. Unguided stays cost $112 per night per person; guided hikes are $744 for 4 nights (including breakfast and dinner). Due to the huge popularity of these camps, management books reservations by lottery. They accept applications from October 15 to November 30, hold the lottery in December, and notify winners by the end of March.

**The Ahwahnee Hotel** ★★★    A National Historic Landmark noted for its granite-and-redwood architecture, the six-story Ahwahnee is one of the most romantic and beautiful hotels in California, with a VIP guest list that ranges from Winston Churchill and John F. Kennedy to Greta Garbo and Queen Elizabeth. With its soaring lobby, cathedral-like dining room, outstanding views, and steep prices, it's definitely worthy of the most special occasions. Try to reserve one of the more spacious cottages, which cost the same as rooms in the main hotel. For the price you're paying, the guest rooms—though pleasant, in warm woods and Indian-motif fabrics—may seem simple to the point of austerity. On the other hand, where else in the world can you look out your window and see Half Dome, Yosemite Falls, or Glacier Point? The **Ahwahnee Restaurant** is a colossal, impressive chamber highlighted by 50-foot-tall, floor-to-ceiling leaded windows. It's more noteworthy for its ambience, however, than for its expensive cuisine.

© 559/252-4848. Fax 559/456-0542. www.yosemitepark.com. 99 units, 24 cottages. $379–$835 double. Children 12 and under stay free in parent's room. Extra person $21. AE, DC, DISC, MC, V. Pets are not accepted, but they can board in the kennel at the park stables. **Amenities:** Restaurant and lounge; heated outdoor pool; nearby golf course; 2 tennis courts; Jacuzzi; concierge; tour desk; room service; babysitting (need 2 weeks notice; child must be potty-trained and at least 2 years old). *In room:* A/C (ceiling fan in cottages), TV, fridge in cottages, coffeemaker, hair dryer, iron.

**Curry Village** *Kids* Celebrating its 107th birthday in 2006, Curry Village is best known as a mass of more than 400 white canvas tents tightly packed together on the valley's south slope. It was founded in 1899 as cheap lodgings, at a mere $2 a day, although guests can kiss those days goodbye. Still, it's an economical place to crash, and it lends you the feeling of a camping vacation without the hassle of bringing your own tent. One downside is that these tents are basically canvas affairs, and this is bear country, so you'll need to lock up all foodstuffs and anything that bears might think is food (even toothpaste) in bear-proof lockers. They're free, but they may be a healthy walk from your tent-cabin. Curry Village also has more than 100 attractive wood cabins with private bathrooms; about 80 wood cabins that, like the tent-cabins, share a large bathhouse; and a number of motel rooms. Canvas tents have wood floors and sleep two to four people, with beds, bedding, dressers, and electrical outlets. The wood cabins are much more substantial and comfortable, and the motel rooms are functional and adequate. *Note:* If Curry Village is full, inquire about available canvas tents-cabins at Tuolumne Meadows Lodge or White Wolf Lodge.

© 559/252-4848. Fax 559/456-0542. www.yosemitepark.com. 628 units. $69–$113 double. Children 12 and under stay free in parent's room. Extra person $9–$11, tent cabins $4. AE, DC, DISC, MC, V. **Amenities:** Buffet-style dining from spring to fall; fast-food court; heated outdoor pool; nearby golf course; bike rental; tour/activities desk. *In room:* No phone.

**Wawona Hotel** ⋆ Six stately white buildings, set near towering trees in a green clearing, make up this classic, Victorian-style hotel. Don't be surprised if a horse and buggy rounds the driveway by the fishpond—it's that kind of place. What makes it so wonderful? Maybe it's the wide porches, the nearby 9-hole golf course, or the vines of hops cascading from one veranda to the next. The entire place was designated a National Historic Landmark in 1987. Clark Cottage is the oldest building, dating back to 1876, and the main hotel was built in 1879. Rooms are comfortable and quaint with a choice of a double and a twin bed, a king bed, or one double bed. (Most of the latter share bathrooms.) All rooms open onto wide porches and overlook green lawns. Clark Cottage is the most intimate. The main hotel has the widest porches and plenty of Adirondack chairs, and at night a pianist performs in the downstairs sunroom. *Note:* Nonguests attend the Saturday-evening summer lawn barbecues or Sunday brunch.

© 559/252-4848. www.yosemitepark.com. 104 units, 52 w/private bathroom. $115 double without private bathroom; $170 double w/private bathroom. Children 12 and under stay free in parent's room. Extra person $16. AE, DC, DISC, MC, V. **Amenities:** Restaurant; outdoor pool; golf course; tennis court. *In room:* Iron, no phone.

---

*Tips* **A Cottage in the Woods**

The key to a relaxing time at Yosemite National Park is to stay clear of the crowds, and one sure way to achieve this is to rent a private home or cottage in the park—but away from Yosemite Valley. A company called **Yosemite West Reservations** (*©* 559/642-2211) rents a variety of privately owned accommodations, ranging from fairly simple rooms with one queen-size bed and kitchenette (suitable for one or two people) to luxurious vacation homes with full-size kitchens, two bathrooms, living rooms, and beds for as many as eight people. Kitchens and kitchenettes are fully equipped, all bedding is provided, TVs and VCRs are on hand, and outdoor decks allow you to soak up the verdant views. All units also have gas or wood-burning fireplaces. The homes are in a forested section of the park, about 10 miles from Yosemite Valley and 8 miles from Badger Pass. Most units range from $99 to $265 per night. For more information, call or log onto www.yosemitewestreservations.com.

---

**Yosemite Lodge**   The next step down in valley accommodations, Yosemite Lodge is not actually a lodge but a large, more modern complex with two types of accommodations. The larger "Lodge" rooms with outdoor balconies have striking views of Yosemite Falls. Indeed the largest bonus—and curse—is that every room's front yard is the valley floor, which means you're near glorious, larger-than-life natural attractions and equally gargantuan crowds.

*©* 559/252-4848. www.yosemitepark.com. 245 units. $104–$161 double. Children 12 and under stay free in parent's room. Extra person $10–$12. AE, DC, DISC, MC, V. **Amenities:** 2 restaurants; bar; food court; heated outdoor pool; nearby golf course; bike rental; tour/activities desk; babysitting.

## WHERE TO DINE IN THE PARK

You certainly won't go hungry here; you'll find plenty of dining options in or near the park. You won't discover many bargains, however, so bring a full wallet.

### IN THE VALLEY

**Ahwahnee Dining Room**  ★★ AMERICAN/INTERNATIONAL   Dining here takes your breath away. Even if you are a died-in-the-wool, sleep-under-the-stars backpacker, the Ahwahnee Dining Room will not fail to impress you. It's where the great outdoors meets four-star cuisine, and it's a wonderful place to celebrate a special occasion. With understated elegance, the cavernous dining room, with its candelabra chandeliers hanging from the 34-foot beamed ceiling, seems intimate once you're seated. (Don't be fooled—it actually seats 350.) The walk from the entrance to the table is a long stroll that establishes the restaurant's grand openness. The menu changes frequently, with a good variety of creative yet recognizable dishes, such as herb-crusted halibut with lobster risotto, a veal chop with spinach ravioli, and pan-seared filet mignon with forest mushroom ragout, a potato cake, and truffle sauce. The dinner menu includes suggested wines (from an extensive wine list) for each entree. Breakfast includes a variety of egg dishes, hotcakes, and the like, plus specialties such as a thick apple crepe filled with spiced apples and raspberry purée. Lunch choices include a grilled turkey quesadilla and grilled portobello mushrooms on a sun-dried tomato roll; and a variety of plates and salads. An evening dress code requires men to wear a coat and long pants (ties are optional).

Ahwahnee Hotel, Yosemite Valley. © **209/372-1489.** Dinner reservations required. Breakfast $7.50–$17; lunch $7.50–$16; dinner $20–$31; Sun brunch $32 adults, $17 children. DC, DISC, MC, V. Mon–Sat 7–10am, 11:30am–3pm, and 5:30–9:15pm; Sun 7am–3pm and 5:30–9:15pm. Shuttle bus stop no. 3.

**Curry Dining Pavilion** *Kids* AMERICAN  A good spot for the very hungry. All-you-can-eat breakfast and dinner buffets offer a wide variety of well-prepared basic American selections at fairly reasonable prices.

Curry Village. Breakfast $9.25 adults, $5.50 children; dinner $12 adults, $6.25 children. DC, DISC, MC, V. Daily 7–10am and 5:30–8pm. Shuttle bus stops nos. 12, 13, 14, and 19.

**Curry Taqueria Stand** MEXICAN  A good place for a quick bite, this taco stand peddles spicy tacos, burritos, taco salads, beans, and rice.

Curry Village. $3–$6. No credit cards. Mon–Thurs 11am–5pm; Fri–Sun 8am–5pm. Closed in winter. Shuttle bus stops nos. 12, 13, 14, and 19.

**Curry Village Coffee Corner** COFFEE SHOP  Specialty coffees and fresh-baked pastries are the fare here. You can also buy ice cream after 11am.

Curry Village, Yosemite Valley. Most items $1–$3. DC, DISC, MC, V. Daily 6am–10pm. Shuttle bus stops nos. 12, 13, 14, and 19.

**Curry Village Pizza Patio** ★ *Kids* PIZZA  Need to watch ESPN? This is the place, but you may have to wait in line. One of the park's few big screens awaits inside, and if you're a sports buff, this is the place to be. The scenic outdoor patio offers large umbrellas, table service, and a great view of Mother Nature, plus or minus a hundred kids. The lounge also taps a few brews—nothing special, but a mix aimed to please. This is a great place to chill after a long day.

Curry Village, Yosemite Valley. Pizza $8–$16. DC, DISC, MC, V. Daily noon–9pm. Shuttle bus stop nos. 12, 13, 14, and 19.

**Degnan's Cafe** AMERICAN  Adjacent to Degnan's Deli, this cafe offers specialty coffee drinks, fresh pastries, wrap sandwiches, and ice cream. It's a good place for a quick bite when you're in a hurry.

Yosemite Village. Most items $1–$4. DC, DISC, MC, V. Daily 7am–7pm. Shuttle bus stop nos. D, 2, and 8.

**Degnan's Deli** ★★ *Value* DELI  A solid delicatessen with a large selection of generous sandwiches made to order, this is our top choice for a quick, healthy lunch or supper. Sometimes the line gets long, but it moves quickly. Half market and half deli, Degnan's also sells a selection of prepared items such as soups, salads, sandwiches, desserts, and snacks. The beer and wine selection is also good.

Yosemite Village. $3–$8. DC, DISC, MC, V. Daily 7am–7pm. Shuttle bus stops nos. D, 2, and 8.

**Degnan's Loft** *Kids* ITALIAN  This cheery restaurant, with a central fireplace and high-beamed ceilings, is adjacent to Degnan's Deli and Degnan's Cafe. It's a good choice for families, with a kid-friendly atmosphere and a menu that features pizza, calzones, lasagna, salads, and desserts.

Yosemite Village. Entrees $4.25–$21. DC, DISC, MC, V. Daily noon–9pm. Shuttle bus stop nos. D, 2, and 8.

**Mountain Room Restaurant** AMERICAN  The best thing about this restaurant is the view. The food's good too, but the floor-to-ceiling windows overlooking Yosemite Falls are spectacular, and there's not a bad seat in the house. We suggest the grilled chicken breast, which is flavorful and moist, as is the rainbow trout almondine and the Pacific salmon. Meals come with vegetables and bread. Soup or salad is extra.

The menu includes entrees for vegetarians, and the dessert tray is amazing. The Mountain Room also has a good wine list, and the Mountain Room Bar and Lounge (open 4–10pm Mon–Fri and noon–10pm Sat–Sun) has an a la carte menu.

Yosemite Lodge. Entrees $17–$29. DC, DISC, MC, V. Daily 5:30–9pm. Shuttle bus stop no. 6.

**Village Grill** AMERICAN    The Village Grill is a decent place to pick up fast food. It offers burgers, chicken sandwiches, and the like, and has outdoor seating.

Yosemite Village. Most items $3.75–$5.25. No credit cards. Daily 11am–5pm. Closed in winter. Shuttle bus stop nos. 1, 2, and 8.

**Yosemite Lodge Food Court** AMERICAN    You'll find breakfast, lunch, and dinner at this busy restaurant, which serves about 2,000 meals each day. A vast improvement over the traditional cafeteria, it's set up with a series of food stations, where you pick up your choices before heading to the centralized cashier. You can eat inside or in the outside seating area, which features tables with umbrellas and good views of Yosemite Falls. Food stations specialize in pasta (with a choice of sauces), pizza, deli sandwiches and salads, a grill (offering burgers, hot dogs, and hot sandwiches), meat-based and vegetarian entrees, desserts and baked goods, and beverages. A hot breakfast food station serves traditional American breakfast items.

Yosemite Lodge. Entrees $5–$14. DC, DISC, MC, V. Daily 6:30–10am, 11:30am–2pm, and 5–8:30pm. Shuttle bus stop no. 8.

## ELSEWHERE IN THE PARK

**Tuolumne Meadows Lodge** AMERICAN    One of the two restaurants in the high country, this lodge has something for everyone. The breakfast menu features the basics, including eggs, pancakes, fruit, oatmeal, and granola. Dinners always include a beef, chicken, fish, pasta, and vegetarian special, all of which change frequently. The quality can swing, but the prime rib and New York steak are consistently good.

Tuolumne Meadows, CA 120. ( 209/372-8413. Reservations required for dinner. Breakfast $3.55–$6.95; dinner $8.65–$19. DC, DISC, MC, V. Daily 7–9am and 6–8pm.

**Wawona Hotel Dining Room** ★★ AMERICAN    Like the hotel, the Wawona dining room is wide open, with lots of windows and sunlight, and the food is great. For breakfast, choose from a variety of items, including the Par Three, a combo of French toast or pancakes, eggs, and bacon or sausage—to fuel you up before you hit the golf course. Lunch features a variety of sandwiches and salads. Dinner appetizers are amazing, and a number of entrees are exceptional—such as brown sugar–rubbed pork loin with apple-onion relish and bourbon sauce, prime rib, or several seafood and veggie dishes. The cumin-crusted *ahi,* roasted whole garlic, and rock shrimp and potato risotto are sumptuous.

Wawona Hotel, Wawona Rd. ( 209/375-1425. Breakfast $3–$8; lunch $5–$10; dinner $14–$25. Sun buffets $9.95 breakfast, $16 brunch. DC, DISC, MC, V. Mon–Sat 7:30–10am, 11:30am–1:30pm, 5:30–9pm; Sun 7:30am–10am (breakfast buffet), 10:30am–1:30pm (brunch buffet), 5:30–9pm.

**White Wolf Lodge** AMERICAN    This casual restaurant has a mountain lodge atmosphere and a changing menu, serving generous portions of a variety of American standards. Breakfast choices include eggs, pancakes, omelets, or biscuits and gravy; and dinner always includes beef, chicken, fish, pasta, and vegetarian dishes. Takeout lunches are also available from noon to 2pm.

White Wolf, Tioga Rd. ( 209/372-8416. Reservations required for dinner. Breakfast $3.85–$6.95; dinner $7–$17. DC, DISC, MC, V. Daily 7:30–9:30am and 5–8:30pm.

## 3 Mammoth Lakes ✶✶

40 miles E of Yosemite; 319 miles E of San Francisco; 325 miles NE of Los Angeles

High in the Sierra, just southeast of Yosemite, Mammoth Lakes is surrounded by glacier-carved, pine-covered peaks that soar up from flower-filled meadows. It's an alpine region of sweeping beauty and one of California's favorite playgrounds for hiking, biking, horseback riding, skiing, and more. It's also home to one of the top-rated ski resorts in the world. At an elevation of 11,053 feet, Mammoth Mountain is higher than either Squaw or Heavenly, so the snow stays firm longer in the year for spring skiing. You won't find the long lift lines that you find at Tahoe, either—just more mountain and fewer people.

### ESSENTIALS

**GETTING THERE**    It's a 6-hour drive from San Francisco via Highway 120 over the Tioga Pass in Yosemite (closed in winter); 5 hours north of Los Angeles via Highway 14 and U.S. 395; and 3 hours south of Reno, Nevada, via U.S. 395. In winter, Mammoth is accessible via U.S. 395 from the north or the south.

**Mammoth Air Charter** (© 760/934-4279) offers charter flights to the area. It services Mammoth Lakes Airport on U.S. 395. The closest international airport is Reno-Tahoe Airport (© 775/328-6400). See "Lake Tahoe" in chapter 9 for airlines that service the Reno-Tahoe International Airport.

**VISITOR INFORMATION**    Contact the **Mammoth Lakes Visitors Bureau,** Highway 203 (P.O. Box 48), Mammoth Lakes, CA 93546 (© 888/466-2666 or 760/934-2712; www.visitmammoth.com).

### OUTDOOR PURSUITS

At the heart of several wilderness areas, Mammoth Lakes is cut through by the San Joaquin and Owens rivers. Mammoth Mountain overlooks the Ansel Adams Wilderness Area to the west and the John Muir Wilderness Area to the southeast, and beyond to the Inyo National Forest and the Sierra National Forest.

The **Mammoth Mountain Ski Area** ✶✶ (© 800/626-6684 or 760/934-2571; www.mammothmountain.com) is the central focus for both summer and winter activities. Visitors can ride the lifts just to see panoramic vistas, but those who want an active adventure have many options. If you do hit the slopes in winter, you can use the free **Mammoth Area Shuttle** or **Mammoth Sierra Express** taxi service (© 760/934-8294; www.mammothlakestransportation.com) for transportation between town and the ski area. The shuttle makes many stops and eliminates the long wait that may befall you if you drive yourself.

The state-of-the-art **Panorama Gondola** provides great viewing every day, in winter or summer, weather permitting. The gondola carries eight passengers and stops midway up the mountain and at the summit with 360-degree views. In summer, you can use it to access the hiking and biking trails on the mountain. Tickets are $16 for adults, $8 kids 6 to 12; kids under 6 ride free.

In addition to the most popular activities listed below, adventurers can go hot-air ballooning with **Mammoth Balloon Adventures** (© 760/937-UPUP; www.mammothballoonadventures.com). And golfers can play at **Snowcreek Golf Course,** Old Mammoth Road (© 760/934-6633).

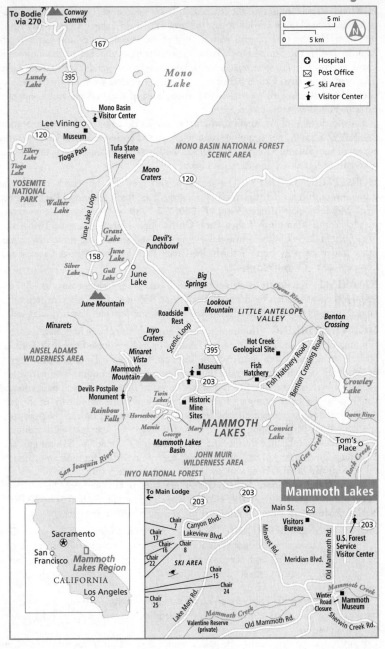

# Mammoth Lakes Region

To Bodie via 270
Conway Summit

167

Lundy Lake
395
Mono Lake

**Mono Basin National Forest Scenic Area**

Mono Basin Visitor Center

Lee Vining
120
Museum

Ellery Lake
Tioga Lake
Tioga Pass
Tufa State Reserve

**YOSEMITE NATIONAL PARK**
Walker Lake

Mono Craters
120

June Lake Loop
Grant Lake
Devil's Punchbowl

June Lake
158
Silver Lake
Gull Lake
June Lake

Big Springs

June Mountain

Lookout Mountain
**LITTLE ANTELOPE VALLEY**

Owens River

**Minarets**

Roadside Rest
Inyo Craters

Scenic Loop
395

Benton Crossing

**ANSEL ADAMS WILDERNESS AREA**

Minaret Vista
Mammoth Mountain

Hot Creek Geological Site

Fish Hatchery

Fish Hatchery Road
Benton Crossing Road

Crowley Lake

Devils Postpile Monument

Museum
203

Rainbow Falls

Twin Lakes
Horseshoe
Mamie
George
Mary

Historic Mine Sites

**MAMMOTH LAKES**

Owens River

Mammoth Lakes Basin

Convict Lake

McGee Creek

Tom's Place

Rock Creek

San Joaquin River

**JOHN MUIR WILDERNESS AREA**

**INYO NATIONAL FOREST**

### Legend
- ✛ Hospital
- ✉ Post Office
- ⛷ Ski Area
- ⚐ Visitor Center

0   5 mi
0   5 km
N

**California inset**
Sacramento
San Francisco
Mammoth Lakes Region
CALIFORNIA
Los Angeles

# Mammoth Lakes

To Main Lodge
203

203

Chair 7
Canyon Blvd.
Lakeview Blvd.
Chair 17
Chair 16
Chair 8
Chair 22
**SKI AREA**
Chair 15
Chair 24
Chair 25

Main St.
Visitors Bureau

Minaret Rd.
Meridian Blvd.

Old Mammoth Rd.

U.S. Forest Service Visitor Center
203

Mammoth Creek

Winter Road Closure
Mammoth Museum

Lake Mary Rd.
Valentine Reserve (private)
Mammoth Creek
Old Mammoth Rd.
Sherwin Creek Rd.

**HIKING** Trails abound in the Mammoth Lakes Basin area. They include the half-mile **Panorama Dome Trail,** just past the turnoff to Twin Lakes on Lake Mary Road, leading to the top of a plateau with a view of the Owens Valley and Lakes Basin. Another trail is the 5-mile **Duck Lake Trail,** starting at the end of the Coldwater Creek parking lot with switchbacks across Duck Pass past several lakes to Duck Lake. The head of the **Inyo Craters Trail** is accessible via a gravel road, off the Mammoth Scenic Loop Road. This trail takes you to the edge of these craters and a sign that explains how they were created.

For additional trail information and maps, contact the **Mammoth Ranger Station** (✆ 760/924-5500). For equipment and maps, go to **Footloose Sports Center,** at the corner of Canyon and Minaret (✆ 760/934-2400; www.footloosesports.com), which also rents in-line skates and mountain bikes.

**HORSEPACKING TRIPS** The region is also great for horseback riding, and numerous outfitters offer pack trips. Among them are **Red's Meadows Pack Station,** Red's Meadows, past Minaret Vista (✆ 800/292-7758 or 760/934-2345; www.reds meadow.com); **Mammoth Lakes Pack Outfit,** Lake Mary Road, past Twin Lakes (✆ 760/934-2434), with 1- to 6-day riding trips and semiannual horse drives, plus other wilderness workshops; and **McGee Creek Pack Station,** McGee Creek Road, Crowley Lake (✆ 760/935-4324).

**KAYAKING** Kayaks are available at Crowley Lake from **Caldera Kayaks** (✆ 760/934-1691; www.calderakayak.com), starting at $35 per day. This outfitter offers guided tours on Crowley and Mono lakes for $65, and provides instruction as well.

**MOUNTAIN BIKING** In summer, the mountain becomes one huge bike park and climbing playground. The bike park is famous for its **Kamikaze Downhill Trail,** an obstacle arena and slalom course where riders can test their balance and skill. Plenty of other trails accommodate gentler folk who just want to commune with nature and get a little exercise, and one area is designed for kids. Bike shuttles will haul you and your bike to the lower mountain trails if you want to skip the uphill part, or the gondola will take you to the summit and let you find your own way down. The park operates daily from 9am to 6pm, during summer months. A 1-day pass with unlimited access to the gondola, bike shuttle, and trail system is $32 for adults, $18 for kids ages 12 and under. A variety of rent-and-ride packages are available; for more information, call ✆ 800/MAMMOTH or visit www.mammothmountain.com.

In town, the **Footloose Sports Center** rents mountain bikes, at the corner of Canyon and Minaret (✆ 760/934-2400; www.footloosesports.com). The **NORBA National Mountain Bike Championships** take place here in summer.

**SKIING & SNOWBOARDING** In winter, Mammoth Mountain has more than 3,500 skiable acres, a 3,100-foot vertical drop, 150 trails (32 with snowmaking), and 30 lifts, including seven high-speed quads. The terrain is 30% beginner, 40% intermediate, and 30% advanced. It's known for power sun, ideal spring skiing conditions, and anywhere from 8 to 12 feet of snow.

**Tamarack Lodge** (✆ 760/934-2442; www.tamaracklodge.com) runs a cross-country ski center, and offers snowmobiling, dog-sledding, snowshoeing, and sleigh rides for nonskiers.

If you're renting equipment, you'll save money if you do it in town instead of the resort. We recommend **Footloose Sports Center,** at the corner of Canyon and Minaret

(© **760/934-2400;** www.footloosesports.com), and **Wave Rave Snowboard Shop,** on Main Street (Hwy. 203; © **760/934-2471**), for snowboards and accessories.

The **June Mountain Ski Area** ☆ (© **888/JUNEMTN** or 760/648-7733; www. junemountain.com), 20 minutes north of Mammoth, is smaller but offers many summer activities as well as 500 skiable acres, a 2,590-foot vertical drop, 35 trails, and eight lifts, including high-speed quads. The terrain is 35% beginner, 45% intermediate, and 20% advanced. It's at the center of a chain of lakes—Grant, Silver, Gull, and June—visible from the scenic driving loop around Highway 158. It's especially beautiful in the fall when the aspens are ablaze with gold.

**TROUT FISHING**   Mammoth Lakes Basin sits in a canyon, a couple miles west of town, with lakes that have made the region known for trout fishing: Mary, Mamie, Horseshoe, George, and Twin. Southeast of town, Crowley Lake is also famous for trout fishing, as are the San Joaquin and Owens rivers, but you can spin your reel at plenty of other nearby lakes as well. For more fishing information and guides, contact **Rick's Sport Center,** at Highway 203 and Center Street (© **760/934-3416**); **The Trout Fitter,** in the Shell Mart Center at Main Street and Old Mammoth Road (© **760/924-3676**); or **Kittredge Sports,** Main Street and Forest Trail (© **760/934-7566**), which rents equipment, supplies, and guides, teaches fly-fishing, and offers backcountry trips.

## EXPLORING THE SURROUNDING AREA

**Bodie** ☆ (www.bodie.net), one of the most authentic ghost towns in the West, is about an hour's drive north of Mammoth, past the Tioga Pass entrance to Yosemite. In 1870, more than 10,000 people lived in Bodie, mining $32 million in gold; today

---

### *Tips*  Winter Driving in the Sierra

Winter driving in the Sierra Nevada Range can be dangerous. The most hazardous roads are often closed, but others are negotiable only by vehicles with four-wheel-drive or tire chains. Be prepared for sudden blizzards, and protect yourself by taking these important precautions:

- Check road conditions before you set out by calling © **800/427-7623.**
- Let the rental-car company know you're planning to drive in snow, and ask whether the antifreeze is prepared for cold climates.
- Make sure your heater and defroster work.
- Always carry chains. In a blizzard, the police will not allow vehicles without chains on some highways. If you don't know how to put them on, you'll have to pay about $40 to have someone "chain up" your car at the side of the road.
- In your trunk, stow an ice scraper, a small shovel, sand or burlap for traction if you get stuck, warm blankets, and an extra car key (motorists often lock their keys in the car while chaining up).
- Don't think winter ends in March. At the end of last April, snow was up to 7 feet high on the sides of the roads leading to the valley, and cold temperatures made more snowfall more than plausible.

it's an eerie shell full of ghost stories. En route to Bodie, you'll pass **Mono Lake** ⭐ (pronounced *Mow*-no), near Lee Vining, which has startling tufa towers arising from its surface—limestone deposits formed by underground springs. It's a major bird-watching area—about 300 species nest or stop here during their migrations. Right off Highway 395 is the **Mono Basin Scenic Area Visitors Center** (✆ 760/647-3044; www.monolake.org; open every day in summer, Thurs–Mon in winter), with scheduled guided tours and a terrific environmental and historical display of this hauntingly beautiful 60-square-mile desert salt lake. After touring the visitors center, head for the **South Tufa Area,** at the southern end of the lake, and get a closer look at the tufa formations and briny water. FYI: Mono means "flies" in the language of the Yokuts, the Native Americans who live south of this region; get to the lake's edge and you'll see why the nickname is suitable.

## WHERE TO STAY

If you stay at the resort, you'll be steps from the lifts. If you opt for the town, you're closer to the restaurants and nightlife. Regardless, they're within a 5-minute drive of one another, so you can never be too far from the action.

More than 700 campsites service the area. They open on varying dates in June, depending on the weather. The largest are at Twin Lakes and Cold Water (both in the Mammoth Lakes Basin), Convict Lake, and Red's Meadow. For additional information, call the **Mammoth Ranger Station** (✆ 760/924-5500).

**Fern Creek Lodge** *Value*   You'll have to drive about 25 miles north of Mammoth to get the best lodging deal in the region. Less than a mile from the June Mountain ski areas, the Fern Creek Lodge is a spread of simple, fully furnished cabins on the sunrise side of the Eastern High Sierra. Built in 1927, it has seen its ups and downs, but thanks to the latest owners—the Hart family—the year-round fishing and skiing resort is better than ever. The least expensive cabins are small, with just enough room for a bed, a table and chairs, and a bathroom. All have fully equipped kitchens, and most have fireplaces. The units are all so different your best bet is to call and tell them what you're looking for. Rooms don't have phones, but guests may use a pay phone on the premises.

4628 Hwy. 158, June Lake, CA 93529. ✆ 800/621-9146 or 760/648-7722. www.ferncreeklodge.com. 10 cabins, 4 apts. $65 cabin for 2; $80–$150 cabin for 4; $235 cabin for 8; $90 apt for 4. Extra person $10. AE, DISC, MC, V. Certain pets allowed ($10 extra). **Amenities:** Common barbecue area; full kitchen; grocery and sporting-goods store. *In room:* TV w/HBO.

**Holiday Inn** ⭐   This faux-alpine lodge is one of Mammoth's newest hotels. A woodsy exterior with a river-rock base gives the three-story hotel a rustic appeal, although the interior feels contemporary. The generically decorated guest rooms contain all the comfort and amenities you could want, and come in variety of configurations, including a King/Kid suite with bunk beds. The suites offer a little extra room and Jacuzzi tubs. A spacious honeymoon suite caters to those seeking romance in the great outdoors.

3236 Main St. (behind the Chevron station), Mammoth Lakes, CA 93546. ✆ 800/HOLIDAY or 760/924-1234. Fax 760/934-3626. www.holiday-inn.com. 72 units. $129–$349 double and suite. Packages available. AE, DC, DISC, MC, V. **Amenities:** Cafe; bar; indoor heated pool; nearby golf course; exercise room; Jacuzzi; room service; coin-op laundry. *In room:* A/C, TV (VCR in some units), dataport, kitchenette in some units, fridge, coffeemaker, hair dryer, iron.

**Mammoth Mountain Inn** ⭐ *Kids*   Opposite the ski lodge at the base of the ski resort, this inn opened in 1954 as only one building, but was expanded a decade later into a larger, glossier complex. Though it was remodeled in the early 1990s, it retains the rugged appeal you'd expect from a mountain resort. The guest rooms, which were recently upgraded with new carpets and furnishings, are well equipped and pleasantly furnished. The best are the junior suites with a view of the ski area. Families love this place for its large condo units, day-care activities, cribs, playground, box lunches and picnic tables, and game room. An array of sports facilities includes bicycles, fishing or hiking guides, downhill or cross-country skiing, sleighing, horseback riding, and hay-wagon rides. Extras include free airport transportation and occasional entertainment. The downside is the 10-minute drive into town, but skiers can't get any closer to the slopes.

Minaret Rd. (P.O. Box 353), Mammoth Lakes, CA 93546. © **800/228-4947** or 760/934-2581. Fax 760/934-0701. www.mammothmountain.com. 173 units, 40 condos (some suitable for up to 13 people). Winter $125–$225 double, from $220–$535 condo; summer $99–$150 double, from $150 condo. Ski and mountain-biking packages available. AE, MC, V. **Amenities:** Restaurant; bar; heated outdoor pool; nearby golf course; 2 indoor and 1 outdoor whirlpool spas; mountain-bike rental; day-care center; game room; video arcade; concierge; 24-hr. room service; babysitting; coin-op laundry; executive-level rooms. *In room:* TV (VCR in 1- and 2-bedroom units), dataport, kitchen in some units, coffeemaker, hair dryer, iron.

**Motel 6** (Value)    The rooms may be small, but they're the nicest around in this price range. Factor in the pool, vending machines, and free coffee in the lobby, and you've got all you need to set up camp.

3372 Main St. (P.O. Box 1260), Mammoth Lakes, CA 93546. © **800/4-MOTEL6** or 760/934-6660. Fax 760/934-6989. www.motel6.com. 151 units. Winter $62–$86 double; summer from $55 double. Extra person $6. AARP discounts. AE, DC, DISC, MC, V. Pets accepted (1 pet per room). **Amenities:** Heated outdoor pool (summer only); coin-op laundry. *In room:* A/C, TV, dataport.

**Sherwin Villas** (Value)    Just outside the center of town on Old Mammoth Road, this cluster of woodsy condos is perfect for families or groups of friends traveling together. You'll find one- to four-bedroom units, each with a fully stocked kitchen, fireplace, linens, and access to a free ski shuttle that will take you to the slopes (a 5-min. drive away). Considering how many people you can pack into these apartments it's a good deal—and if you stay 4 weekday nights, the 5th night is free. When making reservations, specify exactly what you're looking for: Each condo is independently owned and varies dramatically in both decor and quality; you can view a few photos of each condo on the website.

362 Old Mammoth Rd. (P.O. Box 2249), Mammoth Lakes, CA 93546. © **760/934-4773**. www.sherwinvillas.com. 70 condos. 1-bedroom unit for up to 4 people $100–$120 winter, from $95 summer; 2-bedroom loft for up to 6 people $140–$190 winter, from $115 summer; 3-bedroom unit for up to 8 people $155–$220 winter, from $135 summer; 4-bedroom unit for up to 10 people $195–$260 winter, from $155 summer. Extra person $10. MC, V. **Amenities:** Outdoor pool; tennis courts; 2 Jacuzzis; Finnish sauna; game room. *In room:* TV, kitchen, phone on request.

**Sierra Lodge** (Value)    In the heart of Mammoth Lakes, this two-story inn offers contemporary lodgings without a trace of rusticity. The large guest rooms are pleasantly decorated with framed blond-wood furnishings, modern prints, track lighting, big beds, kitchenettes, and small patios or balconies with partial mountain views. The two-bedroom suite—equipped with two queen beds and a full-size pull-out sofa—is ideal for groups or families. Facilities include an outdoor Jacuzzi and a fireside room for relaxing. Other perks include ski lockers, free covered parking, continental breakfast, free shuttle service right out front, and a short walk to Mammoth's best restaurant, Nevados (see review below).

3540 Main St. (Hwy. 203; P.O. Box 9228), Mammoth Lakes, CA 93546. © **800/356-5711** or 760/934-8881. Fax 760/934-7231. www.sierralodge.com. 36 units. $89–$159 double. Rates include continental breakfast. AE, DISC, MC, V. Pets accepted for $10 per night w/$100 deposit. **Amenities:** Nearby golf course; outdoor Jacuzzi. *In room:* TV, dataport, kitchenette, fridge, hair dryer.

**Tamarack Lodge & Resort** The lodge and cabin accommodations at this lakeside retreat are nothing fancy, but that's what has kept guests coming here since the 1920s. The cabins dotted around the 6-acre property accommodate two to nine people, and they come in a variety of configurations: from studios with wood-burning stoves and showers to two-bedroom/two-bathroom quarters with fireplaces. The best units are the lakefront cabins; try to request one with a lake view. The least expensive rooms, in the main lodge, come with private or shared bathrooms. **The Lakefront Restaurant** is romantic with a seasonally changing menu. Entrees range from grilled medallions of elk filet to seared sea scallops and fresh Hawaiian ahi (tuna) flown in daily. In the winter, the lodge opens its popular cross-country ski center with more than 25 miles of trails and skating lanes, ski rentals, and a ski school. Boat and canoe rentals are also available.

Twin Lakes Rd., off Lake Mary Rd. (P.O. Box 69), Mammoth Lakes, CA 93546. © **800/MAMMOTH** or 760/934-2442. Fax 760/934-2281. www.tamaracklodge.com. 11 units, 6 w/private bathroom; 27 cabins. $84–$275 double; $125–$475 cabin. AE, MC, V. **Amenities:** Restaurant; nearby golf course. *In room:* Fax, kitchen in cabins, fridge, coffeemaker, iron.

## WHERE TO DINE

**Berger's Restaurant** *(Value)* *(Kids)* AMERICAN If, after a full day of skiing, you need a hearty American meal at a fair price, head down the mountain to Berger's. Its cabin-like interior, with local photos on the wooden walls, suits the surroundings. Portions are huge and include an array of burgers, steak, ribs, chicken, and sandwiches, as well as a few hefty salads. Entrees come with salad, garlic bread, and either fries or a baked potato. Sandwiches, which cost up to $8 and come with salad and fries, will also easily fill you up without emptying your wallet. The children's menu is the ultimate bargain, offering a selection of kid-friendly feasts for under $6. The daily lunch specials are most coveted by locals, but if you want to try one, come early—they almost always sell out.

6118 Minaret Rd. © **760/934-6622.** Reservations recommended. Main courses $8.25–$15. MC, V. Daily 11am–9:30pm.

**Grumpy's Saloon and Eatery** *(★)* *(Kids)* AMERICAN For more than 2 decades, Grumpy's has been Mammoth's main "sports restaurant"—a log building with 35 TVs, pool tables, pinball machines, video games, and foosball tables. The bar has a great selection of beers on tap, and the hearty, affordable grub features burgers (go for the Grumpy Burger), tasty barbecued ribs, homemade chili, a handful of Mexican items, and the famous quarter-pound Dogger, an unbelievably enormous hot dog. Everything on the menu comes with a choice of fries, coleslaw, or barbecued baked beans, just to make certain that nobody leaves hungry. Stop by for happy hour, which usually features a free buffet of hors d'oeuvres that may include Buffalo wings, cheese and crackers, or mini-quesadillas.

361 Mammoth Rd. © **760/934-8587.** www.grumpysmammoth.com. Main courses $6.25–$16. AE, MC, V. Mon–Sun 11am–10pm; bar stays open until 2am.

**Nevados** *(★★)* EUROPEAN/CALIFORNIA Nevados is one of Mammoth Lakes' best restaurants and a longtime favorite with the locals and Los Angelenos on their annual ski or summer holiday. Owner/host Tim Dawson is usually on hand nightly to ensure that everyone's satisfied with the innovative cuisine and house-baked breads. Most everyone orders the prix-fixe three-course meal, which may consist of a strudel appetizer of wild mushrooms and rabbit with roasted shallots and grilled scallions; a main course of braised Provimi veal shank with roasted tomatoes and garlic mashed potatoes; and a warm pear-and-almond tart sweetened with caramel sauce and vanilla-bean ice cream for dessert. Throw in the casual, sweet ambience (white tablecloths, candles, and French country murals) and the extensive selection of wines, single-malt scotches, and single-batch bourbons, and it's no wonder this is the hangout of choice for ski instructors and race coaches.

Main St. (at Minaret Rd.). © 760/934-4466. Reservations recommended. Main courses $19–$25; fixed-price meal $40. AE, DC, DISC, MC, V. Daily 5:30–9:30pm.

**The Restaurant at Convict Lake** ☆☆ CONTINENTAL/FRENCH    For years, this restaurant on the edge of Convict Lake was a local secret, but the word got out when *Wine Spectator* featured it. Now you'd better make reservations if you want to enjoy a meal in this plank-sided cabin with an open-beam ceiling, wood floors, copper-hooded free-standing fireplace, and mountain views. Five miles south of Mammoth Lakes, it's well worth the drive to spend a romantic evening feasting on duck confit flavored with sun-dried cherry sauce, Chilean sea bass with mango-pineapple-cilantro relish, or lamb loin in a hazelnut-and-rosemary sauce. Linger a bit longer to savor the bananas Foster flambé or meringue topped with kiwi fruit and whipped cream.

Convict Lake Rd. © 760/934-3803. www.convictlake.com. Reservations recommended. Main courses $15–$30. AE, MC, V. Summer daily 11am–2pm; year-round daily 5:30–9:30pm.

**Shogun** ☆ JAPANESE    Sushi and tempura in an alpine setting may seem out of context, but this authentic Japanese restaurant, on the second floor of a strip mall, consistently packs in both tourists and locals. Diners at the eight-seat sushi bar sup on sashimi, hand rolls, and a variety of sushi creations. Delicate tempura, sweet and tangy teriyaki dishes, and grilled *yakitori* skewers come a la carte or as combination dinners. Hearty eaters can order the Boat Dinner, which includes beef and chicken teriyaki, tempura, *tonkatsu,* sashimi or salmon, and dessert for $21 per person (minimum two people). Sake, beer, and cocktails are also available.

Old Mammoth Rd. (in the Sierra Center Mall). © 760/934-3970. Reservations recommended. Main courses $8.95–$18. AE, DC, DISC, MC, V. Mon–Sun 5–9:30pm.

**Skadi** ☆☆ ECLECTIC    Suitably named after the Viking goddess of skiing and hunting, Skadi is the domain of chef-owner Ian Algerøenof, a former chef at Nevados. It's the perfect place for an après-ski cocktail at the 14-seat bar, a snack from the substantial selection of appetizers and desserts, or a full dinner. Skadi's big-city, post-modern aura is a welcome change after all that local alpine simplicity. Main courses include dishes such as pan-roasted crispy-skin salmon served with mashed potatoes and roasted beets, or braised lamb shanks with rosemary-garlic mashed potatoes and a side of garlic confit. Finish the evening with the wild honey–roasted strawberries or house-made chocolates.

587 Old Mammoth Rd. (in the Sherwin Plaza III shopping mall). © 760/934-3902. www.restaurantskadi.com. Reservations recommended. Main courses $22–$28. AE, MC, V. Wed–Sun 5:30–10pm.

**Whiskey Creek** ☆ AMERICAN    If you favor surf-and-turf fare combined with alpine atmosphere and a swinging nightlife scene, you'll want to make a reservation here. Whiskey Creek's wraparound windows proffer a pretty view of the snow-clad mountains, and the menu is known for its excellent South Carolina pork chops, bacon-wrapped meatloaf, and barbecued pork spareribs, all served with a heaping side of roasted garlic mashed potatoes. The dining room may be peaceful, but the upper-level brewpub is a different world. If you're not too stuffed, head upstairs to hear live music every night from 9pm until at least 1am, making it the number-one spot in town to hear cheesy pickup lines.

24 Lake Mary Rd. (at Minaret Rd.). ✆ 760/934-2555. Reservations recommended. Main courses $16–$25. AE, DC, DISC, MC, V. Daily 5–10pm (summer 5:30pm); bar stays open until 2am.

## 4 Devils Postpile National Monument ✿

10 miles W of Mammoth; 50 miles E of Yosemite's eastern boundary

Just a few miles outside the town of Mammoth Lakes, Devils Postpile National Monument is home to one of nature's most curious geological spectacles. Formed when molten lava cracked as it cooled, the 60-foot-high, blue-gray basalt columns that form the postpile look more like an enormous, eerie pipe organ or a jumble of string cheese than anything you'd expect to see made from stone. The mostly six-sided columns formed underground and were exposed when glaciers scoured the valley during the last ice age, some 10,000 years ago. Similar examples of columnar basalt are found in Ireland and Scotland.

Because of its high elevation (7,900 ft.) and heavy snowfall, the monument is open only from summer until early fall. The weather in summer is usually clear and warm, but afternoon thundershowers can soak the unprepared. Nights are still cold, so bring good tents and sleeping bags if you'll be camping. The Mammoth Lakes region is famous for its beautiful lakes—but unfortunately all that water attracts lots of mosquitoes. Plan for them.

### GETTING THERE

From late June to early September, cars are prohibited in the monument between 7:30am and 5:30pm, because the roads can't handle the traffic. Visitors must take a shuttle bus to and from locations in the monument. Although it takes some planning, the resulting peace and quiet warrant the trouble and make you wonder why the park service hasn't implemented similar programs at Yosemite Valley and other traffic hot spots.

**VISITOR INFORMATION** For information before you go, call ✆ **760/934-2289** during open season, or ✆ **760/872-4881** from November to May. You'll also find plenty of info at **www.nps.gov/depo/depomain.htm**.

### HIKING

Devils Postpile is more than a bunch of rocks, no matter how impressive those rocks might be. On the banks of the San Joaquin River, amid granite peaks and crystalline mountain lakes, the 800-acre park is a gateway to a hiker's paradise. Short paths lead from here to the top of the postpile and to **Soda Springs,** a spring of cold carbonated water.

A longer hike (about 1.3 miles) from the separate Rainbow Falls Trail head will take you to spectacular **Rainbow Falls** ✿, where the middle fork of the San Joaquin plunges 101 feet from a lava cliff. From the trail, a stairway and short trail lead to the base of the falls and swimming holes below.

The **Pacific Crest Trail** and the **John Muir Trail** (which connects Yosemite National Park with Kings Canyon and Sequoia national parks) run through here. Named after the conservationist and author who is largely credited with saving Yosemite and popularizing the Sierra Nevada as a place worth preserving, the 211-mile

John Muir Trail traverses some of the most difficult, remote parts of the Sierra. You can access it from two points in Devils Postpile, either near the ranger station, or from the Rainbow Falls Trail head. From here, you can hike as far as your feet will take you north or south. *Note:* Mountain bikes are not permitted on trails.

## CAMPING

While most visitors stay in or around Mammoth Lakes, the monument does maintain a 21-site campground with piped water, flush toilets, fire pits, and picnic tables on a first-come, first-served basis. Rates are $8 per night. Bears are common in the park, so take proper food-storage measures. Leashed pets are permitted on trails and in camp. Call the **National Park Service** (© **760/934-2289,** or 760/872-4881 Nov–May; www.nps.gov/depo/depomain.htm) for details. Other nearby U.S. Forest Service campgrounds include **Red's Meadow** and **Upper Soda Springs.**

## 5 En Route to Sequoia & Kings Canyon

Though **Visalia** is the official "gateway" and the city closest to Sequoia and Kings Canyon national parks, it's still 40 minutes to the park entrance. Much closer is the small town of **Three Rivers,** which until recently had a few mediocre restaurants, coffee shops, and motels for visitors. That's changing with the opening of the **Shoshone Inn,** which has added 60 more hotel rooms in Visalia, in addition to its two restaurants.

### ESSENTIALS

**GETTING THERE**    If you're driving from San Francisco, take I-580 east to I-5 south to Highway 198 east. The trip takes about 5 hours.

   **Amtrak** (© **800/USA-RAIL;** www.amtrak.com) stops at nearby Hanford, and a shuttle runs from there to Visalia.

**VISITOR INFORMATION**    Contact the **Visalia Chamber of Commerce,** 720 W. Mineral King Rd., Visalia, CA 93291 (© **559/734-5876;** www.visaliachamber.org).

### WHERE TO STAY

In Three Rivers, try the **Holiday Inn Express,** 40820 Sierra Dr. (Hwy. 198), Three Rivers, CA 93271 (© **800/HOLIDAY** or 559/561-9000). For other options, contact **The Reservation Centre** (© **866/561-0410** or 559/561-0410; www.rescentre.com).

**Ben Maddox House** ★★   On a residential street of Victorian homes, 4 blocks from the town's main street, the Ben Maddox House is an impressive sight: Its triangular gable is punctuated with a round window and two tall palm trees looming over the front yard. The house, built in 1876, is built of redwood, and its rooms retain their original dark-oak trim and white-oak floors. The six guest rooms have 18th- and 19th-century furnishings, and the two front rooms have French doors leading to two small porch/sitting areas. A full made-to-order breakfast is part of the experience.

601 N. Encina St., Visalia, CA 93291. © **800/401-9800** or 559/739-0721. Fax 559/625-0420. www.benmaddox house.com. 6 units. $110–$120 double. Rates include breakfast. AE, DISC, MC, V. **Amenities:** Outdoor pool; nearby golf course. *In room:* A/C, TV w/free movies, dataport, fridge, hair dryer, iron.

**Buckeye Tree Lodge** ★ (Value   Just a half mile from the entrance to Sequoia National Park, this motel is a good choice for almost anyone. Not only does it offer affordable, attractive rooms, but the property also has rolling lawns that lead down to a picturesque river, and every room has a patio or balcony with splendid views. Rooms are clean, basic, motel units, with a king bed or two queen beds. Eight rooms have showers only; the rest have shower/tub combos. Another option is the separate cottage, which sleeps up to five.

46000 Sierra Dr., Three Rivers, CA 93271. © **559/561-5900.** www.buckeyetree.com. 12 units. $55–$130 double; $148–$205 cottage. Rates include continental breakfast. AE, DC, DISC, MC, V. Pets accepted but must be declared when making reservations. **Amenities:** Outdoor pool. *In room:* A/C, TV, VCR (video rentals available), fridge, coffeemaker, microwave (in some rooms).

**Lake Elowin Resort** ★★ Undoubtedly one of the best places to stay in the Sierra, this is what a mountain resort should be—a place to get away from it all, without the distraction of phones and televisions. Rustic, clean cabins under huge trees look out at Lake Elowin, a small body of water where guests can fish, above the Kaweah River. Milton Melkonian purchased the resort in the 1970s with the idea of creating a place to coexist with nature, and he is fastidious about his property, which now attracts all sorts of creative types, such as writers and artists. Cabins can accommodate two to six people. We especially like cabin no. 1, which sits close to the lake and has a delightful view from the kitchen window; and Master Cabin, with a fireplace, a deck, and a Jacuzzi. All cabins include linens and towels, pots and pans, kitchen utensils, and barbecues. You bring the food, sunblock, and good attitude. The entire property is nonsmoking; guests must actually sign a contract that they will not smoke here.

43840 Dineley Dr., Three Rivers, CA 93271 © **559/561-3460.** Fax 559/561-1300. www.lake-elowin.com. 10 cabins w/showers only. $120–$300 double. AE, DISC, MC, V. From eastbound Sierra Dr. in Three Rivers, about 2½ miles before the park entrance, turn left on Dineley Dr. (the street sign says DINLEY) and drive across a bridge. Bear right, and it's less than ½ mile to the resort's driveway. **Amenities:** Swimming hole; free canoe rental. *In room:* A/C.

**Plantation Bed & Breakfast** ★★★ Step into the Old South at this fun bed-and-breakfast, where the inspiration for the room names and decor comes from *Gone with the Wind.* Those seeking a quietly conservative atmosphere will want to request the Ashley Wilkes Room, which has a king bed, while honeymooners might enjoy the luxurious Scarlett O'Hara Room, with a king bed, velvet love seat, fireplace, and marble bathroom with a Jacuzzi and separate shower. Our favorite is the Belle Watling Room, done up in an elegant bordello style, with a king-size bed with an enormous mirror next to it, a red crystal chandelier, and a claw-foot bathtub with a tasteful, Renaissance-style nude painted on the side. Two rooms have showers only, while the others have showers and tubs.

33038 Hwy. 198, Lemon Cove, CA 93244 (on Hwy. 198, 16 miles west of the park entrance). © **800/240-1466** or 559/597-2555. Fax 559/597-2551. www.plantationbnb.com. 7 units. A/C. $139–$229 double. Rates include full breakfast. AE, DC, DISC, MC, V. **Amenities:** Large pool; Jacuzzi. *In room:* TV, VCR (most rooms), no phone.

## WHERE TO DINE

**The Vintage Press** ★★ AMERICAN/CONTINENTAL This has long been considered the best restaurant in a 100-mile radius, a bastion of culinary merit in the gastronomic wasteland between Los Angeles and San Francisco. The design is reminiscent of a *fin de siècle* gin mill in Gold Rush San Francisco, with a bar imported from that city, manufactured by the Brunswick Company (of bowling-alley fame); lots of antiques bought at local auctions; and glittering panels of leaded glass and mirrors. The place is big enough (250 seats) to feed a boatload of Gold Rush hopefuls, and it has a bustling bar and lounge where a pianist presents live music Thursday through Saturday from 5:30 to 9pm.

The menu is supplemented by daily specials, such as a zesty rack of lamb roasted in a cabernet sauce with rosemary and pistachios. The regular menu offers about a dozen meat and fish dishes, with steaks as well as choices such as red snapper with lemon, almonds, and capers, or pork tenderloin with Dijon mustard, red chile, and honey. To start, I recommend farm-raised fresh oysters on the half shell or the wild mushrooms with cognac in puff pastry. The restaurant's wine cellar, a winner of the *Wine Spectator* Award of Excellence, offers more than 1,000 selections

216 N. Willis St., Visalia. ℂ 559/733-3033. www.thevintagepress.com. Reservations recommended at dinner. Main courses $8.95–$15 lunch, $12–$25 dinner. AE, DC, MC, V. Mon–Thurs 11:30am–2pm and 6–10pm; Fri–Sat 11:30am–2pm and 6–11pm; Sun 10am–2pm and 5–9pm.

## 6 Sequoia & Kings Canyon National Parks ★★

30 miles E of Visalia

Only 200 road miles separate Yosemite from Sequoia and Kings Canyon national parks, but they're worlds apart. While the National Park Service has taken every opportunity to modernize, accessorize, and urbanize Yosemite, resulting in a frenetic tourist scene, at Sequoia and Kings Canyon, they've treated the wilderness with respect and care. Only one road, the Generals Highway, loops through the area, and no road traverses the Sierra here. The park service recommends that vehicles over 22 feet long avoid the steep and windy stretch between Potwisha Campground and the Giant Forest in Sequoia National Park. Generally speaking, the park is much less accessible by car than most, but spectacular for those willing to head out on foot.

The Sierra Nevada tilts upward as it runs south. **Mount Whitney,** at 14,494 feet (the highest point in the lower 48 states), is just one of many high peaks in Sequoia and Kings Canyon. The **Pacific Crest Trail** also reaches its highest point here, crossing north to south through both parks. In addition to snow-covered peaks, Sequoia and Kings Canyon are home to the largest groves of giant sequoias in the Sierra Nevada, as well as the headwaters of the Kern, Kaweah, and Kings rivers. A few high-country lakes are home to some of the only remaining pure-strain golden trout. Bears, deer, and numerous smaller animals and birds depend on the parks' miles and miles of wild habitat for year-round breeding and feeding grounds.

Technically, Sequoia and Kings Canyon are two separate but contiguous parks, managed jointly from the park headquarters at Ash Mountain, just past the entrance on Highway 198 east of Visalia.

### ESSENTIALS

Most visitors make a loop through the parks by entering at Grant Grove and leaving through Ash Mountain, or vice versa.

**VISITOR INFORMATION**    The parks have three major visitor centers open year-round, some seasonal facilities, and a museum where you can buy books and maps and discuss your plans with park rangers. In Sequoia National Park, the largest visitor center is **Foothills Visitor Center** (ℂ 559/565-3135), just inside the Ash Mountain Entrance on Highway 198. Exhibits focus on the Sierran foothills, a biologically diverse ecosystem. The **Giant Forest Museum** (ℂ 559/565-4480) is housed in a historic building and offers extensive exhibits on giant sequoias. **Lodgepole Visitor Center** (ℂ 559/565-4436) includes exhibits on geology, wildlife, air quality, and park history. It's 4½ miles north of Giant Forest Village, and it's closed Tuesday through

> **Tips**  **National Parks vs. National Forests:**
> **What You Don't Know Can Cost You**
> _____
>
> Sierra, Inyo, and Sequoia national forests surround Kings Canyon and Sequoia
> national parks. What's the difference between a national park and a national
> forest? National parks are intended to preserve natural and historic features,
> in addition to providing recreation areas that are easy on the land. National
> forests, on the other hand, operate under a multiple-use concept and some-
> times allow for the harvesting of commodities such as lumber and minerals.
> National parks and national forests have different rules, and you should know
> them. An activity that's legal in a forest can earn you a fine in a park.
>
> Parks forbid hunting; forests usually allow it. Dogs can walk on forest
> trails, but not in parks. You can only camp in numbered sites in designated
> areas in parks; in the forest it's either in campgrounds or, unless posted oth-
> erwise, near roadsides. You can ride your bike on a forest trail; in parks you
> must stay on the roads, and helmets are required for persons 18 and
> younger. To protect the ecosystem in parks, you can't disturb anything—
> plants, pinecones, or rocks; in the forest, collecting a few things for personal
> use is permitted.
>
> For more information, contact the **National Park Service** at © 559/565-3341,
> or the **Forest Service** at © 559/784-1500.

Thursday in winter. The visitor center in **Grant Grove,** Kings Canyon National Park
(© **559/565-4307**), includes exhibits on logging and the role of fire in the forests.
Open only in summer, a small visitor center at **Cedar Grove** in Kings Canyon and a
ranger station at Sequoia's **Mineral King** dispense backcountry permits as well as
information.

To research before you go, log on to www.nps.gov/seki, www.sequoia-kingscanyon.
com, www.sequoiahistory.org, or www.visitsequoia.com, or call © **559/565-3341.**

**FEES & PERMITS**    A $10 fee per car is good for 7 days' entry at any park entrance.
An annual pass costs $20; the Golden Age pass offers lifetime access for seniors 62 and
over for $10; and blind visitors or others with permanent disabilities get free entry
with the Golden Access pass.

Wilderness permits are required for overnight backpacking in the parks. You can
reserve the $10 permits in advance by downloading an application from the national
park website at www.fs.fed.us/r5/inyo and mailing or faxing it to the **Wilderness Permit Office,** 351 Pacu Lane, Suite 200, Bishop, CA 93514 (© **760/873-2485;** fax
760/873-2484). A phone reservation system © **760/873-2483** is open 8am to 4pm,
7 days a week, from June 1 to October 1, and weekdays the rest of the year. If you
plan to climb Mount Whitney, you must enter a lottery for a permit. You'll need to
fill out an application, which you can download and print from the park website
(www.fs.fed.us/r5/inyo). Send it to the Wilderness Permit Office, 351 Pacu Lane,
Suite 200, Bishop, CA 93514. Applications for the Mount Whitney trail are $15 a
person.

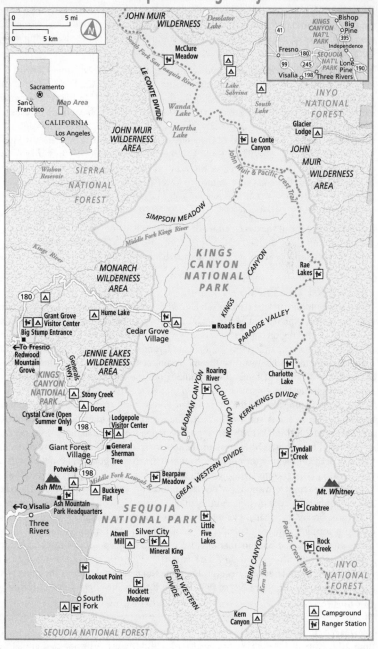

SEQUOIA NATIONAL FOREST

**REGULATIONS** Mountain bikes and dogs are forbidden on all park trails (dogs are permitted in developed areas but must be leashed). The park service allows firewood gathering at campgrounds, although supplies can be scarce. Removing wood from living or standing trees is forbidden.

**THE SEASONS** In the high altitudes, where most Sequoia and Kings Canyon visitors are headed, the summers are short and the winters cold. Snow in July and August, although rare, is not unheard of. At mid-elevations, where the sequoias grow, spring can come as early as April or as late as June. Afternoon showers are occasional. In winter, only the main roads into the parks are usually open; the climate can range from bitter cold to pleasant and can change minute by minute. The Generals Highway between Sequoia and Kings Canyon closes for plowing during and after snowstorms. Be ready for anything if you head into the backcountry on skis. In summer, poison oak and rattlesnakes are common in lower elevations, and mosquitoes are plentiful in all wet areas.

**AVOIDING THE CROWDS** To escape the crowds and see less-used areas of the parks, enter on one of the dead-end roads to Mineral King or Cedar Grove (both open only in summer), or South Fork. The lack of through traffic makes these parts of the parks incredibly peaceful even at full capacity, and they're gateways to some of the best hiking.

## EXPLORING THE PARKS

The second-oldest national park in the United States, Sequoia National Park was created, in 1890, at the request of San Joaquin Valley residents concerned with the conservation of the region's giant redwoods. The park has some 75 groves of giant sequoias, but the easiest places to see them are **Grant Grove** ⚝, in Kings Canyon, near the park entrance on Highway 180 from Fresno, or **Giant Forest** ⚝, a huge enclave of trees with 40 miles of footpaths, 16 miles from the entrance to Sequoia National Park on Highway 198.

The 2-mile **Congress Trail** loop in Giant Forest starts at the base of the **General Sherman Tree** ⚝, the largest living tree in the world. Single branches of this monster are more than 7 feet thick. Each year it grows enough wood to make a 60-foot-tall tree of normal dimensions. Other trees in the grove are nearly as large; many of them, however peaceful-looking they may be, bear militaristic and political monikers such as General Lee. Longer trails lead to remote reaches of the grove and nearby meadows.

Unlike the coast redwoods, which reproduce by sprouting or by seeds, giant sequoias only reproduce by seed. Adult sequoias rarely die of diseases and are protected from most fire by thick bark. The huge trees have surprisingly shallow roots, and most die from toppling when their roots are damaged and can no longer support them. These groves, like the ones in Yosemite, were explored by conservationist and nature writer John Muir, who named the Giant Forest.

Besides the sequoia groves, Sequoia and Kings Canyon are home to the most pristine wilderness in the Sierra Nevada. At **Road's End** on the Kings Canyon Highway

---

*Tips* **Fill 'Er Up**

Note that neither park has a single gas station, so be sure to fill up your gas tank before you enter.

(open late May to early Nov), you can stand by the banks of the Kings River and stare up at granite walls rising thousands of feet above the river, the deepest canyon in the United States.

Near Giant Forest Village, **Moro Rock** is a 6,725-foot-tall granite dome formed by the exfoliation of rock layers. A quarter-mile trail scales the dome for a spectacular view of the adjacent Canyon of the Middle Fork of the Kaweah. The trail gains 300 feet in 400 yards, so be ready for a climb.

**Crystal Cave** is 15 miles from the Highway 198 park entrance; cave parking is an additional 7 miles. Here you can take a 50-minute tour of Crystal's beautiful marble interior. The tour is $8 for adults, $6 for seniors, $4 for children ages 6 to 12, and free for kids 6 and under. Tickets are not sold at the cave and must be purchased at the Lodgepole or Foothills visitor centers at least 1½ hours in advance. Be sure to wear sturdy shoes and bring a jacket. For information, call © **559/565-3759** or log on to www.sequoiahistory.org. The cave is open mid-May to late September daily from 11am to 4pm.

**Boyden Cavern,** on Highway 180 in neighboring Sequoia National Forest, is a cave where, for a fee, you can take a 45-minute tour to see stalactites and stalagmites. Call © **209/736-2708** for details or visit www.caverntours.com. The cave is open April through October daily from 10am to 5pm.

## HIKING THE PARKS

Hiking and backpacking are what these parks are all about. Some 700 miles of trails connect canyons, lakes, and high alpine meadows and snowfields.

When traveling overnight inside parks boundaries, overnight and/or day-use permits are required. If you want to do serious overnight backpacking, see "Fees & Permits" under "Essentials" above.

Some of the park's most impressive hikes start in the **Mineral King** section in the southern end of Sequoia. Beginning at 7,800 feet, trails lead onward and upward to destinations such as Sawtooth Pass, Crystal Lake, and the old White Chief Trail to the now-defunct White Chief Mine. Once an unsuccessful silver-mining town in the 1870s, Mineral King was the center of a battle in the late 1970s when developers sought to build a huge ski resort. They were defeated when Congress added Mineral King to Sequoia National Park, and the wilderness remains.

The **John Muir Trail,** which begins in Yosemite Valley, ends at Mount Whitney. For many miles it coincides with the **Pacific Crest Trail** as it skirts the highest peaks in the park. This is the most difficult part of the Pacific Crest, above 10,000 feet most of the time and crossing 12,000-foot-tall passes.

---

> *Fun Fact* **A Question of Size**
>
> Until recently, the National Park Service claimed that the General Sherman Tree was the largest living thing on earth. Technically, however, this may not be true; now the claim is that it's the largest living *tree*—which, after all, is still quite a distinction. The reason for the change? Park officials say some underground fungi may actually be larger, and groves of aspen trees share a common root system, making them one living thing, also bigger than the General.

---

Other hikers like to explore the northern part of Kings Canyon from **Cedar Grove** and **Road's End.** The **Paradise Valley Trail,** leading to beautiful Mist Falls, is a fairly easy day trip by park standards. The **Copper Creek Trail** immediately rises into the high wilderness around Granite Pass at 10,673 feet, one of the most strenuous day hikes in the parks.

If the altitude and steepness are too much for you at these trail heads, try some of the longer hikes in **Giant Forest** or **Grant Grove.** These forests are woven with interlocking loops that allow you to take as short or as long a hike as you want. The 6-mile **Trail of the Sequoias** in Giant Forest will take you to the grove's far-eastern end, where you'll find some of the finest trees. In Grant Grove, a 100-foot walk through the hollow trunk of the **Fallen Monarch** makes a fascinating side trip. The tree has been used for shelter for more than 100 years and is tall enough inside that you can walk through without bending over.

Perhaps the most traversed trail to the park is the **Whitney Portal Trail.** It runs from east of Sequoia near Lone Pine, through Inyo National Forest, to Sequoia's boundary, the summit of Mount Whitney. Though it's a straightforward walk to the summit and it's possible to do it in a long day hike, you'd better be in tip-top shape before attempting it. Almost half the people who attempt Whitney, including those who camp partway up, don't reach the summit. Weather, altitude, and fatigue can stop even the most prepared party. For more information, contact the **Mount Whitney Ranger Station** at © 760/876-6200. For wilderness permits, see "Fees & Permits" at the beginning of this section.

The official park map and guide has good road maps for the parks, but for serious hiking you'll want to check out *Sierra South: 100 Back-Country Trips,* by Thomas Winnett and Jason Winnett (Wilderness Press). Another good guide is *Kings Canyon Country,* a hiking handbook by Ginny and Lew Clark. The Grant Grove, Lodgepole, Cedar Grove, Foothills, and Mineral King visitor centers sell a complete selection of maps and guidebooks. Books and maps are also available by mail through the **Sequoia Natural History Association** (© 559/565-3759; www.sequoiahistory.org).

## OTHER OUTDOOR PURSUITS

**FISHING**   The **Kaweah** drainage, the parks' lakes, and a section of the south fork of the **Kings River** are open all year for trout fishing, including rainbow, brook, German brown, and golden trout. Most other waters are open for trout fishing from late April to mid-November, and for other species year-round. California fishing licenses (available at stores in the park) are required for anglers 16 and older, and you should also get a copy of the National Park Service's fishing regulations, available at visitor centers.

**HORSEBACK RIDING**    Concessionaires in both parks and the adjacent national monument during the summer offer guided horseback and mule rides and overnight pack trips. In Kings Canyon, **Cedar Grove Pack Station** (© 559/565-3464 summer, 559/337-2314 winter) is about 1 mile east of Cedar Grove Village; and **Grant Grove Stables** (© 559/335-9292 summer, 559/337-2314 winter) is near Grant Grove Village. In Giant Sequoia National Monument, **Horse Corral Pack Station** is on Big Meadows Road, 10 miles east of Generals Highway (© 559/565-3404 summer, 559/564-6429 winter; www.horsecorralpackers.com). The pack stations offer hourly rides as well as overnight treks, while the stables offer day-rides only. Rates range from $25 to $30 for a 1-hour ride, to $75 to $100 for a full day in the saddle; call for current charges for pack trips

**RAFTING & KAYAKING**    Only fairly recently have professional outfitters begun taking experienced rafters and kayakers down the Class IV and V Kaweah and Upper Kings rivers outside the parks. Check **The Reservation Center** website at **www.res centre.com/rafting.htm** for a good list of companies running trips. Rafting and kayaking here are only for the very adventurous.

**SKIING & SNOWSHOEING**    **Wolverton,** 2 miles north of the General Sherman tree, has a snow-play and cross-country ski area. You can rent skis and snowshoes at the Lodgepole Market. About 50 miles of marked, cross-country trails run through the **Giant Forest** and **Grant Grove** areas. Rangers offer naturalist talks and snowshoe walks some weekends. Rental equipment (including snowshoes) and lessons are available at the Grant Grove Market. For more information on cross-country skiing, sledding, or snowshoeing at Grant Grove, call the park service at © **559/335-5500;** for Wolverton, call © **559/565-3435.** Kids can sled and play in the snow-play areas near Wolverton and at Big Stump, Columbine, and Azalea in Grant Grove.

The Sequoia Natural History Association operates the **Pear Lake Ski Hut** for snowshoers and cross-country skiers, which can accommodate up to 10 people. Use of the facility is by lottery. For further information, call © **559/565-3759.**

**WHITE-WATER BOATING**    The **Kaweah** and **Upper Kings** rivers in the parks are not open to boating (neither kayaks nor inflatable rafts), but several companies run trips just outside the parks. You're guaranteed to get wet, but this roller-coaster ride through the rapids is thrilling, and a great way to experience these scenic rivers. **Kaweah White Water Adventures** (© 800/229-8658 or 559/561-1000; www.kaweah whitewater.com) runs class III, IV, and V trips (rated moderate to difficult) on the Merced River. Trips are run in inflatable kayaks or rafts from spring to early fall. Prices range from about $50 per person for a 3-hour trip to $130 per person (including lunch) for a full day. **Whitewater Voyages** (© 800/400-7238; www.whitewatervoyages. com) offers trips on the Kaweah, Kings, Kern, and Merced rivers, with rates that range from $89 to $170 (including lunch) for full-day trips; multiday trips are also available (call for rates). **Kings River Expeditions** (© 800/846-3674 or 559/233-4881; www.kingsriver.com) specializes in rafting trips on the Kings. For 1-day trips, they charge $90 to $150 in spring, and $130 to $225 from mid-May until the season ends. Overnight trips are also available (call for rates)

## CAMPING

Backpackers will find numerous camping opportunities in and around Sequoia and Kings Canyon national parks. It's important to remember that when camping in this area, proper food storage is *required*—for the sake of the black bears as well as your safety. See local bulletin boards for instructions.

## IN SEQUOIA NATIONAL PARK

The only national park campgrounds that accept reservations are Dorst and Lodgepole (© **800/365-2267;** http://reservations.nps.gov), which will do so up to 5 months in advance; the other campgrounds are first-come, first-served. Additional information on the national park campgrounds (but not reservations) can be obtained by calling the general Sequoia/Kings Canyon information line at © **559/565-3341.**

The two biggest campgrounds in the park are in the Lodgepole area. The **Lodgepole Campground,** with flush toilets, is often crowded, but it's pretty and near some spectacular big trees. Nearby backcountry trails offer some solitude. Close to the ground are a grocery store, restaurant, visitor center, children's nature center, evening ranger programs, and gift shop. From Giant Forest, drive 5 miles northeast on the Generals Highway.

**Dorst Campground,** 14 miles northwest of Giant Forest via the Generals Highway, is a high-elevation campground with easy access to Muir Grove and some pleasant backcountry trails. It has flush toilets and evening ranger programs. Group campsites are also available here by reservation.

In the Foothills area, **Potwisha Campground** is small, with well-spaced sites tucked beneath oak trees along the Marble Fork of the Kaweah River. The campground has flush toilets, but it gets very hot in summer. From the Ash Mountain Entrance, drive 3 miles northeast on the Generals Highway to the campground entrance. The **Buckeye Flat Campground** ⭐, open to tents only, is also set among oaks along the Middle Fork of the Kaweah River. Although it also gets hot in summer, it's among our favorites, for its scenery. Recently rehabilitated, it has flush toilets. From the Ash Mountain Entrance, drive about 6 miles northeast on the Generals Highway to the Hospital Rock Ranger Station. From there, follow signs to the campground, which is several miles down a narrow, winding road. **South Fork Campground** is the smallest and most remote campground in the park, just inside Sequoia's southwestern boundary. It is set along the South Fork of the Kaweah River and has pit toilets only. From the town of Three Rivers go east on South Fork Road 23 miles to the campground.

The two campgrounds in the Mineral King area are open to tents only—no RVs or trailers. **Atwell Mill Campground** is a pretty, small campground near the East Fork of the Kaweah River, at Atwell Creek. It has pit toilets. From Three Rivers, take Mineral King Road east for 20 miles to the campground. **Cold Springs Campground,** which also has pit toilets, is a beautiful place to stay, but it's not very accessible. Once you get there, however, you'll be rewarded with beautiful scenery. It's also a good starting point for many backcountry hikes, given its proximity to the Mineral King Ranger Station. From Three Rivers, take Mineral King Road east for 25 miles to the campground.

## IN KINGS CANYON NATIONAL PARK

All the campgrounds in Kings Canyon are first-come, first-served (no reservations), and all have flush toilets. More information can be obtained by calling the general Sequoia/Kings Canyon information line at © **559/565-3341.**

The Grant Grove area has three attractive campgrounds near the big trees—**Azalea, Crystal Springs,** and **Sunset.** All have a nice woodsy feel, they're close to park facilities, and they offer evening ranger programs. To get to them from the Big Stump Entrance, take Highway 180 east about 1¾ miles.

The Cedar Grove Village area has several campgrounds, all accessed from Highway 180. All are fairly close to the facilities in Cedar Grove Village. **Sentinel,** the first to open for the season, fills up quickly. **Moraine** is the farthest from the crowds. **Sheep Creek,** along picturesque Sheep Creek, opens as needed.

## WHERE TO STAY IN THE PARKS

**Cedar Grove Lodge** ★ This motel offers comfortable rooms on the bank of the Kings River. Getting here is half the fun—it's a 36-mile drive down a winding highway with beautiful vistas along the way. The rooms here are standard motel accommodations—clean and comfortable, but nothing special. What you're really paying for is the location, surrounded by tall trees with a pretty river running by. Most of the rooms are above the Cedar Grove Café with communal decks with river views. I prefer the three smaller, less attractively appointed rooms on the ground level, with private patios looking onto the river.

Hwy. 180, Cedar Grove, Kings Canyon National Park (mail: Sequoia Kings Canyon Park Services Co., 5755 E. Kings Canyon Rd., Ste. 101, Fresno, CA 93727). ☏ **866/522-6966** or 559/452-1081. Fax 559/452-1353. www.sequoia-kingscanyon.com. 18 units. $109–$125 double. AE, DISC, MC, V. Closed Nov–Apr. *In room:* A/C, no phone; ground-floor rooms have fridge, microwave.

**Grant Grove Cabins** *Value* Although all the accommodations here are cabins, they offer a wide range of amenities and prices, from handsomely restored cabins that ooze history, with private bathrooms, to primitive tent-cabins that simply provide a comfortable bed and shelter at a very low price. Those who want to "rough it" in style should reserve one of the nine cabins, built in the 1920s, that have electricity, indoor plumbing, and full private bathrooms. A bit less modern, but still quite comfortable, the 43 basic cabins have kerosene lanterns for light and a shared bathhouse. Some are wooden; others, available in summer only, have wood floors and walls but canvas roofs. All cabins have full linen service. It's a 10-minute walk from the cabins to the Grant Grove visitor center, and the Grant Grove Restaurant is also nearby.

Hwy. 180, Grant Grove Village, Kings Canyon National Park (mail: Sequoia Kings Canyon Park Services Co., 5755 E. Kings Canyon Rd., Ste. 101, Fresno, CA 93727). ☏ **866/522-6966** or 559/452-1081. Fax 559/452-1353. www.sequoia-kingscanyon.com. 53 units (9 w/private bathroom). $57–$115 cabins. Register at Grant Grove Village Registration Center, between the restaurant and gift shop. AE, DISC, MC, V.

**John Muir Lodge** ★★ This handsome log lodge, built in 1998, looks perfect in its beautiful national-park setting. It's an excellent choice for visitors who want quiet, comfortable, modern rooms, with full bathrooms and coffeemakers, in a forest environment. Standard rooms have two queen-size beds and wonderful views of the surrounding forest. A mountain lodge atmosphere prevails. Suites consist of two connecting standard rooms, but one of the rooms has a queen bed and a queen sofa sleeper instead of two queens.

Hwy. 180, Grant Grove Village, Kings Canyon National Park (mail: Sequoia Kings Canyon Park Services Co., 5755 E. Kings Canyon Rd., Ste. 101, Fresno, CA 93727). ☏ **866/522-6966** or 559/452-1081. Fax 559/452-1353. www.sequoia-kingscanyon.com. 36 units. $160 rooms; $260 suites. Register at Grant Grove Village Registration Center, between the restaurant and gift shop. AE, DISC, MC, V.

**Silver City Mountain Resort** ★ Three types of cabins are available here, with a variety of bed combinations (some cabins sleep up to eight) and wood stoves for heat. Wood is provided, along with blankets and pillows, but guests need to bring their own sheets, pillowcases, bath and kitchen towels, paper towels, and tall trash bags. The top-of-the-line Swiss Chalets are finished in knotty pine with completely equipped kitchens, full bathrooms, Internet access, and an outdoor barbecue. The midlevel units, dubbed Comfy Cabins, are two-bedroom units with complete kitchens, propane wall lamps and kerosene lanterns, small restrooms with toilets but no showers (you'll have to make do with the centrally located bathhouse), and decks with barbecue grills. Rustic Cabins, which were built in the 1930s, are the most basic units, with light from kerosene and propane lamps; a camp kitchen with a gas stove and an oven; a cold-water sink; and an outdoor deck with barbecue.

Mineral King, Sequoia National Park (mail: 2570 Rodman Dr., Los Osos, CA 93402). (C) **559/561-3223**, or 805/528-2730 in winter. Fax 805/528-8039. www.silvercityresort.com. 14 cabins, 7 w/shared central bathhouse. $75–$275 double. Discounts June 1–15 and after Sept 18. MC, V. Closed Nov–May. Take Hwy. 198 through Three Rivers to the Mineral King turnoff. Silver City is a little more than halfway between Lookout Point and Mineral King. **Amenities:** Restaurant; bakery; breakfast bar; store.

# 11

# Sacramento, the Gold Country & the Central Valley

*by Matthew Richard Poole*

On the morning of January 24, 1848, carpenter James Marshall was working on John Sutter's mill in Coloma when he stumbled upon a gold nugget on the south fork of the American River. Despite Sutter's wishes to keep it a secret, word leaked out—a word that would change the fate of California almost overnight: *Gold!*

The news spread like wildfire, and a frenzy seized the nation: The Gold Rush was on. Within 3 years, the population of the state grew from 15,000 to more than 265,000. Most of these newcomers were single men under the age of 40, and not far behind were the merchants, bankers, and women who made their fortunes catering to the miners, most of whom went bust in their search for wealth.

Sacramento quickly grew as a supply town at the base of the goldfields. The Gold Country boom lasted less than a decade; the supply was quickly exhausted, and many towns shrank or disappeared. Sacramento, however, continued to grow as the fertile Central Valley south of it exploited another source of wealth, becoming the vegetable-and-fruit garden of the nation.

A trip along Highway 49 from the northern mines to the southern mines conveys a sense of what life was like on the mining frontier. Many of the towns along this route seem frozen in time, down to Main Street with its raised wooden sidewalks, double porches, saloons, and Victorian storefronts. Each town tells a similar story of sudden wealth and explosive growth, yet each has also left behind its own unique imprint. Any fan of movie westerns will recognize the setting, given that hundreds, perhaps even thousands, of films have been shot in these parts.

At the base of the Gold Country's hills is the sprawling, flat Central Valley. Some 240 miles long and 50 miles wide, it's California's agricultural breadbasket, the source of bounty shipped across the nation and overseas. A lot of state history has revolved around the struggle for control of the water used to irrigate the valley and make this inland desert bloom. Yes, despite its aridity, a breathtaking panorama of orange and pistachio groves, grapevines, and strawberry fields stretches uninterrupted for miles.

## 1 Sacramento ★

90 miles E of San Francisco; 383 miles N of Los Angeles

Sacramento, with a metro-area population of nearly 1.8 million, is one of the state's fastest-growing areas. In addition to being the state capital, it is a thriving shipping and processing center for the fruit, vegetables, rice, wheat, and dairy goods produced in the

Central Valley. In the past decade, it's also become an area of high-tech spillover from Silicon Valley, and more recently, a suburb for Bay Area workers seeking affordable homes. The quantity and quality of downtown restaurants—such as the Esquire Grill and The Waterboy—have improved as well. This prosperous and politically charged city has broad, tree-shaded streets lined with some impressive Victorians and well-crafted bungalows. At its heart sits the capitol—Sacramento's most visible attraction—in a large park replete with flower gardens, memorial statuary, and curious squirrels. Inside the capitol, visitors strain to get a glimpse of California's movie star governor, Arnold "The Terminator" Schwartznegger.

Sacramento is far from a tourist town, but it does have its share of touristy activities. Visitors and locals alike enjoy spending the day walking through Old Sacramento, floating down the American River, or biking the shady paths along the Sacramento and American rivers. Locals fondly refer to their water-bordered town as "River City." And did I mention that in summer the weather is seriously hot? So much so that San Franciscans drive to Sacramento just to thaw out.

## ESSENTIALS

**GETTING THERE** If you're driving from San Francisco, Sacramento is about 90 miles east on I-80. From Los Angeles, take I-5 through the Central Valley directly into Sacramento. From North Lake Tahoe, get on I-80 west, and from South Lake Tahoe take U.S. 50.

**Sacramento International Airport** (© **916/929-5411**), 12 miles northwest of downtown Sacramento, is served by about a dozen airlines, including Alaska Airlines, American, America West, Continental, Delta, Northwest, Southwest, and United. **SuperShuttle** (© **800-258-3826**) will get you from the airport to downtown; it charges a flat rate of $14 to the capital, a bargain compared to the $25 a conventional taxi would cost.

**Amtrak** (© **800/USA-RAIL;** www.amtrak.com) trains serve Sacramento daily. The Greyhound terminal is at Seventh and L streets.

**VISITOR INFORMATION** The **Sacramento Convention and Visitors Bureau,** 1303 J St., Sacramento, CA 95814 (© **916/264-7777;** www.discovergold.org) provides plenty of information for travelers. It's open Monday through Friday from 8am to 5pm. Once in the city, you can also stop by the **Old Sacramento Visitor Center,** 1002 Second St. (© **916/442-7644**), in Old Sacramento; it's usually open daily from 10am to 5pm. The city's major daily paper is the *Sacramento Bee* (www.sacbee.com).

**ORIENTATION** Suburbia sprawls around Sacramento, but its downtown area is relatively compact. Getting around the city is made easy by a gridlike pattern of streets designated by numbers or letters. The capitol, on 10th Street between N and L streets, is the key landmark. From the front of the capitol, M Street—at this point called Capitol Mall—runs 10 straight blocks to Old Sacramento, the oldest section of the city.

## WHAT TO SEE & DO

In town, you'll want to stroll around **Old Sacramento** ⊕, 4 square blocks at the foot of the downtown area that have become a major tourist attraction. These blocks contain more than 100 restored buildings (California's largest restoration project), including restaurants and shops. Although the area has cobblestone streets, wooden sidewalks, and authentic Gold Rush–era architecture, the high concentration of T-shirt shops and other gimmicky stores has turned it into a sort of historical amusement park. Nonetheless,

# Downtown Sacramento

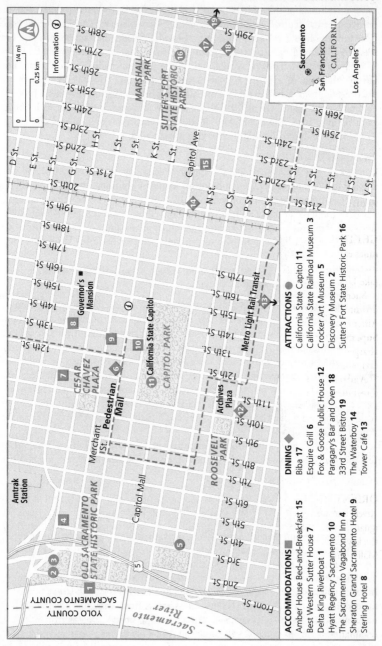

**ACCOMMODATIONS** ■
Amber House Bed-and-Breakfast **15**
Best Western Sutter House **7**
Delta King Riverboat **1**
Hyatt Regency Sacramento **10**
The Sacramento Vagabond Inn **4**
Sheraton Grand Sacramento Hotel **9**
Sterling Hotel **8**

**DINING** ◆
Biba **17**
Esquire Grill **6**
Fox & Goose Public House **12**
Paragary's Bar and Oven **18**
33rd Street Bistro **19**
The Waterboy **14**
Tower Café **13**

**ATTRACTIONS** ●
California State Capitol **11**
California State Railroad Museum **3**
Crocker Art Museum **5**
Discovery Museum **2**
Sutter's Fort State Historic Park **16**

329

there are interesting things to see, such as where the Pony Express ended and the transcontinental railroad—and the Republican Party—began. The **California State Railroad Museum** (see below) is loved by railroad buffs, and the **Sacramento Jazz Festival,** mostly Dixieland, attracts more than 100 bands from around the world for 4 days of madness over Memorial Day weekend. While you're meandering, stop at the **Discovery Museum & History Center** ⚓ at 101 I St. (🕐 **916/264-7057;** www.the discovery.org), which houses exhibits of California's history, highlighting the valley's agricultural Gold Rush as well as the real one in 1849. It's open Tuesday through Sunday from 10am to 5pm. Admission is $5 for adults, $4 for seniors over 60 and kids ages 13 to 17, $3 for kids 4 to 12, and free for kids 3 and under.

## THE MAIN ATTRACTIONS

**California State Capitol** ★★★    Closely resembling a scale model of the U.S. Capitol in Washington, D.C., the beautiful, domed California state capitol was built in 1869 and renovated in 1976. Sacramento's most distinctive landmark, the capitol has been the stage of many political dramas in California history. The 1-hour guided tours provide insight into the architecture and the workings of the government it houses. *Note:* Security will ask you to put your purse or backpack through a metal detector.

10th St. (between N and L sts.). 🕐 **916/324-0333.** Free admission. Daily 9am–5pm. Tours offered every hour on the hour until 4pm. Closed Thanksgiving, Dec 25, and Jan 1.

**California State Railroad Museum** ★★★ *Kids*    Well worth visiting, this museum is the highlight of Old Sacramento. You won't miss much if you bypass the memorabilia displays and head straight for the museum's 105 shiny locomotives and rail cars, beautiful antiques that are true works of art. Afterward, you can watch a 20-minute film on the history of the western railroads that's quite good, then peruse related exhibits that tell the amazing story of the building of the transcontinental railroad. This museum is not just for train buffs: Over half a million people visit each year, and even the hordes of schoolchildren that typically mob this place shouldn't dissuade you from visiting one of the largest and best railroad museums in the country. Allow about 2 hours to see it all.

From April to September, on weekends and holidays from 11am to 5pm, **steam locomotive rides** carry passengers 6 miles along the Sacramento River. Trains depart

---

⌒*Kids*    **Where the Wild Things Are**
_____

The best place to take little kids to let them tear around on a sunny afternoon is **Fairytale Town,** at William Land Park, Land Park Drive and Sutterville Road (🕐 **916/264-5233**). Although the slides and other climbing toys are pretty basic and showing their age, little ones seem to think it's the best place in the world. After you've explored every nook and cranny, cross the street to the **Sacramento Zoo** (🕐 **916/264-5885**), buy some cotton candy, and see the animals. Adjacent to Fairytale Town, there's also the small but pleasant **Funderland** amusement park (🕐 **916/456-0115**) with kid-size rides, open all week in summer months and on spring and fall weekends, weather permitting.

on the hour from the Central Pacific Freight Depot in Old Sacramento, at K and Front streets. Fares are $6 for adults and children ages 13 and older, $3 for children 6 to 12, and free for children under 6.

125 I St. (at Second St.). ℂ **916/445-6645.** Fax 916/327-5655. www.californiastaterailroadmuseum.org. Admission $6 adults 18 and older, $2 children 6–17, free for children 5 and under. Daily 10am–5pm. Closed Thanksgiving, Dec 25, and Jan 1.

**Crocker Art Museum** ✶ This museum houses an outstanding collection of California art, as well as changing exhibits from around the world. It's in an imposing century-old Italianate building, with an ornate interior of carved and inlaid woods. The Crocker Mansion Wing, the museum's most recent addition, is modeled after the Crocker family home and contains works by Northern California artists from 1945 to the present. Plan to spend about an hour here.

216 O St. (at Third St.). ℂ **916/264-5423.** www.crockerartmuseum.org. Admission $6 adults, $4 seniors 65 and over, $3 students w/ID, free for children 6 and under. Tues–Wed and Fri–Sun 10am–5pm; Thurs 10am–9pm. Closed major holidays.

**Sutter's Fort State Historic Park** ✶ John Sutter established this outpost in 1839, and the park, restored to its 1846 appearance, aims to recapture the spirit of 19th-century California. Exhibits include a blacksmith's forge, cooperage, bakery, and jail—and a self-guided audio tour is available. Demonstrations and reenactments in costume are staged daily Memorial Day to Labor Day.

2701 L St. ℂ **916/445-4422.** Admission $4 adults, $2 for children 6–16, free for children 5 and under. Daily 10am–5pm.

## OUTDOOR PURSUITS

**BICYCLING** One good thing about a town that's as flat as a tortilla: It's perfect for exploring on a bike. One of the best places to ride is through Old Sacramento and along the 22-mile American River Parkway, which runs right through it. If you didn't bring your own wheels, the friendly guys at **City Bicycle Works,** 2419 K St., at 24th Street (ℂ **916/447-2453**), will rent you one for about $15 a day.

**RIVER RAFTING** Sacramento lies at the confluence of the American and Sacramento rivers, and rafting on the clear blue water of the American is popular, especially on warm weekends. Several Sacramento-area outfitters rent rafts for 4 to 15 persons, along with life jackets and paddles for about $15 to $25 per person. Their shuttles drop you and your entourage upstream and meet you 3 to 4 hours later at a predetermined point downstream. A recommended outfitter is **American River Raft Rentals,** 11257 S. Bridge St. (at Sunrise Ave.), Rancho Cordova (ℂ **888/338-RAFT** or 916/635-6400; www.raftrentals.com).

## WHERE TO STAY
### EXPENSIVE

**Amber House Bed-and-Breakfast** ✶✶ Just 8 blocks from the capitol on a quiet street, Amber House offers lovely, individually decorated rooms possessing all the amenities you could wish for. Named for famous musicians, and writers, accommodations are in historic houses located across the street from each other: the Poet's Refuge, a 1905 home with five rooms, and an old colonial revival home called the Musician's Manor. Its Mozart Room is the B&B's best, with a four-poster queen bed, a heart-shaped Jacuzzi, a private patio, and three bay windows overlooking the tree-shaded street. A living room and library are available for guests' use. A full breakfast is served at the time and location you request—either in your room, in the large dining room, or outside on the veranda. Coffee and a newspaper are brought to your door each morning, as are freshly baked cookies every afternoon.

1315 22nd St., Sacramento, CA 95816. © 800/755-6526 or 916/444-8085. Fax 916/552-6529. www.amberhouse.com. 10 units. $149–$319 double. Rates include breakfast. AE, DC, DISC, MC, V. **Amenities:** Concierge; in-room massage; laundry service; same-day dry cleaning. *In room:* A/C, TV/VCR, DSL, hair dryer, iron.

**Hyatt Regency Sacramento** ★★ Sacramento's top hotel is in the heart of downtown, across from the state capitol and adjacent to the convention center. It's the high-status address for visiting politicos and is popular with conventioneers as well, as its facilities and services are unmatched in the city. While the rooms themselves are not terribly distinctive, they conform to a high standard and come with all the amenities you expect from Hyatt. The best are the corner units with views facing the state capitol.

1209 L St., Sacramento, CA 95814. © 800/233-1234 or 916/443-1234. Fax 916/321-3799. www.sacramento. hyatt.com. 503 units. $220–$260 double w/weekend specials from $109; from $375 suite. AE, DC, DISC, MC, V. Self-parking $12; valet parking $18. **Amenities:** 2 restaurants; bar; heated outdoor pool; nearby golf course; health club; Jacuzzi; concierge; business center; wireless Internet throughout the hotel; full-service salon; room service; in-room massage; babysitting; laundry service; same-day dry cleaning; executive-level rooms. *In room:* A/C, TV w/pay movies, dataport, minibar, fridge upon request, coffeemaker, hair dryer, iron.

**Sheraton Grand Sacramento Hotel** ★ This convention hotel, which opened in 2001, is praised for its high-tech amenities, a million-dollar public art collection, and the preservation of a beloved landmark. The hotel's 503 rooms are in a new 26-story building adjoining a three-story building that was originally Sacramento's public market from 1920 to the 1960s. This historic structure, designed by Julia Morgan, architect for Hearst Castle, was a favorite gathering place for three generations of Sacramentans. Now housing the lobby, bar, and two restaurants, the site is again a downtown focal point for residents and travelers alike. The accommodations are convention-type hotel rooms—a mite anonymous, but not unpleasant.

1230 J St., Sacramento, CA 95814. © 800/325-3535 or 916/447-1700. Fax 916/477-1701. www.sheraton.com. 503 units. $119–$289 double; from $350 suite. AE, DC, DISC, MC, V. Self-parking $13; valet parking $21. **Amenities:** 2 restaurants; bar; heated outdoor pool; health club; concierge; car-rental desk; business center; wireless Internet in hotel only; room service; in-room massage; babysitting; laundry service; same-day dry cleaning; club-level rooms. *In room:* A/C, TV w/pay movies, dataport, DSL, minibar, coffeemaker, hair dryer, iron.

**Sterling Hotel** ★★ In the heart of Sacramento, 3 blocks from the capitol, this inn occupies a white-fronted Victorian mansion built in the 1890s and heavily renovated in 1995. The Sterling has all the charm of a small, well-managed, sophisticated inn, with a carefully tended flowering yard, tasteful decor, designer furnishings, Italian marble, and a Jacuzzi in every room. **The Chanterelle,** which serves well-prepared California regional cuisine in a dignified setting, is one of Sacramento's better restaurants.

1300 H St., Sacramento, CA 95814. © 800/365-7660 or 916/448-1300. Fax 916/448-8066. www.sterlinghotel.com. 17 units. Sun–Thurs $179–$199 double, $325 suite; Fri–Sat $199–$249 double, $325 suite. Rates include continental breakfast. AE, DISC, MC, V. **Amenities:** Restaurant; Jacuzzi; room service. *In room:* A/C, TV w/pay movies, dataport, fridge in most units, hair dryer, iron.

## MODERATE

***Delta King* Riverboat** ★ The *Delta King* carried passengers between San Francisco and Sacramento in the 1930s. Permanently moored in Sacramento since 1984, the riverboat is now a somewhat gimmicky but charming hotel. Staying here can be a novelty, but the staterooms in a boat are cozy and may bother landlubbers, especially if you're planning to spend a lot of time in your room. All units are newly decorated, with private baths and typical low shipboard ceilings. The captain's quarters, a fancy suite, is a unique, mahogany-paneled stateroom, complete with an observation platform, private deck, and wet bar.

The **Pilothouse Restaurant** has unparalleled river views. When the weather is nice, many loyal patrons dine on outside decks. Live entertainment is presented below decks in two venues on Friday and Saturday nights. In the Mark Twain Salon, "Suspect's Murder Mystery Dinner Theatre," an interactive whodunit, challenges the audience to reveal the true murderer. It's $38 per person to attend, but that includes dinner. Drinks, tax and gratuity are extra. Or for $16 to $25 a person, you can see a local production of a Broadway play in the 110-seat Delta King Theatre.

1000 Front St., Old Sacramento, CA 95814. © 800/825-5464 or 916/444-5464. www.deltaking.com. 44 units. Sun–Thurs $139 double, $550 captain's quarters; Fri–Sat $169 double, $550 captain's quarters. Riverside rooms are $15 extra. Rates include continental breakfast. AE, DC, DISC, MC, V. **Amenities:** Restaurant; lounge; laundry service; same-day dry cleaning. *In room:* A/C, TV, dataport, wireless Internet, hair dryer, iron.

### INEXPENSIVE

**Best Western Sutter House** *(Value)*    You would never know from the plain, motel-like exterior that this is one of the best values in Sacramento. Rooms here are as up-to-date as any offered by upscale hotels such as the Hilton or the Hyatt, including well-coordinated furnishings and lots of amenities. There's a pool in the courtyard, guest passes to a nearby fitness center, free covered parking, and complimentary coffee and pastries are served each morning in the lobby.

1100 H St., Sacramento, CA 95814. © 800/830-1314 or 916/441-1314. Fax 916/441-5961. www.thesutterhouse.com. 98 units. $85–$150 double. Rates include continental breakfast. AE, DC, DISC, MC, V. **Amenities:** Solar-heated outdoor pool; access to fitness center; wireless Internet; room service; same-day dry cleaning; executive-level rooms. *In room:* A/C, TV, fax, dataport, coffeemaker, hair dryer, iron.

**The Vagabond Inn Executive** *(Value)*    A reliable choice within walking distance of the state capitol and one block from historic Old Sacramento, the Vagabond Inn has a host of free features, including local phone calls, weekday newspapers, and continental breakfast. Bedrooms are clean and comfortable—it's the economical rates and the convenient location that make it worth your while. There's an adjoining 24-hour Denny's restaurant as well.

909 Third St., Sacramento, CA 95814. © 800/522-1555 or 916/446-1481. Fax 916/448-0364. www.vagabond inns.com. 108 units. $91–$99 double. Extra person $10. Children 18 and under stay free in parent's room. Rates include continental breakfast. AE, DC, DISC, MC, V. **Amenities:** Restaurant; heated pool; nearby golf course; exercise room; spa; business center w/computers; laundry service; same-day dry cleaning. *In room:* A/C, TV, fridge, coffeemaker, hair dryer, iron, microwave.

## WHERE TO DINE
### EXPENSIVE

**Biba** *(★★★)* ITALIAN    Locals flock to this neo–Art Deco restaurant to sample the classical Italian cuisine of Bologna-born owner Biba Caggiano, who has published nine cookbooks. Although the menu changes seasonally, you can expect to find about 10 pastas and an equal number of main courses. There might be a delicate pappardelle with a fresh-seafood sauce, or a more pungent spaghetti *alla Siciliana,* which combines eggplant, tomatoes, capers, garlic, and anchovies. For a main course, the classic *osso* *buco* Milanese served with a soft, creamy polenta is excellent, but save room for the double-chocolate trifle made with dark and white chocolate, Grand Marnier–soaked pound cake, and raspberry purée.

2801 Capitol Ave. ℂ 916/455-2422. www.biba-restaurant.com. Reservations recommended. Main courses $18–$28. AE, DC, MC, V. Mon–Fri 11:30am–2:30pm; Mon–Thurs 5:30–9:30pm; Fri–Sat 5:30–10pm.

## MODERATE

**Esquire Grill** ✦ AMERICAN GRILL    Next door to Sacramento's convention center and a short walk from the capitol, Sheraton Grand, and the Hyatt Regency, the Esquire Grill was a hit as soon as it opened its handsome doors. The Michael Guthrie architectural group designed the restaurant using rich woods and warm colors. Sacramento has been struggling for years to revive its downtown area and this urbane place is one giant step toward creating the revitalized scene the city planners are hoping for. The bar is always lively with well-dressed folks sipping martinis and Cosmopolitans, and the restaurant's food is classic American grill. It's also considered one of the city's best sites for Arnold-watching. Dinner specialties might include a mixed fry of calamari, fennel, and onions; or spit-roasted pork chops with buttermilk onion rings and house-made applesauce. Some folks come just for the onion rings.

1221 K St. ℂ 916/448-8900. Main courses $15–$46 ($46 for porterhouse steak for 2). AE, DC, DISC, MC, V. Mon–Fri 11am–2:30pm; Sun–Thurs 4:30–10:30pm; Fri–Sat 4:30–11:30pm. Limited menu Mon–Fri 2:30–4:30pm.

**Paragary's Bar and Oven** ✦✦ MEDITERRANEAN    With two dining rooms, Paragary's is widely considered one of the best moderately priced restaurants in Sacramento's trendy midtown scene. In good weather the best seats are outside amid the gorgeous fountains and plantings of the courtyard; other seating options include the formal fireplace room and the brightly lit cafe. The same menu is served no matter where you sit, with some of the best dishes coming from the kitchen's wood-burning pizza oven. But this is more than a gourmet pizza parlor, as evidenced by the grilled rib-eye steak with mashed potatoes, portobello mushrooms, and grilled leeks; or the hand-cut rosemary noodles with seared chicken, pancetta, artichokes, leeks, and garlic.

1401 28th St. ℂ 916/457-5737. Main courses $12–$20. AE, DC, DISC, MC, V. Mon–Thurs 11:30am–10pm; Fri 11:30am–11pm; Sat 4:30–11pm; Sun 4:30–9pm.

**33rd Street Bistro** ✦ BISTRO    Seattle transplants Fred Haynes (chef) and his brother Matt (manager) have taken an old brick building and transformed it into a hugely successful bistro. It's popular for all the right reasons—the food is good (and priced right), the staff is friendly, and the ambience is cheerful. Selections might include a variety of Italian grilled sandwiches and house favorites such as cedar plank–roasted salmon with toasted-hazelnut butter and fruit purée, Uncle Bum's Jerk Ribs with Jamaican barbecue sauce and Key lime crème fraîche, and a variety of wood-fired pizzas and calzone.

3301 Folsom Blvd. (at 33rd St.). ℂ 916/455-2282. Main courses $8–$19. AE, MC, V. Sun–Thurs 8am–10pm; Fri–Sat 8am–11pm.

**The Waterboy** ✦✦ COUNTRY FRENCH/ITALIAN    Until recently, Sacramento had a slim list of really good restaurants, but no more. At the top of everybody's list is The Waterboy. It's got everything going for it: an appealing, airy but unpretentious atmosphere; friendly and knowledgeable servers; and, best of all, outstanding food cooked perfectly. Chef/owner Rick Mahan uses Niman Ranch naturally raised meats

> ## Value  An Insider's Guide to Sacramento's Budget Dining Bests
>
> I used to live in Sacramento as a starving writer, so I'm well acquainted with the city's best dining deals. Here are five of my favorites that you won't find in any other travel guide:
>
> - **Best Burger: Willie's Burgers,** 2415 16th St., between Broadway and X Street (© **916/444-2006**), slathers food in so much chili and cheese that heavy-duty paper towel dispensers are mandatory. It's open late most nights.
> - **Best Coffee Joint:** A tough one, but **Java City** (© **916/444-5282**), at the corner of Capitol Avenue and 18th Street, has been popular forever. Sure, there are a few street people around, but at least they keep the yuppies at bay.
> - **Best Mexican: Taco Loco Taqueria,** 2326 J St., at 24th Street (© **916/447-0711**). Try the charbroiled black-tip shark taco, a big ole shrimp burrito, or snapper ceviche tostada, all so fresh the restaurant doesn't even own a freezer. Wash it all down with a Los Cabos margarita while soaking up the sun on the front patio.
> - **Best Breakfast:** At the **Cornerstone Restaurant,** 2330 J. St., at 24th Street (© **916/441-0948**), the choices are all standard American, but the servings are huge, the service is friendly, and the price is right. A four-egg omelet with home fries, toast, and fruit costs less than $6. My dad eats here once a week.
> - **Best Brewery:** The **Rubicon Brewing Company,** 2004 Capitol Ave., at 20th Street (© **916/448-7032**), still remains my favorite hangout. A pitcher of India Pale and a side of fries is de rigueur.

and local organic produce, and he offers a particularly fine selection of wines. Main courses change every 4 weeks but include dishes such as saffron risotto, cassoulet, chicken *al mattone,* or boneless squab with a very crispy skin, served on a bed of sautéed greens with a squash polenta, figs, and a reduction of squab stock. Rick always has a traditional American favorite on the menu. On my last visit it was a great chili cheese dog.

20th St. and Capitol Ave. © **916/498-9891.** Main courses $16–$22. AE, DC, DISC, MC, V. Tues–Fri 11:30am–2:30pm; Tues–Thurs 5–9:30pm; Fri–Sat 5–10:30pm; Sun 5–9pm.

## INEXPENSIVE

**Fox & Goose Public House** ★★ *Value* ENGLISH PUB   The Fox is your classic British pub, down to the dartboard, picture of the queen, and numerous beers from across the pond. The soups at lunch are excellent, and the specials often include bangers and mash, Welsh rarebit, and Cornish pasties. The burnt-cream dessert is famous. Arrive early for lunch or be prepared for a wait, as locals love this place (no reservations are taken and they won't even seat you until all the members of your party have arrived). Equally popular breakfasts include kippers, grilled tomatoes, and crumpets, as well as waffles, omelets, and French toast. There's live entertainment by local bands 6 nights a week, as well as pub grub like fish and chips and hamburgers Monday through Friday from 2 to 9:30pm.

1001 R St. (at 10th St.). ℂ **916/443-8825.** Reservations not accepted. Main courses $4–$7. AE, MC, V. Mon–Sun 7am–2pm. Bar stays open until midnight Mon–Thurs, until 2am Fri–Sat.

**Tower Café** INTERNATIONAL   The Tower Café gets its name from the building in which it's located: a grand old 1939 movie house with a tall Art Deco spire. The restaurant occupies the same space where a small mom-and-pop music store once stood. The former resident, Tower Records, has since grown into America's second-largest record retailer. While it's unlikely that Tower Café will share the phenomenal success of its predecessor, it's popular with locals. The multicultural decor—kind of Art Deco meets *National Geographic*—is a feast for the eyes. Dishes reflect a variety of international flavors, from the Jamaican jerk chicken to Chinese chicken salad. Usually the food is good, especially the desserts, but once in a while you get something that makes you wonder what's going on in the kitchen. On warm days it seems as if everyone in the city is lunching here on the large outdoor patio (past patrons have included serious foodie Bill Clinton), so people-watching can be a real treat. The movie house typically shows good foreign films, and Tower Records is just across the street. These are all great places to round out a lazy River City afternoon.

1518 Broadway. ℂ **916/441-0222.** Main courses $8–$14. AE, MC, V. Sun–Thurs 8am–11pm; Fri–Sat 8am–midnight, w/dessert and drinks only until midnight.

## 2 The Gold Country ★★

Cutting a serpentine swath for nearly 350 miles along Highway 49, the Gold Country stretches from Sierra City to the foothills of Yosemite. Mining sites, horse ranches, ghost towns, Gold Rush–architecture, and Wild West saloons are common sights in these rugged parts.

The town of Placerville, 44 miles east of Sacramento at the intersection of U.S. 50 and Highway 49, is in the approximate center of the Gold Country. To the north are the old mining towns of Grass Valley and Nevada City, while in the central and southern Gold Country are such well-preserved towns as Amador City, Sutter Creek, Columbia, and Jamestown, to name a few.

In fact, the Gold Country is so immense that it would take weeks to thoroughly explore. But rather than provide an exhaustive list of every town, I have narrowed my coverage to include three of my favorite regions, each of which can be explored in just 2 or 3 days: the charismatic side-by-side towns of Nevada City and Grass Valley to the north; the well-preserved Gold Rush communities of Amador City, Sutter Creek, and Jackson in the central Gold Country; and at the southern end of the Gold Country, the wonderfully authentic neighboring mining towns of Angels Camp, Murphys, Columbia, Sonora, and Jamestown.

Any of these regions will provide an excellent base for exploring and experiencing the Gold Country, whether you're intent on panning for gold, exploring old mines and caverns, or rafting the area's many white-water rivers. In fact, the Gold Country is one of the most underrated and least congested tourist destinations in California, a winning combination of Old West ambience, adorable (and affordable) bed-and-breakfasts, and outdoor adventures galore.

# The Gold Country

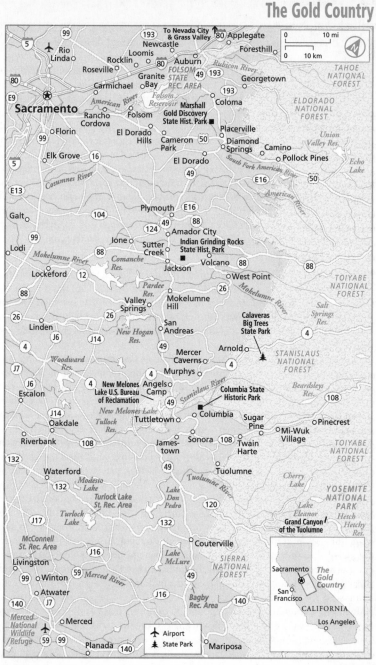

To Nevada City & Grass Valley

Applegate

Foresthill

193 Newcastle

80

Rio Linda

99

Loomis

Rocklin

Roseville

Carmichael

Granite Bay

80

Auburn

FOLSOM STATE REC. AREA

49

193

Georgetown

E9

Sacramento

American River

Rancho Cordova

Folsom

Folsom Reservoir

Marshall Gold Discovery State Hist. Park

193

Coloma

Placerville

ELDORADO NATIONAL FOREST

TAHOE NATIONAL FOREST

Florin

99

El Dorado Hills

Cameron Park

50

Diamond Springs

Camino

Union Valley Res.

Elk Grove

16

El Dorado

Pollock Pines

E16

Echo Lake

5

49

South Fork American River

50

E13

Cosumnes River

American River

Galt

104

Plymouth

E16

99

Ione

124

49

88

Amador City

Indian Grinding Rocks State Hist. Park

Lodi

88

Sutter Creek

Jackson

Volcano

88

TOIYABE NATIONAL FOREST

Lockeford

12

Comanche Res.

Mokelumne River

West Point

88

Pardee Res.

26

Mokelumne River

Salt Springs Res.

Valley Springs

Mokelumne Hill

26

88

26

Linden

New Hogan Res.

San Andreas

Calaveras Big Trees State Park

4

J6

J14

49

Mercer Caverns

Arnold

STANISLAUS NATIONAL FOREST

J7

Woodward Res.

Murphys

4

J6

Escalon

4

New Melones Lake U.S. Bureau of Reclamation

Angels Camp

49

Stanislaus River

Columbia State Historic Park

Beardsleys Res.

108

J14

Oakdale

New Melones Lake

Tulloch Res.

Tuttletown

Columbia

Sugar Pine

Pinecrest

Riverbank

108

Jamestown

Sonora

108

Twain Harte

Mi-Wuk Village

TOIYABE NATIONAL FOREST

132

Waterford

Modesto Lake

49

Tuolumne

Cherry Lake

132

Turlock Lake St. Rec. Area

Lake Don Pedro

Tuolumne River

120

YOSEMITE NATIONAL PARK

J17

Turlock Lake

132

Lake Eleanor

Hetch Hetchy Res.

McConnell St. Rec. Area

J16

Couterville

Grand Canyon of the Tuolumne

Livingston

59

Merced River

Lake McLure

SIERRA NATIONAL FOREST

Winton

99

49

140

Atwater

J7

J16

Bagby Rec. Area

140

Merced National Wildlife Refuge

59

99

Merced

Planada

140

Mariposa

✈ Airport
★ State Park

0        10 mi
0        10 km

Sacramento

The Gold Country

San Francisco

CALIFORNIA

Los Angeles

# THE NORTHERN GOLD COUNTRY: NEVADA CITY & GRASS VALLEY

About 60 miles northeast of Sacramento, Nevada City and Grass Valley are far and away the top tourist destinations of the northern Gold Country.

These two historic towns were at the center of the hard-rock mining fields of Northern California. Grass Valley was California's richest mining town, producing more than a billion dollars worth of gold. Both are attractive, although I usually spend most of my time in smaller Nevada City. Its wealth of Victorian homes and storefronts makes it one of the most appealing small towns in California, particularly in the fall when the maple trees are ablaze with color. (In fact, its entire downtown has been designated a National Historic Landmark.)

It's easy to get here. If you're driving from San Francisco, take I-80 to the Highway 49 turnoff in Auburn and follow the signs heading north. For information about the area, contact the **Grass Valley & Nevada County Chamber of Commerce,** 248 Mill St., Grass Valley (© **800/655-4667** in California or 530/273-4667; www.grassvalley chamber.com), or the **Nevada City Chamber of Commerce,** 132 Main St., Nevada City (© **800/655-NJOY** or 530/265-2692; www.nevadacitychamber.com).

## NEVADA CITY ★★

Rumors of miners pulling a pound of gold a day out of Deer Creek brought thousands of fortune seekers to the area in 1849. Within a year, Nevada City was a boisterous town of 10,000, the third-largest city in California. In its heyday, everyone who was anyone visited this rollicking Western outpost with its busy red-light district. Mark Twain lectured here in 1866, and former president Herbert Hoover also lived and worked here as a gold miner.

Pick up a walking-tour map at the **Chamber of Commerce,** 132 Main St., and stroll the streets lined with impressive Victorian buildings, including the **Firehouse Number 1 Museum,** 214 Main St. (© **530/265-5468**), with bell tower, gingerbread decoration, a small museum that displays mementos from the Donner Party, a Maidu Indian basket collection, and an altar from a temple originally located in the Chinese section of Grass Valley. Admission is free. It's open in summer daily from 11am to 4pm; from November 1 to May 1 hours are Thursday through Sunday from 11:30am to 4pm. The **National Hotel** (built 1854–56) is here (the Gold Rush–era bar serves a spicy bloody mary), as is the **Nevada Theatre** (1865), one of the oldest theaters in the nation still operating as such. Today it's home to the Foothill Theatre Company.

If you want to see the source of much of the city's wealth, visit **Malakoff Diggins State Historic Park** ★, 23579 N. Bloomfield Rd. (© **530/265-2740**), 28 miles northeast of Nevada City. Once the world's largest hydraulic gold mine, it's an awesome (some say disturbing) spectacle of hydraulic mining: Nearly half a mountain has been washed away by powerful jets of water, leaving behind a 600-foot-deep canyon of exposed rock. In the 1870s, North Bloomfield, then located in the middle of this park, had a population of 1,500. Some of the buildings have been reconstructed and refurnished to show what life was like then. The 3,000-acre park also offers several hiking trails, swimming at Blair Lake, and 30 campsites that can be reserved through **ReserveAmerica** (© **800/444-7275;** www.reserveamerica.com). The museum is open daily in summer from 10am to 5pm, in winter on weekends only from noon to 4pm. To reach the park, take Highway 49 toward Downieville for 11 miles. Turn right onto Tyler-Foote Crossing Road for 17 miles. The name changes several times, but just stay on the pavement. Turn right onto Derbec Road, then right on North Bloomfield Road, which takes you to the park entrance. The fee is $6 per car, $5 for seniors.

Another 6 miles up Highway 49 from the Malakoff Diggins turnoff brings you to Pleasant Valley Road, the exit that will take you (in about 7 miles) to one of the nation's most impressive **covered bridges.** Built in 1862, it's 225 feet long and was crossed by many a stagecoach (in fall, it makes for a spectacular photo opportunity).

## Where to Stay

### Deer Creek Inn Bed & Breakfast ★
An 1860 three-floor Victorian overlooking Deer Creek and within walking distance of downtown Nevada City, this inn feels like a warm home-away-from-home. The individually decorated rooms, most with private verandas facing the creek or town, are furnished with antiques and four-poster or canopy beds with down comforters. Three bathrooms have claw-foot tubs. A full breakfast is served either on the deck or in the formal dining room. Guests are invited to try a little panning, fish, or simply relax and enjoy the lawn and landscaped rose gardens along the creek.

116 Nevada St., Nevada City, CA 95959. (℃ **800/655-0363** or 530/265-0363. Fax 530/265-0980. www.deercreek inn.com. 6 units. $160–$215 double. Rates include breakfast. MC, V. **Amenities:** Nearby golf course; bike rental. *In room:* A/C, wireless Internet.

### Emma Nevada House ★★
One of the finest B&Bs in the Gold Country, Emma Nevada House is a picture-perfect Victorian that was the childhood home of 19th-century opera star Emma Nevada. You'll like everything about it: the quiet location, sun-drenched decks, wraparound porch, understated decor, and breakfast served in the hexagonal Sun Room. The guest rooms range from small and intimate to large and luxurious; all have private bathrooms and queen-size beds. Top choice for honeymooners is the Empress's Chamber, with its wall of windows, ivory and burgundy tones, and—of course—the Jacuzzi tub for two. You'll also like the fact that the shops and restaurants of Nevada City's Historic District are only a short walk away.

528 E. Broad St., Nevada City, CA 95959. (℃ **800/916-EMMA** or 530/265-4415. Fax 530/265-4416. www.emma nevadahouse.com. 6 units. $157–$220 double. Rates include breakfast. AE, DISC, MC, V. **Amenities:** Concierge. *In room:* A/C, wireless Internet, hair dryer, iron, phone on request.

### National Hotel
You can't miss this classic three-story Victorian, the oldest hotel in continuous operation west of the Rocky Mountains. Some folks feel this makes it more historic and authentic; others may opt for more upscale and restored lodgings, though the hotel has begun to renovate the rooms and facade. It's near what was once the center of the town's red-light district. The lobby is full of mementos from that era, hence the grandfather clock and early square piano. The suites are replete with Gold Rush–era antiques and large, cozy beds. Most rooms have private bathrooms, and some come with canopy beds and romantic loveseats. A definite bonus during typically sweltering summers is the swimming pool filled with cool mountain water.

The hotel's Victorian dining room and bar, which serves traditional items such as prime rib, steaks, lobster tails, and homemade desserts, also has a Gold Rush atmosphere; tables, for example, are lit with coal-oil lamps. The hotel provides live entertainment on Friday and Saturday nights. There's also a popular Sunday brunch, one of the best in the county.

211 Broad St., Nevada City, CA 95959. (℃ **530/265-4551.** Fax 530/265-2445. www.thenationalhotel.com. 42 units, 30 w/private bathroom. $79–$123 double king or queen w/bathroom; $123–$130 suite w/bathroom; $50 double with shared bath (on walk-in basis only). AE, MC, V. **Amenities:** Restaurant; bar; outdoor pool; business center; room service. *In room:* A/C, TV, dataport.

**Nevada City Inn** *Value* Surely no forty-niner had it this good: his own cabinlike motel room cooled by the shade of a small tree-lined park equipped with barbecues and picnic tables. Granted, the rooms are small and simple at this restored 1940s motor lodge, but considering that you get all the standard amenities for a really low price, the cash-conscious traveler could hardly ask for more. The inn also rents seven fully furnished cottages with kitchens, popular with families and groups. They're a good deal for such a prime location, about a half mile from Nevada City's historic district.

760 Zion St., Nevada City, CA 95959. ⓒ 800/977-8884 or 530/265-2253. www.nevadacityinn.com. Fax 530/265-3310. 27 units. $69–$99 double room; $115–$189 cottage. Rates include continental breakfast. AE, DC, DISC, MC, V. *In room:* A/C, TV, fridge in cottages.

**Red Castle Inn Historic Lodgings** ✸ This elegant, comfortable hillside inn occupies a four-story Gothic Revival brick house built in 1860 in a secluded spot with a panoramic view of the town. The house retains its original woodwork, plaster moldings, ceiling medallions, and much of the handmade glass. It lacks modern intrusions like TVs and phones. Guests enjoy five-course buffet breakfasts and relax on the verandas that encircle the first two floors of the house and overlook the rose gardens. My favorite rooms are the Garden Room, with a canopy bed and French doors leading into the gardens, and the three-room garret suite tucked under the eaves, with sleigh beds and Gothic arched windows.

109 Prospect St., Nevada City, CA 95959. ⓒ 800/761-4766 or 530/265-5135. www.redcastleinn.com. 7 units. $120–$170 double. Rates include breakfast. MC, V. *In room:* A/C, no phone.

## Where to Dine

**Citronée Bistro & Wine Bar** ✸✸ REGIONAL AMERICAN/INTERNATIONAL It took a review by the *New York Times* to get California foodies to turn their appetites from Napa and San Francisco to Nevada City's Citronée. And owner/chef Robert Perez's restaurant is worth exploring. At lunch the barbecued-brisket sandwich topped with white-cheddar on chipotle focaccia served with cayenne-dusted waffle potato chips is a must. The evening menu ranges from oven roasted leg of domestic lamb with asparagus, chanterelles, pearl onions, and golden raisins in a tomato, white wine, and mint dressing, drizzled with potato butter, to the highly acclaimed rare seared *ahi* tuna with poached oysters, romaine lettuce oyster emulsion, and confit of baby fennel. And if that isn't enough, ask for the menu *gastronomique*, a five-course surprise menu specially chosen each night.

320 Broad St. ⓒ 530/265-5697. Reservations recommended. Main courses $15–$28. AE, MC, V. Mon–Fri 11:30am–2pm; Mon–Thurs 5:30–9:30pm; Fri–Sat 5–10pm.

**Country Rose Café** ✸ COUNTRY FRENCH The flowery country-French atmosphere of this popular Nevada City restaurant belies a serious (and seriously priced) menu put together by owner and chef Michael Johns. Dinner selections, written on a huge board that's lugged over to your table after you've been seated, are mostly French with a dash of Italian, Mexican, and American dishes. Skip the typical pastas and head straight for John's specialty—fresh fish prepared in a myriad of classic styles such as filet of sole doré, swordfish Oskar, and sea bass with garlic-basil sauce. Other regular menu items include filet mignon, lobster, rack of lamb, and roast game hen. Both lunch and dinner are served on the pretty walled-in patio in the summer, so be sure to request alfresco seating when making a reservation.

300 Commercial St. ⓒ 530/265-6252. Reservations recommended. Main courses $14–$31. AE, DC, MC, V. Tues–Thurs and Sun 11am–9pm; Fri–Sat 11am–10pm.

**New Moon Café** ★★ AMERICAN/INTERNATIONAL   Nevada City's favorite chef, Peter Selaya, offers a menu of imaginatively prepared items that feature free-range and antibiotic-free meats and poultry, house-baked breads, house-made pastas using organic flours and grains, and local organic vegetables, when available—which is often in this hotbed of natural foodstuffs. So not only is the food healthy, it tastes great. Dinner entrees include the likes of a Niman Ranch *coulotte* steak grilled with a roast-garlic, zinfandel, and rosemary sauce, or fresh line-caught wild salmon pan-seared with julienne vegetables and a beurre blanc verjuice. The raviolis are made fresh daily, as are the desserts. The fresh strawberry Napoleons we had were beyond delicious. Nevada City's balmy climate makes the front deck a great place to dine and people-watch.

203 York St. © 530/265-6399. Reservations recommended. Main courses $15–$25. DC, MC, V. Tues–Fri 11:30am–2pm; Tues–Sun 5–8pm (or later).

## GRASS VALLEY ★

In contrast to Nevada City's "tourist town" image, Grass Valley is the commercial and retail center of the region. The **Empire Mine State Historic Park** ★, 10791 E. Empire St., Grass Valley (© **530/273-8522**), the largest and richest gold mine in California, is just outside of town. This mine, which once had 367 miles of shafts, produced an estimated 5.8 million ounces of gold between 1850 and 1956. You can look down the shaft of the mine, walk around the mine yard, and stroll through the owner's gardens. From March to November, tours are given daily, and a mining movie is shown. You can also enjoy picnicking, cycling, mountain biking, or hiking in the 784-acre park. It's open year-round except for Thanksgiving, Christmas, and New Year's Day. Admission to the park, tour, and museum costs $1 for adults and children, and dogs are free.

In town, visitors can pick up a walking-tour map at the **Chamber of Commerce,** 248 Mill St. (© **530/273-4667;** www. grassvalleychamber.com), and explore the historic downtown area along Mill and Main streets. Two museums will appeal to California-history and gold-mining buffs: the **Grass Valley Museum,** 410 S. Church St., adjacent to St. Joseph's Cultural Center (© **530/273-5509**), and the **North Star Mining Museum,** at the south end of Mill Street at Allison Ranch Road (© **530/ 273-4255;** open May–Oct).

Grass Valley was, for a time, the home of **Lola Montez,** singer, dancer, and paramour of the rich and famous. A fully restored home that she bought and occupied in 1853 can be viewed at 248 Mill St., now the site of Grass Valley's chamber of commerce. **Lotta Crabtree,** Montez's famous protégée, lived down the street at 238 Mill St., now an apartment house. Also pop into the **Holbrooke Hotel,** 212 Main St., to see the signature of Mark Twain, who stayed here, as did five U.S. presidents. The saloon has been in continuous use since 1852, and it's the place to meet the locals and have a tall cold one.

The surrounding region offers many recreational opportunities on its rivers and lakes and in the Tahoe National Forest. You can enjoy fishing, swimming, and boating at **Scotts Flat Lake** near Nevada City (east on Hwy. 20) and at **Rollins Lake** on Highway 174, between Grass Valley and Colfax. White-water rafting is available on several rivers. **Tributary Whitewater Tours,** 20480 Woodbury Dr., Grass Valley, CA 95949 (© **800/ 672-3846** or 530/346-6812; www.whitewatertours.com), offers half- to 3-day trips March through October. The region is also ideal for mountain biking. The chambers of commerce publish a trail guide, but there's nowhere to rent a bike in Nevada City or Grass Valley, so bring your own wheels. For regional hiking information, contact **Tahoe**

**National Forest Headquarters,** at Coyote Street and Highway 49 in Nevada City (© **530/265-4531;** www.r5.fs.fed.us/tahoe).

## Where to Stay

**Grass Valley Courtyard Suites** If you like to lounge poolside with a good book, you'll appreciate the Courtyard Suites, and if you have your little dog Toto with you, he'll appreciate the canine cuddler (fuzzy little blanket) he's provided when you check in. In a quiet neighborhood, a block from downtown Grass Valley, this place offers enough amenities to cover your every need, including a year around heated pool and spa, fitness facility, and sauna. There's a generous continental breakfast, including oatmeal, in the morning, and California wines and hors d'oeuvres in the evening. Some suites have fully equipped kitchens and fireplaces, and there's also a coin-operated guest laundry facility in case you decide to linger longer and want to suds your undies.

210 N. Auburn St., Grass Valley, CA 95945. © **530/272-7696.** www.gvcourtyardsuites.com. 33 units. $130–$150 double; $175–$245 suite. Rates include continental breakfast. AE, DISC, V. **Amenities:** Outdoor heated pool; fitness facility; spa; sauna; coin-op laundry; covered parking. *In room:* A/C; HBO; fridge; coffeemaker; hair dryer; iron; safe; robes; voice mail.

**Holbrooke Hotel** ⭐ This Victorian-era white-clapboard building was a saloon during the Gold Rush days, and then evolved into a place for miners to "rack out." The oldest and most historic hotel in town, it's hosted a number of legendary figures: Mark Twain and presidents Ulysses Grant, Benjamin Harrison, and Grover Cleveland, among others. Seventeen of the rooms lie within the main building. The remainder are in an adjacent annex, a house occupied long ago by the hotel's owner. Each guest room is decorated with a collection of Gold Rush–era furniture and antiques. All have cable TVs in armoires, and most bathrooms have claw-foot tubs. If you can, reserve one of the larger Veranda rooms that face Main Street and have access to the balconies; it's well worth the few extra dollars. A continental breakfast is served in the library.

212 W. Main St., Grass Valley, CA 95945. © **800/933-7077** or 530/273-1353. Fax 530/273-0434. www.holbrooke.com. 28 units. $75–$115 double; $130–$175 suite. Rates include breakfast. AE, DC, DISC, MC, V. **Amenities:** Restaurant; saloon; business center; wireless Internet. *In room:* A/C, TV.

## Where to Dine

**Tofanelli's** Value INTERNATIONAL If a diet of meat and potatoes isn't your cup of tea, head to Tofanelli's, which specializes in good—and good for you—entrees for brunch, lunch, and dinner. You'll like the setting—a bright, cheery trio of dining areas (atrium, outdoor patio, and dining room) separated by exposed brick walls and decorated with beautiful prints and paintings. Specials on the menu, such as Gorgonzola ravioli topped with garlic-cream sauce, or pad Thai noodles with fresh ginger and marinated beef, change quarterly, but you can always rely on Tofanelli's classics like Noni's Famous Lasagna and the popular veggie burger. And yes, they serve good ol' New York steak, too. Don't you dare depart without a slice of Katherine's chocolate cake.

302 W. Main St. (across from the Holbrooke Hotel). © **530/272-1468.** Main courses $12–$20. AE, DISC, MC, V. Mon–Fri 11:30am–8:30pm; Sat 11:30am–9pm; Sun brunch 9:30am–3pm, dinner 5–8:30pm.

**212 Bistro at the Holbrooke** AMERICAN This lovely old hotel dining room with its venerable brick and stone walls is the most elegant place in town—an ironic twist, given its past life as a Gold Rush saloon and a flophouse for drunken miners. In its way, it's the most authentic and nostalgic restaurant in a town filled with worthy competitors. Items on the ever-changing menu range from mesquite-smoked prime rib, Cajun-rubbed New York steak, and seared salmon filet encrusted with a cashew-coconut herb and lime-hibiscus sauce. For lunch try smoked prime rib French dip sandwich, Holbrooke Hamburger, or the Chinese chicken salad.

212 W. Main St. (in the Holbrooke Hotel). © **530/273-1353.** www.holbrooke.com. Reservations recommended Fri–Sat nights. Main courses $15–$25. AE, DC, DISC, MC, V. Mon–Sun 10am–2pm and 5:30–9pm.

## THE CENTRAL GOLD COUNTRY: AMADOR CITY, SUTTER CREEK, JACKSON & ENVIRONS

Though Placerville is technically the center of the Gold Country, it's the small trio of towns a few miles to the south—Amador City, Sutter Creek, and Jackson—that are far and away the most appealing destination in this region of rolling hills, dotted with solitary oaks and granite outcroppings. When the mining boom went bust, most of the towns were abandoned; nowadays, most of these restored Gold Rush towns rely solely on tourism (hence the conversion of many Victorian homes into B&Bs), though a few mines have reopened recently.

One of the advantages of staying in this area, 55 miles southeast of Sacramento, is that both the northern and southern regions of the Gold Country are only a few hours' drive away (via very winding roads, however). If you're intent on seeing as much of the Gold Country as possible in a few days' time, any one of these three towns will suffice as a good home base.

To reach Amador City, Sutter Creek, or Jackson from Placerville, head south along Highway 49 past Plymouth and Drytown. If you're coming straight here from Sacramento, take U.S. 50 to Placerville and head south on Highway 49; Highway 16 from Sacramento is another option, but only slightly faster. For more information about any of these towns, contact the **Amador County Chamber of Commerce,** 125 Peek St., Jackson (© **800/649-4988** or 209/223-0350; www.amadorcountychamber.com).

### AMADOR CITY ⚭

Once a bustling mining town, Amador City is now devoted mostly to dredging up tourist dollars. Although Amador City sounds impressive, it's the smallest incorporated city in California. Local merchants have made the most of a refurbished block-long boardwalk, converting the historic false-fronted buildings into a gallery of sorts; the stores sell everything from early 1900s antiques and folk art to handcrafted furniture, Gold Rush memorabilia, rare books, and Native American crafts. Parking can be difficult, however, especially in summer.

### Where to Stay & Dine

**Imperial Hotel** ⚭⚭  At the foot of Main Street overlooking Amador City, this stately 1879 brick hotel and restaurant has been beautifully restored and manages to be both elegant and whimsical. The individually decorated rooms, all with private bathrooms, are furnished with brass, iron, or pine beds and numerous antiques; two come with private balconies. Room 6 is the quietest, but Room 1—with its high ceiling, hand-painted queen-size canopy bed, Art Deco appointments, and French doors that open onto a private balcony overlooking Main Street—is the most requested. The smart and chic Oasis Bar has been newly renovated and is stocked with a large selection of spirits and California and imported wines and beers. Breakfast is served downstairs, in your room, or on the patio or balcony. The Imperial Hotel restaurant, serving California cuisine—for instance, glazed pork loin with spiced onion marmalade, or fresh Alaskan halibut with olive tarragon bread crumbs—has a sterling reputation.

Guests can take advantage of room service from 5 to 9pm, when it's open. The restaurant is worth a detour, even if you aren't staying here.

14202 Hwy. 49 P.O. Box 212, Amador City, CA 95601. © 209/267-9172. Fax 209/267-9249. www.imperialamador.com. 6 units. $100–$140 double. Rates include breakfast. AE, MC, V. **Amenities:** Restaurant; bar. *In room:* A/C, hair dryer, no phone.

## SUTTER CREEK ✦

The self-proclaimed "nicest little town in the Mother Lode," Sutter Creek was named after sawmill owner John Sutter, employer of James Marshall (whose discovery of gold triggered the 1849 Gold Rush). Railroad baron Leland Stanford made his fortune at Sutter Creek's Lincoln Mine, and then invested his millions to build the transcontinental railroad and fund his successful California gubernatorial campaign.

The town is a charmer, lined with beautiful 19th-century buildings in pristine condition, including **Downs Mansion,** the former home of the foreman at Stanford's mine (now a private residence on Spanish St., across from the Immaculate Conception Church), and the landmark **Knight's Foundry,** 81 Eureka St., off Main Street, the last water-powered foundry and machine shop in the nation. There are also numerous shops and galleries along Main Street, though finding a free parking space can be a real challenge on summer weekends.

### Where to Stay

**The Foxes** ✦✦ This 1857 clapboard house is Sutter Creek's most elegant hostelry. The seven rooms are all unique, each with a queen-size bed and down comforters. Five rooms, including the Garden Room and the Fox Den, have gas-burning fireplaces. The Fox Den has a little library of its own, while the Anniversary Room features a 9-foot-tall Renaissance Revival bed and a sitting room. All have private bathrooms. Breakfast, cooked to order and delivered on silver service, can be served in your room or in the gazebo in the flower-filled garden. Located on Main Street, the inn is only steps away from Sutter Creek's shops and restaurants.

77 Main St. (P.O. Box 159), Sutter Creek, CA 95685. © 800/987-3344 or 209/267-5882. Fax 209/267-0712. www. foxesinn.com. 7 units. $160–$229 double. Rates include breakfast. DISC, MC, V. *In room:* A/C, TV/VCR, fridge, hair dryer, no phone.

**Grey Gables Inn** ✦ The Grey Gables Inn is a postcard-perfect replica of a Victorian manor. The two-story B&B is surrounded by terraces of gardens and embellished with fountains and vine-covered arbors. Each of the plushly carpeted guest rooms is named after a British poet; the Byron Room features hues of deep green and burgundy, dark-wood furnishings, and a four-poster king bed. All rooms have queen or king beds, gas-log fireplaces, armoires, and private bathrooms (a few with claw-foot tubs). Breakfast, delivered on English bone china, is served in the formal dining room adjacent to the Victorian parlor or in your room. The only flaw is the proximity to heavily traveled Highway 49, but once inside, you'll hardly notice. The shops and restaurants of Sutter Creek are within walking distance.

161 Hanford St., Sutter Creek, CA 95685. © 800/473-9422 or 209/267-1039. Fax 209/267-0998. www.grey gables.com. 8 units. $110–$190 double. AE, DC, DISC, MC, V. *In room:* A/C, hair dryer, no phone.

### Where to Dine

**Zinfandels** ✦✦ CALIFORNIA Greg West's Zinfandels has received kudos since it first opened in 1996. Greg, a 6-year veteran of Greens (San Francisco's most famous vegetarian restaurant; see p. 112), makes and bakes just about everything in-house, including the breads and pastries. Though the emphasis is on low-fat vegetarian fare such as butternut-squash risotto with pancetta, leeks, crimini mushrooms, and spinach, West also offers a trio of fresh fish, chicken, and beef dishes ranging from cannelloni filled with lamb sausage, chard, and smoked mozzarella to Petrale sole with a citrus-ginger *beurre blanc*. The menu changes monthly to take advantage of seasonal produce from local farms, and even the wines—paired with each dish—are provided by local wineries such as Sobon and Dillian

51 Hanford St. 𝄢 209/267-5008. www.zinfood.com. Reservations recommended. Main courses $17–$25. AE, DISC, MC, V. Thurs–Sun 5:30–closing.

## What to Do

**Sutter Gold Mine**   One of the most entertaining and educational attractions in the Gold Country, the **Sutter Gold Mine Tours** (𝄢 866/762-2837 or 209/736-2708; www.suttergold.com) lead visitors on an hour-long excursion into the bowels of a modern hard-rock gold mine. The tour starts with a ride on a mining shuttle to the mine, where visitors "tag in" and go through the safety training room, as did the miners. Wearing your hardhat, you'll proceed deep into the mine, learning about geology and the history while marveling at the gems and gold embedded in the quartz of the Comet Vein (you'll even learn to distinguish real gold from "fool's gold").

After the tour, be sure to buy a bag of mining ore—about $5 per bag—head over to the wood sluice, grab one of the gold pans or sluice boxes, and pan for real gold. Each bag is guaranteed to hold either gold or gemstones (emeralds, amethysts, topaz, and many other birthstones), and an assistant is on hand to show you how it's done. The kids get a kick out of this. Other diversions include the Company Store gift shop filled with a huge assortment of inexpensive semiprecious gems and minerals, and a 1-hour documentary about the Gold Rush and a half-hour movie about modern gold mining (a heavy-machinery flick that kids will love). And if you're truly a gold-mine enthusiast, go deep into the mine on the 3- to 4-hour Deep Mine Experience, tour by reservation only.

13660 Hwy. 49, about half mile south of Amador City, just north of Sutter Creek. Daily 9am–5pm in summer, 10am–4pm October–May. 1-hour Family Tour $15 for adults, $13 for AAA members and seniors 55 and older, and $10 for kids 4–13; kids under 4 are not allowed on the tour. The Family Tours take place on the hour and reservations are not necessary.

## COLOMA ⭐

On Highway 49 between Auburn and Placerville, the town of **Coloma** ⭐ is so small and unpretentious it's hard to imagine the significant role it played in the rapid development of California and the West. It was here that James Marshall first discovered that there was gold aplenty in the foothills of California. Over the next 50 years, 125 *million* ounces of gold were taken from the Sierra foothills, an amount worth a staggering $50 billion today.

Although Marshall and Sutter tried to keep the discovery secret, word soon leaked out. Sam Brannan, who ran a general store at Fort Sutter, secured some gold samples himself—as well as significant amounts of choice Coloma real estate—and then headed for San Francisco, where he ran through the streets shouting, "Gold! Gold! Gold! From the American River!" San Francisco rapidly emptied as men rushed off to seek their fortunes at the mines.

Coloma was quickly mined out, but its boom brought 10,000 people to the settlement and lasted long enough for residents to build a schoolhouse, a gunsmith, a general store, and a tin-roofed post office. The miners also planted oak and mimosa trees that shade the street during hot summers. About 70% of this quiet, pretty town lies in the **Marshall Gold Discovery State Historic Park** (© 530/622-3470; www.coloma. com/gold), which preserves the spot where Marshall discovered gold on the banks of the south fork of the American River.

Farther up Main Street is a replica of the mill Marshall was building when he made his discovery. The largest building in town, the mill is powered by electricity during the summer. Other attractions include the **Gold Discovery Museum,** which relates the story of the Gold Rush, and a number of Chinese stores, all that remain of the once-sizable local Chinese community. The park also has three picnic areas, four trails, recreational gold panning, and a number of buildings and exhibits relating the way of life that prevailed here in the 19th century. Admission is $5 per vehicle, $4 for seniors; hours are daily from 10am to 3pm, except on major holidays.

Folks also visit for white-water thrills on the American River. (Coloma is a popular launching point.) **White Water Connection,** in Coloma (© 530/622-6446; www. whitewaterconnection.com), runs half- to 2-day trips down the frothy forks of the American River. It's great fun and one of the Gold Country's best outdoor attractions.

## JACKSON ✸

Jackson, the county seat of Amador County, is far livelier than its neighboring towns to the north. (It was the last place in California to outlaw prostitution.) Be sure to stroll through the center of town, browsing in the stores and admiring the Victorian architecture. Although the Kennedy and Argonaut mines ultimately produced more than $140 million in gold, Jackson initially earned its place in the Gold Rush as a supply center. That history is apparent in the town's wide Main Street, lined by tall buildings adorned with intricate iron railings.

Make no mistake: This is not a ghost town, but rather a modern minicity that has worked to preserve its pre-Victorian influence. At the southern end of the street, the **National Hotel,** 2 Water St., at Main Street (© 209/223-0500), is one of California's oldest continuously operating hotels, since 1862. Will Rogers, John Wayne, Leland Stanford, and many other celebrities and politicos once stayed here. Today the hotel's **Louisiana House Bar**—a cool, dark establishment with live music on Fridays and Saturdays—does a brisk business (alas, the guest rooms aren't nearly as enjoyable).

The **Amador County Museum,** a huge brick building at 225 Church St. (© 209/ 223-6386), is where Will Rogers filmed *Boys Will Be Boys* in 1920. Today the former home of Armistead Calvin Brown and his 11 children is filled with mining memorabilia and information on two local mines, the Kennedy and the Argonaut, that were among the deepest and richest in the nation. Within the museum is a working large-scale model of the Kennedy. The museum is open Wednesday through Sunday from 10am to 4pm; admission is by a contribution of any amount. Tours of the Kennedy Mine model cost $2 and are offered Saturday and Sunday on the hour from 11am to 3pm.

If you would rather see the real thing, head to the **Kennedy Tailing Wheels Park,** site of the Kennedy and Argonaut mines, the deepest in the Mother Lode. The mines have been closed for years, but the tailing wheels and head frames, used to convey debris over the hills to a settling pond, remain. To reach the park, take Main Street to Jackson Gate Road, just north of Jackson (no phone).

A few miles south of Jackson on Highway 49 is one of the most evocative towns of the region: **Mokelumne Hill** ✸. The town consists of one street overlooking a valley with a few old buildings, and somehow its sad, abandoned air has the mark of authenticity. At one time, the hill was dotted with tents and wood-and-tar paper shacks, and the town housed a population of 15,000, including an old French quarter and a Chinatown. But now many of its former residents are memorialized in the town's Protestant, Jewish, and Catholic cemeteries.

## Where to Stay & Dine

**Buscaglia's Ristorante**    This capacious, recently renovated Italian Tuscan restaurant is situated in a building that was originally a tavern for miners and locals in 1905. The miners probably weren't eating sautéed fresh Atlantic salmon with champagne dill sauce or braised pork shank on a bed of cheese polenta, but they might have had the historically popular spaghetti and meatballs or hearty vegetable soup (aka minestrone). The menu features a wide variety of pasta, fish, meat, and pizza selections to accommodate the crankiest family member. There's patio dining in fair weather and a pianist on Friday and Saturday nights.

1218 Jackson Gate Rd. ✆ 209/223-9992. Main courses $10–$23. MC, V. Wed–Fri 11:30am–2:30pm; Wed–Sat 5–9 pm; Sun 4–8 pm.

**The Gate House Bed and Breakfast Inn**    About a mile from downtown Jackson and a short walk to the Kennedy Tailing Wheels park, the Gate House offers an assortment of accommodations in an historic mansion surrounded by landscaped lawns, garden, and open countryside. Besides the two rooms and two suites in the main house, all decorated with Victorian furnishings, there's a small cottage with a wood-burning stove and a Jacuzzi tub for two, and another two-bedroom cottage with a living room, kitchen/dining area, covered porch, and a gas barbeque. Breakfast is a full-scale affair with homemade bread or muffins, sausage, fresh fruit, and an entree such as quiche, breakfast casserole, or the inn's specialty, baked French toast. In the afternoon, they serve fresh cookies and beverages. And if you're still hungry, it's close to some nice restaurants.

1330 Jackson Gate Rd., Jackson, CA 95642. ✆ 800/841-1072 or 209/223-3500. www.gatehouseinn.com. 6 units. $140–$215 double. Rates include breakfast. AE, DISC, MC, V. **Amenities:** Pool (summer only); local airport shuttle service. *In room:* A/C, hair dryer, robes.

**Mel and Faye's Diner**  *Value*  AMERICAN    How can anybody not love a classic old roadside diner? In business since 1956, Mel and Faye have been cranking out the best diner food in the Gold Country for so long that it's okay not to feel guilty for salivating over the thought of a sloppy double Moo Burger smothered with onions and special sauce and washed down with a chocolate shake. And could you please add a large side of fries with that? And how much is a slice of pie? It's a time-honored Jackson tradition, so forget about your diet.

205 Hwy. 49 (at Main St.). ✆ 209/223-0853. Menu items $4–$8. MC, V. Daily 4:45am–10pm.

## VOLCANO

About a dozen miles east of Jackson on Highway 88 is the enchantingly decrepit town of **Volcano** ⟨✦⟩, one of the most authentic ghost towns in the central Sierra. The town got its name in 1848, after miners mistook the origins of the craggy boulders that lie in the center of town. The dark rock and the blind window frames of a few backless, ivy-covered buildings give the town's main thoroughfare a haunted look. Sprinkled between boarded-up buildings, about 100 residents do business in the same sagging storefronts that a population of 8,000 frequented nearly 150 years ago.

The tiny, now-quiet burg has a rich history: Not only was this boomtown once home to the state's first lending library and astronomical observatory, but Volcano gold also supported the Union during the Civil War. Residents smuggled a huge cannon to the front lines in a hearse (it was never used). The story goes that had the enthusiastic blues actually fired it, it was so overcharged that "Old Abe" would have exploded. The cannon sits in the town center today, under a rusting weather vane.

Looming over the small buildings is the stately **St. George Hotel** ⚔ (© 209/ **296-4458;** www.stgeorgehotel.com), a three-story, balconied building that testifies to the $90 million in gold mined in and around the town. Its ivy-covered brick and shuttered windows will remind you of colonial New England. In 1998 new owners took over the run-down 20-room hotel and have totally turned it around. The restaurant serves brunch on Sunday, and dinner Thursday through Sunday. Even if you're not hungry, stop in for a libation at the classic old bar, the Whiskey Flat Saloon.

In summer the **Volcano Theatre Company** performs locally written and produced comedies and mysteries at the town's outdoor amphitheater, hidden behind stone facades on Main Street, a block north of the St. George Hotel. It's a wonderful Gold Country experience. For information on performances, call © **209/223-4663** or visit www.volcanotheatre.org. And in early spring, people come from all around to picnic amid the nearly half-million daffodils in bloom on **Daffodil Hill,** a 4-acre ranch 3 miles north of Volcano (follow the sign on Ram's Horn Grade).

Volcano is also the site of one of the National Park Service's National Natural Landmark—the **Black Chasm** (© **866/762-2837**), a cave with a wide variety of stalactites, stalagmites, flowstones, and rare helictite crystals. There's a 50-minute Landmark Family Tour that leaves every 45 minutes throughout the day, open year around, adults $12, children $6, which follows a series of platforms, stairs, and walkways to preserve the cave environment. Above ground, kids can mine for gemstones at a mining flume, guaranteed to find some real gemstones, $5 for a small bag. The new Visitors Center provides information on the cave's history and contents as well as on Black Chasm's connection to the Matrix trilogy. The cave site is located at 15701 Pioneer-Volcano Rd.

## THE SOUTHERN GOLD COUNTRY: ANGELS CAMP, MURPHYS, COLUMBIA, SONORA & JAMESTOWN

No other region in the Gold Country offers more to see and do than these towns in the south, 86 miles southeast of Sacramento. From exploring caverns to riding in the stagecoach and panning for gold, the neighboring towns of Angels Camp, Murphys, Columbia, Sonora, and Jamestown offer a cornucopia of Gold Rush–related sites, museums, and activities. It's a great place to bring the family (kids love roaming around the dusty car-free streets of Columbia), and the region offers some of the best lodgings and restaurants in the Gold Country. In short, if you're the Type A sort who needs to stay active, the southern Gold Country is for you. For information about lodging, dining, events, and the arts and entertainment in the area, contact the **Tuolumne County Visitors Bureau,** P.O. Box 4020, Sonora, California 95370; (© **800/446-1333** or 209/533-4420; www.tcvb.com).

To reach any of these towns from Sacramento, head south on Highway 99 to Stockton, then take Highway 4 east into Angels Camp. (From here, it's a short, scenic drive to the other towns.) For a longer but more scenic route, take U.S. 50 east to Placerville and head south on Highway 49, which takes you to Angels Camp.

## ANGELS CAMP ✪

You've probably heard of Angels Camp, the town that inspired Mark Twain to pen "The Celebrated Jumping Frog of Calaveras County." This pretty, peaceful community is built on hills honeycombed with tunnels. In the 1880s and 1890s, five mines were located along Main Street—Sultana, Angel's, Lightner, Utica, and Stickle—and the town echoed with noise as more than 200 stamps crushed the ore. Between 1886 and 1910, the mines generated close to $20 million.

But a far-more lasting legacy than the town's gold production is the **Jumping Frog Jubilee,** started in 1928 to mark the paving of the town's streets. The ribbiting competition takes place every third weekend in May. The record, 21 feet, 5¾ inches, was set in 1986 by Rosie the Ribbiter, beating the old record by 4½ inches. Livestock exhibitions, pageants, cook-offs, arm-wrestling tournaments, live music, carnival rides, a rodeo, and plenty of beer and wine keep the thousands of spectators entertained between jump-offs. (You can even rent a frog if you forgot to pack one.) For more information and entry forms (around $5 per frog), call the Jumping Frog Jubilee headquarters at ✆ **209/736-2561** or log on to their website at www.frogtown.org.

### Where to Stay

**Cooper House Bed & Breakfast Inn** ✪    Once the home and office of a prominent physician, Dr. George P. Cooper, the Cooper House is now Angels Camp's only B&B. This small Arts and Crafts home is positioned well away from the hustle and bustle of the town's Main Street. The innkeeper maintains three units, all with private bathrooms. The Zinfandel Suite has its own private entrance and deck, and the Chardonnay Suite has a king-size bed, antique claw-foot bathtub, and a private deck. The third bedroom, the Cabernet Suite, is midsize, with a queen bed, adjoining sunroom, and pretty garden view.

1184 Church St. (P.O. Box 1388), Angels Camp, CA 95222. ✆ **800/225-3764**, ext. 326, or 209/736-2145. 3 units. $125 double. Rate includes breakfast. No credit cards. **Amenities:** Complementary wine 4–6pm. *In room:* A/C.

### Where to Dine

**Camps** ✪✪ *(Kids)* CALIFORNIAN    Located on the edge of a golf resort on the western fringes of Angels Camp is Camps, the culinary feather in the cap of Greenhorn Creek golf resort. The restaurant's architects have integrated the building into its natural surroundings by constructing the outer walls with locally mined rhyolite and painting it in natural earth tones. The interior is furnished with leather armchairs, wicker, and antique woods. The best seats in the house are on the veranda overlooking the golf course, particularly on warm summer nights. Though the menu changes seasonally, a typical dinner may start with house salad with field greens, toasted pistachios, julienned red onions, and a raspberry vinaigrette, followed by macadamia-crusted halibut with a mandarin orange beurre blanc or crisp roasted duck with kumquat and sun-dried tomatoes. The lengthy wine list has been given *Wine Spectator*'s Award of Excellence for 5 years running. The restaurant also offers kids' meals for about $7.

676 McCauley Ranch Rd. (½ mile west of Hwy. 4/Hwy. 49 junction off Angel Oaks Dr.). ✆ **209/729-8181**. www.greenhorncreek.com. Reservations recommended. Main courses $17–$25. AE, MC, V. Wed–Sun 5–9pm; bistro menu Wed–Fri noon–9pm; Sat–Sun brunch 10am–2pm.

**Crusco's Ristorante** ✪ ITALIAN    The sign at the entrance says it all: RELAX AND ENJOY. THIS IS NOT FAST FOOD. The point being that the overall experience is as important as the cuisine at Crusco's, a family-run restaurant headed by Celeste Lusher, the amiable chef/owner who oversees the kitchen along with her daughter Sarah, while her husband and son-in-law cater to their customers. In the heart of old-town Angels Camp, the restaurant's decor is an attractive balance of 19th-century Gold Rush architecture—wood beams, 1½-foot-thick stone walls, dark-wood furnishings—and old-world Mediterranean objets d'art such as faux columns and bas-relief sculptures. It's an apropos setting for Lusher's classic Italian menu, made from scratch using generations of family recipes. Each meal begins with house-made focaccia served with olive oil and balsamic vinegar; then come the tough choices: pan-seared tenderloin steak finished with a sweet brandy demi glace, sautéed apples and prunes, the creamy polenta, or the popular penne *rigate*. For lunch, Celeste recommends the New York steak with garlic french fries. Sampling a few of the house-made desserts is highly advised as well.

1240 S. Main St. (℗ 209/736-1440. www.goldrush.com/~ciao. Reservations recommended. Main courses $15–$23. DISC, MC, V. Thurs–Mon 11:30am–3pm and 5–9pm (closed mid-May to June—call ahead).

## MURPHYS ✦

From Angels Camp, a 20-minute drive east along Highway 4 takes you to Murphys, one of my favorite Gold Country towns. Legend has it Murphys started as a former trading post set up by brothers Dan and John Murphy in cooperation with local Indians (John married the chief's daughter). These days, tall locust trees shade gingerbread Victorians on narrow streets. Be sure to stroll down Main Street, stopping in **Grounds** (℗ 209/728-8663) for a bite, or a cool draft of Grizzly Brown Ale—direct from the **Snowshoe Brewing Company** in nearby Arnold—at the saloon within Murphys Historic Hotel and Lodge at 457 Main St.

While you're here, you might also want to check out **Ironstone Vineyards,** 1894 Six Mile Rd., 1 mile south of downtown Murphys (℗ **209/728-1251;** www.iron stonevineyards.com), a veritable wine theme park built by the Kautz family. It's open daily from 10am to 6pm.

Also in the vicinity—just off Highway 4, 1 mile north of Murphys off Sheep Ranch Road—are the **Mercer Caverns** (℗ **209/728-2101;** www.mercercaverns.com). These caverns, discovered in 1885 by Walter Mercer, contain a variety of geological formations—stalactites and stalagmites—in a series of chambers. Tours of the well-lit caverns take nearly an hour. From Memorial Day to Labor Day hours are Sunday through Thursday from 9am to 5pm, Friday and Saturday from 9am to 6pm; from Labor Day to Memorial Day hours are 10am to 4:30pm daily. Admission is $11 for adults, $6.50 for children ages 5 to 12, and free for children under 5.

Fifteen miles east of Murphys up Highway 4 is **Calaveras Big Trees State Park** ✦ (℗ **209/795-2334;** www.parks.ca.gov), where you can see giant sequoias that are among the biggest and oldest living things on earth. It's a popular summer retreat that offers camping, swimming, hiking, and fishing along the Stanislaus River. It's open daily; admission is $6 per car for day use.

### Where to Stay

**Dunbar House, 1880** ✦✦   This Italianate home, built in 1880 for the bride of a local businessman, is one of the finest B&Bs in the Gold Country. The front porch, which overlooks the exquisite gardens, is decorated with wicker furniture and hanging baskets of ivy. Inside, the emphasis is on comfort and elegance. The guest rooms are furnished with quality antiques and equipped with every possible amenity. Beds have Egyptian cotton linens and down comforters, and each room has a fridge stocked with mineral water and a complimentary bottle of local wine. My favorite room, the Cedar, is a fabulous two-room suite with a private sun porch, whirlpool tub, and complimentary champagne. I also like the Sugar Pine suite, with its private balcony in the trees. Lemonade and cookies are offered in the afternoon, appetizers and wine in the early evening. Breakfast is served in your room, the dining room, or the garden.

271 Jones St., Murphys, CA 95247. ℂ 800/692-6006 or 209/728-2897. Fax 209/728-1451. www.dunbarhouse.com. 5 units. $175–$260 double. Rates include breakfast and afternoon appetizers. AE, DISC, MC, V. *In room:* A/C, flatscreen TV/DVR, wireless Internet, DSL, hair dryer, iron.

## Where to Dine

**Firewood** ★ (Value) AMERICAN   Local restaurateur River Klass opened this order-at-the-counter cafe just down the street from his Grounds restaurant (see below). The open-air establishment specializes in fast, inexpensive, and darn good dishes such as Baja-style fish tacos, drippingly juicy "not healthy" burgers, baby back ribs with house-made barbecue sauce, and superb gourmet pizzas baked in a wood-burning oven (the prosciutto and arugula, shrimp and feta, and sausage and pepperoni versions are all big hits). Good microbeer and local wine selections are available as well.

420 Main St. ℂ 209/728-3248. Reservations not accepted. Main courses $5–$10. MC, V. Wed–Fri 11am–8pm; Sat–Sun 11am–9pm.

**Grounds** ★★ ECLECTIC   When River Klass moved here from the East Coast to open his own place, Murphys's restaurant-challenged residents heaved a sigh of relief. Its nickname is the "Rude Boy Cafe," after Klass's acerbic wit, but you'll find happy smiles and friendly service. The majority of Grounds's business is with the locals, who have become addicted to the potato pancakes that come with every made-to-order omelet. For lunch, try the killer BLT with avocado on a house-baked French roll or the grilled eggplant sandwich stuffed with smoked mozzarella and fresh basil. Typical dinner choices include fresh breaded halibut with house-made lentil salsa served over garlic mashed red potatoes, or a roasted end-bone pork chop with demi glace, cannelini beans, and grilled vegetables. The wine list is impressive (and reasonably priced). The long, narrow dining rooms are bright and airy with pine-wood furnishings, wood floors, and an open kitchen. On sunny days, request a table on the back patio.

402 Main St. ℂ 209/728-8663. Reservations recommended. Main courses $12–$23. AE, DISC, MC, V. Daily 7am–3pm; Wed–Thurs and Sun 5:30–8pm; Fri–Sat 5:30–9pm.

## COLUMBIA

Though a little hokey, **Columbia State Historic Park** ★★ (ℂ 209/532-3184; www.columbiacalifornia.com) is the best-maintained Gold Rush town in the Mother Lode (as well as one of the most popular, so expect crowds in the summer). At one point, this boisterous mining town was the state's second-largest city (and only two votes shy of becoming the state capital). When gold mining no longer panned out in the late 1850s, most of the town's 15,000 residents departed, leaving much of the mining equipment and buildings in place. In 1945 the entire town was turned into a historic park.

As a result, Columbia has been preserved and functions much as it did in the 1850s, with stagecoach rides, Western-style Victorian hotels and saloons, a newspaper office, a blacksmith's forge, a Wells Fargo express office, and numerous other relics of California's early mining days. Cars are banned from its streets, giving the shady town an authentic feel. Merchants still do business behind some storefronts, as horse-, stagecoach-, and pedestrian traffic wanders by.

If Columbia's heat and dust get to you, pull up a stool at the **Jack Douglass Saloon** on Main Street (no phone), open daily from 10am to 5pm. Inside the swinging doors of the classic Western bar, you can sample homemade sarsaparilla and wild cherry, drinks the saloon has been serving since 1857, and it serves dinners on Friday night. The storefront's large shuttered windows open onto a dusty main street, so put up your boots, relax awhile, and watch the stagecoach go by.

Free historical tours of the park depart from the Main Museum Friday and Saturday at 11am. Every second Saturday the park presents Gold Rush Days from 1 to 4pm when costumed docents take you down Main Street and into dusty old structures that are off-limits to the general public. Special docent-led tours are available by reservation for $2 per person.

### Where to Stay & Dine

**City Hotel** 🄀 *(Kids)*    Established in 1856, the City Hotel was restored in 1975 by the State of California, the nonprofit City Hotel Corporation, and Columbia College. Now the college runs it as a training center for hospitality-management students (hence the eager-to-please staff). It's a big, beautiful building, complete with a stately parlor furnished with Victorian sofas, antiques, and Oriental rugs. The largest guest rooms have two balconies overlooking Main Street; the units off the parlor are also spacious. The hallway rooms are smaller but still nicely furnished with Renaissance Revival beds and antiques. Each room has a sink and toilet, but the shower rooms are separate. A buffet breakfast is served in the dining room. The hotel also runs a fine-dining restaurant serving classic Continental cuisine (roast rack of lamb, grilled salmon, and smoked duck breast) Tuesday through Sunday, as well as the What Cheer saloon. Noise from the saloon—though it's not so loud as it was when the customers packed pistols—does travel upstairs. If you're a light sleeper, bring earplugs.

Main St. (P.O. Box 1870), Columbia State Park, CA 95310. © **800/532-1479** or 209/532-1479. Fax 209/532-7027. www.cityhotel.com. 10 units (all w/shared shower rooms). $110–$130 double. Rates include breakfast. AE, DISC, MC, V. **Amenities:** Restaurant; saloon; nearby golf courses. *In room:* A/C, no phone.

**Fallon Hotel** 🄀 *(Kids)*    Opened in 1857, this hotel has been restored and decorated to evoke the 1890s. The two-story building retains many of its original antiques and furniture. The largest rooms are those along the front upper balcony. Only one unit has a full bathroom; the rest have a private sink and toilet, and showers are down the hall. Rooms are furnished with high-backed Victorian beds, marble-topped dressers, and rockers. A full breakfast is served in the downstairs parlor.

Washington St. (P.O. Box 1870), Columbia State Park, CA 95310. © **800/532-1479** or 209/532-1470. Fax 209/532-7027. www.cityhotel.com. 14 units, 13 w/shared bathroom. $65–$130 double. Rates include breakfast. AE, DISC, MC, V. **Amenities:** Ice-cream parlor; nearby golf course. *In room:* A/C, no phone.

### SONORA

A few miles south of Columbia, Sonora is the largest town in the southern Gold Country. (You'll know you've arrived when traffic starts to crawl.) In Gold Rush days, Sonora and Columbia were the two richest towns in the Mother Lode. Dozens of stores and cafes line the main thoroughfare. If you can find a parking space, it's worth your while to spend an hour or two checking out the sites, like the 19th-century **St. James Episcopal Church,** at the top of Washington Street, and the **Tuolumne County Museum and History Center,** 158 W. Bradford Ave. (© **209/532-1317**), in the 1857 County Jail. Admission is free, and it's open daily year-round from 10am to 4pm, closed some holidays.

## Where to Stay

**Gunn House Hotel** ⭐ *Value*     Built in 1850 by Dr. Lewis C. Gunn, the Gunn House was the first two-story adobe structure in Sonora, built to house his family, who sailed around Cape Horn from the East Coast to join him in the Gold Rush. Painstakingly restored, it's now one of the best moderately priced hotels in the Gold Country. It's easy to catch the forty-niner spirit here, as the entire hotel and grounds are brimming with quality antiques and turn-of-the-20th-century artifacts. Rare for a building this old, each guest room has a private bathroom and air-conditioning. What really makes the Gunn House one of my favorites, though, is the hotel's beautiful pool and patio, surrounded by lush vegetation and admirable stonework. It's in a convenient location as well, right in downtown Sonora.

286 S. Washington St., Sonora, CA 95370. ℂ **209/532-3421.** 20 units. $76–$109 double. Rates include breakfast. AE, MC, V. **Amenities:** Outdoor heated pool. *In room:* A/C, TV.

## Where to Dine

**Diamondback Grill** *Value* AMERICAN     For more than a decade, this modest family-owned diner has whipped up the Gold Country's best burger: the Diamondback—a grilled-to-order half-pounder that comes with the works, including fries. There are about a dozen other burgers, as well as gourmet sandwiches (go for the grilled eggplant with fresh tomato and mozzarella), house-made soups and pecan pies, a zesty black-bean-and-steak chili, and great daily specials listed. There's also a good selection of beer and wine by the glass.

110 S. Washington St. ℂ **209/532-6661.** Main courses $5–$10. No credit cards. Mon–Sat 11am–9pm; Sun 11am–5pm.

## JAMESTOWN ⭐

About 4 miles southwest of Sonora on Highway 49 is Jamestown, a 4-block-long town of old-fashioned storefronts and two rustic turn-of-the-20th-century hotels. There's

---

*Fun Fact*  **How to Pan for Gold**

Find a gold pan, ideally a 12- to 15-inch steel pan. Place the pan over an oven burner, or better yet, in a campfire. This will darken the pan, making it easier to see any flakes of placer gold (many gold pans come already blackened). Find some gravel, sand, or dirt in a stream that looks promising or feels lucky. Scoop dirt into the pan until it's nearly full, then place it under water and keep it there while you break up the clumps of mud and clay and toss out any stones. Then grasp the pan with both hands. Holding it level, rotate it in swirling motions. This will cause the heavier gold to loosen and settle to the bottom of the pan. Drain off the dirty water and loose stuff. Keep doing this until gold and heavier minerals called "black sand" are left in the pan. Carefully inspect the black sand for nuggets or speck traces of gold. Who knows? You just might get lucky.

If this all seems too much to try on your own, you can sign up for a lesson with Jamestown's **Gold Prospecting Adventures** (ℂ **800/596-0009** or 209/984-4653; www.goldprospecting.com). The hour-long class costs about $15, and yes, you get to keep any gold you might find.

gold in these parts, too, as the marker commemorating the discovery of a 75-pound nugget attests (panning nearby Woods Creek is a popular pastime among both locals and tourists). If Jamestown looks eerily familiar to you, that's probably because you've seen it in the movies or on television. It's one of Hollywood's favorite Western movie sets; scenes from such films as *Butch Cassidy and the Sundance Kid* were shot here.

Jamestown's most popular attraction is the **Railtown 1897 State Historic Park** ★, a train buff's paradise featuring three Sierra steam locomotives. These great machines were used in many a movie and television show, including *High Noon, Little House on the Prairie, Bonanza,* and *My Little Chickadee.* The trains at the roundhouse are on display daily year-round. Call for information on weekend rides and guided tours. The Depot Store and Museum are open daily from 9:30am to 4:30pm (10am–3pm Nov–Mar). The park is located near the center of town, on Fifth Avenue at Reservoir Road (② **209/984-3953;** www.csrmf.org/railtown).

## Where to Stay & Dine

**Jamestown Hotel & Restaurant** ★  The most worked-over building in town, the Jamestown was originally built in 1858; it burned down and was rebuilt twice before 1915. To achieve the old-fashioned, brick-fronted Victorian look it sports today, a lot of stucco and Spanish-revival paraphernalia had to be removed. Most of the lower floor is devoted to the front office, bar, and restaurant. The second floor contains a cadre of cozy bedrooms outfitted with antiques. All of the spacious rooms are loaded with nostalgic charm; a few have sitting rooms and TVs with VCRs, and all have private bathrooms (some with claw-foot tubs, several with spa tubs). The most popular has its own balcony. The dining room serves upscale American dishes such as New York steak, grilled and served with a roasted tomato demi glace and grilled scallions, rack of Australian lamb, and fresh fish flown in twice a week.

If you're staying for the weekend, be sure to attend the hotel's popular Sunday champagne brunch.

18153 Main St. (P.O. Box 539), Jamestown, CA 95327. ② **800/205-4901** or 209/984-3902. Fax 209/984-4149. www.jamestownhotel.com. 8 units. $90–$175 double. Rates include full breakfast. AE, MC, V. **Amenities:** Restaurant; bar; activities desk; business center. *In room:* A/C, TV/VCR, hair dryer, iron.

**National Hotel & Restaurant** ★  In the center of town, this two-story classic Western hotel has been operating since 1859, making it one of the 10 oldest continuously operating hotels in the state. The saloon has its original 19th-century redwood bar, and you can imagine what it must have been like when miners traded gold dust for drinks. The guest rooms blend 19th-century details (handmade quilts, oak furnishings, lace curtains, brass beds) with 20th-century comforts such as private bathrooms. All guests have access to the authentic Soaking Room, a private room equipped with a sort of 1800s claw-foot Jacuzzi for two (when cowboys longed for a good, hot soak). Brunch, lunch, and dinner are served to the public in the handsome old-fashioned dining room or pretty garden courtyard. Dishes, many with a Mediterranean flavor, range from steak, veal and prime rib to chicken, seafood, pasta dishes, and house-made desserts.

77 Main St. (P.O. Box 502), Jamestown, CA 95327. ② **800/894-3446** or 209/984-3446. Fax 209/984-5620. www. national-hotel.com. 9 units. $95–$150 double. Rates include large buffet breakfast. AE, DC, DISC, MC, V. Pets accepted w/$10-per-night fee. **Amenities:** Restaurant; saloon; nearby golf course; concierge; tour/activities desk; business center; wireless DSL throughout hotel; secretarial services; room service; in-room massage. *In room:* A/C, TV, dataport, coffeemaker, hair dryer.

## 3 The Central Valley & Sierra National Forest

The Central Valley (also known as the San Joaquin Valley) is about as far as you can get from movie stars in stretch limos. This hot, flat strip of farms, dairies, fast-food joints, cheap motels, and truck stops stretches for 225 miles from Bakersfield to Redding. The 18,000-square-mile valley is central to the economy of the Golden State, in part because of its cultivated and irrigated fields, orchards, pastures, and vineyards.

The major traffic arteries through the valley are Highway 99 and I-5. Highway 99 links the agricultural communities, while I-5 provides access routes to the attractions in the valley. Rivers cutting through the valley offer fishing, boating, house boating on the delta, and white-water rafting on the rapids. And once you get off the freeways, the valley's spectacular landscapes provide unrivaled natural beauty. Many visitors drive through in spring just to view the orchards in bloom.

The Central Valley also stands on the doorstep of some of America's greatest attractions, the most well known being Yosemite National Park. The Central Valley town of Visalia is the gateway to Sequoia & Kings Canyon National Park, while Fresno is a popular overnight stay for travelers heading in and out of the Sierra National Forest.

### FRESNO

The running joke in California is that Fresno is the "gateway to Bakersfield." For most visitors, Fresno, 185 miles southeast of San Francisco, is just a place to pass through en route to the state parks; it can, however, be a good place to stop for food and lodging, and it makes a good base for exploring the Sierra National Forest (see below).

Founded in 1874 in the geographic center of the state, Fresno is in the heart of the Central Valley and has experienced incredible growth in recent years. Like most growing cities, it has seen increases in crime, drugs, and urban sprawl.

As the seat of Fresno County, the city handles more than $3 billion annually in agricultural production. It also contains Sun Maid, the world's largest dried-fruit packing plant, and Guild, one of the country's largest wineries.

If you have any reason at all to be in Fresno, try to visit between late February and late March so you can drive the **Fresno County Blossom Trail** . This 62-mile, self-guided tour takes in the beauty of California's agrarian bounty at its peak. The trail courses through fruit orchards in full bloom and citrus groves with lovely orange blossoms and a heady natural perfume. The **Fresno Convention and Visitors Bureau,** 847 M St., Third Floor, in Fresno (© **800/788-0836** or 559/621-4700; www.fresno cvb.org), supplies full details, including a map.

### WHERE TO STAY

**San Joaquin** *   On the northern edge of Fresno, this full-service hotel was conceived as an apartment complex in the 1970s. Around 1985 a lobby was added, the floor plans were adjusted, and the place was reconfigured as an all-suite hotel. Suites range from junior one-bedroom suites to three-bedroom suites with kitchens, and each is outfitted in a slightly different style, with light, contemporary colors and furniture. Room service is available from a restaurant down the street.

1309 W. Shaw Ave., Fresno, CA 93711. © **800/775-1309** or 559/225-1309. Fax 559/225-6021. www.sjhotel.com. 68 suites. $99–$205 suite. Rates include continental breakfast. AE, DC, DISC, MC, V. **Amenities:** Outdoor pool; Jacuzzi; business center; limited room service; laundry service. *In room:* A/C, TV/VCR, dataport, kitchen, fridge, coffeemaker, hair dryer, iron.

## WHERE TO DINE

**Veni, Vidi, Vici** ⋆ CALIFORNIA CUISINE  The most innovative and creative restaurant in Fresno occupies a prominent position about 6 miles south of the commercial center, in a funky neighborhood known as the Tower District. The place's rustic exterior strikes an interesting contrast to the polished and artful interior on the other side of the 15-foot doors, where the decor is accented with exposed-brick walls, mirrors, and chandeliers fashioned from twisted wire and metal leaves. The menu changes often but might include roasted loin of pork with Chinese black beans and citrus-flavored glaze, served with grilled portobello mushrooms, sun-dried tomatoes, risotto, and red-pepper coulis; or a wild-mushroom lasagna with preserved tomato sauce. There are also fresh-fish specials nightly. This is the only restaurant in Fresno that makes its own ice cream (the flavor of the day when I arrived was Technicolor lime sorbet). Have a scoop or two with the restaurant's perennial dessert favorite: bittersweet chocolate cake.

1116 N. Fulton St. ⓒ **559/266-5510.** Reservations recommended. Main courses $20–$29. AE, DC, DISC, MC, V. Tues–Fri 11am–2pm; Tues–Sun 5–10pm (late-night menu Fri–Sat 10pm–midnight).

## SIERRA NATIONAL FOREST ⋆⋆

Leaving Fresno's taco joints, used-car lots, and tract houses behind, an hour's drive and 45 miles northeast gets you to the Sierra National Forest, a land of lakes and coniferous forests between Yosemite, Sequoia, and Kings Canyon national parks. The entire eastern portion of the park is unspoiled wilderness protected by the government. Development—some of it, unfortunately, beside the bigger lakes and reservoirs—is confined to the western side.

The 1.3-million-acre forest contains 528,000 acres of wilderness. The Sierra's five wilderness areas include Ansel Adams, Dinkey Lakes, John Muir, Kaiser, and Monarch (see below). The forest offers plenty of opportunities for fishing, swimming, sailing, boating, camping, water-skiing, white-water rafting, kayaking, and horseback riding, all regulated by certain guidelines. Downhill and cross-country skiing, as well as hunting, are also available, depending on the season. Backpackers looking to retreat to the wilderness will find solace here, as some 1,100 miles of forest hiking trails traverse the park.

### ESSENTIALS

**GETTING THERE**  After visiting the ranger station at Oakhurst, take Highway 41 to Highway 49, the major road into the northern part of the national forest. This is more convenient for visitors approaching the park from Northern California. Highway 168 via Clovis is the primary route from Fresno if you're headed for Shaver Lake. There is no approach road from the eastern Sierra, only from the west.

**VISITOR INFORMATION & PERMITS**  To learn about hiking, camping, or other activities, or to get the fire and wilderness permits, visit one of the ranger stations in the park's western section. These include **Bass Lake Ranger District,** 57003 North Fork (ⓒ **559/877-2218**); and the **High Sierra Ranger District,** 29688 Auberry Rd., Prather (ⓒ **559/855-5355**).

**SUPPLIES**  Shaver Lake is one place where you can stock up on goods and supplies if you're going into the wilderness, but stores in Fresno carry much of the same stuff at lower prices. Cheaper supplies are also available in Clovis, outside Fresno (which you must pass through en route to the forest), at the **Peacock Market,** at Tollhouse Road (Third St.) and Sunnyside Avenue (ⓒ **559/299-6627**).

**WEATHER**   In the lower elevations, summer temperatures can frequently reach 100°F (38°C), but in the higher elevations, more comfortable temperatures in the 70s and 80s (20s Celsius) are the norm.

## THE MAJOR WILDERNESS & RECREATION AREAS

**ANSEL ADAMS WILDERNESS**   Divided between the Sierra and Inyo national forests, this wilderness area covers 228,500 acres. Elevations range from 3,500 to 13,157 feet. The frost-free period extends from mid-July to August, the best time for a visit to the park's upper altitudes.

Ansel Adams is dotted with alpine vistas, including steep-walled gorges and granite peaks. There are several glaciers in the north and some large lakes on the eastern slope of the Ritter Range. This wilderness has excellent stream and lake fishing, especially for rainbow, golden, and brook trout, and offers challenging mountain climbing on the Minarets Range. The wilderness is accessed by the Tioga Pass Road in the north, U.S. 395 and Reds Meadow Road in the east, the Minarets Highway in the west, and Highway 168 to High Sierra in the south.

**DINKEY LAKES WILDERNESS**   The 30,000-acre Dinkey Lakes area, created in 1984, occupies the western slope of the Sierra Nevada, southeast of Huntington Lake and northwest of Courtright Reservoir. Most of the timbered, rolling terrain here is 8,000 feet above sea level, reaching its apex (10,619 ft.) at Three Sisters Peak. Sixteen lakes are clustered in the west-central region. You can reach the area on Kaiser Pass Road (north), Red/Coyote Jeep Road (west), Rock Creek Road (southwest), or Courtright Reservoir (southeast), generally from mid-June to late October.

**JOHN MUIR WILDERNESS**   Occupying 584,000 acres in the Sierra and Inyo national forests, John Muir Wilderness—named after the naturalist—extends southeast from Mammoth Lakes along the crest of the Sierra Nevada for 30 miles before forking around the boundary of Kings Canyon National Park to Crown Valley and Mount Whitney. Elevations range from 4,000 to 14,496 feet at Mount Whitney, with many of the area's peaks surpassing 12,000 feet. The wilderness can be accessed from numerous points west of U.S. 395 between Mammoth Lake and Independence.

Split by deep canyons, the wilderness is also a land of meadows (especially beautiful when wildflowers bloom), lakes, and streams. The south and middle forks of the San Joaquin River, the north fork of Kings River, and many creeks draining into Owens Valley originate in the John Muir Wilderness. Mountain hemlock, red and white fir, and white-bark and western pine dot the park's landscape. Temperatures vary wildly throughout any 24-hour period: Summer temperatures range from 25° to 85°F (–4° to 29°C), and the only really frost-free period is between mid-July and August. The higher elevations are marked by barren expanses of granite splashed with many glacially carved lakes.

**KAISER WILDERNESS**   North of Huntington Lake and 70 miles northeast of Fresno, Kaiser is a 22,700-acre forest tract commanding a view of the central Sierra Nevada. It was named after Kaiser Ridge, which divides the area into two regions. Four trail heads provide access to the wilderness, but the northern half is much more open than the forested southern half; the primary point of entry is the Sample Meadow Campground. All other lakes are approached cross-country. Winter storms begin to blow in late October, and the grounds are generally snow-covered until early June.

**MONARCH WILDERNESS** Monarch is at the southern end of the John Muir Wilderness, on the western border of Sequoia and Kings Canyon National Parks, 65 miles east of Fresno via Highway 180. The area extends across 45,000 acres in the Sierra and Sequoia national forests. The Sierra National Forest portion of the region—about 21,000 acres—is rugged and hard to traverse. Steep slopes climb from the middle and main forks of Kings River, with elevations increasing from 2,400 to more than 10,000 feet. Rock outcroppings are found throughout Monarch, and most of the lower elevations are chaparral covered with pine stands near the tops of the higher peaks. Monarch is located at the southern end of the John Muir Wilderness, on the western border of Sequoia and Kings Canyon national parks, approximately 65 miles east of Fresno via Highway 180.

**HUNTINGTON LAKE RECREATION AREA** At 7,000 feet, this area is a 2-hour drive east of Fresno via Highway 168. The lake is one of the reservoirs in the Big Creek Hydroelectric System and has 14 miles of shoreline. It's a popular recreational area, offering camping, hiking, picnicking, sailing, swimming, windsurfing, fishing, and horseback riding—or you can just appreciate the beauty. The main summer season stretches from Memorial Day to Labor Day. There are seven campgrounds and four picnic areas in the Huntington Lake Basin, plus numerous hiking and riding trails.

**NEIDER GROVE OF GIANT SEQUOIAS** 🌲 This 1,540-acre tract in the Sierra National Forest contains 101 mature giant sequoias in the center of the Sequoia Range, south of Yosemite National Park. A **visitor center** stands near the Neider Grove Campground, with historical relics and displays, including two restored log cabins. The Bull Buck Tree—at one time thought to be the largest in the world—is 246 feet high and has a circumference at ground level of 99 feet. There's a mile-long, self-guided walk along the "Shadow of the Giants" National Recreational Trail in the southwest corner of the grove.

## OUTDOOR PURSUITS

**CAMPING** The Sierra National Forest seems like one vast campsite. Options range from primitive wilderness camps to developed and often crowded campgrounds with snack bars, flush toilets, bathhouses, and RV hookups. For information and reservations, call the **National Recreation Reservation Service** toll-free at © **877/444-6777,** or visit its website at www.reserveusa.com.

The major campgrounds are the Shaver Lake area; the Huntington Lake area (which has seven family campgrounds open from the end of June to Labor Day that must be reserved in advance); the Florence and Edison Lake area (first-come, first-served); the Dinkey Creek area (family and group camping); the Wishon and Court-right area (four campgrounds; first-come, first-served); the Pine Flat Reservoir (in the Sierra foothills, with two first-come, first-served campgrounds); and Upper Kings River, east of Pine Flat Reservoir (family campgrounds; first-come, first-served).

**FISHING** The many streams of the Sierra are home to rainbow, golden, brown, and brook trout. The best freshwater angling is in the Pineridge and Kings River Rangers District. At the lower elevations, Shaver Lake, Bass Lake, and Pine Flat reservoirs are known for their black-bass fishing. Questions about fishing in the national forest can be directed to the **California Department of Fish and Game,** 1234 E. Shaw Ave., Fresno, CA 93710 (© **559/243-4005**).

**SKIING**    Sixty-five miles northeast of Fresno on Highway 168 in the Sierra National Forest, the **Sierra Summit Ski Area** offers mildly challenging alpine skiing and marked trails for cross-country skiing and snowmobiling. The resort has two triple and three double chairlifts, plus four surface lifts and 30 runs, the longest of which extends for 2¼ miles. The vertical drop-off is 1,600 feet. Other facilities include a lodge, snack bar, cafeteria, restaurant, and bar, open daily from mid-November until mid-April. For resort information or a ski report, call ✆ **559/893-3311.**

The **Pineridge Ranger Station** (✆ **559/855-5360**) maintains several marked cross-country trails along Highway 168, ranging from a 1-mile tour for beginners to a 6-mile trail for more advanced skiers.

**WHITE-WATER RAFTING**    The Upper Kings River, east of Pine Flat Reservoir, offers a 10-mile rafting run through Garnet Dike to Kirch Flat Campground. Rafting season is from late April to mid-July, with the highest waters in late May and early June. To get there, take Belmont Avenue in Fresno east (toward Pine Flat Reservoir) for about 63 miles. For more information about guided rafting trips on the Kings River, call **Kings River Expeditions** (✆ **559/233-4881;** www.kingsriver.com).

# The Monterey Peninsula & the Big Sur Coast

*by Matthew Richard Poole*

The Monterey Peninsula and the Big Sur coast comprise one of the world's most spectacular shorelines, skirted with cypress trees, rugged shores, and crescent-shaped bays. Monterey reels in visitors with its world-class aquarium and array of outdoor activities. Pacific Grove is so peaceful that the butterflies choose it as their yearly mating ground. Pebble Beach attracts the golfing elite, and although it's packed with tourists who come for the beaches, shops, and restaurants, tiny Carmel-by-the-Sea is still romantic and sweet. Big Sur's dramatic and majestic coast, backed by pristine redwood forests and rolling hills, is one of the most breathtaking and tranquil environments on earth. If you're traveling on Highway 1 (which you should be), the coastline will guide you all the way through the region.

This chapter begins with Santa Cruz, at the northwestern end of Monterey Bay—one of my favorite destinations on the coast, and home of the Santa Cruz Beach Boardwalk. Across Monterey Bay at the northern tip of the Monterey Peninsula are the seaside communities of Monterey and Pacific Grove, while Pebble Beach and Carmel-by-the-Sea hug the peninsula's south coast along Carmel Bay. Between the north and south coasts, which are only about 5 miles apart, are many golf courses, some of the state's most stunning homes and hotels, and the 17-Mile Drive, one of the most scenic coastal roads in the world.

Inland lies Carmel Valley, with its elegant inns and resorts, golf courses, and guaranteed sunshine, even when the coast is socked in with fog. Farther down the coast along Highway 1 is Big Sur, a stunning 90-mile stretch of coast south of the Monterey Peninsula and west of the Santa Lucia Mountains.

## 1 Santa Cruz ★ ★

77 miles SE of San Francisco

For a small bayside city, Santa Cruz has a lot to offer. The main show, of course, is the Beach Boardwalk, the West Coast's only seaside amusement park, which attracts millions of visitors each year. But past the arcades and cotton candy is a surprisingly diverse and energetic city that has a little something for everyone. Shopping, hiking, mountain biking, sailing, fishing, kayaking, surfing, wine tasting, golfing, whale-watching—the list of things to do here is almost endless, making Santa Cruz one of the premier family destinations on the California coast.

## ESSENTIALS

**GETTING THERE**   Santa Cruz is 77 miles southeast of San Francisco. The most scenic route to Santa Cruz is along Highway 1 from San Francisco, which, aside from the "you fall, you die" stretch called Devil's Slide, allows you to cruise at a steady 50 mph. Faster but less romantic is Highway 17, which is accessed near San Jose from I-280, I-880, or U.S. 101, and ends at the foot of the boardwalk. The exception to this rule is on weekend mornings, when Highway 17 tends to logjam with beach-goers while Highway 1 remains relatively uncrowded.

**VISITOR INFORMATION**   For information, contact the **Santa Cruz County Conference and Visitors Council,** 1211 Ocean St., Santa Cruz, CA 95060 (© **800/ 833-3494** or 831/425-1234; www.santacruzca.org), open Monday through Saturday from 9am to 5pm, Sunday from 10am to 4pm.

**SPECIAL EVENTS**   Special events include **Shakespeare Santa Cruz** in July and August (© **831/459-2121**), and the **Cabrillo Music Festival** in August (© **831/ 426-6966**).

## WHAT TO SEE & DO
### BEACHES, HIKING & FISHING IN SANTA CRUZ

One of the few old-fashioned amusement parks left in the world, the **Santa Cruz Beach Boardwalk** ★★ (© **831/426-7433**) draws more than three million visitors a year to its 30 rides and arcades, shops, and restaurants. The park has two national landmarks—a 1924 wooden Giant Dipper roller coaster and a 1911 carousel with hand-carved wooden horses and a 342-pipe organ band. It's open daily in the summer (from Memorial Day weekend to Labor Day) and on weekends and holidays through-out the spring and fall, from 11am (noon sometimes in winter). Admission to the boardwalk is free, but an all-day "unlimited rides" pass will set you back $27. Check the boardwalk calendar (© **831/423-5590;** www.beachboardwalk.com) for discounts, concerts and events, and up-to-date info on hours, which can often vary.

Here, too, is **Neptune's Kingdom,** 400 Beach St. (© **831/426-7433;** www.beach boardwalk.com), an enormous indoor family recreation center whose main feature is a two-story miniature golf course. Also on Beach Street is the **Municipal Wharf** (© **831/420-6025**), lined with shops and restaurants—a beachfront strip that is serenaded by the sea lions below. You can also crab and fish from here. Most shops are open daily from 7am to 9pm; the wharf is open daily from 5am to 2am. **Stagnaro's** (© **831/427-2334;** www.stagnaros.com) operates fishing and whale-watching trips from the wharf year-round, as well as hour-long narrated bay cruises for a mere $10 for adults, $5 for kids under 14.

Farther down on West Cliff Drive, you'll come to a favorite surfing spot, **Steamer Lane,** where you can watch pro surfers shredding the waves. If you want to find out more about this local sport that's been practiced here for more than 100 years, go to the **Santa Cruz Surfing Museum,** at the lighthouse (© **831/420-6289;** www.santa cruzparksandrec.com), open Thursday through Monday from noon to 4pm. Antique surfboards, videos, photographs, and other memorabilia depict the history and evolution of surfing around the world.

Continue along West Cliff and you'll reach **Natural Bridges State Beach,** 2531 W. Cliff Dr. (© **831/423-4609;** www.scparkfriends.org), a large sandy beach with nearby tide pools and hiking trails. It's also home to a large colony of monarch butterflies that cluster and mate in the nearby eucalyptus grove.

Other Santa Cruz beaches worth noting are **Bonny Doon,** at Bonny Doon Road and Highway 1, an uncrowded sandy beach and a major surfing spot accessible by a steep walkway; **Pleasure Point Beach,** East Cliff Drive at Pleasure Point Drive; and **Twin Lakes State Beach,** which is ideal for sunning and also provides access to Schwann Lagoon, a bird sanctuary.

In addition to hosting many cultural and sporting events, the University of California at Santa Cruz also features the **Seymour Marine Discovery Center** at the Long Marine Laboratory, 100 Shaffer Rd., at the northwest end of Delaware Avenue (© 831/459-3800; www2.ucsc.edu/seymourcenter), where you can observe the activities of marine scientists and the species in tide-pool touch tanks and aquariums. Visitors get to learn how marine research aids in the conservation of the world's oceans. Hours are Tuesday through Saturday from 10am to 5pm, and Sunday from noon to 5pm; admission is $5 for adults, $3 for children ages 6 to 16, and free for kids under 6 (free admission for the first Tues of each month).

The **Santa Cruz Harbor,** 135 Fifth Ave. (© 831/475-6161; www.santacruzharbor. org), is the place to head for boat rentals, open-boat fishing (cod, shark, and salmon), and whale-watching trips. Operators include **Santa Cruz Sportfishing Inc.** (© 831/ 426-4690; www.santacruzsportfishing.com) and **Shamrock Charters,** 2210 E. Cliff Dr. (© 831/476-2648). Even if you're not into fishing, it's worth a walk down the harbor to browse the many shops and restaurants.

Bikes—mountain, kids', tandem, hybrid—are available by the hour, day, or week from various bike-rental shops in convenient locations around the city. For a list of shops, call the **Santa Cruz Visitors Council** at © 800/833-3494, or check the website at www.santacruzca.org. It's about $25 a day, with helmets, locks, and packs.

The **Pasatiempo Golf Club,** at 18 Clubhouse Rd. (© 831/459-9155; www. pasatiempo.com) is rated among the top 100 courses in the U.S. Greens fees are $140 Monday through Friday, $165 Saturday, Sunday, and holidays.

Kayaking is also an option. Outfitters include **Kayak Connection,** 413 Lake Ave. No. 4 (© 831/479-1121; www.kayakconnection.com), and **Venture Quest Kayaking** (© 831/427-2267; www.kayaksantacruz.com), which rent single, double, and triple kayaks at Building No. 2 on the wharf and at 125 Beach St. Classes, wildlife tours, and moonlight paddles are also available.

You can rent surfing equipment at the **Cowell's Beach 'n' Bikini Surf Shop,** 109 Beach St. (© 831/427-2355), and from the **Club Ed Surf School** (© 800/287-SURF or 831/464-0177; www.club-ed.com), on Cowell Beach in front of the West Coast Santa Cruz Hotel. Both offer lessons: Club Ed's are $85 for a 2-hour group session and $95 for private lessons (equipment included); Cowell's are $70 for 2-hour group lessons including a board and wet suit.

## IN NEARBY CAPITOLA & APTOS

South along the coast, the small community of **Capitola** ✿ at the mouth of the Soquel Creek, is a spawning ground for steelhead and salmon. You can fish without a license from the **Capitola Wharf,** 1400 Wharf Rd., or rent a boat from **Capitola Boat and Bait** (© 831/462-2208; www.santacruzboatrentals.net).

**Capitola Beach** fronts the bustling Esplanade. Surf fishing and clamming are popular pastimes at Capitola's **New Brighton State Beach,** 1500 State Park Dr. (© 831/ 464-6330), where camping is allowed. Another popular activity is **antiquing** in the stores along Soquel Drive between 41st and Capitola avenues.

Farther south around the bay is **Aptos** ✿, home to the 10,000-acre **Forest of Nisene Marks State Park** (✆ 831/763-7063), with hiking trails that wind through redwoods and past abandoned mining camps. Mountain bikers and leashed dogs are welcome. This was the infamous epicenter of the 1989 earthquake. It's at the end of Aptos Creek Road off Soquel Drive, and it's open year-round from sunrise to sunset.

In the redwood-forested mountains behind Santa Cruz, there are quite a few **wineries,** although visitors may not be familiar with the labels because the output is small and consumed locally. Most are clustered around Boulder Creek and Felton or around Capitola. All offer tours by appointment; some feature tastings, including the **Bargetto Winery,** 3535 N. Main, Soquel (✆ 800/422-7438 or 831/475-2258; www.bargetto.com), which has a courtyard wine-tasting area overlooking the creek. For information, contact the **Santa Cruz Mountains Winegrowers' Association** (✆ 831/479-WINE; www. scmwa.com).

## WHERE TO STAY
### IN SANTA CRUZ

Two **Travelodges** (✆ 800/578-7878; www.travelodge.com), two **Best Westerns** (✆ 800/528-1234; www.bestwestern.com), two **Super 8s** (✆ 800/800-8000; www. super8.com), and an **Econo Lodge** (✆ 800/553-2666; www.hotelchoice.com) provide moderate- and budget-priced accommodations in addition to the more individual choices below.

**Babbling Brook Bed & Breakfast Inn** ✿✿   With charm to spare, the rooms in this popular inn are like treehouses over and around a brook running through an acre of gardens, pines, and redwoods. It's on a busy street, but what you hear from your room is running water cascading over falls and a waterwheel. The guest rooms are tasteful and simple, with lots of windows, skylights, open-beam ceilings, balconies, and decks; most have gas fireplaces. The inn is within a mile of the beach and boardwalk and a short walk from downtown Santa Cruz. Breakfast is served in the comfortable lobby, and wine and snacks are also served there from 5:30 to 7:30pm.

1025 Laurel St., Santa Cruz, CA 95060. ✆ 800/866-1131 or 831/427-2456. Fax 831/427-2457. www.babbling brookinn.com. 13 units. $189–$295 double. Rates include full country-breakfast buffet. AE, DISC, MC, V. **Amenities:** Nearby golf. *In room:* TV, VCR in some units.

**Casa Blanca Inn**   Across from the wharf in a heavily trafficked area, this motel along the waterfront was once the Mediterranean-style Cerf Mansion, dating from 1918. Other motel-style accommodations have grown up around the main building. Originally the home of a federal judge, it offers individually decorated bedrooms, some with brass beds and velvet draperies. Some units contain fireplaces and terraces, and all have microwaves. Most of the rooms have views of the ocean. Casa Blanca Restaurant serves California-Continental cuisine in a romantic oceanview setting.

101 Main St. (at the corner of Beach St.), Santa Cruz, CA 95060. ✆ 800/644-1570 or 831/423-1570. Fax 831/423-0235. www.casablanca-santacruz.com. 39 units. High season $96–$300 double; low season $78–$295 double. AE, DC, DISC, MC, V. **Amenities:** Restaurant; bar; nearby golf course; room service; laundry service. *In room:* TV, dataport, kitchen in some units, minibar, fridge, coffeemaker, hair dryer, iron, safe.

**Darling House** ✿   This stately Spanish-style house, designed in 1910 by William Weeks (architect of Santa Cruz's Coconut Grove), has a panoramic view of the Pacific Ocean and is in a residential area within walking distance of the boardwalk and lighthouse. The gardens are fragrant with citrus and orchids, and contain some palms as well. From the tiled front veranda, guests enter an elegant interior, the focal point of which is the dining room handcrafted from tiger oak. The house boasts fine architectural features, such as beveled glass, antiques, and handsome fireplaces. Each of the eight rooms is individually decorated; although all have sinks, only two come with private bathrooms. The Pacific Ocean room, decorated like a captain's quarters, features a fireplace, telescope, and one of the finest ocean views in Santa Cruz. Breakfast includes fresh breads and pastries, fruit, and granola made with walnuts from the Darling's own farm.

314 W. Cliff Dr., Santa Cruz, CA 95060. (C) 831/458-1958. www.darlinghouse.com. 8 units, 2 w/bathroom. $95 double without bathroom; $260 double w/bathroom. Rates include breakfast. AE, DISC, MC, V. **Amenities:** Concierge.

**Edgewater Beach Motel**   If the other three inns listed here are booked, consider the Edgewater Beach Motel. It looks like a time capsule from the 1960s, which, oddly enough, makes it all the more appealing (how they kept the furnishings in such prime condition is a mystery). The motel offers a range of accommodations, from family suites with kitchens to rooms with fireplaces; most have microwaves. The Edgewater also sports a nice pool, sun deck, and barbecue area, but the bonus is the location—the Santa Cruz Beach Boardwalk is a block away. *Tip:* Inquire about the Edgewater's off-season minivacation packages, which can save you a bundle. Smoking is not permitted in any of the rooms.

525 Second St., Santa Cruz, CA 95060. (C) 888/809-6767 or 831/423-0440. www.edgewaterbeachmotel.com. 17 units. Winter $85–$219 double; summer $139–$299 double. AE, DC, DISC, MC, V. **Amenities:** Outdoor heated pool. *In room:* TV/VCR, fully equipped kitchen in suites, fridge, coffeemaker.

**Fern River Resort** ★ *Finds*   This nifty mountain retreat is 4 miles from Santa Cruz down a curvy redwood-lined road. The "resort" consists of 13 furnished and equipped cabins on 4 forested acres with lawn, garden, or river views. There you will find a gaggle of outdoor toys to keep you amused, including badminton, Ping-Pong, tetherball, horseshoes, and 20 miles of hiking and mountain-biking trails in nearby Henry Cowell Park. You'll also find an enclosed spa tub and a private beach on the San Lorenzo River for sunning, swimming, and fishing. The cabins range in size from studios to some that sleep up to six and have equipped kitchens, but if you plan on cooking, you might want to bring some pots and pans.

5250 Hwy. 9, Felton, CA, 95018. (C) 831/335-4412. www.fernriver.com. 13 units. High season $80–$135 double; low season $60–$105 double. AE, MC, V. **Amenities:** Jacuzzi. *In room:* TV.

## IN NEARBY CAPITOLA

**The Inn at Depot Hill** ★★★   A few blocks from the bay front, this converted 1910-era railroad station has been designed and decorated with artful attention to detail—which explains why Martha Stewart chose to stay here during her coastal tour a few years ago. Sporting fine fabrics and linens, all rooms and suites have wood-burning fireplaces, stereos, bathrobes, two-person showers, and full bathrooms. Most have private patios with private Jacuzzis (guests in the other rooms share a common Jacuzzi). Perhaps you'll check into the Portofino Room, patterned after an Italian villa right down to the frescoes and stone cherub, or the Stratford-on-Avon, a replica of an English cottage. The evening wine and hors d'oeuvres and the breakfast are of similar prime quality, and can be enjoyed either in your room or out back in the garden courtyard on wrought-iron tables shaded by market umbrellas.

250 Monterey Ave. (near Park Ave.), Capitola, CA 95010. (C) 800/572-2632 or 831/462-3376. Fax 831/462-3697. www.innatdepothill.com. 12 units. $235–$355 double. Rates include breakfast, afternoon tea or wine, hors d'oeuvres, and after-dinner dessert. AE, DC, DISC, MC, V. **Amenities:** Jacuzzi; room service. *In room:* A/C, TV/VCR, fax, dataport, hair dryer.

**Pleasure Point Inn** ★★ With the amenities of a modern hotel and the casual atmosphere of a B&B, the four-room Pleasure Point Inn has the right combination of everything you want in a romantic coastal getaway: a beautiful ocean view overlooking Monterey Bay, a quiet neighborhood location, contemporary design and decor, and a rooftop deck that you will never want to leave. Basically, it's the seaside vacation house you've always wanted. It's named for the Pleasure Point beach and surf break that's right across the street, where local long-boarders provide viewing entertainment from sunrise to sunset. Each guest room is impeccably clean and outfitted with custom furnishings, wood flooring, hand-painted tiles, private bathrooms, down comforters, a gas fireplace, and private entrances. An expanded continental breakfast is served in the oceanview dining/lounge area (I spotted a grey whale while munching on a bagel); after breakfast, guests can stroll the paved coastal path down to Capitola, walk to the beach, or relax on the sunny rooftop deck (top-side toys include an eight-person hot tub, chaise longue chairs, and surround-sound music).

2-3665 East Cliff Dr., Santa Cruz, CA 95062. ℂ 831/475-4657. www.pleasurepointinn.com. 4 rooms. $220–$265 double. Rates include continental breakfast. MC, V. **Amenities:** Hot tub, rooftop deck. *In room:* TV, wireless Internet, minibar, fridge, coffeemaker, safe.

## WHERE TO DINE
### IN SANTA CRUZ

**The Crepe Place** *Value* CREPES/ECLECTIC Beloved by locals, particularly as a late-night hangout, The Crepe Place has been in business for more than a quarter of a century. Choose from 15 styles of crepes (the Spinach Supreme, Salsa, and Jambalaya are the local favorites, or create your own combination), and then sit your booty in the wood-paneled dining room or outdoor garden area. Other menu items include soups, salads (good clam chowder), oven-baked whole-wheat honey bread, and a popular dessert called a Tunisian Doughnut, a yeasty concoction cooked to order with your choice of toppings. On weekends, all kinds of egg dishes are served at brunch in addition to the regular menu.

1134 Soquel Ave. (at Seabright Ave.) ℂ 831/429-6994. Main courses $5–$12. AE, MC, V, local checks only. Mon–Thurs 11am–midnight; Fri–Sun 10am–1am.

**O'Mei** ★★ PROVINCIAL SZECHUAN O'Mei's (pronounced "Oh-*may*") minimall location may not be very inviting, but the fantastic food more than makes up for it. Named after a mountain in the Sichuan province of China, O'Mei's menu features some unusual specialties such as Chengdu-bean curd sea bass in a spicy *dou-ban* sauce (a rich, velvety wine-chile sauce), apricot-almond chicken, and lichee *pi-pa* bean-curd balls, along with more familiar dishes like chicken with cashews or beef with asparagus. The most popular dish is *gang pung chicken*—battered chicken with wood ear mushrooms, ginger, and cilantro, served with a sweet and slightly spicy sauce, but I usually order the rock cod in black bean–and–sweet pepper sauce. Dinner starts with a dim sum–style tray of exotic vegetarian offerings such as sesame-cilantro-eggplant salad or pan-roasted peppers with feta cheese. Cool things off with a bowl of black-sesame ice cream.

2316 Mission St. (where Hwy. 1 turns into Mission St.) ℂ 831/425-8458. www.omeifood.com. Reservations recommended. Main courses $9.25–$19. AE, MC, V. Mon–Fri 11:30am–2pm; Sun–Thurs 5–9pm; Fri–Sat 5–10pm. www.omeifood.com

### IN NEARBY CAPITOLA & APTOS
**Bittersweet Bistro** ★★ CALIFORNIA What started out as a tiny operation in a small strip development has grown into one of the most popular restaurants in the

Santa Cruz region. Its relocation to bigger digs in Rio Del Mar hasn't tarnished chef and owner Thomas Vinolus's reputation for serving exceptional cuisine. The menu offers a wide array of carefully crafted dishes, ranging from pizzas from the wood-fired oven to grilled lamb porterhouse in a sun-dried-cranberry demiglace. Fresh fish is Vinolus's forte, however, such as the Monterey Bay halibut, baked in parchment over fresh vegetables, or the roasted Chelis River wild sturgeon finished with an exotic mushroom sauce. Co-proprietor and wine director Elizabeth Vinolus has put together an exceptional wine list and often hosts winemaker dinners. Bistro Hour is from 3 to 6pm every afternoon, featuring half-price specials on gourmet pizzettas and special pricing on all wines by the glass, beer, and spirits.

787 Rio Del Mar Blvd., Aptos (about 10 miles southeast of Santa Cruz on Hwy. 1). ⓒ 831/662-9799. www.bittersweet bistro.com. Reservations recommended. Main courses $18–$24. AE, MC, V. Daily 5:30–10pm.

**Shadowbrook** ⚜ AMERICAN/CONTINENTAL    Shadowbrook, one of Capitola's most venerable and romantic restaurants, occupies a serene setting above Soquel Creek. To reach it, diners have to take the cable-driven "hillavator" down or walk the long, steep steps beside a running waterfall. At the bottom is a log cabin built in the 1920s, which has been enlarged and now contains a series of dining rooms on different levels: the wood-paneled Wine Cellar, the airy Garden Room, the Fireplace Room, and the creekside Greenhouse.

The menu doesn't hold many surprises, featuring thick-cut prime rib and steaks along with seafood such as scampi and grilled trout, plus pasta dishes including shellfish linguine and porcini ravioli. Prawn cocktail, deep-fried artichoke hearts, and baked brie are among the appetizers. Standout desserts are the mud pie and chocolate torte with raspberry sauce. If you don't have the time, appetite, or budget for a big dinner, grab a seat in the lounge and nosh on appetizers and light entrees prepared in the restaurant's wood-fired oven.

1750 Wharf Rd., Capitola. ⓒ 800/975-1511 or 831/475-1511. www.shadowbrook-capitola.com. Reservations recommended. Main courses $13–$24. AE, DC, DISC, MC, V. Mon–Fri 11:30am–9:30pm; Sat 4:30–10:30pm; Sun 10am–2:30pm and 4:30–9pm.

## A SIDE TRIP TO MISSION SAN JUAN BAUTISTA

On U.S. 101, **San Juan Bautista** ⚜ is a charming mission town that works hard to honor its pioneer heritage by retaining the flavor of a 19th-century village. The mission complex is perched in a picturesque farming valley, surrounded by the restored buildings of the original city plaza.

From U.S. 101, take Highway 156 east (south) to the center of town to the mission itself, which was founded in 1797. Here you'll see the largest church in the mission chain and the only one in continuous service since its founding. The padres here inspired many Native Americans to convert, creating one of the largest congregations in all of California. The small museum contains many musical instruments and transcriptions, evidence of the mission's musical focus—it once boasted a formidable Native American boys' choir. Mission San Juan Bautista is open daily year-round from 9:30am to 4:45pm. The suggested donation is $1 per person. For more information, call ⓒ 831/623-4528 or see www.oldmissionsjb.org or www.san-juan-bautista.ca.us.

East of the church, at the edge of an abrupt drop created by the movement of the San Andreas Fault, a marker points out the path of the old **El Camino Real.** Seismographic measuring equipment and an earthquake science exhibit accompany the marker.

In addition to the mission, there's much to see on the restored city plaza. Be sure to visit the **San Juan Bautista State Historic Park.** The park is comprised of not only the old Plaza Hotel with its frontier barroom and furnished rooms, but also the Plaza Hall, its adjoining stables and blacksmith shop, and the Castro House, where the Breen family lived after traveling here with the ill-fated Donner Party in 1846. Allow 1½ to 2 hours to see the entire plaza. Admission to the park buildings is $2 for adults, $1 for children ages 6 to 12 (separate from your charge to the mission). Hours are daily from 10am to 4:30pm. For further information (including event schedules), call © 831/623-4526.

## 2 Monterey ★★

45 miles S of Santa Cruz; 116 miles S of San Francisco; 335 miles N of Los Angeles

Monterey is now famous as the site of the world's longest running jazz festival (p. 27, in the Calendar of Events), which draws nearly 50,000 visitors annually for performances by the likes of Tony Bennett, Sonny Rollins, and Branford Marsalis. The town itself, however, is much older than that—and no less significant to state history. Settled in 1770 as one of the West Coast's first European outposts, Monterey was the capital of California under Spanish, Mexican, and American rule. The state constitution was drafted here in 1849, which paved the way for admission to the Union a year later. Many early colonial buildings still stand. A major whaling center in the 1800s, Monterey eventually became the sardine capital of the Western Hemisphere when the first packing plant was built in 1900. By 1913, the boats were bringing in 25 tons of sardines a night to the 18 canneries. The gritty lives of the mostly working-class residents were captured by local hero John Steinbeck in his 1945 novel *Cannery Row.*

After the sardines disappeared, Monterey was forced to fish for tourist dollars instead; hence, an array of boutiques, knickknack stores, and theme restaurants now reside in converted sardine factories along the bay. Granted, plenty of history and heritage remains along Cannery Row, but you'll have to weed through the tourist schlock to find them. Its saving grace is the world-class aquarium and beautiful Monterey Bay, where sea lions and otters still frolic in abundance.

As you distance yourself from the Row, however, you'll discover Monterey is a pleasant seaside community with magnificent vistas, historic architecture, stately Victorians, and a number of quality lodgings and restaurants. More important, Monterey is only a short drive from Pacific Grove, Carmel, Pebble Beach, and Big Sur, and the lodgings here are far less expensive, which makes it a great place to set up base while exploring the Monterey coast.

## ESSENTIALS

**GETTING THERE**   The region's most convenient runway, at the **Monterey Peninsula Airport** (© 831/648-7000), is 3 miles east of Monterey on Highway 68. American Eagle, Northwest, United, and US Airways offer daily flights in and out of Monterey. Many area hotels offer free airport shuttle service. If you take a taxi, it will cost about $10 to $15 to get to a peninsula hotel. Several national car-rental companies have airport locations, including **Dollar** (© 800/800-3665; www.dollar.com) and **Hertz** (© 800/654-3131; www.hertz.com).

**VISITOR INFORMATION**   The **Monterey Peninsula Visitors and Convention Bureau** (© 888/221-1010 or 831/649-1770; www.montereyinfo.org) has two visitor centers: one located in the lobby of the Maritime Museum at Custom House Plaza

# The Monterey Peninsula

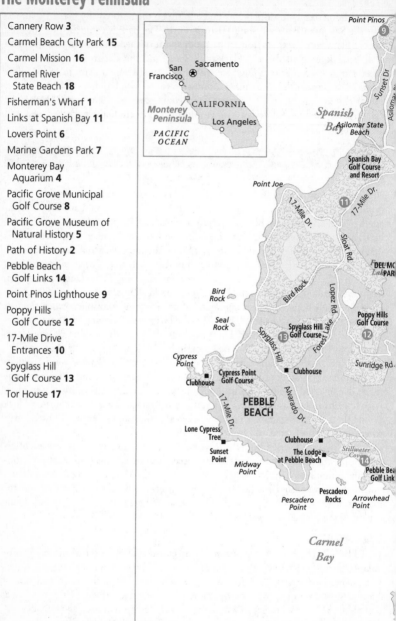

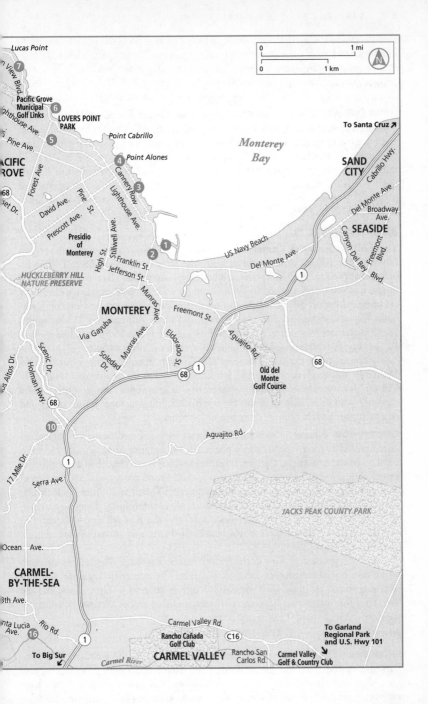

near Fisherman's Wharf, and the other at Lake El Estero on Camino El Estero. Both locations, open daily, offer an array of good maps, as well as free pamphlets and publications, including an excellent visitors' guide and the magazine *Coast Weekly*. Two other good sources for Monterey information are the **Monterey Peninsula On-Line Guide** at www.monterey.com and **Monterey-Carmel.com** (www.monterey-carmel.com).

**GETTING AROUND**    The **Waterfront Area Visitor Express (WAVE)** shuttle operates each year from Memorial Day weekend to Labor Day and takes passengers to and from the aquarium and other waterfront attractions. The free shuttle departs from the downtown parking garages at Tyler Street and Del Monte Avenue every 10 to 12 minutes and operates all day between 9am and 6pm. Other WAVE stops include many hotels and motels in Monterey and Pacific Grove, which eliminates the stress of parking in crowded downtown. For further information, call **Monterey Salinas Transit** at ✆ 831/899-2555.

## WHAT TO SEE & DO

The **National Steinbeck Center** 🔎 isn't in town, but if you're a fan of the author, you can make the 20-mile drive northeast from Monterey on Highway 68 to 1 Main St. in Salinas (✆ **831/796-3833;** www.steinbeck.org). The modern $11-million, 37,000-square-foot museum—opened in 1998—features walk-through interactive exhibits, a changing exhibition gallery, an orientation theater presenting a short video on Steinbeck's life, educational programs, a gift shop, and a cafe. Admission is $11 for adults, $8.95 for seniors over 62, $7.95 for children ages 13 to 17, $5.95 for children 6 to 12, and free for children under 6. Hours are daily from 10am to 5pm.

If you're traipsing through Monterey on a Tuesday afternoon, check out the **Old Monterey Marketplace** on Alvarado Street, from Pearl to Del Monte streets (✆ **831/655-8070;** www.oldmonterey.org), open from 4 to 8pm (until 7pm in winter). More than 100 vendors participate in this farmers market, bringing food, music, crafts, and entertainment together for an afternoon of festivities.

**Cannery Row** *Overrated*    Once the center for an industrial sardine-packing operation immortalized by John Steinbeck as "a poem, a stink, a grating noise, a quality of light, a tone, a habit, a nostalgia, a dream," this area today is better described as a strip congested with tourists, tacky gift shops, overpriced seafood restaurants, and an overall parking nightmare. What changed it so dramatically? The silver sardines suddenly disappeared from Monterey's waters in 1948 as a result of overfishing, changing currents, and pollution. Fishermen left, canneries closed, and the Row fell into disrepair. But curious tourists continued to visit Steinbeck's fabled area, and where there are tourists, there are capitalists.

After visiting Cannery Row in the 1960s, Steinbeck wrote, "The beaches are clean where they once festered with fish guts and flies. The canneries that once put up a sickening stench are gone, their places filled with restaurants, antique shops, and the like. They fish for tourists now, not pilchards, and that species they are not likely to wipe out." And I couldn't put it any better.

Between David and Drake aves. ✆ 831/373-1902. www.canneryrow.com.

**Fisherman's Wharf**    Like its counterpart in San Francisco, this wooden pier is jam-packed with crafts and gift shops, boating and fishing operations, fish markets, and seafood restaurants—all trawling for tourist dollars. But Monterey's wharf does have redeeming qualities: If you cast your view toward its stupendous view, with bobbing boats and sea lions, you might not notice the hordes of tourists around you. Grab some clam chowder in a sourdough-bread bowl and find a seaside perch along the pier. Or, when the wind picks up, find a bayfront seat at one of the seafood restaurants (see "Where to Dine" later in this section).

Boats departing regularly from Fisherman's Wharf will lead you on a number of ocean adventures. See "Outdoor Pursuits" below for details.

99 Pacific St. ℂ **831/649-6544.** www.montereywharf.com.

**Monterey Bay Aquarium** ★★★ *(Kids)*   Attracting nearly two million visitors each year, the site of one of the world's most spectacular aquariums was not chosen at random. On the border of one of the largest underwater canyons on earth (wider and deeper than the Grand Canyon), it's surrounded by incredibly diverse marine life. The Monterey Bay Aquarium is one of the best exhibit aquariums in the world, and one of the largest—home to more than 350,000 marine animals and plants. One of the main exhibits is a three-story, 335,000-gallon tank with clear acrylic walls that offer a stunning view of leopard sharks, sardines, anchovies, and other sea creatures swimming through a towering kelp forest. The outstanding Outer Bay exhibit features creatures that inhabit the open ocean. This million-gallon tank houses yellowfin tuna, large green sea turtles, barracuda, sharks, the very cool giant ocean sunfish, and schools of bonito. The Outer Bay's jellyfish exhibit is guaranteed to amaze, and kids will love Flippers, Flukes, and Fun, a learning area for families.

My favorite exhibit at the aquarium is "Sharks: Myth and Mystery," which features nearly two dozen species of sharks and rays from around the world. The Splash Zone exhibit (designed for families with kids up to 9 years old) features daily programs and exhibits of black-footed penguins, invertebrates, and fish whose habitats are coral reefs and the cooler waters and rocky shores of Northern California. Additional exhibits re-create other undersea habitats found in Monterey Bay. Everyone falls in love with the sea otters playing in their two-story exhibit. There are also coastal streams, tidal pools, a sand beach, and a petting pool, where you can touch living bat rays and handle sea stars. Visitors can also watch a live video link that transmits from a deep-sea research submarine thousands of feet below the surface of Monterey Bay.

*Tip:* You can avoid lines at the gate by ordering tickets in advance ℂ **800/ 756-3737** (or 831/648-4888 outside California). On weekdays, arrive in the afternoon, after the hoards of uber-exuberant school kids have departed.

886 Cannery Row. ℂ **800/756-3737** or 831/648-4800. Fax 831/648-4810. www.mbayaq.org. Admission $20 adults, $18 students and seniors 65 and over, $11 visitors w/disabilities and children 3–12, free for children under 3. AE, MC, V. Daily 10am–6pm.

## FOLLOWING THE PATH OF HISTORY

The dozen or so historic buildings around Fisherman's Wharf and the adjacent town constitute the "Path of History" tour, which examines the 19th-century way of life and its architecture. Many buildings are part of the **Monterey State Historic Park** ★, 20 Custom House Plaza (ℂ **831/649-7118**). Highlights include the **Custom House,** the state's oldest government building (built around 1827), and the **Maritime Museum of Monterey,** 5 Custom House Plaza (ℂ **831/372-2608;** www.montereyhistory.org), which showcases ship models and other collections related to the area's seafaring history—including a two-story, 10,000-pound Fresnel lens, used for nearly 80 years at the Point Sur lighthouse. Admission is $5 for adults, $2.50 for seniors and children ages 13 to 18, and free for children 12 and under; it's open Tuesday through Sunday from 11am to 5pm.

You can go the self-guided route by picking up a free tour booklet at the Monterey Peninsula Visitors and Convention Bureau (see above), the Cooper-Molera Adobe (at the corner of Polk and Munras sts.), and various other locations. You may also opt to take the free guided tour, which departs several times daily. Call © **831/649-7118** for details, or visit the **State Park Visitor Center** at Stanton Center, 5 Custom House Plaza. A free film on the history of Monterey is shown here every 20 minutes.

## MONTEREY WINE COUNTRY

The congestion and price of Napa and Sonoma vineyards and the increasing popularity of winemaking have forced newcomers to plant their grapes elsewhere. Fortunately, much of the California coast offers ideal growing conditions. Nowadays, any area between Monterey and Santa Barbara affords easy access to new appellations and a variety of boutique vintners making respectable wines. Stop by **A Taste of Monterey,** 700 Cannery Row (© **888/646-5446** or 831/646-5446; www.tastemonterey.com), daily between 11am and 6pm, to learn about and taste local wines in front of huge bayfront windows. This is also the place to get a map and winery touring information.

## OUTDOOR PURSUITS

Along with excellent scuba diving, the waters off Monterey are teeming with game fish. Among the public fishing boats are **Chris' Fishing Trips,** 48 Fisherman's Wharf (© **831/375-5951;** www.chrissfishing.com), which offers party boats. Cod and salmon are the main catches, with separate boats leaving daily. Call or log on to the website for a price list and departure schedule. Check-in is 45 minutes prior to departure, and equipment rental costs a bit extra.

Several outfitters rent kayaks for a spin around the bay. Contact **Monterey Bay Kayaks,** 693 Del Monte Ave. (© **800/649-5357** or 831/373-5357; www.monterey kayaks.com), on Del Monte Beach north of Fisherman's Wharf, which offers instruction as well as natural-history tours that introduce visitors to the Monterey Bay National Marine Sanctuary and nearby Elkhorn Slough, one of the last remaining estuaries in California (see "The Otters, Seals & Birds of the Elkhorn Slough" on p. 373). Prices start at $55 for the tours, from $30 for rentals.

For bike rentals, as well as kayak tours and rentals, contact **Adventures by the Sea,** 299 Cannery Row (© **831/372-1807;** www.adventuresbythesea.com). Bikes cost $6 per hour or $24 per day, and kayaks are $30 per person or $50 for a 2½-hour tour. Adventures by the Sea also has another location at 201 Alvarado Mall (© **831/648-7235**), at the Doubletree Hotel.

Experienced scuba divers can contact **Monterey Bay Dive Center,** 225 Cannery Row (© **800/60-SCUBA** or 831/656-0454; www.montereyscubadiving.com), which arranges personal dives with a dive master and has scheduled weekend dives. **Aquarius Dive Shop,** 2040 Del Monte Ave. (© **831/375-1933;** www.aquariusdivers.com), also has regularly scheduled trips and dive masters. Certification cards are required.

If the kids need to let off some steam, take them to the **Dennis the Menace Playground** ⊛ at Camino El Estero and Del Monte Avenue, near Lake Estero (© **831/646-3860**), an old-fashioned playground created by Pacific Grove resident and cartoonist Hank Ketcham. It has bridges, tunnels, and an authentic Southern Pacific Railroad engine teeming with wannabe conductors. There's also a hot-dog-and-burger stand, and a big lake where you can rent paddleboats or feed the ducks. The park is open daily from 10am to sunset.

**_Finds_** The Otters, Seals & Birds of the Elkhorn Slough

One of my favorite stops along the coast is Moss Landing, 25 minutes north of Monterey on Highway 1, home of Captain Yohn Gideon's **Elkhorn Slough Safari.** For $28 for adults or $20 for children 3 to 14, friendly Cap'n Gideon loads guests onto a 27-foot pontoon boat (safe for old and young) and embarks on a 2-hour tour of the Elkhorn Slough Wildlife Reserve, which is like jumping into a _National Geographic_ special. It's not uncommon to see a "raft" of up to 50 otters feet up and sunning themselves, harbor seals, and hundreds of species of waterfowl and migratory shorebirds. An onboard naturalist answers questions, Cap'n Gideon educates on the surroundings, and binoculars are available. For reservations and information, call ⓒ **831/633-5555** or check out www.elkhornslough.com.

## WHERE TO STAY

Monterey has three types of lodgings: lace-and-flowers B&Bs, large corporate hotels, or run-of-the-mill motels. Consider where you'd like to be and how much you want to spend, then check out the options below or contact **Resort 2 Me** (ⓒ **800/757-5646;** www.resort2me.com), a local reservations service that offers free recommendations of Monterey Bay–area hotels in all price ranges.

### EXPENSIVE

In addition to the choices below, there are two chain hotels, popular with business travelers and conventioneers, near Fisherman's Wharf: The **Monterey Marriott,** 350 Calle Principal, at Del Monte Boulevard (ⓒ **888/236-2427** or 831/649-4234; www.marriott.com), offers some rooms with bay views, an outdoor pool, health club, Jacuzzi, and saunas. Less central but great for families and golfers, the **Hyatt Regency Monterey** resort, 1 Old Golf Course Rd. (ⓒ **800/233-1234** or 831/372-1234; www.hyatt.com) adjoins the Del Monte Golf Course, with three pools, two Jacuzzis, a gym, tennis courts, and two restaurants.

**Hotel Pacific** ★★    Although the Hotel Pacific isn't waterfront (it's close to the wharf and across the street from the Monterey Conference Center), it's still my favorite upscale choice in Monterey. Beyond the Spanish-Mediterranean architecture in the common areas, each unit is in 1 of 16 buildings clustered around courtyards and compact gardens with spas and fountains. The junior suites have down comforters and four-poster feather beds (some with canopies), stylish Southwestern decor, terra cotta–tiled floors, fireplaces surrounded by cushy couches and seats, and private patios or terraces overlooking the gardens. _Tip:_ Ask for a room on the fourth level with a panoramic view of the bay.

300 Pacific St., Monterey, CA 93940. ⓒ **800/554-5542** or 831/373-5700. Fax 831/373-6921. www.hotelpacific.com. 105 suites. $229–$409 suite for 2. Rates include continental breakfast and afternoon tea. AE, DC, DISC, MC, V. **Amenities:** Nearby golf course; 2 Jacuzzis; room service; in-room massage; laundry service; same-day dry cleaning. In room: TV/VCR, dataport, minibar, coffeemaker, hair dryer, iron.

**Monterey Plaza Hotel and Spa** ★★    One of the most formal hotels in town, the Monterey Plaza comprises three buildings—two on the water and one across the street—connected by a second-story enclosed "skywalk." The public areas are elegantly decorated with marble, Brazilian teak, and attractive artwork. The bedrooms are more upscale-corporate than most around town and have double or king beds, decor reminiscent of 19th-century Biedermeier, and Italian marble bathrooms. Many have balconies overlooking the water (sea otters included in the view). The least desirable rooms are across the street from the ocean. There's also an 11,000-square-foot European-style spa, the **Duck Club Restaurant** serving American regional cuisine by the sea, and the adjacent **Schooner's Bistro,** which serves lighter fare.

400 Cannery Row, Monterey, CA 93940. ℭ **800/334-3999** or 831/646-1700. Fax 831/646-5937. www.woodsidehotels. com. 290 units. $185–$505 double; $510–$2,500 suite. Children 17 and under stay free in parent's room. Packages available. AE, DC, DISC, MC, V. Parking $14 per day. From Hwy. 1, take the Soledad Dr. exit and follow the signs to Cannery Row. **Amenities:** 2 restaurants; nearby golf course; full fitness center; full-service European-style spa; Jacuzzi; dry sauna; concierge; tour desk; business center; secretarial services; shopping arcade; 24-hr. room service; in-room massage; laundry service; same-day dry cleaning; executive-level rooms. *In room:* TV w/pay movies, dataport, fully stocked minibar, fridge, coffeemaker, hair dryer, iron.

Old Monterey Inn ★★   Proprietors Ann and Gene Swett masterfully converted their three-story family home into a vine-covered Tudor-style country inn. Although it's away from the surf, it's a perfect choice for romantics, with rose gardens, a bubbling brook, and oak-shaded, brick-and-flagstone walkways. All but one guest room have garden views and cozy beds with goose-down comforters and pillows. Most have feather beds and wood-burning fireplaces, and two open onto private patios. All the guest rooms are unique; two of my favorites are the Library and the Serengeti Room. Special touches include fresh fruit, flowers, and candies, sachets by the pillow, and books and magazines. The private cottage has an English country look and a double Jacuzzi, linen-and-lace-draped king-size bed, wood-burning fireplace, sitting area, and private patio.

Gene's breakfasts are stellar—consisting of perhaps orange French toast, soufflés, or Belgian waffles—and served in your room, the dining room, or the rose garden. The Swetts also provide blankets and towels for the beach. At 5pm, guests can retire to the living room for wine and hors d'oeuvres in front of a fire.

500 Martin St. (off Pacific Ave.), Monterey, CA 93940. ℭ **800/350-2344** or 831/375-8284. Fax 831/375-6730. www.oldmontereyinn.com. 9 units, 1 cottage. $240–$390 double; from $450 cottage. Rates include full breakfast and evening wine and hors d'oeuvres. MC, V. Free parking. From Hwy. 1, take the Soledad Dr. exit and turn right onto Pacific Ave., then left onto Martin St. **Amenities:** Nearby golf course; passes to nearby health club; Jacuzzi; concierge; tour desk; in-room massage. *In room:* TV/VCR, dataport, hair dryer, iron.

Spindrift Inn ★   In the middle of honky-tonk Cannery Row, on a narrow stretch of beach, this four-story hotel is an island of Continental style in a sea of commercialism. It's elegant and well maintained, and the rooms are decorated with feather beds (a few with canopies), hardwood floors, wood-burning fireplaces, and cushioned window seats or private balconies. The bathrooms have marble and brass fixtures. Extras include terry robes and two phones. The ocean views are worth the extra cost, particularly from one of the corner rooms with cushioned window seats.

652 Cannery Row, Monterey, CA 93940. ℭ **800/841-1879** or 831/646-8900. Fax 831/646-5342. www.spindriftinn.com. 42 units. $199–$329 double w/Cannery Row view; $329–$459 double w/ocean view. Rates include continental breakfast delivered to your room and afternoon wine and cheese. AE, DC, DISC, MC, V. Parking $14. **Amenities:** 2 restaurants; bar; nearby golf course; room service; in-room massage; same-day dry cleaning. *In room:* TV/VCR, fully stocked minibar, hair dryer.

## MODERATE

Munras Avenue and northern Fremont Avenue are lined with moderate and inexpensive family-style motels, some independently owned and some chains. They're not as central as the downtown options, and atmosphere is seriously lacking on Fremont Avenue, but if transportation's not an issue, you can save a bundle by staying in one of these areas. If the selections below are full, try calling **Best Western** (© **800/528-1234**) for several other options. There's also the **Cypress Gardens Inn,** 1150 Munras Ave. (© **877/922-1150** or 831/373-2761; www.cypressgardensinn.com), with a pool, Jacuzzi, free movie channels, and continental breakfast (dogs are welcome); or the newly remodeled **Monterey Fireside Lodge,** 1131 10th St. (© **800/722-2624**; or 831/373-4172; www.montereyfireside.com) near Fisherman's Wharf and downtown.

**Casa Munras Garden Hotel**    Casa Munras was built around the original hacienda of Don Esteban Munras, the last Spanish diplomat to California. Accommodations are scattered among 11 one- and two-story buildings along the 4.5-acre landscaped property. Each is decorated with an armoire, comfy furnishings, and sweet window shutters. All guests have access to the outdoor pool, and there's an on-site restaurant called the **Casa Café & Bar** that's a good place to have breakfast. *Tip:* Spend a few extra bucks and get a room with a gas fireplace—it gets chilly at night in Monterey.

700 Munras Ave., Monterey, CA 93940. © 800/222-2558 in the U.S. except California, 800/222-2446 in California, or 831/375-2411. Fax 831/375-1365. www.casamunras-hotel.com. 166 units. $139–$209 double. AAA and entertainment discounts available. AE, DC, MC, V. **Amenities:** Outdoor pool; access to nearby health club. *In room:* TV, dataport, iron.

**The Jabberwock Bed & Breakfast** ★    One of the better B&Bs in the area, the Jabberwock (named after a poem in Lewis Carroll's *Through the Looking Glass*) is 4 blocks from Cannery Row. It's centrally located but tranquil; its half-acre garden with waterfalls is a respite from downtown. The seven rooms are individually furnished, some more elegantly than others; all have goose-down comforters and pillows, and three have Jacuzzi tubs for two, fireplaces, and king beds. The Toves Room has a huge walnut Victorian bed, the Borogrove has a fireplace and a view of Monterey Bay, the Mimsey has an ocean view from its window seat, and the Wabe has an Austrian carved bed. A full breakfast is served in the dining room or in your room. Evening hors d'oeuvres are offered on the veranda, and a wooden Vorpal rabbit dispenses cookies, served with milk.

598 Laine St., Monterey, CA 93940. © 888/428-7253 or 831/372-4777. Fax 831/655-2946. www.jabberwockinn.com. 7 units, 5 w/bathroom. $155–$275 double. Rates include full breakfast, afternoon aperitifs, and bedtime cookies. MC, V. **Amenities:** Nearby golf course; Jacuzzi; concierge; activities desk; in-room massage. *In room:* Hair dryer, no phone.

## INEXPENSIVE

Motels offer the best rates in town. Some reliable options are **Motel 6** (© 800/4-MOTEL6), **Super 8** (© 800/800-8000), and **Best Western** (© 800/528-1234).

**Cypress Tree Inn** *Value*    Although it's 2 miles from downtown, if you're on a budget and have transportation, you won't be sorry to stay here. The staff is friendly, the large rooms are spotless, and all but one has a combination tub/shower. Nine rooms even have Jacuzzis. There are no designer soaps or other in-room treats (other than the taffy left by the maid), but the hostelry does have a handy coin-op laundry. RV spaces are also available.

2227 N. Fremont St., Monterey, CA 93940. © 800/446-8303 or 831/372-7586. Fax 831/372-2940. www.cypress treeinn.com. 55 units. $55–$135 double. Rates include continental breakfast. AE, DC, DISC, MC, V. **Amenities:** Nearby golf course; Jacuzzi; sauna; coin-op laundry. *In room:* TV, dataport, kitchen or kitchenette in some units, fridge, hair dryer, iron.

## WHERE TO DINE

**Bubba Gump Shrimp Co. Restaurant & Market** *Overrated* AMERICAN    Culinary cognoscenti will flee at the sight of this tourist haven, but lots of people love this place. It could be the boatyard decor or location—near the aquarium, with a million-dollar, unobstructed bayfront view—that attract visitors in droves. More likely, it's the enter-tainment value, because Gump's (as in *Forrest Gump*) is packed with movie gimmicks and memorabilia. Foodwise, you're in for a lot of greasy, fried and buttered-up seafood—as the roll of paper towels at each table suggests. The Bucket of Boat Trash, for example, is shrimp and lobster tails cooked and served in a bucket with a side of fries and coleslaw. There are also pork chops, a veggie dish, salads, and burgers. The "market" is a gift shop with T-shirts, caps, and, of course, boxes of chocolate.

720 Cannery Row (at Prescott). 🕿 831/373-1884. Fax 831/373-1139. www.bubbagump.com. Main courses $7.95–$25. AE, DC, DISC, MC, V. Sun–Thurs 11am–10pm; Fri–Sat 11am–11pm.

**Cafe Fina** 🛦 ITALIAN/SEAFOOD    Other pier-side restaurants lure tourists with little more than a sea view, but Cafe Fina's mesquite-grilled meats, well-prepared fresh fish, brick-oven pizzas, and an array of delicious salads and pastas give even locals a reason to head here. Hidden behind the facade of a to-go pizza counter, the special-ties at this little jewel are the seafood and pasta dishes, but anything that comes out of the wood broiler or wood-fired brick oven is a winner. Be sure to request a table by the back window to watch the sea otters and sea lions playing in the kelp.

47 Fisherman's Wharf. 🕿 800/THE-FINA or 831/372-5200. www.cafefina.com. Reservations recommended. Main courses $14–$19. AE, DC, DISC, MC, V. Mon–Fri 11:30am–2:30pm; Sat–Sun 11:30am–3pm; daily 5–9:30pm.

**Montrio** 🛦🛦 AMERICAN BISTRO    Big-city sophistication meets old Monterey in this converted 1910 firehouse. The enormous dining room is the sharpest in town, a playfully chic expanse with clouds hanging from the ceiling and curvaceous walls. Order anything cooked in the open kitchen's oak-fired rotisserie grill, such as the crispy Dungeness crab cakes with spicy rémoulade or a roasted portobello mushroom with polenta and ragout of vegetables. The wine list, which received *Wine Spectator* magazine's Award of Excellence, includes numerous vintages by the glass.

414 Calle Principal (at Franklin). 🕿 831/648-8880. www.montrio.com. Reservations recommended. Main courses $12–$25. AE, DISC, MC, V. Sun–Thurs 5–10pm; Fri–Sat 5–11pm.

**Rosine's** *Value* AMERICAN    Everything served at Rosine's is filling and fairly priced, which explains why this local favorite is always busy. Aside from the large, airy window seats, the place has an upscale cafeteria feel, but its menu, filled with standard entrees, aims to please all tastes. Lunch features an extensive list of salads and sand-wiches, and dinner offers an array of pastas, burgers, and more expensive items such as charbroiled pork chops with applesauce and mashed potatoes ($15) and prime rib ($17, Fri–Sat only). Other than steak and seafood, most entrees hover around $8 and

---

### Monterey's Best Seafood Buffet

If I had all the money in the world, I'd still have lunch the same way every day in Monterey. I'd walk down **Old Fisherman's Wharf** and snack on all those small cups of fresh seafood at the numerous faux fish markets. Priced at a couple of bucks each, fresh mussels, octopus, shrimp, crab, oysters, ceviche, and clam chowder let you dine alfresco for a fraction of what you'd pay at a sit-down restaurant. You can either eat on foot as you head down the wharf, or make a picnic of it, by carting your cups to the benches at the end of the pier (just to the left of Rappa's restaurant).

include side salads and/or potatoes. Sugar fiends will appreciate the huge cakes behind glass as you walk in the front door (yes, you can buy them by the slice).

434 Alvarado St. (at Franklin St.). ⓒ **831/375-1400.** www.rosinesmonterey.com. Breakfast $3.50–$8.25; lunch $5.50–$7.95; most dinner dishes $5.75–$8.50. AE, DC, DISC, MC, V. Sun–Thurs 8am–9pm; Fri–Sat 8am–10pm.

**Stokes Restaurant and Bar** ★★ CALIFORNIA/MEDITERRANEAN    This historic adobe and board-and-batten house, built in 1833 for the town doctor, has been converted into one of Monterey's finest restaurants. It's a handsome establishment, consisting of a bar and several large dining rooms, all outfitted with terra-cotta floors, bleached-wood-plank ceilings, and Southwestern-style wood chairs and tables. It's the perfect rustic-yet-contemporary showcase for chef Brandon Miller's California-Mediterranean fare: butternut-squash soup with apple cider and maple crème fraîche; cassoulet of duck confit and homemade currant sausage with chestnut beans. Everything from Miller's wood-burning oven—chicken, fish, pizza, clams—is recommended. Desserts are dreamy, and the wine list is excellent.

500 Hartnell St. (at Madison St.). ⓒ **831/373-1110.** Fax 831/373-1202. www.stokesrestaurant.com. Reservations recommended. Main courses $12–$23. AE, DC, DISC, MC, V. Mon–Fri 11:30am–2pm and 5:30–10pm; Sat–Sun 5:30–10pm.

**Tarpy's Roadhouse** ★★ AMERICAN    A mandatory stop in Monterey, this lively Southwestern-style restaurant is worth the detour a few miles east of downtown. The soothing dining room has stylish yet rustic decor. On sunny afternoons, patrons relax under market umbrellas on the outdoor patio, sip margaritas and munch on Tarpy's locally renowned Caesar salad. Come nightfall, the place fills with tourists and locals who pile in for the hefty plate of bourbon-molasses pork chops or Dijon-crusted lamb loin. There's a modest selection of fresh fish, shellfish, and vegetable dishes, but it's the good ol' meat 'n' potato mainstays that sell the best. (The juicy meatloaf with garlic mashers and fresh vegetables is a bargain at $13.)

2999 Monterey-Salinas Hwy. (at Hwy. 68 and Canyon del Rey near the Monterey Airport). ⓒ **831/647-1444.** Fax 831/647-1103. www.tarpys.com. Reservations recommended for dinner. Most main courses $14–$30. AE, DISC, MC, V. Daily 11:30am–10pm.

## 3 Pacific Grove ★★

42 miles S of Santa Cruz; 113 miles S of San Francisco; 338 miles N of Los Angeles

Some compare 2½-square-mile Pacific Grove—the locals call it "PG"—to Carmel as it was about 20 years ago. Although tourists wind their way through here on oceanfront trails and dining excursions, the town remains quaint and peaceful—amazing considering that Monterey is a stone's throw away (a quarter of the Monterey Bay Aquarium is actually in Pacific Grove). Although neighboring Monterey is comparatively congested and cosmopolitan, Pacific Grove is a community sprinkled with historic homes, flowers, and the kind of tranquility that inspires butterflies to flutter about and deer to meander fearlessly across the road in search of another garden to graze.

## ESSENTIALS

**VISITOR INFORMATION**    Although the town is small, there is a **Pacific Grove Chamber of Commerce,** at the corner of Forest and Central avenues (ⓒ **800/656-6650** or 831/373-3304; www.pacificgrove.org).

**ORIENTATION**    Lighthouse Avenue is the Grove's principal thoroughfare, running from Monterey to the lighthouse at the point of the peninsula. Lighthouse Avenue is bisected by Forest Avenue, which runs from Highway 1 (where it's called Holman Hwy., or Hwy. 68) to Lover's Point, an extension of land that sticks out into the bay in the middle of Pacific Grove.

## WHAT TO SEE & DO

Pacific Grove is a town to be strolled, so park the car, don your walking shoes, and make an afternoon of it. Meander around George Washington Park and along the waterfront around the point.

The **Point Pinos Lighthouse** ⚓, at the tip of the peninsula on Ocean View Boulevard (𝒞 **831/648-5716**), is the oldest working lighthouse on the West Coast. Its 50,000-candlepower beacon has illuminated the rocky shores since 1855, when Pacific Grove was little more than a pine forest. The museum and grounds are open and free to visitors, Thursday through Sunday from 1 to 4pm.

**Marine Gardens Park** ⚓, a stretch of shoreline along Ocean View Boulevard on Monterey Bay and the Pacific, is renowned not only for its ocean views and colorful flowers, but also for its tide-pool seaweed beds. Walk out to **Lover's Point** (named after Lovers of Jesus, not groping teenagers) and watch the sea otters playing in the kelp beds and cracking open an occasional abalone.

An excellent shorter alternative, or complement, to the 17-Mile Drive (see "Pebble Beach & the 17-Mile Drive" later) is the scenic drive or bike ride along Pacific Grove's **Ocean View Boulevard** ⚓. This coastal stretch starts near Monterey's Cannery Row and follows the Pacific around to the lighthouse point. Here it turns into Sunset Drive, which runs along secluded **Asilomar State Beach** ⚓ (𝒞 **831/648-3130**). Park on Sunset and explore the trails, dunes, and tide pools of this sandy stretch of shore. You might find purple shore crabs, green anemone, sea bats, starfish, and limpets, as well as all kinds of kelp and algae. The 11 buildings of the conference center established here by the YWCA in 1913 are landmarks that were designed by noted architect Julia Morgan. If you follow this route during winter, a furious sea rages and crashes against the rocks.

To learn more about the region, stop in at the **Pacific Grove Museum of Natural History,** 165 Forest Ave. (𝒞 **831/648-5716;** www.pgmuseum.org). It has displays on monarch butterflies and their migration, stuffed examples of the local birds and mammals, and temporary exhibits and special events. Admission is free; hours are Tuesday through Saturday from 10am to 5pm.

Pacific Grove is widely known as "Butterfly Town, USA," a reference to the thousands of **monarch butterflies** that migrate here from November to February, traveling from as far away as Alaska. Many settle in the Monarch Grove sanctuary, a eucalyptus stand on Grove Acre Avenue off Lighthouse Avenue. George Washington Park, at Pine Avenue and Alder Street, is also famous for its "butterfly trees." To reach these sites, the butterflies may travel as far as 2,000 miles, covering 100 miles a day at an altitude of 10,000 feet. *Collectors beware:* The town imposes strict fines for disturbing the butterflies.

Just as Ocean View Boulevard serves as an alternative to the 17-Mile Drive, the **Pacific Grove Municipal Golf Course,** 77 Asilomar Ave. (𝒞 **831/648-5777**), serves as a reasonable alternative to the high-priced courses at Pebble Beach. The back 9 of this 5,500-yard, par-70 course overlooks the sea and offers the added challenge of coping with the winds. Views are panoramic, and the fairways and greens are better maintained than most semiprivate courses. There's a restaurant, pro shop, and driving range. Eighteen holes start at $32 Monday through Thursday and $38 Friday through Sunday and holidays; twilight rates are available. Optional carts cost $28.

The **American Tin Cannery Factory Premium Outlets,** 125 Ocean View Blvd., around the corner from the Monterey Bay Aquarium (© **831/372-1442**), is a converted warehouse housing 40 factory-outlet shops, including Bass Shoes, OshKosh B'Gosh, Samsonite, and Izod. It's open Monday through Saturday from 10am to 7pm, Sunday from 10am to 6pm.

## WHERE TO STAY

If you're having trouble finding a vacancy, try calling **Resort 2 Me** (© **800/757-5646;** www.resort2me.com), a local reservations service that offers free recommendations of Monterey Bay–area hotels in all price ranges.

### EXPENSIVE

**Martine Inn** ★★ One glance at the lavish Victorian interior and the bay views and you'll know why this Mediterranean-style inn is one of the best B&Bs in the area. Built in 1899 for James and Laura Parke (of Parke-Davis Pharmaceuticals fame), each room has a view of the ocean or the garden courtyard; most have wood-burning fireplaces. Request a room with a bathtub if it matters to you; some have only a shower. The inn also maintains an adjacent Victorian cottage, which has been converted into a luxury suite. A full breakfast is served at lace-covered tables in the front room; hors d'oeuvres are served in the evening. Guests also have access to two additional common rooms: a room downstairs overlooking the ocean and a larger room with shelves of books.

255 Ocean View Blvd., Pacific Grove, CA 93950. © 800/852-5588 or 831/373-3388. Fax 831/373-3896. www.martine inn.com. 24 units. $185–$335 double. Rates include full breakfast and evening hors d'oeuvres. AE, DISC, MC, V. **Amenities:** Nearby golf course; Jacuzzi; game room; concierge; tour desk; room service; in-room massage; babysitting. *In room:* Fridge, hair dryer.

**Seven Gables Inn** ★★★ This is one of the most opulent B&Bs I've ever seen. Named after the seven gables that cap the inn, the compound of Victorian buildings was built in 1886 by the Chase family (as in Chase Manhattan Bank). Outside is the coast road overlooking the sea; inside is a collection of mostly European antiques. Everything here is luxurious and gilded, including the oceanview rooms, which are scattered among the main house, cottages (including a two-bedroom option), and the guesthouse. The accommodations are linked by gardens filled with roses and marble sculpture. If the hotel's booked, ask about the Grand View Inn, a slightly less ornate but comparable B&B next door that's run by the same owners.

555 Ocean View Blvd., Pacific Grove, CA 93950. © 831/372-4341. www.pginns.com. 14 units. $175–$385 double. Rates include breakfast and afternoon tea. 2-night minimum on weekends. MC, V. **Amenities:** Nearby golf course. *In room:* Kitchenette in 1 unit, fridge in some units, hair dryer, no phone.

### MODERATE

**Butterfly Grove Inn** *Kids* Despite the name, this place is more like a motor lodge than an inn. Located right at the very tip of the Monterey Peninsula, accommodations here are run-of-the-mill, but the amenities are not; some rooms come with refrigerators, kitchenettes, Jacuzzi tubs, and/or fireplaces, and guests have access to the property's pool, spa, Jacuzzi, and shuffleboard, croquet, and volleyball courts. Folks traveling with the family should opt for one of the six family units tucked into a Victorian house. The hotel is located in one of the quieter parts of Pacific Grove, so just meander out your door and you're likely to see a soiree of butterflies (during winter), who migrate here each year, as well as deer who frequently wander the streets.

1073 Lighthouse Ave., Pacific Grove, CA 93950. © **800/337-9244** or 831/373-4921. Fax 831/373-7596. www.butterfly groveinn.com. 31 units. Summer $99–$299 double; winter $79–$249 double. Children under 18 stay free in parent's room. AE, DISC, MC, V. **Amenities:** Outdoor pool; Jacuzzi. *In room:* TV/VCR, dataport, fridge, coffeemaker, hair dryer, iron, microwave.

**Centrella Inn** 👉 A couple blocks from the waterfront and from Lover's Point Beach, the two-story Centrella is a turreted Victorian built as a boardinghouse in 1889. Today the rooms are decorated in Victorian style, but they're somewhat plain—iron beds, side table, floor lamp, and armoire—although the bathrooms do have claw-foot tubs. In the back, connected to the house by walkways, several cottages and suites have fireplaces, separate bedrooms, and bathrooms. Two have private decks; the others offer decks facing the rose garden and patio, which is set with umbrella tables and chairs.

612 Central Ave., Pacific Grove, CA 93950. © **800/233-3372** or 831/372-3372. Fax 831/372-2036. www.centrella inn.com. 26 units. $129–$259 double; $199–$310 suites and cottages. Rates include buffet breakfast and evening hors d'oeuvres. AE, DISC, MC, V. **Amenities:** Nearby golf course. *In room:* TV in cottages, fridge, hair dryer, iron.

**Gosby House** 👉 Originally a boardinghouse for Methodist ministers, this Victorian was built in 1888, 3 blocks from the bay. It's still one of the most charming Victorians in town, with individually decorated rooms, floral-print wallpapers, lacy pillows, and antique furnishings. Twelve guest rooms have fireplaces, and all come with the inn's trademark teddy bears. Especially noteworthy are the two Carriage House rooms, which come with a TV/VCR, fridge and coffeemaker, fireplace, balcony, and bathroom with spa tub. The house has a separate dining room and parlor, where guests gather for breakfast and complimentary wine and hors d'oeuvres in the afternoon. Other amenities include a complimentary newspaper, twice-daily maid service, and bicycles.

643 Lighthouse Ave., Pacific Grove, CA 93950. © **800/527-8828** or 831/375-1287. Fax 831/655-9621. www.four sisters.com. 22 units, 20 w/bathroom. $95–$195 double. Rates include full breakfast and afternoon wine and hors d'oeuvres. AE, DC, MC, V. From Hwy. 1, take Hwy. 68 to Pacific Grove, where it turns into Forest Ave.; continue on Forest to Lighthouse Ave., turn left, and go 3 blocks. **Amenities:** Nearby golf course; complimentary bike use. *In room:* Hair dryer.

**Green Gables Inn** 👉 This 1888 Queen Anne–style mansion, decorated like an English country inn, forgoes opulence (and in some cases private bathrooms) to allow for reasonable rates and less formal accommodations. The rooms are divided between the main building and the carriage houses behind it. The Carriage House rooms, which are better for families, have large private bathrooms with Jacuzzi tubs. All accommodations are individually decorated with period furnishings, including some antiques and an occasional poster bed. Most rooms in the original home have ocean views and share two immaculate bathrooms. Complimentary wine, tea, and hors d'oeuvres are served each afternoon in the parlor, with an antique carousel horse.

301 Ocean View Blvd., Pacific Grove, CA 93950. © **800/722-1774** or 831/375-2095. Fax 831/375-5437. www.four sisters.com. 11 units, 7 w/bathroom. $120–$155 double without bathroom; $170–$260 double w/bathroom; $200–$260 suite. Rates include full breakfast and afternoon wine and hors d'oeuvres. AE, MC, V. From Hwy. 1, take the Pacific Grove exit (Hwy. 68) and continue to the Pacific Ocean; turn right on Ocean View Blvd. and drive ½ mile to Fifth St. **Amenities:** Complimentary bike use. *In room:* Iron.

### INEXPENSIVE

**The Wilkies Inn** (*Value* This motel consistently charges less than the other hotels in town, gets an A+ for service, and is on a tree-lined street with a resident deer who often drops by for breakfast. The motel boasts well-kept furnishings and carpets, and stylish bedspreads. All the squeaky-clean rooms come with free HBO and local calls; some have partial ocean views. Putting up with occasionally noisy plumbing and thin walls might be worth the money saved.

1038 Lighthouse Ave., Pacific Grove, CA 93950. ℂ **866/372-5960** or 831/372-5960. Fax 831/655-1681. 25 units. $77–$210 double. Extra person $10. 2-night minimum on weekends. Rates include continental breakfast. Packages available. AE, DISC, MC, V. **Amenities:** Nearby golf course. *In room:* TV/VCR, dataport, coffeemaker, hair dryer, iron.

## WHERE TO DINE
### EXPENSIVE

**Fandango** ✦✦ MEDITERRANEAN   Provincial Mediterranean specialties from Spain to Greece to North Africa spice up the menu with such offerings as seafood paella with North African couscous (the recipe has been in the owner's family for almost 200 years), cassoulet maison, cannelloni niçoise, and a Greek-style lamb shank. You'll feel transported to Europe in one of the five upstairs and downstairs dining rooms, cozied by roaring fires, wood tables, and antiqued walls. There's an award-winning international wine list with 450 options and a dessert menu that includes a Grand Marnier soufflé with fresh raspberry purée sauce and profiteroles. In winter ask to be seated in the fireplace dining room, and in summer request the terrace room— but whenever you come, expect everything here to be lively and colorful, from the decor to the owner himself.

223 17th St. ℂ **831/372-3456**. www.fandangorestaurant.com. Reservations recommended. Main courses $11–$24. AE, DC, DISC, MC, V. Mon–Sat 11:30am–2:30pm and 5–9:30pm; Sun 10am–2pm and 5–9:30pm. From Hwy. 1, take the Pacific Grove exit (Hwy. 68), turn left on Lighthouse Ave., and continue a block to 17th St.

**Joe Rombi's** ✦ ITALIAN   In an area where most restaurants pack 'em in, Joe Rombi's offers a refreshingly intimate dining room with dimmed lights and antique French posters. The food here is very fresh (lasagnas and pastas are made that day). Once seated at 1 of the 11 tables, you'll immediately be served a basket of fresh house-made focaccia to munch on while you peruse the limited menu of appetizers, soups, salads, pastas, and four main courses (some of which come with soup and salad). Go with the fish of the day—I had a halibut dish that any upscale San Francisco restaurant would be proud to serve.

208 17th St. (at Lighthouse Ave.). ℂ **831/373-2416**. Fax 831/373-2106. Reservations recommended. Main courses $12–$21. AE, MC, V. Wed–Sun 5–10pm.

**The Old Bath House** ✦ CONTINENTAL   Romance is in the air at this restored Victorian restaurant, on the edge of the earth overlooking Lover's Point. It may be pricey and frequented by tourists, but dinner here is a stately affair with knockout bay views, superb service, and competently prepared cuisine. A popular starter is the grilled prawns and wild-boar sausage appetizer. Main courses range from oak-grilled filet mignon to scallops on lemon risotto. The signature dish is the duck merlot, served with a dried cherry-merlot reduction and risotto. End your decadent dinner with a plate of hot pecan ice cream fritters.

620 Ocean View Blvd. ℂ **831/375-5195**. www.oldbathhouse.com. Reservations required. Main courses $20–$40. AE, DC, DISC, MC, V. Mon–Fri 5–10:30pm; Sat–Sun 4–10:30pm.

### MODERATE

**The Fishwife at Asilomar Beach** ✦ *Kids* SEAFOOD   The Fishwife is the ideal dining spot for anyone looking for a casual, affordable, and quality meal. The restaurant dates from the 1830s, when a sailor's wife started a small food market that became famous for its Boston clam chowder. Today locals still return for the soup as well as some of the finest seafood in Pacific Grove. Two bestsellers are calamari steak sautéed with shallots, garlic, tomatoes, and white wine; and prawns Belize, served sizzling with red onions, tomatoes, fresh Serrano chiles, jicama, lime juice, and cashews. Steak and pasta dishes are also available, and all main courses come with vegetables, bread, black beans, and rice or potatoes. Kids get their own menu, which has smaller portions for less than $6.

1996½ Sunset Dr. (at Asilomar Beach). ✆ **831/375-7107.** www.fishwife.com. Main courses $8.95–$15. AE, DISC, MC, V. Mon–Sat 11am–10pm; Sun 10am–10pm. From Hwy. 1, take the Pacific Grove exit (Hwy. 68) and stay left until it becomes Sunset Dr.; the restaurant will be on your left about 1 mile ahead as you approach Asilomar Beach.

**Peppers Mexicali Café** ✪ MEXICAN/LATIN AMERICAN   Peppers is a casual, festive place serving good food at reasonable prices. The inviting dining room has wooden floors and tables, pepper art visible from every vantage point, and a perpetual crowd who come to suck up beers and savor spicy specialties such as well-balanced seafood tacos and fajitas or house-made tamales and chiles rellenos. Other fire-starters include the snapper Yucatán, which is cooked with chiles, citrus cilantro, and tomatoes; and grilled prawns with lime-cilantro dressing. More than a dozen daily specials are offered as well, such as Mexican seafood paella and grilled mahimahi tacos. Add a substantial selection of *cervezas,* an addicting compilation of chips and salsa, and a friendly staff, and your taste buds are bound to bellow *"Olé!"*

170 Forest Ave. ✆ **831/373-6892.** Fax 831/373-5467. Reservations recommended. Main courses $7–$15. AE, DC, DISC, MC, V. Mon and Wed–Thurs 11:30am–10pm; Fri–Sat 11:30am–10:30pm; Sun 4–10pm.

## INEXPENSIVE

**First Awakenings** ✪ *Value* AMERICAN   What was once a dank canning factory is now a bright, huge, open restaurant with one of the cheapest and healthiest breakfasts in the area. Eye-openers include eight varieties of omelets; granola with nuts, fruit, and yogurt; walnut and wheat pancakes; "gourmet" pancakes; and raisin French toast. At lunch there's a fine choice of salads and a slew of sandwiches ranging from albacore to zucchini. On sunny days, take advantage of the outdoor patio tables.

In the American Tin Cannery, 125 Ocean View Blvd. ✆ **831/372-1125.** Reservations not accepted. Breakfast $3–$7; lunch $5–$7. AE, DISC, MC, V. Daily 7am–2:30pm. From Hwy. 1, take the Pacific Grove exit (Hwy. 68) and turn right onto Lighthouse Ave.; after a mile, turn left onto Eardley Ave., and take it to the corner of Ocean View.

**Thai Bistro** ✪ THAI   One of the most popular Thai restaurants in the area is this small white house with blue trim. Inside you'll find a modern, congenial dining room that's usually filled with locals. The menu is a minimanifesto, with more than 60 options. Some of the most popular dishes are the Panang curry (a heavenly blend of spices and coconut milk with your choice of meat or seafood), *Tom kha Gai* soup (chicken in coconut milk), and pad Thai. There's a full vegetarian menu as well. It's all accompanied by local wines and French desserts.

159 Central Ave. (between David Ave. and Eardley St.). ✆ **831/372-8700.** Reservations required on weekends. Most main courses $8–$12. AE, DISC, MC, V. Daily 11:30am–9:30pm.

**Toastie's Cafe** AMERICAN   While most restaurants' success depends not only on food but also on clever decor and elaborate presentation, Toastie's shrugs its traditional-style shoulders and continues to pack 'em in. What's the attraction? A good old-fashioned meal served in a no-frills casual dining room. Some rave about the eggs Benedict (with roasted potatoes), while others swear by the hefty, sinful waffles. One thing's for sure: This place serves up what everyone wants from breakfast—lots of selections, good service, endless coffee refills, and heaping plates of food. Weekend dinner is an equally homey affair and includes chicken and prawn Marsala, teriyaki steak, seafood pasta, and stuffed chicken.

702 Lighthouse Dr. © 831/373-7543. Breakfast and lunch dishes $5.95–$7.25; dinner main courses $9–$12. MC, V. Mon–Sat 6:30am–3pm; Sun 7am–2pm; Fri–Sat 5–8pm.

## 4 Pebble Beach & the 17-Mile Drive 👉👉👉

Pebble Beach is a world unto itself. Polo shirts, golf shoes, and big bankrolls are standard, and if you have to ask how much accommodations and greens fees are, you definitely can't afford them. In this elite golfers' paradise, endless grassy fairways are interrupted only by luxury resorts and cliffs where the ocean meets the land. In winter it's also the site of the AT&T Pebble Beach National Pro-Am, a celebrity tournament originally launched in 1937 by crooner Bing Crosby.

### THE 17-MILE DRIVE 👉👉

Set aside an afternoon, pack a picnic, fork over $8 to enter, and prepare to see some of the most exclusive real estate in California. The drive is accessible from any of five gates: two from Pacific Grove to the north, one from Carmel to the south, or two from Monterey to the east. The most convenient entrance from Highway 1 is off the main road at the Holman Highway exit. You may beat traffic by entering at the Carmel Gate and doing the tour backwards. Admission to the drive includes an informative map with 26 points of interest. Other highlights include **Seal and Bird Rocks,** where you can see countless gulls and cormorants, as well as seals and sea lions; and **Cypress Point Lookout,** with a 20-mile view to the Big Sur Lighthouse, on a clear day. From afar, you can also admire the famous **Lone Cypress** tree, inspiration to many artists and photographers (although it's no longer accessible on foot). The drive also traverses the **Del Monte Forest,** thick with tame black-tailed deer and often described as some "billionaire's private game preserve." *Note:* One of the best ways to see 17-Mile Drive is by bike. For further information, call the **Pebble Beach Resort** at © **831/624-3811** or visit www.pebblebeach.com/17miledrive.html.

### GREAT GOLF COURSES

Locals tell me it's almost impossible to get a tee time unless you're staying at the golf resort. If you're one of the lucky few, you can choose from several famous courses along the 17-Mile Drive.

**PEBBLE BEACH GOLF LINKS** 👉👉👉  The most famous course is Pebble Beach Golf Links (© **800/654-9300**) at The Lodge at Pebble Beach (p. 385). It's home each year to the AT&T Pebble Beach National Pro-Am, a celebrity-laden tournament televised worldwide. Jack Nicklaus has said, "If I could play only one course for the rest of my life, this would be it." He should know: He won the 1961 U.S. Amateur and the 1972 U.S. Open here. Indeed, 10 national championships have been decided here. Herbert Warren Wind, dean of 20th-century golf writers, said, "There is no finer seaside golf course in creation"—and that includes the Old Course at St. Andrews. Built in 1919, this 18-hole course is 6,799 yards and par 72. It's precariously perched over a rugged ocean. Greens fees are a staggering $425, and that doesn't include the cart fee.

**SPYGLASS HILL GOLF COURSE** 👉👉  Also frequented by celebrities is this course at Stevenson Drive and Spyglass Hill Road (© **800/654-9300**). Its slope rating of 143 means it's one of the state's toughest courses. It's justifiably famous at 6,859 yards and par 72 with five oceanfront holes. The rest reach deep into the Del Monte Forest. Greens fees are $290 plus cart. Reservations for non-guests should be made a month in advance. The excellent Grill Room restaurant is on the grounds.

**POPPY HILLS** ★★    This 18-hole, 6,219-yard course on 17-Mile Drive (© 831/625-2035) was named one of the world's top 20 by *Golf Digest*. It was designed by Robert Trent Jones, Jr., in 1986. One golf pro said the course is "long and tough on short hitters." Fees are $125 Monday through Thursday and $150 Friday through Sunday, plus $30 for the cart rental. You can make reservations 30 days in advance.

**THE LINKS AT SPANISH BAY** ★★    On the north end of 17-Mile Drive at the Pebble Beach Resort and Inn at Spanish Bay (© 800/654-9300), this is the most easily booked course. Serious golfers say it's the most challenging of the Pebble Beach links. Robert Trent Jones, Jr., Tom Watson, and Frank Tatum (former USGA president) designed it to duplicate a Scottish links course. Its fescue grasses and natural fairways lead to rolls and unexpected bounces. Greens fees are $230 plus a cart fee. Reservations accepted 60 days in advance.

**DEL MONTE GOLF COURSE** ★    At 1300 Sylvan Rd. (© 831/373-2700) lies the oldest course west of the Mississippi, charging some of the most "reasonable" greens fees: $100 per player, plus a cart rental of $20. The course, often cited in magazines for its "grace and charm," is relatively short—only 6,339 yards. This seldom-advertised course, located at the Hyatt east of Monterey, is part of the Pebble Beach complex, but is not along the 17-Mile Drive.

## WHERE TO STAY & DINE

**Casa Palmero Resort** ★★★    The Casa Palmero is a small, ultraluxury resort on the first tee of the Pebble Beach Golf Links. The two-story villa is the newest gem in the sister properties, which include the Inn at Spanish Bay and The Lodge at Pebble Beach. The most intimate and private of the three, Casa Palmero is fashioned as a European villa with stucco walls, window boxes dripping bougainvillea, every modern comfort, and a staff to anticipate your every wish. It has 24 cottages and suites with amenities that include French doors opening onto private garden spas, oversize window-box sofas, wood-burning fireplaces, and soaking tubs that open to the main room. "Convivial" areas, where you can hang out, include a trellised patio, library, billiards parlor, living room, private dining room, executive boardroom and small conference room, intimate courtyards with fountains, and lavish outdoor pool pavilion.

1518 Cypress Dr. (on 17-Mile Dr.), Pebble Beach, CA 93953. (© 800/654-9300 or 831/622-6650. Fax 831/622-6655. www.pebblebeach.com. 24 units. $705–$2,325 cottage or suite. $20 gratuity added. Rates include continental breakfast and evening hors d'oeuvres and cocktails. AE, MC, V. From Hwy. 1 south, turn west onto Hwy. 68 and south onto 17-Mile Dr., and follow the coastal road to the hotel. **Amenities:** 3 restaurants; outdoor heated pool; golf course; 12 tennis courts; health club; full-service spa; Jacuzzi; sauna; bike rental; concierge; 24-hr. room service; in-room massage; babysitting; laundry service; same-day dry cleaning; executive-level rooms. *In room:* TV/VCR w/pay movies, dataport, minibar, fridge, coffeemaker, hair dryer, iron, safe.

**The Inn at Spanish Bay** ★★★    Surrounded by the renowned Links at Spanish Bay golf course, the Inn at Spanish Bay is a plush three- and four-story low-rise on 236 manicured acres 10 miles north of The Lodge at Pebble Beach. Approximately half the rooms face the ocean and are more expensive than their counterparts, which overlook the forest. Each unit contains about 600 square feet of floor space and has a private fireplace and either an outdoor deck or a patio. The bathrooms are finished in Italian marble; the custom-made furnishings include four-poster beds with down comforters.

My favorite time here is dusk, when a bagpiper strolls the terrace with a skirling tribute to Scotland.

2700 17-Mile Dr., Pebble Beach, CA 93953. © 800/654-9300 or 831/647-7500. Fax 831/644-7960. www.pebblebeach.com. 270 units. $505–$685 double; from $935 suite. $20 gratuity added. AE, DC, MC, V. From Hwy. 1 south, turn west onto Hwy. 68 and south onto 17-Mile Dr.; the hotel is on your right, just past the toll plaza. **Amenities:** 3 restaurants; bar/lounge; heated outdoor pool; golf course; 8 outdoor tennis courts (2 night-lit); health club; full-service spa; Jacuzzi; sauna; bike rental; concierge; tour desk; business center; shopping arcade; 24-hr. room service; in-room massage; babysitting; laundry service; same-day dry cleaning; executive-level rooms. *In room:* TV/VCR w/pay movies, dataport, minibar, fridge, coffeemaker, hair dryer, iron, safe in most units.

**The Lodge at Pebble Beach** ★★  For the combined cost of greens fees and a room here, you could easily create a professional putting green in your own backyard—and still have money left over. But even if you're a dedicated hacker, you've got to play here at least once. Look on the bright side—at least you can expect ultraplush rooms equipped with every conceivable amenity, including wood-burning fireplaces. Most are in two-story cottage clusters, with anywhere from 8 to 12 units in each. Those opening onto the ocean have the highest prices.

1700 17-Mile Dr., Pebble Beach, CA 93953. © 800/654-9300 or 831/624-3811. Fax 831/625-8598. www.pebblebeach.com. 161 units. $585–$975 double; from $1,525 suite. $15 gratuity added. AE, MC, V. From Hwy. 1 south, turn west on Hwy. 68, turn south onto 17-Mile Dr., and follow the coastal road to the hotel. **Amenities:** 4 restaurants; bar/lounge; heated outdoor pool; golf course; 12 tennis courts; health club; full-service spa; Jacuzzi; sauna; bike rental; concierge; business center; shopping arcade; 24-hr. room service; in-room massage; babysitting; laundry service; same-day dry cleaning. *In room:* TV/VCR w/pay movies, dataport, minibar, fridge, coffeemaker, hair dryer, iron, safe in most units.

## 5 Carmel-by-the-Sea ★★

5 miles S of Monterey; 121 miles S of San Francisco; 33 miles N of Big Sur

Carmel began as a seaside artists' colony that attracted such luminaries as Sinclair Lewis, Robert Louis Stevenson, and Ansel Adams. Residents resisted assigned street numbers and lighting, and carried lanterns, which they considered more romantic. Although it's still intimate enough that addresses remain unnumbered—Carmel's inns, restaurants, boutiques, and galleries identify their locations by cross streets—the ragtag bohemian village of yesteryear is long gone. Carmel is now a tourist hot spot, where weekend traffic can be intolerable and lodging rates grossly inflated. But thousands of annual visitors are so taken with the eclectic dwellings, quaint cafes, majestic cypresses, and silky white beaches that they don't seem to mind the modern inconveniences.

### ESSENTIALS

The **Carmel Business Association,** P.O. Box 4444, Carmel (© **831/624-2522;** www.carmelcalifornia.org), is on San Carlos Street between Fifth and Sixth streets. It distributes local maps, brochures, and publications. You'll want to pick up the *Guide to Carmel* and a schedule of events. Hours are Monday through Friday from 9am to 5pm. On weekends, an information booth is set up from 11am to 3pm at Carmel Plaza, on Ocean Avenue between Junipero and San Carlos streets.

### WHAT TO SEE & DO

A wonderful stretch of white sand backed by cypress trees, **Carmel Beach City Park** ★★ is a bit o' heaven on earth (though the jammed parking lot can feel more like a visit to a car rally). There's room for families, surfers, and dogs with their owners (yes, pooches are allowed to run off-leash). If the parking lot is full, there are some spaces on Ocean

Avenue, but take heed: They're generally good for 90-minute parking, and you will get a ticket if you park for the day.

Farther south around the promontory, **Carmel River State Beach** 🌟 is less crowded, with white sand and dunes, plus a bird sanctuary with brown pelicans, black oystercatchers, cormorants, gulls, curlews, godwits, and sanderlings.

The **Mission San Carlos Borromeo del Río Carmelo** 🌟🌟, on Basilica Rio Road at Lasuen Drive, off Highway 1 (© **831/624-1271;** www.carmelmission.org), is the burial ground of Father Junípero Serra and the second-oldest of the 21 Spanish missions he established. Founded in 1771 on a site overlooking the Carmel River, it's one of the largest and most interesting of California's missions. The stone church, with its Moorish bell tower and curving walls covered with a lime plaster made of burnt seashells, was begun in 1793. The kitchen, the first library in California, the high altar, and the flower gardens are all worth visiting. More than 3,000 Native Americans are buried in the adjacent cemetery; their graves are decorated with seashells. The mission is open June through August, Monday through Saturday from 9:30am to 7:30pm, Sunday from 10:30am to 7:30pm; in other months, Monday through Saturday from 9:30am to 4:30pm, Sunday from 10:30am to 4:30pm. A $2 donation is requested.

One of Carmel's prettiest homes and gardens is **Tor House** 🌟, 26304 Ocean View Ave. (© **831/624-1813;** www.torhouse.org), built by poet Robinson Jeffers. On Carmel Point, the house dates from 1918 and includes a 40-foot tower containing stones from around the world embedded in the walls (there's even one from the Great Wall of China). Inside, an old porthole is reputed to have come from the ship on which Napoleon escaped from Elba in 1815. No photography is allowed. Admission is by guided tour only, and reservations are requested. It's $7 for adults, $4 for college students, and $2 for high-school students (no children under 12). It's open on Friday and Saturday from 10am to 3pm.

If the tourists aren't lying on the beach in Carmel, then they're probably **shopping**—the sine qua non of Carmel activities. You'll be surprised at the number of shops packed into this small town—more than 500 boutiques offering unique fashions, baskets, housewares, imported goods, and a veritable cornucopia of art galleries. Most of the commercial action is packed along the small stretch of Ocean Avenue between Junipero and San Antonio avenues.

If you want to tour the **galleries,** pick up a copy of the *Carmel Gallery Guide* from the Carmel Business Association (see "Essentials," above).

Serious shoppers should also head south a few miles to the **Crossroads Shopping Center** (from Hwy. 1 south, take the Rio Rd. exit west for 1 block and turn right onto

---

**⌒ *Tips* Carmel Walking Tours**

The main tourist activity in Carmel is walking around town, so you might as well do it with the pros: **Carmel Walks.** The tour company offers 2-hour guided walks through Carmel's gardens, hidden pathways, fairytale-like cottages and homes of famous writers, artists, and washed-up movie stars. During the walk you'll learn about Carmel's seemingly endless spirits, unusual customs, and juicy gossip. For $20 it's a good deal. The tours run every Saturday at 10am and 2pm, and Tuesday through Friday at 10am. For reservations, call © **831/642-2700** or visit their website at www.carmelwalks.com.

Crossroads Blvd.). As far as malls go, this is a great one, with oodles of shopping and a few good restaurants.

## WHERE TO STAY

Most Carmel lodgings are booked solid from May to October, so make your reservations as far in advance as possible. If you're traveling with pets, your best bet is **The Cypress Inn,** Lincoln and Seventh (P.O. Box Y), Carmel-by-the-Sea, CA 93921 (© **800/443-7443** or 831/624-3871; www.cypress-inn.com), which is a moderately priced option run by owner and actress Doris Day.

### EXPENSIVE

**Carriage House Inn** ★★  Luxurious atmosphere and pampering make this one of my top picks in the "downtown" area. Each room comes with a wood-burning fireplace and king-size bed with a down comforter. Most of the second-floor rooms have sunken tubs and vaulted beam ceilings; first-floor rooms have single whirlpool tubs. Not only is breakfast delivered to guests' rooms, but there are also wine and hors d'oeuvres served in the afternoon and cappuccino, wine, and cheese in the evening. While almost all choices in the area are frill-and-lace, the Carriage House is a more mature, formal, yet cozy environment.

Junipero St., between Seventh and Eighth aves. (P.O. Box 1900), Carmel, CA 93921. © **800/433-4732** or 831/625-2585. Fax 831/624-0974. www.ibts-carriagehouse.com. 13 units. $229–$385 double. Rates include continental breakfast and afternoon wine and hors d'oeuvres. AE, DISC, MC, V. Free parking. From Hwy. 1, exit onto Ocean Ave. and turn left onto Junipero St. **Amenities:** Nearby golf course; concierge. *In room:* TV/VCR, minibar, coffeemaker, fridge, hair dryer, iron, safe.

**Highlands Inn, Park Hyatt Carmel** ★★  Four miles south of Carmel on a 12-acre cliff above Point Lobos, this inn has attracted everyone from celebrities—Madonna, Walt Disney, Marlon Brando—to honeymooners and business executives. It's rustic yet luxurious, with wildflowers gracing its pathways, plenty of character, and a rather exclusive atmosphere. The old-style main lounge dates from 1916 and has panoramic coastal vistas. The guest rooms are distributed throughout a cluster of buildings terraced into the hillside; most units have decks or balconies and wood-burning fireplaces. The suites come with Jacuzzi tubs and fully equipped kitchens; four rooms have showers only.

120 Highlands Dr., Carmel, CA 93923. © **800/682-4811** or 831/620-1234. Fax 831/626-8105. www.highlands inn.hyatt.com. 142 units. $205 double; $260–$695 spa suite; $485–$1,025 2-bedroom, full oceanview spa suite. AE, DC, DISC, MC, V. **Amenities:** 2 restaurants; lounge; outdoor heated pool; nearby golf course; exercise room; 3 outdoor Jacuzzis; complimentary bike use; concierge; tour/activities desk; business center; secretarial services; room service; in-room massage; babysitting; laundry service; same-day dry cleaning. *In room:* TV w/pay movies, VCR on request, kitchen in suites, fridge, coffeemaker, hair dryer, iron, safe, CD player.

**La Playa** ★  The four-story La Playa is a romantic, Mediterranean-style villa 2 blocks from the beach and within walking distance of town. Norwegian artist Christopher Jorgensen ordered its construction, in 1904, for his bride, an heiress of the Ghirardelli chocolate dynasty. The stylish lobby is elegant, with terra-cotta floors, Oriental rugs, and marble fireplace. In the courtyard, walkways lead through beautifully landscaped grounds surrounding a heated pool. Compared to the lobby and grounds, the standard guest rooms are disappointing, with thin walls and perfunctory furnishings. The luxury cottages are a (costly) improvement—with kitchens, wet bars, garden patios, limited room service and, in most cases, wood-burning fireplaces.

Camino Real and Eighth Ave. (P.O. Box 900), Carmel, CA 93921. 🕿 **800/582-8900** or 831/624-6476. Fax 831/624-7966. www.laplayahotel.com. 80 units. $175–$315 double; $375–$475 suite or cottage. Complimentary valet parking. AE, DC, MC, V. **Amenities:** Restaurant; bar; outdoor heated pool; nearby golf course; bike rental; concierge; business center; room service; babysitting; same-day dry cleaning. *In room:* TV, fridge, hair dryer, iron.

**Mission Ranch** ★★   If you want to stay off the beaten track, consider this converted 1850s dairy farm, restored by Clint Eastwood to preserve the vista of the nearby wetlands stretching to the bay. Accommodations are scattered amid different structures, both old and new, and surrounded by wetlands and grazing sheep. Guest rooms range from "regulars" in the main barn (less desirable) to meadow-view units with a vista across the fields to the bay. Rooms are decorated in a provincial style, with carved wooden beds bedecked with handmade quilts. Most are equipped with whirlpool baths, fireplaces, and decks or patios. The Martin Family farmhouse has six units, all arranged around a central parlor, while the Bunkhouse (the oldest structure on the property) contains separate living and dining areas, bedrooms, and a fridge. Even if you're not staying here, call for a table at **The Restaurant at Mission Ranch** (p. 391).

26270 Dolores St., Carmel, CA 93923. 🕿 **800/538-8221** or 831/624-6436. Fax 831/626-4163. www.missionranch carmel.com. 31 units. $110–$290 double. Rates include continental breakfast. AE, MC, V. **Amenities:** Restaurant; 6 tennis courts; exercise room; babysitting; laundry service; dry cleaning. *In room:* TV, dataport, fridge in some units, coffeemaker, hair dryer, iron.

## MODERATE
**Carmel Sands Lodge** ★   The Sands is a motor lodge, but it's decorated better than most on a quiet street in Carmel. The modern rooms have pretty bedspreads and updated furnishings; some have fireplaces and wet bars. There's a small pool, but it's practically in the center courtyard parking lot. Several restaurants are nearby. I like the quiet location here better than that of the comparable Carmel Village Inn (see below).

San Carlos and Fifth (P.O. Box 951), Carmel, CA 93921. 🕿 **800/252-1255** or 831/624-1255. Fax 831/624-2576. www.carmelsandslodge.com. 38 units. $85–$199 double. AE, DC, DISC, MC, V. From Ocean Ave., take a right onto San Carlos and go 2 blocks. **Amenities:** Restaurant; heated outdoor pool (seasonal); nearby golf course. *In room:* TV, minibar, fridge, coffeemaker, in some units hair dryer .

**Cobblestone Inn** ★   The Cobblestone may not be Victorian like other properties owned by the Four Sisters Inns, but it's just as flowery, well kept, and cute, with hand-stenciled wall decorations, fireplaces, and a trademark abundance of teddy bears. The first floor is built of stones taken from the Carmel River (hence the inn's name), and the rooms encircle a slate courtyard; some look out onto the brick patio where breakfast is occasionally served. The guest rooms vary in size; some can be small, and only the Honeymoon Suite comes with a bathtub and VCR, but the largest units include a wet bar, sofa, and separate bedroom. Guests have the use of a comfortable living room with a large stone fireplace. Extras include daily maid and turndown service and a morning newspaper.

Junipero St. (between Seventh and Eighth aves., 1½ blocks from Ocean Ave.; P.O. Box 3185), Carmel, CA 93921. 🕿 **800/833-8836** or 831/625-5222. Fax 831/625-0478. www.foursisters.com. 24 units. $125–$260 double. Rates include full breakfast and afternoon wine and hors d'oeuvres. AE, DC, MC, V. **Amenities:** Complimentary bike use. *In room:* TV, dataport, fridge, hair dryer.

**Normandy Inn** ★   Three blocks from the beach, this French Provençal–style hotel is like something out of a storybook, with an array of colorful flowers that brighten up the property. Some of the guest rooms are showing their age a little, but they're well appointed with French country decor, feather beds, and down comforters. Some have fireplaces and/or kitchenettes. The tiny heated pool is banked by a flower garden. The three large family-style units are an especially good deal and accommodate up to eight; each has three bedrooms, two bathrooms, a fully equipped kitchen, a dining room, a living room with a fireplace, and a back porch. Reserve well in advance, especially in summer.

Ocean Ave., between Monte Verde and Casanova sts. (P.O. Box 1706), Carmel, CA 93921. © 800/343-3825 or 831/624-3825. Fax 831/624-4614. www.normandyinncarmel.com. 48 units. $98–$220 double; $165–$500 suite or cottage. Rates include continental breakfast. Extra person $10. AE, DC, MC, V. From Hwy. 1, exit onto Ocean Ave. and continue straight for 5 blocks past Junipero St. **Amenities:** Outdoor pool (seasonal); nearby golf course. *In room:* TV, kitchenette in some units, coffeemaker, hair dryer, iron.

**Pine Inn Hotel**    Built in 1889, the three-story Pine Inn, which claims to be the oldest hotel in Carmel, looks like a set out of *Wild, Wild West*. The ornate deep-red and mahogany lobby and library (with fireplace) is a fun departure from the beachy alternatives (think turn-of-the-20th-century bordello meets the Far East). Doubles, however, are very small; pay a bit more to secure a larger room with a half-canopy. The hotel's in a good location, just a few blocks from the beach on Carmel's main strolling street. Room service hails from adjoining **Il Fornaio** (© **831/622-5100**) from 7am to 10:30pm. One big bummer: no elevators.

Ocean Ave., between Monte Verde and Lincoln (P.O. Box 250), Carmel-by-the-Sea, CA 93921. © **800/228-3851** or 831/624-3851. Fax 831/624-3030. www.pine-inn.com. 49 units. $135–$260 double. AE, DC, DISC, MC, V. **Amenities:** Restaurant. *In room:* TV.

**Sandpiper Inn by the Sea** ⚐    A garden of flowers welcomes visitors to this quiet, relaxing, midscale Carmel standby that's been in business for more than 60 years. The inn's rooms, from which you can hear the surf, offer a range of well-kept accommodations. The highest priced are corner rooms with four-poster beds and plenty of windows framing the ocean view. All are decorated with handsome country antiques and fresh flowers that are changed daily; three have fireplaces. Carmel's fabled white-sand beaches are a mere 100 yards away.

2408 Bay View Ave., Carmel, CA 93923. © **800/590-6433** or 831/624-6433. Fax 831/624-5964. www.sandpiper-inn.com. 17 units. $135–$250 double. Rates include extended continental breakfast and afternoon sherry/tea. AE, DISC, MC, V. **Amenities:** Nearby golf course; concierge; tour desk. *In room:* No phone.

**Vagabond House** ⚐    In typical Carmel style, oodles of attention have been paid to every element of this English Tudor inn—from the lobby adorned with knickknack antiques and a welcoming decanter of sherry to the wonderfully lush garden courtyard that's draped with greenery and dotted with blooms. Each room is warm and homey, decorated in country decor, and has a private entrance; all have wood-burning fireplaces except two, which means the least expensive rooms book quickly, so call ahead if you want one. Guests are welcomed with a basket of fruit, and the extended continental breakfast is delivered to your room, but you'll most likely prefer to enjoy it on the garden patio.

Fourth and Dolores (P.O. Box 2747), Carmel-by-the-Sea, CA 93921. © **800/262-1262** or 831/624-7738. Fax 831/626-1243. www.vagabondshouseinn.com. 12 units. $125–$265 double. Rates include continental breakfast. 2-night minimum on weekends. AE, DISC, MC, V. Pets allowed for a fee. *In room:* TV, dataport, fridge, coffeemaker, hair dryer, iron.

## WHERE TO DINE
### EXPENSIVE
**Anton & Michel** ⚐ CONTINENTAL    This elegant restaurant, across from Carmel Plaza, serves traditional French cuisine in one of the most formal rooms in town. By day, it's best to dine fountainside or on the glass-encased terrace. The view is equally

alluring in the evening, when the courtyard is lit and the fountain's water sparkles. Decorated with French chandelier lamps and oil paintings, the main dining room is formal—but, as in most restaurants in town, patrons' attire need not match it. Appetizers include crab cakes with cilantro-pesto aioli or delicate ravioli filled with ricotta cheese and spinach. Specialties include rack of lamb with an herb-Dijon mustard au jus and more eclectic items such as a chicken breast Jerusalem, sautéed with olive oil, white wine, cream, and artichoke hearts. The wine list is impressive.

At Court of the Fountain, Mission St. (between Ocean and Seventh aves.). ⓒ 831/624-2406. www.carmelsbest.com. Reservations recommended. Main courses $17–$33. AE, DC, DISC, MC, V. Daily 11:30am–3pm and 5:30–9:30pm.

Casanova ⭐ NORTHERN ITALIAN/COUNTRY FRENCH European ambience has drawn locals and tourists to Casanova for over a quarter of a century. The building, which once belonged to Charlie Chaplin's cook, is divided into three Belgian chalet–style dining rooms that serve as the perfect setting for leaning over a bottle of red wine and creating vacation memories. More festive folk step back to the bustling, old-world-style covered patio. Because all dinner entrees include antipasto and a choice of appetizers (such as baked stuffed eggplant with rice, herbs, cheese, and tomatoes), prices here are not a bad deal (at least in overpriced Carmel). The menu features typical Mediterranean cuisine: paella, homemade pastas, meats, and fish. Casanova also boasts a *Wine Spectator* award–winning wine cellar featuring more than 1,600 French, California, German, and Italian wines.

Fifth Ave. (between San Carlos and Mission sts.). ⓒ 831/625-0501. www.casanovarestaurant.com. Reservations recommended. 3-course dinner $22–$43. MC, V. Daily 11:30am–3pm and 5–10pm. From Hwy. 1, take the Ocean Ave. exit and turn right on Mission, then left onto Fifth Ave.

Flying Fish Grill ⭐⭐ PACIFIC RIM/SEAFOOD I always feel more confident when a restaurant's owner runs the kitchen—and a dinner here will confirm that chef/proprietor Kenny Fukumoto is in the house. Dark, romantic, and Asian-influenced, the dining room has an intimate atmosphere with redwood booths (built by Kenny) and fish hanging (flying?) from the ceiling. The cuisine features fresh seafood with exquisite Japanese accents. Start with sushi, tempura, or any of the other exotic taste teasers. Main-course favorites include a rare peppered *ahi* (tuna), blackened and served with mustard-and-sesame-soy vinaigrette and angel-hair pasta; and a pan-fried almond sea bass with whipped potatoes, Chinese cabbage, and rock shrimp stir-fry.

In Carmel Plaza, Mission St. (between Ocean and Seventh aves.). ⓒ 831/625-1962. Reservations recommended. Main courses $15–$24. AE, DISC, MC, V. Wed–Mon 5–10pm.

Grasing's Coastal Cuisine ⭐ CALIFORNIA When chef Kurt Grasing and renowned Bay Area restaurateur Narsai David teamed to open Grasing's Coastal Cuisine, the result was one of Carmel's best restaurants. The bright, split-room dining area is simple yet stylish, with buttercup-yellow walls, beaded lamps, and colorful artwork. Grasing's menu also reflects a stylish simplicity; ultrafresh ingredients gleaned from California's coast and Central Valley are displayed in a modest fashion that belie an intense combination of textures and flavors. The warm Napa salad, for example, appears ordinary enough, but "when I took it off the menu," says Grasing, "I still made 30 a night." Two other dishes that have generated interest are the lobster risotto made with pearl pasta (rather than arborio rice, for a smoother texture) and the bronzed salmon served in a garlic cream sauce. Even the bread, which comes fresh from Gail's Bakery in Aptos, is fantastic. When the sun's out, request a table at the dog-friendly patio, and be sure to inquire about the very reasonable prix-fixe meal.

Sixth St. (at Mission St.). © **831/624-6562.** www.grasings.com. Reservations recommended. Main courses $17–$26. AE, MC, V. Daily 11am–4pm and 5–10pm.

**The Restaurant at Mission Ranch** ★★ AMERICAN   Clint Eastwood bought this rustic property in 1986 and restored the ranch-style building to its original integrity. The chance of seeing him brings in some folk, but it's the views, quality food, and merry atmosphere that make the place special. The wooden building is encased with large windows that accentuate the wonderful view of the marshlands, grazing sheep, and bay. Warm days make the patio the prime spot, but the key time to come is at sunset, when the sky is transforming and happy hour is in full swing. You'll find some of the cheapest drinks around, and Clint often stops by when he's in town. As you'd expect from the ranch motif, meat is king here: Burgers are freshly ground on-site, and prime rib with twice-baked potato and vegetables is the favored dish. There are, of course, wonderful seafood, chicken, and vegetarian options as well; and all dinners include soup or salad. Entertainment is provided at the piano bar, where locals and tourists have been known to croon their favorites. The Sunday buffet brunch with live jazz piano is also hugely popular; be sure to reserve a table.

At Mission Ranch, 26270 Dolores St. © **831/625-9040.** www.missionranchcarmel.com. Reservations recommended. Most main courses $17–$29. DC, MC, V. Daily 5–9:30pm; Sun brunch 10am–1:30pm; bar stays open until midnight.

## MODERATE

**Caffè Napoli** ★ Value ITALIAN   The decor here is so quintessentially Italian—with flags, gingham tablecloths, garlic, and baskets overhead—that I expected a flour-coated, pot-bellied Padrino Napoli to emerge from the kitchen, embrace me, and exclaim, *"Mangia! Mangia!"* as he slapped down a bowl overflowing with sauce-drenched pasta. Of course, there is no Padrino here, and I received no welcoming hug, but I did indulge in the fine Italian fare that keeps locals coming back for more.

Ocean Ave. (between Dolores and Lincoln). © **831/625-4033.** Reservations recommended. Main courses $10–$20. MC, V. Daily 11:30am–9pm.

**Club Jalapeño** ★★ MEXICAN   Follow the divine aroma wafting down San Carlos Avenue and you'll end up at Club J, tearing into in a plate of Oaxacan enchiladas drizzled with rich mole sauce. The fried and battered Baja fish tacos are just like the ones in Tijuana (love that salsa and lime-cilantro dressing). The coconut-encrusted fish is lightly fried then topped with spicy chipotle sauce and fruit salsa. A righteous meal for two is Club J's spicy shrimp fajitas served with a side of fresh-fruit salsa. You'll like the decor as well—faux-hacienda-rustic with dark-wood flooring, exposed beams, iron furnishings, textured walls, soft lighting, dried hanging chilies, and a sexy little corner bar serving soothing shots of pure agave tequila.

San Carlos (between Fifth and Sixth in the courtyard). ©**831/626-1997.** www.clubjalapeno.com. Main courses $10–$18. AE, MC, V. Wed–Mon noon–10pm; Tues 5–10pm.

**The Hog's Breath Inn** AMERICAN   Clint Eastwood's involvement with this restaurant made it famous, but it's a rare day that he visits (better odds are at the Mission Ranch restaurant). No matter: The patio with tree-trunk tables and plastic chairs is ideal for taking in beer and good ol' American standbys—if you don't mind the usual wait. (Tables in the wood-paneled dark-and-rustic dining room fill up, too, though they're not as lively as outdoor seats.) The food—burgers, nachos, and such—is unremarkable, but the small dark sports bar is the best place to pull up a stool and kick back on a rainy day (or a sunny one for that matter). Come for lunch, when it's more affordable.

San Carlos St. (between Fifth and Sixth aves.). © 831/625-1044. www.hogsbreathinn.net. Reservations not accepted. Main courses $9.50–$23. AE, DC, MC, V. Daily 11:30am–10pm. From Hwy. 1, take the Ocean Ave. exit and turn right onto San Carlos St.

**La Bohème** ★ FRENCH COUNTRY  Like a set from Disney's "It's a Small World," La Bohème mimics a French street with cartoony asymmetrical shingled house facades and a painted blue sky overhead. Thankfully, the similarity stops with the decor, and there are no singing dolls. Dinner here is romantic French cuisine, served at cramped tables set with floral-print cloths in bright colors, hand-painted dinnerware, and vibrant bouquets. Dinner is a three-course, fixed-price feast consisting of a large salad, a tureen of soup, and a main dish (perhaps roast breast of duckling with green-peppercorn sauce). Vegetarian specials are also available. Homemade desserts and fresh coffee are sold separately, and are usually worth the extra expense.

Dolores St. and Seventh Ave. © 831/624-7500. www.laboheme.com. Reservations not accepted. Prix-fixe 3-course dinner $24. MC, V. Daily 5:30–10pm. From Hwy. 1, exit onto Ocean Ave. and turn left onto Dolores St.

**Rio Grill** ★★ AMERICAN  Serious food and a festive atmosphere (with vibrant art, including a cartoon mural of famous locals Clint Eastwood and the late Bing Crosby), have kept this place popular for the past several years. The whimsical nature of the modern Santa Fe–style dining room belies the kitchen's ambitious preparations, which include homemade soups; a rich quesadilla with almonds, cheeses, and smoked-tomato salsa; barbecued baby back ribs from a wood-burning oven; and fresh fish from an open oak grill. The good wine selection includes some rare California vintages and covers a broad price range.

Crossroads Shopping Center, 101 Crossroads Blvd. © 831/625-5436. www.riogrill.com. Reservations recommended. Main courses $8–$25. AE, DISC, MC, V. Sun–Thurs 11:30am–10pm; Fri–Sat 11:30am–11pm. From Hwy. 1, take the Rio Rd. exit west for 1 block and turn right onto Crossroads Blvd.

**Tommy's Wok** ★★ *Value* CHINESE  Far be it for Carmel to have just an ordinary Chinese restaurant. Instead, chef/owner Tommy Mao has eschewed the typical flaming-red-and-gold color scheme for a far more subdued—almost Japanese in its austerity—decor at this Carmel newcomer. The small 12-table restaurant—with its soothing pastel hues, rice-paper posters, semi-open kitchen, and glossy wood floor—is an apt setting for Mao's stylish presentations and unique combinations of Szechuan, Hunan, and Mandarin dishes. Mao's make-it-all-from-scratch philosophy is evident in all his dishes: potstickers made with fresh Napa cabbage, mu shu vegetables with house-made pancakes, tea-smoked duck marinated for 48 hours. All these dishes are proven winners, as are the Hot & Spicy String Beans, Pinenut Chicken, marinated Lover's Prawns, and Mongolian Lamb (okay, now I'm hungry). The combo lunch plates are a real bargain, and a modest dim sum menu is offered for lunch as well.

Mission (between Ocean and Seventh, next to the Wells Fargo ATM). © 831/624-8518. Main courses $7–$14. AE, DISC, MC, V. Tues–Sun 11:30am–2:30pm and 4:30–9:30pm.

**INEXPENSIVE**

**Little Swiss Cafe** CONTINENTAL  This quirky little spot is designed to look like a Swiss cottage. Kids may love the decor (old-fashioned Grandma cute) but the grown-ups come for the best homemade blintzes and pancakes in town. Breakfast is served all day. Lunch is affordable and features sandwiches, which are served with potato salad, mixed green salad, or soup ($5–$7); salads; and an array of unusual entrees such as Swiss sausage with smothered onions, calves' liver sauté, and fillet of red snapper with a rémoulade sauce.

Sixth Ave. (between Lincoln and Mission). ℂ **831/624-5007.** Reservations not accepted. $5–$9. No credit cards. Mon–Sat 7:30am–3pm; Sun 8am–2pm.

**Neilsen Brothers Market** DELI    Why squander precious midday vacation minutes indoors when you can dine alfresco on the sands of Carmel Beach? Duck a few blocks off the main drag to Neilsen Brothers market for everything you could want to fill your picnic basket, including sandwiches, barbecued chicken and ribs, pasta salads, and a vast selection of cheeses. You can even get french fries or veggie and meat burgers (noon–6pm), but expect a 10-minute wait—they cook to order. Call and order by phone or drop in.

San Carlos St. (at Seventh). ℂ **831/624-6263** (deli), or 831/624-6441 (market). Picnic items $3–$5. MC, V. Mon–Sat 8am–8pm; Sun 10am–7pm.

## 6 Carmel Valley

3 miles SE of Carmel-by-the-Sea

Inland from Carmel stretches Carmel Valley, where wealthy folks retreat beyond the reach of the coastal fog and mist. It's a scenic and perpetually sunny valley of rolling hills dotted with manicured golf courses and many a tony pony ranch.

Hike the trails in **Garland Regional Park,** 8 miles east of Carmel on Carmel Valley Road (dogs are welcome off-leash). The sun bakes you out here, so bring lots of water. You can also sign up for a trail ride or riding lesson at **The Holman Ranch,** 60 Holman Rd. (ℂ **831/659-2640;** www.theholmanranch.com), 12 miles east of Highway 1. And several resorts and courses in the valley offer golf—notably **Quail Lodge,** 8205 Valley Green Dr. (ℂ **888/828-8787** or 831/624-2888; www.quaillodge.com), and **Rancho Cañada Golf Club,** Carmel Valley Road (ℂ **800/536-9459** or 831/624-0111; www.ranchocanada.com).

While you're in the area, taste the wines at the **Château Julien Winery,** 8940 Carmel Valley Rd. (ℂ **831/624-2600;** www.chateaujulien.com), which is open Monday through Friday from 8am to 5pm, Saturday and Sunday from 11am to 5pm. Tours are available by reservation.

### WHERE TO STAY

**Bernardus Lodge** ★★★    On the Top 20 list of just about every luxury travel publication is this 57-room boutique "lodge" in scenic Carmel Valley. Bernardus Pon, who owns the Bernardus Winery & Vineyard, must have spent a small fortune to build his eponymous resort, which consists of a main lodge, nine adobe-style guest houses, two restaurants, a meditation garden, a croquet lawn and bocce court, two tennis courts, and a pool. The gorgeous main lodge resembles a French country home, with heavy wood beams, hand-plastered walls, copper chandeliers, antique wrought-iron, and limestone fireplaces. The guest suites are similar, with stone wood-burning fireplaces, vaulted ceilings, arched windows, feather beds with Italian linens, and French doors that open to private decks with mountain or garden views. Although Carmel is only a 15-minute drive westward, your time is far better spent indulging in the resort's full-service spa, playing golf at nearby Quail Lodge (Benardus' sister resort; see below), or having a leisurely breakfast or lunch at the outdoor terrace, followed by an impromptu wine tasting. As for dinner arrangements, stay put: under the helm of chef Cal Stamenov, the lodge's Marinus restaurant offers exquisite California-natural cuisine and a Wine Spectator award-winning wine list.

415 Carmel Valley Rd., Carmel Valley, CA 93924. ℂ **888/648-9463** or 831/648-3400. Fax 831/659-3529. www.
bernardus.com. 57 units. $375–$750 double. AE, DC, DISC, MC, V. **Amenities:** 2 restaurants; heated outdoor pool; 2
tennis courts; 24-hour exercise room; full spa; sauna; concierge; room service; bocce court; croquet lawn. In room:
A/C, TV/DVD, minibar, fridge, coffeemaker, hair dryer, iron, safe, CD player.

**Quail Lodge Resort and Golf Club** ★★　In the foothills of the Santa Lucia
Range, Quail Lodge has received Mobil's five-star ratings for more than 20 years. Its
pastoral setting encompasses more than 850 acres of lakes, woodlands, meadows, an
18-hole championship golf course, and a full-service spa. The guest rooms are in two-
story balconied wings, with terraces overlooking the pool or 1 of the 10 man-made
lakes, or in cottages holding five units each. Executive villas are the most expensive,
luxurious digs. The guest rooms are decorated in earth tones with striped and checkered patterns. Higher-priced accommodations, on the upper floors, have cathedral
ceilings. Every room has a separate dressing area and French doors opening to an
ample balcony; some have fireplaces and wet bars. All have coffeemakers, supplied
with freshly ground beans; a fresh-fruit plate is delivered to each room daily as well.

8205 Valley Greens Dr., Carmel, CA 93923. ℂ **888/828-8787** or 831/624-2888. Fax 831/624-3726. www.quail
lodge.com. 97 units. $225–$435 double; $325–$565 suite. Extra person $35. Call for winter specials. Packages avail-
able. AE, DC, DISC, MC, V. From Hwy. 1 north, past the Carmel exits (after which the highway narrows to 2 lanes),
turn east on Carmel Valley Rd. and continue 3½ miles to Valley Greens Dr. Pets accepted w/$100 fee per stay; $25 fee
per extra pet. Pet amenities and doggie treats included. **Amenities:** 3 restaurants; 2 bars; 2 outdoor pools (1 heated);
golf course; 4 tennis courts; exercise room; full spa services; Jacuzzi; bike rental; concierge; business center; room
service; in-room massage; babysitting; laundry service; same-day dry cleaning; executive-level rooms. In room: TV
w/pay movies, dataport, minibar, coffeemaker, hair dryer.

## 7 The Big Sur Coast ★★★

3 miles S of Carmel-by-the-Sea; 123 miles S of San Francisco; 87 miles N of Hearst Castle

Big Sur is more than a drive along one of the most dramatic coastlines on earth or
a peaceful repose amid a forest of California redwoods. It's a stretch of wilderness so
overwhelmingly beautiful—especially when the fog glows in the moonlight—that it
enchants everyone who visits. It's also home to a particular breed of nature lover
who prefers a rustic lifestyle to the rest of California's offerings. When the 1997 and
1998 El Niño storms caused landslides and major road damage, cutting the area off
from civilization for months, reports from Big Sur were unusual: Some residents
fled, vowing never to return. The remaining residents rejoiced in the temporary solitude; Post Ranch, the area's ultimate luxury resort, shared the impromptu intimacy
with deep-pocketed guests by flying them in via helicopter (for an extra fee, of
course). Such is the price paid for living amid the California wilderness. The
reopened roads are packed again, and driving through the region is slow; rubber-
neckers admiring the view and nervous Nellies fearing the cliffs drive with their foot
on the brakes.

Although there is an actual Big Sur Village 25 miles south of Carmel, "Big Sur"
refers to the entire 90-mile stretch of coastline between Carmel and San Simeon,
blessed on one side by the majestic Santa Lucia Range and on the other by the rocky
Pacific coastline. It's one of the most romantic, relaxing places in California. There's
little more to do than explore the mountains and beaches, and take in the sea air—
but spend a few days here and you won't need to do much else.

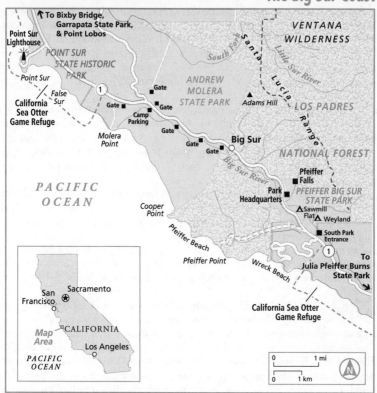

## ESSENTIALS

**VISITOR INFORMATION**   Contact the **Big Sur Chamber of Commerce** (© **831/ 667-2100;** www.bigsurcalifornia.org) for specialized information on places and events in Big Sur.

**ORIENTATION**   Most of this stretch is state park, and Highway 1 runs its entire length, hugging the ocean the whole way. Restaurants, hotels, and sights are easy to spot—most are situated directly on the highway—but without major towns as reference points, their addresses can be obscure. For the purposes of orientation, I'll use the River Inn as a mileage guide. Located 29 miles south of Monterey on Highway 1, the inn is generally considered to mark the northern end of Big Sur.

## EXPLORING THE BIG SUR COAST

Big Sur's tranquility and natural beauty are ideal for hiking, picnicking, camping, fishing, and beachcombing. The first settlers arrived only a century ago, and the present highway, built in 1937, first made the area accessible by car. (Electricity followed in the 1950s, but it's still not available in the remote inland mountains.) Big Sir's mysterious, misty beauty has inspired several modern spiritual movements (the Salem Institute was the birthplace of the human potential movement). Even the tourist bureau bills the area as a place in which "to catch up with your soul." Take the board's advice and take your time.

The region affords bountiful wilderness adventure opportunities. The inland **Venting Wilderness,** run by the U.S. Forest Service, has 167,323 acres straddling the Santa Lucia Mountains. Steep ridges separated by V-shaped valleys characterize it. The streams throughout the area have waterfalls, deep pools, and thermal springs. The wilderness offers 237 miles of hiking trails that lead to 55 designated trail camps—a backpacker's paradise. One of the easiest trails to access is the **Pine Ridge Trail** at Big Sur station (© 831/667-2315).

From Carmel, the first stop along Highway 1 is **Point Lobos State Reserve** ★★ (© 831/624-4909), 3 miles south of Carmel. Sea lions, harbor seals, sea otters, and thousands of seabirds reside in this 1,276-acre reserve. Between December and May you can also spot migrating California gray whales offshore. Trails follow the shoreline and lead to hidden coves. Note that parking is limited; on weekends especially, you need to arrive early to secure a place.

From here, cross the Soberanes Creek, passing **Garrapata State Park** (© 831/624-4909), a 2,879-acre preserve with 4 miles of coastline. It's unmarked and undeveloped, but the trails are maintained. To explore them, park at one of the turnouts on Highway 1 near Soberanes Point and hike in.

Ten miles south of Carmel, you'll find North Abalone Cove. From here, Palo Colorado Road leads back into the wilderness to the first of the Forest Service camping areas at **Bottchers Gap** ($12 to camp, $5 to park overnight; © 805/995-1976; www.campone.com).

Continuing south, about 13 miles from Carmel, you'll cross the **Bixby Bridge** and see the **Point Sur Lighthouse** off in the distance. The Bixby Bridge, one of the world's highest single-span concrete bridges, towers nearly 270 feet above Bixby Creek Canyon, with canyon and ocean views from observation alcoves at intervals along the bridge. The lighthouse, which sits 361 feet above the surf on a volcanic rock promontory, was built in 1889, when only a horse trail provided access to this part of the world. Tours, which take 2 to 3 hours and involve a steep half-mile hike each way, are scheduled on weekends year-round and Wednesday and Thursdays during the summer. For information, call © 831/625-4419, or visit www.pointsur.org. Moonlight tours are offered as well; check the website for specific dates. Admission is $8 for adults, $4 for youths ages 6 to 17, and free for kids 5 and under.

About 3 miles south of the lighthouse is **Andrew Molera State Park** (© 831/667-2315; www.bigsurcalifornia.org), the largest state park on the Big Sur coast, at 4,800 acres. It's much less crowded than Pfeiffer–Big Sur (see below). Miles of trails meander through meadows and along beaches and bluffs. Hikers and cyclists use the primitive trail camp about a third of a mile from the parking area. The 2½-mile-long beach, sheltered from the wind by a bluff, is accessible via a mile-long path flanked in spring by wildflowers, and offers excellent tide pooling. You can walk the length of the beach at low tide; otherwise, take the bluff trail above the beach. Trails run through the park for horseback riders of all levels. **Molera Big Sur Trail Rides** (© 800/942-5486 or 831/625-5486; www.molerahorsebacktours.com) offers coastal trail rides daily from April to December, or until the rains come. The cost varies but starts at about $25 for a 1-hour ride along the beach. The park also has campgrounds.

Back on Highway 1, you'll reach the village of Big Sur, with commercial services. About 26 miles south of Carmel is **Big Sur Station** (© 831/667-2315), where you can pick up maps and information about the region. It's a quarter mile past the entrance to **Pfeiffer–Big Sur State Park** ★ (© 831/667-2315; www.bigsurcalifornia.org), an

810-acre park with 218 camping sites along the Big Sur River (call © **800/444-7275** for camping reservations), picnicking, fishing, and hiking. It's a scenic park of redwoods, conifers, oaks, and meadows, and it gets very crowded. **The Big Sur Lodge** in the park has cabins with fireplaces and other facilities (p. 398 and the "Camping in Big Sur" box below). Admission is $5 per car, and it's open daily from dawn to dusk.

Just over a mile south of the entrance to Pfeiffer–Big Sur State Park is the turnoff to Sycamore Canyon Road (unmarked), which will take you 2 winding miles down to beautiful **Pfeiffer Beach** ✦, a great place to soak in the sun on the wide expanse of golden sand. It's open for day-use only, there's no fee, and it's the only beach accessible by car (but not motor homes).

Back on Highway 1, the road travels 11 miles past Sea Lion Cove to Julia Pfeiffer Burns State Park. High above the ocean is the famous **Nepenthe** restaurant (p. 402), the retreat bought by Orson Welles for Rita Hayworth in 1944. A few miles farther south is the **Coast Gallery** (© **800/797-6869** or 831/667-2301; www.coastgalleries. com), the premier local art gallery, which displays lithographs of works by the late writer and, yes, artist Henry Miller. The gallery's Coast Cafe offers simple serve-your-self lunches of soup, sandwiches, baked goods, and coffee. Miller fans will also want to stop at the **Henry Miller Memorial Library** (© **831/667-2574**; www.henry miller.org) on Highway 1, 30 miles south of Carmel and a quarter mile south of Nepenthe restaurant. The library displays and sells books and artwork by Miller and houses a permanent collection of first editions. It also serves as a community art center, hosting concerts, readings, and art exhibitions (check for upcoming events on the website). The rear gallery room is a video-viewing space where films about Henry Miller can be seen. There's a sculpture garden, plus tables on the adjacent lawn where visitors can rest and enjoy the surroundings. Admission is free; hours are Thursday through Sunday from 11am to 6pm.

**Julia Pfeiffer Burns State Park** ✦✦ (© **831/667-2315**; www.bigsurcalifornia.org) encompasses some of Big Sur's most spectacular coastline. To get a closer look, take the trail from the parking area at McWay Canyon, which leads under the highway to a bluff overlooking the 80-foot-high McWay Waterfall dropping directly into the ocean. It's less crowded here than at Pfeiffer–Big Sur, and there are miles of trails to explore in the 3,580-acre park. Scuba divers can apply for permits to explore the 1,680-acre underwater reserve.

From here, the road skirts the Ventana Wilderness, passing Anderson and Marble Peaks and the Esalen Institute before crossing the Big Creek Bridge to Lucia and several campgrounds farther south. **Kirk Creek Campground** ✦, about 3 miles north of Pacific Valley, offers camping with ocean views and beach access. Beyond Pacific Valley, the **Sand Dollar Beach** ✦ picnic area is a good place to stop and enjoy the coastal view and take a stroll. A half-mile trail leads down to the sheltered beach, with a fine view of Cone Peak, one of the coast's highest mountains. Two miles south of Sand Dollar is **Jade Cove,** a popular spot for rock hounds. From here, it's about another 27 miles past the Piedras Blancas Light Station to San Simeon.

## WHERE TO STAY

Only a handful of Big Sur's accommodations offer the kind of pampering and luxury you'd expect in a fine urban hotel; even direct-dial phones and TVs (often considered gauche in these parts) are rare. Big Sur hotels are especially busy in summer, when advance reservations are required. There are more accommodations than those listed here, so if you're having trouble securing a room or a site, contact the chamber of commerce (listed in the "Essentials" section above) for other options.

**Big Sur Lodge** *Kids* A family-friendly place, the Big Sur Lodge is *in* the park and sheltered by towering redwoods, sycamores, and broad-leafed maples. The rustic motel-style cabins are huge, with high peaked cedar- and redwood-beamed ceilings. They're clean and heated, and have private bathrooms and reserved parking spaces. Some have fireplaces. All offer porches or decks with views of the redwoods or the Santa Lucia Range. An advantage to staying here is that you're entitled to free use of all the facilities of the park, including hiking, barbecue pits, and picnic areas. In addition, the lodge has its own grocery store.

In Pfeiffer–Big Sur State Park, Hwy. 1 (P.O. Box 190), Big Sur, CA 93920. © 800/424-4787 or 831/667-3100. Fax 831/667-3110. www.bigsurlodge.com. 61 cottages. $99–$179 cottage for 2; $129–$219 w/kitchen or fireplace; $149–$229 w/kitchen and fireplace; park entrance fee included. AE, MC, V. From Carmel, take Hwy. 1 south 26 miles. **Amenities:** Restaurant; heated outdoor pool in season. *In room:* Coffeemaker, kitchen in some units, no phone.

**Deetjen's Big Sur Inn** ★ In the 1930s, before Highway 1 was built, this homestead in a redwood canyon was an overnight stopping place on the coastal wagon road. Norwegian homesteader Helmuth Deetjen built the original units from hand-hewn logs and lumber. Folks either love or hate them. They're cozy and adorable, with old-fashioned furnishings and a down-home feel (the hand-hewn doors don't have locks), but those who want creature comforts should go elsewhere, or at least reserve a cabin with a private bathroom. Single-wall construction rooms aren't soundproof, so children under 12 are allowed only if families reserve both rooms of a two-room building. And they're uninsulated, so prepare to crank up the fire or wood-burning stove. *Tip:* The cabins by the river are the most private. If you stay in one of the two-story units, request the quieter upstairs rooms. The restaurant (p. 401) is a local favorite and consists of four intimate, English country inn–style rooms lit by candlelight.

Hwy. 1, Big Sur, CA 93920. © 831/667-2377. www.deetjens.com. 20 units, 15 w/bathroom. $75–$180 double w/shared bathroom; $110–$195 double w/private bathroom. MC, V. **Amenities:** Restaurant. *In room:* No phone.

**Post Ranch Inn** ★★★ This is one of my very favorite places to stay on the planet. Perched on 98 acres of seaside ridges 1,200 feet above the Pacific, this romantic resort opened in 1992 and was instantly declared one of the world's finest retreats. What's the big deal? The Post Ranch doesn't attempt to beat its stunning natural surroundings, but to join them. The wood-and-glass guest cottages are built around existing trees—some are elevated to avoid damaging the delicate redwood root structures—and the ultraprivate Ocean and Coast cottages are so close to the edge of the earth, you get the impression that you've joined the clouds (imagine that from your private spa tub). Other cottages face the woodlands and are as impressive in design. Each room has a fireplace, terrace, massage table, and wet bar filled with complimentary goodies. The bathrooms, fashioned out of slate and granite, feature spa tubs. Also on the premises are the best Jacuzzi I've ever encountered (it's on a cliff and seems to join the sky), an infinity pool, and sun decks. The only drawback is that the vibe can be stuffy, which is due more to the clientele than the staff (my Subaru was sneered at). The **Sierra Mar** restaurant is open to guests-only for continental breakfast, and to the public for dinner. It, too, has floor-to-ceiling views of the ocean.

Hwy. 1 (P.O. Box 219), Big Sur, CA 93920. © 800/527-2200 or 831/667-2200. Fax 831/667-2824. www.post ranchinn.com. 30 units. $495–$960 double. Rates include continental breakfast. AE, MC, V. **Amenities:** Restaurant; bar/lounge; outdoor heated pool; exercise room; spa services; cliffside Jacuzzi; game room; concierge; activities desk; room service; in-room massage. *In room:* A/C, minibar, coffeemaker, hair dryer, iron, safe, CD player.

## *Tips*  Camping in Big Sur

Big Sur is one of California's most spectacular camping destinations. One of the most glorious settings is **Pfeiffer–Big Sur State Park,** on Highway 1, 26 miles south of Carmel (© 831/667-2315). The 810-acre state park has 218 secluded sites amid hundreds of acres of redwoods. Hiking trails, streams, and the river are steps from your sleeping bag, and the most modern amenities are the 25¢ showers (for 3 min.), and water faucets between sites. Each spot has a picnic table and fire pit but no RV hookups or electricity. Riverfront sites are most coveted, but others promise more seclusion among the shaded hillsides. Campfire programs and nature walks are also offered. At the entrance are a store, gift shop, restaurant, and cafe. Fees are $14 for regular sites, $26 for group sites; call © **800/444-7275** or log on to www.reserveamerica.com for reservations. Senior discounts are available, and leashed dogs are permitted ($1 per night extra).

The entrance to the **Ventana Campground,** on Highway 1, 28 miles south of Carmel and 4¼ miles south of the River Inn (© **831/667-2712;** www. ventanawildernesscampground.com), is adjacent to the Ventana Resort entrance, but the comparison stops there. This is pure rusticity. The 80 campsites, on 40 acres of a redwood canyon, are spaced well apart on a hillside and shaded by towering trees. Each has a picnic table and fire ring but no electricity, RV hookups, or river access. Three conveniently located bathhouses have hot showers (25¢ fee). Reserve a space with a credit card (MasterCard or Visa) for 1 night's deposit. Or mail a deposit check, the dates you'd like to stay, and a stamped, self-addressed envelope at least 2 weeks in advance (earlier during peak months). Rates are $28 for a site for two with one vehicle; $35 per night weekends. An additional person is $5 extra, and it'll cost you $5 to bring Fido. Rates include the entrance fee for your car. Open April through October.

**Big Sur Campground and Cabins** is on Highway 1, 26 miles south of Carmel (half mile south of the River Inn; © 831/667-2322; www.bigsurcalifornia.org/ camping.html). The sites are cramped, so the feel is more like a camping village than an intimate retreat. However, it's very well maintained and perfect for families, who love the playground, river swimming, and inner-tube rentals. Each campsite has its own wood-burning fire pit, picnic table, and freshwater faucet within 25 feet of the pitching area. There are also RV water and electric hookups. Facilities include bathhouses with hot showers, laundry facilities, an aged volleyball/basketball court, and a grocery store. There are 81 tent sites (30 RV-ready with electricity and water hookup), plus 13 cabins (all with shower). The all-wood cabins are adorable, with stylish country furnishings, wood-burning ovens, patios, and full kitchens. Rates are $27 for a tent site for two or an RV hookup (plus $4 extra for electricity and water), $57 for a tent cabin (bed, but no heat or plumbing) for two, or $105 to $221 for a cabin for two. Rates include the entrance for your car. MasterCard and Visa are accepted. Pets cost $4 for campsites and $12 for tent cabins; pets are not allowed in the other cabins. It's open year-round.

**Ventana Inn and Spa** ★★★ Luxuriously rustic and utterly romantic, Ventana has been a popular wilderness outpost for more than 20 years, and with good reason. Located on 243 mountainous oceanfront acres, Ventana has an elegance that's atypical of the region, and has attracted famous guests such as Barbra Streisand, Goldie Hawn, and Francis Ford Coppola since opening in 1975.

The accommodations, in 12 one- and two-story natural-wood buildings along winding wildflower-flanked paths, blend in with the magical Big Sur countryside. The extensive grounds are dotted with hammocks and hand-carved benches, strategically located under shady trees and at vista points. The guest rooms are divinely decorated in warm, cozy luxury, with private terraces or balconies overlooking the ocean or forest. Most rooms offer wood-burning fireplaces, and some have Jacuzzis and cathedral ceilings. A small fitness center offers the basics—but you'll be more inspired to hike the grounds, where you'll not only find plenty of pastoral respite, but also a pool, a rustic library, and clothing-optional tanning decks and spa tubs. This, along with Post Ranch, is one of the best retreats in the region, if not the state. But I can't say which is better. I prefer the rooms at Post Ranch but the laid-back energy and the grounds at Ventana. *Families take heed:* Children are permitted but not exactly embraced. Ventana's restaurant, **Cielo** (p. 401), is a romantic and first-rate dining experience.

Hwy. 1, Big Sur, CA 93920. © 800/628-6500 or 831/667-2331. Fax 831/667-2287. www.ventanainn.com. 62 units. $350–$985 double; from $585 suite. Rates include continental breakfast and afternoon wine and cheese. AE, DC, DISC, MC, V. **Amenities:** Restaurant; 2 heated outdoor pools; exercise room; full spa w/2 Japanese hot baths; sauna; concierge; room service; in-room massage; laundry service; executive-level rooms. *In room:* A/C, TV/VCR, minibar, fridge, coffeemaker, hair dryer, iron, safe.

## WHERE TO DINE

In addition to the following choices, you should try the **Big Sur Bakery and Restaurant** on Highway 1, just past the post office and a mile south of Pfeiffer–Big Sur State Park (© 831/667-0520). It offers friendly service and healthy fare, ranging from wood-fired pizzas and portobello-mushroom burgers at lunch to salmon, tuna, and chicken selections at dinner. All the pastries are freshly baked on the premises, along with hearth-baked breads. It's open Tuesday through Sunday from 8am to 10pm; they close early on Monday.

**Big Sur River Inn** CALIFORNIA/AMERICAN Popular with everyone from families to bikers, the River Inn is an unpretentious, rustic, down-home restaurant that has something for all tastes. Trying to seat a small army? No problem. Want to watch sports on TV at a local bar? Pull up a stool. Looking to snag a few rays from a deck right beside the Big Sur River? Break out the suntan lotion. In winter the wooden dining room is the prime spot; on summer days, some folks grab their patio chairs and cocktails and hang out literally midstream. Along with the local color, attractions include a full bar and good ol' American breakfasts (steak and eggs, omelets, pancakes, and so on, plus espresso, with most dishes for around $6), lunches (an array of salads, sandwiches, and baby back ribs, or fish and chips), and dinners (fresh catch, pastas, burgers, or ribs). I usually order the Black Angus Burger with a side of beer-battered onion rings, or a big platter of the Roadhouse Ribs served with cowboy beans.

On Hwy. 1, 2 miles north of Pfeiffer–Big Sur State Park. © 831/667-2700. Fax 831/667-2743. www.bigsurriverinn.com. Main courses $8.75–$15 lunch, $8.95–$28 dinner. AE, DC, MC, V. Daily 8am–10pm; 8am–9pm in winter.

**Café Kevah** SOUTHWEST/CALIFORNIA One level below Nepenthe (see below), Café Kevah offers the same celestial view at a fraction of the price, a more casual environment, and—depending on your taste—better food. Seating is entirely outdoors—a downside when the biting fog rolls in, but perfect on a clear day. You can order breakfast (served all day) or lunch from the shack of a kitchen, then grab an umbrella-shaded table, and enjoy the feast for your eyes and taste buds. Fare here is more eclectic than Nepenthe's, with such choices as homemade granola, baby greens with broiled salmon and papaya, chicken brochettes, omelets, and new-potato hash. It ain't cheap, but innovative cuisine, the view, and a decent mocha make it worthwhile. Don't forget to bring a coat.

On Hwy. 1, 29 miles south of Carmel (5 miles south of the River Inn). ⓒ 831/667-2345. www.nepenthebigsur.com. Appetizers $6.25–$12; main courses $11–$18. AE, MC, V. Daily 9am–4pm; closes when it rains.

**Cielo Restaurant** ✿✿ NEW AMERICAN   Like the resort, Ventana's "heaven" restaurant is a woodsy but extravagant place to dine alfresco at lunch or for a romantic dinner. The airy cedar interior is divided into two spaces: the lounge, where a wooden bar and cocktail tables look onto a roaring fire and through picturesque windows; and the dining room, which overlooks the mountains and/or the ocean. But in summer it's the outdoor patio, with its views of the ocean expanse and 50 miles of Big Sur coast, that's the coveted lunch spot. Unlike some costly restaurants in the area, a meal here is as gratifying as the surroundings. Lunch offers sandwiches, burgers, and an array of gourmet salads, as well as main courses such as grilled Atlantic salmon; dinner includes stellar starters like a perfectly dressed Caesar salad and a well-balanced chanterelle-mushroom risotto, and main courses such as oak-grilled Kansas City steak au poivre, caramelized Maine Diver scallops in a red Thai curry–coconut milk broth, and summer vegetable risotto with English peas and summer squash.

At Ventana Inn and Spa, Hwy. 1, Big Sur. ⓒ 831/667-4242. www.ventanainn.com. Reservations recommended for dinner. Main courses $11–$17 lunch, $23–$32 dinner. AE, DC, DISC, MC, V. Daily noon–3:30pm and 6–9pm.

**Deetjen's Big Sur Inn Restaurant** ✿ AMERICAN   With the feel of an English farmhouse—white-painted wood walls, wood-burning stove, dimly lit old-fashioned lamps, country antiques—this cozy, country setting is the perfect venue for the delicious comfort food and friendly service you'll find here. Mornings start off with a cup of strong coffee and breakfast: omelets and eggs Benedict piled high with potatoes, pancakes, and granola. Dinner is highly regarded by locals, and might include grilled chicken with mushrooms and a garlic Marsala sauce; roasted rack of lamb with a panko crust; prime New York steak with macadamia-nut risotto; and roast duckling with brandy, peppercorn, and molasses sauce.

On Hwy. 1. ⓒ 831/667-2377. www.deetjens.com. Reservations recommended. Main courses $4.25–$12 breakfast, $15–$33 dinner. MC, V. Daily 8am–noon and 6–9pm.

---

### *Tips*  A Big Sur Picnic

**The Big Sur Center Deli** sells fresh-baked goods, salads, wine, beer, coffee drinks, and a slew of more substantial options including calzones, enchiladas, and barbecued chicken—all made on the premises. Sandwiches are made to order, with some ready-made options. It's on Highway 1, 26½ miles south of Carmel, next to the Big Sur Post Office, and is open daily from 7:30am to 8:30pm; ⓒ 831/667-2225.

Nepenthe AMERICAN   Stop by Nepenthe if only to admire the view and pay homage to Henry Miller, who wrote some of his most significant works here. At 808 feet above sea level along the cliffs overlooking the ocean, the view is celestial—especially when fog lingers above the water. On a warm day, join the crowds on the terrace. On colder days, stay indoors. The redwood and adobe structure—with a wood-burning fireplace, redwood ceilings, and bayfront windows—has been a sanctuary for writers, artists, and travelers since 1949. Unfortunately, the food is another story; elsewhere, I would scoff at an $11 mediocre burger (sans fries!), $16 swordfish sandwich, and $4 draft Budweiser. Here, though, I consider it a nominal admission to dine at heights only birds usually enjoy. Come for lunch and spend big dinner bucks elsewhere.

Hwy. 1, 29 miles south of Carmel (5 miles south of the River Inn). © 831/667-2345. www.nepenthebigsur.com. Reservations accepted only for parties of 5 or more. Main courses $9–$25. AE, MC, V. Daily 11:30am–10pm.

## 8 Pinnacles National Monument 🄲

58 miles SE of Monterey

A little-known outpost 10 years ago, the 24,000-acre Pinnacles National Monument is now one of the most popular weekend hiking and climbing destinations in central California. In Steinbeck Country, southeast of Salinas, the mild-winter climate and plentiful routes make it an ideal off-season training ground for climbers. It's also a haven for campers, bird watchers, and nature lovers. One of the world's most unusual chaparral ecosystems, it supports a community of plants and animals, including six endangered California condors—the largest bird in North America, with a wingspan of nearly 10 feet—and one of California's largest breeding populations of raptors. Bring binoculars!

The Pinnacles themselves—hundreds of towering crags, spires, ramparts, and hoodoos—are seemingly out of place in the rolling hills of the coast range. And they are, in fact, out of place, part of the eroded remains of a volcano formed 23 million years ago, 195 miles south in the middle of the Mojave Desert. The movement of the San Andreas Fault, which runs just east of the park, carried them here. (The other half of the volcano remains in the Mojave.)

You could spend days here, but it's possible to cover the most interesting features in a weekend. With a single hike, you can go from the oak woodland around the Bear Gulch Visitor Center to the dry, desolate crags of the high peaks, then back down through a half-mile-long cave with underground waterfalls.

### ESSENTIALS

**GETTING THERE**   Two entrances lead to the park: The **West Entrance** from Soledad and U.S. 101 is a dusty, winding single-lane road (not suitable for trailers) with the best drive-up view. Exit at Front St. in Soledad, turn right and then left onto Hwy 46 heading east (it doesn't connect with the east side entrance). The west gate is open daily from 7:30am to 8pm (until 6pm in winter).

The alternative route is via the **East Entrance.** Unless you're coming from nearby, take the longer drive on Highway 25 through Gilroy and Hollister to enter through the east. Because most of the peaks of the Pinnacles face east and the watershed drains east, most of the interesting hikes and geologic features are on this side. The east gate is open 24 hours a day. No road crosses the park.

**FEES**   Park entrance fees, good for 7 days, are $2 per person or $5 per car.

**VISITOR CENTER**   The first place you should go when entering from the east is the **Bear Gulch Visitor Center** (© **831/389-4485**), open daily from 9am to 5pm. This small center is rich with exhibits on the park's history, wildlife, and geology, with a great selection of nature handbooks and climbing guides for the Pinnacles. Climbers should check with rangers about closures and other information before heading out: Many routes are closed during hawk- and falcon-nesting season, and rangers like to know how many climbers are in the park.

Adjacent to the visitor center, the Bear Gulch picnic ground is a great place to fuel up before setting out on a hike. Don't leave before gazing up at the dramatic spires of the high peaks (the ultimate spot is from the west side).

For more information, log on to the park's website at **www.nps.gov/pinn**.

**REGULATIONS & WARNINGS**   Beware of poison oak, particularly in Bear Gulch. Rattlesnakes are common but rarely seen. Bikes and dogs are prohibited on all trails, and no backcountry camping is allowed in the park.

Hiking through this variety of landscapes demands versatility. Come prepared with a good pair of hiking shoes, snacks, lots of water, and a flashlight.

Daytime temperatures often exceed 100°F (38°C) in summer, so the best time of year to visit is spring, when the wildflowers are blooming, or in the fall. Crowds are common during spring weekends.

## HIKING & EXPLORING THE PARK

To see most of the park in a single, moderately strenuous morning, take the **Condor Gulch Trail** from the visitor center. As you climb out of the parking area, the Pinnacles' wind-sculpted spires seem to grow taller. In less than 2 miles, you're among them, and Condor Gulch intersects with the **High Peaks Trail.** The view from the top spans miles: the Salinas Valley to your west, the Pinnacles below, and miles of coast to the east. And it's the most likely place to spot the elusive California condor. (Look for the white-triangle markings on the undersides of their wings.) After traversing the high peaks (including stretches of footholds carved in steep rock faces) for about a mile, the trail drops back toward the visitor center via a valley filled with eerie-looking hoodoos.

In another 1.5 miles you'll reach the reservoir marking the top of **Bear Gulch Cave,** which closes occasionally; in 1998 it closed due both to storm damage and to accommodate migrating Townsend bats, who in the past several years have come here to have their babies. It's usually open, but if you want to explore, you'll need your flashlight and you might get wet; still, this half-mile-long talus cave is a thrill. From the end of the cave, you're just a short walk (through the most popular climbing area of the park) away from the visitor center. It's also possible to hike just Bear Gulch and the cave, then return via the **Moses Spring Trail.** It's about 2 miles round-trip, but you'll miss the view from the top.

If you're coming from the West Entrance, the **Juniper Canyon Trail** is a short (1.25 miles), but very steep, blast to the top of the high peaks. You'll definitely earn the view. Otherwise, try the short **Balconies Trail** to the monument's other talus cave, **Balconies Cave.** Flashlights are required here, too.

## WHERE TO STAY

**The Inn at the Pinnacles** ★ *Finds*   Unless you intend to camp, the only place to stay at the Pinnacles National Monument is this sprawling hacienda-style inn a half-mile from the west park entrance. Built in 2002 in the heart of a working vineyard—Chalone

Vineyards—the six-room inn has unblemished vistas of rolling vineyards and the Gabilan Mountain Range. Each of the individually decorated guest rooms has a private entrance, ceramic tile flooring, private patio with a gas grill and vineyard views, and a sitting area with gas fireplace; all but one have a two-person whirlpool tub (heaven after a long day of hiking). The inn's sprawling patio is a popular spot to sip wine under a shade umbrella with panoramic views of the surrounding hillsides and Pinnacles National Monument. The staff serves a full breakfast each morning (in the dining room, patio, or guest rooms), and wine and cheese every evening. The nearest restaurants are 10 miles away, so you can either bring your own food to grill or make advance arrangements for the innkeepers to serve dinner for about $35 per person. *Note:* The inn is normally only open on weekends.

32025 Stonewall Canyon Rd., Soledad, CA 93960. (© 831/678-2400. www.innatthepinnacles.com. 6 units. $200–$225 double. Rates include continental breakfast and afternoon wine and cheese. MC, V. **Amenities:** Bocce court; gas grills. *In room:* A/C, wet bar, fridge, microwave, Jacuzzi (in 5 rooms).

## CAMPING

The park's campground on the west side was demolished by El Niño storms in 1997 and 1998 and is not scheduled for repair. Now the only campground is the privately run **Pinnacles Campground, Inc.,** on the east side ((© 831/389-4462; www.pinn camp.com), which charges $7 per person. It's just outside the park (off Hwy. 25, 32 miles south of Hollister), with lots of privacy and space between sites, plus showers, a store, and a large pool. It's close enough so you can hike into the park from the campground, though it will add a few miles to your outing. Though private campgrounds are often overdeveloped, the surroundings here are natural. Dogs are not recommended, but you can bring them if you're willing to pay a $10 leash deposit. *Note:* No other animals are allowed at Pinnacles.

# 13

# The Central Coast

*by Matthew Richard Poole*

California's Central Coast—a gorgeous amalgam of beaches, lakes, rolling hills, and mountains—is the state's most diverse region. The narrow strip that runs for more than 100 miles from San Simeon to Ventura spans several climate zones and is home to an eclectic mix of college students, middle-class workers, wealthy retirees, winemakers, strawberry farmers, ranchers, immigrant labor, and fishermen. The ride along Highway 1, which follows the ocean cliffs, is almost always packed with rental cars, RVs, and bicycles on summer weekends, but the scenery is so gorgeous that nobody seems to mind a little traffic.

The Central Coast is also coming into its own as a major wine region, and offers another excuse to visit some of the state's most scenic countryside. Wine snobs might tell you that Central Coast wines cannot compare to those from the northern appellations, where vintages can age to sublime flavor and astronomical price, but if you're in the market for bottles in the $20-to-$30 range that are ready to drink within a couple of years, you'll love what this up-and-coming wine destination has to offer.

Whether you're driving up from Los Angeles or down from San Francisco, Highway 1 is the most scenic and leisurely route. (U.S. 101 is faster but less picturesque.) Most bicyclists pedal from north to south, the direction of the prevailing winds. Those in cars may prefer to drive south to north so they can get a better look at the coastline as it unfolds toward the west. No matter which direction you drive, break out the camera—you're about to experience unparalleled beauty, California-style.

## 1 San Simeon: Hearst Castle ★★★

250 miles S of San Francisco (via Hwy. 1); 250 miles NW of Los Angeles

Few buildings on earth are as elaborate as **Hearst Castle.** The 165-room estate of publishing magnate William Randolph Hearst, high above the village of San Simeon atop a hill he called La Cuesta Encantada ("the Enchanted Hill"), is an ego trip *par excellence.* One of the last great estates of America's Gilded Age, it's an over-the-top monument to wealth—and to the power that money brings.

Hearst Castle is a sprawling compound, constructed over 28 years in a Mediterranean Revival style and never fully completed. The focal point of the estate is **Casa Grande,** a 100-plus-room mansion filled with art and antiques that you have to see to believe. Hearst acquired most of his collection via New York auction houses, where he bought entire rooms (including walls, ceilings, and floors) and shipped them here. The result is an old-world-style castle in a mix-and-match style. You'll see 400-year-old Spanish and Italian ceilings, 500-year-old mantels, 16th-century Florentine bedsteads, Renaissance paintings, Flemish tapestries, and innumerable other treasures.

Three opulent "guesthouses" also contain magnificent works of art. A lavish private movie theater was used to screen first-run films twice nightly—once for employees, and again for the guests and host.

And then there are the swimming pools. The Roman-inspired indoor pool has intricate mosaic work, Carrara-marble replicas of Greek deities, and alabaster globe lamps that create the illusion of moonlight. The breathtaking outdoor Greco-Roman Neptune pool, flanked by marble colonnades that frame the distant sea, is one of the mansion's most memorable—and photographed—features.

In 1957, in exchange for a massive tax write-off, the Hearst Corporation donated the estate to the state of California (while retaining ownership of approximately 80,000 acres). The California Department of Parks and Recreation now administers it as a State Historic Monument and officially refers to it as the rather unpoetic Hearst San Simeon State Historical Monument.

## ESSENTIALS

**GETTING THERE**   Hearst Castle is on Highway 1, about 42 miles north of San Luis Obispo, 94 miles south of Monterey, 250 miles north of Los Angeles, and 250 miles south of San Francisco. From San Francisco or Monterey, take U.S. 101 south to Paso Robles, then Highway 46 west to Highway 1, and Highway 1 north to the castle. From Los Angeles, take U.S. 101 north to San Luis Obispo, then Highway 1 north to the castle. Park in the visitor center lot; a bus takes guided tour guests up the hill to the estate. The movie theater and visitor center adjoin the parking lot and are easily accessible without heading up to the actual estate.

**VISITOR INFORMATION**   To get information about Hearst Castle, call ℂ **800/ 444-4445** or 805/927-2020, or log on to **www.hearstcastle.org**. For more information on nearby Cambria (see below), check out **www.cambria-online.com** or stop into the **Cambria Chamber of Commerce**'s visitor center at 767 Main St., in the west village (ℂ **805/927-3624;** www.cambriachamber.org).

## TOURING THE ESTATE

Hearst Castle can be visited only by guided tours, conducted daily beginning at 8:20am, except on New Year's Day, Thanksgiving, and Christmas. Two to six tours leave every hour, depending on the season. Allow 2 hours between starting times if you plan on taking more than one tour. You can buy tickets right at the visitor center, but you have no guarantee that they'll be available—a day's slate of tours can easily sell out. You pay no fee for advance reservations, and you can make them from 1 hour to 8 weeks in advance. Tickets can be purchased by phone or online at California Reservations (ℂ **800/444-4445;** www.hearstcastle.org). If you're ordering tickets from outside the United States, call ℂ **916/414-8400,** ext. 4100.

Four different daytime tours run on a daily basis, each lasting 1 hour 45 minutes, including the 15-minute bus ride to and from the castle. Docents dress in 1930s period costume and assume a variety of roles, enhancing the living history experience.

I strongly recommend setting aside 2 full days to enjoy the castle at a leisurely pace. If you're just coming to see the castle, 1 day will do, but expect it to be a longish one and sandwich it between a 2-night stay. Also, children under 6 may find walking and climbing hundreds of steps for almost 2 hours a bit overwhelming.

Tickets for the daytime tours are $24 for adults and $12 for kids 6 to 17. The Evening Tour is $30 for adults and $15 for kids. Children under 6 are free. Prices are a few bucks cheaper during the off-season, September 16 to May 14.

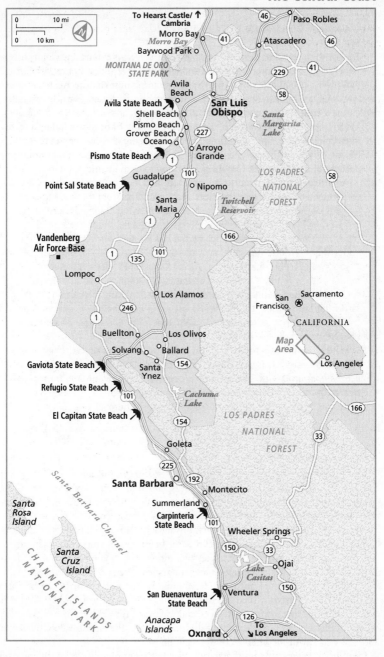

# The Central Coast

0     10 mi
0     10 km

To Hearst Castle/ Cambria

Paso Robles

Morro Bay
*Morro Bay*
Baywood Park

46

41

Atascadero

46

*MONTANA DE ORO STATE PARK*

229

41

Avila Beach

58

Avila State Beach

**San Luis Obispo**

*Santa Margarita Lake*

Shell Beach

227

Pismo Beach
Grover Beach
Oceano

Arroyo Grande

*LOS PADRES*

Pismo State Beach

1

101

*NATIONAL*

58

Guadalupe

Nipomo

*FOREST*

Point Sal State Beach

Santa Maria

*Twitchell Reservoir*

1

166

**Vandenberg Air Force Base**

1

135

101

Lompoc

Los Alamos

San Francisco

Sacramento

246

**CALIFORNIA**

1

Buellton

Los Olivos

Solvang

Ballard

*Map Area*

154

Gaviota State Beach

Santa Ynez

Los Angeles

Refugio State Beach

101

*Cachuma Lake*

El Capitan State Beach

154

*LOS PADRES*

166

Goleta

*NATIONAL*

225

33

**Santa Barbara**

192

*FOREST*

Montecito

*Santa Rosa Island*

*Santa Barbara Channel*

Summerland

Carpinteria State Beach

101

Wheeler Springs

*Santa Cruz Island*

150

33

Ojai

*CHANNEL ISLANDS NATIONAL PARK*

*Lake Casitas*

150

San Buenaventura State Beach

Ventura

*Anacapa Islands*

126

To Los Angeles

**Oxnard**

407

---

*Fun Fact*   Weekends at "the Ranch"

The lavish palace that William Randolph Hearst always referred to simply as "the ranch" took root in 1919. William Randolph ("W.R." to his friends) had inherited 275,000 acres from his father, mining baron George Hearst, and was well on his way to building a formidable media empire. He often escaped to a spot known as "Camp Hill" on his lands in the Santa Lucia Mountains above the village of San Simeon, the site of boyhood family outings. Complaining that "I get tired of going up there and camping in tents," Hearst hired architect Julia Morgan to design the retreat that would become one of the most famous private homes in the world.

An art collector with indiscriminate taste and inexhaustible funds, Hearst overwhelmed Morgan with interiors and furnishings from the ancestral collections of Europe. Each week, railroad cars carrying fragments of Roman temples, lavish doors and carved ceilings from Italian monasteries, Flemish tapestries, hastily rolled paintings by the old masters, ancient Persian rugs, and antique French furniture arrived—5 tons at a time—in San Simeon. Orson Welles's 1941 masterpiece *Citizen Kane,* which depicts a Hearst-like mogul with a similarly excessive estate called Xanadu, has a memorable scene of hoarded priceless treasures warehoused in dusty piles, stretching as far as the eye can see. Like Kane, Hearst, once described as a man with an "edifice complex," purchased so much that only a fraction of what he bought was ever installed in the estate.

In 1925 Hearst separated from his wife and began to spend time in Los Angeles overseeing his movie company, Cosmopolitan Pictures. His principal actress, Marion Davies, also became his constant companion and hostess at Hearst Castle. The ranch soon became a playground for the Hollywood crowd as well as for dignitaries like Winston Churchill and playwright

---

**The Experience Tour (Tour 1)** is ideal for first-time visitors and is the first to get filled up. In addition to the swimming pools, this tour visits several rooms on the ground floor of Casa Grande, including Hearst's private theater, where you'll see some home movies taken during the castle's heyday. **Tour 2** focuses on Casa Grande's upper floors, including Hearst's opulent library, private suite of rooms, and lots of fabulous bathrooms. Tour 2 is a perfectly fine choice for first-timers if you're only planning to take one tour, particularly if your interest lies more in the home's private areas. **Tour 3,** which delves into the construction and subsequent alterations of Hearst Castle, is fascinating for architecture buffs and detail hounds, but it shouldn't be the first and only tour if you've never visited the castle before. From April to October, **Tour 4** is dedicated to the estate's gardens, terraces, and walkways, the Casa del Mar guesthouse, the wine cellar of Casa Grande, and the dressing rooms at the Neptune Pool. This tour does not visit any of the interiors of the main house.

**Evening tours** are held most Friday and Saturday nights during spring and fall, and usually nightly around Christmas (when the house, decked out for the holidays, is

George Bernard Shaw, who is said to have wryly remarked of the estate, "This is the way God would have done it if He had the money."

Despite its opulence, Hearst promoted "the ranch" as a casual weekend home. He regularly laid the massive refectory table in the dining room with paper napkins and bottled ketchup and pickles to evoke a rustic camplike atmosphere. In Hearst's beautiful library, his priceless collection of ancient Greek pottery—one of the greatest collections of its kind in the world—is arranged casually among the rare volumes, like knickknacks.

W. R. Hearst and Marion Davies hosted frequent costume parties at the ranch, which were as intricately planned as a movie production. The most legendary, the Circus Party, was held to celebrate W.R.'s 75th birthday on April 29, 1938. Much of Hollywood attended to honor the tycoon, including grande dame Bette Davis—dressed as a bearded lady. The Hollywood crowd would take Hearst's private railway car from Los Angeles to San Luis Obispo, where a fleet of limousines waited to transport them to San Simeon. Those who didn't come by train were treated to a flight on Hearst's private plane from the Burbank airport (MGM head Irving Thalberg and his wife, Norma Shearer, preferred this mode of transportation). Hearst, an avid aviator, had a landing strip built; Charles Lindbergh used it when he flew up for a visit in the summer of 1928.

Oh, if the walls could talk. . . . Atop one of the castle's towers are the hexagonal Celestial Suites. One was a favorite of Clark Gable and Carole Lombard, who would be startled out of their romantic slumber by the clamor of 18 carillon bells overhead. David Niven, a frequent guest, was one of the unknown number who defied Hearst's edict against liquor in private rooms: Niven was called upon more than once to explain the "empties" under the bed (which Cardinal Richelieu once owned) in his customary suite.

magical). Thirty minutes longer than the daytime tours, they visit highlights of the main house, the most elaborate guesthouse, and the illuminated pools and gardens.

No matter how many tours you take in a day, you must return to the visitor center each time and ride the bus back to the top of the hill with your tour group, so allow at least 2 hours between tours when you buy your tickets. You'll find plenty to keep you busy at the visitor center before, after, and in between tours: an observation deck of the Enchanted Hill, two gift shops, ball-park-quality food vendors, and a good small museum. The permanent William Randolph Hearst Exhibit focuses on the castle's history, art, and architecture.

You can visit the giant-screen **Hearst Castle National Geographic Theater** regardless of whether you take a tour. Larger-than-life films include the 40-minute Hearst Castle: Building the Dream and other films in five-story-high iWERKS format (just like IMAX) with seven-channel surround sound. Shows begin every 45 minutes throughout the day. The movie is included in the price of Tour One; by itself it's $8 for adults, $6 for kids 6 to 17. For current information, call © **805/927-6811** or visit their website at www.ngtheater.com.

Wear comfortable shoes—you'll walk about a half-mile per tour, each of which includes 150 to 400 steps. (Wheelchair tours are available by calling © **800/444-4445** or 805/927-2020, with 10 days notice.)

## WHAT TO SEE & DO IN NEARBY CAMBRIA ⭐

After driving for close to an hour without passing anything but lush green hills (especially from Hwy. 46 off U.S. 101), it's a pleasant surprise to roll into the endearing coastal town of Cambria (pronounced "*Cam*-bree-uh"), 6 miles south of San Simeon. Not quite Northern Californian and not quite Southern California, not quite coastal and not quite inland, this charming artists' colony is so appealing that the town itself is reason enough to make the drive. With little more than 4 blocks worth of shops, restaurants, and a handful of B&Bs, Cambria is the perfect place to escape the everyday, enjoy the endless expanses of pristine coastal terrain, and meander through little shops selling local artwork and antiques.

Cambria has three distinct parts. Along Main Street is "the Village," which is divided into two sections: the **West Village** and the **East Village.** The West Village is the newer, somewhat more touristy end of town where you'll find the visitor information center. The more historic East Village is a bit quieter, more locals-oriented, and a tad more sophisticated than the West Village. If you cross Highway 1 to the coastal side at the far west end of town (or the north end, if you're considering how the freeway runs), you'll reach Cambria's third part, **Moonstone Beach.** Lined with motels, inns, and a few restaurants on the inland side of the street, ocean-facing Moonstone Beach Drive is my favorite place to stay in Cambria.

Before you set out, pick up the Cambria Historical Society's brochure at your hotel and take a simple, fun **self-guided tour** of the historical buildings in the East Village. You'll not only get a history lesson about this picturesque village, but you'll also discover a few places you may have overlooked otherwise, such as the **blacksmith shop** at 4121 Burton Dr. or the **Santa Rosa Chapel and Cemetery** at 2352 Main St.

An overnight stay in Cambia also allows visitors to see the coastal region's "new" attraction: a spring (yes, that's the correct term—I looked it up) of elephant seals sunning themselves on the beaches year-round. Once thought to be extinct, since 1990 these 3,000-pound mammals have returned to Piedras Blancas, an **elephant seal rookery** 12 miles north of Cambria. Today more than 2,000 of these magnificent, prehistoric-looking beasts are counted here annually. Breeding takes place here December through March; molting occurs August through September. Keep your distance from the elephant seals: They're a protected species and can be dangerous if approached. Finding the beach is easy: Just stop at the packed parking lot 4.5 miles north of Hearst Castle and follow the crowds along the short, sandy walk for a good vantage. Docents wearing blue jackets are usually on hand to answer questions. The beaches and coves are also great places for humans to cavort as well. For more information log onto www.beachcalifornia.com/piedras.html.

### SHOPPING

Shopping is a major pastime in the village. Boutique owners are hyper-savvy about keeping their merchandise current—and priced just a hair lower than L.A. or San Francisco. This close-knit community has always attracted artists and artisans. For the finest handcrafted glass artworks, from affordable jewelry to investment-scale sculpture, head to **Seekers Collection & Gallery,** 4090 Burton Dr. (© **800/841-5250;** www.seekers glass.com). Nearby, at **Moonstones Gallery,** 4070 Burton Dr. (© **805/927-3447**), you'll find a selection of works ranging from woven crafts to jewelry and an exceptional collection of woodcarvings and other crafts. The shopping highlight of the West Village is **Home Arts**, 727 Main St. (© **805/927-2781;** www.home-arts.com), which offers an appealingly eclectic mix of country and contemporary home fashions and gifts. If a visit to the nearby Paso Robles wine country has inspired you, **Fermentations,** 4056 Burton Dr. (© **800/446-7505;** www.fermentations.com), has wines, wine accessories, and gifts, plus wine country gourmet goodies open for tasting. **Heart's Ease,** 4101 Burton Dr. (© **800/266-4372** or 805/927-5224), is inside a historic cottage and is packed with an abundance of garden delights, apothecary herbs, and custom-blended potpourris.

If Cambria has aroused your artistic instincts, a few miles south is another charming, tiny artists colony, **Harmony.**

## WHERE TO STAY

Because of its proximity, most people use Cambria as the jumping-off point for a visit to San Simeon. Cambria's popularity in summertime and on holiday weekends makes advance planning necessary. If my favorites are full, try one of these alternatives: **Captain's Cove Inn,** 6454 Moonstone Beach Dr. (© **800/781-COVE** or 805/927-8581; www.captainscoveinn.com), is a small beachfront B&B whose motel-style exterior belies the array of creature comforts provided by the family owners. The **Ragged Point Inn,** 19019 Hwy. 1 (© **805/927-4502;** www.raggedpointinn.com), is 21 miles north of Cambria, with ocean views from every room. It's a great choice if you're planning to explore both Hearst Castle and the Big Sur Coast from one perch.

If you want a cheaper choice, try the **Creekside Inn,** 2618 Main St., Cambria (© **800/269-5212** or 805/927-4021; www.cambriacreeksideinn.com). It's basic, but the village location is extremely convenient and the rates are considerably lower—$69 to $159 double, year-round. Still too expensive? One mile north is **San Simeon State Beach** (© **800/444-7275** or 805/927-2020), a 133-site beachfront campground.

*Note:* If you can't find a vacancy anywhere in Cambria, the tiny town of San Simeon, 6 miles north, has numerous run-of-the-mill motels lining both sides of Highway 1, but I only recommend staying here as a last resort.

### Best Western Cavalier Oceanfront Resort ★ *Kids*    Of the dozen or so budget and midrange motels along Highway 1 near Hearst Castle, this surprisingly nice chain is the only one that's oceanfront. Sprawled across a slope, the family-owned hotel invites guests to huddle around cliff-side bonfires each evening. Every room—whether you choose a basic double or opt for a fireplace, ocean view, wet bar, or oceanfront terrace—features an array of amenities. On-site extras include two heated pools, a Jacuzzi, an exercise room, two restaurants, and a coin-op laundry, plus video rentals next door. The motel welcomes pets, and it's a terrific choice for castle-bound families.

9415 Hearst Dr. (Hwy. 1), San Simeon, CA 93452. © **800/826-8168** or 805/927-4688. Fax 805/927-6472. www. cavalierresort.com. 90 units. $139–$279 double. AE, DC, DISC, MC, V. Pets accepted. **Amenities:** 2 restaurants; 2 outdoor heated pools; Jacuzzi; exercise room; concierge; room service (7am–9pm); coin-op laundry. *In room:* TV/DVD, dataport, minibar, fridge, coffeemaker, hair dryer, iron.

### Cambria Pines Lodge ★    On a mountain just above town on 25 acres of mostly landscaped grounds dotted with Monterey pines, the Cambria Pines is equal parts vacation lodge and summer camp. Accommodations are in 31 different buildings, and range from rustic, secluded cabins to contemporary hotel-style units. At the heart is the main lodge, a re-creation of the original 1927 building. Nearly all the rooms have

fireplaces; dedicated bargain hunters can snag the lowest rates by choosing an older cabin without one. Bonus points for the awesome, nearly Olympic-size pool.

2905 Burton Dr., Cambria, CA 93428. ℂ **800/445-6868** or 805/927-4200. Fax 805/927-4016. www.cambriapines lodge.com. 125 units. $109–$299 double. Rates include buffet breakfast. AE, DC, DISC, MC, V. **Amenities:** Restaurant; large heated pool; Jacuzzi; massage. In room: A/C, TV, fridge, coffeemaker, hair dryer, iron.

## FogCatcher Inn ★

You'll spot the FogCatcher by its faux English Tudor architecture (though a contemporary hotel), that fits right in with the mishmash of styles on funky Moonstone Beach. The U-shaped building is situated so many rooms have unencumbered views of the crashing waves across the street; some gaze oceanward over a sea of parked cars, and others are hopelessly landlocked—be sure to inquire when reserving. Rates vary wildly according to view, but each room interior has identical amenities and comforts. Immaculately maintained and furnished in a comfy cottage style with pine furniture, each room is made cozier by a gas fireplace and also has a microwave oven. Unlike many comparably priced Moonstone Beach lodgings, the FogCatcher has a heated swimming pool and Jacuzzi. Stop by the breakfast room in the morning for basic coffee, juice, and muffins to start the day.

6400 Moonstone Beach Dr., Cambria, CA 93428. ℂ **800/425-4121** or 805/927-1400. Fax 805/927-0204. www. fogcatcherinn.com. 60 units. $199–$279 double; from $369 suites. Rates include continental breakfast. AE, DISC, MC, V. Pets accepted in select rooms w/$25 fee per night. **Amenities:** Outdoor heated pool; Jacuzzi. In room: TV, minibar, fridge, coffeemaker, hair dryer, iron, fireplace.

## J. Patrick House ★

Hidden in a pine-filled neighborhood overlooking Cambria's village, this B&B is cozy, elegant, and welcoming. The main house is a two-story log cabin, where each afternoon innkeepers Ann and John host wine and hors d'oeuvres next to the living room fireplace, and each morning serve breakfast by windows overlooking a hummingbird-filled garden. Most guest rooms are in the adjacent carriage house and all feature wood-burning fireplaces, feather duvets, bedtime milk and cookies, and knotty pine, bent-twig furniture, calico prints, and hand-stitched quilts. Amenities like phone, fax, and guest fridge are in the common area.

2990 Burton Dr., Cambria, CA 93428. ℂ **800/341-5258** or 805/927-3812. Fax 805/927-6759. www.jpatrickhouse. com. 8 units. $155–$195 double. Rates include full breakfast, afternoon wine/hors d'oeuvres, and evening milk and cookies. Seasonal discounts and packages available. DISC, MC, V. In room: Hair dryer, iron, CD/radio, no phone.

## Olallieberry Inn ★★

This 1873 Greek Revival house is my favorite B&B in the area. In the afternoon the aromas of baked brie and homemade bread (served during the wine hour) waft through the main house, and the staff does everything imaginable to make your stay special. They also have a passion for cooking and gardening, but the decor doesn't fall by the wayside: A countrified berry motif reigns, and the guest rooms are lovingly and individually appointed. Each has its own private bathroom, although some are across or down the hall. Rooms in an adjoining building overlook a creek and have a fireplace and private deck. The full breakfast—accompanied by olallieberry jam, of course—is gourmet all the way. Amenities like phone, fax, and guest fridge are available in the common area.

2476 Main St., Cambria, CA 93428. ℂ **888/927-3222** or 805/927-3222. Fax 805/927-0202. www.olallieberry.com. 9 units. $115–$210 double. Rates include full breakfast and evening wine and hors d'oeuvres. AE, MC, V. **Amenities:** Massage. In room: Hair dryer, iron available upon request, no phone.

## WHERE TO DINE

Tiny Cambria boasts an unusual concentration of superb restaurants. In addition to the restaurants listed below, consider **Moonstone Beach Bar & Grill,** 6550 Moonstone

Beach Dr. (© **805/927-3859;** www.moonstonebeach.com), whose incredible view must be what accounts for prices on the expensive side for this tasty but casual restaurant—stick to breakfast or lunch; or local institution **Linn's Main Binn Restaurant,** 2277 Main St. (© **805/927-1499;** www.linnsfruitbin.com), a casual all-day farmhouse restaurant/bakery/gift shop featuring homemade pot pies, fresh-from-the-farm salads, breakfast treats, and Linn's famous olallieberry fruit pies.

**Mustache Pete's** *Kids* ITALIAN    The friendly, casual atmosphere makes this a great place for families. The main menu attraction is the gourmet pizzas, a staple that seems indigenous to California/Italian eateries. You won't be disappointed by the variety, however. Also on the menu are traditional pasta dishes that come in big portions and are served with soup or salad.

4090 Burton Dr., Cambria © 805/927-8589. www.mustachepetes.com. Main courses $6–$16. AE, DISC, MC, V. Mon–Sat 11am–10pm; Sun 10am–10pm.

**Robin's** ✦ INTERNATIONAL    Robin's is a restaurant with something for everyone, from exotic dishes from Mexico, Thailand, India, and beyond to more straightforward preparations like a tasty salad, a juicy steak, and a nightly vegetarian dish, along with tofu and tempeh specials. Offerings include a salmon bisque appetizer; artichoke and Gorgonzola ravioli in a spinach-cream sauce; and other combinations such as tandoori prawns with basmati brown rice, fruit chutney, and *chapati;* and *roghan josh,* Indian lamb curry mixed with yogurt, almonds, and toasted coconut. Don't miss dessert—try the espresso-soaked cake with mascarpone mousse and shaved chocolate or vanilla-custard bread pudding.

4095 Burton Dr., Cambria. © 805/927-5007. www.robinsrestaurant.com. Reservations recommended. Main courses $7–$13 lunch, $11–$18 dinner. MC, V. Daily 11am–9pm (later in summer).

**Sea Chest Oyster Bar** ✦ SEAFOOD    Feeling like a dozen other seaside old-salt hangouts, the strangely familiar Sea Chest is a must for seafood lovers. Sporting nautical kitsch and warm, welcoming atmosphere, this gray clapboard cottage even has a game-filled lounge complete with cribbage, checkers, and chess to keep you amused during the inevitable wait for a table. Oysters are the main attraction: on the half shell, oyster stew, oysters Casino, oysters Rockefeller, or "devils on horseback" (with wine, garlic, and bacon). The menu is also filled with fresh seafood from local and worldwide waters: steamed New Zealand green-lipped mussels, clams in several preparations, halibut, salmon, lobster, scampi, plus whatever looked good off the boats that morning. There's a respectable list of microbrewed and imported beers, along with a selection of Central Coast wines. *Note:* If you don't enjoy seafood, stay away—there's not even a token steak on this menu!

6216 Moonstone Beach Dr. © 805/927-4514. Reservations not accepted. Main courses $11–$22. No credit cards. Daily 5:30–9pm (closed Tues Sept–May).

**Sow's Ear Café** ✦✦ AMERICAN/SEAFOOD    Despite the porcine moniker, this tiny old cottage at the center of the village is a rather warm and romantic hideaway. The best tables are in the fireside front room, lit just enough to highlight its rustic wood-and-brick decor. Pigs appear everywhere, in oil paintings, as ceramic or cast-iron models, and the logo is a woodcut sow. Though the menu features plenty of contemporary California cuisine, the most popular dishes are American favorites given a contemporary lift; these include a warmly satisfying chicken-fried steak with gravy, chicken and dumplings, and zesty baby pork ribs. Other standouts are parchment-wrapped salmon, and pork loin glazed with chunky olallieberry chutney. Every meal begins with the restaurant's signature marbled bread baked in terra-cotta flowerpots, and the wine list is among the area's best. *Tip:* Early birds (5–6pm nightly) choose from eight dinners from $12 to $20.

2248 Main St. ℂ **805/927-4865.** www.thesowsear.com. Reservations recommended. Main courses $14–$23. DISC, MC, V. Daily 5–9pm (open later in summer).

## 2 Morro Bay

124 miles S of Monterey; 235 miles S of San Francisco (via Hwy. 1); 220 miles N of L.A.

Morro Bay is separated from the ocean by a long peninsula of towering sand dunes. It's best known for dramatic **Morro Rock,** an enormous egg-shaped monolith that juts 576 feet above of the water at the entrance to Morro Bay. Across from the rock, a huge oceanfront electrical plant mars the visual appeal of the otherwise pristine bay, which is filled with birds, sea mammals, and calm water offering plenty of recreational activities such as fishing, surfing, kayaking, bird watching (Morro Rock is a protected falcon sanctuary), and beachcombing.

Other than gawking at the "Gibraltar of the Pacific," there's not all that much to see in the town itself. Tourist-trade motels, shops, and seafood restaurants line the waterfront Embarcadero and adjacent blocks, but the town's best feature is its setting: The beaches, bay, and wildlife sanctuaries are the main reason to visit.

### ESSENTIALS

Morro Bay is on U.S. 101 (itself only four lanes on this stretch). The **Morro Bay Visitors Center & Chamber of Commerce,** 845 Embarcadero Rd., Morro Bay, CA 93442 (ℂ **800/231-0592** or 805/772-4467; www.morrobay.org), offers lots of information on their website. The visitor center is open Monday through Friday from 8:30am to 5pm and Saturday from 10am to 3pm. For additional online information log onto **www.morrobay.com**.

### EXPLORING THE AREA

Most visitors come to Morro Bay to ogle **Morro Rock,** the much-photographed Central Coast icon that anchors the mouth of the waterway. This ancient landmark, whose name comes from the Spanish word for a Moorish turban, is a volcanic remnant inhabited by the peregrine falcon and other migratory birds.

**BEACHES**   Popular **Atascadero State Beach,** just north of Morro Rock, has gentle waves and pretty views. Restrooms, showers, and dressing rooms are available. Just north of Atascadero is **Morro Strand State Beach,** a long, sandy stretch with normally gentle surf. Restrooms and picnic tables are available. Morro Strand has its own campgrounds; for information, call ℂ **805/772-2560,** or reserve through **ReserveAmerica** (ℂ **800/444-7275;** www.reserveamerica.com).

**STATE PARKS**   Cabrillo Peak, in the **Morro Bay State Park** (ℂ **805/772-7434**), makes a terrific day hike and offers 360-degree views from its summit. There's a zigzagging trail, but the best way to reach the top is by bushwhacking straight up the gentle slope—a hike that takes about 2 hours round-trip. To reach the trail head, take Highway 1 south and turn left at the Morro Bay State Park/Montana de Oro State Park exit. Follow South Bay Boulevard for three-quarters of a mile, then take the left fork another half a mile to the Cabrillo Peak dirt parking lot on your left. The park also offers camping and the oceanside **Morro Bay Golf Course** (aka "Poor Man's Pebble Beach"), which charges only $41 for weekend greens fees (ℂ **805/782-8060**).

South of Morro Bay in Los Osos is **Montana de Oro State Park** ("Mountain of Gold"), known as "petite Big Sur" because of its stony cliffs and rugged terrain. There's great swimming at Spooner's Cove and lots of easy hiking trails, including some that lead to coastal vistas or forest streams. The Hazard Reef Trail will take you up on the Morro Bay Sandspit dunes. The park's campground is in the trees, across from the beach, and is worth the detour, if you have a reservation in summer. For information, call the park rangers (© **805/528-0513**), or reserve a spot through **ReserveAmerica** (© **800/444-7275;** www.reserveamerica.com).

**ON THE WATER**    You can take a kayak tour around the bay with **Kayak Horizons of Morro Bay,** 551 Embarcadero (© **805/772-6444;** www.kayakhorizons.com).

**IN TOWN**    The Embarcadero is also home to the **Giant Chessboard,** whose 3-foot-tall, 18- to 20-pound redwood pieces were inspired by open-air boards in Germany. If you're up for a game, contact the Rec & Parks Dept for reservations at © **805/772-6278.** Nearby is the **Morro Bay Aquarium,** 595 Embarcadero (© **805/772-7647**), a modest operation notable for the injured or abandoned sea otters, seals, and sea lions it rescues and rehabilitates. During their stay, animals learn to perform tricks for a morsel of food (admission is $2 for adults, $1 for children 5–11).

## WHERE TO STAY

**Baywood Bed & Breakfast Inn** *Finds*    South of Morro Bay in Baywood Park, facing out onto Morro's "back bay," this two-story gray inn is a 1970s garden-style office building with B&B suites, each furnished in a distinctive (over-the-top) theme and Grandma-style flair. Every room has a private entrance, gas fireplace, and microwave (plus a fridge stocked with complimentary sodas and snacks); all but a few have bay views. Included in your stay is a full breakfast each morning and a late-afternoon wine-and-cheese reception highlighted by a room tour. If you're looking for solitude, Baywood Park fits the bill. There are a couple of decent restaurants on the block, and pretty Montana de Oro is close by.

1370 Second St. (2½ blocks south of Santa Ysabel Ave.), Baywood Park, CA 93042. © **805/528-8888.** Fax 805/528-8887. www.baywoodinn.com. 18 units. $90–$170 double; from $110–$180 suite. Extra person $15. Rates include full breakfast and afternoon wine and cheese. MC, V. *In room:* TV/VCR, kitchenette, minibar, fridge, coffeemaker, hair dryer.

**The Inn at Morro Bay**    This comfortable, moderately priced resort is smart enough to let its natural surroundings be the focus. Right on the water, the inn's two-story Cape Cod–style buildings have contemporary interiors amid a quiet garden setting. Rates vary according to view; the best rooms have unobstructed views of Morro Rock; addition upgrades include private balcony Jacuzzis and bayfront sun decks. Those in back face the swimming pool, gardens, and eucalyptus-forested golf course at Morro Bay State Park (see above). The hotel has a bayside lounge and California/Mediterranean restaurant, and a full-service spa and wellness center. Beach cruisers are lent out free to guests, and even the range balls are complimentary.

60 State Park Rd., Morro Bay, CA 93442. © **800/321-9566** or 805/772-5651. Fax 805/772-4779. www.innatmorrobay.com. 98 units. $159–$379 double. Midweek and seasonal discounts available. AE, DISC, MC, V. Take Main St. south, past park entrance. **Amenities:** 2 restaurants; lounge; outdoor heated pool; nearby golf and water recreation; full-service spa; complimentary bikes; room service (7am–10pm); massage; babysitting. *In room:* TV, dataport, fridge, coffeemaker, hair dryer, iron, CD player.

## WHERE TO DINE

**Hofbrau** *Value* *Kids* GERMAN/AMERICAN   When you're hungry in Morro Bay and want something other than fish and chips, Hofbrau is the place. Although they do serve the standard wharfside fare, the star here is the roast beef French Dip (their strategically placed carving station ensures its popularity). Those in the know order the minisandwich, which is a dollar less and just an inch shorter. As the name would suggest, they have a good selection of beers as well as a kids' menu.

901 Embarcadero. © 805/772-2411. Reservations not accepted. Most items $4.25–$8.75. AE, DISC, MC, V. Daily 11am–9pm.

**Windows on the Water** ☞ CALIFORNIA   If you're looking for a special meal in town, your best bet is this seaside restaurant that takes full advantage of prime waterfront views with its airy, high-ceilinged, multilevel space. The cuisine emanating from the open kitchen is a California/French/Mediterranean hybrid that incorporates local fresh seafood and produce. On a given evening the menu might include seared halibut in a Dijon crust offset by sweet-tangy orange marmalade and tequila sauce, shellfish braised in champagne and tossed with house-made fettuccine, or pheasant breast enveloped in prosciutto and brie atop a Riesling reduction sauce. The first-rate wine list includes choice Central Coast vintages and select French bottles. *Tip:* Tuesday is oyster night: fresh, fried, or "shootered," they're 65 cents each all evening.

699 Embarcadero (in Marina Sq.). © 805/772-0677. www.windowsonthewater.net. Reservations recommended. Main courses $17–$27. AE, DC, DISC, MC, V. Daily 5–10pm.

## 3 San Luis Obispo ☞

38 miles S of Cambria; 226 miles S of San Francisco; 198 miles N of L.A.

Because the town of San Luis Obispo is not visible from U.S. 101, even many Californians don't know that it's more than another fast-food-and-gasoline stopover on the highway. But its "secret" location is part of what helps this relaxed yet vital college town keep its charm and character intact—it has much of the appeal that defined Santa Barbara a few decades ago.

San Luis Obispo (SLO to locals) is tucked into the mountains halfway between San Francisco and Los Angeles. It's surrounded by green, pristine mountain ranges and filled with a mix of college kids attending California Polytechnic University (Cal Poly for short), big-city transplants, and agricultural folk.

The town grew up around an 18th-century mission, and its dozens of historic landmarks, Victorian homes, shops, and restaurants are its primary attractions for visitors. Today it's still kinda quaint, almost undiscovered, and best ventured around on foot. It also makes a good base for exploration of the region as a whole. To the west of town, a short drive away, are some of the state's prettiest swimming beaches; to the north and south you'll find the Central Coast's wine country, home to dozens of respectable wineries and bucolic scenery.

### ESSENTIALS

**GETTING THERE**   U.S. 101, one of the state's primary north-south roadways, runs through San Luis Obispo; it's the fastest land route here from anywhere. If you're driving down along the coast, Highway 1 is the way to go for its natural beauty and oceanfront cliffs. If you're entering the city from the east, take Highway 46 or 41 to U.S. 101, then go south. **Amtrak** (© **800/USA-RAIL;** www.amtrak.com) offers daily service into SLO from Oakland and Los Angeles.

**VISITOR INFORMATION** At the **San Luis Obispo Visitors Center,** 1039 Chorro St. (© **805/781-2777;** www.visitslo.com), downtown between Monterey and Higuera streets, you can pick up the colorful, comprehensive *Visitors Guide* and self-guided *Points of Interest Walking Tour.* It's open Sunday and Monday from 10am to 5pm, Tuesday and Wednesday from 8am to 5pm, Thursday from 8am to 8pm, Friday from 8am to 7pm, and Saturday from 10am to 7pm.

**ORIENTATION** San Luis Obispo is about 10 miles inland, at the junction of Highway 1 and U.S. 101. The downtown is laid out in a grid, roughly centered on the historic mission and its Mission Plaza (see below). Most of the main tourist sights are around the mission, within the small triangle created by U.S. 101 and Santa Rosa and Marsh streets.

## EXPLORING THE TOWN

Before heading downtown, make a pit stop at the perpetually pink **Madonna Inn,** 100 Madonna Rd., off U.S. 101 (© **805/543-3000;** p. 419), if for no other reason than to use its unique public restrooms (the men's has a waterfall urinal; the women's is a barrage of crimson and pink). Every inch of this place is an exercise in excess, from the dining room, complete with pink leather booths, pink table linens, and colored sugar that's—you guessed it—piquantly pink, to the rock-walled, cavelike guest rooms. And if you think it's as gaudy as it gets, you should see it around Christmas time.

Once downtown, you can ride the free trolley that repeats a loop through downtown every 15 minutes daily from noon to 5pm. (Stops are well marked.)

**Ah Louis Store** *Finds* Mr. Ah Louis was a Cantonese immigrant who was lured to California by gold fever in 1856. Emerging from the mines empty-handed, he began a lucrative career as a labor contractor, hiring and organizing Chinese crews that built the railroad. In 1874 he opened this store. Today the store is rarely open, but if it is, you can browse the clutter of Asian merchandise. Don't be afraid to call—this is a worthwhile gem.

800 Palm St. (at Chorro St.). © 805/543-4332. Hours vary; serious shoppers phone in advance.

**Farmers Market** ☆ If you're in town on a Thursday, be sure to take an evening stroll down Higuera Street, when the county's largest weekly street fair fills 4 downtown city blocks. You'll find much more here than fresh-picked produce—there's an ever-changing array of street entertainment, open-pit barbecues, food stands, and market stalls selling flowers, cider, and other seasonal farm-fresh items. Surrounding stores typically stay open until 9pm.

Higuera St. (between Osos and Nipomo sts.). © 805/781-2777. Thurs 6–9pm (weather permitting).

**Mission San Luis Obispo de Tolosa** Founded by Father Junípero Serra in 1772, California's fifth mission was built with adobe bricks by Native American Chumash people. It remains one of the prettiest, most interesting structures in the Franciscan chain. Serra chose this valley for the site of his fifth mission based on tales of friendly natives and bountiful food. Here the traditional red-tile roof was first used atop a California mission, after the original thatched tule roofs repeatedly fell to hostile Native Americans' burning arrows. The former padres' quarters are now an excellent museum chronicling both Native American and missionary life through all eras of the mission's use. Allow about 30 to 45 minutes to tour the mission and its grounds.

**Mission Plaza,** a garden with brick paths and park benches fronting a creek in which children love to wade, still functions as San Luis Obispo's town square. It's the focal point for local festivities and activities, from live concerts to poetry readings and dance and theater productions. Check at the visitor center (see "Essentials," above) to find out what's on when you're in town.

At the south end of Mission Plaza, the **San Luis Obispo Art Center's** (© 805/543-8562), galleries display and sell an array of California-made art. Admission is free; hours are 11am to 5pm Wednesday through Monday (open daily July–Aug).

751 Palm St. © 805/781-8220. www.missionsanluisobispo.org. Free admission ($2 donation requested). Summer daily 9am–5pm (sometimes later); winter daily 9am–4pm.

## ATTRACTIONS OUTSIDE OF TOWN

Dozens of **wineries** offer tastings and tours daily and make for a fun diversion. See "The Central Coast Wine Country: Paso Robles & the Santa Ynez Valley," later in this chapter for further details. If you don't have time to tour the wineries or would like more information before heading out to taste, you can visit **Central Coast Wines,** 712 Higuera St. in downtown SLO (© 805/784-9463), a wine shop specializing in central coast wines, and offering daily wine tastings and weekly winemaker pourings.

## WHERE TO STAY

In addition to what's listed below, there's a pristine branch of **Holiday Inn Express** (© 800/465-4329 or 805/544-8600), and a reliable **Motel 6** (© 800/4-MOTEL-6 or 805/541-6992).

**Apple Farm Inn** ★★   Ultrapopular, the Apple Farm Inn is a peaceful getaway in a Disney-plantation kind of way. Every square inch of the immaculate Victorian-style farmhouse is adorable, with floral wallpaper, fresh flowers, and sugar-sweet colorful touches. No two rooms are alike, although each has a gas fireplace, large well-equipped bathroom, pine antiques, lavish country decor, and either a canopy four-poster or brass bed. Some bedrooms open onto cozy turreted sitting areas with romantic window seats; others have bay windows and a view of San Luis Creek, where a working mill spins its huge wheel to power an apple press. The outstanding service here includes nightly turndown and a morning wake-up knock, delivered with complimentary coffee or tea and a newspaper. Other features include complimentary cribs and train and airport shuttle service, as well as a full-service spa. The hotel shares a name with their on-site restaurant, one of Highway 101's best-loved pit stops.

Budget travelers can opt for the adjoining motel-style **Apple Farm Trellis Court,** which shares the inn's wonderful grounds. Rooms are smaller but well decorated, with gas fireplaces. Rates include continental breakfast and cost $139 to $239.

2015 Monterey St., San Luis Obispo, CA 93401. © 800/255-2040 or 805/544-2040. Fax 805/546-9495. www.apple farm.com. 104 units. $139–$359 double. Rates include complimentary morning coffee/tea and afternoon wine. AE, DISC, MC, V. **Amenities:** Restaurant; outdoor heated pool; Jacuzzi; room service (6am–11pm); laundry service; dry cleaning. *In room:* A/C, TV w/pay movies, dataport, hair dryer, iron.

**Garden Street Inn** ★   SLO's prettiest (and most-polished) bed-and-breakfast is this gracious Italianate/Queen Anne downtown. Built in 1887 and restored in 1990, the house is a monument to gentility and good taste. Each bedroom and suite is decorated with well-chosen antique armoires, fabric or paper wall coverings, and vintage memorabilia, and all have private baths. Choose one with a claw-foot tub, fireplace, whirlpool tub, or private deck—whatever suits your fancy. Breakfast is served in the stained-glass morning room, and each evening wine and cheese are laid out for guests. A well-stocked Goldtree Library is always available.

1212 Garden St. (between Marsh and Pacific), San Luis Obispo, CA 93401. © **800/488-2045** or 805/545-9802. Fax 805/545-9403. www.gardenstreetinn.com. 13 units. $145–$205 double. Rates include full breakfast and evening wine and cheese. AE, MC, V. *In room:* A/C, dataport.

**Madonna Inn** This one you've got to see for yourself. The creative imaginations of owners Alex (now deceased) and Phyllis Madonna gave birth to the wildest—and most superfluously garish—fantasy world this side of Graceland. For more than 45 years the only consistency throughout the hotel has been its color scheme: perpetual pink. Beyond that, it's a free-for-all. Although tongue-in-cheek, this place can seem tired and tacky, and some of the rooms could use updating. However, the lobby men's room with its rock-waterfall urinal and clamshell sinks is a must-see. One guest room features a trapezoidal bed—it's 5 feet long on one side and 6 feet long on the other. "Rock" rooms with zebra- or tiger-patterned bedspreads and stonelike showers and fireplaces conjure up thoughts of a Flintstones's Playboy palace. There are also blue rooms, red rooms, and over-the-top Spanish, Italian, Irish, Alps, Currier and Ives, Native American, Swiss, and hunting rooms. The cocktail lounge and steakhouse are also outlandishly ornate. Even if you don't stay here, stop by for a liquid refresher and check it out, particularly around Christmastime. *One caveat:* The Madonna Inn, surprisingly, lacks a swimming pool.

100 Madonna Rd. (off U.S. 101), San Luis Obispo, CA 93405. © **800/543-9666** or 805/543-3000. Fax 805/543-1800. www.madonnainn.com. 109 units. $147–$248 double; from $210 suite. AE, DISC, MC, V. **Amenities:** Restaurant; coffee shop; 2 lounges; massage center. *In room:* A/C, TV, coffeemaker, hair dryer, iron.

**Petit Soleil Bed et Breakfast** 🐸 Formerly known as the Adobe Inn, new owners John and Dianne Conner have taken this old motor inn and renovated it in a French country atmosphere in the spirit of their other BetB in France. Each room has quirky additions such as painted cupboards or a window-side reading nook; all have private bathrooms and phones for free local calls. Breakfast is served in a dining area that faces the street, but coffee snobs will delight in the strong, locally roasted blend, and hot offerings like quiche or caramel-apple French toast are a treat.

1473 Monterey St., San Luis Obispo, CA 93401. © **800/676-1588** or 805/549-0321. Fax 805/549-0383. www.petit soleilslo.com. 15 units. $129–$159 double. Rates include breakfast. Extra person $10. AE, DISC, MC, V. **Amenities:** Complimentary bikes. *In room:* TV, dataport, coffeemaker, hair dryer, iron, CD player.

## WHERE TO DINE

**Big Sky Cafe** 🐸 AMERICAN The folk-artsy fervor of San Luis shines at this Southwestern mirage, where local art and a blue, star-studded ceiling surround diners who come for fresh, healthy food. The menu is self-classified "modern food," a category that here means a dizzying international selection including Caribbean shrimp tacos with chipotle-lime yogurt, Thai curry pasta tossed with sautéed tiger shrimp, chilled sesame-ginger noodles, and breakfast's red-flannel turkey hash—a beet-fortified ragout topped with basil-Parmesan-glazed eggs. Big Sky's owner also runs L.A.'s funky Gumbo Pot, whose Cajun-Creole influences spice up the menu at every turn. In fact, this might be the only Central Coast outlet for decent jambalaya, gumbo, or authentically airy beignets.

1121 Broad St. © 805/545-5401. www.bigskycafe.com. Main courses $10–$17; lunch $6–$11; breakfast $5–$10. AE, MC, V. Mon–Sat 7am–10pm; Sun 8am–9pm.

**Buona Tavola** ★★ NORTHERN ITALIAN   Most choices in town are burger-and-sandwich casual, Buona Tavola offers well-prepared Italian food in a more upscale setting. You can stroll in wearing jeans, but the dining room, with checkerboard floors and original artwork, is warmer and more intimate than other spots in town. On the backyard terrace, you can enjoy your meal surrounded by magnolias, ficus, and grapevines. The menu boasts a number of salads on the antipasti list. Favorite pastas include *agnolotti de scampi allo zafferano*, house-made pockets filled with scampi, then served in a cream-saffron sauce; *linguini fra diavolo* served with Manila clams, mussels, and river shrimp in a spicy tomato sauce; or the classic *timballo di parma*, a vegetarian delight baked with two cheeses.

1037 Monterey St. ⓒ 805/545-8000. www.btslo.com. Reservations recommended. Main courses $12–$23. AE, DISC, MC, V. Mon–Fri 11:30am–2:30pm; Sun–Thurs 5:30–9:30pm; Fri–Sat 5:30–10pm.

**Mondéo Pronto** (*Value*) (*Kids*) INTERNATIONAL   Mondéo Pronto provides patrons an affordable bite of international fillings in a burrito-type wrap. But unlike most "wrap" restaurants in California, this place pays attention to presentation and freshness. Choices range from American versions like the Mardi Gras (a tomato tortilla with Cajun sausage, rock shrimp, Creole veggies, and jambalaya sauce) to Mediterranean selections like the Sicilian, with grilled portobello mushrooms, herb polenta, veggies, goat cheese, olives, capers, and sun-dried tomato pesto. "Fusion bowls" are satisfying, with such combinations as basil scampi, a shrimp dish over bowtie pasta with pesto, marinara, pine nuts, and herbs. Everything on the kids' menu is under $3, and as the menu states, "Substitutions and sides are no problem."

893 Higuera St. (in the plaza). ⓒ 805/544-2956. Most items $5–$7. MC, V. Sun–Wed 11am–9pm; Thurs–Sat 11am–10pm.

**Mo's Smokehouse BBQ** ★ BARBECUE   Just about everyone in SLO is a devotee of this place, whose reputation and great barbecue belie its humble ambience. It's not fancy, but you name it, they've got it—pork or baby back ribs, barbecued beef, and chicken in either a mild or hot sauce, accompanied by baked beans, bread, potato salad, or coleslaw. Practically everything on the menu is under $10.

970 Higuera St. (at Osos St.). ⓒ 805/544-6193. www.mosbbq.com. Most items $4.95–$13. AE, MC, V. Sun–Wed 11am–9pm; Thurs–Sat 11am–10pm.

## 4 Pismo Beach

13 miles S of San Luis Obispo

Just outside San Luis Obispo, on Pismo's 23-mile stretch of prime beachfront, flip-flops are the shoes of choice and surf wear is the dominant fashion. It's all about beach life here, so bring your bathing suit, your board, and a good book.

If building sand castles or tanning isn't your idea of fun, you can explore isolated dunes, cliff-sheltered tide pools, and old pirate coves. Bring your dog (Fido's welcome here) and play an endless game of fetch. Or go fishing—it's permitted from Pismo Beach Pier, which also offers arcade entertainment, bowling, and billiards. Pismo is also the only beach in the area that allows all-terrain vehicles on the dunes.

Because the town itself consists of little more than tourist shops and surf-and-turf restaurants, nearby San Luis Obispo is a far more charming place to stay. But if all you want are a few lazy days on a beautiful beach at half the price of an oceanfront room in Santa Barbara, Pismo is the perfect choice.

## ESSENTIALS

The **Pismo Beach Chamber of Commerce and Visitors Bureau,** 581 Dolliver St., Pismo Beach, CA 93449 (© **800/443-7778** or 805/773-4382; www.pismochamber. com), offers free brochures and information on local attractions, lodging, and dining. The office is open Monday through Saturday from 9am to 5pm and Sunday from 10am to 4pm. You can peruse their tourist information online at **www.classiccalifornia.com**.

## WHAT TO SEE & DO

**Beaches** in Pismo are exceptionally wide, making them some of the best in the state for sunning and playing. The beach north of Grand Avenue is popular with families and joggers. North of Wadsworth Street, the coast becomes dramatically rugged as it rambles northward to Shell Beach and Pirates Cove.

Pismo Beach was once one of the most famous places in America for **clamming,** but the famed "Pismo clam" reached near-extinction in the mid-1980s due to over-harvesting. If you'd like to dig for bivalves, you'll need to obtain a license and follow strict guidelines. Or come for the annual **Clam Festival:** Held at the pier each October since 1946, the celebration features a chowder cook-off, sand-sculpture contest, and Miss Pismo Beach pageant.

### The Rare Golden Sand Dunes of Guadalupe

The California coast was once rich in dramatic, windswept sand dunes, sheltered valleys of wildflowers and willows, and lakes full of pond turtles, red-legged frogs, muskrats, and nesting birds. San Francisco's dunes are now covered in part by Golden Gate Park, while Los Angeles's dunes were leveled to create beach towns and the airport. But travelers cruising the central coast have the chance to visit what's now a rare sight at the **Guadalupe-Nipomo Dunes Preserve** just north of the tiny agricultural hamlet of Guadalupe, about 20 minutes south of Pismo.

The preserve comprises 18 miles of the largest, most biodiverse coastal dune-lagoon ecosystem on the planet. They have been the subject of photographers such as Ansel Adams and Brett Weston; home to the Dunites, a utopian group of artists founded in 1931; and the setting for Cecil B. DeMille's spectacular 1923 film, *The Ten Commandments.* Designated by the Nature Conservancy as number one in its "Last Great Places on Earth" campaign, these dunes are now permanently protected for wildlife and passive recreation.

The **Dunes Center interpretive facility** (1055 Guadalupe St., Hwy. 1, Guadalupe; © **805/343-2455;** www.dunescenter.org), in a restored 1910 Craftsman-style home, is open Tuesdays through Sundays from 10am to 4pm, and a schedule of guided walks is available on the website.

The Dunes are accessible at the southern end by driving on West Main St. (Hwy. 166) to a parking lot just below Mussel Rock Dunes, the highest coastal dunes in the world. The middle of the dunes are accessible off Highway 1, 3 miles north of Guadalupe. Turn west onto Oso Flaco Lake Road, pay a small parking fee, and walk along a rare riparian corridor to a bridge that crosses Oso Flaco Lake. A 1-mile boardwalk leads you to the ocean through one of the best examples of coastal dune scrub in the country.

If **fishing** is more your style, you'll be pleased to know that no license is required to fish from Pismo Beach Pier. Catches here are largely bottom fish like red snapper and lingcod. There's a bait-and-tackle shop on the pier.

**Livery Stables,** 1207 Silver Spur Place (© **805/489-8100**), in Oceano (about 5 min. south of Pismo Beach), is one of the few places in the state that rents horses for riding on the beach. Horses go for about $20 per hour and can be ridden at your own pace, or you can opt for a guided ride.

From late November to February, thousands of migrating **monarch butterflies** take up residence in the area's eucalyptus and Monterey-pine-tree groves. The butterflies form dense clusters on the trees, each hanging with its wings over the one below it, providing warmth and shelter for the entire group. During the monarchs' stay, naturalists at Pismo State Beach conduct 45-minute narrated walks every Saturday and Sunday at 11am and 2pm (call © **805/772-2694** for tour information). The Butterfly Grove is on Highway 1, between Pismo Beach and Grover Beach, to the south.

## WHERE TO STAY

**Cottage Inn by the Sea** ⭐ One of Pismo Beach's newer cliffside lodgings, the Cottage Inn is a good, moderately priced choice for couples and families. With its thatched roofs and Laura Ashley–style decor, the country charm is evident inside and out. Rooms, refreshingly clean and spacious, range both in price and style from traditional to oceanview. All come with the amenities of a romantic inn (including fireplaces) as well as modern conveniences (like in-room microwaves). This seaside retreat is one of the best in town.

2351 Price St., Pismo Beach, CA 93449. © **888/440-8400** or 805/773-4617. Fax 805/773-8336. www.cottage-inn. com. 79 units. $179–$279 double. Rates include deluxe continental breakfast. Extra person $10. AE, DC, DISC, MC, V. Pets accepted w/$10-per–night fee. **Amenities:** Oceanfront heated pool and Jacuzzi. *In room:* TV w/pay movies and Nintendo, fridge, coffeemaker, hair dryer, iron, safe.

**Kon Tiki Inn** *Value* The over-the-top Polynesian architecture of this three-story gem is easy to spot from the freeway, and evokes memories of 1960s Waikiki hotels. Rooms are modest, small, and simply furnished with unremarkable faux bamboo furniture, yet each has an oceanfront balcony or patio. Outside, vast lawns slope gently toward the cliffs, broken only by the shielded, kidney-shaped swimming pool flanked by twin Jacuzzis. This humble hotel—which is privately owned and does no advertising—has a sandy beach with stairway access, and lacks the highway noise that plagues many neighbors.

1621 Price St., Pismo Beach, CA 93449. © **888/KON-TIKI** or 805/773-4833. Fax 805/773-6541. www.kontikiinn.com. 86 units. $99–$152 double. Extra person $16. AE, DISC, MC, V. **Amenities:** Outdoor heated pool; free access to adjacent health club; 2 Jacuzzis; laundry service. *In room:* TV w/pay movies, dataport, fridge, coffeemaker.

**The Sea Venture Resort** ⭐ If luxury accommodations overlooking the beach and an outdoor spa on your private deck sound like heaven to you, head for Sea Venture, a resort providing the most luxurious accommodations along Pismo Beach. Once in your room, you need only drag your tired feet through the thick forest-green carpeting and past the white country furnishings and feather bed, and turn on your gas fireplace to begin a relaxing stay. Rent a movie from the video library, schedule a massage, or bathe your weary bones in your own outdoor hydrotherapy spa tub. With the beach right outside your door, there's not much more you could ask for—although there is, in fact, more provided: plush robes, a wet bar, continental breakfast delivered to your room, and a restaurant on the premises with a tapas bar and Sunday brunch. Most rooms have ocean views and many have a private balcony overlooking the beach.

100 Ocean View Ave., Pismo Beach, CA 93449. © **800/760-0664** or 805/773-4994. Fax 805/773-0924. www.sea venture.com. 50 units. $179–$449 double. Rates include continental breakfast. AE, DC, DISC, MC, V. Take U.S. 101 to the Price St. exit, turn west onto Ocean View (at the beach). **Amenities:** Restaurant; outdoor heated pool; complimentary bikes; room service (5–9pm); massage center; laundry service; dry cleaning. *In room:* TV/VCR, dataport, minibar, coffeemaker, hair dryer, iron.

## WHERE TO DINE

Local icon **F. McLintocks** has a lock on Pismo with two crowd-pleasing oceanview restaurants: **F. McLintocks Saloon & Dining House,** 750 Mattie Rd. (across Hwy. 101; © **805/773-1892**), serves stick-to-your-ribs, ranch-style meals in an Old West setting. **Steamers of Pismo,** 1601 Price St. (© **805/773-4711**) serves "Miles of Clams" with options for landlubbers too.

**Giuseppe's Cucina Italiana** ⚘ SOUTHERN ITALIAN   This is the region's best southern Italian restaurant—would you believe owner Giuseppe DiFronza started it as his senior project at Cal Poly University? It's true, and DiFronza's love of cuisine from the Pugliese region (an Adriatic seaport) continues to bring diners a taste of the Italian countryside. Along with the homemade bread baked in a wood-burning oven imported from Italy, Giuseppe's fare uses authentic recipes, imported ingredients, and organically grown produce; the large menu of antipasti, salads, pizzas, pastas, fish, and steak makes it easy to find something you like. Highlights of the meal included linguine with shrimp, scallops, pancetta, and garlic in a vodka cream sauce, and seared *ahi* (tuna) with a peppercorn crust and garlic-caper aioli.

891 Price St. © **805/773-2870**. www.giuseppesrestaurant.com. Reservations not accepted. Main courses $7–$14 lunch, $9.50–$24 dinner. AE, DISC, MC, V. Mon–Fri 11:30am–3pm; nightly 4:30–10pm (until 11pm Fri–Sat).

**Splash Cafe** AMERICAN   This beachy burger stand, with a short menu and a few tables, gets high marks for its award-winning clam chowder in a sourdough bread bowl—more than 10,000 gallons a year are served. Fish and chips, burgers, hot dogs, and grilled ahi sandwiches are also available. Far-flung aficionados know that Splash ships its chowder frozen, overnight, anywhere in the U.S. (sourdough loaves, too). There's often a line, but it usually moves quickly.

197 Pomeroy St. (near Pismo Beach Pier). © **805/773-4653**. www.splashcafe.com. Most items $3–$7. MC, V. Daily 10am–8pm.

## 5 The Central Coast Wine Country: Paso Robles & the Santa Ynez Valley

Paso Robles: 29 miles N of San Luis Obispo; Solvang: 60 miles S of San Luis Obispo

When people talk about California wines, we usually assume they mean those from the Napa and Sonoma regions north of San Francisco. But here in California—and increasingly across the country thanks to the Academy award-winning comedy *Sideways*—wine lovers are becoming increasingly aware of quality vintages coming from the sun-drenched valleys of San Luis Obispo and Santa Barbara counties.

The truth is that the Central Coast Wine Country is the oldest of California's winegrowing regions. The old Franciscan missions strung along the coast, and just inland by it, attest to the area's heritage when early Spanish settlers planted grapevines and olive trees. But the area's wine production went into decline during Prohibition, and after it was repealed, Napa and Sonoma valleys shot ahead as the leading and best-known producers.

But in the last 25 years, the Central Coast has experienced a boom in grape production and winemaking, and with the new growth in winemaking has come general growth, much of it geared to visitors: hotels, spas, golf courses, restaurants, art galleries, museums, antiques stores, and even a Vegas-style casino attract a mostly well-over-40 clientele who appreciate the relaxed pace and beauty of the region (little of this area—except perhaps for the bakeries in Solvang—will thrill your kids).

The principal parts of the Central Coast Wine Country are **Paso Robles** (the town of this name and the surrounding countryside), **San Luis Obispo** (again, the town of the same name plus the nearby areas of Edna Valley and Arroyo Grande), and **northern Santa Barbara County** (the Santa Maria and Santa Ynez valleys). The great news for visitors is that these areas are distinct but sufficiently close together to make visiting all of them practical on even a short timetable. And staying in Paso Robles or San Luis Obispo is also a convenient option for visiting Hearst Castle (p. 405), offering more to do (or, at least, more to drink) than quaint Cambria.

## PASO ROBLES

Paso Robles ("pass of the oaks") is suitably named for the clusters of oak trees scattered throughout the rolling hills of this inland region. The town has a faintly checkered past: It was established in 1870 by Drury James, uncle of outlaw Jesse James (who hid out in tunnels under the original Paso Robles Inn). In 1913, pianist Ignace Paderewski came to live in Paso Robles, where he brought zinfandel vines for his ranch—Paderewski played often in the Paso Robles Inn, which today maintains a small exhibit in his honor in the lobby. He really wasn't here for long, returning to Poland after World War I, but the town today treats Paderewski like a native son.

Arriving in downtown Paso Robles is like taking a step back in time and right into a movie set. The main town square is surrounded by blocks of venerable Victorian-era buildings such as the public library, a neoclassical edifice from 1907. It's worth taking a leisurely stroll around the square before heading out into the rolling vineyards for an afternoon of wine tasting.

### ESSENTIALS

**GETTING THERE/ORIENTATION**    Paso Robles is on U.S. 101; there's an exit for the town's main thoroughfare, Spring Street. Highway 46 intersects, and briefly joins, U.S. 101. **Amtrak** (© **800/USA-RAIL;** www.amtrak.com) offers daily service to Paso Robles from Oakland and Los Angeles.

Many wineries are on the winding roads off Highway 46 on either side—try to cluster your visit according to this destination, visiting one side and then the other. You'll be able to feel how the weather on the western side, which is cooler due to higher elevations and frequent coastal fog, differs from the hotter east side, on a flat plain leading inland; winemakers bicker constantly over which conditions are better for growing wine grapes.

**VISITOR INFORMATION**    For a list of area wineries, tasting rooms, and seasonal events, contact the **Paso Robles Vintners and Growers Association,** 744 Oak St., Paso Robles, CA 93446 (© **800/549-WINE** or 805/239-8463; www.pasowine.com). Additional information on the area is offered by the **Paso Robles Chamber of Commerce and Visitors & Conference Bureau,** 1225 Park St., Paso Robles, CA 93446 (© **800/ 406-4040** or 805/238-0506; fax 805/238-0527; www.pasorobleschamber.com).

## TOURING THE LOCAL WINERIES

Growers have been tending vines in Paso Robles's fertile foothills since the turn of the century—the 19th century, that is. For decades, wine aficionados overlooked the area, even though in 1983 it was granted its own "Paso Robles" appellation (the official government designation of a recognized wine-producing region; "Napa Valley" and "Sonoma County" are probably more familiar). Around 1992, wine grapes surpassed lettuce as San Luis Obispo County's primary cash crop, and the region now has at least 75 wineries and more than 100 vineyards (which grow grapes but do not produce their own wine from them).

Paso Robles is reminiscent of Napa Valley way back in the '70s before it became a major tourist destination. Because not all wine enthusiasts are wine experts, an advantage of the area is its friendly attitude and small crowds, which make it easy to learn more about the winemaking process as you go along. Enjoy the relaxed rural atmosphere along two-lane country roads, driving leisurely from winery to winery and, more often than not, chatting with the winemaker while tasting his or her product.

**Eberle Winery**    Owner Gary Eberle, who's been making Paso Robles wine since 1973, is sometimes called the "grandfather of Paso Robles's Wine Country," because many of the new vintners in the area honed their craft working under his tutelage. A visit to Eberle Winery includes a tour through its underground caves, where hundreds of aging barrels share space with the Wild Boar Room, site of Eberle's monthly winemaker dinners featuring guest chefs from around the country (always held on Sat nights; the prix-fixe meal is around $110, including wine). Call for current events.

Hwy. 46 E. (3½ miles east of U.S. 101). ✆ **805/238-9607**. www.eberlewinery.com. Complimentary tastings daily 10am–5pm (until 6pm in summer).

**EOS Estate Winery at Arciero Vineyards**    Follow the checkered flag to the 700 acres of wine grapes owned by former race-car driver Frank Arciero, Sr. Arciero was drawn to the area by its resemblance to his native Italy; he passed through on his way to Laguna Seca, a racetrack near Salinas. (Trivia buffs know it as James Dean's intended destination in 1955, when he was killed in nearby Cholame while driving his Porsche.) The label specializes in Italian varietals *(nebbiolo, sangiovese)* and blends. The facility includes a self-guided tour, a race-car exhibit, rose gardens, a Mediterranean marketplace, and picnic area.

5625 Hwy. 46 E. (6 miles east of U.S. 101). ✆ **805/239-2562**. www.eosvintage.com. Complimentary tastings daily 10am–5pm (until 6pm summer weekends).

**Justin Vineyards & Winery** ★★★    At the end of a scenic country road lies Justin and Deborah Baldwin's boutique winery, and even a casual glance shows how much love and dedication the ex–Los Angelenos have put into their operation. The tasting room, dining room, offices, and even winemaking barns have a stylish Tuscan flair. Justin's flagship wine is a 2002 Isosceles, a Bordeaux-style blend that—at about $55 a bottle—is pricier than most area wines but exudes sophistication—and earns *Wine Spectator* raves. Also worth a try is their port-style dessert wine, called Obtuse. Tours of the winery are available by appointment only at 10:30am and 2:30pm and can be arranged via the reservation desk at ✆ 805/238.6932, ext. 300.

For a special treat, the winery has a luxurious four-suite B&B called the **JUST Inn.** Impeccably outfitted, the romantic inn has an undeniable serenity. Room rates are $295 to $395. Nightly dinners and weekend lunches are also offered to both guests and day-trippers—call ✆ 805/238-6932, ext.300, for advance reservations.

11680 Chimney Rock Rd. (15 miles west of U.S. 101). © **800/726-0049** or 805/237-4149. www.justinwine.com. Tastings daily 10am–5pm. Tasting fee $4, includes souvenir glass.

**Meridian Vineyards** ★ The local vintner with the largest profile is also the Central Coast's best-known label, producing more cases each year than all the other Paso wineries combined. Veteran winemaker Chuck Ortman brought a respected Napa Valley pedigree to Meridian; as a result, here's where you'll get the most Napa-like tasting experience. In addition to the beautiful natural stone winery there's a man-made lake surrounded by rolling lawns, majestic oak trees, and landscaped herb and flower gardens. Picnicking is encouraged.

7000 Hwy. 46 E. (7 miles east of U.S. 101). © **805/226-7133**. www.meridianvineyards.com. Complimentary tastings daily 10am–5pm.

**Summerwood Winery & Inn** ★★ There's a spit and polish about this sleek player in the Paso wine game. The former Treana Winery's elegant tasting room (Treana's still in business, crafting wonderful red blends at a different location with no public tastings) now features a gourmet deli for picnickers, plush fireside chairs for relaxed sipping, and the luxurious Summerwood Inn bed-and-breakfast set among the vines (see review below). With the help of internationally experienced winemaker Scott Hawley, Summerwood is turning out some of the best reds around, including cabernet and syrah from pedigreed estate vineyards.

2175 Arbor Rd. (at Hwy. 46 W., 1 mile west of U.S. 101). © **805/227-1365**. www.summerwoodwine.com. Complimentary tastings daily 10am–5:30pm (till 6pm in summer).

**Tobin James Cellars** ★★ Winemaker Tobin James is a walking contradiction. A lifelong wine expert who claims to wear the same pair of khaki shorts every day, Toby has patterned his winery in the spirit of local bad boys, the James Gang. The tasting room has a Wild West theme, a 100-year-old saloon bar, and plays country music, all serving to dispel the wine-snob atmosphere that prevails at so many other wineries. Tobin James's expertise lies in the production of a "user-friendly" zinfandel; the late-harvest dessert wine from zinfandel grapes is smooth and spicy.

8950 Union Rd. (at Hwy. 46 E., 8 miles east of U.S. 101). © **805/239-2204**. www.tobinjames.com. Complimentary tastings daily 10am–6pm.

**York Mountain Winery** *Finds* If you're impressed by "firsts" and "onlys," don't miss York Mountain. It was the first winery in the area (begun in 1882 by Andrew York, on land originally deeded by President Ulysses S. Grant) and is the oldest continuously operating vintner, as well as the only producer in the "York Mountain" viticulture appellation. In the century-old stone tasting room, look for a dry chardonnay with a complex, spicy aroma, and award-winning cabernet sauvignons, the best of which are the reserve bottlings from hand-chosen grapes.

7505 York Mountain Rd. (off Hwy. 46 W., 7 miles west of U.S. 101). © **805/238-3925**. www.yorkmountainwinery. com. Tasting fee $1. Tastings Thur–Mon 11am–4pm.

## WHERE TO STAY

Also see Justin Vineyards & Winery (p. 425) for lodging.

**Adelaide Inn** *Value* Tended with loving care that's rare among lower-priced accommodations, the Adelaide Inn stands out from other motels. Although it's adjacent to gas stations and coffee shops, attention has been paid to isolate this quiet, lushly landscaped property from its surroundings. The rooms are clean and comfortable with extra warmth, and the motel has a welcoming ambience. Unexpected comforts include complimentary newspaper and fruit and muffins. Facilities include summertime water diversions and even a putting green.

1215 Ysabel Ave., Paso Robles, CA 93446. ℂ 800/549-PASO or 805/238-2770. Fax 805/238-3497. www.adelaide inn.com. 67 units. $55–$89 double. Extra person $6. Rates include morning coffee and muffins. AE, DC, DISC, MC, V. From U.S. 101, exit Hwy. 46 E. Turn west at 24th St.; the hotel is just west of the freeway. **Amenities:** Heated outdoor pool; Jacuzzi; sauna; coin-op laundry and laundry service; dry cleaning. *In room:* A/C, TV w/pay movies, dataport, fridge, coffeemaker, hair dryer, iron.

**Paso Robles Inn**   This Mission Revival–style inn was built to replace the 1891 Stanford White masterpiece, El Paso De Robles Hotel, that burned in 1940. Photos of the landmark in its heyday line the Spanish-tiled lobby and adjacent dining room and cocktail lounge. A creek meanders through the oak-shaded property, and two-story motel units are scattered across the tranquil grounds. Well shielded from street noise, these rooms are simple but boast creature comforts (shiny bathrooms, gas fireplaces, and microwaves in many rooms) added in a 2000 update that, unfortunately, removed much of their nostalgic charm. The best rooms are worth the extra bucks: "Mineral Spa Rooms" with fireplaces and shielded outdoor Jacuzzis supplied by the property's mineral springs. Carports are located behind each building. The inn also has a steakhouse, retro-flavored coffee shop, and the Cattleman's Lounge, a local hot spot featuring live entertainment on weekends. *Tip:* Avoid room numbers beginning with 1 or 2—they're too close to the street.

1103 Spring St., Paso Robles, CA 93446. ℂ 800/676-1713 or 805/238-2660. www.pasoroblesinn.com. 100 units. $155–$175; spa room $245. Extra person $10. AE, MC, V. **Amenities:** 2 restaurants; lounge; outdoor heated pool; Jacuzzi; business center; room service (6am–9pm); laundry service; dry cleaning. *In room:* A/C, TV w/pay movies, dataport, fridge, coffeemaker, hair dryer, iron.

**The Summerwood Inn** ✪   The guest book at this elegant B&B sports more than its share of honeymooners drawn by the beautiful 46-acre setting and luxurious treatment. On the grounds of Summerwood Winery (p. 426), this three-story clapboard house looks like a cross between Queen Anne and Southern-plantation styles, but it's furnished in formal English country. It's a contemporary building, though, so rooms are spacious and bathrooms ultramodern; the main floor (including two guest rooms) is wheelchair accessible. Every room has a private balcony overlooking the vineyards, a gas fireplace, fresh flowers, and terry robes; morning coffee is left outside your door in insulated carafes.

2130 Arbor Rd. (P.O. Box 3260), Paso Robles, CA 93447. ℂ 805/227-1111. www.summerwoodinn.com. 9 units. $260–$310 double; $360 suite. Extra person $65. Rates include full breakfast, afternoon wine and hors d'oeuvres, and evening cookies. MC, V. From U.S. 101, exit Hwy. 46 W. Continue 1 mile to Arbor Rd. *In room:* A/C, TV, hair dryer.

**Villa Toscana Bed & Breakfast** ✪✪✪   This new all-suites inn, in the rolling vineyards at the Martin & Weyrich winery east of downtown, is fashioned after a lavish Spanish villa, with a colonnade-rimmed courtyard and fountains galore. The suites, each named after Martin & Weyrich wine, are quite spacious and individually decorated with a profusion of elegant frills of various colors (I prefer the rich moss green, purple and wheat tones of the Viognier suite, but that may be a guy thing). The beds are smartly set into recessed alcoves, and all guest rooms have Jacuzzi tubs, wood-beamed ceilings, kitchenettes, fireplaces, and expansive vineyard views. In-room spa treatments are also available. An excellent full breakfast is served either in-room, within the Bistro Kitchen, or outside in the sun-filled courtyard. Despite the beauty, what's offered may not be worth the high rack rates, but special deals are frequently offered on the Internet.

4230 Buena Vista Dr. (½ mile north of Circle B Rd.), Paso Robles, CA 93447. ⓒ 805/238-5600. Fax: 805/238-5605. www.myvillatoscana.com. 8 units. $360–$390 double; winemaker's residence $1,700–$1,900. AE, DISC, MC, V. *In room:* A/C, TV w/DVD/VCR, high-speed Internet, kitchenette, hair dryer, free DVD rental.

## WHERE TO DINE

You should also consider Paso's branch of the San Luis Obispo favorite, **Buona Tavola,** 943 Spring St. (ⓒ **805/237-0600;** www.btslo.com), whose house-made pastas and fresh-from-the-fields northern Italian cuisine are a welcome addition to town (see p. 420 for full review).

**Bistro Laurent** ★★ COUNTRY FRENCH   Executive chef/owner Laurent Grangien's sophisticated bistro caused quite a stir in this town unaccustomed to such innovations as a chef's tasting menu. But once the dust settled, everyone kept returning for the unpretentious neighborhood atmosphere, superb cuisine, and reasonable (at least by L.A. or San Francisco standards) prices. Whet your appetite with the crispy crab risotto hors d'oeuvre (the crispy tarts are addictive as well) and warm potato and goat cheese salad before plunging into main dishes such as rosemary-garlic chicken, venison *osso buco,* or shrimps and scallops served in puff pastry with asparagus and creamy tomato sauce. *Note:* The Bistro serves dinner only, but its sister restaurant next door, Le Petit Marcel (ⓒ **805/226-9750**), offers lunch fare in an open patio setting.

1202 Pine St., Paso Robles. ⓒ 805/226-8191. Reservations recommended. Main courses $15–$23. MC, V. Mon–Sat 4:30–10pm.

**McPhee's Grill** ★★ *Kids* CALIFORNIA GRILL   When Ian McPhee left Ian's Restaurant in Cambria and launched this one, it didn't take long for word to get out. McPhee's is worth the short drive to the historic town of Templeton. The converted old saloon features contemporary country decor, an open kitchen, and indoor and outdoor dining. The menu offers half a dozen appetizers such as a duck *carnitas* quesadilla, and seared ahi tuna on crispy sesame won-ton crackers with wasabi cream and pickled ginger. Gourmet pizza, pasta, an amazing macadamia-crusted Alaskan halibut, and four varieties of tender, juicy steaks cooked to perfection round out the Americana-with-a-twist-style menu. Especially impressive are the prices—it's rare that a restaurant "dedicated to great food and great service" offers the majority of its dishes for under $20. A champagne buffet brunch is offered on Sundays. McPhee's is one of the very best in the region, and families will appreciate the economical kids' menu.

416 Main St., Templeton. ⓒ 805/434-3204. www.mcphees.com. Reservations recommended. Main courses $9–$12 lunch, $15–$34 dinner; brunch $19 adults, $9 for kids under 10. MC, V. Mon–Sat 11:30am–2pm and 5–9pm; Sun 10am–2pm and 5–9pm.

**Odyssey World Café** *Value Kids* CONTINENTAL   Odyssey offers an eclectic range of foods reflecting world influences in a cozy, casual atmosphere at affordable prices. Lunch choices include salads, pizzas, pastas, sandwiches, wraps, gyros, oriental bowls, and rotisserie chicken, with full dinners available in the evening. The kids menu offers four choices they're sure to eat, each at $4.95. This is also the best place in Paso Robles to stock up on picnic foods.

1214 Pine St. (at 12th St.). ⓒ 805/237-7516. www.odysseyworldcafe.com. Reservations not accepted. Main courses $7–$15. AE, MC, V. Sun–Thurs 11am–8:30pm; Fri–Sun 11am–9pm.

## THE SANTA YNEZ VALLEY

The Santa Ynez Valley presents a soothing and intriguing blend of Arabian horses standing beside pristine vineyards, rolling pastures dotted with spreading oaks, graceful

Victorian farmhouses and barns beside cutting-edge wineries, all surrounded by imposing mountains. This is beautiful country, where the clear blue sky achieves a brilliance rarely seen in the smog-clogged cities to the south. In the Santa Ynez Valley the pace is slower and the locals friendlier, but don't expect to find yokels gnawing on hay—this is gentleman-farmer country, where some of the nicest ranches are gated and have video surveillance, and even Disney's Davy Crockett is a respected winemaker. This balance of old-fashioned living and modern amenities is what makes the area so enjoyable: You can read in the shade of an oak tree one day and go on a wine tasting adventure the next. Just minutes away from one another, Los Olivos, Ballard, and Solvang each make an excellent base for touring the wineries of this fertile area.

## ESSENTIALS

**GETTING THERE**    To reach the Santa Ynez Valley from the north, take Highway 101 to Highway 154 at Los Olivos. Tiny Ballard lies 3 miles south off Baseline Road. The turnoff for Solvang is just beyond, west on Highway 246, while a straight jaunt on Highway 154 will take you through the spectacular San Marcos Pass and onto Highway 101 toward Santa Barbara.

From the south, take Highway 154 off Highway 101 at Goleta (just north of Santa Barbara), up through the San Marcos Pass. A left turn heading west on Highway 246 takes you into Solvang; continuing straight along Highway 154 takes you through Los Olivos and onto Highway 101 towards San Lois Obispo.

**VISITOR INFORMATION**    Contact the **Santa Ynez Valley Visitors Association,** P.O. Box 1918, Santa Ynez, CA 93460 (© **800/742-2843;** www.syvva.com), for general visitors information. The local and comprehensive website, www.solvangca.com, also carries information about the entire valley, as well as Santa Barbara, Lompoc, and Santa Maria. Always a definitive authority for activity in the Santa Maria and Santa Ynez valleys is the **Santa Barbara County Vintners' Association,** 3669 Sagunto St., Unit 101 (P.O. Box 1558), Santa Ynez, CA 93460 (© **800/218-0881** or 805/688-0881; www.sbcountywines.com), which also publishes a *Winery Touring Map.* Hours are Monday through Friday from 9am to 5pm. The **Solvang Conference & Visitors Bureau,** 1511 Mission Dr., at Fifth Street (P.O. Box 70), Solvang, CA 93464 (© **800/468-6765** or 805/688-6144; www.solvangusa.com or www.solvang.org), has additional information on the Santa Ynez Valley, including maps and brochures. It's open daily from 10am to 4pm (a satellite visitor information office is at 1639 Copenhagen Dr.).

**ORIENTATION**    U.S. 101, Highway 246, and Highway 154 form a triangle around the six towns of the Santa Ynez Valley, all residing within a 10-mile radius. Highway 246 becomes Mission Drive within Solvang city limits, then continues east past the mission toward Santa Ynez. Alamo Pintado Road connects Solvang with Los Olivos, whose commercial stretch is along 3 blocks of Grand Avenue. This geographic arrangement may sound confusing but in reality it all blurs together gracefully, and the friendly residents are always handy with directions.

## TOURING THE LOCAL WINERIES

Santa Barbara County has a 200-year tradition of growing grapes and making wine— an art originally practiced by Franciscan friars at the area's missions—but only in the past 20 to 30 years have wine grape fields begun to approach the size of other crops that do so well in these fertile inland valleys.

Geography makes the area well suited for vineyards: The Santa Ynez and San Rafael mountain ranges are transverse (east-west) ranges, which allows ocean breezes to flow through, keeping the climate temperate. Variations in temperature and humidity within the valley create many microclimates, and vintners have learned how to cultivate nearly all the classic grape varietals. But it's the chardonnay, pinot noir, and syrah that draw the most acclaim, and you'll find more than 50 wineries in the Santa Ynez Valley area, most of which have tasting rooms—a few offer tours as well. If you'd like to start with a winery tour to acquaint yourself with viticulture, Gainey Vineyard or Firestone Vineyard are good bets (see below). And if you'd like to sample wines without driving around, head to **Los Olivos Tasting Room & Wine Shop,** 2905 Grand Ave. (© **805/688-7406;** www.losolivoswines.com), in the heart of town, or **Los Olivos Wine & Spirits Emporium,** 2531 Grand Ave. (© **888/ SB-WINES** or 805/ 688-4409; www.sbwines.com), a friendly barn in a field half a mile away. Both offer a wide selection of vintners, including those—such as Au Bon Climat and Qupé— who don't have their own tasting rooms.

**Fess Parker Winery & Vineyard** ✦ You loved him as a child, now see what Hollywood's Davy Crockett/Daniel Boone is up to. Fess Parker has made a name for himself in Santa Barbara County, with resort hotels, cattle ranches, and now an eponymous winery that's turning out some critically acclaimed syrahs, among other varietals. Look for the syrah and chardonnay American Tradition Reserve vintages in the tasting room. Parker's grandiose complex, shaded by the largest oak tree I've ever seen, also features picnic tables on a terrace and an extensive gift shop where you can even buy (you guessed it) coonskin caps.

6200 Foxen Canyon Rd., Los Olivos. © 800/841-1104 or 805/688-1545. www.fessparker.com. Tastings Mon–Fri 11am–5pm and Sat–Sun 10am–5pm; tours daily at 11am, 1pm, and 3pm. Tasting fee $7, includes souvenir glass.

**The Gainey Vineyard** ✦ This slick operation is one of the most visited wineries in the valley, thanks to its prime location on Highway 246 and its in-depth tours, offered daily. It has every hallmark of a visitor-oriented winery: a terra cotta–tiled tasting room, plenty of logo merchandise, and a deli case for impromptu lunches at the picnic tables in a secluded vineyard garden. It bottles the most popular varietals— chardonnay, cabernet sauvignon, pinot noir, sauvignon blanc—and offers them at moderate prices.

3950 E. Hwy. 246, Santa Ynez. © 888/424-6398. www.gaineyvineyard.com. Tastings daily 10am–5pm; tours daily 11am and 1, 2, and 3pm. Tasting fee $5, includes souvenir glass.

**Sunstone Vineyards and Winery** ✦✦✦ Take a rambling drive down to this locally known winery, whose wisteria-wrapped stone tasting room belies the dirt road you take to reach it. Sunstone sits in an oak grove overlooking the river, boasting a splendid view from the lavender-fringed picnic courtyard. Inside, try its flagship merlot or treasured reserve vintages; there's also a fine selection of gourmet foods, logo ware, and cigars. The pretty setting and attractive tasting room, combined with excellent products, make this a quintessentially enjoyable wine-touring experience.

125 Refugio Rd., Santa Ynez. © 800/313-WINE or 805/688-WINE. www.sunstonewinery.com. Tastings daily 10am–4pm. Tasting fee $5, includes souvenir glass.

**Zaca Mesa Winery** ✦✦ One of the region's old-timers, Zaca Mesa has been in business since 1972, so one can forgive the hippie/New Age mumbo-jumbo pleasantly interwoven with the well-honed vintages. Situated on a unique plateau that the Spanish named *la zaca mesa* (the restful place), this winery's 750 acres are uniquely beautiful, with two easy nature trails for visitors. You'll also find picnic tables and a giant lawn chessboard. Inside, look for the usual syrah and chardonnay offerings jazzed up with experimental Rhône varietals like *grenache, roussanne,* and *voignier.*

6905 Foxen Canyon Rd., Los Olivos. ⓒ 800/350-7972 or 805/688-9339. www.zacamesa.com. Complimentary tastings daily 10am–4pm (until 5pm Fri–Sat); call for tour schedule.

## SOLVANG: A TOURISTY TASTE OF DENMARK

The valley's largest community is also one of the state's most popular tourist towns, with more than a million tourists each year. Founded in 1911 by Danish immigrants longing for plenty of sunny weather, Solvang takes a lot of flack for being a Disneyfied version of its founders' vision, where everything that *can* be Danish *is* Danish ("More Danish than Denmark!" is the oft-heard local mantra). You've never seen so many windmills, cobblestone streets, flying flags, wooden shoes, and gingerbreadtrimmed bakeries (even the trash cans look like little Danish farmhouses with pitchedroof lids). In fact, the whole town looks like a Thomas Kinkade painting, so it's no wonder that America's most populist painter has an outlet on the main drag, **Thomas Kinkade Places in the Heart Gallery,** 1576 Copenhagen Dr. (ⓒ 805/693-8739).

To reach Solvang from U.S. 101 south, turn east (left) onto Highway 246 at Buellton. It's a well-marked 20-minute drive along a scenic two-lane road. From Santa Barbara, take U.S. 101 north to Highway 154, a truly breathtaking 45-minute drive over San Marcos Pass. For a destination guide or hotel information, contact the **Solvang Conference & Visitors Bureau** (ⓒ 800/468-6765 or 805/688-6144; www.solvang usa.com and www.solvang.org).

One of the biggest attractions in Solvang is the conspicuous abundance of baked goods such as Danishes, Sarah Bernhardts, kringles, and *kransekage,* making walkingfriendly Solvang a great place to stop for a leg stretch and a sugar rush between Hearst Castle and Santa Barbara. **Olsen's Danish Village Bakery,** 1529 Mission Dr. (ⓒ 800/ 621-8238; www.olsensdanishbakery.com), is the town's best bakery.

Solvang is also full of Danish import shops stuffed with Royal Copenhagen collectibles, lace, and carvings. **Gerda's Iron Art Gift Shop,** 1676 Copenhagen Dr. (ⓒ 805/688-3750), the **Royal Copenhagen Shop,** 1683 Copenhagen Dr. (ⓒ 805/ 688-6660), and **Gaveaesken,** 433 Alisal Rd. (ⓒ 805/686-5699), all offer a large selection of china, cookware, potholders, and Danish gift items, while **Lemos Feed and Pet Supply,** 1511-C Mission Dr. (ⓒ 805/693-8180), has a great selection of gifts for pets. Antiques hounds will find plenty to admire and buy at the **Solvang Antique Center,** 486 First St. (ⓒ 805/686-2322), with more than 50 dealers.

**Windhaven Glider Rides,** Santa Ynez Airport (ⓒ 805/688-2517; www.glider rides.com) runs hang glider rides over the gorgeous valley. For a different kind of thrill you can try your luck at the **Chumash Casino,** a huge Las Vegas–style casino on Highway 246 in Santa Ynez (ⓒ 877/248-6274; www.chumashcasino.com).

If you feel the need to wedge some history and culture between bites of pastries and sips of wine, the valley is the home of the historic, tragic **Mission Santa Ines,** 1760 Mission Dr. (ⓒ 805/688-4815; www.missionsantaines.org; winter hours: Mon–Fri 9am–5:30pm, Sat–Sun 9am–5pm; summer hours: daily 9am–7pm), with its interpretive display of Chumash, religious, and Spanish artifacts, paintings, and documents. Built in 1804, the mission fell into disuse and disrepair after a series of natural and man-made disasters, but near-divine intervention—in the form of Capuchin monks—helped resurrect the mission, which now serves Mass and hosts an annual fiesta in midsummer.

## Miniature Horses and More

Miniature horses supposedly make great house pets, but you may not want to mention that to your kids until you are far, far away from **Quicksilver Miniature Horse Ranch,** 1555 Alamo Pintado Rd. (℃ **800/370-4002** or 805/686-4002). No more than 34 inches high, these four-legged Lilliputians can be petted and played with during visiting hours. If you prefer full-sized equines, visit **Day Dream Arabians,** 2065 Refugio Rd. (℃ **805/688-9106**) for a presentation, tour, and the opportunity to stroll with and feed the mares and foals. For more exotic animals, call in advance and book a tour at the **Flying V Llama Ranch and Llama Memories Gift Shop,** 6615 E. Hwy. 246, Lompoc (℃ **805/735-3577**), 6½ miles west of Buellton (technically just outside of the Santa Ynez Valley). If birds are more your bag, **Ostrich Land,** 610 E. Hwy. 246, Buellton (℃ **805/686-9696**) lets you view the 8½-foot-tall, 350-pound bipeds from a safe distance, and then buy some low-fat ostrich meat (which surprisingly tastes like beef).

Dedicated to documenting and preserving America's flora and fauna, the small yet wonderful **Wildling Museum,** 2329 Jonata St. Los Olivos (℃ **805/688-1082;** www.wildlingmuseum.org; Wed–Sun 11am–5pm; $2 donation requested for admission) is solely supported by donations. Its three rooms offer a changing display of photographs and paintings depicting the history of our vanishing lands and wildlife, and it's truly a labor of love.

Both the **Hans Christian Andersen Museum,** 1680 Mission Dr., upstairs (℃ **805/688-2052;** daily 10am–5pm), and the **Elverhoj Museum,** 1624 Elverhoj Way (℃ **805/686-1211;** www.elverhoj.org; Wed–Sun 1–4pm) cater to children—especially the Elverhoj, which is designed to stimulate children to celebrate the life of Denmark's most famous citizen. Downstairs is the Bookloft and Kaffe Hus, with a reading area for children.

### LOS OLIVOS: A QUIET WINE COUNTRY TOWN

Los Olivos is a good ol' fashioned country town in the middle of the Central Coast Wine Country, complete with a flagpole at the town's main intersection. If you saw TV's *Return to Mayberry,* that was Los Olivos standing in for Andy Griffith's sentimental Southern hamlet. But these days, the town's storefronts feature numerous art galleries, stylish cafes, and wine-tasting rooms. If cutesy and congested Solvang is definitely not your kind of scene, make the short, scenic drive over here along Alamo Pintado Road and spend a few hours browsing the town's 3 short blocks, then enjoy an alfresco lunch at the Los Olivos Café or Panino gourmet sandwich shop (see "Where to Dine," below). If you're looking for a place to stay, Fess Parker (remember Daniel Boone?) runs a beautiful inn and spa here (p. 433).

### CACHUMA LAKE: A BALD-EAGLE HABITAT

Created in 1953 by damming the Santa Ynez River, this picturesque reservoir running along Highway 154 is the primary water source for Santa Barbara County. It's also the centerpiece of a 6,600-acre county park with a flourishing wildlife population and well-developed recreational facilities. Cachuma has, through both agreeable climate and diligent ranger efforts, become a notable habitat for resident and migratory birds, including rarely sighted bald eagles, which migrate south from as far as Alaska in search of food.

One of the best ways to appreciate this fine-feathered bounty is to take one of the naturalist-led **Eagle Cruises** of the lake, offered between November and February. The 48-foot *Osprey* was specially designed for wildlife observation, with unobstructed views from nearly every seat. During the rest of the year, rangers lead **Wildlife Cruises** around the lake, helping you spot resident waterfowl, deer, and the elusive bobcats and mountain lions that live here. Eagle Cruises depart Wednesday through Sunday at 10am, with additional cruises Friday and Saturday at 2pm. Wildlife Cruises run Friday and Saturday at 3pm, and Saturday and Sunday at 10am. All cruises are 2 hours long. In addition to the park day-use fee of $5 per car, the fare is $15 for adults and $7 for children 12 and under. Reservations are recommended; call the **Santa Barbara County Parks Department** (© **805/686-5050;** www.sbparks.com).

The recreational opportunities also offer campers, boaters, and fishermen abundant facilities. Contact the **Lake Cachuma Recreation Area** (© **805/686-5054**) for recorded information.

## WHERE TO STAY

**The Ballard Inn & Restaurant** ★★   This two-story inn may look 100 years old, but it's actually of modern construction, offering both contemporary comforts and charming country details like wicker rockers on a wraparound porch. The entry and parlors are tastefully furnished with a comfortable mix of antiques and reproductions. Sumptuous wallpaper and fabrics lend a cozy touch, and hand-hooked rugs, bent-twig furniture, and vintage accessories lend character to the house. The guest rooms upstairs are unique—some have fireplaces and/or private balconies, and all have well-stocked bathrooms, many featuring a separate antique washbasin in the bedroom. The best (and most expensive) unit is the Mountain Room, a minisuite decorated in rich forest-green and outfitted with a fireplace and private balcony. In addition to cooked-to-order breakfast and a wine-and-hors d'oeuvres reception, you'll be treated to evening coffee and tea, plus addictive chocolate cookies on your nightstand at bedtime.

The inn's upscale restaurant, tucked into a cozy room downstairs by a crackling fire, has garnered much praise since Chef Budi Kazali took over recently. Dishes from his globally inspired menu range from seared tuna with cucumber wakame salad to pan seared Sonoma duck breast with sweet potato purée, and wild striped bass with potato artichoke hash. *Note:* The inn staff doesn't accept gratuities; instead, a 10% service charge is added at checkout.

2436 Baseline Ave., Ballard, CA 93463. © **800/638-2466** or 805/688-7770. Fax 805/688-9560. www.ballardinn. com. 15 units. $225–$305 double. Rates include full breakfast, afternoon wine and hors d'oeuvres, and evening coffee and tea. AE, MC, V. Take Alamo Pintado Rd. to Baseline; the inn is half a block east of the intersection. **Amenities:** Restaurant; bike rental; activities desk; in-room massage. *In room:* A/C, hair dryer, iron.

**Fess Parker's Wine Country Inn & Spa** ★★   Yes, that Fess Parker—Daniel Boone and Davy Crockett, both. But when he's not playing pioneer legends, he's a big local developer. This sprawling eponymous inn is a deep lap of luxury, with each room uniquely decorated by "Mrs. Marcy Parker" herself. The rooms are certainly pristine and comfortable, and each comes with a fireplace, cushy beds with down comforters, and even a lavender turndown service. Other welcoming perks include complimentary mountain bikes, a wine-and-cheese reception, complimentary full American breakfast, and a free wine tasting for two at the adjoining winery. There is also a full spa, a pool and Jacuzzi, and by the time you read this, the inn's new restaurant, Wine Cask of Los Olivos (see the review of the Santa Barbara location on p. 444), should be open. And if you haven't already, buy property in these parts—this region is exploding.

2860 Grand Ave (at Hollister St.), Los Olivos, CA 93441. © 800/446-2455 or 805/688-778. Fax: 805/688-1942. www.fessparker.com. 21 units. $265–$465 double. AE, DISC, MC, V. **Amenities:** Restaurant; pool; spa; bike rental. *In room:* A/C, TV, hair dryer, iron, fireplace.

**Inn at Petersen Village** ★  If you think every hotel in Solvang has a kitschy Danish theme, then step into this quiet, tasteful hotel. Rooms are decorated in a European country motif, with print wallpaper, canopy beds, and mahogany-hued furniture. But it's the little touches that impress the most, like lighted magnifying mirrors, bathroom lights controlled by dimmers, free coffee and tea service to your room, and the complimentary food that's nearly always laid out in the hotel's friendly piano lounge. Some rooms overlook a bustling courtyard of shops, while others face Solvang's scenic hills. All are designed so everyone's happy: Smaller units have private balconies, those with noisier views are more spacious, and so on. Note that rates include a complete dinner for two and a European buffet breakfast.

1576 Mission Dr., Solvang, CA 93463. © 800/321-8985 or 805/688-3121. Fax 805/688-5732. www.peterseninn.com. 42 units. $220–$340 double. Extra person $15. Rates include full dinner and breakfast buffet. AE, MC, V. **Amenities:** Restaurant; piano/wine bar; room service (7am–11pm). *In room:* A/C, TV, dataport, hair dryer, iron.

**Royal Scandinavian Inn**  If you're looking for a traditional, full-service hotel, this attractive and comfortable mainstay in Solvang is away from the congested main drag. Popular with conventions and leisure groups, the Royal Scandinavian has an all-day restaurant and cocktail lounge and is within walking distance of downtown Solvang; the championship Alisal River Golf Course is next door. Ask for a room overlooking the courtyard—the view extends to the foothills beyond. The hotel's restaurant, **Meadows,** is one of the better options in the area, with an attractive patio for dining—equipped with heaters for cool nights and misters for hot days.

400 Alisal Rd. (P.O. Box 30), Solvang, CA 93464. © 800/624-5572 or 805/688-8000. Fax 805/688-0761. www.royal scandinavianinn.com. 133 units. $114–$214 double; from $229 suite. Extra person $15. AE, DC, DISC, MC, V. **Amenities:** Restaurant; lounge; outdoor pool; nearby golf; fitness room; Jacuzzi; business center; room service (7am–10pm); laundry service; dry cleaning. *In room:* A/C, TV w/pay movies, fax, fridge, coffeemaker, hair dryer, iron.

**Solvang Gardens Lodge** *Value*  Solvang's oldest motel is also one of the best values in the entire Santa Ynez Valley. The rooms are all nonsmoking and comfortably sized, with floral prints and marble bathrooms. Nine rooms have full kitchens and seating areas, and the lodge offers weekly and monthly rates, as well as dinner, golf, and theater packages. The meticulously manicured grounds are replete with gardens and fruit trees, and hidden in the backyard is a billiard cottage where guests can play pool, darts, and board games.

293 Alisal Rd., Solvang, CA 93464. © 888/688-4404 or 805/688-4404. Fax 805/688-9975. www.solvanggardens.com. $89–$149 double; $109–$189 suite. DISC, MC, V. **Amenities:** Billiard cottage. *In room:* A/C, TV, wireless Internet.

## WHERE TO DINE

For a quick sandwich or burger on the porch—or to select prepared salads, breads, and artisan cheeses for a picnic to go—you'll be quite pleased with **Los Olivos Grocery,** 2621 W. Hwy. 154 (© 805/688-5115; www.losolivosgrocery.com). This small gourmet country store, open daily from 7am to 8pm, has a great selection of fine wine and foods made from scratch.

If you're looking for traditional Danish fare, head for **Bit o' Denmark,** 473 Alisal Rd. (© 805/688-5426). Its smorgasbord may not be the largest in town, but it's the freshest and highest quality; you can also order from the regular menu. It's open daily from 11:30am to 9pm. **The Hitching Post,** 406 E. Hwy. 246, Buellton (© 805/688-0676), is the valley's mecca for meat lovers. Within these Western-themed surroundings, steaks are grilled to perfection over an oak-wood pit, and—fittingly—the house label wine is better than you'd expect.

**Brothers Restaurant at Mattei's Tavern** ★ AMERICAN/CONTINENTAL Mattei's is proud of its stagecoach past. Built in 1886 by Swiss-born Felix Mattei to service waiting stage coach passengers, the tavern remained in business until 1914 when the Model-A Ford put the coaches out of business. Rumors abound of high-stakes poker games in Mattei's back room, where many an early rancher literally "lost the farm." As soon as you step inside this rambling white Victorian submerged in wisteria you'll be impressed by how successfully it has retained its historic charm. The restaurant is known throughout the county for its signature reduction sauces and house-made ice cream. You'll find thick steaks on the menu, along with honey-glazed Iowa pork chops, prime rib with garlic mashed potatoes, and Australian lobster tail. Bust a pant button with the sinful fudge brownie sundae with banana ice cream, then saddle up and mosey along.

2350 Railway Ave. (just east of Grand Ave. on Hwy. 154), Los Olivos. ☎ 805/688-4820. Reservations recommended on weekends. Dinner $15–$32. AE, MC, V. Daily 5–9pm; bar open daily from 4pm.

**Los Olivos Café** ★ CALIFORNIA/MEDITERRANEAN The patio is so ensconced with wisteria that it's easy to walk right past this popular cafe and not notice it (I did it twice). The sunny patio is ideal for lunch, the inside is warm and beckoning with its massive concrete fireplace, and the food is so consistently good that even locals eat here regularly. The menu offers mostly Mediterranean-style gourmet sandwiches, salads, and pastas—think grilled eggplant and ham on hearth bread, pesto ravioli, basil pesto pizza, and butternut-squash-and-cranberry salad. And, but of course, you can sample local wines with your meal. Don't leave without a bottle of their signature olive oil.

2879 Grand Ave., Los Olivos. ☎ 805/688-7265. www.losolivoscafe.com. Reservations recommended. Main courses $9–$12 lunch, $14–$27 dinner. AE, DISC, MC, V. Daily 11am–9pm.

**Paula's Pancake House** ★ *Kids* AMERICAN/DANISH Morning means one thing in Solvang—Paula's three-page menu of breakfast treats. Paula's is friendly and casual, in the heart of town where patio diners can watch the world go by. So, should we order the wafer-thin Danish pancakes served plain and simple or sweet and fruity? Better include some sausage and eggs with that, and a side of buttermilk pancakes. No, make that a side of whole-wheat honey pancakes, a waffle, and sourdough French toast. Hmmm, an omelet sounds pretty good too. More coffee, please.

1531 Mission Dr., Solvang. ☎ 805/688-2867. Most dishes under $7. AE, DISC, MC, V. Daily 6am–3pm.

---

⌐*Tips* **Picnicking in the Santa Ynez Valley**

On a sunny summer day there's no better way to enjoy lunch than having an impromptu picnic anywhere in the valley. Some of the best sandwiches in the region are made daily at **Panino**, 2900 Grand Ave., Los Olivos (☎ 805/688-9304), a small gourmet sandwich shop where you can choose from about 30 varieties of sandwiches—I usually order the grilled chicken with sun-dried tomatoes, fresh basil, and provolone on fresh walnut bread—all served on Panino's fresh-baked Italian-style bread. It's open Monday through Friday from 10am to 4pm, Saturday and Sunday from 9am to 5pm. There's even a small, grassy picnic area with tables right across the street.

## 6 Santa Barbara ✸✸✸

45 miles S of Solvang; 105 miles S of San Luis Obispo; 92 miles NW of L.A.

Between palm-lined Pacific beaches and the foothills of the Santa Ynez Mountains, Santa Barbara's mosaic of whitewashed stucco and red-tile roofs and gracious, relaxed attitude have earned it the sobriquet "American Riviera." It's ideal for kicking back on white-sand beaches, prowling the shops and galleries that line the village's historic streets, and relaxing over a meal in one of many top-notch cafes and restaurants.

Downtown Santa Barbara is distinctive for its Spanish-Mediterranean architecture. But it wasn't always this way. Santa Barbara had a thriving Native American Chumash population for hundreds, if not thousands, of years. The European era began in the late 18th century, around a Spanish *presidio* (fort) that's been reconstructed in its original spot. The earliest architectural hodgepodge was destroyed in 1925 by a powerful earthquake that leveled the business district. Out of the rubble rose the Spanish-Mediterranean town of today, a stylish planned community that continues to enforce strict building codes.

Visit Santa Barbara's waterfront on a Sunday and you're sure to see the weekly **Waterfront Arts and Crafts Show,** one of the city's best-loved traditions. Since 1965, artists, craftspeople, and street performers have been lining grassy Chase Palm Park, along Cabrillo Boulevard.

### ESSENTIALS

**GETTING THERE** By car, U.S. 101 runs right through Santa Barbara. It's the fastest and most direct route from north or south (1½ hr. from L.A., 6 hr. from San Francisco).

The **Santa Barbara Municipal Airport** (© 805/683-4011; www.flysba.com) is in Goleta, about 10 minutes north of downtown Santa Barbara. Airlines serving Santa Barbara include **AmericaWest Express** (© 800/235-9292; www.americawest.com), **Delta Connection** (© 800/221-1212; www.delta.com), **Horizon Air** (© 800/547-9308; www.horizonair.com), and **United Express** (© 800/241-6522; www.united.com). **Yellow Cab** (© 805/965-5111) and other metered taxis line up outside the terminal; the fare is about $24 (without tip) to downtown.

By train, **Amtrak** (© **800/USA-RAIL;** www.amtrak.com) offers daily service to Santa Barbara (five daily from L.A., one a day from Oakland and the Bay Area). Trains arrive and depart from the **Santa Barbara Rail Station,** 209 State St. (© **805/963-1015**). Fares start at $34 (round-trip) from Los Angeles.

**VISITOR INFORMATION** Stop by the **Santa Barbara Visitor Information Center,** at 1 Garden St., Santa Barbara, CA 93101 (© **805/965-3021;** www.sbchamber. org). The center distributes maps, brochures, an events calendar, and information. It's open Monday through Saturday from 9am to 4pm and Sunday from 10am to 4pm. The **Santa Barbara Conference & Visitors Bureau and Film Commission,** 1601 Anacapa St., Santa Barbara, CA 93101 (© **800/676-1266** or 805/965-3021; www. santabarbaraca.com), does not offer a walk-up facility, but will send out a visitors guide in advance of your visit; request it through © 800/927-4688.

Pick up a copy of the *Independent,* Santa Barbara's free weekly, for events listings; the local daily newspaper is the *Santa Barbara New-Press.* Two good online sources for events listings are the *Independent*'s website, www.independent.com, and **SantaBarbara.com** (www.santabarbara.com).

# Santa Barbara

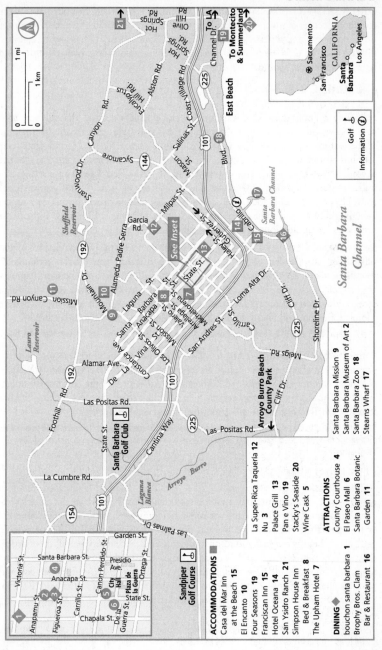

**CALIFORNIA**

Sacramento

San Francisco

**Santa Barbara**

Los Angeles

Golf

Information

**Santa Barbara Channel**

Santa Barbara Channel

**Sandpiper Golf Course**

**Santa Barbara Golf Club**

## ACCOMMODATIONS

Casa del Mar Inn at the Beach **15**
El Encanto **10**
Four Seasons **19**
Franciscan Inn **15**
Hotel Oceana **14**
San Ysidro Ranch **21**
Simpson House Inn Bed & Breakfast **8**
The Upham Hotel **7**

## DINING

bouchon santa barbara **1**
Brophy Bros. Clam Bar & Restaurant **16**
La Super-Rica Taquería **12**
Nu **3**
Palace Grill **13**
Pan e Vino **19**
Stacky's Seaside **20**
Wine Cask **5**

## ATTRACTIONS

County Courthouse **4**
El Paseo Mall **6**
Santa Barbara Botanic Garden **11**
Santa Barbara Mission **9**
Santa Barbara Museum of Art **2**
Santa Barbara Zoo **18**
Stearns Wharf **17**

**ORIENTATION** State Street, the city's primary commercial thoroughfare, is the geographic center of town. It ends at Stearns Wharf and Cabrillo Street; the latter runs along the ocean and separates the city's beaches from touristy hotels and restaurants. Electric shuttles (25¢ fare) provide frequent service along these two routes if you'd rather leave the car behind.

## EXPLORING THE TOWN
### HISTORIC DOWNTOWN

Following a devastating 1925 earthquake, city planners decreed that all new construction would follow codes of Spanish and Mission-style architecture. In time, the adobe-textured walls, rounded archways, artfully glazed tile work, and terra-cotta rooftops would come to symbolize the Mediterranean ambience that characterizes Santa Barbara. The architecture also gave a name to the **Red Tile Tour,** a self-guided walking tour of historic downtown. The visitor center (see "Visitor Information" above) has a map and guide of the tour, which can take anywhere from 1 to 3 hours, including time to visit some of the buildings, and covers about 12 blocks. Some of the highlights are destinations in their own right.

**Santa Barbara County Courthouse** ★ Built in 1929, this grand "palace" is considered the local flagship of Spanish colonial revival architecture (you've undoubtedly seen its facade on TV during the Michael Jackson trial). It's certainly the most flamboyant example, with impressive facades, beamed ceilings, striking murals, an 85-foot-high observation clock tower, and formal sunken gardens. Free guided tours are offered on Monday, Tuesday, and Friday at 10:30am, and Monday through Saturday at 2pm.

1100 Anacapa St. ✆ 805/962-6464. Free admission. Mon–Fri 8am–5pm; Sat–Sun, and holidays 10am–4:45pm.

**Santa Barbara Museum of Art** ★ This little jewel of a museum feels more like the private gallery of a wealthy collector. Its leaning is toward early-20th-century Western American paintings and 19th- and 20th-century Asian art, but the best displays might be the antiquities and Chinese ceramics. In addition, there are often visiting exhibits featuring small but excellent collections from other establishments.

1130 State St. ✆ 805/963-4364. www.sbmuseart.org. Admission $9 adults, $7 seniors 65 and over, $6 students and children ages 6–17, free for children under age 6; free for everyone Thurs and the 1st Sun of each month. Tues–Sun 11am–5pm.

### ELSEWHERE IN THE CITY

**Ganna Walska Lotusland** *Finds* This secluded, lavishly landscaped estate is renowned for exotic plants and mysterious garden paths. Named for the estate's vivacious European-born mistress and the romantic, lotus-filled ponds in her gardens, the estate reflects the late Madame Walska's eccentricity and the skill of her prestigious gardeners. She was especially fond of succulents and cacti, interspersing them artistically among native plants and decorative objects. Assembled when money was no object and import regulations were lenient (mostly in the 1940s), the garden contains priceless rare specimens—even prehistoric plants that are extinct in the wild. Reservations are required six months in advance. Montecito is a 5-minute freeway drive south of downtown Santa Barbara.

695 Ashley Rd., Montecito. ✆ 805/969-9990. www.lotusland.org. Admission $15 adults, $8 children 2–10. 2-hour guided tours mid-Feb to mid-Nov Wed–Sat 10am and 1:30pm.

**Santa Barbara Botanic Garden** *Finds* The Botanic Garden is devoted to indigenous California plants. More than 5½ miles of meandering trails on 65 acres offer glimpses of cacti, redwoods, wildflowers, and much more, many arranged in representational habitats or landscapes. The gardens were established in 1926. You'll catch the very best color and aroma just after spring showers.

1212 Mission Canyon Rd. (a short drive uphill from the mission). © 805/682-4726. www.sbbg.org. Admission $7 adults, $4 children 13–18, $5 seniors 60 and over, $1 children 5–12, free for children under 5. Mon–Fri 9am–5pm; Sat–Sun 9am–6pm.

**Santa Barbara Mission** ★ Established in 1786 by Father Junípero Serra and built by the Chumash Indians, this is a rare example in physical form of the blending of Indian and Hispanic spirituality. This hilltop structure is called the Queen of the Missions for its twin bell towers and beauty. It overlooks the town and the Channel Islands beyond. Self-guided tour booklets are available in six languages.

2201 Laguna St. (at Los Olivos St.). © 805/682-4149. www.sbmission.org. Admission $4 adults, free for children under 12. Daily 9am–5pm.

**Santa Barbara Zoo** ★ *Kids* When you're driving around the bend on Cabrillo Boulevard, look up—you might spot the head of a giraffe poking through the palms. This zoo is an appealing, pint-size place, where all 700 animals can be seen in about 30 minutes. Most live in natural, open settings. There are also a children's Discovery Area, a miniature train ride, and a small carousel. The picnic areas (with barbecue pits) are underused and especially recommended.

500 Niños Dr. (off Cabrillo Blvd.). © 805/962-5339 or 805/962-6310 for recorded information. www.santabarbara zoo.org. Admission $9 adults, $7 seniors and children 2–12, free for children under 2. Daily 10am–5pm; last admission is 1 hr. before closing. Closed Thanksgiving and Christmas. Parking $3.

**Stearns Wharf** ★ California's oldest working wharf attracts visitors for strolling, shopping, and dining. There's also a Sea Center with aquariums, an outdoor touch-tank, and other exhibits. Although the wharf no longer functions for passenger and freight shipping as it did when built in 1872 by local lumberman John C. Stearns, you might still see local fishing boats unload their daily catch. Consider taking a narrated sunset harbor cruise aboard the *Harbour Queen* at **Captain Don's** (© 805/969-5217). Parking, free with merchant validation, is available on the wharf.

At the end of State St.

## BEACHES

**East Beach** is Santa Barbara's favorite beach, stretching from the Zoological Gardens to Chase Palm Park and the wharf. Nearer the pier you can enjoy manicured lawns, tall palms, and abundant facilities; to the east are many volleyball courts, plus the Cabrillo Pavilion, a recreational center, bathhouse, and architectural landmark dating from 1925. Picnic areas with barbecue grills, showers, and clean, well-patrolled sands make this beach a good choice for everyone. **West Beach,** between the wharf and the harbor, has recently been dredged to create a kid-friendly water-play lagoon, conveniently located across the street from some of Santa Barbara's best family-choice hotels.

On the other side of Santa Barbara Harbor is **Leadbetter Beach,** less sheltered than those to the south, and thus popular with surfers. It's reached by following Cabrillo Boulevard after it turns into Shoreline Drive. This beach is also a great place to watch pleasure boats entering or leaving the harbor. Leadbetter has basic facilities, including restrooms, picnic areas, and a metered parking lot. Two miles west of Leadbetter is the secluded but popular **Arroyo Burro Beach County Park,** also known as Hendry's Beach. This gem has a grassy park beneath the cliffs and a white crescent beach with great waves for surfing and bodysurfing. There are volleyball nets, picnic areas, restrooms, and a free parking lot.

## OUTDOOR ACTIVITIES

**BIKING & SURREY CYCLING**  A relatively flat, palm-lined 2-mile coastal pathway, perfect for biking, runs along the beach. More adventurous riders can pedal through town (where painted bike lanes line many major routes, including one up to the mission). These routes and many more are outlined in the *Santa Barbara County Bike Map,* a free and comprehensive resource available at the visitor center or by calling Traffic Solutions at ℂ **805/963-7283.**

**Wheel Fun Rentals,** 101 State St. (just off Cabrillo Blvd.; ℂ **805/966-2282;** www.wheelfunrentals.com), rents well-maintained beach cruisers, mountain bikes, tandem bikes, and an Italian 4-wheel surrey that seats three adults; rates vary. It's open daily from 8am to 8pm.

**BOATING**  The **Santa Barbara Sailing Center,** 133 Harbor Way at the Santa Barbara Harbor (ℂ **800/350-9090** or 805/962-2826; www.sbsail.com), rents sailboats from 21 to 50 feet in length, as well as paddleboats, kayaks, and motorboats. Both skippered and bareboat charters are available by the day or hour. Sailing instruction for all levels of experience is also available. Coastal, island, whale-watching, dinnercruise, and adventure tours are offered on the 50-foot sailing catamaran *Double Dolphin.* It's open daily from 9am to 6pm.

**GOLF**  The **Santa Barbara Golf Club,** 3500 McCaw Ave., at Las Positas Rd. (ℂ **805/687-7087**), has a great 6,009-yard, 18-hole course and a driving range. Unlike many municipal courses, the Santa Barbara Golf Course is well maintained and presents a moderate challenge for average golfers. Fees are $30 Monday through Friday and $40 on weekends. Optional carts are $25 for 18 holes, and $15 for 9.

The 18-hole, 7,000-yard **Sandpiper,** at 7925 Hollister Ave. (ℂ **805/968-1541;** www.sandpipergolf.com), is a scenic oceanside course that's rated as one of the top public course in the U.S. It also has a driving range. Weekend greens fees are $130, and the cart fee is $15.

**HIKING**  The foothill trails in the Santa Ynez Mountains above Santa Barbara are perfect for day hikes. In general, they aren't overly strenuous. Trail maps are available at **Pacific Travelers Supply,** 12 W. Anapamu St. (at State St.; ℂ **888/PAC-TRAV** or 805/963-4438), at the visitor center (see "Visitor Information," above), and from **Traffic Solutions** (ℂ **805/963-7283**).

One of the most popular hikes is the **Seven Falls/Inspiration Point Trail,** an easy trek that begins on Tunnel Road, passes the mission, and skirts the edge of Santa Barbara's Botanic Garden (which also has some pleasant hiking trails).

**SKATING**  The paved beach path that runs along Santa Barbara's waterfront is perfect for rollerblading. **Wheel Fun Rentals,** 101 State St. (just off Cabrillo Blvd.; ℂ **805/966-2282;** www.wheelfunrentals.com), rents skates and all the requisite protective gear. It's open daily from 8am to 8pm.

**WHALE-WATCHING**  Whale-watching cruises are offered between late December and late March, when Pacific gray whales pass by on migratory journeys from their breeding lagoons in Baja California, Mexico, to their Alaskan feeding grounds. **Shoreline Park,** west of the harbor, has high bluffs ideal for land-based whale-spotting. Sea excursions are offered by both **Captain Don's Harbor Tours** (ℂ **805/969-5217;**

www.captdon.com), on Stearns Wharf, and **The Condor** (© **888/77-WHALE** or 805/882-0088; www.condorcruises.com), at 301 W. Cabrillo Blvd. in the Santa Barbara Harbor.

## SHOPPING

**State Street** from the beach to Victoria Street is the city's main thoroughfare and has the largest concentration of shops. Many specialize in T-shirts and postcards, but there are a number of boutiques as well. If you get tired of strolling, hop on one of the electric shuttle buses (25¢) that run up and down State Street.

Also check out **Brinkerhoff Avenue** (off Cota St., between Chapala and De La Vina sts.), Santa Barbara's "antiques alley." Most shops here are open Tuesday through Sunday from 11am to 5pm. **El Paseo** (814 State St.) is a picturesque shopping arcade reminiscent of an old Spanish street. It's built around an 1827 adobe home and is lined with charming shops and art galleries. **Paseo Nuevo,** on the other side of State Street, is a modern outdoor mall, featuring familiar chain stores and cafes, and anchored by a Nordstrom department store.

## WHERE TO STAY

Before you even begin calling around for reservations, keep in mind that Santa Barbara's accommodations are expensive—especially in summer. Then decide whether you'd like to stay beachside (even more expensive) or downtown. Santa Barbara is small, but not small enough to happily stroll between the two areas.

The reservations service **Hot Spots** (© **800/793-7666** or 805/564-1637; www.hotspotsusa.com) maintains an availability list for about 90% of the area's hotels, motels, inns, and B&Bs. The service will have the latest information on who might be looking to fill last-minute vacancies at reduced rates. Reservationists are available for free Monday through Saturday from 9am to 9pm and Sunday from 9am to 4pm.

### VERY EXPENSIVE

**Four Seasons Resort Santa Barbara** ★★★    This gem of the American Riviera manages to adhere to the most elegant standards of hospitality without making anyone feel unwelcome. It's easy to sense the ghosts of golden-age Hollywood celebs like Greta Garbo, Errol Flynn, and Bing Crosby, who used to play croquet or practice putting on the hotel's perfectly manicured lawns and then head over to the private Coral Casino Beach & Cabana Club—because that's exactly what today's privileged guests are *still* doing! The Four Seasons company acquired this Spanish-style hacienda (ca. 1927) in 1987 and restored the 20-acre property without spoiling a bit of its historic charm. Rooms have an airy feel, heightened by white plantation shutters, light-wood furnishings, and full marble bathrooms with all the modern amenities. Guests can amuse themselves with a putting green, shuffleboard courts, and croquet lawn. In addition to two acclaimed dining rooms, the Biltmore offers a no-holds-barred Sunday brunch that draws folks from 100 miles away. The hotel's most recent addition is The Spa, a multimillion-dollar, 10,000-square-foot new Spanish-style annex that houses numerous treatment rooms, a swimming pool and two huge whirlpool baths, a state-of-the-art fitness center, and, for the big spenders, 10 oceanview deluxe suites with fireplaces, in-room bars, changing rooms, and twin massage tables (essentially, your own private treatment room).

1260 Channel Dr. (at the end of Olive Mill Rd.), Santa Barbara, CA 93108. © **800/819-5053** or 805/969-2261. Fax 805/565-8323. www.fourseasons.com/santabarbara. 209 units. $450–$750 double; from $1,250 suite. Extra person $55. Children age 18 and under stay free in parent's room. Special midweek and package rates available. AE, DC, MC, V. Valet parking $20; free self-parking. **Amenities:** 4 restaurants; 2 lounges; 2 outdoor heated pools; 3 lit tennis courts; health club; salon/spa services; whirlpool; complimentary bicycles; salon; 24-hr. room service; laundry service; dry-cleaning service. *In room:* A/C, TV/VCR w/pay movies, high-speed dataport, minibar, hair dryer, iron, safe, complimentary morning paper, robes.

## EXPENSIVE

**El Encanto Hotel & Garden Villas** ★★   This romantic hillside retreat, whose very name means "enchantment," was built in 1915 and is made up of Craftsman cottages and Spanish bungalows. Uphill from the mission and surrounded by an exclusive older residential community, El Encanto features a spectacular ocean view, secluded nooks, gardens and lily ponds, and lush landscaping. The hotel's discreetly attentive service has made it a favorite among privacy-minded celebs. The spacious rooms are decorated in a European country style, with bathrobes and refrigerators; many have fireplaces, balconies, or patios.

1900 Lasuen Rd., Santa Barbara, CA 93103. (*C*) 800/393-5315 or 805/687-5000. Fax 805/687-3903. www.elencanto hotel.com. 77 units. $189–$299 double; from $299 suite. AE, DC, MC, V. Take Mission Rd. past the mission, forking right and then turning left onto Lasuen Rd. **Amenities:** Restaurant; lounge; outdoor heated pool; outdoor tennis court; concierge; room service (6am–10pm); in-room massage. *In room:* TV, dataport, minibar, coffeemaker, hair dryer, iron.

**Simpson House Inn Bed & Breakfast** ★★★   Rooms within the 1874 Historic Landmark main house are decorated to Victorian perfection, with extras ranging from a claw-foot tub and antique brass shower to skylight and French doors opening to the manicured gardens; romantic cottages are scattered throughout the grounds. The rooms have everything you could possibly need, but most impressive are the extras: the gourmet Mediterranean hors d'oeuvres and Santa Barbara wines served each afternoon, the enormous video library, and the full gourmet breakfast (delivered, for detached cottages, on delicate china). Fact is, the Simpson House goes the distance— and then some—to create the perfect stay. Although this property is packed into a relatively small space, it still manages an ambience of country elegance and exclusivity—especially if you book one of the cottages.

121 E. Arrellaga St. (between Santa Barbara and Anacapa sts.), Santa Barbara, CA 93101. (*C*) 800/676-1280 or 805/963-7067. Fax 805/564-4811. www.simpsonhouseinn.com. 14 units. $235–$615 double; $595–$605 suite and cottage. 2-night minimum on weekends. Rates include full gourmet breakfast, evening hors d'oeuvres, and wine. AE, DISC, MC, V. **Amenities:** Complimentary bicycles; concierge; in-room massage. *In room:* A/C, TV/VCR, minibar, hair dryer, iron, robes.

## MODERATE

**Casa del Mar Inn at the Beach** *Value*   A half block from the beach (sorry, no views), Casa del Mar is an excellent-value Spanish-architecture motel with one- and two-room suites. The largish rooms have relatively new furnishings, with plenty of pastels. The flower-sprinkled grounds are well maintained, with an attractive sun deck (but no swimming pool), and the staff is eager to please. Many rooms have kitchenettes, and a dozen different room configurations guarantee something to suit your needs (especially families). Guests get discounts at a nearby day spa, and golf packages can be arranged. *Tip:* Despite the hotel's multitude of rates, rooms can often be an unexpected bargain. Also check the website for Internet-only specials.

18 Bath St., Santa Barbara, CA 93101. (*C*) 800/433-3097 or 805/963-4418. Fax 805/966-4240. www.casadelmar.com. 21 units. $194–$234 double; from $249 suite. Rates include continental breakfast and wine-and-cheese social. Extra person $10. AE, DC, DISC, MC, V. Free parking. From northbound U.S. 101, exit at Cabrillo, turn left onto Cabrillo, and head toward the beach; Bath is the 2nd street on the right after the wharf. From southbound U.S. 101, take the Castillo exit and turn right on Castillo, left on Cabrillo, and left on Bath. Pets accepted w/$10 fee. **Amenities:** Jacuzzi; in-room massage; laundry service; dry cleaning. *In room:* TV, kitchen or kitchenette and fridge in some units, coffeemaker, hair dryer, iron.

**Hotel Oceana** ★★ If you're going to vacation in Santa Barbara, you might as well stay in style and on the beach—ergo the Hotel Oceana, a "beach chic" hotel with an oceanfront setting. The 2.5-acre Spanish mission–style property consists of four adjacent motels built in the 1940s that have been merged and renovated into one sprawling hotel. The result is a wide range of charmingly old-school accommodations—everything from apartments with real day beds (great for families) to inexpensive courtyard rooms and deluxe oceanview suites—with bright modern furnishings. Each guest room, decorated by renowned interior designer Kathryn Ireland, is smartly appointed with soft Frette linens, down comforters (the beds are fantastic), ceiling fans, CD players, cozy duvets, and Aveda bath products. Along with the size and location of your room, you get to choose from four color schemes—soothing blue or green, racy red, and a cheery yellow (my preferred choice). The beach and jogging path are right across the street, and there's a huge lawn area that's perfect for picnic lunches.

202 W. Cabrillo Blvd., Santa Barbara, CA 93101. © **800/965-9776** or 805/965-4577. Fax 805/965-9937. www.hotel oceana.com. 122 units. $185–$360 double. 2-night minimum for weekend reservations. AE, DC, DISC, MC, V. **Amenities:** Denny's restaurant adjacent; 2 swimming pools; fitness room; spa; whirlpool; large lawn area; sun deck. In room: A/C, TV, high-speed wireless Internet access, fridge, hair dryer, iron, CD player.

**The Upham Victorian Hotel and Garden Cottages** This conveniently located inn combines the intimacy of a B&B with the service of a small hotel. Built in 1871, the Upham is the oldest continuously operating hostelry in Southern California. Somewhere the management made time for upgrades, though, because guest accommodations are complete with all the modern comforts. The hotel is constructed of redwood, with sweeping verandas and a Victorian cupola on top. It also has a warm lobby and a cozy restaurant.

1404 De La Vina St. (at Sola St.), Santa Barbara, CA 93101. © **800/727-0876** or 805/962-0058. Fax 805/963-2825. www.uphamhotel.com. 50 units. $165–$245 double; from $275 suite and cottage. Rates include continental breakfast and afternoon wine and cheese. AE, DC, MC, V. **Amenities:** Restaurant; laundry/dry-cleaning service. In room: TV.

**INEXPENSIVE**

All the best buys fill up fast in the summer months, so be sure to reserve your room—even if you're just planning to stay at the decent, reliable **Motel 6,** 443 Corona del Mar Dr. (© **800/466-8356** or 805/564-1392; www.motel6.com), near the beach.

**Franciscan Inn** The Franciscan is situated in a quiet neighborhood just a block from the beach, near Stearns Wharf. This privately owned and meticulously maintained hotel is an affordable retreat with enough frills that you'll still feel pampered. The small but comfy rooms feature a country-tinged decor and finely tiled bathrooms. Services include morning newspaper and free local calls. Most second-floor rooms have unobstructed mountain views, and some suites feature fully equipped kitchenettes. The inn stacks up as a great family choice that's classy enough for a romantic weekend, too.

109 Bath St. (at Mason St.), Santa Barbara, CA 93101. © **800/663-5288** or 805/963-8845. Fax 805/564-3295. www.franciscaninn.com. 53 units. Summer (mid-May to mid-Sept) $150–$170 double, $175–$195 suite; winter $120–$150 double, $135–$165 suite. Extra person $8. Rates include continental breakfast and afternoon snacks. AE, DC, MC, V. Free parking. **Amenities:** Heated outdoor pool; whirlpool; coin-op laundry; laundry/dry-cleaning service. In room: A/C, TV/VCR, dataport, coffeemaker, hair dryer, iron.

## WHERE TO DINE
### EXPENSIVE

**bouchon** ★★ CALIFORNIA As suggested by its name (*bouchon* is the French word for "wine cork"), this warm, inviting restaurant is passionate about wine. And not just any wines, but those from Santa Barbara County. Fifty Central Coast wines are available by the glass, and knowledgeable servers will help you have some fun by enhancing each course with a different glass (or half glass) of wine. The seasonally composed, regionally inspired menu has included dishes such as smoked Santa Barbara albacore carpaccio, arranged with a tangy vinaigrette and shaved imported Parmesan; luscious sweetbread and chanterelle ragout cradled in a potato-leek basket; local venison sliced and laid atop cumin *spaetzle* in a shallow pond of green peppercorn-Madeira demiglace; or monkfish saddle fragrant with fresh herbs and accompanied by a creamy fennel-Gruyère gratin. Request a table on the heated front patio, and don't miss the signature chocolate soufflé for dessert.

9 W. Victoria St. (off State St.). ℂ 805/730-1160. www.bouchonsantabarbara.com. Reservations recommended. Main courses $22–$30. AE, DC, MC, V. Daily 5:30–10pm.

**Nu** ★★ CALIFORNIA CUISINE  *Nu* is French for naked, which explains why the entire staff here works totally naked. Just kidding! Proprietor and executive chef David Cecchini picked the name to convey that his restaurant "strips away" any preconceived notions you may have about dining in Santa Barbara. Metaphors aside, I love everything about Nu, from its pleasant, woodsy neo-Tuscan decor to the exceptional service, plant-filled courtyard seating, and weekend jazz sessions. But the food is really the thing here. You might want to start with lobster risotto, featuring a carrot-infused crème fraîche and orange demiglace, or the yellowfin tuna tartare, then move on to a citrus-spiced swordfish, served with beet-infused toasted quinoa, cabbage fondue, shiitake mushrooms, and saffron nage. If all this sounds slightly fussy, it is; yet it works, and beautifully. *Tip:* If you're not in the mood for a full sit-down dinner, visit the cocktail lounge, with its own menu of appetizers, including great pizzas made in a wood-burning oven.

1129 State St., Santa Barbara. ℂ 805/965-1500. www.restaurantnu.com. Main courses $10–$11 lunch, $22–$28 dinner. AE, DC, DISC, MC, V. Mon–Thurs and Sun 5:30–10pm; Fri–Sat 5:30–11pm.

**Wine Cask** ★★ CALIFORNIA/ITALIAN  Take a 20-year-old wine shop, a large 1920s landmark dining room with a big stone fireplace, an outdoor dining patio, and outstanding Italian fare, and mix them with an attractive staff and clientele, and you've got the Wine Cask—the most popular upscale dining spot in Santa Barbara. Here you'll be treated to such comforting creations as braised oxtail with crème fraîche mashed potatoes and roasted seasonal vegetables. Other options include potato and prosciutto–wrapped local halibut in cioppino sauce, Niman Ranch pork cheek ravioli, and butternut-squash risotto with a fig glaze and Parmesan crisp. The wine list reads like a novel, with more than 1,000 wines ($14–$1,400), and has deservedly received the *Wine Spectator* award for excellence. There's also a happy hour at the beautiful maple bar from 4 to 6pm daily.

In El Paseo Center, 813 Anacapa, Santa Barbara. ℂ 800/436-9463 or 805/966-9463. www.winecask.com. Reservations recommended. Main courses $29–$36 dinner, $12–$17 lunch. AE, DC, MC, V. Mon–Fri 11:30am–2pm; Sun–Thurs and 5:30–10pm; Fri–Sat 5:30–11pm.

## MODERATE

**Brophy Bros. Clam Bar & Restaurant** ★★ SEAFOOD  This place is most known for its unbeatable view of the marina, but the dependable fresh seafood keeps tourists and locals coming back. Dress is casual, portions are huge, and favorites include New England clam chowder, cioppino, and any one of an assortment of seafood salads. The scampi and garlic-baked clams are consistently good, as is all the fresh fish, which comes with soup or salad, coleslaw, and pilaf or french fries. A great deal is the hot-and-cold shellfish combo platter for $13. Ask for a table on the narrow deck overlooking the harbor. **Be forewarned:** The wait at this small place can be up to 2 hours on a weekend night.

119 Harbor Way (off Cabrillo Blvd. in the Waterfront Center). © **805/966-4418.** Reservations not accepted. Main courses $9–$19. AE, MC, V. Sun–Thurs 11am–10pm; Fri–Sat 11am–11pm.

**Palace Grill** ★ CAJUN/CREOLE   Strolling by this restaurant, just a stone's throw from State Street, you'll see why the atmosphere at the Palace Grill garners descriptions like "rollicking" and "hot as the food." The scene extends to the sidewalk, where waiting diners thirst after Mason jar Cajun martinis and Caribbean rum punch. Inside you'll find yourself part of the loud fun; this is not the place for meaningful dinner conversation. Try a platter of spicy blackened steak and seafood, a rich crawfish étouffée, or a Creole jambalaya pasta. Save room for the renowned Southern desserts, including sweet potato–pecan pie, Florida Key lime pie, and the Louisiana bread pudding soufflé, laced with Grand Marnier and whiskey cream sauce.

8 E. Cota St., Santa Barbara. © **805/963-5000.** www.palacegrill.com. Reservations accepted. Dinner main courses $9–$25; lunch $5–$13. AE, MC, V. Daily 11am–3pm and 5:30–10pm (until 11pm Fri–Sat). Valet parking.

**Pan e Vino** ★ ITALIAN   This perfect Italian trattoria offers food as authentic as you'd find in Rome. The simplest spaghetti topped with basil-tomato sauce is so delicious it's hard to understand why diners would want to occupy their taste buds with more complicated concoctions. But this kitchen is capable of almost anything. Pasta puttanesca, with tomatoes, anchovies, black olives, and capers, is always tops. Pan e Vino also gets high marks for its reasonable prices, service, and casual atmosphere. Although many diners prefer to eat outside on the patio, some of the best tables are in the charming, cluttered dining room.

1482 E. Valley Rd., Montecito (a 5-min. drive south of downtown Santa Barbara). © **805/969-9274.** Reservations required. Main courses $10–$22. AE, MC, V. Mon–Thurs 11:30am–9pm; Fri–Sat 11:30am–9:30pm; Sun 5–9pm.

### INEXPENSIVE

**La Super-Rica Taqueria** ★★ MEXICAN   Looking at this humble street-corner shack, you'd never guess it's blessed with an endorsement by Julia Child. The tacos here are authentic and no-nonsense, with generous portions of filling piled onto fresh, grainy corn tortillas. My favorites are the *adobado* (marinated pork), *gorditas* (thick corn *masa* pockets filled with spicy beans), and the flank steak. A dollop of housemade salsa and green or red hot sauce is the only adornment required. You might catch Julia lining up for Sunday's special, *pozole,* a stew of pork and hominy in red chili sauce. On Friday and Saturday, the specialty is freshly made tamales (if the Dover sole tamales are one of the specials, order them—they're incredible. **Tip:** Always check the daily specials—those pieces of paper taped to the glass partition—first, and be sure to ask for extra tortillas, no matter what you order.

622 N. Milpas St. (between Cota and Ortega sts.), Santa Barbara. © **805/963-4940.** Most menu items $3–$7. No credit cards. Sun–Thurs 11am–9pm; Fri–Sat 11am–9:30pm.

**Stacky's Seaside** SANDWICHES   This ivy-covered shack filled with fishnets, surfboards, and local memorabilia has been a local favorite for years. A classic seafood dive, its menu of sandwiches is enormous, as are most of their pita pockets, hoagies, and club sandwiches. A sign proudly proclaims HALF OF ANY SANDWICH, HALF PRICE— NO PROBLEM, and Stacky's has made a lot of friends because of it. Choices include the

Santa Barbaran (roasted tri-tip and melted jack cheese on sourdough), the Rincon pita (jack and cheddar cheeses, green Ortega chiles, onions, and ranch dressing), and a hot pastrami hoagie with Swiss cheese, mustard, and onions. Heck, they even serve a PB&J for $2.99. And if you like fish and chips, they nail it here. Stacky's also serves breakfast, featuring scrambled-egg sandwiches and south-of-the-border egg dishes. An order of crispy fries is enough for two.

2315 Lillie Ave., Summerland (5 min. on the freeway from Santa Barbara—take the Summerland exit, turn left under the freeway, and then take the 1st right). (C) **805/969-9908**. Most menu items under $8. AE, DISC, MC, V. Mon–Fri 6:30am–7:30pm; Sat–Sun 7am–7:30pm.

## 7 The Ojai Valley (★)

35 miles E of Santa Barbara; 88 miles NW of L.A.

In a crescent-shaped valley between Santa Barbara and Ventura, surrounded by mountain peaks, lies Ojai (pronounced "*Oh*-hi"). It's a magical place, selected by Frank Capra as Shangri-La, the legendary utopia of his 1936 classic *Lost Horizon*. The spectacularly tranquil setting has made Ojai a mecca for artists and a large population of New Age spiritualists, drawn by the area's mystical beauty.

Life is low-key in the Ojai Valley. Perhaps the most excitement generated all year happens during the first week of June when the **Ojai Music Festival** draws world-renowned classical artists to perform in the Libbey Bowl amphitheater (for more information, call (C) **805/646-2094** or visit www.ojaifestival.org).

### ESSENTIALS

**GETTING THERE**   The 45-minute drive south from Santa Barbara to Ojai is along two-lane Highway 150, a road that's as curvaceous as it is stunning. From Los Angeles, take U.S. 101 north to Highway 33, which winds through eucalyptus groves to meet Highway 150—the trip takes about 90 minutes. Highway 150 is called Ojai Avenue in the town center and is the village's primary thoroughfare.

**VISITOR INFORMATION**   The **Ojai Valley Chamber of Commerce & Visitors Bureau,** 150 W. Ojai Ave., Ojai, CA 93023 ((C) **805/646-8126;** www.ojaichamber. org), has free area maps, brochures, and the *Visitor's Guide to the Ojai Valley,* which lists galleries and events. It's open Monday through Friday from 9:30am to 4:30pm, Saturday and Sunday from 10am to 4pm.

### EXPLORING THE TOWN & VALLEY

Ojai is home to more than 35 artists working in a variety of media; most have home studios and are represented in one of several galleries in town. The best for jewelry and smaller pieces is **HumanArts,** 310 E. Ojai Ave. ((C) **805/646-1525**). It also has a home-accessories annex, **HumanArts Home,** 246 E. Ojai Ave. ((C) **805/646-8245**). Artisans band together each October for an organized **Artists' Studio Tour** ((C) **805/646-8126** or www.ojaiarttour.com for information). It's fun to drive from

### Fun Fact

While in Ojai, you're bound to hear folks wax poetically about the "pink moment"—a phenomenon first noticed by the earliest Native American valley dwellers, when the brilliant sunset over the nearby Pacific is reflected onto the mountainside, creating an eerily beautiful pink glow.

studio to studio at your own pace, meeting artists and perhaps purchasing some of their work. Ojai's most famous artist was world-renowned Beatrice Wood, who worked until her death in 1998 at 104. Her whimsical sculpture and luminous pottery are internationally acclaimed, and her spirit is still a driving force in Ojai.

Strolling the Spanish arcade shops downtown and the surrounding area will yield a treasure trove, including open-air **Bart's Books,** Matilija Street at Canada Street (© **805/646-3755**), an Ojai fixture for many years. Antiques hounds head for **Treasures of Ojai,** 110 N. Signal St. (© **805/646-2852**), an indoor antiques mall packed to the rafters with treasures, trash, and everything in between.

Residents of the Ojai Valley *love* their equine companions—miles of bridle paths are painstakingly maintained, and HORSE CROSSING signs are everywhere.

Ojai has long been a haven for several esoteric sects of metaphysical and philosophical beliefs. The **Krotona Institute and School of Theosophy,** Highway 33 and Highway 150 at Hermosa Road (© **805/646-2653**), has been in the valley since 1926, and visitors are welcome at their library and bookstore.

In the **Lake Casitas Recreation Area** (© **805/649-2233** for visitor information), the beautiful Lake Casitas boasts nearly 32 miles of shoreline and was the site of the 1984 Olympic canoeing and rowing events. You can rent rowboats and small powerboats year-round from the **boathouse** (© **805/649-2043**) or enjoy picnicking and camping by the lakeside. Because the lake serves as a domestic water supply, swimming is not allowed. From Highway 150, turn left onto Santa Ana Road, and then follow the signs to the recreation area.

When Ronald Coleman saw **Shangri-La** in *Lost Horizon,* he was really admiring the Ojai Valley. To visit the spot where he stood for his view, drive east on Ojai Avenue, up the hill, and stop at the stone bench near the top—the sight is spectacular.

## WHERE TO STAY

**Blue Iguana Inn** ★ *Kids* *Value*   The Mission-style architecture, colorful Southwestern decor, and artwork by local artists (most of which are for sale) are just a few of the highlights of this small, charming hotel. The double rooms at the Blue Iguana are reasonably priced, and the fact that they are also equipped with clean, modern kitchens makes the inn an even bigger value for cook-at-home types. There's even a detached, private two-bedroom bungalow with one-and-a-half bathrooms and a full kitchen starting at $180. Kids can play croquet on the large open lawn while parents take a breather under the shady oaks; on hot summer days it's straight to the pool for everyone. The icing on the cake is the friendly, helpful staff, which makes the Blue Iguana an excellent all-around choice. Heck, they even offer spa treatments. *Tip:* Be sure to visit their website for package deals.

11794 N. Ventura Ave., Ojai, CA 93023. © 805/646-5277. www.blueiguanainn.com. 23 units. Rates $95–$145 double; $139–$209 suite; $179–$229 cottage. AE, DC, DISC, MC, V. **Amenities:** Pool; spa services. *In room:* A/C, TV, kitchen, fridge, coffeemaker.

**Ojai Valley Inn & Spa** ★★★   In 1923, Hollywood architect Wallace Neff designed the clubhouse that's now the focal point of this quintessentially Californian, Spanish Colonial–style resort. The inn has carefully kept a sprawling Mediterranean estate ambience while providing gracious, elegant service and amenities, along with an oak-studded Senior PGA Tour golf course. The jewel of the resort is 31,000 square-foot Spa Ojai, where stylish spa treatments—some modeled after Native American traditions—are administered inside a beautifully designed, exquisitely tiled Spanish-Moorish complex.

Mind- and body-fitness classes, art classes, nifty workout machines, and a sparkling outdoor pool complete the relaxation choices. Many guest rooms have fireplaces, and most have sofas, writing desks, and secluded terraces or balconies that open onto expansive views of the valley and the mountains. Take advantage of the scenery via wooded jogging trails and horseback riding facilities.

905 Country Club Rd. (off Hwy. 33), Ojai, CA 93023. © **888/697-8780** or 805/646-5511. Fax 805/646-7969. www.ojairesort.com. 305 units. $400–$550 double; from $525 suite. AE, DC, DISC, MC, V. Free self- and valet parking. Pets accepted w/$35-per–night fee and advance notice. **Amenities:** Restaurant; outdoor heated 60-ft. lap pool; championship golf course; 4 tennis courts; fitness center; full-service spa; Jacuzzi; complimentary bikes; concierge; in-room massage; laundry service; dry cleaning. *In room:* A/C, TV w/pay movies and Nintendo, fax, dataport, minibar, coffeemaker, hair dryer, iron, safe.

## WHERE TO DINE
### EXPENSIVE

In addition to the choices below, check out **Deer Lodge,** 2261 Maricopa Hwy. (© **805/646-4256**), the latest incarnation of Ojai's favorite hippie-biker hangout on Highway 33, a few minutes north of Ojai. In the valley's gorgeous foothills, the building dates back to the Depression, when it served as a country store with bait and hunting supplies for local sportsmen, but new owners have been busy sprucing the place up and expanding to include a live stage in the bar, enclosed outdoor dining, and a hearty lodge menu with enough contemporary touches to bring in an upscale—yet adventuresome—clientele.

**L'Auberge** ★★ FRENCH/BELGIAN    Possibly the most romantic restaurant in the Ojai Valley, L'Auberge is in a 1910 mansion with a fireplace, chandeliers, and a terrace with an excellent view of Ojai's famous sunset "pink moment." The dinner menu is traditional, with scampi, frogs' legs, trout filet, tournedos of beef, sweetbreads, and duckling *a l'orange.* The weekend brunch menu offers a selection of crepes. Service is expert and friendly, and this elegant house is an easy walk from downtown.

314 El Paseo (at Rincon St.). © **805/646-2288.** Reservations recommended. Main courses $18–$27. AE, MC, V. Sat–Sun 11am–2:30pm; daily 5:30–9pm.

**The Ranch House** ★★★ CALIFORNIA    This restaurant has been placing an emphasis on the freshest vegetables, fruits, and herbs since opening its doors in 1965, long before this practice became a national craze. Freshly snipped sprigs from the restaurant's lush herb garden will aromatically transform your simple meat, fish, or game dish into a work of art. From an appetizer of cognac-laced liver pâté served with its own chewy rye bread to desserts such as fresh raspberries with sweet Chambord cream, the ingredients always shine through. And you'll love the setting, for the Ranch House offers alfresco dining year-round on the wooden porch facing the scenic valley, as well as in the romantic garden amid twinkling lights and stone fountains.

S. Lomita Ave. © **805/646-2360.** www.theranchhouse.com. Reservations recommended. Main courses $20–$32; Sun brunch $21. AE, DC, DISC, MC, V. Tues–Sat 5:30–8:30pm; Sun 11am–7:30pm. From downtown Ojai, take Hwy. 33 north to El Roblar Dr. Turn left, then left again at Lomita Ave.

**Suzanne's Cuisine** ★★ CONTEMPORARY EUROPEAN    Enjoy a great meal in a comfortably sophisticated setting at this local favorite, where every little touch bespeaks a preoccupation with quality details. Ask for a table on the covered outdoor patio, where lush greenery frames a casual setting warmed by a fireplace; when it rains, a plastic curtain descends to keep water out without losing that airy garden feel. Favorites from a seasonal menu include the lunch-only Southwest salad (wild, brown, and jasmine rice tossed with smoked turkey, feta cheese, veggies, and green chiles) and pepper-and-sesame encrusted ahi, served at dinner sautéed or seared (your choice). From seafood specialties to Italian recipes from chef and owner Suzanne Roll's family, everything is fresh and natural. Veggies are crisply al dente, and even the occasional cream sauce tastes light and healthy. Don't skip dessert.

502 W. Ojai Ave. © 805/640-1961. www.suzannescuisine.com. Reservations recommended. Main courses $8–$16 lunch, $15–$28 dinner. MC, V. Wed–Mon 11:30am–3pm and 5:30–8:30pm.

## MODERATE

**Boccali's** ★ ITALIAN   This small, wood-frame restaurant among citrus groves is a pastoral spot where patrons eat at picnic tables under umbrellas and oak trees, or inside at tables covered with red-and-white checked oilcloths. Pizza is the main dish served, topped California-style with the likes of crab, garlic, shrimp, and chicken. I think Boccali's lasagna (served piping hot *en casserole*) would win a statewide contest hands down. Fresh lemonade, from fruit plucked from local trees, is the drink of choice. Come hungry, and plan on sharing.

3277 Ojai–Santa Paula Rd. © 805/646-6116. Reservations recommended for dinner. Pizza $9–$23; pasta $7–$16. No credit cards. Mon–Tues 4–9pm; Wed–Sun 11:45am–9pm.

**Oak Pit BBQ** *Kids* BARBECUE   This stick-to-your-ribs joint on the road between Ojai and Ventura is worth building up an appetite for. The rust-colored shack doesn't have much going for it—just some gingham curtains, a few tables indoors and out, and stacks of wood for firing up the barbecue—but generous portions of slowly oak-smoked meats will have dedicated carnivores coming back for more. Barbecue tri-tip brisket, ham, pork, Cajun sausage, and chicken—they're all served up in sandwiches or full dinners, with available sides of coleslaw, potato salad, fries, baked beans, and corn on the cob.

820 N. Ventura Ave. (Hwy. 33), Oak View. © 805/649-9903. Reservations not accepted. Sandwiches $6; main courses $9–$13. AE, DISC, MC, V. Tues–Thurs and Sun 11:30am–8:30pm; Fri–Sat 11am–9pm.

## 8 En Route to Los Angeles: Ventura

15 miles SW of Ojai; 74 miles NW of L.A.

Snugged between rolling foothills and the sparkling blue Pacific Ocean, Ventura may not have the cultural and gastronomic appeal of Los Angeles or even Santa Barbara, but it does boast the picturesque setting and clean sea breezes typical of California coastal towns. Southland antiques hounds have long reveled in Ventura's quirky collectible markets, but trendy home-decor shops, coffeehouses, wine bars, and fashionable restaurants are providing another lure for time-pressed vacationers who zip up from L.A. to charming bed-and-breakfasts. Ventura is also the headquarters and main point of embarkation for Channel Islands National Park (see below).

Most travelers don't bother exiting U.S. 101 for a closer look. But think about stopping to while away a few hours around lunchtime. Ventura's unforced charm might even convince you to spend a night.

### ESSENTIALS

**GETTING THERE**   If you're traveling northbound on U.S. 101, exit at California Street; southbound, take the Main Street exit. If you're coming west on Highway 33 from Ojai, there's also a Main Street exit. By the way, don't let the directions throw you off; because of the curve of the coastline, the ocean is not always to the west, but often southward.

**VISITOR INFORMATION** For a visitor's guide and genial answers to any questions you might have, stop in at the **Ventura Visitors & Convention Bureau,** 89-C S. California St., Ventura, CA 93001 (🕐 **800/483-6214** or 805/648-2075; www.ventura usa.com).

## EXPLORING THE TOWN

Much of Ventura's recent development has taken place along the **Main Street,** the town's historic center, which grew outward from the Spanish mission of San Buenaventura (see below). The best section for strolling is between the mission (to the north) and Fir Street (to the south). While many of the antique and thrift stores are no more, you'll find plenty of window-shopping opportunities in the revitalized downtown area.

Ventura stretches south to one of California's most picturesque harbors (the departure point for the Channel Islands; see section 9, below), but the town also has its own **pier** at the end of California Street. Well maintained and favored by area fishers, the picturesque wooden pier is the longest of its kind in the state.

**Mission San Buenaventura** Founded in 1782 (current buildings date from 1815) and still in use for daily services, this whitewashed and red-tile church lent its style to the contemporary civic buildings across the street. Step back in time by touring the mission's inside garden, where you can examine the antique water pump and olive press once essential to daily life here. The mission is small and near the rest of Ventura's action. Pick up a self-guided tour brochure in the adjacent gift shop for the modest donation of $1 per adult, 50¢ per child.

225 E. Main St. 🕐 **805/643-4318.** www.sanbuenaventuramission.org. Free admission; donations appreciated. Mon–Fri 10am–5pm; Sat 9am–5pm; Sun 10am–4pm.

**San Buenaventura City Hall** This majestic neoclassical building was built in 1912 as the Ventura County Courthouse. It sits on the hillside, overlooking old downtown and the ocean. To either side on Poli Street are some of Ventura's best-preserved and most ornate late-19th- and early-20th-century houses. Notice the carved heads of Franciscan friars adorning the facade inside and out.

501 Poli St. 🕐 **805/658-4726.** www.ci.ventura.ca.us.

**Ventura County Museum of History & Art** This museum is worth visiting for its Native American Room, filled with Chumash treasures, and its Pioneer Room, which contains a collection of artifacts from the Mexican-American War (1846–48). The art gallery features exhibits of local painters and photographers, and the museum has an enormous archive (20,000 and counting) of photos of Ventura County from its origins to the present. There is also a small archaeological museum across Main Street from the main building. Allow 1 to 2 hours for your visit.

100 E. Main St. 🕐 **805/653-0323.** www.venturamuseum.org. Admission $4 adults, $3 seniors 62 and over, $1 kids 6–17, free for children under 6. Tues–Sun 10am–5pm.

## WHERE TO STAY

**Bella Maggiore Inn** The Bella Maggiore is an intimate Italian-style small hotel whose simply furnished rooms (some with fireplaces, balconies, or bay-window seats) overlook a romantic courtyard or roof garden. The style is Mediterranean casual, with shuttered windows, ceiling fans, and fresh flowers in every room. An open-air center courtyard is the inn's focal point, with stone fountains and flowering trees. Complimentary breakfast is served downstairs at Nona's Courtyard Cafe, which also offers dinner and weekday lunches and a wine bar. A kind of European elegance pervades all but the reasonable rates here.

67 S. California St. (half block south of Main St.), Ventura, CA 93001. © **800/523-8479** or 805/652-0277. 24 units. $85–$145 double; $185 suite. Extra person $10. Rates include full breakfast and afternoon refreshments and appetizers. AE, DISC, MC, V. **Amenities:** Restaurant; wine bar; laundry service; dry cleaning. *In room:* TV, dataport.

**The Brakey House Bed & Breakfast** ✦   Perfect for a romantic getaway, Brakey House is an 1890 Cape Cod–style home with a great view of the ocean from the parlor and two of the seven guest rooms, each individually furnished with a variety of amenities and named after the Channel Islands. The Santa Barbara, for example, has a cast-iron fireplace and 6-foot Jacuzzi tub, while the Anacapa hideaway has an antique sunken bathtub. The Santa Catalina is romantic, with its canopy-draped king-sized bed and sweeping ocean views from inside or the balcony. The B&B is ideally situated on a hill overlooking the shops and restaurants along Main Street, which are a short walk away— *if* you can get past the inviting front lawn graced with a shaded rocking sofa.

411 Poli St. (at Oak St.), Ventura, CA 93001. © **805/643-3600.** Fax 805/653-7329. www.brakeyhouse.com. 5 units (4 w/private entrance). $115–$205 double. Rates include buffet breakfast and complimentary wine. AE, DISC, MC, V. No children accepted. **Amenities:** DVD library. *In room:* TV w/DVD player, hair dryer.

## WHERE TO DINE

**Deco** ✦ CALIFORNIA/CONTINENTAL CUISINE   In the historic, stately Bank of Italy building, Deco is a sterling addition to Ventura's gastronomic scene. The handsome dining room is bedecked with dark woods and modern painting and sculpture, but you'll spend most of your time looking at your plate: The contemporary California/Continental specialties are first-rate. The organic lamb bolognese served over penne pasta is among the best I've had, as is the pork *osso buco* with a rosemary and garlic demiglace. If you are not in the mood for a full-service dinner, Deco offers a wonderful Patio & Bar menu that's a mere $7 per dish.

394 E. Main St. © **805/667-2120.** www.decorestaurant.com. Main courses $15–$22. AE, MC, V. Mon–Thur 5:30–9:30pm; Fri–Sat 5:30–10pm; Sun 5:30–9pm.

**71 Palm Restaurant** ✦ COUNTRY FRENCH   Situated in a beautifully restored 1910 Craftsman, this country-French restaurant is a pleasant change of pace. Upstairs tables have an ocean view, while downstairs a crackling wood fire warms diners. Chef Didier Poirier hails from Le Mans, France, and takes an earnest approach to traditional specialties like steak au poivre with *pommes frites,* New Zealand rack of lamb Provençal style, or homemade pâté served with crusty bread and tangy cornichons. Poirier also dabbles with vegetarian dishes and pastas, and every night the cuisine of a different region of France is highlighted.

71 N. Palm St. (between Main and Poli sts.). © **805/653-7222.** www.71palm.com. Reservations recommended. Main courses $11–$23; lunch $5–$12. AE, DC, DISC, MC, V. Mon–Fri 11:30am–2:30pm and 5–9:30pm; Sat 5–9:30pm.

**Taquería Vallarta** *Value* MEXICAN   There's no better place to find a snapshot of Ventura than at the Taquería Vallarta, where young, old, rich, poor, Anglo, and Latino come for Mexican-style comfort food. There's nothing fancy here—it's your standard order-at-the-counter then slide-into-your-Formica-booth kind of joint, but that's no problem. The *carnitas* are among the best you'll find anywhere, perfect in a burrito, and the *carne asada* is best in the enchiladas. Don't forget to dress up your dishes with the fresh salsas, limes, and chile peppers available at the condiment bar. For fans of great, cheap Mexican food, Taquería Vallarta's a must.

278 E. Main St. ⓒ **805/643-3037.** Main courses $4–$8. DC, DISC, MC, V. Mon–Fri 9:30am–9pm; Sat–Sun 7:30am–9pm.

## 9 Channel Islands National Park ⓒ

Approximately 40 miles W (offshore) of Ventura

There's nothing like a visit to the Channel Islands for discovering the sense of awe explorers must have felt more than 400 years ago. It's miraculous what 25 miles of ocean can do, for compared to the mainland, this is wild and empty land, and only 55,000 visitors a year come to the islands. Whether you approach them by sea or air, you'll be bowled over by how untrammeled they remain despite neighboring Southern California's teeming masses.

Channel Islands National Park encompasses the five northernmost islands of the eight-island chain: Santa Barbara, Anacapa, Santa Cruz, Santa Rosa, and San Miguel. The park also protects the ocean 1 nautical mile offshore from each island, thereby prohibiting oil drilling, shipping, and other industrial uses.

The islands are the meeting point of two distinct marine ecosystems: The cold waters of Northern California and the warmer currents of Southern California swirl together here, creating an awesome array of marine life. On land, the isolation from mainland influences has allowed distinct species—including the island fox and the night lizard—to evolve and survive here. The islands are also the most important seabird-nesting area in Southern California and home to one of the biggest seal- and sea-lion-breeding colonies in the United States.

### ESSENTIALS

**VISITOR INFORMATION**    Each of the five islands is distinct and takes some forethought to reach. Odds are, you're only going to visit one island on a given trip, so it's a good idea to study your options before going. Visit the **Channel Islands National Park Headquarters and Visitor Center,** 1901 Spinnaker Dr., Ventura, CA 93001 (ⓒ **805/658-5730;** www.nps.gov/chis), to get acquainted with the programs and individual personalities of the islands through maps and displays. Rangers run interpretive programs both on the islands and at the center year-round.

**GETTING THERE    Island Packers,** near the visitor center at 1691 Spinnaker Dr. (ⓒ **805/642-7688** for recorded information, 805/642-1393 for reservations; www.islandpackers.com), is the park's main concessionaire for boat transportation to and from the islands. Daylong tours are offered daily year-round to Anacapa and Santa Cruz; the price to Anacapa is $42 for adults, $38 for seniors, and $25 for children ages 3 to 12 (Santa Cruz is slightly higher). A half-day trip is also offered to Anacapa on Saturdays. Trips to Santa Rosa and San Miguel operate weekly May through October; boats to Santa Barbara Island are less frequent. Boats to Anacapa leave from the Channel Islands Harbor in Oxnard, 15 minutes south of Ventura. Also see Santa Barbara–based **Truth Aquatics,** under "Diving" below.

Another option, for visiting Santa Rosa Island only, is **Channel Islands Aviation,** 305 Durley Ave., Camarillo (ⓒ **805/987-1301;** www.flycia.com), which flies nine-passenger, fixed-wing aircraft. Day trips are scheduled every Saturday and every other Sunday (year-round, weather permitting); flying time to Santa Rosa is 25 minutes. The fare is $130 per person, which includes a guided island tour with a ranger via four-wheel-drive. Campers (that is, people camping) are flown over for about $200 round-trip (these flights scheduled on demand).

**THE WEATHER** The climate is mild, with little variation in temperature year-round, but the weather is still unpredictable; 30-mph winds can blow for days, fog banks can settle in and smother the islands for weeks, and winter rains can turn trails into mud baths. In general, plan on wind, lots of sun (bring sunscreen), cool nights, and the possibility of hot days. Water temperatures are in the 50s and 60s (10s–20s Celsius) year-round. If you're camping, bring a good tent. (If you don't know the difference between a good and a bad tent, the island wind will gladly demonstrate it for you.)

**CAMPING** Camping is legal on all the park-owned islands but limited to a certain number of campers per night, depending on the island. Fires and pets are prohibited on all the islands. You must bring everything you'll need; there are no supplies on any of the islands. To reserve camping permits for any of the islands, call © **800/365-CAMP** or log on to http://reservations.nps.gov. The rate is $10 per night, per site.

## EXPLORING THE ISLANDS

**ANACAPA** Most people who visit the park come to Anacapa. It's 14 nautical miles from Ventura, an easy day trip—it takes about an hour to reach by boat. At only 1¼ square miles, Anacapa—actually three small islets divided by narrow stretches of ocean—is only marginally larger than Santa Barbara and, consequently, not a place for those who need a lot of space. Only East Anacapa is open to visitors, as the other two islets are important brown-pelican breeding areas. Several trails on the island will take you to beautiful overlooks of clear-watered coves and wild ocean. **Arch Rock,** a natural land bridge, is visible from the landing cove, where you'll clamber up 154 stairs to the island's flat top.

Camping is allowed on East Anacapa year-round, but don't bring more than you can carry the half mile from the landing cove. Bring earplugs and steer clear of the foghorn, which can cause permanent hearing damage. Most of the waters around the island, including the landing cove, are protected as a National Marine Preserve, where divers can look but not take anything. Pack a good wet suit, mask, fins, and snorkel; you can dive right off the landing-cove dock.

**SANTA CRUZ** By far the biggest of the islands—nearly 100 square miles—Santa Cruz is also the most diverse. It has huge canyons, year-round streams, beaches, cliffs, the highest mountain in the Channel Islands (2,450 ft.), now-defunct early cattle and sheep ranches, and Native American Chumash village sites—2,000 Chumash were probably living on the island when Cabrillo first visited in 1542. The island also hosts seemingly endless displays of flora and fauna, including 680 species of plants, 45 of which are multi-island endemics and 8 of which are single-island endemics; 140 land-bird species; and a small group of other land animals, including the island fox.

Most of the island is still privately owned: The Nature Conservancy holds the western three-quarters. When the park service took over the eastern end from the Gherini family, owners of a sheep ranch here, it eliminated the island's formerly exorbitant landing and camping fees, but it also eliminated the Channel Islands' only noncamping overnight options; the Gherinis currently use the ranch house and adobe bunkhouse at Scorpion Ranch under a special-use-and-occupancy permit.

**Valdez Cave** (aka Painted Cave for its colorful rock types, lichens, and algae) is one of the largest and deepest known sea caves in the world. The huge cave stretches nearly a quarter of a mile into the island and is nearly 100 feet wide. The entrance ceiling rises 160 feet, and in the spring, a waterfall tumbles over the opening. On the northwest end of the island, the cave can only be entered via dinghy or kayak.

**SANTA ROSA** The second-largest of the chain, windy Santa Rosa also has a ranching past—one that ended in 1998 in a storm of controversy that pitted the National Park Service against both environmental groups and the 97-year-old Vail & Vickers cattle ranch. The cows are all gone now, taking with them a slice of California history. In the meantime, the island's native vegetation has begun to recover. Santa Rosa is home to a large concentration of endangered plant species, 34 of which occur only on the islands. And like Santa Cruz, Santa Rosa is home to the diminutive island fox, a tiny cousin of the gray fox that has become nearly fearless as it has evolved in the predator-free island environment. They'll walk right through your camp if you let them. Santa Rosa also has great beaches, a benefit somewhat outweighed by the nearly constant winds.

**SAN MIGUEL** People often debate what's the wildest place left in the lower 48 states. They bat around names like Montana, Colorado, and Idaho, but rarely does anyone consider San Miguel, 55 miles off Ventura. They should, for this 9,325-acre island is a wild, wild place. The wind blows constantly, and the island can be shrouded in fog for days at a time. Human presence is definitely not the status quo here.

Visitors land at Cuyler Harbor, a half-moon-shaped cove on the island's east end. Arriving here is like arriving on earth the day it was made: perfect water, perfect sand, outrageously blue water. Seals bask on the offshore rocks. The island's two most interesting features are the **Caliche Forest,** which sort of petrified when the wind exposed sandstone casts of trees that once stood on the island, and **Point Bennett,** the outrageous-sounding (and smelling) breeding ground of four species of seals and sea lions. In winter up to 50,000 pinnipeds carpet the beach; their barking is deafening.

The waters around San Miguel are the richest and most dangerous of all the islands. The island's 27 miles of rocky coastline is exposed to wave action from all sides—many ships have sunk here. A 3-foot-tall stone cross stands in memory of Juan Rodríguez Cabrillo, the Spanish explorer credited with discovering the Channel Islands in 1542. Although his grave has never been found, Cabrillo is believed to be buried at sea, near Catalina Island.

**SANTA BARBARA** As you come upon Santa Barbara Island after a typical 3-hour crossing, you'll think that someone took a single, medium-size, grassy hill, ringed it with cliffs, and plunked it down in the middle of the ocean. When you drop anchor, you'll realize that your initial perception is basically on target. Landwise, there's just not a lot here. But the upside is that, of all the islands, Santa Barbara gives you the best sense of what it's like to be stranded on a desert isle. Being on Santa Barbara, far enough out to sea that the mainland is almost invisible, gives you an idea of just how immense the Pacific really is.

Other than the landing cove, there's no access to the water's edge. The snorkeling in the chilly cove is great. You can hike the entire 639-acre island in a few hours; then it's time to stare out to sea. You won't be let down. The cliffs and rocks are home to elephant seals, sea lions, and swarms of seabirds such as you'll never see on the mainland. There's also a small campground, pit toilets, and a tiny museum chronicling island history.

## THE EXTRA MILE: EXPLORING THE COASTLINE & WATERS OFF THE CHANNEL ISLANDS

**DIVING** A good portion of Channel Islands National Park is underwater. In fact, almost as many visitors come to dive the waters as ever set foot *on* the islands. Divers come from all over to explore stunning kelp forests, pinnacles, and underwater caves, all with the best visibility in California. Everything from sea snails and urchins to orcas and great white sharks call these waters home.

**Truth Aquatics,** in Santa Barbara (© **805/962-1127;** www.truthaquatics.com), is the best provider of single- and multiday dive trips to all the islands. They also offer single- and multiday hiking, kayaking, and fishing tours. **Ventura Dive & Sport** (© **805/650-6500;** www.venturadive.com) also leads trips, including a Discover Program for novice and uncertified divers accompanied by an instructor. **Channel Islands Scuba** in Thousand Oaks (© **805/230-9995;** www.channelislandsscuba.com) and **Pacific Scuba** in Oxnard (© **805/984-2566;** www.pacificscuba.com) also lead regular trips, as do boats from San Pedro and other Southern California ports.

**SEA KAYAKING**    One of the best ways to explore the fascinating coastline of the islands is by sea kayak. The excursions allow you to explore sea caves and rock gardens. Fares generally run about $175 per person for full-day trips; channel crossing by charter boat, equipment, and brief lessons are included. Two- and 3-day adventures to Santa Rosa—campsite, camp gear, and guide included—are offered for $265 to $330 (you'll need to bring your own food, sleeping bag, and tent). **Aquasports** (© **800/ 773-2309** or 805/968-7231; www.islandkayaking.com) operates most trips out of Ventura Harbor, and **Paddle Sports of Santa Barbara** (© **888/254-2094** or 805/ 899-4925; www.kayaksb.com) leads similar excursions.

# 14

# Los Angeles

*by Matthew Richard Poole*

The allure of Los Angeles, like that of nearby Las Vegas, is undeniable, however fleeting and vain. Los Angelenos know their city will never have the sophisticated style of Paris or the historical riches of London, but they cheerfully lay claim to living in the most entertaining city in the United States, if not the world. It really is warm and sunny most days of the year, movie stars actually do live and dine among the commoners, and you can't swing a cellphone without hitting a roller-blading blonde at the beach.

This part of the L.A. mystique—however exaggerated it may be—does exist, and it's not hard to find. It's fitting that L.A. is

home to the world's first amusement park, because it regularly feels like one, and the line between fantasy and reality is often obscured. From the unattainable, anachronistic glamour of Beverly Hills to the vibrant street energy of the Venice Boardwalk, each of the city's diverse neighborhoods is like a mini–theme park, offering its unique kind of adventure. Drive down Sunset Boulevard and you'll see what I mean: The billboards are racier, the fashions trendier, the cars fancier, the bodies sexier, the sun brighter, and the energy higher than in any place you've ever been. Darlin', you ain't in Kansas anymore—you're in La-La Land. So let's go play.

## 1 Orientation

### GETTING THERE
### BY PLANE
### LAX & the Other Los Angeles–Area Airports

The Los Angeles area has five airports. Most visitors fly into **Los Angeles International Airport** (© 310/646-5252; www.lawa.org/lax), better known as LAX. This behemoth—ranked fourth in the world for number of passengers—is situated oceanside, between Marina del Rey and Manhattan Beach. LAX is a convenient place to land, within minutes of Santa Monica and the beaches, and not more than a half-hour from Downtown, Hollywood, and the Westside. Despite its size, the eight-terminal airport has a straightforward, easy-to-understand design. Free blue, green, and white **shuttle buses** connect the terminals and stop in front of each ticket building. Special minibuses accessible to travelers with disabilities are also available. **Travelers Aid of Los Angeles** (© 310/646-2270; www.travelersaid.org) operates booths in each terminal. You can find extensive information about LAX—including maps, parking and shuttle-van information, and links to weather forecasts—online at **www.lawa.org**. All car-rental agencies are in the neighborhood surrounding LAX, within a few minutes' drive via complimentary shuttles to and from the airport.

For some travelers, one of the area's smaller airports might be more convenient than LAX. **Bob Hope Airport** (2627 N. Hollywood Way, Burbank; © 818/840-8840;

www.bobhopeairport.com) is the best place to land if you're headed for Hollywood or the valleys, and it's closer to Downtown than LAX. The small airport has especially good links to Las Vegas and other southwestern cities. **Long Beach Municipal Airport** (4100 Donald Douglas Dr., Long Beach; ✆ **562/570-2600;** www.lgb.org), south of LAX, is the best place to land if you're visiting Long Beach or northern Orange County and want to avoid the city. **John Wayne Airport** (19051 Airport Way N., Anaheim; ✆ **949/252-5200;** www.ocair.com) is closest to Disneyland, Knott's Berry Farm, and other Orange County attractions. **Ontario International Airport** (Terminal Way, Ontario; ✆ **909/937-2700;** www.lawa.org/ont) is not a popular airport for tourists; businesspeople use it to head to San Bernardino, Riverside, and other inland communities. However, it's convenient if you're heading to Palm Springs, and also a viable choice if you're staying in Pasadena.

## Getting into Town from LAX

**BY CAR**   To reach **Santa Monica** and other northern beach communities, exit the airport, take Sepulveda Boulevard north, and follow the signs to Highway 1 (Pacific Coast Hwy., or PCH) north. You *can* take the I-405 north, but you'll be sorry you did; that stretch of freeway is always heavily congested. To reach **Redondo, Hermosa, Newport,** and the other southern beach communities, take Sepulveda Boulevard south and then follow the signs to Highway 1 (Pacific Coast Hwy., or PCH) south. To reach **Beverly Hills** or Hollywood, exit the airport via Century Boulevard and then take I-405 north to Santa Monica Boulevard east. To reach **Downtown** or **Pasadena,** exit the airport, take Sepulveda Boulevard south, then take I-105 east to I-110 north.

**BY SHUTTLE**   Many city hotels provide free shuttles for their guests; ask when you make reservations. **SuperShuttle** (✆ **800/258-3826** or 310/782-6600; www.super shuttle.com) offers regularly scheduled minivans from LAX to any location in the city. The fare ranges from $15 to $35 per person. It's cheaper to cab it to most places if you're with a group of three or more, but you might have to stop at other passengers' destinations first. Reservations are required for return trips to the airport but not for arrivals.

**BY TAXI**   Metered taxis line up outside each terminal on the lower level. Expect to pay about $35 to Hollywood and Downtown, $25 to Beverly Hills, $20 to Santa Monica, and $45 to $60 to the Valley and Pasadena, *including* a $2.50 service charge for rides originating at LAX.

**BY RAIL**   Budget travelers bound for Downtown, Universal City, or Long Beach can take L.A.'s Metro Rail service from LAX. An airport shuttle will take you to the Green Line light-rail station, which connects with the Blue, Gold, and Red lines; ask your hotel for the closest station. The service operates from 5am to midnight, and the combined fare is under $2, but prepare to spend 1 to 2 hours in transit. Call the **Los Angeles County Metropolitan Transit Authority (MTA)** at ✆ **800/COMMUTE,** or see www.mta.net for information.

---

*Tips* **Don't Rush!**

If you're renting a car at the LAX airport, avoid arriving during the midweek rush hour—morning or evening—particularly if you have to drive dreaded I-405. You'll save yourself several hours of stop-and-go misery.

---

# Southern California at a Glance

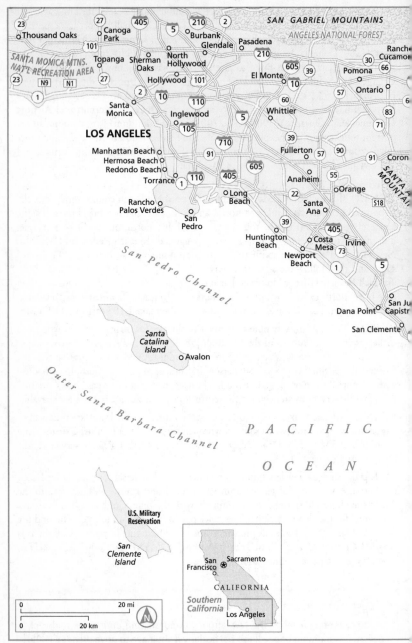

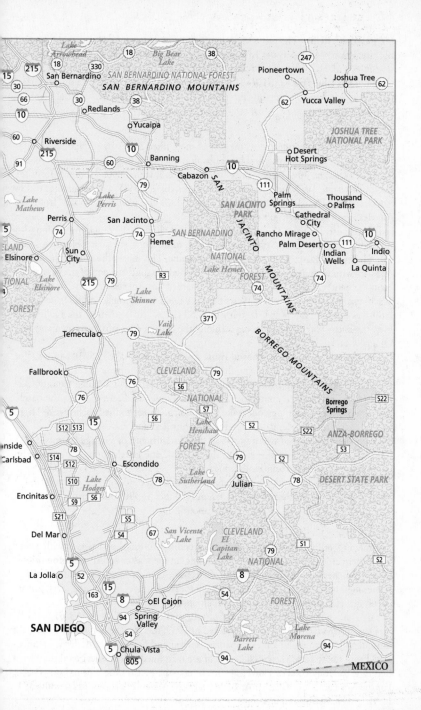

459

**BY PUBLIC BUS** The city's MTA buses also run between LAX and many parts of the city. Phone **MTA Airport Information** (✆ **800/COMMUTE;** www.mta.net) for schedules and fares. If you're arriving at LAX and staying in Santa Monica, hop aboard the city's **Big Blue Bus** (✆ **310/451-5444;** www.bigbluebus.com). It's a slow ride, but the 75¢ fare is hard to beat. Bus information is available in the baggage claim area of each LAX terminal.

### BY CAR

Los Angeles is well connected to the rest of the United States by several major highways; in fact, L.A. has the highest rate of bank robberies in the U.S. because it's so easy to make a fast getaway. Among them are Interstate 5, which enters the state from the north; Interstate 10, which originates in Jacksonville, Florida, and terminates in Los Angeles; and U.S. 101, a scenic route that follows the western seaboard from Los Angeles north to the Oregon state line.

If you're driving **from the north,** you have two choices: the quick route, along I-5 through the middle of the state, or the scenic route along the coast. Heading south along I-5, you'll pass a small town called Grapevine. This marks the start of the mountain pass with the same name. Once you've reached the southern end of the pass, you'll be in the San Fernando Valley, which is the start of Los Angeles County. To reach the beach communities and L.A.'s Westside, take I-405 south (hello, traffic!); to get to Hollywood, take Highway 170 south to U.S. 101 south (known as the Hollywood Fwy. the entire way); I-5 will take you along the eastern edge of Downtown and into Orange County.

If you're taking the **scenic coastal route** from the north, take U.S. 101 to I-405 or I-5, or stay on U.S. 101, following the instructions above to your destination.

If you're approaching **from the east,** you'll be on I-10. For Orange County, take Highway 57 south. I-10 continues through Downtown and terminates at the beach. If you're heading to the Westside, take I-405 north. To get to the beaches, take Highway 1 (PCH) north or south, depending on your destination.

**From the south,** head north on I-5 at the southern end of Orange County. I-405 splits off to the west; take this road to the Westside and beach communities. Stay on I-5 to reach Downtown and Hollywood.

*Driving times:* From Phoenix, it's about 350 miles (a 6- to 7-hr. drive) via I-10; Las Vegas is 265 miles northeast (4–5 hrs.); San Francisco is 390 miles north on I-5 (6–7 hrs.); and San Diego is 115 miles south (about 2 hrs.).

### BY TRAIN

**Amtrak** (✆ **800/USA-RAIL;** www.amtrak.com) connects Los Angeles with about 500 American cities. Fares fluctuate depending on the season and special promotions. In general, heavily restricted advance tickets are competitive with similar airfares. Remember, however, that those low fares are for coach travel in reclining seats; private sleeping accommodations cost substantially more.

The L.A. train terminus is **Union Station,** 800 N. Alameda (✆ **213/617-0111**), on Downtown's northern edge. Completed in 1939, this was the last of America's great train depots—a unique blend of Spanish Revival and Streamline Moderne architecture. From the station, you can take one of the taxis lined up outside, board the Metro Red Line to Hollywood or Universal City, or take the Metro Blue Line to Long Beach. For the San Fernando Valley or Anaheim, take the **Metrolink** trains; call ✆ **800/371-LINK** (www.metrolinktrains.com).

## BY BUS

Bus travel is an inexpensive and often flexible option. **Greyhound** (© **800/229-9424;** www.greyhound.com) can get you to L.A. from anywhere in the U.S. and offers several money-saving multiday passes. The main station for arriving buses is Downtown at 1716 E. Seventh St., east of Alameda.

## VISITOR INFORMATION

### INFORMATION CENTERS

The **Los Angeles Convention and Visitors Bureau** (aka **LA INC.;** © **800/366-6116** or 213/689-8822; www.visitLAnow.com) maintains an informative Internet site, answers telephone inquiries, sends free visitor's kits, and runs a **walk-in visitor center** at 685 S. Figueroa St., Downtown (Mon–Fri 9am–5pm). Many Los Angeles–area communities also have their own information centers and detailed, colorful websites loaded with timely information. These include the following:

- The **Beverly Hills Visitors Bureau,** 239 S. Beverly Dr. (© **800/345-2210** or 310/248-1015; www.beverlyhillscvb.com), is open Monday through Friday from 8:30am to 5pm.

- The **Hollywood Arts Council,** P.O. Box 931056, Dept. 1995, Hollywood, CA 90093 (© **323/462-2355;** www.discoverhollywood.com), publishes the magazine *Discover Hollywood,* a biannual publication that contains listings and schedules for the area's many theaters, galleries, music venues, and comedy clubs; the current issue is always available online. You can also load up on visitor information at the **Hollywood Visitor Center,** 6801 Hollywood Blvd., Suite 237 (© **323/467-6412**), on the second level of the Hollywood & Highland mall (between Babylon Court and Awards Walk).

- The **West Hollywood Convention and Visitors Bureau,** 8687 Melrose Ave., M-26, West Hollywood, CA 90096 (© **800/368-6020** or 310/289-2525; www.visitwest hollywood.com), is located in the Pacific Design Center and is open Monday through Friday from 9am to 6pm.

- The **Santa Monica Convention and Visitors Bureau** (© **800/544-5319** or 310/393-7593; www.santamonica.com) is the best source for information about Santa Monica. The Palisades Park walk-up center is near the Santa Monica Pier, at 1400 Ocean Ave. (between Santa Monica Blvd. and Broadway); open daily from 10am to 4pm. Also check out **www.malibu.org** for information about Malibu, to the northwest.

- The **Pasadena Convention and Visitors Bureau,** 171 S. Los Robles Ave. (© **626/795-9311;** www.pasadenacal.com), is open Monday through Friday from 8am to 5pm and Saturday from 10am to 4pm.

## OTHER INFORMATION SOURCES

Several city-oriented newspapers and magazines offer the most up-to-date information regarding dining, culture, and nightlife. *L.A. Weekly* (www.laweekly.com), an excellent free listings magazine, is packed with details on current events around town. It's available from sidewalk news racks and in many stores and restaurants around the city; it also has a lively website.

The *Los Angeles Times* **"Calendar"** section of the Sunday paper, an excellent guide to entertainment in and around L.A., includes listings of what's doing and where to do it. The *Times* also maintains a comprehensive website, at **www.calendarlive.com,** with departments such as "Southland Scenes," "Tourist Tips," "Family & Kids," and

"Recreation & Fitness." Information, culled from the newspaper's many departments, is always up-to-date. For L.A.'s most immediate hard news, see the *Times*'s main website: **www.latimes.com**.

*Los Angeles* magazine (**www.lamag.com**) is a glossy monthly full of real news and pure gossip, plus guides to L.A.'s art, music, and food scenes. Its calendar of events has been getting better, with an excellent overview of goings-on at museums, galleries, musical venues, and other places. The magazine is available at newsstands around town and in other major U.S. cities; you can also access stories and listings from the current issue on the Internet. Cybersurfers should visit **At L.A.**'s website, **www.at-la. com**; its exceptional search engine provides links to more than 23,000 sites relating to the L.A. area, including many destinations covered in chapter 15, "Side Trips from Los Angeles."

## CITY LAYOUT

Los Angeles is a sprawling suburbia encompassing dozens of disparate communities on the ocean or the flatlands of a huge desert basin. Ocean breezes push the city's infamous smog inland and through mountain passes into the sprawl of the San Fernando and San Gabriel valleys. Downtown Los Angeles is in the center of the basin, about 12 miles east of the Pacific Ocean. Most visitors spend the bulk of their time along the coast or on the ever-trendy Westside (see "Neighborhoods in Brief," below, for complete details on all of the city's sectors).

### MAIN ARTERIES & STREETS

L.A.'s extensive system of toll-free, high-speed freeways connects the city's patchwork of communities. The system works well to get you where you need to be, although rush-hour (roughly 6–9am and 4–7pm) traffic is often bumper-to-bumper. Here's an overview (best read with an L.A. map in hand):

**U.S. 101** (aka the Ventura Fwy. in the San Fernando Valley, and the Hollywood Fwy. in town) runs across L.A. in a northwest-southeast direction, from the San Fernando Valley to Downtown. Heavy rush-hour traffic. **Highway 134** continues as the Ventura Freeway after U.S. 101 turns into the city and becomes the Hollywood Freeway. This branch of the Ventura Freeway continues directly east, through the valley towns of Burbank and Glendale, to I-210 (the Foothill Fwy.), which runs through Pasadena and out toward the eastern edge of Los Angeles County.

**I-5** (aka the Golden State Fwy. north of I-10, and the Santa Ana Fwy. south of I-10) bisects Downtown on its way from Sacramento to San Diego.

**I-10** (aka the Santa Monica Freeway west of I-5, and the San Bernardino Freeway east of I-5) is the city's major east-west freeway, connecting the San Gabriel Valley with Downtown and Santa Monica.

**I-405** (aka the San Diego Fwy.) runs north-south through the Westside, connecting the San Fernando Valley with LAX and southern beach areas. *Tip:* This is one of the area's busiest freeways; steer clear of it when possible—and avoid it like the plague during rush hour.

**I-105** (aka the Century Fwy.), Los Angeles's newest highway, extends from LAX east to I-605.

**I-110** (aka the Harbor Fwy.) starts in Pasadena as Highway 110 (the Pasadena Fwy.); it becomes an interstate in Downtown Los Angeles and runs directly south, where it dead-ends in San Pedro. The section that is now the Pasadena Freeway was Los Angeles's first freeway, known as the Arroyo Seco when it opened in 1940.

---

**Tips**  **Stay Away from Santa Monica Boulevard**

If you're driving to or from Santa Monica and Beverly Hills, West Hollywood, or Century City, try to avoid Santa Monica Boulevard. It's under construction and almost always jammed. Wilshire and Pico boulevards, which run parallel to Santa Monica, are usually less congested and smoother.

---

**I-710** (aka the Long Beach Fwy.) runs north-south through East Los Angeles and dead-ends at Long Beach. Crammed with big rigs leaving the port in San Pedro in a rush, this is the ugliest and most dangerous freeway in California.

**I-605** (aka the San Gabriel River Fwy.) runs from the I-405 near Seal Beach to the I-210 interchange at Duarte. It follows the San Gabriel River, paralleling I-710 to the east, through the San Gabriel Valley up to the edge of the San Gabriel Mountains.

**Highway 1** (aka the Pacific Coast Highway, or simply PCH) is more of a scenic, oceanside parkway linking all of L.A.'s beach communities, from Malibu to the Orange Coast. It's often slow going, but far more scenic than the freeways.

A complex web of surface streets complements the freeways. From north to south, the major east-west thoroughfares connecting Downtown to the beaches are **Sunset, Santa Monica, Wilshire, Olympic, Pico,** and **Venice boulevards.**

## NEIGHBORHOODS IN BRIEF

Los Angeles confuses newcomers in that Downtown isn't the center point of the city. The city itself is more of a juxtaposition of disparate communities that loosely form a metropolis (67 suburbs searching for a city, so they say). The best way to grasp the geography is to break it into six regions: Santa Monica and the beaches, L.A.'s Westside and Beverly Hills, Hollywood and West Hollywood, Downtown, Pasadena, and—beyond the Hollywood Hills—the San Fernando Valley ("The Valley" to locals). Each encompasses a more-or-less distinctive patchwork of city neighborhoods and independently incorporated communities.

### Santa Monica & the Beaches

These L.A. communities get my highest recommendation as the premier place to book a hotel during your vacation. The 60-mile beachfront stretching from Malibu to the Palos Verdes peninsula has milder weather and less smog than the inland communities, and traffic is nominally lighter, except on summer weekends. Each of the coastal towns listed below, from north to south, has a distinct mood and charm, and most are connected via a walk/bike path.

**Malibu,** at the northern border of Los Angeles County, 25 miles from Downtown, was once a privately owned ranch—purchased in 1857 for 10¢ an acre and now the most expensive real estate in L.A. Today its 27 miles of wide

beaches, beachfront cliffs, sparsely populated hills, and relative remoteness from the inner city make it popular with rich recluses such as Cher and Mel Gibson. Indeed, the resident lists of Malibu Colony and nearby Broad Beach—oceanfront strips of closely packed mansions—read like a who's who in Hollywood. With plenty of green space and dramatic rocky outcroppings, Malibu's rural beauty is unsurpassed in L.A., and surfers flock to "the 'Bu" for great, if crowded, waves.

**Santa Monica,** Los Angeles's premier beach community, is known for its festive ocean pier, stylish oceanfront hotels, artsy atmosphere, and large number of homeless residents (it's an oxymoron, but true). Shopping is king

# Santa Monica & the Beaches

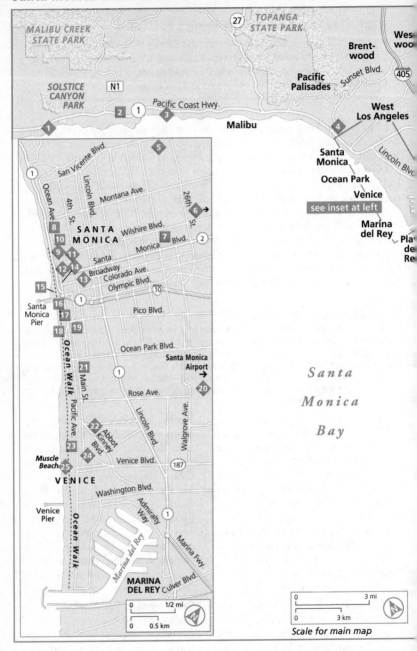

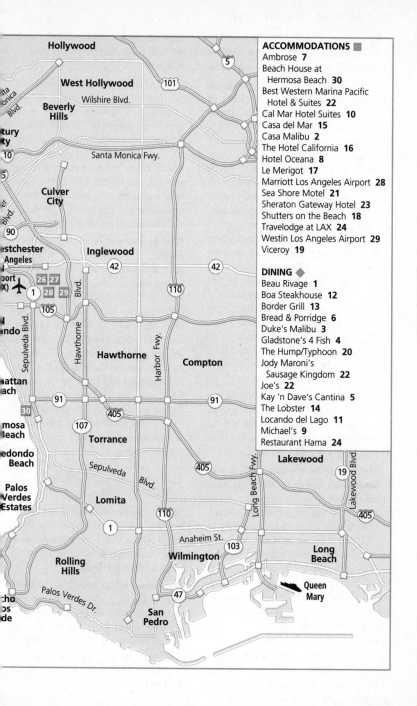

**ACCOMMODATIONS** ■
Ambrose **7**
Beach House at
  Hermosa Beach **30**
Best Western Marina Pacific
  Hotel & Suites **22**
Cal Mar Hotel Suites **10**
Casa del Mar **15**
Casa Malibu **2**
The Hotel California **16**
Hotel Oceana **8**
Le Merigot **17**
Marriott Los Angeles Airport **28**
Sea Shore Motel **21**
Sheraton Gateway Hotel **23**
Shutters on the Beach **18**
Travelodge at LAX **24**
Westin Los Angeles Airport **29**
Viceroy **19**

**DINING** ◆
Beau Rivage **1**
Boa Steakhouse **12**
Border Grill **13**
Bread & Porridge **6**
Duke's Malibu **3**
Gladstone's 4 Fish **4**
The Hump/Typhoon **20**
Jody Maroni's
  Sausage Kingdom **22**
Joe's **22**
Kay 'n Dave's Cantina **5**
The Lobster **14**
Locando del Lago **11**
Michael's **9**
Restaurant Hama **24**

here, especially along the Third Street Promenade, a pedestrian-only outdoor mall lined with shops and restaurants.

**Venice Beach** was created by tobacco mogul Abbot Kinney, who set out in 1904 to transform a worthless marsh into a resort town modeled after Venice, Italy—hence, the series of narrow canals connected by one-lane bridges that you'll see as you explore this eclectic community. It was once infested with grime and crime, but regentrification has brought scores of great restaurants, boutiques, and rising property values for the canalside homes and apartment duplexes. Even the movie stars are moving in: Dennis Hopper, Anjelica Huston, and Julia Roberts reside in this pseudo-bohemian community. Some of L.A.'s most innovative and interesting architecture lines funky Main Street, but Venice Beach is best known for its Ocean Front Walk, a nonstop Mardi Gras of skaters, vendors, fortunetellers, street musicians, and the like.

**Marina del Rey,** just south of Venice, is a somewhat quieter, more upscale waterside community best known for its man-made small-craft harbor (the largest of its kind in the world).

**Manhattan, Hermosa,** and **Redondo beaches** are laid-back, mainly residential neighborhoods with modest homes (except for the oceanfront real estate), mild weather, and residents happy to have fled the L.A. hubbub. You'll find excellent beaches for volleyball, surfing, and tanning here, but when it comes to cultural activities, pickings can be slim. The restaurant scene, while limited, has been improving steadily, and some great new bars and clubs have opened near their respective piers.

### L.A.'s Westside & Beverly Hills

The **Westside,** sandwiched between Hollywood and the city's coastal communities, includes some of Los Angeles's most prestigious neighborhoods, virtually all with names you're sure to recognize:

**Beverly Hills** is politically distinct from the rest of Los Angeles—a famous enclave best known for its palm tree–lined streets of palatial homes, famous residents (Jack Nicholson, Warren Beatty, Annette Bening), and high-priced shops. But it's not all glitz and glamour; the healthy mix of the filthy rich, wannabes, and tourists in downtown Beverly Hills creates a unique—and often snobby-surreal—atmosphere.

**West Hollywood** is a key-shape community, the epicenter of which is the intersection of Santa Monica and La Cienega boulevards. Between Beverly Hills and Hollywood, this politically independent—and blissfully fast-food–free—town is home to some of the area's best restaurants, clubs, shops, and art galleries. WeHo, as it's come to be known, is also the center of L.A.'s gay community; you'll know you've arrived when you see the risqué billboards. Encompassing about 2 square miles, it's a pedestrian-friendly place with plenty of metered parking. Highlights include the 1½ miles of Sunset Boulevard known as Sunset Strip, the chic Sunset Plaza retail strip, and the liveliest stretch of Santa Monica Boulevard.

**Bel Air** and **Holmby Hills,** in the hills north of Westwood and west of Beverly Hills, are old-money residential areas featured prominently on most maps to the stars' homes.

**Brentwood** is best known as the backdrop to the O. J. Simpson melodrama. If Starbucks ever designed a neighborhood, it would look like this generic, upscale mix of track homes, restaurants, and strip malls. The Getty Center looms over Brentwood from its hilltop next to I-405.

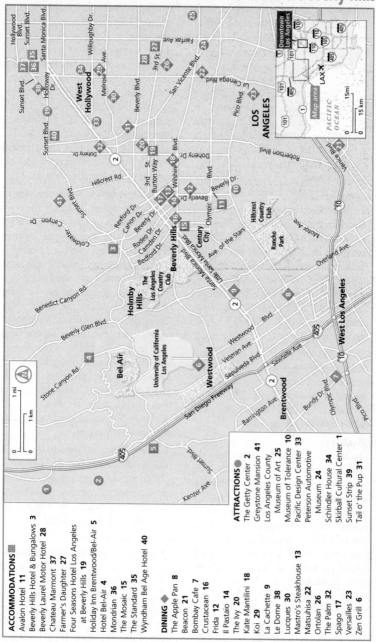

**ACCOMMODATIONS**

Avalon Hotel **11**
Beverly Hills Hotel & Bungalows **3**
Beverly Laurel Motor Hotel **28**
Chateau Marmont **37**
Farmer's Daughter **27**
Four Seasons Hotel Los Angeles at Beverly Hills **19**
Holiday Inn Brentwood/Bel-Air **5**
Hotel Bel-Air **4**
Mondrian **36**
The Mosaic **15**
The Standard **35**
Wyndham Bel Age Hotel **40**

**DINING** ◆

The Apple Pan **8**
Beacon **21**
Bombay Cafe **7**
Crustacean **16**
Frida **12**
Il Pastaio **14**
The Ivy **20**
Kate Mantilini **18**
Koi **29**
La Cachette **9**
Le Dome **38**
Lucques **30**
Mastro's Steakhouse **13**
Matsuhisa **22**
Ortolan **26**
The Palm **32**
Spago **17**
Versailles **23**
Zen Grill **6**

**ATTRACTIONS** ●

The Getty Center **2**
Greystone Mansion **41**
Los Angeles County Museum of Art **25**
Museum of Tolerance **10**
Pacific Design Center **33**
Peterson Automotive Museum **24**
Schindler House **34**
Skirball Cultural Center **1**
Sunset Strip **39**
Tail o' the Pup **31**

**Westwood,** an urban village founded in 1929 and home to the University of California at Los Angeles (UCLA), used to be a hot destination for a night on the town, but it lost much of its appeal in the past decade due to over-crowding and even some minor street violence. Although Westwood is unlikely to regain its old charm, the vibrant new culinary scene has brought new life to the village. Combined with the high concentration of movie the-aters, it's now the premier L.A. destina-tion for dinner and a flick.

**Century City** is a compact and rather bland high-rise area between West Los Angeles and Beverly Hills. Its primary draws are the 20th Century Fox studios, Shubert Theatre, and the Westside Pavil-ion, a huge open-air shopping mall. Century City's three main thoroughfares are Century Park East, Avenue of the Stars, and Century Park West.

**West Los Angeles** encompasses every-thing that isn't one of the other West-side neighborhoods. It's basically the area south of Santa Monica Boulevard, north of Venice Boulevard, east of Santa Monica and Venice, and west and south of Century City.

## Hollywood

Yes, they still come to the mecca of the film industry—young hopefuls with stars in their eyes gravitate to this his-toric heart of L.A.'s movie production like moths fluttering to the glare of neon lights. But today's Hollywood is more illusion than industry. Many of the neighborhood's former movie stu-dios have moved to more spacious ven-ues in Burbank, the Westside, and other parts of the city.

Despite the downturn, visitors con-tinue to flock to Hollywood's landmark attractions, such as the star-studded Walk of Fame and Grauman's Chinese Theatre. Now that the city's $1-billion,

30-year revitalization project is in full swing, Hollywood Boulevard is, for the first time in decades, rising out of a seedy slump, with refurbished movie houses and stylish restaurants and clubs making a fierce comeback. The center-piece Hollywood & Highland complex anchors the neighborhood, with shop-ping, entertainment, and a luxury hotel built around the beautiful Kodak The-atre, designed to host the Academy Awards (really, you'll want to poke your head into this gorgeous theater).

**Melrose Avenue,** scruffy but fun, is the city's funkiest shopping district. It caters to often-raucous youth with sec-ondhand and avant-garde clothing shops, and several good restaurants.

The stretch of Wilshire Boulevard running through the southern part of Hollywood is known as the **Mid-Wilshire** district, or the Miracle Mile. It's lined with tall, contemporary apartment houses and office buildings. The section just east of Fairfax Avenue, known as Museum Row, is home to almost a dozen museums, including the Los Angeles County Museum of Art, the La Brea Tar Pits, and that shrine to L.A. car culture, the Petersen Automotive Museum.

**Griffith Park,** up Western Avenue in the northernmost part of Hollywood, is one of the country's largest urban parks, home to the Los Angeles Zoo, the famous Griffith Observatory, and the outdoor Greek Theater.

## Downtown

Despite the fairly recent construction of numerous cultural centers (such as the Walt Disney Concert Hall and Cathedral of Our Lady of the Angels) and a handful of trendy restaurants, Downtown isn't the tourist hub that it would be in most cities. When it comes to entertaining visitors, the Westside, Hollywood, and beach com-munities are all far more popular.

# Hollywood

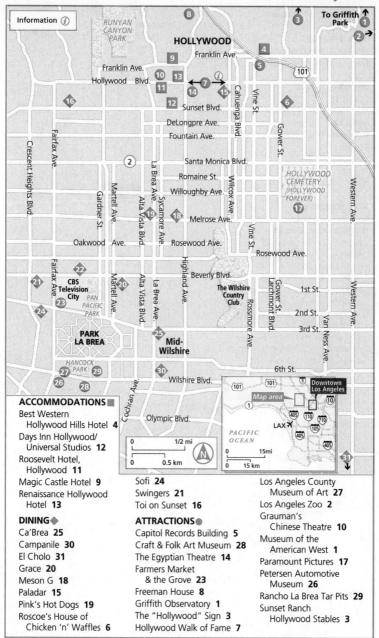

**Information** ⓘ

RUNYAN CANYON PARK

**HOLLYWOOD**

Franklin Ave.

Franklin Ave.

Hollywood Blvd.

Sunset Blvd.

DeLongpre Ave.

Fountain Ave.

Santa Monica Blvd.

Romaine St.

Willoughby Ave.

Melrose Ave.

Oakwood Ave.

Rosewood Ave.

Rosewood Ave.

Beverly Blvd.

CBS Television City

PAN PACIFIC PARK

The Wilshire Country Club

1st St.

2nd St.

3rd St.

**PARK LA BREA**

**Mid-Wilshire**

HANCOCK PARK

Wilshire Blvd.

6th St.

Olympic Blvd.

To Griffith Park

101

Vine St.

Gower St.

HOLLYWOOD CEMETERY (HOLLYWOOD FOREVER)

Western Ave.

Crescent Heights Blvd.

Fairfax Ave.

Gardner St.

Martell Ave.

Alta Vista Blvd.

Sycamore Ave.

La Brea Ave.

Highland Ave.

Wilcox Ave.

Vine St.

Rossmore Ave.

Gower St.

Larchmont Blvd.

Van Ness Ave.

Cahuenga Blvd.

Cochran Ave.

**Downtown Los Angeles**

Map area

PACIFIC OCEAN

LAX ✈

| 0 | 1/2 mi |
| 0 | 0.5 km |

| 0 | 15mi |
| 0 | 15 km |

## ACCOMMODATIONS ■

Best Western
  Hollywood Hills Hotel **4**
Days Inn Hollywood/
  Universal Studios **12**
Roosevelt Hotel,
  Hollywood **11**
Magic Castle Hotel **9**
Renaissance Hollywood
  Hotel **13**

## DINING ◆

Ca'Brea **25**
Campanile **30**
El Cholo **31**
Grace **20**
Meson G **18**
Paladar **15**
Pink's Hot Dogs **19**
Roscoe's House of
  Chicken 'n' Waffles **6**

Sofi **24**
Swingers **21**
Toi on Sunset **16**

## ATTRACTIONS ●

Capitol Records Building **5**
Craft & Folk Art Museum **28**
The Egyptian Theatre **14**
Farmers Market
  & the Grove **23**
Freeman House **8**
Griffith Observatory **1**
The "Hollywood" Sign **3**
Hollywood Walk of Fame **7**

Los Angeles County
  Museum of Art **27**
Los Angeles Zoo **2**
Grauman's
  Chinese Theatre **10**
Museum of the
  American West **1**
Paramount Pictures **17**
Petersen Automotive
  Museum **26**
Rancho La Brea Tar Pits **29**
Sunset Ranch
  Hollywood Stables **3**

# Downtown Los Angeles

**ACCOMMODATIONS** ■
Hotel Figueroa **25**
Hotel Stillwell **23**
Millennium Biltmore Hotel Los Angeles **21**
Westin Bonaventure Hotel & Suites **19**

**DINING** ◆
Ciudad **18**
The Original Pantry Cafe **24**
Patina **12**
Philippe the Original **5**
R23 **10**
Tantra **2**
Traxx **7**
Water Grill **22**

**ATTRACTIONS** ●
Angelino Heights **3**
The Bradbury Building **16**
California Science Center **25**
Cathedral of Our Lady of the Angels **11**
Central Library **20**
Chinatown **4**
City Hall **13**
Dodger Stadium **1**
El Pueblo de Los Angeles Historic District
  (Olvera Street) **6**
Grand Central Market **17**
Japanese American National Museum **9**
Museum of Contemporary Art/
  Geffen Contemporary at MOCA **8**
  Main Building **15**
Natural History Museum
  of Los Angeles County **27**
Performing Arts Center of L.A. County **14**
Staples Center **26**
Union Station **7**
University of Southern California (USC) **27**
Walt Disney Concert Hall **12**

Information (i)
Parking P

W. Temple St.
S. Virgil Ave.
Commonwealth Ave.
Hoover St.
Benton Way
Rampart Blvd.
LAFAYETTE PARK
MACARTHUR PARK
Westmoreland Ave.
S. Hoover St.
W. 8th St.
San Marino St.
W. 9th St.
Westlake Ave.
S. Burlington Ave.
Bonnie Brae St.
S. Union Ave.
W. 11th St.
Magnolia Ave.
W. 12th St
W. Pico Blvd.
W. Venice Blvd.
W. Washington Blvd.
W. 20th St.
Santa Monica Freeway
W. 23rd St.

Map area
PACIFIC OCEAN
LAX

0    15mi
0    15 km

0    1/2 mi
0    1/2 km

Easily recognized by the tight cluster of skyscrapers bolstered by earthquake-proof technology, the business center is eerily vacant on weekends and evenings. The outlying residential communities, however—such as Koreatown, Little Tokyo, Chinatown, and Los Feliz—are vibrant. If you want a tan, head to Santa Monica, but if you want an enticing dose of non-90210 culture, come here.

**El Pueblo de Los Angeles Historic District,** a 44-acre ode to the city's early years, is worth a visit. **Chinatown** is small and touristy, but it's fun for souvenir hunting or traditional dim sum. **Little Tokyo,** on the other hand, is a genuine gathering place for the Southland's Japanese population, with a wide array of shops and restaurants with an authentic flair.

**Silver Lake,** a residential section north of Downtown and adjacent to **Los Feliz,** just to the west, has arty areas with unique cafes, theaters, graffiti, and art galleries—all in equally plentiful proportions. The local music scene has been burgeoning of late.

**Exposition Park,** south and west of Downtown, is home to the Los Angeles Memorial Coliseum, the L.A. Sports Arena, the Natural History Museum, the African-American Museum, and the California Science Center. The University of Southern California (USC) is next door.

**East** and **South Central L.A.,** just east and south of Downtown, are home to the city's large barrios. This is where the 1992 L.A. riots were centered; it was here, at Florence and Normandie avenues, that a news station reporter, hovering above in a helicopter, videotaped Reginald Denny being pulled from the cab of his truck and beaten. These neighborhoods are unique, but they contain few tourist sites, save the Watts Towers. This can be a rough part of town, so avoid looking like a tourist if you decide to visit, particularly at night.

## The San Fernando Valley

The San Fernando Valley, known locally as "The Valley," was nationally popularized in the 1980s by the mall-loving "Valley Girl" stereotype. Between the Santa Monica and the San Gabriel mountain ranges, most of The Valley is residential and commercial—thus off the beaten track for tourists. But some of its attractions are bound to draw you over the hill. **Universal City,** located west of Griffith Park between U.S. 101 and Highway 134, is home to Universal Studios Hollywood and the shopping and entertainment megacomplex City-Walk. The only reason to go to **Burbank,** west of these other suburbs and north of Universal City, is to see one of your favorite TV shows being filmed at NBC or Warner Brothers Studios. Ventura Boulevard has a few good restaurants and shops, in and around Studio City.

**Glendale** is a largely residential community north of Downtown between the Valley and Pasadena. Here you'll find Forest Lawn, the city's best cemetery for very retired movie stars.

## Pasadena & Environs

Best known as the site of the Tournament of Roses Parade each New Year's Day, **Pasadena** was spared from the teardown epidemic that swept L.A., so it has a refreshing old-time feel. Once upon a time, Pasadena was every Angeleno's best-kept secret: A quiet community whose slow and careful regentrification meant nonfranchise restaurants and boutique shopping without the crowds, in a revitalized downtown respectful of its old brick and stone commercial buildings. Although the area's natural and architectural beauty still shines through—so much so that Pasadena remains Hollywood's favorite backyard

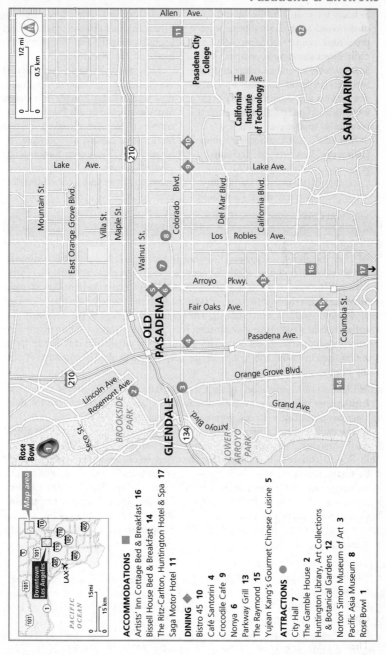

Pasadena & Environs

ACCOMMODATIONS
Artists' Inn Cottage Bed & Breakfast 16
Bissell House Bed & Breakfast 14
The Ritz-Carlton, Huntington Hotel & Spa 17
Saga Motor Hotel 11

DINING
Bistro 45 10
Café Santorini 4
Crocodile Cafe 9
Nonya 6
Parkway Grill 13
The Raymond 15
Yujean Kang's Gourmet Chinese Cuisine 5

ATTRACTIONS
City Hall 7
The Gamble House 2
Huntington Library, Art Collections & Botanical Gardens 12
Norton Simon Museum of Art 3
Pacific Asia Museum 8
Rose Bowl 1

473

location for countless movies and TV shows—Old Town has become a pedestrian mall similar to Santa Monica's Third Street Promenade, complete with huge crowds, midrange chain eateries, and standard-issue mall stores. It still gets our vote as a scenic alternative to the congestion of central L.A., but it has lost much of its small-town charm.

Pasadena is also home to the famous **California Institute of Technology** (CalTech), which boasts 22 Nobel Prize winners among its alumni. The CalTech-operated Jet Propulsion

Laboratory was the birthplace of America's space program, and CalTech scientists were the first to report earthquake activity worldwide.

The residential neighborhoods in Pasadena and its adjacent communities—**Arcadia, La Cañada–Flintridge, San Marino,** and **South Pasadena**—are renowned for well-preserved historic homes, from humble bungalows to lavish mansions. These areas feature public gardens, historic neighborhoods, house museums, and quiet bed-and-breakfast inns.

## 2 Getting Around

### BY CAR

Need I tell you that Los Angeles is car-crazed? Although L.A. *has* public transportation, you really need a set of wheels to get around easily. An elaborate network of well-maintained freeways connects this urban sprawl, but you have to learn how to make sense of the system and cultivate some patience with the traffic (those plastic-covered fold-out maps are a smart investment). The golden rule of driving Los Angeles is this: Allow more time to get to your destination than you think you'll need, especially during morning and evening rush hours (40 min. of leeway usually suffices). For an explanation of the city layout and details on the freeway system, see "Orientation," earlier in this chapter.

**RENTALS**   Los Angeles is one of the cheapest places in America to rent a car. Major national car-rental companies usually rent economy- and compact-class cars for about $35 per day and $120 per week, with unlimited mileage.

All the major car-rental agencies have offices at the airport and in the larger hotels. If you're thinking of splurging on a dig-me road machine such as a Maserati, Ferrari, Rolls-Royce, Lamborghini, or Hummer, the places to call are either **Budget Beverly Hills Car Collection,** 9815 Wilshire Blvd. (© **800/227-7117** or 310/881-2335; www.budgetbeverlyhills.com), or **Beverly Hills Rent-A-Car,** 9732 Little Santa Monica Blvd., Beverly Hills (© **800/479-5996** or 310/337-1400; www.bhrentacar.com). Both car-rental companies have additional locations in Santa Monica, LAX, Orange County, and Newport Beach, and both offer complimentary delivery to local hotels or pickup service at LAX.

### BY PUBLIC TRANSPORTATION

Some visitors manage to successfully tour Los Angeles via public transportation (and I believe I've met them both . . . ), but we don't recommend that plan for most readers. L.A. is a metropolis that has grown up around the automobile, and many areas are inaccessible without one. Still, if you're visiting for a short time, on a very tight budget, or if you don't expect to move around a lot, public transport *might* work for you. The **Los Angeles County Metropolitan Transit Authority (MTA;** © **213/922-2000;** www.mta.net) runs the city's trains and buses; brochures and schedules are available at every area visitor center.

## BY BUS OR SHUTTLE

Spread-out stops, sluggish service, and frequent transfers make extensive touring by bus impractical. For short hops and occasional jaunts, however, buses are economical and environmentally correct. However, I don't recommend riding buses late at night. The basic bus fare is $1.25 for all local lines, with transfers costing 25¢. Express buses, which travel along the freeways, and buses on intercounty routes charge higher fares; phone for information.

The **Downtown Area Short Hop (DASH)** shuttle system operates buses throughout Downtown, Hollywood, and the west side of L.A. Service runs every 5 to 20 minutes, depending on the time of day, and costs just 25¢. Contact the Department of Transportation (ⓒ **213/808-2273;** www.ladottransit.com) for schedules and route information; request a weekday *and* weekend map.

The **Cityline** shuttle is a great way to get around West Hollywood on weekdays (9am–4pm) and Saturday (10am–7:30pm). For 50¢, it'll take you to most of the major shops and restaurants throughout WeHo (very handy if you park your car in a flat-fee lot). For more information, call ⓒ **800/447-2189.**

## BY RAIL & SUBWAY

The **MetroRail** system is a sore subject in town. For years, the MTA has been digging up the streets, sucking up tax money, and pushing exhaust vents up through peaceful parkland—and for what? Let's face it, L.A. will never have New York's subway or San Francisco's BART. Today the system is still in its infancy, mainly popular with commuters from outlying suburbs. Here's an overview of what's currently in place:

The **Metro Blue Line,** an aboveground rail line, connects Downtown Los Angeles with Long Beach. Trains runs daily from 6am to 9pm; the fare is $1.35.

The **Metro Red Line,** L.A.'s first subway, has been growing since 1993 and opened a highly publicized Hollywood–Universal City extension in 2000. The line begins at Union Station, the city's main train depot, and travels west underneath Wilshire Boulevard, looping north into Hollywood and the San Fernando Valley. The fare is $1.35; discount tokens are available at Metro service centers and many area convenience stores.

The **Metro Green Line** runs for 20 miles along the center of the new I-105, the Glenn Anderson (Century) Freeway, and connects Norwalk in eastern Los Angeles County to LAX. A connection with the Blue Line offers visitors access from LAX to Downtown L.A. or Long Beach. The fare is $1.35.

The **Metro Gold Line** is a 13¾-mile link between Pasadena and Union Station in Downtown L.A. Stops include Old Pasadena, the Southwest Museum, and Chinatown. The fare is $1.35.

Weekly Metro passes are $14 at Metro Customer Centers and local convenience and grocery stores. For more information—including construction updates and details on purchasing tokens or passes—call **MTA** at ⓒ **213/922-2000.** Better yet, log onto their handy website at www.mta.net.

## BY TAXI

Distances are long in Los Angeles, and cab fares are high; even a short trip can cost $10 or more. Taxis currently charge $1.90 at the flag drop, plus $1.60 per mile, but it will probably go up by the time you read this. A service charge is added to fares originating at LAX.

Except in the heart of Downtown, cabs usually won't pull over when hailed. Cabstands are found at airports, Downtown's Union Station, and major hotels. To ensure a ride, order a taxi in advance from **Checker Cab** (📞 323/654-8400), **L.A. Taxi** (📞 213/627-7000), or **United Taxi** (📞 213/483-7604).

## FAST FACTS: Los Angeles

*American Express* In addition to those at 327 N. Beverly Dr., Beverly Hills (📞 310/274-8277), and at the Beverly Connection, 8493 W. Third St., Los Angeles (📞 310/659-1682), offices are located throughout the city. To locate one nearest you, call 📞 800/221-7282.

*Area Codes* Within the past 20 years, L.A. has gone from a single area code (213) to a whopping seven. Even residents can't keep up. At press time, here's the layout: Areas west of La Cienega Boulevard, including Beverly Hills and the beach communities, use **310**. Portions of Los Angeles County east and south of the city, including Long Beach, use **562**. The San Fernando Valley uses **818**, while points east—including parts of Burbank, Glendale, and Pasadena—use the new **626** code. What happened to 213, you ask? Downtown still uses it, but all other numbers, including Griffith Park, Hollywood, and parts of West Hollywood (east of La Cienega Blvd.) now use the new **323**. When in doubt, call directory assistance at 📞 **411**.

*Babysitters* If you're staying at one of the larger hotels, the concierge can usually recommend a reliable babysitter. If not, contact the **Baby-Sitters Guild** in Glendale (📞 310/837-1800 or 818/552-2229), L.A.'s oldest and largest babysitting service.

*Camera Repair* On-site repairs are the specialty at family-owned **General Camera Repair,** 2218 E. Colorado Blvd., Pasadena (📞 626/449-4533); they opened in 1964 at this spot on the Rose Parade route.

*Dentists* For a local recommendation, call the **Dental Referral Service** (📞 800/422-8338).

*Doctors* See "Hospital," below.

*Emergencies* For police, fire, highway patrol, or life-threatening medical emergencies, dial 📞 **911**. No coins are needed at payphones.

*Hospital* The centrally located (and world-famous) **Cedars-Sinai Medical Center,** 8700 Beverly Blvd., Los Angeles (📞 310/423-3277), has a 24-hour emergency room staffed by some of the country's finest MDs.

*Liquor Laws* Liquor and grocery stores, and most restaurants, nightclubs, and bars can sell alcoholic beverages between 6am and 2am. The legal age for purchase and consumption is 21; proof of age is required.

*Newspapers & Magazines* **World Book & News Co.,** at 1652 N. Cahuenga Blvd. (📞 323/465-4352), near Hollywood and Vine and Grauman's Chinese Theatre, stocks lots of out-of-town and foreign periodicals. Customers may browse through magazines but not newspapers. It's open 24 hours.

*Pharmacies* **Horton & Converse** (www.hortonandconverse.com) has locations around L.A., including 2001 Santa Monica Blvd., Santa Monica (📞 310/829-3401);

9201 Sunset Blvd., Beverly Hills (© **323/272-0488**); and 11600 Wilshire Blvd., West Los Angeles (© **310/478-0801**). Hours vary, but the West L.A. location is open until 2am. Chances are good that there's either a **Walgreens** (www.walgreens. com) or a **Rite Aid** (www.riteaid.com) within a mile of where you're staying.

*Police*  In an emergency, dial © **911.** For nonemergency police matters, call © **213/485-2121;** in Beverly Hills, dial © **310/550-4951.**

*Post Office*  Call © **800/ASK-USPS** to find the one closest to you.

*Taxes*  The combined Los Angeles County and California state sales taxes amount to 8.25%; hotel taxes add 12% to 17% to room tariffs.

*Taxis*  See "Getting Around," earlier in this chapter.

*Time Zone*  Los Angeles is in the Pacific Standard Time zone, 8 hours behind Greenwich Mean Time and 3 hours behind Eastern Standard Time.

*Weather*  Call **Los Angeles Weather Information** (© **213/554-1212**) for the daily forecast. For beach conditions, call the **Zuma Beach Lifeguard** recorded information (© **310/457-9701**).

## 3 Where to Stay

Due to space constraints, I've had to limit the number of hotels included here. For dozens of additional options, check out *Frommer's Los Angeles 2006.*

**CHOOSING A LOCATION**   In sprawling Los Angeles, location is everything; the neighborhood you choose as a base can make or break your vacation. If you plan to spend your days at the beach but stay Downtown, for example, you're going to lose a lot of valuable relaxation time on the freeway. For business travelers, choosing a location is easy: Pick a hotel near your work. For vacationers, though, the decision is more difficult. Consider where you want to spend your time before you book a room. Wherever you stay, though, count on driving a good bit—no hotel in Los Angeles is convenient to everything.

The relatively smog-free beach communities such as **Santa Monica** and **Venice** are popular with visitors; just about everybody loves to stay at the beach. Book ahead because hotels fill up quickly, especially in summer.

If they're not at one of the beach communities, most visitors stay on the city's **Westside,** a short drive from the beach and close to most of L.A.'s colorful sights. The most elegant, expensive accommodations are in **Beverly Hills** and **Bel Air;** a few of the hotels in these neighborhoods have become visitor attractions unto themselves. The focal point of L.A. nightlife, **West Hollywood,** is home to the greatest range of hotels, from $300-plus-per-night boutiques to affordably priced motels.

**Hollywood** has fewer hotels than you might expect. Accommodations are generally moderately priced and well maintained but unspectacular. Centrally located between Downtown and Beverly Hills, just a stone's throw from Universal Studios, Hollywood makes a convenient base if you're planning to explore, but it has more tourists and less visual appeal than other neighborhoods.

**Downtown** hotels are generally business-oriented, but thanks to direct Metro (L.A.'s subway) connections to Hollywood and Universal Studios, the demographic has begun to shift. The top hotels offer excellent deals on weekend packages. But chances are good that Downtown doesn't embody the picture of L.A. you've been dreaming of; you need a coastal or Westside base for that.

Families might want to head to the **Universal City** to be near Universal Studios, or straight to **Anaheim and Disneyland** (see chapter 15). **Pasadena** offers historic charm, small-town ambience, easy access to downtown L.A., and picture-postcard beauty, but driving to the beach can take forever.

To locate the hotels reviewed below, see the individual neighborhood maps in section 1, "Orientation."

**RATES** The following **rates** are the rack rates—the maximum that a hotel charges for rooms. Rack rates are only guidelines, though, and you can usually find ways around them. *Always* check hotel websites for package deals and special Internet rates. The hotels in this section provided their best estimates for 2006, and all rates were correct at press time. **Be aware that rates can change at any time,** subject to availability, seasonal fluctuations, and plain old increases.

## SANTA MONICA & THE BEACHES
### VERY EXPENSIVE

**Casa del Mar** ★★★ In a former 1920s Renaissance Revival beach club, this Art Deco stunner is a real dream of a resort hotel—equal to its sister resort across the street, Shutters (see below). Whereas Shutters is outfitted like a chic East Coast beach house, Casa del Mar is an impeccable, U-shaped, villalike structure that radiates period glamour. Most of the guest rooms have ocean views; unfortunately, windows don't open more than an inch or two (giving Shutters a slight advantage). You're unlikely to be disappointed, though, given the gorgeous, summery, European-inspired decor in golds and sea-grass hues, sumptuously dressed beds, and big Italian marble bathrooms with extra-large whirlpool tubs and separate showers. Rooms are laid out for relaxation, not business, so travelers with work on their minds should stay elsewhere.

Downstairs you'll find the big, elegant living room with ocean views, a stylish lounge, and the **Oceanfront** restaurant, which has earned kudos and more than a few celebrity fans for its beautiful setting, great service, and seafood-heavy California cuisine. Outdoors, the Mediterranean-evocative Palm Terrace boasts a gorgeous Roman-style pool and Jacuzzi with spectacular ocean views. The Spa is one of L.A.'s finest and most expensive, featuring the exclusive product line of Dr. Howard Murad—one of the country's foremost authorities on skin care.

1910 Ocean Way (next to the Santa Monica Pier), Santa Monica, CA 90405. ℂ **800/898-6999** or 310/581-5533. Fax 310/581-5503. www.hotelcasadelmar.com. 129 units. $405–$650 double; from $975 suite. AE, DC, DISC, MC, V. Valet parking $21. **Amenities:** Restaurant; bar/lounge; café; tearoom; lobby lounge for cocktails and light fare; alfresco cafe for daytime dining; heated outdoor Roman-style pool; plunge pool; state-of-the-art health club w/spa services; Jacuzzi overlooking Santa Monica Beach; 24-hr. concierge; business center; 24-hr. room service; laundry service; dry cleaning. *In room:* A/C, TV/VCR, dataport, minibar, hair dryer, iron, laptop-size safe, CD player.

**Hotel Oceana** ★★ *Kids* Many advertising execs and others who could stay anywhere make the Oceana their choice for long-term stays. Across the street from the ocean, this all-suite hotel sits alongside low-rise, high-rent condos on a gorgeous stretch of Ocean Avenue, several blocks north of the Santa Monica hubbub. With their bright, Matisse-style interiors and cushy IKEA-style furniture, the wonderful apartmentlike suites are colorful, modern, and amenity laden: Goodies run the gamut from comfy robes, multiple TVs, and CD players to full gourmet kitchens stocked with Wolfgang Puck microwavable pizzas, Häagen-Dazs pints, and bottles of California Merlot. The enormous suites make the Oceana terrific for families or shares.

Oceanview suites feature balconies and two-person whirlpools in the mammoth bathrooms, but don't feel the need to stretch your budget for a view, as all units sit garden-style around the courtyard with its cushiony chaises and boomerang-shape pool. The primary colors and playful modern style suit the beach location perfectly, and service is excellent.

849 Ocean Ave. (south of Montana Ave.), Santa Monica, CA 90403. © 800/777-0758 or 310/393-0486. Fax 310/458-1182. www.hoteloceana.com. 63 units. $380 studio suite; $390–$500 1-bedroom suite; $750–$800 2-bedroom suite. AE, DC, DISC, MC, V. Valet parking $21. **Amenities:** Outdoor heated pool; exercise room; access to nearby health club; watersports equipment; concierge; business center; 24-hr. room service; room service from Wolfgang Puck Cafe (7am–10pm); in-room massage; babysitting; laundry service; dry-cleaning service. *In room:* A/C; TV/VCR w/pay movies, video games, Internet access, dataport, kitchen, minibar, fridge, coffeemaker, hair dryer, iron, safe, microwave, CD player.

**Shutters on the Beach** ★★★    This Cape Cod–style luxury hotel enjoys one of the city's most prized locations—on the beach, 1 block from Santa Monica Pier. Only relative newcomer Casa del Mar (above) can compete, but Shutters bests it by attaching alfresco balconies to every guest room and having a more personal boutique hotel-like feel. The views and sounds of the ocean are the most outstanding qualities of the spacious, luxuriously outfitted, Cape Cod–inspired rooms, some of which have fireplaces and/or whirlpool tubs; all have floor-to-ceiling windows that open. The elegant marble bathrooms come with generous counter space, waterproof radios, and toy whales. A relaxed ambience pervades the contemporary art–filled public spaces, which feel like the common areas of a deluxe Montauk beach house. The small swimming pool and sunny lobby lounge are great perches for spotting the many celebrities who swear by Shutters. **One Pico,** the hotel's premier restaurant, serves modern American cuisine in a seaside setting; the best meals at the more casual **Pedals Cafe** come from the wood-burning grill. The hotels recently opened a spa called **ONE,** which offers guests facials, massages, body scrubs and body treatments, manicures, pedicures, and waxing. *Tip:* The beach-cottage rooms overlooking the sand are more desirable and no more expensive than those in the towers.

1 Pico Blvd., Santa Monica, CA 90405. © 800/334-9000 or 310/458-0030. Fax 310/458-4589. www.shuttersonthe beach.com. 198 units. $405–$650 double; from $905 suite. AE, DC, DISC, MC, V. Valet parking $26. **Amenities:** Restaurant; cafe; lobby lounge; outdoor heated pool and Jacuzzi; health club w/spa services; sauna; extensive beach equipment rentals; concierge; activities desk; courtesy car; business center w/secretarial services; 24-hr. room service; babysitting; laundry service; dry-cleaning; video library. *In room:* A/C, TV/VCR, dataport, hair dryer, iron, safe, CD player, mini–wine cellar.

## EXPENSIVE

**Beach House at Hermosa Beach** ★★ *Finds*    With a Cape Cod style that suits its location on the sand, this luxurious, romantic inn is a network of beautifully designed split-level studio suites. Every bright, sunny unit comes with a plush, furnished living room with a wood-burning fireplace (Duraflame logs provided) and entertainment center; a micro-kitchen with china and flatware for four; an elevated sleeping niche with a down-dressed king bed, a second TV, and a generous work area; an extralarge bathroom with an extradeep soaking tub, a separate shower, cotton robes, and Aveda products; and a furnished balcony, many of which overlook the beach. (And it's worth the extra money to score a beachfront room.) Although sofas convert into second beds, the unit configuration is best suited to couples; more than three is too many. Despite the summertime carnival atmosphere of the Strand, the Beach House stays serene with double-paned windows and noise-insulated walls. An excellent light breakfast is served in the sunny breakfast room, and the staff is attentive yet easygoing. L.A.'s city center is at least a half-hour drive away, but Hermosa is airport-convenient and ideal for a beach getaway.

1300 The Strand, Hermosa Beach, CA 90254. © **888/895-4559** or 310/374-3001. Fax 310/372-2115. www.beach-house.com. 96 units. $224–$349 double. Rates include continental breakfast. AE, DC, DISC, MC, V. Valet parking $17. **Amenities:** Concierge; room service from nearby restaurant; laundry service; dry cleaning. *In room:* A/C, 2 TVs, data-port, stocked kitchenette w/microwave and stovetop, fridge, coffeemaker, hair dryer, iron, stereo w/5-disk CD changer, menu of spa services.

**Le Merigot** ★★  Le Merigot is a low-key luxury hotel and spa that doesn't try to be anything other than a comfortable place to spend your seaside vacation. Ideally situated on the sandy side of Ocean Avenue in the heart of Santa Monica's beach scene, the 175-room property is essentially a business hotel that doubles as a resort, complete with a well-regarded French-California restaurant, **Cézanne,** and the 5,500-square-foot SPA Le Merigot, which offers a full range of services along with an outdoor pool and a state-of-the-art fitness center. Most of the contemporary-style guest rooms offer ocean views, and all are plushly furnished with thick carpeting, marble-tiled baths, oversized lounge chairs, and "Cloud Nine" beds topped with Frette linens, down comforters, and feather pillows. What I really like about this hotel, however, are the clever package deals, such as the "California Dreamin'," which includes your choice of a convertible Porsche Boxster or a BMW Z4 Roadster rental car, and the "California Surfin' Safari," a deluxe package that includes a full breakfast for two, a 2-hour surf lesson, a rejuvenating full-session Swedish massage, and celebratory Blue Crush graduation martinis (how very L.A.).

1740 Ocean Ave., Santa Monica, CA 90401. © **800/228-9290** or 310/395-9700. Fax 310/395-9200. www.lemerigot hotel.com. 175 units. $299–$499 double; from $800 suite. AE, DISC, MC, V. Valet parking $28. **Amenities:** Full-service restaurant; lobby bar; outdoor pool; fitness facilities and spa; concierge; business services; gift shop; 24-hr. room service; choice of morning newspaper. *In room:* A/C, cable TV, 3 dual-line phones w/voice mail, fax machine on request, high-speed Internet access, minibar, iron/roning board, laptop safe.

**Viceroy** ★★  This fairly new, überchic hotel, on the sea side of Santa Monica, is still at the top of L.A.'s "in" list. Of course, part of being "in" is breaking new ground, and that's certainly what designer Kelly Wearstler achieved with her "Modern Colonialism" makeover. As you enter the lobby, the startling color scheme first grabs your attention—a rather unorthodox blend of parrot green, charcoal gray, and glossy white with chrome, silver, and ebony highlights. Then there's the dish thing: hundreds of custom-made china pieces arranged in symmetrical patterns throughout the hotel and guest rooms (Where's The Who when you really need them?). The array of white patent-leather chaises in the lobby seem more for form than function; most guests prefer more conventional seating in the Cameo bar or private poolside cabanas. The edgy-English theme applies to each guest room as well, rigged with an array of high-tech toys (27-inch flat-screen TV, another flat-screen TV in the marble-laden bathrooms, a CD/DVD player, and T1 Internet access), custom-made furnishings, and luxurious Frette linens and bathrobes, Molton Brown products, and down comforters and pillows. The restaurant **Whist** serves superb contemporary cuisine. You'll enjoy the location as well—a short walk to the beach and in the thick of the shopping, entertainment, and restaurant scene. Full spa services by Fred Segal Beauty are offered either in-room or at the poolside spa tent. *Tip:* Splurge for an oceanview room; your only other choice is the hotel parking lot.

1819 Ocean Ave., Santa Monica, CA 90401. ℂ **800/670-6185** or 310/260-7500. Fax 310/260-7515. www. viceroysantamonica.com. 170 units. $249–$339 double; from $689 suite. AE, DC, DISC, MC, V. Valet parking $24. **Amenities:** Restaurant; bar; lounge; 2 heated outdoor pools; fitness center; concierge; 24-hr. room service; in-room massage; laundry service; dry cleaning; newspaper delivery; videos available. *In room:* TV w/pay movies and video games, dataport and high-speed Internet connection, minibar, hair dryer, safe, CD/DVD player.

## MODERATE

**The Ambrose** ★★ *Value*    If a soothing, peaceful environment is more important to you than being steps from the ocean, I've found your hotel. In a residential Santa Monica neighborhood, the new 77-room Ambrose is quickly becoming a favorite boutique hideaway for CEOs who are tired of the megahotel experience and want a relaxing place to hang their coats and unwind. The Ambrose's unique architecture blends the Arts and Crafts movement with soothing Asian influences—a tranquil Japanese garden, a koi pond, trickling fountains, beautiful artwork, and a profusion of dark woods and mossy palates. The majority of the guest rooms are small—if you're not satisfied with the elbow room, feel free to ask for another—but they're luxuriously appointed with Matteo Italian bedding, Frette cotton kimonos and bath linens, oversize goose-down pillows, and surround-sound CD-DVD music systems. Studio rooms are the most ample, with a large private deck with partial ocean views and a fireplace. It's the many complimentary amenities, however, that really sold me on the Ambrose: underground parking with direct elevator access, wireless Internet access, access to the community computer, breakfast by local gourmet Hans Rockenwagner, a 24-hour fitness room filled with top-of-the-line equipment, and shuttle service around Santa Monica via the hotel's London taxi, which is cute as all get out. Other perks include a 24-hour in-room dining menu and Aveda products. Rack rates start at a very reasonable $175, so book a room fast while it's still a bargain.

1255 20th St. (at Arizona), Santa Monica, CA 90404. ℂ **310/315–1555.** Fax 310/315-1556. www.ambrosehotel.com. 77 units. $175–$300 double. Rates include continental breakfast. AE, DC, DISC, MC, V. Valet parking free. **Amenities:** Fitness center; complimentary local transportation; 24-hr. room service. *In room:* TV/VCR, free dataport and wireless high-speed Internet connection, minibar, hair dryer, safe, CD/DVD surround sound, daily newspaper.

**The Hotel California** ★ *Finds*    On an enviable piece of real estate along Ocean Avenue—right next door to the behemoth Loews—this welcoming hacienda-style beachfront motel has the surfer/sun-worshiper vibe you'd expect from Santa Monica lodgings. The well-tended complex sits above and across an alley from the beach with excellent views and direct access to the sand via a private path. The inn offers cheery, newly renovated rooms with California-themed decor—including beds with down comforters, Egyptian-cotton sheets, and surfboard headboards—hardwood floors, and Spanish-tiled bathrooms. Five one-bedroom suites also have kitchenettes and pullout sofas that make them great for families or longer stays; all rooms have minifridges, 27-inch TVs, and ceiling fans, as well a free wireless Internet and local calls. A handful of rooms have showers only in the bathrooms, so request a room with a tub if it matters to you. And no, this place is not the hotel from the Eagle's hit—*that* hotel is rumored to be in Mexico, and it's the Beverly Hills Hotel on the album cover. *Tip:* Pay a few bucks extra for a courtyard view, because the cheapest rooms face the parking lot and noisy Ocean Avenue. And check the website for specials.

1670 Ocean Ave. (south of Colorado Ave.), Santa Monica, CA 90401. ℂ **866/571-0000** or 310/393-2363. Fax 310/ 393-1063. www.hotelca.com. 26 units. $169–$279 double or suite. AE, DISC, MC, V. Self-parking $15. **Amenities:** Jacuzzi; activities desk; discount car-rental desk; high-speed Internet access, fax/copier, and coffeemaker in front office. *In room:* TV/VCR, dataport, fridge, hair dryer, iron.

## INEXPENSIVE

**Best Western Marina Pacific Hotel & Suites** ✦ *Kids*   This bright, four-story hotel is a haven of smart value. Just off the Venice boardwalk and 200 feet from the beach, spacious rooms are brightened with beachy colors, and equipped with chain-standard furnishings, fridges, and two-line phones. The one-bedroom suites are terrific for families: Master bedrooms have king-size beds, fully outfitted kitchens with microwave and dishwasher, dining areas, queen-size sofa sleepers, balconies, and fireplaces. Photos of local scenes and rock-'n'-roll legends, along with works by local artists, give the public spaces a cool L.A. vibe. Many rooms have at least partial ocean views (the best are from the top-floor facing the ocean). Additional perks include complimentary continental breakfast, free local shuttles, and secured, covered parking. Stay elsewhere if you need a lot in the way of service or if you don't relish the party-hearty human carnival of Venice Beach. (Santa Monica is quieter and more refined.)

1697 Pacific Ave. (at 17th Ave.), Venice, CA 90291. © **800/786-7789** or 310/452-1111. Fax 310/452-5479. www.mphotel.com. 88 units. $109–$159 double; $169–$269 suite. Rates include continental breakfast. Extra person $10. Children 12 and under stay free in parent's room. Ask about AAA, senior, and other discounts; weekly and monthly rates also available. AE, DC, DISC, MC, V. Self-parking $9. **Amenities:** Continental breakfast; free shuttle to Santa Monica and Marina del Rey; coin-op laundry; laundry service; dry cleaning. *In room:* A/C, cable TV w/HBO, free high-speed dataport, fridge, coffeemaker, hair dryer, iron/ironing board.

**Cal Mar Hotel Suites** ✦ *Value*   In a residential neighborhood 2 blocks from the ocean, this garden apartment complex delivers a lot of bang for your buck. Each unit is an apartment-style suite with a living room and pullout sofa, a full-size kitchen with utensils, and a separate bedroom; most are spacious enough to accommodate four in comfort. The building was constructed in the 1950s with an eye for quality (with attractive tile work and large closets). The furnishings aren't luxurious, but they're modern and clean, and everything is well kept. It's easy to stay comfortably here for a week or more. It's well located—a block from Third Street shopping and a short walk to the beach—and covered parking is free. The staff is attentive and courteous, which helps account for the high rate of repeat guests. The garden courtyard has a swimming pool and chaises for lounging. *Tip:* Request a room on the second floor to avoid the sound of stomping feet.

220 California Ave., Santa Monica, CA 90403. © **800/776-6007** or 310/395-5555. Fax 310/451-1111. www.calmarhotel.com. 36 units. $109–$169 suite. Extra person $10. Children under 10 stay free in parent's room. AE, DC, DISC, MC, V. Free parking. **Amenities:** Heated outdoor pool; coin-op laundry. *In room:* TV, full kitchen w/fridge and coffeemaker, hair dryer, iron, CD sound system.

**Casa Malibu** ✦✦ *Finds*   On its very own beach, this leftover jewel from Malibu's golden age doesn't try to play the sleek resort game. Instead, the modest, low-rise inn has a cozy, timeless California-beach-cottage look. Wrapped around a palm-studded inner courtyard with well-tended flower beds and climbing *cuppa d'oro* vines, the 21 rooms are comfortable and thoughtfully outfitted. Many have been upgraded with tile bathrooms, air-conditioning (almost never necessary on the coast), and VCRs or DVDs, but even the older units are in great shape, with top-quality bedding and bathrobes. Depending on which you choose, you might also find a fireplace, a kitchenette (in a half dozen or so), a CD player (in suites), a tub (instead of shower only), and/or a private deck over the sand. The upstairs Catalina Suite (Lana Turner's old hideout) has the best view, and the gorgeous Malibu Suite—the best room in the house, right on the beach—offers state-of-the-art pampering. More than half the rooms have ocean views, and even those facing the courtyard are quiet, with easy access to the beach (raked smooth each morning), via wooden stairs. The handsome, wind-shielded brick sun deck extends directly over the sand. Book well in advance for summer; this one's a favorite among locals and visitors alike.

22752 Pacific Coast Hwy. (about ¼ mile south of Malibu Pier), Malibu, CA 90265. ℂ 800/831-0858 or 310/456-2219. Fax 310/456-5418. 21 units. $99–$189 garden or oceanview double; $229–$249 beachfront double; $229–$379 suite. Rates include continental breakfast. Extra person $15. AE, MC, V. Free parking. **Amenities:** Access to nearby private health club; room service for lunch and dinner; in-room massage; laundry service; dry cleaning; private beach; hotelwide wireless access. *In room:* TV, 2-line telephone w/dataport, fridge, coffeemaker, hair dryer, iron.

**Sea Shore Motel** ★ *Finds*    In the heart of Santa Monica's Main Street dining and shopping sector, this small, friendly, family-run motel is one of the best bargains near the beach. Arranged around a parking courtyard, rooms are small and unremarkable from the outside, but the conscientious management has done a nice job with the interiors, installing attractive terra-cotta floor tiles, granite countertops, and conveniences like voice mail and data-jack phones. Complete with a living room and full kitchen, the four new 800-square-foot suites are a phenomenal deal; book them as far in advance as possible. With a full slate of restaurants out the front door and the Santa Monica Pier and beach a couple of blocks away, it's a terrific bargain base for exploring the sandy side of the city.

2637 Main St. (south of Ocean Park Blvd.), Santa Monica, CA 90405. ℂ 310/392-2787. Fax 310/392-5167. www.seashoremotel.com. 24 units. $75–$95 double; $150–$225 suite. Extra person $5. Children under 12 stay free in parent's room. Midweek discounts available. AE, DISC, MC, V. Free parking. Pets accepted for $10-per-night fee. **Amenities:** Deli; coin-op laundry; sun deck. *In room:* TV, dataport, fridge, coffeemaker, iron.

## NEAR LAX

If you have an early-morning flight and you need an airport hotel, the **Westin Los Angeles Airport,** 5400 W. Century Blvd. (ℂ **800/937-8461** or 310/216-5858; www.westin.com/losangelesairport), is a cut above the rest, with its patented Westin Heavenly Beds. Two other good, moderately priced choices are the **Sheraton Gateway Hotel,** 6101 W. Century Blvd., near Sepulveda Boulevard (ℂ **800/325-3535** or 310/642-1111; www.sheratonlosangeles.com), a comfortable, California-style hotel that literally overlooks the runway; and the **Marriott Los Angeles Airport,** 5855 Century Blvd. (ℂ **800/228-9290** or 310/641-5700; www.marriott.com), a reliable choice for travelers on the fly.

An inexpensive option is the **Travelodge at LAX,** 5547 W. Century Blvd. (ℂ **800/ 421-3939** or 310/649-4000; www.travelodgelax.com), an otherwise standard member of the reliable chain with a surprisingly beautiful tropical garden surrounding the pool area.

## L.A.'S WESTSIDE & BEVERLY HILLS
### VERY EXPENSIVE

**Beverly Hills Hotel and Bungalows** ★★★    Behind the famous facade (remember the Eagles' *Hotel California* album?), legends are still made in this historically celebrity-studded haven. In Hollywood's golden days, The "Pink Palace" was center stage for both deal- and star-making. Today, actors and other industry hotshots—"all the current rulers of the universe," as one staff member joked—lounge around the Olympic-size pool (into which Katharine Hepburn once dove fully clothed), or dig into Dutch apple pancakes in the iconic **Polo Lounge** (where Ozzy Osbourne has been known to take his afternoon tea). I had the pleasure of staying here recently and was so impressed with the entire experience that the Beverley Hills Hotel has become my new favorite in L.A. It's a world-class landmark, and improvements over the years have only added to its luster.

Following a $100-million restoration, the grand lobby and impeccably landscaped grounds retain their glory. And the lavish guest rooms—each uniquely decorated in a subdued palate of pinks, greens, apricots, and yellows—have every state-of-the-art luxury, including extralarge bathrooms with double Grecian marble sinks and TVs. Management has assembled an unpretentious, service-oriented staff bent on guest comfort, while retaining the best original services, such as butler service at the touch of a button. Many rooms feature private patios, Jacuzzi tubs, kitchens, and/or dining rooms. The 21 bungalows are more luxurious than ever, and the lush, tropical-like grounds are brimming with exotic trees and divinely aromatic flowers. The outdoor pathways are even carpeted, to reduce noise. *Tip:* The inexpensive, informal **Fountain Coffee Shop,** open daily from 7am to 7pm, is a great stop for an hour; you never know who might be slurping down a chocolate malt on the stool next to you.

9641 Sunset Blvd. (at Rodeo Dr.), Beverly Hills, CA 90210. ℂ **800/283-8885** or 310/276-2251. Fax 310/887-2887. www.beverlyhillshotel.com. 203 units. $395–$485 double; from $835 suite or bungalow. AE, DC, MC, V. Parking $23. Pets accepted in bungalows only. **Amenities:** 3 restaurants (Polo Lounge, Fountain Coffee Shop, alfresco Cabana Club Cafe); 2 lounges (Sunset Lounge for high tea and cocktails, bar in Polo Lounge); Olympic-size outdoor heated pool; 2 outdoor tennis courts (lit for night play); fitness center; whirlpool; concierge; car-rental desk; courtesy limo; business center w/computers; salon services; 24-hr. room service; in-room or poolside massage; babysitting; laundry/dry-cleaning service; video rentals. *In room:* A/C, TV/VCR, fax/copier/scanner, DSL dataport, minibar, hair dryer, safe, CD player.

**Four Seasons Hotel Los Angeles at Beverly Hills** ⭐⭐ This intimate-feeling 16-story hotel attracts a mix of A-list Four Seasons loyalists and L.A. showbiz types who cherish the hotel as an *après*-event gathering place. The small marbled lobby is always anchored by a stunning floral extravaganza, and lush gardens will help you forget you're in the heart of the city. Four Seasons runs terrific hotels, with a concierge that's famously well connected and service that goes the distance. Guest rooms are sumptuously furnished in traditional style and pastel hues. Luxuries include custom extra-stuffed Sealy mattresses with heavenly linens and pillows, marble baths with vanity TV, and French doors leading to private balconies. Room rates rise with the elevator, so bargain hunters need to sacrifice the view; ask for a corner room to get extra space at no additional cost. Since you're already in for a penny, get the pounding as well: a California Sunset Massage at one of the private candlelit poolside cabanas. Along with a full-service spa, the fourth-floor deck features great views, a lap pool, a grill, and a glass-walled fitness center. **Gardens** is a refined and excellent California-French restaurant often overlooked by locals.

300 S. Doheny Dr. (at Burton Way), Los Angeles, CA 90048. ℂ **800/819-5053,** 800/332-3442, or 310/273-2222. Fax 310/859-3824. www.fourseasons.com/losangeles. 285 units. $375–$470 double; from $600 suite. AE, DC, DISC, MC, V. Valet parking $21; free self-parking. Pets under 15 lb. welcomed (no charge). **Amenities:** Restaurant and lounge; poolside grill; rooftop heated pool; exercise room; full-service spa; Jacuzzi; children's program; concierge; courtesy limo within 5-mile radius; business center; 24-hr. room service; in-room massage; laundry service; dry-cleaning service. *In room:* A/C, TV/VCR w/pay movies (suites have DVD), dataport, minibar, hair dryer, iron, safe, CD player.

**Hotel Bel-Air** ⭐⭐⭐ Spread over 12 luxuriant garden acres, this stunning Mission-style hotel is one of the most beautiful, romantic, exclusive, all-around impressive hotels in California. This opulent early-20th-century castle wins a stream of praise for its faultless service, luxurious accommodations, and magical ambience. The parklike grounds—rich with ancient trees, fragrant flowers, bubbling fountains, playful statuary, and swan-graced ponds—are enchanting, and the welcoming, richly traditional public rooms are filled with fine antiques. Rooms, villas, and garden suites are individually decorated and stunning; some have Jacuzzis, many have private patios and wood-burning fireplaces, and all have romantic country French decor.

The hotel is a natural for honeymooners and other celebrants, but families might be put off by the Bel-Air's relative formality, which is geared to the jet set, CEO types, and ladies who lunch. Even if you don't stay here, you might consider a cocktail at the cozy bar or brunch, lunch, or dinner at the highly regarded, ultraromantic restaurant or on the woodsy outdoor terrace.

701 Stone Canyon Rd. (north of Sunset Blvd.), Los Angeles, CA 90077. © **800/648-4097** or 310/472-1211. Fax 310/476-5890. www.hotelbelair.com. 91 units. $465–$555 double; $700–$3,500 suite. AE, DC, DISC, MC, V. Parking $20. **Amenities:** Indoor/outdoor restaurant; lounge w/pianist nightly; outdoor heated pool; exercise room; concierge; business center; 24-hr. room service; in-room massage; babysitting; laundry/dry-cleaning service; video library. *In room:* A/C, digital TV/VCR w/pay movies, fax, dataport and high-speed connection, minibar, hair dryer, laptop-size safe, CD player.

**Mondrian** ✹✹ Superhotelier Ian Schrager has created a theatrical, sophisticated, coveted space from a once-drab apartment building. Working with his regular partner, French designer Philippe Starck (as he did at Miami's Delano and Manhattan's Royalton and Hudson hotels), Schrager used the Mondrian's breathtaking views (from every room) as the starting point for his vision of a "hotel in the clouds." Purposely underlit hallways lead to bright, clean rooms done in shades of white, beige, and pale gray outfitted with simple furniture casually slipcovered in white; about three-quarters of the rooms and suites have fully outfitted kitchenettes. And the accommodations are secondary; stay here if you want to be part of a superhip, star-studded scene. Set poolside and in a magical treehouse, **Skybar** is still one of L.A.'s hottest watering holes, and booking a room guarantees admission. (Soundproof windows on the entire south side of the building have already dealt with a troublesome noise problem in rooms overlooking the raucous late-night scene.) Guests can dine in the terrific, ultrahip Asian-Latin fusion restaurant, **Asia de Cuba,** or at a quirky communal table in the lobby, where sushi and light meals are served. Service isn't optimal, but the staff is beautiful enough that you won't mind.

8440 Sunset Blvd., West Hollywood, CA 90069. © **800/606-6090** or 323/650-8999. Fax 323/650-5215. www.mondrianhotel.com. 237 units. $310–$560 double; from $385 suite. Weekend rates available. AE, DC, DISC, MC, V. Valet parking $23. **Amenities:** Restaurant (Asia de Cuba); sushi bar in lobby (Seabar); alfresco bar (Skybar); outdoor pool; exercise room w/sauna and Jacuzzi; Agua Spa; concierge; business center; 24-hr. room service; in-room massage; laundry/dry-cleaning service; video, DVD, and CD libraries. *In room:* A/C, TV/VCR, dataport, minibar, coffeemaker, hair dryer, iron, safe, CD player.

## EXPENSIVE

**Avalon Hotel** ✹✹ *Finds* The first style-conscious boutique hotel on the L.A. scene, this mid-20th-century–inspired gem in the heart of Beverly Hills still leads the pack. With a soothing, sherbet-hued palette and classic Atomic Age furnishings—Eames cabinets, Heywood-Wakefield chairs, Nelson bubble lamps—mixed with smart custom designs, every room looks like a *Metropolitan Home* spread. Fashion isn't at the sake of function, however; luxury comforts and amenities are abundant enough to please design-blind travelers, too.

The property comprises the former Beverly-Carlton (seen on *I Love Lucy,* and once home to Marilyn Monroe and Mae West) and two neighboring 1950s-era apartment houses. The main building is the hub of a chic, low-key scene, but I prefer the quieter Canon building, where many of the units have kitchenettes and/or furnished terraces. All rooms are gorgeous, restful cocoons with terry bathrobes, Frette linens, and easy access to the sunny courtyard with its retro, amoeba-shape pool, the fitness room, and the groovy *Jetsons*-style restaurant and bar. Service is friendlier than in other style-minded hotels. *Note:* I've received complaints of noisy pool parties that have kept guests up at night. If you're a light sleeper, request a room away from the pool area.

9400 W. Olympic Blvd. (at Beverly Dr.), Beverly Hills, CA 90212. © 800/670-6183 or 310/277-5221. Fax 310/277-4928. www.avalonbeverlyhills.com. 86 units. $220–$300 double; from $259 junior or 1-bedroom suite. Extra person $25. AE, DC, MC, V. Valet parking $17. **Amenities:** Restaurant; lounge; courtyard pool; in-room spa and massage; concierge; 24-hr. room service; laundry/dry-cleaning service. *In room:* A/C, TV/VCR w/pay movies and video games, fax, dataport, minibar, coffeemaker, hair dryer, iron, safe, CD player.

**Chateau Marmont** ★★ Secreted away in a curve above the Sunset Strip, this château, modeled after an elegant Loire Valley castle, is a landmark from 1920s-era Hollywood; step inside and you expect to find John Barrymore or Errol Flynn holding inebriated court in the baronial living room (reputedly haunted). Greta Garbo regularly checked in as Harriet Brown, and Jim Morrison was one of many celebrities to call this home in later years. This historical landmark built its reputation on exclusivity and privacy, which John Belushi shattered when he overdosed in Bungalow No. 2. Now, under the guiding hand of boutique hotelier Andre Balazs (also lord of The Standard [below] and New York's Mercer Hotel), this funky, luxury oasis is hipper and more exclusive than ever. No two antiques-filled accommodations are alike: The poolside Spanish-style garden cottages are outfitted in Arts and Crafts style, and suites and bungalows may have a 1950s look or a Gothic style. Many units have fireplaces and CD stereos, and all but 11 have kitchenettes or full kitchens.

Beautifully kept, eternally chic, faultlessly service-oriented, and overflowing with Hollywood and rock-'n'-roll lore and celebrities, the Chateau Marmont is not for everybody. Quirkiness rules, so don't expect traditional luxuries. For those with left-of-center attitudes and a penchant for Hollywood romanticism, don't stay anywhere else; this will be the highlight of your vacation.

8221 Sunset Blvd. (between La Cienega and Crescent Heights boulevards), West Hollywood, CA 90046. © 800/242-8328 or 323/656-1010. Fax 323/655-5311. www.chateaumarmont.com. 63 units. $260–$335 double; from $385 suite; from $420 cottage; from $885 bungalow. AE, DC, MC, V. Valet parking $21. Pets accepted w/$100-per-pet fee. **Amenities:** Restaurant (serves in lobby, garden, and dining room); bar (Bar Marmont); outdoor heated pool w/brick sun deck; exercise room; access to nearby health club; 24-hr. concierge; business center; secretarial services; 24-hr. room service; in-room massage; babysitting; same-day laundry and dry cleaning; CD library. *In room:* A/C, TV/VCR, dataport, minibar, fridge, coffeemaker, hair dryer, iron, laptop-size safe, CD player.

**The Mosaic** ★★★ *Finds* I've seen hundreds of hotel renovations in my travels, but none have impressed me as much as this boutique Beverly Hills hotel. The new owners pumped $3 million into renovating the entire premises (formerly the Beverly Hills Inn), and the result is spectacular. The lobby is a showcase of functional art, with gleaming tile mosaics, fabrics in deep, rich tones, and a profusion of artfully arranged orchids. Following a recent trend, they removed a wall to allow direct access from the check-in desk to the bar and lounge, where guests are encouraged to sample the house special—a Mosaic sake martini. The guest rooms are equally impressive, in soothing earth tones with 300-count Frette linens, goose-down comforters, piles of pillows, windows that open onto the quiet neighborhood street or garden courtyard, minibars with Wolfgang Puck snacks and libations, and sparkling bathrooms with Bulgari products and huge showerheads. Other perks include free high-speed Internet access, poolside cabanas, CD players, DVD players in the suites, late room service from the hotel restaurant, a fitness room, and covered parking. *Tip:* The corner deluxe rooms are worth the extra $15.

125 S. Spalding Dr., Beverly Hills, CA 90212. ℂ 800/463-4466 or 310/278-0303. Fax 310/278-1728. www.innat
beverlyhills.com. 49 units. $225–$450 double; from $600 2-bedroom suite. AE, DC, MC, V. Parking $15. Small pets
accepted. **Amenities:** Restaurant; full bar; heated outdoor pool; exercise room w/sauna; tour desk; business services;
full room service menu until 10pm; laundry/dry-cleaning service. *In room:* A/C, TV, high-speed dataport, fridge, hair
dryer, iron, cordless phone, CD player.

**Wyndham Bel Age Hotel** ★★ *(Kids* *(Value*    This high-rise all-suite hotel is one of
West Hollywood's best. The Bel Age has it all: huge, amenity-laden suites, excellent
service, terrific rooftop sun deck with pool and Jacuzzi, and A-1 location—half a block
off Sunset Strip, yet removed from the congestion and noise. What's more, thanks to
an excellent art collection (assembled by the hotel's original owners) in the public spaces
and guest rooms, the hotel has far more personality than your average chain.

Accommodations hardly get better for the money. The monster-size suites offer
contemporary decor with a few classic touches and a soothing palette of navy, burgundy, and gray. Selected to suit every need—including those of families and business
travelers—luxuries include pillow-top mattresses with cushioned headboards and
plush bedding, a sleeper sofa in the living area that opens into a queen bed, plus an
excellent work desk with an ergonomically correct Herman Miller desk chair. The
bathrooms come with generous counter space and robes. The best rooms face south;
on a clear day, you can see all the way to the Pacific. Be sure to make reservations
before you leave home for a special meal at the Franco-Russian **Diaghilev** restaurant.

1020 N. San Vicente Blvd. (between Sunset and Santa Monica boulevards), West Hollywood, CA 90069. ℂ 800-
WYNDHAM or 310/854-1111. Fax 310/854-0926. www.wyndham.com. 200 units. $199–$339 suite (accommodates
up to 4 at no extra charge). Ask about weekend rates, holiday specials, and discounts on longer stays. AE, DC, DISC,
MC, V. Valet parking $18. **Amenities:** Restaurant; bar and grill w/live entertainment; rooftop outdoor heated pool
and Jacuzzi; exercise room; concierge; salon; room service (6am–2am); laundry/dry-cleaning service. *In room:* A/C,
TV/VCR (w/pay movies, Sony Playstation, and onscreen Internet access), dataport and high-speed connection, minibar, coffeemaker, hair dryer, iron, CD player.

**MODERATE**

**Holiday Inn Brentwood/Bel-Air**    This L.A. landmark is the last of a vanishing
breed of circular hotels from the 1960s and 1970s. It's beside the city's busiest freeway,
a short hop from the popular Getty Center, and it's centrally located between the
beaches, Beverly Hills, and the San Fernando Valley. Completely refurbished in 2000,
each pie-shape room boasts a private balcony and double-paned glass to keep the noise
out. Little extras such as Nintendo games, in-room bottled water, and great views add
panache to otherwise-unremarkable chain-style accommodations. You'll also enjoy the
360-degree view from the top-floor restaurant, **West,** which serves a casual cuisine; the
adjoining cocktail lounge features live piano nightly. Popular with older travelers and
museum groups, the hotel provides complimentary shuttle service to the Getty Center and Westwood.

170 N. Church Lane (at intersection of Sunset Blvd. and I-405), Los Angeles, CA 90049. ℂ 800/HOLIDAY or
310/476-6411. Fax 310/472-1157. www.holiday-inn.com/brentwood-bel. 211 units. $159–$199 double; from $285
suite. Inquire about AAA and AARP discounts, breakfast packages, and "Great Rates," often as low as $129. AE, DC,
DISC, MC, V. Valet parking $12; self-parking $10. Small pets accepted for $50-per-pet nonrefundable fee. **Amenities:**
Rooftop restaurant and lounge; heated outdoor pool and Jacuzzi; exercise room; concierge; activities desk; free shuttle to Getty Center and within a 3-mile radius; room service (6am–10pm); coin-op laundry; laundry/dry-cleaning service. *In room:* A/C, TV w/pay movies and Nintendo, dataport, coffeemaker, hair dryer, iron.

**The Standard** ★★    If Andy Warhol had gone into the hotel business, The Standard
would've been the end result. Designed to appeal to the under-35 "it" crowd, Andre
Balazs's swank West Hollywood neo-motel is sometimes absurd, sometimes brilliant,

and always provocative (not to mention crowded!). It's a scene worthy of its Sunset Strip location: Shag carpeting on the lobby ceiling, blue Astroturf around the swimming pool, a DJ spinning ambient sounds, a performance artist showing more skin than talent poses in a display case behind the check-in desk—this place is definitely left of center.

The good news is that The Standard is more than an attitude. Look past the retro clutter and raucous party scene, and you'll find a level of service more often associated with hotels costing twice as much. Constructed from the bones of a vintage 1962 motel, it boasts comfortably sized rooms outfitted with cobalt-blue indoor-outdoor carpeting, silver beanbag chairs, safety-orange tiles in the bathrooms, and Warhol's poppy-print curtains, plus private balconies and minibars whose contents include goodies like sake, condoms, and animal crackers. On the downside, the cheapest rooms face noisy Sunset Boulevard, and the scene is tiring if you're not into it.

*Note:* The 12-story **Downtown Standard,** 550 S. Flower St. (© **213/892-8080**), opened in mid-2002, brings a similar dose of retro-future style and cool attitude to Downtown. The Cheap Rooms—yes, that's what they call them—run about $100 on weekends. It's worth visiting just to check out the retro-glam rooftop bar with its vibrating waterbed pleasure pods, movies projected onto neighboring buildings, and hot waitresses.

8300 Sunset Blvd. (at Sweetzer Ave.), West Hollywood, CA 90069. © **323/650-9090**. Fax 323/650-2820. www. standardhotel.com. 139 units. $109–$235 double; from $470 suite. AE, DC, DISC, MC, V. Valet parking $18. Pets under 30 lb. accepted for $100-per-pet fee. **Amenities:** 24-hr. coffee shop; poolside cafe; bar/lounge; outdoor heated pool; access to nearby health club; concierge; business center; barbershop; 24-hr. room service; in-room massage; babysitting; laundry/dry-cleaning service. *In room:* A/C, TV/VCR w/pay movies, dataport and high-speed connection, minibar, CD player.

### INEXPENSIVE

**Beverly Laurel Motor Hotel** *Value* Touted by the *New York Times* for its Gen-X appeal and value, the Beverly Laurel is a great choice for wallet-watching travelers who want a central location and a room with more style than your average motel. Overlooking the parking lot, the budget-basic but well-kept rooms are smartened up with diamond-print spreads and eye-catching artwork; other features include a minifridge, microwave, and ample closet space, and a large kitchenette for an extra 10-spot. The postage-stamp-size outdoor pool is a little public for carefree sunbathing, but it does the job on hot summer days. Best of all is the motel's own excellent coffee shop, **Swingers** (p. 512). Nobody serves burgers and malts better, and you may spot your favorite alt-rocker tucking into a 3pm breakfast in the vinyl booth next to yours.

8018 Beverly Blvd. (between La Cienega Blvd. and Fairfax Ave.), Los Angeles, CA 90048. © **800/962-3824** or 323/651-2441. Fax 323/651-5225. 52 units. $89–$94 double. AAA and senior discounts may be available. AE, DC, MC, V. Free parking. **Amenities:** Heated outdoor pool; access to nearby health club; car-rental desk; laundry service. *In room:* A/C, TV, dataport, minifridge, microwave, hair dryer.

**Farmer's Daughter** *Value* Most people end up at the Farmer's Daughter hotel because they're waiting to be the next contestant on *The Price is Right*. The CBS Studios across the street recommends the budget motel to its game show fans, but I'm recommending it just because I dig this chic little lodge. It's cheery from the moment you walk in the lobby. Bright yellows and cool blues mix well with the country-kitsch theme: rooster wallpaper, faded barn-wood paneling, denim bedspreads, cow-skin rugs, and a parade of inflatable animals that float around the pool. It's obvious that someone with smart fashion sense and a little money turned a dumpy motel into an oasis of stylish affordability for people like me who drive Jettas and wear flip-flops in winter. Money-saving perks include free Internet hookup, free parking, a free DVD library, and across-the-street access to an entire Farmers Market of inexpensive food-stuffs (p. 519). *Tip:* Book a room facing the alley—the view is terrible, but you're spared the 24-hour noise off Fairfax Avenue.

115 S. Fairfax Ave. (between Beverly Dr. and Third St.), Los Angeles, CA 90036. © **800/334-1658** or 323/937-3930. Fax 323/932-1608. www.farmersdaughterhotel.com. 66 units. $115–$135 double; from $159 suite. AE, DISC, MC, V. Free on-site parking. **Amenities:** Restaurant; bar; morning coffee and tea service; pool; concierge; daily laundry and dry cleaning. *In room:* A/C, TV/DVD and CD player, complimentary DVD library, free high-speed Internet access, minifridge, coffeemaker, personal safe, telephone w/voice mail.

## HOLLYWOOD
### EXPENSIVE

**Renaissance Hollywood Hotel** ⭐    Part of the $615 million-Hollywood & Highland project to restore Hollywood to the glory of its heyday, the Renaissance Hollywood opened in late 2001. The hotel now serves as Oscar-night headquarters for the frenzy of participants and paparazzi attending the Academy Awards in the Kodak Theatre next

---

### *Kids* Family-Friendly Hotels

**Best Western Marina Pacific Hotel & Suites** (p. 482) gives families a place to stay just off the carnival-like **Venice Boardwalk.** The suites are a terrific choice for the brood—each with a full kitchen, dining area, pullout sofa, and connecting door to an adjoining room that lets you form an affordable two-bedroom, two-bathroom suite.

**Beverly Garland's Holiday Inn** (p. 493) is a terrific choice for wallet-watching families: Rates are low, the **North Hollywood** location is close to Universal Studios (a free shuttle ride away), and kids stay and eat free.

The **Roosevelt Hotel, Hollywood** (p. 490) in the heart of gentrified **Hollywood,** makes an excellent base for families who want access to the Walk of Fame. Request a ground-level room, with a porch facing the pool.

**Hotel Oceana** (p. 478) offers big apartment-style suites with all the conveniences of home. Kids will love the bright colors, the cushy furniture, the video games, and the location—across the street from the beach.

**Magic Castle Hotel** (p. 491) is a good budget choice, with roomy apartment-style suites and proximity to **Hollywood Boulevard's** family-friendly attractions.

**Sheraton Universal Hotel** (p. 494) enjoys a terrifically kid-friendly location, adjacent to **Universal Studios** and the fun CityWalk mall. Babysitting services are available, and there's a game room on the premises.

**Wyndham Bel Age Hotel** (p. 487) is a terrific all-suite hotel whose mega-size suites feature everything a family requires, including a king-size sleeper sofa in the living area, VCR and PlayStation, and a wet bar with fridge that allows for easy prep of morning cereal. There's no extra-person charge for kids (rates include up to four per unit).

door. Despite its high profile, the hotel is principally a convention property and not quite as elite or elegant as the media hype might have you believe. Nonetheless, its commitment to the history of the area infuses it with far more personality than most chain hotels. Guest rooms are like swinging '50s bachelor pads, with wood-paneled headboards and Technicolor furniture (think *The Jetsons* meets IKEA). Rooms on the seventh floor and up offer impressive views. One-third look toward the Pacific Ocean, one-third face the skyline of Downtown L.A., and one-third take in the lush Hollywood Hills (yes, you can see the sign).

The location makes getting around on foot a cinch, in a town where most destinations require navigating L.A.'s notorious freeway system. Sightseeing is virtually unavoidable, since the hotel shares the same block as two of the city's most famous landmarks—the Hollywood Walk of Fame and Grauman's Chinese Theatre. The Hollywood Bowl is less than a mile away (check with the concierge about shuttle service), and the subway stops under the hotel complex, offering access to Universal Studios and destinations farther afield.

1775 N. Highland Ave., Hollywood, CA 90028. ℂ **800/HOTELS-1** or 323/856-1200. Fax 323/856-1205. www. renaissancehollywood.com. 637 units. $259 double; $269 executive bedroom; 1-bedroom suite $310; other suites from $320 and way up. Discount rates and packages available. AE, DC, DISC, MC, V. Valet parking $22. **Amenities:** Restaurant; 2 bars (lobby and poolside); outdoor pool; small fitness room; concierge; business center; shopping complex; 24-hr. room service; dry cleaning. *In room:* A/C, TV w/pay movies, dataport, high-speed Internet access, 2-line cordless phone, minibar, coffeemaker, hair dryer, iron, safe, robes, CD player.

## MODERATE

**Roosevelt Hotel, Hollywood** ⭐ *Kids* This 12-story landmark is on an unabashedly touristy but no longer seedy section of Hollywood Boulevard—across from Grauman's Chinese Theatre and along the Walk of Fame. Host to the first Academy Awards in 1929—not to mention a few famous-name ghosts—this national landmark is Hollywood's only historic hotel still in operation today. It celebrated its 75th anniversary with a $15-million renovation that has harmoniously melded historical highlights with modern luxuries. Much of the 1927 Spanish-influenced sunken lobby remains the same—the hand-crafted columns and dramatic arches are magnificent—but the guest rooms have been completely, tastefully renovated, with colorful, extralarge bathrooms, dark-wood platform beds, luxurious Frette linens, and all the latest high-tech accessories. Rooms on the upper floors have unbeatable skyline views, while cabana rooms have a balcony or patio overlooking the Olympic-size pool, with a mural by David Hockney. **Theodore's Restaurant** serves breakfast, lunch, and progressive American cuisine for dinner daily. **Cinegrill,** a cool, dark, tier-leveled supper club is also on-site. *Tip:* Request the Steven Spielberg room on the ninth floor, with a fantastic view of Hollywood Boulevard.

7000 Hollywood Blvd., Hollywood, CA 90028. ℂ **800/950-7667** or 323/466-7000. Fax 323/462-8056. www. hollywoodroosevelt.com. 302 units. $189–$299 double; from $310 suite. Ask about AAA, senior, business, government, and other discounted rates (as low as $159 at press time). Children under 18 stay free in parent's room. AE, DC, DISC, MC, V. Valet parking $18. **Amenities:** Restaurant (steakhouse); cocktail lounge; cabaret and nightclub (Feinstein's at the Cinegrill); outdoor pool and Jacuzzi; spa and fitness center; concierge; activities desk; room service (6am–11pm); babysitting; laundry/dry-cleaning service; executive-level rooms. *In room:* A/C, TV w/pay movies and video games, high-speed dataport, minibar, coffeemaker, hair dryer.

## INEXPENSIVE

**Best Western Hollywood Hills Hotel** ⭐ Location is a big selling point for this family-owned (since 1948) member of the reliable Best Western chain: It's just off U.S. 101; a Metro Line stop 3 blocks away means easy, car-free access to Universal

Studios; and the famed Hollywood and Vine intersection is just a 5-minute walk away. The hotel was recently renovated in a contemporary style, and all the spiffy guest rooms come with a refrigerator, coffeemaker, microwave, and wireless Internet. The rooms in the back building are my favorites; they sit back from busy Franklin Avenue and face the gleaming blue-tiled, heated outdoor pool, with a view of the neighboring hillside. A major convenience is the **101 Hills Coffee Shop** off the lower lobby.

6141 Franklin Ave. (between Vine and Gower sts.), Hollywood, CA 90028. Ⓒ **800/287-1700** or 323/464-5181. Fax 323/962-0536. www.bestwestern.com/hollywoodhillshotel. 86 units. $89–$139 double. AAA and AARP discounts available. AE, DISC, MC, V. Free covered parking. Small pets accepted w/$25-per-night fee. **Amenities:** Coffee shop; heated outdoor pool; access to nearby health club; tour desk; coin-op laundry. *In room:* A/C, TV, dataport, wireless Internet, fridge, coffeemaker, hair dryer, iron, microwave.

**Days Inn Hollywood** It's east of the prime Sunset Strip action, but this freshly renovated motel is safe and convenient. Free underground parking and continental breakfast make it an especially good value. Doubles are large enough for families. Some rooms have microwaves, fridges, and coffeemakers; if yours doesn't have a hair dryer or an iron, they're available at the front desk. It's usually easy to snare an under-$100 rate; for maximum bang for your buck, ask for a room overlooking the pool.

7023 Sunset Blvd. (between Highland and La Brea aves.), Hollywood, CA 90028. Ⓒ **800/329-7466** or 323/464-8344. Fax 323/962-9748. www.daysinn.com. 72 units. $92–$170 double; $135–$210 Jacuzzi suite. Rates include continental breakfast. Ask about AAA, AARP, and other discounted rates (as low as $83 at press time). AE, DC, DISC, MC, V. Free secured parking. **Amenities:** Heated outdoor pool; laundry/dry-cleaning service. *In room:* A/C, TV.

**Magic Castle Hotel** ★ *(Kids* *(Value* A stone's throw from Hollywood Boulevard attractions, this garden-style hotel/motel at the base of the Hollywood Hills offers L.A.'s best cheap sleeps; it's ideal for wallet-watching families or long-term stays. You won't see the Magic Castle Hotel in *Travel + Leisure* anytime soon—the rooms are done in high Levitz style—but the newly refurbished units are spacious, comfortable, and well kept. Named for the Magic Castle, the illusionist club just uphill, the hotel was once an apartment building, and it still feels private and insulated from Franklin Avenue's constant traffic. The units are situated around a center swimming pool. Most are large apartments with fully equipped kitchens complete with a microwave and coffeemaker; grocery shopping service is available as well.

7025 Franklin Ave. (between La Brea and Highland aves.), Hollywood, CA 90028. Ⓒ **800/741-4915** or 323/851-0800. Fax 323/851-4926. www.magiccastlehotel.com. 49 units. $129 double; $149–$239 suite. Extra person $10. Off-season and other discounts available. AE, DC, DISC, MC, V. Parking $8. **Amenities:** Outdoor heated pool; full-service or coin-op laundry. *In room:* A/C, TV, dataport, coffeemaker, hair dryer, iron, safe.

## DOWNTOWN
### EXPENSIVE/MODERATE

Traditionally the domain of business folk and convention attendees, Downtown L.A. is becoming increasingly attractive to leisure travelers for several reasons: a Rudy Giuliani–style cleanup in the late 1990s; a growing number of cultural attractions and destination dining; excellent-value weekend packages at luxury hotels that empty out once the workweek ends; and easy, car-free access via the Metro Line to Hollywood and Universal Studios. Every freeway passes through Downtown, so it's a breeze to hop in the car and head to other neighborhoods, except during rush hour. Consider yourself forewarned, however: Despite low weekend rates, Downtown L.A. can feel like a ghost town, particularly after dusk. And all the hoopla about urban revival? Let's just say Downtown has had more comebacks than Richard Gere.

**Figueroa Hotel** ★★ *Finds*   With an artistic eye and a heartfelt commitment to creating an anti-corporate-style accommodation, owner Uno Thimansson has transformed a 1925-vintage former YWCA residence into L.A.'s best moderately priced hotel—my top pick for Downtown lodging. This enchanting, 12-story property sits in an increasingly gentrified corner of Downtown, within shouting distance of the STAPLES Center. The big, airy lobby exudes a romantic Spanish Colonial–Gothic vibe with beamed ceilings and soaring columns, tile flooring, ceiling fans, Moroccan chandeliers, and medievalist furnishings such as big floor pillows made of Kurdish grain sacks, Persian kilims, and exotic fabrics draped from the ceiling. Elevators lead to equally artful, comfortable guest rooms that are a bit dark and small. Each comes with a firm, well-made bed with a wrought-iron headboard or canopy and a Georgia O'Keeffe–reminiscent spread, a Mexican-tiled bathroom, and Indian fabrics that double as blackout drapes. My favorite room is no. 1130, a large double-queen with a Spanish terra cotta–print chaise, but you can't go wrong with any room. The Casablanca Suite is a Moroccan pleasure den, ideal for romance. Out back you'll find a gorgeous desert-garden deck with a mosaic-tiled pool and Jacuzzi, and the Verandah Bar, the poolside place to go on warm Southern California nights for a minty *mojito*.

939 S Figueroa St. (at Olympic Blvd.), Los Angeles, CA 90015. © 800/421-9092 or 213/627-8971. Fax 213/689-0305. 285 units. $104–$134 double; $205 Casablanca Suite. www.figueroahotel.com. AE, DC, MC, V. Parking $10. **Amenities:** Restaurant; bar; outdoor pool area w/lounge chairs and Jacuzzi; laundry/dry-cleaning service. *In room:* A/C, TV, dataport, minifridge.

**Millennium Biltmore Hotel Los Angeles** ★★   The Biltmore is one of those hotels that's worth a visit even if you're not staying here. Built in 1923 and encompassing an entire square block, this Italian-Spanish Renaissance landmark is the grande dame of L.A. hotels. Chances are you've seen it in many movies, including *The Fabulous Baker Boys, Chinatown, Ghostbusters, Bugsy, Beverly Hills Cop,* and Barbra Streisand's *A Star Is Born.* The hotel lobby—JFK's campaign headquarters during the 1960 Democratic National Convention—appeared upside-down in *The Poseidon Adventure.* Always in fine shape and host to world leaders and luminaries, the former Regal Biltmore is now under the guiding hand of the Millennium Hotels and Resorts group, and the sense of refinement and graciousness endures. The "wow" factor ends at guest rooms, however, which are small and less eye-popping than the public spaces. Bathrooms are small too, but peach-toned marble adds a luxurious touch.

A range of dining and cocktail outlets includes **Sai Sai** for Japanese cuisine. Pretty, casual **Smeraldi's** serves homemade pastas and lighter California fare. Off the lobby is the stunning **Gallery Bar,** named by *Los Angeles* magazine as one of the sexiest cocktail lounges in L.A. Afternoon tea and cocktails are served in the **Rendezvous Court,** the hotel's original lobby, which resembles the interior of a Spanish cathedral, with a Moorish ceiling of carved beams and an altarlike Baroque doorway. Spend the few bucks to appreciate the Art Deco health club, with its gorgeous Roman-style pool.

506 S. Grand Ave. (between Fifth and Sixth sts.), Los Angeles, CA 90071. © 800/245-8673 or 213/624-1011. Fax 213/612-1545. www.millennium-hotels.com. 683 units. $185–$330 double; $469–$729 suite. Weekend discount packages available. AE, DC, DISC, MC, V. Parking $22. **Amenities:** 3 restaurants; 2 lounges; health club w/original 1923 inlaid pool, Jacuzzi, steam, and sauna; concierge; Enterprise car-rental desk; courtesy car; business center; salon; 24-hr. room service; in-room massage; babysitting; laundry/dry-cleaning service; executive-level rooms. *In room:* A/C, TV w/pay movies, dataport, minibar, hair dryer, laptop-size safe.

**Westin Bonaventure Hotel & Suites** ★   This 35-story, 1,354-room monolith is the hotel that locals love to hate. The truth is that the Bonaventure is a terrific hotel.

It's certainly not for travelers who want intimacy or personality in their accommodations—but with more than 20 restaurants and bars, a full-service spa, a monster health club, a Kinko's-size business center, and much more on hand, you'll be hard-pressed to want for anything here (except maybe some individualized attention). After a recent $35-million renovation, this convention favorite has never looked fresher.

The hotel's five gleaming glass silos encompass a square block, forming one of Downtown's most distinctive landmarks. The six-story lobby houses fountains and trees (and, surprise, a Starbucks). A tangle of concrete ramps and 12 high-speed glass elevators lead to the extensive array of shops and services. Highlights include the rooftop **L.A. Prime Steak House** and revolving **BonaVista lounge,** both with unparalleled views, and even a **Krispy Kreme Donut Stand.** The pie-shape guest rooms are small, but a wall of windows and Westin's unparalleled Heavenly Bed make for a comfy cocoon. With an executive work station, fax, and wet bar, guest office suites are great for business travelers. Tower suites—with a living room, an extra half-bathroom, a minifridge, a microwave, and two TVs—are ideal for families.

404 S. Figueroa St. (between Fourth and Fifth sts.), Los Angeles, CA 90071. (C) **800/WESTIN-1** or 213/624-1000. Fax 213/612-4800. www.starwood.com/westin. 1,354 units. $237–$289 double; $297–$559 suite. Ask about theater packages. AE, DC, DISC, MC, V. Valet parking $19. **Amenities:** 17 restaurants and fast-food outlets; 5 bars and lounges; outdoor heated lap pool; 15,000-sq.-ft. full-service spa w/exercise room, running track, and access to adjacent 85,000-sq.-ft. health club; Westin Kids Club; concierge; tour desk; Dollar Rent-a-Car desk; full-service business and copy center; shops; salon; 24-hr. room service; babysitting; laundry/dry-cleaning service. *In room:* A/C, TV w/pay movies and video games, high-speed Internet dataport, coffeemaker, hair dryer, iron, laptop-size safe.

### INEXPENSIVE

**Hotel Stillwell**    The Stillwell is far from fancy, but its modestly priced rooms are a good option in this generally pricey neighborhood. Built in 1906, this once-elegant 250-room hotel is convenient, near the STAPLES Center, the Civic Center, and the Museum of Contemporary Art. Rooms are clean, basic, and simply decorated with decent furnishings. The hotel is quiet, and hallways feature East Indian artwork. I much prefer the Hotel Figueroa, but this is a less eccentric and perfectly reasonable choice. The lobby-level Indian restaurant is a popular lunch spot for Downtown office workers; other options include a casual Mexican restaurant and **Hanks Cocktail Lounge,** so old it's retro.

838 S. Grand Ave. (between Eighth and Ninth sts.), Los Angeles, CA 90017. (C) **800/553-4774** or 213/627-1151. Fax 213/622-8940. www.hotelstillwell.com. 250 units. $79 double; $85–$115 suite. AE, DC, DISC, MC, V. Parking $4.50. **Amenities:** 2 restaurants; lounge; activities desk; business center; coin-op laundry; laundry/dry-cleaning service. *In room:* A/C, TV, fax, fridge, iron.

## SAN FERNANDO VALLEY & UNIVERSAL CITY

### MODERATE

**Beverly Garland's Holiday Inn** *(Kids*    Grassy areas and greenery abound at this 258-room North Hollywood Holiday Inn, a virtual oasis in the concrete jungle. The Mission-influenced buildings are a bit dated, but if you grew up with *Brady Bunch* reruns, this only adds to the charm; the spread looks like something Mike Brady would have designed. (If you were a fan of *My Three Sons,* even better, because "Beverly Garland" is the actress who played Fred MacMurray's wife.) Southwestern-themed fabrics complement the natural-pine furnishings in the spacious guest rooms, distracting you from the painted cinder-block walls. On the upside, all the well-outfitted rooms have balconies overlooking pleasant grounds, which include a pool and two lighted tennis courts. With Universal Studios just down the street and a free shuttle to the park, the location can't be beat for families. Since proximity to the 101 and 134 freeways also means the constant buzz of traffic, ask for a room facing Vineland Avenue for maximum quiet. *Tip:* If you're bringing the kids, be sure to inquire about the "KidSuites," an adjoining room designed just for the young ones.

4222 Vineland Ave., North Hollywood, CA 91602. © **800/BEVERLY** or 818/980-8000. Fax 818/766-0112. www.beverly garland.com. 255 units. $149–$179 double; from $209 suite. Ask about AAA, AARP, corporate, military, Great Rates, weekend, and other discounted rates (from $109 at press time). Kids 12 and under stay free in parent's room and eat free. AE, DC, DISC, MC, V. Free parking. **Amenities:** Restaurant; heated outdoor pool; lighted tennis courts; sauna; carrental desk; complimentary shuttle to Universal Studios. *In room:* A/C, TV, coffeemaker, hair dryer, iron.

**Sheraton Universal Hotel** ★ *Kids* Despite the addition of the sleekly modern Hilton just uphill, the 21-story Sheraton is still considered the Universal City hotel of choice for tourists, businesspeople, and industry folk visiting the studios' production offices. On the back lot of Universal Studios, it has a spacious 1960s feel, with updated styling and amenities. Although the Sheraton does its share of convention/ event business, the hotel feels more leisure-oriented than the Hilton next door (an outdoor elevator connects the two properties). Choose a Lanai room for balconies that overlook the lushly planted pool area, or a Tower room for stunning views and solitude. The hotel is close to the Hollywood Bowl, and you can practically roll out of bed into the theme park (via a continuous complimentary shuttle). An extra $35 per night buys a Club Level room—worth the money, for the extra in-room amenities, free continental breakfast, and afternoon hors d'oeuvres. Business rooms also feature a movable workstation and a fax/copier/printer.

333 Universal Hollywood Dr., Universal City, CA 91608. © **800/325-3535** or 818/980-1212. Fax 818/985-4980. www.sheraton.com/universal. 436 units. $149–$219 double; $350–$650 suite. Children stay free in parent's room. Ask about AAA, AARP, and corporate discounts; also inquire about packages that include theme-park admission. AE, DC, DISC, MC, V. Valet parking $16; self-parking $11. **Amenities:** Casual indoor/outdoor restaurant; lobby lounge w/pianist; Starbucks coffee cart in lobby; outdoor pool and whirlpool; health club; game room; concierge; free shuttle to Universal Studios every 15 minutes; business center; room service (6am–midnight); babysitting; laundry/drycleaning service; executive-level rooms. *In room:* A/C, TV w/pay movies and video games, dataport, minibar, hair dryer and iron in club-level rooms, safe.

### INEXPENSIVE

**Best Western Mikado Hotel** This Asian-flavored garden hotel has been a Valley fixture for 40-plus years. A 1999 renovation muted but didn't obliterate the kitsch value, which extends from the pagoda-style exterior to the sushi bar (the Valley's oldest) across the driveway. Two-story motel buildings face two well-maintained courtyards, one with a koi pond and wooden footbridge, the other with a shimmering blue-tiled pool and hot tub. The face-lift stripped most of the Asian vibe from guest rooms, which are suitably comfortable and well outfitted. Furnished in 1970s-era chic (leather sofas, earth tones), the one-bedroom apartment is a steal, with enormous rooms and a full-size kitchen. Rates include a full breakfast.

12600 Riverside Dr. (between Whitsett and Coldwater Canyon), North Hollywood, CA 91607. © **800/780-7234** or 818/763-9141. Fax 818/752-1045. www.bestwestern.com/mikadohotel. 58 units. $129–$139 double; $175 1-bedroom apartment. Rates include full breakfast. Ask about AAA, senior, and other discounted rates (as low as $98 at press time). Extra person $10. Children under 12 stay free in parent's room. Rates include full American breakfast. AE, DC, DISC, MC, V. Free parking. **Amenities:** Japanese restaurant and sushi bar; cocktail lounge; outdoor pool and Jacuzzi; fax and copying services at front desk. *In room:* A/C, TV, dataport, coffeemaker, hair dryer, iron.

## PASADENA & ENVIRONS
### VERY EXPENSIVE

**The Ritz-Carlton, Huntington Hotel & Spa** ★★★ Originally built in 1906, the opulent Huntington Hotel was one of America's grandest hotels, but not the most earthquake-proof. No matter—the hotel was rebuilt and opened on the same spot in 1991 with such astonishing authenticity many patrons from the early days are fooled. This Spanish-Mediterranean beauty sits on 23 spectacularly landscaped acres a world apart from L.A., though Downtown is only 20 minutes away. Each oversize guest room is dressed in conservatively elegant Ritz-Carlton style, softened by English garden textiles and a palette of celadon, cream, and butter yellow. Luxuries include Frette linens, marble bathrooms, thick carpets, and terry robes. You might consider spending a few extra dollars on a club-level room, with featherbeds, down comforters, CD players, morning coffee delivered with your wake-up call, and access to the club lounge with dedicated concierge and complimentary gourmet spreads all day (including breakfast).

The 12,000-square-foot, full-service Ritz-Carlton Spa makes the Huntington an ideal place for a therapeutic getaway. Both guests and locals enjoy dining in the casual elegance of **The Dining Room,** but I prefer the more casual California-style **Terrace Restaurant,** which also serves patrons at umbrella-covered tables by the Olympic-size pool (Southern California's first). High tea is served in the Lobby Lounge.

1401 S. Oak Knoll Ave., Pasadena, CA 91106. (C) **800/241-3333** or 626/568-3900. Fax 626/568-3700. www.ritzcarlton. com. 392 units. $330–$450 double; from $435–$855 suite. Discount packages always available. AE, DC, MC, V. Valet parking $21. Pets accepted for $125 non-refundable fee. **Amenities:** 2 restaurants; 2 lounges (bar, Lobby Lounge for high tea); Olympic-size heated outdoor pool and Jacuzzi; 3 lighted tennis courts; fitness center; full-service spa w/whirlpool, sauna, and steam room; concierge; business center; salon; 24-hr. room service; in-room massage; babysitting; laundry/dry-cleaning service. *In room:* A/C, TV w/pay movies, dataport, high-speed Internet connection, minibar, hair dryer, iron, laptop-size safe, CD player.

## MODERATE

**Artists' Inn & Cottage Bed & Breakfast** Pleasantly unpretentious and furnished with wicker throughout, this yellow-shingled Victorian-style inn was built in 1895 as a farmhouse and expanded to include a neighboring 1909 home. Each of the 10 rooms is decorated to reflect the style of a particular artist or period: the country-cozy New England–style Grandma Moses room; the soft, pastel-hued Degas suite; and the bold-lined, primary-hued Expressionist suite. Every room is thoughtfully arranged with a private bathroom (many with period fixtures, three with Jacuzzi tubs), phone, fresh roses from the front garden, port wine, and chocolates. Most rooms have TVs; if yours doesn't, the innkeeper will provide one if you want it. The quiet residential location is just 5 minutes from the heart of Old Town Pasadena.

1038 Magnolia St., South Pasadena, CA 91030. (C) **888/799-5668** or 626/799-5668. Fax 626/799-3678. www. artistsinns.com. 10 units. $125–$225 double. Rates include full breakfast and afternoon tea. Check for midweek specials. Extra person $20. AE, MC, V. Free parking. *In room:* A/C, TV (upon request), dataport, hair dryer.

**Bissell House Bed & Breakfast** (★) If you enjoy B&Bs, you'll love the Bissell House, an 1887 gingerbread Victorian filled with antiques. Hidden behind hedges from busy Orange Grove Avenue, this former home of the Bissell vacuum heiress (now owned by hosts Russell and Leonore Butcher) offers a taste of life on what was once Pasadena's "Millionaire's Row." Outfitted in a traditional chintz-and-cabbage-roses style, all individually decorated rooms have private bathrooms (one with an antique claw-foot tub, one with a whirlpool, and two with showers only), individual heating and air-conditioning (a B&B rarity), Internet access, and very comfortable beds. If you don't mind stairs, request one of the more spacious top-floor rooms. The modern world doesn't interfere with the mood in these romantic sanctuaries, but the downstairs library features a TV with VCR and a telephone/fax machine for guests' use. The beautifully landscaped grounds have an inviting pool, Jacuzzi, and deck with lounge chairs. Included in the room rate is an elaborately prepared breakfast served in the large dining room, as well as an afternoon tea, cookie, and wine service.

201 Orange Grove Ave. (at Columbia St.), South Pasadena, CA 91030. ℂ 800/441-3530 or 626/441-3535. Fax 626/441-3671. www.bissellhouse.com. 5 units. $150–$225 double. Rates include full breakfast. AE, MC, V. Free parking. **Amenities:** Outdoor pool and Jacuzzi; CD and video libraries. *In room:* A/C, hair dryer, iron.

### INEXPENSIVE

**Saga Motor Hotel** *Value*    This 1950s relic of old Route 66 has far more character than most motels in its price range. The rooms are small, clean, and simply furnished with the basics. The double/doubles are spacious enough for shares, but budget-minded families will prefer the extra-large configuration, which has a king and two doubles. The best rooms are in the front building surrounding the gated swimming pool; they're shielded from the street and inviting in warm weather. The grounds are attractive and well kept, if you don't count the Astroturf "lawn" on the pool deck. The location is very quiet and very good, just off the Foothill (210) Freeway about a mile from the Huntington Library and within 10 minutes of both the Rose Bowl and Old Pasadena.

1633 E. Colorado Blvd. (between Allen and Sierra Bonita aves.), Pasadena, CA 91106. ℂ 800/793-7242 or 626/795-0431. Fax 626/792-0559. www.thesagamotorhotel.com. 70 units. $74–$92 double; $110–$130 family suite. Rates include continental breakfast. AE, DC, DISC, MC, V. Free parking. **Amenities:** Outdoor heated pool; free self-serve laundromat; laundry/dry-cleaning service. *In room:* A/C, TV, dataport.

## 4 Where to Dine

All cities are defined by their restaurants, and as one of the world's cultural crossroads, Los Angeles is an international atlas of exotic cuisines: Afghan, Argentinean, Armenian, Burmese, Cajun, Cambodian, Cuban, Ethiopian, Jewish, Korean, Lebanese, Moroccan, Oaxacan, Peruvian, Persian, Spanish, Vietnamese, and so on. Whatever you're in the mood for, this town has got it. All you need to join the dinner party is an adventurous palate, because half the fun of visiting Los Angeles is experiencing worldly dishes that only a major metropolis can provide.

The famous celebrity chef and celebrity-owned restaurants attract most of the limelight, but most of L.A.'s best dining experiences are courtesy of its neighborhood haunts and minimalls—the kind of restaurants you'd never find unless someone let you in on the city's dining secrets. This section is full of such places, although limited space has forced me to eliminate some great finds. For a greater selection, pick up *Frommer's Los Angeles 2006.* For additional late-night dining options, see "Late-Night Bites" under "Los Angeles After Dark," later in this chapter. To locate the restaurants reviewed below, see the individual neighborhood maps in section 1, "Orientation."

### SANTA MONICA & THE BEACHES
#### EXPENSIVE

**Boa Steakhouse** ★★ STEAKHOUSE    Combine the best quality steaks with a sexy decor, lively bar, and a key corner location in Santa Monica and you'll do well. Very well. Cashing in on American's steak craze, the owners of the original Boa in West Hollywood opened this suave steakhouse at the foot of Santa Monica Boulevard. The sophisticated decor eschews the traditional dim steakhouse ambience in favor of a warm, sleek interior highlighted with floor-to-ceiling windows that allow natural light to filter in. The menu makes for some tough decisions: Do I order the bone-in filet mignon, petite filet mignon, Kobe filet mignon, 35-day dry-aged New York strip, bone-in rib-eye, flat iron steak, or porterhouse? Do I want it prepared with a foie gras crust, tri-peppercorn rub, or whole-grain mustard? You purchase sides separately; the most popular are the home-made crispy fries, truffle macaroni and cheese, and roasted garlic whipped potatoes. As for appetizers, I love their Dungeness crab cake with shaved fennel–and–mustard aioli. For dessert, try the refreshing blackberry crush cocktail, a *mojito*-like mixture made with fresh fruit and top-shelf vodka. *Note:* A second Boa steakhouse is open on the Sunset Strip at 8462 W. Sunset Blvd., West Hollywood (© **323/650-8383**).

101 Santa Monica Blvd. (at Ocean Ave.), Santa Monica. © 310/899-4466. www.boasteak.com. Reservations recommended. Main courses $25–$39. AE, DC, DISC, MC, V. Daily 11:30am–11:30pm. Valet parking $4.

**The Lobster** ★★ SEAFOOD   The Lobster has sat on the Santa Monica Pier since 1923—making it almost as old as the pier itself. Its revival in 2000 brought a new sophistication to this perpetually crowded seafood shack. The interior is completely rebuilt but still accentuates the seaside location and million-dollar ocean view with floor-to-ceiling windows. Chef Allyson Thurber, formerly of Downtown's Water Grill, brought her impressive pedigree to the kitchen and revamped the menu as well. Although the namesake crustacean from Maine is a great choice—grilled, steamed, or roasted—the menu consistently presents a multitude of ultrafresh fish with thoughtful and creative preparation. Specialties range from spicy Louisiana prawns with dirty rice to jumbo lump crab cakes. Creative appetizers include *ahi* carpaccio with tangy *tobiko* wasabi, or steamed mussels and Manila clams with applewood bacon. Try the decadent *kasu*-marinated sea bass with a bottle of dry chardonnay from the well-stocked cellar. The menu offers a couple of fine steaks for landlubbers, and the practiced bar serves lots of bloody marys garnished with jumbo shrimp to dedicated locals. For dessert, the strawberry shortcake and devil's food cake are terrific. *Tip:* Request a table on the deck for a 180-degree view of the Pacific.

1602 Ocean Ave. (at Colorado), Santa Monica. © 310/458-9294. www.thelobster.com. Reservations recommended. Main courses $15–$32. AE, DC, DISC, MC, V. Mon–Thurs 11:30am–3pm and 5–10pm; Fri–Sat 11:30am–3pm and 5–11pm. Valet parking $4.

**Michael's** ★★ CALIFORNIA   Owner Michael McCarty, L.A.'s answer to Alice Waters, is considered by many to be the father of California cuisine. Since Michael's opened in 1979 (when McCarty was only 25), several top L.A. restaurants have caught up to it, but this fetching Santa Monica venue remains one of the city's best. The dining room is filled with contemporary art by Michael's wife, Kim McCarty, and the restaurant's garden is Santa Monica's most romantic setting for always-inventive menu choices such as Baqueta sea bass with a chanterelle mushroom ragout and fresh Provençal herbs, or grilled pork chop sweetened with sweet-potato purée and anise–pinot noir sauce. Don't miss Michael's famous warm mushroom salad, tossed with crumbled goat cheese, watercress, caramelized onion, and mustard-sage vinaigrette. The dry-aged New York strip and *frites* are also fantastic.

1147 Third St. (north of Wilshire Blvd.), Santa Monica. © 310/451-0843. www.michaelssantamonica.com. Reservations recommended. Dinner main courses $28–$39; lunch $14–$23. AE, DC, DISC, MC, V. Mon–Fri 11:30am–2:30pm and 6–10:30pm; Sat 6–10:30pm. Valet parking $5.50.

## MODERATE

**Border Grill** ★★ MEXICAN   Before Mary Sue Milliken and Susan Feniger spiced up cable TV with *Too Hot Tamales,* they started this hugely popular haute Mexican restaurant in West Hollywood. Since then the Border Grill has moved to a vibrantly painted, cavernous, and loud space in Santa Monica that's packed every night with locals and tourists.

---

### Finds L.A.'s Best Sushi & Stir-Fried Crickets

If you want to start a heated argument with L.A.'s foodies, just claim that you know where the best sushi in the city is served. Well, let the tongue-fu begin, because I'm claiming that **The Hump** ★★★ (© 310/313-0977; www.typhoon-restaurant.com) serves L.A.'s best sushi. If I'm ever on death row, I want my last meal to be a giant plate of sushi prepared by these master chefs. Much of the seafood is flown in daily from Tokyo's Tsukijii and Fukuoka fish markets in oxygen-filled containers. It's so fresh management posted a sign to deter the faint-of-heart from sitting at the sushi bar—because much of what's sliced there is still moving at the time.

Alongside Santa Monica Airport's runway, this small wedge-shape Japanese restaurant is ranked among the top sushi restaurants in America, but it has only nine tables, so be sure to make a reservation a few days in advance. Specialties include the *dengaku* (stuffed eggplant and avocado with seafood and miso sauce), live baby squid, live whitefish served in martini grass with a vinegar broth, hairy crab, live red snapper, and the most tender, flavorful baby *hamachi* I've ever had. Dine Ozzie-style and order the $220 snapping turtle (the blood goes well with a rich cabernet or port), the snake sake (with, yes, a snake in the bottle), and the blowfish (to die for). If the menu's all Greek to you, say *"omakase"* and get ready for a chef's choice, seven-course seafood adventure. Skip the rolls—they're huge and fill you up too fast. And don't be surprised if you spot a celebrity: Regulars include Harrison Ford, Calista Flockhart, Kurt Russell, Goldie Hawn, Dustin Hoffman, and Meryl Streep.

Directly below The Hump, the much larger **Typhoon** ★★ (© 310/390-6565; www.typhoon-restaurant.com) is a popular, high-energy Pan-Asian restaurant where stir-fried Taiwanese spicy crickets, dried Manchurian ants, and Thai-style crispy white sea worms punctuate a family-style menu filled with less exotic fare from Southeast Asia. The huge open kitchen serves everything from Burma-style chicken wings (outrageously hot) to Filipino fried squid, Mongolian lamb, and Thai-style deep-fried frogs' legs. Most items are $7 to $12. The well-stocked bar even offers a Chinese herb-infused vodka reputed to have aphrodisiac qualities. Both restaurants are on the second and third floors of the airport's administration building at 3221 Donald Douglas Loop Rd. in Santa Monica. Call or visit the website for directions and hours.

---

Let's get one thing straight: This is not your Combo #7 kind of place. The duck tamale appetizer I ordered the last time I visited was *the* most flavorful and unique Mexican dish I've ever had: freshly made corn *masa* filled with tender roast duck, *guajillo* chile sauce, and roasted sweet peppers, then topped with an exquisite cranberry salsa (I could have eaten 10). Other favorite small plates are the plantain empanadas with *chipotle* salsa and Mexican *crema,* and the übertender roasted lamb tacos with poblano chiles and manchego. The best meatless dish is the *mulitas,* a layering of portobello mushrooms, roasted peppers, and pickled onions. For dessert, try the *Tres Leches* (a milk cake with passion fruit and prickly pear sauces) or a slice of Aztec chocolate cake. And start with one of their superb margaritas or *mojitos.*

1445 Fourth St. (between Broadway and Santa Monica Blvd.), Santa Monica. ℂ 310/451-1655. www.bordergrill. com. Reservations recommended. Main courses $13–$25. AE, DC, DISC, MC, V. Mon 5–10pm; Tues–Thurs 11:30am–10pm; Fri–Sat 11:30am–11pm; Sun 11:30am–10pm. Metered parking lots; valet parking $4.

**Joe's Restaurant** ★★ *Value* AMERICAN ECLECTIC    This is one of L.A.'s best dining bargains. Chef/owner Joeseph Miller excels in simple New American cuisine, particularly grilled fish and roasted meats accented with piquant herbs. Formerly a tiny, quirky storefront with humble elbow room, Joe gutted and completely remodeled the entire restaurant, adding a far more spacious dining room and display wine room (though the best tables are still tucked away on the trellised outdoor patio complete with a gurgling waterfall). Despite the upscale additions, Joe's remains a hidden treasure for those with a champagne palate and seltzer pocketbook. Case in point: For lunch, an autumn vegetable platter of butternut-squash purée, braised greens, grilled portobello mushrooms, and Brussels sprout leaves wilted with truffle oil and wild mushrooms goes for a mere $12. And this includes a fresh mixed green salad or one of Miller's exquisite soups. Dinner entrees are equally sophisticated: beet risotto with grilled asparagus or fallow deer wrapped in bacon (served in a black-currant sauce with a side of roasted root vegetables). A double whammy is Joe's grilled ahi tuna *and* Hudson Valley foie gras appetizer served with *rösti* potatoes and a red-wine herb sauce. Desserts are equally fantastic. *Tip:* Joe's four-course, prix-fixe menu is a bargain for under $40.

1023 Abbot Kinney Blvd., Venice. ℂ 310/399-5811. www.joesrestaurant.com. Reservations required. Main courses $18–$25 dinner, $8–$15 lunch. AE, MC, V. Tues–Thurs noon–2:30pm and 6–10pm; Fri noon–2:30pm and 6–11pm; Sat 11am–2:30pm and 6–11pm; Sun 11:30am–2:30pm and 6–10pm. Free street parking or valet parking in rear of building.

**Locanda del Lago** ★★ NORTHERN ITALIAN    In a sea of mediocre restaurants along Santa Monica's Third Street Shopping Promenade, this corner trattoria reminds you why Italians are the world's best cooks. Locanda del Lago (Trattoria of the Lake) is the only restaurant in Los Angeles that specializes in cuisine from Northern Italy's Lombardy region. Both the co-owner and executive chef were born in Milan, worked in Bellagio, and share a passion for food that hasn't waned since this warm, friendly restaurant opened more than 14 years ago. I dined there with my chef friend recently, and we both agreed that the house-made whole wheat pappardelle tossed in a duck ragout was the best pasta dish we've ever had; unfortunately it's not on the regular menu but I'm lobbying for it. On sunny days, there's no better place to people-watch than at the trattoria's outdoor patio. Savor a glass of Chianti while tucking into the house specialty, *Ossobuco alla Milanese*, a veal shank slow-cooked in white wine and vegetables, topped with traditional gremolata and served with saffron risotto. The butternut-squash risotto with seared scallops is also excellent. After a hard day's shopping, there's no better place to relax on the Promenade than Lago.

231 Arizona Ave. (at Third St.), Santa Monica. ℂ 310/451-3525. www.lagosantamonica.com. Reservations recommended. Main courses $14–$30. AE, DC, DISC, MC, V. Mon–Thurs 11:30am–10pm; Fri–Sat 11am–11pm; Sun 11:30am–10pm. Valet parking $5.

**Restaurant Hama (Hama Sushi)** ★★ *Finds*    It's called a sushi "bar" for a reason—it's where people gather to socialize, drink, and have a good time. Unfortunately, too many sushi bars in California focus more on presentation than salutation. So imagine my surprise when I walked into Hama Sushi for the first time and was greeted with a chorus of "HEEEEEYYYYY!" from the six jolly chefs behind the bar, along with a few well-juiced regulars. Everybody's a somebody here, and it's only a matter of time before you, too, are cheering newcomers and buying those madcap chefs another round of Sapporos.

In Venice at the town's only roundabout, the restaurant is usually packed with regulars, so expect to wait before diving into Hama's melt-in-your-mouth yellowtail, albacore, *unagi,* and specialty rolls. Standard Japanese hot plates such as chicken teriyaki, grilled Chilean sea bass, and excellent grilled marinated squid are available as well, with a wide selection of premium chilled sake. If it's your first visit, pass on the outside patio dining area and request a stool at the sushi bar to get the full Hama effect. *Tip:* Stay long enough to close the place down and you'll be in for a singing surprise.

213 Windward Ave. (at Main St.), Venice. ℂ 310/396-8783. Main courses $6–$13. AE, DC, DISC, MC, V. Mon–Thurs 11:30am–2:30pm and 6–10:30pm; Fri 11:30am–2:30pm and 5:30–11pm; Sat 5:30–11pm; Sun 5–10pm. Valet parking $3.

## INEXPENSIVE

**Bread & Porridge** *Value* INTERNATIONAL/BREAKFAST This neighborhood cafe has only a dozen tables, but steady streams of locals mill outside, reading their newspapers and waiting for a vacant seat. Once inside, surrounded by the vintage fruit-crate labels adorning the walls and tabletops, you can sample delicious breakfasts, fresh salads and sandwiches, and superaffordable entrees. The menu has a vaguely international twist, leaping from breakfast quesadillas and omelets served with black beans and salsa, to the Southern comfort of Cajun crab cakes and coleslaw, to typical Italian pastas adorned with Roma tomatoes and plenty of garlic. All menu items are truck-stop cheap but with an inventive elegance that makes this a best-kept secret. And go ahead, order a short stack of one of five pancake varieties with any meal; this place thoughtfully serves breakfast all day.

2315 Wilshire Blvd. (3 blocks west of 26th St.), Santa Monica. ℂ 310/453-4941. Main courses $6–$9. AE, MC, V. Mon–Fri 7am–2pm; Sat–Sun 7am–4pm. Metered street parking.

**Jody Maroni's Sausage Kingdom** *Finds* SANDWICHES Your cardiologist might not approve, but Jody Maroni's all-natural, preservative-free "haute dogs" are some of the best wieners served anywhere. The grungy walk-up (or in-line skate-up) counter looks fairly foreboding—you wouldn't know that aging hot dog stand facade was serving gourmet fare, including at least 14 different grilled-sausage sandwiches. Bypass the traditional hot Italian sausage and try the Toulouse garlic, Bombay curried lamb, all-chicken apple, or orange-garlic-cumin. Each is served on a freshly baked onion roll and smothered with onions and peppers. Burgers, BLTs, and rotisserie chicken are also served, but why bother? *Note:* Other locations include the Valley's Universal CityWalk (ℂ 818/622-5639) and LAX Terminals 3, 4, and 6, where you can pick up some last-minute vacuum-packed sausages for home. Jody's now boasts a humorous cookbook, and a website with franchising opportunities as well.

2011 Ocean Front Walk (north of Venice Blvd.), Venice. ℂ 310/822-5639. www.maroni.com. Sandwiches $4–$6. No credit cards. Daily 10am–sunset.

**Kay 'n Dave's Cantina** *Kids* BREAKFAST/MEXICAN A beach community favorite since 1991, Kay 'n Dave's is well known for big portions of healthy Mexican food at low prices. Come early—and be prepared to wait—for breakfast, as local devotees line up for five kinds of fluffy pancakes (my favorite is the cinnamon swirl), zesty omelets, or breakfast burritos (among L.A.'s best). Grilled tuna Veracruz, spinach and chicken enchiladas in tomatillo salsa, and other Mexican specialties come in huge portions, making this mostly locals minichain a great choice for a day of sightseeing. Bring the family—there's a kids' menu and plenty of crayon artwork.

*Moments* Sea Breezes & Sunsets: Oceanview Dining in Malibu

**Beau Rivage,** 26025 Pacific Coast Hwy. (at Corral Canyon; © **310/456-5733;** www.beaurivagerestaurant.com). Although it's on the *other* side of PCH from the beach, this romantic Mediterranean restaurant (whose name means "beautiful shore") has nearly unobstructed ocean views. The baby-pink villa and its flagstone dining patio are overgrown with flowering vines. The place is prettiest at sunset; romantic lighting takes over after dark. The menu is composed of country French and Italian dishes with plenty of moderately priced pastas, many with seafood. Other main courses are more expensive; they include chicken, duck, rabbit, and lamb, traditionally prepared. An older, nicely dressed crowd dines at this special-occasion place. It's open Monday through Saturday from 5 to 10pm, and Sunday from 11am to 10pm. Valet parking is $4 (Fri–Sat only; otherwise, free self-parking). *Tip:* Sunday's brunch menu, which isn't limited to breakfast dishes, is a less pricey alternative to dinner.

**Duke's Malibu** ☆, 21150 Pacific Coast Hwy. (at Las Flores Canyon; © **310/ 317-0777;** www.dukesmalibu.com). Lovers of Hawaii and all things Polynesian will thrive in this outpost of the Hawaiian chain. Imagine a South Pacific T.G.I. Fridays where the food is secondary to the decor, then add a rocky perch above breaking waves, and you have this surfing-themed crowd-pleaser. It's worth a visit for the memorabilia alone—the place is named for Hawaiian surf legend "Duke" Kahanamoku. Duke's offers pretty good food at inflated but not outrageous prices. You'll find plenty of fresh fish prepared in the Hawaiian regional style, hearty surf and turf, a smattering of chicken and pasta dishes, and plenty of poo-poos to accompany Duke's Day-Glo tropical cocktails. It's open Monday through Thursday from 11:30am to 10pm, Friday and Saturday from 11:30am to 10:30pm, and Sunday from 10am to 10pm. Valet parking is $2 (dinner and weekends only; otherwise, free self-parking).

**Gladstone's 4 Fish,** 17300 Pacific Coast Hwy. (at Sunset Blvd.; © **310/454-3474;** www.gladstones.com). A local tradition, Gladstone's is totally immersed in the Malibu scene. It shares a parking lot with a public beach, so the wood deck has a constant view of surfers and bikini-clad sunbathers. At busy times, Gladstone's even sets up picnic-style tables on the sand. Prices are moderate, and the atmosphere is casual. The menu offers several pages of fresh fish and seafood, augmented by a few salads and other meals for landlubbers—mostly fried tourist food, but the large portions get the job done. Gladstone's is popular for afternoon/evening drinks and offers nearly 20 seafood appetizer platters; it's also known for decadent chocolate dessert, the Mile High Chocolate Cake, large enough for the whole table. It's open Monday through Thursday from 11am to 11pm, Friday from 11am to midnight, Saturday from 7am to midnight, and Sunday from 7am to 11pm. Parking is $3.50.

262 26th St. (south of San Vicente Blvd.), Santa Monica. ✆ **310/260-1355**. Reservations not accepted. Main courses $5–$10. AE, MC, V. Mon–Thurs 11am–9:30pm; Fri 11am–10pm; Sat 8:30am–10pm; Sun 8:30am–9:30pm. Metered street parking.

## L.A.'S WESTSIDE & BEVERLY HILLS
### EXPENSIVE

**Crustacean** ★★ SEAFOOD/VIETNAMESE   It's an amazing story how this Beverly Hills restaurant came to be. Helene An, matriarch and executive chef of the An family restaurants, is a Vietnamese princess, great-granddaughter of the vice king of Vietnam. When she and her family fled penniless from Saigon in 1975, they relocated to San Francisco, purchased a deli, and introduced the city to their now-legendary recipe: An Family's Famous Roast Crab and Garlic Noodles. This single dish spawned a Horatio Alger story and a family restaurant dynasty. The Beverly Hills location is pure drama from the moment you walk in: You're immediately scrutinized by the patrons to see 1) if you're a somebody and 2) what you're wearing. But you're too busy admiring the Indochina-themed decor—a curvaceous copper bar, balcony seating, a bamboo garden, a waterfall, and an 80-foot-long "stream" topped with glass and filled with exotic koi—to notice. What you won't see is the Secret Kitchen (it's even off-limits to most of the staff), where the An family's signature dishes such as roasted lobster in tamarind sauce or roast Dungeness crab are prepared (all quite good, but heavy on the butter). I prefer the lighter sea bass dish with ginger and garlic–black bean sauce. On weekend nights, Helene (a sweetheart and timeless beauty) often holds court, making sure your dining experience is faultless.

9646 Little Santa Monica Blvd. (at Bedford St.), Beverly Hills. ✆ **310/205-8990**. www.anfamily.com. Reservations suggested. Main courses $19–$26. AE, DC, DISC, MC, V. Mon–Thurs 11:30am–2:30pm and 5:30–10:30pm; Fri 11:30am–2:30pm and 5:30–11:30pm; Sat 5:30–11:30pm. Valet parking $4.50.

**The Ivy** ★★ NEW AMERICAN   If you're willing to pay lots for a perfect meal and endure the cold shoulder to ogle celebrities, The Ivy can be enjoyable. This snobby place attracts one of the most industry-heavy crowds in the city and treats celebrities and nobodies as differently as Brahmans and untouchables. Just past the cool reception lie two disarmingly countrified dining rooms filled with rustic antiques, comfortably worn chintz, and hanging baskets of fragrant flowers. Huge roses bloom everywhere, including the brick patio, where the highest-profile patrons are seated, dutifully ignoring the stares. And the food is excellent. The Ivy's Caesar salad is perfect, as are the plump and crispy crab cakes. Recommended dishes include spinach linguine with a peppery tomato-basil sauce, or tender lime-marinated grilled chicken. The burger and fried chicken are even great. The wine list is notable, and the variety of dessert is terrific—not least of all the chocolate chip cookies to go.

113 N. Robertson Blvd. (between Third St. and Beverly Blvd.), West Hollywood. ✆ **310/274-8303**. Reservations recommended on weekends. Main courses $22–$38 dinner, $10–$25 lunch. AE, DC, DISC, MC, V. Mon–Thurs 11:30am–10:30pm; Fri 11:30am–11:30pm; Sat 11am–11:30pm; Sun 10:30am–10:30pm. Valet parking $4.50.

**La Cachette** ★★★ FRENCH   Widely considered one of the most influential French chefs in America, Jean François Meteigner literally wrote the book on *Cuisine Naturelle*, a revolutionary approach to fine French cuisine that eschews heavy creams, butter, and complex recipes in favor of simple, light, flavorful fare, 90% free of cream and butter. Meteigner began his career as a chef in France, moved to Los Angeles in 1980 to serve as executive chef at L'Orangerie, and then opened La Cachette ("The Hideaway") in 1994. Situated on the edge of a residential neighborhood in Century

City, the elegant, romantic, white-on-white dining room is a bit hard to find—you have to access it from an alley off Little Santa Monica Boulevard—but it only adds to the restaurant's charm. As a fan of rich lobster bisque, I found Meteigner's dairy-free crab and lobster bisque intensely flavorful but lacking the richness that only heavy cream can provide (cream is optional, however). The escargot was also bland, but all was forgiven as I devoured my entree: braised Kurobuta black pork shank with braised baby back ribs and Banyul vinegar sauce, served with roasted apples and Yukon mashed potatoes. The wine list has earned the *Wine Spectator* Award of Excellence, and the warm fruit tart is a fitting finale—light and flavorful.

10506 Santa Monica Blvd. (between Beverly Glen Blvd. and Overland Ave.), Century City. ✆ 310/470-4992. www. lacachetterestaurant.com. Reservations recommended. Main courses $26–$35 dinner, $15–$32 lunch. AE, DC, MC, V. Lunch Mon–Fri noon–2pm; dinner Mon–Thurs 6–9:30pm, Fri–Sat 5:30–10:30pm, Sun 6–9pm. Valet parking $3.50.

**Le Dôme** ★★ WORLD CUISINE   For more than 25 years, Le Dôme was where eye-popping starlets hung out by the circular bar, hoping to be noticed by regulars such as Frank Sinatra, Kirk Douglas, Gregory Peck, Sly Stallone, and Richard Gere. The menu and decor got tired, and it closed in 2002 for a year-long, $2-million makeover by designer *du moment* Dodd Mitchell and Executive Chef Sam Marvin. The result is a hybrid of old and new, and the word about town is that Le Dôme is back on again. That explains why Kobe Bryant was seated nearby on my last visit, and why the lunch hour is a sure bet for celebrity spotting on the outdoor terrace. Marvin's eclectic, enticing menu is a work-in-progress, with Le Dôme classics—Mediterranean fish soup, pasta with vodka and caviar—and trendier plates such as Japanese black pig baby back ribs and Kumamoto oysters. I've also happily tried the filet mignon steak tartar on walnut toast, the Maine diver scallops with asparagus risotto, and the rack of Colorado lamb rubbed with a minty Moroccan oil, served with couscous and Barolo wine sauce. The Harlequin chocolate soufflé with Grand Marnier sauce and Chantilly cream had me crooning. Stop in just for this.

8720 Sunset Blvd. (at N. Sherbourne Dr.), West Hollywood. ✆ 310/659-6919. www.ledomerestaurant.com. Reservations recommended. Main courses $22–$60 dinner, $16–$26 lunch. AE, DC, MC, V. Tue–Thurs 6–10:30pm; Fri–Sat 6–11pm. Valet parking $5.

**Lucques** ★★ FRANCO-MEDITERRANEAN   Once Los Angeles became accustomed to this restaurant's unusual name—a kind of French olive, pronounced "Luke"—local foodies fell hard for this quietly, comfortably sophisticated home of former Campanile chef Suzanne Goin. The old brick building, once silent star Harold Lloyd's carriage house, is decorated in muted, clubby colors with subdued lighting that extends to the handsome enclosed patio. Goin cooks with bold flavors, produce fresh from the farm, and an instinctive feel for Mediterranean food. The short, oft-changed menu makes the most of unusual ingredients such as salt cod and oxtails. Standout dishes include Tuscan bean soup with tangy greens and pistou, braised beef short ribs with potato purée and horseradish cream, and a perfect vanilla *pòt de crème* for dessert. Lucques's bar menu, featuring steak *frites* béarnaise, omelets, and tantalizing hors d'oeuvres (olives, warm almonds, sea salt, chewy bread), is a godsend for late-night diners, and the bartenders make a mean vodka collins. *Tip:* On Sundays, Lucques offers a bargain $35 prix-fixe three-course dinner from a weekly changing menu.

8474 Melrose Ave. (east of La Cienega), West Hollywood. ✆ 323/655-6277. www.lucques.com. Reservations recommended. Main courses $18–$30. AE, DC, MC, V. Mon 6–11pm; Tues–Sat noon–2:30pm and 6–11pm; Sun 5:30–10pm. Metered street parking or valet ($3.50).

---

**Tips** **The ABCs of Restaurant Cleanliness**

There's something far more valuable to Wolfgang Puck than luring movie stars to his world-famous Spago restaurant. If he doesn't earn an "A" from the city's health department, he might as well "86" his hoity-toity Beverly Hills business. Here's the scoop: The L.A. County Department of Health Services started issuing report cards on restaurants' cleanliness and food-handling practices in the late 1990s, and now all of L.A.'s 37,000 retail food establishments are required to post their letter grades prominently or face closure. Anything less than a big blue "A" means bad business for a restaurant owner, since only about one in four residents will dine at a "B" restaurant. (I've never even seen a "C" placard.) Inevitably, those "A" placards have become a hot commodity, so much so that restaurateurs with "B" or "C"s are stealing the "A"s. Offenses include hair in food, chipped dishware, and waitstaff with dirty fingernails.

---

**Mastro's Steakhouse** ★★★ STEAKS/SEAFOOD  Down the street from Spago—so you know it's expensive—this is one of the best steakhouses in Southern California. Typical of an upscale steakhouse, the dimly lit dining room on the first floor has a dark, leathery, serious men's club feel to it. Request a table on the second floor, where the bar and live music are located. Slide into a plush black leather booth, order a Mastro Dry Ice Martini (which comes with the shaker, so it takes only one to get a groove on), and start off the feast with an Iced Seafood Tower—a massive pyramid of crab legs, lobster, shrimp, clams, and oysters the size of your palm. And I've found the beef: Fred Flintstone–size slabs of hand-cut USDA beef on sizzling plates heated to 400°F (204°C), so your steak stays warm and juicy throughout the meal. The only side you need is the Mastro Mash, a big bowl of creamy mashed potatoes mixed with sour cream, chives, bacon, and butter ("I'll have a Diet Coke with that"). The bad news: A bone-in rib-eye is $50. The good news: One will feed three normal-size people. The white-jacketed waiters are friendly and attentive, and manager Jin Yu has some great stories to tell about this celebrity-filled joint.

246 N. Canon Drive (between Dayton Way and Wilshire Blvd.), Beverly Hills. © 310/888-8782. www.mastrossteakhouse.com. Reservations suggested. Main courses $26–$84. AE, DC, MC, V. Daily 5–11pm. Valet parking $7.

**Matsuhisa** ★★★ JAPANESE/PERUVIAN  Japanese chef/owner Nobuyuki Matsuhisa arrived in Los Angeles via Peru in 1987 and opened what may be the most creative restaurant in the city. A true master of fish cookery, Matsuhisa creates unusual dishes by combining Japanese flavors with South American spices and salsas. (He was the first to introduce Americans to yellowtail sashimi with sliced jalapeños.) Broiled sea bass with black truffles, miso-flavored black cod, and tempura sea urchin in a *shiso* leaf are just a few examples of his masterfully prepared dishes, in addition to thickly sliced nigiri and creative sushi rolls. Matsuhisa is perennially popular with celebrities and hard-core foodies, so reserve well in advance. The small, crowded main dining room suffers from poor lighting and precious lack of privacy; many big-name patrons are ushered to private dining rooms. Expect a bit of attitude from the staff as well. *Tip:* If you're feeling adventurous, ask for *omakase* and the chef will personally compose a selection of eccentric dishes.

129 N. La Cienega Blvd. (north of Wilshire Blvd.), Beverly Hills. © 310/659-9639. www.nobumatsuhisa.com. Reservations recommended. Main courses $15–$50; sushi $4–$13 per order; full *omakase* dinner from $65. AE, DC, MC, V. Mon–Fri 11:45am–2:15pm; daily 5:30–10:15pm. Valet parking $3.50.

**Ortolan** ★★ FRENCH   Named after a small bird that has been savored to near extinction by French gourmands (now an outlawed delicacy), this wonderful new restaurant is a partnership between former L'Orangerie chef Christophe Emé and Jeri Ryan, the beautiful *Boston Public* actress and puberty-inducing "7-of-9" character in Star Trek (ask your son). The restaurant is cleverly divided into four separate sections to match your mood: a glamorous main dining room with creamy leather booths and crystal chandeliers; a smaller dining room with Pennsylvania barn-plank flooring and a long communal table where patrons dine family-style; a small, dimly lit bar with dark woods, potted herbs, and a pewter bar top; and a cozy fireplace lounge for small dinner parties or swooning couples. Emé's sophisticated French cuisine is cleverly arranged as well: bread dippings arrive in a trio of test tubes; John Dory is served on a hot river stone; dessert arrives in baby ice cream cones. His most popular dishes include crayfish and rabbit meatballs with creamy rosemary gnocchi, a superb lamb *pasilla* wrapped in filo and served in thick slices, and the most tender squab I've ever tasted. For dessert, the chocolate cake with praline *mille-feuille* is a must. Jeri, a wonderfully warm person who loves being a restaurateur, is around most nights to greet guests. *Tip:* If you don't have a reservation, join the dinner party at the enormous communal table, where less expensive small plates are served nightly.

8338 W. Third St. (at N. Kings Rd.), Los Angeles. ☏ 323/653-3300. Reservations recommended. Main courses $16–$39. AE, DISC, MC, V. Mon–Thurs 6–10pm; Fri–Sat 6–10:30pm (bar open until midnight). Valet parking $4.

**The Palm** ★★ STEAKS/LOBSTER   Every major American city has a renowned steakhouse; in L.A. it's The Palm. The child of the famous New York restaurant of the same name, The Palm is widely regarded by local foodies as one of the best traditional American restaurants in the city. The glitterati seem to agree, as stars and their handlers are regularly in attendance. Like its New York forebear, this restaurant is brightly lit, bustling with energy, and playfully decorated with dozens of celebrity caricatures on the walls. Live Nova Scotia lobsters are flown in almost daily, broiled over charcoal, and served with big bowls of melted butter. Most are enormous (3–7 lb.) and, although they're obscenely expensive, can be shared. The steaks and swordfish are similarly sized, perfectly grilled to order, and served a la carte by cheeky waiters in white jackets who have been around since the Nixon administration. Diners also swear by the creamed spinach and celebrated Gigi Salad—a mixture of lettuce, shrimp, bacon, green beans, pimento, and avocado. For dessert, stick with The Palm's perfect New York cheesecake, flown in from the Bronx.

9001 Santa Monica Blvd. (between Doheny Dr. and Robertson Blvd.), West Hollywood. ☏ 310/550-8811. www.the palm.com. Reservations recommended. Main courses $17–$41 dinner, $10–$19 lunch; lobsters $18 per pound. AE, DC, MC, V. Mon–Fri noon–10:30pm; Sat 5–10:30pm; Sun 5–9:30pm. Valet parking $4.

**Spago Beverly Hills** ★★★ CALIFORNIA   Wolfgang Puck is more than a great chef; he's a masterful businessman and publicist who has made Spago one of the best-known restaurants in the United States. Despite all the hoopla—and 24 years of stiff competition—Spago remains one of L.A.'s top-rated restaurants and continues to live up to the hype. Talented Puck henchman Lee Hefter presides over the kitchen, delivering the culinary sophistication demanded by an upscale Beverly Hills crowd. This high-style indoor/outdoor space glows with the aura of big bucks, celebrities, and California cuisine that helped set the standard. Spago is also one of the last places in L.A. where men will feel most comfortable in jacket and tie (suggested, but not required). All eyes may be on the romantic, twinkle-lit outdoor patio (with the most coveted tables), but the food takes center stage. You can't choose wrong, but highlights include the foie gras "three ways"; slow-roasted Sonoma lamb with braised greens; and rich Austrian dishes such as spicy beef goulash or perfect veal schnitzel.

176 N. Canon Dr. (north of Wilshire). © 310/385-0880. www.wolfgangpuck.com. Reservations required. Jacket and tie advised for men. Main courses $18–$34; tasting menu $85. AE, DC, DISC, MC, V. Mon–Thurs 11:30am–2:30pm and 6–10:30pm; Fri–Sat 11:30am–2:30pm and 5:30–11:30pm; Sun 6–10:30pm. Valet parking $4.50.

## MODERATE

**Beacon** ★★★ *Value* ASIAN FUSION    Ranked No. 1 in a recent Top 25 Restaurants article in *Los Angeles Magazine,* Beacon is the best thing to happen to the Culver City dining scene in years. For more than a decade Chef Kazuto Matsusaka has worked in the kitchen of some of L.A.'s top restaurants (Spago, Chinois on Main), mastering the art of fusion cooking. Along with his wife Vicky Fan (she's the GM), the duo recently opened this small, minimally decorated cafe in the Helms Bakery complex, and it has been packed ever since. On most nights you'll see a stern-faced Kazuto in the open kitchen (he's actually hilarious) while Vicky oversees the L-shaped dining room. The reasonably priced cuisine is simple yet superb, combining fresh California ingredients with traditional Asian cooking styles and a dash of Vicky's family recipes. You have to start with the outstanding Kaki Fry appetizer—warm crispy oysters in cool lettuce cups topped with *yuzu* tartar sauce (a steal at $5.75)—and the stir-fried mushroom salad, a heavenly mix of organic mushrooms, mixed greens, manchego, and tangy *yuzu* dressing. Other fantastic dishes include miso-marinated black cod with sesame-tossed green beans, tender grilled hangar steak with wasabi relish, and *kakuni udon*—thick wheat-flour noodles flavored with a generous cut of braised pork belly, bamboo shoots, baby bock choy, and warm broth. For dessert, the green tea and white chocolate cheesecake with fresh raspberry sauce is a must. *Tip:* On sunny days request a table at the back patio.

3280 Helms Ave. (at Washington Blvd.), Culver City. © 310/838-7500. www.beacon-la.com. Reservations recommended. Main courses $13–$20. AE, DISC, MC, V. Mon 11:30am–2:15pm; Tues–Wed 11:30am–2:15pm and 5:30–9:15pm; Thur–Sat 11:30am–2:15pm and 5:30–10:15pm; Sun 5:30–9:15pm. Free lot parking.

**Bombay Café** ★★ INDIAN    This friendly sleeper may be L.A.'s best Indian spot, serving excellent curries and *kurmas* typical of South Indian street food. Once seated, immediately order *sev puri* for the table; these crispy little chips topped with chopped potatoes, onions, cilantro, and chutneys are the perfect accompaniment to what's sure to be an extended menu-reading session. Also recommended are the burrito-like "frankies," juicy little bread rolls stuffed with lamb, chicken, or cauliflower. The best dishes come from the tandoor and include spicy yogurt-marinated swordfish, lamb, and chicken. While some dishes are authentically spicy, plenty of others have a mellow flavor. This restaurant is phenomenally popular and gets its share of celebrities.

12021 W. Pico Blvd. (at Bundy Dr.). © 310/473-3388. Reservations recommended for dinner. Main courses $9–$17. MC, V. Mon–Thurs 11:30am–3pm and 5–10pm; Fri 11:30am–3pm and 5–11pm; Sat 5–11pm; Sun 5–10pm. Metered street parking (lunch); valet parking $3.50 (dinner).

**Frida** ★★ *Finds* MEXICAN    The last time I had Mexican food this good I was living on the shores of Lake Chapala near Guadalajara. Made from recipes handed down by the owner's ancestors, the cuisine is the kind of food you find when you're so far south of Tijuana the culture appears more Mayan than Mexican. The friendly owner and waiters proudly present dishes as patrons eagerly tuck into handmade soft tacos brimming with sautéed shrimp bathed in a dark, tangy *pasilla*-orange sauce (fantastic), or *carnitas* in an annatto-seed sauce topped with onion-habañero relish and served over fresh corn tortillas. With so many ceviches, *sopas, ensaladas,* moles, *pescados, carnes,* and other dishes you've probably never heard of, it helps to enlist the advice of the waitstaff. Trust me on a couple, though: the dark, rich chicken mole simmered in ground pumpkin-seed sauce, and the Filete Tentacion (charbroiled filet mignon on a bed of dry chile and Mexican truffle sauce, topped with goat cheese and jalapeno sauce, and served with a side of grilled chayote squash). The wide selection of superb margaritas is the perfect accompaniment to the spicy dishes. Even the velvety refried beans were the best I've ever had. If you like authentic Mexican cuisine, *achiwawa* will you love Frida's.

236 S. Beverly Dr. (between Charleville Blvd. and Gregory Way), Beverly Hills. ℭ 310/278-7666. Fax 310/278-9699. www.fridarestaurant.com. Reservations recommended. Main courses $6–$27 dinner, $6–$32 lunch. AE, DC, MC, V. Mon–Sat 11am–10pm; Sun 4–9pm. Valet parking $5.

**Il Pastaio** ★★ NORTHERN REGIONAL ITALIAN   Sicilian-born chef/owner Giacomino Drago (scion of L.A.'s well-known Drago restaurateur family) hit the jackpot with this hugely successful, value-priced trattoria, on a busy corner in the shopping district of Beverly Hills. All day long, Giacomino's fans take a break from work or shopping and converse over glasses of Chianti and plates of oh-so-authentic pasta. With 57 menu items to choose from, I haven't come close to trying everything, but I can tell you with certainty that you will swoon over the *arancini,* breaded rice cones filled with mozzarella cheese and peas, then fried crispy brown; the pumpkin tortelloni in a light sage-and-cream sauce; and for dessert, the *panna cotta* (the silkiest in the south). There's almost always a wait—and not much room to wait in—but by meal's end it always seems worth it.

400 N. Canon Dr. (at Brighton Way), Beverly Hills. ℭ 310/205-5444. www.celestinodrago.com. Main courses $16–$25 dinner, $8–$14 lunch. AE, DC, MC, V. Mon–Sat 11:30am–11pm; Sun 5:30–11pm.

**Koi** ★★ ASIAN-FUSION   If your goal is to spot A-list celebrities, make a reservation at Koi, the current fave of L.A.'s glam scene: George Clooney, Jennifer Garner, the Osbournes, Madonna, Demi and Ashton, Jessica and Nick, Liv Tyler, J.Lo, and Martin Lawrence come here with regularity. Or just make a reservation because the food is so damn good. Either way, you won't be disappointed. Incorporating feng shui elements of trickling water, votive candles, open-air patios, and soft lighting, the minimalist earthen-hued interior has a calming effect that is a welcome relief from the hectic Melrose scene just outside the ornately carved gates. Exec chef Stephane Chevet's brilliant fusions of Japanese and Californian cuisine accounts for the repeat clientele. Start with the refreshing cucumber *sunomono* tower flavored with sweet vinegar and edible flowers, followed by baked crab roll with edible rice paper, the tuna tartare and avocado on crispy wontons, and the house special: black cod bronzed with miso that's warm-butter soft and exploding with sweetness. *Tip:* Request one of the horseshoe booths on the back patio amid Buddha statues and candlelight.

730 N. La Cienega Blvd. (between Melrose Ave. and Santa Monica Blvd.), West Hollywood. ℭ 310/659-9449. www. koirestaurant.com. Reservations recommended. Main courses $13–$27. AE, MC, DISC, DC, V. Mon–Thurs 6–11pm; Fri–Sat 6pm–midnight; Sun 6–10pm. Valet parking $5.

**Zen Grill & Sake Lounge** ★★ PAN-ASIAN   L.A.'s rising star of interior design, Dodd Mitchell, has wowed them again by introducing elements of the earth to restaurant design, at this new Westwood Village hot spot. Bathed in a soothing amber glow, it takes a few moments for the eye to take in all of Mitchell's Asian-inspired design elements: dark ebony woods, lacquered cement walls, enigmatic images of Buddhist temples and koi ponds, and a sweeping staircase with Chinese abacus railings—it's like dining in the world's hippest opium den. The pan-Asian menu has Thai, Indian, Japanese, Korean, and Chinese influences. Dishes are served family-style; recommended starters are the shrimp dumplings, tuna rice tower, Mongolian lamb with jasmine rice, and my favorite dish, Chilean sea bass simmered in a light caramelized sauce. It took a couple of Happy Buddhas—a refreshing cocktail made with *schochu* Japanese vodka, cranberry, pineapple juice, and herbal tonic—to awaken my inner self, but nobody's in a hurry to leave this Asian oasis. After a dessert of sautéed bananas topped with ice cream and drizzled with chocolate and caramel sauce, head upstairs to the sake loft and order a sweet/strong glass of unfiltered nigiri.

1051 Broxton Ave. (at Weyburn Ave.), Westwood Village. ✆ **310/209-1994.** www.zengrillsakelounge.com. Reservations recommended. Main courses $8–$26 dinner, $8–$10 lunch. AE, DC, MC, V. Tues–Thurs 11:30am–2:30pm and 5–10:30pm; Fri 11:30am–2:30pm and 5–11:30pm; Sat 5:30–11:30pm; Sun 5–10:30pm. Valet parking $4.

### INEXPENSIVE

**The Apple Pan** ⭐ SANDWICHES/AMERICAN   This classic American burger shack, a hugely popular L.A. landmark, has no tables, just a U-shaped counter. Open since 1947, The Apple Pan is a diner that looks and acts the part. It's famous for juicy burgers, grumpy service, and an authentic frills-free atmosphere. The hickory burger is best, though the tuna sandwich also has its share of fans. Ham, egg-salad, and Swiss-cheese sandwiches round out the menu. Definitely order fries and, if you're in the mood, the house-baked apple pie. Expect to wait a bit during the lunch rush, but don't worry—that line moves fast.

10801 Pico Blvd. (east of Westwood Blvd.). ✆ **310/475-3585.** www.applepan.com. Most menu items under $6. No credit cards. Tues–Thurs and Sun 11am–midnight; Fri–Sat 11am–1am. Free parking.

**Versailles** ⭐ *Value* CARIBBEAN/CUBAN   With Formica tabletops and the general appearance of an ethnic IHOP, Versailles feels much like any number of Miami restaurants that cater to the Cuban community. The menu reads like a survey of Havana-style cookery and includes specialties such as "Moors and Christians" (black beans with white rice) and *ropa vieja* (a stringy beef stew). Anybody who has eaten here will tell you the same thing: "Order the shredded roast pork." Tossed with the restaurant's trademark garlic-citrus sauce, it's highly addictive. Equally fetching is the garlic chicken—succulent, slow roasted, and smothered in onions and garlic-citrus sauce. Almost everything is served with black beans and rice, and wine and beer are available. Meals are good, bountiful, and cheap, so expect a bit of a wait.

1415 S. La Cienega Blvd. (south of Pico Blvd.). ✆ **310/289-0392.** Main courses $5–$11. AE, MC, V. Daily 11am–10pm. Free parking.

## HOLLYWOOD
### EXPENSIVE

**Campanile** ⭐⭐⭐ BREAKFAST/CALIFORNIA-MEDITERRANEAN   Built as Charlie Chaplin's private offices in 1928, this Tuscan-style building has a multilevel layout with flower-bedecked interior balconies, a bubbling fountain, and a skylight through which diners can see the campanile (bell tower). The kitchen, headed by Spago alumnus chef/co-owner Mark Peel, gets a giant leg up from pastry chef/co-owner (and wife) Nancy Silverton, who also runs the now-legendary La Brea Bakery next door. Consistently ranked as one of L.A.'s finest restaurants, a meal here might begin with fried zucchini flowers drizzled with melted mozzarella or lamb carpaccio surrounded by artichoke leaves—a dish that arrives looking like one of van Gogh's sunflowers. Chef Peel is particularly known for his grills and roasts; try the wood-grilled prime rib

---

/ *Fun Fact*  **Grilled Cheese Night**

Every Thursday evening, acclaimed pastry chef Nancy Silverton hosts a hugely popular Grilled Cheese Night at her restaurant, Campanile (see review above). The menu offers 12 different gourmet sandwiches along with appetizers.

---

smeared with black-olive tapenade, the pappardelle with braised rabbit, roasted tomato, and collard greens, or the cedar-smoked trout with fennel salad. And don't skip desserts: Nancy's many fans have turned her dessert book into a bestseller (the sour cherry brioche is fabulous). The weekend brunch is a terrific way to appreciate this beautiful space on a budget. *Tip:* On Monday nights, Campanile offers a $35 three-course, family-style themed menu that *Los Angeles Magazine* voted "Best Monday Night Dinner."

624 S. La Brea Ave. (north of Wilshire Blvd.). *C* **323/938-1447.** www.campanilerestaurant.com. Reservations required. Main courses $26–$38. AE, DC, DISC, MC, V. Mon–Fri 11:30am–2:30pm; Mon–Sat 5:30–11pm; Sat–Sun brunch 9:30am–1:30pm. Valet parking $3.50.

**Grace** ★★★ NEW AMERICAN   I'm going to start an argument here by stating that Grace is the best restaurant in Los Angeles. I had dinner here last night with two friends and everything was flawless: the service, the cuisine, the wine, the decor—even the patrons were well dressed, well behaved, and unpretentious (a rarity in this town). High ceilings, well-spaced tables, and soothing earth tones of orange, green, brown, and rose inspire relaxation. And you'll want to sit back and slowly savor each dish created by executive chef and co-owner Neal Fraser, a veteran of Iron Chef and a culinary scion of Wolfgang Puck, Thomas Keller, and Joachim Splichal. Our memorable dinner started with plump *kumamoto* oysters with a trio of superb dipping sauces, a roast beet salad with grilled radicchio and onion marmalade, pumpkin risotto with sea urchin and sweet Maine shrimp, and the most beautiful fois gras I've ever seen, served both as a pâté and sautéed with pistachio cocoa nib crust and a dab of huckleberry compote. Entrees included wild-boar tenderloin with violet mustard sauce, and slow-braised pork shank with smoked shallots and cider-sage sauce—both paired with an excellent pinot noir by the glass. The piece de résistance was a sublime, warm Cajeta bread pudding topped with pumpkin seed ice cream. It's expensive, but if you're going to splurge on a meal in L.A., Grace is where I'd recommend you go.

7360 Beverly Blvd. (at N. Fuller Ave.), Los Angeles. *C* **323/934-4400.** www.gracerestaurant.net. Reservations recommended. Main courses $20–$33. AE, DC, DISC, MC, V. Tues–Thurs 5:30–11pm; Fri–Sat 5:30pm–midnight; Sun 5–10pm. Valet parking $4.50.

**Meson G** ★★ GLOBAL   If you're a fan of small plates, you will love Meson G, a new Melrose Avenue restaurant that is both visually striking and immensely satisfying. The stylish retro '70s decor artfully blends incongruent design elements such as tufted orange banquettes, rosewood furnishings, and pebble flooring, and the large dining room affords plenty of space between tables. Executive Chef Josef Centeno's globally inspired cuisine is unlike anything I've experienced before, and I found myself becoming increasingly intrigued and impressed as dinner progressed. The "spontaneous and seasonal" chef's tasting menu started with a superb English pea soup and turnip soup, followed by crunchy *kaboucha* squash poppers that literally exploded with flavor as I bit into them. The delicate, slightly sweet Maine scallop ceviche was followed by an equally wonderful salt cod fritter, but both were eclipsed by a fois gras *panna cotta* that literally melts in your mouth. And from there it only got better. Centeno is constantly experimenting with whatever catches his eye at the farmers' market, and the best place to be when he's concocting new creations is at the marble "chef's table" facing the glimmering open kitchen—dinner and a cooking show—plus he's a pleasure to converse with. If you're pairing wines with the small plates expect to spend well over $100 per person for dinner, but it's worth the expense; you'll relish this dining experience long after it's over. *Tip:* If you're dining during lunch, request a table in the front patio area.

6703 Melrose Ave. (at Highland Ave.), Los Angeles. (C) 323/525-1415. www.mesongrestaurant.com. Reservations recommended. Main courses $12–$18. AE, DC, DISC, MC, V. Mon–Fri 11am–3pm; daily 6–11pm. Valet parking $5.50.

## MODERATE

**Ca' Brea** ★★ NORTHERN ITALIAN When Ca' Brea opened in 1990, its talented chef/owner, Antonio Tommasi, was catapulted into a public spotlight shared by only a handful of L.A. chefs—Wolfgang Puck, Michel Richard, and Joachim Splichal. Since then, Tommasi has opened two other celebrated restaurants—**Locanda Veneta** in Hollywood and **Ca' Del Sole** in the Valley—but for many Ca' Brea remains tops. The Venetian-style trattoria's bright two-story dining room is cheerful, hung with colorful, oversize contemporary paintings and backed by an open prep kitchen where you can watch as your seafood cakes are sautéed and your Napa cabbage is braised. Booths are the most coveted seats, but with only 20 tables in all, be thankful you're sitting anywhere. Detractors might complain that Ca' Brea isn't what it used to be since Tommasi began splitting his time among three restaurants, but Tommasi stops in daily and watches over his handpicked staff. Consistently excellent dishes include the roasted pork sausage, the butter squash–stuffed ravioli, and a different risotto each day—always rich, creamy, and decadent.

346 S. La Brea Ave. (north of Wilshire Blvd.). (C) 323/938-2863. www.cabrearestaurant.com. Reservations recommended. Main courses $9–$21 dinner, $7–$20 lunch. AE, DC, MC, V. Mon–Thurs 11:30am–2:30pm and 5:30–10:30pm; Fri 11:30am–2:30pm and 5:30–11pm; Sat 5:30–11pm. Valet parking $3.50.

**El Cholo** ★ MEXICAN L.A.'s oldest Mexican restaurant (Gary Cooper and Bing Crosby were regulars, and Jack Nicholson and Warren Beatty still are), El Cholo has been serving up authentic Mexican cuisine in this pink adobe hacienda since 1925, even though the once-outlying mid-Wilshire neighborhood around it has since turned into Koreatown. El Cholo's *muy* strong margaritas, invitingly messy nachos—the first served in the U.S.—and classic combination dinners don't break new culinary ground, but the kitchen has perfected these standards over 80 years. (I wish they bottled their rich enchilada sauce.) Other specialties include seasonally available green-corn tamales and creative sizzling vegetarian fajitas that go beyond eliminating the meat. The atmosphere is festive, as people from all parts of town dine happily in the many rambling rooms that compose the restaurant. There's valet parking as well as a free self-park lot directly across the street. Westsiders head to El Cholo's Santa Monica branch at 1025 Wilshire Blvd. at 11th Street ((C) 310/899-1106). *Note:* Be prepared for a long wait on weekends.

1121 S. Western Ave. (south of Olympic Blvd.). (C) 323/734-2773. www.elcholo.com. Reservations suggested. Main courses $8–$14. AE, DC, DISC, MC, V. Mon–Thurs 11am–10pm; Fri–Sat 11am–11pm; Sun 11am–9pm. Free self-parking or valet parking $4.

**Paladar** ★★ CUBAN In Cuba, *paladares* are small, privately owned restaurants in people's homes that offer authentic, home-cooked meals at affordable prices. This explains Paladar's unique "room-within-a-room" design, effected with ornate steel-grill partitions. The stylish illusion is meant to make guests feel as if they're dining in different parts of a house. Currently one of L.A.'s "in" restaurants, this Hollywood hot spot is all about Nuevo Cubano, from the unique plaster-and-tobacco-leaf wallpaper to the Afro-Cuban-American menu. If you like pork chops, you're in luck: Their specialty is an inch-and-a-half-thick grilled chop topped with mango/quince chutney and served with a side of *boniato* sweet-potato mash. Other standout dishes are the boiled yucca salad with spiced onion and a citrus *mojo* vinaigrette, the oxtail soup, and the grilled octopus served over a plantain-and-cranberry bean salsa. Some arrangements work better than others, but the overall experience is worth the pesos. All entrees come with traditional sides such as plantains, yucca mash, and rice and beans. *Tip:* After dinner, head to the small bar in the back and warm your *chichis* with a few Key lime *mojitos*.

1651 Wilcox Ave. (at Hollywood Blvd.), Hollywood. (C) 323/465-7500. www.paladar.cc. Main courses $8–$13. AE, DC, DISC, MC, V. Mon–Fri 11am–midnight; Sat–Sun 6pm–midnight. Valet parking $4.50.

**Sofi** ⭐ *Finds* GREEK   Look for the black awning over the narrow passageway that leads from the street to this hidden Aegean treasure. Ask for a table on the patio amid twinkling lights, and immediately order a plate of their thick, satisfying *tsatziki* accompanied by a basket of warm pita for dipping. Other specialties (recipes courtesy of Sofi's grandmother) include herbed rack of lamb with rice, fried calamari salad, and *saganaki* (kasseri cheese flamed with ouzo). Sofi's odd, off-street setting, near the Farmers Market in a popular part of town, has made it an insiders' secret.

8030¾ W. Third St. (between Fairfax Ave. and Crescent Heights Blvd.). (C) 323/651-0346. Reservations recommended. Main courses $7–$14. AE, DC, MC, V. Mon–Sat 11:30am–2:30pm; daily 5:30–11pm. Metered street parking or valet parking $3.

## INEXPENSIVE

**Pink's Hot Dogs** ⭐ *Kids* SANDWICHES/BURGERS/HOT DOGS   Pink's isn't your usual guidebook recommendation, but then again, this crusty corner stand isn't your typical hot dog shack. Name another hot dog stand that has its own valet who deftly parks the stream of Rolls-Royces and Mercedes that pull up regularly. This L.A. icon grew around the late Paul and Betty Pink, who opened for business in 1939 selling 10¢ wieners from a used hot dog cart. Now 2,000 of them are served every day on Pink's soft steamed rolls. Twenty-four varieties of dogs are available, many of them coined by the celebrities who order them. Martha Stewart once stopped her caravan to order a 10-incher with mustard, relish, onions, chopped tomatoes, sauerkraut, bacon, and sour cream, and now you too can order a "Martha Stewart" dog. The

---

*Tips* **Hallelujah!: A Brunch Worth Singing About**

Have mercy and say "Hallelujah!" for the Gospel Brunch at the **House of Blues** (8430 Sunset Blvd., West Hollywood; www.hob.com). For more than a decade, it has been a Sunday tradition at the HOB to feed both the body and soul with inspiring gospel performances and heaping plates of all-you-can-eat Southern home cooking. Every week different gospel groups from around the region perform uplifting and energetic music that invariably gets the crowd on its feet and raising the roof. Seatings are every Sunday at 10am and 1pm. Tickets are $33, including tax and gratuity, and are available only through the HOB Sunset Strip box office; call (C) 323/848-5100.

heartburn-inducing chili dogs (made from Betty's secret chili formula) are craved by even the most upstanding, health-conscious Angelenos. Lots of folklore emanates from this wiener shack: Bruce Willis reportedly proposed to Demi Moore in the parking lot, and Orson Welles holds the record for the most hot dogs consumed in one sitting (18). Expect to wait in line even at midnight—when it's a true crossroads of Los Angeles cultures. Pray that greedy developers spare this little nugget of Americana.

709 N. La Brea Ave. (at Melrose Ave.). ✆ 323/931-4223. www.pinkshollywood.com. Chili dog $2.65. No credit cards. Sun–Thurs 9:30am–2am; Fri–Sat 9:30am–3am.

**Roscoe's House of Chicken 'n' Waffles** ✪ BREAKFAST/SOUTHERN    It sounds like a bad joke—fried chicken and waffles on the same plate. But Roscoe's is one of those places that you have to visit at least once to see how it works (and judging by the wait, it definitely works). This Hollywood institution's proximity to CBS Television City has turned this Harlem-inspired restaurant into a kind of de facto commissary for the network. A chicken-and-cheese omelet isn't everyone's ideal way to begin the day, but it's de rigueur at Roscoe's. At lunch, few calorie-unconscious diners (and they come in all colors here) can resist the juicy fried chicken smothered in gravy and onions, a house specialty that's served with waffles or grits and biscuits. Large chicken-salad bowls and chicken sandwiches also provide plenty of cluck for the buck. Homemade corn bread, sweet-potato pie, homemade potato salad, and corn on the cob are available as side orders. Granted, the waffles are of Eggo quality and come with enough whipped butter to stop your heart, but the Southern-fried chicken is addictive. *Tip:* The waffles tend to come a bit undercooked, so ask for them crispy.

1514 N. Gower St. (at Sunset Blvd.). ✆ 323/466-7453. Main courses $4–$11. No credit cards. Sun–Thurs 9am–midnight; Fri–Sat 8:30am–4am. Metered street parking.

**Swingers** ✪ AMERICAN/TRADITIONAL/BREAKFAST    Resurrected from a motel coffee shop, Swingers was transformed by a couple of L.A. hipster nightclub owners into a 1990s version of comfy Americana. The interior seems like a slice of the 1950s until you notice the plaid upholstery and Warhol-esque graphics, which contrast nicely with the retro red-white-and-blue Swingers logo adorning *everything.* Guests at the attached Beverly Laurel Motor Hotel chow down alongside body-pierced industry hounds from nearby record companies, while a soundtrack that runs the gamut from punk rock to *Schoolhouse Rock* plays in the background. It's not all attitude, though—you'll enjoy a menu of high-quality diner favorites with trendy crowd-pleasers, including Steel-cut Irish oatmeal, *challah* French toast, grilled Jamaican jerk chicken, and a selection of tofu dishes. Sometimes I swing by just for a malt or milkshake to go—they're among the best in town. *Note:* A second location is in Santa Monica at 802 Broadway (at Lincoln Ave.; ✆ 310/393-9793).

8020 Beverly Blvd. (west of Fairfax Ave.). ✆ 323/653-5858. www.swingersdiner.com. Most items less than $8. AE, DISC, MC, V. Daily 6am–4am. Metered street parking.

**Toi on Sunset** ✪ ⓥalue THAI    Because it's open *really* late, a few blocks from the Sunset Strip, Toi has become a post-clubbing fave of Hollywood hipsters such as Sean Penn and Woody Harrelson. After all the hype, I was surprised to find what's possibly L.A.'s best authentic bargain Thai food, served in portions so generous the word *enormous* seems inadequate. Menu highlights include hot-and-sour chicken, coconut soup, and the house specialty: chicken curry *somen,* a spicy dish with green curry–and-mint sauce spooned over thin Japanese rice noodles. Vegetarians will love the vast selection of meat-free items such as *pad kee mao,* rice noodles served spicy with tofu, mint, onions, peppers, and chile. The interior is a noisy amalgam of cultish movie posters, rock-'n'-roll memorabilia, and industrial-issue dinette sets; and the coffee-shop issue plates, flatware, and glasses. It's all about the food and the scene; neither will disappoint.

Westsiders can opt for Toi on Wilshire, 1120 Wilshire Blvd., Santa Monica (© 310/394-7804), open daily from 11am to 3am; or Toi on Vine, 1360 N. Vine St., Hollywood (© 323/467-8378), open daily until 2am.

7505½ Sunset Blvd. (at Gardner St.). © 323/874-8062. www.toirockinthaifood.com. Reservations accepted only for parties of 6 or more. Main courses $6–$11. AE, DISC, MC, V. Daily 11am–4am.

## DOWNTOWN
### EXPENSIVE

**Patina** ★★★ FRENCH   When celebrity L.A. restaurateur Joachim Splichal moved his flagship Patina restaurant from Melrose Avenue to the new Walt Disney Concert Hall, it raised one pertinent question: "Is it as good as the old Patina?" If you arrived after a performance ended, you wouldn't hear the answer anyway. Billowing walls of laser-cut walnut and floor-to-ceiling glass panels only augment the hubbub as droves of smartly clad fans of the performing arts dine on Splichal's signature dishes of wild game and the ahi tuna appetizer. The après-show performances continue with a trio of carts—mounds of caviar, giant rib-eye steaks for two, and expensive cheeses—criss-cross the dining room. My dinner started with soft, thin slices of *hamachi* matched with green-apple granite and mango, followed by seared foie gras atop caramel-poached apples, and segued into an entree of crispy skinned yellowtail snapper served on a bed of fava bean puree. Dishes I reluctantly passed on included a puff pastry–encrusted grouse with caramelized endive and black-olive reduction sauce. Vegetarian dishes and wine pairings are also available, as are prix-fixe theater menus. Jackets are suggested but not required for dinner, and valet service is recommended, as it's a bit of a hike from the nearest pay lot. *Tip:* If you want a quiet, romantic dinner, ask the hostess to schedule it at the *start* of a performance.

141 S. Grand Ave. (near First St.), Los Angeles. © 213/972-3331. Reservations recommended. Main courses $31–$39 dinner, $15–$29 lunch. AE, DC, MC, V. Daily 11:30am–1:30pm and 5–9:30pm (till 11pm on performance evenings). Valet parking $8.

**Water Grill** ★★★ SEAFOOD   Widely considered by L.A. foodies to be the best seafood house in the city, Water Grill is popular with the suit-and-tie crowd at lunch and with concertgoers en route to the Music Center at night. The dining room is a stylish and sophisticated fusion of wood, leather, and brass, but it gets a lighthearted lift from papier-mâché fish that play against an aquamarine ceiling painted with bubbles. The restaurant is known for its shellfish; among the appetizers are a dozen different oysters, Nantucket Bay scallops with Queensland blue pumpkin, and crispy sweetbreads with crayfish, chanterelles, and roasted asparagus. Main courses are influenced by the cuisines of Hawaii, the Pacific Northwest, New Orleans, and New England. A good start is the appetizer seafood platter, a mouthwatering assortment served with well-made aioli. Other selections range from Santa Barbara spot prawns with fingerling potato salad, to line-caught pan-roasted Alaskan halibut with Niman Ranch bacon and sweet-pea tendril juice. For dessert, try the mascarpone with figs and cherries, or the chocolate bread pudding. Better yet, splurge on the $85 seven-course tasting menu.

544 S. Grand Ave. (between Fifth and Sixth sts.). © 213/891-0900. www.watergrill.com. Reservations recommended. Main courses $19–$31. AE, DC, DISC, MC, V. Mon–Fri 11:30am–9:45pm; Sat 5–9:45pm; Sun 4:30–9pm. Valet parking $4.

## MODERATE

**Ciudad** ★★ LATIN   The latest L.A. venture of celebrity chefs Susan Feniger and Mary Sue Milliken, this intriguing restaurant in the heart of Downtown is a nod to the partners' long-ago venture City Restaurant (*ciudad* meaning "city" in Spanish). Here, amid juicy sherbet pastel walls and Miro-esque abstract designs, exuberant crowds gather to revel in a menu that brings together cuisines from the world's great Latin urban centers: Havana, Rio de Janeiro, Barcelona, and so on. Standout dishes include the Honduran ceviche in a martini glass accented with tropical coconut and pineapple and a Brazilian *moqueca*—shrimp, mussels, and other seafood in a coconut-lime broth over coconut rice. Between 3 and 7pm on weekdays, Ciudad presents happy hour *cuchifrito*, traditional Latin snacks served at the bar; it's easy to make a meal of several, choosing from *papas rellenos* (mashed-potato fritters stuffed with oxtail stew), plantain gnocchi in tomatillo sauce, and more. **Tip:** Ciudad provides free shuttle service to the Music Center, the Walt Disney Concert Hall, and selected STAPLES Center events.

445 S. Figueroa St., at Fifth St. ℭ 213/486-5171. www.marysueandsusan.com. Reservations recommended. Main courses $12–$23; *cuchifrito* $5–$8. AE, MC, V. Mon–Fri 11:30am–3pm and 5–10:30pm; Sat–Sun 5–10:30pm. Day parking $2 w/validation; valet parking (after 5pm) $5.

**R23** ★★ *Finds* JAPANESE/SUSHI   This gallery-like space in Downtown's out-of-the-way warehouse/artist loft district has consistently ranked as one of the city's top sushi restaurants. At the back of R23's single, large, exposed-brick dining room, the 12-seat sushi bar shines like a beacon; what appear at first to be ceramic wall ornaments are really stylish sushi platters hanging in wait for large orders. More functional art reveals itself in the corrugated cardboard chairs designed by renowned architect Frank Gehry; they're funky yet far more comfortable than wood. Genial sushi wizards stand in wait, cases of the finest fish before them. Salmon, yellowtail, shrimp, tuna, and scallops are among the always-fresh selections; an excellent and unusual offering is seared *toro*, in which the rich belly tuna absorbs a faint and delectable smoky flavor from the grill. R23's sublimely perfect sushi is the star, but the short, inventive menu includes pungent red miso soup, finely sliced beef "sashimi," and several other choices. Browse a wide selection of premium wines and sakes (try the addictively sweet nigiri).

923 E. Second St. (between Alameda St. and Santa Fe Ave.). ℭ 213/687-7178. www.r23.com. Reservations recommended. Main courses $12–$20; sushi $4–$8. AE, DC, DISC, MC, V. Mon–Fri 11:30am–2pm and 5:30–10pm; Sat 5:30–10pm. Free parking.

**Tantra** ★★ INDIAN   Tantra owner Navraj Singh hired a studio design company to create an Indian restaurant unlike anything ever seen. Hammered copper doors, iron-and-silk light fixtures, curtains of oxidized metals, murals of gender-fused beings, and black-and-white Bollywood movies shown on a giant plasma screen are just a few of the unorthodox props that vie for your attention. Part restaurant and part nightclub, Tantra is one of L.A.'s current "in" destinations, both for its scene and its cuisine. The gym-size building is equally divided: Veer right at the foyer and join the Silver Lake hipsters sipping too-cool cocktails such as Tears of Ganesha and Shiva's Revenge while the DJ spins vinyl; veer left and behold Lord Ganesha, god of prosperity, perched high above the temple-style dining room. Just about all of the curries, stir-frys, masalas, and kebobs are expertly prepared, but two are standouts: Coconut-curry shrimp flavored with caraway and stir-fried with palm vinegar, red onions, and peppers, and then finished with tomato coconut broth; and the *mumbai* crepes—chickpea-and-corn crepes with a tangy cream cheese filling and topped with mango sauce.

3705 W. Sunset Blvd., Silver Lake. © **323/663-8268.** Reservations for parties of 6 or more. Main courses $11–$16. AE, MC, V. Tues–Wed 5–11pm; Thurs–Sat 5pm–midnight; Sun 4–11pm (bar open until 2pm). Valet parking $3.50.

## INEXPENSIVE

**The Original Pantry** AMERICAN/BREAKFAST    An L.A. institution in a city that thrives on change, this bastion of blue-collar cooking has been serving huge portions of comfort food around the clock since 1924. (Because it's always open, there isn't even a key to the front door.) Owned by former L.A. mayor and botched governor contender Richard Riordan, the cash-only Pantry is popular with politicos, who come here for weekday lunches, and with conference-goers en route to the nearby L.A. Convention Center. The well-worn restaurant is also a welcoming beacon to clubbers after hours, when Downtown becomes a virtual ghost town. A bowl of celery stalks, carrot sticks, and whole radishes greets you at your Formica table, and creamy coleslaw and sourdough bread come free with every meal. The menu? It's a chalkboard hanging on the wall. Famous for quantity rather than quality, the Pantry serves huge T-bone steaks, densely packed meatloaf, macaroni and cheese, and other American favorites to an already overfed crowd. A typical breakfast—served all day—consists of a huge stack of hotcakes, a slab of sweet cured ham, home fries, and coffee.

877 S. Figueroa St. (at Ninth St.). © **213/972-9279.** Main courses $6–$11. No credit cards. Daily 24 hr. Free parking across the street w/validation.

**Philippe The Original** *Value* BREAKFAST/SANDWICHES    Good old-fashioned value is what this legendary landmark cafeteria is all about. Popular with both South Central project residents and Beverly Hills elite, Philippe's unspectacular dining room with sawdust floors is one of the few places in L.A. where everyone can get along. Philippe's claims to have invented the French-dipped sandwich at this location in 1908; it remains the most popular menu item. Patrons push trays along the counter and watch while their choice of beef, pork, ham, turkey, or lamb is sliced and layered onto crusty French bread that's been dipped in meat juices. Other menu items include house-made beef stew, navy bean soup, chili, and pickled pigs' feet. A hearty breakfast, served daily from 6 to 10:30am, is worthwhile if only for Philippe's uncommonly good cinnamon-dipped French toast. Beer and wine are available. For added entertainment, request a booth in the Train Room, which houses the nifty Model Train Museum.

1001 N. Alameda St. (at Ord St.). © **213/628-3781.** www.philippes.com. Most menu items under $7. No credit cards. Daily 6am–10pm. Free parking.

## SAN FERNANDO VALLEY & UNIVERSAL CITY
### EXPENSIVE

**Pinot Bistro** ★★ *Kids* CALIFORNIA/FRENCH    When the Valley crowd doesn't want to drive to Patina, they pack into Pinot Bistro, one of Joachim Splichal's cadre of successful restaurants. The Valley's only great bistro is designed with dark woods, etched glass, and cream-colored walls that scream "trendy French" almost as loudly as

---

*Value* **Budget Brew**

The price of a regular coffee at **Philippe The Original** is the same as it was when the diner opened in 1924: 9¢. That explains why the restaurant serves more than 20,000 cups per week.

---

the rich, straightforward cooking. The menu, a symphony of California and Continental elements, includes a beautiful warm potato tart with smoked whitefish, and baby lobster tails with creamy polenta—both studies in culinary perfection. The most popular dish is the French-ified Tuscan bean soup, infused with oven-dried tomatoes and roasted garlic, served over crusty *ciabatta* bread. The generously portioned main dishes continue the gourmet theme, including baby lobster risotto and braised oxtail with parsley gnocchi. The service is attentive and unobtrusive. At lunch, a less expensive menu is served to a more easygoing crowd of regulars.

12969 Ventura Blvd. (west of Coldwater Canyon Ave.), Studio City. ( 818/990-0500. www.patinagroup.com. Reservations required. Main courses $16–$22 dinner, $7–$13 lunch. AE, DC, DISC, MC, V. Mon–Fri noon–2pm; dinner Mon 6–9pm, Tues–Thurs 6–9:30pm, Fri 6–10pm, Sat 5:30–10pm, Sun 5:30–9:30pm. Valet parking $3.50.

## MODERATE

**Jerry's Famous Deli** ★ *Kids* BREAKFAST/DELICATESSEN   Here's a simple yet sizable deli where the Valley hipsters go to relieve their late-night munchies. This place probably has one of the largest menus in America—a tome that spans cultures and continents, from Central America to China to New York. From salads to sandwiches to steak-and-seafood platters, everything—including breakfast—is served all day. Jerry's is consistently good at lox and eggs, pastrami sandwiches, potato pancakes, and all the deli staples. It's also an integral part of L.A.'s cultural landscape and a favorite of the show-business types who populate the adjacent foothill neighborhoods. It even has a full bar.

12655 Ventura Blvd. (just east of Coldwater Canyon Ave.), Studio City. ( 818/980-4245. www.jerrysfamousdeli. com. Dinner main courses $9–$14; breakfast $2–$11; sandwiches and salads $4–$12. AE, MC, V. Daily 24 hr. Free parking.

**Miceli's** *Kids* TRADITIONAL ITALIAN   *Mostaccioli* marinara, lasagna, thin-crust pizza, and eggplant parmigiana are indicative of the Sicilian-style fare at this cavernous, stained-glass-windowed Italian restaurant adjacent to Universal City. The waitstaff sings show tunes or opera favorites in between serving dinner (and sometimes instead of); make sure you have enough Chianti to get into the spirit of it all. This is a great place for kids but it's too rollicking for romance.

3655 Cahuenga Blvd. (east of Lankershim), Los Angeles. ( 323/851-3344. www.micelisrestaurant.com. Main courses $7–$12; pizza $9–$15. AE, DC, MC, V. Mon–Thurs 11:30am–midnight; Fri 11:30am–1am; Sat 4pm–1am; Sun 4–11pm. Parking $2.50.

## INEXPENSIVE

**Du-par's Restaurant & Bakery** ★ AMERICAN/TRADITIONAL/BREAKFAST   It has been called a "culinary wax museum," the last of a dying breed, the kind of coffee shop Donna Reed took the family to for blue-plate specials. This isn't a trendy new theme place, it's the real deal—and that motherly waitress who calls everyone under 60 "hon" has probably been slinging hash here for 20 or 30 years. Du-par's is popular among old-timers who made it part of their daily routine decades ago, show business denizens who eschew the industry watering holes, and a new generation that appreciates a tasty, cheap meal. It's common knowledge that Du-par's makes the best buttermilk pancakes in town, though some prefer the eggy, perfect French toast (extra crispy around the edges, please). Inexpensive, mouth-watering pies (blueberry cream cheese, coconut cream, and more) line the front display case.

12036 Ventura Blvd. (1 block east of Laurel Canyon Blvd.), Studio City. ( 818/766-4437. www.dupars.com. All items under $11. AE, DC, DISC, MC, V. Sun–Thurs 6am–1am; Fri–Sat 6am–4am. Free parking.

## PASADENA & ENVIRONS
### EXPENSIVE

**Bistro 45** ★★ CALIFORNIA-FRENCH    All class, yet never stuffy, Bistro 45 is a favorite among Pasadena's old guard and nouvelle riche. The restaurant's warm, light ambience and gallery-like decor are an unexpected surprise beyond the ornately historic Art Deco exterior (the building is a former bank); it's a romantic backdrop for owner Robert Simon's award-winning cuisine. The seasonally inspired menu changes often; dishes might include rock shrimp risotto with saffron, pan-roasted monkfish with garlic polenta, roasted veal loin filled with Roquefort, and Nebraska pork with figs. For dessert, try the "chocolate soup," a creamy soufflé served with chocolate-kirsch sauce and vanilla ice cream. The knowledgeable waitstaff can answer questions about the excellent wine list (Bistro 45 appears regularly on *Wine Spectator*'s Best Of lists, and hosts special-event wine dinners).

45 S. Mentor Ave. (between Colorado and Green), Pasadena. ℂ **626/795-2478.** www.bistro45.com. Reservations recommended. Main courses $17–$27 dinner, $11–$16 lunch. AE, DC, MC, V. Tues–Thurs 11:30am–2:30pm and 6–9pm; Fri 11:30am–2:30pm and 6–9:30pm; Sat 6–9:30pm; Sun 5–9pm. Valet parking $4.

**Parkway Grill** ★★ CALIFORNIA    This vibrant, quintessential Southern California restaurant has been one of L.A.'s top-rated spots since 1985, quickly gaining a reputation for avant-garde flavor combinations and gourmet signature pizzas to rival Spago's. Although some critics find many dishes too fussy, others thrill to appetizer innovations such as lobster-stuffed cocoa crepes or Dungeness crab cakes with ginger cream and two salsas. Take my advice and start with the hot cheese-pear-walnut flatbread and the roasted beet salad, followed by any main dish from the iron mesquite grill. The richly sweet and substantial desserts can easily satiate two appetites. With free valet parking, where the old Arroyo Seco Parkway glides into an ordinary city street, the Parkway Grill is a couple minutes' drive from Old Pasadena.

510 S. Arroyo Pkwy. (at California Blvd.), Pasadena. ℂ **626/795-1001.** Reservations recommended. Main courses $8–$27. AE, DC, MC, V. Mon–Thurs 11:30am–2pm and 5–10pm; Fri 11:30am–2pm and 5:30–11pm; Sat 5–11pm; Sun 5–10pm. Free valet parking.

**The Raymond** ★★ NEW AMERICAN/CONTINENTAL    Easy to miss, in a sleepy part of Pasadena, the Raymond is a jewel few locals even know about. This Craftsman cottage was once the caretaker's house for a grand Victorian hotel called The Raymond. The city has grown to surround it, but the place maintains an enchanting air of seclusion, romance, and serenity. Chef Renée Guilbault, of Le Cordon Bleu in Paris, brings a romantic sensibility and impeccable culinary instincts to dishes that are mostly haute American with a European flair. The menu changes seasonally: A typical dinner may start with a pancetta-wrapped shrimp appetizer tossed in an orange reduction sauce, followed by roast Long Island duckling with raspberry Port sauce, followed by chocolate Moelleux soufflé cake with a melted chocolate center served with vanilla ice cream. Tables are scattered throughout the house and in the lush English garden, and free, nonvalet parking is plentiful (you won't find *that* on the Westside). *Note:* If you're a fan of finger sandwiches, afternoon tea here, from noon to 4pm, is a great excuse to drink champagne under the sun.

1250 S. Fair Oaks Ave. (at Columbia St.), Pasadena. ℂ **626/441-3136.** www.theraymond.com. Reservations required. Main courses $30–$34 dinner, $13–$20 lunch. AE, DC, DISC, MC, V. Tues–Fri 11:30am–2:30pm and 5:30–10pm; Sat 10am–2:30pm and 5:30–10pm; Sun 10am–2:30pm and 5–9pm; afternoon tea Tues–Sun noon–4pm. Free parking.

## MODERATE

**Café Santorini** ⊯ GREEK   In Pasadena's crowded Old Town shopping mecca, this second-story gem has a secluded Mediterranean ambience—due in part to its historic brick building with patio tables overlooking the plaza below but insulated from it. In the evening, lighting is subdued and romantic, but the ambience is casual; many diners are coming from or going to an adjacent movie-theater complex. The food is terrific and affordable, featuring grilled meats and kebabs, pizzas, fresh and tangy hummus, plenty of warm pita, and other staples of Greek cuisine. The menu includes regional flavors such as lamb, feta cheese, spinach, or Armenian sausage; the vegetarian baked butternut squash is filled with fluffy rice and smoky roast vegetables.

64–70 W. Union St. (main entrance at the shopping plaza at the corner of Fair Oaks and Colorado), Pasadena. ✆ 626/564-4200. www.cafesantorini.com. Reservations recommended on weekends. Main courses $9–$22. AE, DC, DISC, MC, V. Mon–Thurs 11:30am–10pm; Fri–Sat 11:30am–midnight; Sun 11:30am–10pm. Valet or self-parking $4.

**Nonya** ⊯⊯ *Finds* CHINESE/MALAYSIAN/PERANAKAN   Peranakan cuisine (aka Nonya) was developed in the 15th century by Peranakans, a people whose heritage stems from the intermarriage between Chinese settlers of Singapore and the local Malaysians. It's a complex and sophisticated style of cooking, involving exotic ingredients and a layering of flavors. Only a few chefs in the Western world—including Nonya's executive chef Tony Pat, a Hong Kong native—know the authentic techniques. Pungent roots such as ginger, turmeric, and galangal are used liberally along with aromatic and often spicy seasonings. *Mangga ikan* salad is a light, flavorful dish made with fresh mango, tender halibut, thinly sliced red onions, and a lemon grass–lime vinaigrette. *Khaj panggang* is thin slices of chicken breast marinated in chili and grilled in banana leaves. The seafood dishes are equally enticing: red snapper spiced with turmeric and tamarind, cooked in banana leaves and served with house-pickled vegetables, or whole Dungeness crab sautéed with curry leaves and black pepper. Owner Simon Tong, who owned Asian restaurants in London for 25 years until recently settling in Pasadena, hired designer Dodd Mitchell to create a gorgeous dining room, replete with glimmering hardwoods, metals, and lush foliage that surround a tranquil elevated pond. Both sexy and soothing, this is a perfect date place.

61 N. Raymond St. (at Union St.), Pasadena. ✆ 626/583-8398. www.nonyarestaurant.com. Reservations suggested. Main courses $9–$42. AE, MC, V. Mon–Thurs 11:30am–2:30pm and 5–10pm; Fri 11:30am–2:30pm and 5–11pm; Sat 5–11pm; Sun 11:30am–3pm and 5–11pm. Valet parking $4.

**Yujean Kang's Gourmet Chinese Cuisine** ⊯⊯ CHINESE   Many Chinese restaurants put the word *gourmet* in their name, but few really mean it—or deserve it. Not so at Yujean Kang's, where Chinese cuisine is taken to an entirely new level. A master of fusion cuisine, the eponymous chef/owner snatches techniques and flavors from both China and the West, commingling them in an entirely fresh way. Can you resist such provocative dishes as "Ants on Tree" (beef sautéed with glass noodles in chile and black sesame seeds), or lobster with caviar and fava beans? Kang is also a wine aficionado and has assembled a magnificent cellar of Californian, French, and particularly German wines. Try pairing a German Spätlese with tea-smoked duck salad. The red-wrapped dining room is less subtle than the food, but just as elegant.

67 N. Raymond Ave. (between Walnut St. and Colorado Blvd.), Pasadena. ✆ 626/585-0855. Reservations recommended. Main courses $8–$19. AE, MC, V. Daily 11:30am–2:30pm and 5–10pm. Street parking.

## INEXPENSIVE

**Crocodile Cafe** AMERICAN/TRADITIONAL/INTERNATIONAL    Casual and colorful, this offshoot of Pasadena's groundbreaking Parkway Grill builds a menu around simple crowd-pleasers (pizza, pasta, burgers, salads) prepared with fresh ingredients and jazzed up with creative marinades, vinaigrettes, and salsas. It's a formula that works; this Lake Avenue branch is the original location, but siblings have sprung up throughout the San Fernando and San Gabriel Valleys—even as far away as Santa Monica. Popular selections include the oakwood-grilled burger with curly french fries, the Croc's signature blue-corn chicken tostada with warm black beans and fresh guacamole, wood-grilled gourmet pizzas in the California Pizza Kitchen style, excellent chili, zesty tortilla soup, and ooey-gooey desserts.

140 S. Lake Ave., Pasadena. © **626/449-9900.** www.crocodilecafe.com. Main courses $8–$18. AE, MC, V. Daily 11am–10pm (till midnight Fri–Sat). Free self-parking.

## 5 L.A.'s Top Attractions

**Farmers Market and The Grove** ★ *Kids*    Entering its 8th decade, the original market was once little more than a field with wood stands set up during the Depression. Eventually, permanent buildings grew up, including the trademark shingled 10-story clock tower. Today the sprawling marketplace with a carnival atmosphere is a kind of "turf" version of San Francisco's Fisherman's Wharf. About 100 restaurants, shops, and grocers cater to a mix of workers from the CBS Television City complex, locals, and tourists by the busload. Retailers sell greeting cards, kitchen implements, candles, and souvenirs, but everyone comes for the food stands, which offer oysters, hot donuts, Cajun gumbo, fresh-squeezed orange juice, corned-beef sandwiches, fresh-pressed peanut butter, and all kinds of international fast foods. You can still buy produce here too; it's no longer a farm-fresh bargain, but the selection's better than at the grocery store. Don't miss **Kokomo** (© **323/933-0773**), a "gourmet" outdoor coffee shop that has become a power breakfast spot for showbiz types. Red turkey hash and sweet-potato fries are the dishes that keep them coming back. The seafood gumbo and gumbo *ya ya* at the **Gumbo Pot** (© **323/933-0358**) are also very popular.

At the eastern end of the Farmers Market is **The Grove,** a massive 575,000-square-foot Vegas-style retail complex composed of various architectural styles ranging from Art Deco to Italian Renaissance. Miniature streets link The Grove to the Market via a double-deck electric trolley. Granted, it's all a bit Disney-gaudy, but the locals love it. Where else can you power-shop until noon, check all your bags at a drop-off station, get a spa treatment at **Amadeus Spa** (© **323/297-0311**), see a movie at the 14-screen **Grove Theatre,** have an early dinner at **Maggiano's Little Italy** (© **323/965-9665**), and be home by 7pm?

6333 W. Third St. (at Fairfax Ave.), Hollywood. © **323/933-9211.** www.farmersmarketla.com or www.thegrovela.com. Mon–Fri 9am–9pm; Sat 9am–8pm; Sun 10am–7pm.

**J. Paul Getty Museum at the Getty Center** ★★ *Kids*    Since opening in 1997, the Richard Meier–designed Getty Center has quickly assumed its place in the L.A. landscape as the city's cultural acropolis and international mecca. Headquarters for the Getty Trust's research, education, and conservation concerns, the postmodernist complex on a hillside in the Santa Monica Mountains is most frequently visited for the displays of J. Paul Getty's enormous art collection. Always known for antiquities, expanded galleries now allow for the display of Impressionist paintings, truckloads of glimmering French furniture and decorative arts, fine illuminated manuscripts, contemporary photography, and previously overlooked graphic arts. Each gallery is specially designed to complement the works on display, and a sophisticated system of programmable window louvers allows many works (particularly paintings) to be displayed in the natural light in which they were created. One of these is van Gogh's *Irises,* one of the museum's finest and most popular holdings. The museum spent $53.9 million to acquire this painting; suitably, it's displayed in a complex, swathed in Italian travertine marble, that cost roughly $1 *billion* to construct.

Visitors park at the base of the hill and ascend via a cable-driven electric tram. On clear days, the sensation is of being in the clouds, gazing across Los Angeles and the Pacific Ocean. I recommend getting one of the new GettyGuides—a handheld multimedia system that looks like an orange iPod—at the information desk. The nifty device tracks a visitor's location and provides various ready-to-go tours, and when you dock it into any GettyGuide computer station you can get more in-depth info on specific art objects. The 45-minute human-led architectural tours, offered throughout the day, are also worth looking into. Dining options include several espresso/snack carts, a cafeteria, a self-service cafe, and the elegant (though informal) "Restaurant" offering table service for lunch (Tues–Sun) and dinner (Fri–Sat), with breathtaking views overlooking the ocean and mountains (reservations are recommended, though walk-ins are accepted; call ✆ **310/440-6810** or make reservations online at www.getty.edu).

The center provides several clever programs for kids—including a Family Room filled with puzzles, computers, picture books, and games; weekend family workshops; and self-guided audio tours made specifically for families.

Entrance to the Getty Center is free. Cameras and video cams are permitted, but only if you use existing light (flash units are verboten).

1200 Getty Center Dr., Los Angeles. ✆ **310/440-7300.** www.getty.edu. Free admission. Tues–Thurs and Sun 10am–6pm; Fri–Sat 10am–9pm. Closed major holidays. Parking $7.

**Grauman's Chinese Theatre** ⭐ This is one of the world's great movie palaces and one of Hollywood's best landmarks. The theater was opened in 1927 by impresario Sid Grauman, a brilliant promoter who's credited with originating the paparazzi-packed movie "premiere." Outrageously conceived, with both authentic and simulated Chinese embellishments, Grauman's theater was designed to impress. Original Chinese heavenly doves top the facade, and two of the theater's columns once propped up a Ming dynasty temple. Visitors by the millions flock to the theater for its famous entry court, where stars such as Elizabeth Taylor, Paul Newman, Ginger Rogers, Humphrey Bogart, Frank Sinatra, Marilyn Monroe, and about 160 others set their signatures and hand-/footprints in concrete (a tradition started when actress Norma Talmadge accidentally stepped in wet cement during the premiere of Cecil B. DeMille's *King of Kings*). You'll also find Betty Grable's leg; the hoofprints of Gene Autry's horse, Champion; Jimmy Durante's nose; and George Burns's cigar.

6925 Hollywood Blvd. (between Highland and La Brea Ave.). ✆ **323/464-MANN or 323/461-3331.** www.mann theaters.com. Movie tickets $10. Call for show times.

**Griffith Observatory** ⭐ Made world-famous by *Rebel Without a Cause,* Griffith Observatory's bronze domes have been Hollywood Hills landmarks since 1935. Most visitors don't actually go inside; they come to this spot on the south slope of Mount Hollywood for unparalleled city views. On warm nights, with the lights twinkling below, it's one of the most romantic places in L.A.

The main dome houses a **planetarium,** where narrated projection shows reveal the stars and planets hidden from the naked eye. Other shows take you into space to search for extraterrestrial life, or to examine the causes of earthquakes.

The adjacent **Hall of Science** holds exhibits on galaxies, meteorites, and other cosmic objects, including a telescope trained on the sun, a Foucault pendulum, and earth and moon globes 6 feet in diameter. On clear nights, you can gaze at the heavens through the powerful 12-inch telescope.

*Note:* The entire Griffith Observatory area is closed for a major renovation and expansion and will not reopen until May 14, 2006 (so they say). However, a temporary Griffith Observatory Satellite, just south of the Los Angeles Zoo at 4800 Western Heritage Way, hosts planetarium shows, a modest display of astronomy exhibits, and a telescope for viewing the moon and planets at night; public access is free. It's open Tuesday through Friday 1 to 10pm, and Saturday and Sunday 10am to 10pm. Call © **323/664-1181** for more information.

2800 E. Observatory Rd. (in Griffith Park, at the end of Vermont Ave.). © **323/664-1181,** or 323/663-8171 for the Sky Report, a recorded message on current planet positions and celestial events. www.griffithobs.org.

**The Hollywood Sign** ★    These 50-foot-high white sheet-metal letters have come to symbolize the movie industry and the city itself. The sign was erected on Mount Lee in 1923 as an advertisement for a real-estate development. The full text originally read HOLLYWOODLAND, lined with thousands of 20-watt bulbs around the letters (changed by a caretaker who lived in a small house behind the sign). The sign gained notoriety when actress Peg Entwistle leapt to her death from the "H" in 1932. The LAND section was damaged by a landslide, and the entire sign fell into major disrepair until the Hollywood Chamber of Commerce spearheaded a campaign to repair it. (Hugh Hefner, Alice Cooper, Gene Autry, and Andy Williams were all major contributors.) Officially completed in 1978, the 450-foot-long installation is now protected by a fence and motion detectors. The best view is from down below, at the corner of Sunset Boulevard and Bronson Avenue.

**Hollywood Walk of Fame** ★ *(Kids)*    When the Hollywood honchos realized how limited the footprint space was at the Grauman's Chinese Theatre, they came up with another way to pay tribute to the stars. Since 1960, more than 2,000 TV, film, radio, theater, or recording personalities have been honored along the world's most famous sidewalk with bronze medallions, set into the center of a terrazzo star. Although about a third of these celebrities are now as obscure as Michael Jackson's sexual preference, millions of visitors thrill to the sight of the famous names, such as **James Dean** (1719 Vine St.), **John Lennon** (1750 Vine St.), **Marlon Brando** (1765 Vine St.), **Rudolph Valentino** (6164 Hollywood Blvd.), **Marilyn Monroe** (6744 Hollywood Blvd.), **Elvis Presley** (6777 Hollywood Blvd.), **Greta Garbo** (6901 Hollywood Blvd.), and **Louis Armstrong** (7000 Hollywood Blvd.). **Gene Autry** earned five different stars (a sidewalk record), one in each category.

---

*Fun Fact*  **Body Double**

Here's a really cheap and easy way to get a great seat at a fancy Hollywood award ceremony: Log on to Seatfiller.com and sign up to be one of those people who make sure all the front seats are occupied.

---

**⟨Tips⟩  Seeing the Getty without the Crowd**

Avoid the masses at the Getty Center by visiting in the late afternoon or evening. The center is open until 9pm Friday and Saturday, and the nighttime view is breathtaking.

---

The Hollywood Chamber of Commerce has been sprucing up the pedestrian experience with filmstrip crosswalks, swaying palms, and more. At least one weekend a month, a group of fans calling themselves Star Polishers busy themselves scrubbing tarnished medallions. And the legendary sidewalk is continually adding new names. The public is invited to attend dedication ceremonies; the honoree—who pays a whopping $15,000 for the eternal upkeep—is usually in attendance. Contact the **Hollywood Chamber of Commerce,** 6255 Sunset Blvd., Suite 911, Hollywood, CA 90028 (✆ **323/469-8311**), for information on who's being honored this week.

Hollywood Blvd., between Gower St. and La Brea Ave.; and Vine St., between Yucca St. and Sunset Blvd. ✆ **323/ 469-8311.** www.hollywoodcoc.org.

**La Brea Tar Pits and Page Museum** ★★ *Kids*   An odorous swamp of gooey asphalt oozes to the earth's surface in the middle of Los Angeles. No, it's not a low-budget horror-movie set—it's the La Brea Tar Pits, a truly bizarre primal pool on Museum Row where hot tar has been bubbling from the earth for more than 40,000 years. The bubbling pools may look like a fake Disney set, but they're the real thing and have enticed thirsty animals throughout history. Nearly 400 species of mammals, birds, amphibians, and fish—many of which are now extinct—walked, crawled, landed, swam, or slithered into the sticky sludge, got stuck in the worst way, and stayed forever. In 1906, scientists began a systematic removal and classification of entombed specimens, including giant vultures and mastodons, a Starbucks, and prehistoric relatives of today's super-rats. It's one of the world's richest excavation sites for Ice Age fossils. The best are on display in the adjacent **Page Museum at the La Brea Tar Pits,** with the largest, most diverse collection of Ice Age plants and animals in the world. Archaeological work is ongoing; you can watch as scientists clean, identify, and catalog new finds in the Paleontology Laboratory, or view the entertaining, 15-minute film documenting the recoveries.

5801 Wilshire Blvd. (east of Fairfax Ave.), Los Angeles. ✆ **323/934-PAGE.** www.tarpits.org. Museum admission $7 adults, $4.50 seniors 62 and older and students w/ID, $2 children ages 5–12, free for kids under 5; free for everyone the 1st Tues of every month. Mon–Fri 9:30am–5pm; Sat–Sun 10am–5pm (museum). Parking $6 w/validation.

**Mulholland Drive** ★   Los Angeles is the only major city in the world divided by a mountain range, and the road on top of this range is the famous Mulholland Drive. It travels 21 miles along the peaks and canyons of Hollywood Hills and the Santa Monica mountains, separating the Los Angeles basin from the San Fernando Valley. The winding road provides amazing views of the city (particularly at night) and offers many opportunities to pull over and enjoy the view 1,400 feet above sea level.

Completed in 1924, it's named after William Mulholland, the engineer of the aqueduct connecting L.A. and the Valley. Yes, celebrities live up in them thar hills, but you'll never find them, as most of the mansions are well hidden. You don't need to drive the whole road to get the full effect. From Cahuenga Boulevard (near the Hollywood Bowl), take the Mulholland Drive turnoff heading west. After about a mile, you'll see

## Stargazing in L.A.: Top Spots for Sighting Celebrities

Celebrities pop up everywhere in L.A. If you spend enough time here, you'll surely bump into a few of them, but if you're in the city for only a short time, it's best to go on the offensive.

Restaurants are your surest bet. Dining out is such a popular recreation among Hollywood's elite that you sometimes wonder whether frequently sighted folks such as Johnny Depp, Nicole Kidman, Kobe Bryant, Bridget Fonda, Harrison Ford, Nicolas Cage, and Cindy Crawford ever actually eat at home. **Matsuhisa, The Ivy, The Palm, Le Dome, Koi,** and **Spago Beverly Hills** can almost guarantee sightings any night of the week. Stylish hotels are also good bets: the poolside cabanas at the **Viceroy** in Santa Monica; **Mondrian**'s dining room, **Asia de Cuba,** and **Skybar** lounge; **Shutters'** lobby lounge and **One Pico** restaurant; and the **Beverly Hills Hotel.** A couple of cocktails will run you about $26, but a late-afternoon visit to the outdoor lounge at **Chateau Marmont** is almost a sure thing (I scored a trifecta on my last visit). The trendiest clubs and bars—**Whiskey Bar, House of Blues, Viper Room,** and **Skybar**—are all good for star sighting, but cover charges can be astronomical and the velvet rope gauntlet oppressive. And it's not always Mick, Quentin, and Madonna; a recent night on the town turned up Yanni, Ralph Macchio, and Judge Judy.

Often the best places to see A-list stars are **Tower Records** and the **Virgin Megastore,** along Sunset Boulevard, or chichi shops within the **Beverly Center** mall. **Book Soup,** that browser's paradise across the street from Tower, is usually good for a star or two. A midafternoon stroll along **Melrose Avenue** might also produce a familiar face; likewise for the chic European-style shops of **Sunset Plaza** or the **Beverly Center.**

Or you can seek out celebrities on the job. It's not uncommon for movie productions to use L.A.'s diverse cultural landscape for **location shots;** in fact, it's such a regular occurrence that locals are usually less impressed with an A-list presence than perturbed about the precious parking spaces lost to all those equipment trucks and dressing-room trailers. On-the-street movie shoots are part of what makes L.A. unique, and onlookers gather wherever hastily scrawled production signs point to a hot site. For the inside track on where the action is, check the **Daily Shoot Sheet** at www.eidc.com. It's a strictly legit online listing of every filming permit applied for within the city limits. Entries are classified by type (commercial advertisement, feature film, student film, TV program) and working title, and the site lists production hours and exact street addresses.

If you're intent on seeing as many stars as possible, log onto **www.seeing-stars.com,** which keeps tabs on where stars shop, eat, stay, and play in L.A.

the scenic view area on your left (look for the black iron fence). Park at the small paved parking lot and then drive a few miles farther west until you spot the other scenic view area on your right (dirt this time) overlooking the San Fernando Valley. The whole trip should take you less than an hour. *Tip:* Don't drive here after 3pm on the weekdays—

the rush hour traffic in this area is horrible. Also, no matter what your map says, U.S. 101 doesn't have a Mulholland Drive exit; you have to get on Cahuenga Blvd.

Between Coldwater Canyon Dr. and U.S. 101.

**Santa Monica Pier** ★★ *Kids*    Piers have been a tradition in Southern California since its 19th-century seaside resort days. Many have long since disappeared (like Pacific Ocean Park, an amusement park perched on offshore pilings), and others have been shortened by battering storms and are now mere shadows (or stumps) of their former selves. You can still experience those halcyon days of yesteryear, however, at the Santa Monica Pier.

Built in 1908 for passenger and cargo ships, the Santa Monica Pier recaptures the glory days of Southern California. The wooden wharf is now home to seafood restaurants and snack shacks, a touristy Mexican cantina, and a gaily colored, turn-of-the-20th-century indoor wooden carousel (which Paul Newman operated in *The Sting*). Summer evening concerts, which are free and range from big band to Miami-style Latin, draw crowds, as does the small amusement area halfway down. **Pacific Park** (© 310/260-8744; www.pacpark.com) hearkens back to the granddaddy pier amusement park in California, Pacific Ocean Park; this updated version has a solar-powered Ferris wheel, a mild-mannered roller coaster, and 10 other rides, plus a high-tech arcade shoot-out. Anglers still head to the end to fish, and nostalgia buffs to view the photographic display of the pier's history. This is the last of the great pleasure piers, with rides, romance, and perfect panoramic views of the bay and mountains.

The pier is about a mile up Ocean Front Walk from Venice; it's a great round-trip stroll. Parking is available for $6 to $8 on both the pier deck and the beachfront nearby. Limited short-term parking is also available. For information on twilight concerts (generally held Thurs between mid-June and the end of Aug), call © 310/458-8900 or visit www.santamonicapier.org.

Ocean Ave. at the end of Colorado Blvd., Santa Monica.

**Six Flags California (Magic Mountain and Hurricane Harbor)** ★★ *Kids*    What started as a countrified little amusement park with a couple of relatively tame coasters in 1971 has been transformed by Six Flags into a daredevil's paradise called The Xtreme Park. The 16 world-class roller coasters (more than at any other place in the world) make it enormously popular with teenagers and young adults, and the children's playland—Bugs Bunny World—creates excitement for kids under 48 inches tall. Bring an iron constitution; rides with names such as Goliath, Déjà Vu, Ninja, Viper, Colossus, and Psyclone will have your cheeks flapping with the G-force. Some rides are themed to action-film characters (such as Superman The Escape and The Riddler's Revenge); others are loosely tied to their themed surroundings, such as a Far East pagoda or Gold Rush mining town. The newest thrill rides are Scream!, where riders are strapped into a "flying chair" and raced upside down seven times at 65 mph, and X, the world's first and only coaster that rotates riders 360 degrees forward and backward. Arcade games and summer-only entertainment (stunt and animal shows, parades) round out the park's attractions. About 20 to 30 minutes north of Universal Studios, Six Flags Magic Mountain is open year-round.

**Hurricane Harbor** is Six Flags's tropical paradise, right next door to Magic Mountain, open May through September. You can't see both parks in 1 day, but combo tickets allow you to return sometime before the end of the season. Bring your own swimsuit; the park has changing rooms with showers and lockers. Like Magic Mountain, areas have themes such as a tropical lagoon or an African river (complete with ancient temple ruins). The primary activities are swimming, going down the 23 water slides, rafting, playing volleyball, and lounging; many areas are designed especially for little "buccaneers."

Magic Mountain Pkwy. (off Golden State Fwy. [I-5 N]), Valencia. © 661/255-4100 or 818/367-5965. www.sixflags. com. Magic Mountain $48 adults, $30 seniors 55 and older and children age 2 to 48 inches high, free for kids under 2; Hurricane Harbor $24 adults, $17 seniors and children; combo ticket $58. Magic Mountain daily Apr to Labor Day, and weekends and holidays the rest of the year; Hurricane Harbor daily Memorial Day to Labor Day, weekends May and Sept, closed Oct–Apr. Both parks open at 10am, and closing hours vary between 6pm–midnight. Parking $9. All prices and hours are subject to change without notice, so please call before you arrive.

**Sunset Boulevard & The Sunset Strip** ★★    The most famous of L.A.'s many legendary boulevards, Sunset Boulevard winds dozens of miles over prime real estate as it travels from Downtown to the beach, taking its travelers on both a historic and microcosmic journey that defines Los Angeles as a whole—from tacky strip malls and historic movie studios to infamous strip clubs and some of the most coveted zip codes on earth. In fact, driving the stretch from U.S. 101 to the Pacific should be a prerequisite for all first-time visitors because it provides so perfectly what L.A. is all about: instant gratification.

From the start, you'll see the original **CBS Studios,** from where *The Jack Benny Show* emanated; the **Hollywood Palladium,** where Lawrence Welk and the Dorsey Brothers performed; the **Sahara Hotel,** of many a movie shoot; the Guitar Center's **Hollywood RockWalk,** where superstars such as Chuck Berry, Little Richard, Santana, and the Van Halen brothers left handprints or signatures; the **"Riot Hyatt,"** where The Doors, Led Zeppelin, and Guns N' Roses crashed and smashed from the '60s through the '80s; and **Chateau Marmont,** where Greta Garbo lived and John Belushi died.

And you've barely even started. Once you pass the Chateau Marmont, you're officially cruising the **Sunset Strip**—a 1¾-mile stretch of Sunset Boulevard from Crescent

---

*Moments* **Topanga Canyon: Nature's Solution to L.A.'s Noise Pollution**

When you've had enough of cellphones, cement, and Mercedes, it's time to take the short drive from L.A. to Topanga Canyon to bargain-shop, drink margaritas, and play cowgirl for a day. Here's the game plan: Call **Escape on Horseback** (see "Horseback Riding" below) and make a reservation for a guided horseback ride in the late afternoon. Next, take the winding drive up Topanga Canyon Boulevard to tiny **Topanga,** one of the last art communities left in Southern California and the perfect antidote to the dig-me L.A. scene. Spend an hour or so picking through the treasure trove of vintage clothes, accessories, and antiques at the funky little **Hidden Treasures** (154 S. Topanga Canyon Blvd; © 310/455-2998). After the scenic horseback ride through the boulder-strewn Topanga canyons lined with oaks, sycamores, chaparral, and sage, finish off your relaxing day with a leisurely dinner in Topanga at **Abuelitas** (137 S. Topanga Canyon Rd.; © 310/455-8788), a popular Mexican restaurant, or the romantic **Inn of the Seventh Ray** (128 Old Topanga Canyon Rd.; © 310/455-1311; www.innoftheseventhray.com).

Heights Boulevard to Doheny Drive. The tour continues with **The Comedy Store,** where Robin Williams and David Letterman rose to stardom; Dan Aykroyd's ramshackle **House of Blues; Tower Records,** the largest record store in the world; the **Argyle Hotel,** where Clark Gable, Marilyn Monroe, and John Wayne once lived; the ultraexclusive **Skybar** within the Mondrian hotel; Johnny Depp's **Viper Room,** where River Phoenix overdosed in 1993; **Whisky A Go-Go,** where The Doors were once a house band; and the **Rainbow Bar & Grill,** where Jimi Hendrix, Bruce Springsteen, and Bob Marley became legends.

Once you emerge from the strip, things calm down considerably as you drive through the tony neighborhoods of **Beverly Hills, Bel Air, Brentwood,** and **Pacific Palisades.** By the time you've reached **Malibu** and the beach where *Baywatch* is filmed, you'll have seen a vivid cross-section of the city and gotten a pretty good idea of what L.A. is all about.

**Universal Studios Hollywood and CityWalk** ★★ *Kids*  Believing that filmmaking itself is a bona fide attraction, Universal Studios began offering tours to the public in 1964. The concept worked: Today Universal is more than just one of the largest movie studios in the world—it's one of the largest amusement parks as well. By integrating shows and rides with behind-the-scenes presentations on movie-making, Universal created a new genre of theme park, stimulating a number of clone and competitor parks.

The main attraction continues to be the **Studio Tour,** a 1-hour guided tram ride around the company's 420 acres. En route you pass stars' dressing rooms and production offices before visiting famous back-lot sets that include an eerily familiar Old West town, the famous town square from *Back to the Future,* and newer sets such as *Curse of the Mummy's Tomb* and *The Grinch.* Along the way, the tram encounters several staged "disasters," which I won't divulge here lest I ruin the surprise (they're all very tame). Each tram carries several hundred people and departures are frequent, so the line moves quickly.

Other attractions are more typical of high-tech theme-park fare, but all have a film-oriented slant. The newest ride, **Revenge of the Mummy,** is a super-high-tech indoor roller coaster that whips you backwards and forwards through a dark Egyptian tomb filled with creepy Warrior Mummies. **Jurassic Park—The Ride** is short in duration but long on dinosaur animatronics; riders in jungle boats float through a world of five-story-tall T-rexes and airborne raptors, and culminates in a pitch-dark vertical drop with a splash ending. **Terminator 2: 3D** is a high-tech cyberwar show that combines live action along with triple-screen 3-D technology, explosions, spraying mists, and laser fire (Arnold prevails, of course). **Shrek 4D** is one of the park's best attractions, a multisensory animated show that combines 3-D effects, a humorous storyline, and "surprise" special effects (such as the wild flying dragon chase). **Back to the Future** is a virtual-reality ride within a bucking simulation chamber. As a guest in Doc Brown's lab, you're caught up in a high-speed DeLorean chase through a million years.

Several live shows run daily. At the new *Fear Factor Live* show—based upon the NBC hit—park guests compete against each other in a progression of extreme stunts. *Waterworld* is an entertaining, fast-paced outdoor theater presentation featuring stunts and special effects performed around a small man-made lagoon. (Most performances are sold out, so arrive at the theater at least 15 minutes before the show time listed in the handout park map.) In *Backdraft,* guests move from theater to theater amid realistic ruptured fuel lines, melting metal, and scorching warehouse scenes. *Animal Planet Live!* stars trained monkeys, pigs, hawks, and other animals doing various entertaining tricks. And be sure to check out the **Wardrobe Dept.**, a new retail store offering an eclectic array of men's and women's clothing from popular television and movie productions, such as *Will and Grace* and *Crossing Jordan*. Each item is accompanied by a Certificate of Authenticity, documenting the television or movie production on which the item was originally worn (all surprisingly affordable). Straight ahead of the park's main entrance on Main Street is the **Audiences Unlimited ticket booth,** where you can obtain free tickets to join the audience for any TV shows that are taping during your visit (subject to availability).

Universal Studios is an exciting place for kids and teens, but as with any theme park, lines can be brutally long; the wait for a 5-minute ride can sometimes last more than an hour. In summer, the stifling Valley heat can dog you all day. To avoid the crowds, try not to visit on weekends, school vacations, and Japanese holidays. If you're willing to pay extra money to save the hassle of standing in line, the park offers a "Front of Line" pass with front-of-the-line privileges, as well as VIP passes (essentially private tours). You can also save time by purchasing and printing your tickets online. See the website for more information.

Just outside the gate of Universal Studios Hollywood, **Universal CityWalk** (© **818/622-4455;** www.citywalkhollywood.com) is Universal Studio's version of Downtown Disney. If you have any money left from the amusement park, you can spend it at this 3-block-long pedestrian promenade crammed thick with flashy name-brand stores (Fossil, Skechers), nightclubs (B. B. King's, Howl at the Moon dueling piano bar, Rumba Room Latin dance club), restaurants (Daily Grill, Jerry's Famous Deli), a six-story 3-D IMAX theater, an 18-screen cinema, a 6,200-seat amphitheater, NASCAR virtual racing, and even a bowling alley. Entrance to CityWalk is free; it's open until 9pm on weekdays and until midnight Friday and Saturday. *Tip:* The sushi at the Wasabi at Citywalk restaurant (© **818/622-7224**) was surprisingly good and very reasonably priced.

Hollywood Fwy. (Universal Center Dr. or Lankershim Blvd. exits), Universal City. © **800-UNIVERSAL** or 818/662-3801. www.universalstudioshollywood.com. Admission $53 adults, $43 children under 48 inches tall, free for kids under 3. Parking $10. Winter hours 10am–6pm; summer hours 9am–7pm.

## Venice Beach's Ocean Front Walk ★★★ Kids

A must-visit for any first-time tourist, Venice was inspired by its Italian namesake at the turn of the last century. Authentic gondolas plied miles of inland waterways lined with rococo palaces. In the 1950s, Venice became the stomping grounds of Jack Kerouac, Allen Ginsberg, William S. Burroughs, and other beats. In the 1960s, this was the epicenter of L.A.'s hippie scene. Today, Venice it's still one of the world's most engaging bohemian locales. No visit to L.A. would be complete without a stroll along the famous paved beach path, an almost surreal assemblage of every L.A. stereotype and then some. Among stalls and stands selling cheap sunglasses, Mexican blankets, and "herbal ecstasy" pills swirls a carnival of humanity that includes bikini-clad in-line skaters, tattooed bikers, tan hunks pumping iron at Muscle Beach, panhandling vets, beautiful wannabes, and plenty of tourists and gawkers. On any given day, you're bound to come across all kinds of performers: mimes, break-dancers, stoned drummers, chain-saw jugglers, talking parrots, and the occasional apocalyptic evangelist.

On the beach, between Venice Blvd. and Rose Ave, Venice. www.venicebeach.com.

## Walt Disney Concert Hall ★★★

The strikingly beautiful Walt Disney Concert Hall isn't just the new home of the Los Angeles Philharmonic; it's a key element in an urban revitalization effort now underway Downtown. The Walt Disney family insisted on the best and, with an initial gift of $50 million to build a world-class performance venue, that's what they got: A masterpiece of design by world-renown architect Frank Gehry, and an acoustical quality that equals or surpasses the best concert halls in the world. Similar to Gehry's Guggenheim Museum in Bilbao, the concert hall's dramatic stainless-steel exterior consists of a series of undulating curved surfaces that partially envelop the entire building, presenting multiple glimmering facades to the surrounding neighborhood. Within, the dazzling, 2,273-seat auditorium is replete with curved woods and an array of organ pipes (also designed by Gehry), as well as Joachim Splichal's Patina restaurant, the hip Concert Hall Cafe, a bookstore, and a gift shop.

The 3½-acre Concert Hall is open to the public for viewing, but to witness it in its full glory, do whatever it takes to attend a concert by the world-class Los Angeles Philharmonic (p. 569). Also highly recommended are the $10 audio tours, which lead visitors through the Concert Hall's history from conception to creation. The 45-minute self-guided tour is narrated by actor John Lithgow and includes interviews with Frank Gehry, Los Angeles Philharmonic music director Esa-Pekka Salonen, and acoustician Yasuhisa Toyota, among others. One big caveat is that you see just about everything except the auditorium: A rehearsal is almost always in progress, and the acoustics are so good there's no discreet way to sneak a peak. The audio tours are available on nonmatinee days from 9am to 3pm and matinee days from 9am to 10:30am.

111 S. Grand Ave (at First St). ℂ **323/850-2000**. www.musiccenter.org or www.laphil.com.

## 6 Exploring the City

To locate the attractions discussed below, see the individual neighborhood maps in section 1, "Orientation."

## MUSEUMS & GALLERIES
### L.A.'S WESTSIDE & BEVERLY HILLS

**Museum of Tolerance** ⭐ The Museum of Tolerance is designed to expose prejudices, bigotry, and inhumanity while teaching racial and cultural tolerance. Since its opening in 1993, it has hosted 4 million visitors from around the world, including King Hussein of Jordan and the Dalai Lama. It's located in the Simon Wiesenthal Center, an institute founded by the legendary Nazi hunter. While the Holocaust figures prominently here, this is not just a Jewish museum; it's an academy that broadly campaigns for a world where people live and let live. Tolerance is an abstract idea that's hard to display, so most of this $50-million museum's exhibits are high-tech and conceptual in nature. Fast-paced, interactive displays are designed to touch the heart as well as the mind, and engage everyone from heads of state to the MTV generation.

9786 W. Pico Blvd. (at Roxbury Dr.). ℂ **310/553-8403**. www.museumoftolerance.com. Admission $10 adults, $8 seniors 62 and above, $7 students w/ID, $7 children ages 3–12, free for children age 2 and under. Advance purchase recommended; photo ID required for admission. Mon–Thurs 11:30am–4pm; Fri 11:30am–3pm (to 1pm Nov–Mar); Sun 11am–5pm. Closed Sat and many Jewish and secular holidays; call for schedule.

**UCLA Hammer Museum** ⭐ Created by the former chairman and CEO of Occidental Petroleum, the Hammer Museum is ensconced in a two-story Carrara marble building attached to the oil company's offices. It's better known for its high-profile and often provocative visiting exhibits, such as the opulent prerevolution treasures of Russian ruler Catherine the Great. In conjunction with UCLA's Wight Gallery—a feisty gallery with a reputation for championing contemporary political and experimental art—the Hammer continues to present daring and usually popular special exhibits. It's definitely worth calling ahead to find out what will be there during your visit to L.A. The permanent collection (Armand Hammer's personal collection) consists mostly of traditional western European and Anglo-American art, and contains noteworthy paintings by Toulouse-Lautrec, Rembrandt, Degas, and van Gogh.

10899 Wilshire Blvd. (at Westwood Blvd.). © **310/443-7000**. www.hammer.ucla.edu. Admission $5 adults, $3 students and seniors 55 and over, free for kids age 17 and under; free for everyone Thurs. Tues–Wed and Fri–Sat 11am–7pm; Thurs 11am–9pm; Sun 11am–5pm. Parking $2.75 for first 3 hr. w/validation.

## HOLLYWOOD

**Craft & Folk Art Museum**   This gallery, housed in a prominent Museum Row building, has grown into one of the city's largest. "Craft and folk art" encompasses everything from clothing, tools, religious artifacts, and other everyday objects to wood carvings, papier-mâché, weaving, and metalwork. The museum displays folk objects from around the world, but its strongest collection is masks from India, America, Mexico, Japan, and China. The museum is also known for its annual International Festival of Masks, held each October in Hancock Park, across the street. Be sure to stop in the funky, eclectic Museum Shop (© **323/857-4677**) to peruse the wearable art, folk art books, and various handmade crafts.

5814 Wilshire Blvd. (between Fairfax and La Brea aves.). © **323/937-4230**. www.cafam.org. Admission $3.50 adults, $2.50 seniors and students, free for children under age 12, free to all the 1st Wed each month. Museum exhibits Wed–Sun 11am–5pm; museum shop Tues–Sun 11am–5pm.

**Los Angeles County Museum of Art** ★★   For more than 50 years the LACMA has been one of the nation's finest art museums, with its 110,000-piece collection of works by Degas, Rembrandt, Hockney, Monet, and others. The largest visual arts museum west of the Mississippi, this huge complex was designed by three very different architects over a span of 30 years. The architectural fusion can be migraine inducing, but this city landmark is well worth exploring.

The **Japanese Pavilion** has exterior walls made of Kalwall, a translucent material that, like shoji screens, permits the entry of soft natural light. Inside is a collection of Japanese Edo paintings rivaled only by the holdings of the emperor of Japan. The **Anderson Building,** the museum's contemporary wing, is home to 20th-century painting and sculpture. Here you'll find works by Matisse, Magritte, and a good number of Dada artists. The **Ahmanson Building** houses the rest of the museum's permanent collections—everything from 2,000-year-old pre-Columbian Mexican ceramics, to 19th-century portraiture, to a unique glass collection spanning centuries. Other displays include one of the nation's largest holdings of costumes and textiles, and an important Indian and Southeast Asian art collection. The **Hammer Building** is primarily used for major special-loan exhibitions. Free guided tours covering the museum's highlights depart on a regular basis from here. Be sure to visit the museum's website to see what special exhibits are currently on display.

5905 Wilshire Blvd. © **323/857-6000**. www.lacma.org. Admission $9 adults, $5 students and seniors age 62 and over, free for children 17 and under; regular exhibitions free for everyone after 5pm and all day the 2nd Tues of each month. Mon–Tues and Thurs noon–8pm; Fri noon–9pm; Sat–Sun 11am–8pm. Parking $5.

**Museum of the American West** ★★   Located north of Downtown in Griffith Park, this is one of the country's finest and most comprehensive museums of the American West. More than 78,000 artifacts showcase the history of the region west of the Mississippi River. Evocative exhibits illustrate the everyday lives of early pioneers, not only with antique firearms, tools, saddles, and the like, but with many hands-on displays that successfully stir the imagination and the heart. You'll find footage from Buffalo Bill's Wild West Show, movie clips from the silent days, contemporary films, the works of Wild West artists, and plenty of memorabilia from Gene "The Singing Cowboy" Autry's film and TV projects. The Hall of Merchandising displays Roy Rogers bedspreads, Hopalong Cassidy radios, and other items from the collective consciousness—and material collections—of baby boomers. Provocative visiting exhibits usually focus on cultural or domestic regional history. Docent-led tours are generally scheduled on Saturdays at 11am and noon. *Tip:* You can purchase a $12 two-site ticket that also includes entry into the Southwest Museum of the American Indian; it's valid for 3 months.

4700 Western Heritage Way (in Griffith Park). (C) 323/667-2000. www.museumoftheamericanwest.org. Admission $7.50 adults, $5 seniors 60 and over and students ages 13–18, $3 children ages 2–12, free for kids under age 2; free to all Thurs after 4pm. Tues–Sun 10am–5pm (Thurs until 8pm). Parking free.

**Petersen Automotive Museum** ★ *Kids*   When the Petersen opened in 1994, many locals were surprised that it had taken this long for the city of freeways to salute its most important shaper. Indeed, this museum says more about the city than probably any other in L.A. Named for Robert Petersen, the publisher responsible for *Hot Rod* and *Motor Trend* magazines, the four-story museum displays more than 200 cars and motorcycles, from the historic to the futuristic. Cars on the first floor are exhibited chronologically in period settings. Other floors are devoted to frequently changing shows of race cars, early motorcycles, famous movie vehicles, and celebrity wheels such as Jack Benny's old Chrysler Imperial. On the third floor, the Discovery Center is a 6,500-square-foot, "hands-on" learning center that teaches kids and women the basic scientific principles of auto mechanics. Past shows have included a comprehensive exhibit of "woodies" and surf culture, Hollywood "star cars," and the world's fastest, most valuable cars.

6060 Wilshire Blvd. (at Fairfax Ave.). (C) 323/930-CARS. www.petersen.org. Admission $10 adults, $5 seniors and students, $3 children ages 5–12, free for kids age 4 and under. Tues–Sun 10am–6pm. Parking $6.

## DOWNTOWN

**California Science Center** ★★ *Kids*   A $130-million renovation has turned the former Museum of Science and Industry into Exposition Park's most popular attraction. Using high-tech sleight-of-hand, the center stimulates kids of all ages with questions, answers, and lessons about the world. One of the museum's highlights is Tess, a 50-foot animatronic woman whose muscles, bones, organs, and blood vessels are exposed, showing how the body reacts to a variety of stimuli. Another highlight is the **Air and Space Gallery,** a seven-story space where real air- and spacecraft are suspended overhead.

Nominal fees range from $2 to $5 for the science center's more thrilling attractions. You can pedal a bicycle across a high-wire suspended 43 feet above the ground (demonstrating the principle of gravity and counterweights) or get strapped into the Space Docking Simulator for a virtual-reality taste of zero gravity. There's plenty more, and plans for expansion are always in the works. The IMAX theater boasts a screen seven stories high and 90 feet wide, with state-of-the-art surround sound and 3-D technology. Films, screened throughout the day until 9pm, are nearly always breathtaking (even the two-dimensional ones).

700 State Dr., Exposition Park. ⓒ **323/724-3623;** IMAX theater ⓒ **213/744-7400.** www.casciencectr.org. Free admission to the museum; IMAX theater $7.50 adults, $5.50 seniors over 60 and children ages 13–17, $4.50 ages 4–12. Multishow discounts available. Daily 10am–5pm. Closed Thanksgiving, Christmas, and New Year's Day. Parking $6.

**Japanese American National Museum** ⚡ *Finds* In an architecturally acclaimed modern building in Little Tokyo, this soaring 85,000-square-foot pavilion—designed by renowned architect Gyo Obata—is a private nonprofit institute created to document and celebrate the history of the Japanese in America. The permanent and rotating exhibits chronicle Japanese life in the United States, highlighting distinctive aspects of Japanese-American culture ranging from the internment camp experience during the early years of World War II to the lives of Japanese Americans in Hawaii. The experience is made even more poignant by the personal accounts of the docents, many of whom are elderly Japanese-American citizens who were interred in these camps during the war. It's a very popular museum, attracting more than 150,000 annual visitors. *Tip:* Don't miss the museum store, which carries excellent gift items ranging from hand-fired sake sets to mini Zen gardening kits.

369 E. First St. (at Central Ave.). ⓒ **213/625-0414.** www.janm.org. Admission $8 adults, $5 seniors, $4 students and kids 6–17, free for kids age 5 and under; free to all the 3rd Thurs of each month and every Thurs after 5pm. Tues–Sun 10am–5pm (Thurs till 8pm).

**Museum of Contemporary Art/Geffen Contemporary at MOCA** ★★ MOCA is Los Angeles's only institution devoted to art from 1940 to the present. Displaying works in a variety of media, it's strong in works by Cy Twombly, Jasper Johns, and Mark Rothko, and shows are often superb. For many experts, MOCA's collections are too spotty to be considered world class, and the conservative museum board blushes when offered controversial shows (they passed on a Whitney exhibit that included photographs by Robert Mapplethorpe). Nevertheless, I've seen some excellent exhibitions here.

MOCA is housed in three buildings: The Grand Avenue main building (250 S. Grand Ave., Los Angeles) is a contemporary red sandstone structure by renowned Japanese architect Arata Isozaki. The museum restaurant, **Patinette** (Mon and Fri 11am–5pm; Wed 11am–2pm; Thurs 11am–8pm; Sat–Sun 11am–6pm; ⓒ **213/626-1178**), is the casual-dining creation of celebrity chef Joachim Splichal (see Patina, p. 513). The museum's second space, on Central Avenue in Little Tokyo (152 North Central Ave., Los Angeles), was the "temporary" Contemporary while the Grand structure was being built and now houses a superior permanent collection in a warehouse-type space that's been renamed for entertainment mogul and art collector David Geffen. An added feature is a detailed timeline corresponding to the progression of works. Unless there's an exceptional visiting exhibit at the main museum, I recommend that you start at the Geffen building, where it's also easier to park. The third gallery is in the compact building next to the Pacific Design Center (8687 Melrose Ave., West Hollywood). Unlike the other two, admission to this galley is free, and emphasis is on contemporary architecture and design, and new work by emerging and established artists.

Main MOCA information line: ⓒ **213/626-6222.** www.moca-la.org. Admission $8 adults, $5 seniors 65 and over and students, free for children age 11 and under; admission to Melrose Ave. branch is always free. Free admission to all MOCA galleries every Thurs. Mon 11am–5pm; Thurs 11am–8pm; Fri 11am–5pm; Sat–Sun 11am–6pm.

**Natural History Museum of Los Angeles County** ⚡ *Kids* The "Fighting Dinosaurs" are not a high school football team, but the trademark symbol of this massive museum: *Tyrannosaurus rex* and triceratops skeletons poised in a stance so realistic that every kid feels inspired to imitate their *Jurassic Park* bellows (think Calvin & Hobbes). Opened in 1913 in a beautiful domed Spanish Renaissance building, this massive museum is a 35-hall warehouse of Earth's history; it chronicles the planet and its inhabitants from 600 million years ago to the present day, and houses more than 33 million specimens and artifacts. The array of exhibits on prehistoric fossils, bird and marine life, gems and minerals, and North American mammals is mind-numbing. The kid-friendly Discovery Center entertains children via hands-on, interactive exhibits: Kids can make fossil rubbings, dig for fossils, and view live animals such as snakes and lizards. The best permanent displays include the world's rarest shark, a walk-through vault of priceless gems (including the largest collection of gold in the United States), and an Insect Zoo.

The Dinosaur Shop sells ant farms and exploding volcano and model kits, the Ethnic Arts Shop has unique folk art and jewelry from around the world, and the bookstore has a wide selection of scientific titles and hobbyists' field guides.

900 Exposition Blvd., Exposition Park. ℂ 213/763-DINO. www.nhm.org. Admission $9 adults; $6.50 children ages 13–17, seniors, and students w/ID; $2 children ages 5–12; free for kids under 5; free for everyone the 1st Tues of each month. Mon–Fri 9:30am–5pm; Sat–Sun 10am–5pm.

## SANTA MONICA & THE BEACHES

**Bergamot Arts Station and Santa Monica Museum of Art** ★★     One of L.A.'s primary cultural destinations is the Bergamot Arts Station. Home to the **Santa Monica Museum of Art,** this campuslike complex is hugely popular for visitors from around the world. The location dates from 1875, when it was a stop for the Red Line trolley, and retains its industrial, rustic look. Filled with 20 galleries, the unique installations on display here range from photography and sculpture to interactive pieces. Its central location allows visitors to park and spend the day seeing art rather than driving from one gallery to the next, and many pieces are available for purchase. A must-see for the arts lover.

2525 Michigan Ave., Santa Monica. ℂ 310/829-5854. www.bergamotstation.com. Free admission. Most galleries open Tues–Sat 11am–6pm.

## PASADENA & ENVIRONS

**Norton Simon Museum of Art** ★★ *Finds*     Named for a food-packing king and financier who reorganized the failing Pasadena Museum of Modern Art, the Norton Simon displays one of the finest private collections of European, American, and Asian art in the world (yet another feather in the cap of architect Frank Gehry, who redesigned the interior space). Comprehensive collections of masterpieces by Degas, Picasso, Rembrandt, and Goya are augmented by the sculptures of Henry Moore and Auguste Rodin, including *The Burghers of Calais,* which greets you at the gates. The "Blue Four" collection of works by Kandinsky, Jawlensky, Klee, and Feininger is impressive, as is a superb collection of Southeast Asian sculpture. *Still Life with Lemons, Oranges, and a Rose* (1633), an oil by Francisco de Zurbarán, is one of the museum's most important holdings. Perhaps the most popular piece is *The Flower Vendor/Girl with Lilies,* by Diego Rivera, followed by Goya's *Disasters of War.* The collection of paintings, sculptures, pastels, and prints by French Impressionist Edgar Degas is among the best in the world. *Tip:* Unless you're an art expert, you'll probably want to take the "Acoustiguide" audio tour; it's $3 well spent.

411 W. Colorado Blvd., Pasadena. ℂ 626/449-6840. www.nortonsimon.org. Admission $8 adults, $4 seniors, free for students and kids 17 and under. Free for everyone the 1st Fri of each month 6–9pm. Wed–Mon noon–6pm (Fri till 9pm). Free parking.

**Pacific Asia Museum** The most striking aspect of this museum is the building itself. Designed in the 1920s, in Chinese Imperial Palace style, it's rivaled in flamboyance only by Grauman's Chinese Theatre in Hollywood (see "L.A.'s Top Attractions," earlier in this chapter). Rotating exhibits of 14,000 rare Asian and Pacific Islands artworks and artifacts span the centuries, from 100 B.C. to now. This manageably sized museum is worth a visit, particularly if you're an adherent of Buddhism.

46 N. Los Robles Ave., Pasadena. ⓒ 626/449-2742, ext. 10. www.pacificasiamuseum.org. Admission $7 adults, $5 students and seniors; free for children under 12; free for everyone the 4th Fri of each month. Wed–Thurs and Sat–Sun 10am–5pm; Fri 10am–8pm. Free parking.

## ARCHITECTURAL HIGHLIGHTS

Los Angeles is a veritable Disneyland of architecture (and not too far from the real Disneyland). The city is home to an amalgam of styles—from Art Deco to Spanish Revival to coffee-shop kitsch to suburban ranch to postmodern, and much more. Over-the-top styles that would be out of place in other cities—from the oversize hot dog that is Tail o' the Pup to the mansions lining the streets of Beverly Hills—are perfectly at home. The newest gem on the scene is the Frank Gehry–designed **Walt Disney Concert Hall,** at the intersection of First Street and Grand Avenue in the historic Bunker Hill area (see p. 527 for information on tickets and tours of the state-of-the-art facility).

### SANTA MONICA & THE BEACHES

When you're strolling the historic canals and streets of Venice, be sure to check out the **Chiat/Day** offices at 340 Main St. What would otherwise be an unspectacular contemporary office building is made fantastic by a **three-story pair of binoculars** that frames the entrance. The sculpture is modeled after a design created by Claes Oldenburg and Coosje van Bruggen.

When you're on your way in or out of LAX, be sure to stop for a moment to admire the **Control Tower** and **Theme Building.** The space-age, *Jetsons*-style Theme Building, which has always loomed over LAX, has been joined by a more recent silhouette. The main control tower, designed by local architect Kate Diamond to evoke a stylized palm tree, is tailored to present Southern California in its best light. You can go inside

---

### *Moments* Greystone Mansion

If you've seen *The Witches of Eastwick* or *War and Remembrance,* then you know how beautiful and opulent the Greystone Mansion and surrounding gardens are. On a slope overlooking Beverly Hills, the 18½-acre park is a prime filming location where dozens of TV episodes, movies *(Spiderman, X-Men, Batman, Ghostbusters, The Bodyguard),* commercials, and music videos are filmed annually. It's worth a visit just to admire this matriarch of Beverly Hills mansions and her meticulously groomed gardens. A self-guided tour takes you through the Formal Gardens, Mansion Gardens, and Lower Ground Estate. Picnics are welcome in designated areas (as are dogs), and **Afternoon Tea on the Terrace** is offered one Saturday per month from May through August at 4pm. The price is $34 for nonresidents and includes musical entertainment and a tour of the mansion's first floor. Tickets must be purchased in advance by calling ⓒ 310/550-4796. The park is at 905 Loma Vista Dr., just off Doheny, and is open daily from 10am to sunset. Admission is free. For more information, log on to www.beverlyhills.org.

to enjoy the view from the Theme Building's observation deck, or have a cocktail at the Technicolor bachelor pad that is the **Encounter at LAX** restaurant.

## L.A.'S WESTSIDE & BEVERLY HILLS

In addition to the sights below, don't miss the **Beverly Hills Hotel and Bungalows** (p. 483), and be sure to wind your way through the streets of Beverly Hills off Sunset Boulevard.

**Pacific Design Center**  The bold architecture and overwhelming scale of the Pacific Design Center, by Argentinean architect Cesar Pelli, aroused controversy when it was erected in 1975. Sheathed in gently curving cobalt-blue glass, the seven-story building houses more than 750,000 square feet of wholesale interior-design showrooms, known to locals as "the blue whale." When the property for the design center was acquired in the 1970s, almost all the small businesses that lined this stretch of Melrose Avenue were demolished. Only Hugo's Plating, which still stands in front of the center, successfully resisted the wrecking ball. In 1988, a second boxlike structure, dressed in equally dramatic Kelly green, was added to the design center and surrounded by a protected outdoor plaza.

8687 Melrose Ave., West Hollywood. ✆ 310/657-0800. www.pacificdesigncenter.com.

**Schindler House** ✪  A protégé of Frank Lloyd Wright and contemporary of Richard Neutra, Austrian architect Rudolph Schindler designed this innovative modern house for himself in 1921 and 1922. It's now home to the Los Angeles arm of Austria's Museum of Applied Arts (MAK Center for Art and Architecture L.A.). The house is noted for its complicated interlocking spaces; the interpenetration of indoors and out; simple, unadorned materials; and technological innovations. Docent-guided tours are conducted at no additional charge on weekends only.

The MAK Center offers guides to L.A.-area buildings by Schindler and other Austrian architects, and presents visiting related exhibitions and creative arts programming. Call for schedules.

835 N. Kings Rd. (north of Melrose Ave.), West Hollywood. ✆ 323/651-1510. www.makcenter.com. Admission $5 adults, free to children age 12 and under. Free to all every Fri after 4pm, Sept 10 (Schindler's birthday), May 24 (International Museum Day), and Dec 1. Wed–Sun 11am–6pm.

**Tail o' the Pup**  At first glance, you might not think twice about this hot dog–shaped bit of kitsch just across from the Beverly Center. But locals adored this closet-size wiener dispensary so much that when it was threatened by the developer's bulldozer, they spoke out en masse to save it. One of the last remaining examples of 1950s representational architecture, the "little dog that could" still serves up a great Baseball Special.

329 N. San Vicente Blvd. (between Beverly Blvd. and Melrose Ave.), West Hollywood. ✆ 310/652-4517.

## HOLLYWOOD

In addition to the buildings listed below, don't miss the **Griffith Observatory** (p. 520), **Grauman's Chinese Theatre** (p. 520), and the **Roosevelt Hotel, Hollywood** (p. 490).

**Capitol Records Building**  Opened in 1956, this 13-story tower, just north of the legendary intersection of Hollywood and Vine, is one of the city's most recognizable buildings. The world's first circular office building is often, but incorrectly, said to have been made to resemble a stack of 45s under a turntable stylus (it kinda does, though). Nat "King" Cole, songwriter Johnny Mercer, and other 1950s Capitol artists

> **Fun Fact  Not Quite S.O.S., but . . .**
>
> The light on the rooftop spire of the Capitol Records building flashes "H-O-L-L-Y-W-O-O-D" in Morse code. Really, it does.

figure into a giant exterior mural. Look down and you'll see the sidewalk stars of Capitol's recording artists, including John Lennon. In the lobby, numerous gold albums are on display.

1750 Vine St. ✆ 323/462-6252.

**The Egyptian Theatre**  Conceived by grandiose impresario Sid Grauman, the Egyptian Theatre is just down the street from his better-known Chinese Theatre. Compared to the Chinese, it remains less altered from its original design, which was based on the then-headline news discovery of hidden treasures in Pharaohs' tombs (hence the hieroglyphic murals and enormous scarab decoration above the stage). Hollywood's first movie premiere, *Robin Hood,* starring Douglas Fairbanks, was shown here in 1922, followed by the premiere of *The Ten Commandments* in 1923. The building recently underwent a sensitive restoration by American Cinematheque, which now screens rare, classic, and independent films here.

6712 Hollywood Blvd. ✆ 323/466-FILM. www.egyptiantheatre.com.

**Freeman House**  Frank Lloyd Wright's Freeman House, built in 1924, was designed as an experimental prototype of mass-produced affordable housing. The home's richly patterned "textile-block" exterior was Wright's invention and is the most famous aspect of the home's design. On a dramatic site overlooking Hollywood, Freeman House is built with the world's first glass-to-glass corner windows. Dancer Martha Graham, bandleader Xavier Cugat, art collector Galka Sheye, photographer Edward Weston, and architects Philip Johnson and Richard Neutra all lived or spent significant time at this house, which became known as an avant-garde salon. The house is currently closed for restoration; call ahead to see if it's open.

1962 Glencoe Way (off Hillcrest, near Highland and Franklin aves.). ✆ 323/851-0671.

## DOWNTOWN

For a taste of what downtown's Bunker Hill was like before the bulldozers, visit the residential neighborhood of **Angelino Heights,** near Echo Park. Entire streets are still filled with stately gingerbread Victorian homes; most still enjoy the beautiful views that led early L.A.'s elite to build here. The 1300 block of Carroll Avenue is the best preserved. Don't be surprised if a film crew is scouting locations while you're there; these blocks appear often on the silver screen.

**The Bradbury Building**  This National Historic Landmark, built in 1893 and designed by George Wyman, is Los Angeles's oldest commercial building and one of the city's most revered architectural achievements. Legend has it that an inexperienced draftsman named George Wyman accepted the $125,000 commission after communicating with his dead brother through a Ouija board. Capped by a five-story skylight, Bradbury's courtyard combines glazed brick, ornate Mexican tile floors, Belgian marble, Art Nouveau grillwork, handsome oak paneling, and lacelike wrought-iron railings. It's one of the great interior spaces of the 19th century. The glass-topped atrium

## Stargazing in L.A., Part II: The Less-Than-Lively Set

Almost everybody who visits L.A. hopes to see a celebrity—they are, after all, our most common export. But celebrities usually don't cooperate, failing to gather in readily viewable herds. There is, however, an absolutely guaranteed method to come within 6 feet of many famous stars. Cemeteries are *the* place for star (or at least headstone) gazing: The star is always available, and you're going to get a lot more up close and personal than you probably would with anyone who's actually alive. Here is a guide to the most fruitful cemeteries, listed in order of their friendliness to stargazers. If you're looking for someone in particular, log onto www.findagrave.com (they have a website for *everything*).

Weathered Victorian and Art Deco memorials add to the decaying charm of **Hollywood Forever** ⭐ (formerly Hollywood Memorial Park), 6000 Santa Monica Blvd., Hollywood (© **323/469-1181**; www.hollywoodforever.com). Fittingly, there's a terrific view of the HOLLYWOOD sign over the graves, as many of the community founders rest here. The most notable tenant is Rudolph Valentino, who rests in an interior crypt. Outside are Tyrone Power, Jr.; Douglas Fairbanks, Sr.; Cecil B. DeMille (facing Paramount, his old studio); Carl "Alfalfa" Spritzer from *The Little Rascals* (the dog on his grave is not Petey); Hearst mistress Marion Davies; John Huston; and a headstone for Jayne Mansfield (she's really buried in Pennsylvania with her family). In 2000, Douglas Fairbanks, Jr., joined his dad at Hollywood Forever.

The catholic **Holy Cross Cemetery,** 5835 W. Slauson Ave., Culver City (© **310/836-5500**), founded in 1939, hands out maps to the stars' graves. In one area, within mere feet of each other, lie Bing Crosby, Bela Lugosi (buried in his Dracula cape), and Sharon Tate; not far away are Rita Hayworth and Jimmy Durante. Also here are "Tin Man" Jack Haley and "Scarecrow" Ray Bolger, Mary Astor, John Ford, and Gloria Morgan Vanderbilt. More recent arrivals include John Candy and Audrey Meadows.

The front office at **Hillside Memorial Park,** 6001 Centinela Ave., Baldwin Hills (© **800/576-1994**; www.hillsidememorial.com), can provide a guide to this Jewish cemetery, which has an L.A. landmark: the behemoth tomb of Al Jolson. His rotunda, complete with a bronze reproduction of Jolson and cascading fountain, is visible from I-405. Also on hand are Jack Benny, Eddie Cantor, Vic Morrow, and Michael Landon.

You just know developers get stomachaches looking at **Westwood Village Memorial Park,** 1218 Glendon Ave., Westwood (© **310/474-1579**; the staff

is often used as a movie and TV set; you've probably seen it before in *Chinatown* and *Blade Runner.*

304 S. Broadway (at Third St.). © **213/626-1893.** Mon–Fri 9am–6pm; Sat–Sun 9am–5pm.

**Cathedral of Our Lady of the Angels** ⭐ Completed in September 2002 at a cost of $163 million and built to last 500 years, this ultracontemporary cathedral is one of L.A.'s newest architectural treasures and the third-largest cathedral in the world. It was can direct you around), smack-dab in the middle of some of L.A.'s priciest real estate (behind the AVCO office building south of Wilshire Blvd.). But it's not going anywhere, especially when you consider its most famous resident: Marilyn Monroe (entombed in a simple wall crypt, number 24). It's also got Truman Capote, Roy Orbison, John Cassavetes, Armand Hammer, Donna Reed, and Natalie Wood. Walter Matthau and Jack Lemmon are buried here as well, a fitting ending for the Odd Couple.

**Forest Lawn Glendale,** 1712 S. Glendale Ave. (© **800/204-3131;** www. forestlawn.com), likes to pretend it has no celebrities. The most prominent of L.A. cemeteries, it's also the most humorless. The place is full of bad art, all part of the continuing vision of founder Huburt Eaton, who thought cemeteries should be happy places. So he banished those gloomy upright tombstones and monuments in favor of flat, pleasant, character-free, flush-to-the-ground slabs. Contrary to urban legend, Walt Disney was *not* frozen and placed under Cinderella's castle at Disneyland. His cremated remains are in a little garden to the left of the Freedom Mausoleum. Turn around, and just behind you are Errol Flynn and Spencer Tracy. In the Freedom Mausoleum itself are Nat "King" Cole, Chico Marx, Gummo Marx, and Gracie Allen—finally joined by George Burns. In a columbarium near the Mystery of Life is Humphrey Bogart. Unfortunately, some of the best celebs—such as Clark Gable, Carole Lombard, and Jean Harlow—are in the Great Mausoleum, which you often can't get into unless you're visiting a relative.

You'd think a place that encourages people to visit for fun would understand what the attraction is. But no—Forest Lawn Glendale won't tell you where any of their illustrious guests are, so don't ask. This place is immense—and, frankly, dull in comparison to the previously listed cemeteries, unless you appreciate the kitsch value of the Forest Lawn approach to art.

**Forest Lawn Hollywood Hills,** 6300 Forest Lawn Dr. (© **800/204-3131;** www.forestlawn.com), is slightly less anal than the Glendale branch, but the same basic attitude prevails. On the right lawn, near the statue of George Washington, is Buster Keaton. In the Courts of Remembrance are Lucille Ball, Charles Laughton, and the not-quite-gaudy-enough tomb of Liberace. Outside, in a vault on the Ascension Road side, is Andy Gibb. Bette Davis's sarcophagus is in front of the wall, to the left of the entrance to the Courts. Gene Autry is also buried here, almost within earshot of the museum that bears his name.

designed by award-winning Spanish architect Jose Rafael Moneo and features a 20,000-square-foot plaza, more than 6,000 crypts and niches (making it the largest crypt mausoleum in the U.S.), Mission-style colonnades, biblically inspired gardens, and work by world-acclaimed artists. While most Angelenos admit that the exterior of this austere, sand-colored structure is rather uninspiring and uninviting (the church doors don't face the street but rather a private plaza in back surrounded by fortresslike

**Moments Divine Vibrations**

Every Wednesday from 12:45 to 1:15pm, the Cathedral of Our Lady of the Angels—the city's new $163-million architectural jewel—hosts an **organ recital** that is open to the public and free of charge. The power of the 42-ton organ's 6,019 pipes makes the cathedral vibrate, enabling you to not only hear the music but also feel it, making the experience physically poignant well as emotionally moving. See above for more information.

walls), the view from the inside is breathtaking. Soaring heights, 12,000 panes of translucent alabaster, and larger-than-life tapestries lining the walls create an awe-inspiring sense of magnificence and serenity. The bronze doors, created by sculptor Robert Graham, pay homage to Ghiberti's bronze baptistery door in Florence. The cathedral now serves as the Mother Church of the Archdiocese of L.A.

555 W. Temple St. (at Grand Ave.), Los Angeles. © 213/680-5200. www.olacathedral.org.

**Central Library** ★★ This is one of L.A.'s early architectural achievements and the third-largest library in the U.S. The city rallied to save the library when arson nearly destroyed it in 1986; the triumphant restoration has returned much of its original splendor. Working in the early 1920s, architect Bertram G. Goodhue employed the Egyptian motifs and materials popularized by the discovery of King Tut's tomb, and combined them with a more modern use of concrete block to great effect. Walking tours are the best way to explore this old beauty; they run Monday through Friday at 12:30pm, Saturday at 11am and 2pm, and Sunday at 2pm. *Warning:* Parking in this area can involve a heroic effort. Try visiting on the weekend and use the Flower Street parking entrance; the library will validate your ticket and you can escape for only $2.

630 W. Fifth St. (between Flower St. and Grand Ave.). © 213/228-7000. www.lapl.org.

**City Hall** Built in 1928, the 27-story, triangular Los Angeles City Hall was the tallest building in the city for more than 30 years. The structure's distinctive ziggurat roof was featured in the film *War of the Worlds,* but it is probably best known as the headquarters of the *Daily Planet* in the *Superman* TV series. When it was built, City Hall was the sole exception to an ordinance outlawing buildings taller than 150 feet. On a clear day (yeah, right), the top-floor observation deck offers views to Mount Wilson, 15 miles away.

200 N. Spring St. © 213/485-2121. www.lacityhall.org. Observation deck open Mon–Fri 10am–4pm.

**El Alisal** ★ El Alisal is a small, two-story "castle," built between 1889 and 1910 from large rocks and telephone poles purchased from the Santa Fe Railroad. The architect and creator was Charles F. Lummis, a Harvard graduate, archaeologist, and writer, who walked from Ohio to California and coined the slogan "See America First." A fan of Native American culture, Lummis is credited with popularizing the concept of the "Southwest," referring to New Mexico and Arizona. He often lived the lifestyle of the Indians, and he founded the Southwest Museum, a repository of Indian artifacts. Lummis held fabulous parties for the theatrical, political, and artistic elite; his guest list often included Will Rogers and Theodore Roosevelt. The outstanding feature of his house is the fireplace, which was carved by Mount Rushmore creator Gutzon Borglum. The lawn is now an experimental garden of water-conserving plants.

200 E. Ave. 43, Highland Park. © 323/222-0546. www.socalhistory.org. Free admission. Fri–Sun noon–4pm.

**Union Station** ★   Union Station, completed in 1939, is one of the finest examples of California Mission-style architecture and one of the last of America's great rail stations. It was built with the opulence and attention to detail that characterize 1930s WPA projects. The cathedral-size, richly paneled ticket lobby and waiting area of this cream-colored structure stand sadly empty most of the time, but the MTA does use Union Station for Blue Line commuter trains. When you're strolling through these grand historic halls, it's easy to imagine the glamorous movie stars who once boarded *The City of Los Angeles* and *The Super Chief* to journey back east during the glory days of rail travel; it's also easy to picture the many joyous reunions between returning soldiers and loved ones following the victorious end to World War II, in the station's heyday. Movies shot here include *Bugsy* and *Blade Runner*. The station has always housed a restaurant; the latest to occupy this unusually beautiful setting is **Traxx.**

800 N. Alameda St. (at Cesar E. Chavez Ave.).

**US Bank Tower (aka Library Tower)**   Designed by renowned architect I. M. Pei, L.A.'s most distinctive skyscraper (it's the round one) is the tallest building between Chicago and Singapore. Built in 1989 at a cost of $450 million, the 76-story monolith is both square and rectangular, rising from its Fifth Street base in a series of overlapping spirals and cubes. The Bunker Hill Steps wrapping around the west side of the building were inspired by Rome's Spanish Steps. Gee Whiz Fact: The glass crown at the top—illuminated at night—is the highest helipad in the world.

633 W. Fifth St. at S. Grand Ave.

**Watts Towers & Art Center**   Watts became notorious as the site of riots in the summer of 1965, during which 34 people were killed and more than 1,000 injured. Today a visit to Watts is a lesson in inner-city life. It's a high-density land of gray strip malls, well-guarded check-cashing shops, and fast-food restaurants; but it's also a neighborhood of hardworking families struggling to survive in the midst of gangland. Although there's not much for the casual tourist here, the Watts Towers are truly a unique attraction, and the adjoining art gallery illustrates the fierce determination of area residents to maintain cultural integrity.

The Towers—the largest piece of folk art created by a single person—are colorful, 99-foot-tall cement and steel sculptures ornamented with mosaics of bottles, seashells, cups, plates, pottery, and ceramic tiles. They were completed in 1955 by folk artist Simon Rodia, an immigrant Italian tile-setter who worked on them for 33 years in his spare time. True fans of decorative ceramics will enjoy the fact that Rodia's day job was at the legendary Malibu Potteries (are those fragments of valuable Malibu tile encrusting the Towers?). Closed since 1994 due to earthquake damage, the towers were triumphantly reopened in 2001 and now attract 20,000 visitors annually. Tours are offered every half-hour on a first-come, first-served basis.

*Note:* Next to these designated Cultural Landmarks is the Art Center, which has an interesting collection of ethnic musical instruments as well as several visiting art exhibits throughout the year.

1727 E. 107th St., Los Angeles. ✆ **213/847-4646.** www.wattstowers.net. Gallery open Tues–Sat 10am–4pm; Sun noon–4pm.

## PASADENA & ENVIRONS

See "Sightseeing Tours" on p. 544 for more information on touring the many well-preserved historic neighborhoods in Pasadena. For a quick but profound architectural fix, stroll past Pasadena's grandiose and baroque **City Hall,** 100 N. Garfield Ave., 2 blocks north of Colorado Boulevard; closer inspection will reveal its classical colonnaded courtyard, formal gardens, and spectacular tiled dome.

**The Gamble House** ★★ The huge, two-story Gamble House, built in 1908 as a California vacation home for the wealthy family of Procter and Gamble fame, is a sublime example of Arts and Crafts architecture. The interior, designed by the famous Pasadena-based Greene and Greene architectural team, abounds with handcraftsmanship, including intricately carved teak cornices, custom-designed furnishings, elaborate carpets, and a fantastic Tiffany glass door. No detail was overlooked. Every oak wedge, downspout, air vent, and switch plate contributes to the unified design. Admission is by 1-hour guided tour only, which departs every 15 minutes. Tickets go on sale on tour days in the bookstore at 10am Thursday through Saturday, and at 11:30am on Sunday. No reservations are necessary, but tours are often sold out, especially on weekends by 2pm. And don't wear high heels or they'll make you put on slippers.

If you can't fit the tour into your schedule but have an affection for Craftsman design, visit the well-stocked bookstore and museum shop in the former garage (you can also see the exterior and grounds of the house this way). The bookstore is open Tuesday through Saturday 10am to 5pm, and Sunday 11:30am to 5pm.

Additional elegant Greene & Greene creations (still privately owned) abound 2 blocks away along **Arroyo Terrace,** including nos. **368, 370, 400, 408, 424,** and **440.** The Gamble House bookstore can give you a walking-tour map or conduct guided neighborhood tours by appointment.

4 Westmoreland Place (in the 300 block of N. Orange Grove Blvd.), Pasadena. ℭ 626/793-3334. www.gamble house.org. Tours $8 adults, $5 students and seniors 65 and over, free for children under 12. Tours Thurs–Sun noon–3pm. Closed holidays.

## PARKS & GARDENS

In addition to the two examples of urban parkland below, check out **Pan Pacific Park,** a hilly retreat near the Farmers Market and CBS Studios, named for the Art Deco auditorium that unfortunately no longer stands at its edge.

**Griffith Park** ★★ *Kids* Mining tycoon Colonel Griffith J. Griffith donated these 4,107 acres to the city in 1896 as a Christmas gift. Today Griffith Park is the largest urban park in America. There's a lot to do here, including 53 miles of hiking trails (the prettiest is the Fern Dell trail near the Western Ave. entrance, a shady hideaway cooled by waterfalls and ferns), horseback riding, golfing, swimming, biking, and picnicking (see "Outdoor Pursuits" later in this chapter). For a general overview of the park, drive the mountainous loop road that winds from the top of Western Avenue, past Griffith Observatory, and down to Vermont Avenue. For a more extensive foray, turn north at the loop road's midsection, onto Mt. Hollywood Drive. To reach the golf courses, the **Museum of the American West** (p. 529), or **Los Angeles Zoo** (p. 543), take Los Feliz Boulevard to Riverside Drive, which runs along the park's western edge.

Near the zoo, in a particularly dusty corner of the park, you can find the **Travel Town Transportation Museum,** 5200 Zoo Dr. (ℭ 323/662-5874), a little-known outdoor museum with a small collection of vintage locomotives and old airplanes. Kids love the miniature train ride that circles the perimeter of the museum. The museum is open Monday through Friday from 10am to 4pm, and Saturday and Sunday from 10am to 5pm; admission is free. Griffith Park entrances are along Los Feliz Boulevard, at Riverside Drive, Vermont Avenue, and Western Avenue (Hollywood; ℭ 323/913-4688; www.cityofla.org/RAP/grifmet/gp). Park admission is free.

**Huntington Library, Art Collections & Botanical Gardens** ★★ The Huntington Library is the jewel in Pasadena's crown. The 207-acre hilltop estate was once home to industrialist and railroad magnate Henry E. Huntington (1850–1927), who bought books at the same massive scale on which he acquired businesses. The continually expanding collection includes dozens of Shakespeare's first editions, Benjamin Franklin's handwritten autobiography, a Gutenberg Bible from the 1450s, and the earliest known manuscript of Chaucer's *Canterbury Tales.* Although some rare works are available only to visiting scholars, the library has a regularly changing (and always excellent) exhibit showcasing different items in the collection.

If you prefer canvas to parchment, Huntington also put together a terrific 18th-century British and French art collection. The most celebrated paintings are Gainsborough's *The Blue Boy* and *Pinkie,* a companion piece by Sir Thomas Lawrence depicting the youthful aunt of Elizabeth Barrett Browning. These and other works are displayed in the stately Italianate mansion on the crest of this hillside estate, so you can also get a glimpse of its splendid furnishings. American art and Renaissance paintings are exhibited in two additional galleries.

It's the **botanical gardens** that draw most locals to the Huntington. The Japanese Garden comes complete with a traditional open-air Japanese house, koi-filled stream, and serene Zen garden. The cactus garden is exotic, the jungle garden is intriguing, the lily ponds are soothing—and many benches are scattered about so you can sit and enjoy the surroundings.

Because the Huntington surprises many with its size and wealth of activities to choose from, first-timers might want to start with a tour. One-hour garden tours are offered daily; no reservations or additional fees are required. Times vary, so check at the information desk upon arrival. I also recommend that you tailor your visit to include the popular English high tea served Tuesday through Friday from noon to 4:30pm, and Saturday and Sunday from 10:45am to 4:30pm (last seating at 3:30pm). The **tearoom** overlooks the Rose Garden (home to 1,000 varieties displayed in chronological order of their breeding). Given that the finger sandwiches and desserts are served buffet style, it's a genteel bargain even for hearty appetites at $15 per person (please note that museum admission is a separate required cost). Phone ✆ **626/683-8131** for tearoom reservations, which are required and should be made at least 2 weeks in advance.

1151 Oxford Rd., San Marino. ✆ 626/405-2100. www.huntington.org. Admission $15 adults, $12 seniors 65 and over, $10 students and children age 12 and over, $6 children ages 5-11, free to children under 5; free to all the 1st Thurs of each month. Sept–May Tues–Fri noon–4:30pm, Sat–Sun 10:30am–4:30pm; June–Aug Tues–Sun 10:30am–4:30pm. Closed major holidays.

**Will Rogers State Historic Park** Will Rogers State Historic Park was once Will Rogers's private ranch and grounds. Willed to the state of California in 1944, the 168-acre estate is now both a park and a historic site, supervised by the Department of Parks and Recreation. Visitors may explore the grounds, the former stables, and the 31-room house filled with the original furnishings, including a porch swing in the living room and many Native American rugs and baskets. Charles Lindbergh and his wife, Anne Morrow Lindbergh, hid out here in the 1930s during part of the craze that followed the kidnap and murder of their first son. The park has picnic tables, but no food vendors.

Who's Will Rogers, you ask? He was born in Oklahoma in 1879 and became a cowboy in the Texas Panhandle before drifting into a Wild West show as a folksy, speechifying roper. The "cracker-barrel philosopher" performed lariat tricks while carrying on

## ⸨Value⸩ Free Culture

To beef up attendance and give indigent travel writers a break, almost all of L.A.'s art galleries and museums are open free to the public 1 day of the week or month (or both), and several charge no admission at all. Use the following list to plan your week around the museums' free-day schedules; refer to the individual attractions listings in this chapter for more information on most of these museums.

**Free Every Day**
- J. Paul Getty Museum at the Getty Center
- Museum of Television and Radio (donation suggested)
- Los Angeles County Museum of Art, *after* 5pm
- California Science Center
- Bergamot Arts Station & Santa Monica Museum of Art

**Free Every Thursday**
- Museum of Contemporary Art (MOCA), from 11am to 8pm
- Museum of the American West, from 4 to 8pm
- UCLA Hammer Museum, from 11am to 9pm
- Japanese American National Museum, from 5 to 8pm
- Skirball Cultural Center, from noon to 9pm
- Geffen Contemporary at MOCA, from 5 to 8pm

**Free Every Friday**
- Schindler House, from 4 to 6pm

**Free Every First Tuesday**
- Natural History Museum of Los Angeles County, from 9:30am to 5pm
- Page Museum at La Brea Tar Pits, from 9:30am to 5pm

**Free Every First Wednesday**
- Craft & Folk Art Museum, from 11am to 5pm

**Free Every First Thursday**
- Huntington Library, Art Collections & Botanical Gardens, from noon to 4:30pm

**Free Every First Friday**
- Norton Simon Museum of Art, from 6 to 9pm

**Free Every Second Tuesday**
- Museum of the American West, from 10am to 5pm
- Los Angeles County Museum of Art, from noon to 8pm

**Free Every Third Tuesday**
- Japanese American National Museum, from 10am to 8pm

**Free Every Fourth Friday**
- Pacific Asia Museum, from 10am to 5pm

a humorous deadpan monologue on current events. The showman moved to Los Angeles in 1919, where he become a movie actor as well as the author of numerous books detailing his down-home "cowboy philosophy."

1501 Will Rogers State Park Rd., Pacific Palisades (between Santa Monica and Malibu). 📞 310/454-8212. Park entrance $6 per vehicle. Daily 8am–sunset. House opens daily 10am–5pm; guided tours can be arranged for groups of 10 or more. From Santa Monica, take the Pacific Coast Hwy. (Hwy. 1) north, turn right onto Sunset Blvd., and continue to the park entrance.

## THE ZOO

**Los Angeles Zoo** ⛲ *Kids*   The L.A. Zoo, which shares its parking lot with the Museum of the American West, has been welcoming visitors and busloads of school kids since 1966. In 1982, the zoo inaugurated a display of cuddly koalas, still one of its biggest attractions. Although it's smaller than the world-famous San Diego Zoo, the L.A. Zoo is surprisingly enjoyable and easy to fully explore. As much an arboretum as a zoo, the grounds are thick with mature shade trees from around the world that help cool the once-barren grounds, and new habitats are light-years ahead of the cruel concrete roundhouses originally used to exhibit animals (though you can't help feeling that, despite the fancy digs, all the creatures would rather be in their natural habitat). Highlights include the **Chimpanzees of the Mahale Mountains** habitat, where visitors can see plenty of primate activity; **the Red Ape Rain Forest,** a natural orangutan habitat; the entertaining **World of Birds** show; the **Pachyderm Forest** (climate-controlled digs for the elephants and hippos, complete with an underwater viewing area); the new mandrills exhibit (the world's largest and most colorful baboons); and the **silverback gorilla exhibit.** The gargantuan Andean condor had me enthralled as well (the facility is renowned in zoological circles for the successful breeding and releasing of California condors, and occasionally it has some of these majestic and endangered birds on exhibit).

The zoo's latest attraction (one they're rightfully proud of) is the **Winnick Family Children's Zoo,** a fantastic and forward-thinking children's zoo that contains a petting area, exhibition animal care center, Adventure Theater storytelling and puppet show, and other kid-hip exhibits and activities. *Tip:* To avoid the busloads of rambunctious school kids, arrive after noon.

5333 Zoo Dr., Griffith Park. 📞 323/644-4200. www.lazoo.org. Admission $10 adults, $7 seniors 62 and over, $5 kids ages 2–12, free to children under 2. Daily 10am–5pm (till 6pm July 1 to Labor Day). Closed Christmas Day. Free parking.

## ORGANIZED TOURS
### STUDIO TOURS

**NBC Studios** *Kids*   According to a security guard, John Wayne and Redd Foxx once got into a fight here after Wayne refused to ride in the same limo as Foxx, who called the movie star a "redneck." Well, your NBC tour will probably be a bit more docile than that. The guided, 70-minute indoor walking tour, which departs every half-hour, includes a behind-the-scenes unstaged look at *The Tonight Show with Jay Leno* set (see p. 547 on how to get free tickets); wardrobe, makeup, and set-building departments; and several sound studios. In fact, NBC is the only TV studio that offers the public a behind-the-scenes look at the inner workings of its television operation, and it's a lot less expensive than the competition's studio tours. It doesn't have the cachet of a major motion picture studio tour, but it's entertaining nonetheless. *Note:* Tours are sold on a first-come, first-served basis and sell out early during peak vacation season, so arrive early. Also, this is one of the few studio tours without a minimum age requirement.

3000 W. Alameda Ave., Burbank. 📞 818/840-3537. www.studioaudiences.com/tvstudios. Tours $7.50 adults, $6.75 seniors 60 and over, $4 children ages 5–12, free for children under 5. Mon–Fri 9am–3pm (open weekends and extended hours during summer and holiday season—call for current schedule).

**Paramount Pictures** ⭐   Paramount is the only major studio still located in Hollywood, which makes the 2-hour walking tour around its Hollywood headquarters far more historically enriching than the modern studios in Burbank (even the wrought-iron gates Gloria Swanson motored through in *Sunset Boulevard* are still there) The tour is both a historical ode to filmmaking and a real-life, behind-the-scenes look at a working movie and television facilities in day-to-day operation; ergo, no two tours are alike, and chances of spotting a celebrity are pretty good. Visits typically include a walk-through of the soundstages of TV shows or feature films, though you can't enter while taping is taking place. The $35 tours depart Monday through Friday on a first-come, first-served basis at10am, 11am, 1pm, and 2pm. You need to be 12 or older to take the tour, and cameras and recording equipment are verboten. *Tip:* After the tour, have lunch at the Paramount Studio's world-famous Commissary; you never know who might drop in for a bite, and the food's pretty darn good.

5555 Melrose Ave. ℂ **323/956-1777**. www.paramount.com. Tours $35 per person. Mon–Fri 10am–2pm.

**Sony Pictures Studio Tour**   Although it doesn't have quite the historical cachet as Warner Brothers or Paramount, this Culver City lot has also seen its share of movie history. The 2-hour walking tour includes stops at classic stage scenes such as the Yellow Brick Road winding through Munchkinland, sets from modern thrillers such as *Spiderman,* and the chance to drop in on the *Jeopardy!* or *Wheel of Fortune* sets. But the main reason for the tour is the chance to catch a glimpse at the stars who work here, one of the world's busiest studio lots.

Sony Picture Studios, 10202 W. Washington Blvd., Culver City. ℂ **323/520-TOUR**. www.sonypicturesstudios.com. Advance reservations required; children under 12 not admitted. Tours $20 per person, departing Mon–Fri 9am–3pm. Photo ID required.

**Universal Studios** ⭐   Universal offers daily tram tours of their studio lot every day as part of the general admission price to their amusement park. See listing on p. 526 for more information.

**Warner Brothers Studios**   The Warner Brothers tour takes visitors on a 2¼-hour informational drive-and-walk jaunt around the studio's faux streets. After a brief introductory film, you'll pile into glorified golf carts and cruise past parking spaces marked "Clint Eastwood," "Michael Douglas," and "Sharon Stone," and then walk through film and television sets such as *ER, The Drew Cary Show,* and *West Wing.* Whether it's an orchestra scoring a film or a TV show being taped or edited, you'll get a glimpse of how it's done (nothing is staged for the tour). Stops may include the wardrobe department or the mills where sets are made. Reservations are required; children under 8 are not admitted. Bring valid photo ID.

WB Studio Gate 3, 4301 W. Olive Ave. (at Hollywood Way), Burbank. ℂ **818/846-1403**. www.wbstudiotour.com. Advance reservations recommended. Tours $35 per person, departing every 20 min. Mon–Fri 9am–4pm (9am–3pm winter).

## SIGHTSEEING TOURS
### Bus/Van Tours

**L.A. Tours** (ℂ **800/881-7715** or 323/460-6490; www.latours.net) operates regularly scheduled tours of the city. Plush shuttle buses (27 passengers maximum) pick up riders from major hotels for morning or afternoon tours of Sunset Strip, the movie studios, the Farmers Market, Hollywood, homes of the stars, and other attractions. Different itineraries are available, from Downtown and the Music Center to Disneyland, Universal Studios, or Six Flags Magic Mountain. Tours vary in length from a

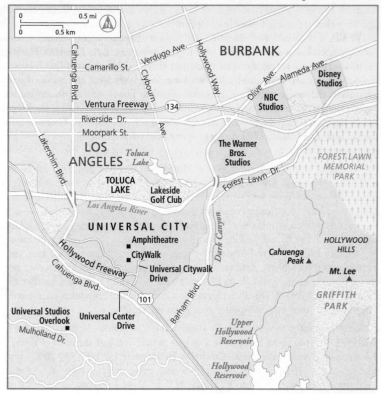

half-day Beaches & Shopping tour to a full-day Grand City tour. Advance reservations are required.

The other major tour company in L.A. is **Starline Tours** (© **800/959-3131;** www. starlinetours.com); you'll see their air-conditioned minibuses all over the city. Since 1935, it has been offering a wide selection of L.A. tours, including the first-ever Movie Stars' Homes tour. Its most popular tour, the 2-hour neighborhood jaunt, departs every half-hour from the front of Grauman's Chinese Theatre between 9:30am and 5:30pm (you'll see the Starline kiosk to the right of the theater entrance at 6925 Hollywood Blvd.). If you really like driving tours, sign up for the piece d' resisténce: the 5½-hour Grand Tour of L.A. See the website for more tour information.

## Walking Tours

**Red Line Tours** (© **323/402-1074;** www.redlinetours.com) runs the best class Hollywood walking tour, with daily sightseeing expeditions to all the famous (and infamous) landmarks. Its unique "live-audio" system allows customers to hear the tour guide over city noise. Customers wear an audio headset receiver while the tour guide wears a headset microphone transmitter (pretty clever, actually). Trips depart from the Stella Adler Academy & Theatres (6773 Hollywood Blvd.) at 10am, noon, 2pm, and 4pm 7 days a week. Rates are $20 for adults, $18 for students and seniors, and $15 for children ages 9 to 15. Tours of downtown L.A. are available as well. Log onto the Red Line Tour website for more information.

The **L.A. Conservancy** (② 213/623-2489; www.laconservancy.org) conducts about a dozen entertaining walking tours of historic Downtown L.A. **Pasadena Heritage** (② 626/441-6333; www.pasadenaheritage.org) offers a walking tour of Old Pasadena.

The free **Beverly Hills Public Art Walking Tour** takes place at 1pm on the first Saturday of the month from May through September. The 60-minute docent-led tour departs from the front of City Hall (450 Crescent Dr.). Highlights include the Municipal Gallery, City Hall, the Beverly Gardens Park, and several galleries. For more information, call ② 310/288-2202 or log onto www.beverlyhills.org.

### Bicycle Tours

For an aerobic way to see L.A., stop in at **Hollywood Pro Bicycles,** 6731 Hollywood Blvd., Hollywood (② 888/775-BIKE or 323/466-5890; www.hollywoodprobicycles. com), and rent a bicycle for the day. With your rental, you'll receive a free tour map along with plenty of advice and tips from the staff. It's a great way to spend a day—tooling around Hollywood or Beverly Hills, or pushing on for longer excursions to the Getty Center, Venice Beach, and Griffith Park. Rates are from $25 for a 24-hour period and $15 for each additional day. Every rental comes with a safety helmet, a bike lock, and a handlebar bag for storage. Reservations are encouraged for all rentals. Another good choice if you're staying in the Santa Monica/Venice Beach area is **Blazing Saddles Bike Rentals** (② 310/393-9778), at the Santa Monica Pier, which rents bikes for about $30 a day but gives away nifty self-guided tour maps for free.

### Helicopter Tours

Touring L.A. from above is certainly a unique perspective. Just the thrill of riding in a helicopter is worth the price. **Celebrity Helicopters** (② 877/999-2099; www. celebheli.com) offers a wide array of themed trips, ranging from a 35-minute Celebrity Home Tour ($155) to a 25-miniute flyby of the L.A. coastline ($95). If you really want to impress your partner, opt for the fly-and-dine Night Tour, which starts with a 25-minute city tour and ends with a thrilling landing on top of a Downtown skyscraper and dinner ($189). Other tour packages are available as well; check their website for more information.

### Jogging Tours

**Off 'N Running Tours** (② 310/246-1418; www.offnrunningtours.com) combines sporting with sightseeing, taking joggers on guided runs through Los Angeles. The themed tours are customized to take in the most entertaining areas around the city and can accommodate any skill level for 4 to 12 miles. One of the most popular routes is up to Holmby Hills, past the Playboy Mansion and Aaron and Candy Spelling's massive estate. It's a fun way to get the most out of your morning jog. Tours cost about $45 and include a T-shirt, a light breakfast, snacks, and plenty of water.

### Beverly Hills Trolley Tours

The city of Beverly Hills offers two inexpensive trolley tours that detail the city's history as well as little-known facts and celebrity tidbits. The **Sites and Scenes Trolley Tour** take visitors on a 40-minute, docent-led tour through the tony avenues of Beverly Hills, including Rodeo Avenue and the Golden Triangle. The summer schedule is Tuesday through Saturday on the hour from noon to 5pm (call for winter schedule). The 50-minute docent-led **Art and Architecture Trolley Tour** visits Beverly Hills' architectural highlights, including the Creative Artists Agency, Museum of Television and Radio, and the Gagosian Art Gallery. It runs May through December Saturday at 11am. Fares for both tours are $5, and both depart at the Trolley Stop at the intersection of Rodeo Drive and Dayton Way. For more information, call ℂ **310/285-2438** or log onto www.beverlyhills.org.

## 7 TV Tapings

Being part of the audience for the taping of a television show might be the quintessential L.A. experience. This is a great way to see Hollywood at work, to find out how your favorite sitcom or talk show is made, and to catch a glimpse of your favorite TV personalities. Timing is important—remember that most series go on hiatus between March and July. Tickets to top shows such as *Joey* or *Will & Grace* are in greater demand than others, so getting your hands on them takes advance planning—and maybe waiting in line.

Request tickets as far in advance as possible. Several episodes may be shot on a single day, so you may be required to remain in the theater for up to 4 hours (in addition to the recommended 1-hr. early check-in). If you phone at the last moment, you may luck into tickets for your top choice. More likely, however, you'll be given a list of shows that are currently filming, and you won't recognize many of the titles; studios are always taping pilots, few of which end up on the air. But you never know who may be starring in them—look at all the famous faces that have launched new sitcoms in the past couple of years. Tickets are always free, are usually limited to two per person, and are distributed on a first-come, first-served basis. Many shows don't admit children under the age of 10; in some cases, no one under the age of 18 is admitted.

Tickets are sometimes given away to the public outside popular tourist sites such as Grauman's Chinese Theatre in Hollywood and Universal Studios in the Valley; L.A.'s visitor information centers in Downtown and Hollywood often have tickets as well. But if you're determined to see a particular show, contact the following suppliers:

**Audiences Unlimited, Inc.** (ℂ **818/753-3470**; www.tvtickets.com), is a good place to start. It distributes tickets for most of the top sitcoms, including *That '70s Show, Will & Grace, The King of Queens, Joey,* and many more. This service is organized and informative (as is their website), and fully sanctioned by production companies and networks. ABC, for example, no longer handles ticket distribution directly, but refers all inquiries to Audiences Unlimited, Inc. **TVTIX.COM** (ℂ **323/653-4105;** www.tvtix.com) also distributes tickets for numerous talk and game shows, including *The Tonight Show with Jay Leno* and *Jeopardy!*

You also may want to contact the networks for information on a specific show, including some whose tickets are not available at the above agencies. At **ABC,** all ticket inquiries are referred to Audiences Unlimited (see above), but you may want to check out ABC's website at **www.abc.com** for a colorful look at their lineup and links to specific show sites.

For **CBS Television City,** 7800 Beverly Blvd., Los Angeles, CA 90036, call ℂ **323/575-2458** between Monday and Friday from 9am to 5pm to see what's being filmed while you're in town. Tickets for CBS tapings are distributed on a first-come, first-served basis; you can write in advance to reserve them or pick them up at the studio up to an hour before taping. Tickets for many CBS sitcoms are also available from Audiences Unlimited (see above). For tickets to *The Price Is Right,* call the 24-hour ticket hot line at ℂ **323/575-2449** or log onto www.cbs.com/daytime/price/tickets.

For **NBC,** 3000 W. Alameda Ave., Burbank, CA 91523 (© **818/840-3537**), call to see what's on while you're in L.A. Tickets for NBC tapings, including *The Tonight Show with Jay Leno* (minimum age to attend this show is 16), can be obtained in two ways: Either pick them up at the NBC ticket counter on the day of the show (they're distributed on a first-come, first-served basis at the ticket counter off California Ave. starting at 8am, two tickets per person), or, at least 6 weeks before your visit, send a self-addressed, stamped envelope with your ticket request to the address above. Be sure to include show name, number of tickets (four per request), and dates desired. All the NBC shows are represented online at either www.nbc.com or www.tvtickets.com.

**Paramount Studios** also offers free tickets to its live audience shows. All you need to do is call one of the friendly employees at Paramount Guest Relations (© **323/ 956-1777**) between 9am and 6pm on weekdays, find out which shows are being filmed or taped while you're in town, and make a reservation (you might want to log onto www.paramount.com to see what shows they're currently taping; click on "Show Tickets"). **Universal Studios** (© **800/UNIVERSAL;** www.universalstudios.com) also offers free tickets to their live audience shows. At the amusement park's **Audiences Unlimited ticket booth,** you can obtain free tickets to join the audience for any TV shows that are taping during your visit (subject to availability).

## 8 Beaches

Los Angeles County's 72-mile coastline sports more than 30 miles of beaches, most of which the **Department of Beaches & Harbors,** 13837 Fiji Way, Marina del Rey (© **310/305-9503**) oversees. County-run beaches usually charge for parking ($4–$8). Alcohol, bonfires, and pets are prohibited. For recorded **surf conditions** (and coastal weather forecast), call © **310/457-9701.** The following are the county's best beaches, listed from north to south.

**EL PESCADOR, LA PIEDRA & EL MATADOR BEACHES** *Finds* These rugged and isolated beaches front a 2-mile stretch of the Pacific Coast Highway (Hwy. 1) between Broad Beach and Decker Canyon roads, a 10-minute drive from the Malibu Pier. Picturesque coves with unusual rock formations are great for sunbathing and picnicking, but swim with caution; no lifeguards tend the shore. The beaches can be difficult to find; only small signs on the highway mark them. There are a limited number of parking spots atop the bluffs. Descend to the beach via stairs that cling to the cliffs.

**ZUMA BEACH COUNTY PARK** ★ Jam-packed on warm weekends, L.A. County's largest beach park sits off the Pacific Coast Highway (Hwy. 1), a mile past Kanan Dume Road. While it can't claim to be the most scenic beach in the Southland, Zuma has the most comprehensive facilities: plenty of restrooms, lifeguards, playgrounds, volleyball courts, and snack bars. The southern stretch, toward Point Dume, is Westward Beach, separated from the noisy highway by sandstone cliffs. A trail leads over the point's headlands to Pirate's Cove, once a popular nude beach.

**PARADISE COVE** This private beach in the 28000 block of the Pacific Coast Highway (Hwy. 1) charges $15 to park and $5 per person if you walk in. Changing rooms and showers are included in the price. The beach is often full by noon on weekends.

**MALIBU LAGOON STATE BEACH** ★★ Not just a pretty white-sand beach but an estuary and wetlands area as well, Malibu Lagoon is the historic home of the Chumash Indians. The entrance is on the Pacific Coast Highway (Hwy. 1) south of Cross Creek Road, and there's a small admission charge. Marine life and shorebirds teem where the creek empties into the sea, and the waves are always mild. The historic **Adamson House** is here, a showplace of Malibu tile now operating as a museum.

**SURFRIDER BEACH** Without a doubt, L.A.'s best waves roll ashore here. One of the city's most popular surfing spots, this beach is between the Malibu Pier and the lagoon. In surf lingo, few "locals-only" wave wars are ever fought here; surfing is not as territorial here as it can be in other areas, where out-of-towners can be made to feel unwelcome. Surfrider is surrounded by all of Malibu's hustle and bustle; don't come here for peace and quiet as the surf is always crowded.

**TOPANGA STATE BEACH** Highway noise prevents solitude at this short, narrow strip of sand where Topanga Canyon Boulevard emerges from the mountains. Why go? Ask the surfers who wait in line to catch Topanga's excellent right point breaks. The beach has restrooms, lifeguard services and, across the street, one of the best fresh-fish restaurants around.

**WILL ROGERS STATE BEACH** Three miles of the Pacific Coast Highway (Hwy. 1), between Sunset Boulevard and the Santa Monica border, are named for the American humorist whose ranch-turned-state-historic-park (see "Parks & Gardens," earlier in this chapter) is nestled above the palisades that rise above this popular beach. A pay parking lot extends the length of Will Rogers, and facilities include restrooms, lifeguards, and a snack hut in season. While the surfing is not the best, the waves are friendly for swimmers, and competitive volleyball games are a staple activity.

**SANTA MONICA STATE BEACH** (Kids) The beaches on either side of the Santa Monica Pier (see "L.A.'s Top Attractions," earlier in this chapter) are popular for their white sands, accessibility, and ease of use—with big parking lots, cafes, and well-maintained restrooms. A paved beach path runs along here, allowing you to walk, bike, or skate to Venice and points south. Colorado Boulevard leads to the pier; turn north on the Pacific Coast Highway (Hwy. 1) below the coastline's bluffs, or south along Ocean Avenue; you can find parking in both directions.

**VENICE BEACH** (★★) Moving south from the city of Santa Monica, the paved pedestrian Promenade becomes Ocean Front Walk and gets progressively weirder until it reaches an apex at Washington Boulevard and the Venice fishing pier. Although people do swim and sunbathe here, Venice Beach is defined by the sea of humanity on the Ocean Front Walk, and the bevy of boardwalk vendors and old-fashioned pedestrian streets a block away (see "L.A.'s Top Attractions," earlier in this chapter). Park on the side streets or in the plentiful lots west of Pacific Avenue.

**MANHATTAN STATE BEACH** The Beach Boys used to hang out at this wide, friendly beach backed by beautiful oceanview homes. Plenty of parking on 36 blocks of side streets (between Rosecrans Ave. and the Hermosa Beach border) draws weekend crowds from the L.A. area. Manhattan has some of the best surfing around, restrooms, lifeguards, and volleyball courts. Manhattan Beach Boulevard leads west to the fishing pier and adjacent seafood restaurants.

**HERMOSA CITY BEACH** (★★) My favorite beach, this very wide stretch of white sand is one of the best in Southern California. Hermosa extends to either side of the pier and includes "The Strand," a wide, smooth pedestrian lane that runs its entire length. Main access is at the foot of Pier Avenue, lined with interesting shops and cafes with outdoor seating. There's plenty of street parking, as well as restrooms, lifeguards, volleyball courts, a fishing pier, playgrounds, and good surfing.

# L.A.'s Beaches & Coastal Attractions

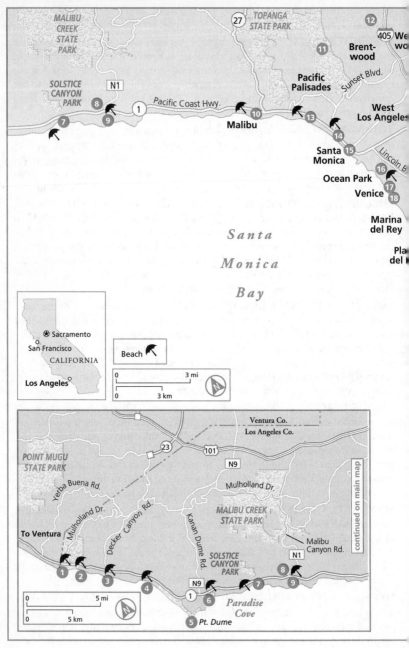

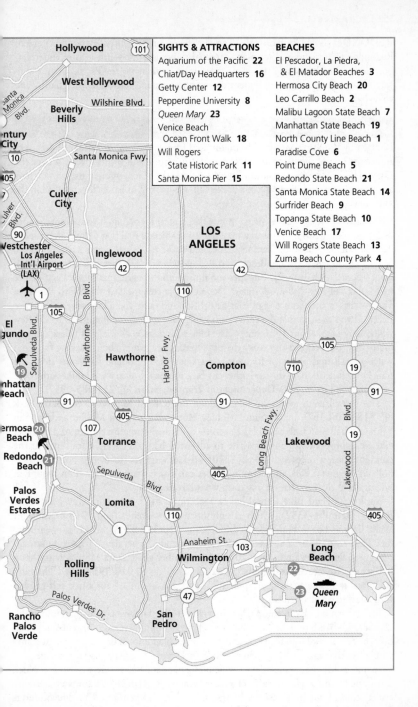

Hollywood 101

West Hollywood

Wilshire Blvd.

Beverly Hills

Century City 10

Santa Monica Fwy.

405

Culver City

90

Westchester
Los Angeles Int'l Airport (LAX) 1

105

El Segundo

Sepulveda Blvd.

19
Manhattan Beach

91

Hermosa 20 Beach

Redondo 21 Beach

107

Palos Verdes Estates

Rancho Palos Verde

Palos Verdes Dr.

Inglewood 42

Hawthorne Blvd.

Hawthorne

405

Torrance

Sepulveda Blvd.

Lomita

110

1

Rolling Hills

San Pedro

47

LOS ANGELES

42

Harbor Fwy.

110

Compton

91

405

Anaheim St.

Wilmington 103

105

710

Long Beach Fwy.

Lakewood

405

Long Beach

22

23 Queen Mary

19

91

19

Lakewood Blvd.

405

**SIGHTS & ATTRACTIONS**
Aquarium of the Pacific **22**
Chiat/Day Headquarters **16**
Getty Center **12**
Pepperdine University **8**
*Queen Mary* **23**
Venice Beach
  Ocean Front Walk **18**
Will Rogers
  State Historic Park **11**
Santa Monica Pier **15**

**BEACHES**
El Pescador, La Piedra,
  & El Matador Beaches **3**
Hermosa City Beach **20**
Leo Carrillo Beach **2**
Malibu Lagoon State Beach **7**
Manhattan State Beach **19**
North County Line Beach **1**
Paradise Cove **6**
Point Dume Beach **5**
Redondo State Beach **21**
Santa Monica State Beach **14**
Surfrider Beach **9**
Topanga State Beach **10**
Venice Beach **17**
Will Rogers State Beach **13**
Zuma Beach County Park **4**

**REDONDO STATE BEACH**    Popular with surfers, bicyclists, and joggers, Redondo's white sand and ice-plant-carpeted dunes are just south of tiny King Harbor, along "The Esplanade" (S. Esplanade Dr.). Get there via the Pacific Coast Highway (Hwy. 1) or Torrance Boulevard. Facilities include restrooms, lifeguards, and volleyball courts.

## 9 Outdoor Pursuits

Bisected by the Santa Monica Mountains and fronted by long stretches of beach, Los Angeles is one of the best cities in the world for nature and sports lovers. Where else can you hike in the mountains, in-line-skate along the beach, swim in the ocean, enjoy a gourmet meal, and then take in a basketball, ice-hockey, or baseball game—all in the same day?

**BICYCLING**    Los Angeles, being mostly flat, is great for biking. If you're into distance pedaling, you can do no better than the flat, paved bicycle trail that follows along about 22 miles of state beaches, harbors, LAX, and laid-back beach towns such as Venice, Manhattan Beach, Hermosa Beach, and Redondo Beach. The first stretch starts at Will Rogers State Beach in Pacific Palisades and runs south through Santa Monica and Venice to Marina del Rey—about 8 miles. The second stretch—called the South Bay Bike Trail—starts at the south end of Marina del Rey and takes you all the way to Torrence Beach. If you want to ride the entire path you'll have to detour around Marina del Rey, which only takes about 15 minutes. The bike path attracts all levels of riders and gets pretty busy on weekends, so ixnay the time trials. Don't worry about packing food and water—you'll find plenty of fountains, snack stands, and public restrooms along the trail. For information on this and other city bike routes, log onto **www.labikepaths.com** or phone the **Los Angeles Department of Transportation** (© 213/485-9957).

The best place to mountain-bike is along the trails of **Malibu Creek State Park** (© 818/880-0367), in the Santa Monica Mountains between Malibu and the San Fernando Valley in Calabasas. Fifteen miles of trails rise to a maximum of 3,000 feet and are appropriate for intermediate to advanced bikers. Pick up a trail map at the park entrance, 4 miles south of U.S. 101 off Las Virgenes Road, just north of Mulholland Highway. Park admission is $5 per car. For more information on mountain bike trails in the L.A. region, log onto **www.latrails.com**.

**Spokes 'N Stuff Bike Rental** has two locations: 4175 Admiralty Way, Marina del Rey (© 310/306-3332), which is only open on weekends, and 1715 Oceanfront Walk, behind Loews Hotel, Santa Monica (© 310/395-4748), which is open every day. They rent 10-speed cruisers for $7 per hour and $16 per day; 15-speed mountain bikes rent for $8 per hour and $20 per day. Another good Santa Monica rental shop is **Blazing Saddles Bike Rentals** (Santa Monica Pier; © 310/393-9778). The rates are about the same as those at Spokes 'N Stuff. Be sure to ask for a free **self-guided tour map** (it's really handy).

In Hollywood, **Hollywood Pro Bicycles** (6731 Hollywood Blvd., Hollywood; © 888/775-BIKE or 323/466-5890; www.hollywoodprobicycles.com) rents mountain bikes at $25 for a 24-hour period and $15 for each additional day. Every rental comes with a free tour map, a safety helmet, a bike lock, and a handlebar bag for storage.

In the South Bay, bike rentals—including tandem bikes—are available 1 block from The Strand at **Hermosa Cyclery,** 20 13th St. (© 310/374-7816; www.hermosacyclery.com). Cruisers are $7 per hour; tandems are $13 per hour. FYI, The Strand is an excellent car-free path that's tailor-made for a leisurely bike ride.

**FISHING** **Del Rey Sport Fishing,** 13759 Fiji Way, Marina del Rey (✆ **310/822-3625;** www.marinadelreysportfishing.com), has three deep-sea boats departing daily on half- and full-day ocean fishing trips. Of course, it depends on what's running when you're out, but bass, barracuda, halibut, and yellowtail are the most common

*Tips* **Spectator Sports**

The **Los Angeles Dodgers** (✆ 323/224-1448; http://losangeles.dodgers.mlb. com), winner of eight National League championships and five World Series, play at Dodger Stadium, at 1000 Elysian Park near Sunset Boulevard. Watching a game at this old-school ballpark is a great way to spend the day, chomping on Dodger Dogs and basking in the sunshine. Tickets are reasonably priced, too. The team's website offers everything from game schedules to souvenir merchandise online. The 2002 World Series champion **Los Angeles Angels of Anaheim** (✆ 888/796-HALO; http://losangeles.angels.mlb. com) play American League ball at Anaheim Stadium, at 2000 S. State College Blvd. (near Katella Ave.), about 30 minutes from Downtown L.A. The regular Major League Baseball season runs from April to October. See either team's website for ticket information.

Los Angeles has two NBA franchises: the **Lakers** (www.lakers.com), who have won 14 NBA titles, and the hapless **Clippers** (www.clippers.com), who haven't made the playoffs for 8 years running. Both teams play in the **STAPLES Center** in Downtown L.A., 1111 S. Figueroa St. Celebrity fans such as Jack Nicholson, Leonardo DiCaprio, Heather Locklear, and Dyan Cannon have the best tickets, but this 20,000-seater should have room for you—that is, if you have the big bucks for a Lakers ticket or the interest in watching a Clippers game. The season runs from October to April, with 2 months of playoffs following. For tickets to either team call ✆ **213/742-7340** or log onto www.staplescenter.com.

Los Angeles suffers from an absence of major-league football, but it gets by just fine with two popular college teams and an Arena League team. The college season runs September through November; to check out a game, contact **UCLA Bruins Football** (✆ 310/825-2101; www.uclabruins.com) or **USC Trojan Football** (✆ 213/740-2311; www.usctrojans.com). Described as "fun, fast, and furious," Arena League football tends to be action-packed and exciting, and it sure costs a lot less than its NFL counterpart. The local team is the **L.A. Avengers** (✆ 888/283-6437 or 310/788-7744; www.la avengers.com); games run from April through July and are played Downtown at the STAPLES Center.

Since its inaugural season in 1996, the **Los Angeles Galaxy** (✆ 310/630-2200; www.lagalaxy.com) has already won the Major League Soccer Cup of 2002 and earned a reputation as a major force in MLS. Visitors can catch a game at the Home Depot Center stadium at 18400 Avalon Blvd. in Carson. Tickets for individual games are available through the Galaxy box office and Ticketmaster.

## Polo Anyone?

Way back in 1930, cowboy humorist Will Rogers got a hankering to play some polo, so he cleared the field in front of his Pacific Palisades home for a friendly match with his ponies and celebrity pals. Shortly after, he started his famed **Will Rogers Polo Club,** and of the 25 polo organizations that existed at the time, his polo field is the only one that remains. Matches are still held on weekends from mid-April through early October, and the bucolic setting of wide green fields, whitewashed fences, and majestic oaks is ideal for a leisurely picnic lunch and a respite from the city. The polo field is at 1501 Will Rogers State Park Rd. in Pacific Palisades, off West Sunset Boulevard. For more information call the club at ℂ **310/573-5000** or see the website at www.willrogerspolo.org.

catches on these party boats. Excursions cost from $30 to $540; tackle rental is available. Phone for reservations.

No permit is required to cast from shore or drop a line from a pier. Local anglers will hate me for giving away their secret spot, but the **best saltwater fishing** in all of L.A. is at the foot of Torrance Boulevard in Redondo Beach.

**GOLF**    The greater Los Angeles area has more than 100 golf courses, which vary in quality from abysmal to superb. Most of the city's public courses are administered by the Department of Recreation and Parks, which follows a complicated registration/reservation system for tee times. While visitors cannot reserve start times in advance, you're welcome to play any of the courses by showing up and getting on the call sheet. Expect to wait for the most popular tee times, but try to use your flexible vacationer schedule to avoid the morning rush.

Of the city's seven 18-hole and three 9-hole courses, you can't get more central than the **Rancho Park Golf Course,** 10460 W. Pico Blvd. (ℂ **310/838-7373;** www.rpgc.org), smack-dab in the middle of L.A.'s Westside. The par-71 course has lots of tall trees, but not enough to block the towering Century City buildings next door. For the money it's a bargain (heck, even Bill Clinton golfed here). Rancho also has a 9-hole, par-3 course.

For a genuinely woodsy experience, try one of the three courses inside Griffith Park, northeast of Hollywood ("Parks & Gardens," earlier in this chapter). The courses are extremely well maintained, challenging without being frustrating, and (despite some holes alongside I-5) a great way to leave the city behind. Bucolic pleasures abound, particularly on the 9-hole **Roosevelt,** on Vermont Avenue across from the Greek Theatre; early morning wildlife often includes deer, rabbits, raccoons, and skunks (fore!). **Wilson** and **Harding** are each 18 holes and start from the main clubhouse off Riverside Drive, the park's main entrance.

Greens fees on all city courses are $22 Monday through Friday, and $29 on weekends and holidays; 9-hole courses cost $13 on weekdays and $17 on weekends and holidays. For details on other city courses, or to contact the starter directly by phone, call the Department of Recreation and Parks at ℂ **888/527-2757** or log onto the city's parks website at www.laparks.org.

**Industry Hills Golf Club,** 1 Industry Hills Pkwy., City of Industry (© 626/ 810-4653; www.ihgolfclub.com), has two 18-hole courses designed by William Bell. Together they encompass eight lakes, 160 bunkers, and many long fairways. The Eisenhower Course, consistently ranked among *Golf Digest*'s top 25 public ranges, has extra-large, undulating greens and the challenge of thick *Kikuyu* rough. An adjacent driving range is lit for night use. Greens fees are $63 Monday through Thursday and $93 Friday through Sunday, including a cart; call in advance for tee times.

For more information on regional golf courses, log onto www.golfcalifornia.com.

**HIKING** The **Santa Monica Mountains,** a small range that runs only 50 miles from Griffith Park to Point Mugu, on the coast north of Malibu, makes Los Angeles a great place for hiking. The mountains, which peak at 3,111 feet, are part of the Santa Monica Mountains National Recreation Area, a contiguous conglomeration of 350 public parks and 65,000 acres. Many animals live in this area, including deer, coyote, rabbit, skunk, rattlesnake, fox, hawk, and quail. The hills are also home to almost 1,000 drought-resistant plant species, including live oak and coastal sage.

Hiking is best after spring rains, when the hills are green, flowers are in bloom, and the air is clear. Summers can be very hot; hikers should always carry fresh water. Beware of poison oak, a hearty shrub that's common on the West Coast. Usually found among oak trees, poison oak has leaves in groups of three, with waxy surfaces and prominent veins. If you come into contact with this itch-producing plant, you'll end up with a California souvenir that you'll soon regret.

**Santa Ynez Canyon,** in Pacific Palisades, is a long and difficult climb that rises steadily for about 3 miles. At the top, hikers are rewarded with fantastic views over the Pacific. At the top is **Trippet Ranch,** a public facility providing water, restrooms, and picnic tables. From Santa Monica, take Pacific Coast Highway (Hwy. 1) north. Turn right onto Sunset Boulevard and then left onto Palisades Drive. Then continue for 2½ miles, turn left onto Verenda de la Montura, and park at the cul-de-sac at the end of the street, where you can find the trail head.

**Temescal Canyon,** in Pacific Palisades, is far easier than the Santa Ynez trail and far more popular, especially among locals. This is one of the quickest routes into the wilderness. Hikes here are anywhere from 1 to 5 miles. From Santa Monica, take Pacific Coast Highway (Hwy. 1) north; turn right onto Temescal Canyon Road, and follow it to the end. Sign in with the gatekeeper, who can also answer your questions.

**Will Rogers State Historic Park,** Pacific Palisades, is also a terrific place for hiking. An intermediate-level hike from the park's entrance ends at Inspiration Point, a

---

## Segway Rentals in Santa Monica

**Segway Los Angeles** rents those weird-looking, forward-pitching, upright scooters you've probably seen on TV. The two-wheeled "Human Transporter" is an ingenious electric-powered transportation device that uses gyroscopes to emulate human balance. Lean forward, go forward; lean back, go back; stand up, stop: Simple. After the free 25-minute lesson it become intuitive, then you're on your own to scoot around the paved shoreline path around Venice Beach and the Santa Monica Pier (*everyone* checks you out). It's the closest you'll come to being a celebrity and a bargain at only $45 for lessons and a full hour's rental. *Note:* You have to be at least 21 to rent one. Segway is at 1660 Ocean Ave., 1 block south of the pier, Santa Monica (© 310/395-1395; www.segway.la).

---

*Moments* Sunset Margarita Horse Rides

Every Friday night, the Sunset Ranch Hollywood Stables company hosts the **Friday Night Dinner Ride.** They saddle you up on a big ol' horse, and then y'all take a scenic 1½-hour ride through Griffith Park—with the city lights shining far below—to the Viva Fresh Mexican restaurant in Burbank. After dinner and a few margaritas, you mount up and ride back to the ranch, arriving at about 11pm. Anyone under 250 pounds can go, and no reservations are required (it's strictly first come, first served). The ride costs $50, not including dinner and drinks. Sign-up begins at 4:30pm and the ride leaves at 5:30pm. Consider yourself warned, however: Many a sore derriere has wished it hadn't been subjected to 180 minutes in the saddle. The ranch is at the very end of Beachwood Drive off of Franklin Avenue, just under the HOLLYWOOD sign. For more information, call ✆ **323/469-5450** or log onto www.sunsetranchhollywood.com.

---

plateau from which you can see a good portion of L.A.'s Westside. See "Parks & Gardens," earlier in this chapter, for complete information.

For more information on hiking in the L.A. region, log onto **www.latrails.com**.

**HORSEBACK RIDING** **Griffith Park Horse Rental,** 480 Riverside Dr. (in the Los Angeles Equestrian Center), Burbank (✆ **818/840-8401;** www.la-equestrian center.com), rents horses hourly for Western or English riding through Griffith Park's hills. It's $20 for 1 hour; the maximum rental is 2 hours ($35). The stables are open daily from 8am to 4pm, and you must be at least 7 years old to ride. If you have a rider younger than 7, you can either opt for the pony rides in Griffith Park (p. 540), or arrange for a private 1-hour lesson by calling ✆ **818/569-3666.**

Another popular horseback-riding outfit is **Sunset Ranch,** at 3400 Beachwood Dr. off of Franklin Avenue, just under the HOLLYWOOD sign. Horse rentals are offered daily from 9am to 5pm for all levels of riders. The ranch is on the edge of Griffith Park with access to 52 miles of trails. Also available are private night rides (very romantic), dinner rides (see the "Sunset Margarita Horse Rides" box, above), and riding lessons. Rates are $20 per hour with a $10 deposit. No reservations are required. For more information, call ✆ **323/469-5450** or log on to www.sunsetranchhollywood.com.

Closer to the ocean in the Topanga Canyon is **Los Angeles Horseback Riding** (2623 Old Topanga Canyon Rd., Topanga; ✆ **818/591-2032;** www.lahorseback riding.com), a small, friendly outfit that offers guided Western-style trail rides for beginners to advanced riders. It's at the top of an 1,800-foot ridgeline—about a 25-minute drive from Santa Monica—with panoramic views of the ocean and San Fernando Valley (best seen on one of the sunset or full-moon rides). What I like about this outfit is that, if the guide feels the group is experienced enough, she'll pick up the pace to a canter. Although same-day reservations are sometimes possible, try to book at least 3 days in advance. Kids 6 and older are welcome, and kids under 16 must wear helmets (bring a bike helmet, if possible). Prices start at $55 for a guided 70-minute ride, plus tip; 2-hour canyon rides are available as well.

**SAILING** Marina del Rey, the largest man-made marina in the world, is the launching point for L.A.'s sailboat charters such as **Free Spirit Sailing Adventures,** which offers trips ranging from a 2-hour harbor tour (about $80 per person) to full-day outings along the coast and even 4-day voyages to the Channel Islands. Your host is Captain Larry, and the boat is the *Carmina Mare*, a 46-foot cutter-rigged motorsailor. You can either bring your own food and drinks or have Captain Larry prepare lunch and dinner for you. Bring your own rods and tackle and you can even go deep-sea fishing. For more information call Captain Larry's cellphone number, © **310/780-3432,** or log onto www.capt larry.com.

**SEA KAYAKING**    Sea kayaking is all the rage in Southern California, a simple and serene way to explore the southern coastline. **Southwind Kayak Center** (17855 Skypark Circle, Irvine; © **800/768-8494** or 949/261-0200; www.southwindkayaks.com) rents sea kayaks for use in the bay or open ocean at their Newport Beach and Dana Point rental bases; rates are $50 per day; instructional classes are available on weekends only. The center also conducts several easy-going guided outings, including a $55 Back to Nature trip that highlights the marine life around Dana Point. Visit the website for more details.

**SKATING**    The 22-mile-long South Beach Trail that runs from Pacific Palisades to Torrance is one of the premier skating spots in the country. In-line skating is especially popular, but conventional skates are often seen here, too. Skating is allowed just about everywhere bicycling is, but be advised that cyclists have the right of way. **Spokes 'N Stuff,** 4175 Admiralty Way, Marina del Rey (© **310/306-3332;** open weekends only), is just one of many places to rent wheels near the Venice portion of Ocean Front Walk. In the South Bay, in-line skate rentals are available 1 block from the Strand at **Hermosa Cyclery,** 20 13th St. (© **310/374-7816;** www.hermosacyclery.com). Skates cost $6 per hour ($18 for the day); kneepads and wrist guards come with every rental.

**SURFING**    George Freeth (1883–1918), who first surfed Redondo Beach in 1907, is widely credited with introducing the sport to California. But surfing didn't catch on until the 1950s, when CalTech graduate Bob Simmons invented a more maneuverable lightweight fiberglass board. The Beach Boys and other surf-music groups popularized Southern California in the minds of beach babes and dudes everywhere. The rest, as they say, is history.

If you're a first-timer eager to learn the sport, contact **Learn to Surf L.A.** (© **310/ 920-1265;** www.learntosurfla.com). This highly respected school features a team of experienced instructors who will supply all necessary equipment and get you up and riding a foam board on your first day (trust me, it's a blast). Private lessons are $100, and group lesson are $70.

If you want to try it on your own, surfboards are available for rent at shops near all top surfing beaches in the L.A. area. **Zuma Jay Surfboards,** 22775 Pacific Coast Hwy., Malibu (© **310/456-8044**), Malibu's oldest surf shop, is about a quarter-mile south of Malibu Pier. Rentals are about $20 per day, plus $8 for wet suits in winter. For more information about surfing in Southern California, log on to www.surfline.com.

---

*Fun Fact*  **The Surfing Rabbi**

*Only* in L.A.: Surfing instructor and orthodox rabbi Nachum Shifren hosts "Surf and Soul" sermons-on-the-sand in Santa Monica. Not only will the rabbi teach you how to surf, his wise words will empower you to succeed in this competitive world we live in. Gentiles are welcome (© **310/877-1482;** www.surfingrabbi.com).

**TENNIS**   Although soft-surface courts are more popular on the East Coast, hard surfaces are most common in California. If your hotel doesn't have a court and can't suggest any nearby, try the well-maintained, well-lit **Griffith Park Tennis Courts,** on Commonwealth Road, just east of Vermont Avenue (© 323/662-7772). Call or log onto the website of the **City of Los Angeles Department of Recreation and Parks** (© 888/527-2757; www.laparks.org) for a long list of free tennis courts or make a reservation at a municipal court near you. *Tip:* Spectators can watch free collegiate matches at the UCLA campus's L.A. Tennis Center from October through May. For a schedule of tournaments, call © 310/206-6831.

## 10 Shopping

Whether you're looking for trend-setting fashions or just some tourist schlock mementos, Los Angeles has your shopping needs covered like no other place in the world. Heck, Los Angeles practically *invented* the shopping mall.

Here's a rundown of the primary shopping areas, with descriptions of a few of their best stores. The sales tax in Los Angeles is 8%, but savvy out-of-state shoppers know how to have more expensive items shipped directly home, thereby avoiding the tax.

### L.A.'S WESTSIDE & BEVERLY HILLS

**BEVERLY BOULEVARD** (from Robertson Blvd. to La Brea Ave.) ⭐   Beverly is L.A.'s premier boulevard for mid-20th-century furnishings. Expensive showrooms line the street, but the one that started it all is **Modernica,** 7366 Beverly Blvd. (© 323/933-0383). You can still find vintage Stickley and Noguchi pieces, but Modernica has become best known for the authentic—and more affordable—replicas they offer (Eames storage units are one popular item).

**Every Picture Tells a Story** (7525 Beverly Blvd.; © 310/451-2700), a gallery devoted to the art of children's literature, displays antique children's books as well as the works of more than 100 illustrators, including lithos of *Curious George, Eloise,* and *Charlotte's Web.* Across the street from Cedars-Sinai Medical Center, the **Mysterious Bookshop** (8763 Beverly Blvd., between Robertson and San Vicente boulevards; © 310/209-0415), carries more than 20,000 used, rare, and out-of-print titles in the field of mystery, espionage, detective stories, and thrillers. Author appearances and other special events are regularly scheduled. If you can name more than three tenors, then the pleasantly cluttered **Opera Shop of Los Angeles,** 8384 Beverly Blvd. (3 blocks east of La Cienega Blvd.; © 323/658-5811), is for you. Everything imaginable with an opera theme is available: musical motif jewelry, stationery, T-shirts, opera glasses, and tapes, videos, and CDs of your favorite productions.

If you complain that they just don't make 'em like they used to, be sure to drop by **Re-Mix,** 7605½ Beverly Blvd. (between Fairfax and La Brea aves.; © 323/936-6210). This shop sells only vintage (1940s–'70s)—but brand-new (as in unworn)—shoes for men and women, such as wingtips, Hush Puppies, Joan Crawford pumps, and 1970s platforms. It's more like a shoe-store museum. A rack of unworn vintage socks all display their original tags and stickers, and the prices are downright reasonable. Celebrity hipsters and hep cats from Madonna to Roseanne are often spotted here. Other vintage wares are found at **Second Time Around Watch Co.,** 8840 Beverly Blvd. (west of Robertson Blvd.; © 310/271-6615). The city's best selection of collectible timepieces includes dozens of classic Tiffanys, Cartiers, Piagets, and Rolexes, plus rare pocket watches. Priced for collectors, but a fascinating browse for the Swatch crowd, too.

**LA BREA AVENUE** (north of Wilshire Blvd.) ⭐ This is L.A.'s artiest shopping strip. La Brea is anchored by the giant **American Rag, Cie** alterna-complex, and is also home to lots of great urban antiques stores dealing in Art Deco, Arts and Crafts, 1950s modern, and the like. You'll also find vintage clothiers, furniture galleries, and other warehouse-size stores, and some of the city's hippest restaurants, such as Campanile (p. 508).

Bargain hunters find flea-market furnishings at **Nick Metropolis,** 100 S. La Brea Ave. (© **323/934-3700**), while more upscale seekers of home decor head to **Mortise & Tenon,** 446 S. La Brea Ave. (© **323/937-7654**), where hand-crafted wood pieces sit next to overstuffed velvet-upholstered sofas and vintage steel desks. The best place for a snack is Nancy Silverton's **La Brea Bakery,** 624 S. La Brea Ave. (© **323/939-6813;** www.labreabakery.com), which foodies know from gourmet markets and the attached Campanile restaurant.

Stuffed to the rafters with hardware and fixtures from the past 100 years, **Liz's Antique Hardware,** 453 S. La Brea Ave. (© **323/939-4403;** www.lahardware.com), thoughtfully keeps a canister of wet wipes at the register. (Believe us, you'll need one after sifting through bags and crates of doorknobs, latches, finials, and any other home hardware you can imagine.) Perfect sets of Bakelite drawer pulls and antique ceramic bathroom fixtures are some of the more intriguing items. Be prepared to browse for hours, whether you're redecorating or not. There's a respectable collection of coordinating trendy clothing for men and women, too. Hipsters also head up the street to **Yellowstone** for vintage duds, and souvenir seekers know to visit **Moletown** for studio merchandise featuring logo graphics from the hottest new movies.

**RODEO DRIVE & BEVERLY HILLS' GOLDEN TRIANGLE** (between Santa Monica Blvd., Wilshire Blvd., and Crescent Dr., Beverly Hills) ⭐⭐ Everyone knows about Rodeo Drive, the city's most famous shopping street. Couture shops from high fashion's Old Guard are located along these 3 hallowed blocks, along with plenty of newer high-end labels. Two Beverly Hills minimalls are more insular and attractive than the national average: the **Rodeo Collection,** 421 N. Rodeo Dr, a contemporary center with towering palms; and **2 Rodeo,** a cobblestoned Italianate piazza at Wilshire Boulevard. The 16-square-block area surrounding Rodeo Drive is known as the Golden Triangle. Shops off Rodeo are generally not as name-conscious as those on the strip, so you might actually be able to afford something there, but they're still plenty upscale. Little Santa Monica Boulevard has a particularly colorful line of specialty stores, and Brighton Way is as young and hip as relatively staid Beverly Hills gets. Parking is a bargain, with nine city-run lots offering 2 hours of free parking and a flat fee of $2 after 2pm.

The big names to look for are **Bulgari,** 201 N. Rodeo Dr. (© 310/858-9216); **Giorgio Beverly Hills,** 327 N. Rodeo Dr. (© 800/GIORGIO); **Gucci,** 347 N. Rodeo Dr. (© 310/278-3451); **Hermès,** 434 N. Rodeo Dr. (© 310/278-6440);

---

*Tips* **Window Shopping—L.A. Style**

The gorgeous Bulgari jewelry store at the corner of Rodeo Drive and Wilshire Boulevard—former home of the Brown Derby restaurant—displays many of the priceless (literally) jewels worn by the stars at the big awards ceremonies. Look wealthy? They might even invite you upstairs for an espresso.

**Louis Vuitton,** 295 N. Rodeo Dr. (© 310/859-0457); **Polo/Ralph Lauren,** 444 N. Rodeo Dr. (© 310/281-7200); and **Tiffany & Co.,** 210 N. Rodeo Dr. (© 310/273-8880). The newest arrivals are the ultrachic clothiers **Dolce & Gabbana,** 312 N. Rodeo Dr. (© 310/888-8701), and **Badgley Mischka,** 202 Rodeo Dr. (© 310/248-3750); British plaid palace **Burberry Limited,** 9560 Wilshire Blvd. (© 310/550-4500); and **NikeTown,** on the corner of Wilshire Boulevard and Rodeo Drive (© 310/275-9998), a behemoth shrine to the reigning athletic-gear king.

Wilshire Boulevard is also home to New York–style department stores (each in spectacular landmark buildings), such as **Saks Fifth Avenue,** 9600 Wilshire Blvd. (© 310/275-4211); **Barneys New York,** 9570 Wilshire Blvd. (© 310/276-4400); and **Neiman Marcus,** 9700 Wilshire Blvd. (© 310/550-5900).

**THE SUNSET STRIP** (between La Cienega Blvd. and Doheny Dr., West Hollywood)   The monster-size billboards advertising the latest rock god make it clear this is rock-'n'-roll territory. So it makes sense that you'll find legendary **Tower Records** in the heart of the action. Tower insists that it has L.A.'s largest selection of compact discs (more than 125,000 titles)—despite the Virgin Megastore's contrary claim—and it's open 365 days a year. At the east end of the strip sits the gigantic **Virgin Megastore.** Some 100 CD "listening posts" and an in-store "radio station" make this place a music-lover's paradise. Virgin claims to stock 150,000 titles, including an extensive collection of hard-to-find artists.

The Strip is lined with trendy restaurants, industry-oriented hotels, and dozens of shops offering outrageous fashions and stage accessories. One anomaly is Sunset Plaza, an upscale cluster of Georgian-style shops resembling Beverly Hills at its snootiest. You'll find **Billy Martin's,** 8605 Sunset Blvd. (© **310/289-5000**), founded by the legendary Yankees manager in 1978. This chic men's Western shop—complete with fireplace and leather sofa—stocks hand-forged silver and gold belt buckles, Lucchese and Liberty boots, and stable staples such as flannel shirts. Next door the fine-jewelry store **Philip Press, Inc.,** 8601 Sunset Blvd. (© **310/360-1180**), specializes in platinum and diamonds, handcrafted to evoke ornate estate jewelry. If you want to commemorate a special occasion or want the best selection, this is the place to go. **Book Soup** has long been one of L.A.'s most celebrated bookshops, selling mainstream and small-press books and hosting book signings and readings.

**WEST THIRD STREET** (between Fairfax and Robertson boulevards)  ⭐  You can shop until you drop on this trendy strip, anchored on the east end by the **Farmers Market and The Grove** (see "L.A.'s Top Attractions" earlier). Many of Melrose Avenue's shops have relocated here, along with terrific up-and-comers, several cafes, and the much-lauded restaurant Locanda Veneta. *Fun* is more the catchword here than *funky,* and the shops (including the vintage clothing stores) are a bit more refined than those along Melrose. **The Cook's Library** is where the city's top chefs find classic and offbeat cookbooks, wine guides, and other food-oriented tomes. Browsing is welcomed, even encouraged, with tea, tasty treats, and rocking chairs. **Traveler's Bookcase** is one of the best travel bookshops in the West, stocking a huge selection of guidebooks and travel literature, as well as maps and travel accessories. Nearby **Memory Lane,** 8387 W. 3rd St. (© **323-655-4571**), is filled with 1940s, 1950s, and 1960s collectibles.

There's lots more to see along this always-growing street. Refuel at **Chado Tea Room,** 8422 W. Third St. (© **323/655-2056**). Chado is designed with a nod to Paris's renowned Mariage Frères tea purveyor; one wall is lined with nooks full of brown tins filled with more than 250 different varieties of tea from around the world.

Among the choices are 15 kinds of Darjeeling, Indian teas blended with rose petals, and ceremonial Chinese and Japanese blends. You can also get tea meals here, featuring delightful sandwiches and individual pots of any loose tea in the store.

## HOLLYWOOD

**HOLLYWOOD BOULEVARD** (between Gower St. and La Brea Ave.)   One of Los Angeles's most famous streets is, for the most part, a cheesy tourist strip. But along the Walk of Fame, between the T-shirt shops and greasy pizza parlors, you'll find some excellent poster shops, souvenir stores, and Hollywood-memorabilia dealers worth getting out of your car for—especially if you can get your hands on that long-sought-after Ethel Merman autograph or *200 Motels* poster.

Some long-standing purveyors of memorabilia include **Hollywood Book City Collectibles,** 6631 Hollywood Blvd. (ⓒ **323-466-0120;** www.hollywoodbookcity. com), which has more than 70,000 color prints of past and present stars, along with a good selection of famous autographs. **Hollywood Book and Poster Company,** 6562 Hollywood Blvd. (ⓒ **323/465-8764;** www.hollywoodbookandposter.com), has an excellent collection of posters (from about $15 each), strong in horror and exploitation flicks. Photocopies of about 5,000 movie and television scripts are sold for $10 to $15 each (*Pulp Fiction* is just as good in print, by the way), and the store also carries music posters and photos. The **Collector's Book Store,** 6225 Hollywood Blvd. (ⓒ **323/467-3296**), is a movie buff's dream, with enough printed memorabilia for an afternoon of browsing; vintage copies of *Photoplay* and other fan mags cost $2 to $5, and the selection of biographies is outstanding.

**LARCHMONT BOULEVARD** (between Beverly Blvd. and Second St.)   Neighbors congregate on this old-fashioned street just east of busy Vine Avenue. As the surrounding Hancock Park homes become increasingly popular with artists and young industry types, the shops and cafes lining Larchmont get more stylish. Sure, chains such as Jamba Juice and The Coffee Bean are infiltrating this former mom-and-pop terrain, but plenty of unique shopping awaits amid charming elements such as diagonal parking, shady trees, and sidewalk bistro tables.

One of L.A.'s landmark independent bookstores is **Chevalier's Books,** 126 N. Larchmont Blvd. (ⓒ **323/465-1334**), a 60-year Larchmont tradition. If your walking shoes are letting you down, stop into **Village Footwear,** 240 N. Larchmont Blvd. (ⓒ **323/461-3619**), which specializes in comfort lines such as Josef Siebel.

**MELROSE AVENUE** (between Fairfax and La Brea aves.) ★★   It's showing some wear—some stretches have become downright ugly—but this is still one of the most exciting shopping streets in the country for cutting-edge fashions and people-watching. Melrose is always an entertaining stroll, dotted with plenty of hip restaurants and funky shops selling the latest in clothes, gifts, jewelry, and accessories that are sure to shock. Where else could you find green patent-leather cowboy boots, a working 19th-century pocket watch, an inflatable girlfriend, and glow-in-the-dark condoms on the same block? From east to west, here are some highlights.

**l.a. Eyeworks,** 7407 Melrose Ave. (© 323/653-8255), revolutionized eyeglass designs from medical supply to stylish accessory, and now their brand is nationwide. **Retail Slut,** 7308 Melrose Ave. (© 323/934-1339), is a rock-'n'-roll shop carrying new clothing and accessories for men and women. The unique designs are for a select crowd (the name says it all), so don't expect to find anything for your next PTA meeting here. **Betsey Johnson Boutique,** 8050 Melrose Ave. (© 323/852-1534), is a favorite among the young and pencil-thin; the New York–based designer has brought to L.A. her brand of fashion: Trendy, cutesy, body-conscious women's wear in colorful prints and faddish fabrics. Across the street, **Off the Wall,** 7325 Melrose Ave. (© 323/930-1185), is filled with neon-flashing kitsch collectibles, from vintage Wurlitzer jukeboxes to life-size fiberglass cows. The L.A. branch of a Bay Area hipster hangout, **Wasteland,** 7428 Melrose Ave. (© 323/653-3028), has an enormous steel-sculpted facade. There's a lot of leather and denim, and some classic vintage—but mostly funky 1970s-style garb, both vintage and contemporary. More racks of vintage treasures (and trash) are found at **Aardvark's Odd Ark,** 7579 Melrose Ave. (© 323/655-6769), which stocks everything from suits and dresses to neckties, hats, handbags, and jewelry. This place also manages to anticipate some of the hottest new street fashions.

## SANTA MONICA & THE BEACHES

**MAIN STREET** (between Pacific St. and Rose Ave., and Santa Monica and Venice boulevards) ★ An excellent street for strolling, Main Street is crammed with a combination of mall standards as well as upscale, left-of-center individual boutiques. You can also find plenty of casually hip cafes and restaurants. The primary strip connecting Santa Monica and Venice, Main Street has a relaxed, beach-community vibe that sets it apart from similar strips. The stores here straddle the divide between upscale trendy and beach-bum edgy. Highlights include **Obsolete,** 222 Main St. (near Rose Ave; © 310/399-0024), the most hip antiques store I've ever seen. Collectibles range from antique carnival curios to 19th-century anatomical charts from Belgium (you'd be amazed at how much some of that junk in your attic is worth). **CP Shades,** 2937 Main St. (between Ashland and Pier sts.; © 310/392-0949), a San Francisco ladies' clothier whose loose and comfy cotton and linen line is carried by many department stores and boutiques. **Horizons West,** 2011 Main St. (south of Pico Blvd.; © 310/392-1122), sells brand-name surfboards, wet suits, leashes, magazines, waxes, lotions, and everything else you need to catch the perfect wave. If you're looking for some truly sophisticated, finely crafted eyewear, the friendly **Optical Shop of Aspen,** 2904 Main St. (between Ashland and Pier sts.; © 310/392-0633), is for you. Ask for frames by

---

**Tips Cinderella Complex: Custom Shoes**

If you're still searching for The Perfect Pair of Shoes, why not have them custom made just for your feet? **Stanners & Kent,** a tiny shoe shop at 800 B 14th St. (at Montana Ave.; © 310/656-2720), creates custom-designed shoes in whatever style you desire. Prices start at about $200.

> *Tips* **Celebrity-Cloned Clothing**
>
> If your dream is to dress like a celebrity fresh off the red carpet, visit **A.B.S. by Allen Schwartz.** As soon as an award event is over (think Golden Globes, SAG Awards, Oscars), A.B.S. has already produced knock-offs of the evening's dresses that are every bit as lovely, but much more affordable. A.B.S. is at 1533 Montana Ave. (at 15th St.; © **310/393-8770**).

cutting-edge L.A. designers Bada and Koh Sakai. For aromatherapy nirvana, it's **Cloud's,** 2719 Main St., (© **310/399-2059**), where Jill Cloud (happily assisted by her lovely mom) carries the most heavenly scented candles. Then there's **Arts & Letters,** 2665 Main St. (© **310/314-7345**), a stationery haven that includes invitations by the owner herself, Marilyn Golin. Outdoors types will get lost in 5,600-square-foot **Patagonia,** 2936 Main St. (© **310/314-1776;** www.patagonia.com), where climbers, surfers, skiers, and hikers can gear up in the functional, colorful duds that put this environmentally friendly firm on the map.

**MONTANA AVENUE** (between 7th & 17th sts., Santa Monica; www.montana ave.com)   This breezy stretch of slow-traffic Montana has gotten a lot more pricey than in the late 1970s, when tailors and laundromats ruled the roost, but the specialty shops still outnumber the chains. Look around and you can see upscale moms with strollers and cellphones shopping for designer fashions, country home decor, and gourmet takeout.

Montana is still original enough for residents from across town to make a special trip here, seeking out distinctive shops such as **Shabby Chic,** 1013 Montana Ave. (© 310/394-1975), a much-copied purveyor of slipcovered sofas and flea-market furnishings, while clotheshorses shop for designer wear at minimalist **Savannah,** 706 Montana Ave. (© 310/458-2095); ultrahip **Jill Roberts,** 920 Montana Ave. (© 310/260-1966); and sleekly professional **Weathervane,** 1209 Montana Ave. (© 310/393-5344). For more grown-up style, head to **Ponte Vecchio,** 702 Montana Ave. (© 310/394-0989), which sells Italian hand-painted dishes and urns, or to **Cinzia,** 1129 Montana Ave. (© 310/393-7751), which features a smattering of both Tuscan and English home accessories. If Valentine's Day is approaching, duck into **Only Hearts,** 1407 Montana Ave. (© 310/393-3088), for heart-themed gifts and seductively comfortable intimate apparel. And don't forget the one-of-a-kind shops such as **Sun Precautions,** 1600 Montana Ave. (© 310/451-5858), specializing in 100% UV protection apparel, and the second largest **Kiehl's** store outside of NYC, 1515 Montana Ave. (© 310/255-0055). Enjoy a meal at the local favorite, **Café Montana,** 1534 Montana Ave. (© 310/829-3990), for great people-watching through its floor-to-ceiling glass windows.

**THIRD STREET PROMENADE** *Overrated*   Packed with those ubiquitous corporate chain stores, restaurants, and cafes (gee, *another* Starbucks), Santa Monica's pedestrians-only section of Third Street is the most popular shopping area in the city and, certainly, the least original. (Picture a suburban shopping mall without a roof and you've got it.) The Promenade (Third St. from Broadway to Wilshire Blvd., Santa Monica; www.downtownsm.com) bustles all day and well into the evening with a seemingly endless assortment of street performers, shoppers, bored teens, and homeless drifters.

### GR8 Finds in West L.A.'s J-Town

What started off as a magazine has spawned two of L.A.'s most talked-about new stores: **GR2,** 2062 Sawtelle Blvd. (© 310/445-9276), and **Giant Robot,** 2015 Sawtelle Blvd. (© 310/478-1819). Across the street from each other in West L.A.'s Japantown (at Sawtelle and Olympic boulevards), both specialize in a wide range of Asian-American pop-culture items including T-shirts, books, music, stationery, toys, art, and accessories (check out the Tadashi Murakami pins and felt pins by Saejean Oh). Several other cool shops and restaurants line this 1½-block stretch as well. One of my favorite stores is **Happy Six,** 2115 Sawtelle Blvd. (© 310/479-5363), which looks like Hello Kitty on acid and sells playful apparel and accessories for men and women. If you're hungry, my favorites along Sawtelle are **Manpuku,** 2125 Sawtelle Blvd. (© 310/473-0580); **Sawtelle Kitchen,** 2024 Sawtelle Blvd. (© 310/445-9288); and **Hurry Curry,** 2131 Sawtelle Blvd. (© 310/473-1640). Or you can pop into **Nijiya Market,** 2130 Sawtelle Blvd. (© 310/575-3300), and grab a bento (Japanese boxed lunch) to go.

A few shopping gems are squeezed between the Abercrombie & Fitches and Old Navies. You can easily browse for hours at **Hennessey+Ingalls,** 214 Wilshire Blvd. (© 310/458-9074; www.hennesseyingalls.com), a bookstore devoted to art and architecture. **Midnight Special Bookstore,** 1450 2nd St. (© 310/393-2923), is a medium-size general bookshop known for its good small-press selection and regular poetry readings. **Restoration Hardware,** 1221 Third Street Promenade (© **310/458-7992**), is still the retro-current leader for reproduction home furnishings and accessories. **Puzzle Zoo,** 1413 Third Street Promenade (© **310/393-9201**), voted "Best in L.A." by *Los Angeles* magazine, is where you'll find the double-sided World's Most Difficult Puzzle and many other brain-teasing challenges. Music lovers can get CDs and vinyl at **Hear Music,** 1429 Third Street Promenade (© 310/319-9527), and **Pyramid Music,** 1340 Third Street Promenade (© 310/393-5877). Stores stay open late (often till 1 or 2am on the weekends) for the movie-going crowds, and there's plenty of metered parking in six structures along Second and Fourth streets between Broadway and Wilshire Boulevard, so bring lots of quarters.

### DOWNTOWN

Since the late lamented Bullock's department store closed in 1993 (its Art Deco masterpiece salons were rescued to house the Southwestern Law School's library), Downtown has become less of a shopping destination than ever. Although many of the once-splendid streets are lined with cut-rate luggage and electronics stores, shopping here can be a rewarding—albeit gritty—experience for the adventuresome.

Savvy Angelenos still go for bargains in the garment and fabric districts; florists and bargain hunters arrive at the vast Flower Mart before dawn for the city's best selection of fresh blooms; and families of all ethnicities stroll the **Grand Central Market** ★★, 317 S. Broadway (between Third and Fourth sts.; © **213/624-2378;** www.grandcentral square.com). Opened in 1917, this bustling market has watched the face of Downtown L.A. change, while changing little itself. Today its sawdust-covered aisles serve Latino families, enterprising restaurateurs, and cooks in search of unusual ingredients—stuffed goat heads, mole, plantains, deep-fried smelt, Mexican cane alcohol—and bargain-priced produce. On weekends you'll be greeted by a mariachi band at the Hill Street entrance, near my favorite market feature, the fruit-juice counter, which dispenses 20 fresh varieties from wall spigots and blends the tastiest, healthiest "shakes" in town. Farther into the market you'll find produce sellers and prepared-food counters, spice vendors straight out of a Turkish bazaar, and a grain and bean seller who'll scoop out dozens of exotic rice and dried legumes. It's open 9am to 6pm daily.

Another of my favorite Downtown shopping zones is **Olvera Street** ⚘ (© 213/628-1274; www.olvera-street.com), a lively brick pedestrian lane near Union Station that has been lined with stalls selling Mexican wares since the 1930s. Everything that's sold south of the border is available here, including custom leather accessories, huarache sandals, maracas, and—but of course—freshly baked *churros*. On weekends, you're bound to see strolling bolero musicians, mariachis, folk dancers, and performances by Aztec Indians. It's open daily from 10am to about 7pm.

If you're looking to find *the* best shopping deals on handbags, luggage, shoes, costume jewelry, and trendy fashions, then try your best to find a parking meter or park in one of the parking structures from Olympic Boulevard to 12th Street and explore **Santee Alley,** located in the alley between Santee Street and Maple Avenue. Often referred to as the heart of the fashion district, it's got everything you've ever wanted at bargain prices. Go early on Saturday mornings if you want to blend in with the locals.

You have to wake up a little early to experience the **Southern California Flower Mart,** 742 Maple Ave. between Seventh and Eighth streets (© 213/627-2482; open to the public Tues, Thurs, and Sat 6am–noon; Mon, Wed, and Fri 8am–noon). If you do it right, though—wear comfortable shoes, bring cash, and a cup o' joe—walking through the myriad flower stalls is a tranquil experience. Besides the usual buds and

---

### Abbot Kinney Boulevard: L.A.'s Antithesis to Rodeo Drive

When you're fed up with the Rodeo Drive attitude and megamall conformity, drive to Venice and stroll the eclectic shops along **Abbot Kinney Boulevard.** This antiestablishment stretch has the most diverse array of shops, galleries, and restaurants in Los Angeles. You can easily spend the entire afternoon here poring over vintage clothing, antique furniture, vintage Vespas, local art, and amusing gifts. For one-of-a-kind designed jewelry, check out **Nagual,** 1326 Abbott Kinney Blvd. (© 310/396-8500), whose "metals with an edge" have caught the eye of many celebrities. Or if you're looking for a unique gift, walk into the shop of **Strange Invisible Perfumes,** 1209 Abbot Kinney Blvd. (© 310/314-1505), where they can custom-make a scent to match your musk. Then there's **Firefly,** 1413 Abbot Kinney Blvd. (© 310/450-6288), that one store where you can find a great baby gift, stationery, books, quirky handbags, and cool clothing. **DNA Clothing Company,** 411 Rose Ave. (© 310/399-0341), is the motherlode for the coolest, most current styles for men and women at great prices (numerous stylists and costumers use DNA for sitcoms and feature films). You'll find major brands as well as DNA's private label wear, and fresh stock arrives weekly. When you're ready to sit down and look over your loot, take a break to eat at one of the boulevard's many restaurants, including **Joe's** (the best California cuisine in L.A.; see p. 499), **Primitivo, Axe, Lilly's, Massimo's, Jin's Patisserie, French Market Café** and, of course, **Hal's Bar & Grill,** with its live jazz music. Two hours of street parking are free.

stems you see in *Sunset Magazine,* you'll find tropicals such as torch ginger, protea, and bird of paradise. You can purchase flowers by the bundles at amazingly low prices.

## 11 Los Angeles After Dark

Your best bet for current entertainment info is the *L.A. Weekly* (www.laweekly.com), a free paper available at sidewalk stands, shops, and restaurants. It has all the most up-to-date news on what's happening in Los Angeles's playhouses, cinemas, museums, and live-music venues. The Sunday **"Calendar"** and Thursday **"Weekend"** sections of the *Los Angeles Times* (www.calendarlive.com) are also a good source of information on what's going on throughout the city.

To purchase tickets in advance, first try buying them directly from the venue to avoid paying a surcharge. If that doesn't work, log onto **Good Time Tickets'** website at www.goodtime-tickets.com or call ✆ **800/464-7383.** Based in Hollywood for more than 30 years, the privately owned company specializes in tickets to sporting, theater, music, and other entertainment events throughout Los Angeles—at a markup, of course. If all else fails, take out a loan and call **Ticketmaster** (✆ **213/480-3232;** www.ticketmaster.com), but beware of their absurdly high processing fees.

### THEATER

Tickets for most plays usually cost $10 to $35, although big-name shows at the major theaters can fetch up to $75 for the best seats. The **Theatre League Alliance** (✆ **213/614-0556;** www.TheatreLA.org), an association of live theaters and producers in Los Angeles, offers same-day, half-price tickets via **Web Tix,** an Internet-only service at www.TheatreLA.org. Tickets are available Tuesday through Saturday from 4 to 11pm; purchase them online with a credit card and they'll be waiting for you at the box office. The site features a frequently updated list of shows and availability; you can also sign up for e-mail alerts. If you didn't bring your computer, log on at any public library, Internet cafe, or office service store.

### MAJOR THEATERS & COMPANIES

The all-purpose **Music Center of Los Angeles County,** 135 N. Grand Ave., Downtown, houses the city's top two playhouses: the **Ahmanson Theatre** and **Mark Taper Forum.** They're both home to the Center Theater Group (www.taperahmanson.com), as well as traveling productions (often Broadway- or London-bred). Each season, the Ahmanson Theatre (✆ **213/628-2772**) hosts a handful of high-profile shows, such as Andrew Lloyd Webber's *Phantom of the Opera;* the Royal National Theatre's production of Ibsen's *Enemy of the People,* starring Sir Ian McKellan; and the Adventures in Motion Pictures presentation of Matthew Bourne's *Cinderella. Tip:* The best seats are in the mezzanine section.

The **Mark Taper Forum** (✆ **213/628-2772;** www.marktaperforum.com) is a more intimate theater with a thrust stage—where the audience is seated on three sides of the acting area—that performs contemporary works by international and local playwrights. Neil Simon's humorous and poignant *The Dinner Party* and Tom Stoppard's witty and eclectic *Arcadia* are among the more popular productions performed on this internationally recognized stage, which has won three Pulitzer Prizes and 18 Tony Awards.

One of L.A.'s most venerable landmarks, the **Orpheum Theatre,** 842 S. Broadway (at Ninth St.; ✆ **213/749-5171;** www.laorpheum.com), recently reopened after a 75-year hiatus. Built in 1926, this renowned venue has hosted an array of theatrical productions, concerts, film festivals, and movie shoots—from Judy Garland's 1933

---

*Tips*  **Great Theater, Cheap Tickets**

Two hours before curtain time, the Ahmanson Theatre and Mark Taper Forum offer specially priced $12 tickets, which must be purchased in person at the box office with cash. All performances are subject to availability with restrictions.

---

vaudeville performance to *Ally McBeal.* The 2,000-seat theater is home to the Mighty Wurlitzer, one of three original theater organs left in Southern California theaters.

Across town, the moderately sized **Geffen Playhouse,** 10886 Le Conte Ave., Westwood (℃ **310/208-5454;** www.geffenplayhouse.com), presents dramatic and comedic work by prominent and emerging writers. UCLA purchased the theater—which was originally built as a Masonic temple in 1929, and later served as the Westwood Playhouse—back in 1995 with a little help from philanthropic entertainment mogul David Geffen. This striking venue is often the West Coast choice of many acclaimed off-Broadway shows, and also attracts locally based TV and movie actors eager for the immediacy of stage work. One recent production featured Annette Bening in Ibsen's *Hedda Gabler.* Always audience-friendly, the Playhouse prices tickets in the $28 to $43 range.

You've probably already heard of the **Kodak Theatre,** 6834 Hollywood Blvd. (℃ 323/308-6300; www.kodaktheatre.com), home of the Academy Awards. The crown jewel of the Hollywood & Highland entertainment complex, this modern beauty hosts a wide range of international performances, musicals, and concerts ranging from Alicia Keys and Elvis Costello to the Moscow Stanislavsky Ballet and *Grease* starring Frankie Avalon. Guided tours are given 7 days a week from 10:30am to 2:30pm.

The recently restored **Pantages Theatre,** 6233 Hollywood Blvd. between Vine and Argyle (℃ 323/463-4367), reflects the full Art Deco glory of L.A.'s theater scene. Opened in 1930, this historical and cultural landmark was the first Art Deco movie palace in the U.S. and site of the Academy Awards from 1949 to 1959. The theater recently presented the run of Disney's *The Lion King* and Mel Brooks' smash hit *The Producer,* with Jason Alexander and Martin Short.

At the foot of the Hollywood Hills, the 1,245-seat outdoor **John Anson Ford Amphitheatre** (℃ 213/974-1343; www.lacountyarts.org/ford.html) is in a county regional park, set against a backdrop of cypress trees and chaparral. It's an intimate setting, with no patron more than 96 feet away from the stage. Music, dance, film, theater, and family events run from May through September. The indoor theater, a cozy, 87-seat space that was extensively renovated in November 1998 and renamed **[Inside] The Ford,** features live music and theater year-round.

One of the most highly acclaimed professional theaters in L.A., the **Pasadena Playhouse,** 39 S. El Molino Ave., near Colorado Boulevard, Pasadena (℃ 626/356-7529; www.pasadenaplayhouse.org), is a registered historic landmark that has served as the training ground for many theatrical, film, and TV stars, including William Holden and Gene Hackman. Productions take place on the main theater's elaborate Spanish Colonial Revival stage.

For a schedule at any of the above theaters, check the listings in *Los Angeles* magazine (www.lamag.com), available at most area newsstands, or the "Calendar" section of the Sunday *Los Angeles Times* (www.calendarlive.com), or call the box offices at the numbers listed above.

## SMALLER PLAYHOUSES & COMPANIES

On any given night, there's more live theater to choose from in Los Angeles than in New York City, due in part to the surfeit of ready actors and writers chomping at the bit to make it in Tinseltown. Many of today's familiar faces from film and TV spent plenty of time cutting their teeth on L.A.'s busy theater circuit, which is home to nearly 200 small and medium-size theaters and companies, ranging from the 'round-the-corner, neighborhood variety to high-profile, polished troupes of veteran actors. With so many options, navigating the scene to find the best work can be a monumental task. A good bet is to choose one of the theaters listed below, which have established excellent reputations for their consistently high-quality productions; otherwise, consult the *L.A. Weekly* (www.laweekly.com), which advertises most current productions, or call **Theatre LA** (© 213/614-0556) for up-to-date performance listings.

The **Colony Studio Theatre,** 555 N. Third St., Burbank (© **818/558-7000;** www.colonytheatre.org), formed in 1975, has developed from a part-time ensemble of TV actors longing for their theatrical roots into a nationally recognized company. The company produces plays in all genres at the 276-seat Burbank Center Stage, which they share with other performing arts groups.

**Actors Circle Theater,** 7313 Santa Monica Blvd., West Hollywood (© 323/ 882-8043), is a 47-seater that's as acclaimed as it is tiny. Look for original contemporary works throughout the year.

The **Actor's Gang Theater,** 6201 Santa Monica Blvd., Hollywood (© **323/465-0566),** is not one to shy from irreverence. Back in 1997, the in-house company, a group of UCLA alums, presented *Bat Boy: The Musical,* based on a story in the bizarre tabloid *Weekly World News.*

Founded in 1965, **East West Players,** 120 N. Judge John Aiso St., Los Angeles (© **213/625-7000;** www.eastwestplayers.org), is the oldest Asian American theater company in the United States. It has been so successful that the company moved from a 99-seat venue to the 200-seat David Henry Hwang Theater in Downtown L.A.'s Little Tokyo.

The 25-year-old **L.A. Theatre Works** (© 310/827-0889) is renowned for its marriage of media and theater and has performed more than 200 plays and logged more than 350 hours of on-air programming. Performances are held at the Skirball Cultural Center, nestled in the Sepulveda Pass near the Getty Center. In the past, personalities such as Richard Dreyfuss, Julia Louis-Dreyfus, Jason Robards, Annette Bening, and John Lithgow have given award-winning performances of plays by Arthur Miller, Neil Simon, Joyce Carol Oates, and more. For nearly a decade, the group has performed simultaneously for viewing and listening audiences in its radio theater series. Tickets are usually around $35; a full performance schedule can be found online at **www.skirball.org**.

Founded in 1981, the **West Coast Ensemble Theater,** 522 N. La Brea Ave. (between Melrose and Beverly), Hollywood (© **323/876-8723;** www.wcensemble.org), is a nonprofit multiethnic assemblage of professional actors, writers, and directors. The ensemble has collected accolades from local critics, as well as many awards for its excellent production quality. Expect to see well-written, well-directed, and socially relevant plays performed by a talented and professional cast. Ticket prices range from $15 to $22.

## CLASSICAL MUSIC & OPERA

While L.A. is best known for its pop realms (see later in this chapter), other types of music here consist of top-flight orchestras and companies—both local and visiting—

to fulfill the most demanding classical music appetites; scan the papers to find out who's performing while you're in the city.

The world-class **Los Angeles Philharmonic** (© 323/850-2000; www.laphil.org) is the only major classical music company in Los Angeles, and it just got a whole lot more popular with the completion of its incredible new home: the Walt Disney Concert Hall, at the intersection of First Street and Grand Avenue in the historic Bunker Hill area (see "L.A.'s Top Attractions," earlier in this chapter). Designed by world-renowned architect Frank O. Gehry, this exciting addition to the Music Center of L.A. includes a breath-taking 2,265-seat concert hall, outdoor park, restaurant, cafe, bookstore, and gift shop.

The Philharmonic's Finnish-born music director, Esa-Pekka Salonen, concentrates on contemporary compositions; despite complaints from traditionalists, he does an excellent job attracting younger audiences. Tickets can be hard to come by when celebrity players such as Itzhak Perlman, Isaac Stern, Emanuel Ax, and Yo Yo Ma are in town. In addition to performances at the Walt Disney Concert Hall, the Philhar-monic plays a summer season at the **Hollywood Bowl** (see "Concerts Under the Stars" below) and a chamber music series at the **Skirball Cultural Center.**

Slowly but surely, the **Los Angeles Opera** (© 213/972-8001; www.losangeles opera.com), which performs at the **Dorothy Chandler Pavilion,** is gaining respect and popularity with inventive stagings of classic pieces, modern operas, visiting divas, and the contributions from high-profile artistic director Plácido Domingo. The 120-voice **Los Angeles Master Chorale** sings a varied repertoire that includes classical and pop compositions. Concerts are held at the **Walt Disney Concert Hall** (© 213/972-7200) October through June.

The **UCLA Center for the Performing Arts** (© 310/825-2101; www.performing arts.ucla.edu) has presented music, dance, and theatrical performances of unparalleled quality for more than 60 years and continues to be a major presence in the local and national cultural landscape. Presentations occur at several different theaters around Los Angeles, both on and off campus. UCLA's **Royce Hall** is the Center's pride; it has even been compared to New York's Carnegie Hall. Recent standouts from the Center's busy calendar included the famous Gyuto Monks Tibetan Tantric Choir and the Cin-derella story *Cendrillon,* with an original score by Sergei Prokofiev.

## CONCERTS UNDER THE STARS

**Hollywood Bowl** ★★★ *Moments*    Built in the early 1920s, the Hollywood Bowl has just undergone a major overhaul. The elegant Greek-style natural outdoor amphithe-ater is cradled in a small mountain canyon and is the summer home of the Los Ange-les Philharmonic and Hollywood Bowl orchestras. The space often hosts internationally known conductors and soloists on Tuesday and Thursday nights. Fri-day and Saturday concerts typically feature orchestral swing or pops concerts. The summer season also includes a jazz series; past performers have included Natalie Cole, Dionne Warwick, and Chick Corea. Other events, from standard rock-'n'-roll acts such as Radiohead to Garrison Keillor programs, summer fireworks galas, and the annual Mariachi Festival, are often on the season's schedule.

To round out an evening at the Bowl, many concertgoers use the occasion to enjoy a picnic dinner and a bottle of wine—one of L.A.'s grandest traditions. You can pre-pare your own or order a picnic basket with a choice of hot and cold dishes and a selec-tion of wines and desserts from Patina's on-site catering department, which also provides delivery to box seats: Call © 323/850-1885 by 4pm the day before you go

---

Finds  **Free Morning Music at Hollywood Bowl**

The Bowl's summer morning rehearsals are open to the public and free. On Tuesday, Thursday, and Friday from 9:30am to 12:30pm, you can see the program scheduled for that evening. So bring some coffee and doughnuts (the concession stands aren't open) and enjoy the best seats in the house (© 323/ 850-2000; www.hollywoodbowl.org).

---

to place your food order. Arrive a couple of hours before the show starts to dine while listening to the orchestra or band tune up.

2301 N. Highland Ave. (at Pat Moore Way), Hollywood. © 323/850-2000. www.hollywoodbowl.org.

## THE CLUB & MUSIC SCENE

Los Angeles is more or less the center of the entertainment industry, so on any given night, it's a snap to find something to satisfy any musical taste. From acoustic rock to jazz fusion, from Judas Priest cover bands to Latin funk, from the up-and-coming to the already gone, L.A. has something for everyone. For a listing of shows, check the websites of the *LA Weekly* (www.laweekly.com) and the *Los Angeles Times* "Calendar" section (www.calendarlive.com).

**The Avalon Hollywood**    Formerly known as The Palace, this 1,200-capacity theater and nightclub—just across Vine from the famed Capitol Records tower—was the site of numerous significant alternative-rock shows throughout the late '90s and recently received a much-needed makeover. Its lounge, the Spider Club, acts as the VIP room/late-night oasis and makes for an excellent place to see and be seen, imbibe, dance, and cavort until the wee hours of the morning. Club nights feature famous DJs such as Paul Oakenfeld. 1735 N. Vine St., Hollywood. © 323/462-8900. www.avalonhollywood.com.

**Babe's & Ricky's Inn** ⭐ Finds    In South Central L.A.'s up-and-coming Leimert Park, this blues club stands out as an original, a place where you can imagine B. B. King himself would have played before he became famous. Mama Laura Gross is the cultivator of the fabulous, endangered sound and the house goddess of this intimate bar. Great guitarists are the rule, not the exception here. 4339 Leimert Blvd., Leimert Park. © 323/295-9112. www.bluesbar.com.

**B. B. King's Blues Club**    Hidden in Universal CityWalk's commercial plaza, this three-level club/restaurant hosts plenty of great local and touring national blues acts and is a testament to the establishment's venerable namesake. There's no shortage of good seating, but if you find yourself on the top two levels, it's best to grab a table adjacent to the railing to get an ideal view of the stage. The ribs alone are worth the trip. CityWalk, Universal City. © 818/622-5464.

**Forty Deuce**    Owner Ivan Kane reopened this suave nightclub, formerly known as Kane. Designed as "back-alley, striptease lounge," the low bar, lounge-chair seating, vintage brass registers, and cocktail tables with chic lamps all chip in to create a sexy, burlesque-esque vibe. Models use the bar as a runway, so watch your cocktail. 5574 Melrose Ave., Hollywood. © 323/466-6263. www.fortydeuce.com.

**House of Blues** ⭐    With three great bars, cutting-edge Southern art, and a key Sunset Strip location, the House of Blues gives music fans and industry types plenty of reasons to keep coming back. Night after night, audiences are dazzled by performances from nationally and internationally acclaimed acts as diverse as Duran Duran, B. B. King, and Queensryche. The food in the upstairs restaurant can be great (reservations are a must), and the Sunday gospel brunch, though a bit pricey, puts a mean raise on the roof. 8430 Sunset Blvd., West Hollywood. © 323/848-5100. www.hob.com.

**King King** ⭐   I'm not normally keen on Hollywood clubs (too much überhip dig-me crap), but King King is a refreshing change of venue. The warehouse-sized spot feels more SoHo than L.A.: exposed brick walls and ceilings, dark lighting, black velvet curtains, and a square bar on wheels that's moved to accommodate whatever's going on. The last time I was there I watched a rather disturbing play followed by a sensational rockabilly band. 6555 Hollywood Blvd. (between Hudson and Whitley aves.), Hollywood. © 323/960-9234. Cover $5–$10.

**The Knitting Factory**   The West Coast branch of the legendary New York City music emporium has arrived, in the redeveloping Hollywood Boulevard nightlife district. The Main Stage was inaugurated by a Posies performance and sees such diverse bookings as Kristin Hersh, Pere Ubu, and Jonathan Richman; a secondary AlterKnit stage has sporadic shows. The Factory is totally wired for digital, including interactive online computer stations throughout the club. 7021 Hollywood Blvd., Hollywood. © 323/463-0204. www.knittingfactory.com.

**Roxy**   Veteran record producer/executive Lou Adler opened this Sunset Strip club in the mid-1970s with concerts by Neil Young and a lengthy run of the stage version of *Rocky Horror Show.* Since then, it has remained among the top showcase venues in Hollywood. Although the revitalized Troubadour and such new entries as the House of Blues challenge its preeminence among cozy clubs, national acts will pop in as well as great local bands. 9009 Sunset Blvd. © 310/276-2222.

**Spaceland** ⭐   Wall-to-wall mirrors and shiny brass posts create the feeling that, in a past life, Spaceland must've been a seedy strip joint, but the club's current personality offers something entirely different. Having hosted countless performances by cutting-edge artists such as Pavement, Mary Lou Lord, Elliot Smith, and the Eels, this hot spot on the fringe of east Hollywood has become one of the most important clubs on the L.A. circuit. 1717 Silver Lake Blvd., Silver Lake. © 323/661-4380. www.clubspaceland.com.

**The Troubadour**   Since the 1960s, this West Hollywood mainstay has seen 'em all. Audiences of all ages are consistently treated to memorable shows from the already-established or young-and-promising acts that take the stage. But bring earplugs—they like it loud at this beer- and sweat-soaked club. 9081 Santa Monica Blvd., West Hollywood. © 310/276-6168. www.troubadour.com.

**Viper Room**   This world-famous club on the Strip has been king of the hill since actor Johnny Depp and co-owner Sal Jenco first opened it back in 1993. With an intensely electric and often star-filled scene, the intimate club is also known for unforgettable late-night surprise performances from powerhouses such as the late Johnny Cash, Iggy Pop, Tom Petty, Slash, and Trapt (to name but a few), after they play headline gigs elsewhere in town. 8852 Sunset Blvd., West Hollywood. © 310/358-1881. www.viperroom.com.

**Whisky A Go-Go** ⭐   This legendary bi-level venue embodies L.A. rock history, from Jim Morrison and X to Guns N' Roses and Beck. Every trend has passed through this club, and it continues to be the most vital venue of its kind. With the hiring of an in-house booker a few years ago, the Whisky began showcasing local talent on free-admission Monday nights. 8901 Sunset Blvd., West Hollywood. © 310/652-4202. www.whiskyagogo.com. All ages.

## One-Stop Night Out

If your big night on the town involves dinner, a movie, DJs, and dancing, **Cine-Space** has you covered. Every Thursday through Saturday this stylish, intimate Hollywood supper club serves contemporary American cuisine—and stiff cocktails—while screening recent hits, indies, classics, and shorts. When the film's over, the DJ party starts at around 10pm and goes until 2pm. Not only is the movie free, but you don't need to stand in line or pay cover when the nightclub opens. Check the CineSpace event calendar online to see what's playing, then call to make a reservation. It's located in the heart of Hollywood at 6356 Hollywood Blvd. at Ivar Street on the second level (© **323/817-3456;** www.cine-space.com).

### DANCE CLUBS

**The Conga Room** Attracting Latin-music luminaries such as Pucho & The Latin Soul Brothers, this one-time health club on the Miracle Mile has quickly become *the* nightspot for live salsa and merengue. Break up the evening of heart-melting, sexy Latin dancing with a trip to the dining room, where the chef serves savory Cuban fare in a setting that conjures the romance of pre-Castro Cuba, or indulge yourself in the Conga Room's stylish cigar lounge. 5364 Wilshire Blvd., Los Angeles. © **323/938-1696.** www.congaroom.com.

**The Derby** This class-A east-of-Hollywood club has been at ground zero of the swing revival since the very beginning. At a former Brown Derby site, the club was restored to its original luster and detailed with a heavy 1940s edge. With Big Bad Voodoo Daddy as the onetime house band and regular visits from Royal Crown Revue, hep guys and dolls knew that The Derby was money even before *Swingers* transformed it into one of the city's most happenin' hangs. If you come on the weekends, expect a wait. Once you're inside, dance space is at a premium. 4500 Los Feliz Blvd., Los Feliz. © **323/663-8979.** www.the-derby.com. Cover $7–$10.

**El Floridita** *Finds* This tiny Cuban restaurant-and-salsa club is hot, hot, hot. Despite its modest strip-lot locale, it draws the likes of Jennifer Lopez, Sandra Bullock, Jimmy Smits, and Jack Nicholson, in addition to a festive crowd of Latin-dance devotees who groove well into the night. The hippest nights continue to be Mondays, when Johnny Polanco and his swinging New York–flavored salsa band get the dance floor jumpin'. 1253 N. Vine St., Hollywood. © **323/871-8612.** Cover $10.

**Hollywood Athletic Club** Built in 1924, this pool hall, restaurant, and nightclub is home to some groovin' dance clubs. Saturdays feature a lively mix of progressive house music spun by DJs Drew Down and Dave Audé. On Sundays, Latin house, merengue, hip-hop, and salsa fill the air. The Hollywood Athletic Club also hosts concerts from internationally known DJs and bands as diverse as Mono and the Wu Tang Clan. 6525 Sunset Blvd., Hollywood. © **323/462-6262** or 323/957-0722. Cover $10–$20.

**Nacional** *★* At what is quickly becoming Hollywood's most desirable dance floor, you'll find a hip and gorgeous crowd engaging in an orgiastic celebration of youth. It also has a well-designed balcony where you can watch all the flirting in a lively outdoor smoking area. So grab a *mojito* and mingle among the young, beautiful, and unshakably self-assured. And remember: Even the rest of us can have fun here. 1645 Wilcox Ave., Hollywood. © **323/962-7712.**

## BARS & COCKTAIL LOUNGES

**Beauty Bar**    It's a proven concept in New York, Las Vegas, and San Francisco: a cocktail lounge/beauty salon. Decorated with vintage salon gear, with a hip-retro vibe, the Beauty Bar is campy and trendy. Where else can you actually get a manicure while sipping cocktails with names like Blue Rinse (made with blue Curaçao) or Prell (their version of a grasshopper)? 1638 N. Cahuenga Blvd., Hollywood. ✆ 323/464-7676. www.beautybar.com.

**The Dresden Room** ⭐    Hugely popular with L.A. hipsters because of its longevity, location, often-overlooked cuisine, and elegant ambience, "The Den" was pushed into the mainstream of L.A. nightlife thanks to its inclusion in the movie *Swingers*. It's the timeless lounge act of Marty and Elayne (the couple has been performing there up to 5 nights a week since 1982), however, that has proven that this place is cool, fad or no fad. Sidle up to the bar for a blue glass of the house classic, Blood and Sand—a space-age margarita of sorts. 1760 N. Vermont Ave., Hollywood. ✆ 323/665-4294.

**Good Luck Bar**    Until they installed a flashing neon sign outside, only locals and hipsters knew about this Kung Fu–themed room in the Los Feliz/Silver Lake area. The dark-red windowless interior has Oriental ceiling tiles, fringed Chinese paper lanterns, sweet-but-deadly drinks such as the Yee Mee Loo (translated as "blue drink"), and a jukebox with selections ranging from Thelonius Monk to Cher's "Half Breed." The spacious sitting room, furnished with mismatched sofas, armchairs, and banquettes, provides a great atmosphere for conversation or romance. Arrive early to avoid the throng of L.A. scenesters. 1514 Hillhurst Ave. (between Hollywood and Sunset boulevards), Los Angeles. ✆ 323/666-3524.

**Hank's Bar** ⭐    Although the original grand old man behind the bar (Henry "Hank" Holzer) is no longer with us, his legacy endures at this classic Downtown watering hole, on the ground floor of the Stillwell Hotel. Its battered booths and well-liquored patrons who have been elbowing up to the bar here for a decade mingle nicely with the drop-in customers riding the surge of Downtown's recently reinvigorated night life. 840 S. Grand Ave., Los Angeles. ✆ 213/396-7718.

**Skybar** *Overrated*    Since its opening in hotelier Ian Schraeger's refurbished Sunset Strip hotel, Skybar has been a favorite among L.A.'s most fashionable residents. This place was at one time so hot that even the agents to the stars needed agents to get in.

---

### Stars, Whiskey & Cigars

Just off the Third Street Shopping Promenade in Santa Monica is a small cigar shop called the **Lone Wolf Cigar Company,** where local cigar aficionados—including many celebrities—congregate for a guilt-free smoke and scotch among friends. Founded in 1996 by Chuck Norris and James Belushi, it's now owned and run by David Weiss, whose love for fine cigars is infectious: Pedestrians wander in out of curiosity and end up staying for hours, talking shop with David while savoring a mild Lone Wolf Signature Select made from top-grade Dominican Republic tobacco. David also carries a large selection of other premium cigar brands and beautiful lighters—the perfect gift for the guy who has it all. Even if you don't know a Montecristo from a Swisher Sweet, stop in, say hello, fire up a smoke, and relax for a while. It's at 223-B Broadway Blvd., between Second and Third sts., Santa Monica (✆ 800/577-9653; www.lonewolfcigars.com).

---

(Rumor has it that one agent was so desperate to enter that he promised one of the servers a contract.) With a little image overhaul—affect the right look, strike the right pose, and look properly uninterested—you might get to rub elbows with some of the faces that regularly appear on the cover of *People* (please, though, don't stare). 8440 W. Sunset Blvd., West Hollywood. (*C*) **323/848-6025.**

**The Standard Downtown** ✰✰  This rooftop bar atop the Standard Hotel in Downtown L.A. (formerly Superior Oil Headquarters) is surrounded by high office towers and helipads, and the view is magnificent. The skyscrapers act like strangely glowing lava lamps in the night sky, as exotic ladies sip exotic cocktails amid waterbeds and bent-plastic loungers. 550 S. Flower St. (*C*) **213/892-8080.** www.standardhotel.com.

**Star Shoes** ✰  From the same club gurus who run Beauty Bar around the corner, Star Shoes is a combo shoe store and dance club. It's usually packed with trendy young clubsters who bump around the narrow dance floor while a projectionist plasters the walls with vintage celluloid (a stony effect). The scene here is far more energetic than at the Beauty Bar, and the DJs are among the best in town. 6364 Hollywood Blvd., Hollywood. (*C*) **323/462-7827.** www.starshoes.org.

**360**  This 19-story, penthouse restaurant and lounge is a winning place to romance your special someone. It's all about the view here—all 360 degrees of it. The understated, softly lit, sleek interior emphasizes the scene beyond the plentiful, large windows, including a spectacular vista of the famed HOLLYWOOD sign. 6290 Sunset Blvd., Hollywood. (*C*) **323/871-2995.** www.360hollywood.com.

**Whiskey Blue**  Upon ascending the dramatic, backlit staircase and entering the dimly lit, seductive interior, it's hard to believe Whiskey Blue in the W Hotel is situated on UCLA's Sorority Row. The atmosphere is as chic as the decor, which features high screen partitions, low cushioned couches, sleek private rooms, and a row of carved stumps of wood where manicured martinis may be set. Patrons are encouraged to dress their best, especially on the weekends when the Westside's glitterati come to this scene to be seen. Hotel guests are given priority entrance. 930 Hilgard Ave., Westwood. (*C*) **310/443-8232.**

**White Lotus** ✰  Previously known as the Crush Bar, this new spot has quickly become hot; limos regularly clog the street outside, and tabloids report on sightings inside. A dramatic white-peaked roof shrouds statues of Buddha on the crowded patio. Inside, a dining room, sushi bar and several sexy VIP rooms are filled with Asian antiques. Co-executive chefs Andrew Pastore (of the Sunset Room and Pig 'n Whistle) and Hiroji Obayashi (of Hirozen) collaborate on a menu loaded with influences from Japan, China, Thailand, and France. The sushi is excellent, and the dim sum—morsels accompanied by nontraditional reduction sauces—are sublime. The bar stocks an impressive collection of sakes and the staff is knowledgeable enough to introduce you to various styles. Make reservations for the restaurant in advance, which automatically gets you access to the hot nightclub. 1743 N. Cahuenga Blvd., Hollywood. (*C*) **323/463-0060.** www.whitelotushollywood.com.

## COMEDY CLUBS

**Comedy Store** ✰  You can't go wrong here: New comics develop their material, and established ones work out their kinks at this landmark owned by Mitzi Shore (Pauly's mom). The **Best of the Comedy Store Room,** which seats 400, features professional stand-ups continuously on Friday and Saturday nights. Several comedians each do about a 15-minute stint. The talent is always first-rate and includes comics who regularly appear on the *Tonight Show* and other shows. The **Original Room** features a dozen or so comedians back-to-back nightly. Sunday night is amateur night: Anyone with enough guts can take the stage for 3 minutes, and Lord only knows what you'll see. 8433 Sunset Blvd., West Hollywood. ℂ **323/650-6268**. www.comedystore.com. Sun, Mon free before 9pm, $10 cover after 9pm; Tues–Thurs $15 cover; Fri–Sat $20 cover. Additional two-drink minimum daily.

**Groundling Theater** ✸    L.A.'s answer to Chicago's Second City has been around for more than 25 years, yet it remains the most innovative and funny group in town. The skits change every year or so, but they take new improvisational twists every night and the satire is often savage. The Groundlings were the springboard to fame for Pee-Wee Herman and former *Saturday Night Live* stars Jon Lovitz, Phil Hartman, and Julia "It's Pat" Sweeney. Phone for show times and reservations. 7307 Melrose Ave., Los Angeles. ℂ **323/934-9700**. www.groundlings.com. Tickets $11–$20.

**The Improv**    A showcase for top stand-ups since 1975, the Improv offers something different each night. Although it used to have a fairly active music schedule, the place is now mostly doing what it does best—showcasing comedy. Owner Budd Freedman's buddies—such as Jay Leno, Billy Crystal, and Robin Williams—hone their skills here more often than you would expect. Even if the comedians on the bill are unknowns, you can bet they won't be for long. Shows are at 8pm Sunday through Thursday, and at 8:30 and 10:30pm Friday and Saturday. 8162 Melrose Ave., West Hollywood. ℂ **323/651-2583**. www.improvclubs.com. Tickets usually $10 Sun–Thurs, $15 Fri and Sat. Additional 2-item minimum daily.

## LATE-NIGHT BITES

Finding places to dine in the wee hours is getting easier in L.A., as each year sees the opening of more 24-hour and after-midnight restaurants and diners.

**The Apple Pan** ✸✸    This classic American burger shack (p. 508), an L.A. landmark, hasn't changed much since 1947—and its burgers and pies continue to hit the spot. Open until 1am Friday and Saturday, and until midnight other nights; closed Monday. 10801 W. Pico Blvd., West L.A. ℂ **310/475-3585**.

**Canter's Fairfax Restaurant, Delicatessen & Bakery**    This 24-hour Jewish deli has been a winner with late-nighters since it opened more than 66 years ago. If you show up after the clubs close, you're sure to spot a bleary-eyed celebrity or two alongside the rest of the after-hours crowd, chowing down on a giant pastrami sandwich, matzo-ball soup, potato pancakes, or other deli favorites. Try a potato knish with a side of brown gravy—trust me, you'll love it. 419 N. Fairfax Ave., West Hollywood. ℂ **323/651-2030**.

**Dolores's**    One of L.A.'s oldest surviving coffee shops, Dolores's offers just what you might expect: Naugahyde, laminated counters, lots of linoleum, and comforting predictability. Expect the usual coffee-shop fare of pancakes, burgers, and eggs at this 24-hour joint. 11407 Santa Monica Blvd., Los Angeles. ℂ **310/477-1061**.

**Du-par's Restaurant & Bakery** ✸    During the week, this popular Valley coffee shop (p. 516) serves blue-plate specials until 1am; on the weekend, they're slinging hash until 4am. 12036 Blvd. (1 block east of Laurel Canyon), Studio City. ℂ **818/766-4437**.

**Fred 62**    Silver Lake/Los Feliz hipsters hankering for a slightly demented take on classic American comfort grub skulk into Fred around the clock. 1850 N. Vermont, Los Angeles. ℂ **323/667-0062**.

**Jerry's Famous Deli** ✸    Valley hipsters head to 24-hour Jerry's (p. 516) to satiate the late-night munchies. 12655 Ventura Blvd. (east of Coldwater Canyon Ave.), Studio City. ℂ **818/980-4245**.

**Kate Mantilini** ⭐ Kate's serves stylish nouveau comfort food in a striking setting. It's open until midnight Sunday and Monday, Tuesday through Friday until 1am, and Saturday until 2am. 9101 Wilshire Blvd. (at Doheny Dr.), Beverly Hills. ℂ 310/278-3699.

**Mel's Drive-In** Straight from an episode of *Happy Days*, this 24-hour 1950s diner on the Sunset Strip attracts customers ranging from chic shoppers during the day to rock 'n' rollers at night. The fries and shakes here are among the best in town. 8585 Sunset Blvd. (west of La Cienega), West Hollywood. ℂ 310/854-7200.

**101 Coffee Shop** A retro coffee shop right out of the early '60s with rock walls, funky colored tiles, comfy booths, and cool light fixtures, all pulled together nicely in a hip yet subdued fashion. Count on tasty grinds until 3am (try the breakfast burritos). 6145 Franklin Ave., Hollywood. ℂ 323/467-1175.

**Original Pantry Cafe** Owned by former Los Angeles mayor Richard Riordan, this Downtown diner (p. 515) has been serving huge portions of comfort food around the clock for more than 60 years; in fact, they don't even have a key to the front door. 877 S. Figueroa St. (at Ninth St.), Downtown. ℂ 213/972-9279.

**Pink's Hot Dogs** Many a woozy hipster has awakened with the telltale signs of an after-party trip to this greasy street-side hot-dog stand (p. 511)—the oniony morning-after breath and chili stains on your shirt are dead giveaways. Open Friday and Saturday until 3am, and all other nights until 2am. 709 N. La Brea Ave., Los Angeles. ℂ 323/931-4223.

**Swingers** ⭐ This hip coffee shop (p. 512) keeps L.A. scene-stealers happy with its retro comfort food. Open from 6:30am until 4am daily except Tuesday (when they close at 2am). In addition to the Hollywood location, there's another Swingers at 802 Broadway, with only slightly more limited hours (at Lincoln Ave., Santa Monica (ℂ 310/393-9793). 8020 Beverly Blvd. (west of Fairfax Ave., Santa Monica. ℂ 323/653-5858.

**Toi on Sunset** ⭐ Those requiring a little more *oomph* from their late-night snack should come here. At this colorful and *loud* hangout (p. 512), garbled pop-culture metaphors mingle with the tastes and aromas of "rockin' Thai" cuisine until 4am nightly. 7505 Sunset Blvd. (at Gardner), Hollywood. ℂ 323/874-8062.

## MOVIES

This being the heart of the film industry, L.A. is saturated with megaplexes catering to high-budget, high-profile flicks featuring the usual big-ticket lures such as Hanks, Willis, and Leonardo. At times, though, those polished Hollywood-studio stories just won't do. Below are some nonmainstream options that play movies from bygone eras or those with an indie bent. Consult the *L.A. Weekly* (www.laweekly.com) to see what's playing when you're in town.

During a weeklong event in April, the **Los Angeles Film Festival** (ℂ 888/ETM-TIXS or 310/432-1200) looks at what's new in American indies, short films, and music videos. Each July since 1982, the **Gay and Lesbian Film Festival** (ℂ 213/480-7088; www.outfest.org), also known as Outfest, has aimed to bring high-quality gay, lesbian, bi, and transgender films to a wider public awareness. In 1998, the festival became Los Angeles's largest, with 31,000 audience members.

The **American Cinematheque** in Hollywood (ℂ 323/466-3456; www.egyptian theatre.com) presents rare videos and films, ranging from the wildly arty to old classics. Since relocating to the historic, beautifully refurbished 1923 **Egyptian Theatre,**

## The Most Private Public Theater

Part of L.A. culture is to avoid standing in line—presumably because you're far too important and busy—so it was only a matter of time before someone created a movie theater where everyone is treated like a VIP. **ArcLight Cinemas** (② 323/464-4226; www.arclightcinemas.com) is designed for anyone who abhors rude patrons (ushers keep it quiet), late arrivals (forbidden), searching for seats (reserved in advance by customer preference), uncomfortable chairs (think Lazyboy), neck strain (the first rows start 25 ft. from the screen), pimply teenage employees (most of the staff are struggling actors or film students), crappy popcorn (real butter and freshly made caramel popcorn), and paying for parking (4 free hr. are included in the ticket price). And it only gets better at the bar and lounge with appetizers and themed cocktails such as the Mordor.

The ArcLight shows a mix of indie and Hollywood films, and ticket prices are higher than the industry average ($11 for matinees and $14 on weekend nights). But the rewards are worth the occasional splurge. The sound and picture quality are so good that filmmakers come here to host Q&A sessions (George Clooney on *Confessions of a Dangerous Mind*), and celebrities such as Leonardo DiCaprio prefer the ArcLight's reserved seating system. Be sure to review the "Now Playing" and "Coming Soon" sections on ArcLight's website to see what's scheduled. It's located at 6360 W. Sunset Blvd., between Vine and Ivar streets.

6712 Hollywood Blvd. in Hollywood, American Cinematheque has hosted several film events, including a celebration of contemporary flicks from Spain, a tribute to the femme fatales of film noir, and a retrospective of the films of William Friedkin. Events highlighting a specific individual are usually accompanied by at least one in-theater audience Q&A session with the honoree.

**The Leo S. Bing Theater** at the **L.A. County Museum of Art,** 5905 Wilshire Blvd., Los Angeles (② 323/857-6010), presents a themed film series each month. Past subjects have ranged from 1930s blonde bombshell films to Cold War propaganda flicks and contemporary British satire (complete with a 3-day *Monty Python's Flying Circus* marathon).

Despite being a multiplex in a bright outdoor mall, **Laemmle's Sunset 5,** 8000 Sunset Blvd., West Hollywood (② 323/848-3500; www.laemmle.com), features independent art films that most theaters of its ilk won't even touch. They also show a selection of gay-themed movies.

**The Nuart Theater,** 11272 Santa Monica Blvd., Los Angeles (② 310/478-6379), plumbs its archives for real classics, ranging from campy to cool. They also feature frequent appearances and Q&A sessions from stars and filmmakers, and screen *The Rocky Horror Picture Show* every Saturday at midnight.

Silent-movie fans will enjoy the **Silent Movie Theatre,** 611 N. Fairfax Ave. (half block south of Melrose), near the Miracle Mile (② 323/655-2520 for recorded information, or 323/655-2510 for office; www.silentmovietheatre.com). Tickets are $8 ($6 for kids and seniors), but it's only open for social events and once-a-month movies when the new owner fancies.

If TV's more your thing, the **Museum of Television and Radio,** 465 N. Beverly Dr., Beverly Hills (© **310/786-1000**), celebrates this country's long relationship with the tube. The museum often features a movie of the month and shows free selections from past television programs.

# 15

# Side Trips from Los Angeles

*by Matthew Richard Poole*

The area within a 100-mile radius of Los Angeles is one of the most diverse regions in the world. Here, you can find arid deserts, rugged mountains, historic towns, alpine lakes, and even an island paradise. In the following pages, I've included a variety of the best attractions outside of Los Angeles County, such as the smog-free mountain communities of Big Bear and Lake Arrowhead, the world-famous Disneyland and Knott's Berry Farm amusement parks, SoCal beach towns like Newport and Huntington Beach, and the ultimate L.A. weekend getaway, Catalina Island. From L.A., you can reach most of these scenic side trips in less than an hour by car or boat—an easy and refreshing diversion from the big-city scene.

## 1 Santa Catalina Island

22 miles W of mainland Los Angeles

*by Trisha Clayton*

After an unhealthy dose of the mainland's soupy smog and freeway gridlock, you'll appreciate an excursion to Santa Catalina Island, with its clean air, crystal-clear water, and the blissful absence of traffic. In fact, there isn't a single traffic light on the entire island. Conditions like these can fool you into thinking that you're miles away from the hustle and bustle the city, but the reality is that you're only 22 miles off the Southern California coast and *still* in L.A. County.

Because of its relative isolation, out-of-state tourists tend to ignore Santa Catalina—which everyone calls simply Catalina—but those who do make the crossing have plenty of elbow room to boat, fish, swim, scuba, and snorkel. There are also miles of hiking and biking trails, plus golf, tennis, and horseback riding, but the main sport here seems to be bar-hopping.

Catalina is so different from the mainland that it almost seems like a different country, remote and unspoiled. In 1919, the island was purchased by William Wrigley, Jr., the chewing-gum magnate, who had plans to develop it into a fashionable pleasure resort. To publicize the new vacation land, Wrigley brought big-name bands to the Avalon Ballroom and moved the Chicago Cubs, which he owned, to the island for spring training. His marketing efforts succeeded and Catalina soon became a world-renowned playground, luring such celebrities as Laurel and Hardy, Cecil B. DeMille, John Wayne, and even Winston Churchill.

In 1975, the Santa Catalina Island Conservancy—a nonprofit operating foundation organized to preserve and protect the island's nature habitat—acquired about 88% of Catalina Island, protecting virtually all of the hilly acreage and rugged coastline that make up what is known as the interior. In fact, some of the most spectacular outlying areas can only be reached by arranged tour (see "Exploring the Island," below).

# ESSENTIALS

**GETTING THERE**    The most common way to get to and from the island is on the **Catalina Express** ferryboat (© 800/481-3470; www.catalinaexpress.com), which operates up to 30 daily departures year-round from Long Beach, San Pedro and Dana Point. All Catalina Express terminals offer high-speed catamaran service, as well as fast mono-hull boats. The trip takes about an hour. Round-trip fares are $49 for adults, $44 for seniors 55 and over, $38 for children ages 2 to 11, and $3 for infants. Fares for Dana Point are $2 more, except for infants. In San Pedro, the Catalina Express departs from the **Sea/Air Terminal,** Berth 95; take the Harbor Freeway (I-110) south to the Harbor Boulevard exit, and then follow signs to the terminal. In Long Beach, boats leave from the **Catalina Landing;** take the 710 Freeway south into Long Beach. Stay to the left, follow signs to downtown, and exit Golden Shore. Turn right at the stop sign and follow around to the terminal on the right. Parking is in the parking structure on the left. Call ahead for reservations. *Note:* Check-in at the ticket window is required and begins 1 hour prior to each departure. Passengers must be checked in, holding tickets, and ready to board at 15 minutes prior to departure or the reservation will be canceled and the credit card will be charged for the full amount of the round-trip fare. Luggage is limited to 70 pounds per person; reservations are necessary for bicycles, surfboards, and dive tanks; and there are restrictions on transporting pets. You can leave your car at designated lots at each departure terminal; the parking fee is around $10 per 24-hour period.

The **Catalina Flyer,** 400 Main St., Balboa (© 949/673-5245; www.catalina info.com), the largest passenger-carrying catamaran on the West Coast, departs daily from Newport Beach's historic Balboa Pavilion. The boats leaves once a day at 9 a.m. and returns to Newport at 4:30 p.m. daily. Travel time is about 75 minutes each way. Round-trip fares are $44 for adults, $27 for children 3 to 12, $41 for seniors, and $3 for infants. Pets are not allowed.

**Island Express Helicopter Service,** 900 Queens Way Dr., Long Beach (© 800/2-AVALON or 310/510-2525; www.islandexpress.com), flies from Long Beach or San Pedro to Avalon in about 15 minutes. The expense is definitely worth the thrill and convenience, particularly if you're prone to seasickness. It flies on demand between 8am and sunset year-round, charging $74 plus tax each way. The weight limit for luggage, however, is a mere 25 pounds. It also offers brief air tours over the island; prices vary. The heliport is located a few hundred yards southwest of the Queen Mary.

**VISITOR INFORMATION**    The **Catalina Island Chamber of Commerce and Visitors Bureau,** P.O. Box 217, Avalon, CA 90704 (© 310/510-1520; fax 310/510-7606; www.catalinachamber.com), located on the Green Pleasure Pier, distributes brochures and information on island activities, hotels, and transportation. Call for a

---

## *Fun Fact* Cart Culture

One of the first things you'll notice when you arrive in Avalon is the abundance of golf carts in a comical array of styles and colors. Since Avalon is the only city in California authorized by the state legislature to regulate the number of vehicles allowed to drive on city streets, there are no rental cars and only a handful of privately owned vehicles.

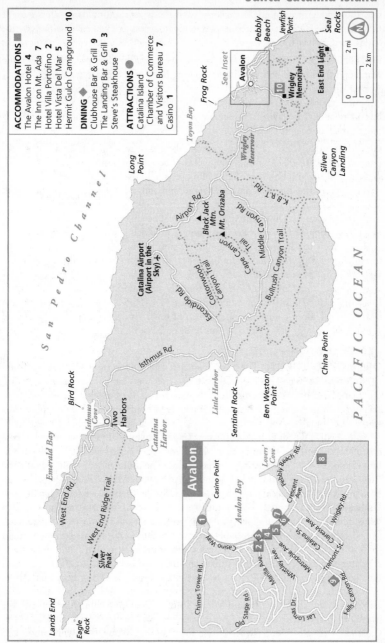

# Santa Catalina Island

San Pedro Channel

PACIFIC OCEAN

Pebbly Beach
Jewish Point
Seal Rocks
East End Light
Wrigley Memorial
See Inset
Avalon
**10**

2 mi
2 km

Frog Rock

Toyon Bay

Wrigley Reservoir

Silver Canyon Landing

Long Point

Airport Rd.
Black Jack Mtn.
Mt. Orizaba
Cape Canyon Trail
Middle Canyon Rd.
K.B.R.T Rd.
Bullrush Canyon Trail

Catalina Airport (Airport in the Sky)

Cottonwood Canyon Trail
Escondido Rd.

Isthmus Rd.

Bird Rock

Isthmus Cove
Two Harbors

Catalina Harbor

Little Harbor

Sentinel Rock

Ben Weston Point

China Point

Emerald Bay

West End Rd.

West End Ridge Trail

Silver Peak

Lands End

Eagle Rock

## Avalon

Casino Point

Avalon Bay

Lovers' Cove

Pebbly Beach Rd.

Crescent Ave.

**8**

Wrigley Rd.

Catalina St.

Claressa Ave.

Tremont St.

Metropole Ave.

Whittley Ave.

Sumner Ave.

**1**

**2 3**
**4**
**5 6**
**7**

**9**

Casino Way

Chimes Tower Rd.

Old Stage Rd.

Las Lomas Dr.

Falls Canyon Rd.

free 100-page visitors' guide. Its colorful website, **www.catalina.com**, offers current news from the *Catalina Islander* newspaper, in addition to updated activities, events, and general information.

**ORIENTATION**  The picturesque town of **Avalon** is both the port of entry for the island and the island's only city. From the ferry dock, you can wander along Crescent Avenue, the main road along the beachfront, and easily explore adjacent side streets.

Northwest of Avalon is the village of **Two Harbors,** accessible by boat or shuttle bus. Its twin bays are favored by pleasure yachts from L.A.'s various marinas, so there's more camaraderie and a less touristy ambience overall.

**GETTING AROUND**  Once in Avalon, take a taxi from the **Catalina Cab Company** (② 310/510-0025) from the heliport or dock to your hotel, and enjoy the quick and colorful trip through town (don't blink or you'll miss it). Only a limited number of cars is permitted on the island; visitors are not allowed to drive cars on the island, and most residents motor around in golf carts (many of the homes only have golf cart–size driveways). Don't worry, though—you'll be able to get everywhere you want to go by renting a cart yourself or just hoofing it, which is what most visitors do.

If you want to explore the area around Avalon beyond where your feet can comfortably carry you, rent a mountain bike or tandem from **Brown's Bikes,** 107 Pebbly Beach Rd. (② 310/510-0986). If you'll be exploring, you'll want to rent a gas-powered golf cart from **Cartopia Golf Cart Rentals** on Crescent Avenue at Pebbly Beach Road (② 310/510-2493), or **Island Rentals** (② 310/510-1456), across from the boat terminal. Both companies offer a map of town for a self-guided tour. Rates are about $30 per hour plus a deposit. You must be 25 or older to drive.

## EXPLORING THE ISLAND

**ORGANIZED TOURS**  The Santa Catalina Island Company's **Discovery Tours** (② 800/626-1496 or 310/510-TOUR; www.scico.com) has a ticket and information office on Crescent Avenue across from the Green Pier. It offers the greatest variety of excursions from Avalon; many last just a couple of hours and don't monopolize your whole day. Tours are available in money-saving combo packs; inquire when you call.

Noteworthy excursions include the new **Cape Canyon** that takes you into the heart of Catalina's "outback" in an open-air 4WD Mercedes Benz Unimog Vehicle, driven by a Catalina Island Conservancy–trained guide. The tour's rugged route includes the American Bald Eagle and Catalina Island Fox habitats at Middle Ranch, lunch at Airport-in-the-Sky and plenty of photo stops ($89 per person, includes lunch); the **Undersea Tour,** a leisurely 45-minute cruise of Lover's Cove Marine Preserve in a semisubmerged boat that allows you to sit 5 feet under the water in a climate-controlled cabin where you comfortably observe Catalina's kelp forests by day or night ($33 adults, $17 kids, $30 seniors); the **Casino Tour,** a fascinating 1-hour look at the style and inventive engineering of this elegant ballroom (see "Catalina's Grand Casino" box, below; $14 adults, $6.75 kids, $12 seniors); nighttime **Flying Fish Boat Trips,** a 50-minute Catalina tradition in searchlight-equipped open boats ($21 adults, $10 kids, $19 seniors); and the **Inland Motor Tour,** a 32-mile, 4-hour jaunt through the island's rugged interior, including a stop at the **Airport-in-the-Sky, Little Harbor** on Catalina's west coast (our favorite locale for camping, hiking, and swimming), and Wrigley's **El Rancho Escondido,** a working ranch where some of America's finest Arabian horses are raised and trained ($50 adults, $25 kids, $45 seniors).

## Catalina's Grand Casino

No trip to Catalina is complete without taking the **Casino Tour** (see "Organized Tours," above). The Casino Building, Avalon's world-famous Art Deco landmark, is not—and never was—a place to gamble your vacation money away (*casino* is an Italian word for a place of entertainment or gathering). Rather, the incredibly ornate structure (the craftsmanship inside and out is spectacular) is home to the island's only movie theater and the world's largest circular ballroom. Virtually every big band in the '30s and '40s played in the 158-ft.-diameter ballroom, carried over CBS radio since its grand opening in May 1929. Today it's a coveted venue for elaborate weddings, dances, gala dinners, and the Catalina Jazz Festival. The 3-week **JazzTrax Festival** (© 866/872-9849; www.jazztrax.com) takes place every October. To experience the festival, be sure to book your tickets and accommodations as far in advance as possible.

**VISITING TWO HARBORS**    If you want to get a better look at the rugged natural beauty of Catalina and escape the throngs of beachgoers, head over to Two Harbors, the quarter-mile "neck" at the island's northwest end that gets its name from the "twin harbors" on each side, known as the Isthmus and Cat harbors. An excellent starting point for campers and hikers, Two Harbors also offers just enough civilization for the less-intrepid traveler.

The **Banning House Lodge** (© 310/510-2800; www.scico.com) is an 11-room bed-and-breakfast overlooking the Isthmus. The clapboard house was built in 1910 for Catalina's pre-Wrigley owners and has seen duty as on-location lodging for movie stars like Errol Flynn and Dorothy Lamour. Peaceful and isolated, the simply furnished but comfortable lodge has spectacular views of both harbors. Rates range from $179 to $269 including deluxe continental breakfast (Jun–Sept), and they'll even give you a lift from the pier.

Everyone eats at **The Harbor Reef Restaurant** (© 310/510-4215) on the beach. This nautical, tropical-themed saloon/restaurant serves breakfast, lunch, and dinner, the latter consisting of hearty steaks, ribs, swordfish, chicken teriyaki, and buffalo burgers in summer. The house drink is sweet "buffalo milk," a potent concoction of vodka, crème de cacao, banana liqueur, milk, whipped cream, and nutmeg.

**WHAT TO SEE & DO IN AVALON**    Walk along horseshoe-shaped Crescent Avenue, past private yachting and fishing clubs, toward the landmark **Casino** building. You can see the Art Deco **theater** for the price of a movie ticket any night. Also on the ground floor is the **Catalina Island Museum** (© 310/510-2414), which explores 7,000 years of island history including fascinating exhibits of archaeology, steamships, big bands, and natural history. The museum has a contour relief map of the island that's helpful to hikers. Admission is $2.50 for adults, $1 for kids and $2 for seniors; it's included in the price of Discovery's Casino Tour (see above).

Around the point from the Casino lies **Descanso Beach Club** (© 310/510-7410), a mini–Club Med in a private cove. While you can get on the beach year-round, the club's facilities (including showers, restaurant/bar, sandy beach, volleyball lawns, dance area, and thatched beach umbrellas) are only open from Easter to September 30. Admission is $1.50.

About 1½ miles from downtown Avalon is the **Wrigley Memorial and Botanical Garden** (© 310/510-2288). The specialized gardens, a project of Ada Wrigley, showcase plants endemic to California's coastal islands. It's open daily from 8am to 5pm; admission is $5, children under 12 are free.

## DIVING, SNORKELING & SEA KAYAKING ⍟

Snorkeling, scuba diving, and sea kayaking are among the main reasons mainlanders head to Catalina. Catalina Island's naturally clean water and giant kelp forests teeming with marine life have made it a renowned diving destination that attracts experts and beginning divers alike. **Casino Point Marine Park,** Southern California's first city-designated underwater park, was established in 1965 and is located behind the Casino. Due to its convenient location, it can get outrageously crowded in the summer (just like everything else at that time of year).

**Catalina Divers Supply** (© 800/353-0330 or 310/510-0330; www.catalinadivers supply.com) runs two full-service dive shops: One from a large trailer behind the Casino at the edge of Avalon's underwater park, where they offer guided snorkeling tours and introductory scuba dives; and another at the Green Pier, where they launch boat dives aboard the Scuba Cat. The three best locations for snorkeling are **Lover's Cove Marine Preserve, Casino Point Marine Park,** and **Descanso Beach Club. Catalina Snorkeling Adventures,** at Lover's Cove (© 877/SNORKEL), offers snorkel gear rental. Snorkeling trips that take you outside of Avalon depart from **Joe's Rent-a-Boat** (© 310/510-0455), on the Green Pier.

At Two Harbors, stop by **West End Dive Center** (© 310/510-2800). Excursions range from half-day introductory dives to complete certification courses and multiday dive packages. It also rents snorkel gear and offers kayak rental, instruction, and tours.

## HIKING & BIKING

When the summer crowds become overwhelming, it's time to head on foot for the peacefulness of the interior, where secluded coves and barren, rolling hills soothe frayed nerves. Visitors can obtain a free **hiking permit** at the Conservancy Office (125 Claressa Ave.; © 310/510-2595; www.catalinaconservancy.org), where you'll find maps, wildlife information, and friendly assistance from Conservancy staffers who love to share their knowledge of the interior. It's open daily from 9am to 5pm, and closed for lunch on weekends. Among the sights you may see are the many giant buffalo roaming the hills, scions of movie extras that were left behind in 1929 and have since flourished.

**Mountain biking** is allowed on the island's designated dirt roads, but requires a $60-per-person permit ($85 per family) that must be purchased in person at the Conservancy Office. Permits are valid for 1 year and include coverage for accident, liability, and life insurance.

## BEACHES

Unfortunately, Avalon's beaches leave much to be desired. The town's central beach, located off Crescent Avenue, is small and completely congested in the busy season. Be sure to claim your spot early in the morning before it's full. **Descanso Beach Club** offers the best beach in town but also gets crowded very quickly. Your best bet is to kayak out to a secluded cove where you have the beach virtually to yourself.

## WHERE TO STAY

If you plan to stay overnight, be sure to reserve a room in advance because most places fill up pretty quickly during the summer and holiday seasons. There are only a handful of hotels whose accommodations and amenities actually justify the rates that they charge. Some are downright scary, so be sure to book as far in advance as possible to get a room that makes the trip worthwhile. Don't stress too much over your accommodations, as you'll probably spend most of your time outdoors. Keep in mind that the best time to visit is in September or October when the water is warm, the crowds have somewhat subsided, and hotel occupancy is easier to find. If you're having trouble finding a vacancy, try calling the **Convention and Visitors Bureau** (© **310/510-1520**); they keep tabs on last-minute cancellations. **Catalina Island Accommodations** (© **310/510-3000**) might be able to help you out in a pinch; it's a reservations service with updated information on the whole island. When booking, ask the hotel agent about money-saving packages that offer discounted room rates, boat or helicopter fare, and tours.

### VERY EXPENSIVE

**The Inn on Mt. Ada** ★★   When William Wrigley, Jr., purchased Catalina Island in 1921, he built this ornate hilltop Georgian colonial mansion as his summer vacation home; it's now one of the finest small hotels in California. The opulent inn—considered to be the best in town for its luxury accommodations and views—has several ground-floor salons, a club room with a fireplace, a deep-seated formal library, and a wickered sunroom where tea, cookies, and fruit are always available. The best guest room is the Grand Suite, fitted with a fireplace and a large private patio. Amenities include bathrobes and the use of a golf cart during your stay. TVs are available on request, but there are no phones in the rooms. A hearty full breakfast, a light deli-style lunch, appetizers, fresh fruit, freshly baked cookies, soft drinks, beers, wines, and champagne are included in the rate. *Tip:* Even if you find that they're sold out or too pricey to fit your budget, make a lunch reservation and enjoy amazing views from the Inn's spectacular balcony.

398 Wrigley Rd. (P.O. Box 2560), Avalon, CA 90704. © **800/608-7669** or 310/510-2030. Fax 310/510-2237. www.catalina.com/mtada. 6 units. Nov–May Mon–Thurs $320–$475 double, $560 suite; June–Oct and Fri–Sun year-round $360–$560 double, $675 suite. Rates include 2 meals daily. AE, MC, V. **Amenities:** Courtesy car. *In room:* TV, hair dryer, iron, no phone.

### EXPENSIVE

**The Avalon Hotel**   Catalina's newest boutique hotel is all about the details. The lot was originally developed in the late 1800s as The Pilgrim Club, a gentleman's club that vanished in the great fire of 1915. After many incarnations, the dilapidated property was acquired in 2003 by locals Rock and Kathleen Gosselin, who have transformed it into one of the Island's most luxurious hideaways. The cozy Craftsman-style hotel is decked out in rich, hand-carved mahogany and imported slate tastefully accented with handmade tile and local artwork. Catalina's silhouette is artfully etched into the slate, stained glass and light fixtures while shadowboxes showcase Island memorabilia throughout the hotel's homey public space. Guest rooms, which come in a variety of sizes, feature garden or ocean views (some with balconies), gleaming white bathrooms with natural skin-care products, and an incredibly comfy queen- or king-size Supple-Pedic memory foam bed. *Caution:* The Gosselins are Supple-Pedic mattress dealers so don't be surprised if you find yourself ordering your own before checking out.

---

**_Tips_ For Travelers Who Use Wheelchairs**

Visitors who use wheelchairs should request a room at **Hotel Metropole** (© 800/541-8528 or 310/510-1884). One of the most modern properties in Avalon, it has an elevator, a large sun deck that overlooks Avalon Bay, a shopping complex, and a very convenient location in the heart of Avalon.

---

124 Whittley Ave. (P.O. Box 706), Avalon, CA 90704. © 310/510-7070. www.theavalonhotel.com. 15 units. Mid-Nov to mid-March and Mon–Thurs year-round $195–$395 double; mid-June to mid-Sept and Fri–Sun year-round $295–$495 double. Rates include continental breakfast, complimentary taxi pickup from the boat or helicopter, nightly turn-down service. AE, MC, V. **Amenities:** Rooftop deck w/360-degree views, beautifully furnished garden patio w/fountain, laptops and DVDs to borrow at front desk. _In room:_ Flatscreen TV (in most rooms) w/DVD, high-speed Internet connection, fridge w/refreshments, coffeemaker, hair dryer, microwave, nature-based bath products, Supple-Pedic memory foam mattresses, fresh flowers, local artwork.

### MODERATE

**Hotel Villa Portofino** ⋆  Enjoy European elegance on the ocean front from your courtyard room or harborview suite after a warm welcome from the hotel's efficient and friendly staff. The hotel boasts recently renovated rooms and well-appointed bathrooms, some with Alacante-colored Spanish marble, and fantastic views overlooking the bay. There's also a spacious rooftop deck that's perfect for people-watching, sunbathing, and cocktail sipping. Some rooms have luxurious touches like fireplaces, deep soaking tubs, and separate showers. Just outside the front door is all of Avalon Bay's activity.

111 Crescent Ave. (P.O. Box 127), Avalon, CA 90704. © 800/35-62326 or 310/510-0555. Fax 310/510-0839. www.hotelvillaportofino.com. 35 units. May–Oct $135–$249 double, from $335 suite; winter $85–$195 double, from $235 suite. Rates include continental breakfast, beach towels, and chairs. AE, DC, MC, V. **Amenities:** Award-winning restaurant; adjacent art gallery. _In room:_ A/C, TV, fridge, coffeemaker, hair dryer, iron/board.

### INEXPENSIVE

Our recommended choices for inexpensive lodgings are the **Pavilion Lodge** (© 800/ 414-2754 or 310/510-2500), which recently completed an extensive renovation on all guest rooms, which are basic but affordable and clean (a great alternative when budgets and availability are tight); **Hotel Catalina** (© 800/540-0184 or 310/510-0027), a well-maintained Victorian-style hotel just a half-block from the beach, with tons of charm, family cottages, a courtyard with beautiful stained glass, and large verandas with bay views; **Zane Grey** (© 310/510-0966), a Hopi-style pueblo built in 1926 and former home of American author Zane Grey, situated above town and equipped with a cozy living room with fireplace and piano, free shuttle service, and a swimming pool; and **Hermit Gulch Campground,** Avalon's only campground, which can be crowded and noisy in peak season. Campsites can be tough to secure, especially when hotels are booked, so it's a good idea to make reservations in advance. The walk to town and back can be draining, so hop on the green-and-white tram that runs you back and forth to town for a dollar each way.

### WHERE TO DINE

Along with the choices below, recommended Avalon options include **The Busy Bee** on Crescent Ave. (© 310/510-1983), an always-crowded waterfront diner with a heated and wind-protected patio. On the Two Harbors side of the island, **The Harbor Reef Restaurant** is the place to eat; see "Exploring the Island," above.

## EXPENSIVE

**Clubhouse Bar & Grille** ✦ CALIFORNIA    You'll find some of Avalon's most elegant meals at this landmark Catalina Country Club, whose stylish Spanish-Mediterranean clubhouse was built by William Wrigley, Jr., during the 1920s. Recently restored, it exudes a chic and historic atmosphere; the menu is peppered with archival photos and vintage celebrity anecdotes. Sit outdoors in an elegant tiled courtyard, or inside the intimate, clubby dining room. Much of the menu, including gourmet sandwiches, tasty appetizers, and soups, is served throughout the afternoon. Dinner offerings include fresh local fish as well as free-range veal, lamb, and chicken that are cooked to perfection. The club is a few blocks uphill, so shuttle service is available from Island Plaza (on Sumner Ave.) on weekends.

1 Country Club Dr. (above Sumner Ave.). ✆ 310/510-7404. Reservations recommended. Main courses $9–$18 lunch, $26–$35 dinner. AE, DISC, MC, V. Daily 11:30am–2:30pm and 5–9pm (closing hr. will vary seasonally).

## MODERATE

**The Landing Bar and Grill** AMERICAN    With a secluded and heated deck overlooking the harbor, The Landing is one of the most romantic dining spots in Avalon. It boasts beautiful Spanish-style architecture located in the historic El Encanto Center that manages to attract as many jeans-clad vacationers as dressed-up islanders. The menu is enticing, with local seafood offerings, pasta, Mexican cuisine, and gourmet pizzas that can be delivered to your hotel room if you wish.

Intersection of Crescent and Marilla. ✆ 310/510-1474. Reservations recommended. Main courses $11–$22. AE, DISC, MC, V. Daily 11am–3pm and 4–10pm (subject to changes in winter).

**Steve's Steakhouse** AMERICAN    Step up above the busy bayside promenade into a fantastic collage of museum-quality photos capturing the Avalon of old. This setting overlooking Avalon Bay feels just right for the hearty menu of steaks, seafood, and pasta—all of which can be ordered from the full bar as well as the dining room. Catalina swordfish is their specialty, along with excellent cuts of meat. You can also make a respectable repast from the many appetizer selections, especially the fresh oysters and sashimi.

417 Crescent Ave. (directly across from the Green Pier, upstairs). ✆ 310/510-0333. Reservations recommended on weekends. Main courses $7–$15 lunch, $15–$25 dinner. AE, DISC, MC, V. Daily 11am–3pm and 5–10pm.

## INEXPENSIVE

*Note:* Street addresses are useless in a town as small as Avalon, but all these restaurants are near each other on the main strip. Our three favorites for a low-bucks meal are **Rosie's Fish and Chips** (✆ 310/510-0197), on the Green Pier, which serves fresh seafood favorites like fish and chips and seafood cocktails; **Casino Dock Café** (✆ 310/510-2755), with live summertime entertainment, marina views from the sun-drenched deck, breakfast burritos loaded with homemade salsa, and kicking bloody marys; and **Lori's Good Stuff** (✆ 310/510-2489), a tiny spot with fresh, healthy sandwiches, smoothies, and milkshakes—the best around.

## BARHOPPING

*Note:* Avalon doesn't have listed street addresses, but all these bars are within stumbling distance of each other on the main drag. The **Chi Chi Club** (✆ 310/510-2828), the "noisy bar in Avalon" referred to in Crosby, Stills, and Nash's song "Southern Cross," is the island's only dance club and quite a scene on summer weekend evenings—the DJ spins an eclectic mixture of dance tunes. **Luau Larry's** (✆ 310/510-1919) is Avalon's signature bar that everyone must visit; its tacky Tiki theme and signature Wicky Wack drink kicks you into island mode as soon as you step inside—sure to stumble out. Or go where the locals go and swill beers at **The Marlin Club** (© 310/510-0044), Avalon's oldest drinking hole; catch the Dodgers game at **J. L.'s Locker Room** (© 310/510-0258); and recover from your hangover with a spicy bloody mary at the rustic bar inside **The Busy Bee** (© 310/510-1983).

## 2 Big Bear Lake & Lake Arrowhead

100 miles NE of L.A.

These two deep-blue lakes lie close to each other in the San Bernardino mountains and have long been favorite year-round alpine playgrounds for city-weary Angelenos.

**Big Bear Lake** has always been popular with skiers as well as boaters (it's much larger than Arrowhead, and equipment rentals abound), and in the past decade the area has been given a much-needed face-lift. Big Bear Boulevard was widened to handle high-season traffic, and downtown Big Bear Lake (the "Village") was spiffed up without losing its woodsy charm. In addition to two excellent ski slopes less than 5 minutes from town, you can enjoy the comforts of a real supermarket and several video-rental shops, all especially convenient if you're staying in a cabin. Most people choose Big Bear over Arrowhead because there's so much more to do, from boating, fishing, and hiking to snow sports, mountain biking, and horseback riding. The weather is nearly always perfect at this 7,000-foot-plus elevation: If you want proof, ask Caltech, which operates a solar observatory here to take advantage of nearly 300 days of sunshine per year.

**Lake Arrowhead** has always been privately owned, as is apparent from the affluence of the surrounding homes, many of which are gated estates rather than rustic mountain cabins. The lake and the private docks lining its shores are reserved for the exclusive use of homeowners, but visitors can enjoy Lake Arrowhead by boat tour or use of the summer-season beach clubs, a privilege included in nearly all private-home rentals. Reasons to choose a vacation at Lake Arrowhead? The roads up are less grueling than the winding ascent to Big Bear Lake and, being at a lower elevation, Arrowhead gets little snow (you can forget those pesky tire chains). It's very easy and cost effective to rent a luxurious house from which to enjoy the spectacular scenery, crisp mountain air, and relaxed resort atmosphere—and if you do ski, the slopes are only a half-hour away.

### ESSENTIALS

**GETTING THERE**    Lake Arrowhead is reached by taking Highway 18 from San Bernardino. The last segment of this route takes you along the aptly named **Rim of the World Highway,** offering a breathtaking view over the valley below on clear days. Highway 18 then continues east to Big Bear Lake, but to get to Big Bear Lake, it's quicker to bypass Arrowhead by taking Highway 330 from Redlands, which meets Highway 18 in Running Springs. During heavy-traffic periods, it can be worthwhile to take scenic Highway 38, which winds up from Redlands through mountain passes and valleys to approach Big Bear from the other side.

*Note:* Nostalgia lovers can revisit legendary **Route 66** on the way from Los Angeles to the mountain resorts, substituting scenic motor courts and other relics of the "Mother Road" in place of impersonal I-10. For a complete driving tour, see "Get Your Kicks on Historic Route 66" in chapter 16.

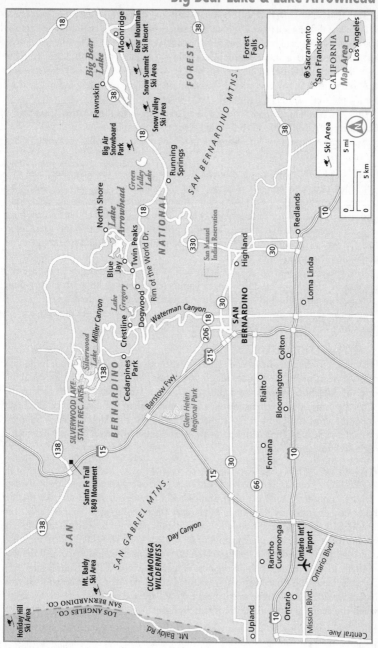

**VISITOR INFORMATION**    National ski tours, mountain-bike races, and one of Southern California's largest Oktoberfest gatherings are just some of the events held year-round—which may either entice or discourage you from visiting when they're on. Contact the **Big Bear Lake Resort Association,** 630 Bartlett Rd., Big Bear Lake Village (✆ **800/4BIG-BEAR** or 909/866-7000; www.bigbearinfo.com), for schedules and information. They also provide information on sightseeing and lodging and will send you a free visitors guide.

In Lake Arrowhead, contact the **Lake Arrowhead Communities Chamber of Commerce** (✆ **800/337-3716** for the Lodging Information Line, or 909/337-3715; www.lakearrowhead.net). The visitor center is located in the Lake Arrowhead Village lower shopping center.

**ORIENTATION**    The south shore of Big Bear Lake was the first resort area to be developed here and remains the most densely populated. Highway 18 passes first through the city of Big Bear Lake and its downtown village; then, as Big Bear Boulevard, it continues east to Big Bear City, which is more residential and suburban. Highway 38 traverses the north shore, home to pristine national forest and great hiking trails, as well as a couple of small marinas and a lakefront bed-and-breakfast inn (see the Windy Point Inn on p. 594).

Arrowhead's main town is Lake Arrowhead Village, located on the south shore at the end of Highway 173. The village's commercial center is home to factory-outlet stores, about 40 chain and specialty shops, and the Lake Arrowhead Resort (p. 595). Minutes away is the town of Blue Jay (along Hwy. 189), where the Blue Jay Ice Castle skating rink is located (see "Winter Fun" below).

## ENJOYING THE OUTDOORS

In addition to the activities described below, there's a great recreation spot for families near the heart of Big Bear Lake: **Magic Mountain,** on Highway 18/Big Bear Boulevard (✆ **909/866-4626;** www.bigbear.com), has a year-round bobsled-style Alpine Slide, a splashy double water slide open from mid-June to mid-September, and bunny slopes for snow tubing from November to Easter. The dry Alpine Slide is $4 a ride, the water slide is $1 (or $12 for a day pass), and snow play costs $20 per day including tube and rope tow.

### WATERSPORTS

**BOATING**    You can rent all kinds of boats—including speedboats, rowboats, paddleboats, pontoons, sailboats, and canoes—at a number of Big Bear Lake marinas. Rates vary only slightly from place to place: A 14-foot dinghy with an outboard runs around $15 per hour or $35 for a half-day; pontoon (patio) boats that can hold large groups range in size and price from $50 to $60 per hour or $140 to $150 for a half-day. **Pine Knot Landing** (✆ **909/866-2628;** www.pineknotlanding.com) is the most centrally located marina, behind the post office at the foot of Pine Knot Boulevard in Big Bear Lake. **Big Bear Marina,** Paine Road at Lakeview (✆ **909/866-3218;** www. bigbearmarina.com), is close to Big Bear Lake Village and provides take-along dinners when you rent a pontoon boat for a sunset cruise.

**FISHING**    Big Bear Lake brims with rainbow trout, bass, and catfish in spring and summer, the best fishing seasons. Pine Knot Landing, Gray's Landing, and Big Bear Marina (see "Boating" above) all rent fishing boats and have bait-and-tackle shops that sell licenses.

**JET-SKIING**    Personal Water Craft (PWCs) are available for rent at **Big Bear Marina** (see "Boating" above) and **Pleasure Point Landing,** 603 Landlock Landing Rd. (℃ **909/866-2455**), where you can rent a single-rider Sea-Doo for $35 an hour, or opt for a two-seat WaveRunner at $55 per hour. **North Shore Landing,** on Highway 38, 2 miles west of Fawnskin (℃ **909/878-4-FUN;** www.800bigbear.com), rents jet skis and two- and three-person WaveRunners at rates ranging from $55 to $65 per hour. Call ahead to reserve your craft and check age and deposit requirements.

**WATER-SKIING & WAKE BOARDING**    Big Bear Lake, Pine Knot Landing, North Shore Landing, and Big Bear Marina (see above) all offer water-ski and wakeboard lessons and speedboat rentals. Lake Arrowhead is home to the **McKenzie Water Ski School,** dockside in Lake Arrowhead Village (℃ **909/337-3814;** www.mckenzie skischool.com), famous for teaching Kirk Douglas, George Hamilton, and other Hollywood stars to ski. It's open from Memorial Day to the end of September and offers group lessons for $45 per hour, short pulls for $40, and boat charters (including instruction) for $155 an hour.

## OTHER WARM-WEATHER ACTIVITIES

**GOLF**    The **Bear Mountain Golf Course,** Goldmine Drive, Big Bear Lake (℃ **909/ 585-8002;** www.bigbearmountainresorts.com), is a 9-hole, par-35, links-style course that winds through a gently sloping meadow at the base of the Bear Mountain Ski Resort. The course is open daily April through November. Weekend greens fees are about $32 and $44 for 9 and 18 holes, respectively. Both riding carts and pull carts are available. Call ahead for tee times.

**HIKING**    Hikers love the **San Bernardino National Forest.** The gray squirrel is a popular native so you may see them scurrying around gathering acorns or material for their nests. You can sometimes spot deer, coyotes, and American bald eagles, which come here with their young in winter. The black-crowned Steller's jay and the talkative red, white, and black acorn woodpecker are the most common of the great variety of birds in this pine forest.

The best choice for a short mountain hike is the **Woodland Trail,** which begins near the ranger station. The best long hike is a section of the **Pacific Crest Trail,** which travels 39 miles through the mountains above Big Bear and Arrowhead lakes. The most convenient trail head is located at Cougar Crest, a half mile west of the Big Bear Ranger Station.

The best place to begin a hike in Lake Arrowhead is at the **Arrowhead Ranger Station** (℃ **909/337-2444**), in the town of Skyforest on Highway 18 a quarter mile east of the Lake Arrowhead turnoff (Hwy. 173). The staff will provide you with maps and information on the best area trails, which range from easy to difficult. The **Enchanted Loop Trail,** near the town of Blue Jay, is an easy half-hour hike. The **Heaps Peak Arboretum Trail** winds through a grove of redwoods; the trail head is on the north side of Highway 18, at an auxiliary ranger kiosk west of Running Springs.

The area is home to a **National Children's Forest,** a 20-acre area developed so that children, people in wheelchairs, and the visually impaired can enjoy nature. To get to the Children's Forest from Lake Arrowhead, take Highway 330 to Highway 18 east, past Deer Lick Station; when you reach a road marked IN96 (open only in summer), turn right and go 3 miles.

**HORSEBACK RIDING**    **Baldwin Lake Stables,** southeast of Big Bear City (℃ **909/ 585-6482;** www.baldwinlakestables.com), conducts hourly, lunch, and sunset rides along a wide variety of terrains and trails—all with spectacular vistas—including the Pacific Crest Trail, which includes expansive views of the Mojave Desert. It's open year-round.

**MOUNTAIN BIKING**    Big Bear Lake has become a mountain-biking center, with most of the action around the Snow Summit ski area (see "Winter Fun," below), where a $10 lift ticket will take you and your bike to a web of trails, fire roads, and meadows at about 8,000 feet. Call its **Summer Activities Hot Line** (① **909/866-4621**). The lake's north shore is also a popular destination; the forest-service ranger stations (see "Hiking," above) have maps to the historic Gold Rush–era Holcomb Valley and the 2-mile Alpine Pedal Path (an easy lakeside ride).

**Big Bear Bikes,** 41810 Big Bear Blvd. (① **909/866-6588**), rents quality mountain bikes for about $10 an hour or $50 a day, as does **Bear Valley Bikes,** 40298 Big Bear Blvd. (① **909/866-8000**). **Team Big Bear** is located at the base of Snow Summit (① **909/866-4565;** www.teambigbear.com); it rents bicycles and provides detailed maps and guides for all Big Bear–area trails.

At Lake Arrowhead, bikes are permitted on all hiking trails and back roads except the Pacific Crest Trail. See the local ranger station for an area map. Gear can be rented from the **Lake Arrowhead Resort** (① **909/336-1511**) or **Above & Beyond Sports,** 32877 Hwy. 18, Running Springs (① **909/867-5517**).

## WINTER FUN

**SKIING & SNOWBOARDING**    When the L.A. basin gets wintertime rain, skiers rejoice, for they know snow is falling up in the mountains. The last few seasons have seen abundant natural snowfall at Big Bear, augmented by snowmaking equipment. While the slopes can't compare with those in Utah or Colorado, they do offer diversity, difficulty, and convenience.

**Snow Summit** at Big Bear Lake (① **909/866-5766;** www.bigbearmountainresorts. com) is the skiers' choice, especially because it installed its second high-speed quad express from the 7,000-foot base to the 8,200-foot summit. There are also green (easy) runs, even from the summit, so beginners can also enjoy the Summit Haus lodge and breathtaking lake views from the top. Advanced risk-takers will appreciate three double black-diamond runs. The resort offers midweek, beginner, half-day, night, and family specials, as well as ski and snowboard instruction. Other helpful Snow Summit phone numbers include advance lift-ticket sales (① **909/866-5841**), and a snow report (① **800/BEAR-MTN**).

The **Bear Mountain Resort** at Big Bear Lake (① **909/866-5766;** www.bigbear mountainresorts.com) has the largest beginner area, but experts flock to the double-black-diamond Geronimo run from the 8,805-foot Bear Peak. Natural-terrain skiers and snowboarders will enjoy legal access to off-trail canyons, but the limited beginner slopes and kids' areas get pretty crowded in season. One of two high-speed quad expresses rises from the 7,140-foot base to 8,440-foot Goldmine Mountain; most runs from here are intermediate. Bear Mountain has a ski-and-snowboard school, abundant dining facilities, and a well-stocked ski shop.

The **Snow Valley Ski Resort** in Arrowbear, midway between Arrowhead and Big Bear (① **909/867-2751;** www.snow-valley.com), has improved its snowmaking and facilities to be competitive with the other two major ski areas, and is the primary choice of skiers staying at Arrowhead. From a base elevation of 6,800 feet, Snow Valley's 13 chairlifts (including five triples) can take you from the beginner runs all the way up to black-diamond challenges at the 7,898-foot peak. Lift tickets cost $44 for adults; children's programs, night skiing, and lesson packages are available.

**ICE-SKATING**   The **Blue Jay Ice Castle,** at North Bay Road and Highway 189 (© 909/337-0802; www.icecastle.us), near Lake Arrowhead Village, is a training site for world champion Michelle Kwan and boasts Olympic gold medalist Robin Cousins on its staff. Several public sessions each day—as well as hockey, broomball, group lessons, and private parties—give nonpros a chance to enjoy this impeccably groomed "outdoor" rink (it's open on three sides to the scenery and fresh air).

## ORGANIZED TOURS

**LAKE TOURS**   The *Big Bear Queen* (© 909/866-3218; www.bigbearmarina.com), a midget Mississippi-style paddle-wheeler, cruises Big Bear Lake on 90-minute tours daily from late April to the end of November. The boat departs from Big Bear Marina (at the end of Paine Ave.). Tours are $11 for adults, $10 for seniors 65 and older and children ages 3 to 12, and free for kids under 3. Call for reservations and information on the special Sunday brunch, champagne sunset, and dinner cruises.

Fifty-minute tours of Lake Arrowhead are offered year-round on the *Arrowhead Queen* (© 909/336-6992), a sister ship that departs hourly each day between 10am and 6pm from Lake Arrowhead Village. Tours are $12 for adults, $10 for seniors, $7.50 for children 2 to 12, and free for kids under 2. It's about the only way to really see this alpine jewel, unless you know a resident with a boat.

## WHERE TO STAY
### BIG BEAR LAKE

Vacation rentals are plentiful in the area, from cabins to condos to private homes. Some can accommodate up to 20 people and can be rented on a weekly or monthly basis. For a wide range of rental properties, all pictured in detail online, contact **Big Bear Mountain Rentals** (© 888/306-9618 or 909/878-2233; www.bigbearmountainrentals.com). The **Village Reservation Service** (© 800/693-0018 or 909/866-9689; www.village reservations.net) can arrange for everything from condos to lakefront homes, or call the **Big Bear Lake Resort Association** (© 909/866-7000; www.bigbear.com) for referrals on all types of lodgings.

Besides the places below, other choices I recommend are **Apples Bed & Breakfast Inn,** 42430 Moonridge Rd. (© 909/866-0903; www.applesbedandbreakfast.com), a crabapple-red New England–style clapboard that blends hotel-like professionalism with B&B amenities (and lots of frilly touches); and **Gold Mountain Manor,** 1117 Anita Ave. (© 800/509-2604 or 909/585-6997; www.goldmountainmanor.com), a woodsy 1920s lodge that's now an ultracozy (and affordable) B&B.

**Grey Squirrel Resort** *Kids*   This is the most attractive of the many cabin-cluster-type motels near the city of Big Bear Lake, offering a wide range of rustic cabins, most with fireplace and kitchen. They're adequately, if not attractively, furnished—the appeal is the flexibility and privacy afforded large or long-term parties. Facilities include a heated pool that's enclosed in winter, a fire pit and barbecues, volleyball and basketball courts, and completely equipped kitchens.

39372 Big Bear Blvd., Big Bear Lake, CA 92315. © 800/381-5569 or 909/866-4335. Fax 909/866-6271. www. greysquirrel.com. 18 cabins. $85–$115 1-bedroom cabin; $115–$145 2-bedroom cabin; $155–$275 3-bedroom cabin. Value rates available; higher rates on holidays. AE, DISC, MC, V. Pets accepted w/$10-per-day fee. **Amenities:** Heated indoor/outdoor pool; Jacuzzi; coin-op laundry. *In room:* TV/VCR, kitchen in some units.

**Best Western Big Bear Chateau** *(Kids)*    This European-flavored property is one of only two traditional full-service hotels in Big Bear. Its location—just off Big Bear Boulevard at the base of the road to Bear Mountain—makes the Chateau a popular choice for skiers and families (kids 17 and under stay free in their parent's room, and there are also children's activities). The rooms are modern but more charming than your average Best Western, with tapestries, brass beds, antique furniture, gas fireplaces, and marble bathrooms with heated towel racks and many with whirlpool tubs. The compound is surrounded by tall forest. The Le Bistro restaurant (which provides room service) is advertised as "casually elegant," which means you can dine on upscale California cuisine in après-ski duds.

42200 Moonridge Rd. (P.O. Box 1814), Big Bear Lake, CA 92315. ⓒ **800/232-7466** or 909/866-6666. Fax 909/866-8988. www.bestwestern.com. 80 units. Winter $99–$180 double; summer $89–$160 double. Children 17 and under stay free in parent's room. Extra person $10. Winter-ski and summer-fun packages available. AE, DISC, MC, V. **Amenities:** Restaurant; lounge; heated outdoor pool; Jacuzzi; children's activities; limited room service. *In room:* A/C, TV, dataport, coffeemaker, hair dryer, iron.

**Knickerbocker Mansion Country Inn** *(★)*    Innkeepers Thomas Bicanic and Stan Miller faced quite a task reviving this landmark log house; when they moved in, it was empty of all furnishings and suffered from years of neglect. But Knickerbocker Mansion has risen to become the most charming and sophisticated inn on the lake's south side; chef Bicanic, who honed his craft in L.A.'s culinary temple Patina restaurant, even has plans to begin serving intimate gourmet dinners. The pair scoured antiques stores in Big Bear and Los Angeles for vintage furnishings, creating a warm and relaxing ambience in the grand-yet-quirky, house of legendary local character Bill Knickerbocker, who assembled it by hand almost 90 years ago. Today's guest rooms are a cedar-paneled dream, with luxury bed linens, cozy bathrobes, modern marble bathrooms with deluxe Australian showerheads, and refreshing mountain views. After Bicanic's memorable breakfast, you can spend the day relaxing on veranda rockers or garden hammocks; Big Bear's village is also an easy walk away.

869 Knickerbocker Rd. (P.O. Box 1907), Big Bear Lake, CA 92315. ⓒ **877/423-1180** or 909/878-9190. Fax 909/878-4248. www.knickerbockermansion.com. 11 units. $110–$155 double; $200–$225 suite. Rates include full gourmet breakfast and all-day refreshments and snacks. AE, DISC, MC, V. *In room:* TV/VCR, dataport, hair dryer, iron.

**Windy Point Inn** *(★)*    A contemporary architectural showpiece on the scenic north shore, the Windy Point is the only shorefront B&B in Big Bear; ergo, all guest rooms have a view of the lake. Hosts Val and Kent Kessler's attention to detail is impeccable—if you're tired of knotty pine and Victorian frills, here's a grown-up place for you, with plenty of romance and all the pampering you can stand. Every room has a wood-burning fireplace, feather bed, private deck, and DVD player (borrow DVDs from the inn's plentiful collection); some also feature whirlpool tubs and luxurious state-of-the-art bathrooms. The welcoming great room features a casual sunken fireplace nook with floor-to-ceiling windows overlooking the lake, a telescope for stargazing, a baby grand, and up-to-date menus for every local eatery. You might not want to leave the cocoon of your room after Kent's custom gourmet breakfast, but if you do, you'll find a wintertime bald-eagle habitat just up the road, and the city of Big Bear Lake is only a 10-minute drive around the lake.

39015 N. Shore Dr., Fawnskin, CA 92333. ⓒ **909/866-2746.** Fax 909/866-1593. www.windypointinn.com. 5 units. $155–$265 double. Rates include welcome cookies, lavish full breakfast, and afternoon hors d'oeuvres. Midweek discounts available. AE, DISC, MC, V. *In room:* TV/DVD, fridge, coffeemaker, hair dryer, CD player in some units, no phone.

## LAKE ARROWHEAD

There are far more private homes than tourist accommodations in Arrowhead, but rental properties abound, from cozy cottages to mansions; many can be economical for families or other groups. Two of the largest agencies are **Arrowhead Cabin Rentals** (© **800/244-5138** or 909/337-2403; www.arrowheadrent.com) and **Arrowhead Mountain Resorts Rentals** (© **800/743-0865** or 909/337-4413; www.lakearrowheadrentals.com). Overnight guests in rentals enjoy some resident lake privileges—ask when you reserve.

Two other options are **Chateau du Lac,** 911 Hospital Rd. (© **909/337-6488;** www.chateau-du-lac.com), an elegant and contemporary five-room B&B with stunning views of the lake; and the **Saddleback Inn,** 300 S. Hwy. 173 (© **800/858-3334** or 909/336-3571; www.saddlebackinn.com), an inn and restaurant that still boasts historic charm while offering up-to-date amenities, all at a prime location in the center of the village.

### Bracken Fern Manor *Finds*

This "House of Now Fine Repute" is equally proud of its registered historical marker *and* its checkered past. The present owners work hard at evoking the inn's 1930s heyday: They've preserved the downstairs public rooms, along with many well-maintained antiques, and named each guest room for one of the "girls." There are many quiet corners for relaxing, including a game room, hidden library, whirlpool gazebo, and wood-lined sauna. Rooms are decorated in a fresh country style and have private bathrooms, a feature not originally included in the house. A detached cottage sleeps four and rents for $380 for 2 nights.

815 Arrowhead Villas Rd. (P.O. Box 1006), Lake Arrowhead, CA 92352. © 888/244-5612 or 909/337-8557. Fax 909/337-3323. www.brackenfernmanor.com. 10 units. $80–$185 double. Rates include full breakfast. MC, V. Located half mile north of Hwy. 18. **Amenities:** Jacuzzi; sauna. *In room:* No phone.

### Lake Arrowhead Resort *Kids*

This sprawling resort has been upgraded somewhat since it was part of the Hilton chain, but location is still its most outstanding feature, coupled with unparalleled (for the mountains) service and facilities. Situated on the lakeshore adjacent to Lake Arrowhead Village, the hotel has its own beach, plus docks that are ideal for fishing. The rooms are fitted with good-quality, bulk-purchased contemporary furnishings, and most have balconies, king-size beds, and fireplaces. The suites, some in private cottages, are equipped with full kitchens and whirlpool tubs.

The hotel caters primarily to groups, and sports a businesslike ambience during the week. A full program of supervised children's activities, ranging from nature hikes to T-shirt painting, is offered on weekends year-round.

27984 Hwy. 189, Lake Arrowhead, CA 92352. © 800/800-6792 or 909/336-1511. Fax 909/336-1378. www.lakearrowheadresort.com. 177 units. $109–$229 double; $325–$475 suite. Inquire about auto-club discounts. AE, DC, DISC, MC, V. **Amenities:** 2 restaurants; outdoor pool (summer only); 2 lit rooftop tennis courts; health club; Jacuzzi; children's programs; video arcade; business center; salon; babysitting; laundry service; dry cleaning. *In room:* A/C, TV w/pay movies, dataport, minibar, coffeemaker, hair dryer.

### Pine Rose Cabins *Kids*

Pine Rose Cabins is a good choice for families. On 5 forested acres about 3 miles from the lake, the wonderful free-standing cabins offer lots of privacy. Innkeeper Tricia Dufour has 15 cabins, ranging in size from romantic studios to a large five-bedroom lodge, each decorated in a different theme: The Indian cabin has a tepeelike bed; the bed in Wild Bill's cabin is covered like a wagon. Multibedroom units have fully stocked kitchens and separate living areas; for all cottages, daily maid service is available at an additional charge. There are plenty of fun and games on the premises, including swing sets, croquet, tetherball, and Ping-Pong.

25994 Hwy. 189 (P.O. Box 31), Twin Peaks, CA 92391. © **800/429-PINE** or 909/337-2341. Fax 909/337-0258. www. lakearrowheadcabins.com. 17 units. $59–$179 studio for 2; $69–$179 1-, 2-, and 3-bedroom cabins for up to 10 people; $395–$450 large-group lodges. Ski packages available. AE, DISC, MC, V. Pets accepted w/$10 fee per night and $100 refundable deposit. **Amenities:** Outdoor heated pool; Jacuzzi. *In room:* TV/VCR, kitchen, coffeemaker.

# WHERE TO DINE
## BIG BEAR LAKE
A reliable option for all-day dining is **Stillwell's,** 40650 Village Dr. (© **909/866-3121,** ext. 3). You might otherwise pass right by, because Stillwell's is the dining room for convention-friendly Northwoods Resort at the edge of the village; despite the unmistakable hotel feel, though, its something-for-everyone American/Continental menu is surprisingly good, with noted attention to detail and fair prices (rare in this mountain resort town).

**The Captain's Anchorage** STEAK/SEAFOOD    Historic and rustic, this knotty-pine restaurant has been serving fine steaks, prime rib, seafood, and lobster since 1947. Inside, the dark, nautical decor and fire-warmed bar are just right on blustery winter nights. It's got one of those mile-long soup-and-salad bars, plus some great early-bird and weeknight specials.

Moonridge Way at Big Bear Blvd., Big Bear Lake. © **909/866-3997.** Reservations recommended. Full dinners $15–$29. AE, MC, V. Sun–Thurs 4:30–9pm; Fri–Sat 4:30–10pm.

**Madlon's** AMERICAN/CONTINENTAL    One of the few non-retro-fare dining rooms at the mountain resorts, Madlon's brings a bit of European flair to this fairytale cottage. A variety of creative croissant sandwiches at lunch are complemented by dinner selections like black-pepper filet mignon with mushroom-and-brandy sauce, and lemon-pepper-marinated chicken breast over pasta, all of which are prepared with a sophisticated touch.

829 W. Big Bear Blvd., Big Bear City. © **909/585-3762.** Reservations recommended. Main courses $12–$25. DC, DISC, MC, V. Sat–Sun 8am–1:30pm; Tues–Fri 11am–1:30pm; Tues–Sun 5–9pm.

**Old Country Inn** DINER/GERMAN    The Old Country Inn has long been a favorite for hearty preski breakfasts and stick-to-your-ribs dinners. The restaurant is casual and welcoming, and the adjacent cocktail lounge is raucous on weekends. At breakfast, enjoy German apple pancakes or colossal omelets. Lunch includes salads, sandwiches, and burgers. At lunch or dinner, feast on Wiener schnitzel, sauerbraten, and other gravy-topped German standards, as well as grilled steaks and chicken.

41126 Big Bear Blvd., Big Bear Lake. © **909/866-5600.** Main courses $6–$28. AE, DC, DISC, MC, V. Sun–Thurs 8am–9pm; Fri–Sat 8am–10pm.

## LAKE ARROWHEAD
For an affluent residential community, there are surprisingly few dining options around Lake Arrowhead. Not surprisingly, what's there tends to run toward pricey elegance—relative to a rustic mountain resort, that is. Although the town has both a California/Continental restaurant and a casual family place in the Lake Arrowhead Resort (p. 595), you might want to venture out to some of the local haunts. These include the **Chef's Inn & Tavern,** 29020 Oak Terrace, Cedar Glen (© **909/336-4488**), a moderate to expensive Continental restaurant in a former bordello; the **Antler's Inn,** 26125 Hwy. 189, Twin Peaks (© **909/337-4020**), serving prime rib, seafood, and buffalo in a log lodge; the **Royal Oak,** 27187 Hwy. 189, Blue Jay Village (© **909/337-6018**), an expensive American/Continental steakhouse with a pub; and **Belgian Waffle Works,**

dockside at Lake Arrowhead Village (© **909/337-5222**), a bargain coffee shop with Victorian decor, known for crispy waffles with tasty toppings.

## 3 The Disneyland Resort ✶✶✶

30 miles SE of downtown L.A.

Florida, Tokyo, France, and Hong Kong have newer and larger Disneyland parks, but the original, and the inspiration for all of them, still opens its gates in Anaheim, California, every day, proudly proclaiming itself "The Happiest Place on Earth." Smaller than Walt Disney World, Disneyland—which opened in 1955 on a 107-acre tract surrounded almost exclusively by orange groves—has always capitalized on being the world's first family-oriented mega theme park. Nostalgia is a big part of the original park's appeal, and despite many advancements, changes, and expansions over the years, Disneyland remains true to the vision of founder Walt Disney.

While the Disneyland Resort is the undisputed frontrunner in family-friendly vacation destinations in Southern California, I've also included another appealing amusement park option that's a short drive away from Disneyland: Knott's Berry Farm. Hosting a far better selection of high-speed roller coasters, it's hugely popular with teens who crave thrill rides.

### ESSENTIALS

**GETTING THERE**   To reach the Disneyland Resort by car from LAX, take I-105 east to I-605 north, then I-5 south. From Los Angeles, take I-5 south until you see signs for Disneyland. Dedicated off-ramps from I-5 lead to the attraction's parking lots and surrounding streets (follow signs leading to THEME PARKS). The drive from LAX takes approximately 40 minutes with no traffic (right).

If Anaheim is your first—or only—destination and you want to avoid L.A. altogether, consider flying directly into **John Wayne Airport** in Santa Ana (© **949/252-5200;** www.ocair.com), Orange County's largest airport. It's about 15 miles from Disneyland at the intersection of I-405 and California 55. Check to see if your hotel has a free shuttle to and from either airport (some will pick you up at LAX), or call one of the following commercial shuttle services (fares are generally $12–$14 one-way from John Wayne): **Xpress** (© **800/427-7483;** www.xpressshuttle.com), **Prime Time** (© **800/ 733-8267;** primetimeshuttle.com), or **SuperShuttle** (© **800/258-3826;** www.super shuttle.com). Car-rental agencies located at the John Wayne Airport include **Budget** (© **800/527-0700;** www.budget.com) and **Hertz** (© **800/654-3131;** www.hertz.com). To reach Anaheim from the airport, take California 55 north to I-5 north, and then take the Harbor Boulevard exit and follow signs leading to THEME PARKS. You can also catch a ride with **American Taxi** (© **888/482-9466**), whose cabs queue up at the Ground Transportation Center on the lower level; reservations are not necessary. Expect the fare to Disneyland to cost about $30.

**VISITOR INFORMATION**   For information on the **Disneyland Resort,** including show schedules and ride closures that apply to the specific day(s) of your visit, call © **714/781-4565** for automated information or © **714/781-7290** to speak to Guest Relations (but expect a long wait). Better yet, log onto the Disneyland Resort's official website at **www.disneyland.com.**

For general information on the entire Anaheim region, contact the **Anaheim/ Orange County Visitor and Convention Bureau,** 800 W. Katella Ave., inside the Anaheim Convention Center (© **714/765-8888;** www.anaheimoc.org). It's open

## CityPass Savings

If your vacation includes a visit to San Diego, look into purchasing a **Southern California CityPass** (www.citypass.com), which can be added to any Walt Disney Travel Company vacation package. It includes a 3-Day Park Hopper ticket to Disneyland and Disney's California Adventure, plus a 1-Day admission to Knotts Berry Farm, SeaWorld Adventure Park, and the San Diego Zoo. It costs $172 for adults and $129 for children, and if you visit all these attractions you'll save more than $70.

Monday to Friday from 8:30am to 5:30pm. Staffers can fill you in on area activities and shopping, as well as send you their *Official Visitors Guide* and the AdventureCard, which offers discounts at dozens of local attractions, hotels, restaurants, and shops.

You can find out everything you need to know about the Disneyland Resort online, beginning with the official site, **www.disneyland.com**, which contains the latest information on park improvements and additions, plus special offers (sometimes on airfare or reduced admission) and an interactive trip planner that lets you build a custom Disney vacation package. If you prefer human interaction, contact a Walt Disney Travel Company specialist at © 877/700-DISNEY and ask about money-saving package deals.

There are numerous unofficial Disney websites as well, which provide very detailed—and often judgmental—information about the Disneyland Resort. The best we've found are: **IntercotWest.com**, an active and friendly website filled with detailed information on every corner of the Disneyland Resort; **LaughingPlace.com** and **MouseInfo.com**, which both feature daily updated headlines and columns on all things Disney; **Mouseplanet.com**, a comprehensive Disneyland information resource that offers features and reviews by guest writers; and **MouseSavers.com**, which offers in-depth information on Disney theme parks and helps users save money on lodging and admissions.

**ADMISSION, HOURS & INFORMATION**   Admission to *either* Disneyland or Disney's California Adventure, including unlimited rides and all festivities and entertainment, is $53 for adults and children over 10, $43 for children 3 to 9, and free for children under 3. Parking is $8. A 1-Day Park Hopper ticket is $73 for adults and $63 for children. A 2-day Park Hopper ticket, which allows you to go back and forth as much as you'd like each day, is $105 for adults and children over 9, and $85 for children 3 to 9. Other multiday, multipark combination passes are available as well. In addition, many area accommodations offer lodging packages that include admission for 1 or more days. Be sure to check the Disney website, www.disneyland.com, for seasonal ticket specials.

If you plan on arriving during a busy time (when the gates open in the morning, or between 11am and 2pm), purchase your tickets in advance and get a jump on the crowds at the ticket counters. Advance tickets may be purchased through Disneyland's website (www.disneyland.com), at Disney stores in the United States, by calling the ticket mail-order line (© **714/781-4043**), at any nearby Disneyland Resort Good Neighbor Hotel, or as part of your travel package.

Disneyland and Disney's California Adventure are open every day of the year, but operating hours vary, so be sure to call for information that applies to the specific

---

**Value    The Art of the (Package) Deal**

If you intend to spend 2 or more nights in Disney territory, it pays to investigate packaged vacation options. Log onto www.disneyland.com and click "Parks & Hotels" for standard package offers, a virtual tour of Disney hotel properties, and online price quotes for customized, date-specific packages, including airline tickets. The packages have abundant flexibility, and rates are highly competitive, considering each package includes multiday and multipark admission, souvenirs, preferred seating at Disney shows, Disney pocket guides, and coupon books. If you're staying in a non-Disney hotel (even in L.A. or San Diego), ask if they sell Disneyland admission packages. To ensure you're getting the best deal, call the official Disney travel agency, **Walt Disney Travel Co.** (© 877/700-DISNEY or 714/520-5050) and compare their packages with others you've found.

---

day(s) of your visit (© **714/781-7290**). The same information, including ride closures and show schedules, can also be found online at **www.disneyland.com**. Generally speaking, the parks are open from 9 or 10am to 6 or 7pm on weekdays, fall to spring; and from 8 or 9am to midnight or 1am on weekends, holidays, and during winter, spring, or summer vacation periods. *Tip:* The park's operating hours can give you some idea of what kinds of crowds Disney planners are expecting: The later the parks close, the more people will be there.

**WHEN TO GO**    The Disneyland Resort is busiest in summer (between Memorial Day and Labor Day), on holidays (Thanksgiving week, Christmas week, President's Day weekend, Easter week, and Japan's Golden Week in early May), plus weekends year-round. All other periods are considered off season. Peak hours are from noon to 5pm; visit the most popular rides before and after these hours, and you'll cut your waiting times substantially. If you plan to arrive during a busy time, buy your tickets in advance and get a jump on the crowds at the ticket counters. Advance tickets may be purchased through Disneyland's website (www.disneyland.com), at Disney stores in the United States, or by calling the ticket mail-order line (© **714/781-4043**).

Attendance falls dramatically during the winter, so the park offers discounted (about 25% off) admission to Southern California residents, who may buy up to five tickets per zip code verification. If you'll be visiting the park with someone who lives here, be sure to take advantage of this Resident Salutes promotion.

Another secret time-saving tip is to enter Disneyland from the turnstile at the Monorail Station in Downtown Disney. The line is usually shorter and the Monorail will take you straight into Tomorrowland (but it doesn't stop in Disney's California Adventure). Once in the park, many visitors tackle Disneyland (or Disney's California Adventure) systematically, beginning at the entrance and working their way clockwise around the park. My advice: Arrive early and run to the most popular rides—the Indiana Jones Adventure, Star Tours, Big Thunder Mountain Railroad, Splash Mountain, the Haunted Mansion, and Pirates of the Caribbean rides in Disneyland; and Twilight Zone Tower of Terror, Soarin' Over California, California Screamin', Grizzly

River Run, and *It's Tough to Be a Bug* rides in Disney's California Adventure. Waits for these rides can last an hour or more in the middle of the day.

This time-honored plan of attack may eventually become obsolete, thanks to Disney's complimentary **FASTPASS** system. Here's how it works: Say you want to ride Space Mountain, but the line is long—*so* long the current wait sign indicates a 75-minute standby. Instead, you can head to the automated FASTPASS ticket dispenser, where you pop in your park ticket to receive a free voucher listing a computer-assigned boarding time later that day. When you return at the assigned time, you enter through the FASTPASS gate and only have to wait about 10 minutes (to the envy of everyone in the slowpoke line). The hottest features at Disney's California Adventure had FASTPASS built in from the start; for a complete list for each park, check your official map/guide when you enter and look for the red FP symbol. *Note:* You can obtain a FASTPASS for only one attraction at a time. Also, the FASTPASS system doesn't eliminate the need to arrive at the theme park early because there's only a limited supply of FASTPASSes available for each attraction on a given day. So, if you don't show up until the middle of the afternoon, you might find that all the FASTPASSes have been distributed to other guests.

### DISNEYLAND ★★★

Disneyland is divided into eight subareas or "lands" arranged around a central hub, each of which has a number of rides and attractions that are, more or less, related to that land's theme. Be sure to pick up a free park map on the way in or you'll probably get lost almost immediately.

**MAIN STREET U.S.A.**   At the park's entrance, Main Street U.S.A. is an idealized version of a turn-of-the-20th-century American small-town street inspired by Marceline, Missouri (Walt Disney's childhood home), and built on a ⅞ scale. Many visitors are surprised to discover that all the buildings are real, not elaborate props. Attention to detail here is exceptional—interiors, furnishings, and fixtures conform to the period. As with any real Main Street, the Disney version is essentially a collection of shops and eating places, with a city hall, a fire station, and an old-time silent cinema. Live performances include piano playing at the Carnation ice-cream parlor and the Dapper Dan's barbershop quartet along the street. A mixed-media attraction combines a presentation on the life of Walt Disney *(The Walt Disney Story)* with a patriotic remembrance of Abraham Lincoln. Horse-drawn trolleys, fire engines, and horseless carriages give rides along Main Street and transport visitors to the central hub (properly known as the Central Plaza).

Because there are no major rides, it's best to tour Main Street during the middle of the afternoon, when lines for rides are longest, and in the evening, when walkways can be packed with visitors viewing parades and shows. Stop at the information booth to the left of the Main Entrance for a schedule of the day's Main Street events.

**ADVENTURELAND**   Inspired by the most exotic regions of Asia, Africa, India, and the South Pacific, Adventureland is home to several popular rides. Here's where you can cavort inside **Tarzan's Treehouse,** a climb-around attraction based on the animated film. Its African-themed neighbor is the **Jungle Cruise,** where passengers board a large authentic-looking Mississippi River paddleboat and float along an Amazon-like river; a spear's throw away is the **Enchanted Tiki Room,** one of the most sedate attractions in Adventureland. Inside, you can sit down and watch a 20-minute musical comedy featuring electronically animated tropical birds, flowers, and "Tiki gods."

The **Indiana Jones Adventure** is Adventureland's star ride. Based on the Steven Spielberg films, this ride takes adventurers into the Temple of the Forbidden Eye, in joltingly realistic all-terrain vehicles. Riders follow Indy and experience the perils of bubbling lava pits, whizzing arrows, fire-breathing serpents, collapsing bridges, and the familiar cinematic tumbling boulder (an effect that's very realistic in the front seats).

**NEW ORLEANS SQUARE**   A large, grassy green dotted with gas lamps, New Orleans Square is home to the **Haunted Mansion,** where the dated effects are more funny than scary. Even more fanciful is **Pirates of the Caribbean,** one of Disneyland's most popular rides. Visitors float on boats through mock underground caves, entering an enchanting world of swashbuckling, rum-running, and buried treasure. Even in the middle of the afternoon you can dine by moonlight and to the sound of crickets in the **Blue Bayou** restaurant, in the middle of the ride itself.

**CRITTER COUNTRY**   An ode to the backwoods, Critter Country is a sort of Frontierland without those pesky settlers. Older kids and grown-ups head straight for **Splash Mountain,** one of the largest water flume rides in the world. Loosely based on the Disney movie *Song of the South,* the ride is lined with about 100 characters that won't stop singing "Zip-A-Dee-Doo-Dah." Be prepared to get wet, especially if someone sizable is in the front seat of your log-shape boat. **The Many Adventures of Winnie the Pooh** is a new children's attraction based on Winnie the Pooh and his friends from the Hundred-Acre Wood—Tigger, Eeyore, Piglet, et al. The attraction is of the kindler, gentler sort, where you board "hunny bee-hives" and take a slow-moving journey through the Hundred-Acre Wood on an endless pursuit of "hunny." The high-tech gadgetry and illusions are spellbinding for kids and mildly entertaining for adults. (***Tip:*** It's a very popular attraction, so be sure to arrive early or make use of FASTPASS.) While it may not be the fastest ride in the park, **Davy Crockett's Explorer Canoes** allows folks to row around Tom Sawyer Island. It's the only ride where you actively control your boat (no underwater rails!). Hop into replica canoes, grab a paddle, and away you go.

**FRONTIERLAND**   Inspired by 19th-century America, Frontierland features a raft to **Tom Sawyer's Island,** a do-it-yourself play area with balancing rocks, caves, and a rope bridge. You'll also find the **Big Thunder Mountain Railroad,** a runaway roller coaster that races through a deserted 1870s gold mine. Children will dig the petting zoo, and there's an Abe Lincoln–style log cabin; both are great for exploring with the little ones. This is also where you board one of two large-capacity riverboats—*Mark Twain* and the *Sailing Ship Columbia*—that navigate the waters around Tom Sawyer Island and Fort Wilderness. A beautiful craft, the *Mark Twain* provides a lofty perch from which to see Frontierland and New Orleans Square. The *Sailing Ship Columbia,* however, has far more historic and aesthetic appeal. As with the other river craft, the riverboats suspend operations at dusk.

When it's showing (it's a seasonal presentation), head to Frontierland's **Rivers of America** after dark to see the *FANTASMIC!* show. It mixes magic, music, 50 live performers, floats, and sensational special effects. Just as he did in *The Sorcerer's Apprentice,* Mickey Mouse battles evil and conjures good, using his magical powers to create giant water fountains, enormous flowers, and fantasy creatures. There's plenty of pyrotechnics, lasers, and fog, as well as a 45-foot-tall dragon that breathes fire and sets the water of the Rivers of America aflame.

**MICKEY'S TOONTOWN**   This is a colorful, whimsical world inspired by the "Roger Rabbit" films—a wacky, gag-filled land populated by 'toons. It even looks like a cartoon come to life, a trippy, smile-inducing world without a straight line or right angle in sight. In addition to serving as a place where guests can be certain of finding Disney characters at any time during the day, Mickey's Toontown also serves as an elaborate interactive playground where it's okay for the kids to run, climb, and let off steam. There are several rides and play areas, including **Roger Rabbit's CarToonSpin, Donald's Boat, Chip 'n' Dale's Treehouse, Gadget's Go Coaster, Goofy's Bounce House,** and **Mickey's House & Minnie's House.** *Tip:* Because of its popularity with families, Toontown is most crowded during the day but often deserted after dinnertime.

**FANTASYLAND** With a storybook theme, this is the catchall "land" for stuff that doesn't quite fit anywhere else. Most of the rides are geared to the under-6 set, including the **King Arthur Carrousel, Mad Tea Party, Dumbo the Flying Elephant ride,** and the **Casey Jr. Circus Train.** Some, like **Mr. Toad's Wild Ride** and **Peter Pan's Flight,** appeal to grownups as well, and are the original attractions from opening day in 1955. You'll also find **Alice in Wonderland, Snow White's Scary Adventures, Pinocchio's Daring Journey,** and more.

The most lauded attraction is **it's a small world,** a slow-moving indoor river ride through a saccharine nightmare of all the world's children singing the song everybody loves to hate. (Perhaps the ride would be more entertaining if each person got four softballs on the way in?) For a different kind of thrill, try the **Matterhorn Bobsleds,** a zippy roller coaster through chilled caverns and drifting fog banks. It's one of the park's most popular rides and the world's first steel tubular track roller coaster.

**TOMORROWLAND** Conceived as an optimistic look at the future, Tomorrowland employs an angular, metallic look popularized by futurists like Jules Verne. Longtime Tomorrowland favorites include the newly revamped **Space Mountain** (a pitch-black indoor roller coaster that assaults your equilibrium and ears), and **Star Tours,** the original Disney–George Lucas joint venture. It's a 40-passenger Star-Speeder that encounters a space-load of misadventures on the way to the Moon of Endor, achieved with wired seats and video effects—not for the queasy.

Other Tomorrowland attractions include: the new **Buzz Lightyear Astro Blasters,** where guests pilot their own Star Cruiser through a comical interactive space mission to conquer the Evil Emperor Zurg; *Honey, I Shrunk the Audience,* an interactive 3-D movie based on the popular movie series featuring Rick Moranis in the role of Wayne Szalinski; the **Disneyland Monorail,** a "futuristic" elevated monorail that takes you to Downtown Disney and back again (and offers the only practical opportunity for escaping the park during the crowded lunch period and early afternoon); and **Innoventions,** a huge, busy collection of industry-sponsored hands-on exhibits. Exhibits, many of which change each year, demonstrate such products as virtual reality games, high-definition TV, voice-activated appliances, and various CD-ROM applications, among others.

## DISNEY'S CALIFORNIA ADVENTURE 🎡🎡

With a grand entrance designed to resemble one of those "Wish you were here" scenic postcards, the 55-acre Disney's California Adventure starts out with a bang. You walk beneath the scale model of the Golden Gate Bridge (keep watching—the monorail will pass overhead) into **Sunshine Plaza,** which is anchored by a perpetual wave fountain and an enormous gold titanium "sun" that shines all day (it's illuminated by six computerized heliostats that follow the real sun's path). From this point, visitors can head into four themed "districts," each containing rides, interactive attractions, live-action shows, and plenty of dining, snacking, and shopping opportunities.

**THE GOLDEN STATE**    This multidimensional area represents California's history, heritage, and physical attributes. Sound boring? Actually, the park's splashiest attractions are here. **Condor Flats** is a tribute to daring aviators; inside a weathered corrugated test-pilots' hangar is **Soarin' Over California,** the simulated hang-glider ride that immediately rose to the top on everyone's "ride first" list (it's equipped with FASTPASS, and I highly recommend using it). It uses cutting-edge technology to combine elevated seats with a spectacular IMAX-style surround-movie—riders literally "soar" over California's scenic lands, feeling the Malibu ocean breeze and smelling the Central Valley orange groves and Yosemite pines.

Nearby, California Adventure's iconic Grizzly Peak towers over the **Grizzly River Run,** a splashy gold-country ride through caverns, mine shafts, and water slides; it culminates with a wet plunge into a spouting geyser. Kids can cavort nearby on the **Redwood Creek Challenge Trail,** a forest playground with smoke-jumper cable slides, net climbing, and swaying bridges.

**Pacific Wharf** was inspired by Monterey's Cannery Row and features mouthwatering demonstration attractions by **Boudin Sourdough Bakery, Mission Tortillas,** and **Lucky Fortune Cookies.** If you get hungry, each has a food counter where you can enjoy soup in a sourdough bowl; tacos, burritos, and enchiladas; and teriyaki bowls, egg rolls, and wonton soup.

**PARADISE PIER**    Journey back to the glory days of California's beachfront amusement piers—remember Santa Monica, Santa Cruz, and Belmont Park?—on this fantasy boardwalk. Highlights include **California Screamin',** a classic roller coaster that replicates the whitewashed wooden white-knucklers of the past—but with state-of-the-art steel construction and a smooth, computerized ride that catapults you from 0 to 55mph in less than 5 seconds, then take a loop-de-loop through a silhouette of Mickey Mouse's ears. There's also the **Maliboomer,** a trio of towers (giant strongman sledgehammer tests) that catapult riders to the tip-top bell and then lets them down bungee-style with dangling feet; the **Orange Stinger,** a whooshing swing ride inside an enormous orange, complete with orange scent piped in; **Mulholland Madness,** a wacky, wild trip along L.A.'s precarious hilltop street that is way scarier than it looks; and the **Sun Wheel Carousel,** featuring unique zigzagging cars that bring a new twist to the familiar ride.

There are all the familiar boardwalk games (complete with stuffed prizes); guilty-pleasure fast foods like pizza, corn dogs, and burritos; plus a full-service over-water restaurant called **Ariel's Grotto.**

**HOLLYWOOD PICTURES BACKLOT**    If you've visited Disney in Florida, you might recognize many elements of this trompe l'oeil re-creation of a Hollywood movie studio lot. Pass through a classic studio archway flanked by gigantic golden elephants and you'll find yourself on a surprisingly realistic Hollywood Boulevard. The Resort's hottest new attraction is the **Twilight Zone Tower of Terror.** This truly scary ride has been a huge hit since its debut at Walt Disney World. Legend has it that during a violent storm on Halloween night 1939, lightning struck the Hollywood Tower Hotel, causing an entire wing and an elevator full of people to disappear and you're about to retrace their steps from that fateful night as you become the star in a special Disney episode of . . . *The Twilight Zone.* In this once glamorous but now eerily vacant hotel, you tour the lobby, library, boiler room, and ultimately board the elevator to plunge 13 stories to the fifth dimension and beyond.

The Backlot's other main attraction is *Playhouse Disney—Live on Stage!,* starring the characters from the popular *Playhouse Disney* kid's program on the Disney Channel. It's a hugely popular high-energy show where Bear in the Big Blue House, Jo Jo of *Jo Jo's Circus,* Stanley, and other television characters entertain kids with songs, music, and stories of friendship. Another popular show is *Jim Henson's MuppetVision 3D,* an onscreen comedy romp featuring Kermit, Miss Piggy, Gonzo, Fozzie Bear—and even hecklers Waldorf and Statler. Although it's not nearly as entertaining as *It's Tough to Be a Bug,* it has its moments and won't scare the bejeezus out of little kids.

At the end of the street, the replica movie palace **Hyperion Theater** presents Broadway-caliber live-action shows of classic Disney films such as *Aladdin—A Musical Spectacular.* In the **Disney Animation** building, visitors can participate in different interactive galleries and learn how stories become animated features as told by Disney artists in the Drawn to Animation studio.

**A BUGS LAND** The bug-themed **"a bug's land"** encompasses *It's Tough to Be a Bug,* **Flik's Fun Fair,** and **Bountiful Valley Farm.** Inspired by the movie *A Bug's Life, It's Tough to Be a Bug* uses 3D technology to lead the audience on an underground romp in the insect kingdom with bees, termites, grasshoppers, stink bugs, spiders, and a few surprises that keep everyone hopping, ducking, and laughing along (I could see how little kids might find the show rather terrifying, however). The **Flik's Fun Fair** area features bug-themed rides and a water playground designed especially for little ones ages 4 to 7—but sized so their parents can ride along, too. **Bountiful Farm** pays tribute to California's agriculture (a real ho-hum if you're a Californian). Exhibits include a demonstration vineyard, mission-style "aging room" (with "Seasons of the Vine," a film presented by Robert Mondavi on the art of winemaking), wine bars, and the park's most upscale eatery, the **Vineyard Room,** a great place to sip champagne and watch Disney's Electrical Parade.

## DOWNTOWN DISNEY DISTRICT ⊛

Borrowing a page from central Florida's successful Disney compound, the **Downtown Disney District** is a colorful (and very sanitized) "street scene" filled with restaurants, shops, and entertainment for all ages. Options abound: Window-shop with kids in tow, have an upscale dinner for two, or party into the night. The promenade begins at the amusement park gates and stretches toward the Disneyland Hotel; there are nearly 20 shops and boutiques, and a dozen-plus restaurants, live music venues, and entertainment options.

Highlights include **House of Blues,** the blues-jazz restaurant/club that features Delta-inspired cuisine, big-name musicians, and a raucous Sunday Gospel Brunch; **Ralph Brennan's Jazz Kitchen,** a spicy mix of New Orleans traditional foods and live jazz; **ESPN Zone,** the ultimate sports dining and entertainment experience, including an interactive game room with a rock climbing wall; and **World of Disney,** one of the biggest Disney shopping experiences anywhere, with a vast and diverse range of toys, souvenirs, and collectibles. There is also an AMC Theatres 12-screen multiplex, the LEGO Imagination Center, a Sephora cosmetics store, and much more.

## WHERE TO STAY
### VERY EXPENSIVE
**Disney's Grand Californian Hotel** ⊛⊛⊛ *(Kids)*   Disney didn't miss the details when they constructed this enormous version of an Arts and Crafts–era lodge (think Yosemite's Awhanee and Pasadena's Gamble House), hiring craftspeople throughout the state to

contribute one-of-a-kind tiles, furniture, sculptures, and artwork. Taking inspiration from California's redwood forests, mission pioneers, and plein-air painters, designers managed to create a nostalgic yet state-of-the-art high-rise hotel that has its own private entrance into Disney's California Adventure Park and Downtown Disney District.

Enter through subtle (where's the door?) stained-glass sliding panels to the hotel's centerpiece, a six-story "living room" with a William Morris–designed marble "carpet," an angled skylight seen through exposed support beams, display cases of Craftsman treasures, and a three-story walk-in "hearth" whose fire warms Stickley-style rockers and plush leather armchairs.

Guest rooms are spacious and smartly designed, carrying through the Arts and Crafts theme surprisingly well considering the hotel's grand scale. The best ones overlook the park, but you'll pay for that view. Despite the sophisticated air of the Grand Californian, this is a hotel that truly caters to families, with a bevy of room configurations including one with a double bed plus bunk beds with a trundle. Since the hotel provides sleeping bags (rather than rollaways) for kids, this standard-size room will sleep a family of six—but you have to share the bathroom. *Tip:* Ask for a free upgrade to a room with a view of the park when you check in—they're pretty generous about this.

The hotel's two main restaurants are the upscale **Napa Rose** and the **Storytellers Cafe,** a "character dining" restaurant that's always bustling with excited kids who pay more attention to Chip and Dale than their eggs and bacon (be sure to make a breakfast reservation).

1600 S. Disneyland Dr., Anaheim, CA 92802. ✆ **714/956-MICKEY** (central reservations), or 714/635-2300. For vacation packages, call the Walt Disney Travel Company at 877/700-DISNEY. Fax 714/956-6099. www.disneyland.com. 745 units. $205–$335 double; from $345 suite. AE, DC, DISC, MC, V. Free self-parking; valet $6. **Amenities:** 3 restaurants; lounge; 2 outdoor pools; health club w/massage therapy; whirlpool; children's center; game room/arcade; concierge; business center; 24-hour room service; laundry/dry-cleaning service; concierge-level rooms. *In room:* A/C, TV, dataport, minibar, coffeemaker, hair dryer, iron, safe, robes, portable crib.

## EXPENSIVE

### The Disneyland Hotel ★★ *Kids*
The holy grail of Disney-goers has always been this, the "Official Hotel of the Magic Kingdom." A monorail connection via Downtown Disney means you'll be able to return to your room anytime, whether to take a much-needed nap or to change your soaked shorts after riding Splash Mountain. The theme hotel is an attraction unto itself and is the best choice for families with small children. The rooms aren't fancy, but they're comfortably furnished and all have balconies. In-room amenities include movie channels (with free Disney Channel, naturally) and even Disneyland-themed toiletries and accessories such as Sneezy on the tissue box. When you turn out the lights in the guest room, the wall paper glows with Tinker Bell's pixie dust. This all-inclusive resort offers several restaurants (see the full review of **Goofy's Kitchen** later in this chapter), snack bars, and cocktail lounges; every kind of service desk imaginable; a video game center; and the Never Land Pool Complex with a white-sand beach and separate adult pool nearby.

1150 W. Magic Way, Anaheim, CA 92802. ✆ **714/956-MICKEY.** Reservations fax 714/956-6582. www.disneyland. com. 990 units. $170–$310 double; from $265 suite. AE, MC, V. Parking $10. **Amenities:** 4 restaurants; 3 lounges; 3 outdoor pools; health club; whirlpool; children's programs; game room; concierge; shopping arcade; room service; babysitting; laundry/dry-cleaning service. *In room:* A/C, TV, dataport, minibar, hair dryer, safe.

### Paradise Pier Hotel ★ *Kids*
The whimsical beach boardwalk theme of this 15-story hotel ties in with the Paradise Pier section of Disney's California Adventure park across the street. The surfer theme salutes the heyday of seaside amusement parks with

nautical and beach decor in the guest rooms, nostalgic California artwork, and a new water slide modeled after the wooden roller coasters of yesteryear. Book a room at this smallest Disney property only if the other two are full—it's not as "magical" as the original Disneyland Hotel and it's soundly trounced by the superlative Grand Californian. It's also not as centrally located as the other two hotels, which could be a problem if you're not fond of walking. It does, however, offer new "family suites" that comfortably accommodate families of six or more, as well as Lilo & Stitch's Aloha Breakfast featuring island songs and tableside visits at the hotel's **PCH Grill.** Kids even get to make their own pizzas. *Tip:* Request a room that overlooks the Paradise Pier section of California Adventure or has direct access to the poolside cabanas.

1717 S. Disneyland Dr., Anaheim, CA 92802. ⓒ 714/956-MICKEY. For vacation packages, call the Walt Disney Travel Company at 877/700-DISNEY. Reservations fax 714/956-6582. www.disneyland.com. 489 units. $170–$310 double; from $265 suite. AE, MC, V. Parking $10. **Amenities:** 2 restaurants; lounge; outdoor pool; fitness center; whirlpool; children's programs; game room; concierge; shopping arcade; room service; babysitting; laundry/dry-cleaning service. *In room:* A/C, TV w/pay movies, dataport, minibar, coffeemaker, hair dryer, safe.

**Sheraton Anaheim Hotel** ⚜ This hotel rises to the festive theme-park occasion with its fanciful English Tudor architecture; it's a castle that lures business conventions, Disney-bound families, and local high school proms. The public areas are quiet and elegant—intimate gardens with fountains and koi ponds, and a plush lobby and lounges—which can be a pleasing touch after a frantic day at the amusement park. The rooms are modern and unusually spacious, but otherwise not distinctive. A large swimming pool sits in the center of the complex, surrounded by attractive landscaping. Don't be put off by the high rack rates; rooms commonly go for $100 to $130, even on busy summer weekends.

900 S. Disneyland Dr. (at I-5), Anaheim, CA 92802. ⓒ 800/331-7251 in CA, 800/325-3535 or 714/778-1700 in the U.S. Fax 714/535-3889. www.sheraton.com. 489 units. $200–$235 double; $290–$360 suite. AE, DC, MC, V. Parking $10; free Disneyland shuttle. **Amenities:** 2 restaurants; lounge; outdoor pool; fitness center; whirlpool; concierge; 24-hr. room service; coin-op laundry; laundry/dry-cleaning service. *In room:* A/C, TV w/pay movies, dataport, minibar, coffeemaker, hair dryer, iron.

## MODERATE
**The Anabella Hotel** ⚜ Uniting several formerly independent low-rise hotels across the street from Disney's California Adventure, The Anabella started from scratch, gutting each building to create carefully planned rooms for park-bound families and business travelers alike. The complex features a vaguely mission-style facade of whitewashed walls and red-tiled roofs, though guest room interiors are strictly contemporary in style and modern in appointments. Bathrooms are generously sized and outfitted in honey-toned granite; most have a tub-shower combo—just a few are shower-only. Though parking areas dot the grounds, you'll also find a pleasant garden around the central swimming pool and whirlpool; a separate adult pool hides out next to the street-side fitness room. Business travelers will appreciate the in-room executive desks with high-speed Internet access, while families can take advantage of "kids suites" complete with bunk beds and separate bedrooms. There's a pleasant indoor-outdoor all-day restaurant, and the hotel is a stop on both the Disney and Convention Center shuttle routes. *Note:* Rooms and rates vary wildly in terms of room size, layout, and occupancy limits; extra time spent at the hotel's website and with the reservationist will pay off in the most comfortable room for your needs.

1030 W. Katella Ave., Anaheim, CA 92802. ⓒ 800/863-4888 or 714/905-1050. Fax 714/905-1054. www.anabella hotel.com. 360 units. $89–$309 double. AE, DC, DISC, MC, V. Free parking. **Amenities:** Restaurant; lounge; 2 outdoor heated pools; exercise room; whirlpool; concierge; activities desk; business center; room service (7am–11pm); self-service laundromat; laundry/dry-cleaning service; nail salon. *In room:* A/C, TV w/pay movies/Web TV/Sony Playstation, dataport, fridge, coffeemaker, hair dryer, iron, safe.

**Anaheim Plaza Hotel & Suites** ⭐ *(Value)*   Although it's located across the street from the Disneyland Resort's main gate, you'll appreciate the way this hotel's clever design shuts out the noisy world. In fact, the seven two-story garden buildings remind me more of 1960s Waikiki than busy Anaheim (maybe it's the palm trees). A key feature is the Olympic-size heated outdoor pool and whirlpool. The furnishings are motel-bland but you won't be spending much time here anyway. On the plus side, little has changed about the friendly rates, which often drop as low as $59.

1700 S. Harbor Blvd., Anaheim, CA 92802. ☎ 800/631-4144 or 714/772-5900. Fax 714/772-8386. www.anaheimplaza hotel.com. 300 units. $89–$160 double; from $195 suite. Rates include continental breakfast. AE, DC, DISC, MC, V. Free parking and Disneyland shuttle. **Amenities:** Restaurant; lounge; outdoor pool; whirlpool; room service (8am–11pm); coin-op laundry; laundry/dry-cleaning service. *In room:* A/C, TV, coffeemaker, hair dryer.

**Portofino Inn & Suites** ⭐ *(Kids)*   Emerging from the rubble of the former Jolly Roger Hotel renovation, this complex of low- and high-rise all-suite buildings sports a cheery yellow exterior and family-friendly interior. The location couldn't be better—directly across the street from California Adventure's backside. You can either walk or take the ART (Anaheim Resort Transit) to the front gate. Designed to work as well for business travelers from the nearby Convention Center as for Disney-bound families, the Portofino offers contemporary, stylish furnishings as well as vacation-friendly rates and suites for any family configuration. Families will want a Kids Suite, which features bunk beds and a sleeper sofa, plus a TV, fridge, and microwave—and that's just in the kids' room; Mom and Dad have a separate bedroom with grown-up comforts like a double vanity, shower massage, and their own TV. There's even a Kid Eat Free program at the inn's cafe.

1831 S. Harbor Blvd. (at Katella), Anaheim, CA 92802. ☎ 800/398-3963 or 714/782-7600. Fax 714/782-7619. www. portofinoinnanaheim.com. 190 units. $94–$159 double; $109–$219 suite. Midweek, off-season, and other discounts available. AE, DC, DISC, MC, V. Free parking and Disneyland shuttle. **Amenities:** Restaurant; outdoor pool; fitness center; whirlpool; game room; tour desk; wireless Internet; coin-op laundry; laundry/dry-cleaning service. *In room:* A/C, TV, dataport, coffeemaker, hair dryer, iron.

### INEXPENSIVE

**Candy Cane Inn** ⭐ *(Value)*   Take your standard U-shape motel court with outdoor corridors, spruce it up with cobblestone drives and walkways, old-time street lamps, add in flowering vines engulfing room balconies, and you have the Candy Cane. The face-lift worked, making this gem near Disneyland's main gate a treat for the stylish bargain hunter. The rooms are decorated in bright floral motifs with comfortable furnishings, including queen beds and a separate dressing and vanity area. Breakfast is served in the courtyard, where you can also splash around in a heated pool, spa, or kids' wading pool. If you feel like splurging request one of the Premium Rooms with extended checkout and nightly turndown service.

1747 S. Harbor Blvd., Anaheim, CA 92802. ☎ 800/345-7057 or 714/774-5284. Fax 714/772-1305. www.candy caneinn.net. 172 units. $82–$159 double. Rates include expanded continental breakfast. AAA discount available. AE, DC, DISC, MC, V. Free parking and Disneyland shuttle. **Amenities:** Outdoor pool; whirlpool; coin-op laundry; laundry/dry-cleaning service. *In room:* A/C, TV, fridge, coffeemaker, hair dryer.

## WHERE TO DINE

There's nothing quite like an energetic family vacation to build an appetite, and sooner or later you'll have to make the inevitable Disney dining decisions: Where, when, and

---

*Value* **Super-Cheap Sleeps**

When you simply must shave a few more dollars off the hotel tariff, try these bargain-priced chains within easy reach of Disneyland. The **Anaheim at the Park Travelodge,** 1166 W. Katella Ave (© 800/578-7878 or 714/774-7817; www.anaheimatthepark.com), makes up for being a long walk from the resort (no shuttle) by offering regular rates of only $60–$100; AAA members and seniors can stay for as low as $52. This basic chain motel does, however, boast a nice swimming pool with separate whirlpool, kids' pool, and small playground. There's also a **Super 8 Motel** about 1½ blocks from the Disneyland Resort at 415 W. Katella Ave. (© 800/777-7123 or 714/778-6900). It's a large, impersonal budget property that's very basic but offers little extras such as a heated swimming pool. Room rates range from about $60 to $80 (AAA and senior discounts are available).

---

for how much? The expanded Disneyland Resort, with something for everyone, can easily meet your needs for the duration of the typical visit. Until recently, dining options were pretty sparse, limited to those inside Disneyland and some old standbys at the Disneyland Hotel. But Disney's big expansion upped the ante with national theme/concept restaurants along Downtown Disney and competitive dining options at the resort hotels. The best of the bunch are reviewed below. For dining reservations at any place throughout the Disneyland Resort call © 714/781-DINE.

## EXPENSIVE

**Granville's Steak House** ★★ STEAKHOUSE   Deep inside the Disneyland Hotel tower, this classic steakhouse specializes in thick-cut steaks and seafood in a men's club–style ambience replete with dark-wood paneling, beveled glass, richly colored carpeting, and scenic paintings depicting the American Southwest. It's perfectly suited for meat lovers with big appetites and a penchant for fine wines. Dinner starts with a loaf of sourdough bread on a cutting board; a waitperson then brings a small display of the various cuts of beef available—porterhouse, filet mignon, New York—to your table, along with a chart to determine your particular taste for doneness. Although the prices are expensive—a meal for two will set you back about $150—the tender cuts are very generous, as are the classic steakhouse sides such as baked potatoes, creamed spinach, and Caesar salad. Granville's is also one of the few places where you can get a brief respite from the Disney theme; as such, it's not recommended for children. Dress is casual, though you may feel a bit out of place in your Mickey T-shirt.

1150 W. Magic Way (in the Disneyland Hotel). © 714/956-6755. www.disneyland.com. Reservations recommended. Main courses $24–$31. AE, DC, DISC, MC, V. Daily 5–10pm.

**Napa Rose** ★★★ CALIFORNIA   Inside the upscale Grand Californian Hotel, Napa Rose is the first really serious (read: on "foodie" radar) restaurant at the Disneyland Resort. Its warm and light dining room mirrors the Arts and Crafts style of the hotel, down to Frank Lloyd Wright stained-glass windows and Craftsman-inspired seating throughout the restaurant and adjoining lounge. Executive chef Andrew Sutton was lured away from the Napa Valley's chic Auberge du Soleil, bringing with him a wine-country sensibility and passion for fresh California ingredients and inventive preparations. You can see him busy in the impressive open exhibition kitchen, showcasing specialty items like Sierra golden trout, artisan cheeses from Humboldt County and the Gold Country, and the Sonoma rabbit in Sutton's signature braised mushroom-rabbit tart. The tantalizing Seven Sparkling Sins starter platter (for two) features jewel-like portions of *foie gras*, caviar, oysters, lobster, and other exotic delicacies; the same attention to detail is evident in seasonally composed main-course standouts like grilled yellowtail with tangerine-basil fruit salsa atop savory couscous, or free-range veal *osso buco* in rich bacon-forest mushroom ragout. Leave room for dessert, to at least share one of pastry chef Jorge Sotelo's creative treats; our favorites are Sonoma goat-cheese flan with Riesling-soaked tropical fruit, and chocolate crepes with house-made caramelized banana ice cream. Napa Rose boasts an impressive and balanced wine list, with 60 by-the-glass choices (and 40-plus sommeliers, the most of any restaurant in the world); and outdoor seating is arranged around a rustic fire pit, gazing out across a landscaped arroyo toward California Adventure's distinctive Grizzly Peak. *Tip:* My favorite place to sit is at the counter facing the exhibition kitchen. Also, you can skip all the pomp and circumstance of a full sit-down meal by dining at the restaurant's lounge, which offers full menu service.

1600 S. Disneyland Dr. (in Disney's Grand Californian Hotel). ℰ **714/300-7170.** www.disneyland.com. Reservations strongly recommended. Main courses $19–$30. AE, DC, DISC, MC, V. Daily 11:30am–2pm and 5:30–10pm.

**Yamabuki** ★★ JAPANESE    Often ignored by all but their thriving clientele of Asian tourists and business folk—plus in-the-know expense account suits from surrounding Orange County—Yamabuki has been tucked away for years in the low-profile former Pacific Hotel (now reinvented as Disney's Paradise Pier Hotel). With an upscale and quietly traditional Japanese aesthetic, Yamabuki—the name of a Japanese rose—has a rich interior of deep-red lacquer, delicate porcelain vases, discreet teak shutters, and translucent rice-paper screens that together impart a sense of very un-Disney nobility. The staff is elegantly kimono-clad—even at lunch, when the fare includes casual bento boxes, lunch specials, and sushi/sashimi selections (try the Crunchy Roll). At dinner, tradition demands a languorous procession of courses, from refreshing seafood starters and steaming noodle bowls to grilled teriyaki meats or table-cooked specialties like sukiyaki or *shabu shabu*. The menu, in Japanese and English, rates each dish as contemporary, traditional, or very traditional, presenting the opportunity to try unusual squid, soybean, and pickled-root dishes common in the East. If you're willing to spend the time—and the money—Yamabuki is a cultural trip across the globe.

1717 S. Disneyland Dr. (in Disney's Paradise Pier Hotel). ℰ **714/239-5683,** or reservations 714/956-6755. www. disneyland.com. Reservations recommended at dinner. Main courses $7.50–$11 lunch, $14–$30 dinner. AE, DC, DISC, MC, V. Mon–Fri 11:30am–2pm; daily 5:30–10pm.

**MODERATE**

**Catal Restaurant/Uva Bar** ★★ MEDITERRANEAN/TAPAS    Branching out from acclaimed Patina restaurant in Los Angeles, high-priest-of-cuisine Joachim Splichal brings us this Spanish-inspired Mediterranean concept duo at the heart of Downtown Disney. The main restaurant, Catal, features a series of intimate second-floor rooms that combine rustic Mediterranean charm with fine dining. Complemented by an international wine list, the menu is a collage of flavors that borrow from France, Spain, Italy, Greece, Morocco, and the Middle East—all united in selections that manage to be intriguing but not overwhelming. Though the menu will vary seasonally, expect to find selections that range from seared sea scallops over saffron risotto or chorizo-spiked Spanish paella to herb-marinated rotisserie chicken or Sicilian rigatoni with ricotta cheese.

The Uva Bar (*uva* means "grape" in Spanish) is a casual tapas bar in an outdoor courtyard in the middle of the Downtown Disney walkway. Martinis are a stand-out here; there are also 40 different wines by the glass. The affordable menu features the same pan-Mediterranean influence, even offering many items from the Catal menu; standouts include cabernet-braised short ribs atop horseradish mashed potatoes, marinated olives and cured Spanish ham, and Andalusian gazpacho with rock shrimp.

1580 Disneyland Dr. (at Downtown Disney). ⓒ 714/774-4442. Reservations recommended Sun–Thurs, not accepted Fri–Sat for Catal; not accepted for Uva Bar. Main courses $14–$24; tapas $5–$8. AE, DC, DISC, MC, V. Mon–Thurs 11am–11pm; Fri–Sun 11am–midnight.

**Goofy's Kitchen** *(Kids)* AMERICAN   Your younger kids will never forgive you if they miss an opportunity to dine with their favorite Disney characters at this colorful, lively restaurant inside the Disneyland Hotel. Known for its entertainment and wacky and off-center Toontown-esque decor, Goofy's Kitchen features tableside visits by Disney characters (Goofy, Alice, Geppetto Pocahontas, Aladdin, the Beast) who thrill the youngsters with dancing, autograph signing, and up-close-and-personal encounters. Meals are buffet-style and offer an adequate selection of crowd pleasers and reliable standbys, from bacon and eggs at breakfast to fried chicken, Caesar salad, deli sandwiches, and Italian pastas at lunch and dinner. The most popular kid food is the peanut butter and jelly pizza (even for breakfast), the buffet of gummy worms, Mickey Mouse–shaped waffles, and Mickey ear–shaped chicken nuggets. This place isn't really about the food, though, and is definitely *not* for kidless grownups (unless you're trying to make up for a deprived childhood). Bring a camera and Disney autograph book for capturing the family's "candid" encounters. *Tip:* Make reservations for an early or late breakfast or dinner to avoid the mayhem.

1150 Magic Way (inside the Disneyland Hotel). ⓒ 714/956-6755 or 714/781-DINE. www.disneyland.com. Reservations recommended. Buffet prices (child/adult) $10/$17 breakfast, $10/$18 lunch, $10/$27 dinner. AE, DC, DISC, MC, V. Daily 7am–9pm.

**House of Blues** ⚐ AMERICAN/SOUTHERN   For years, fans have been comparing the House of Blues to Disneyland, so this celeb-backed restaurant/nightclub fits right into the Disney compound. Locations in Las Vegas, L.A., Orlando, and so forth all sport a calculated backwoods-bayou-meets-Country-Bear-Jamboree appearance that fits right into the Disneyfied world. The Anaheim HOB follows the formula, filled with made-to-look-old found objects, amateur paintings, uneven wood floors, seemingly decayed chandeliers, and a country-casual attitude. The restaurant features Delta-inspired stick-to-your-ribs cuisine like Louisiana crawfish cakes, Creole seafood jambalaya, cornmeal-crusted catfish, baby back ribs glazed with Jack Daniels sauce, and spicy Cajun meatloaf—plus some out-of-place Cal-lite stragglers like seared *ahi* and pesto pasta. Sunday's Gospel Brunch is an advance-ticket event of hand-clapping, foot-stomping proportions. The adjacent Company Store offers logo ware interspersed with selected pieces of folk art. HOB's state-of-the-art Music Hall is a welcome addition to the local music scene (advance tickets are highly recommended for big-name bookings).

1530 S. Disneyland Dr. (at Downtown Disney). ⓒ 714/778-2583. www.hob.com. Reservations not accepted for restaurant (tickets required for performance). Main courses $8–$17. AE, DC, DISC, MC, V. Daily 11am–midnight (open from 10am Sun).

**Naples Ristorante e Pizzeria** ⚐ ITALIAN   The eye-catching entrance of this better-than-expected Italian concept eatery features a larger-than-life harlequin with an impish expression, wielding a pizza and beckoning you to step inside. Designed to be sophisticated enough for discerning palates while still appropriate for casual families, Naples features a colorful, high-ceilinged dining room filled with padded loveseats and comfy chairs. Busy chefs work the white-tiled open kitchen's wood-burning oven, while a floor-to-ceiling cherry-wood bar anchors the other side of the room. Naples also boasts some of the most scenic outdoor seating in Downtown Disney—request a patio table when reserving. At dinner, you can also opt for the quieter ambience of the upstairs dining room. Piedmontese executive chef Corrado Gionatti is a master of the thin-crust Neapolitan pizza and uses an appropriately light hand saucing the menu's selection of pastas. Salads, antipasti, and calzone round out the menu; everything is very good, and—be forewarned—portions are quite large. *Tip:* Napolini, Naples' sister cafe next door, offers quick grab-and-go sandwiches and salads.

1550 Disneyland Dr. (at Downtown Disney). ✆ **714/776-6200.** Reservations strongly recommended. Main courses $11–$16. AE, DC, DISC, MC, V. Daily 11am–11pm.

**Rainforest Cafe** (Kids) INTERNATIONAL    Designed to suggest ancient temple ruins in an overgrown Central American jungle, this national chain favorite successfully combines entertainment, retail, and family-friendly dining in one fantasy setting. There are cascading waterfalls inside and out, a canopy of lush vegetation, simulated tropical mists, and even a troupe of colorful parrots beckoning shoppers into the Retail Village. Once seated, diners choose from an amalgam of wildly flavored dishes inspired by Caribbean, Polynesian, Latin, Asian, and Mediterranean cuisines. Masquerading under exotic-sounding names like Jungle Safari Soup (a meaty version of minestrone) and Mojo Bones (barbecue pork ribs), the food is really fairly familiar: A translated sampling includes Cobb salad, pita sandwiches, potstickers, shrimp-studded pasta, and charbroiled chicken. Fresh-fruit smoothies and tropical specialty cocktails are offered, as is a best-shared dessert called the Giant Chocolate Volcano. After your meal, you can browse through logo items, environmentally educational toys and games, stuffed jungle animals and puppets, straw safari hats, and other themed souvenirs in the lobby store. There's a children's menu, and the Rainforest Cafe is one of the few Downtown Disney eateries to have full breakfast service.

1515 S. Disneyland Dr. (at Downtown Disney). ✆ **714/772-0413.** www.rainforestcafe.com. Reservations recommended for peak mealtimes. Main courses $9–$21. AE, DC, DISC, MC, V. Sun–Thurs 7am–11pm; Fri–Sat 7am–midnight.

**Ralph Brennan's Jazz Kitchen** ✦ CAJUN-CREOLE    If you always thought Disneyland's New Orleans Square was just like the real thing, wait till you see this authentically Southern concept restaurant at Downtown Disney. Ralph Brennan, of the New Orleans food dynasty responsible for NOLA landmarks like Commander's Palace and a trio of Big Easy hot spots, commissioned a handful of New Orleans artists to create the handcrafted furnishings that give the Jazz Kitchen its believable French Quarter ambience. Lacy wrought-iron grillwork, cascading ferns, and trickling stone fountains enhance three separate dining choices: The upstairs Carnival Club is an elegant dining salon with silk-draped chandeliers and terrace dining that overlooks the "street scene" below; casual Flambeaux is downstairs, where a bead-encrusted grand piano hints at the nightly live jazz that sizzles in this room; and the Creole Cafe is a quick stop for necessities like muffulettas or beignets. Expect traditional Cajun-Creole fare with heavy-handed seasonings and rich, heart-stopping sauces—now *that's* authentically New Orleans.

1590 S. Disneyland Dr. (at Downtown Disney). ℭ **714/776-5200.** www.rbjazzkitchen.com. Reservations strongly recommended. Main courses $16–$25; cafe items $4–$8. AE, DC, DISC, MC, V. Daily 11am–3pm and 5–11pm.

## INEXPENSIVE

**La Brea Bakery Express & Cafe** BAKERY/MEDITERRANEAN   Fresh from the ovens of L.A.'s now nationally known artisan bakery, this La Brea Bakery duo occupies a coveted position at the beginning of Downtown Disney, right across from the theme parks' ticket kiosks. Each morning, still-groggy early-bird park-goers stumble from the parking-lot tram and head straight to La Brea's cafeteria-style Express for a caffeinated pick-me-up or a meal to start the day. Light breakfast items are served in addition to creator Nancy Silverton's irresistible breads and pastries. The outdoor patio is comfortably outfitted with woven bistro chairs (plus heat lamps for brisk mornings) and provides a relaxing setting before braving the Disney throngs. Throughout the day, folks stop in for a lunch of sandwiches, filled brioche, or herb-laden focaccia. The kids' menu offers less-grown-up choices like grilled cheese and PB&J.

1556 Disneyland Dr. (at Downtown Disney). ℭ **714/490-0233.** www.labreabakery.com. Reservations recommended for Cafe. Light fare under $5 (Express); main courses $10–$20 (Cafe). AE, DISC, MC, V. Daily 8am–11pm (Express) and 11am–11pm (Cafe).

## 4 Knott's Berry Farm

30 miles SE of downtown L.A.

Although destined to always be in the shadow of Mickey's megaresort, the reality is that Knott's doesn't even attempt to compete with the Disney empire: Instead, it targets Southern California thrill-seekers (droves of them) by offering a far better selection of scream-inducing thrill rides.

Like Disneyland, Knott's Berry Farm has a history. In 1920, Walter Knott began farming 20 acres of leased land on Highway 39 (now Beach Blvd.). When things got tough during the Depression, Mrs. Knott set up a roadside stand, selling pies, preserves, and home-cooked chicken dinners. Within a year, she was selling 90 meals a day. Lines became so long that Walter decided to create an Old West Ghost Town—America's first theme park—in 1940 as a diversion for waiting customers. Today Knott's amusement park offers a whopping 165 shows, attractions, and state-of-the-art rides that are far more intense than Disneyland's swirling teacups.

## ESSENTIALS

### GETTING THERE

Knott's Berry Farm is at 8039 Beach Blvd. in Buena Park. It's about a 10-minute ride north on I-5 from Disneyland. From I-5 or California 91, exit south onto Beach Boulevard. The park is about half a mile south of California 91.

### VISITOR INFORMATION

The **Buena Park Convention and Visitors Office,** 6601 Beach Blvd., Suite 200, Buena Park (ℭ **800/541-3953** or 714/562-3560; www.buenapark.com/cvo), provides specialized information on the area, including Knott's Berry Farm. To learn more about the amusement park before you arrive, call ℭ **714/220-5200** or log onto **www. knotts.com**.

### ADMISSION PRICES & OPERATING HOURS

Admission to the park, including unlimited access to all rides, shows, and attractions, is $45 for adults and children 12 and over; $35 for seniors 60 or older, nonambulatory visitors, and expectant mothers; $15 for kids 3 to 11; and free for children under 3. Admission after 4pm (any day the park is open past 6pm) is $22 for adults and seniors 60 or older, and $15 for kids 3 to 11. Parking is $9. Tickets can also be purchased at many Southern California hotels, where discount coupons are sometimes available.

Like Disneyland, Knott's offers discounted admission—$31 for adults and $15 for kids 3 to 11—for Southern California residents with zip codes 90000 through 93599, so if you're bringing local friends or family members along, try to take advantage of the bargain. Also like Disneyland, Knott's Berry Farm's hours vary from week to week, so call ahead. The park generally is open during the summer daily from 10am to midnight. The rest of the year, it opens at 10am and closes at 6 or 8pm, except Saturday, when it stays open until 10pm. Knott's is closed December 25. Special hours and prices are in effect during Knott's Scary Farm in October. Stage shows and special activities are scheduled throughout the day. Pick up a schedule at the ticket booth.

## TOURING THE PARK

Despite all the high-tech multimillion-dollar rides, Knott's Berry Farm maintains much of its original Old West motif and also features the Peanuts gang: Snoopy, Charlie Brown, Woodstock, and pals are the official costumed characters of Knott's. The park is divided into six themed areas, each one of which features at least one of the thrill roller coasters that are the Knott's claim to fame. The California MarketPlace is located adjacent to, but outside of, the theme park, featuring 14 unique shops and restaurants, including the original favorite, Mrs. Knott's Chicken Dinner Restaurant and the new TGI Friday's franchise.

### GHOST TOWN

The park's original attraction is a collection of authentic 19th-century buildings relocated from deserted Old West towns in Arizona and California. You can pan for gold, ride an authentic stagecoach, take rickety train cars through the Calico Mine, and get held up aboard the Calico Railroad. If you love wooden roller coasters, don't miss the clackity GhostRider.

**Ghost Town Artisans** ★ *Finds*    An entertaining holdover from the earliest days of the park, these living history booths present old-time crafts and tall tales presented by costumed blacksmiths, woodcarvers, a spinner, and storytellers who help bring Ghost Town to life for curious kids and history buffs.

**Calico Railroad**    Board this 1881 narrow-gauge steam-engine train—once part of the Denver and Rio Grande Southern Line—for a round-trip tour of half the theme park, interrupted by "bandit" holdups.

**GhostRider** ★★★    Looming 118 feet high, this coaster is the single largest attraction in park history and one of the longest and tallest wooden roller coasters in the world. Riders enter through a replica mine and are strapped into gold, silver, or copper mining cars for an adventure that twists and careens through sudden dips, banked turns, and cheek-flattening G-forces. The ride isn't nearly as smooth and quiet as the steel roller coasters, and that's part of the thrill. Worldwide coaster enthusiasts worship this classic ride.

**Silver Bullet** ★★    Brand new in 2005, this inverted coaster dangles riders from the steel track that weaves its way through the center of the park. Flying over Reflection Lake from the edge of the stagecoach stop to the top of the Log Ride mountain at a height of 146 feet, this high-speed thriller sends riders head over heels six times with cobra rolls, spirals, corkscrews, and other whacked-out whirls.

**Timber Mountain Log Ride** 🎯 Riders emerge from a dark and twisting "sawmill" waterway and plummet down a 42-foot flume for the grand splash. Compared to the other water rides in the park, this one leaves you only slightly sprinkled.

**Wild West Stunt Show** This wild and woolly stunt spectacular is a raucous salute to the Old West presented throughout the day in the open-air Wagon Camp Theater.

## FIESTA VILLAGE

Here you'll find a south-of-the-border theme—festive markets and an ambience that suggests old Spanish California. A cluster of carnival-style rides (in addition to the roller coasters listed below) includes a 100-year-old merry-go-round, plus Knott's version of Disneyland's Tea Cups, where you can sit-and-spin in your own sombrero. You can stroll the paths of Fiesta Village, which are lined with old-time carnival games and state-of-the-art electric arcades.

**The Revolution** 🎯 A real stomach-churner, this new ride both spins you in circles while swinging back and forth more than 65 feet in the air. It's like being in the rinse cycle of a washing machine that's swinging from a rope.

**Jaguar!** 🎯🎯 Loosely themed around a tropical jungle setting, this wild roller coaster includes two heart-in-the-mouth drops and a view of Fiesta Village from high above. It's a good family roller coaster for first-timers or the easily frightened.

**Montezooma's Revenge** 🎯 Blasting from 0 to 60mph in 5 seconds, this not-for-the-fainthearted thriller then propels riders through a giant 360-degree loop both forward and backward.

## THE BOARDWALK

The park's most recently renovated area is a salute to Southern California's beach culture, where colorful architecture and palm trees are the backdrop for a trio of thrill rides. Other amusements include arcade and boardwalk games, the **Dinosaur Discover Center,** and the **Charles M. Schulz Theatre,** where seasonal productions include a *Snoopy* ice show or holiday pageant (check the marquee or park entertainment schedule for show times).

**Xcelerator** 🎯🎯🎯 It's scary just looking at this stomach-churner. One of the resort's newest attractions, this super-high-tech 1950s–themed roller coaster launches you from 0 to 82mph in 2⅓ seconds, and then whips you straight up 20 stories (with a half-twist thrown in for added addling) and almost straight back down again. It's like riding on the outer edge of a gigantic paperclip.

**Boomerang** 🎯 This corkscrew scream machine sends you twisting through three head-over-heels loops in less than a minute—but it doesn't end there, since you're sent through the track again . . . backward.

**Lazer Invaders** *Kids* In this adaptation of the classic Lazer Runner, participants equipped with phasers and fiber-optic vests battle for supremacy in a richly evocative atmosphere. Each combatant must make use of protective walls and laser power to vanquish opponents.

**Perilous Plunge** 🎯🎯 Just 34 feet shorter than Niagara Falls, this wet adventure sends riders to a height of 127 feet and then drops them down a 115-foot water chute at a 75-degree angle—15 degrees from a sheer vertical. Prepare for a thorough soaking (a boon on hot days, but best experienced before nightfall).

**Sky Cabin** ⚓ Just when you were thinking all the rides were for hard-core adrenaline-seekers (most are, actually), this quiet ride offers the same spectacular views at a calmer pace. The slowly rotating "cabin" ascends Knott's vertical tower, providing panoramic views of the park and surrounding area.

**Supreme Scream** ⚓⚓ They could've called this one the "Evil Elevator:" Seated and fully exposed riders are hoisted straight up a 30-story tower with their feet dangling in the air, then held at the top just long enough to rattle the nerves before plunging downward faster than gravity at more than 60mph. The whole descent takes only a bowel-shaking 3 seconds. It's one of the tallest (and most unnerving) thrill rides in the world.

## CAMP SNOOPY

This will probably be the youngsters' favorite area. The first-ever theme park area dedicated solely for kids, it's meant to re-create a wilderness camp in the High Sierras. Six rustic acres are the playgrounds of Charles Schulz's beagle and his pals, Charlie Brown and Lucy, who greet guests and pose for pictures. There are over a dozen rides in the Camp; several kid-size rides are made especially for the younger set, while the entire family can enjoy others. Scaled-down stock cars, locomotives, steamboats, 18-wheeler semis, hot-air balloons, and even the Peanuts gang's school bus give kids a playland of their own. There's also a child-size version of Supreme Scream, called Woodstock's Airmail, and Joe Cool's GR8 SK8, a minithrill ride for the whole family. Interactive attractions include the new **Camp Snoopy Theatre** starring the Peanuts gang (little kids are transfixed by this show).

## WILD WATER WILDERNESS

This $10-million, 3½-acre area is styled like a turn-of-the-20th-century California wilderness park with a raging white-water river, cascading waterfalls, soaring geysers, and old-style ranger stations.

**Bigfoot Rapids** ⚓⚓ The centerpiece of Wild Water Wilderness is this outdoor white-water river raft ride, the longest of its kind in the world. Climb aboard a six-seat circular raft, and prepare to be bounced, buffeted, tossed, spun, and splashed along fast-moving currents, under cascading waterfalls, and around soaring geysers. Let there be no doubt: You will get *extremely* wet on this one.

**Mystery Lodge** ⚓⚓ This amazing high-tech, trick-of-the-eye tribute to the magic of Native American storytelling is a theater attraction for the whole family. The Old Storyteller takes the audience on a mystical, multisensory journey into the culture of local tribes by employing centuries-old legends passed down through oral history.

## INDIAN TRAILS

Explore the ride-free Indian Trails cultural area, which offers daily demonstrations of native dance and music by authentically costumed Native American and Aztec dancers, singers, and musicians performed in the round on the Indian Trails stage. In addition, the compound showcases a variety of traditional Native American structures from the Pacific Northwest, Great Plains, and Southwest. The area includes four towering totem poles, standing from 15 to 27 feet high; three authentic tepees, representing the Arapaho, Blackfoot, and Nez Perce tribes; and more. The arts and crafts of Native American tribes from the western part of North America are also demonstrated and displayed.

While exploring Indian Trails, visitors can enjoy a sampling of Native American foods, including Navajo tacos, Indian fry bread, and fresh-roasted ears of corn.

## WHERE TO STAY

**Knott's Berry Farm Resort Hotel** ★ *Kids*   Within easy walking distance of Knott's Berry Farm, this nine-story hotel is the only accommodation located near the amusement park. Despite the hotel's lengthy moniker, the exterior and lobby have the look of a business hotel. I especially like two things about this hotel: the Peanuts-themed rooms with Snoopy tuck-in service and bedtime stories told via the in-room phone by the bed, and free shuttle service to Disneyland, 7 miles away. There's also a large family pool with a children's water play structure, and an arcade. Be sure to inquire about special rates and Knott's multiday-vacation package deals.

7675 Crescent Ave. (at Grand), Buena Park, CA 90620. © 866/752-2444 or 714/995-1111. Fax 714/828-8590. www.knottshotel.com. 320 units. $149 single; $159 double. Discount packages available. AE, DC, DISC, MC, V. Parking $9 per night; free Disneyland shuttle. **Amenities:** Restaurant; lounge; outdoor pool; 2 outdoor tennis and basketball courts (lit for night play); fitness center; whirlpool; video arcade; concierge; wireless Internet access; room service; self-service laundry; laundry/dry-cleaning service. *In room:* A/C, TV w/pay movies and video games, fax, dataport, hi-speed Internet access (for a fee), coffeemaker, hair dryer, iron, safe.

## WHERE TO DINE

**Mrs. Knott's Chicken Dinner Restaurant** *Kids* AMERICAN   Knott's Berry Farm got its start as a roadside diner in 1934, and you can still get a filling—albeit unhealthful—all-American meal without even entering the theme park. Cordelia Knott's down-home cooking was so popular that her husband created a few humble attractions to amuse patrons. Today more than 1.5 million annual patrons line up around the building to experience Cordelia's original recipe (very similar to the Colonel's, I must admit), served by sweet waitresses built more for comfort than speed. Looking just as you'd expect—country cute, with window shutters, old black-and-white photos of the original diner, and calico prints aplenty—the restaurant serves up its featured attraction of the original fried chicken dinner, complete with soup, salad, warm buttermilk biscuits, mashed potatoes and chicken gravy, and a slice of famous pie (the boysenberry pie is fantastic). Country-fried steak, pot roast, roast turkey, and pork ribs are options, as are sandwiches, salads, and a terrific chicken potpie. Boysenberries

---

*Tips* **Getting Soaked at Knott's**

Surf's up at **Knott's Soak City Water Park**, a 13-acre water park next door to Knott's Berry Farm. Water thrill-seekers of all ages can get soaked on 21 water rides and attractions, to the theme of surf woodies and long boards of the 1950s Southern California coast. The fun includes tube and body slides, speed slides, an artificial wave lagoon, and an area for youngsters with their own pool and beach shack fun house. The park is located at 8039 Buena Park (© 714/220-5200; www.soakcityusa.com). Admission prices are $26 for adults, $15 for kids 3 to 11, and free to children under 3; parking is $9. Ask about special promotions and discount coupons (or check the website). The park is open weekends in May and September, and then daily between Memorial Day and Labor Day. Soak City Water Park opens at 10am and closes between 6 and 8pm, based on the season.

abound, from breakfast jam to traditional double-crust pies, and there's even an adjacent take-out shop that's always crowded. If you're not visiting the amusement park, park in the lot that offers 3 free hours.

8039 Beach Blvd. (near La Palma), Buena Park. (*C*) **714/220-5080.** Reservations not accepted. Main courses $7–$10; complete dinners $13. DC, DISC, MC, V. Sun–Thurs 7am–9pm, Fri–Sat 7am–9:30pm; the restaurant closes ½-hour earlier between Labor Day and Memorial Day.

## 5 The Orange Coast

Seal Beach is 36 miles S of Los Angeles; Newport Beach, 49 miles; Dana Point, 65 miles

Whatever you do, don't say "Orange County" here. The mere name evokes images of smoggy industrial parks, cookie-cutter housing developments, and the staunch Republicanism that prevails behind the so-called "orange curtain." We're talking instead about the Orange Coast, one of Southern California's best-kept secrets—a string of seaside jewels that have been compared with the French Riviera or the Costa del Sol. Forty-two miles of beaches offer pristine stretches of sand, tide pools teeming with marine life, ecological preserves, secluded coves, picturesque pleasure-boat harbors, and legendary surf breaks. My advice? Make it a day trip from L.A.—hit the road early for a scenic cruise down the Pacific Coast Highway starting at Seal Beach, stop for lunch at Laguna Beach (the prettiest of all the SoCal beach towns), continue south to Dana Point where the *really* expensive resorts reside, then take the freeway back to L.A. (I-5 to I-405).

### ESSENTIALS

**GETTING THERE**   See "Getting There" in chapter 2 for airport and airline information. By car from Los Angeles, take I-5 or I-405 south. The scenic, shore-hugging Pacific Coast Highway (Hwy. 1, or just PCH to the locals) links the Orange Coast communities from Seal Beach in the north to Capistrano Beach just south of Dana Point, where it merges with I-5. To reach the beach communities directly, take the following freeway exits: **Seal Beach,** Seal Beach Boulevard from I-405; **Huntington Beach,** Beach Boulevard/California 39 from either I-405 or I-5; **Newport Beach,** California 55 from either I-405 or I-5; **Laguna Beach,** California 133 from I-5; **San Juan Capistrano,** Ortega Highway/California 74 from I-5; and **Dana Point,** Pacific Coast Highway/California 1 from I-5.

**VISITOR INFORMATION**   The **Seal Beach Chamber of Commerce,** 201 Eighth St., Suite 120, next to City Hall (*C* **562/799-0179;** www.sealbeachchamber. com), is open Monday through Friday from 10am to 4pm.

The **Huntington Beach Conference & Visitors Bureau,** 301 Main St., Suite 208 (*C* **800/729-6232** or 714/969-3492; www.hbvisit.com), offers copious information and personal anecdotes about the area. It's open Monday through Friday 9am to 5pm.

The **Newport Beach Conference & Visitors Bureau,** 110 Newport Center Dr., Suite 120 (*C* **800/94-COAST** or 949/719-6100; www.newportbeach-cvb.com), distributes brochures, sample menus, a calendar of events, and the free *Visitor's Guide.* Call or stop in Monday through Friday from 8am to 5pm (plus weekends in summer).

The **Laguna Beach Visitors Bureau,** 252 Broadway (*C* **800/877-1115** or 949/ 497-9229; www.lagunabeachinfo.org), is in the heart of town and distributes lodging, dining, and art gallery guides. It's open Monday through Friday from 9am to 5pm, and Saturday from 10am to 4pm (plus Sun in summer).

The **San Juan Capistrano Chamber of Commerce,** Franciscan Plaza, 31781 Camino Capistrano, Suite 306 (*C* **949/493-4700;** www.sanjuancapistrano.com), is within walking distance of the mission and offers a walking tour guide to historic sites. It's staffed Monday through Friday from 9am to 5pm.

The **Dana Point Chamber of Commerce Visitor Center,** located in the Clocktower Building at the LaPlaza Center (© **800/290-DANA** or 949/496-1555; www.danapoint-chamber.com), is open Monday through Friday from 9am to 5pm (closed noon–1pm for lunch) and carries some restaurant and lodging information, as well as a comprehensive recreation brochure.

## DRIVING THE ORANGE COAST

You'll most likely be exploring the coast by car, so the beach communities are covered in order, from north to south. Keep in mind, however, that if you're traveling between Los Angeles and San Diego, the Pacific Coast Highway (Hwy. 1) is a breezy, scenic detour that adds less than an hour to the commute—so pick out a couple of seaside destinations and take your time.

**Seal Beach,** on the border between Los Angeles and Orange counties, and a neighbor to Long Beach's Naples Harbor, is geographically isolated by both the adjacent U.S. Naval Weapons Station and the self-contained Leisure World retirement community. As a result, the beach town appears untouched by modern development—it's Orange County's version of small-town America. Take a stroll down Main Street for a walk back in time, culminating in the Seal Beach Pier. Although the clusters of sunbathing, squawking seals that gave the town its name aren't around any more, old-timers still fish, lovers still stroll, and families still cavort by the seaside, enjoying great food and retail shops or having a cold drink at Hennessey's tavern.

**Huntington Beach**—or Surf City, as it's known—is the largest Orange Coast city; it stretches quite a ways inland and has seen the most urbanization. To some extent, this has changed the old boardwalk and pier to a modern outdoor mall where cliques of teens coexist with families and the surfers who continue to flock here, drawn by Huntington's legendary place in surf lore. Hawaiian-born George Freeth is credited with bringing the sport here in 1907, and some say the breaks around the pier and Bolsa Chica are the best in California. The world's top wave riders flock to Huntington each August for the rowdy but professional **U.S. Open of Surfing.** If you're around at Christmas time, try to see the gaily decorated marina homes and boats in Huntington Harbor by taking the **Cruise of Lights,** a 45-minute narrated sail through and around the harbor islands. The festivities generally last from mid-December until Christmas; call © **714/840-7542** for schedules and ticket information.

The name **Newport Beach** conjures comparisons to Rhode Island's Newport, where the well-to-do enjoy seaside living with all the creature comforts. That's the way it is here, too, but on a less grandiose scale. From the million-dollar Cape Cod–style cottages on sunny Balboa Island to elegant shopping complexes like Fashion Island and South Coast Plaza (an übermall with valet parking, car detailing, limo service, and concierge), this is where fashionable socialites, right-wing celebrities, and business mavens can all be found. Alternatively, you could explore **Balboa Peninsula**'s historic Pavilion and old-fashioned pier or board a passenger ferry to Catalina Island.

**Laguna Beach,** whose breathtaking geography is marked by bold elevated headlands, coastal bluffs, pocket coves, and a very inviting beach, is known as an artists' enclave, but the truth is that Laguna has became so "in" (read: expensive) that it's driven most of the true bohemians out. Their legacy remains with the annual **Festival of Arts and Pageant of the Masters** (see "A Special Arts Festival," above), as well as a proliferation of art galleries mingling with high-priced boutiques along the town's

# Anaheim Area & Orange Coast Attractions

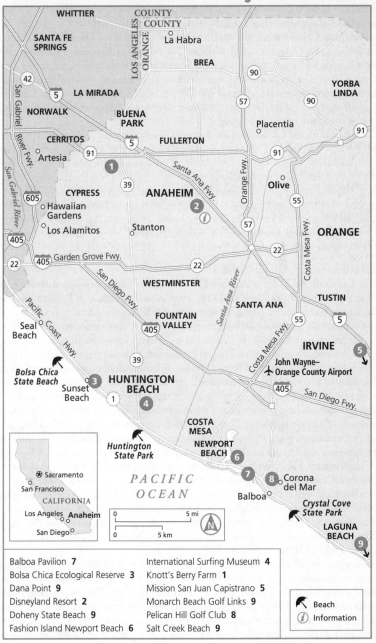

Balboa Pavilion 7
Bolsa Chica Ecological Reserve 3
Dana Point 9
Disneyland Resort 2
Doheny State Beach 9
Fashion Island Newport Beach 6

International Surfing Museum 4
Knott's Berry Farm 1
Mission San Juan Capistrano 5
Monarch Beach Golf Links 9
Pelican Hill Golf Club 8
Salt Creek Beach 9

Beach
Information

cozy streets. In warm weather, Laguna Beach has an overwhelming Mediterranean-island ambience, which makes *everyone* feel beautifully, idly rich.

**San Juan Capistrano,** in the verdant headlands inland from Dana Point, is defined by Spanish missions and its loyal swallows. The mission architecture is authentic, and history abounds. Think of San Juan Capistrano as a compact, life-size diorama illustrating the evolution of a small western town—from Spanish-mission era to secular rancho period, statehood, and into the 21st century. Surprisingly, Mission San Juan Capistrano (see "Seeing the Sights," below) is once again the center of the community, just as the founding friars intended 200 years ago.

**Dana Point,** the last town south, has been called a "marina development in search of a soul." Overlooking the harbor stands a monument to 19th-century author Richard Henry Dana, who gave his name to the area and described it in *Two Years Before the Mast.* Activities generally center on yachting and Dana Point's beautiful harbor. Nautical themes are everywhere, particularly the streets named for old-fashioned shipboard lights—a hodgepodge that includes Street of the Amber Lantern, Street of the Violet Lantern, Street of the Golden Lantern, and so on. Bordering the harbor is Doheny State Beach (see "Beaches & Nature Preserves," below), one of the very best for its seaside park and camping facilities.

## ENJOYING THE OUTDOORS

**BEACHES & NATURE PRESERVES**   The **Bolsa Chica Ecological Reserve,** in Huntington Beach (© 714/846-1114; www.bolsachica.org), is a 900-acre restored urban salt marsh that's a haven to more than 200 bird species, as well as a wide variety of protected plants and animals. Naturalists come to spot herons and egrets as well as California horn snails, jackknife clams, sea sponges, common jellyfish, and shore crabs. An easy 1.5-mile loop trail begins from a parking lot on the Pacific Coast Highway (Hwy. 1) a mile south of Warner Boulevard; docents lead a narrated walk the first Saturday of every month. The trail heads inland, over Inner Bolsa Bay and up Bolsa Chica bluffs. It then loops back toward the ocean over a dike that separates the Inner and Outer Bolsa bays and traverses a coastal sand-dune system. This beautiful hike is a terrific afternoon adventure. The Bolsa Chica Conservancy has been working since 1978 on reclaiming the wetlands from oil companies that drill here. It's an ongoing process, and you can still see those "seesaw" drills dotting the outer areas of the reserve.

**Huntington City Beach,** adjacent to Huntington Pier, is a haven for volleyball players and surfers; dense crowds abound, but so do amenities like outdoor showers, beach rentals, and restrooms. Just south of the city beach is 3-mile-long **Huntington State Beach.** Both popular beaches have lifeguards and concession stands seasonally. The state beach also has restrooms, showers, barbecue pits, and a waterfront bike path. The main entrance is on Beach Boulevard, and there are access points all along the Pacific Coast Highway (Hwy. 1).

**Newport Beach** runs for about 5 miles and includes both Newport and Balboa piers. It has outdoor showers, restrooms, volleyball nets, and a vintage boardwalk that just may make you feel as though you've stepped 50 years back in time. **Balboa Bike and Beach Stuff** (© 949/723-1516), at the corner of Balboa and Palm near the pier, rents a variety of items, from pier fishing poles to bikes, beach umbrellas, and body boards. The **Southwind Kayak Center,** 17855 Sky Park Circle, Irvine (© 800/768-8494 or 949/261-0200; www.southwindkayaks.com), rents sea kayaks for use in the bay or open ocean at rates starting at $40 per day; instructional classes are available on weekends, with some midweek classes in summer. The center also conducts several easygoing guided outings, including a $55 Back to Nature trip that highlights the marine life around Dana Point.

**Crystal Cove State Park,** which covers 3 miles of coastline between Corona del Mar and Laguna Beach and extends into the hills around El Moro Canyon, is a good alternative to the more popular beaches for seekers of solitude. (There are, however, lifeguards and restrooms.) The beach is a winding, sandy strip, backed with grassy terraces; high tide sometimes sections it into coves. The entire area offshore is an underwater nature preserve. There are four entrances, including Pelican Point and El Moro Canyon. For information, call © **949/494-3539.**

**Salt Creek Beach Park** lies below the palatial Ritz-Carlton Laguna Niguel; guests who tire of the pristine swimming pool can venture down the staircase on Ritz-Carlton Drive to wiggle their toes in the sand. The setting is spectacular, with wide white-sand beaches looking out toward Catalina Island (which explains why the Ritz-Carlton was built here). The park has lifeguards, restrooms, a snack bar, and convenient parking near the hotel.

**Doheny State Beach** in Dana Point, just south of Dana Point Marina (enter off Del Abispo St.), has long been known as a premier surfing spot and camping site. Doheny has the friendly vibe of beach parties in days gone by: Tree-shaded lawns give way to wide beaches, and picnicking and beach camping are encouraged. There are 121 sites that can be used for either tents or RVs, plus a state-run visitor center featuring several small aquariums of sea and tide-pool life. For more information and camping availability, call © **949/492-0802.**

**BICYCLING**   Biking is the most popular beach activity up and down the coast. A slower-paced alternative to driving, it allows you to enjoy the clean, fresh air and notice smaller details of these laid-back beach towns and harbors. The Newport Beach visitor center (see "Visitor Information," above) offers a free *Bike Ways* map of trails throughout the city and harbor. Bikes and equipment can be rented at **Balboa Bike & Beach Stuff,** 601 Balboa Blvd., Newport Beach (© **949/723-1516**), and **Laguna Beach Cyclery,** 240 Thalia St. (© **949/494-1522;** www.lagunacyclery.net).

**GOLF**   Many golf-course architects have used the geography of the Orange Coast to its full advantage, molding challenging and scenic courses from the rolling bluffs. Most courses are private, but two outstanding ones are open to the public. **The Links at Monarch Beach,** 33033 Niguel Rd., Dana Point (© **949/240-8247**), is particularly impressive. This hilly, challenging course, designed by Robert Trent Jones, Jr., offers great ocean views. Afternoon winds can sneak up, so accuracy is essential. Weekend greens fees are $185 ($160 weekdays). The rates after 1pm drop to $125 weekends and $99 weekdays.

Another challenge is the **Pelican Hill Golf Club,** 22651 Pelican Hill Rd. S., Newport Beach (© **949/760-0707;** www.pelicanhill.com), with two Tom Fazio–designed courses. The Ocean North course is heavily bunkered, while the Ocean South course features canyons and ravines; both have large, multi-tier greens. Weekend greens fees are $250; weekday fees are $175. And remember—when putting near the ocean, the break is always toward the water.

## SEEING THE SIGHTS

Beyond the sights listed below, an excellent attraction is **Balboa Island** (www.balboa island.com). The charm of this pretty little neighborhood isn't diminished by knowing that the island was man-made—and it certainly hasn't affected the price of real estate (it's hard to believe that the original property lots sold for $250). Tiny clapboard cottages in the island's center and modern houses with two-story windows and private docks along the perimeter make a colorful and romantic picture. You can drive onto the island on Jamboree Road to the north or take the three-car ferry from Balboa Peninsula ($1.50 per vehicle; $1 per pedestrian). It's generally more fun to park and take the 30-minute ferry ride as a pedestrian, since the island is crowded and lacks parking, and the tiny alleys they call streets are more suitable for strolling. **Marine Avenue,** the main commercial street, is lined with small shops and cafes that evoke a New England fishing village. Shaved ices sold by sidewalk vendors will relieve the heat of summer.

**Balboa Pavilion** ★ *Kids*   This historic cupola-topped structure, a California Historical Landmark, was built in 1905 as a bathhouse for swimmers in their ankle-length bathing costumes. Later, during the Big Band era, dancers rocked the Pavilion doing the "Balboa Hop." Now it serves as the terminal for Catalina Island passenger service, harbor and whale-watching cruises, and fishing charters. The surrounding boardwalk is the Balboa Fun Zone, a collection of carnival rides, game arcades, and vendors of hot dogs and cotton candy. For Newport Harbor or Catalina cruise information, call ℂ **949/673-5245;** for sportfishing and whale-watching, call ℂ **949/673-1434.**

400 Main St., Balboa, Newport Beach. ℂ **949/673-5245.** From Hwy. 1, turn south onto Newport Blvd. (which becomes Balboa Blvd. on the peninsula); turn left at Main St.

**Laguna Art Museum**   This beloved local institution is working hard to position itself as the artistic cornerstone of the community. In addition to a small but interesting permanent collection, the museum presents installations of regional works definitely worth

---

## Biplane, Air Combat & Warbird Adventures: Aerial Thrills

For anyone with a thirst for adrenaline-pumping excitement, have I got a recommendation for you. At a small airport in the coastal town of Carlsbad, about 30 miles north of San Diego, is a company called Biplane, Air Combat & Warbird Adventures, run by husband-and-wife team Kate and Tom. This cheerful duo offers a mind-blowing opportunity to fly either a World War II fighter plane or a modern combat aircraft (or both!).

Couples wearing soft leather headgear and goggles (think Snoopy vs. The Red Baron) sit side-by-side at the front of the open cockpit while the pilot—seated in back—flies a leisurely route along the sunny coast. At your request, the pilot will perform a few dips and lazy eights to add a touch of excitement, but nothing compares to the loops and rolls you can perform yourself (yes, *you,* even if you've never flown a plane in your life) in their big blue AT-6 Texan, a 600-horsepower killer aircraft equipped with machine-gun barrels. "Okay, it's your plane," are four words you'll remember forever as the pilot (seated in front on this ride), calmly talks you through the aerobatic procedures, which are surprisingly easy to perform. (It's one of the most incredible things I've ever done.)

For more information about Biplane, Air Combat & Warbird Adventures, call ℂ **800/SKY-LOOP** or 760/930-0903. And be sure to visit their website—www.barnstorming.com—for special Internet rates and package deals.

a detour. Past examples include a display of surf photography from the coast's 1930s and 1940s golden era, and dozens of plein-air Impressionist paintings (ca. 1900–30) by the founding artists of the original colony. The museum is also open during Laguna Beach Artwalk, the first Thursday each month, when all are admitted free.

307 Cliff Dr., Laguna Beach. © **949/494-8971**. www.lagunaartmuseum.org. Admission $9 adults, $7 students and seniors, free for kids under age 12. Daily 11am–5pm.

**Mission San Juan Capistrano**   The 7th of the 21 California coastal missions, Mission San Juan Capistrano is continually being restored. The mix of old ruins and working buildings is home to small museum collections and various adobe rooms that are as quaint as they are interesting. The intimate mission chapel with its ornate baroque altar is still used for religious services, and the mission complex is the center of the community, hosting performing arts, children's programs, and other cultural events year-round.

This mission is best known for its **swallows,** which are said to return to nest each year at their favorite sanctuary. According to legend, the birds wing their way back to the mission annually on March 19, St. Joseph's Day, arriving at dawn; they are said to take flight again on October 23, after bidding the mission farewell. In reality, you'll probably see the well-fed birds here any day of the week, winter or summer.

Ortega Hwy. (Hwy. 74), San Juan Capistrano. © **949/234-1300**. www.missionsjc.com. Admission $6 adults, $5 seniors, $4 children. Daily 8:30am–5pm.

## WHERE TO STAY

Also consider the **Seal Beach Inn** (© **800/HIDEAWAY** or 562/493-2416; fax 562/799-0483; http://sealbeachinn.com), a romantic 23-room bed-and-breakfast inn 1 block from the beach in a quiet Seal Beach residential neighborhood.

### VERY EXPENSIVE

**Montage Resort & Spa** ★★★   The rich have it good when it comes to vacationing. Spend a few minutes walking around the new 30-acre Montage resort in Laguna Beach and you'll see why. Unfazed by the two luxury resorts—the St. Regis and the Ritz-Carlton Laguna Niguel—just down the road, the investors behind this Arts and Crafts beauty have created yet another reason for big spenders to unwind along the Orange Coast. You can barely see it from the PCH, and the front entrance is rather understated, but as you walk through the lobby and onto the balcony overlooking the . . . oh my. The change of scenery is so breathtakingly abrupt that it takes composure not to sprint down to the gorgeous mosaic-tiled pool or run barefoot along the sun-kissed beach. It's the same view from the balcony of every room, and you never tire of it.

The Montage Resort is all about style. You don't even check in at the front desk— as soon as you arrive you're warmly greeted and given a well-rehearsed tour of the resort by attractive khaki-clad employees wearing tailored jackets. The tour ends at the neo-Craftsman–style guestrooms, which are spacious, immaculate, and tastefully decorated with muted color schemes, museum-quality plein-air artwork, huge marble bathrooms with oversize tubs and plush robes, 27-inch flatscreen TVs with DVD players, quality dark-wood furnishings, feather-top beds with goose-down pillows, and very inviting balconies. But don't get too attached: You'll be spending very little time here as you lounge by the infinity-edged pool sipping a lemonade, spend hours exploring the tide pools, stroll through the hotel's impeccably manicured park and pristine beaches, spoil yourself rotten with skin treatments and massages at the oceanfront Spa Montage, and then feast on chef James Boyce's superb Mediterranean-style cuisine at the resort's signature restaurant, **Studio.** There's plenty for kids to do as well: They have their own pool and several fun-filled programs to keep them entertained (and, of course, there's the beach). Montage is in a better location than the St. Regis (but no golf course) and has far superior facilities compared to the Ritz-Carlton, so if the higher rate doesn't matter then, well, there you have it.

30801 S. Coast Highway, Laguna Beach, CA 92651. © **888/715-6700** or 949/715-6000. Fax 949/715-6100. www.montagelagunabeach.com. 262 units. $475–$735 double; from $1,100 suite. AE, DISC, MC, V. Valet parking $25. **Amenities:** 3 restaurants and lobby lounge w/live entertainment; outdoor heated Olympic-sized pool; ocean-front fitness facilities and spa with outdoor heated lap pool; concierge; business services; 24-hr. room service; daily laundry/valet service; newspaper delivery. *In room:* A/C, flatscreen TV and DVD/CD player, 3 multiline phones w/voice mail, high-speed Internet access, minibar, hair dryer, iron/board, personal safe.

**Ritz-Carlton Laguna Niguel** ★★★   The Old World meets the Pacific Rim at this regal Dana Point grande dame. Although it's the oldest and most outdated (for now) of the three major resorts in this region—the other two being the St. Regis and the Montage—it has one major trump card: the region's most spectacular setting. It's perched right on the edge of a 150-foot-high bluff that fronts an idyllic 2-mile-long beach where some of the world's best surfers play in the waves (truly, you can spend hours on your balcony admiring the ocean view). Lush terraces and colorful flower gardens abound throughout the well-tended property. The service, in typical Ritz-Carlton style, is unassuming and impeccable. The spacious rooms are outfitted with sumptuous furnishings and fabrics, and all come with a terrace, an Italian marble bathroom equipped with a double vanity, and the most comfortable feather beds I've ever slept in; some suites even have fireplaces. Garden tours, beach shuttles, and excellent kids programs are available as well.

If elegant European ambience and unobstructed ocean views are your criteria, the Ritz property is a better choice than the nearby St. Regis, but if you prefer a more modern and trend-setting hotel, both the St. Regis and Montage are hard to beat. *Please note:* A massive $40-million renovation of almost the entire property is scheduled for completion by 2006. I've seen a peek of the new look and it's surprisingly modish—far more chic and contemporary than your typical Ritz decor.

1 Ritz-Carlton Dr., Dana Point, CA 92629. © **800/241-3333** or 949/240-2000. Fax 949/240-0829. www.ritzcarlton. com. 393 units. From $345 gardenview/poolview double; $495 oceanview double; from $525 suite. Children age 17 and under stay free in parent's room. Midweek and special packages available. AE, DC, DISC, MC, V. Parking $25. **Amenities:** 4 restaurants; 2 lounges; 4 outdoor tennis courts; health club; whirlpool; sauna; children's programs; concierge; business center; 24-hr. room service; in-room massage; babysitting; laundry/dry-cleaning service; executive-level rooms; regular shuttle to/from the beach and the golf course. *In room:* A/C, TV w/pay movies, minibar, hair dryer, iron, safe, robes.

**St. Regis Monarch Beach Resort & Spa** ★★★   Let's cut to the chase: The St. Regis Monarch Beach Resort is one of the finest luxury hotels I have ever had the pleasure of reviewing—and I've reviewed a *lot* of luxury hotels. They nailed it with this one, setting a standard for all other resort hotels to follow. Everything oozes with indulgence here, from the stellar service to the striking artwork, high-tech electronics, absurdly comfortable beds, stellar restaurants, and a 30,000-square-foot spa that will blow your mind. The $240-million, 172-acre resort opened on July 30, 2001, with a massive star-studded gala and has since been wooing the wealthy with its gorgeous Tuscan-inspired architecture and soothing ocean views.

Perfection is all in the details, and the St. Regis is full of them: a three-lane lap pool with an underwater sound system; a yoga, spinning, and "movement" studio; a full-service Vogue salon; private poolside cabanas; incredible contemporary cuisine at the **Aqua** ★★★ restaurant; couples spa treatment rooms with whirlpool baths and fireplaces; an 18-hole Robert Trent Jones, Jr., golf course; and even a private beach club. Then there are the guest rooms, loaded with beautiful custom-designed furniture, 32-inch Sony Vega flatscreen TVs with CD-DVD audio systems and a 300-DVD library, huge marble-laden bathrooms with glass shower doors that must weigh 100 pounds, and the most comfortable bathrobe I've ever worn.

The resort's only caveat is that it's near the beach, but unlike the Ritz-Carlton Laguna Niguel and Montage (see reviews above), it's not on it. Your view is of the terraced pool area and golf course, and complimentary shuttle service is needed to get to the beach. However, hotel guests have exclusive access to the St. Regis Beach Club, where beach attendants set up beach chairs, towels, and umbrellas, and also take food and beverage (including alcohol) orders. You can even hire a "Surf Butler," who will take your measurements for a wet suit, bring out a long board, and give you surfing lessons. *Tip:* Even if it's a bit beyond your price range, give yourself one heckuva birthday present this year and book a room on the Astor Floor, which comes with your own private butler (trust me, you'll be spoiled for life).

1 Monarch Beach Rd., Dana Point, CA 92629. **©** **800/722-1543** or 949/234-3200. Fax 949/234-3201. www.stregis monarchbeach.com. 400 units. From $450 resortview double; from $550 oceanview double; from $875 suites. Golf and spa packages available as well. AE, DC, DISC, MC, V. Valet parking $25. **Amenities:** 6 restaurants; lounge; 3 pools; 18-hole golf course; 3 tennis courts (lit for night play); Spa Gaucin and a fitness center; 2 hot tubs; Kid's Club; concierge; complimentary local shuttle; 24-hr. business center; retail shops; 24-hr. room service; in-room massage; babysitting; laundry/dry-cleaning service; executive-level rooms; morning paper; 24-hr. butler service; wine-cellar tasting room. *In room:* A/C, TV w/CD-DVD and DVD library, 3 phones, high-speed Internet access, minibar, hair dryer, safe, robes.

**Surf and Sand Resort** ★★   Perhaps the most beloved hotel on the Orange Coast, the Surf and Sand has come a long way since it started in 1948 as a beachside motor lodge with 13 units. Still occupying the same fantastic oceanside location, it now features 165 top-of-the-line rooms that, despite their simplicity and standard size, feel enormously decadent. They're all very bright and beachy; each is done entirely in white and has a private balcony with a dreamy ocean view, a marble bathroom accented handsomely with granite, and plush cotton terry robes. All have whirlpool tubs as well. *Tip:* Try getting one of the deluxe corner rooms, affording an expanded 90-degree view of the California coastline—it's well worth the additional $40. Also, be sure to check their website for special package deals. The hotel's Mediterranean-style **Aquaterra Spa** offers a tantalizing array of personalized massage, skincare, and body treatments. You'll find the requisite ocean-inspired treatments, but personal choice is the rule here: The menu features eight different specialty massages, each with your choice of four aromatherapy oils. The spa's four Couples Rituals offer themed body treatments followed by a bubble bath for two (the tub has an ocean view) and a massage to finish. **Splashes** restaurant serves three meals daily in a beautiful ocean-front setting; the rich Mediterranean cuisine is perfect against a backdrop of sunlight and crashing waves.

1555 S. Coast Hwy. (south of Laguna Canyon Rd.), Laguna Beach, CA 92651. **©** **888/869-7569** or 949/497-4477. Fax 949/494-2897. www.surfandsandresort.com. 165 units. Doubles high season (July 1–Sept 6) $430–$530; doubles low season (Sept 7–June 30) $350–$450; suites year-round $680–$1,100. AE, DC, DISC, MC, V. **Amenities:** Restaurant; bar; outdoor heated pool; fitness room; full-service spa; whirlpool; summer children's programs; concierge; business center; room service (6:30am–10pm); in-room massage; babysitting; laundry/dry-cleaning service; concierge-level rooms. *In room:* TV w/pay movies and video games, minibar, hair dryer, iron, safe, robes, CD player.

## SoCal Surfing Lessons

Some of the best beginner surf breaks in California are located around the Dana Point region. If you're interested in taking a beginner surfing lesson—no, really, it's easy and a lot of fun—contact **Monarch Adventures** at ℂ **949/ 254-8139** or paul.grosveld@stregis.com. The ever-so-patient surf instructors are wizards at getting everyone to stand up and ride on those big, padded learner surfboards. The company also offers kayaking, body boarding, and body surfing lessons, as well as hiking tours and beach activity rentals. It's located at 500 Monarch Bay Drive in Dana Point.

### EXPENSIVE

**Portofino Beach Hotel** ⭐   This oceanfront inn, built in a former seaside rail station, is steps away from the Newport Pier, along a stretch of bars and equipment-rental shacks; the beach is across the parking lot. The place maintains a calm, European air even in the face of the midsummer beach frenzy. Although it can get noisy in summer, there are advantages to being at the center of the action. The hotel has its own enclosed parking, and sunsets are spectacular viewed from a plush armchair in the upstairs parlor. Guest rooms, furnished with antique reproductions, are on the second floor—the first is occupied by a guests-only bar and several cozy sitting rooms—and most have luxurious skylit bathrooms.

2306 W. Ocean Front, Newport Beach, CA 92663. ℂ **800/571-8749** or 949/673-7030. Fax 949/723-4370. www. portofinobeachhotel.com. 20 units. $159–$349 double. Rates include continental breakfast. Free parking. AE, DC, DISC, MC, V. **Amenities:** Whirlpool; coin-op laundry; laundry/dry-cleaning service. *In room:* A/C, TV.

### MODERATE

**Blue Lantern Inn** ⭐⭐   A three-story New England–style gray clapboard inn, the Blue Lantern is a pleasant cross between romantic B&B and modern, sophisticated small hotel. Almost all the rooms, which are decorated with reproduction traditional furniture and plush bedding, have a balcony or deck overlooking the harbor. All have a fireplace and whirlpool tub. You can have your breakfast here in private (clad in the fluffy robe provided), or go downstairs to the sunny dining room that also serves complimentary afternoon tea. There's also an exercise room and a cozy lounge with menus for many area restaurants. The friendly staff welcomes you with home-baked cookies at the front desk.

34343 St. of the Blue Lantern, Dana Point, CA 92629. ℂ **800/950-1236** or 949/661-1304. Fax 949/496-1483. www.foursisters.com. 29 units. $175–$500 double. Rates include full breakfast and afternoon wine and hors d'oeuvres. AE, DC, MC, V. **Amenities:** Exercise room; whirlpool; complimentary bicycles; laundry/dry-cleaning service. *In room:* A/C, TV/VCR, minibar, coffeemaker, hair dryer.

**Casa Laguna Inn** ⭐   Once you see this romantic terraced complex of Spanish-style cottages amid lush gardens and secluded patios—which offers all the amenities of a B&B *and* affordable prices—you might wonder what's the catch? Well, the noise of busy PCH wafts easily into Casa Laguna, which might prove disturbing to sensitive ears and light sleepers. Still, the Casa has been a favorite hideaway since Laguna's early days and now glows under the watchful eye of a terrific owner, who's upped the comfort ante by adding a spa. Some rooms—especially the suites—are downright luxurious, with fireplace, kitchen, bathrobes, CD player, VCR, and other in-room goodies. Throughout the property, Catalina tile adorns fountains and bougainvillea spills into paths; each room has an individual charm. Breakfast is served in the sunny morning room of the Craftsman-style Mission House, where a cozy living room also invites relaxation and conversation.

2510 S. Coast Hwy., Laguna Beach, CA 92651. ℂ **800/233-0449** or 949/494-2996. Fax 949/494-5009. 21 units. $140–$320 double; from $250 suite. Rates include breakfast, afternoon wine, and hors d'oeuvres. Off-season and midweek discounts available. AE, DISC, MC, V. **Amenities:** Heated outdoor pool; spa; whirlpool. *In room:* TV.

### Doryman's Inn Bed & Breakfast ★

The rooms at Doryman's Inn are both luxurious and romantic, making this one of the nicest B&Bs to be found along the coast. The rooms are outfitted with French and American antiques, floral textiles, beveled mirrors, and cozy furnishings. Every room has a working fireplace and a sunken marble tub (some have whirlpool jets). King- or queen-size beds, lots of plants, and good ocean views round out the decor. The location, directly on the Newport Beach Pier Promenade, is also enviable, though some may find it a bit too close to the action. Breakfast includes fresh pastries and fruit, brown eggs, yogurt, cheeses, and international coffees and teas.

2102 W. Ocean Front, Newport Beach, CA 92663. ℂ **949/675-7300.** www.dorymansinn.com. 10 units. $190–$380 double; from $265 suite. Rates include continental breakfast. AE, MC, V. Free parking. **Amenities:** Restaurant. *In room:* A/C, TV.

## WHERE TO DINE

Options in Seal Beach are limited, but a good choice for seafood is **Walt's Wharf,** 201 Main St. (ℂ **562/598-4433**), a bustling, polished restaurant featuring market-fresh selections either plain or with Pacific Rim accents.

### EXPENSIVE

**Five Feet** ★★ CALIFORNIA/ASIAN   While Five Feet may no longer break culinary ground, the kitchen still combines the best in California cuisine with Asian technique and ingredients. The restaurant has a minimalist, almost-industrial decor that's brightened by a friendly staff and splendid cuisine. Menu selections run the gamut from tea-smoked filet mignon topped with Roquefort cheese and candied walnuts to a hot Thai-style mixed grill of veal, beef, lamb, and chicken stir-fried with sweet peppers, onions, and mushrooms in curry-mint sauce. The menu changes daily, but you can always find the house specialty, whole braised catfish.

328 Glenneyre, Laguna Beach. ℂ **949/497-4955.** Reservations recommended. Main courses $18–$49. AE, DC, DISC, MC, V. Sun–Thurs 5–10pm; Fri–Sat 5–11pm.

### Roy's of Newport Beach ★★ HAWAIIAN REGIONAL/PACIFIC RIM

Any foodie who's been to Hawaii in the past decade knows the name Roy Yamaguchi, father of Hawaiian Regional Cuisine (HRC) and the islands' answer to Wolfgang Puck. Roy's empire expanded to Southern California in 1999 with the opening of this dinner-only restaurant on the fringe of Fashion Island shopping center. Yamaguchi developed a menu that represents his groundbreaking East/West/Polynesian cuisine but can be reliably executed by chefs in far-flung kitchens. Most of each night's specials are fresh Pacific fish, given the patented HRC touch with Japanese, Thai, and even Latin accents. Signature dishes include island-style *ahi poke,* spicy Mongolian-glazed rack of lamb, and blackened yellowfin tuna in soy-mustard-butter sauce. The bar whips up "vacation" cocktails in tropical colors, and the chocolate soufflé is to die for.

453 Newport Center Dr., Fashion Island. ℂ **949/640-7697.** www.roysrestaurant.com. Reservations suggested. Main courses $18–$32. AE, DC, DISC, MC, V. Sun–Thurs 5–10pm; Fri–Sat 5–11pm.

## MODERATE

**Crab Cooker** SEAFOOD   Since 1951, folks in search of fresh, well-prepared seafood have headed to this bright-red former bank building. Also a fish market, the Crab Cooker has a casual atmosphere of humble wooden tables, uncomplicated smoked and grilled preparations, and meticulously selected fresh fare. The place is especially proud of its Maryland crab cakes; clams and oysters are also part of the repertoire.

2200 Newport Blvd., Newport Beach. (C) **949/673-0100.** www.crabcooker.com. Main courses $10–$25 dinner, $8–$19 lunch. AE, MC, V. Sun–Thurs 11am–9pm; Fri–Sat 11am–10pm.

**Harbor Grill** SEAFOOD/STEAK   In a business/commercial mall in the center of the Dana Point Marina, the Harbor Grill is enthusiastically recommended by locals for mesquite-broiled ocean-fresh seafood. Hawaiian mahimahi with a mango-chutney baste is on the menu, along with Pacific swordfish, crab cakes, and beef steaks.

34499 St. of the Golden Lantern, Dana Point. (C) **949/240-1416.** www.harborgrill.com. Reservations recommended. Main courses $10–$23. AE, DC, DISC, MC, V. Daily 11:30am–10pm; Sun brunch 9am–2pm.

**Las Brisas** *(Moments* MEXICAN SEAFOOD   Las Brisas's breathtaking view of the Pacific (particularly at sunset) and potent margaritas are a surefire combination for a *muy romantico* evening. In fact, it's so popular that it can get pretty crowded during the summer months, so be sure to make a reservation. Affordable during lunch but pricey at dinner, the menu consists mostly of seafood recipes from the Mexican Riviera. Even the standard enchiladas and tacos get a zesty update with crab or lobster meat and fresh herbs. Calamari steak is sautéed with bell peppers, capers, and herbs in a garlic-butter sauce, and king salmon is mesquite-broiled and served with a creamy lime sauce. Although a bit on the touristy side, Las Brisas can be a fun part of the Laguna Beach experience.

361 Cliff Dr. (off Hwy. 1 north of Laguna Canyon), Laguna Beach. (C) **949/497-5434.** www.eltorito.com/lasbrisas. Reservations recommended. Main courses $10–$24. AE, DC, DISC, MC, V. Mon–Thurs 8am–10pm; Fri–Sat 8am–11pm; Sun 9am–10pm. Valet parking $3 lunch, $4 dinner.

**Ramos House Cafe** *(★★* REGIONAL AMERICAN   Hidden away in the historic Rios district next to the train tracks, this converted 1881 cottage brings the flavor of a simpler time to busy Orange County. The small seasonal menu of regional American favorites uses garden-grown herbs, house-baked breads, and hand-turned ice cream. The all-purpose breakfast/lunch menu (dinner only for special events) features warmly satisfying cinnamon-apple beignets, wild mushroom and sun-dried tomato omelets, fried green tomatoes sauced with goat cheese, Southern fried chicken salad in pumpkin seed–buttermilk dressing, shrimp and sourdough bread pudding, an always changing but always superb fresh soup, and more comfort food faves with a Southern flair. Seating is outside, on a tree-shaded brick garden patio that invites leisure.

31752 Los Rios St. (off Del Obispo St.), San Juan Capistrano. (C) **949/443-1342.** www.ramoshouse.com. Main courses $9–$16. AE, DC, DISC, MC, V. Tues–Sun 8:30am–3pm.

# 16

# The Southern California Desert

*by Harry Basch*

To the casual observer, the Southern California desert might seem like a desolate expanse under an unrelenting sun. Its splendor is subtle, though; you have to discover its beauty in your own time.

If it looks as though nothing but insects could survive here, look again: You're bound to see a roadrunner or a tiny gecko dart across your path. Close your eyes and listen for the cry of a hawk or an owl. Check the ground for coyote or bobcat tracks. Notice the sparkle of fish in the streams running through palm oases. Check the road signs, which warn of desert tortoise crossings (the tortoise being one of many endangered species found only here, where it's protected by the federal government in a wildlife sanctuary). Visit in spring, when the ground throughout the Lancaster area is carpeted with the brilliant golds and oranges of the poppy, California's state flower (which, like the autumn leaves in New England, draw seasonal tourists in droves).

Let your eyes adjust to take in the lushness of trees, flowering cacti, fragrant shrubs, and other singular plants that have adapted to this harsh climate—such as the gnarly Joshua tree, ugly to some but noble and eerily beautiful to many veteran explorers of the Mojave Desert.

If the beauty you seek is that of personal renewal, you're likely to find that too—if not in the shadow of purple-tinged mountains and otherworldy rock formations, then in a chaise longue beside a sparkling, impossibly blue swimming pool. Destinations here range from gloriously untouched national parks to luxurious resorts—united by the fact that it's a rare day when the sun doesn't shine.

## 1 En Route to the Palm Springs Resorts

If you're making the drive from Los Angeles via I-10, your first hour or so will be spent just, well, getting out of the L.A. metropolitan sprawl. Soon you'll leave the Inland Empire auto plazas behind, sail past the last of the bedroom-community shopping malls, and edge ever closer to the snowcapped (if you're lucky) San Bernardino and San Jacinto mountain ranges. (Coming from San Diego via I-15, the area discussed below is east of the junction with I-10.)

For frequent travelers on this stretch of highway, there are certain unmistakable signposts. Roadside attractions are part of what makes every moment of the vacation enjoyable. Below are three of our favorites.

**Hadley's Fruit Orchards**   Since 1931, this friendly emporium has been a fixture here, packed with folks shopping for dates, dried fruits, nuts, honey, preserves, and other regional products. A snack bar serves the beloved date shake; there are also plenty of gift-packed treats to carry home. (For more about the date mystique, see "Sweet Treat of the Desert: The Coachella Valley Date Gardens," on p. 641.)

48980 Seminole Dr. (off I-10), Cabazon. © **800/854-5655** or 951/849-5255. www.hadleyfruitorchards.com. Mon–Thurs 9am–7pm; Fri–Sun 8am–8pm (call to verify).

**Windmill Tours** (Finds)  For years, travelers through the San Gorgonio Pass have been struck by an awesome, otherworldly sight: never-ending, ever-expanding fields of windmills that harness the force of the breezes gusting through this passage and convert them to electricity to power air-conditioners throughout the Coachella Valley. If you get a charge from them, consider a guided tour offering a look into this alternative energy source. Learn how designers have improved the efficiency of wind turbines (technically they're not windmills), and measure those long rotors against the average human height (about 10 people could lie along one span).

Interstate 10 (Indian Ave. exit), Palm Springs. © **877/449-WIND** or 760/320-1365. www.windmilltours.com. Admission $23 adults, $20 seniors, $10 kids under 14. Tours Wed–Sat at 9am, 11am, and 2pm (varies seasonally).

## 2 Get Your Kicks on Historic Route 66

Until the final triumph of the multilane interstate system in the early 1960s, 2,300-mile-long Route 66 was the only automobile route between the Chicago shores of Lake Michigan and L.A.'s golden Pacific beaches. "America's Main Street" rambled through eight states, and today, in each one, organizations exist, such as Route 66 Tourism, just to preserve its remnants. California has a lengthy stretch of the original highway, many miles of which still proudly wear the designation "California State Highway 66." It's not just weed-split abandoned blacktop, either. These are active streets, often the main commercial drag of the community. Many stretches have become clusters of new developments, shopping centers, and fast-food chains. Pretty mundane—until you round a curve and unexpectedly see a vintage wood-frame house, perhaps from a pre–Great Depression ranch. There's poignancy here: That house was probably set way back from the road, amidst a shady grove, before highway workers buried the front yard under asphalt.

Other picturesque relics of that era—single-story motels, two-pump gas stations—exist beside their modern neighbors, inviting nostalgia for a time when the vacation began the moment you backed out of the driveway.

### ESSENTIALS

**THE ROUTE**  Our drive begins in Pasadena and ends in downtown San Bernardino, 56 miles west of Palm Springs. In San Bernardino, I-215 intersects Route 66; take it 4 miles south to rejoin I-10 and continue east.

*Note:* This detour works equally well if your destination is Lake Arrowhead or Big Bear Lake; take I-215 north 3 miles to Hwy. 30 and continue into the mountains. For more information, see chapter 15, "Side Trips from Los Angeles." The drive will take anywhere from 2 hours to 3 hours for your trip, depending on how many relics and photo opportunities you stop to enjoy. Some suitably retro meal suggestions are included in case you want to stop for lunch.

**VISITOR INFORMATION**  For more information, contact the **National Historic Route 66 Federation,** in the Los Angeles area (© **909/336-6131;** www.national66. com). There's also a quarterly *Route 66 Magazine* (4 issues, $18; © **702/299-0856;** www.route66magazine.com).

## LET'S HIT THE ROAD!

Although Route 66 officially ended at the picturesque Pacific, there are very few reminders left in the heart of L.A. Besides, I assume you've already seen the city, so Pasadena is the best point to begin your time-warp experience.

One of my favorite places is the **Fair Oaks Pharmacy,** Fair Oaks Avenue and Mission Street, 1½ miles south of Colorado Boulevard (© **626/799-1414**), a fixture on this corner since 1915. If you're in the mood for a treat, try an authentic ice-cream soda, a sparkling phosphate, a "Route 66" sundae, or an old-fashioned malt (complete with the frosty mixing can), all served by fresh-faced soda jerks from behind the marble counter. They also serve soup, sandwiches, and snacks. The Fair Oaks is still a pharmacy and offers a variety of gifts, including an abundance of Route 66–themed items. It's open Monday through Friday from 9am to 7pm, Saturday 9am to 5pm, and Sunday from 9am to 2pm. Pharmacy is closed on Sunday.

Perhaps you'd like some driving music. Then, reverse and go north on Fair Oaks to Colorado and turn right. There's no better place than **Canterbury Records,** 805 E. Colorado Blvd., a block west of Lake Avenue (© **626/792-7184**). It has L.A.'s finest selection of big bands and pop vocalists on CDs; perhaps you'll choose one of the many renditions of the late Bobby Troup's "(Get Your Kicks on) Route 66." The store is open Monday through Saturday from 9am to 9pm and Sunday from 10am to 7pm.

As you continue east on Colorado Boulevard, keep your eyes peeled for **motels** like the Saga Motor Hotel, Vagabond, Astro (fabulous *Jetsons*-style architecture), and Hi-Way Host. In fact, lodgings have proven the hardiest post-66 survivors, and you'll be seeing many frozen-in-time motor courts on the way.

Turn left on Rosemead Boulevard, passing under the freeway (boo, hiss) to Foothill Boulevard. Turning right, you'll soon be among the tree-lined streets of **Arcadia,** home to the Santa Anita Racetrack and the Los Angeles Arboretum, the picturesque former estate of "Lucky" Baldwin, whose Queen Anne cottage has been the setting for many movies and TV shows. Passing into Monrovia, look for the life-size plastic cow on the southeast corner of Mayflower. It marks the drive-thru called **Mike's Dairy**— a splendid example of this auto-age phenomenon. If you're observant, you'll see many drive-thru dairies along my route (mostly Alta-Dena brand). Mike's has all the typical features, including the refrigerated island display case still bearing a vintage DRIFT-WOOD DAIRY PRODUCTS price sign.

Next, look for Magnolia Avenue and the **Aztec Hotel** on the northwest corner. Opened in 1925, the Aztec was a local showplace, awing guests with its overscale, dark, Native American–themed lobby, Mayan murals, and exotic Brass Elephant bar. The arcade of shops once held the city's most prominent barbershop, beauty salon, and pharmacy. Little has changed about the interior, and a glance behind the front desk reveals the original cord-and-plug telephone switchboard still in use. If you care to wet your whistle, stop into the bar before continuing on.

Leaving the Aztec, you'll pass splendid Craftsman bungalows and other historic homes. Turn right on Shamrock Avenue and ogle the old gas station with its classic (if ornamental) gas pumps on the northwest corner of Almond Avenue; continue onward 2 more blocks, then make a left turn on Huntington Drive. Now you're in **Duarte,** where Huntington is lit by graceful and ornate double street lamps on the center median. This stretch also has many fabulous old motor courts; see if you can spot the Ranch Inn, Evergreen, Oak Park, Duarte Inn, and Capri. Check out the **Justice**

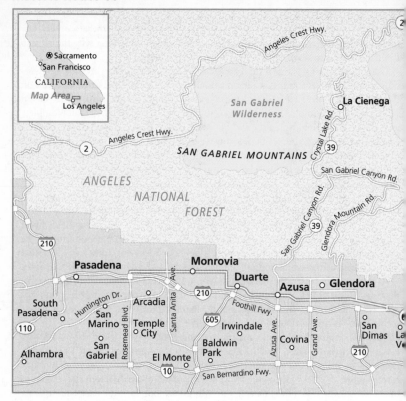

**Brothers Racing Museum,** 2734 E. Huntington Dr. in an officelike building at the east edge of town just before the river (open Mon–Fri 8am–5pm).

As you cross over the wide but nearly dry San Gabriel River, glance right from the bridge to see cars streaming along the interstate that supplanted Route 66. In Irwindale—which smells just like the industrial area it is, with plants ranging from a Miller brewery to Health Valley Foods—the street resumes the Foothill Boulevard name. At Irwindale Avenue the 30-mile "neon cruise" begins. You'll pass into **Azusa,** with its elegant 1932 **Azusa City Hall and Auditorium,** with vintage lampposts and a Moorish fountain enhancing a charming courtyard.

Our route swerves right onto Alosta Avenue at the **Foothill Drive-In Theater,** Southern California's last single-screen drive-in. As you cruise by, think of the days when our cars were an extension of our living rooms (with the great snacks Mom wouldn't allow at home), and the outdoor theaters were filled every summer evening by dusk. Alas, the drive-in awaits demolition, but the new owners may donate it to the city, relocate it, and refurbish the marquee.

Continuing on Alosta, you'll enter Glendora, named in 1887 by founder George Whitcomb for his wife, Ledora. Look for the **Palm Tropics,** one of the best-maintained old motels along the route. Farther along on the left-hand side is the **Golden Spur,** which began 70 years ago as a ride-up hamburger stand for the equestrian

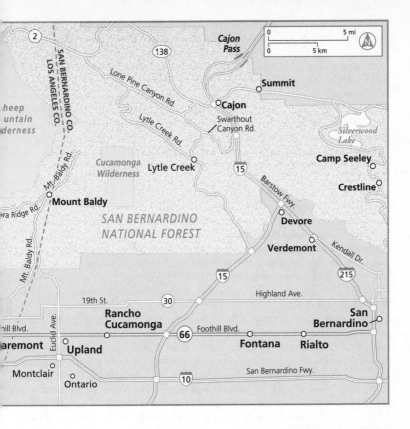

crowd. Unfortunately, the restaurant has been remodeled in boring stucco, leaving only the original sign, with its neon cowboy boot, as a reminder of its colorful past. At the corner of Cataract Avenue, a covered wagon announces the **Pinnacle Peak** restaurant, guarded by a giant steer atop the roof. In a mile or two, you'll pass quickly through San Dimas, a ranchlike community where you must pay attention to the HORSE CROSSING street signs.

Foothill Boulevard enters **La Verne** as you pass underneath the ramps to the I-30 freeway. In a large mall, you'll find a **Route 66 Gift Shop** inside the Cash Plus, between Vons and Target, 2418 Foothill Blvd. (© **909/592-2090**). **La Paloma** Mexican cafe, a fixture on the route for years, is on your left as you leave town. Continue on to Claremont, known these days for the highly respected group of **Claremont Colleges.** You'll pass several of them along this eucalyptus-lined boulevard. In days gone by, drivers would cruise along this route for mile upon mile, through orchards and open fields, the scenery punctuated only by ambling livestock or a rustic wood fence.

At Benson Avenue in Upland, a classic **1950s-style McDonald's** stands on the southeast corner, its golden arches flanking a low, white, walk-up counter with outdoor stools. The fast-food chain has its roots in this region: Richard and Maurice McDonald opened their first burger joint in San Bernardino in 1939. The brothers expanded their business, opening locations throughout Southern California, until entrepreneur Ray Kroc purchased the chain in 1955 and franchised McDonald's nationwide. Farther along, look north at the intersection of Euclid Avenue for the regal **monument to pioneer women.**

Pretty soon you'll be cruising through Rancho Cucamonga, whose fertile soil still yields a reliable harvest. You might see **produce stands** springing up by the side of the road; stop and pick up a fresh snack. If you're blessed with clear weather, gaze north at the gentle slope of the **San Gabriel Mountains** and you'll understand how Foothill Boulevard got its name. The construction codes in this community are among the most stringent in California, designed to respect the region's heritage and restrict runaway development. All new buildings are Spanish-Mediterranean in style and amply landscaped. At the corner of San Bernardino Road, the architectural bones of a wonderful old service station now stand forsaken. Across the street is the **Sycamore Inn,** in a grove of trees, looking like an old-style stagecoach stop. This reddish-brown wooden house, dating from 1848, has been a private home and gracious inn; today, it serves the community of Cucamonga as a restaurant and civic hall.

Rancho Cucamonga has preserved two historic wineries. First you'll see the **Thomas Vineyards,** at the northeast corner of Vineyard Avenue, established in 1839. Legend holds that the first owner mysteriously disappeared, leaving hidden treasure still undiscovered on the property. The winery's preserved structures now house a restaurant, coffeehouse, country crafts store, and a garden-supply boutique in the former brandy still tower.

Continuing on to Hellman Avenue, look for the **New Kansan Motel** (on the northeast corner). With that name, it must have seemed welcoming to Dust Bowl refugees. Near the northwest corner of Archibald Avenue, you'll find remnants of a **1920s-era gas station.** Empty now, those service bays have seen many a Ford, Studebaker, and Packard in need of a helping hand. Nearby, on the left, is **Route 66 Memories,** 10150 Foothill Blvd. (© **909/476-3843**), in a three-story classic house with a collection of metallic dinosaurs in the front yard, and a gift shop for antiques and rustic furniture. Next you'll pass the **Virginia Dare Winery,** at the northwest corner of Haven Avenue, whose structures now house part of a business park/mall, but retain the flourish of the original (1830s) winery logo.

Soon you'll pass the I-15 junction and be driving through Fontana, whose name in Italian means "fountain city." Slow down to have a look at the **motor-court hotels** lining both sides of the road. They're of various vintages, all built to cater to the once-vigorous stream of travelers passing through. Today they're dingy, but the melody of their names conjures up those glory days: Oasis, Rose Motel, Moana, El Rey, Rex, Fiesta, Dragon, Sand & Sage, and Sunset.

As you enter **San Bernardino,** be on the lookout for Meriden Avenue, site of the **Wigwam Motel.** Built in the 1950s (along with an identical twin motor court in Holbrook, Arizona), the whimsy of these stucco tepees lured many a road-weary traveler in for the night. Its catchy slogan, "Sleep in a wigwam, get more for your wampum," has been supplanted today by the more to-the-point "Do it in a teepee." But, as with many of the motor courts we'll pass, you need only picture a few large, shiny Buicks, T-bird convertibles, and "woodie" station wagons pulling in for the night and your imagination will drift back to days gone by.

Soon Foothill Boulevard will become Fifth Street, where the San Bernardino sign must have been a welcome sight for hot and weary westbound travelers emerging from the Mojave Desert. Route 66 wriggled through the steep Cajon Pass into a land fragrant with orange groves, where agricultural prosperity had quickly earned this region a lasting sobriquet: "the Inland Empire."

The year 1928 saw the grand opening of an elegant movie palace, the **California Theatre,** 562 W. Fourth St., only a block from Route 66. From Fifth Street east, turn right at E Street, then make a right on Fourth Street, where you can pull over to view the theater. Lovingly restored and still popular for nostalgic live entertainment and the rich tones of its original Wurlitzer pipe organ, the California was a frequent site of Hollywood "sneak previews." Humorist Will Rogers made his last public appearance here, in 1935. (Following his death, the highway was officially renamed the Will Rogers Memorial Hwy.) Notice the intricate relief of the theater's stone facade, and peek into the lobby to see the red velvet draperies, rich carpeting, and gold-banistered double staircase leading up to the balcony.

The theater is the last stop on your time-warp driving tour. Continue west on Fourth Street to the superslab highway only 2½ blocks away—that's I-215, your entry back to the present (see "Essentials" above).

## 3 The Palm Springs Desert Resorts

120 miles E of L.A.; 135 miles NE of San Diego

Palm Springs had been known for years as a golf-course-studded retirement mecca that's invaded annually by hordes of libidinous college kids on spring break. Well, the city of Palm Springs has been quietly changing its image and attracting a whole new crowd. Former mayor (the late) Sonny Bono's revolutionary "anti-thong" ordinance in 1991 halted the spring-break migration by eliminating public display of the bare derrière, and the upscale fairway-condo crowd now congregates in the outlying resort cities of Rancho Mirage, Palm Desert, Indian Wells, and La Quinta.

These days, no billboards are allowed in Palm Springs; all the palm trees in the center of town are backlit at night, and you won't see the word "motel" on any establishment. Seniors are everywhere, dressed to the nines in leisure suits and keeping alive the retro-kitsch establishments from the days when Elvis, Liberace, and Sinatra made the desert a swingin' place. But they're not alone: Baby boomers and yuppies nostalgic for the kidney-shaped swimming pools and backyard luaus of the Eisenhower/Kennedy glory years are buying ranch-style vacation homes and restoring them to their 1950s splendor. Hollywood's young glitterati are returning, too. Today, the city fancies itself a European-style resort with a dash of good ol' American small town thrown in—think *Jetsons* architecture and the crushed-velvet vibe of piano bars with the colors and attitude of a laid-back Aegean village. One thing hasn't changed: Swimming, sunbathing, golfing, and playing tennis are still the primary pastimes.

Another important presence in Palm Springs has little to do with socialites and Americana. The Agua Caliente Band of Cahuilla Indians settled in this area 1,000 years before the first golf ball was ever teed up. Recognizing the beauty and spirituality of this wide-open space, they lived a simple life around the mineral springs on the desert floor, migrating into the cool canyons during the summer months. Under a treaty with the railroad companies and the U.S. government, the tribe owns half the land on which Palm Springs is built and works to preserve Native American heritage. It's easy to learn about the American Indians during your visit, and it will definitely add to your appreciation of this part of California.

## ESSENTIALS

**GETTING THERE**    Airlines that service the **Palm Springs International Airport,** 3400 E. Tahquitz Canyon Way (℡ 760/323-8161), include **Alaska Airlines** (℡ 800/426-0333; www.alaskaair.com), **American** and **American Eagle** (℡ 800/433-7300; www.aa.com), **America West Express** (℡ 800/235-9292; www.americawest.com), **Continental Express** (℡ 800/525-0280; www.continental.com), **Delta** and **Delta Connection** (℡ 800/221-1212; www.delta.com), **Horizon Air** (℡ 800/547-9308; www.horizonair.com), **Northwest** (℡ 800/225-2525; www.nwa.com), and **United Airlines** and **United Express** (℡ 800/241-6522; www.united.com). Flights from Los Angeles take about 40 minutes.

If you're driving from Los Angeles, take I-10 east to the Highway 111 turnoff to Palm Springs. You'll breeze into town on North Palm Canyon Drive, the main thoroughfare. The trip from downtown L.A. takes about 2 hours if traffic is light. If you're driving from San Diego, take I-15 north to I-10 east; it takes a little more than 2 hours.

**VISITOR INFORMATION**    Be sure to pick up *Palm Springs Life* magazine's free monthly, *Desert Guide.* It contains tons of visitor information, including a comprehensive calendar of events. Copies are distributed in hotels and newsstands and by the **Palm Springs Desert Resorts Convention & Visitors Authority,** 70-100 Hwy. 111, Rancho Mirage, CA 92270 (℡ **800/937-3767** or 760/770-9000). The bureau's office staff can help with maps, brochures, and advice Monday through Friday from 8:30am to 5pm. They also operate a website (www.palmspringsusa.com).

The **Palm Springs Visitors Information Center,** 2901 N. Palm Canyon Dr., Palm Springs, CA 92262 (℡ **800/34-SPRINGS;** www.palm-springs.org), offers maps, brochures, advice, souvenirs, and a free hotel reservation service. The office is open Monday through Saturday from 9am to 5pm and Sunday from 8am to 4pm.

Another site worth browsing is **www.thedesertsun.com**, an offshoot of the local newspaper the *Desert Sun* that has information for locals as well as visitors.

**ORIENTATION**    The commercial downtown area of Palm Springs stretches about half a mile along North Palm Canyon Drive between Alejo and Ramon streets. The street is one-way southbound through the heart of town, but its northbound counterpart is Indian Canyon Drive, 1 block east. The mountains lie west and south, while the rest of Palm Springs is laid out in a grid to the southeast. Palm Canyon forks into South Palm Canyon (leading to the Indian Canyons) and East Palm Canyon (the continuation of Hwy. 111) traversing the towns of Cathedral City, Rancho Mirage, Palm Desert, Indian Wells, and La Quinta before looping up to rejoin I-10 at Indio. Desert Hot Springs is north of Palm Springs, straight up Gene Autry Trail. Tahquitz Canyon Way creates North Palm Canyon's primary intersection, tracking a straight line between the airport and the heart of town.

## WHAT TO SEE & DO
### GREAT GOLF COURSES

The Palm Springs Desert Resorts are a mecca for golfers (see "Fairways & Five-Irons, Desert-Style" below), with 114 public, semiprivate, and private courses in the area. If you're the kind who starts polishing your irons the moment you begin planning your vacation, you're best off staying at one of the valley's many golf resorts, where you can enjoy the proximity of your hotel's facilities as well as smart package deals that can give you a taste of country-club membership. On the other hand, if you'd like to fit a round of golf into an otherwise varied trip and you aren't staying at a hotel with its own links,

# The Palm Springs Desert Resorts

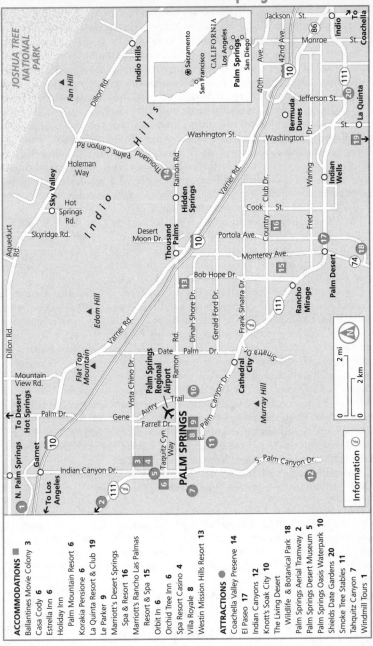

**ACCOMMODATIONS** ■
Ballantines Movie Colony **3**
Casa Cody **6**
Estrella Inn **6**
Holiday Inn
  Palm Mountain Resort **6**
Korakia Pensione **6**
La Quinta Resort & Club **19**
Le Parker **9**
Marriott's Desert Springs
  Spa & Resort **16**
Marriott's Rancho Las Palmas
  Resort & Spa **15**
Orbit In **6**
Orchid Tree Inn **6**
Spa Resort Casino **4**
Villa Royale **8**
Westin Mission Hills Resort **13**

**ATTRACTIONS** ●
Coachella Valley Preserve **14**
El Paseo **17**
Indian Canyons **12**
Knott's Soak City **10**
The Living Desert
  Wildlife & Botanical Park **18**
Palm Springs Aerial Tramway **2**
Palm Springs Desert Museum **5**
Palm Springs Oasis Waterpark **10**
Shields Date Gardens **20**
Smoke Tree Stables **11**
Tahquitz Canyon **7**
Windmill Tours **1**

courses at all levels are open to the public, many in Palm Springs, with others down the valley in Cathedral City, Palm Desert, Indian Wells, La Quinta, and Indio. Call ahead to see which will rent gear on short notice.

Beginners will enjoy **Tommy Jacobs' Bel-Air Greens,** 1001 El Cielo, Palm Springs (© 760/322-6062; www.tommyjacobsbelairgreens.com), a 9-hole, par-32 executive course that challengers golfers with water and sand traps while allowing for a few confidence-boosting successes. Generally flat fairways and trees characterize the relatively short (3,350-yd.) course. Greens fees range from $15 to $19.

Slightly more intermediate amateurs will want to check out the **Tahquitz Creek Golf Resort,** 1885 Golf Club Dr., Palm Springs (© 760/328-1005), whose two diverse courses both appeal to mid-handicappers. The Legend's wide, water-free holes will appeal to anyone frustrated by the "target" courses popular with many architects, while the Ted Robinson–designed Resort course offers all those accuracy-testing bells and whistles more common to lavish private clubs. Greens fees, including cart, range from $50 to $109, depending on the day of the week.

The **Palm Springs Country Club,** 2500 Whitewater Club Dr. (© 760/323-2626), is the oldest public-access golf course in the city of Palm Springs and is popular with budget-conscious golfers, as greens fees are only $35 to $45 with a cart, $23 to walk. The challenge of bunkers and rough can be amplified by the oft-blowing wind along the 5,885 yards of this unusually laid-out course.

One of our favorite desert courses is the **PGA West TPC Stadium Course,** La Quinta Resort & Club, 49499 Eisenhower Dr., La Quinta (© 760/564-4111), which received *Golf* magazine's 1994 Gold Medal Award for the total golf-resort experience. The par-3 17th has a picturesque island green where Lee Trevino made Skins Game history with a spectacular hole in one. The rest of Pete Dye's 7,261-yard design is flat, with huge bunkers, lots of water, and severe mounding throughout. It's one of the most difficult courses in the U.S. Also open for semiprivate play is the **Mountain Course at La Quinta,** another Dye design that regularly appears on U.S. top-100 lists. It's set dramatically against the rocky mountains, which thrust into fairways to create tricky doglegs, and its small Bermuda greens are well guarded by boulders and deep bunkers. Greens fees for nonguests vary seasonally, from $65 to $195. Also at La Quinta Resort is the Pete Dye–designed **Dunes Course,** the (Jack) **Nicklaus Tournament Course,** and the (Greg) **Norman Resort Course.**

A complete **golfer's guide** is available from the Palm Springs Desert Resorts Convention & Visitors Authority (see "Visitor Information" above).

## MORE OUTDOOR FUN

The Coachella Valley Desert is truly a playground, and what follows is but a sampling of the opportunities that allow visitors to enjoy its abundant sunshine. But the strong sun and dry air that are so appealing can also sneak up on you in the form of sunburn and heat exhaustion. Especially during the summer, but even in milder times, always carry and drink plenty of water.

**BALLOONING** This is perhaps the most memorable way to see the desert: floating above the landscape in a colorful hot-air balloon. Choose from specialty themes like sunrise, sunset, or romantic champagne flights. Rides are offered by **Dream Flights** (© 800/933-5628 or 760/321-5154; www.dreamflights.com), and **Fantasy Balloon Flights** (© 800/GO-ABOVE or 760/568-0997; www.fantasyballoonflights.com). Rates range from $145 to $150 per person for a 60- to 90-minute flight (two per day), including champagne and hors d'oeuvres.

## Here's the Rub: Two Bunch Palms Desert Spa

Since the time of the Native American Cahuilla, who knew how great it felt to soak in the Coachella Valley's natural hot springs, this desert has drawn stressed-out masses seeking relaxation, rejuvenation, and the sigh-inducing pleasure only a health spa can deliver. My number-one choice is heavenly **Two Bunch Palms.** Posh yet intimate, this spiritual sanctuary in Desert Hot Springs (about 20 min. north of Palm Springs) has been drawing weary city dwellers since Chicago mobster Al Capone hid out here in the 1930s. Two Bunch Palms later became a playground for the movie community, but today it's a friendly and informal haven offering renowned spa services, bungalows on lush grounds, and lagoons of steaming mineral water. Service is famously—and excellently—discreet; and legions of return guests will attest that the outstanding spa treatments (nine varieties of massage, mud baths, body wraps, facials, salt rubs, and more) and therapeutic waters are what make the luxury of Two Bunch Palms irresistible. Room rates start at $175 (including breakfast) in the high season, with midweek and substantial off-season discounts available. Spa treatments typically cost between $75 and $100 per hour, and money-saving room/meal/spa packages are offered. Don't want to stay over? Then book one of Two Bunch's 6-hour Day Spa packages. The resort is off Palm Drive (Gene Autry Trail) at 67-425 Two Bunch Palms Trail (© **800/472-4334** or 760/329-8791; www.twobunchpalms.com).

**BICYCLING**   The clean, dry air just cries out to be enjoyed—what could be better than to pedal your way around town or into the desert? **Adventure Bike Tours** (© **760/328-0282**) will outfit you with a bike, helmet, water bottle, and certified guide. Three-hour tours, which meet at local hotels, start at about $50, and bike rentals are $10 per hour or $30 for the day. If you're just looking to rent some wheels and a helmet, **Tri a Bike Rental,** 44841 San Pablo Ave., Palm Desert (© **760/340-2840**), rents road and mountain bikes for the hour ($8–$12), the day ($15–$30), or the week ($45–$99), and offers children's and tandem models. The **Bighorn Bicycle Rental & Tour Company,** 302 N. Palm Canyon (© **760/325-3367**), has hourly ($6–$12) and daily ($20–$40) rental rates in addition to guided bike treks (a 2–4-hr. guided ride/hike is $35–$49 per person including all equipment and snacks). It's closed on Wednesday.

**A FAMILY WATER PARK** 🅚🆒   **Knott's Soak City,** off I-10 south on Gene Autry Trail between Ramon Road and East Palm Canyon Drive (© **760/327-0499**; www. knotts.com/soakcity/ps/index.shtml), is a 16-acre water playground with 12 water slides, body- and board surfing, a wave pool, and more. Dressing rooms, lockers, and private beach cabanas (with food service) are available. Admission is $26 for adults, $15 for kids 3 to 11, and free for kids under 3; rates are discounted after 3pm. The park is open daily mid-March through August, and weekends through October, from 11am to 5pm.

**GUIDED ALL-TERRAIN EXCURSIONS**   **Desert Adventures** (© **888/440-JEEP** or 760/324-JEEP; www.red-jeep.com) offers four-wheel-drive eco-tours led by naturalist guides. Your off-road adventure may take you to a replica of an ancient Cahuilla village, the Santa Rosa Mountain roads overlooking the Coachella Valley, or picturesque ravines on the way to the San Andreas Fault. Tours range in duration from 2 to 4 hours and in price from $69 to $99. Advance reservations are required. The company's trademark red Jeeps depart from the Desert Adventures Ranch on South Palm Canyon near the entrance to the Indian Canyons, but most of the longer excursions include hotel pickup and return.

**HIKING**   The most popular spot for hiking is the nearby **Indian Canyons,** at the end of South Palm Canyon Drive (© **800/790-3398** or 760/325-3400; www.aguacaliente.org). The Agua Caliente tribe made their home here centuries ago, and remnants of their lifestyle can be seen among the streams, waterfalls, and palm groves in Andreas, Murray, and Palm canyons. Striking rock formations and herds of bighorn sheep and wild ponies will probably be more appealing than the Trading Post in Palm Canyon, but it does sell detailed trail maps. This is Indian land, and the Tribal Council charges admission of $6 per adult, $4.50 for students, seniors, and military, and $2 for kids ages 6 to 12. The canyons are closed to visitors from late June to early September. The canyons are open 8am to 5pm, and guided hiking tours and ranger lectures are also available.

Don't miss the opportunity to explore **Tahquitz Canyon,** 500 W. Mesquite, west of Palm Canyon Drive, also an Agua Caliente territory. This scenic canyon, which features the waterfall filmed for the classic *Lost Horizon,* was closed to the public for nearly 30 years after it became an all-night party zone for hippies, who vandalized land considered sacred—serious injuries also plagued careless canyon squatters. But now the vegetation is renewed and decades' worth of dumping cleaned up, and in 2001 the tribe began offering 2½-hour ranger-led hikes into their most spiritual and beautiful place. The 2-mile round-trip hike is of moderate difficulty; hikes depart daily at 8am, 10am, noon, and 2pm. The fee is $13 for adults, $6 for children ages 6 to 12; call © **800/790-3398** for recorded information, © **760/416-7044** for reservations (recommended).

Ten miles east of Palm Springs is the 13,000-acre **Coachella Valley Preserve** (© **760/343-1234**), open daily from sunrise to sunset. It has springs, mesas, both hiking and riding trails, the Thousand Palms Oasis, a visitor center, and picnic areas.

If you're heading up to Joshua Tree National Park (see later in this chapter), consider stopping at the **Big Morongo Canyon Preserve** (© **760/363-7190**), which was once an Indian village and later a cattle ranch. It's open Wednesday through Sunday from 7:30am to sundown. The park's high water table makes it a magnet for birds and other wildlife; the lush springs and streams are an unexpected desert treat.

**HORSEBACK RIDING**   Equestrians from novice to advanced can experience the solitude and quiet of the desert on horseback at **Smoke Tree Stables** (© **760/327-1372**). Located south of downtown and ideal for exploring the nearby Indian Canyon trails, Smoke Tree offers guided rides for $35 per hour, $70 for 2 hours; the 2-hour tour includes admission to an Aguacaliente Indian reservation. But don't expect your posse leader to be primed with facts on the nature you'll encounter—this is strictly a do-it-yourself experience. Open daily 8am to 4pm. No credit cards.

**TENNIS**   Virtually all the larger hotels and resorts have tennis courts; but if you're staying at a B&B, you might want to play at the **Plaza Racquet Club,** 1300 Baristo Rd. (© **760/323-8997**). It has nine courts and offers day and evening clinics for adults, juniors, and seniors, and ball machines for solo practice. USPTA pros are on hand.

If you'd like to play for free, the night-lit courts at **Palm Springs High School,** 2248 E. Ramon Rd., are open to the public on weekends, holidays, and in summer.

There are also eight free night-lit courts in beautiful **Ruth Hardy Park** at Tamarisk and Caballero streets.

## EXPLORING THE AREA

**The Living Desert Zoo & Gardens** 🐾 *Kids*    This 1,200-acre desert reserve, museum, zoo, and educational center is designed to acquaint visitors with the unique habitats that make up the Southern California deserts. You can walk or take a tram tour through sectors that re-create life in several distinctive desert zones. See and learn about a dizzying variety of plants, insects, and wildlife, including bighorn sheep, mountain lions, rattlesnakes, lizards, owls, golden eagles, and the ubiquitous road-runner. It's a nonstuffy learning experience for kids, and an interesting way for any-one to learn about the surrounding landscape.

47-900 Portola Ave., Palm Desert. ℂ 760/346-5694. www.livingdesert.org. Admission $11 adults, $9.50 seniors/military, $6.50 children 3–12, free for kids under 3. Reduced summer rates. Daily 9am–5pm (last entrance 4pm); summer (mid-June to Aug) 8am–1:30pm.

**Palm Springs Aerial Tramway** 🎿🎿    To gain a bird's-eye perspective on the Coachella Valley, take this 14-minute ascent up nearly 5,900 feet to the upper slopes of Mount San Jacinto. While the Albert Frey–designed boarding stations retain their 1960s ski-lodge feel, newly installed Swiss funicular cars are sleekly modern and rotate during the trip to allow each passenger a panoramic view. There's a whole other world once you arrive: alpine scenery, a ski-lodge-flavored restaurant and gift shop, and

---

### Sweet Treat of the Desert: The Coachella Valley Date Gardens

In a splendid display of both wishful thinking and clever engineering, the Coachella Valley has grown into a rich agricultural region, known interna-tionally for grapefruit, figs, and grapes—but mostly for dates. Entrepre-neurs, fascinated with Arabian lore and fueled by the Sahara-like conditions of the desert around Indio, planted the area's date palm groves in the 1920s. Launched with just a few parent trees imported from the Middle East, the groves now produce 95% of the world's date crop.

Farmers hand-pollinate the trees, and the resulting fruit is bundled in wind-protective paper while still on the tree, which makes an odd sight indeed. You'll see them along Highway 111 through Indio, where the road is sometimes referred to as the "Date Highway."

There's no more picturesque place in the valley to sample dates than **Oasis Date Gardens**, 59111 Hwy. 111 (ℂ 800/827-8017 or 760/399-5665), started in 1912 with nine Moroccan trees and now one of the largest com-mercial date groves in the United States. It's a drive—about 40 minutes from downtown Palm Springs—but there's a lot to do here. Picnic tables dot an inviting lawn, videos illustrate the history and art of date cultivation, and there's a cool palm arboretum and cactus exhibit, plus a petting zoo for youngsters. Many varieties of dates are laid out for free tasting. Oasis also sells date shakes, ice cream, date pie by the slice, homemade chili and sand-wiches, and gourmet food gifts from all over the Southwest. Open daily (except Christmas) from 8am to 5pm.

temperatures typically 40° cooler than the desert floor. The most dramatic contrast is during the winter, when the mountaintop is a snowy wonderland, irresistible to hikers and bundled-up kids with saucers. The excursion might not be worth the expense during the rest of the year. Guided mule rides and cross-country ski equipment are available at the top. An upscale restaurant, **Elevations,** serves cuisine designed by Anthony Gusich. Appetizers begin at $12, entrees $29. Wait and take the tram to the top after 3pm for a lower rate. Elevations is open noon to 3pm and 4 to 8pm daily and reservations are recommended (© **760/327-1590**).

Tramway Rd. off Hwy. 111, Palm Springs. © **888/515-TRAM** or 760/325-1391. www.pstramway.com. Tickets $21 adults, $19 seniors, $14 children 3–12, free for kids under 3. Mon–Fri 10am–8pm; Sat–Sun 8am–8pm. Tram runs every 30 min., last tram down at 9:45pm.

**Palm Springs Desert Museum** ⭐    Unlikely though it may sound, this well-endowed museum is worth a look. Exhibits include world-class Western and Native American art collections, the natural history of the desert, and an outstanding anthropology department, primarily representing the local Cahuilla tribe. Traditional Indian life as it was lived for centuries is illustrated by tools, baskets, and other relics. Check local schedules to find out about visiting exhibits (which are usually excellent). Plays, lectures, and other events are presented in the museum's **Annenberg Theater.**

101 Museum Dr. (just west of the Palm Canyon/Tahquitz intersection), Palm Springs. © 760/325-7186. www.ps museum.org. Admission $7.50 adults, $6.50 seniors 62 and over, $3.50 military and children 6–17, free for children under 6. Free for all each Thurs after 4pm. Tues–Wed and Fri–Sat 10am–5pm; Thurs noon–8pm; Sun noon–5pm.

## SHOPPING

Downtown Palm Springs revolves around **North Palm Canyon Drive;** many art galleries, souvenir shops, and restaurants are here, along with a couple of large-scale hotels and shopping centers. This wide one-way boulevard is designed for pedestrians, with many businesses set back from the street—don't be shy about poking around the little courtyards you'll encounter. On Thursday nights from 6 to 10pm, the blocks between Amado and Baristo roads are transformed into **VillageFest,** a town street fair. Handicrafts vendors and aromatic food booths compete for your attention with wacky street performers and even wackier locals shopping at the mouthwatering fresh-produce stalls.

The northern section of Palm Canyon is becoming known for collectibles and is being touted as the **Antique and Heritage Gallery District.** Check out **Antiques Collector,** 798 N. Palm Canyon Dr. (© **760/323-4443**), a discriminating mall-style store whose 35 dealers display wares ranging from vintage linens to handmade African crafts to prized Bakelite jewelry. The **111 Antique Mall** with vintage furnishings, art and lighting is now in two locations: 2500 N. Palm Canyon Drive in Palm Springs (© **760/864-9390**); and at 68-401 E. Palm Canyon Drive in Cathedral City (© **760/202-0215**).

Down in Palm Desert lies the delicious excess of **El Paseo,** a cornucopia of high-rent boutiques, salons, and upscale eateries reminiscent of Rodeo Drive in Beverly Hills, along with over a dozen major shopping malls.

Put a spring in your step with sandals, running shoes, and boots from **Z-Coil of the Desert,** 80150 Hwy. 111 at Jefferson, Indio (© **760/775-1933**). A coiled spring at the heel cushions walking and standing. Prices range from $180 to $200. While there, pick up a pair of "soft socks."

**Factory-outlet shopping** is 20 minutes away in Cabazon (see "En Route to the Palm Springs Resorts," earlier in this chapter).

## GAY & LESBIAN LIFE IN PALM SPRINGS

Don't think the chamber of commerce doesn't recognize that the Palm Springs area is among America's top destinations for gay and lesbian travelers. After just a short while in town, it's easy to see how the gay tourism dollar is courted as aggressively as straight spending. Real-estate agents cater to gay shoppers for vacation properties, while entire condo communities are marketed toward the gay resident. Advertisements for these and scores of other gay-owned businesses can be found in the *Bottom Line* (www. psbottomline.com), the desert's free biweekly magazine of articles, events, and community guides for the gay reader, which is available at hotels, at newsstands, and from select merchants.

Throughout the year, events are held that transcend the gay community to include everyone. In March the **Desert AIDS Walk** benefits the Desert AIDS Project, while one of the world's largest organized gathering of lesbians—the **Dinah Shore Weekend** (www.clubskirts.com)—coincides with the LPGA's **Kraft Nabisco Championship** in mid-March. The predominantly men's **White Party** (www.jeffreysanker. com), the area's largest circuit party event, takes place Easter weekend. **Greater Palm Spring Pride** occurs the first weekend in November, with a parade and 2-day cultural fair (© **760/416-8711;** www.pspride.org).

There are more than two dozen gay hotels, many concentrated on Warm Sands Drive south of Ramon. Known simply as "Warm Sands," this area holds many of the private resorts—mostly discreet and gated inns, many of them clothing-optional. Try the **East Canyon Hotel & Spa,** 288 E. Camino Monte Vista (© **877/324-6835** or 760/320-1928; www.eastcanyonps.com), a men's luxury resort and full-service spa; or **Casitas Laquita,** 450 E. Palm Canyon Dr. (© **760/416-9999;** www.casitaslaquita. com), one of two all-women resorts in town.

The **Palm Springs Visitor and Hotel Information Center** publishes an **Official Gay Visitors Guide.** Obtain it and additional information at their office at 2781 N. Palm Canyon Dr. (© **888/866-2744;** www.palm-springs.org).

## WHERE TO STAY

The city of Palm Springs offers a wide range of accommodations, but we particularly like the inns that have opened as new owners renovate the many fabulous 40- to 60-year-old cottage complexes in the wind-shielded Tennis Club area west of Palm Canyon Drive. The other desert resort cities offer mostly sprawling complexes, many boasting world-class golf, tennis, or spa facilities and multiple on-site restaurants. Most are destinations in and of themselves, offering activities for the whole family (including a whole lot of relaxing and being pampered). So if you're looking for a good base from which to shop or sightsee, Palm Springs is your best bet.

Regardless of your choice, remember that the rates given below are for high season (winter, generally Nov–May). During the hotter summer months, it's common to find $300 rooms going for $99 or less as part of off-season packages. Even in high season, discounts for midweek stays are common.

### PALM SPRINGS
#### Expensive
**Le Parker Meridien Palm Springs** ★★★ The newest arrival on the super luxury Palm Springs hotel scene, known simply as The Parker, is a $27-million renovation of the former Gene Autry Melody Ranch and then the Merv Griffin Givenchy Resort and Spa. If you have been to either of these you won't recognize the make-over. The

13-acre property has 131 rooms, 12 one-bedroom villas, and the original Gene Autry house. Two restaurants serve your every desire: Norma's has breakfast all day long for late sleepers, served indoors on an outdoor terrace; Mister Parker's presents a daily changing dinner menu in an intimate atmosphere. Are you ready for a $1,000 sevruga caviar–and-lobster omelet? Activities center around four red clay tennis courts, four pools (two of them heated), and the Palm Springs Yacht Club spa to revive the jet-lagged body and a 24-hour gym to get it back in shape. Golfers will be able to use the next door Seven Lakes Country Club's 18-hole golf course, where President Dwight D. Eisenhower once scored his only hole in one.

4200 E. Palm Canyon Dr., Palm Springs, CA 92264. ℂ **760/770-5000.** www.theparkerpalmsprings.com. 131 units. Doubles $315–$625 Oct–May, $139–$500 June–Sept; 12 private villas $875–$2,000 Oct–May, $700–$800 June–Sept. There is a $25 resort fee. Guests under 30 can stay in the staff quarters for much less; call for details. AE, DC, DISC, MC, V. **Amenities:** 2 restaurants; lobby bar; 4 pools (2 heated); 4 red-clay tennis courts; 24-hr gym; spa; Jacuzzi; steam and sauna rooms; 24-hr room service and free morning coffee delivery upon request; twice-daily maid service; DVD library; helipad, daily newspaper. *In Room:* A/C, CD/DVD/MP3 player, Wi-Fi Internet access, minibar, fridge.

**Orbit In** ★★ This much-hyped renovation of a classic 1950s motel gets our vote as grooviest digs in town, exceeding everyone's expectations with a cocktails-by-the-pool Rat Pack aesthetic and almost scholarly appreciation of the architects and designers responsible for Palm Springs's reign as a mecca of vintage modernism. Serious connoisseurs of interior design will find a museum's worth of furnishings in these rooms, each of which adheres to its theme (Martini Room, Atomic Paradise, and so on) right down to customized lounge-music CDs for your listening pleasure. Contemporary comforts are provided, from cushy double pillow-top mattresses to poolside misters that create an oasis of cool even during midsummer scorchers. Kitchenettes all boast charming restored fixtures, as do the candy-pink-tiled original bathrooms, which have only stall showers but make up for the lack of tubs by being surprisingly spacious—and naturally sunlit. Guests gather at the poolside "boomerang" bar, or in the **Albert Frey Lounge** (homage to the late, great architect whose unique home sits midway up the mountain backdrop); a central "movies, books, and games" closet encourages old-fashioned camaraderie amidst this chic atmosphere. Nearby is the eight-unit **Hideaway**, a quieter, more secluded hospice with a large saltwater pool; no Jacuzzi but access to the Orbit amenities is available.

562 W. Arenas Rd., Palm Springs, CA 92262. ℂ **877/99-ORBIT** or 760/323-3585. Fax 760/323-3599. www.orbitin. com. 10 units. $199–$299 double. Rates include deluxe continental breakfast. AE, DISC, MC, V. Free parking. **Amenities:** Outdoor heated saltwater pool; spa facilities; Jacuzzi; complimentary Schwinn cruiser bikes; private patios. *In room:* A/C, TV/VCR, dataport, kitchenette, fridge, coffeemaker, hair dryer, iron, safe, CD player.

**Viceroy Palm Springs** ★★ Once the choice of Hollywood celebrities, this outstanding historic hotel, formerly the Estrella, is quiet and secluded yet wonderfully close to the action. It's composed of three distinct properties from three different eras, which benefited from a chic transformation in 2002—sort of a Grecian-meets-modern Regency style popular during Palm Springs's golden era. Guest rooms vary widely in terms of size and amenities—some have fireplaces and/or full kitchens, others have wet bars or private balconies—the color scheme is very black-and-white with dramatic lemon-yellow accents. The real deals are the studio bungalows, even though they have tiny 1930s bathrooms. Lavish landscaping completes the elegant ambience. The restaurant, **Citron**, serves lunch and dinner (entrees $24–$34) and has a full bar. There is also pool food service.

415 S. Belardo Rd. (south of Tahquitz Way), Palm Springs, CA 92262. (C) **800/237-3687** or 760/320-4117. Fax 760/ 323-3303. www.viceroypalmsprings.com. 74 units. $279 double; $300–$459 suite; $500–$700 villa. AE, DC, MC, V. Free parking. No pets. **Amenities:** 3 outdoor heated pools (including children's pool); fitness room; full-service spa; 2 Jacuzzis. *In room:* A/C, TV, DVD player, fridge, hair dryer.

## Moderate

**Korakia Pensione** ★★ If you can work within the Korakia's rigid deposit-cancellation policy, you're in for a special stay at this Greek-Moroccan oasis a few blocks from Palm Canyon Drive. This former artist's villa from the 1920s draws a hip international crowd of artists, writers, and musicians. The simply furnished rooms and spacious suites are peaceful and private, surrounded by flagstone courtyards and flowering gardens. Rooms are divided between the main house, a second restored villa across the street, and guest bungalows. Most have kitchens; many have fireplaces. All beds are blessed with thick duvets, and the windows are shaded by flowing white-canvas Mediterranean-style draperies. You also get a sumptuous breakfast served in your room or poolside. *Korakia* is Greek for "crow," and a tile mosaic example graces the pool bottom. *Note:* You must pay a deposit when booking a room, there's a 2-night minimum on weekends, and you have to give at least 2 weeks' cancellation notice (*45 days'* advance notice for holidays) or you'll lose your deposit.

257 S. Patencio Rd., Palm Springs, CA 92262. (C) **760/864-6411.** Fax 760/864-4147. www.korakia.com. 29 units. $139–$199 double; $399–$600 suite. Rates include breakfast. MC, V. Free parking. **Amenities:** 2 outdoor heated pools; in-room massage. *In room:* A/C, fridge, coffeemaker, hair dryer and iron on request, safe.

**Movie Colony Hotel** ★ Take one classic 1930s hotel (designed by prolific renowned area architect Albert Frey) and remodel it with black-and-white 1935 Moderne suites, some two-storied, and you've got a flashback into the reel world.

726 N. Indian Canyon Dr., Palm Springs, CA 92262. (C) **888/953-5700** or 760/320-6340. Fax 760/320-1640. www. moviecolonyhotel.com. 16 units. Doubles Jan–May $189–$289, June–Aug $129–$229; Sept–Dec $169–269. Rates include continental breakfast and evening wine. AE, MC, V. Free parking. **Amenities:** Hotel bar w/glass fire pit; outdoor heated pool; Jacuzzi; complimentary bicycles; massage; private patio or balcony. *In room:* A/C, TV w/DVD, minibar, fridge, hair dryer, iron, robes.

**Villa Royale** ★★ This charming inn, 5 minutes from the hustle and bustle of downtown, evokes a European cluster of villas, complete with climbing bougainvillea and rooms filled with international antiques and artwork. Uniform luxuries (down comforters and other pampering touches) appear throughout. Rooms vary widely in size and ambience; larger isn't always better, as some of the inn's most appealing rooms are in the smaller, more affordable range. Many rooms have fireplaces, private patios, full kitchens, and a variety of other amenities. A full breakfast is served in an intimate garden setting surrounding the main pool. This is a genuine desert oasis. The hotel's romantic restaurant, **Europa** (p. 648), is a sleeper, offering some of Palm Springs's very best meals.

1620 Indian Trail (off E. Palm Canyon), Palm Springs, CA 92264. (C) **800/245-2314** or 760/327-2314. Fax 760/322-3794. www.villaroyale.com. 31 units. $150–$225 double; $250–$375 suite. Rates include full breakfast. AE, DC, DISC, MC, V. Free parking. **Amenities:** Restaurant; 2 outdoor heated pools; Jacuzzi; in-room massage; morning newspaper. *In room:* A/C, TV, dataport, hair dryer, iron.

## Inexpensive

**Casa Cody** ★ Once owned by "Wild" Bill Cody's niece, this 1920s casa with a double courtyard (each with swimming pool) has been restored to fine condition. It now sports a Southwestern decor and peaceful grounds marked by large lawns and mature, blossoming fruit trees. You'll feel more like a houseguest than a hotel client at the Casa

Cody. It's located in the residential "Tennis Club" area of town, a couple of easy blocks from Palm Canyon Drive. Many units here have fireplaces and full-size kitchens. Breakfast is served poolside, as are complimentary wine and cheese on Saturday afternoons. Kids are welcome.

175 S. Cahuilla Rd. (between Tahquitz Way and Arenas Rd.), Palm Springs, CA 92262. ℂ **800/231-2639** or 760/320-9346. Fax 760/325-8610. www.casacody.com. 23 units. $89–$159 double; $159–$199 suite; $359 2-bedroom house. Rates include expanded continental breakfast. AE, DC, DISC, MC, V. Pets accepted for $10 extra per night. **Amenities:** 2 outdoor heated pools; Jacuzzi; in-room massage. *In room:* A/C, TV, fridge.

**Orchid Tree Inn** Billed as a "1930s desert garden retreat," the Orchid Tree is a sprawling complex of buildings from the 1920s to 1950s, just a block from Palm Canyon Drive in the "Tennis Club" district. Dedicated family ownership ensures that the place is impeccably maintained. The inn truly feels like a retreat. The grounds are rich with flowering shrubs, citrus trees, and multitudes of hummingbirds, sparrows, and quail drawn by bird feeders and birdbaths. The rooms are nicer than you'd expect at this price, in keeping with the grace and excellence of the entire neighborhood. Room types range from simple, hotel-style doubles to charming bungalows to pool-front studios with sliding-glass doors.

261 S. Belardo Rd. (at Baristo Rd.), Palm Springs, CA 92262. ℂ **800/733-3435** or 760/325-2791. Fax 760/325-3855. www.orchidtree.com. 42 units. $110–$145 double; $175–$360 suite. Extra person $15. Rates include expanded continental breakfast (Nov–May only). AE, DC, DISC, MC, V. **Amenities:** 3 swimming pools; 2 Jacuzzis. *In room:* A/C, TV, hair dryer.

**Palm Mountain Resort and Spa** *Kids* Within easy walking distance of Palm Springs's main drag, this former Holiday Inn welcomes kids under 18 free in their parent's room, making it a good choice for families. The rooms are in the two- or the three-story wing, and many have a patio or balcony, with a view of the mountains or the large Astroturf courtyard. Midweek and summer rates can be as low as $99. For the best rates, book online or ask for "Great Rates."

155 S. Belardo Rd., Palm Springs, CA 92262. ℂ **800/622-9451** or 760/325-1301. Fax 760/323-8937. www.palmmountainresort.com. 119 units. June–April $119–$189, May–Sept $69–$139, Oct–Dec $99–$169. Rates include continental breakfast. Children 17 and under stay free in parent's room. AE, DC, DISC, MC, V. Free parking. **Amenities:** Restaurant; ; lounge; heated pool; day spa. *In room:* A/C, TV, fridge, coffeemaker, hair dryer, iron.

## RANCHO MIRAGE

**Marriott's Rancho Las Palmas Resort & Spa** ★★ The early-California charm of this relaxing Spanish hacienda makes Rancho Las Palmas one of the least pretentious luxury resorts in the desert. Dedicated golfers come to play on the adjoining country club's 27 holes; tennis buffs flock to the 25 hotel courts (three of them red clay); everybody enjoys the world-class health spa plus a separate pool with water slide. Guest rooms are arranged in a complex of low-rise, tile-roofed structures, and the public areas have an easygoing elegance, filled with flower-laden stone fountains, smooth terra-cotta tile floors, and rough-hewn wood trim. Each room has a balcony or patio.

41000 Bob Hope Dr., Rancho Mirage, CA 92270. ℂ **800/I-LUV-SUN** or 760/568-2727. Fax 760/568-5845. www.rancholaspalmas.com. 450 units. $285–$400 double; from $489 suite. Children 17 and under stay free in parent's room. AE, DISC, MC, V. Self-parking. **Amenities:** 2 restaurants; cocktail lounge; 2 outdoor heated pools; night-lit outdoor tennis courts; health club; full-service spa; 2 Jacuzzis; children's programs; concierge; business center; room service (6am–11pm); babysitting; laundry/dry-cleaning service. *In room:* A/C, TV w/pay movies, dataport, minibar, coffeemaker, hair dryer, iron, safe.

**Westin Mission Hills Resort** ★★ Designed to resemble a Moroccan palace surrounded by pools, waterfalls, and lush gardens, this self-contained resort stands on 360 acres. It's an excellent choice for families and for travelers who take their golf game seriously. (Regular desert visitors will note the Westin is situated so Palm Springs and Palm Desert are equally accessible without driving on congested Highway 111.) Rooms are arranged around the grounds in a series of two-story buildings, with accommodations that range from basic to palatial. All have terraces and come with an array of creature comforts befitting this price range—including the Westin trademark Heavenly Bed, an ultracomfy white confection so popular many guests order one for home.

Though the Westin has the business demeanor of a practiced group-and-meeting hotel, it offers a multitude of recreation options for leisure travelers, gamblers attracted to the nearby Agua Caliente Casino, or professionals after the day's business is concluded. In addition to their championship golf course, you'll find a running track, bike trails, lawn games, and the freshly expanded Spa at Mission Hills, a boutiquelike oasis whose treatments range from sports massage to pampering Hawaiian body treatments.

71-333 Dinah Shore Dr. (at Bob Hope Dr.), Rancho Mirage, CA 92270. ℂ 800/WESTIN-1 or 760/328-5955. Fax 760/321-2955. www.starwood.com. 512 units. $300–$480 double; from $400 suite. Extra person $35. Children under 18 stay free in parent's room. Golf, spa, and family packages available. AE, DC, DISC, MC, V. Free valet and self-parking. **Amenities:** Excellent restaurant serving breakfast all day; 2 lounges; 3 poolside cabana bars; multiple outdoor heated pools and Jacuzzis; night-lit outdoor tennis courts; health club; full-service spa; bike rental; children's activity center; concierge; business center; 24-hr. room service; in-room massage; babysitting; dry-cleaning/laundry service; water slide. *In room:* A/C, TV w/pay movies, dataport, minibar, coffeemaker, hair dryer, iron, safe.

## PALM DESERT

### Desert Springs—A JW Marriott Resort & Spa *Kids* ★★    A tourist attraction in its own right, Marriott's Desert Springs resort is worth a peek even if you're not lucky enough to stay here. Most of the guests are attracted by the golf and tennis facilities, and the luxurious, full-service spa is an added perk. Visitors enter this artificial desert oasis via a sweeping palm-tree-lined road wending its way past a small pond that's home to a gaggle of pink flamingos. Once inside, guests are greeted by a shaded marble lobby "rainforest" replete with interior moat and the squawk of tropical birds; gondolas even ply the lobby's waterways.

While the rooms here are not as fancy as the lobby would lead you to believe, they're exceedingly comfortable, decorated with muted pastels and contemporary furnishings. All have terraces with views of the golf course and the San Jacinto Mountains. Recreational options include a jogging trail, 36 holes of golf, driving range, a unique 18-hole putting range, basketball courts, lawn croquet, and a sunbathing "beach" with volleyball court—you don't have to ever leave the premises if you don't want to.

74855 Country Club Dr., Palm Desert, CA 92260. ℂ 800/331-3112 or 760/341-2211. Fax 760/341-1872. www.desertspringsresort.com. 886 units. $350–$400 double; from $600 suite. Children 17 and under stay free in parent's room. AE, DC, DISC, MC, V. **Amenities:** 5 restaurants; 4 snack bars; 2 lounges; 5 heated outdoor pools; 20 tennis courts (hard, clay, and grass; 7 lit); full-service spa and health club; 5 outdoor Jacuzzis; bike rental; children's programs; game room; concierge; tour desk; car-rental desk; business center; shopping arcade; salon; room service; in-room massage; babysitting; dry-cleaning/laundry service. *In room:* A/C, TV w/pay movies, dataport, minibar, coffeemaker, hair dryer, iron, safe.

## LA QUINTA

### La Quinta Resort & Club ★★★    A luxury resort amid citrus trees, towering palms, cacti, and desert flowers at the base of the Santa Rosa Mountains, La Quinta is *the* place to be if you're serious about your golf or tennis. The resort is renowned for its five championship golf courses—including one of California's best, Pete Dye's PGA West TPC Stadium Course. All guest rooms are in single-story, Spanish-style buildings throughout the grounds. Each has its own patio and access to one of several dozen small

---

> ## Tips A La Quinta Bed & Breakfast Hideaway
>
> Devotees of bed-and-breakfasts or boutique inns might find the La Quinta Resort's 900-plus rooms a little daunting, but there's a way to enjoy this quiet, affluent end of the valley with a little more intimacy. Check out the hidden-secret **Lake La Quinta Inn**, 78-120 Caleo Bay (© **888/226-4546** or 760/564-7332; www.lakelaquintainn.com), a 13-room Norman-style B&B on the shores of a man-made lake (surrounded by homes) just blocks from the famous resort. Exquisitely outfitted rooms, delightful hosts, on-site massage, and a 24-hour pool and Jacuzzi complete the fantasy. Rates range from $209 to $449; suites are $399 to $449.

---

pools, enhancing the feeling of privacy at this retreat. Some units have a fireplace or private Jacuzzi. The tranquil lounge and library in the original hacienda hearken back to the early days of the resort, when Clark Gable, Greta Garbo, Frank Capra, and other luminaries chose La Quinta as their hideaway. The resort includes Spa La Quinta, a Mission-style complex with 35 treatment rooms for every pampering luxury.

49499 Eisenhower Dr., La Quinta, CA 92253. © **800/598-3828** or 760/564-4111. Fax 760/564-7656. www.laquintaresort.com. 800 units. $445–$485 double; from $675 suite. $15 resort fee per night. Extra person $25. Children 17 and under stay free in parent's room. Packages available. AE, MC, V. Free self-parking; valet parking $15. **Amenities:** 5 restaurants (including Azur by Le Bernadin for fine dining and Adobe for Mexican); 3 bars (2 featuring entertainment); 41 outdoor pools w/Jacuzzis; 23 outdoor tennis courts (10 night-lit); full-service spa; bike rental; children's programs; concierge; business center; 24-hr. room service; in-room massage; babysitting; laundry service. *In room:* A/C, TV/VCR w/pay movies, dataport, minibar, coffeemaker, hair dryer, iron, safe.

## WHERE TO DINE
### PALM SPRINGS
#### Expensive

**Europa Restaurant** ★★ CALIFORNIA/CONTINENTAL    Long advertised as the "most romantic dining in the desert," Europa is a sentimental favorite of many regulars among an equally gay and straight clientele. This European-style hideaway exudes charm and ambience. Whether you sit under the stars on Europa's garden patio or in subdued candlelight indoors, you'll savor dinner prepared by one of Palm Springs's most dedicated kitchens and served by a discreetly attentive staff. Standout dishes include a tender *osso bucco* that falls off the bone, filet mignon on a bed of crispy onions with garlic butter, and a show-stopping salmon baked in parchment with crème fraîche and dill. For dessert, don't miss the signature chocolate mousse—smooth, grainy, and addictive.

1620 Indian Trail (at the Villa Royale). © **760/327-2314.** Reservations recommended. Main courses $22–$34. AE, DC, DISC, MC, V. Tues–Sun 6–9pm; Sun 11:30am–2pm.

#### Moderate

**Edgardo's Café Veracruz** ★ MEXICAN    The pleasant but humble ambience at Edgardo's is a welcome change from touristy Palm Springs. The expert menu features authentic Mayan, Huasteco, and Aztec cuisine. The dark interior boasts an array of colorful masks and artwork from Central and South America, but the postage-stamp-size front patio with a fountain is the best place to sample Edgardo's tangy quesadillas, desert cactus salad, and poblano chiles rellenos—and perhaps even an oyster-tequila shooter from the oyster bar!

494 N. Palm Canyon (at W. Alejo Rd.). ⒞ **760/320-3558.** Reservations recommended for weekend dinner. Main courses $8–$22 dinner, $7–$11 lunch. AE, DC, DISC, MC, V. Daily 11am–10pm. Free parking.

## Inexpensive
### Murph's Gaslight  PAN-FRIED CHICKEN   Join those in the know at this budget-saving lunch-and-dinner rendezvous where the chicken just keeps coming and coming. There are all the trimmings: black-eyed peas, mashed potatoes, corn bread, hot biscuits, country gravy, and fruit cobbler. Call ahead for takeout or join this family-style restaurant on a first-come, first-served basis. There's an early-bird special at 5pm for $8. If there's a wait, relax in Murph's Irish Pub.

79-860 Ave. 42, next to the airport in Bermuda Dunes near Jefferson. ⒞ **760/345-6242.** $15 for full dinner. MC, V. Tues–Sat 11am–3pm and 5–9pm; Sun 3–9pm.

### Sherman's Deli and Bakery  KOSHER DELI   Join the locals at this indoor and outdoor-patio eatery with 2-inch-thick deli sandwiches, lox and bagels, and a bakery with some of the richest and most delicious cakes and pastries that will put any calorie-conscious dieter into trauma. Iced tea is the drink of the day, but wine and beer are also available. A full lunch can be had on the Lite Lunch Special: chicken or matzo ball soup with a half sandwich of any of the regular deli variety. Sherman's has a second branch in Palm Desert (73–161 Country Club Dr.; ⒞ **760/568-1350**).

401 Tahquitz, Palm Springs. ⒞ **760/325-1199.** Breakfast omelets $5.95–$8.95; deli sandwich board $7.95–$12 (includes potato salad); dinner $14–$19, early-bird dinner $11. AE, DC, DISC, MC, V. Daily 7am–9pm.

### Simba's BARBECUE   For the best barbecued ribs in the desert, check out Simba's Ribhouse in Palm Springs. You'll find chicken and dumplings, black-eyed peas, barbecued beans, corn bread, hush puppies, and sweet-potato pie.

190 N. Sunrise Way, in a former bank building. ⒞ **760/778-7630.** $11–$15. MC. V. Tues–Fri 11am–2pm and 5–10pm; Sat–Sun 3–10pm.

## PALM DESERT
### Louise's Pantry  COFFEE SHOP/DINER   A real old-fashioned luncheonette, Louise's has been a fixture in Palm Springs since opening as a drugstore lunch counter in 1945. The original location on Palm Canyon Drive fell victim to skyrocketing property values, but not before establishing this welcome offshoot decorated with vintage photos of Louise's heyday. Devoted patrons—young and old—still flock in for premium-quality comfort foods such as Cobb salad, Reuben and French dip sandwiches, chicken and dumplings, hearty breakfasts with biscuits and gravy, and tasty fresh-baked pies. A new branch, on Washington in La Quinta, is serving the same menu through dinner, open 7am until 8pm (47-150 Washington [south of Hwy. 111]; ⒞ **760/771-3330**).

44491 Town Center Way (at Fred Waring Dr. north of Hwy. 111). ⒞ **760/346-9320.** Reservations not accepted. Most menu items under $10. MC, V. Daily 7am–3pm. Menu items $4–$14. Beer and wine available.

### Palmie  CLASSIC FRENCH   Martine and Alain Clerc's cozy bistro is filled with Art Deco posters of French seaside resorts. Chef Alain sends out masterful traditional French dishes such as bubbling cheese soufflé, green lentil salad dotted with pancetta, steak au poivre rich with cognac sauce, and lobster raviolis garnished with caviar. In fact, every carefully garnished plate is a work of art. To the charming background strains of French chanteuses, hostess and manager Martine circulates between tables, determined that visitors should enjoy their meals as much as do the loyal regulars she greets by name. Don't leave without sampling dessert: Our favorite is the trio of petite crème brûlées, flavored with ginger, vanilla, and Kahlúa.

44-491 Town Center Way, Suite G, Palm Desert. ℂ **760/341-3200.** Reservations recommended. Main courses $15–$30. AE, DC, MC, V. Mon–Sat 5:30–9pm.

**Tommy Bahama's Tropical Cafe** CARIBBEAN   If all this desert makes you long for *de islands, mon,* step upstairs from fashionable Tommy Bahama's boutique for a dose of Caribbean relaxation. The decor alone is worth a visit: a fantasy port of call, around 1940, with ceiling fans, plenty of rattan and palms, and upholstery in TB's signature tropical prints. Enormous umbrellas shade patio seating with valley views, and spacious indoor booths make for easy relaxing over a series of sweet umbrella drinks. The food is a delicious change of pace, its Caribbean zing not overly spiced; check out coconut shrimp with mango dip, conch fritters, mango shrimp salad, Boca Chica chicken, Jamaican jerk pork, and Key lime pie for dessert. Diners are an entertaining mix of fresh-from-the-courts socialites, always-on-vacation retirees, and well-heeled shoppers.

73595 El Paseo (at Larkspur Ave.). ℂ **760/836-0288.** Reservations recommended in season. Main courses $8–$16 lunch, $16–$35 dinner. AE, MC, V. Daily 11am–10pm.

## THE DESERT RESORTS AFTER DARK

Every month a different club or disco is the hot spot in the Springs, and the best way to tap into the trend is by consulting the *Desert Guide,* the *Bottom Line* (see "Gay & Lesbian Life in Palm Springs," earlier in this chapter), or one of the many other free newsletters available from area hotels and merchants. **VillageFest** (see "Shopping," earlier in this chapter) turns Palm Canyon Drive into an outdoor party every Thursday night. Below, I've described a couple of the enduring arts and entertainment attractions around the desert resorts.

The **Fabulous Palm Springs Follies,** at the Plaza Theatre, 128 S. Palm Canyon Dr., Palm Springs (ℂ **760/327-0225;** www.psfollies.com), a vaudeville-style show filled with production numbers, is a long-running hit in the historic Plaza Theatre in the heart of town. With a cast of retired showgirls, singers, dancers, and comedians, the revue is hugely popular. The season runs November through May; call for exact schedule. Tickets range from $39 to $89. Matinees at 1:30pm, Evening at 7pm.

The **McCallum Theatre for the Performing Arts,** 73000 Fred Waring Dr., Palm Desert (ℂ **760/340-ARTS**), offers the only cultural high road around. Frequent symphony performances with visiting virtuosos such as conductor Seiji Ozawa or violinist Itzhak Perlman; musicals like *Cats, Chicago,* and *Riverdance;* and pop performers like Olivia Newton John or Michael Finestein are among the theater's recent offerings. Call for upcoming event information.

## CASINOS

Native American gaming has been around in the desert for years now, but recently the industry seems to have joined the major leagues, with a professionalism and polish that create a "virtual Vegas."

The best-known and most centrally located casino is the **Spa Resort Casino** in the heart of Palm Springs. The gaming rooms that used to be almost an afterthought now share the spotlight with the hot springs. Attendees at the hotel's conference center can often be found playing hooky from business at one or both!

And it was only a matter of time before Donald Trump came to mine gold in the California desert: His operation Trump 29 is now operated by the owning Indian tribe and is called Spotlight 29, 46-200 Harrison Place, Coachella (ℂ **866/878-6729**, about a half-hour from Palm Springs. The land may be tribal-owned, but this sophisticated complex is Vegas all the way, from the big-name shows and a high-roller players club to 24-hour fine dining and even one of those all-you-can-eat prime-rib buffets.

## 4 Joshua Tree National Park ⭐

40 miles NE of Palm Springs; 128 miles E of L.A.

The Joshua trees in this national park are merely a jumping-off point for exploring this seemingly barren desert. Viewed from the roadside, the dry land only hints at hidden vitality, but closer examination reveals a giant mosaic of intense beauty and complexity. From lush oases teeming with life to rusted-out relics of man's attempts to tame the wilderness, from low plains of tufted cacti to mountains of exposed, twisted rock, the park is much more than a tableau of the curious tree for which it is named.

The Joshua tree is said to have been given its name by early Mormon settlers traveling west, for its upraised limbs and bearded appearance reminded them of the prophet Joshua leading them to the promised land. Other observers were not so kind. Explorer John C. Frémont called it "the most repulsive tree in the vegetable kingdom."

That's harsh criticism for this hardy desert dweller, really not a tree but a variety of yucca and member of the lily family. The relationship is apparent when pale-yellow, lilylike flowers festoon the limbs of the Joshuas when they bloom in March, April, or May (depending on rainfall). When Mother Nature cooperates, the park also puts on quite a wildflower display, and you can get an updated report on prime viewing sites by calling the park ranger (see "Essentials" below).

The park, which reaches the southernmost boundary of this special tree's range, straddles two desert environments. There's the mountainous, Joshua tree–studded Mojave Desert forming the northwestern part of the park, while the Colorado Desert—hotter, drier, lower, and characterized by a wide variety of desert flora, including cacti, cottonwood, and native California fan palms—comprises the southern and eastern sections of the park. Between them runs the "transition zone," displaying characteristics of each.

The area's geological timeline is fascinating, stretching back 8 million years to a time when the Mojave landscape was one of rolling hills and grasslands; horses, camels, and mastodons abounded, preyed upon by saber-toothed tigers and wild dogs. Displays at the Oasis Visitor Center show how resulting climatic, volcanic, and tectonic activity have created the park's signature cliffs and boulders and turned Joshua Tree into the arid desert you see today.

Human presence has been traced back nearly 10,000 years with the discovery of Pinto Man, and evidence of more recent habitation can be seen in the form of Native American pictographs carved into rock faces throughout the park. Miners and ranchers began coming in the 1860s, but the boom went bust by the turn of the 20th century. Then a Pasadena doctor, treating World War I veterans suffering from respiratory and heart ailments caused by mustard gas, prescribed the desert's clean, dry air—and the town of Twentynine Palms was (re)born.

In the 1920s, cactus gardens were very much in vogue. Entrepreneurs hauled truckloads of desert plants into Los Angeles for quick sale or export, and souvenir hunters removed archaeological treasures. Incensed that the beautiful Mojave was in danger of being picked clean, Los Angeles socialite Minerva Hoyt organized a conservation movement and successfully lobbied for the establishment of Joshua Tree National Monument in 1936. The park got an unexpected boost when the first rock-climbing route was put up in 1956, near Jumbo Rock. The sport didn't take off until the late

# Joshua Tree National Park

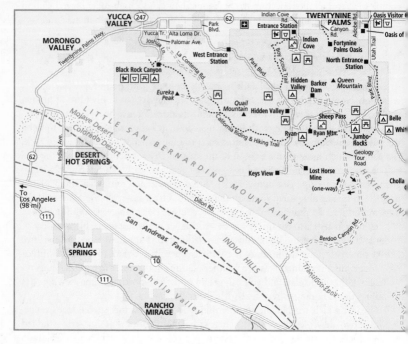

1960s, but today the park is considered Southern California's best rock-climbing area, and in winter (when places like Yosemite are embraced by cold weather), Joshua Tree is crawling with climbers.

In 1994, under provisions of the federal California Desert Protection Act, Joshua Tree was "upgraded" to national park status and expanded to nearly 800,000 acres. The park is popular with everyone from campers to wildflower lovers and even RVers just cruising through. It's a must-see for nature and geology lovers visiting during temperate weather, and more "user-friendly" than the other two hard-core desert parks.

## ESSENTIALS

**GETTING THERE**    From metropolitan Los Angeles, the usual route to the **Oasis Visitor Center** in Joshua Tree National Park is via I-10 to its intersection with Highway 62 (some 92 miles east of downtown). Highway 62 (the Twentynine Palms Hwy.) leads northeast for about 43 miles to the town of Twentynine Palms. Total driving time is around 2½ hours. In town, follow the signs at National Park Drive or Utah Trail to the visitor center and ranger station. Admission to the park is $10 per car (good for 7 days). Camping fees: $5 with no water, $10 with water.

**WHEN TO GO**    The park is busiest—relatively speaking, since it rarely feels crowded—in winter (Nov–Mar). Rock climbers flock to Joshua Tree in winter and spring, along with day-trippers drawn by brilliant wildflower displays (if winter rainfall was sufficient) in March, April, and May. And the sizzling summer months are popular with international visitors curious about the legendary extremes of temperature, and hardy campers looking for the solitude of balmy evenings.

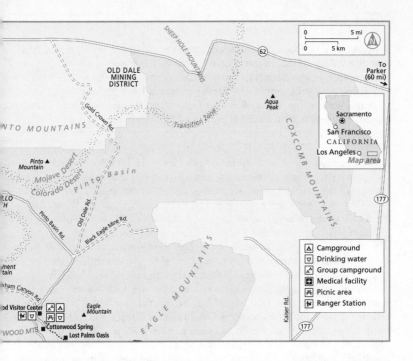

**VISITOR CENTERS & INFORMATION**  In addition to the main **Oasis Visitor Center** (© 760/367-5500) at the Twentynine Palms entrance, **Cottonwood Visitor Center** is at the south entrance, and the privately operated **Park Center** is located in the town of Joshua Tree, close to the West Entrance, unofficially also the portal for rock climbers.

The Oasis Visitor Center is open daily (except Christmas) from 8am to 5pm. Check here for a detailed map of park roads, plus schedules of ranger-guided walks and interpretive programs. Ask about the weekend tours of the Desert Queen Ranch, once a working homestead and now part of the park.

For information before you go, contact the **Park Superintendent's Office,** 74485 National Park Dr., Twentynine Palms, CA 92277 (© 760/367-5500; www.nps.gov/jotr). The **Joshua Tree National Park Association** is another good resource; reach them at © 760/367-5500 (www.joshuatree.org). Another outfit focused on the surrounding communities is **www.desertgold.com**.

## EXPLORING THE PARK

An excellent first stop, outside the park's north entrance, is the main **Oasis Visitor Center,** located alongside the Oasis of Mara, also known as the Twentynine Palms Oasis. For many generations, the native Serrano tribe lived at this "place of little springs and much grass." Get maps, books, and the latest in road, trail, and weather conditions before beginning your tour.

From the Oasis Center, drive south to **Jumbo Rocks,** which captures the essence of the park: a vast array of rock formations, a Joshua tree forest, and the yucca-dotted

---

### Tips  Load Up on Everything

No restaurants, lodging, gas stations, or stores are found within Joshua Tree National Park. In fact, water is only available at five park locations: Cottonwood Springs, the Black Rock Canyon Campground, the Indian Cove Ranger Station, the West Entrance (the hamlet of Joshua Tree), and the Oasis Visitor Center. Joshua Tree, Twentynine Palms, and Yucca Valley have lots of restaurants, markets, motels, and B&Bs.

---

desert, open and wide. Check out Skull Rock (one of the many rocks in the area that appear to resemble humans, dinosaurs, monsters, cathedrals, or castles) via a 1.5-mile nature trail that provides an introduction to the park's flora, wildlife, and geology.

At Cap Rock Junction, the main park road swings north toward the **Wonderland of Rocks,** 12 square miles of massive jumbled granite. This curious maze of stone hides groves of Joshua trees, trackless washes, and several small pools of water. To the south is Keys View Road, which dead-ends at mile-high **Keys View.** From the crest of the Little San Bernardino mountains, enjoy grand desert views that encompass both the highest (Mt. San Gorgonio) and lowest (Salton Sea) points in Southern California.

Don't miss the contrasting Colorado Desert terrain found along Pinto Basin Road—to conserve time, you might plan to exit the park via this route, which ends up at I-10. You'll pass both the **Cholla Cactus Garden** and spindly **Ocotillo Patch** on your way to vast, flat **Pinto Basin,** a barren lowland surrounded by austere mountains and punctuated by trackless sand dunes. The dunes are an easy 2-mile round-trip hike from the backcountry camping board (one of the few man-made markers along this road and one of the only designated parking areas), or simply continue to **Cottonwood Springs,** near the southern park entrance. Besides a small ranger station and well-developed campground, Cottonwood has a cool, palm-shaded oasis that is the trail head for a tough hike to Lost Palms Oasis.

## KING, BIKING & CLIMBING

**HIKING & NATURE WALKS**  The national park holds a variety of nature trails ranging in difficulty from strenuous challenges to kid-friendly interpretive walks—two of these (**Oasis of Mara** and **Cap Rock**) are paved and wheelchair-accessible. A favorite of the 11 short interpretive trails is **Cholla Cactus Garden,** smack-dab in the middle of the park, where you stroll through dense clusters of the deceptively fluffy-looking "teddy bear cactus."

For the more adventurous, **Barker Dam** is an easy 1-mile loop accessible by a graded dirt road east of Hidden Valley. A small, man-made lake is framed by the majestic Wonderland of Rocks. In addition to scrambling atop the old dam, it's fun to search out Native American petroglyphs carved into the base of cliffs lining your return to the trail head.

The challenging **Lost Horse Mine Trail** near Keys View leads through rolling hills to the ruins of a successful gold-mining operation; once here, a short, steep hike leads uphill behind the ruins for a fine view into the heart of the park.

When you're ready for a strenuous hike, try the **Fortynine Palms Oasis Trail,** accessible from Canyon Road in Twentynine Palms. After a steep, harsh ascent to a cactus-fringed ridge, the rocky canyon trail leads to a spectacular oasis, complete with palm-shaded pools of green water and abundant birds and other wildlife. Allow 2 to 3 hours for the 3-mile round-trip hike.

Another lush oasis lies at the end of **Lost Palms Oasis Trail** at Cottonwood Springs. The first section of the 7.5-mile trail is moderately difficult, climbing slowly to the oasis overlook; from here, a treacherous path continues to the canyon bottom, a remote spot that the elusive bighorn sheep find attractive.

**MOUNTAIN BIKING**    Much of the park is designated wilderness, meaning that bicycles are limited to roads (they'll damage the fragile ecosystem if you venture off the beaten track). None of the paved roads have bike lanes, but rugged mountain bikes are a great tool to explore the park via unpaved roads, where there aren't many cars.

Try the 18-mile **Geology Tour Road,** which begins west of Jumbo Rocks. Dry lake beds contrast with towering boulders along this sandy downhill road, and you'll also encounter abandoned mines.

A shorter but still rewarding ride begins at the **Covington Flats** picnic area. A steep 4-mile road climbs through Joshua trees, junipers, and pinyon pines to Eureka Peak, where you'll be rewarded with a panoramic view. For other bike-friendly unpaved and four-wheel-drive roads, consult the official park map.

**ROCK CLIMBING**    From Hidden Valley to the Wonderland of Rocks, the park has emerged as one of the state's premier rock-climbing destinations. The park offers some 4,000 climbing routes, ranging from the easiest of bouldering to some of the sport's most difficult climbs. November through May is the prime season to watch lizardlike humans scale sheer rock faces with impossible grace. Beginners can get into the act with the **Joshua Tree Rock Climbing School** (© **800/890-4745** or 760/366-4745; www.rockclimbingschool.com), which has been operating since 1988 and offers weekend and 4-day group lessons ($110 for 1 day, $195 for 2 days, and $390–$490 for 4 days, including equipment), plus private guiding ($275–$295 per person, per day). **Nomad Adventures** in Joshua Tree (© **760/366-4684**) is the local climbing store for gear sales and shoe rentals ($7.50 a day). Open weekdays from 8am to 6pm, weekends 8am to 8pm.

## WHERE TO STAY

If you're staying in the Palm Springs area, it's possible to do the national park as a day trip. But if you'd like to stay close by or spend more time here, Twentynine Palms, just outside the north boundary of the national park on Highway 62, offers budget-to-moderate lodging; there are also accommodations in Blackrock and Joshua Tree (West Entrance). For a complete listing of Twentynine Palms lodging, contact the **29 Palms Chamber of Commerce,** 6455 Mesquite Rd., Twentynine Palms, CA 92277 (© **760/ 367-3445;** www.29chamber.com). Blackrock information is available through the **Yucca Valley Chamber of Commerce,** 56711 Twentynine Palms Hwy., Yucca Valley, CA 92284 (© **760/365-6323;** www.yuccavalley.org). For Joshua Tree (West Entrance), contact the **Joshua Tree Chamber of Commerce,** 61325 Twentynine Palms Hwy. #F, Joshua Tree, CA 92252 (© **760/366-3723;** www.joshuatreechamber.org).

Near the visitor center in the Oasis of Mara is the rustic **29 Palms Inn** (© **760/ 367-3505;** www.29palmsinn.com), a cluster of adobe cottages and old cabins from the 1920s; its garden-fresh restaurant is the best in town. The 100-room **Best Western Garden Inn** (© **760/367-9141;** www.bestwestern.com), is also a comfortable base from which to maximize your outdoor time. Also recommended in Twentynine

Palms is the 53-room **Holiday Inn Express Hotel and Suites,** 71809 Twentynine Palms Hwy. (② **760/361-4009**).

Nine **campgrounds** scattered throughout the park offer pleasant though often spartan accommodations, with just picnic tables and pit toilets for the most part. Only two—**Black Rock Canyon** and **Cottonwood Springs**—have potable water and flush toilets, for a $10 overnight fee. Indian Cove and West Entrance have water at the ranger station, less than 2 miles from their closest campgrounds. You can make reservations online at **http://reservations.nps.gov** or by calling ② **800/365-2267.** Hot showers are available at **Coyote Corner,** 6535 Park Blvd. in Joshua Tree (② **760/366-9683**); they also rent climbing and camping gear.

## 5 Anza-Borrego Desert State Park 🖈

90 miles NE of San Diego; 31 miles E of Julian

The 600,000-acre Anza-Borrego Desert State Park, the nation's largest contiguous state park, lies mostly within San Diego County, and getting to it is almost as much fun as being there. From Julian, the first 20 minutes of the winding hour-long drive feel as if you're going straight downhill; in fact, it's a 7-mile-long drop called Banner Grade. A famous scene from the 1954 movie *The Long, Long Trailer* with Lucille Ball and Desi Arnaz was shot on the Banner Grade, and countless Westerns have been filmed in the Anza-Borrego Desert. An easier access is from Indio, go south on Highway 86 to Salton City and west on County Road S22 into Borrego Springs.

The desert is home to fossils and rocks dating from 540 million years ago; human beings arrived only 10,000 years ago. The terrain ranges in elevation from 15 feet to 6,100 feet above sea level. It incorporates dry lakebeds, sandstone canyons, granite mountains, palm groves fed by year-round springs, and more than 600 kinds of desert plants. After the spring rains, thousands of wildflowers burst into bloom, transforming the desert into a brilliant palette of pink, lavender, red, orange, and yellow. The rare bighorn sheep can sometimes be spotted navigating rocky hillsides, and an occasional migratory bird stops off on the way to the Salton Sea. A sense of timelessness pervades this landscape; travelers tend to slow down and take a long look around.

When planning a trip here, keep in mind that temperatures rise to as high as 115°F (46°C) in summer. Winters days are very comfortable with temperatures in the low to mid 70s (mid 20s Celsius), but note that nighttime temps can drop to freezing—hypothermia is as big a killer out here as the heat.

### ESSENTIALS

**GETTING AROUND**    You don't need a four-wheel-drive vehicle to tour the desert, but you'll probably want to get off the main highways and onto the jeep trails. The Anza-Borrego Desert State Park Visitor Center staff can tell you which jeep trails are in condition for two-wheel-drive vehicles. A Back Country Permit is issued free of

---

*Moments*   **The Desert in Bloom**

From mid-March to the beginning of April, the desert wildflowers and cacti are usually in bloom—a hands-down, all-out natural special event that's not to be missed. It's so extraordinary, there's a hot line to let you know when the blossoms are expected to burst forth: ② **760/767-4684.**

charge and is required to camp or use the jeep trails in the park. The Ocotillo Wells area of the park has been set aside for off-road vehicles such as dune buggies and dirt bikes. To use the jeep trails, a vehicle has to be licensed for highway use.

**ORIENTATION & VISITOR INFORMATION**   In Borrego Springs, the shopping center known as "the Mall" is on Palm Canyon Drive, the main drag. Christmas Circle surrounds a grassy park at the entry to town. The **Anza-Borrego Desert State Park Visitor Center** (© 760/767-4205; www.anzaborrego.statepark.org) lies just west of the town of Borrego Springs. It supplies information, maps, and two 15-minute audiovisual presentations, one on the desert's changing faces and the other on wildflowers. The visitor center is open October through May daily from 9am to 5pm, June through September weekends from 9am to 5pm. You might also stop by the **Desert Natural History Association,** 652 Palm Canyon Dr. (© 760/767-3098; www.abdnha.org), whose sleek Borrego Desert Nature Center and Bookstore features an impressive selection of guidebooks, historical resources, educational materials for kids, native plants and regional crafts, and a small museum display that includes a frighteningly real stuffed bobcat. This is also your best source for information on the nearby Salton Sea. It's open daily 9am to 5pm.

For information on lodging, dining, and activities, contact the **Borrego Springs Chamber of Commerce,** 786 Palm Canyon Dr., Borrego Springs, CA 92004 (© **800/559-5524** or 760/767-5555; www.borregosprings.org).

## EXPLORING THE DESERT

Remember that when you're touring in this area, hydration is of paramount importance. Whether you're walking, cycling, or driving, always have a bottle of water at your side. If you will be out after dusk, or anytime during January and February, warm clothing is also essential.

You can explore the desert's terrain on one of its trails or on a self-guided driving tour; the visitor center can supply maps. For starters, the **Borrego Palm Canyon self-guided hike** (1.5 miles each way) starts at the campgrounds near the visitor center. It is beautiful and easy to do, leading to a waterfall and massive fan palms in about 30 minutes. There is a $4 to $6 per vehicle day-use fee.

View spectacular canyons, fossil beds, ancient Native American sites, caves, and more in excursions by **La Casa del Zorro Desert Tours,** 3845 Yaqui Pass Rd., Borrego Springs, CA 92004 (© 760/767-2882). Tours go to the awesome viewpoint at Font's Point, where you can look out on the Badlands—named by the early settlers because it was an impossible area for moving or grazing cattle. A variety of itineraries vary during the week and prices range from $75 per person for a half-day tour to $150 for a full day. A minimum of four persons is required. Tours leave from La Casa del Zorro lobby. *Note:* Don't miss the sunset from Font's Point (accessible via four-wheel drive; check at the visitor center)—plan ahead and bring champagne and beach chairs for the nightly ritual.

## WHERE TO STAY

Borrego Springs is small, but there are enough accommodations to suit all travel styles and budgets. Peak season corresponds with the most temperate weather and wildflower viewing—mid-January through mid-May. Other decent options include **Palm Canyon Resort,** 221 Palm Canyon Dr. (© **800/242-0044** or 760/767-5341; www.pcresort.com), a large complex that includes a moderately priced hotel, RV park, restaurant, and recreational facilities; and **Borrego Valley Inn,** 405 Palm Canyon Dr.

(© **800/333-5810** or 760/767-0311; www.borregovalleyinn.com), a luxury South-western complex featuring sand-colored pueblo-style rooms and upscale bed-and-breakfast amenities. High season rates are $150 to $235.

**La Casa del Zorro Desert Resort** ★★    This pocket of heaven on earth was built in 1937, and the tamarisk trees that were planted then have grown up around it. So have the many charming tile-roofed casitas, originally neighboring homes bought by the resort's longtime owners, San Diego's Copley newspaper family. Over time the property has grown into a cohesive blend of discreetly private cottages and luxurious two-story hotel buildings—each blessed with personalized service and unwavering standards—that make La Casa del Zorro unequaled in Borrego Springs. Courtesy carts ferry you around the lushly planted grounds, and to the resort's stunning new pool area by the resurfaced tennis courts. It's easy to understand why repeat guests book their favorite casita year after year; some have a fireplace or pool, every bedroom has a separate bathroom, and they all have minifridges and microwaves (though a lack of dishes and utensils is calculated to get you into the Spanish-style main lodge's fine dining room). Outdoor diversions include horseshoes, Ping-Pong, volleyball, jogging trails, basketball, shuffleboard, and a life-size chess set. By the way, *zorro* means fox, and you'll find subtle fox motifs throughout the property.

3845 Yaqui Pass Rd., Borrego Springs, CA 92004. © **800/824-1884** or 760/767-5323. Fax 760/767-5963. www. lacasadelzorro.com. 79 units. $255–$415 double; casitas from $290. AE, DC, DISC, MC, V. **Amenities:** Restaurant (jackets required Oct–May); lounge; 5 outdoor pools; 9-hole putting green; 6 tennis courts; health club and spa; 4 whirlpools; bike rental; activities desk; courtesy car to golf; business center; salon; room service (7am–11pm); in-room massage; babysitting. *In room:* A/C, TV/VCR w/pay movies, dataport, minibar, coffeemaker, hair dryer, iron.

**The Palms at Indian Head** ★★ *Finds*    It takes a sense of nostalgia and an active imagination for most visitors to appreciate Borrego Springs's only bed-and-breakfast. Its fervent owners, David and Cynthia Leibert, have renovated the once-chic resort. Originally opened in 1947, then rebuilt after a fire in 1958, the Art Deco–style hill-top lodge was a favorite hideaway for San Diego's and Hollywood's elite. It played host to stars like Bing Crosby, Clark Gable, and Marilyn Monroe. The Leiberts rescued it from disrepair in 1993, uncovering original wallpaper, light fixtures, and priceless memorabilia. As soon as they'd restored several rooms in luxurious Southwestern style, they began taking in guests.

Now up to 12 rooms, the inn also boasts a restaurant, the **Krazy Coyote** (see "Where to Dine" below), that's a culinary breath of fresh air in town. Also restored is the 42×109-foot pool, soon to be joined by the original subterranean grotto bar behind viewing windows at the deep end. The inn occupies the most envied site in the valley—shaded by palms, adjacent to the state park, with a view across the entire Anza-Borrego region. A hiking trail begins steps from the hotel. The Palms at Indian Head rewards you with charm, comfort, and convenience.

2220 Hoberg Rd., Borrego Springs, CA 92004. © **800/519-2624** or 760/767-7788. Fax 760/767-9717. www.thepalms atindianhead.com. 12 units. $169–$219 double. Extra person $20. Rates include continental breakfast. DC, DISC, MC, V. Take S22 into Borrego Springs; at Palm Canyon Dr., S22 becomes Hoberg Rd. Continue north half mile. **Amenities:** Restaurant; bar; fantastic outdoor pool; room service (8am–8pm); in-room massage; laundry service. *In room:* A/C, TV, fridge, coffeemaker.

## CAMPING

The park has two developed campgrounds. **Borrego Palm Canyon,** with 117 sites, is 2½ miles west of Borrego Springs, near the visitor center. Full hookups are available, and there's an easy hiking trail. **Tamarisk Grove,** at Highway 78 and County Road

S3, has 27 sites. The overnight rate at both ranges $12 to $20. Both have restrooms with pay showers (bring quarters!) and a campfire program; reservations are a good idea. The park allows open camping along all trail routes. For more information, check with the visitor center (© **760/767-4205;** www.anzaborrego.statepark.org).

## WHERE TO DINE

Pickings are slim, but your best bet—if you're not willing to break the bank at La Casa del Zorro's classy dining room (dinner $20–$50)—is the surprisingly good **Krazy Coyote,** which presents a new menu of steaks and seafood. The **Badlands Market & Cafe,** 561 Palm Canyon Dr., in the Mall (© **760/767-4058**), offers a daily board of gourmet light meals that are great for picnics, plus a prepared-foods deli and store that features imported mustards, marinated sun-dried tomatoes, delicate desserts, and other sophisticated treats; it's open Sunday through Thursday from 7:30am to 4pm, and Friday and Saturday until 7pm. Or you could follow legions of locals into downtown mainstay **Carlee's Place,** 660 Palm Canyon Dr. (© **760/767-3262**), a casual bar and grill with plenty of neon beer signs, a pool table, and fuzzy-sounding jukebox. It's easy to understand why Carlee's is the watering hole of choice for motorcycle brigades that pass through town on recreational rides—and the food is tasty, hearty, and priced just right. If you have a sweet tooth, check out the **Fudge Factory,** 202 Palm Canyon (© **760/760-05407**), for a wide variety of fudge, ice creams, pastries and espresso. It's open Tuesday through Sunday 8am to 4pm.

**Bernard's** ✿ GERMAN   For a change of pace in desert dining drop in to Bernard's for some authentic German food such as Hassler Wiener schnitzel ($14) or Alsatian *choucroute* (sauerkraut, Polish sausage, pork, and brisket). Other daily specials run from $7 to $13. A full bar is served in a separate area.

In the Mall at #503. (© 760/767-5666). MC, V. Daily 11am–9pm.

**Krazy Coyote Saloon & Grille** ✿ SURF AND TURF   The same style and perfectionism that pervades David and Cynthia Leibert's bed-and-breakfast is evident in this restaurant, overlooking the inn's swimming pool and the desert beyond. The menu includes prime steaks, New Zealand rack of lamb or lobster, shrimp scampi, and salmon. The evening ambience is welcoming and romantic, as the sparse lights of tiny Borrego Springs twinkle on the desert floor below.

In the Palms at Indian Head, 2220 Hoberg Rd. © 760/767-7788. Dinner $7–$50. AE, MC, V. Open daily; call for seasonal hours.

**The Red Ocotillo** OLD-FASHIONED DINER   For hearty breakfast (served all day) or a casual lunch, join the crowd at the Red Ocotillo. Dining is casual indoors or in the patio. Eggs Benedict and omelets go for $9.95 while sandwiches are $8.95. Beer and wine are available.

818 Palm Canyon (as you enter town). © 760/767-7400. Daily 7am–2pm.

## 6 Mojave National Preserve

235 miles E of L.A.; 125 miles SW of Las Vegas

Two decades of park politicking ended in 1994 when President Bill Clinton signed into law the California Desert Protection Act, which created the Mojave National Preserve. Thus far, the Mojave's elevated status has not attracted hordes of sightseers, and devoted visitors are happy to keep it that way. Unlike a fully protected national park, the "national preserve" designation allows hunting and certain commercial land uses, and the continued grazing and mining within the preserve's boundaries are a sore spot for ardent environmentalists.

To most Los Angelenos, the East Mojave is that vast, bleak, interminable stretch of desert to be crossed as quickly as possible while leaving California via I-15 or I-40. Few realize that these highways are the boundaries of what some have long considered the crown jewel of the California desert.

This land is hard to get to know—unlike more developed desert parks, it has no lodgings or concessions, few campgrounds, and only a handful of roads suitable for the average passenger vehicle. It takes a special love of the desert to fully appreciate this stark, spare, spartan, barren terrain. But hidden within this natural fortress are some true gems—the preserve's 1.6 million acres include the world's largest Joshua tree forest; abundant wildlife; spectacular canyons, caverns, and volcanic formations; nationally honored scenic back roads and footpaths to historic mining sites; tabletop mesas; and a dozen mountain ranges.

## ESSENTIALS

**GETTING THERE** I-15, the major route between the Southern California metropolis and the state line for Las Vegas–bound travelers, extends along the northern boundary of Mojave National Preserve. I-40 is the southern access route to the East Mojave. It's a 3½-hour drive from Los Angeles to Kelso Depot, roughly in the center of the preserve. The closest major airport is in Las Vegas.

**WHEN TO GO** Spring is a splendid time to visit this desert (autumn is another). From March to May the temperatures are mild, the Joshua trees are in bloom, and the lower Kelso Dunes are bedecked with yellow and white desert primrose and pink sand verbena.

**VISITOR CENTERS & INFORMATION** You can visit the preserve online at **www.nps.gov/moja**. The best source for up-to-date weather conditions and a free topographical map is the **Mojave Desert Information Center,** 72157 Baker Blvd., Baker (under the "World's Tallest Thermometer"; ⓒ **760/733-4040**), which is open daily from 9am to 5pm and also has a superior selection of books for sale. Additional information and maps are available inside the preserve at the **Hole-in-the-Wall Visitor Center** (ⓒ **760/928-2572**), which is open Wednesday to Sunday for most of the year, Friday to Sunday in summer. An additional visitor center was scheduled to open in **Kelso Depot** in late 2005 and become the park's main visitor hub.

## EXPLORING THE PARK

One of the preserve's spectacular sights is the **Kelso Dunes,** the most extensive dune field in the West. The 45-square-mile formation of magnificently sculpted sand is famous for "booming": Visitors' footsteps cause miniavalanches and make the dunes go "sha-boom-sha-boom-sha-boom." Geologists speculate that the extreme dryness of the East Mojave Desert, combined with the wind-polished, rounded nature of the individual sand grains, has something to do with their musicality. Sometimes the low rumbling sound resembles a Tibetan gong; other times it sounds like a 1950s doo-wop musical group.

A 10-mile drive from the Kelso Dunes is **Kelso Depot,** built by the Union Pacific in 1924. The Spanish Revival–style structure was designed with a red-tile roof, graceful arches, and a brick platform. The depot continued to be open for freight-train crew use through the mid-1980s, although it ceased to be a railroad stop for passengers after World War II.

# Mojave National Preserve

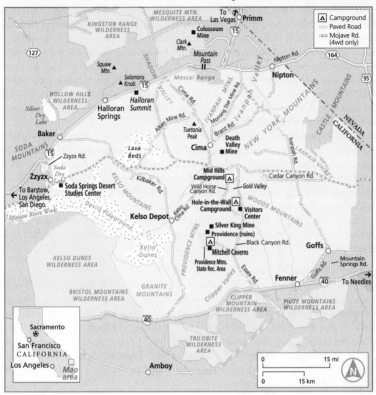

On and around **Cima Dome,** a rare geological anomaly, grows the world's largest and densest Joshua tree forest. Botanists say Cima's Joshuas are more symmetrical than their cousins elsewhere in the Mojave. The dramatic colors of the sky at sunset provide a breathtaking backdrop for Cima's Joshua trees, some more than 25 feet tall and several hundred years old.

Tucked into the Providence Mountains, in the southern portion of the preserve, is a treat everyone should try to see. The **Mitchell Caverns** ★, contained in a state recreation area within the national preserve, is a geological oddity exploited for tourism but still quite fascinating. Regular tours are conducted of these cool rock "rooms"; in addition to showcasing stalactites, stalagmites, and other limestone formations, the caves have proven to be rich in Native American archaeological finds.

**Hole-in-the-Wall** and **Mid Hills** are the centerpieces of Mojave National Preserve. Both locales offer diverse desert scenery, fine campgrounds, and the feeling of being in the middle of nowhere. The preserve's best drive links the two sites. In 1989 **Wildhorse Canyon Road,** which loops from Mid Hills Campground to Hole-in-the-Wall Campground, was declared the nation's first official "Back Country Byway," an honor federal agencies bestow upon America's most scenic back roads. The 11-mile, horseshoe-shaped road crosses wide-open country dotted with cholla and, in season, purple, yellow, and red wildflowers. Volcanic slopes and flattop mesas tower over the low desert.

Mile-high Mid Hills, so named because of its location halfway between the Providence and New York mountains, recalls the Great Basin Desert topography of Nevada and Utah. Mid Hills Campground offers a grand observation point from which to gaze out at the creamy, coffee-colored Pinto Mountains to the north and the rolling Kelso Dunes shining on the western horizon.

Hole-in-the-Wall is the kind of place Butch Cassidy and the Sundance Kid would have chosen as a hideout. This twisted maze of rhyolite rocks is a form of crystallized red-lava rock. A series of iron rings aids descent into Hole-in-the-Wall; they're not particularly difficult for those who are reasonably agile.

Kelso Dunes, Mitchell Caverns, Cima Dome, and Hole-in-the-Wall are highlights of the preserve that can be viewed in a weekend. But you'll need a week to see all the major sights, and maybe a lifetime to really get to know the East Mojave. And right now, without much in the way of services, the traveler to this desert must be well prepared and self-reliant. For many, this is what makes a trip to the East Mojave an adventure.

If Mojave National Preserve attracts you, you'll want to return again and again to see the wonders of this desert, including **Caruthers Canyon,** a "botanical island" of pinyon pine and juniper woodland, and **Ivanpah Valley,** which supports the largest desert-tortoise population in the California desert.

## HIKING & BIKING

**HIKING**   The free-form ambling climb to the top of the **Kelso Dunes** is 3 miles round-trip. A cool, inviting pinyon pine/juniper woodland is explored by the **Caruthers Canyon Trail** (3 miles round-trip). The longest pathway is **Mid Hills to Hole-in-the-Wall Trail,** a grand tour of basin and range tabletop mesas, large pinyon trees, and colorful cacti; it's 8 miles one-way. If you're not up for a long day hike, the 1-mile trip from **Hole-in-the-Wall Campground** to **Banshee Canyon** and the 5-mile jaunt to **Wildhorse Canyon** offer some easier alternatives. Be sure to pick up trail maps at one of the visitor centers.

**MOUNTAIN BIKING**   Opportunities are as extensive as the preserve's hundreds of miles of lonesome dirt roads. The 140-mile historic **Mojave Road,** a rough four-wheel-drive route, visits many of the most scenic areas in the East Mojave; sections of this road make excellent bike tours. Prepare well: The Mojave Road and other dirt roads are rugged routes through desert wilderness.

## CAMPING

The **Mid Hills Campground** is in a pinyon-pine/juniper woodland and offers outstanding views. This mile-high camp is the coolest in the East Mojave. Nearby **Hole-in-the-Wall Campground** sits above two canyons. Both campgrounds have pit toilets and potable water but no utility hookups. There is a graded dirt road between the two, but it's suitable for two-wheel-drive passenger cars.

There are also some sites at **Providence Mountain State Recreation Area** (Mitchell Caverns; see "Exploring the Park," above).

One of the highlights of the East Mojave Desert is camping in the open desert all by your lonesome, but certain rules apply. Call the **Mojave Desert Information Center** (© 760/733-4040) for suggestions.

## NEARBY TOWNS WITH TOURIST SERVICES

**BARSTOW**   This sizable town has a great many restaurants and motels and is about a 1-hour drive from the center of the preserve. On the east end of Main Street is Barstow

Station, looking like a collection of railway cars, but inside is a rambling shop with an amazing collection of tacky souvenirs: Everything from life-size howling wolves made of plaster of Paris to Marilyn Monroe cookie jars. On the other end of Main Street at the Greyhound bus station is a **Route 66 museum** (© 760/255-1890). It's only open Friday through Sunday from 11am to 4pm, and admission is free. Of the dozen motels in town, the most reliable are the **Best Western Desert Villa,** 1984 E. Main St., Barstow, CA 92311 (© 760/256-1781), and the **Ramada Inn,** 1511 E. Main St., Barstow, CA 92311 (© 760/256-5673).

**BAKER** Accommodations and food are available in this small desert town, which is a good place to fill up your gas tank and purchase supplies before entering Mojave National Preserve. Inexpensive lodging can be secured at the **Bun Boy Motel,** P.O. Box 130, Baker, CA 92309 (© 760/733-4363). The Bun Boy Coffee Shop is open 24 hours. For a tasty surprise, hop across the street to the **Mad Greek** (© 760/733-4354). Order a gyro, Greek salad, souvlaki, or baklava, and marvel at your good fortune for finding such tasty food and pleasant surroundings in the middle of nowhere. You can feast here daily from 6am to midnight.

**NIPTON** This tiny (pop. 30), charming town boasts a "trading post" that stocks snacks, maps, ice, and native jewelry; and the **Hotel Nipton** (© 760/856-2335; www.nipton.com), a B&B with a sitting room, two bathrooms down the hall, and five guest rooms, each for $70 a night. There are also four eco-tents on platforms that are $60 per night and sleep four. Owners Jerry and Roxanne Freeman, a former hard-rock miner who purchased the entire town in 1984, moved from Malibu to the abandoned ghost town and brought it back to life. Nipton is on Nipton Road, a few miles from I-15 near the Nevada state line.

## 7 Death Valley National Park ⍟

290 miles NE of L.A.; 120 miles NW of Las Vegas

Park? Death Valley National Park? The forty-niners, whose suffering gave the valley its name, would have howled at the notion. To them, other four-letter words would have been more appropriate: gold, mine, heat, lost, dead. And when you trace the whole history, you can imagine a host of other four-letter words shouted by teamsters who drove the 20-mule-team borax wagons.

Americans looking for gold in California's mountains in 1849 were forced to cross the burning sands to avoid severe snowstorms in the nearby Sierra Nevada. Some perished along the way, and the land became known as Death Valley.

Mountains stand naked, unadorned. The bitter waters of saline lakes evaporate into bizarre, razor-sharp crystal formations. Jagged canyons jab deep into the earth. Ovenlike heat, frigid cold, and the driest air imaginable combine to make this one of the most inhospitable locations in the world.

But, human nature being what it is, it's not surprising that people have long been drawn to challenge the power of Mother Nature, even in this, her home court. Man's first foray into tourism began in 1925, a scant 76 years after the forty-niners' harrowing experiences (which would discourage most sane folks from ever returning!). It probably would have begun sooner, but the valley had been consumed with lucrative borax mining since the late 1880s.

Death Valley is raw, bare earth, the way it must have looked before life began. Here, forces of the earth are exposed to view with dramatic clarity; just looking out on the landscape, it's impossible to know what year—or what century—it is. It's no coincidence that many of Death Valley's topographical features are associated with hellish images—the Funeral Mountains, Furnace Creek, Dante's View, Coffin Peak, and the Devil's Golf Course. But it can be a place of serenity.

President Herbert Hoover signed a proclamation designating Death Valley a national monument on February 11, 1933. With the stroke of a pen, he not only authorized the protection of a vast and wondrous land but also helped transform one of the earth's least hospitable spots into a tourist destination.

The naming of Death Valley National Monument came at a time when Americans began to discover the romance of the desert. Land that had been considered devoid of life was now celebrated for its spare beauty; places that had been feared for their harshness were now admired for their uniqueness. In 1994, when President Clinton signed the California Desert Protection Act, Death Valley National Park became the largest national park outside Alaska, with over 3.3 million acres. Though remote, it's one of the most heavily visited, and you're likely to hear less English spoken than German, French, and Japanese.

Today's visitor to Death Valley drives in air-conditioned comfort, stays in comfortable hotel rooms or at well-maintained campgrounds, orders meals and provisions at park concessions, even quaffs a beer at the local saloon. You can take a swim in the Olympic-size pool, tour a Moorish castle, shop for souvenirs, and enjoy the landscape while hiking along a nature trail with a park ranger.

## ESSENTIALS

**GETTING THERE**    There are several routes into the park, all of which involve crossing one of the steep mountain ranges that isolate Death Valley from, well, everything. Perhaps the most scenic entry to the park is via Calif. 190, east of Calif. 178 from Ridgecrest. Another scenic drive to the park is by way of Calif. 127 and Calif. 190 from Baker. For a first-time visitor, take the road 1 mile north of Tocopa, marked to Badwater and Death Valley. It's longer and rougher, but you dip down from the hills into the valley and have the full approach into the region. Otherwise, for the shorter route, continue to 190, which will bring you into Death Valley Center. You'll be required to pay a $10-per-car entrance fee, valid for 7 days. The closest major airport is in Las Vegas. *Note:* Top off your gas tank in Tocopa—it's pricey but not as bad as in the valley.

**WHEN TO GO**    Death Valley is popular year-round, with the greatest number of visitors during the temperate winter and spring (Nov–Mar). The heavy rains of 2005 caused road washouts and brought forth a carpet of multicolor wild flowers, and the floor of the desert became a lake, 2 feet deep, offering rare kayak adventures. All disappeared when the summer temperature returned. But the park is never deserted, not even in the scorching months of July, August, and September, as international visitors and extreme-heat seekers come to experience record-breaking temperatures. Even during the "cool" months (when evenings can actually become quite chilly), it's essential to wear sunscreen by day to protect against unfiltered rays, and to drink plenty of water to avoid becoming dehydrated in the ultra-arid climate.

**VISITOR CENTER & INFORMATION**    For camping and road information before you go, contact the Superintendent, Death Valley National Park, Death Valley, CA 92328 (© 760/786-3200; www.nps.gov/deva). The **Furnace Creek Visitor Center & Museum,** 15 miles inside the eastern park boundary on Calif. 190 (© 760/786-3200),

# Death Valley National Park

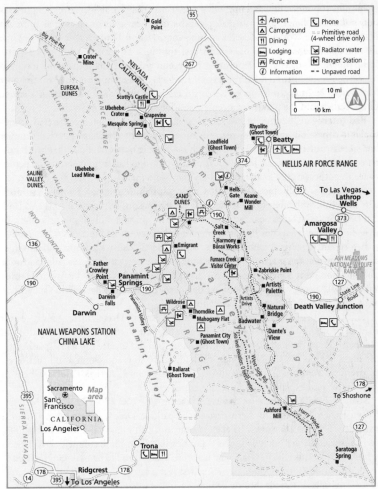

offers interpretive exhibits and an hourly slide program. Ask at the information desk for ranger-led nature walks and evening naturalist programs. The center is open daily from 8am to 6pm in winter (to 5pm in summer). Every November a group called Death Valley 49ers (www.deathvalley49ers.org) gather for 5 days to celebrate the pioneers who first traveled through this harsh environment. A $20 fee per family gives access to hootenannies, hoedowns, covered-wagon parades, gold panning, hiking, and four-wheel drives in the area.

## EXPLORING THE PARK

A good first stop after checking in at the main park visitor center in Furnace Creek is the **Harmony Borax Works**—a rock-salt landscape as tortured as you'll ever find. Death Valley prospectors called borax "white gold," and though it wasn't exactly a glamorous substance, it was a profitable one. From 1883 to 1888, more than 20 million pounds of borax (used to make laundry detergent) were transported from the Harmony Borax Works, and borax mining continued in Death Valley until 1928. A short trail with interpretive signs leads past the ruins of the old borax refinery and some outlying buildings. Transport of the borax was the stuff of legends, too. The famous 20-mule teams hauled the huge loaded wagons 165 miles to the rail station at Mojave. To learn more about this colorful era, visit the Borax Museum at Furnace Creek Ranch and the park visitor center, also located in Furnace Creek.

**Badwater**—at 282 feet below sea level, the lowest point in the Western Hemisphere—is possibly the hottest place in the world, with regularly recorded summer temperatures of 120°F (49°C). Badwater is mostly a curiosity, and not that much hotter or more brutal than the rest of Death Valley; most folks like to make a brief detour to see the otherworldly landscape and say they were there.

Salt Creek is the home of the **Salt Creek pupfish,** found nowhere else on earth. The little fish, which has made some amazing adaptations to survive in this arid land, can be glimpsed from a boardwalk nature trail. In spring a million pupfish might be wriggling in the creek, but by summer's end only a few thousand remain.

Before sunrise, photographers set up their tripods at **Zabriskie Point** and aim their cameras down at the magnificent panoramic view of Golden Canyon's pale mudstone hills and the great valley beyond. For another spectacular vista, check out **Dante's View,** a 5,475-foot viewpoint looking out over the shimmering Death Valley floor, backed by the high Panamint Mountains.

South of Furnace Creek is the 9-mile loop of **Artists Drive,** an easy must-see for visitors (except those in RVs, which can't negotiate the sharp, rock-bordered curves in the road). From the highway, you can't see the splendid palette of colors splashed on the rocks behind the foothills; once inside, though, stop and climb a hill that offers an overhead view, then continue through to aptly named **Artists Palette,** where an interpretive sign explains the source of nature's rainbow.

**Scotty's Castle & the Gas House Museum** (© **760/786-2392**), the Mediterranean hacienda in the northern part of the park, is Death Valley's premier tourist attraction. Visitors are wowed by the elaborate Spanish tiles, well-crafted furnishings, and construction that included solar water heating. Even more compelling is the colorful history of this villa in Grapevine Canyon, brought to life by park rangers dressed in 1930s period clothing. Don't be surprised if the castle cook or a friend of Scotty's gives you a special insight into castle life.

Construction of the "castle"—more officially, Death Valley Ranch—began in 1924. It was to be a winter retreat for eccentric Chicago millionaire Albert Johnson. The insurance tycoon's unlikely friendship with prospector, cowboy, and spinner-of-tall-tales Walter Scott put the $2.3-million structure on the map and captured the public's imagination. Scotty greeted visitors and told them fanciful stories from the early hard-rock mining days of Death Valley.

The 1-hour walking tour of Scotty's Castle is excellent, both for its inside look at the mansion and for what it reveals about the eccentricities of Johnson and Scotty. Tours (9am–5pm daily) fill up quickly; arrive early for the first available spots ($11 adult, $9 senior, and $6 child fee). Its open daily from 9am to 5pm.

Near Scotty's Castle is **Ubehebe Crater.** It's known as an explosion crater—one look and you'll know why. When hot magma rose from the depths of the earth to meet the groundwater, the resultant steam blasted out a crater.

## BIKING & HIKING

**BIKING**  Because most of the park is federally designated wilderness, cycling is allowed only on roads used by cars. Bikes are not allowed on hiking trails. Check © 760/786-3200 for road and trail conditions.

Good routes for bikers include Racetrack (28 miles, mainly level), Greenwater Valley (30 miles, mostly level), Cottonwood Canyon (20 miles), and West Side Road (40 miles, fairly level with some washboard sections). Artists Drive is 8 miles long and paved, with some steep uphills. A favorite is Titus Canyon, a 28-mile one-way route that starts 2¾ miles east of the park boundary on Nevada Highway 374.

**HIKING**  The trails in Death Valley range from the half-mile **Salt Creek Nature Trail,** an easy boardwalk suitable for everyone in the family, to the grueling **Telescope Peak Trail** (14 miles round-trip). Telescope Peak is a day-long, 3,000-foot climb to the 11,049-foot summit. Snow-covered during the winter, the peak is best climbed between May and November.

For hikes of moderate difficulty, try the trail into **Mosaic Canyon,** near Stovepipe Wells, where water has polished the marble rock into mosaics. It's an easy, 2.5-mile scramble through long, narrow walls that provide shade at every turn.

Romping among the **Sand Dunes** on the way to Stovepipe Wells is also fun, particularly for kids. It's a free-form adventure, and the dunes aren't particularly high— but the sun can be merciless. The sand in the dunes is actually tiny pieces of rock, most of them quartz fragments. As with all desert activities, having an adequate water supply is crucial.

Near the park's eastern border, two trails lead from the **Keane Wonder Mill,** site of a successful gold mine. The first is a steep and strenuous 2-mile challenge leading to the mine itself, passing along the way the solid, efficient wooden tramway that carried ore out of the mountain. The 2-mile **Keane Wonder Spring Trail** is much easier. The spring announces itself with a sulfur smell and piping birdcalls.

If you're visiting **Ubehebe Crater,** there's a steep but plain trail leading from the parking area up to the crater's lip and around some of the contours. Fierce winds can hamper your progress, but you'll get the exhilarating feeling that you're truly on another planet.

Park rangers can provide topographical maps and detailed directions to these and a dozen other hiking trails within the national park.

## WHERE TO STAY

The park's nine campgrounds are at elevations ranging from below sea level to 8,000 feet. In Furnace Creek, **Sunset** offers 1,000 spaces with water and flush toilets. **Furnace Creek Campground** has 200 similarly appointed spaces. **Stovepipe Wells** has 200 spaces with water and flush toilets. Reservations can be made online at **http:// reservations.nps.gov** or by calling © 800/365-2267.

The **Furnace Creek Ranch** (© 760/786-2345; www.furnacecreekresort.com), a private in-holding within the park, has 224 no-frills cottage units with air-conditioning and showers ($108–$162). The swimming pool is a popular hangout. Nearby are a coffee shop, saloon, steakhouse, and general store. **Stovepipe Wells Village** (© 760/ 786-2387) has 74 modest rooms with air-conditioning and showers, plus a casual dining room that closes between meals ($83–$103).

The only lodging in the park not run by the official concessionaire is the **Panamint Springs Resort** (© 775/482-7680; www.deathvalley.com), a rustic motel, cafe, and snack shop an hour east of Furnace Creek ($65–$79). Because accommodations in Death Valley are limited and expensive, you might consider the money-saving (but inconvenient) option of spending a night at one of the two gateway towns: **Lone Pine,** on the west side of the park, or **Baker,** on the south. **Beatty, Nevada,** which has inexpensive lodging, is an hour's drive from the park's center. The restored **Amargosa Hotel** (© 760/852-4441) in Death Valley Junction offers 14 rooms in a historic, out-of-the-way place, 40 minutes from Furnace Creek ($50–$65).

*Tip:* Meals and groceries are exceptionally costly due to the remoteness of the park. If possible, consider bringing a cooler with some snacks, sandwiches, and beverages to last the duration of your visit. Ice is easily obtainable, and you'll also be able to keep water chilled.

**Furnace Creek Inn** ★★   Like an oasis in the middle of Death Valley, the inn's red-tiled roofs and sparkling blue mineral-spring-fed swimming pool hint at the elegance within. The hotel has equipped its 66 deluxe rooms and suites with every modern amenity while successfully preserving the charm of this 1930s resort. Stroll the palm-shaded gardens before sitting down to a meal in the elegant dining room, where the food is excellent but the formality a bit out of place. Don tennis whites for a match in the midwinter sunshine, enjoy 18 holes of golf nearby, take an excursion on horse-back—there's even a shuttle from the Furnace Creek airstrip for well-heeled clientele. Reserve early: The inn is booked solid in winter with guests who appreciate a little pampering after a day in the park.

Hwy. 190 (P.O. Box 1), Death Valley, CA 92328. © **800/236-7916** or 760/786-2345. Fax 760/786-2307. www.furnace creekresort.com. 66 units. $250–$385 double; from $350 suite. Extra person $20. AE, DISC, MC, V. **Amenities:** Restaurant; lounge; naturally heated outdoor pool; nearby golf course (greens fees $35–$55, cart $25); 4 night-lit tennis courts; room service (7am–10pm); in-room massage. *In room:* A/C, TV w/pay movies, fridge, hair dryer, iron.

# 17

# San Diego & Environs

*by Mark Hiss*

Once dismissed as a slow-growth, conservative Navy town graced with 70 miles of fabulous sandy coastline, San Diego has been evolving steadily during the past 2 decades. The military link is still a presence today, with a handful of large bases throughout the county. Yet the city—California's first and the nation's seventh largest—now hosts a diversity of neighborhoods and residents to rival Los Angeles. San Diego reflects its Spanish-Mexican heritage in every corner; you won't forget that bustling Tijuana is just across the border, less than 30 minutes away. Despite that city's infamous poverty, San Diego boasts one of the nation's priciest housing markets and a biotech/tourism/telecom economy that's firing on all burners. A full-fledged building boom is transforming formerly seedy downtown neighborhoods and architecturally rich suburbs into upscale wonders. And the stylish young residents and shop owners they attract are, in turn, updating and enriching San Diego's dining, shopping, and entertainment options.

Amid all the change, San Diego is still first and foremost a big outdoor playground. You can still swim, snorkel, windsurf, kayak, bicycle, in-line skate, and partake of other diversions in or near the water, as you like. And top-notch civic attractions still include three world-famous animal parks and Balboa Park, one of the finest urban parks in the country.

So pack a laid-back attitude along with your sandals and swimsuit. Prepare for a warm welcome to California's grown-up beach town.

## 1 Orientation

### GETTING THERE

#### BY PLANE

**San Diego International Airport,** 3707 N. Harbor Dr. (© **619/231-2100;** www.san. org), locally known as Lindbergh Field, is just 2 miles from downtown. All the major domestic carriers fly here, plus **AeroMexico** from Los Cabos and Mexico City. The complex has three passenger buildings, with short local flights departing from the Commuter Terminal, a half-mile away.

**TRANSPORTATION FROM THE AIRPORT**   All the major car-rental agencies have offices at the airport, including **Avis** (© **800/230-4898**), **Budget** (© **800/527-0700**), **Dollar** (© **800/800-3665**), and **Hertz** (© **800/654-3131**). If you're driving to downtown from the airport, take Harbor Drive south to Broadway, the main east-west thoroughfare, and turn left. To reach Hillcrest or Balboa Park, exit the airport toward I-5, and follow the signs for Laurel Street. To reach Mission Bay and the beaches, take I-5 north to I-8 west. To reach La Jolla, take I-5 north to the La Jolla Parkway exit, which turns into Torrey Pines Road.

**Metropolitan Transit System (MTS)** (☏ **619/233-3004;** www.sdcommute.com) bus route no. 992 provides service between the airport and downtown San Diego. Route no. 992 bus stops are located at each of the three terminals. The one-way fare is $2.25. Request a transfer if you're connecting to another bus or to the San Diego Trolley route downtown. Downtown, route no. 992 stops on Broadway. The ride takes about 15 minutes; buses come at 10- to 15-minute intervals. At Broadway and First Avenue is the **Transit Store** (☏ **619/234-1060**), where the staff can answer your transit questions and provide free route maps to help you get where you're going.

**Shuttle** services run regularly from the airport to points around the city; you'll see designated pickup areas outside each terminal. The fare is about $5 per person to downtown; Mission Valley and Mission Beach are $8 to $10; La Jolla and Coronado are $10 to $13—rates to a residence in these areas are usually about double for the first person. **Taxis** line up outside all terminals, and the trip downtown, usually a 10-minute ride, is about $10 (plus tip); budget $20 to $22 for Coronado or Mission Beach, and about $30 to $35 for La Jolla.

## BY CAR

From Los Angeles, you'll enter San Diego via coastal route **I-5.** From points northeast of the city, you'll come down on **I-15** and **Highway 163** south to drive into downtown (where 163 turns into 10th Ave.), or hook up with **I-8** west for the beaches. From the east, you'll come in on I-8, connecting with Highway 163 south. The freeways are well marked, pointing the way to downtown streets.

## BY TRAIN

San Diego is connected to the rest of the country by **Amtrak** (☏ **800/USA-RAIL;** www.amtrak.com), but only via Los Angeles. Trains pull into San Diego's pretty Mission-style **Santa Fe Train Depot,** 1050 Kettner Blvd. (at Broadway), within walking distance of some downtown hotels and 1½ blocks from the Embarcadero. Expect to pay $30 one-way from Los Angeles.

## BY BUS

**Greyhound** (☏ **800/229-9424;** www.greyhound.com) buses from Los Angeles, Phoenix, Las Vegas, and other points in the Southwest U.S. arrive at the station in downtown San Diego at 120 W. Broadway. The one-way fare from Los Angeles is $16. Local buses stop in front, and the San Diego Trolley is nearby.

## VISITOR INFORMATION

You'll find staffed information booths at airport terminals, the train station, and the cruise ship terminal. Downtown, the **San Diego Convention & Visitor Bureau** (☏ **800/350-6205** or 619/236-1212; www.sandiego.org) is at 1040⅓ W. Broadway at Harbor Boulevard (across the street from the cruise ship terminal). The *Official Visitors Pocket Guide* includes information on dining, activities, attractions, tours, and transportation. Be sure to ask for the *San Diego Travel Values* pamphlet, full of discount coupons for hotels, restaurants, and attractions. The center is open Monday through Saturday from 9am to 5pm year-round and, from June through August, it's open on Sundays as well; it is closed on major holidays. There is also a walk-up-only facility (sans phone) at the **La Jolla Visitor Center,** 7966 Herschel Ave., near the corner of Prospect Street. This office is open daily, in summer from 10am to 7pm, with a shortened schedule mid-September through mid-June.

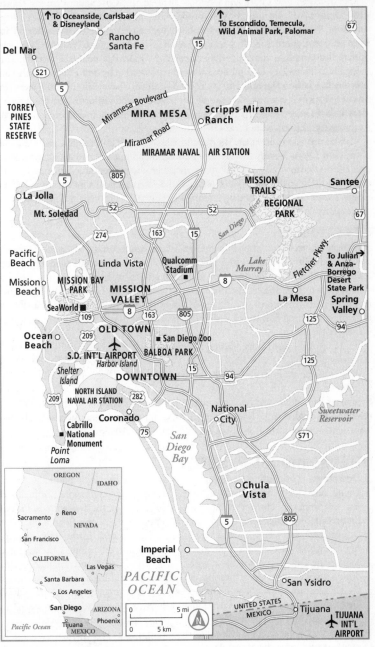

# San Diego Area at a Glance

↑ To Oceanside, Carlsbad & Disneyland

↑ To Escondido, Temecula, Wild Animal Park, Palomar

67

Del Mar

Rancho Santa Fe

S21

15

5

TORREY PINES STATE RESERVE

Miramesa Boulevard

MIRA MESA

Scripps Miramar Ranch

Miramar Road

MIRAMAR NAVAL AIR STATION

805

MISSION TRAILS

Santee

5

La Jolla

52

52

67

Mt. Soledad

San Diego River

REGIONAL PARK

274

163

15

Pacific Beach

Linda Vista

Qualcomm Stadium

Lake Murray

Fletcher Pkwy

→ To Julian & Anza-Borrego Desert State Park

Mission Beach

MISSION BAY PARK

MISSION VALLEY

8

La Mesa

Spring Valley

SeaWorld

109

8

163

805

125

94

Ocean Beach

209

OLD TOWN

✈ S.D. INT'L AIRPORT

Harbor Island

San Diego Zoo

BALBOA PARK

125

Shelter Island

DOWNTOWN

15

94

209

NORTH ISLAND NAVAL AIR STATION

282

National City

Sweetwater Reservoir

Cabrillo National Monument

Coronado

75

San Diego Bay

S71

Point Loma

Chula Vista

OREGON

IDAHO

5

805

Sacramento

Reno

NEVADA

San Francisco

CALIFORNIA

Las Vegas

Imperial Beach

PACIFIC OCEAN

Santa Barbara

Los Angeles

San Diego

ARIZONA

Phoenix

San Ysidro

Pacific Ocean

Tijuana

MEXICO

0    5 mi

0    5 km

N

UNITED STATES

MEXICO

Tijuana

✈ TIJUANA INT'L AIRPORT

Specialized visitor information outlets include the **Coronado Visitors Center,** 1100 Orange Ave., Coronado (✆ **619/437-8788**); and **Promote La Jolla,** 1150 Silverado St. (✆ **858/454-5718;** www.lajollabythesea.com). The **Mission Bay Visitor Information Center,** 2688 E. Mission Bay Dr., San Diego (✆ **619/276-8200;** www.infosandiego.com), is conveniently located on Mission Bay next to I-5 (exit Clairemont Dr./Mission Bay Dr. and head toward the water). The **San Diego North Convention & Visitors Bureau,** 360 N. Escondido Blvd., Escondido (✆ **800/848-3336** or 760/745-4741; www.sandiegonorth.com), can provide information on excursion areas in San Diego County, including Del Mar, Carlsbad, Escondido, Julian, and Anza-Borrego Desert State Park.

To find out what's on at the theater and who's playing in the clubs, pick up a copy of the *San Diego Weekly Reader* (www.sdreader.com), a free newspaper available all over the city every Thursday; in tourist areas it is distributed in a condensed version under the title the *Weekly.* "Night & Day," the entertainment supplement in the *San Diego Union-Tribune* (www.signonsandiego.com), the city's main daily newspaper, appears on Thursday.

## CITY LAYOUT

San Diego has a clearly defined downtown, which is surrounded by several dozen separate neighborhoods—each with its own personality, but all incorporated into the city. The street system is straightforward, so getting around is fairly easy.

Downtown, Broadway is the main street, intersected by Fourth and Fifth avenues (running south and north, respectively). Harbor Drive hugs the waterfront (Embarcadero), connecting downtown with the airport to the northwest and the Convention Center to the south.

The Coronado Bay Bridge leading to Coronado is accessible from I-5 just south of downtown, and I-5 north leads to Old Town, Mission Bay, La Jolla, and North County coastal areas. Balboa Park (home of the San Diego Zoo), Hillcrest, and uptown areas lie north of downtown San Diego. The park and zoo are easily reached by way of Park Boulevard (which would otherwise be 12th Ave.), which leads to the parking lots. Fifth Avenue leads to the Hillcrest and uptown neighborhoods. Highway 163, which heads north from 11th Avenue, leads into Mission Valley.

## NEIGHBORHOODS IN BRIEF

**Downtown** The business, shopping, dining, and entertainment heart of the city encompasses Horton Plaza, the Embarcadero (waterfront), and the Convention Center, sprawling over eight "neighborhoods." This is the most convenient area to stay for those with downtown appointments or meetings at the Convention Center. The **Gaslamp Quarter** is the center of a redevelopment kicked off in the mid-1980s with the opening of the Horton Plaza shopping complex; now, the once-seedy area is jam-packed with boutiques, restaurants, and nightspots. Immediately southeast of the Gaslamp is **PETCO Park,** home of the San Diego Padres. Just northwest, **Little Italy** is an old neighborhood along India Street, between Cedar and Fir, and a great place to find Italian food as well as cutting-edge architecture. Overall, downtown is the easiest place to stay if you don't have your own set of wheels.

**Hillcrest & Uptown** Hillcrest was the city's first self-contained suburb, in the

1920s. Despite the cachet of being close to **Balboa Park** (home of the San Diego Zoo and numerous museums), the area fell into neglect in the 1960s. However, in the late 1970s, legions of preservation-minded residents—particularly its lively gay community—began to restore Hillcrest's charms, making it the local equivalent of a West Hollywood or SoHo in the 1980s and '90s. Centrally located and brimming with popular restaurants and avant-garde boutiques, Hillcrest also offers less expensive and more personalized accommodations than any other area in the city. Other uptown neighborhoods of interest are **Mission Hills** to the west of Hillcrest, **University Heights, Normal Heights, North Park,** and **Kensington,** to the east.

**Old Town & Mission Valley** These two busy areas wrap around the neighborhood of Mission Hills. On one end are the Old Town State Historic Park (where California "began"), Presidio Park, Heritage Park, and numerous museums that recall the turn of the 20th century and the city's beginnings. Shopping and dining here largely target visitors. Not far from Old Town lies the suburban sprawl of Mission Valley, home to gigantic shopping centers. Hotel Circle is an elongated loop road paralleling I-8, where a string of moderately priced and budget hotels offer an alternative to the ritzier neighborhoods. In recent years, several major hotel and convention complexes have opened in Mission Valley, and 1990s condo developments have made the valley a residential area.

**Mission Bay & the Beaches** Here's where they took the picture on the postcard you'll send home. Mission Bay is a watery playground perfect for water-skiing, sailing, and windsurfing. The adjacent communities of **Ocean Beach, Mission Beach,** and **Pacific Beach** are known for their wide stretches of sand, nightlife, and casual dining. Many single San Diegans live here, and once you've visited you'll understand why. The boardwalk, which runs from South Mission Beach to Pacific Beach, is a popular place for skating, biking, people-watching, and sunsets. It's the place to stay if you are traveling with beach-loving children.

**La Jolla** With an atmosphere somewhere between Rodeo Drive and a Mediterranean village, this seaside community is home to an inordinate number of residents wealthy enough to live anywhere. Surrounded by the beach, and the **University of California, San Diego,** La Jolla offers top restaurants, shopping, and medical facilities. Tourists who bed down here can take advantage of the community's attributes without having to buy its high-priced real estate, but they'll share in La Jolla's problematic parking and traffic snarls. There are really two La Jollas: the so-called "village," the original seaside community, and the residential and business areas that have sprouted along La Jolla Village Drive east of I-8, which are of less interest. Public transportation is limited, too, so La Jolla is not an ideal base if you don't have a car.

**Coronado** You might be tempted to think of Coronado as an island, as many San Diegans still do. It does have an isolated, resort ambience and it's most easily accessed by ferry or sweeping bridge, but the city of Coronado is actually on a bulbous peninsula connected to the mainland by a narrow sand spit, the **Silver Strand.** The northern portion—known as "North Island"—is home to a U.S. Naval Air Station, in use since World War I. The southern sector has a history as an elite playground for snowbirds. It's a charming suburban community, home to more retired admirals than any other place in the country. Shops line the main street, Orange Avenue, and the Hotel del Coronado sits astride one of the area's finest beaches.

## 2 Getting Around

### BY CAR

San Diego's traffic woes are increasing. It's not L.A., by any means, but the construction of dense, outlying suburbia over the last 20 years has made morning and evening rush-hour traffic a headache. Aside from that, it's a very car-friendly town and easy to navigate.

Downtown, many streets run one-way, and finding a parking space can be tricky, but some reasonably priced parking lots are centrally located.

**RENTALS** All the large, national car-rental firms have rental outlets at the airport (see "Getting There," earlier), in the major hotels, and at other locations around the city. Some car-rental companies will allow their cars into Mexico as far as Ensenada, provided that you stop before crossing the border to buy Mexican auto insurance. Insurance is also advised if you drive your own car over the border.

**PARKING** Parking meters are common in most San Diego areas, including downtown, Hillcrest, the beaches, and La Jolla. Posted signs indicate operating hours—generally between 9am and 6pm, even on Saturdays; meters devour quarters at a rate of 1 per 12 minutes. Two large parking structures (at Market Street and Sixth Avenue, and K Street and Sixth Avenue) have eased parking problems in the busy Gaslamp Quarter. Free parking is the rule in Balboa Park and Old Town.

### BY PUBLIC TRANSPORTATION

Both city buses and the San Diego Trolley are operated by the **San Diego Metropolitan Transit System (MTS)** (© 619/595-4949; www.sdcommute.com). The website displays timetables, maps, and fares online, and provides information for travelers with disabilities. Or visit the system's **Transit Store,** 102 Broadway at First Avenue (© 619/234-1060), a complete public-transportation information center, supplying travelers with passes, tokens, timetables, maps, and brochures. Get a copy of the useful pamphlet *Way to Go to See the Sights,* which details routes to the city's most popular tourist attractions. The store is open Monday through Friday from 9am to 5pm. If you know your route and just need schedule information—or automated answers to FAQs—call **Info Express** (© 619/685-4900) from any touch-tone phone, 24 hours a day. A $5 **Day-Tripper pass** allows for 1 day of unlimited rides (there's also a 2-day pass for $9, a 3-day for $12, or 4-day for $15); it's available from the Transit Store and at all Trolley ticket vending machines. *Note:* A fare increase as of July 1, 2005, raised the monthly pass price $2.

**BY BUS** San Diego has an adequate bus system encompassing more than 100 routes that will get you to where you're going—eventually. Bus stops are marked by rectangular blue signs every other block or so on local routes, farther apart on express routes. More than 20 bus routes pass through the downtown area. Most fares are $2.25. Buses accept dollar bills, but the driver can't give change. You can request a free transfer as long as you continue on a bus with an equal or lower fare (if it's higher, you pay the difference). Transfers must be used within 90 minutes. You can return to where you started, if you want. Some routes stop at 6pm, while other lines continue to 9pm, midnight, and 2am—ask your bus driver for more specific information. On Saturday a few routes run all night.

**BY TROLLEY**    The San Diego Trolley is great for visitors, particularly if you're staying downtown and plan to visit Tijuana, Old Town, or Mission Valley. Two main routes intersect downtown. The Blue Line travels from the Mexican border north through downtown, Old Town, and then east through Mission Valley. The trip to the border takes 40 minutes from downtown. The Orange Line runs from downtown east through Lemon Grove and El Cajon to the city of Santee. A new extension—the Green Line, from Old Town to San Diego State University and on to El Cajon— opened in July 2005.

Trolleys operate on a self-service fare-collection system; riders buy tickets from machines in stations before boarding. The machines list fares for each destination ($1.25–$3) and dispense change. Tickets are valid for 2 hours from the time of purchase, in any direction. Fare inspectors board trains at random to check tickets. A round-trip ticket is double the price, but it's valid all day between the origination and destination points.

Trolleys run every 15 minutes during the day and every 30 minutes at night; during peak weekday rush hours the Blue Line runs every 10 minutes. The trolleys generally operate daily from 5am to about midnight; the Blue Line runs 24 hours Saturday night/Sunday morning.

**BY TRAIN**    San Diego's express rail commuter service, the **Coaster,** travels between the downtown Santa Fe Depot station and the Oceanside Transit Center, with stops at Old Town, Sorrento Valley, Solana Beach, Encinitas, and Carlsbad. Fares range from $3.75 to $5.25 each way and can be paid by credit card at vending machines at each station. Eligible seniors and riders with disabilities pay half price. The scenic trip between downtown San Diego and Oceanside takes just under an hour. Trains run Monday through Friday about once an hour, with four trains each direction on Saturday (no service Sun); call ✆ **800/COASTER** for the current schedule.

**Amtrak** (✆ **800/USA-RAIL;** www.amtrak.com) trains run between San Diego and downtown Los Angeles about 12 times daily each way. Trains depart from the Santa Fe Depot and stop at Solana Beach, Oceanside, San Juan Capistrano, and Anaheim (Disneyland). A ticket to Los Angeles is $30 each way, or $42 in business class. One-way to Solana Beach is $9.50, to Oceanside $13.

**BY FERRY & WATER TAXI**    Regularly scheduled ferry service runs between San Diego and Coronado (✆ **619/234-4111** for information). Ferries leave from the Broadway Pier (1050 N. Harbor Dr., at the intersection of Broadway) on the hour from 9am to 9pm Sunday through Thursday, and until 10pm Friday and Saturday. They return from the Old Ferry Landing in Coronado to the Broadway Pier every hour on the half-hour from 9:30am to 9:30pm Sunday through Thursday and until 10:30pm Friday and Saturday. The ride takes 15 minutes. The fare is $2.25 each way (50¢ extra if you bring your bike).

Water taxis (✆ **619/235-TAXI**) will pick you up from any dock around San Diego Bay from Monday through Friday between noon and 10pm, Saturday and Sunday 11am to 11pm. If you're staying in a downtown hotel, this is a great way to reach the beach fronting the Hotel del Coronado. Boats are sometimes available on the spur of the moment, but reservations are advised. Fares are $6 per person to most locations.

## BY TAXI

Half a dozen taxi companies serve the area. Rates are based on mileage and can add up quickly in sprawling San Diego; a trip from downtown to La Jolla, for example, will cost $30 to $35. Other than in the Gaslamp Quarter after dark, taxis don't cruise the streets as they do in other cities, so you have to call ahead for quick pickup. If you are waiting at a hotel or restaurant, the front-desk attendant or maitre d' will call one for you. Local companies include **Orange Cab** (© 619/291-3333), **San Diego Cab** (© 619/226-TAXI), **Yellow Cab** (© 619/234-6161), **Coronado Cab Company** (© 935/435-6211), and **La Jolla Cab** (© 858/453-4222).

## BY BICYCLE

San Diego is on the verge of becoming the nation's preeminent bicycling destination, with millions of dollars earmarked for bicycle paths throughout the city and county. But already, San Diego is cyclist friendly, and named as "one of the top 10 cities in the U.S. to bicycle" by *Bicycling* magazine.

Most major thoroughfares offer bike lanes. Bikes are allowed on the San Diego–Coronado ferry, the San Diego Trolley, and most city buses, at no charge. *Cycling San Diego,* by Nelson Copp and Jerry Schad (Sunbelt Publications), is a good resource for bicyclists and is available at most local bike shops. Or to obtain a detailed map by mail of San Diego County's bike lanes and routes, call **Ride Link Bicycle Information** (© 800/COMMUTE or 619/231-BIKE). You might also want to talk to the **City of San Diego Bicycle Coordinator** (© 619/533-3110) or the **San Diego County Bicycle Coalition** (© 858/487-6063).

For information on rentals, see "Outdoor Pursuits," later in this chapter.

---

### FAST FACTS: San Diego

*Area Codes*  San Diego's main area code is **619,** used primarily by downtown, uptown, Mission Valley, Point Loma, Coronado, La Mesa, and El Cajon. The area code **858** is used for northern and coastal areas, including Mission Beach, Pacific Beach, La Jolla, Del Mar, and Rancho Santa Fe. Use **760** to reach the remainder of San Diego County, including Encinitas, Carlsbad, Oceanside, Escondido, Julian, and Anza-Borrego.

*Babysitters*  **Marion's Childcare** (© 888/891-5029) has bonded babysitters available to come to your hotel room. **Panda Services** (© 858/292-5503) is also available.

*Dentists/Doctors*  For dental referrals, contact the **San Diego County Dental Society** at © 800/201-0244, or call 800/DENTIST. Miami-based **Hotel Docs** (© 800/468-3537) is a 24-hour network of physicians, dentists, and chiropractors. They accept credit cards, and their services are covered by most insurance. In a life-threatening situation, dial © **911.**

*Emergencies*  Call © **911** for fire, police, and ambulance.

*Hospitals*  In Hillcrest, near downtown San Diego, **UCSD Medical Center-Hillcrest,** 200 W. Arbor Dr. (© 619/543-6222), has the most convenient emergency room. In La Jolla, **Thornton Hospital,** 9300 Campus Point Dr. (© 858/657-7000), has a good emergency room, and you'll find another in Coronado, at **Coronado**

**Hospital,** 250 Prospect Place, opposite the Marriott Resort (© **619/522-3600**). Twenty-four-hour pharmacies include **Sav-On Drugs,** 313 E. Washington St., Hillcrest (© **619/291-7170**); call for more locations (© 619/531-2000).

*Police* The downtown police station is at 1401 Broadway (© **619/531-2000** or 619/233-3323 for the hearing impaired).

*Post Office* San Diego's main post office is at 2535 Midway Dr., just west of Old Town; it is open Monday from 7am to 5pm, Tuesday through Friday from 8am to 5pm, and Saturday from 8am to 4pm. For branch locations, call © **800/ASK-USPS** or log on to www.usps.gov.

*Safety* Of the 10 largest cities in the United States, San Diego historically has had the lowest incidence of violent crime per capita. Virtually all areas of the city are safe during the day, but caution is advised in Balboa Park, in areas not frequented by regular foot traffic. Homeless transients are common—especially downtown, in Hillcrest, and in beach areas. They are rarely a problem, but can be unpredictable when inebriated. Downtown areas to the east of PETCO Park are sparsely populated and poorly lighted after dusk. The Gaslamp Quarter, Hillcrest, Old Town, Mission Valley, La Jolla, and Coronado are usually safe on foot at night.

*Taxes* Sales tax in restaurants and shops is 7.75%. Hotel tax is 10.5%.

*Useful Telephone Numbers* For the latest San Diego arts and entertainment information, call © **619/238-0700;** for half-price day-of-performance tickets, call © **619/497-5000;** for a beach and surf report, call © **619/221-8824.** For the correct time, call © **853-1212** (works in all area codes). For local **weather,** call © **619/289-1212.**

## 3 Where to Stay

The rates listed below are all "rack," or official, rates—you can almost always do better. Rates tend to be highest in summer at beach hotels, and midweek downtown when a big convention is in town. Remember to factor in the city's 10.5% hotel tax. For good prices in all accommodations categories, contact **San Diego Hotel Reservations** (© **800/SAVE-CASH** or 619/627-9300; www.sandiegohotelres.com). Bed-and-breakfasts are available, and several are listed below. For additional choices, contact the **San Diego Bed & Breakfast Guild** (© **619/523-1300;** www.bandbguild sandiego.org).

### DOWNTOWN

San Diego's downtown is an excellent place for leisure travelers to stay. The nightlife and dining in the Gaslamp Quarter and Horton Plaza shopping are close at hand; Balboa Park, Hillcrest, Old Town, and Coronado are less than 10 minutes away by car; and beaches aren't much farther. It's also the city's public-transportation hub, and thus very convenient for car-free visitors.

Conventions are big business, and the high-rise hotels cater primarily to the meet-and-greet crowd. While they don't offer much personality for leisure travelers, it's not hard to get rooms for 30% to 50% off the rack rates when a convention isn't taking up all the availability. Although their rack rates start in the mid-$300s, chain operations

# San Diego Accommodations & Dining

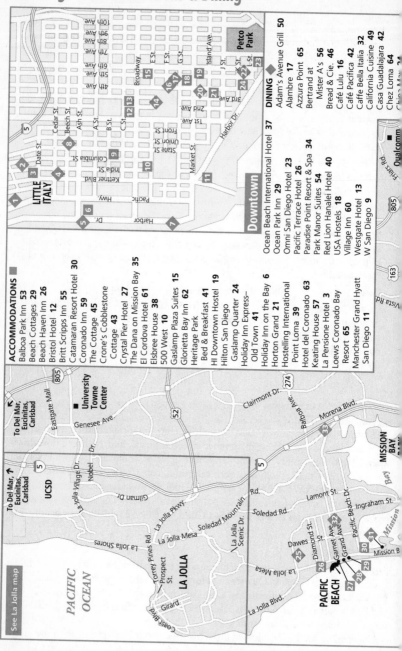

**ACCOMMODATIONS**

Balboa Park Inn **53**
Beach Cottages **29**
Beach Haven Inn **26**
Bristol Hotel **12**
Britt Scripps Inn **55**
Catamaran Resort Hotel **30**
Coronado Inn **59**
The Cottage **45**
Crone's Cobblestone Cottage **43**
Crystal Pier Hotel **27**
The Dana on Mission Bay **35**
El Cordova Hotel **61**
Elsbree House **38**
500 West **10**
Gaslamp Plaza Suites **15**
Glorietta Bay Inn **62**
Heritage Park Bed & Breakfast **41**
HI Downtown Hostel **19**
Hilton San Diego Gaslamp Quarter **24**
Holiday Inn Express–Old Town **41**
Holiday Inn on the Bay **6**
Horton Grand **21**
Hostelling International Point Loma **39**
Hotel del Coronado **63**
Keating House **57**
La Pensione Hotel **3**
Loews Coronado Bay Resort **65**
Manchester Grand Hyatt San Diego **11**

Ocean Beach International Hotel **37**
Ocean Park Inn **29**
Omni San Diego Hotel **23**
Pacific Terrace Hotel **26**
Paradise Point Resort & Spa **34**
Park Manor Suites **54**
Red Lion Hanalei Hotel **40**
USA Hostels **18**
Village Inn **60**
Westgate Hotel **13**
W San Diego **9**

**DINING** ◆

Adam's Avenue Grill **50**
Alambre **17**
Azzura Point **65**
Bertrand at Mister A's **56**
Bread & Cie. **46**
Café Lulu **16**
Café Pacifica **42**
Caffe Bella Italia **32**
California Cuisine **49**
Casa Guadalajara **42**
Chez Loma **64**

678

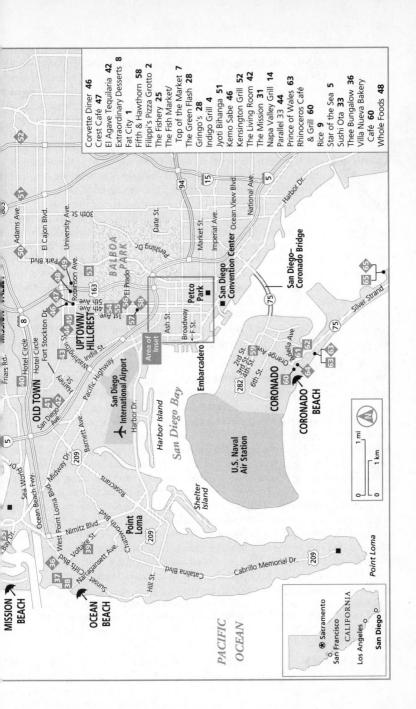

Corvette Diner **46**
Crest Café **47**
El Agave Tequilaria **42**
Extraordinary Desserts **8**
Fat City **1**
Fifth & Hawthorn **58**
Filippi's Pizza Grotto **2**
The Fishery **25**
The Fish Market/
  Top of the Market **7**
The Green Flash **28**
Gringo's **28**
Indigo Grill **4**
Jyoti Bihanga **51**
Kemo Sabe **46**
Kensington Grill **52**
The Living Room **42**
The Mission **31**
Napa Valley Grill **14**
Parallel 33 **44**
Prince of Wales **63**
Rhinoceros Café
  & Grill **60**
Rice **9**
Star of the Sea **5**
Sushi Ota **33**
Thee Bungalow **36**
Villa Nueva Bakery
  Café **60**
Whole Foods **48**

are a good place to test your wheelin'-and-dealin' skills. Start with the city's biggest hotel, the 1,625-room **Manchester Grand Hyatt San Diego** ★★, 1 Market Place (© **800/233-1234** or 619/232-1234; www.hyatt.com), a two-towered behemoth with a 40th-floor cocktail lounge with fabulous views. Then there's the 223-room **Westgate Hotel** ★★★, 1055 Second Ave. (© **800/221-3802** or 619/238-1818; www.westgate hotel.com), where the lobby looks transplanted out of the Palace of Versailles and rooms (remodeled in 2003) are plush, spacious, and bright. A large (306-room) hotel with a boutique feel and a popular rooftop bar, the **San Diego Marriott Gaslamp Quarter** ★★, 660 K St., San Diego (© **619/696-0234**; www.sandiegogaslamphotel. com) opened recently. Another newcomer, **Hotel Solamar** ★★, 435 6th Ave., San Diego (© **877/230-0300**; www.hotelsolamar), a 235-room, stylishly urban Kimpton Hotels property, draws nonguests to revel in its restaurant, Jsix, and bar, Jbar.

A more moderate choice, in terms of price, is the colorful, modern **Bristol Hotel,** 1055 First Ave. (© **800/662-4477** or 619/232-6141; www.bristolhotelsandiego.com), adjacent to the Gaslamp Quarter. In the budget category, the 260-room **500 West,** 500 W. Broadway (© **619/234-5252**), offers small but comfortable rooms for $69 to $89 a night in a seven-story building dating to 1924. It offers contemporary style, history, and a good location, but bathrooms are down the hall. Cheaper still are downtown's two hostels, where double rooms are about $55 and dorm rooms are under $25: **USA Hostels** (© **800/438-8622** or 619/232-3100; www.usahostels.com) is in the heart of the Gaslamp, at 726 Fifth Ave; **HI Downtown Hostel** (© **800/909-4776,** ext. 43, or 619/525-1531; http://sandiegohostels.org) is nearby, at 521 Market St.

## VERY EXPENSIVE

### Hilton San Diego Gaslamp Quarter ★★★

At the foot of the Gaslamp Quarter, immediately across from the Convention Center, this hotel is ideally situated for business travelers. Yet unlike some of its competition, the Hilton doesn't overwhelm with size, making it a great place for guests who want to be close to the action (loads of restaurants, nightlife, and the ballpark are within a few blocks) but stay out of the fray. The hotel opened in 2001 on the site of the old Bridgeworks building, part of San Diego's original wharf of a century ago; much of the brick facade was incorporated into the hotel's polished design. Standard rooms boast upmarket furniture, down comforters, and pillow-top mattresses. There are suites and an executive floor, but the snazzy quarters are in the intimate Enclave wing, a converted office space next to the main building with 30 oversize guest rooms with towering ceilings, custom furnishings, Frette linens, and lavish bathrooms with whirlpool tubs. No two of the Enclave units have the same floor plan, but they are the most handsome accommodations downtown—resembling a swinging loft redo far more than any typical chain hotel room. The open-air terrace between the two buildings has a pool and sunning area and a fitness room.

401 K St. (at Fourth Ave.), San Diego, CA 92101. © **800/HILTONS** or 619/231-4040. Fax 619/231-6439. 282 units. $295 double; from $395 suite. Children under 12 stay free in parent's room. AE, DC, DISC, MC, V. Valet parking $21. Trolley: Gaslamp Quarter. **Amenities:** 2 restaurants; 2 bars; outdoor pool; health club and full-service spa; Jacuzzi; concierge; business center; salon; 24-hr. room service; laundry service. *In room:* A/C, TV w/pay movies, dataport, minibar, coffeemaker, hair dryer, iron.

### W San Diego ★★

The W took the city by storm when it opened in 2003, delivering swanky nightlife beyond the Gaslamp Quarter. The place is still packed on weekends, with lines out the door to get into the hotel bars. Fortunately, rooms are bright and cheery—like mod beach cabanas beamed into downtown, replete with a sexy shower. *Nouveau nautique* is the theme, with elegant aqua and sand tones accenting the whites, a window seat (great idea) for gazing down on this languid corner of downtown, and a beach-ball-shaped pillow, a blunt reminder that this hotel is supposed to be fun. The restaurant **Rice** stumbled out of the gate initially, but an adventurous and playful new menu of contemporary global cuisine has made it a winner. The adjoining bar, **Magnet,** has unveiled a new martini menu. Then there's **Beach,** on the third floor, where the developers let rip: The open-air bar has a sand floor (heated at night), a fire pit, and cabanas. Drinks are served in plastic, allowing you to safely roam the terrace barefoot. The cacophony dies down by Sunday when Los Angelenos depart, and for a few days the W is a proper business hotel—albeit one with a (tiny) pool, a 24-hour open-air gym, and a bank of 18 video screens glowing with an idealized landscape of bubbles floating heavenward. A 1,250-square-foot luxury suite, known as the WoW suite, was added to the 19th floor, with a host of state-of-the-art features and killer skyline views.

421 W. B St. (at State St.), San Diego, CA 92101. ⓒ 888/625-5144 or 619/231-8220. Fax 619/231-5779. www.whotels.com/sandiego. 259 units. $359–$469 double; $700–$3,000 suite. AE, DC, DISC, MC, V. Valet parking $23. Bus: All Broadway routes. Trolley: American Plaza or Civic Center. **Amenities:** Restaurant; 3 lounges; 24-hr. concierge; 24-hr. room service; laundry/dry-cleaning service. *In room:* A/C, TV w/VCR and DVD, dataport, minibar, coffeemaker, hair dryer, iron, CD player.

## EXPENSIVE

**Holiday Inn on the Bay** ★★ *Kids*   Renovated in 2002, this better-than-average Holiday Inn is reliable and nearly always offers great deals. The three-building high-rise complex is on the Embarcadero across from the harbor and the Maritime Museum. This scenic spot is only 1½ miles from the airport (you can watch planes landing and taking off) and 2 blocks from the train station and trolley. Rooms, while basic, always seem to sport clean new furnishings and plenty of thoughtful comforts. Although rooms are identical inside, choose carefully; the bay views are marvelous, but the city views may encompass construction sites—the byproduct of superheated redevelopment. In either case, request the highest floor possible.

1355 N. Harbor Dr. (at Ash St.), San Diego, CA 92101-3385. ⓒ 800/HOLIDAY or 619/232-3861. Fax 619/232-4924. www.holiday-inn.com/san-onthebay. 600 units. $169 double; from $299 suite. Children under 18 stay free in parent's room. AE, DC, MC, V. Self-parking $18; valet $22. Bus: All Pacific Hwy. routes. Trolley: American Plaza. Pets accepted w/$25 fee and $100 deposit. **Amenities:** 4 restaurants; lounge; outdoor heated pool; exercise room; concierge; business center; room service (6–11am and 5–11pm); babysitting; laundry service; self-service laundry. *In room:* A/C, TV w/pay movies, dataport, coffeemaker, hair dryer, iron.

## MODERATE

**Horton Grand** ★ *Finds*   A cross between an elegant hotel and a charming inn, the Horton Grand combines two hotels that date from 1886—the Horton Grand (once an infamous red-light establishment) and the Brooklyn Hotel (which for a time was the Kayle Saddlery Shop where Wyatt Earp resided). Both were saved from demolition, moved to this spot, and connected by an airy atrium lobby filled with white wicker. The facade, with its graceful bay windows, is original. Each room is unique, with vintage furnishings and gas fireplaces; bathrooms are lush with reproduction floor tiles, fine brass fixtures, and genteel appointments. Rooms overlook either the city or the fig-tree-filled courtyard; they're divided between the clubby and darker "saddlery" side and the pastel-toned and Victorian "brothel" side. The suites (really just large studio-style rooms) are located in a newer wing; choosing one means sacrificing historic character for a sitting area/sofa bed and minibar with microwave. If you're lonely, request room no. 309, where resident ghost Roger likes to hang out.

311 Island Ave. (at Fourth Ave.), San Diego, CA 92101. © 800/542-1886 or 619/544-1886. Fax 619/239-3823. www. hortongrand.com. 132 units. $129–$279 double; from $199 suite. Extra person $20. Children under 18 stay free in parent's room. AE, DC, MC, V. Valet parking $20. Bus: 1, 4, 5, 16, or 25. Trolley: Convention Center. **Amenities:** Restaurant (7–10am daily, Sun champain brunch 10am–2pm). *In room:* A/C, TV, dataport, hair dryer.

### INEXPENSIVE

**Gaslamp Plaza Suites** ★★ *Value*    You can't get closer to the center of the vibrant Gaslamp Quarter than this impeccably restored late-Victorian edifice. At 11 stories, it was San Diego's first skyscraper, built in 1913. Crafted of Australian gumwood, marble, brass, and exquisite etched glass, the building originally housed San Diego Trust & Savings. Various other businesses (jewelers, lawyers, doctors, and photographers) set up shop here until 1988, when the elegant structure landed on the National Register of Historic Places and reopened as a boutique hotel. You'll be surprised at the timeless elegance, from the dramatic lobby and wide corridors to guest rooms furnished with European flair. Each bears the name of a writer (Emerson, Swift, Zola, Shelley, Fitzgerald, and so on). Most rooms are spacious and offer luxuries rare in this price range, like pillow-top mattresses and premium toiletries; microwave ovens and dinnerware; and impressive luxury bathrooms. The cheapest rooms on the back side are uncomfortably small. The higher floors boast splendid city and bay views. Despite the noise-muffling windows, don't be surprised to hear street noise, especially when the Quarter gets rockin' on the weekends.

520 E St. (corner of Fifth Ave.), San Diego, CA 92101. © 800/874-8770 or 619/232-9500. Fax 619/238-9945. www.gaslampplaza.com. 64 units. $99–$149 double; from $169 suite. Rates include continental breakfast. AE, DC, DISC, MC, V. Valet parking $18. Bus: 1, 3, or 25. Trolley: Fifth Ave. **Amenities:** Room service (lunch and dinner hours). *In room:* A/C, TV w/VCR, dataport, fridge, coffeemaker, hair dryer, iron, safe, microwave.

**La Pensione Hotel** ★ *Value*    This place has modern style and a convenient location in Little Italy (within walking distance of the business district), a friendly staff, and free parking (a premium for small hotels in San Diego). The four-story Pensione is built around a courtyard and feels like a small European hotel. The decor throughout is modern and streamlined, with plenty of sleek black and metallic surfaces, crisp white walls, and modern wood furnishings. Guest rooms are small but leave you with room to move around. Each room offers a ceiling fan and minifridge; some have a small balcony. *Note:* Rooms don't have air-conditioning. You can open your window, but the street cafes are noisy until midnight on weekends.

606 W. Date St. (at India St.), San Diego, CA 92101. © 800/232-4683 or 619/236-8000. Fax 619/236-8088. www. lapensionehotel.com. 80 units. $75 double. AE, DC, DISC, MC, V. Limited free underground parking. Bus: 5 or 16. Trolley: Little Italy. **Amenities:** Self-service laundry. *In room:* TV, dataport, fridge.

## HILLCREST/UPTOWN

Although they're certainly no longer a secret, the gentrified historic neighborhoods north of downtown are still something of a bargain. They're convenient to Balboa Park and offer easy access to the rest of town. Filled with casual and upscale restaurants, eclectic shops, and upbeat nightlife, the area is also easy to navigate. All of the following accommodations cater to the mainstream market but attract a gay/lesbian clientele as well.

In addition to Keating House (below), several bed-and-breakfasts in elegant, older neighborhoods invite consideration. **Crone's Cobblestone Cottage** ★, 1302 Washington Place (© **619/295-4765;** www.cobblestonebandb.com), is a beautifully restored

Craftsman bungalow in Mission Hills; **The Cottage,** 3829 Albatross St. (ⓒ **619/299-1564;** www.sandiegobandb.com/cottage.htm), is a 1913 home tucked into a quiet cul-de-sac; and the **Britt Scripps Inn** ✦✦, 406 Maple St. (ⓒ **888/881-1991;** www.brittscrippsinn.com) is one of the city's finest Victorian structures, adjacent to Balboa Park in Bankers Hill.

## INEXPENSIVE

**Balboa Park Inn** ✦  Insiders looking for unusual accommodations head for this small pink inn at the northern edge of Balboa Park. It's a cluster of four Spanish colonial–style former apartment buildings in a mostly residential neighborhood a half-mile east of Hillcrest proper. The hotel is popular with gay travelers drawn to Hillcrest's restaurants and clubs, which are several blocks away. All the rooms and suites are tastefully decorated; the specialty suites, however, are over-the-top. There's the Tara suite, as in *Gone With the Wind;* the Nouveau Ritz, which employs every Art Deco cliché, including mirrors and Hollywood lighting; and the Greystoke suite, a jumble of jungle, safari, and tropical themes with a completely mirrored bathroom and Jacuzzi tub. Seven rooms have Jacuzzi tubs, and most have kitchens. All have a private entrance, though the front desk operates 24 hours. From here, you're close enough to walk to the San Diego Zoo and other Balboa Park attractions.

3402 Park Blvd. (at Upas St.), San Diego, CA 92103. ⓒ **800/938-8181** or 619/298-0823. Fax 619/294-8070. www.balboaparkinn.com. 26 units. $99 double; $129–$219 suite. Extra person $10. Children under 12 stay free in parent's room. Rates include continental breakfast. AE, DC, DISC, MC, V. Parking available on street. Bus: 7. From I-5, take Washington St. east, follow signs to University Ave. E. Turn right at Park Blvd. *In room:* TV, fridge, coffeemaker.

**Keating House** ✦✦ *(Finds)*  This grand 1880s Bankers Hill mansion, between downtown and Hillcrest, 4 blocks from Balboa Park, has been meticulously restored by two energetic innkeepers with a solid background in architectural preservation. Doug Scott and Ben Baltic not only know old houses; they're also neighborhood devotees filled with historical knowledge. They celebrate authentic period design throughout, even in the overflowing gardens that bloom on four sides of this local landmark. The house contains a comfortable hodgepodge of antique furnishings and appointments; three additional rooms in the restored carriage house open onto an exotic garden patio. The downstairs entry, parlor, and dining room all have cozy fireplaces; bathrooms—all private—are gorgeously restored with updated period fixtures. Breakfast is served in a sunny, friendly setting, and they cheerfully consider special dietary needs. This classy inn draws a range of guests, from Europeans to businessmen.

2331 Second Ave. (between Juniper and Kalmia sts.), San Diego, CA 92101. ⓒ **800/995-8644** or 619/239-8585. Fax 619/239-5774. www.keatinghouse.com. 9 units. $95–$185 double. Rates include full breakfast. AE, DISC, MC, V. Bus: 1, 3, 11, or 25. From the airport, take Harbor Dr. toward downtown; turn left on Laurel St., then right on Second Ave. *In room:* Hair dryer, no phone.

**Park Manor Suites** ✦ *(Value)*  This eight-story building was built as a full-service luxury hotel in 1926 on a prime corner overlooking Balboa Park. Over time the hotel became a popular stopping-off point for celebrities headed for Mexican vacations in the 1920s and 1930s. Although dated, guest rooms are huge and very comfortable, featuring full kitchens, dining rooms, living rooms, and bedrooms with separate dressing areas. A few have glassed-in terraces; request one when you book. The overall feeling is that of a prewar East Coast apartment building, complete with steam heat and lavish moldings. Park Manor Suites does have its weaknesses, particularly bathrooms that have mostly original fixtures and could use some renovation. But prices are quite reasonable, there's a darkly old-world restaurant on the ground floor, laundry service is also available, and a simple continental breakfast buffet is served in the penthouse banquet room. In fact, the penthouse bar becomes a bustling gay social scene on Friday evenings, drawing a horde—the single elevator gets a real workout that night.

525 Spruce St. (between Fifth and Sixth aves.), San Diego, CA 92103. ℂ 800/874-2649 or 619/291-0999. Fax 619/291-8844. www.parkmanorsuites.com. 74 units. $99–$139 studio; from $139 1-bedroom suite. Extra person $15. Children under 12 stay free in parent's room. Rates include continental breakfast. AE, DC, DISC, MC, V. Free parking. Bus: 1, 3, or 25. Take Washington St. exit off I-5, right on Fourth Ave., left on Spruce. **Amenities:** Restaurant/bar; access to health club ($5); laundry/dry-cleaning service; self-service laundry. *In room:* TV, dataport, kitchen, coffeemaker, hair dryer, iron.

## OLD TOWN & MISSION VALLEY

Old Town is a popular area for families because of its proximity to Old Town State Historic Park and other attractions within walking distance, and SeaWorld and the San Diego Zoo are within a 10-minute drive. Around the corner, in Mission Valley, you'll find the city's largest collection of hotels with rooms under $100 a night. Mission Valley lacks much homegrown personality—this is the spot for chain restaurants and huge shopping malls, not gardens or water views. But it caters to convention groups and leisure travelers drawn by the lower prices and competitive facilities.

Room rates at properties on Hotel Circle are significantly cheaper than those in many other parts of the city. You'll find a cluster of inexpensive chain hotels and motels, including **Best Western Seven Seas** (ℂ 800/328-1618 or 619/291-1300), **Mission Valley Travelodge** (ℂ 800/255-3050 or 619/297-2271), **Motel 6 Hotel Circle** (ℂ 800/4-MOTEL-6 or 619/296-1612), **Ramada Plaza** (ℂ 800/532-4241 or 619/291-6500), and **Vagabond Inn–Hotel Circle** (ℂ 800/522-1555 or 619/297-1691). Although these hotels are a couple miles from the beach, like beach hotels, summer and weekend rates tend to be higher.

### MODERATE

**Heritage Park Bed & Breakfast Inn** ★★  This exquisite 1889 Queen Anne mansion is set in a Victorian park—an artfully arranged cobblestone cul-de-sac lined with historic buildings saved from the wrecking ball and assembled here, in Old Town, as a tourist attraction. Most of the rooms are in the main house, with a handful of equally appealing choices in an adjacent 1887 Italianate companion building. Owner Nancy Helsper is an amiable and energetic innkeeper with an eye for detail, and she's eager to share the homes' fascinating history with guests. A stay here is about surrendering to indulgences such as afternoon tea, candlelight breakfast, and romantic extras (champagne and chocolates, dear?) available for special celebrations. Like the gracious parlors and porches, each room has meticulous period antiques and luxurious fabrics; the small staff provides turndown service and virtually anything else you might require. The fireplaces are all ornamental, but some rooms have whirlpool baths.

2470 Heritage Park Row, San Diego, CA 92110. ℂ 800/995-2470 or 619/299-6832. Fax 619/299-9465. www.heritageparkinn.com. 12 units. $130–$265 double. Extra person $20. Rates include full breakfast and afternoon tea. AE, DC, DISC, MC, V. Free parking. Bus: 5. Trolley: Old Town. Take I-5 to Old Town Ave., turn left onto San Diego Ave., then turn right onto Harney St. *In room:* A/C, hair dryer, iron.

**Holiday Inn Express–Old Town** ★  Just a couple of easy walking blocks from the heart of Old Town, this Holiday Inn has a Spanish colonial exterior that suits the neighborhood. Inside you'll find above-par contemporary furnishings and surprising small touches that make this hotel an affordable option favored by business travelers and families alike. There's nothing spectacular about the adjacent streets, so the hotel is smartly oriented toward the interior; request a room with a patio or balcony that opens onto the pleasant courtyard. Rooms are thoughtfully and practically appointed, with extras like microwave ovens and writing tables. The lobby, surrounded by French doors, features a large fireplace, several sitting areas, and a TV. The hotel entrance, on Jefferson Street, is hard to find but definitely worth the search.

3900 Old Town Ave., San Diego, CA 92110. © 800/451-9846 or 619/299-7400. Fax 619/299-1619. www.ichotels group.com/h/d/hiex/hd/santa. 125 units. $129–$169 double; from $179 suite. Extra person $10. Children under 18 stay free in parent's room. Rates include continental breakfast. AE, DC, DISC, MC, V. Free parking. Bus: 5. Take I-5 to Old Town Ave. exit. **Amenities:** Outdoor pool; whirlpool; laundry/dry-cleaning service. *In room:* A/C, TV, fridge, coffeemaker, microwave.

**Red Lion Hanalei Hotel** ⭐ My favorite hotel along Mission Valley's Hotel Circle has a Polynesian theme and comfort-conscious sophistication that sets it apart. Most rooms are split between two eight-story towers, set back from the freeway and cleverly positioned so the balconies open onto the tropically landscaped pool courtyard or the attractive links of a golf club. A few more rooms are found in the Presidio Building, which is too close to the freeway for my comfort. The heated outdoor pool is large enough for a luau, as is the oversize whirlpool beside it. The hotel boasts an unmistakable 1960s Hawaiian vibe: The restaurant and bar have over-the-top, kitschy decor, with waterfalls, outrigger canoes, and more. But guest rooms are outfitted with contemporary furnishings and conveniences; some have microwaves and refrigerators. Services include a free shuttle to Old Town and the Fashion Valley Shopping Center, plus meeting facilities. Golf packages are also available.

2270 Hotel Circle N., San Diego, CA 92108. © 800/RED-LION or 619/297-1101. Fax 619/297-6049. www.redlion. com. 416 units. $159–$169 double; from $275 suite. Extra person $10. AE, DISC, MC, V. Parking $8. Bus: 6. From I-8, take Hotel Circle exit, follow signs for Hotel Circle N. Pets accepted w/$50 deposit. **Amenities:** 2 restaurants; lounge; outdoor pool; nearby golf course; fitness center; whirlpool; game room; activities desk; 24-hr. business center; room service (6am–10pm); laundry/dry-cleaning service; self-service laundry. *In room:* A/C, TV w/pay movies, dataport, coffeemaker, hair dryer, iron.

## MISSION BAY & THE BEACHES

If the beach and aquatic activities are the focus of your San Diego agenda, this part of town may be for you. Even though the beach communities feel removed from the city, downtown and Balboa Park are only a 15-minute drive away. Some hotels are right on Mission Bay, San Diego's water playground; they're usually good choices for families. Ocean Beach, Mission Beach, and Pacific Beach provide a taste of the transient-beach-bum lifestyle. They can be raucous at times, especially on summer weekends, and dining options are largely limited to chains. If you're looking for a more refined landing, head to La Jolla or Coronado (the sections that follow).

**Hostelling International** has a 53-bed location in **Point Loma** (© **800/909-4776,** ext. 157, or 619/223-4778), 3790 Udall St., about 2 miles inland from Ocean Beach; rates run $19 per person, and private rooms that sleep two are $48. The **Ocean Beach International Hostel,** 4961 Newport Ave. (© **800/339-7263** or 619/223-7873; www.californiahostel.com), has more than 60 beds, just 2 blocks from the beach; bunk rates are $20 per person, and they offer free pickup from the airport, train, or bus station. An extensive collection of DVDs is available for guests, and free barbecues are held Tuesday and Thursday.

Rates listed below are for the peak summer season (July–Aug); rates the rest of the year average 20% to 40% lower. Accommodations here tend to book up solid on summer weekends and even weekdays, but discounts can be had, especially for those who dare to wait until the afternoon of arrival.

## EXPENSIVE

**Catamaran Resort Hotel** ★★ (Kids)   Right on Mission Bay, the Catamaran has its own bay and ocean beaches, complete with watersports facilities. Built in the 1950s, the hotel has been fully renovated to modern standards without losing its trademark Polynesian theme; the atrium lobby holds a 15-foot waterfall and full-size dugout canoe, koi-filled lagoons meander through the property, and the pool is surrounded by a real bamboo fence, rather than a fake metal one. Numerous varieties of bamboo and palms sprout in the lush gardens, tropical birds chirp away, and torches blaze after dark. Guest rooms—in a 13-story building or one of the six 2-story buildings—have subdued South Pacific decor, and each has a balcony or patio. High floors of tower rooms have commanding views, while studios and suites have kitchenettes. A 9,300-square-foot spa was added in 2005, featuring a menu of South Pacific and Asian-inspired treatments. It's steps away from the bay's jogging-and-biking path, and runners with tots in tow can rent jogging strollers at the hotel. The Catamaran is also within a few blocks of Pacific Beach's restaurant-and-nightlife scene. The resort's Mississippi-style stern-wheeler, the *Bahia Belle*, cruises the bay Friday and Saturday evenings (nightly in summer) and is free to hotel guests.

3999 Mission Blvd. (4 blocks south of Grand Ave.), San Diego, CA 92109. ℂ **800/422-8386** or 858/488-1081. Fax 858/488-1387. www.catamaranresort.com. 315 units. $275–$385 double; from $299 suite. Children under 12 stay free in parent's room. AE, DC, DISC, MC, V. Valet parking $11; self-parking $9. Bus: 27 or 34. Take Grand/Garnet exit off I-5 and go west on Grand Ave., then south on Mission Blvd. **Amenities:** Restaurant; 2 bars; outdoor pool; full-service spa and fitness room; Jacuzzi; watersports equipment rental; bike rental; children's programs; concierge; limited room service (5am–11pm); in-room massage; laundry service; dry cleaning. *In room:* A/C, TV w/pay movies, dataport, fridge in most units, coffeemaker, hair dryer, iron.

**Crystal Pier Hotel** ★★ (Kids) (Finds)   When historic charm is higher on your wish list than hotel-style service, head to this unique cluster of cottages over the surf on the vintage Crystal Pier at Pacific Beach. As though you'd rented your own self-contained hideaway, you'll get a separate living room and bedroom, fully equipped kitchen, and private patio with breathtaking ocean views—all within the whitewashed walls of sweet, blue-shuttered, renovated cottages from 1936. Each of the Cape Cod–style units has a deck; the more expensive units farthest out have the most privacy. Six units aren't actually on the pier but offer sunset-facing sea views, and these are cheaper. The sound of waves is soothing, yet the boardwalk action is only a few steps away, and the pier is a great place for watching sunsets and surfers. Guests drive right out and park beside their cottages—a boon on crowded weekends. This operation is strictly BYOBT (beach towels), however, and the office is only open from 8am to 8pm. Reserve for summer and holiday weekends several months in advance.

4500 Ocean Blvd. (at Garnet Ave.), San Diego, CA 92109. ℂ **800/748-5894** or 858/483-6983. Fax 858/483-6811. www.crystalpier.com. 29 units. $225–$320 double. DISC, MC, V. Free parking. Bus: 27, 30, or 34. Take I-5 to Grand/Garnet exit; follow Garnet to the pier. *In room:* TV, kitchen.

**Ocean Park Inn** ★   This modern, oceanfront motor hotel has simple, attractive, spacious rooms with contemporary furnishings. Although the inn is a bit more sophisticated than the norm in this casual, surfer-populated area, you won't find much solitude given the boisterous scene outside. You can't beat the sand access, however, or the view. Most rooms have at least a partial ocean view (the better the view the higher the rate), and all have a private balcony or patio. Units in front are most desirable, but it can get noisy directly above the boardwalk; try for the second or third floor, or pick one of the three junior suites, which have huge bathrooms and pool views.

710 Grand Ave., San Diego, CA 92109. © **800/231-7735** or 858/483-5858. Fax 858/274-0823. www.oceanpark inn.com. 73 units. $109–$224 double; $154–$269 suite. Rates include continental breakfast. AE, DC, DISC, MC, V. Free indoor parking. Bus: 34 or 34A/B. Take Grand/Garnet exit off I-5; follow Grand Ave. to ocean. **Amenities:** Outdoor pool; Jacuzzi; dry cleaning. *In room:* A/C, TV, dataport, fridge, coffeemaker, hair dryer.

### Pacific Terrace Hotel ★★    The best modern hotel on the boardwalk swaggers with

a heavy-handed South Seas–meets–Spanish Colonial ambience. Rattan fans circulate in the lobby and hint at the sunny Indonesian-inspired decor in the guest rooms, which are named after Caribbean islands. Hands-on owners kicked up the luxury factor (and prices) with a 2003 renovation, resulting in a more upscale atmosphere than most of the casual beach pads nearby are able to muster. At the north end of the Pacific Beach boardwalk, it's far from the more rowdy surfers, who tend to stay a few blocks south. Large, comfortable guest rooms each have balconies or terraces and fancy wall safes; bathrooms—designed with warm-toned marble and natural woods—have a separate sink/vanity area. About half the rooms have kitchenettes, and top-floor rooms in this three-story hotel enjoy particularly nice views of the rhythmic waves and determined surfers below. Management keeps cookies, coffee, and iced tea at the ready throughout the day. The lushly landscaped pool and hot tub overlook a relatively quiet stretch of beach. Four nearby restaurants allow patrons to bill meals to the hotel, but there's no on-site restaurant.

610 Diamond St., San Diego, CA 92109. © **800/344-3370** or 858/581-3500. Fax 858/274-3341. www.pacificterrace. com. 75 units. $260–$415 double; from $485 suite. Rates include continental breakfast. AE, DC, DISC, MC, V. Parking $15; limited free parking in off-street lot. Bus: 30 or 34. Take I-5 to Grand/Garnet exit and follow Grand or Garnet west to Mission Blvd., turn right (north), then left (west) onto Diamond. **Amenities:** Pool; access to nearby health club ($5); whirlpool; bike rental nearby; activities desk; room service (11am–10:30pm); in-room massage; laundry/dry-cleaning service; coin-op laundry. *In room:* A/C, TV w/pay movies, dataport, minibar, coffeemaker, hair dryer, iron.

### Paradise Point Resort & Spa ★★ *Kids*    In the middle of Mission Bay, this hotel

complex is almost as much a theme park as its closest neighbor, SeaWorld (a 3-min. drive). Single-story accommodations spread across 44 tropically landscaped acres of duck-filled lagoons, lush gardens, and swim-friendly beaches; all have private lanais (patios) and plenty of thoughtful conveniences. The resort was recently updated to retain its low-tech 1960s charm but lose tacky holdovers, and rooms now have a colorful beach-cottage decor. Despite daunting high-season rack rates, you can usually score a deal here. The upscale waterfront restaurant, Baleen, offers fine dining in a contemporary, fun space. The stunning, Indonesian-inspired spa is a vacation in itself, affording cool serenity and aromatic Asian treatments.

1404 Vacation Rd. (off Ingraham St.), San Diego, CA 92109. © **800/344-2626** or 858/274-4630. Fax 858/581-5924. www.paradisepoint.com. 462 units. $249–$649 double. Extra person $20. AE, DC, DISC, MC, V. Parking $10. Bus: 9. Follow I-8 west to Mission Bay Dr. exit; take Ingraham St. north to Vacation Rd. **Amenities:** 3 restaurants; lounge; pool bar; 3 outdoor pools; 18-hole putting course; tennis courts; fitness center; full-service spa; whirlpool; bike rental; room service (6am–midnight); laundry/dry-cleaning service; croquet; sand volleyball; basketball. *In room:* A/C, TV w/pay movies, dataport, fridge, coffeemaker, hair dryer, iron.

## MODERATE

### The Dana on Mission Bay ★    The Dana completed a $20-million renovation and

expansion in 2004 that added 74 contemporary rooms in a three-story arc around an infinity pool. The original rooms, in two-story buildings, were spruced up at the same time. Some overlook bobbing sailboats in the recreational marina; others face onto a kidney-shaped pool surrounded by gardens lit by tiki torches, with shuffleboard and Ping-Pong facilities. You'll pay a little extra for bay and marina views, although every one of the old rooms is the same size, with plain but well-maintained furnishings. The new rooms are bigger, with water views and reclaimed-redwood beam ceilings. Beaches and SeaWorld are a 15-minute walk away (and there's a complimentary shuttle). Meals and room service (including poolside food and cocktail ministrations) are available through the new restaurants, **Firefly Bar & Grill** and **Blue Pearl.**

1710 W. Mission Bay Dr., San Diego, CA 92109. **©** **800/345-9995** or 619/222-6440. Fax 619/222-5916. www.the dana.net. 270 units. $165–$235 double (sleeps up to 4); from $270 suite. AE, DC, DISC, MC, V. Free parking. Bus: 27 or 34. Follow I-8 west to Mission Bay Dr. exit; take W. Mission Bay Dr. **Amenities:** 2 restaurants; outdoor heated pool and Jacuzzi; fitness room; watersports equipment rental; bike rental; limited room service (7am–8:30pm); coin-op laundry; laundry service; dry cleaning. *In room:* A/C, TV, dataport, fridge, coffeemaker, hair dryer, iron.

**Elsbree House** ★   Katie and Phil Elsbree have turned this modern Cape Cod–style building into an immaculate, exceedingly comfortable B&B, half a block from the water's edge in Ocean Beach. One condo unit with a private entrance rents only by the week; the Elsbrees occupy another. Each of the six guest rooms has a patio or balcony. Guests share the cozy living room (with a fireplace and TV), breakfast room, and kitchen. Although other buildings on this tightly packed street block the ocean view, sounds of the surf and fresh sea breezes waft in open windows, and a charming garden—complete with trickling fountain—runs the length of the house. This Ocean Beach neighborhood is populated by ocean-loving couples, dedicated surf bums, and the occasional contingent of punk skater kids who congregate near the pier. Its strengths are proximity to the beach, a limited but pleasing selection of restaurants that cater to locals, and San Diego's best antiquing (along Newport Ave.).

5054 Narragansett Ave., San Diego, CA 92107. **©** **800/607-4133** or 619/226-4133. www.bbinob.com. 6 units. $100–$135 double; $900–$1,600 per week 3-bedroom condo. Rates include continental breakfast. MC, V. Bus: 23 or 35. From airport, take Harbor Dr. west to Nimitz Blvd. to Lowell St., which becomes Narragansett Ave. *In room:* Hair dryer, iron, no phone.

### INEXPENSIVE

**The Beach Cottages**   This family-owned operation has been around since 1948 and offers a variety of guest quarters, most of them geared to the long-term visitor. It's the 17 cute little detached cottages with patios, steps from the sand, that give it real appeal, although some of them lack a view of any kind. Adjoining apartments are perfectly adequate as well, especially for budget-minded families who want to log major hours on the beach. (All cottages and apartments sleep four or more and have full kitchens.) Standard motel rooms are worn but cheap, and most sleep two. The property is within walking distance of shops and restaurants and provides shared barbecue grills, shuffleboard courts, and table tennis. The cottages themselves aren't pristine but their rustic charm makes them popular with young honeymooners or those nostalgic for the golden age of laid-back California beach culture. Reserve the beachfront cottages well in advance.

4255 Ocean Blvd. (1 block south of Grand Ave.), San Diego, CA 92109-3995. **©** **858/483-7440.** Fax 858/273-9365. www.beachcottages.com. 61 units, 17 cottages. $120–$180 double; from $210 cottages for 4–6. Monthly rates available mid-Sept to Mar. AE, DC, DISC, MC, V. Free parking. Bus: 27, 30, or 34. Take I-5 to Grand/Garnet exit, go west on Grand Ave. and left on Mission Blvd. **Amenities:** Self-service laundry. *In room:* TV, fridge, coffeemaker.

**Beach Haven Inn**   This motel, a block from the sand, is a great spot for beach lovers who can't afford digs right on the beach. Rooms face an inner courtyard, where guests can relax by the pool in seclusion. On the street side, it looks kind of marginal; once on the property, though, you'll find the quarters well maintained, with clean, up-to-date furnishings and eat-in kitchens in nearly all units. Friendly staff members provide free coffee in the lobby and rent VCRs and movies.

4740 Mission Blvd. (at Missouri St.), San Diego, CA 92109. (℃ **800/831-6323** or 858/272-3812. Fax 858/272-3532. www.beachhaveninn.com. 23 units. $69–$205 double. 2-night minimum on weekends. Extra person $5. Children under 12 stay free in parent's room. Rates include continental breakfast. AE, DC, DISC, MC, V. Free parking. Bus: 30 or 34. Take I-5 to Grand/Garnet exit, follow Grand Ave. to Mission Blvd. and turn right. **Amenities:** Outdoor pool; whirlpool. *In room:* A/C, TV, kitchenette (most units).

## LA JOLLA

No one is quite sure, but the name "La Jolla" is probably misspelled Spanish for "the jewel"—a fitting comparison for this section of the city with its beautiful coastline and compact downtown village that makes for a delightful stroll. You'll have a hard time finding bargain accommodations in this upscale, conservative community. But remember, most hotels—even those in our "Very Expensive" category—have occupancy-driven rates, meaning you can score surprising discounts during the off season (winter), when the beds go begging.

All the hotels listed below are moderate in size. For a more intimate experience, check in to the luxe **Hotel Parisi** ★★★, 1111 Prospect St. (℃ **877/4-PARISI** or 858/ 454-1511; www.hotelparisi.com), a sleek 28-room boutique inn amid fashionable clothing boutiques. The Parisi caters to the city-savvy traveler who seeks a bit of Italy tempered with Zen-like calm. Two other moderately priced properties provide relatively good value: **Best Western Inn by the Sea** ★, 7830 Fay Ave. (℃ **800/526-4545** or 858/459-4461; www.bestwestern.com/innbythesea), in the heart of La Jolla's village, a short walk from the cliffs and beach; and the nearby **Empress Hotel of La Jolla** ★, 7766 Fay Ave. (℃ **888/369-9900** or 858/454-3001; www.thegrandecolonial. com), where you'll find spacious quarters with classy traditional furnishings in a 1960s high-rise. On the luxury side, **Estancia La Jolla Hotel and Spa** ★★★, 9700 N. Torrey Pines Rd. (℃ **877/437-8262**; estancialajolla.com), which opened in 2004, is a California rancho-style retreat, built on the remains of a 19th-century horse farm, on 9½ acres near Black's Beach.

### VERY EXPENSIVE

**La Valencia Hotel** ★★★    Within its bougainvillea-draped walls and wrought-iron garden gates, this gracious bastion of gentility resurrects the elegance of Hollywood's Golden Age, when the likes of Greta Garbo and Charlie Chaplin vacationed here alongside the world's moneyed elite. The bluff-top hotel, which looks much like a Mediterranean villa, has been the centerpiece of La Jolla since it opened in 1926. A $10-million renovation in 2000 refined some of the details and added 15 villas and an enlarged pool, without breaking from its historical glamour. Brides still pose in front of the lobby's picture window, well-coiffed ladies lunch in the dappled shade of the garden patio, and neighborhood cronies quaff libations in the clubby **Whaling Bar.**

All rooms are comfortably and traditionally furnished, with lavish appointments and all-marble bathrooms with signature toiletries. Because rates vary wildly according to view (from sweeping to *nada*), my advice is to get a cheaper room and enjoy the scene from one of the many lounges, serene garden terraces, or the amazing pool, which fronts the Pacific and nearby Scripp's Park. Room decor, layouts, and size (starting at a relatively snug 246 sq. ft.) are all over the map, too; a few extra minutes with the reservationist will ensure a custom match for you. If you've got the bucks, spring for one of the newer villas, with fireplaces and butler service. The hotel's 12-table **Sky Room** is one of the city's most celebrated dining rooms

1132 Prospect St. (at Herschel Ave.), La Jolla, CA 92037. © **800/451-0772** or 858/454-0771. Fax 858/456-3921. www.lavalencia.com. 155 units. $300–$1,400 double; from $699 suite or villa. 2-night minimum summer weekends. AE, DC, DISC, MC, V. Valet parking $15. Bus: 30 or 34. Take Torrey Pines Rd. to Prospect Place and turn right. Prospect Place becomes Prospect St. **Amenities:** 3 restaurants; bar; outdoor pool; exercise room w/spa treatments; whirlpool; sauna; concierge; secretarial services; 24-hr. room service; babysitting; laundry/dry-cleaning service. *In room:* A/C, TV w/VCR, wireless Internet access, dataport, minibar, coffeemaker, hair dryer, iron, safe.

**The Lodge at Torrey Pines** ★★★    Ten minutes north of La Jolla proper, this triumphant *trompe l'oeil* creation at the edge of the Torrey Pines Golf Course is the fantasy of a local hotelier, who took his appreciation for Craftsman-style homes and amplified it into a 175-room upscale hotel. Patterned largely after the 1908 Greene and Greene–designed Gamble House (see chapter 14), The Lodge brims with perfectly assembled nuances of the era: clinker-brick masonry, art glass windows and doors, Stickley furniture, and exquisite pottery. Most guest rooms fall into two main categories. The least expensive are an unstinting 520 square feet, lavished with Tiffany-style lamps, period wallpaper, and framed Hiroshige prints, with lots of wood accents. Views face a courtyard carefully landscaped to mimic the rare coastal environment that exists just beyond the hotel grounds. More expensive rooms overlook the golf course and the sea in the distance; most of these have balconies, fireplaces, and giant bathrooms with separate tub and shower. Sumptuous suites are also available.

The 9,500-square-foot spa specializes in treatments utilizing coastal sage and other local plants. An excellent restaurant named after painter A.R. Valentien features superb seasonal vegetables with most entrees. Valentien's wildflower watercolors line the walls, and his personal effects and medals are displayed in glass bookcases. I find the embrace of local artists and the natural environment to be absolutely inspired, making the Lodge San Diego's ultimate luxury destination, where mindful staffers cater to your every whim.

11480 N. Torrey Pines Rd., La Jolla, CA 92037. © **800/656-0087** or 858/453-4420. Fax 858/550-3908. www.lodge torreypines.com. 175 units. $450–$625 double; from $900 suite. Children under 18 stay free in parent's room. AE, DC, DISC, MC, V. $14 self-parking, $17 valet parking. Bus: 301. From I-8 take La Jolla Village Dr. W., bear right (north) onto N. Torrey Pines Rd. **Amenities:** 2 restaurants; outdoor pool; preferential tee times; fitness center; spa; whirlpool; concierge and valet; 24-hr. room service. *In room:* A/C, TV, minibar, coffeemaker, hair dryer, in-room safe, fireplace and balcony in most units.

## EXPENSIVE

**The Grande Colonial** ★★ *Finds*    Possessed of an old-world European flair that's more London or Georgetown than seaside La Jolla, the Grande Colonial earned accolades for the complete restoration in 2001 of its polished mahogany paneling, brass fittings, and genteel library and lounge. During the original heyday of the La Jolla Playhouse, it was the temporary home for everyone from Groucho Marx to Jane Wyatt. Today a large spray of fresh flowers is the focal point in the lounge, where guests gather in front of the fireplace for drinks—often before enjoying dinner at the hotel's **Nine-Ten** restaurant. Guest rooms are quiet and elegantly appointed, with beautiful draperies and traditional furnishings. Relics from the early days include oversize closets, meticulously tiled bathrooms, and heavy fireproof doors suspended in the corridors. The hotel is 1 block from the ocean, but many of the rooms have sea views. Numerous historic photos on the walls illustrate the hotel's story, which started as a full-service apartment hotel in 1913. Among La Jolla's minihorde of deluxe properties, the Grande Colonial is sometimes overlooked. In fact, the centrally located hotel is a sleeper that provides comparatively good value.

# La Jolla

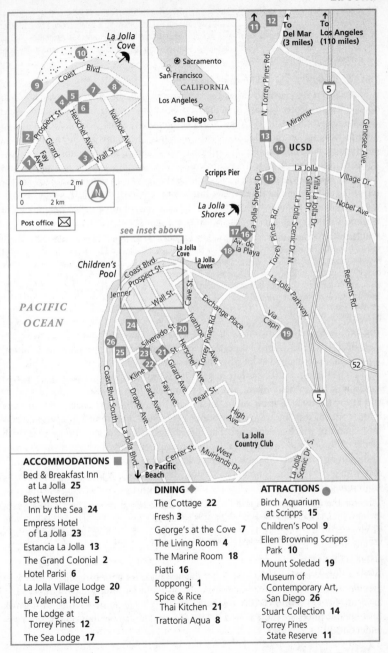

La Jolla Cove

To Del Mar (3 miles) 12

To Los Angeles (110 miles)

CALIFORNIA

Sacramento

San Francisco

Los Angeles

San Diego

Scripps Pier

La Jolla Shores

PACIFIC OCEAN

Children's Pool

La Jolla Cove

La Jolla Caves

UCSD

La Jolla Country Club

To Pacific Beach

Post office

2 mi

2 km

see inset above

## ACCOMMODATIONS

Bed & Breakfast Inn
at La Jolla **25**

Best Western
Inn by the Sea **24**

Empress Hotel
of La Jolla **23**

Estancia La Jolla **13**

The Grand Colonial **2**

Hotel Parisi **6**

La Jolla Village Lodge **20**

La Valencia Hotel **5**

The Lodge at
Torrey Pines **12**

The Sea Lodge **17**

## DINING

The Cottage **22**

Fresh **3**

George's at the Cove **7**

The Living Room **4**

The Marine Room **18**

Piatti **16**

Roppongi **1**

Spice & Rice
Thai Kitchen **21**

Trattoria Aqua **8**

## ATTRACTIONS

Birch Aquarium
at Scripps **15**

Children's Pool **9**

Ellen Browning Scripps
Park **10**

Mount Soledad **19**

Museum of
Contemporary Art,
San Diego **26**

Stuart Collection **14**

Torrey Pines
State Reserve **11**

910 Prospect St. (between Fay and Girard), La Jolla, CA 92037. (C) **800/826-1278** or 858/454-2181. Fax 858/454-5679. www.thegrandecolonial.com. 75 units. $249–$475 double. AE, DC, DISC, MC, V. Valet parking $14. Bus: 30 or 34. Take Torrey Pines Rd. to Prospect Place and turn right. Prospect Place becomes Prospect St. **Amenities:** Restaurant; outdoor pool; access to nearby health club; limited room service (6:30am–10:30pm); laundry service; dry cleaning. *In room:* A/C, TV w/pay movies, dataport, hair dryer, iron, safe.

**The Sea Lodge** (★) (Kids)   This three-story, 1960s hotel in a mainly residential enclave is under the same management as the exclusive La Jolla Beach & Tennis Club next door. It has an identical location on the sand, minus the country club ambience—and without reciprocal privileges. About half the rooms have some view of the ocean, and the rest look out on the pool or a tiled courtyard. The rooms are pretty basic, with perfunctory, outdated furnishings, priced by view and size. Bathrooms feature separate dressing areas with large closets; balconies or patios are standard; and some rooms have fully equipped kitchenettes. From the Sea Lodge's beach you can gaze toward the top of the cliffs, where La Jolla's village hums with activity and traffic. Like the "B&T," the Sea Lodge is popular with families but also attracts business travelers looking to balance meetings with time on the beach or the tennis court.

8110 Camino del Oro (at Avenida de la Playa), La Jolla, CA 92037. (C) **800/640-7702** or 858/459-8271. Fax 858/456-9346. www.ljbtc.com. 128 units. $279–$559 double; $739 suite. Extra person $20. Children under 12 stay free in parent's room. AE, DC, DISC, MC, V. Free covered parking. Bus: 34. Take La Jolla Shores Dr., turn left onto Avenida de la Playa, turn right on Camino del Oro. **Amenities:** Restaurant; swimming pool (plus wading pool for kids); 2 tennis courts; fitness room; whirlpool; babysitting; laundry/dry-cleaning service. *In room:* A/C, TV, dataport, fridge, coffeemaker, hair dryer, iron, safety deposit box.

## MODERATE

**The Bed & Breakfast Inn at La Jolla** (★★) (Finds)   The setting for this cultured, elegant B&B is a 1913 Cubist house, designed by San Diego's first important architect, Irving Gill. Reconfigured as lodging, the house, which John Philip Sousa and his family occupied in the 1920s, has lost none of its charm. Its appropriately unfrilly period furnishings add to the sense of history. The inn also features lovely enclosed gardens and a cozy library and sitting room. Sherry and fresh-cut flowers await guests in every room, some of which feature a fireplace or ocean view. Each unit has a private bathroom, most of which are compact. The furnishings are tasteful and cottage style, with plenty of historic photos of La Jolla. Gourmet breakfast is served wherever you desire—in the dining room, on the patio or sun deck, or in your room. Picnic baskets are available with a day's notice, for an extra charge. Kate Sessions, who created much of the landscaping for Balboa Park, originally planned the gardens surrounding the inn.

7753 Draper Ave. (near Prospect), La Jolla, CA 92037. (C) **800/582-2466** or 858/456-2066. Fax 858/456-1510. www.innlajolla.com. 15 units. $189–$359 double; $399 suite. 2-night minimum on weekends. Rates include full breakfast and afternoon wine and cheese. AE, DISC, MC, V. Bus: 30 or 34. Take Torrey Pines Rd. to Prospect Place and turn right. Prospect Place becomes Prospect St.; proceed to Draper Ave. and turn left. *In room:* A/C, hair dryer, iron.

## INEXPENSIVE

Wealthy, image-conscious La Jolla is not the best place for deep bargains, but if you're determined to stay here on a budget, try the 30-room **La Jolla Village Lodge,** 1141 Silverado St. ((C) **858/551-2001;** www.lajollavillagelodge.com), a motel with small, basic rooms; prices are more than $100 April through October, but otherwise they're under $100.

## CORONADO

The "island" of Coronado is a great escape. It offers quiet, architecturally rich streets, a small-town, Navy-oriented atmosphere, and one of the state's most beautiful, welcoming beaches. Coronado's resorts are especially popular with Southern California and Arizona families for weekend escapes. Although downtown San Diego is just a 10-minute drive or 20-minute ferry-ride away, you may feel pleasantly isolated in Coronado. It isn't your best choice, however, if you plan to spend most of your time in central parts of the city.

The 438-room **Loews Coronado Bay Resort** ★★, 4000 Coronado Bay Rd. (© 800/23-LOEWS or 619/424-4000; www.loewshotels.com), is San Diego's most removed hotel, 6 miles down the Silver Strand. It works for those who want to get away from it all in a self-contained resort; it's good for convention groups as well. The on-site restaurant, Azzura Point, is superb. The vintage **Village Inn**, 1017 Park Place (© 619/435-9318; www.coronadovillageinn.com), is far cheaper but with a central location. You can walk to all of Coronado's sights, and the rates are less than $100 a night. The only drawback is tiny, tiny bathrooms.

## VERY EXPENSIVE

### Hotel del Coronado ★★★ (Kids)

Opened in 1888 and designated a National Historic Landmark in 1977, the "Hotel Del," as it's affectionately known, is the last of California's grand old seaside hotels. This monument to Victorian grandeur boasts tall cupolas, red turrets, and gingerbread trim, spread out over 31 acres. Rooms—almost no two alike—run the gamut from compact to extravagant, and all are packed with antique charm; most have custom-made furnishings. The least expensive are snug with views of a roof or parking lot. The best are junior suites with large windows and balconies fronting one of the state's finest white-sand beaches, but note that even here, bathrooms are modest in size. The nine cottages that line the sand are more private (Marilyn Monroe stayed in the first one during the filming of *Some Like It Hot*). *Note:* Almost half the hotel's rooms are in the seven-story contemporary tower, offering more living space, but none of the historical ambience. Personally, I can't imagine staying here in anything but the Victorian structure, but you pay a premium for the privilege (especially for an ocean view), and 2-night minimums often apply.

Even if you don't stay here, don't miss a stroll through the grand, wood-paneled lobby or along the pristine wide beach. The **Prince of Wales,** remodeled from a dark, clubby room to an airy, elegant salon with oceanfront dining, has received accolades; cocktails and afternoon tea are served in the wood-paneled lobby and adjoining **Palm Court**, and Sunday Brunch in the **Crown Room** is a San Diego tradition.

1500 Orange Ave., Coronado, CA 92118. © 800/468-3533 or 619/435-6611. Fax 619/522-8238. www.hoteldel. com. 688 rooms. $295 double, $400 suites, $705 cottages. Children under 18 stay free in parent's room. Additional person $25. Minimum-stay requirements apply most weekends. AE, DC, DISC, MC, V. Valet parking $23, self-parking $18. Bus: 901 or 902. From Coronado Bridge, turn left onto Orange Ave. **Amenities:** 9 restaurants/bars; 2 outdoor pools; 3 tennis courts; health club and spa; 2 whirlpools; bike rental; children's activities; concierge; shopping arcade; 24-hr. room service; babysitting; laundry/dry-cleaning service. *In room:* A/C, TV w/pay movies, dataport, minibar, hair dryer, iron, safe.

## MODERATE

### El Cordova Hotel ★

This Spanish hacienda across the street from the Hotel del Coronado began life as a private mansion in 1902. By the 1930s, it had become a hotel, the original building augmented by a series of attachments housing retail shops along the ground-floor arcade. Shaped like a baseball diamond and surrounding a courtyard with meandering tiled pathways, flowering shrubs, a swimming pool, and patio seating for Miguel's Cocina Mexican restaurant, El Cordova hums pleasantly with activity. Each room differs from the next—some have a Mexican colonial feel, while others evoke comfy beach cottages. All are no-frills, with ceiling fans and brightly tiled bathrooms. El Cordova is inviting, and its prime location makes it a popular option; make reservations several weeks in advance in summer.

1351 Orange Ave. (at Adella Ave.), Coronado, CA 92118. © **800/229-2032** or 619/435-4131. Fax 619/435-0632. www.elcordovahotel.com. 40 units. $99–$189 double; from $184 suite. Children under 12 stay free in parent's room. AE, DC, DISC, MC, V. Parking in neighboring structure $6/day. Bus: 901 or 902. From Coronado Bridge, turn left onto Orange Ave. **Amenities:** 3 restaurants; barbecue area with picnic table; outdoor pool; shopping arcade; coin-op laundry. *In room:* A/C, TV.

**Glorietta Bay Inn** ★★  Across the street and in the (figurative) shadow of the Hotel Del, this pretty hotel consists of the charmingly historic John D. Spreckels mansion (1908) and several younger, motel-style buildings. Only 11 rooms are in the mansion, which boasts original fixtures, a grand staircase, and old-fashioned wicker furniture; the guest rooms are also decked out in antiques. Rooms and suites in the 1950s annexes are much less expensive but only somewhat better than motel-plain; some have kitchenettes and marina views. The least expensive units are small with views of the parking lot. Extra-helpful staffers will remember your name and happily offer dining and sightseeing recommendations, arrange tee times, and lavish special attention on return guests and families with toddlers. The hotel offers rental bikes and boat rentals on Glorietta Bay across the street, and it's within easy walking distance of the beach, golfing, tennis, watersports, shopping, and dining. Rooms in the mansion fill up early, but they're worth the extra effort and expense.

1630 Glorietta Blvd. (near Orange Ave.), Coronado, CA 92118. © **800/283-9383** or 619/435-3101. Fax 619/435-6182. www.gloriettabayinn.com. 100 units. Double $160; from $255 for suite in the mansion. Extra person $10. Children under 18 stay free in parent's room. Rates include continental breakfast and afternoon refreshment. AE, DC, DISC, MC, V. Self-parking $10. Bus: 901 or 902. From Coronado Bridge, turn left on Orange Ave. After 2 miles, turn left onto Glorietta Blvd.; the inn is across the street from the Hotel del Coronado. **Amenities:** Outdoor pool; whirlpool; in-room massage; babysitting; laundry/dry-cleaning service; coin-op laundry. *In room:* A/C, TV w/pay movies, dataport, fridge, coffeemaker, hair dryer.

## 4 Where to Dine

San Diego's dining scene, once a culinary backwater, has come into its own in the past decade—due, in part, to the bustling economy and the number of people moving here from other cities. Residents have learned to respect the seasonality of vegetables, allowing chefs to revel in San Diego County's bountiful produce, and focus on vegetables when flavors are at their peak, at specialized North County growers like Chino Farm. But don't just take my word for it. In 2003 *Gourmet* magazine announced: "Perhaps for the first time ever, San Diego has a buzzing restaurant scene as engaging as the area's other tourist attractions." Finally, we can be known for something on the table besides tacos and *frijoles.*

Nevertheless, the number-one cuisine is still Mexican food, given the city's history and location. You'll find lots of Americanized but satisfying interpretations of Mexican fare (i.e., combo plates heaped with melted cheddar cheese) along with hidden gems, like El Agave (p. 700), that serve true south-of-the-border cuisine. Don't miss the fish taco, the city's favorite fast food, which gained mass popularity at the locally based chain Rubio's.

What follows is an abbreviated sampling of highlights from San Diego's dining scene, with an emphasis on the best of the best in all price categories, locations, and cuisines. For a greater selection of reviews, see *Frommer's San Diego 2006.* To locate these restaurants, see the "San Diego Accommodations & Dining" map on p. 678, and the "La Jolla" map on p. 691.

## DOWNTOWN

Downtown was turned on its ear when Horton Plaza was redeveloped in 1985 and swank spots began moving in to the Gaslamp Quarter's restored Victorian buildings. Today dozens of restaurants (and nightclubs) have opened within the quarter, with dozens more nearby.

On evenings when the Padres are playing, or when a big convention has filled the hotels, you'll compete for parking. Fortunately, pedicabs—three-wheeled bikes that carry two passengers each—are easy to hire. But if you take a taxi or the trolley downtown on game nights, you'll find most restaurants easy to get into once the first pitch is thrown. Try the excellent bistro **Cafe Chloe** ★★, 721 Ninth Ave. (© **619/232-3242**), which has created a buzz in the ballpark district.

The city's top dessert emporium is aptly named **Extraordinary Desserts** ★★, with locations in Little Italy, 1430 Union St. (© **619/294-7001**), and adjacent to Balboa Park, 2929 Fifth Ave. (same phone number). Proprietor Karen Krasne produces exquisite cakes and pastries garnished with edible gold, flowers, and exotic fruits. Both locations stay open late (midnight Fri–Sat, 11pm Sun–Thurs) to indulge late-night emergency cravings.

### VERY EXPENSIVE

**Star of the Sea** ★★★ SEAFOOD    A bastion of fine dining in the Embarcadero since 1966, the Star of the Sea underwent a millennium makeover and reopened with a new look, new chef, and new name (to differentiate it from the unexceptional waterfront fish houses next door, also in the Anthony's restaurant family). A comfortable, intimate atmosphere and modern decor match the still-glorious harbor view (tables face the 1863 sailing ship *Star of India*). And the food is imbued with sophisticated touches that show the restaurant is in touch with today's gourmands. The menu is seasonally composed and heavy on impeccably fresh seafood; representative dishes include striped sea bass with *picholine* olives and squid, floating in a bisque of Meyer lemons, or perfectly seared diver scallops nuzzling a lobster-and-chanterelle risotto. For carnivores, there's the "duo of beef" (short ribs, grilled filet, and roasted bone marrow), or the seared elk loin. The wine list is reasonably priced, and the welcoming bar has its own abbreviated menu.

1360 N. Harbor Dr. (at Ash St.), Embarcadero. © 619/232-7408. www.starofthesea.com. Reservations recommended. Main courses $26–$38. AE, DC, DISC, MC, V. Daily 5:30–9pm (until 10pm Fri–Sat). Valet parking $8. Bus: All Harbor Dr. routes. Trolley: America Plaza.

### EXPENSIVE

**Chive** ★★★ CALIFORNIA    This Gaslamp venue introduced San Diego to the sleek, chic dining rooms of the East Coast, and to daring kitchen inventions. The culinary adventure starts with a fashionable cocktail, of course: The local martini is embellished with Gorgonzola-stuffed olives, and *mojitos* get a splash of ginger. The menu changes every 6 to 8 weeks, but popular repeat dishes include lamb tagine served with *harissa*, gnocchi, a roasted baby-beet salad, the caramelized-onion-and-potato pastilla, a nightly "noodle" (pasta) of the chef's whim, and salads that balance crispy greens with pungent, creamy cheeses and sweet fruit accents. Don't be surprised to encounter curiosities like foie gras with banana bread and caramelized bananas; diners who take a chance on such eccentricities are usually richly rewarded. The evolving wine list offers many intriguing selections by "cork" or "stem," from all corners of the globe, such as quality bottles from South Africa, Temecula, or Mexico. Chive balances its angular, wide space with cozy lighting, warm fabrics, and a pervasive sense of relaxed fun. One lament: In pursuit of elegant modernity, the cement floors and other hard surfaces amplify the noise level.

558 Fourth Ave. (at Market St.), Gaslamp Quarter. ℭ 619/232-4483. www.chiverestaurant.com. Reservations recommended. Main courses $20–$32. AE, DC, DISC, MC, V. Daily 5–11pm. Live jazz Sat. Bus: 1, 3, 4, 5, 16, or 25. Trolley: Convention Center.

**Indigo Grill** ★★ CALIFORNIA   Chef Deborah Scott's Little Italy adventure showcases bracing "aboriginal" cuisine of the Pacific coast—from Mexico to Alaska. Root veggies, game, and fruit are integral to the menu, with liberal use of unusual spices, served in a dining room with varied textures of wood, stone, metal, and leather. Occasionally, she reaches too far, but dishes are usually a treat for diners who yearn for something original. Start with Oaxaca Fire, a kicky, tequila-based cocktail with a salt-and-pepper rim, and move on to a salad of spinach, spaghetti squash, and strawberries. The alder-wood plank salmon, served with a tangle of squid-ink pasta spotted with smoky Oaxacan cheese, is a wonderful entree. Although the menu is primarily meat- and fish-oriented, there are always a couple excellent vegetarian entrees, a throng of meatless appetizers (big enough that two will make a meal), and the ceviche bar is worth investigating.

Scott made her name in the mid-1990s at **Kemo Sabe** (where Pacific Rim meets Southwestern) and now juggles duties there and at this new venture. If you enjoy one, it's worth checking out the other; Kemo Sabe is at 3958 Fifth Ave., near University Avenue, Hillcrest (ℭ **619/220-6802**).

1536 India St. (at Cedar St.), Little Italy. ℭ 619/234-6802. Reservations recommended. Main courses $9–$13 lunch, $18–$29 dinner. AE, DC, DISC, MC, V. Mon–Fri 11:30am–2pm; Sun–Wed 5–9pm; Thurs 5–10pm; Fri–Sat 5–11pm. Bus: 5 or 16. Trolley: Little Italy.

## MODERATE

**Fat City** AMERICAN   If you need a steak but don't want to deal with the Gaslamp's roster of pricey chophouses, or settle for one of those chains, Fat City is your place. Overlook the vaguely scary name (the owner's name is Tom Fat) and the overly vivid hot-pink paint job (the building is vintage Art Deco), and settle into one of the cushy booths beneath a canopy of Tiffany lamps. Skip the skimpy list of appetizers, since the entrees come with a side of potato or rice, and specials on the blackboard throw in a salad for a couple of bucks more. The steaks are USDA Choice, aged 21 days and grilled to order over mesquite charcoal. Aim for the USDA Prime top sirloin: A hunky, 12-ounce cut is just $19, and miles ahead in flavor of what you get at a Black Angus–type joint. You'll also find teriyaki salmon, chicken in a peppercorn sauce, and a couple of pasta dishes. I haven't tried those, however; I come here for the steaks and haven't found a reason to look farther down the menu.

2137 Pacific Hwy. (at Hawthorn), Little Italy. ℭ 619/232-9303. Main courses $15–$23. AE, MC, V. Daily 5–10pm. Free parking. Bus: 34.

**The Fish Market** ★ *Value* SEAFOOD/SUSHI   Ask any San Diegan where to go for the biggest selection of the freshest fish and they'll send you to the bustling Fish Market at the end of the G Street Pier, on the Embarcadero. Chalkboards announce the day's catches—be it Mississippi catfish, Maine lobster, Canadian salmon, or Mexican yellowtail. They're sold by the pound or available in a number of classic, simple preparations in the casual, always-packed restaurant. Upstairs, the fancy offshoot **Top of the Market** offers sea fare with souped-up presentations (and jacked-up prices). Either way, the fish comes from the same trough, so I recommend having a cocktail in Top's plush, clubby atmosphere, enjoying the panoramic bay views, and then heading downstairs for solidly affordable fare or treats from the sushi and oyster bars.

750 N. Harbor Dr., Embarcadero. ℂ 619/232-FISH. www.thefishmarket.com. Reservations not accepted. Main courses $10–$25 lunch, $13–$32 dinner (Top of the Market main courses $13–$35 lunch, $15–$45 dinner). AE, DC, DISC, MC, V. Daily 11am–10pm. Valet parking $5. Bus: 7/7B. Trolley: Seaport Village.

## INEXPENSIVE

Also noteworthy in the Gaslamp is the hip, bohemian **Café Lulu,** 419 F St. (ℂ **619/ 238-0114**), a coffee bar with light meals; the spot is open until 1am, 3am on Friday and Saturday. Late-night **Alambres**, 756 Fifth Ave. (ℂ **619/233-2838**), serves cheap, tasty Mexican food to famished club-goers from 9am until 3am daily.

**Filippi's Pizza Grotto** *Kids* *Value* ITALIAN   When longtime locals think "Little Italy," Filippi's comes to mind; it was a childhood fixture for many of us. To get to the dining area, decorated with chianti bottles and red-checked tablecloths, you walk through a "cash and carry" Italian grocery store and deli strewn with cheeses, pastas, wines, bottles of olive oil, and salamis. You might even end up eating behind shelves of canned olives, but don't feel bad—this has been a tradition since 1950. The intoxicating smell of pizza wafts into the street; Filippi's has more than 15 varieties (including vegetarian), plus old-world spaghetti, lasagna, and other pasta. Children's portions are available, and kids will feel right at home under the sweeping mural of the Bay of Naples. The line to get in on Friday and Saturday can look intimidating, but it moves quickly. This was the first of a dozen branches throughout the county, including the one in **Pacific Beach** at 962 Garnet Ave. (ℂ **858/695-1441**).

1747 India St. (between Date and Fir sts.), Little Italy. ℂ 619/232-5095. No reservations accepted on weekends. Main courses $5–$13. AE, DC, DISC, MC, V. Sun–Mon 9am–10pm; Tues–Thurs 9am–10:30pm; Fri–Sat 9am–11:30pm. Free parking. Bus: 5. Trolley: Little Italy.

## HILLCREST/UPTOWN

Hillcrest and the other gentrified uptown neighborhoods to its west and east brim with great food for any palate and wallet. Some are old standbys filled nightly with loyal regulars; others are cutting-edge experiments that might be gone next year. Whether they're serving ethnic food, French food, health-conscious bistro fare, retro comfort food, specialty cafes and bakeries, or California cuisine, they seem governed by an innovative panache that suits this part of town.

This is also the place to stock up on Balboa Park picnic supplies. **Bread & Cie. Bakery and Cafe** ★★, 350 University Ave. (ℂ **619/683-9322**), is San Diego's top bakery, in the tradition of European artisan bread-making. Sandwiches here are delicious. The popular **Whole Foods** supermarket, 711 University Ave. (ℂ **619/294-2800**), has a mouthwatering deli and robust salad bar. You can take out or eat at the tables up front. Families should consider a nostalgic crowd-pleaser, the 1950s flashback **Corvette Diner,** 3946 Fifth Ave. (ℂ **619/542-1001**), where chummy waiters lavish kids with entertainment.

## VERY EXPENSIVE

**Bertrand at Mister A's** ★★★ AMERICAN/MEDITERRANEAN   Since 1965, San Diegans have come to high-rise Mister A's for proms, anniversaries, power meals, and other special occasions. Mister A's star began to wane in the '80s, though, despite its unsurpassed views of Point Loma, downtown, and Balboa Park. In 2000, it finally closed—only to reopen four months later, after a reported $1-million makeover under the stewardship of one of San Diego's most successful and charismatic restaurateurs, Bertrand Hug. The original Mister A's, with its dark, red-velvet interiors and cocktail waitresses in campy one-shouldered gowns, was reborn into Bertrand at Mister A's—an elegant, bright, sophisticated space, with an array of modern art. The vistas are still the best in town, although condo towers have sprouted up on the Balboa Park side of the restaurant. Seasonal menus and fresh ingredients are a highlight, and fare may include items such as sautéed boneless frog legs in Riesling sauce, Maine lobster strudel, and paella. Hug is also the proprietor of romantic **Mille Fleurs**, 6009 Paseo Delicias (© **858/756-3085**), in the wealthy North County neighborhood of Rancho Santa Fe.

2550 Fifth Ave. (at Laurel St.), Hillcrest. © 619/239-1377. www.bertrandatmisteras.com. Reservations recommended. Main courses $15–$20 lunch, $20–$45 dinner. AE, DC, MC, V. Mon–Fri 11:30am–2:30pm; Fri–Sat 5:30–11pm; Sun–Thurs 5:30–10pm. Valet parking $6. Bus: 1, 3, or 25.

## EXPENSIVE

**California Cuisine** ★★ CALIFORNIA    The kitchen at this long-popular restaurant underwent an overhaul in 2003. The menu was slimmed down to restore the qualities that landed it on the map when it originally opened in 1982. (Think no freezers, no can openers.) The menu here is once again fresh and contemporary, and the spare, understated dining room and romantic patio set the stage for smoothly professional, respectful staff members to serve fine food at fair prices to a casual crowd. The menu changes regularly but features mouthwatering appetizers such as sesame-seared *ahi* with spicy mango *culée,* or Prince Edward Island mussels in a Thai coconut broth. Main courses are composed with equal care and might include herb-crusted rack of lamb, topped with whole-grain-mustard sherry sauce. Don't miss the scintillating desserts, all made on-site (including the ice creams and sorbets). Allow time to find parking, which can be sparse.

1027 University Ave. (east of 10th St.), Hillcrest. © 619/543-0790. www.californiacuisine.cc. Reservations recommended. Main courses $25–$30. AE, DISC, MC, V. Daily 5–10pm. Bus: 908.

**Parallel 33** ★★ *Finds* INTERNATIONAL    Inspired by a theory that all locales that share San Diego's position along the 33rd parallel might share the culinary traditions of the Tigris-Euphrates Valley (the birthplace of civilization), chef Amiko Gubbins presents a cuisine that combines flavors from Morocco, Lebanon, India, China, and Japan. Sit back and savor the creativity of a menu that leaps enthusiastically from fragrant Moroccan chicken *b'stilla* to oven-roasted *za'atar* chicken with basmati rice, English peas, and *harissa.* The *ahi poke* (raw tuna) appetizer fuses a Hawaiian mainstay with Asian pear and mango and Japanese wasabi. The restaurant is nice but not fancy—just an upscale neighborhood joint easily overlooked by visitors. The Indian/African/Asian decor throws soft shadows throughout, inviting conversation and leisurely dining. The intimate dining room was instantly popular after opening, and in 2004 a stand-alone chill-out lounge, **Blue Lotus,** was added next door. The number of devout fans shows no signs of waning, so you'll want to reserve a table in advance.

741 W. Washington St. (at Falcon), Mission Hills. © 619/260-0033. Reservations recommended. Main courses $18–$27. AE, DISC, MC, V. Mon–Thurs 5:30–10pm; Fri–Sat 5:30–11pm. Bus: 3, 16, or 908.

## MODERATE

**Fifth & Hawthorn** ★ *Value* AMERICAN    You won't find a sign in front of this neighborhood hideaway—just look for the street sign marking the intersection of

Fifth and Hawthorn, a few blocks north of downtown, and aim for the red neon OPEN sign. Inhabited by a slew of regulars, the comfortable room is somewhat dark and vaguely romantic—just enough to take your mind off the sound of planes coming in for a landing overhead. The menu has pretty much stayed the same for 16 years. You won't find anything daring, but you will find lots of well-executed basics, such as a filet mignon in green-peppercorn sauce, or linguine with clams, white wine, and garlic. Fifth & Hawthorn excels at a few fish dishes as well: The mustard-crusted catfish is simple and delicious, and the calamari sautéed "abalone-style" are tender and sweet. The restaurant also offers a terrific four-course meal: appetizer, soup or salad, one of six entrees, and dessert for $50 per couple—*including* a bottle of wine to share.

515 Hawthorn St. (at Fifth Ave.), Banker's Hill. ✆ 619/544-0940. Main courses $15–$25. AE, MC, V. Tues–Fri 11:30am–2pm; Mon–Thurs 5–9pm; Fri–Sat 5–10:15pm; Sun 4:30–8:30pm. Street parking usually available. Bus: 1, 3, or 25.

## INEXPENSIVE

**Crest Cafe** AMERICAN/BREAKFAST    This long-popular Hillcrest diner is a great refuge from sleek designer food and swank settings. The cheery pink interior announces its 1940s style, and the room bubbles with upbeat waiters who dole out comfort food on Fiestaware. Church pew–like booths are comfortable enough, but the small stucco room doesn't do much to mask the clang of plates. Don't miss the "butter burger"—a dollop of herb butter is buried in the patty before cooking (it's even better than it sounds). The East Texas fried chicken breast crusted with hunks of jalapeño peppers is none too subtle either, but it's tasty. A variety of sandwiches and salads, the popular steamed-vegetable basket, and broiled chicken dishes are healthier options. During the early evening, the joint brims with neighborhood bohemians in search of a cholesterol fix, while later the club contingent swoops in; the breakfast of omelets or crème brûlée French toast is a happy eye-opener.

425 Robinson Ave. (between Fourth and Fifth aves.), Hillcrest. ✆ 619/295-2510. www.crestcafe.net. Reservations not accepted. Main courses $5–$14. AE, MC, V. Daily 7am–midnight. Bus: 1, 3, 25, or 908.

## OLD TOWN & MISSION VALLEY

Visitors usually have at least one meal in Old Town, and although this area is San Diego at its most touristy, I can't refute the appeal of dining in California's original settlement. Mexican food reigns supreme at most Old Town restaurants—combo plates and bathtub-size margaritas are the focus, liberally spiced with mariachi music and colorful decor. Old Town is also the gateway to the decidedly less-historic Mission Valley. Here you'll find plenty of chains, both good and bad, in addition to the establishments discussed below.

## EXPENSIVE

**Cafe Pacifica** ★★ CALIFORNIA/SEAFOOD    Inside this cozy Old Town casita, the decor is cleanly contemporary (but still romantic), and the food is anything but Mexican. Established in 1980, Cafe Pacifica serves upscale, imaginative seafood at decent prices, and its kitchen alumni often go on to enjoy local fame. Among the temptations are crab-stuffed portobello mushrooms topped with grilled asparagus, anise-scented bouillabaisse, and daily fresh-fish selections grilled with your choice of five sauces. Signature items include Hawaiian ahi with shiitake mushrooms and ginger butter, griddled mustard catfish, and the "Pomerita," a pomegranate margarita. To avoid the crush, arrive before 6:30pm, and you'll also get to take advantage of the early-bird special: entree with soup or salad for $26.

2414 San Diego Ave., Old Town ✆ **619/291-6666**. www.cafepacifica.com. Reservations recommended. Main courses $16–$29. AE, DC, DISC, MC, V. Mon–Sat 5–10pm; Sun 5–9:30pm. Valet parking $5. Bus: 5/5A. Trolley: Old Town.

**El Agave Tequileria** ★★ MEXICAN Don't be misled by this restaurant's less-than-impressive location above a liquor store. The regional Mexican cuisine at this warm, bustling restaurant leave Old Town's touristy fajitas and *cerveza* joints far behind. El Agave gets its name from the agave plant from which tequilas are derived. Living up to its name, the restaurant sells more than 600 boutique and artisan tequilas and mescals; bottles of every size, shape, and jewel-like hue fill shelves and cases throughout the dining room. Even teetotalers will enjoy the restaurant's authentically flavored mole sauces (from Chiapas, rich with peanuts; tangy tomatillo from Oaxaca; and the more familiar dark mole flavored with chocolate and sesame), along with giant shrimp and sea bass prepared in a dozen variations, or El Agave's signature beef filet with goat cheese and dark tequila sauce. On the other hand, I could almost make a meal out of the warm watercress salad dressed with onions and bacon, folded into tortillas. Lunches are inexpensive, simpler affairs, without the exotic sauces.

2304 San Diego Ave., Old Town. ✆ **619/220-0692**. www.elagave.com. Reservations recommended. Main courses $7–$10 lunch, $16–$32 dinner. AE, MC, V. Daily 11am–10pm. Street parking. Bus: 5. Trolley: Old Town.

## MODERATE

**Casa Guadalajara** ★ *Kids* MEXICAN A block away from the hubbub of Old Town State Historic Park, Casa Guadalajara has an advantage: It's less crowded than those places in the park (although waits of 30 min. or more are not unusual Fri–Sat). Strolling mariachi play nightly, and patrons can dine alfresco in a picturesque courtyard with a 200-year-old pepper tree. Huge margaritas start most meals, but the menu ranges from gourmet Mexican to simpler south-of-the-border fare. My favorite dish is the *tacos de cochinita*—two soft corn tacos bulging with *achiote*-seasoned pork and marinated red onions—but the extensive menu features all the fajita and combo plates most people expect. This place is touristy, but it's where I bring friends from out of town for reliable old-California ambience and food.

4105 Taylor St. (at Juan St. in Old Town). ✆ **619/295-5111**. www.casaguadalajara.com. Reservations recommended. Main courses $8–$16. AE, DC, DISC, MC, V. Sun–Thurs 7am–10pm; Fri–Sat 7am–11pm. Free parking. Bus: 5/5A. Trolley: Old Town.

## INEXPENSIVE

**The Living Room** COFFEE & TEA/LIGHT FARE You're liable to hear the buzz of conversations from students on break from nearby universities, who use this spot as an off-campus study hall. Grab a sidewalk table and enjoy splendid people-watching any time of day. Indoors, you'll find faux antiques, appropriately weathered to give a lived-in feel. I think the pastries and coffee fall a bit short, but the good light meals at this local minichain make it a good choice for early risers and insomniacs alike. Breakfast includes omelets and waffles. Later in the day, try the turkey lasagna, tuna melt, or one of several hearty entree salads. Plus you'll find exotic iced or hot coffees and Italian sodas. Additional locations are in **La Jolla** at 1010 Prospect St. (✆ 858/459-1187), **Hillcrest** at 1417 University Ave. (✆ 619/295-7911), the **Sports Arena** area at 1018 Rosecrans (✆ 619/222-6852), and near **San Diego State University,** at 5900 El Cajon Blvd. (✆ 619/286-8434).

2541 San Diego Ave., Old Town. ✆ **619/325-4445**. www.livingroomcafe.com. Main courses $6–$8; $3–$8 breakfast. AE, MC, V. Sun–Thurs 7am–10pm; Fri–Sat 7am–midnight. Bus: 5. Trolley: Old Town.

## MISSION BAY & THE BEACHES

Generally speaking, dining at the beach is primarily an excuse to sit and gaze at the water. Because this activity is often accompanied by steady drinking, it stands to reason that the food isn't often remarkable. One exception, with modest prices slightly off the beaten track, is **Thee Bungalow** ★★, 4996 W. Point Loma Blvd., Ocean Beach (✆ **619/224-2884**), which features Continental fare and a wine list with some excellent values. If all you need is a beach and a view, **The Green Flash,** 701 Thomas Ave., Pacific Beach (✆ **858/270-7715**), offers a glassed-in patio that is probably the city's best place for people-watching.

### MODERATE

**Caffè Bella Italia** ★★ ITALIAN   Caffe Bella's odd-looking stucco exterior, in a less-than-promising section of PB, looks like a dry cleaner adorned with umbrellas because it once *was* a spot for 1-hour Martinizing. It's lovely inside, however, with romantic lighting, sheer draperies, and earthy walls. Staff members, many with lilting Milanese accents, welcome guests like family. And the food can knock your socks off. It's the best spot in the area for shellfish-laden pasta and wood-fired pizzas. Salmon is endowed with olives, capers, and thick hunks of tomato in wine and garlic. Every item is impeccably fresh and rendered with homemade care. The simplest curled-edge ravioli with ricotta, spinach, and pine nuts is culinary perfection. A second location is in Kearny Mesa, 4411 Mercury St. (✆ **858/278-5367**).

1525 Garnet Ave. (between Ingraham and Haines), Pacific Beach. ✆ **858/273-1224.** www.caffebellaitalia.com. Reservations suggested for dinner. Main courses $8–$13 lunch, $10–$28 dinner. AE, MC, V. Tues–Fri 11am–2:30pm; Tues–Sun 5–10:30pm. Free (small) parking lot. Bus: 9 or 27.

**The Fishery** ★ *Finds* SEAFOOD   You're guaranteed seafood fresh off the boat at this wholesale warehouse and retail fish market with a casual restaurant attached. The decor is clean, calm, and slightly utilitarian, and the prices are fair. Menu favorites include spicy mahimahi, chargrilled and topped with jalapeño butter, or king salmon Oscar, layered with garlic mashed potatoes and grilled asparagus, Dungeness crab, and hollandaise. You can keep it simple at lunch or dinner with bacon-wrapped scallops over a delectable salad, or the reliable fish and chips. The menu is printed fresh daily, and a couple of vegetarian stir-fry entrees are always available. A loyal crowd of followers ventures away from the Mission/Garnet/Grand strips to enjoy this neighborhood haunt.

5040 Cass St. (at Opal, ¾ miles north of Garnet), Pacific Beach. ✆ **858/272-9985.** Reservations accepted. Main courses $6–$21 lunch, $8–$27 dinner. AE, MC, V. Daily 11am–10pm. Street parking usually available. Bus: 9.

**Gringo's** ★ MEXICAN   Aiming for a more accurate reflection of Mexican cooking traditions, Gringo's, at PB's busiest intersection, provides visitors and locals with an option beyond the neighborhood's ubiquitous fast-food emporiums. The discretely upscale space is agreeable, with warm woods, cool flagstone, and trendy lighting. A large patio is primed with heaters and fire pits most evenings. Although the menu does offer a few dishes the average gringo will recognize (quesadillas, fajitas, burritos), flip it over and you'll find regional specialties from all over Mexico—Oaxaca, the Yucatan, and Mexico's Pacific coast. So, a chicken breast is stuffed with goat cheese and corn, then lathered in a sauce of *huitlacoche* (a delicious fungus that grows on corn); or a poblano chile is stuffed with *picadillo* and draped in walnut-cream sauce with a drizzle of pomegranate. The margarita options are worth inspection, as are the selection of Mexican wines; drink specials run Sunday through Thursday. Sunday brunch is available from 10am to 3pm.

4474 Mission Blvd. (at Garnet Ave.), Pacific Beach. ℂ 858/490-2877. www.gringoscantina.com. Reservations suggested for weekends. Main courses $8–$14 lunch, $11–$27 dinner. AE, DISC, MC, V. Sun–Wed 10am–10pm; Thurs–Sat 10am–11am. Bus: 27 or 34.

**Sushi Ota** ★★ SUSHI   Masterful chef-owner Yukito Ota creates San Diego's finest sushi. This sophisticated, traditional restaurant (no Asian fusion here) is a minimalist bento box with stark white walls and black furniture, softened by indirect lighting. The sushi menu is short, because discerning regulars look first to the daily specials posted behind the counter. The city's most experienced chefs, armed with nimble fingers and seriously sharp knives, turn the day's fresh catch into artful bundles. The rest of the varied menu features seafood, teriyaki-glazed meats, tempura, and a variety of small appetizers perfect for accompanying sushi. This restaurant is difficult to find, behind a laundromat and convenience store in the rear of a minimall. It's also in a nondescript part of Pacific Beach, a stone's throw from I-5, but none of that should discourage you from seeking it out.

4529 Mission Bay Dr. (at Bunker Hill), Pacific Beach. ℂ 858/270-5670. Reservations strongly recommended on weekends. Main courses $6–$9 lunch, $9–$20 dinner; sushi $4–$12. AE, MC, V. Tues–Fri 11:30am–2pm; Mon–Thurs 5:30–10:30pm; Fri–Sun 5–10:30pm. Free parking (additional lot behind the mall). Bus: 27.

**INEXPENSIVE**

**The Mission** ★ *Value* BREAKFAST/LIGHT FARE   Alongside the funky surf shops, bikini boutiques, and alternative galleries of bohemian Mission Beach, this is the neighborhood's central meeting place. It attracts more than just locals, however, and now it has siblings near the ballpark and east of Hillcrest. The menu features all-day breakfasts, from traditional pancakes to nouvelle egg dishes to burritos and quesadillas; standouts include tamales and eggs with tomatillo sauce, chicken-apple sausage with eggs and a mound of rosemary potatoes, and cinnamon French toast with blackberry purée. At lunch, the menu expands for sandwiches, salads, and a few Chino-Latino items such as ginger-sesame chicken tacos. Seating is casual, comfy, and conducive to lingering (tons of students, writers, and surfers hang out here), if only with a soup-bowl-size latte. The other locations are at 2801 University Ave., in North Park (ℂ 619/220-8992), and in a historic building at 1250 J St., downtown (ℂ 619/232-7662). Expect waits of half an hour or more on weekends.

3795 Mission Blvd. (at San Jose), Mission Beach. ℂ 858/488-9060. All items $5–$9. AE, MC, V. Daily 7am–3pm. Bus: 27 or 34.

**LA JOLLA**

As befits an upscale community with ample time and money on its hands, La Jolla seems to have more than its fair share of good restaurants. Happily, they're not all expensive, and they're more ethnically diverse than you might expect in a community that still supports a haberdashery called The Ascot Shop.

Other choices include the stylish **Roppongi** ★, 875 Prospect St., at Fay Avenue (ℂ 858/551-5252), where the cuisines of Japan, Thailand, China, Vietnam, and India collide in a creative explosion of flavorful dishes that are perfect for sharing. At **Trattoria Acqua** ★★, 1298 Prospect St. (ℂ 858/454-0709), northern Italian is nurtured with a relaxed ambience and top-drawer wine list (reserve for a table with a sea view).

## VERY EXPENSIVE

**George's at the Cove** ✿✿✿ CALIFORNIA You'll find host and namesake George Hauer at his restaurant's door most nights; he greets loyal regulars by name, and his confidence assures newcomers that they'll leave impressed with this beloved La Jolla institution. Regularly voted San Diego's most popular restaurant, George's wins consistent praise for impeccable service, gorgeous views of the cove, and outstanding cuisine. The menu presents many inventive seafood options, filtered through the myriad influences of chef Trey Foshee, selected as one of America's top 10 chefs by *Food & Wine*. Foshee starts each day with a trek up to Chino Farm to select the evening's produce. Entrees range from the Neiman Ranch pork tasting to roasted lamb loin and braised lamb shoulder with a spicy *medjool*-date couscous and baby spinach. George's signature smoked chicken, broccoli, and black-bean soup is still a mainstay at lunch; he'll even give out the recipe for this local legend. As an alternative to dinner's pricey main courses, try the tasting menu, which offers a seasonally composed five-course sampling for $62 per person ($86 with wine). George's **Ocean Terrace Café** ✿✿ is upstairs, with casual, moderately priced dining on a splendid rooftop terrace.

1250 Prospect St., La Jolla. ℂ **858/454-4244.** www.georgesatthecove.com. Reservations strongly recommended for dinner. Main courses $12–$15 lunch, $26–$45 dinner. AE, DC, DISC, MC, V. Daily 11:30am–2:30pm; Sun–Thurs 5:30–10pm; Fri–Sat 5–10:30pm. Valet parking $8. Bus: 34.

**The Marine Room** ✿✿✿ *Moments* FRENCH/CALIFORNIA For more than 6 decades, San Diego's most celebrated dining room has been this shorefront institution, within kissing distance of La Jolla's waves. It wasn't until the 1994 arrival of executive chef Bernard Guillas of Brittany that the food finally lived up to its glass-fronted room with a view, but today, The Marine Room is the city's top "special occasion" destination. Guillas and *chef de cuisine* Ron Oliver don't hesitate to pursue unusual flavors from other corners of the globe. So, a favored entree includes barramundi, a delicate white fish from Australia, encrusted with a hazelnut fennel pollen, garnished with flowering chive and a lacy crisp of fried lotus root. The vigilant service is deferential, yet never condescending. The Marine Room is filled to the gills on weekends; weekdays it's much easier to score a table. Ideally, schedule your reservation a half-hour or so before sunset, to leave time to watch the scampering sandpipers and fishing pelicans at dusk.

2000 Spindrift Dr., La Jolla. ℂ **858/459-7222.** www.marineroom.com. Reservations recommended, especially weekends. Main courses $14–$25 lunch, $25–$40 dinner; Sun brunch $35. AE, DC, DISC, MC, V. Tues–Sat 11:30am–2pm; Sun brunch 11am–2pm; Sun–Thurs 6–8:30pm; Fri–Sat 5:30–9:30pm. Valet parking $3 lunch, $5 dinner. Bus: 34.

## EXPENSIVE

**Fresh** ✿✿ CALIFORNIA/SEAFOOD La Jolla never quite got the point of the *nuevo latino* cuisine at Tamarindo, so the owners went back to the drawing board and created this fine seafood-plus restaurant, which was a hit right from its 2003 debut. Chef Matthew Zappoli has created a moderately adventurous menu with an emphasis on small plates, such as the mouthwatering lobster Napoleon made with delicate potato chips; pan-seared scallops; soy balsamic-lacquered black cod; shredded duck spring rolls; or spice-rubbed venison. Large-plate entrees include a surprisingly delicate coriander-crusted mahimahi and shellfish-stuffed rainbow trout. The good quantity of "land" offerings includes pepper-seared beef Delmonico; braised lamb *osso buco*; and crisp roasted duck with wild mushroom risotto. Don't miss the flight of three minimartinis or the desserts (also overseen by Zappoli), which are well worth investigating. The dining room underwent a soothing modern redesign, with billowing waves of fabric across the elevated ceilings, and broad windows that successfully integrate the outside dining area. Fresh is one of La Jolla's favorite haunts.

1044 Wall St. (at Hershel), La Jolla. ⓒ 858/551-7575. www.freshseafoodrestaurant.com. Reservations strongly recommended. Main courses $9–$17 lunch, $18–$30 dinner. AE, DISC, MC, V. Daily 11:30am–3pm and 5–9:30pm (Fri–Sat till 10pm). 2-hr. validated parking. Bus: 34.

## MODERATE

**Piatti** ⭐ ITALIAN/MEDITERRANEAN   La Jolla's version of the neighborhood hangout is this pasta-centric trattoria a couple blocks inland from La Jolla Shores. Come here on Friday or Saturday evening, and you're likely to be surrounded by a crew of regulars that pops in once or twice a week and knows all the staff by name. You won't feel left out, however, and the food is well priced. Lemon-herb-roasted chicken, peppercorn-crusted *bistecca* (rib-eye), plus the Thursday night special of *osso buco* with risotto lead the short list of entrees, but it's the pastas that make their way to the most tables. Try *orecchiette* bathed in Gorgonzola or pappardelle "fantasia"— shrimp-crowned ribbons of saffron pasta, primed with garlic, tomato, and white wine. The outdoor patio, beneath the sprawl of an enormous ficus tree, is ideal for dining any night.

2182 Avenida de la Playa. ⓒ 858/454-1589. Reservations recommended. Main courses $13–$25; Sat–Sun brunch $8–$11. AE, DC, DISC, MC, V. Sun–Thurs 11am–10pm; Fri–Sat 11am–11pm. Street parking usually available. Bus: 34.

**Spice & Rice Thai Kitchen** ⭐ THAI   This attractive restaurant is a couple of blocks from the village's traffic crush—far enough to ensure easier parking. The lunch crowd consists of shoppers and curious tourists, while dinner is quieter, after all the local businesses have shut down. The food is excellent, with polished presentations and expert renditions of classics such as pad Thai and glazed duck. The starters often sound as good as the entrees—consider making a grazing meal of house specialties such as prawns with yellow-curry lobster sauce, or crispy calamari flavored with tamarind and chile sauce. The covered front patio has a romantic, secluded-garden feel, and inside tables have indirect lighting.

7734 Girard Ave. ⓒ 858/456-0466. Reservations recommended. Main courses $8.95–$16. AE, DC, DISC, MC, V. Mon–Sat 11am–3pm; Sun–Thurs 5–10pm; Fri–Sat 5–11pm. Bus: 34.

## INEXPENSIVE

**The Cottage** BREAKFAST/CALIFORNIA   La Jolla's best, friendliest breakfast is served at this turn-of-the-20th-century bungalow on a sunny village corner. Newly modernized, the cottage is light and airy, but most diners opt for tables outside, where a white picket fence encloses the trellis-shaded brick patio. Omelets and egg dishes feature Mediterranean, Asian, or classic American touches; my favorite has creamy mashed potatoes, bacon, and melted cheese folded inside. The Cottage bakes its own muffins, breakfast breads, and the best brownies in San Diego. Breakfast dishes are served all day, but toward lunch the kitchen begins turning out freshly made soups, light meals, and sandwiches. Summer dinners (never heavy, always tasty) are a delight, particularly when you're seated before dark on a balmy seaside night. Like what you taste? You're in luck, because The Cottage has its own cookbook, with recipes for its most popular dishes.

7702 Fay Ave. (at Kline St.). ⓒ 858/454-8409. www.cottagelajolla.com. Reservations accepted for dinner only. Main courses $9–$15 dinner, $7–$11 lunch, $6–$9 breakfast. AE, DC, DISC, MC, V. Daily 7:30am–3pm; dinner (June–Sept only) Tues–Sat 5–9:30pm. Bus: 34.

# CORONADO

Befitting this "island's" old-school Navy aura, the dining options on Coronado are reliable and often quite good, but the restaurants aren't breaking new culinary ground. Notable exceptions are the resort dining rooms, which seem to be waging a little rivalry to attract the most prestigious executive chef. **Azzura Point** ★★ at Loews Coronado Bay Resort (© 619/424-4000), has a stylish dining room with great views and wins raves from deep-pocketed San Diegans looking for inventive California-Mediterranean creations. The Hotel del Coronado's fancy **Prince of Wales** ★★ (© 619/522-8490) is equally scenic, with views of the beach across the regal Windsor Lawn; the California menu showcases seasonally fresh ingredients.

## EXPENSIVE

**Chez Loma** ★★ FRENCH   This intimate Victorian cottage filled with antiques and subdued candlelight makes for romantic dining. The house dates from 1889, the French-Continental restaurant from 1975. Tables are scattered throughout the house and on the enclosed garden terrace; an upstairs wine salon, reminiscent of a Victorian parlor, is a cozy spot for coffee or conversation. Among the entrees are salmon with smoked-tomato vinaigrette, and roast duckling with lingonberry, port, and burnt-orange sauce; main courses are served with soup or salad, rice or potatoes, and fresh vegetables. Follow dinner with a silky crème caramel or Kahlúa crème brûlée. California wines and American microbrews are available, in addition to a full bar, and early birds enjoy specially priced meals: $25 for a three-course meal before 6pm. The restaurant's only downfall—predictability—is also its main strength.

1132 Loma (off Orange Ave.), Coronado. © 619/435-0661. www.chezloma.com. Reservations recommended. Main courses $20–$29. AE, DC, MC, V. Daily 5–10pm. Bus: 901, 902, or 904.

## MODERATE

**Rhinoceros Cafe & Grill** AMERICAN   This bright bistro is more casual than it looks from the street and offers large portions, although the kitchen can be a little heavy-handed with sauces and spices. At lunch, every other patron seems to be enjoying the *penne à la vodka* in creamy tomato sauce; favorite dinner specials are Italian cioppino and Southwestern-style meatloaf. Plenty of crispy fresh salads balance out the main courses. The wine list is fair.

1166 Orange Ave., Coronado. © 619/435-2121. Main courses $10–$25. AE, DC, DISC, MC, V. Daily 11am–2:30pm; Sun–Thurs 5–9pm; Fri–Sat 5–10pm. Street parking available. Bus: 901, 902, or 904.

## INEXPENSIVE

**Villa Nueva Bakery Café** ★ (Value) BREAKFAST/LIGHT FARE   Formerly known as Primavera Pastry Caffe, this wonderful little cafe is the best of its kind in Coronado. In addition to fresh-roasted coffee and espresso drinks, it serves omelets, bagels and lox, and other breakfast treats (until 2pm), deli sandwiches on their delicious house bread, and a daily fresh soup. It's the kind of spot where half the customers are greeted by name. Locals rave about the "Yacht Club" sandwich, a croissant filled with yellowfin tuna, and the breakfast croissant, topped with scrambled eggs, ham, and cheddar cheese. Those fat, gooey cinnamon buns are every bit as good as they look.

956 Orange Ave., Coronado. © 619/435-4191. Main courses $5–$8. AE, DC, DISC, MC, V. Daily 6:30am–6pm; summer hours Mon–Sat 6:30am–9pm, Sun 6:30am–6pm. Bus: 901, 902, or 904.

## SPECIAL FINDS IN THE BURBS

Don't limit your dining experience in San Diego to the main tourist zones outlined above. Five minutes north of Mission Valley is the mostly business neighborhood of Kearny Mesa, home to San Diego's best Asian venues. One to try is **Jasmine** ★★, 4609 Convoy St. (© **858/268-0888**), which at lunch showcases wonderful Hong Kong–style dumplings wheeled around the room on carts. Dinners are more elaborate; seafood and Peking duck two ways are good choices. Nearby, **China Max** ★, 4698 Convoy St. (© **858/650-3333**), occupies a nondescript building in an Asian minimall, near the junction of the 805 and 163 freeways. The dining room is spare, but the kitchen exhibits finesse with southern Chinese delicacies and excellent (sometimes pricey) fish specials.

Just east of Hillcrest (south and parallel to Mission Valley), Adams Avenue is one of the city's streets of character, with antiques shops and bistros en route to Kensington. Here you'll find the **Kensington Grill** ★★, 4055 Adams Ave., next to the Ken Cinema (© **619/281-4014**), owned by the same crew in charge of the Gaslamp's hip Chive. Kensington features contemporary American cuisine in a chic setting that draws lots of neighborhood types. In nearby Normal Heights, **Jyoti Bihanga,** 3351 Adams Ave. (© **619/282-4116**), caters to followers of Sri Chinmoy and delivers a vegetarian menu of Indian-influenced salads, wraps, and curries; the "neatloaf" is a winner. All items are priced under $10. Close to Park Boulevard (and Hillcrest) is the **Adams Avenue Grill** ★, 2201 Adams Ave. (© **619/298-8440**), a friendly neighborhood joint that serves comfort food with international accents.

## 5 The Three Major Animal Parks

**San Diego Wild Animal Park** ★★★ *(Kids)*    Located 34 miles north of San Diego, outside of Escondido, this terrific "zoo of the future" will transport you to the African plains and other faraway landscapes. Originally a breeding facility for the San Diego Zoo, the 1,800-acre Wild Animal Park now holds 3,500 animals of 429 different species. Many of the animals roam freely in vast enclosures, allowing giraffes to interact with antelopes, much as they would in Africa. You'll find the largest crash of rhinos at any zoological facility in the world, an exhibit for the endangered California condor, and a mature landscape of exotic vegetation. The San Diego Zoo is "world famous," but many visitors end up preferring the Wild Animal Park.

The central focus is the 5-mile **Wgasa Bush Line Railway**, a 60-minute monorail ride included in the price of admission. Trains leave every 10 minutes or so from the station, and lines build up by late morning, so make this your first or last attraction of the day (the animals are more active anyway). The monorail passes through areas designated as East Africa, South Africa, Asian Plains, and the Eurasian Waterhole, through swaying grasses and along rocky outcrops.

Other exhibits bring you closer to the animals, like the three self-guided **walking tours,** which visit various habitats, including the new **Lion Camp. Nairobi Village** is the commercial hub of the park, but even here animal exhibits are interesting, including the **nursery area,** where young ones can be seen frolicking, bottle-feeding, and sleeping; a **petting station;** the **lowland gorillas;** and the **Bee Eater Aviary.** There are amphitheaters for a bird show and another featuring elephants, scheduled two or three times daily. Nairobi Village has souvenir stores and several spots for mediocre dining. Visitors should be prepared for sunny, often downright hot weather; it's not unusual for temperatures to be 5°–10° warmer here than in San Diego.

If you want to get up-close-and-personal with the animals, take one of the park's **Photo Caravans,** which shuttle groups of eight in flatbed trucks out into the open areas that are inaccessible to the general public. Two different itineraries are available, each 1¾ hours long, and you'll want to make reservations ahead of your visit (© **619/ 718-3050**). The price is $90 per person for one caravan (park admission not included), or $130 for both; children must be at least 8 years old, and ages 8 through 17 must be accompanied by an adult. The new **Cheetah Run Safari** allows a limited number of guests (reservations required, © **619/718-3000**) to watch the world's fastest land mammal in action, sprinting after a mechanical lure. Cost is $69 per person, excluding park admission.

15500 San Pasqual Valley Rd., Escondido. © **760/747-8702.** www.wildanimalpark.org. Admission $29 adults, $26 seniors 60 and over, $18 children 3–11, free for children under 3 and military in uniform. AE, DISC, MC, V. Daily 9am–4pm (grounds close at 5pm); extended hours during summer and Festival of Lights (2 weekends in Dec). Parking $8. Take I-15 to Via Rancho Pkwy.; follow signs for about 3 miles.

**San Diego Zoo** ★★★ *Kids*    More than 4,000 creatures reside at this influential zoo, started in 1916 and run by the Zoological Society of San Diego. In the early days, the zoo's founder, Dr. Harry Wegeforth, traveled the world and bartered native Southwestern animals such as rattlesnakes and sea lions for more exotic species. "Dr. Harry" also brought home plants, which flourish in the zoo's botanical garden, with more than 700,000 plants.

The zoo is one of only four in the U.S. with giant pandas, and many other rare species live here, including Buerger's tree kangaroos of New Guinea, long-billed kiwis from New Zealand, wild Przewalski's horses from Mongolia, lowland gorillas from Africa, and giant tortoises from the Galapagos. The Zoological Society is involved with animal preservation efforts around the world and has engineered many "firsts" in breeding. The zoo was also a forerunner in creating barless, moated enclosures that allow animals to roam in sophisticated environments resembling their natural ones.

The new **Monkey Trails and Forest Tales** is the largest, most elaborate habitat in the zoo's history, re-creating a wooded forest full of endangered species such as the mandrill monkey, clouded leopard, and pygmy hippopotamus. An elevated trail through the treetops allows for close observation of the primate, bird, and plant life that thrives in the forest canopy. **Absolutely Apes** showcases orangutans and siamangs of Indonesia; while next door is **Gorilla Tropics,** where two troops of Western lowland gorillas roam an 8,000-square-foot habitat. Despite the hype, I find the **Giant Panda Research Center** *not* worth the hassle when a long line is in place (lines are shortest first thing in the morning or toward the end of the day). More noteworthy is **Ituri Forest,** which simulates a central African rainforest with forest buffalos, otters, okapis, and hippos, which are viewed underwater from a glassed-in enclosure; and the **Polar Bear Plunge,** where you'll find a 2¼-acre summer tundra habitat populated by Siberian reindeer, yellow-throated martens, and diving ducks, as well as polar bears. The **Children's Zoo** features a nursery with baby animals and a petting area where kids can cuddle up to sheep, goats, and the like. There's also a **sea lion show** at the 3,000-seat amphitheater (easy to skip if you're headed to SeaWorld).

If a lot of walking—some of it on steep hills—isn't your passion, a 40-minute **Guided Bus Tour** provides a narrated overview and covers about 75% of the facility. It costs $10 for adults, $5.50 for children 3 to 11; it's included in the "Best Value" admission package. Since you get only brief glimpses of the enclosures, and animals won't always be visible, you'll want to revisit some areas. Included in the bus ticket is

# San Diego Attractions

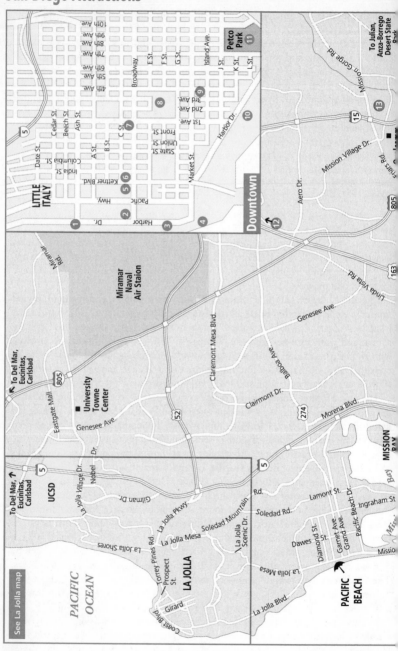

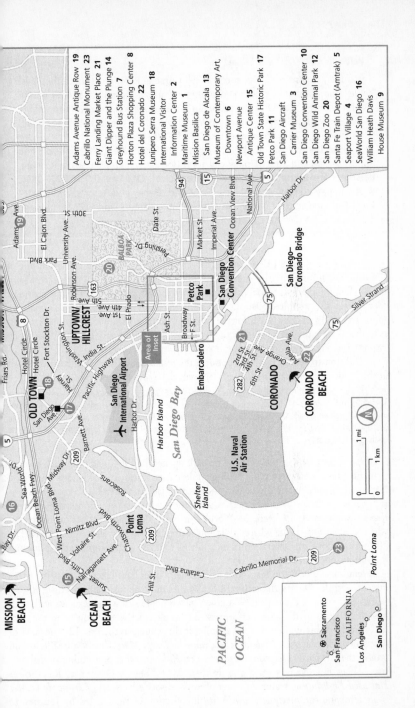

Adams Avenue Antique Row **19**
Cabrillo National Monument **23**
Ferry Landing Market Place **21**
Giant Dipper and the Plunge **14**
Greyhound Bus Station **7**
Horton Plaza Shopping Center **8**
Hotel del Coronado **22**
Junipero Serra Museum **18**
International Visitor
  Information Center **2**
Maritime Museum **1**
Mission Basilica
San Diego de Alcala **13**
Museum of Contemporary Art,
  Downtown **6**
Newport Avenue
Antique Center **15**
Old Town State Historic Park **17**
Petco Park **11**
San Diego Aircraft
  Carrier Museum **3**
San Diego Convention Center **10**
San Diego Wild Animal Park **12**
San Diego Zoo **20**
Santa Fe Train Depot (Amtrak) **5**
Seaport Village **4**
SeaWorld San Diego **16**
William Heath Davis
  House Museum **9**

> **Value** Now *That's* a Deal!
>
> If you plan to visit both the zoo and Wild Animal Park, investigate the "Best Value" zoo package, including Wild Animal Park admission. It's $54 for adults, $34 for children 3 to 11 (a $61/$37 value). You get one visit to each attraction, to be used within 5 days of purchase. Visit SeaWorld in the same 5 days, and it's $99 for adults, $75 children ages 3 to 9 (a $111/$78 value).
>
> The **San Diego Passport** ($79 for adults, $45 for children 3–11), includes zoo admission, an Old Town Trolley city tour, Hornblower bay cruises, and more; passports are sold at the attractions themselves. **City Pass** (© **707/256-0490;** www.citypass.com) covers the zoo, SeaWorld, Disneyland Resorts, and Knott's Berry Farm in Orange County; passes are $185 for adults, and $127 for kids age 3 to 9 (a $266/$184 value), valid for 14 days.

access to the un-narrated **Express Bus,** which allows you to get on and off at one of five different stops along the same route. You can also get an aerial perspective from the **Skyfari,** which costs $3 per person each way, though you won't see many creatures. Ideally, take the complete bus tour first thing in the morning, when the animals are more active. By midday, waits for the bus tour can top an hour. After the bus tour, take the Skyfari to the far side of the park and wend your way back on foot or by Express Bus to revisit animals you missed.

In addition to several fast-food options, the restaurant **Albert's** is a beautiful oasis at the lip of a canyon and a lovely place in which to break up the day.

2920 Zoo Dr., Balboa Park. © **619/234-3153** (recorded info), or 619/231-1515. www.sandiegozoo.org. Admission $21 adults, $14 children 3–11, free for military in uniform. The "Best Value" package (admission, guided bus tour, round-trip Skyfari aerial tram) $32 adults, $29 seniors, $20 children. AE, DISC, MC, V. Sept to mid-June daily 9am–5pm (last ticket sold at 4pm); mid-June to Aug daily 9am–9pm (last ticket sold at 8pm). Bus: 7, 7A/B. Interstate 5 south to Pershing Dr., follow signs.

**SeaWorld San Diego** ★★ *Kids*   The park opened in 1964, and with each passing year the educational pretext increasingly takes a back seat to slick shows and rides. Nevertheless, the aquatic theme park—owned by the Anheuser-Busch corporation—is perhaps the country's premiere showplace for marine life, in a nominally informative atmosphere. At its heart, SeaWorld is a shoreside family entertainment center where the performers are whales, dolphins, otters, sea lions, walruses, and seals. The 20-minute shows run several times each during the day, with visitors cycling through the various open-air amphitheaters.

Several successive 4-ton black-and-white killer whales have taken turns as the park's mascot, and the ***Shamu Adventure*** is SeaWorld's most popular show. Performed in a 5,500-seat stadium, the stage is a 7-million-gallon pool lined with plexiglass walls with magnified views of the huge performers. But think twice before you sit in the seats down front—a highlight of the act is multiple drenchings in the first 12 or so rows of spectators. The slapstick ***Cyde and Seamore in Deep, Deep Trouble*** (sea lions and otters), the fast-paced ***Dolphin Show,*** and *Pets Rule!* are other performing animal routines, all in huge venues seating more than 2,000. The "4-D" movie, ***R.L. Stine's Haunted Lighthouse,*** features a roster of multisensory effects; and ***Cirque de la Mer*** is an acrobatic summertime show. A small collection of rides is led by **Journey to Atlantis,** a 2004 roller coaster and log flume. **Shipwreck Rapids** is a splashy adventure on raftlike inner tubes through caverns, and **Wild Arctic** is a motion simulator heli-copter trip to the frozen North.

Guests disembarking Wild Arctic or using the ride bypass find themselves in the midst of one of SeaWorld's real specialties: carefully simulated marine environments. In this case it's an **arctic research station,** surrounded by beluga whales and polar bears. Other animal environments worth seeing are **Manatee Rescue, Shark Encounter,** and the **Penguin Encounter.** The 2-acre hands-on area called **Shamu's Happy Harbor** encourages kids to handle things—and features a pretend pirate ship with netted towers, tube crawls, and slides.

The **Dolphin Interaction Program** is an opportunity for people to wade waist-deep with dolphins. This program includes some classroom time before participants wriggle into a wet suit and climb into the water for 20 minutes with the dolphins. It costs $150 per person (not including park admission); participants must be age 6 or older.

500 Sea World Dr., Mission Bay. ℂ **800/380-3203** or 619/226-3901. www.seaworld.com. Admission $51 adults, $41 children 3–9, free for children under 3. AE, DISC, MC, V. Daily 10am–5pm; most weekends and in summer the park opens at 9am and stays open until midnight during peak periods. Parking $7. Bus: 9 or 27. From I-5, take Sea World Dr. exit; from I-8, take W. Mission Bay Dr. exit to Sea World Dr.

## 6 Beaches

San Diego County is blessed with 70 miles of sandy coastline and more than 30 indi-vidual beaches, probably the state's best collection. The beaches cater equally to surfers, snorkelers, swimmers, sailors, divers, walkers, volleyballers, sunbathers—you get the drift. Even in winter and spring, when water temps drop to the high 50s (teens Celsius), they are great places to walk and jog, and surfers happily don wet suits to pursue their passion. In summer the beaches teem with locals and visitors alike—the bikinis come out, the pecs are bared, and a spring-break atmosphere is imminent, although common sense and good taste usually prevail in the end. (From mid-May through mid-July, however, prepare for **June Gloom,** a local phenomenon caused as inland deserts heat up at the end of spring and suck the marine layer—a thick bank of fog—inland for a few miles. Expect clammy mornings and evenings.)

Here's a list of San Diego's best stretches of sand, each with its own personality and devotees. They are listed geographically from south to north.

**CORONADO** 🐕 Lovely, wide, and sparkling, this beach is conducive to strolling and lingering, especially in the late afternoon. At the north end, you can watch fighter jets in formation flying from the Naval Air Station, while in the center is the pretty section fronting Ocean Boulevard and the Hotel del Coronado. Waves are gentle here, so the beach draws many Coronado families—and their dogs, which are allowed off-leash at the most northwesterly end. South of the Hotel Del, the beach becomes the beautiful, often deserted, **Silver Strand.**

**OCEAN BEACH** The northern end of Ocean Beach Park is officially known as **Dog Beach,** and it's one of a few in the county where your pooch can roam freely on the sand. Surfers congregate around the O.B. Pier, mostly in the water but often at the snack shack on the end. Rip currents can be strong—check with the lifeguard stations. Facilities at the beach include restrooms, showers, picnic tables, volleyball courts, and plenty of metered parking lots. To reach the beach, take West Point Loma Boulevard all the way to the end.

**MISSION BEACH**   Anchored by the 81-year-old **Giant Dipper** roller coaster, the sands and wide cement "boardwalk" sizzle with activity for most of the year. At the southern end, a volleyball game always seems to be going on. Parking can be tough, with your best bet being the public lots around the Giant Dipper or at the south end of West Mission Bay Drive. This street is the centerline of a 2-block-wide isthmus that leads a mile north to Pacific Beach.

**PACIFIC BEACH**   The action is here, particularly along **Ocean Front Walk**—a paved promenade showcasing a human parade akin to the one at L.A.'s Venice Beach boardwalk. It runs along Ocean Boulevard (just west of Mission Blvd.) to the pier. Surfing is popular year-round, in marked sections, and the beach is well staffed with lifeguards. You're on your own to find street parking. A half-mile north of the pier is **Tourmaline Surfing Park,** where the sport's old guard gathers to surf waters where swimmers are prohibited.

**MISSION BAY PARK**   This *inland,* 4,600-acre aquatic playground contains 27 miles of bay front, picnic areas, children's playgrounds, and paths for biking, in-line skating, and jogging. The bay lends itself to windsurfing, sailing, water-skiing, and fishing. There are dozens of access points; at the southwest corner is **Bonita Cove,** a protected inlet with calm waters, grassy picnic areas, and playground equipment. The water is cleaner for swimming here than in the northeastern reaches. Get there from Mission Boulevard in south Mission Beach.

**LA JOLLA COVE**  ⭐⭐   These protected, calm waters—celebrated as the clearest along the coast—attract snorkelers and scuba divers, along with a fair share of families. The stunning setting offers only a small sandy beach, as well as the **Children's Cove,** inhabited by a colony of harbor seals. Smaller fish huddle in the tide pools between the two beaches. The cove is terrific for swimming, cramped for sunbathing, and accessible from Coast Boulevard; parking nearby is free, if sparse.

**LA JOLLA SHORES**   The wide, flat mile of sand at La Jolla Shores is popular with joggers, swimmers, and beginning body- and board surfers, as well as with families. Weekend crowds can be enormous, quickly occupying both the sand and the metered parking spaces in the lot. There are restrooms, showers, and picnic areas here, as well the grassy, palm-lined Kellogg Park across the street.

**BLACK'S BEACH**  ⭐   The area's unofficial (and illegal) nude beach, 2-mile-long Black's lies north of La Jolla Shores, at the base of steep, 300-foot-high cliffs. It is out of the way and tricky to reach, but it draws scores with its secluded beauty and good swimming conditions. The spectacle of hang gliders launching from the cliffs above adds to the show. To get here, take North Torrey Pines Road, park at the Glider Port, and clamber down the makeshift path, staying alert to avoid one of several false trails. To bypass the cliff descent, you can walk to Black's from beaches north (Torrey Pines) or south (La Jolla Shores). *Note:* Lifeguards are usually present from spring break through October. Citations for nude sunbathing, however, are rarely issued. There are no restroom facilities.

**TORREY PINES**  ⭐   At the north end of Black's Beach, at the foot of the Torrey Pines State Park, this fabulous strand is accessed by a pay parking lot at the entrance to the park. Combining a visit to the park with a day at the beach is my concept of the quintessential insider's San Diego experience. It's rarely crowded, though you need to be aware of high tide (when most of the sand gets a bath). In almost any weather, it's a great beach for walking.

## 7 Exploring the Area

## BALBOA PARK

Like New York's Central Park, San Francisco's Golden Gate, and Philly's Fairmount, 1,200-acre Balboa Park is San Diego's green crown jewel and one of the nation's largest urban parks, established in 1868. Tree plantings began in the late 19th century, and while the initial buildings were created to host the 1915–16 Panama-California Exposition, another expo in 1935–36 brought additional developments. Today Balboa Park's most distinctive features include mature landscaping, the architectural beauty of the Spanish-Moorish buildings lining El Prado, and an outstanding and diverse collection of museums. You'll also find **The Old Globe** theater complex (p. 726) and the **San Diego Zoo** (p. 707).

Entry to Balboa Park is free, as is parking, but most of the museums have admission charges and varying open hours (most are open daily). A free tram will transport you around the park. Get details from the **Balboa Park Visitor Center,** in the House of Hospitality (℗ **619/239-0512;** www.balboapark.org). The visitor center is also the starting point for several free tours of the park that focus on architecture, horticulture, and so on. Top museums include:

**Mingei International Museum** ★★    This captivating museum (pronounced *Min*-gay, meaning "art of the people" in Japanese), offers changing exhibitions one could generally describe as folk art. The rotating exhibits—usually four at a time—feature artists from countries across the globe; displays include textiles, costumes, jewelry, toys, pottery, paintings, and sculpture. The permanent collection includes whimsical contemporary sculptures by the late French artist Niki de Saint Phalle, who made San Diego her home in 1993. As one of only two major museums in the United States devoted to folk crafts on a worldwide scale (the other is in Santa Fe, New Mexico), it's well worth a look.

1439 El Prado, in the House of Charm. ℗ **619/239-0003.** www.mingei.org. Admission $6 adults, $3 children 6–17 and students w/ID, free for children under 6. Free 3rd Tues of each month. AE, MC, V. Tues–Sun 10am–4pm. Bus: 7 or 7A/B.

**Museum of Photographic Arts** ★★    Fans of Ansel Adams and Edward Weston shouldn't miss a sampling of the 7,000-plus images housed by this museum—one of few in the United States devoted exclusively to the photographic arts (encompassing cinema, video, and digital photography as well). Provocative traveling exhibits change every few months, while photos by Alfred Stieglitz, Margaret Bourke-White, Imogen Cunningham, Paul Strand, and Manuel Alvarez Bravo are all in the permanent collection, and the plush cinema hosts special screenings.

---

### Tips    Balboa Park Money-Savers

Most Balboa Park attractions are free one Tuesday each month; the schedule rotates so two or three participate each Tuesday (the visitor center has a schedule). If you plan to visit more than three of the park's museums, buy the **Passport to Balboa Park,** a coupon booklet that allows entrance to 13 major museums; it's valid for 1 week for $30. If you plan to spend a day at the zoo and return for the museums, buy the **Best of Balboa Park Combo,** which provides one ticket to the zoo and 3 days' admission to the 13 museums, for $55. Passports are available at any museum or the visitor center.

---

1649 El Prado. ✆ **619/238-7559.** www.mopa.org. Admission $6 adults; $4 seniors, students, and military; free for children under 12 w/adult; cinema admission $7 adults, $6 seniors, students, and children. Free 2nd Tues of each month. Daily 10am–5pm (Thurs until 9pm). Bus: 7 or 7A/B.

**Reuben H. Fleet Science Center** ⭐ *Kids*   A park highlight for kids, this tantalizing collection of interactive exhibits and rides is designed to provoke the imagination and teach scientific principles. The Virtual Zone includes Deep Sea, a motion simulator ride that lurches you into a virtual ocean floor. The Fleet also houses a 76-foot-high IMAX Dome Theater, and the Fleet has a spiffy simulator for planetarium shows (held the first Wed of each month).

1875 El Prado. ✆ **619/238-1233.** www.rhfleet.org. Fleet Experience admission includes 1 IMAX film and exhibit galleries: $12 adults, $10 seniors 65 and over, $9 children 3–12 (exhibit gallery can be purchased individually). Free 1st Tues of each month (exhibit galleries only). AE, DISC, MC, V. Open daily 9:30am; closing times vary but always until at least 5pm. Bus: 7 or 7A/B.

**San Diego Aerospace Museum** ⭐⭐ *Kids*   The other big kid-pleaser, this facility provides an overview of the nation's air-and-space history, from the days of hot-air balloons to the space age, with plenty of biplanes and military fighters in between. It emphasizes local aviation history, particularly the construction here of the *Spirit of St. Louis.* Highlights include the only GPS satellite on display in a museum, and a World War I–era Spad. The museum is housed in a stunning cylindrical hall built by the Ford Motor Company in 1935 for the park's second international expo.

2001 Pan American Plaza. ✆ **619/234-8291.** www.aerospacemuseum.org. Admission $9 adults, $7 seniors, $4 juniors 6–17, free for active military w/ID and children under 6. Free 4th Tues of each month. Sept–May daily 10am–4:30pm; June–Aug daily 10am–5:30pm. Bus: 7 or 7A/B.

**San Diego Museum of Art** ⭐   This museum is known in the art world for its collection of Spanish baroque painting and possibly the largest horde of Asian Indian paintings outside India. The American collection includes works by Georgia O'Keeffe and Thomas Eakins. Only a small percentage of the 12,000-piece permanent collection is on display at any given time, in favor of varied, often prestigious touring shows. In summer 2006, *Andy Warhol's Dream America* will be the museum's next blockbuster exhibition, presenting a broad overview of the pop art master's career.

1450 El Prado. ✆ **619/232-7931.** www.sdmart.org. Admission $9 adults 25 and older; $7 seniors, military, and youths 18–24; $4 children 6–17; free for children under 6. Admission to traveling exhibits varies. Free 3rd Tues of each month. Tues–Sun 10am–6pm (Thurs until 9pm). Bus: 7 or 7A/B.

**Timken Museum of Art** ⭐ *Finds*   This jewel-like repository houses the Putnam Foundation's collection of 19th-century American paintings and works by European old masters, as well as a worthy display of Russian icons. Yes, it's a small horde, but it's free, and the marquee attractions include Peter Paul Reubens's *Portrait of a Young Man in Armor;* San Diego's only Rembrandt, *St. Bartholomew;* and a masterpiece by Eastman Johnson, *The Cranberry Harvest.* You'll find a spot apiece for works by Bierstadt, Pissarro, Corot, and Cézanne. The petite Timken also makes for an easy introduction to fine art for younger travelers (pick up a copy of the *Children's Gallery Guide* for $2).

1500 El Prado. ✆ **619/239-5548.** www.timkenmuseum.org. Free admission. Tues–Sat 10am–4:30pm; Sun 1:30–4:30pm. Closed Sept and major holidays. Bus: 7 or 7A/B.

Other noteworthy attractions—with their locations shown on the Balboa Park map on p. 715—include:

# Balboa Park

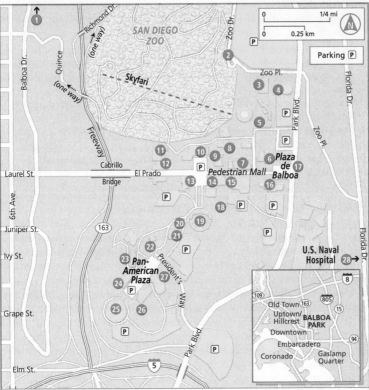

Parking P

| | |
|---|---|
| Balboa Park Municipal Golf Course **28** | Marston House **1** |
| Botanical Building and Lily Pond **8** | Reuben H. Fleet Science Center **16** |
| Carousel **4** | Rose & Desert Gardens **17** |
| Casa de Balboa **15** | San Diego Aerospace Museum **25** |
|   Model Railroad Museum | San Diego Automotive Museum **24** |
|   Museum of Photographic Arts | San Diego Hall of Champions |
|   San Diego Historical Society Museum |   Sports Museum **27** |
| Casa del Prado **7** | San Diego Miniature Railroad **3** |
| The Old Globe Theatres **11** | San Diego Museum of Art **10** |
| Hall of Nations **20** | San Diego Museum of Man **12** |
| House of Charm **13** | San Diego Museum |
|   Mingei International Museum |   of Natural History **6** |
|   SDAI Museum of the Living Artist | San Diego Zoo entrance **2** |
| House of Hospitality **14** | Spanish Village Art Center **5** |
|   Balboa Park Visitors Center | Spreckels Organ Pavilion **19** |
|   Prado Restaurant | Starlight Bowl **26** |
| House of Pacific Relations | Timken Museum of Art **9** |
|   International Cottages **22** | United Nations Building **21** |
| Japanese Friendship Garden **18** | |
| Marie Hitchcock Puppet Theatre **23** | |

- **Botanical Building and Lily Pond** ⚕ (no phone)
- **Japanese Friendship Garden** (© 619/232-2721; www.niwa.org)
- **Marston House Museum** ⚕ (3525 Seventh Ave., at Upas St., in the northwest corner of the park; © 619/298-3142)
- **San Diego Automotive Museum** ⚕ (© 619/231-2886; www.sdautomuseum.org)
- **San Diego Hall of Champions Sports Museum** (© 619/234-2544; www.sdhoc.com)
- **Museum of San Diego History** (© 619/232-6203; www.sandiegohistory.org)
- **San Diego Miniature Railroad and Carousel** (Kids) (619/460-9000)
- **San Diego Model Railroad Museum** ⚕ (Kids) (© 619/696-0199; www.sdmodel railroadm.com)
- **San Diego Museum of Man** (© 619/239-2001; www.museumofman.org)
- **San Diego Natural History Museum** (Kids) (© 619/232-3821; www.sdnhm.org)
- **Spreckels Organ Pavilion** (© 619/702-8138; www.sosorgan.com)

## MORE ATTRACTIONS IN & AROUND SAN DIEGO
### DOWNTOWN & BEYOND

Downtown, you can wander through the turn-of-the-20th-century **Gaslamp Quarter** ⚕⚕, with 16½ blocks of restored historic buildings. You'll find many of San Diego's best restaurants and its most vigorous nightlife scene here. More information about the Gaslamp Quarter, and walking tours on Saturdays at 11am, are available at the **William Heath Davis House,** a museum in downtown's oldest structure and home to the quarter's historical foundation; it's at 410 Island Ave., at Fourth Avenue (© 619/233-4692; www.gaslampquarter.org). At **Horton Plaza** ⚕, you can shop, stroll, dine, and people-watch—all within a playful village framework (p. 724).

In 2004, the city completed the $474-million **PETCO Park.** Mired in litigation and revelations of influence peddling that drove a city councilperson from office, the 42,000-seat ballpark incorporated seven historic structures into the stadium, including the Western Metal Supply building, a four-story brick edifice dating to 1909 that now sprouts left-field bleachers from one side. The San Diego Padres play April through September. PETCO parking is limited, and costly—for a space within a couple blocks of the facility, expect to pay at least $17. Better yet, take the San Diego Trolley. For schedules, information, and tickets, call © 877/374-2784 or 619/795-5000, or visit www.padres.com.

**Cabrillo National Monument** ⚕⚕ Breathtaking views mingle with the early history of San Diego, which began when Juan Rodríguez Cabrillo arrived in 1542. This tip of Point Loma is also a vantage point for migrating Pacific gray whales en route from Alaska to Baja California December through March. A tour of the restored lighthouse (1855) illuminates what life was like here more than a century ago. National Park Service rangers lead walks at the monument, and tide pools at the base of the peninsula beg for exploration. Free 30-minute films on Cabrillo, tide pools, and the whales screen on the hour daily from 10am to 4pm. The drive from downtown takes about a half-hour.

1800 Cabrillo Memorial Dr., Point Loma. © 619/557-5450. www.nps.gov/cabr. Admission $5 per vehicle, $3 for walk-ins. Daily 9am–5:15pm. Take I-8 west to Rosecrans St., right on Canon St., left on Catalina, and follow signs. Bus: 26.

**Maritime Museum** ⚕⚕ (Kids) This flotilla of classic ships is led by the full-rigged merchant vessel *Star of India* (1863), a National Historic Landmark and the world's oldest ship that still goes to sea. The gleaming white San Francisco–Oakland steam-powered ferry *Berkeley* (1898) worked round-the-clock to carry people to safety following the 1906 San Francisco earthquake; you'll find a museum with fine ship models on display. The elegant *Medea* (1904) is one of the world's few remaining large steam yachts, and *Pilot* (1914) was San Diego Bay's official pilot boat for 82 years. Recent additions include the HMS *Surprise*, a painstakingly accurate reproduction of an 18th-century Royal Navy Frigate, which played a supporting role to Russell Crowe in the film *Master and Commander: Far Side of the World*; and a 300-foot-long Cold War–era B-39 Soviet attack submarine. You can board and tour each vessel.

1492 N. Harbor Dr. ℂ **619/234-9153.** www.sdmaritime.com. Admission $10 adults; $8 seniors over 62, youths 13–17, and active military w/ID; $7 children 6–12; free for children under 6. Daily 9am–8pm (till 9pm in summer). Bus: 2, 4, 20, 23, or 29. Trolley: America Plaza.

**San Diego Aircraft Carrier Museum**  The USS *Midway*'s 47-year military history began 1 week after the Japanese surrender of World War II in 1945. By the time *Midway* was decommissioned in 1991, the aircraft carrier had patrolled the Taiwan Straits in 1955, operated in the Tonkin Gulf, and served as the flagship from which Desert Storm was conducted. In all, more than 200,000 men served aboard the warship. The carrier is now moored at the Embarcadero and in 2004 became San Diego's first naval museum. Incomplete paint jobs litter the walls with the occasional graffiti, and the austere bunkers look as though the inhabitants just stepped out. A self-guided audio tour takes visitors to several levels of the ship, telling the story of life onboard. The highlight is climbing up the superstructure to the bridge and gazing down on the 1,001-foot-long flight deck, with various aircraft poised for duty.

910 N. Harbor Dr. (at Navy Pier). ℂ **619/544-9600.** www.midway.org. $15 adults, $10 seniors and veterans, free for children under 5 and military in uniform. Daily 10am–5pm (ticket booth closes at 4pm). $7 parking. Bus: 7/7B. Trolley: American Plaza.

## OLD TOWN & BEYOND: CALIFORNIA'S BEGINNINGS

The birthplace of San Diego—indeed, of California—Old Town takes you back to the Mexican California that existed here until the mid-1800s. Today the spot suffers a daily invasion of tourists, many of them headed to **Plaza del Pasado**, a one-time 1930s-era motel that is now a terrific collection of shops and restaurants for well-chosen south-of-the-border wares and margaritas (see "Where to Dine," earlier in this chapter and "Shopping," later in this chapter).

**Mission Valley,** which starts at Presidio Park and heads straight east, is anything but old; until Highway 8 was built in the 1950s, it was little more than cow pastures with a couple of dirt roads. Shopping malls, motels, a golf course, condos, car dealerships, and a massive sports stadium fill its girth today.

Old Town and Mission Valley are easily accessed via San Diego Trolley.

**Junípero Serra Museum** ★★  On the hill above Old Town, this iconic Spanish Mission-style building built in 1929 overlooks the slopes where, in 1769, the first mission, first presidio (fort), and first non-native settlement on the west coast of the United States and Canada were founded. The museum's exhibits introduce visitors to the Native American, Spanish, and Mexican people who first called this place home. On display are their belongings, from cannons to cookware; a Spanish furniture collection; and one of the first paintings brought to California, which survived an Indian attack. From the 70-foot tower, visitors can compare the spectacular view with historic photos to see how this land has changed over time. Designed by William Templeton Johnson, the structure can be seen from miles around.

2727 Presidio Dr., Presidio Park. ℂ **619/297-3258.** Admission $5 adults; $4 seniors, students, and military; $2 children 6–17; free for children under 6. Daily 10am–4:30pm. Bus: 5, 5A, or 6. Trolley: Old Town. Take I-8 to the Taylor St. exit. Turn right on Taylor, then left on Presidio Dr.

**Mission Basilica San Diego de Alcalá**   This was the first link in a chain of 21 California missions founded by Spanish missionary Junípero Serra (the mission was moved from Old Town to this site in 1774 for agricultural reasons, and to separate Native American converts from the fortress that included the original building). The mission was burned by Indians a year after it was built—Father Serra rebuilt the structure using 5- to 7-foot-thick adobe (mud) walls and clay tile roofs, rendering it harder to burn. In the process he inspired a bevy of 20th-century California architects. A few bricks belonging to the original mission are in Presidio Park in Old Town. Mass is said daily in this active Catholic parish.

10818 San Diego Mission Rd., Mission Valley. ℂ **619/281-8449.** Admission $3 adults, $2 seniors and students, $1 children under 13. Free Sun and for daily Masses. Daily 9am–4:45pm; Mass daily 7am and 5:30pm. Bus: 13. Trolley: Mission San Diego. Take I-8 to Mission Gorge Rd. to Twain Ave., which turns into San Diego Mission Rd.

**Old Town State Historic Park** ⭐   The stars and stripes weren't raised over Old Town until 1846, and this historic park is dedicated to re-creating the city as it was during this era of Mexican influence, from around 1821 to 1872. Seven of the park's 20 structures are original, including the adobe homes. La Casa de Estudillo represents the living conditions of a wealthy family in 1872. Seeley Stables is named after A. L. Seeley, who ran the stagecoach and mail service in these parts from 1867 to 1871. Pick up a map at Park Headquarters, and peruse the model of Old Town as it looked in 1872. On Wednesday and Saturday, costumed park volunteers reenact 19th-century life with cooking and crafts demonstrations, a working blacksmith, and parlor singing. Free 1-hour walking tours leave daily at 11am and on Saturday and Sunday at 2pm from the Robinson-Rose House.

San Diego Ave. at Twiggs St., Old Town. ℂ **619/220-5422.** Free admission (donations welcome). Daily 10am–5pm. Bus: 5, 5A, or 6. Trolley: Old Town.

## MISSION BAY & THE BEACHES

**Mission Bay** is a 4,600-acre aquatic playground created in 1945 when tidal mud flats were dredged and opened to sea water. Today it's a great area for walking, jogging, in-line skating, biking, and boating. The boardwalk connecting **Mission Beach** and **Pacific Beach** is almost always bustling and colorful. A wooden roller coaster, the **Giant Dipper**, still screams away—daily in summer, and on weekends the rest of the year—providing a thrill for $5. Dedicated swimmers head for **The Plunge,** the classic, 175-foot-long indoor pool at the foot of the Giant Dipper. For all of these activities, see "Outdoor Pursuits," below. For **SeaWorld San Diego,** see p. 710.

## LA JOLLA

One of San Diego's most scenic spots—star of postcards for more than 100 years—is **La Jolla Cove** and the **Ellen Browning Scripps Park** on the bluff above it. The walk through the park, along Coast Boulevard, offers some of California's most resplendent coastal scenery, and just south is the **Children's Pool,** a beach where dozens of harbor seals laze in the sun. For a fine scenic drive, follow La Jolla Boulevard to Nautilus Street and turn east to get to 800-foot-high **Mount Soledad** ⭐, with a 360-degree view of the area.

**Birch Aquarium at Scripps** ⭐⭐   This beautiful facility is both aquarium and museum, operated as the interpretive arm of the world-famous Scripps Institution of

Oceanography. To make the most of it, pick up a visitor guide from the information booth just inside the entrance, and take time to read about each of the exhibits. The aquarium affords close-up views of the Pacific Northwest, the California coast, Mexico's Sea of Cortez, and the tropical seas, all presented in 33 marine-life tanks. The giant kelp forest is particularly impressive, replete with sharks and eels. Don't miss the tanks of fanciful white anemones and ethereal moon jellies (which look like living parachutes). The sea-horse propagation program here has met with excellent results, and nine different species of sea horse are on display. The rooftop demonstration tide pool not only shows visitors marine coastal life but also offers an amazing view of Scripps Pier and La Jolla. Free tide-pool talks are offered on weekends, when the aquarium is most crowded. Off-site adventures are conducted year-round.

2300 Expedition Way. (© 858/534-FISH. www.aquarium.ucsd.edu. Admission $10 adults, $8.50 seniors, $7 college students w/ID, $6.50 children 3–17, free for kids under 3. Parking free. AE, MC, V. Daily 9am–5pm. Bus: 34. Take I-5 to La Jolla Village Dr. exit, go west 1 mile, and turn left at Expedition Way.

## Museum of Contemporary Art San Diego ★★
Focusing on works produced since 1950, this museum is known internationally for its permanent collection and thought-provoking exhibitions. The 3,000-plus holdings represent every major art movement of the past half-century, with a strong showing by California artists. You'll see particularly noteworthy examples of minimalism, light and space work, conceptualism, installation, and site-specific sculptures. The museum is on a bluff overlooking the ocean, and the views from the galleries are gorgeous. The original building was the residence of the legendary Ellen Browning Scripps, designed by Irving Gill in 1916. More than a dozen exhibitions are presented each year, and guided docent tours are available daily at 2pm, with a second tour Thursdays at 5:30pm. Admission is free at the small satellite location in downtown San Diego at 1001 Kettner Blvd., across from the Santa Fe depot (© 619/234-1001) which usually features two exhibitions.

700 Prospect St. (© 858/454-3541. www.mcasandiego.org. Admission $6 adults; $2 students, seniors, and military; free for children under 12. Free 1st Sun and 3rd Tues of each month. Fri–Tues 11am–5pm; Thurs 11am–7pm. Bus: 30, 34, or 34A. Take the La Jolla Pkwy. exit off I-5 north or the La Jolla Village Dr. west exit off I-5 south. Take Torrey Pines Rd. to Prospect Place and turn right. Prospect Place becomes Prospect St.

## Stuart Collection ★
This collection of site-related sculptures by leading contemporary artists is scattered throughout UCSD's 1,200-acre campus. Pick up a brochure and map from the information booth (directions below), park in one of the metered spaces, and wend your way through the campus to discover the 16 highly diverse artworks. Among them: Niki de Saint-Phalle's *Sun God,* a jubilant 15-foot-high fiberglass bird on a 15-foot concrete base (an unofficial mascot of the students); Alexis Smith's *Snake Path,* a 560-foot-long slate-tile pathway that winds up the hill from the Engineering Mall to the east terrace of the spectacularly sculptural Geisel Library; and Terry Allen's *Trees,* three eucalyptus trees encased in lead—one emits songs, another poems and stories, and the third stands silent in a grove of living trees. Allow 2 hours to tour the entire collection.

9500 Gilman Dr., University of California, La Jolla (UCSD). (© 858/534-2117. http://stuartcollection.ucsd.edu. Free admission. Bus: 30, 34, 41, or 101. From La Jolla, take Torrey Pines Rd. to La Jolla Village Dr., turn right, go 2 blocks to Gilman Dr., and turn left into the campus; in about a block the information booth will be visible on the right.

## Torrey Pines State Reserve ★★ *Moments*
The rare torrey pine tree grows only two places in the world: Santa Rosa Island 175 miles northwest of San Diego and here, at the north end of La Jolla. If the twisted shape of these awkwardly beautiful trees doesn't move you, the equally rare, undeveloped coastal scenery should. The 1,750-acre

reserve encompasses the 300-foot-high, water-carved limestone bluffs, which provide a precarious footing for the trees. A half-dozen trails, under 1.5 miles in length, travel from the road to the cliff edge or down to the beach. A small visitor center, built in the traditional adobe style of the Hopi Indians, features a lovely, 12-minute video about the park. For a taste of what Southern California's coast looked like a couple hundred years ago, this delicate spot is one of San Diego's unique treasures. *Note:* The park has no facilities for food or drinks.

Hwy. 101, La Jolla. © 858/755-2063. www.torreypine.org. Admission $6 per car, $5 for seniors. Daily 8am–sunset. Bus: 101. From I-5, take Carmel Valley Rd. exit west; left at Hwy. 101.

## CORONADO

It's hard to miss San Diego Bay's most iconic landmark: the **San Diego–Coronado Bay Bridge** ✈. Completed in 1969, this graceful five-lane bridge spans 2¼ miles and links the city and the "island" of Coronado. At 246 feet in height, the bridge is tall enough to allow navy aircraft carriers to pass under it. It still looks more elegant than utilitarian, with a sweeping curve that maximizes the view, encompassing Mexico and the shipyards of National City to the left, the San Diego skyline to the right, and Coronado, the naval station, and Point Loma in front of you. (Designated drivers must promise to keep their eyes on the road!) Bus no. 901 from downtown will also take you across the bridge. The **Hotel del Coronado** ✈✈ is also worth checking out, even if you're not checking in. This turreted Victorian seaside resort remains an enduring, endearing national treasure (p. 693).

## SIGHTSEEING TOURS

**Hornblower Cruises**    These 1- or 2-hour narrated tours lead passengers through the San Diego harbor on one of seven different yachts, ranging from a 40-passenger vessel to a three-deck, 880-passenger behemoth. You'll see the *Star of India,* cruise under the San Diego–Coronado Bridge, and swing by the submarine base and an aircraft carrier or two. Guests can visit the captain's wheelhouse for a photo op, and harbor seals and sea lions on buoys are a regular sighting. Whale-watching trips (mid-Dec through late Mar) are a blast, a 2-hour Sunday (and Sat in summer) champagne brunch cruise departs at 11am, and dinner cruises run nightly.

1066 N. Harbor Dr. © 800/ON-THE-BAY or 619/686-8715. www.hornblower.com. Harbor tours $15–$20 adults; $2 off for seniors and military; half price children 4–12. Brunch cruise $45; whale-watching trips $25 (both $2 off for seniors and military, half price for children). Bus: 2. Trolley: Embarcadero.

**Old Town Trolley Tours**    Not to be confused with the public transit trolley, these narrated excursions are an easy way to get an overview of the city, especially if you're short on time or lacking your own set of wheels. The trackless trolleys do a 30-mile circular route, and you can hop off at any one of eight stops, explore at leisure, and reboard when you please (trolleys run every half-hour). Stops include Old Town, the Gaslamp Quarter, Coronado, the San Diego Zoo, and Balboa Park. You can begin wherever you want, but you must purchase tickets before boarding (not all stops have a ticket kiosk).

Old Town Trolley also operates **Sea and Land Adventures,** a 90-minute tour of the city in amphibious vehicles that hold 50 passengers. After cruising along the Embarcadero, you'll dip into the bay to experience the maritime and military history of San Diego. The trip is $30 for adults and $15 for kids 4 to 12. Or opt for the humorous **Ghosts & Gravestones** tour, a 90-minute twilight excursion to haunted and historical houses that concludes with a walk through one of the city's oldest cemeteries. The tour costs $30 and is restricted to ages 8 and up.

4040 Twiggs St., Old Town. © **619/298-TOUR.** www.historictours.com. $28 adults, $15 for kids 4–12, free for children 3 and under. The route by itself takes about 2 hr. Old Town Trolleys operate 9am–5pm in winter, 9am–6pm in summer.

## 8 Outdoor Pursuits

**BALLOONING & SCENIC FLIGHTS**    A peaceful dawn or dusk balloon ride reveals sweeping vistas of the Southern California coast, the wine country surrounding Temecula (70 min. north of downtown), or rambling estates and golf courses around Rancho Santa Fe (25 min. north of downtown). For a champagne-fueled glimpse of the county at sunrise or sunset, followed by an hors d'oeuvres party, contact **Skysurfer Balloon Company** (© **800/660-6809** or 858/481-6800; www.sandiego hotairballoons.com) or **California Dreamin'** (© **800/373-3359** or 760/438-3344; www.californiadreamin.com). Rates range from $138 to $158 (the higher rates apply on weekends).

**BIKING**    The paths around **Mission Bay** are great for leisurely rides, although the oceanfront **boardwalk** between Pacific Beach and Mission Beach can get very crowded, especially on weekends (and that's half the fun). The road out to **Point Loma** (Catalina Dr.) is moderately hilly with wonderful scenery. Traveling old **State Route 101** (aka the Pacific Coast Hwy.) from La Jolla north to Oceanside yields terrific coastal views, with plenty of places to refuel with coffee, a snack, or a swim.

For rentals, call **Bike Tours San Diego,** 509 Fifth Ave. (© **619/238-2444**), which offers delivery ($5) as far north as Del Mar. Rates for a city/hybrid bike start at $20 for a day, and include helmets, locks, maps, and roadside assistance. Other rental outlets include **Mission Beach Club,** 704 Ventura Place, off Mission Boulevard at Ocean Front Walk (© **858/488-8889**), for one-speed beach cruisers, and **Cheap Rentals** on Mission Boulevard (© **858/488-9070**) for mountain bikes and more. In La Jolla, try **California Bicycle,** 7462 La Jolla Blvd. (© **858/454-0316**), for front-suspended mountain bikes. In Coronado, check out **Bikes and Beyond,** 1201 First St., at the Ferry Landing Marketplace (© **619/435-7180**), for beach cruisers and mountain bikes. Expect to pay $7 and up per hour for bicycles, $30 for 24 hours.

**BIRD-WATCHING**    San Diego's birding scene is huge: More than 480 species have been observed in the county—more than anywhere else in the United States. The area is a haven along the Pacific Flyway—the migratory route along the Pacific Coast—and the diverse range of ecosystems helps to lure a wide range of winged creatures. From the tidal marshes to the desert, it's possible for birders to enjoy four distinct bird habitats in a single day.

Among the best places for bird-watching is the **Chula Vista Nature Center** at **Sweetwater Marsh National Wildlife Refuge** (© **619/409-5900;** www.chulavista naturecenter.org), where you may spot rare residents like the light-footed clapper rail and the western snowy plover, as well as predatory species like the American peregrine falcon and northern harrier. The **Torrey Pines State Reserve** (p. 719) is a protected habitat for swifts, thrashers, woodpeckers, and wrentits. Inland, the **Anza-Borrego Desert State Park** (see chapter 16) makes an excellent day trip from San Diego—268 species of birds have been recorded there.

Obtain the free brochure *Birding Hot Spots of San Diego* through the Port Administration Building, 3165 Pacific Hwy., or at the San Diego Zoo, Wild Animal Park, San Diego Natural History Museum, Birch Aquarium, or on the **Port of San**

**Diego** website at www.portofsandiego.org/sandiego_environment/bird_brochure.asp. The **San Diego Audubon Society** is another great source of birding information: ℂ 619/682-7200; www.sandiegoaudubon.org.

**FISHING**    Summer and fall are ideal for boat fishing, when the waters around **Point Loma** are brimming with bass, bonito, and barracuda; the **Islas los Coronados**, which belong to Mexico but are only about 18 miles from San Diego, are popular for abalone, yellowtail, yellowfin, and big-eyed tuna. Some outfitters will take you deeper into Baja California waters on multiday trips. Fishing charters depart from Harbor and Shelter islands, Point Loma, Imperial Beach, and Quivira Basin in Mission Bay. Participants over age 16 need a California fishing license, but anglers of any age can fish free of charge without a license off any **municipal pier** in the state, including those of Shelter Island, Ocean Beach, and Imperial Beach.

San Diego's sport-fishing fleet consists of more than 75 large commercial vessels and several dozen private charter yachts, and a variety of half-, full-, and multiday trips are available. Rates for trips on a large boat average $35 for half a day or $70 for three-quarters of a day. Or spring $100 for a 20-hour overnight trip to the Islas los Coronados, but call around first and compare prices. Rates are lower for kids, and discounts are often available for twilight sailings; charters or "limited load" rates are also available. The following outfitters offer short or extended outings with daily departures: **H & M Landing,** 2803 Emerson (ℂ 619/222-1144; www.hmlanding.com); **Lee Palm Sportfishers,** 2801 Emerson (ℂ 619/224-3857; www.redrooster3.com); **Point Loma Sportfishing,** 1403 Scott St. (ℂ 619/223-1627; www.pointlomasportfishing.com); and **Seaforth Sportfishing,** 1717 Quivira Rd. (ℂ 619/224-3383; www.seaforthlanding.com).

**GOLF**    San Diego County has 90-plus courses, and more than 50 of them are open to the public. For a full listing of area courses, visit **www.golfsd.com**, or request the *Golf Guide* from the San Diego Convention and Visitors Bureau (ℂ **619/236-1212;** www. sandiego.org). **San Diego Golf Reservations** (ℂ **866/701-4653** or 858/964-5980; www.sandiegogolf.com) can arrange tee times for you at the city's premiere greens. They will consult with you first, charging a $10 per person/per tee time coordination fee.

The city's most famous links are at the **Torrey Pines Golf Course** ★★, a pair of 18-hole championship courses on the cliffs between La Jolla and Del Mar. The biggest challenge, however, at Torrey Pines—home of the Buick Invitational Tournament, and the setting for the 2008 U.S. Open—is getting a tee time. Reservations are taken starting at 7pm, 7 days in advance, by automated telephone. Greens fees on the south course are $185 Monday through Friday, $205 Saturday and Sunday; the north course is $140 Monday through Friday, $150 Saturday and Sunday. Cart rentals are $32, and twilight rates are available. Golf packages double the cost but give you much better odds of actually getting onto the course. Tee times: ℂ **858/570-1234** (ℂ 858/452-3226 for the pro shop and packages; www.torreypinesgolfcourse.com).

Other acclaimed, newer links include the **Four Seasons Resort Aviara Golf Club** in Carlsbad (ℂ 760/603-6900; www.fourseasons.com), **The Grand Del Mar Golf Club** (ℂ 858/792-6200; www.thegrandgolfclub.com), **Maderas Golf Club** in Poway (ℂ 858/451-8100; www.maderasgolf.com), **Barona Creek** in Lakeside (ℂ 619/387-7018; www.barona.com), and **The Auld Course** in Chula Vista (ℂ 619/482-4666; www.theauldcourse.com). More convenient for most visitors is the **Riverwalk Golf Club** (ℂ 619/296-4653; www.riverwalkgc.com), links that wander along the Mission Valley floor. Nonresident greens fees, including cart, are $95 Monday through Thursday, $105 Friday through Sunday; twilight and bargain evening rates are available.

**HIKING & WALKING**    The best **beaches** for walking are Coronado, Pacific Beach, La Jolla Shores, and Torrey Pines, but pretty much any shore is a good choice. You can also walk around most of Mission Bay on a series of connected footpaths. If a four-legged friend is walking with you, head for Dog Beach in Ocean Beach or Fiesta Island in Mission Bay—two of the few areas where dogs can legally go unleashed. The **Coast Walk** offers supreme surf-line views above the bluffs of La Jolla. Other places for hikes listed earlier in this chapter include **Torrey Pines State Reserve** (p. 719) and **Cabrillo National Monument** (p. 716).

The **Sierra Club** sponsors many hikes in the San Diego area, and nonmembers are welcome to participate. Most are free. For a recorded message about outings, call ⓒ **619/299-1744,** or contact the office (ⓒ **619/299-1743**). Volunteers from the **Natural History Museum** (ⓒ **619/255-0203;** www.sdnhm.org) also lead nature walks throughout San Diego County.

**Walkabout International,** 4639 30th St., Suite C, San Diego (ⓒ **619/231-7463;** www.walkabout-int.org), sponsors more than 100 free walking tours every month. Led by local volunteers, they're listed on the website and hit all parts of the county, including the Gaslamp Quarter, La Jolla, and the beaches. Mountain hikes take place most Wednesdays and Saturdays.

**SAILING & MOTOR YACHTS**    Sailors can choose from among the calm waters of 4,600-acre **Mission Bay,** with its 26 miles of shoreline; the exciting **San Diego Bay,** which is one of the most beautiful natural harbors in the world; or the open **Pacific Ocean,** by sailing south to the Islas los Coronados (the trio of uninhabited islets on the Mexico side of the border).

The **Maritime Museum** (ⓒ **619/234-9153;** www.sdmaritime.org) offers sailing trips aboard the *Californian,* the official tall ship of the state, a replica of an 1847 cutter that sailed the coast during the Gold Rush. Half-day sails depart most days at 1pm from the Maritime Museum; cost is $30 for adults, $21 for seniors over 65, juniors ages 13 to 17 and active military, and $17 for kids 12 and under (not recommended for children under 10). Full-day sails, overnight trips to the Catalina Islands and week-long excursions up the coast are also offered; call or check the website for details.

Based at Shelter Island Marina, **Classic Sailing Adventures** (ⓒ **800/659-0141** or 619/224-0800; www.classicsailingadventures.com) offers two 4-hour sailing trips daily aboard *Soul Diversion,* a 38-foot Ericson. The afternoon cruise leaves at 1pm and a champagne sunset sail departs at 5pm. The yacht carries a maximum of six passengers (minimum two), and the $65-per-person price includes beverages and snacks. From mid-December through March the company offers similarly priced whale-watching excursions.

If you have sailing or boating experience, consider a nonchartered rental. **Seaforth Boat Rental,** 1641 Quivira Rd., Mission Bay (ⓒ **888/834-2628** or 619/223-1681; www.seaforthboatrental.com), has a variety of boats for the bay or the ocean. It rents 15- to 240-horsepower powerboats starting at $48 an hour, sailboats starting at $25 an hour, and jet skis starting at $80 an hour. Half- and full-day rates are available. Canoes, kayaks, and pedal boats are also for rent, as are fishing boats and equipment. Seaforth has a location downtown at the Marriott San Diego Hotel, 333 W. Harbor Dr. (ⓒ **619/239-2628**), and in Coronado at 1715 Strand Way (ⓒ **619/437-1514**). **Mission Bay Sportcenter,** 1010 Santa Clara Place (ⓒ **858/488-1004;** www.mission baysportcenter.com), rents sailboats, catamarans, sailboards, kayaks, and motorboats.

Prices range from $18 to $95 an hour, with discounts for 4-hour and full-day rentals. Sailing lessons are $85 per weekend.

**SCUBA DIVING & SNORKELING**   San Diego's underwater scene ranges from the magnificent giant kelp forests of Point Loma to a nautical graveyard off Mission Beach called Wreck Alley, where a 366-foot Canadian destroyer and other ships sit on the sea floor. The aquatic Ecological Reserve off the La Jolla Cove is adequate. Fishing and boating activity are banned in the 533-acre reserve, but diving and snorkeling is welcome. It's a reliable place to spot garibaldi, California's state fish, as well as giant black sea bass. Shore diving here, or at nearby La Jolla Shores, is common, and a number of dive shops will help set you up. Boat dives are the rule, however, particularly to the Islas los Coronados, a trio of uninhabited islets off Tijuana, where seals, sea lions, and eels cavort against a landscape of boulders.

The **San Diego Oceans Foundation** (© 619/523-1903; www.sdoceans.org) is devoted to the stewardship of local marine waters. The website contains good information about local diving opportunities. **San Diego Divers Supply,** 4004 Sports Arena Blvd. (© 619/224-3439) and 1084 Broadway (© 619/224-3228), will set you up with scuba and snorkeling equipment. **Scuba San Diego** (© 800/586-3483 or 619/260-1880; www.scubasandiego.com) is another good outfit.

**SURFING**   San Diego is a popular year-round surf destination. Some of the best spots include La Jolla Shores, Windansea, Pacific Beach, Mission Beach, Ocean Beach, and Imperial Beach. In North County you might consider Carlsbad State Beach and Oceanside. If you didn't bring your own board, they are available for rent at stands at many popular beaches. Local surf shops also rent equipment; they include **La Jolla Surf Systems,** 2132 Avenida de la Playa, La Jolla Shores (© 858/456-2777), and **Emerald City–The Boarding Source,** 1118 Orange Ave., Coronado (© 619/435-6677).

For surfing lessons, check with **San Diego Surfing Academy** (© 800/447-SURF or 760/230-1474; www.surfsdsa.com/index.htm), which offers lessons at Tourmaline in Pacific Beach and San Elijo State Beach in Cardiff by the Sea; and **Surf Diva** (© 858/454-8273; www.surfdiva.com), the world's first surfing school for women and girls, based in La Jolla.

## 9 Shopping

Okay, so San Diegans have embraced the suburban shopping mall with vigor, and many residents do the bulk of their shopping at two massive complexes in Mission Valley. Downtown has even adopted the mall concept at Horton Plaza.

Sales tax in San Diego is 7.75%, but savvy out-of-state shoppers avoid the tax by shipping larger items home at the point of purchase.

### DOWNTOWN

The Disneyland of shopping malls, **Horton Plaza** ⭐, 324 Horton Plaza (© 619/238-1596; www.westfield.com/hortonplaza), is in the heart of the revitalized city center. The multilevel facility has more than 130 specialty shops, including art galleries, clothing and shoe stores, and several fun shops for kids. There's a 14-screen cinema, a performing arts theater, three major department stores, several restaurants, and a roster of short-order cook shops. It transcends its genre with a conglomeration of rambling paths, bridges, towers, piazzas, sculptures, fountains, and live greenery. Designed by the local Jerde Partnership, Horton Plaza opened in 1985 to rave reviews and provided an initial catalyst for the Gaslamp's redevelopment. The parking garage (3 hr. free with validation) is confusing, and temporarily losing your car is part of the Horton Plaza experience.

The ersatz, 14-acre **Seaport Village,** 849 W. Harbor Dr. (© **619/239-8180;** www. seaportvillage.com), alongside San Diego Bay, was built to resemble a small Cape Cod community, but the 57 shops are decidedly Southern California cutesy. Still the waterfront atmosphere is pleasant, and 2 hours' free parking is provided with purchase.

Seekers of serious art, design, and home furnishings should head to Little Italy. The conglomeration of hip stores and galleries along Kettner Boulevard, from Laurel to Date Streets, has become known as the Kettner Art and Design District. Among the highlights are **Vetro** (© **619/546-5120**) for vintage glass art; **Mixture** (© **619/ 239-4788**) for modern furniture and accessories; and **David Zapf Gallery** (© **619/ 232-5004**) and **Scott White Contemporary Art** (© **619/501-5689**), two of the city's most prominent galleries.

## HILLCREST/UPTOWN

Compact Hillcrest is an ideal shopping destination for unique and often wacky shops, with many vintage-clothing stores and memorabilia markets as well as recognizable chains, bakeries, and cafes. Start at the neighborhood's axis, the intersection of University and Fifth Avenues. Street parking is available.

A half-mile east of Hillcrest is the start of the **Adams Avenue Antique Row.** It lies along Park Boulevard (beginning at Robinson Ave.) and on Adams Avenue (extending from Park east to around 40th St.). Antiques and collectibles stores, vintage-clothing boutiques, and dusty used-book stores line this sprawling L-shaped district, providing many hours of happy browsing and treasure hunting. Plenty of coffeehouses, pubs, and small restaurants will break up the excursion. For more information and an area brochure with a map, contact the **Adams Avenue Business Association** (© **619/282-7329;** www.GoThere.com/AdamsAve).

## OLD TOWN & MISSION VALLEY

**Old Town Historic Park** is a restoration of some of San Diego's historic sites and adobe structures, a number of which now house shops that cater to tourists. Many have a "general-store" theme and carry gourmet treats and inexpensive Mexican crafts alongside the obligatory T-shirts, baseball caps, and other San Diego–emblazoned souvenirs. New, but in keeping with the park's old California theme, **Plaza del Pasado,** 2754 Calhoun St. (© **619/297-3100;** www.plazadelpasado.com), encompasses 11 specialty shops, 3 restaurants, and a boutique hotel. Costumed employees, special events and activities, and strolling musicians heighten the festive flavor here.

Mission Valley is home to two giant malls (**Fashion Valley** and **Mission Valley**), with more than enough stores to satisfy any shopper, and free parking. Both can be reached via San Diego Trolley from downtown. Book lovers will find local outposts of **Barnes & Noble,** 7610 Hazard Center Dr. (© **619/220-0175**), and **Borders,** 1072 Camino del Rio N. (© **619/295-2201**).

## MISSION BAY & THE BEACHES

The beach communities all offer laid-back shopping in typical California fashion: plenty of surf shops, recreational gear, and casual garb stores. If you're in need of a new bikini, the best selection is at **Pilar's Beach Wear,** 3745 Mission Blvd., Pacific Beach (© **858/488-3056**), where dozens of racks are meticulously organized. Across the street is **Liquid Foundation Surf Shop,** 3731 Mission Blvd. (© **858/488-3260**), which specializes in board shorts for guys.

San Diego's greatest concentration of antiques stores is in the **Ocean Beach Antique District,** along the 4800 block of Newport Avenue. Several of the stores are mall-style, featuring multiple dealers under one roof. The hundreds of individual sellers cover the gamut—everything from Asian antiquities to vintage watches to mid-20th-century collectibles. A good place to start is the **Newport Ave. Antique Center,** 4836 Newport Ave. (© **619/224-1994**), with 18,000 square feet of retail, and even a small espresso bar. Most of the O.B. antiques stores are open daily from 10am to 6pm, with reduced hours Sunday.

## LA JOLLA

It's clear from the look of La Jolla's village that shopping is a major pastime in this upscale community of moneyed professionals and retirees. Women's-clothing boutiques tend toward conservative and costly, like those lining Girard and Prospect streets (Ann Taylor, Armani Exchange, Polo/Ralph Lauren, Talbots, and Sigi's Boutique), but you'll also find mainstream (that is, less pricey) venues such as Banana Republic and Dansk.

Even if you're not in the market for furnishings and accessories, the many home-decor boutiques make for great window-shopping, as do La Jolla's ubiquitous jewelers: Swiss watches, tennis bracelets, gems, and pearl necklaces sparkle at you from windows along every street.

## 10 San Diego After Dark

Historically, San Diego's cultural scene has lounged in the shadows of Los Angeles and San Francisco, content to take a back seat to the beach, the zoo, and the perfect weather. But the dot-com influence brought new blood and money into the city, and arts organizations reaped the benefits. The biggest winner was the San Diego Symphony, which in 2002 received the largest single donation to a symphony anywhere, ever. But don't think "after-dark" activity in this city is limited to high-falutin' affairs for the Lexus crowd. Night life is also *lively*, with rock and pop concerts, swank martini bars, and nightclubs.

## THE PERFORMING ARTS

For a rundown of major events, the San Diego Convention and Visitors Bureau has an **Art + Sol** campaign which provides a calendar of events and profiles of 11 member institutions; check it out at www.sandiegoartandsol.com. The San Diego Performing Arts League produces *What's Playing?,* a performing-arts guide, every 2 months. You can pick one up at the ARTS TIX booth or write to 110 W. C St., Suite 1414, San Diego, CA 92101 (© **619/238-0700;** www.sandiegoperforms.com).

Half-price tickets to theater, music, and dance events are available at the **ARTS TIX** booth, in Horton Plaza Park at Broadway and Third Avenue. For a daily listing of offerings, call © **619/497-5000** or visit www.sandiegoperforms.com.

The biggest news in San Diego's arts and culture scene is the ongoing development of **NTC Promenade** in Point Loma (© **619/226-1491**; www.ntcpromenade.org), the remnants of a huge Navy base transformed into a flagship hub of creative activity. The project includes office, studio, and performance space for more than a dozen arts groups.

## THEATER

A complex of three performance venues inside Balboa Park, **The Old Globe** ★★ is best known for the 581-seat Old Globe Theatre (fashioned after Shakespeare's), but it also includes the 225-seat Cassius Carter Centre Stage and the 612-seat open-air Lowell Davies Festival Theatre. Between them, they mount 15 plays annually, from world premieres of subsequent Broadway arrivals such as *Dirty Rotten Scoundrels* or *The Full Monty*, to excellent summer Shakespeare. Leading performers regularly grace the stage, and tours are offered Saturday and Sunday at 10:30am ($5 per person). Tickets range from $19 to $55. For more information, call © 619/239-2255 or log on to www.oldglobe.org.

Founded in 1947 by Gregory Peck, Dorothy McGuire, and Mel Ferrer, **La Jolla Playhouse** 🎭🎭 won a 1993 Tony Award for outstanding regional theater. With the recent completion of a third theater and the addition of an on-site restaurant at its UCSD location, the Playhouse plans to host productions, staged readings, and educational programs year-round. Past hits include Matthew Broderick in *How to Succeed in Business Without Really Trying*, and the world premieres of *Thoroughly Modern Millie*, *The Who's Tommy*, and *Big River*. Tickets are $29 to $60, but for each show, one Saturday matinee is a "pay what you can" performance, and every night unsold tickets are $15 each in a "public rush" sale 10 minutes before curtain call. For more information, call © 858/550-1010 (www.lajollaplayhouse.com).

Also noteworthy are **San Diego Repertory Theatre,** which mounts plays and musicals at the Lyceum Theatre in Horton Plaza (© **619/544-1000;** www.san diegorep.com), and **Lamb's Players Theatre** (© **619/437-0600;** www.lambsplayers. org), a professional rep company based in Coronado. Founded in 1948, the **San Diego Junior Theatre,** at Balboa Park's Casa del Prado Theatre (© **619/239-8355;** fax 619/239-5048; www.juniortheatre.com), is the country's oldest continuously producing children's theater. Students make up the cast and crew of nine shows each year.

## CLASSICAL MUSIC, OPERA & DANCE

Like a phoenix from the ashes, the **San Diego Symphony** 🎭 survived disaster with the announcement in 2002 of a $120-million bequest by Joan and Irwin Jacobs (of Qualcomm Inc.). The donation allows the organization—now "placed firmly on the nation's musical landscape" (the *New York Times*)—to lure top talent, including resident conductor, Jahja Ling. The symphony's home is the restored Fox Theatre, a 1929-era, French-rococo-style downtown landmark, now known as Symphony Hall. The season runs October through May, while a Summer Pops series, with programs devoted to an eclectic mix of big band, Broadway, Tchaikovsky, and sundry "pops," is held weekends late June through August at the Embarcadero. Tickets range $12 to $85. For additional information, call © 619/235-0804 (www.sandiegosymphony.com).

The respected **La Jolla Music Society** 🎭 has been bringing marquee names to San Diego since 1968, including Pinchas Zukerman, Emanuel Ax, Joshua Bell, and the American Ballet Theatre. Most of the 40-plus annual shows are held October through May in La Jolla's Sherwood Auditorium, at the Museum of Contemporary Art. The annual highlight is SummerFest, a 3-week series of concerts, forums, open rehearsals, talks, and artist encounters. It's held in early August and broadcast live on National Public Radio. Tickets range from $20 to $105; for more information, call © 858/459-3728 (www.ljms.org).

The **San Diego Opera** 🎭🎭 has grown into one of the community's most successful arts organizations. The annual season runs from late January through mid-May, with five offerings at downtown's 3,000-seat Civic Theatre, ranging from well-trod warhorses like *Madame Butterfly* to new productions such as 2005's *Vanessa*, all performed by local singers and name talent from around the world. Tickets run $20 to $150. For more information, call © 619/533-7000 (box office) or 619/232-7636 (www.sdopera.com).

The **San Diego Dance Alliance** is the umbrella organization for the local dance community (© 619/230-8623; www.sandiegodance.org). The alliance puts on the **Nations of San Diego International Dance Festival,** held each January and spotlighting the city's ethnic dance groups and emerging artists. The website provides links to 45 local dance outfits.

## MOVIES

My favorite venue is Pacific's **Gaslamp Stadium,** Fifth Avenue at G Street, downtown (© 619/232-0400); the 15 theaters all offer stadium seating with large screens and great sound systems. The AMC chain operates swarming complexes in both the **Mission Valley** and **Fashion Valley** shopping centers (call both at © 858/558-2AMC); both have free parking but popular films sell out early on weekends. Current American independent and foreign films play at Landmark's five-screen **Hillcrest Cinema,** 3965 Fifth Ave., Hillcrest, which offers 3 hours of free parking (© 619/294-2021); the **Ken Cinema,** 4061 Adams Ave., Kensington near Hillcrest (© 619/283-5909); and the four-screen **La Jolla Village,** 8879 Villa La Jolla Dr., La Jolla, also with free parking (© 858/453-7831). Only in San Diego, **Movies Before the Mast** (© 619/234-9153) are screened aboard the *Star of India* at the waterfront Maritime Museum. Movies of the nautical genre are shown on a special "screensail" Fridays and Saturdays at 7pm during July and August

## THE CLUB & MUSIC SCENE

The most comprehensive listings are found in the free *San Diego Weekly Reader* (www.sdreader.com), published Thursdays and distributed all over town (in tourist areas, it's a condensed version called the *Weekly*).

### LIVE ROCK, POP, FOLK, JAZZ & BLUES

San Diego's new downtown **House of Blues**, 1055 Fifth Ave. (© 619/299-2583; www.hob.com), features an eclectic lineup of rock, blues, reggae, and world music. You'll find live music nightly at **Croce's Nightclubs,** 802 Fifth Ave. at F Street (© 619/233-4355; www.croces.com), a mainstream gathering place in the Gaslamp. Two separate clubs operate a couple doors apart—one provides a venue for traditional jazz, the other is rhythm and blues on Friday and Saturday. Near Little Italy is **The Casbah,** 2501 Kettner Blvd. at Laurel (© 619/232-HELL; www.casbahmusic.com), which is a total dive but boasts a well-earned rep for showcasing alternative and rock bands that either are, were, or will be famous. In summer, San Diegans flock to **Humphrey's** ☜, 2241 Shelter Island Dr. (© 619/523-1010; www.humphreysconcerts.com), a 1,300-seat outdoor venue on the water. The lineup covers the spectrum of entertainment—rock and jazz to comedy, blues, folk, and international music.

### DANCE CLUBS & DISCOS

The Gaslamp Quarter is the hub of nightlife in San Diego. **On Broadway,** 615 Broadway at Sixth Avenue (© 619/231-0011), is a swanky hangout in a converted 1925 bank building with five rooms and a 90,000-watt sound system pumping out a range of styles. The former vault is now a sushi bar and billiards parlor. This high-end spot, which is open to the public only on Friday and Saturday, may soon have company at the top of the heap. **Stingaree** (454 Sixth Ave.; © 619/544-0867) due to open in late November 2005, is a three-level, 22,000-square-foot megaclub at Sixth Avenue and Island Street. It aims to be *the* place to go for a big night out. Miami South Beach Art Deco flair meets high-tech dance club at **Deco's,** 731 Fifth Ave. (© 619/696-3326), which means candy-colored neon, "VIP beds," and an open-air lounge. **The**

**Bitter End,** 770 Fifth Ave. (© **619/338-9300;** www.thebitterend.com), has three levels for its specialty-martini bar, late-night dance club, and relaxing cocktail lounge. For Latin-themed fun, visit **Olé Madrid,** 751 Fifth Ave. (© **619/557-0146**), a loud, energetic club with tapas and sangria from the adjoining Spanish restaurant; or **Sevilla,** 555 Fourth Ave. (© **619/233-5979**), where you can learn to salsa (lessons Tues–Thurs and Sun at 8pm, followed by live bands) or nibble on tapas.

## BARS & COCKTAIL LOUNGES

**Beach,** the rooftop bar of the W Hotel at 421 B St. downtown (© 619/231-8220), features a heated sand floor, cabanas, and fire pit. **Altitude,** 660 K St. (© 619/696-0234), 22 stories up, and **Jbar,** 616 J St. (© 619/531-8744), join the open-air lounge derby. San Diego's ultimate bar with a view, though, is **Top of the Hyatt,** 1 Market Place, at Harbor Drive (© 619/232-1234). It's on the 40th floor of the West Coast's tallest waterfront building. The **Onyx Room,** 852 Fifth Ave., Gaslamp Quarter (© 619/235-6699), is an underground (literally) club where the atmosphere is lounge, the drinks are up, and the music is cool. Besides the sleek, retro-cool atmosphere at **Airport,** 2400 India St. (© 619/685-3881), the big draw is the back patio where you can practically touch the airplanes as they come in for a landing at nearby Lindbergh Field.

## GAY & LESBIAN CLUBS & BARS

The **Brass Rail,** 3796 Fifth Ave., Hillcrest (© 619/298-2233), is San Diego's oldest gay bar, with energetic dancing, bright lights, and a come-as-you-are attitude. Across the street from one another, **Numbers,** 3811 Park Blvd. (near University Ave.), Hillcrest (© 619/294-9005) and **The Flame,** 3780 Park Blvd. (© **619/295-4163**), are popular dance emporiums with theme nights. **Bourbon Street,** 4612 Park Blvd., University Heights (© **619/291-4043**), is a jazzy and elegant piano bar with a New Orleans–esque patio. Finally, **Rich's,** 1051 University Ave., between 10th and 11th avenues (© 619/295-2195 for upcoming events; http://richs-sandiego.com), is a high-energy, high-image dance club, with house music and a video bar.

## 11 North County Beach Towns

The necklace of picturesque beach towns that dot the coast of San Diego County from Del Mar to Oceanside make great day trips for sun worshipers and surfers. Be forewarned: You'll be tempted to spend the night.

## ESSENTIALS

It's a snap: **Del Mar** is only 18 miles north of downtown San Diego; **Carlsbad** is about 33 miles. If you're driving, follow I-5 north; Del Mar, Solana Beach, Encinitas, Carlsbad, and Oceanside all have freeway exits. The farthest point, Oceanside, will take about 45 minutes. The other choice by car is to wander up the coast road, known along the way as Camino del Mar, the "PCH" (Pacific Coast Hwy.), Old Highway 101, and County Highway S21.

From downtown San Diego, the **Coaster** commuter train provides service to Solana Beach, Encinitas, Carlsbad, and Oceanside, and **Amtrak** stops in Solana Beach—just a few minutes north of Del Mar—and Oceanside. The Coaster makes the trip almost hourly weekdays, four times on Saturday; Amtrak passes through 11 times daily each way. Call © 619/685-4900 for local transit information, or for Amtrak call © **800/ USA-RAIL** (www.amtrak.com).

## DEL MAR 🏖🏖

Just 18 miles up the coast lies Del Mar, a small community with just more than 4,500 inhabitants in a 2-square-mile municipality. The town has adamantly maintained its independence, eschewing incorporation into the city of San Diego. It's one of the most upscale communities in the greater San Diego area, yet Del Mar somehow manages to maintain a casual, small-town personality and charm. Come summer, the town swells as visitors flock in for the thoroughbred horseracing season and the county's San Diego Fair.

The history and popularity of Del Mar are inextricably linked to the **Del Mar Racetrack & Fairgrounds,** 2260 Jimmy Durante Blvd. (© **858/755-1161;** www.delmarfair.com). In 1933, Bing Crosby developed the Del Mar Turf Club, enlisting the help of Pat O'Brien and other celebrity friends. Soon, Hollywood stars like Lucille Ball, Desi Arnaz, Betty Grable, and Bob Hope were seen around Del Mar, and the town experienced a resurgence. The grandstand is built in the Spanish Mission style of the original structure. Racing season is late July through mid-September.

Two excellent beaches flank Del Mar: **Torrey Pines State Beach** to the south and **Del Mar State Beach.** Both are wide, well-patrolled strands popular for sunbathing, swimming, and surfing (in marked areas). The sand stretches north to the mouth of the San Dieguito Lagoon, where people bring their dogs for a romp in the sea. Beyond the surf and the turf, the hub of activities for most residents and visitors is **Del Mar Plaza,** 1555 Camino del Mar, an open-air shopping center with fountains, sculptures palazzo-style terraces, good restaurants and shops, and super views of the sea, especially at sunset.

For more information about Del Mar, contact or visit the **Del Mar Regional Chamber of Commerce Visitor Information Center,** 1104 Camino del Mar #1, Del Mar, CA 92014 (© **858/755-4844;** www.delmarchamber.org), which also distributes a detailed folding map of the area. Open hours vary according to volunteer staffing but usually approximate weekday business hours. The city-run website is www.delmar.ca.us.

### WHERE TO STAY

**Del Mar Motel on the Beach** *Finds* The only property in Del Mar right on the beach, this simply furnished little white-stucco motel has been here since 1946. All rooms are of good size and well kept (except for a number of worn-out lampshades). Upstairs units have one king-size bed; downstairs rooms have two double beds. Most of them have little in the way of a view, but two oceanfront rooms, dressed up with faux plants and larger bathrooms, sit right over the sand. It's a good choice for beach lovers, because you can walk along the shore for miles, and families can be comfortable knowing a lifeguard station is right next door, as are popular seaside restaurants Poseidon and Jake's.

1702 Coast Blvd. (at 17th St.), Del Mar, CA 92014. © **800/223-8449** for reservations, or 858/755-1534. www.del marmotelonthebeach.com. 44 units (upper units w/shower only). $149–$279 double. AE, DC, DISC, MC, V. Take I-5 to Via de la Valle exit. Go west, then south on Hwy. 101 (Pacific Coast Hwy.); veer west onto Coast Blvd. *In room:* A/C, TV, fridge, coffeemaker.

**L'Auberge Del Mar Resort and Spa** 🏖🏖🏖 On the site of the historic Hotel del Mar (1909–69), the luxurious yet intimate L'Auberge manages to attract casual weekenders as well as the rich-and-famous equestrian set, who flock here during summer racing season. In 2002 the resort enhanced the lower-level full-service spa, polished up the poolside, and revamped the dining room. Guest rooms exude the elegance of a European country house, complete with marble bathrooms, architectural accents, well-placed casual seating, and the finest bed linens and appointments. Twenty-five rooms boast fireplaces; all have a private balcony or terrace (several with an unadvertised view of the ocean). The hotel is across the street from Del Mar's main shopping and dining scene, and a short jog from the sand. **J. Taylor's,** the hotel's California/Mediterranean dining room, easily stands as one of Del Mar's finest restaurants.

1540 Camino del Mar (at 15th St.), Del Mar, CA 92014. ℂ **800/245-9757** or 858/259-1515. Fax 858/755-4940. www.laubergedelmar.com. 120 units. $300–$365 double; from $600 suite. AE, DC, DISC, MC, V. Valet parking $19. Take I-5 to Del Mar Heights Rd. west, then turn right onto Camino del Mar Rd. **Amenities:** Restaurant; lounge; 2 swimming pools; tennis courts; indoor/outdoor fitness center; full-service spa; whirlpool; concierge; courtesy van; room service (Sun–Thurs 6am–11pm, Fri–Sat 6am–midnight); laundry/dry-cleaning service. *In room:* A/C, TV w/pay movies, dataport, minibar, coffeemaker, hair dryer, iron.

## WHERE TO DINE

Head to the upper level of the centrally located Del Mar Plaza, at Camino del Mar and 15th Street. Here you'll find **Il Fornaio Cucina Italiana** ⭐ (ℂ **858/755-8876**) for pleasing Italian cuisine and an *enoteca* (wine bar) that is great for ocean views; **Pacifica Del Mar** ⭐⭐ (ℂ **858/792-0476**), which serves outstanding seafood; and **Epazote** ⭐ (ℂ **858/259-9966**), where Southwestern meets Asian, with a terrific house margarita.

**Arterra** ⭐⭐⭐ CALIFORNIA   The name of this restaurant derives from "art of the earth." Under the stewardship of Bay Area chef Bradley Ogden, the name is no mere marketing gimmick. Housed in a drab, modern Marriott hotel, the broad dining room is impressive, cast in gold and purple tones, with accents of glass and copper, and plush leather banquettes. On-site kitchen master Carl Shroeder crafts his menu based on what's on the shelves at Chino or Be Wise, the Encinitas farms specializing in heirloom vegetables. Needless to say, Ogden regularly adapts the menu to meet the schedule of mother earth. You'll never eat rigid hot-house tomatoes in winter, when tomatoes don't grow naturally in San Diego. Come summer, you'll feast on a plate of ravishing heirloom tomatoes lightly garnished with pickled corn and warm goat cheese. Patrons can also sample four-, five- and seven-course chef's tasting meals with wine pairings. The breakfast, by the way, is superlative, and worth the trip by itself.

11966 El Camino Real (next to I-5 in the Marriott Del Mar), Carmel Valley. ℂ **858/369-6032.** www.arterrarestaurant. com. Main courses $21–$32 dinner, $13–$21 lunch, $10–$15 breakfast. AE, DC, DISC, MC, V. Daily 5:30–9:30pm; Mon–Fri 6:30–10:30am and 11:30am–2pm; Sat–Sun 7–11:30am. Free parking w/validation, or $3 for valet parking.

**Jake's Del Mar** ⭐ SEAFOOD/CALIFORNIA   This Hawaiian-owned seafood restaurant with a fabulous view occupies a building originally constructed in 1910. Jake's has a perfect seat beside the sand, and diners get straight-on views of the beach scene—sunbathers, surfers, and the occasional school of dolphins passing by. Lunch here is *Endless Summer,* no matter the weather. The predictable menu can't live up to the panorama, but it's prepared competently and service is swift (too swift, actually—don't let them rush you). At lunch you'll find sandwiches and salads. Dinner brings in the big boys: Maine lobster tails, giant scampi, rack of lamb, and so on. To enjoy the scene without the wallet wallop, come for happy hour when a shorter bar/bistro menu is half price and the mai tais are just $3.

1660 Coast Blvd. (at 15th St.), Del Mar. ℂ **858/755-2002.** Main courses $9–$15 lunch, $16–$42 dinner. AE, DISC, MC, V. Daily 5–9pm; Tues–Sat 11:30am–2:30pm; Sun brunch 11am–2pm. Happy hour Mon–Fri 4–6pm, Sat 2:30–4:30pm. Valet parking $2–$3. Bus: 101.

## SOLANA BEACH, ENCINITAS & CARLSBAD ⍟

North of Del Mar and a 45-minute drive from downtown San Diego, the pretty communities of Solana Beach, Encinitas, and Carlsbad provide many reasons to linger on the California coast: good swimming and surfing beaches, small-town atmosphere, an abundance of antiques and gift shops, and a seasonal display of the region's most beautiful flowers.

Carlsbad was named for Karlsbad, Czechoslovakia, because of the similar mineral waters (some say they're curative) that they both produced, although the town's once-famous artesian well has long been plugged up. Carlsbad is also a noted commercial-flower-growing region, along with its neighbor Encinitas. A colorful display can be seen at **Carlsbad Ranch** (© 760/431-0352) each spring, when 45 acres of solid ranunculus fields bloom into a breathtaking rainbow visible even from the freeway. In December, the nurseries are alive with holiday poinsettias.

The **Solana Beach Visitor Center** is near the train station at 103 N. Cedros (© 858/350-6006; www.solanabeachchamber.com). The **Encinitas Visitors Center** is located in a nondescript shopping mall immediately west of the I-5, at 138 Encinitas Blvd. (© 800/953-6041 or 760/753-6041; www.encinitaschamber.com). The **Carlsbad Visitor Information Center,** 400 Carlsbad Village Dr. (in the old Santa Fe Depot; © 800/227-5722 or 760/434-6093; www.carlsbadca.org), has information on flower fields and nursery touring.

### FUN THINGS TO SEE & DO

Going from south to north, the main area of activity for **Solana Beach** is South Cedros Avenue, parallel to the Pacific Coast Highway, 1 block east. In a 2-block stretch are many of San Diego County's best furniture and home-design shops, antiques stores, art dealers, and boutiques selling imported goods. The **Belly Up Tavern** is an appealing concert venue that often hosts high-profile acts.

In **Encinitas,** everyone flocks to **Moonlight Beach,** where you'll find plenty of facilities, including free parking, volleyball nets, restrooms, showers, picnic tables, and fire grates. The beach entrance is at the end of B Street (at Encinitas Blvd.). A mile south is the appropriately serene **Swami's Beach,** named for the adjacent spiritual retreat (see below). This lovely little beach is surfer central in the winter. It adjoins little-known **Boneyard Beach,** directly to the north. Here, low-tide coves provide shelter for romantics and nudists; this isolated stretch can be reached only from Swami's Beach. There's a free parking lot at Swami's, plus restrooms and a picnic area.

The **Self Realization Fellowship** was founded in 1920 by guru Paramahansa Yogananda, and these exotic-looking domes are what remain of the retreat originally built in 1937 (the rest was built too close to the cliff-edge and tumbled into the sea). Today the site is a spiritual sanctuary for holistic healers and their followers, with meditation gardens and a gift shop that sells Fellowship publications and arts and crafts from India. The serene, immaculate gardens line a cliff, with beautiful flower displays in spring and koi ponds—a terrific place to cool off on a hot day. One enters the gardens at 215 K St., at the south end of Encinitas; they're open Tuesday through Sunday, and admission is free. The bookstore is located at 939 Second St., between J and K streets (© 760/436-7220; www.yogananda-srf.org).

**Carlsbad** is a great place for antiquing. Whether you're a serious shopper or seriously window-shopping, park the car and stroll the 3 blocks of **State Street** between Oak and Beech streets. There are about two dozen shops in this part of town, where diagonal street parking and welcoming merchants lend a village atmosphere. Wares range from estate jewelry to country quilts, from inlaid sideboards to Depression glass.

**Carlsbad State Beach** runs alongside downtown. It's a great place to stroll along a wide concrete walkway, surrounded by like-minded outdoors types walking, jogging, and in-line skating, even at night (thanks to good lighting). Enter on Ocean Boulevard at Tamarack Avenue; there's a $4 fee per vehicle. South of town is **South Carlsbad State Beach,** almost 3 miles of cobblestone-strewn sand. A state-run campground at the north end is immensely popular year-round, and the southern portion is favored by area surfers. There's a $4 fee at the beach's entrance, along Carlsbad Boulevard at Poinsettia Lane.

**LEGOLAND California** ★ *Kids*   The ultimate monument to the world's most famous plastic building blocks, LEGOLAND is the third such theme park—following branches in Denmark and Britain that proved enormously successful. In addition to 5,000 Lego models, the Carlsbad park is beautifully landscaped with 1,360 bonsai trees and other plants from around the world, and features more than 50 rides, shows, and attractions. Attractions include hands-on interactive displays; a life-size menagerie of animals; scale models of international landmarks (the Eiffel Tower, Sydney Opera House, and so on)—all constructed of real LEGO bricks. To give the park a little more weight for older kids, there are three relatively gentle roller coasters, but the park is geared toward children ages 2 to 12. The newest attraction, **Knights' Tournament**, is a "robo-coaster" that allows you to choose the intensity of your ride experience. *A touring tip:* When the park opens, many visitors hop in line at the first rides they encounter, but it's better to head to the back side of the park where lines are shorter for the first hour or so.

1 Legoland Dr. ✆ 877/534-6526 or 760/918-LEGO. www.legoland.com. $47 adults, $39 seniors and kids 3–12, free for children under 3. AE, DISC, MC, V. Summer (late June to Aug) daily 10am–8pm; off season Thurs–Mon 10am–5 or 6pm. Closed Tues–Wed Sept–May, but open daily during Christmas and Easter vacation periods. Parking $8. From I-5 take the Cannon Rd. exit east, following signs for Legoland Dr.

**Quail Botanical Gardens** ★   You don't have to possess a green thumb to be satisfied with an afternoon at this wonderful botanical facility, with the country's largest bamboo collection, plus 30 acres of California natives, exotic tropicals, palms, cacti, Mediterranean, Australian, and other unusual collections. Scenic walkways, trails, and benches crisscross this serene compound. Guided tours take place Saturdays at 10am, and you can shop afterward at the on-site gift shop and nursery. The gardens are free on the first Tuesday of the month.

230 Quail Gardens Dr., Encinitas. ✆ 760/436-3036. www.qbgardens.com. Admission $8 adults; $5 students, seniors, and military; $3 children 3–12; free for children under 3. AE, MC, V. Daily 9am–5pm. From San Diego take I-5 north to Encinitas Blvd.; go half mile east, left on Quail Gardens Dr.

## WHERE TO STAY

**Beach Terrace Inn**   At Carlsbad's only beachside hostelry (others are across the road or a little farther away), the rooms and the swimming pool/whirlpool all have ocean views. This downtown Best Western's scenic location, tucked between rows of high-rent beach cottages, is its best quality. The rooms are extra-large, and although they suffer from generic, "furnished bachelor pad"–style interiors, some have balconies, fireplaces, and kitchenettes. Suites are affordable and have separate living rooms and bedrooms, making this a good choice for families. VCRs and videos are available at the front desk. You can walk everywhere from here—except LEGOLAND, which is a 5-minute drive away.

2775 Ocean St., Carlsbad, CA 92008. (℃ 800/433-5415 or 760/729-5951. Fax 760/729-1078. www.beachterrace inn.com. 49 units. $165 double; from $215 suite. Children 12 and under stay free in parent's room. Extra person $20. Rates include continental breakfast. AE, DC, DISC, MC, V. Free parking. **Amenities:** Outdoor pool; whirlpool; self-service laundry; dry-cleaning service. *In room:* A/C, TV w/pay movies, dataport, fridge, coffeemaker, hair dryer, iron, safe.

**Four Seasons Resort Aviara** ★★★  In 1997 the Four Seasons chain opened its first oceanview golf-and-tennis resort in the continental United States. Aviara quickly won over skeptical local residents, who head here for summer jazz concerts and an exceptional Friday night seafood buffet. When not wielding club or racquet, guests can lie by the dramatically positioned pool, relax in a series of carefully landscaped gardens, or luxuriate in the expanded spa, where treatments incorporate regional flowers and herbs. The hotel's **Vivace** restaurant is also one of the county's most elegant dining destinations. Rooms are decorated with soothing neutrals, with nature prints of the many birds in the surrounding Batiquitos Lagoon. In fact, the name Aviara is a nod to the egrets, herons, cranes, and 130 additional bird species nesting in the protected coastal wetlands. The hotel's Arnold Palmer–designed golf course was designed to keep the wetlands intact, and incorporates native marshlike plants throughout its 18 holes to help blend with the surroundings. The once-barren hills around the Four Seasons have since been built up with multimillion-dollar homes, but you can quickly escape to the wildness of the lagoon on a nature trail with several different access points.

7100 Four Seasons Point, Carlsbad, CA 92009. (℃ 800/332-3442 or 760/603-6800. Fax 760/603-6801. www.four seasons.com/aviara. 329 units. From $395 double; from $620 suite. Kids 17 and under stay free in parent's room. AE, DISC, MC, V. Valet parking $18. From I-5, take Poinsettia Lane east to Aviara Pkwy. S. **Amenities:** 4 restaurants; 2 lounges; 2 outdoor pools; golf course (see above); 6 tennis courts; health club; 15,000-sq.-ft. spa; whirlpool; bike rental; concierge; business center; 24-hr. room service; in-room massage; babysitting; laundry/dry-cleaning service. *In room:* A/C, TV w/pay movies, dataport, minibar, coffeemaker, hair dryer, iron, safe.

**Pelican Cove Inn** ★  Two blocks from the beach, this Cape Cod–style bed-and-breakfast hideaway combines romance with luxury. Hosts Kris and Nancy Nayudu see to your every need, from furnishing guest rooms with soft feather beds and down comforters to providing beach chairs and towels or preparing a picnic basket (with 24-hr. notice). Each room features a fireplace and private entrance; some have private spa tubs. The Pacific room is most spacious, while the airy La Jolla room has bay windows and a cupola ceiling. You can eat breakfast in the garden if weather permits. Courtesy transportation from the Carlsbad or Oceanside train stations is available.

320 Walnut Ave., Carlsbad, CA 92008. (℃ 888/PEL-COVE or 760/434-5995. www.pelican-cove.com. 10 units. $90–$210 double. Rates include full breakfast. Extra person $15. AE, MC, V. Free parking. From downtown Carlsbad, follow Carlsbad Blvd. south to Walnut Ave.; turn left and drive 2½ blocks. *In room:* TV, no phone.

**WHERE TO DINE**

Always crowded, **Fidel's** is known for reliably tasty Mexican food and kickin' margaritas. The restaurant has a location in Solana Beach at 607 Valley Ave. (℃ 858/755-5292), and there's a **Fidel's Norte** branch in Carlsbad at 3003 Carlsbad Blvd. (℃ 760/729-0903).

In Encinitas look for **Vigilucci's,** 505 S. Hwy. 101 ( ℃ 760/942-7332). The fragrance of garlic always draws a crowd here for authentic southern Italy trattoria fare served in a lively atmosphere, accented with old-world touches such as stained glass and a grand mahogany bar. **Meritage** ★, 897 S. Coast Hwy. 101 (℃ 760/634-3350), is an appealing charmer that embraces light California cuisine. On Monday and Wednesday nights, almost all bottles are half off. At **Siamese Basil,** 527 S. Coast Hwy. 101 (℃ 760/753-3940), an innocuous facade and bland interior belie a friendly attitude and well-deserved reputation for zesty Thai food. Spice levels range from toddler-safe 1 to fire-alarm 10.

The architectural centerpiece of Carlsbad is **Neiman's,** 300 Carlsbad Village Drive. (© 760/729-4131; www.neimans.com), a restored Victorian mansion complete with turrets, cupolas, and waving flags. Inside, there's a casual cafe and bar; the Sunday brunch is a vast buffet of breakfast and lunch items, and the daily happy hour (11am–6pm) offers draft beers and well drinks for $2. Most evenings feature live music, a DJ, or karaoke. In the Carlsbad Premium Outlets shopping center, **Belle-fleur,** 5610 Paseo del Norte (© 760/603-1919; www.bellefleur.com), celebrates the "wine country experience," with wood-fired grills, a tasting bar, and glassed-in aging room. Lunchtime sandwiches and salads surpass shopping-mall standards.

## 12  Julian: Gold, Apple Pies & a Slice of Small-Town California

60 miles NE of San Diego; 31 miles W of Anza-Borrego Desert State Park

A trip to Julian (pop. 3,000) is a trip back in time. The old gold-mining town, now best known for its apples, has a handful of cute B&Bs, but its popularity is based on the fact that it provides a chance for city-weary folks to get away from it all. It's at its best on weekdays, when things are a little quieter.

People first ventured into these fertile hills—elevation 4,225 feet—in search of gold in the late 1860s. They discovered it in 1870 near where the Julian Hotel stands today, and 18 mines sprang up like mushrooms. Four cousins—all former Confederate soldiers from Georgia, two with the last name Julian—founded this town. The mines produced up to an estimated $13 million worth of gold in their day.

In October 2003, Julian was virtually engulfed by the devastating Cedar Fires. Firefighters made a stand to protect the town against what seemed insurmountable odds. For a few days it was touch-and-go, and hundreds of homes in the surrounding hillsides were lost. But the central, historic part of Julian was saved, along with all of the town's famed apple orchards. Today you can stand on Main Street again without knowing a catastrophe visited just a few hundred yards away. But keep in mind that most of Julian's residents *do* live on the outskirts, and more than a third lost their homes and livelihoods.

### ESSENTIALS

**GETTING THERE**   The 90-minute drive can be made via Highway 78 or I-8 to Highway 79. Highway 78 traverses open country and farmland, while Highway 79 winds through scenic Cuyamaca Rancho State Park.

**VISITOR INFORMATION**   For a brochure on what to see and do, contact the **Julian Chamber of Commerce,** corner of Main and Washington streets, P.O. Box 1866, Julian, CA 92036 (© 760/765-1857; www.julianca.com), where staffers offer enthusiastic suggestions. The office is open daily 10am to 4pm.

### EXPLORING THE TOWN

This 1880s gold-mining town retains the dusty aura of the Old West. Julian offers an abundance of early California history, Victorian streets filled with apple-pie shops and antiques stores, crisp fresh air, and friendly people. *Be forewarned:* Julian's downtown can be exceedingly crowded during the fall harvest season, so consider making your trip at another time. At an elevation of 4,225 feet, the autumn air is crisp and bracing, and Julian often sees a dusting of snow during the winter months. Don't worry, though: They bake their famous apple pies year-round.

The best way to experience tiny Julian is on foot. The **chamber of commerce** in the old town hall displays vintage photos of Julian in its prime. Across the street, the **Julian Drug Store & Candy Mine,** 2134 Main St. (© 760/765-3753), is an old-style soda fountain serving sparkling sarsaparilla, conjuring images of boys in buckskin and girls in bonnets. The **Eagle and High Peak Mines** (ca. 1870) at the end of C Street (© 760/765-0036), although seemingly a tourist trap, offers an educational look at the town's one-time economic mainstay. The town's **Pioneer Cemetery** is a must-see for graveyard buffs; the eroded older tombstones in this overgrown, hilly burial ground tell the intriguing story of Julian's rough pioneer history.

The Julian hills have lots of **roadside fruit stands** and **orchards;** in autumn they're open all day, every day, but in the off season, many are open only on weekends. Most stands sell apples, pears, peaches, cider, jams, jellies, and other homemade foodstuffs. Many are along Highway 78 between Julian and Wynola; Farmers Road, a scenic country lane leading north from downtown Julian, also has stands.

Apple pie is the town's new mainstay, and the **Julian Pie Company,** 2225 Main St. (© 760/765-2449), is the most charming pie shop of them all. It serves original, Dutch, apple-mountain berry, and no-sugar-added pies, as well as other baked goodies. Another great bakery is the aptly named **Mom's Pies,** 2119 Main St. (© 760/765-2472), with a sidewalk plate-glass window through which you can observe the mom-on-duty rolling crust, filling pies, and crimping edges. Nearby, at the **Julian Cider Mill,** 2103 Main St. (© 760/765-1430), you can see cider presses at work October through March; it offers free tastes of the fresh nectar and sells jugs to take home.

## OUTDOOR PURSUITS

Within 10 miles of Julian, numerous hiking trails traverse rolling meadows, high chaparral, and thick pine forests. All the trails closed by the 2003 fires have reopened. The most spectacular hike is at **Volcan Mountain Preserve,** north of town along Farmers Road; the trail to the top is a moderately challenging hike of around 3.5 miles round-trip, with a 1,400-foot elevation gain. From the top, hikers have a panoramic view of the desert, mountains, and sea.

The 26,000-acre **Cuyamaca Rancho State Park,** along Highway 79 between Julian and the I-8, was badly burned during the October 2003 forest fires. For a map and further information about park status, stop in at **park headquarters,** 12551 Highway 79, Descanso (© 760/765-0755; www.cuyamaca.us).

Eight miles south of Julian, **Lake Cuyamaca** is a tiny community that centers around lake activities, primarily boating and fishing for trout (stocked year-round), plus bass, catfish, bluegill, and sturgeon. There's a general store and restaurant. The fishing fee is $5 per day, $2.50 per day for kids 8 to 15, free for children under 8. A California state fishing license is required and sold here; it's $11 for the day or $33 per year. Rowboats are $15 per day, and motorboat rentals run $35 for the day ($30 after 1pm). You can rent canoes and paddleboats by the hour for $10. For boat rental, fishing information, and RV or tent sites, call © 877/581-9904 or 760/765-0515 or see www.lakecuyamaca.org.

For a different way to tour, try **Llama Trek** (© 800/LAMAPAK or 760/765-1890; www.wikiupbnb.com). You'll lead the llama, which carries packs, for hikes to rural neighborhoods, a historic gold mine, mountain and lake views, and apple orchards. Rates for the 4-hour trips run $95 per person ($75 for children 10 and under) and include lunch.

## WHERE TO STAY

Julian is B&B country, and they fill up months in advance for the fall apple harvest season. Many (but not all) are affiliated with the **Julian Bed & Breakfast Guild** (© 760/765-1555; www.julianbnbguild.com), a terrific resource for personal assistance in locating accommodations. The 15 members also include private cabins and other options.

**Julian Gold Rush Hotel** ✦  Built in 1897 by freed slave Albert Robinson, this frontier-style hotel is a living monument to the area's gold boom days—it's the oldest continually operating hotel in Southern California. The downtown hotel isn't as secluded or plush as some of the many B&Bs, but if you seek historically accurate lodgings in Queen Anne style, this is the place. The 14 rooms and 2 cottages have been authentically restored (with nicely designed private bathrooms added where necessary) with antiques; some rooms are tiny, so claustrophobics should inquire upon reserving! Colorful wallpapers engulf the upstairs rooms. An inviting private lobby is stocked with books, games, literature on local activities, and a wood-burning stove.

2032 Main St. (at B St.), Julian, CA 92036. © **800/734-5854** or 760/765-0201. Fax 760/765-0327. www.julian hotel.com. 16 units. $110–$155 double; $150–$200 cottages. Rates include full breakfast and afternoon tea. AE, MC, V. *In room:* No phone.

**Orchard Hill Country Inn** ✦✦ *(Value)*  Hosts Darrell and Pat Straube offer the most upscale lodging in Julian—a posh, two-story Craftsman lodge and 12 cottages on a hill overlooking the town. The lodge has 10 guest rooms, a guests-only dining room (open 5 nights a week), and a great room with a massive stone fireplace. The 12 cottages spread across 3 acres and offer romantic hideaways. All units feature contemporary country furnishings and snacks. Rooms in the main lodge feel hotel-ish, but the cottage suites are secluded and luxurious, with private porches, fireplaces, wet bars, whirlpool tubs in most, and robes. Several hiking trails lead from the lodge into adjacent woods. Check for midweek specials on the website.

2502 Washington St., at Second St. (P.O. Box 425), Julian, CA 92036. © **800/71-ORCHARD** or 760/765-1700. Fax 760/765-0290. www.orchardhill.com. 22 units. $205–$425 double; from $285 for cottages. Extra person $25. 2-night minimum if including Sat. Rates include breakfast and hors d'oeuvres. AE, MC, V. From Hwy. 79, turn left on Main St., right on Washington St. *In room:* A/C, TV/VCR.

## WHERE TO DINE

Julian has a variety of adequate restaurants, all of which serve apple pie for dessert. In a cozy cottage with lacy draperies, flickering candles, and a warm hearth, the **Julian Grille,** 2224 Main St. (© 760/765-0173), is the town's nicest, with lunches of soups, sandwiches, large salads, charbroiled burgers, and hearty omelets. Dinner features grilled and broiled meats, seafood, and prime rib. In a historic farmhouse off Main Street, **Romano's Dodge House,** 2718 B St. (© 760/765-1003), serves home-style Italian, with red-checkered tablecloths and straw-clad chianti bottles. The signature dish, pork Juliana, is loin chops in a whisky–apple cider sauce.

# Index

# THE NEW TRAVELOCITY GUARANTEE

## EVERYTHING YOU BOOK WILL BE RIGHT, OR WE'LL WORK WITH OUR TRAVEL PARTNERS TO MAKE IT RIGHT, RIGHT AWAY.

*To drive home the point,
we're going to use the word "right" in every single sentence.*

Let's get right to it. Right to the meat! Only Travelocity guarantees everything about your booking will be right, or we'll work with our travel partners to make it right, right away. Right on!

*Here's a picture taken smack dab right in the middle of Antigua, where the guarantee also covers you.*

*The guarantee covers all but one of the items pictured to the right.*

For example, what if the ocean view you booked actually looks out at a downright ugly parking lot? You'd be right to call – we're there for you. And no one in their right mind would be pleased to learn the rental car place has closed and left them stranded. Call Travelocity and we'll help get you back on the right track.

Now, you may be thinking, "Yeah, right, I'm so sure." That's OK; you have the right to remain skeptical. That is until we mention help is always right around the corner. Call us right off the bat, knowing that our customer service reps are there for you 24/7. Righting wrongs. Left and right.

Now if you're guessing there are some things we can't control, like the weather, well you're right. But we can help you with most things – to get all the details in righting,* visit **travelocity.com/guarantee.**

*Sorry, spelling things right is one of the few things not covered under the guarantee.

*I'd give my right arm for a guarantee like this, although I'm glad I don't have to.*

travelocity
*You'll never roam alone.*

**IF YOU BOOK IT, IT SHOULD BE THERE.**

Only Travelocity guarantees it will be, or we'll work with our travel partners to make it right, right away. So if you're missing a balcony or anything else you booked, just call us 24/7. **1-888-TRAVELOCITY.**

traveloci

*You'll never roam*

My, what an inefficient way to fish.

Ring toss, good. Horseshoes, bad.

Faster! Faster! Faster!

We take care of the fiddly bits, from providing over 43,000 customer reviews of hotels, to helping you find our best fares, to giving you 24/7 customer service. So you can focus on the only thing that matters. Goofing off.

**travelocity**
*You'll never roam alone.*™

# AHH, THE SUN
## THE BEACHES, AND THE REALLY LOW RATES

For our absolute lowest rates in California, there's just one place to go.

**Thrifty.com**

*Book Smart.*℠

Get our **Lowest Rate** online.
Or call **1.800.THRIFTY**® or your professional travel agent.